CONGRESS INVESTIGATES
A Documented History
1792–1974

EDITORS

Arthur M. Schlesinger, jr.

Albert Schweitzer Professor in the Humanities
City University of New York

Roger Bruns

National Historical Publications Commission

Volume IV

with an introductory essay by
Arthur M. Schlesinger, jr.

New York
CHELSEA HOUSE PUBLISHERS

in association with
R. R. BOWKER COMPANY
New York and London
1975

Project Editors: Kathryn Hammell, Karyn Browne
Managing Editor: Roberta Morgan
Assistant Editor: Deborah Weiss

Published by Chelsea House Publishers in association
with R. R. Bowker Company (a Xerox Education Company)

Schlesinger, Arthur Meier, 1917–   comp.
Congress investigates.

1.   Governmental investigations—United States—
History. I. Bruns, Roger, joint comp. II. Title.
JK1123.A2S34   328.73'07'452   74-34005
ISBN 0-8352-0795-1

Volume I: 0-8352-0811-7
II: 0-8352-0812-5
III: 0-8352-0813-3
IV: 0-8352-0814-1
V: 0-8352-0816-8

Contents

VOLUME IV

The Pecora Wall Street Exposé, 1934

Donald A. Ritchie

The Nye Munitions Committee, 1934

The Dies Committee, 1938

Michael Wreszin   2923

The Truman Committee, 1941

Teapot Dome
1924

Teapot Dome
1924

by Hasia Diner

Of the corruption-ridden Harding Administration, Frederick Lewis Allen, the popular chronicler of the 1920s, noted in *Only Yesterday,* "the oil cases were the aristocrats among the scandals." For the year and a half that the Senate's Committee on Public Lands and Surveys pondered the perplexities of the Teapot Dome scandal, hundreds of witnesses paraded through the Senate investigating chambers, either answering or refusing to answer questions. When Senator Thomas Walsh (D.-Montana) began to direct the hearing in the Senate on October 24, 1923, few newspapers gave it prominent coverage. Walsh's hearings were expected to be dull, tedious, and short-lived. As the months proceeded, however, and as the Montana senator and the committee attempted to unravel and expose the various strands of the explosive scandal, the inquiry generated intense interest.

The taint of oil and corruption was eventually to stain both parties, causing at least three cabinet-level resignations, inspiring several Supreme Court decisions, and making the name Teapot Dome synonymous with the seamy side of American politics. This scandal also caused political thinkers, constitutional theorists, and government officials to discuss the proper role of Congress in the investigatory procedure.

What was Teapot Dome and the scandal surrounding it, and why should it have engendered such controversy, shattering any number of political careers? Simply, Teapot Dome was a tract of oil-rich land in Wyoming which had been set aside by President Wilson, under the auspices of the Department of the Navy, to be used exclusively by the navy. There were similar tracts of land in California, and Teapot Dome was known as Naval Oil Reserve Number Three. For some time, however, oilmen and developers had hoped to lease parts of the naval oil reserves. Conservationists, both in and out of the government, angrily contested any move to remove oil which they felt should be held in reserve for national emergencies. After a protracted dispute within Wilson's cabinet over the leasing of the oil reserves, a special amendment was pushed through the Congress in 1920 which gave complete control of the naval oil reserves to the secretary of the navy, who was entrusted "to conserve, develop, use and operate the oil reserves . . . directly." Previous to this legislation, the Interior Department maintained control of the lands. Conservationists such as Gifford Pinchot praised this complete transfer of control to the navy because its secretary, Josephus Daniels, was recognized as an ardent supporter of the conservation movement.

The conservationists' celebration was, however, brief. The year 1921 saw not only the end of Wilson's Administration and the return to power of the Republican party, but also the ascension of a number of dubiously qualified individuals to positions of power in the Harding Administration. Of particular concern to conservationists were Albert Fall, secretary of the interior, and Edwin Denby, secretary of the navy. Fall had begun his career as a gold and silver prospector in the southwest and Mexico. Eventually he settled in New Mexico and acquired large mining and land-holding interests. His dealings went beyond amassing land and wealth, and he immersed himself in state politics—but he was a Democrat in Republican territory. Fall, however, switched party affiliations in 1906, anticipating New Mexico's statehood. He quickly became a figure of some importance in Republican circles and after serving in several lower offices, in 1912 he was elected to the Senate by the New Mexico legislature. In the Senate he befriended Warren Harding, then senator from Ohio.

Early in his tenure as secretary of the interior, Fall discussed the possibility of a change in naval oil land policy. Denby agreed with Fall that the Interior Department should have control of the lands rather than the navy, and on May 11, 1921, Fall wrote to Harding, requesting that change. On May 21, after consulting with Denby, Harding issued Executive Order 3474, formally transferring the reserves.

The transfer received little public attention, barely meriting press coverage, although some conservationists were immediately aware of the implications inherent in future land policy. One such person was Harry Slattery, a Washington lawyer and former secretary to Gifford Pinchot, who brought his concerns to Senator Robert La Follette. He confided to the senator his fear that Fall would lease the oil lands for private exploitation. While Slattery had no specific evidence, Fall did have the authority to lease the reserves according to the General Leasing Act of 1920. The legislation permitted the reserves to be leased to prevent drainage from them through private drillings on the peripheries of the government lands. Earlier, Secretary of the Navy Daniels had allowed isolated private leasings, but he had never leased an entire reserve.

Secretary of the Navy Denby had been concerned with the drainage problem. Accordingly, he had been amenable to Fall's suggestion that the oil lands be transferred to the Interior Department. Denby was also concerned with the problems of military security, for he feared that, if a war with Japan developed, the underground oil would be utterly useless: the oil could aid in mobilization only if it were refined and accessible. Fall agreed with Denby and both officials assumed that the transfer of authority was but a prelude to further private exploitation of the oil lands under the auspices of the General Leasing Act.

The first of the private leases granted by the Department of the Interior was to Edward Doheny, head of the Pan-American Petroleum and Transport Company. Doheny was awarded part of Naval Reserve Number One in Elk Hills, California; he won the right to the oil reserves through open, competitive bidding. However, in April 1922, rumors began to circulate that private deals had been made involving private leasing of the oil land, both in Elk Hills and at Teapot Dome. Senator John Kendrick of Wyoming had received numerous communications from constituents about the clandestine leasing of Teapot Dome; Kendrick duly asked for information from the Interior Department. On April 14, 1922, the *Wall Street Journal* carried an article announcing that all of the Teapot Dome had been leased to the business interests of Harry F. Sinclair, president of Mammoth Oil Company. According to the *Journal*, "the arrangement . . . marks one of the greatest petroleum undertakings of the age and signalizes a notable departure on the part of the government in seeking partnership with private capital for the working of government owned natural resources." The next day Kendrick introduced a resolution in the Senate calling for further information on the leasing of the Teapot Dome. Within three days the acting secretary of the interior, Edward Finney, responded, stating that Sinclair's company had been given the lease to develop all of the Teapot Dome and that the Pan-American Petroleum and Transport Company, owned by Doheny, was to get the rest of the rights to the Elk Hills reserve. Shortly thereafter, the Senate was given a copy of the Sinclair lease, accompanied by a frank statement explaining that, because of naval preparedness and national security, there had been no competitive bidding.

While there was still little public attention focused on the issue, conservationists remained concerned with the secrecy of the Sinclair lease—there had been no official announcement of it. La Follette introduced resolutions on April 21 and 28, calling for the Senate Committee on Public Lands and Surveys to look into all leases on naval lands. He then pleaded with Senator Walsh to assume the leadership of the investigation. Although the senator agreed, he was appalled by the drudgery which the task would involve and stunned by the amount of material he would have to examine. In June Fall had ordered a truckload of documents and material sent to the Senate. At the same time Walsh was also informed in a letter by President Harding that the oil policy pursued by Fall and Denby "was submitted to me prior to the adoption thereof, and the policy decided upon and the subsequent acts have at all times had my entire approval."

While Walsh had little reason to question Harding's faith in his appointees, several suspicious events caused him to continue plodding through the reams of documents. For example, shortly after La Follette introduced his resolutions calling for an investigation, La Follette's offices were ransacked. Then, Walsh discovered that someone had been investigating his own past, and he had reason to suspect that his phones were tapped and that his mail was being read. While this was occurring, Walsh was barraged with intriguing rumors, especially those which pointed to Albert Fall's obvious increase in wealth shortly after granting the oil leases. Walsh's curiosity was further triggered in early 1923 when it was announced that Fall was leaving the cabinet to work with the Sinclair oil interests. Later, in the spring, Fall traveled with Harry Sinclair to Russia to obtain oil concessions on the island of Sakhalin. At his final cabinet meeting Fall ironically told reporters that he had "tried to impress upon my friends and associates that my leaving Washington is not a case of saying goodbye, but until we meet again." Seven months later, on October 24, Fall was among the first witnesses to testify in Walsh's investigation of oil, politics, and corruption.

Before Fall appeared in front of the Public Lands Committee, two days of testimony by geologists indicated that the oil from the Teapot Dome reserve was draining out at an alarming rate. One geologist, K. C. Heald, noted: "There is no doubt that from the point of development of the property and recovery of oil from it, it will be much better to develop the property as a unit. . . ." Republican Senator Reed Smoot, one of the staunchest Administration supporters on the committee, observed: "If the reports of the experts are accepted the theory that the Government made a mistake in leasing this . . . reserve has been exploded." This was an ominous beginning for those Democrats who hoped that the hearings would expose unsavory Republican policies and practices. Even the conservationists who were eagerly casting about for a way to discredit Fall and Denby were taken aback by the early geological evidence.

Fall's testimony lasted for two days. He not only defended his oil leasing policy in terms of the problems of oil drainage but in terms of "national security." Claiming that his actions in leasing the lands to Sinclair were part of a campaign for greater energy preparedness if the United States was forced into a war with Japan, Fall emphasized that President Harding had endorsed the leasing policy in his letter to the Senate committee. Walsh could do nothing after the two days of testimony but dismiss Fall with the reminder that he would most likely be called back again. Fall's testimony was followed by that of Denby, who stood behind the secretary of the interior and doggedly maintained that no wrongdoing was involved in the decision to transfer authority to the Interior Department or to lease the various oil reserves.

While Walsh assumed the burden of examining witnesses and ploughing through voluminous pieces of evidence, the officials of the Democratic party, and especially Cordell Hull, the chairman of the Democratic National Committee, began to take an interest in the Teapot Dome hearings. Hull convinced conservationist Slattery to draw up a list of potential witnesses, including Josephus Daniels, Franklin Roosevelt, Attorney General Harry Daugherty, as well as officers of the Departments of the Navy, Justice, and the Interior. The remaining days of October and most of November were taken up with minor witnesses who added very little to Walsh's search for substantive information. However, Walsh began hearing numerous stories about Fall's land deals in New Mexico—deals which had netted him a tidy profit. This put Walsh on a new path. He summoned witnesses from New Mexico, including a news-paper editor from Albuquerque—Carl Magee. Magee informed the com-mittee that after 1923 Fall's Three Rivers ranch had vastly improved in condi-tion. As Magee described it to Senator Walsh: "There had been pillars built up to this road, and beautiful woven wire fence put along, and trees planted, and beautifully concreted gutters, and a very expensive road, as far as I could see, up to the ranch house. . . . The conditions were so changed I couldn't recognize it." Magee contrasted Fall's newly found opulence with his dire economic straits of several years before. This testimony and that of several subsequent witnesses caused committee members to wonder about a possible connection between Fall's economic prosperity and the leasing of the Teapot Dome reserves.

On the same day that Magee testified, Fall's ranch manager appeared before the committee, revealing that Sinclair had been a guest at the Three Rivers ranch in December 1921. At that time Fall received several well-bred hogs and cows from Sinclair, who owned a farm in New Jersey. While Walsh was not interested in Fall's livestock interests, he decided to pursue the reasons why Sinclair might want to thank Fall in some material way. When Republican Senator Irvine L. Lenroot asked Edward Doheny if Fall had prof-ited "in any way, directly or indirectly," through contracts, Doheny tersely answered: "Not yet." Walsh's suspicions were further whetted when Sinclair appeared again, on December 4. At first Sinclair's secretary, G. D. Wahlberg, answered for him, stating that Fall had paid for "seven cows and two bulls." Sinclair admitted, however, that he had been down to Three Rivers, saw that Fall did not have any cows, and that Fall had agreed to accept them as a gift.

As the sessions of 1923 ended and those of 1924 began, Walsh had made little progress. He was bogged down in trivial and circumstantial evidence and there seemed to be no end to the possible number of witnesses. The *New York Times* noted, "Senator Walsh was up against a stone wall. The wise politicos of Washington believed that he had gone as far as he possibly could go."

Walsh's investigatory drive was, however, not dampened, and a major breakthrough occurred on January 8, 1924, when Edward McLean's lawyer, former Attorney General A. Mitchell Palmer, informed the committee that McLean, then living in Florida, would make a full disclosure of a $100,000 loan that he had made to Fall in 1921. Walsh wanted to examine McLean, the publisher of the *Washington Post,* more closely, but McLean, ill with a sinus infection, would not appear in Washington. He did agree, however, to testify from his bed in Florida. Walsh, who was skeptical about the seriousness of McLean's illness, was then appointed as a subcommittee of one and he went to Palm Beach to accept McLean's testimony. On January 12, McLean revealed, much to Walsh's surprise, that Fall never used the money McLean had lent to him and had returned the checks to him uncashed. Walsh suspected that the reason Fall did not accept the money was because he had found some other, more lucrative, source. Walsh immediately asked Fall, who was also in Palm Beach, for a statement about the money. Only under threat did Fall agree to answer Walsh's questions. In a letter he admitted that he had not accepted McLean's loan, "because I found other sources." The whole matter, he quickly added, "was in no way connected with Mr. Sinclair of . . . Teapot Dome or any oil concession." He refused to appear in person before Walsh in Palm Beach, partially because of ill health and more importantly because he thought that he was "right in believing that on his visit here he [Walsh] was empowered only to examine Mr. McLean's confidential secretary. . . . As to the question of where I got the money . . . that is my own private affair. I do not feel called upon to discuss it either with Senator Walsh or any other man."

Fall's refusal to cooperate invigorated the expiring inquiry; journalists suddenly began to demand answers from Fall; newspapers which had previously dismissed the hearings and the work of the Walsh Committee began to report that there was, indeed, some substance to the suspicions they raised. The first major witness to appear before the Senate committee in this revitalized atmosphere, Edward Doheny, told the committee on January 24, 1924, that he had been the one who lent Fall the $100,000. Doheny revealed that his son had carried the total amount in cash to Fall's office "in a little brown satchel." Doheny's statement made it clear that Fall had lied to the committee. While Doheny maintained that "there was no discussion between Mr. Fall and myself as to any contract whatever" and that the loan "had no relation to any of the subsequent transactions," Democrats began to publicly charge a high degree of collusion between the Harding Administration and the oil interests. The Democratic National Committee played up the Republican party's part in the oil frauds and released a pamphlet, *The Land Ye Possess*, chronicling how conservation thrived under the Democrats, while the Harding Administration had mercilessly "raped" Teapot Dome.

The Democrats continued to exploit the proceedings of the Walsh Committee when Archie Roosevelt, son of the late President, testified that he had resigned from his position with the Sinclair oil enterprises because his suspicions of wrongdoings had been substantially confirmed by the findings of the committee. Roosevelt informed the committee that Sinclair's private secretary, G. D. Wahlberg, had admitted to him that $68,000 had been given to Fall's ranch foreman, and that he, Wahlberg, had possession of the canceled checks. Wahlberg then testified that the President's son had misunderstood him. Wahlberg boldly stated that he had told Roosevelt about "six or eight cows, and [Roosevelt] probably understood that to mean $68,000 in some manner," inferring that "thous" had been heard instead of "cows." Walsh could not prod Wahlberg into changing his story.

Fall, questioned in New Orleans, denied ever receiving money from Sinclair. Few observers, however, took his denials seriously, and most newspapers spoke cynically about Fall's cries of innocence. January 1924 saw a dip in favorable public opinion towards the Republicans, and various members of Harding's former cabinet joined in a chorus denying any complicity or any knowledge of the affair. Charles Evans Hughes, secretary of state, publicly announced his shock and claimed that "the question of oil leases had never come up in the Cabinet." Herbert Hoover echoed Hughes's declaration, saying: "My recollection is exactly the same as expressed by Secretary Hughes. There may have been some discussions . . . but if there . . . [were] I don't remember it, and I . . . missed very few Cabinet meetings in the last three years."

Two days after Doheny's explosive testimony a group of Republican congressmen desperately appealed to Calvin Coolidge, who had succeeded to the presidency on Harding's death: "Believe situation demands vigorous action by President in oil lease matter. Public amazed by developments and nothing could increase confidence in administration like use of 'Big Stick' without delay. Think it important hit at once and hit hard." At the same time, at an executive session of the Public Lands Committee, Walsh announced that he intended to offer a resolution on the floor of the Senate authorizing Coolidge to annul the leases of Teapot Dome and Elk Hills, to stop all further removal of oil, and to appoint a special counsel to prosecute those involved in the wrongdoings. Walsh had obviously come to the conclusion that the committee had ploughed through enough material to warrant congressional action, and the time was ripe for criminal prosecution.

Even though Walsh had desired to keep secret the proceedings of the executive session of the committee for several days, news of the committee's decision leaked to President Coolidge. After spending the day consulting with various Republican senators and with various Justice Department officials who had been vigilant observers of the Public Lands Committee hearings, he issued the following statement on January 27, designed no doubt to steal the thunder and the prerogative from Walsh's committee:

> It is not for the President to determine criminal guilt or render judgment in civil causes; that is the function of the courts. It is not for him to prejudge. I shall do neither. But when the facts are revealed to me that require action for the purpose of insuring the enforcement of either civil or criminal liability such action will be taken. That is the province of the Executive.
>
> Acting under my direction, the Department of Justice has been observing the course of the evidence which has been revealed at the hearings . . . which I believe warrants action for the purpose of enforcing the law and protecting the rights of the public. This is confirmed by reports made to me from the committee.
>
> If there has been any crime, it must be prosecuted. If there has been any property of the United States illegally transferred or leased, it must be recovered.
>
> I feel the public is entitled to know that in the conduct of such action no one is shielded for any party, political or other reason. As I understand, men are involved who belong to both political parties, and having been advised by the Department of Justice that it is in accord with the former precedents, I propose to employ special counsel of high rank drawn from both political parties to bring such action for the enforcement of the law. Counsel will be instructed to prosecute these cases in the courts so that if there is any guilt it will be punished; if there is any civil liability it will be enforced; if there is any fraud it will be revealed; and if there are any contracts which are illegal they will be cancelled.
>
> Every law will be enforced. And every right of the people and the government will be protected.

While Coolidge's pronouncement was primarily a criticism of Attorney General Daugherty, Coolidge's move to take the investigation and prosecution of the cases out of the Justice Department was also an attempt to lessen the legislative role in the affair. He quite clearly stated: "That is the province of the Executive." The message to Walsh, the Democrats, and the Senate was explicit.

January ended with a combination of frustration and success for Walsh's efforts. The committee had once again summoned Albert Fall to appear before them, but the former secretary of the interior again used the issue of his health to avoid testifying. Fall presented the testimony of four physicians who stated that they had "carefully examined Hon. A. B. Fall. We find that it would be detrimental to Mr. Fall's health for him to leave his residence in his present condition." While Walsh's efforts to bring Fall to public testimony were thwarted, on the same day, January 29, the Senate began to debate Walsh's resolution. The only obstacle to his proposal was Senator Lenroot, who as a member of the Public Lands Committee praised Walsh's thorough investigation, but condemned the partisan motives behind it. He attempted to amend Walsh's resolution by asking the Senate to express their doubts about the legality of the oil contracts, rather than explicitly labeling them illegal. There was no support except among Republicans for Lenroot's attempt to soften the Walsh resolution. Thus, on January 31, it was unanimously passed by the Senate, who called on Coolidge to begin legal procedures to cancel the oil leases and engage a special prosecutor to examine the situation.

Up to this point, the taint of corruption and collusion had clearly fallen upon the Republicans. Republicans could only accuse the Democrats of crassly exploiting a national disaster for purely partisan motives. Yet by early 1924 Republicans began to use the forum of the Public Lands Committee to implicate Democrats in the oil leasings. The Democrat upon whom they seized and whose political fortunes were destroyed because of his testimony before the committee was William Gibbs McAdoo, son-in-law of the late Woodrow Wilson, and in 1924 a leading candidate for the Democratic nomination for President. It was a Democrat, Senator James A. Reed from Missouri, who publicly linked McAdoo to the Teapot Dome and fatally damaged the aspirations of the former secretary of the treasury. Reed's motivations were more personal than ideological; he wanted the nomination himself. On January 31, after the Senate had passed the Walsh resolution, Reed asked the Public Lands Committee to recall Doheny. Reed suggested that the committee ask Doheny if he had ever "given or contributed any money to any person at the time holding a public position . . . or whether any such official . . . contributed or given any money to him." This was clearly intended to publicize and expose some earlier dealings with McAdoo.

Lenroot, chairman of the committee, conducted most of the Doheny investigation. He asked if Doheny had ever employed any cabinet members after they had retired from the cabinet; Doheny answered affirmatively. He had employed Franklin K. Lane, Wilson's secretary of the interior. He had also employed former Attorney General Thomas Gregory as an attorney "to represent us before the President in regard to a lot of permits that we were trying to get in Mexico. . . ." Finally, Lenroot asked, "Now, have you employed any other ex-Cabinet officers?" "Yes," answered Doheny, "at the time when our properties were greatly menaced in Mexico by the hostile attitude of the Mexican Government I employed ex-Secretary McAdoo." Doheny admitted that he had paid McAdoo $250,000 to represent the interests of the Pan-

American Company in Washington, especially to then President Woodrow Wilson. Senator Holm Bursum of New Mexico then attempted to tie McAdoo's involvement with Doheny to that of Fall. He asked the oil speculator: "How do you compare the value of Mr. Fall's service in relation to Mexican oil interests in which you are interested with the service performed by Mr. McAdoo as to benefits?" The mere mention of McAdoo's name at the hearing and the linking of his name with that of Fall and the whole series of incidents regarding oil policy almost instantly damaged the base of his wide-spread support for the Democratic presidential nomination. One newspaper in South Carolina noted that it "threw McAdoo over immediately [after] the oil touched him. . . . It would be impossible for the Democrats to capitalize the oil scandals to anything like their productive value with McAdoo as leader."

Urged on by his friends and by loyal Democratic supporters, McAdoo attempted to salvage his reputation and his credibility as a presidential candidate. He issued a statement condemning Doheny and stating that Doheny had no reason to bring up his name in the oil lease hearings. McAdoo then asked Walsh for the chance to appear before the Public Lands Committee to clear his name. He had previously written to Lenroot justifying his activities:

> What I have done was within my rights as a lawyer. In my represen-
> tation of the Doheny companies in Mexican matters I never dealt in
> political influence, nor did I ask, or promise, or give, or receive
> political favors or other favors. If my conduct in acting profession-
> ally in these matters is open to criticism, then no lawyer can take a
> Cabinet office unless he be rich enough to give up all professional
> employment in business when he comes out of office. I do not
> believe that any such standard is wise or proper. I believe that the
> spirit of fair play of the honest-minded American people will not
> misunderstand my course in this matter, nor take their minds off of
> those who are guilty of betraying their trust as disclosed in this
> investigation.

That individual who had betrayed the trust of the public was the "real culprit—an ex-member of the Cabinet of this administration who appears to have acted corruptly." McAdoo boldly stated that he was "not willing that the innocent shall be made to suffer in order that the guilty may be protected or shielded by this transparent effort to bring odium upon innocent men connected with a former administration."

On February 11 when McAdoo appeared before the committee, he was treated with respect by the committee members, Republicans as well as Democrats. They readily accepted his records of a straight business transaction with the Pan-American Company. He adamantly insisted that there had been no official collusion between him and Doheny and that he had not had any contact, in fact, had not even met Doheny, until after he had left public office. McAdoo's testimony presented fairly clear evidence that he was not involved in the seamy side of Doheny's activities; McAdoo had taken no part in the illegal aspects of the Teapot Dome. Yet many observers noted that after McAdoo appeared before the committee, his refusal to *offer* to step out of the presidential race ruined his political fortunes. Sadly, or cheerfully, some Democratic politicos contended that McAdoo was no longer a viable candidate since he had accepted fees from Doheny, and according to one party figure, the Democrats "would be on the defensive the moment they would nominate McAdoo."

In the interim between McAdoo's decision to appear before the committee and his actual testimony, new issues and incidents entered into the narrative of the Teapot Dome. One of the major events occurred in early February. A group of physicians appointed by the committee issued a report stating that Albert Fall was now well enough to testify in person. The press, eager for lively print, was gleeful. The *New York Times,* for example, believed that both parties "were awaiting his testimony with ill-concealed nervousness." The *Santa Fe New Mexican,* a major and early critic of Fall, noted that, "the oil lease probe is spreading. The deeper you get into it the more bottomless it appears." And the always liberal *Nation* asserted that the revelations about Teapot Dome were just coming to a head, and the American public was "getting a delightful picture of what a business government really is."

Political commentators and politicians were eager for Fall's testimony. They were, however, once again disappointed. Fall refused to answer any of the committee's questions. Although he eventually refused to respond on the grounds of the Fifth Amendment, he also questioned the legality of the hearings and the right of the Senate committee to conduct its investigation. Fall stated that he did "not consider that acting under those resolutions [Senate Resolutions 282, 294, 434] . . . which authoriz[e] the committee to sit after the expiration of the Sixty-seventh Congress . . . this committee has any authority to conduct the investigation now attempted to be conducted by the addressing of this question to me."

Fall also told the committee that according to its own resolution the President now had sole authority "to prosecute such proceedings, civil and criminal, as may be warranted by the facts in the making of the said leases." The claim that the Senate had no legal authority to compel testimony was also raised by Sinclair at a later date, but Sinclair's refusal brought him a contempt citation. The committee did not take Fall's criticism seriously, but his refusal to provide the senators with any information added to the general confusion. One writer for the Baltimore *Sun* on February 5 speculated: "Neither Republican, Democrat or insurgent leaders [has] the least idea which way the 'cat is going to jump. . . .' All over Washington there is a feeling that the worst is yet to come."

One of the most significant clashes between the Senate and the President in the Teapot Dome imbroglio also occurred in early February 1924. As a result of Fall's refusal to testify and the growing impatience with the endless maze of witnesses, the Senate on February 11, in a basically partisan vote, called upon President Coolidge to request Denby's resignation as secretary of the navy. Coolidge refused to comply, claiming that the proper time for action had not yet come. He was waiting for the special counsel to inform him of the legality of the leases and about the "pertinent facts in the various transactions." Coolidge felt, moreover, it was his prerogative as President to decide who should remain in or who should leave the cabinet. He asserted that the Executive had the final and exclusive authority to remove a cabinet officer, in all cases except impeachment. Coolidge cited various statements by former

Presidents on the rights of the Executive, and he charged that the Senate's wish was a blatant violation of the principle of separation of powers. Most Republicans praised Coolidge's steadfastness, describing his actions in glowing terms of his loyalty to an innocent man and his commitment to the historic role of the presidency. The President's loyalty, however, did not save Denby. On February 18 the secretary tendered his resignation.

Meanwhile, Coolidge was searching for special counsel to take charge of the investigation of the leases, an investigation he hoped would steal the publicity and impetus from the Walsh Committee. At one point in early 1924 Coolidge had suggested Silas Strawn, a Republican from Chicago. Lenroot, always trying to protect the Republican interests on the Public Lands Committee, informed Coolidge that the committee was going to report back negatively on Strawn and advised the President to withdraw his name. Coolidge complied, wishing to avoid further controversy with the Senate committee. He next suggested Owen J. Roberts, a Republican lawyer from Philadelphia, who had been endorsed by Senator George Pepper. Walsh opposed the nomination; for while he was convinced that Roberts was a good lawyer with impeccable credentials, he felt that "the country knows nothing of him." Walsh, at this point, was suspicous of almost anyone, especially a Republican suggested by Calvin Coolidge. After a fairly heated debate over both Roberts and Coolidge's other nominee, Atlee Pomerene, the Senate confirmed both special counsels. Pomerene was approved first, and two days later (when Walsh was absent), Roberts was also confirmed.

Although Coolidge and the Republicans had hoped that the confirmation of the special prosecutors would take much of the initiative and the publicity away from the Public Lands Committee, on February 25, after a two-week recess, the committee once again resumed its hearings. Of the half-dozen witnesses who appeared over the next few days, the most significant was C. Bascom Slemp, Calvin Coolidge's private secretary. Walsh requested Slemp's testimony because Slemp had been in Palm Beach at the same time that Walsh was there questioning Edward McLean. Slemp admitted that he had talked to McLean while in Florida, but that his exchange with McLean had been purely personal and in no way involved McLean's supposed $100,000 loan to Fall. In response to Walsh's question, "Did you have any communication at any time while you were down there with anyone in the city of Washington in relation to the subject?" Slemp stated emphatically that he "had no communications with anyone in Washington at all." He admitted some communication with the White House of a purely personal nature, but also stated that he felt that those "communications that I would make to the White House I would have to reserve as confidential."

In the subsequent week, however, Walsh located and made public a series of bizarre telegrams which had been passed from McLean in Palm Beach to numerous persons in Washington. The telegrams showed that McLean was frantically trying to avoid being questioned by Walsh. Most were written in a secret code which had once been used in the Justice Department. For example, one dated January 11, 1924, read:

Cravingly in dxewoux resurge ledgment aliment fastidious tuck skewered suckled scrag emerse vethousl punctators gob. Virgin lectionary jangler high lander kelder hobgoblin roguery sawbuck hosier bonka gob saline dismounted renominated torso.

Another of January 24, also from Palm Beach, from a William Wiley, continued this garbled line:

Saw apples, and everything fine. Also saw cherries and they were very good. The peaches will be just what you want, and I am sure any change in weather will not affect them.

Buried among the hundred of telegrams which Walsh had taken from two Washington telegraph offices were two wires from Coolidge to McLean. Neither wire was particularly damning. In one, Coolidge told McLean: "Prescott is away. Advise Slemp with whom I shall confer. Acknowledge." The other was even less obvious: "Thank you for your message. You have always been most considerate. . . ." An employee of McLean's, however, told the committee that among those people receiving some of the coded telegrams was Slemp. This series of telegrams piqued the appetites of the Democrats who were hoping to find something to link Coolidge to the various aspects of the Teapot Dome scandal. The rumors which had been making their way out of the Senate investigating chambers were ambiguous and unfounded. To add some substance to these shadowy innuendos, McLean was asked to appear again before the committee in mid-March, but he offered no new material which tied the President to any aspect of Teapot Dome or suggested that the purpose of Slemp's trip to Florida was to directly communicate with Fall or McLean. At the same time, Coolidge felt compelled to clear himself and to justify the two telegrams which clearly bore his name. The first telegram had concerned a routine political appointment, he said, and the second acknowledged a note McLean had sent to Coolidge congratulating him on his refusal to dismiss Denby.

For several weeks anti-Administration newspapers reveled in the linkage. The *Washington Daily News* advised the Walsh Committee that it would be irrational for it not to investigate the implications of a telegram "ambiguous in text, sent by the Chief Executive to one of the most important figures" of the Teapot Dome scandal. A more balanced judgment was rendered by the *New York Times* which said in a March 7 editorial that it was "humiliating to think that we have come to the point where every idle talk and gratuitous suspicion about the President . . . must be given resounding publicity." Democrats in Congress continued to fill the *Congressional Record* with statements questioning the President's role. Senator Norris, an independent, claimed that the entire drift of the Walsh investigations had made him doubt Coolidge's ability to serve as President. Coolidge's association with McLean, "one of the most disreputable characters in . . . Washington—a man who has lived a life of continual debauchery," had convinced the Nebraska senator that Coolidge was the wrong person for the office. Throughout the crisis, Coolidge, true to his public image of the tight-lipped, reticent New Englander, remained publicly unruffled and silent.

But the taint of oil continued to plague the beleaguered President. After Democratic senators attacked Attorney General Daugherty in late February, the Senate on March 1 established a special committee under Senator Burton K. Wheeler to investigate Daugherty's failure to prosecute Fall, Sinclair, Doheny, and others. The investigation featured numerous charges of illegality, graft, and influence-peddling in the Justice Department. On March 28 Harry Daugherty resigned. The Teapot Dome morass had claimed another victim.

Throughout the spring Walsh made a concerted effort to direct the hearings toward the true story of the Teapot Dome, continuing his search for some key to the whole fiasco. On March 8 he began a new tack, which involved the recollections of Gifford Pinchot. Walsh had heard rumors that the collusion surrounding Teapot Dome had begun before the 1920 Republican convention. Originating in a statement that General Leonard Wood had supposedly made to Pinchot, the rumor was that Wood told Pinchot that he would have gotten the Republican nomination had he agreed to turn over to private exploitation the public natural resources. While Pinchot told Walsh explicitly that he could not remember Wood making such a remark to him, Walsh continued to probe the story. On March 8 a front-page article in the *New York Times* claimed that before the 1920 convention certain oil interests had sought to persuade General Wood to appoint Jake Hamon secretary of the interior. In return for the promise of appointing Hamon, Wood was to receive the support of oilmen in his own bid for the nomination.

While Walsh could not subpoena Hamon, who had died several years before, he did bring in a series of witnesses who had some knowledge of this tangent of the investigation. One of the most verbose of these witnesses was Al Jennings, a real estate dealer and former train robber from California, who had announced to the press that his testimony would burst open the whole affair. Jennings, who had accompanied Hamon to the 1920 convention in Chicago, testified that Hamon had told him that "Harding would be nominated the next day, and it had cost him a million dollars." According to Jennings's recollections of the manipulations at the convention, "it had been agreed upon that day by Mr. Daugherty, Will Hays [Republican national chairman], and he named somebody else from Ohio, that he was to be Secretary of the Interior. He said it had all been settled; that Mr. Daugherty at first was in favor of Senator Fall occupying that position, and they had a fight, but he put it all over them, and it cost him a lot of money to do it." Jennings implied that Hays had received part of Hamon's million dollars; the charge was immediately denied by Hays.

The air around the oil leases and the 1920 Republican convention was still clouded and in late March 1924 the *New York Times* published substantial evidence that 75,000 shares of Sinclair oil stock had been used to assist the Republican party with its campaign expenditures. Hays denied this allegation also. He branded the *Times* story, "false in content, as it is libelous in purpose." Hays did admit, however, that Harry Sinclair had made a personal loan of $75,000 to the Republican party, but the gift was not in the form of oil shares. Hays added that he knew nothing about the oil leases at Elk Hills and Teapot Dome until he had read about them in the papers. A steady stream of subsequent witnesses called by Walsh could not flesh out the allegations and innuendos, so by late spring the committee was at a dead end.

Not giving up the battle entirely, Walsh continued to call in geologists, petroleum specialists, and other technical experts. The committee ended the search for political scandal and began looking for more concrete answers about oil drainage and the productive capabilities of the reserves in question. The symbolic end of public interest in the hearings could be dated May 8, when not one spectator came to listen to testimony about the geological features of the Teapot Dome.

As Walsh was having a progressively more difficult time tracking through the web of Teapot Dome testimony, and as interest shifted away from the Senate investigation, most of the work on the scandal was handled by the President's special counsel, Owen Roberts and Atlee Pomerene. Some of the Teapot Dome drama had also moved to the courts. In March 1924 Sinclair was indicted for contempt of the Senate by a Washington, D.C., grand jury. He had refused to answer questions about his 1920 campaign contributions when he appeared before the Walsh Committee on March 23. He did not refuse to testify on the basis of the Fifth Amendment, but because he believed that the Senate committee had no "jurisdiction to question me further regarding . . . lease." Sinclair gave this same response on ten separate occasions, and on March 24 the Senate voted to bring grand jury action against him. The grand jury brought in its indictment on March 31, despite the fact that it had been several decades since a grand jury had indicted an individual on such charges. Sinclair pleaded not guilty. However, nearly three years later he was found guilty by the criminal branch of the Supreme Court in the District of Columbia. After a lengthy appeal to the United States Supreme Court, Sinclair's contempt sentence was upheld and the oilman served a three-month prison term. Sinclair also served a six-month term for a contempt of court citation stemming from his and Fall's conspiracy trial.

There was no doubt that the initiative for the investigation of the Teapot Dome began with Walsh and the Senate Public Lands Committee. Walsh, who had exerted more energy to get to the truth of the allegations and circumstances surrounding the leasing of the naval oil reserves than any other individual, had been the subject of criticism across the country. He had been accused by many of blatantly partisan behavior, of succumbing to rumor and innuendo, and of jumping to rash and unsubstantiated conclusions. Before Walsh and the Public Lands Committee issued their final report based on months of investigation, Walsh summarized his findings for *Outlook* magazine in May 1924. While the magazine did not fully agree with Walsh's "extreme claims," it felt that the public was entitled to hear the judgments of the Montana senator, the person who had inspected and analyzed more material on the subject than had any other public figure. According to Walsh's analysis, the most damning piece of evidence brought in against Fall was the fact that Doheny's lease on the Elk Hills reserve was secured without any kind of competitive bidding. This occurred simultaneously with his grant of $100,000 to Albert Fall. Fall's move from poverty to riches coincided with his awarding the lease of the Teapot Dome reserve to Sinclair. Walsh noted that the evidence of the technical experts, especially the later witnesses, had revealed that the government had been defrauded of its rightful portion of the oil when the reserves were leased out to private individuals. These points which Walsh touched upon in the *Outlook* article served as a synopsis of the majority report which emerged from the committee on June 6.

The report submitted to the Senate was signed by Senator Edwin Ladd of North Dakota, who had assumed the chairmanship of the committee from Lenroot, and the other Democrats and independent Republicans. The final report attacked Fall most severely for his lawlessness and his assumption of authority far beyond the limits of his position. The Senate committee found all the transactions surrounding the leasings to be corrupt, although it admitted that much of the evidence had been inconclusive and that there was no real proof that anyone had profited from advance knowledge about the leases. The committee report also failed to draw any real links between the machinations of the oilmen and the 1920 Republican campaign.

Not everyone was happy with the report. Naturally, the Republicans and the Administration supporters in the press were highly critical. A minority report was issued by Senator Spence of Missouri, claiming that the members had not had sufficient time to read the report and that it had been impossible for them to make any definite conclusions, given how much ephemeral material was presented to the committee. The *Boston Evening Transcript*, a staunch Administration organ, also criticized Walsh's report. Not only had Walsh usurped those powers which the Constitution had intended for the courts when he had declared the leases to be illegal, the *Transcript* declared, but he had been overtly partisan in his attack on the Harding Administration.

From the other end of the political spectrum, from the whole range of Democratic party spokespeople, there were also criticisms of the report. Harry Slattery, the ardent conservationist, thought that the report was much too mild in its complete exoneration of Archie Roosevelt and Secretary of the Navy Denby. Slattery was also convinced that certain aspects of Fall's behavior were not pointed out clearly enough by Walsh. The *Times* noted that the Walsh report was thorough and straight in its coverage of the facts, but "after the thunder and the earthquake, the still small voice. After the months of resounding inquiry . . . the report of Senator Walsh." Other commentators echoed the *Times's* disappointment: the Walsh report lacked drama; it lacked hard and fast conclusions about the web of collusion and conspiracy between government officials, party functionaries, and oil speculators. The official organ of the American Federation of Labor perhaps best summarized the liberal disappointment with the Walsh report: "The single, solemn truth is that the Walsh report is a flat fizzle. It doesn't sound like Walsh."

While Walsh was never able to produce indisputable data on the complex questions of Teapot Dome, Elk Hills, and the oil leasing policy of the Harding years, there was no question that he was able to point it in the right direction. The investigation of the oil scandals continued under the prosecution of Roberts and Pomerene, and indictments and guilty verdicts were handed down for conspiracy, bribery, and illegal transferral of the oil lands. On February 28, 1927, the Supreme Court unanimously decided that the lease upon the oil reserves had, indeed, been illegal. The Court later declared that the lease was a product of the Fall-Sinclair conspiracy, that Denby had purposely acquiesced, and in the process had allowed Fall to act without restraint.

The criminal proceedings against Harry Sinclair which eventually went to the Supreme Court and which centered on Sinclair's contempt of the Senate citation, were an important step in broadening the investigatory powers of the Congress. Sinclair had contended that the interrogations to which he had refused to respond "related to his private affairs and to matters cognizable only in the courts"; thus, the Senate had no jurisdiction. In April 1929 the Court refused to accept Sinclair's position and upheld the right of the Senate to investigate. This decision, *Sinclair* v. *United States,* stretched the purposes for which Congress could conduct its investigations. The Court first affirmed that Congress could dispose of and make all the necessary rules and regulations regarding the oil reserves. It further noted that

> the Senate had power to delegate authority to its committee to investigate and report what had been and was being done by executive departments under the Leasing Act, the Naval Oil Reserve Act, and the President's order in respect of the reserves, and to make any other inquiry concerning the public domain. . . . Congress, in addition to its general legislative power over the public domain, had all the powers of a proprietor and was authorized to deal with it as a private individual may deal with land owned by him. The committee's authority to investigate extended to matters affecting the interest of the United States as owner as well as to those having relation to the legislative function. . . . Moreover, it was pertinent for the Senate to ascertain the practical effect of recent changes that had been made in the laws relating to oil and other mineral lands in the public domain.

The *Sinclair* decision asserted that Congress may investigate in order to understand the effect of its own laws.

Two years before the *Sinclair* decision, in January 1927, the Supreme Court had decided in *McGrain* v. *Daugherty* that the Senate (or House of Representatives) "has power, through its own processes, to compel a private individual to appear before it or one of its committees and give testimony needed to enable it efficiently to exercise a legislative function belonging to it under the Constitution." This decision had also grown out of the Teapot Dome controversy, although it was not a result of the Walsh investigations. It was significant, however, that two of the most sweeping court decisions concerning the rights of Congress to act as an investigative body grew out of the same scandal and out of the efforts of Congress to get a thorough understanding of the activities within the Executive branch. The Walsh hearings cleared the way for a broader definition of the legislature as an investigatory body. While critics inveighed against Walsh and the other members of the Public Lands Committee for usurping the role of the judiciary, the Supreme Court, in two separate decisions, confirmed the growing role of Congress in the investigatory process. The Court resoundingly confirmed this growth by stating: "We are of opinion that the power of inquiry—with process to enforce it—is an essential and appropriate auxiliary to the legislative function." The importance of that growth was earlier asserted by one of the nation's outstanding legal scholars and a future Supreme Court justice. In a 1924 article in the *New Republic,* Felix Frankfurter replied to critics of the congressional investigation:

> The procedure of congressional investigation should remain as it is. No limitations should be imposed by congressional legislation or standing rules. The power of investigation should be left untram-

meled, and the methods and forms of each investigation should be left for the determination of Congress and its committees, as each situation arises. The safeguards against abuse and folly are to be looked for in the forces of responsibility which are operating from within Congress, and are generated from without.

INTRODUCTION OF KENDRICK RESOLUTION
APRIL 12, 1922

Congressional Record, 67th Congress, 2nd Session, 5567–68.

Mr. Kendrick. I offer a resolution of peculiar importance to the people of my State, and I ask unanimous consent for its immediate consideration.

The resolution (S. Res. 277) was read and considered by unanimous consent, as follows:

> Whereas there have recently appeared in the public press statements purporting to have been authorized by the Department of the Interior to the effect that the Secretary of the Interior and the Secretary of the Navy are negotiating with private parties for the operation of lands included in naval petroleum reserve No. 3, Wyoming No. 1, withdrawn by Executive order of the President dated April 30, 1915, known as the Teapot Dome:
>
> *Resolved,* That the Secretary of the Interior and the Secretary of the Navy are hereby requested to inform the Senate, if not incompatible with the public interests, whether such negotiations are pending, and if so the names of all parties, the terms and conditions of all proposed operating agreements, and whether opportunity will be given the public for competitive bidding for the operation of these lands, or whether it is proposed to award a lease or other operating contract or agreement for the entire area to one person, corporation, or association.

Mr. Kendrick. Mr. President, in the subject matter of the resolution there are two questions involved: First, whether there is any present need for the development and operation of the Wyoming naval reserve, known as the Teapot Dome; and, second, if there is such need, whether the interests of the Government would be best preserved by a private or a public sale. I have no doubt that the Department of the Interior and the Department of the Navy have very excellent reasons for any program they may have adopted, and if it is really their intention to permit the operation of the Teapot Dome within the near future, that they have a very good explanation for that intention. I am constrained to believe, however, that the interests of the State of Wyoming and the interests of the people of the United States are so intimately involved in this matter that before any arrangement by contract or otherwise is made for the development of this field, the public should be permitted to have some inkling of the terms upon which it is proposed to act.

It has been announced, apparently on the authority of the Secretary of the Interior, that the policy of the Interior and Navy Departments is now to abandon the storage of oil underground and to store it rather in surface tanks prepared for this purpose on the Atlantic and Pacific coasts. That such a policy would be in all respects a wise and commendable one with respect to the California naval reserves I am ready to agree, if the information which I have received with respect to the condition of those reserves is correct. I am told that oil wells which have been sunk upon private lands within the boundaries of the California reserve would, in a comparatively short time, drain those fields of their contents, and therefore that it is to the interests of the Government to have similar wells drilled upon the land in the same fields which have been reserved for the use of the Navy. But this is not the condition that prevails in the Teapot Dome. There, if I am correctly advised, no wells whatever have been drilled to production, and no wells have been drilled in the vicinity through which by any possibility this reserve could be drained. It would appear, therefore, that there is no danger of the oil in the Teapot Dome being removed until the Government acts. All the land in this field is owned by the Government, and no one may remove the oil until the Secretary of the Interior and the Secretary of the Navy shall consent.

Is it, then, to the interest of the Government to authorize the development of this field at the present time, to pay private operators for drilling the field, to authorize the necessarily heavy expenditures that would have to be met if tanks sufficiently large to store the content of this dome are to be erected, in order that this oil may be taken from its natural storage place to the seaboard? We have just ratified a treaty by which the size of the Navy has been reduced. It is to be presumed, therefore, that unless the use of coal is to be abandoned on our naval vessels, the Navy will have less rather than a greater need for oil in the immediate future. Not only that but the oil fields on the public domain outside of the naval reserve are not now being worked to capacity. The Government derives a royalty of from 12½ per cent to 33⅓ per cent upon all oil removed from the Salt Creek field, which lies immediately north of the Teapot Dome. The Secretary of the Interior is authorized to take this royalty in oil, and in Wyoming he is doing that, but within the past year the drilling requirements of the Government leases in the Salt Creek field have been suspended and the field is producing scarcely more than one-third of its capacity with the present number of wells. It would seem to follow from this that there is no great need for oil at the present time. Of course it may be said that the royalty oil from the lands outside the naval reserve is used by the Shipping Board; but, of course, since the Shipping Board is not using the full amount of the Government oil which could be produced, the difference between what it is using and the capacity of the field, so far as the Government is concerned, could be assigned to the use of the Navy if the Navy needs more oil. I take it, however, that there is no present need for naval fuel oil, because all of the announcements emanating from the Interior Department indicate that if the Teapot Dome is developed its production will be stored for future use. The question, therefore, is simply whether it is wiser and of greater benefit to the Navy to allow this oil to remain stored underground or to remove it across the country to be stored in surface tanks.

If it should appear from the information afforded by the department that it is expedient to develop the Teapot Dome now, there still remains the inquiry whether the interests of the Government would best be preserved by a private or a public sale. There can be no doubt that if these lands are to be let to private interests for development it should only be after all operators have been given a full and complete opportunity by competitive bidding to offer the Government the best possible return.

Only last June approximately 2,000 acres of outside land in the Salt Creek field were sold at public auction under the authority of the Department of the Interior. Although the price of oil at that time was only 50 cents a barrel, the bonuses paid by the operators, who were eager to secure the leases, amounted to the sum of $1,687,000. That the lands in the Teapot Dome are vastly more valuable than these which sold for bonuses of over a million and a half dollars is the general belief of all Wyoming operators, and if these lands were put up at public auction the profit to the Government would be proportionately greater.

SENATE DEBATE OVER LA FOLLETTE RESOLUTION APRIL 28 AND 29, 1922

Congressional Record, 67th Congress, 2nd Session, 6041–47; 6096–97.

Mr. La Follette. Mr. President, on the calendar day of April 21 I submitted a resolution (S. Res. 282) calling upon the Secretary of the Interior for information with regard to the naval oil reserves. When I presented that resolution, sir, I asked that it be printed and that it lie upon the table subject to call. I am not able to call it up this morning, as the unfinished business, the tariff bill, is before the Senate; but I want to give notice now that as soon as I am able to call that resolution before the Senate I am going to avail myself of the right of the introducer of every resolution or bill to perfect it before it is submitted to a vote, and I shall make certain changes in it. As I desire to have those changes appear in the Record in connection with some remarks which I am going to submit at this time upon the resolution, I send to the Secretary's desk the resolution in the form in which, as I am now advised, I shall submit it to the Senate, and ask that it be read.

The Vice President. The Secretary will read the proposed modification of Senate Resolution 282, heretofore submitted by the Senator from Wisconsin.

The reading clerk read as follows:

> *Resolved,* That the Secretary of the Interior is directed to send to the Senate:
>
> (a) Copies of all oil leases made by the Department of the Interior within naval oil reserve No. 1, and, separately, naval oil reserve No. 2, both in the State of California, and naval oil reserve No. 3, in the State of Wyoming, showing as to each the claim upon which the lease was based or issued, the name of the lessee, the date of the lease, the area of the leased property, the amount of the rent royalty,

bonus, and all other compensation paid and to be paid to the United States.

(b) All Executive orders and other papers in the files of the Department of the Interior and its bureaus, or copies thereof if the originals are not in the files, authorizing or regulating such leases, including correspondence or memoranda embodying or concerning all agreements, instructions, and requests by the President or the Navy Department as to the making of such leases and the terms thereof.

(c) All correspondence, papers, and files showing and concerning the applications for such leases and the action of the Department of the Interior and its bureaus thereon and upon all the several claims upon which such leases were based or issued, all in said naval reserves; be it further

Resolved, That the Committee on Public Lands and Surveys be authorized to investigate this entire subject of leases upon naval oil reserves, with particular reference to the protection of the rights and equities of the Government of the United States and the preservation of its natural resources, and to report its findings and recommendations to the Senate.

Mr. La Follette. Mr. President, I wish to submit some observations upon the resolution in the form in which I have modified it this morning.

Mr. Norris. Mr. President—

The Vice President. Does the Senator from Wisconsin yield to the Senator from Nebraska?

Mr. La Follette. I yield.

Mr. Norris. May I inquire of the Senator what was the action of the Senate Committee on Finance as to a duty on petroleum in the tariff bill?

Mr. La Follette. As the Senator will see from an examination of the tariff bill, no duty was placed upon the imports of this product.

I desire especially to refer to the condition in which the country finds itself with regard to the reservations of oil lands made for the protection of the Government in supplying oil as the source of motive power for the modern Navy of to-day.

It will be remembered by Senators that some years ago, beginning with the administration of President Taft, it was decided that oil-burning vessels were likely to displace coal-burning vessels in every navy that sought to keep abreast of the advanced policies of naval construction. As soon as that was understood by our Government, the head of the Navy Department sought information as to whether it would be possible, from the public lands owned by the Government, to supply the oil necessary for the vessels of the Navy. He was informed by the Secretary of the Interior of that time, on the authority of the Geological Survey, that there was an abundance of oil on the public domain. It was then determined that there should be a radical change in all naval construction, and that from that time on we should build oil-burning instead of coal-burning vessels.

As the next step in taking care of the public interests a plan was formulated, and urged upon the President, of withdrawing from sale or entry certain oil-producing lands, as indicated by investigations that had been made by the Geological Survey.

Mr. President, as a result of this understanding between the different departments of the Government certain lands known to contain oil were thereupon withdrawn from sale or public entry and were set apart as Government reservations, known as naval oil reservations Nos. 1 and 2, located in California, and No. 3, located in Wyoming.

It must be confessed, to our humiliation and our shame, that private interests, eager to profit out of the exploitation of any natural resource, at once sought to secure a foothold in these oil reserves that the Government had selected and set apart as a source of supply for the Navy. Under various subterfuges private entries were made upon these lands, and contests were raised as to whether the President had a right to make these reservations for the protection of our Navy, and out of these contests there grew up a controversy which developed into what I might say amounted to a national scandal.

The Navy Department tried to protect the naval reserves. Private interests, great oil companies, intruded upon these reserves, questioned the authority of the Government, through an Executive order by the President, to withdraw them from public entry, and raised technicalities here and there to break down the authority under which the reservations had been made. It is the history of legislation touching this subject that there were men to be found in the Senate of the United States and in the House of Representatives to take the side of the private interests that had invaded these reservations to deprive this Government of the naval reserves that had been thus withdrawn in the public interest.

Mr. Harreld. Mr. President—

The Vice President. Does the Senator from Wisconsin yield to the Senator from Oklahoma?

Mr. La Follette. I yield.

Mr. Harreld. I am not sure that I am right, but my recollection is that the Executive order which set aside these naval reserves provided that they should be controlled by the Secretary of the Navy. I do remember that I called on the Secretary of the Navy once about some proposed leases, and at that time he told me that he had control of the situation. I would like to ask the Senator from Wisconsin how it comes that the Secretary of the Interior is now vested with authority to make these leases?

Mr. La Follette. These naval reserves were under the authority and control of the Secretary of the Navy down to the time when there was a change of administration following the election of 1920.

Some time after the present administration came into control of the Government the public was informed that a movement was on foot to transfer from the Navy Department to the Interior Department the control of the naval oil reserves. The change of policy under the Harding administration goes much further than that. It involves the forests and it involves the coal lands.

I say now, and I sound it as a note of warning to my Republican colleagues, that we can not afford to permit a record to be made here which will parallel the record of Mr. Ballinger, Secretary of the Interior under the Taft administration.

Mr. President, all sorts of looting goes on in a Government as big as ours in spite of anything that can be done to prevent it. The most scandalous gouging of the public by private interests probably occurs during a war period, and the plunderers operate through the War Department. But, sir, in normal peace times the sluiceway for a large part of the corruption to which this Government of ours is subjected is the Department of the Interior. That department has been befouled under all administrations, in greater or less degree, by the corrupting influences which work through it to plunder our great heritage of public lands, of timber, of coal, of iron, of copper, of oil. All of the wealth deposited by the lavish hand of nature in the public domain belongs to the people of this Government, but it is raided by selfish special interests through the Interior Department. . . .

Mr. La Follette. The throwing open of the naval reserves by leasing the lands to oil corporations by this administration came as a distinct shock to the country when it became known a few weeks ago after the transfer of the control of the naval oil reserves to the Interior Department, after they had been handed over by the consent of the Secretary of the Navy to the Secretary of the Interior. Following that the country was startled with the information that practically all the oil in naval reserve No. 1 and naval oil reserve No. 2 in California and naval oil reserve No. 3 in Wyoming had been leased to private interests.

Mr. President, ever watchful of the public interest, the junior Senator from Wyoming [Mr. Kendrick] was the first Member of this body to call attention in a public way to what had been done. I myself had overlooked it, and I have had for many years (very near to my heart) an interest in this branch of the public service. The junior Senator from Wyoming introduced a resolution, calling the attention of the Senate and the country to the leasing of naval reserve No. 3, located in Wyoming, the richest of all the naval reserves. He first informed the public that this lease had been made without open competitive bidding to some favored party.

The Senator from Wyoming promptly demanded information on the subject. He introduced a resolution and made a brief statement on the floor. That brought the matter to my attention. Subsequently I introduced the resolution to which I am now addressing myself.

Mr. President, the policy of 13 years of conserving underground oil in naval oil reserves has been abandoned. The three great naval reserves have recently become private oil reserves.

Within the present month the last of the reserves, and the richest, No. 3, in Wyoming, has been leased in its entirety to one oil corporation. The only possible justification which can be offered for this action by the Interior Department is the one which they have put forward, namely, that these valuable reserves are being depleted by the drilling of wells on adjoining privately owned lands. I shall presently call the attention of the Senate to the opinions of competent authority upon that subject, but for the moment I wish to consider the phases of this situation which led up to the action of the Interior Department.

I was astounded when I learned that the Navy Department had turned the administration of these naval oil reserves over to the Interior Department. It can be said for the present Secretary of the Interior that he has always frankly declared his position on public questions. As a Member of the Senate, his attitude toward the public domain generally, and the naval oil reserves in particular, was well understood during his service as a Member of this body. Upon every measure that involved the conservation of natural resources upon the public lands Senator Fall, from New Mexico, was the aggressive opponent of the policy of conservation as established under Roosevelt and thereafter maintained as a general policy of administration by his successors. His position, as shown by speech and vote while a Member of this body, makes it very plain that he was opposed to strengthening and extending conservation and in favor of weakening and impairing the policy.

During the long fight over the naval oil reserves, which was the subject of sharp contention from time to time on the floor of the Senate, the present Secretary of the Interior, then a Member of the Senate, was not conspicuous as a guardian of naval oil reserves. Everybody familiar with his record will admit that to be true. He voted and spoke against provisions offered to safeguard these valuable reserves.

In view of this record it seems almost unbelievable that the Secretary of the Navy would be willing to turn over to the Secretary of the Interior the administration of the naval oil reserves. Especially is this true when one remembers the strenuous fight which the Navy Department had with the Interior Department during President Wilson's administration to prevent the very disaster which has now occurred. In this connection it is significant to note that every officer of the Navy who had been specially detailed to investigate the naval reserves and who had become especially well informed as to these naval oil reserves and who supported Secretary Daniels in that contest have since the advent of the present administration been ordered to sea or to other parts of the world for duty. I have been informed upon very high naval authority that these changes in personnel detail were made after the present Secretary of the Interior had begun his campaign to secure the transfer of these naval reserves to the Interior Department. In fact, it was after a very stormy interview with the former custodians of the Navy oil that Mr. Fall, Secretary of the Interior, requested the Navy Department to send more "reasonable" officers to represent the Navy in conference with him. These naval officers, equipped and efficient, who had proven their loyalty to the naval reserve, were ordered elsewhere, and others who had not been specially associated with or interested in the former policy of the Navy were named to take their places.

Without access to the records in this case it is somewhat difficult to get at all the facts, but there is sufficient material available to make it plain that the naval reserves are being sacrificed to private exploitation at the hands of favored interests.

On the 28th day of February there was organized under the laws of Delaware the Mammoth Oil Co., with a capital stock of 1,000,000 shares without nominal or par value. The articles of incorporation stated, in article 4, that the actual number of shares with which the corporation commenced business should be 10. The incorporators were T. L. Croteau, of Wilmington, Del., who subscribed for eight shares; M. A. Bruce, of Wilmington, Del., who has one share; C. H. Blaske, of the same place, who also subscribed for one share.

The next record which appears in the files of the secretary of state of Delaware is an amendment to the articles of incorporation of the Mammoth Oil Co., which by this time had blossomed out with a vice president and secretary, who filed the amended articles of incorporation with the secretary of state. They are, respectively, G. C. Wahlberg and H. W. Kenwell. The former appears in the directory of directors of New York City as a director of the Sinclair Central American Oil Corporation.

This amendment increased the authorized shares of capital stock of the Mammoth Oil Co. from 1,000,000 to 2,005,000. There were certain other amendments of the articles of incorporation filed at the same time not material to note at this time.

In passing it may be interesting to observe that this capital stock is divided into two classes—A and B—2,000,000 shares being class A and 5,000 shares constituting class B.

The right to elect directors in this corporation is vested exclusively in the holders of class B stock. This virtually gives these 5,000 shares absolute control of the company.

A conservative estimate of the value of naval reserve No. 3 in Wyoming, known as Teapot Dome, is a half billion dollars. Any Senator with paper and pencil can figure out the value of these 5,000 shares of stock.

At the very time when correspondents of the press were being assured by officials of the Interior Department that no lease of the rich naval reserve No. 3 had been made, a certain gentleman, prominent in oil, racing, and administration circles, published an interview in the New York World in which he asserted that the lease had been made and signed.

Mr. King. That showed that he was swift. He learned to be so in horse racing probably.

Mr. La Follette. Yes. He was very rapid; he was somewhat ahead of the announcement of the Interior Department. This gentleman was none other than Harry Sinclair, of the Sinclair Oil Co.

This lease between the Secretary of the Interior, the Secretary of the Navy, and the Mammoth Oil Co. was signed on April 7, 1922. The fact that this lease had actually been made was not officially admitted until April 21, when its existence was acknowledged in the letter of the Acting Secretary of the Interior and the Secretary of the Navy, in response to Senate resolution of April 15, 1922, introduced by the able and diligent junior Senator from Wyoming [Mr. Kendrick].

During the time between April 7 and 21, when this mystery surrounded the public's business, speculation in Sinclair oil jumped on the New York Exchange in three days' trading over $30,000,000.

Mr. President, if there was a bill before the Senate granting a concession to the Mammoth Oil Co. of naval oil reserve No. 3 in Wyoming, comprising between six and seven thousand acres of the richest oil lands in the United States, worth at least half a billion dollars, the Senate would certainly demand all the facts and details respecting the matter before taking any action upon the bill. It would not accept glittering generalities. It would not be satisfied with the mystery, evasion, and denials that have emanated from the Interior Department for weeks concerning this Mammoth Oil deal. It would not be satisfied with the answers to the resolution of the Senator from Wyoming that duck and dodge the facts in the case. Would not some Members of the Senate want to know who were the real organizers of the Mammoth Oil Co. who were to be favored by the Government with a special privilege in value beyond the dreams of Croesus? Would they not want to know something specific about Mr. Harry F. Sinclair and his associates, to whom it was proposed to transfer this naval oil reserve?

If the lease of No. 3 is as loosely drawn as the one given to other favored companies on the naval reserves in California, copies of which have recently come into my possession, I would want to bring certain provisions of it to the attention of the Senate. In any event the Congress of the United States and the public should have all the facts and information regarding the reversal of a great national policy and the surrender of our naval oil reserves, which may involve the Nation's safety, to say nothing of the question which is raised here of granting to favored individuals public properties worth hundreds of millions of dollars which belong to the people.

I shall confine my remarks to-day to naval reserve No. 3; sometimes called the Teapot Dome, because this is the reserve which has been thrown open to private exploitation most recently. Later on I shall have something to say concerning the department's handling of naval oil reserves 1 and 2 in California.

The only possible defense which the Interior Department can make for leasing the No. 3 reserve is that it is being drained by drilling in the adjoining privately owned Salt Creek field. No other valid reason can be advanced, and some reason of paramount importance for the action taken will have to be proven before the public will accept this reversal of an approved Government policy which has been in force for nearly 13 years.

Mr. Hitchcock. Mr. President, will the Senator yield to me?

The Vice President. Does the Senator from Wisconsin yield to the Senator from Nebraska?

Mr. La Follette. I do.

Mr. Hitchcock. The Senator is making some amazing revelations, and I think that most of the Members of the Senate are not aware of that fact. Will he yield to me in order that I may suggest the absence of a quorum?

Mr. La Follette. I yield to the Senator from Nebraska.

Mr. Hitchcock. Mr. President, I suggest the absence of a quorum.

The Vice President. The Secretary will call the roll. . . .

The Vice President. Fifty-five Senators have answered to their names. A quorum is present.

Mr. La Follette. Mr. President, I repeat that the only possible defense which the Interior Department can make for leasing the No. 3 reserve in Wyoming is that it is being drained by drilling in the adjoining privately owned Salt Creek field. . . .

Mr. La Follette. . . . The excuse that the naval reserve is in danger of depletion by draining into private wells on contiguous lands is as old as the date of its withdrawal. It has ever been the specious plea upon which those desiring to exploit this rich field have based their efforts to secure access to it. But even if the weight of scientific opinion were not against the contention that this field can be drained by outside drilling there is a definite way in which the Government can protect itself against such a ruthless system of pillage. It does not have to surrender to the burglars. The oil in these reserves, under the decision of the Supreme Court of the United States, belongs to the Government. Private interests threaten to draw that oil off by sinking wells on adjoining territory. The policy of the present Secretary of the Interior is to surrender to these pillaging interests. . . .

But, Mr. President, there is a deeper underlying issue involved here than our national safety or the protection of the mere property rights and equities of our Government. It is true that over an unbroken period of more than a decade three Presidents—Roosevelt, Taft, and Wilson—maintained the policy of conservation in respect to the natural resources of the public domain, which has now been repudiated and reversed during the first year of the administration of President Harding. It is true that Admiral George Dewey, as president of the General Board of the Navy, more than a dozen years ago, declared the necessity of an ample oil supply for the Navy, and that Thomas A. Edison, probably the greatest creative technical mind of American history, as chairman of the Naval Consulting Board in 1916, gave his assent to the policy which has now been overthrown. It is true that every competent authority that has written upon the subject in recent years has named oil as the natural resource upon which the industrial and naval strength of the future must depend, and, because of the prodigal waste of our oil resources under the present system of exploitation, that the supply which should have lasted us for a century to come will be exhausted within a brief span of years. . . .

I propose to press this resolution for prompt passage, and I invite Senators upon both sides of the aisle to examine its provisions, and, if they may conscientiously do so, to give it their support. No matter whom it hits or hurts, let us have the facts. The American people will be satisfied with nothing less. . . .

Mr. Smoot. I really have not read the resolution. I would like to have it go over until to-morrow at least, so that I can read it.

Mr. La Follette. All there is of the resolution is that it calls for an investigation with regard to this matter. There are no preambles to the resolution. The Senator can not be ignorant of the fact that we have these reserves. He can not be ignorant of the fact that the public press has carried the announcement of their lease to private interests. I am simply asking for an investigation into the truth of this whole matter.

Mr. Smoot. I may have no objection to it at all when I have an opportunity to read it, but I really want to have it go over so that I can look into it.

Mr. Poindexter. Mr. President, I think that if a request is made for the adoption of the resolution at an early date, it will be adopted.

I may say in connection with the remarks of the Senator from Wisconsin that, of course, it is perfectly obvious that whatever he may say or whatever he may do to preserve the naval oil reserves to the best possible advantage of the Government is in the interest of the public and of the naval service and should have the commendation and support of Congress and the country. . . .

I assert that these propositions are established beyond dispute, and I rely upon unimpeachable authority for that statement. Yet these facts are not the basic fundamental elements involved in this problem after all.

The great issue involved here is whether the Congress of the United States, charged with solemn responsibility under the Constitution as trustees of the public domain, is to take the necessary steps to protect the people of this country from the extension of monopoly control over their natural resources.

The trail of corruption left by the oil monopoly in the pages of American history is not calculated to inspire the confidence of the people in any transaction to which the agents of that monopoly are parties.

Dominated by the Standard Oil Co., the oil monopoly has been the boldest, the most brazen, the most aggressive violator of the law with which any legislative body has ever had to contend. It has forced people all over this country out of business, crushed competition, and driven competitors in many instances to suicide. It has had on its pay rolls the employees of its competitors, who have sold to it the secrets of those competitors.

There are volumes of evidence taken by congressional committees to which I can cite the Senate in support of every statement I make. The oil monopolists have, in a word, corrupted Government servants, ruthlessly seized and exploited the natural resources which Nature gave to man, and systematically robbed the people through extortionate prices. They could not have done that if they did not have servants on this floor and on the floor of the other branch of Congress and in the Cabinets of every administration.

Under the leases which are the subject of the resolutions offered by the Senator from Wyoming and myself, the oil monopolists of the United States have now taken within their grasp the three remaining naval oil reserves of the United States. The great special interests, which are the beneficiaries of these leases, will inevitably withdraw the oil which belongs to the people and sell it back to the Government for its naval vessels at extortionate prices. Not only will oils to the value of hundreds of millions of dollars be lost to the Government, but the oil monopolist will exact his toll whenever the Congress passes an appropriation bill making public money available for the maintenance of the Navy. Moreover, with an increasingly profitable customer, such as the United States Government, bidding against other consumers of oil, the Standard Oil Trust and its allies will find a ready excuse to increase further the already unreasonable prices exacted from the general public.

That is what this conspiracy amounts to, sir. It not only appropriates for private gain the rich natural wealth which the Government holds in trust for the people, but it reaches out and enables the special interests behind this scheme to tighten their grip upon the farmer, the business man, and upon every person who runs a gasoline engine, and upon every family that enjoys the use of an automobile.

I believe I have produced this afternoon the outline of enough evidence to suggest to the minds of Senators that the rights of the Government and the interests of the people are imperiled in these transactions, which involve hundreds of millions of dollars in public property. Congress can not escape its responsibility in this matter. The Ballinger-Pinchot investigation a decade ago, which broke the back of the Taft administration, did not proceed upon more damning evidence that public interests were being violated than is ready at hand at this time bearing upon the leasing of these naval oil reserves.

By that earlier investigation Congress discharged its obligations to the people and set up a precedent, supported by public opinion, which has had a salutary influence upon every administration since then down to the present time.

Congress in the present instance must either call for an investigation which will unearth all the facts, or, by its silence, it must share its responsibility with the executive branch for what has already transpired. There is no escape from that alternative.

The able Senator from Wyoming [Mr. Kendrick] took the initiative in this matter and by his resolution focused upon it the attention of the public. For that action he deserves the gratitude of the country.

I propose to support and sustain him in the stand he has taken. This is not a partisan question. Men of both parties in the Navy and in the Interior Departments in previous administrations have worked together to preserve the public interests and to protect the rights of the Government in these lands. The resolution I have introduced offers Congress the opportunity to ascertain the truth regarding these leases and to perform its duty to the public. . . .

The Vice President. The Senator from Wisconsin asks unanimous consent for the present consideration of Senate Resolution 282, as modified by him. The Secretary will read the resolution, as modified, for the information of the Senate.

The reading clerk read Senate Resolution 282, which had been submitted by Mr. La Follette on April 21, as modified, as follows:

Resolved, That the Secretary of the Interior is directed to send to the Senate:

(a) Copies of all oil leases made by the Department of the Interior within naval oil reserve No. 1, and, separately, naval oil reserve No. 2, both in the State of California, and naval oil reserve No. 3, in the State of Wyoming, showing as to each the claim upon which the lease was based or issued; the name of the lessee; the date of the lease; the area of the leased property; the amount of the rent, royalty, bonus, and all other compensation paid and to be paid to the United States.

(b) All Executive orders and other papers in the files of the Department of the Interior and its bureaus, or copies thereof if the originals are not in the files, authorizing or regulating such leases, including correspondence or memoranda embodying or concerning all agreements, instructions, and requests by the President or the Navy Department as to the making of such leases and the terms thereof.

(c) All correspondence, papers, and files showing and concerning the applications of such leases and the action of the Department of the Interior and its bureaus thereon and upon all the several claims upon which such leases were based or issued, all in said naval reserves.

Resolved further, That the Committee on Public Lands and Surveys be authorized to investigate this entire subject of leases upon naval oil reserves, with particular reference to the protection of the rights and equities of the Government of the United States and the preservation of its natural resources, and to report its findings and recommendations to the Senate.

The Vice President. Is there objection to the immediate consideration of the resolution?

Mr. Smoot. I have no objection at all to the immediate consideration of the resolution, but I wish to call the attention of the Senator from Wisconsin to the fact that there is no provision made in the resolution for the expenses of carrying on the investigation provided for therein if such investigation shall prove to be extensive. I will say, however, to the Senator from Wisconsin that if there should develop any necessity for an appropriation for that purpose we can ask for it at the time when that becomes apparent.

Mr. La Follette. That had already occurred to me, Mr. President. I should like to have present consideration of the resolution if I can get it.

Mr. McCumber. Mr. President——

The Vice President. Does the Senator from Wisconsin yield to the Senator from North Dakota?

Mr. La Follette. I do.

Mr. McCumber. With the understanding that the consideration of the resolution will not lead to any prolonged debate, I have no objection.

Mr. La Follette. I have no desire to extend the debate at all. I am ready for a vote on the resolution at this time.

The Vice President. Is there objection to the immediate consideration of the resolution?

There being no objection, the Senate proceeded to consider the resolution.

The Vice President. The question is on agreeing to the resolution as modified.

Mr. Poindexter. Mr. President, I suggest to the Senator from Wisconsin that, so long as a report is being called for by the resolution on the general subject of naval oil reserves, the resolution might be made somewhat more comprehensive, and ask for a report at the same time upon the contracts for the drilling of oil wells on naval oil reserves, aside from the question of leasing, and the reasons for such contracts; also for a report on the question of the drilling of oil wells on private property adjacent to the naval oil reserves, the number of such wells, and the date when they were drilled. If the Senator from Wisconsin has no objection, I suggest the addition of a subparagraph to read as follows:

(d) And all contracts for drilling wells on naval oil reserves, date and terms of same, reasons therefor, and the number and date of the drilling of wells on private lands adjacent to the naval oil reserves.

Mr. La Follette. I have no objection to such an amendment, Mr. President.

Mr. Poindexter. I offer that amendment to the resolution.

Mr. La Follette. Indeed, I am in favor of broadening the scope of the investigation which is proposed by the resolution to include everything that touches the subject and is material to it.

Mr. Townsend. Mr. President, may I ask whether or not the department would have any information that it could submit to the Senate relative to wells drilled on private property?

Mr. Poindexter. Undoubtedly the department must have such information, since that is the reason assigned for the drilling of wells on the Government property.

Mr. La Follette. If I may be permitted, I will suggest that if the Government is not in the possession of information with respect to that matter, under the resolution, which authorizes the Committee on Public Lands and Surveys to conduct an investigation, the committee would be able to secure such information.

Mr. Townsend. I concede that may be true, but I can understand that possibly the department may have no information relative to such drilling.

Mr. Poindexter. Of course, if the department has no information, it will report that fact. I wish to explain the purpose of my amendment. Entirely outside of the question of the leasing of Government land, in California wells were sunk by private parties adjacent to naval oil reserves; and it was obvious that through those wells the Government supply of oil was being drained off. The only way of meeting that contingency that has been suggested was to drill corresponding wells upon Government land in order to draw from this common pool of underground oil at the same time and in a somewhat similar quantity.

Mr. Nelson rose.

Mr. Poindexter. Just one second. So the Government did proceed to call for the contracts for the drilling of the wells on the Government property because of the fact that wells were being sunk upon private property. Of course, the Government knew about it; the whole proceeding was based upon that knowledge, and I should like to know just what the circumstances are.

Mr. Townsend. I have no objection to securing any information that can be obtained. I was merely wondering if we were asking for something over which the department had no jurisdiction. I concede, of course, that under the authority given by the resolution to conduct an investigation the committee may look into all of these questions.

Mr. Nelson. Mr. President, I simply rose to state that a report has already been submitted by the department concerning this matter, and that report indicates that the Government has considered the question of the oil being drained from Government lands by operations on adjoining private lands. The Government evidently has that information now, and no doubt a report on the subject can be secured.

Mr. La Follette. Mr. President, I ask for a yea-and-nay vote on agreeing to the resolution.

Mr. Poindexter. Mr. President, I should like to know whether the amendment has been agreed to.

Mr. La Follette. I accept the amendment, and I ask to have it stated at the desk, so that it may be clearly understood.

The Vice President. The Secretary will state the amendment.

The Reading Clerk. In the resolution as modified, on page 2, after line 14, it is proposed to insert:

(d) And all contracts for drilling wells on naval oil reserves, date
and terms of same, reasons therefor, and the number and date of the
drilling of wells on private lands adjacent to oil reserves.

The Vice President. The question is on the amendment offered by the Senator from Washington.

The amendment was agreed to.

The Vice President. The question now is on agreeing to the modified resolution as amended, on which question the Senator from Wisconsin has requested the yeas and nays.

The years and nays were ordered, and the reading clerk proceeded to call the roll . . .

TESTIMONY OF ALBERT FALL OCTOBER 24, 1923

U.S. Senate, Leases Upon Naval Oil Reserves, Hearings Before the Committee on Public Lands and Surveys, 68th Congress, 1st Session, Vol. 1, 270–75.

. . . Senator Walsh. Well, what objection was there, if there was any objection, to giving to the public immediately upon the execution of this contract information that the contract was, in fact, executed, inasmuch as the public would necessarily know as soon as Mr. Sinclair began work that he had the lease?

Mr. Fall. Certainly no sinister purpose could have been served by it.

Senator Walsh. Was there any purpose not sinister?

Mr. Fall. Now, you are going into the policy which I had in mind with reference to this thing. I have undertaken to explain that I regarded myself as a business agent of the Secretary of the Navy, acting in what I regarded as a military matter under the President of the United States. I did not propose, so far as I was concerned, to call attention to the fact that contracts providing for enormous storages for future use in a crisis of oil were being made off the coast or in certain parts of this country. That was what I had in the back of my head. If that information should be given out through publicity of the contracts, it must be by the parties who were interested in it more than I was. I did not suggest it to them. It was up to them. I had my own ideas.

Senator Walsh. I did not speak about the matter of the details of the contract. All I inquired about was what objection there was, if any, to making public a statement to the effect that a lease of the Teapot Dome had been executed to Mr. Sinclair and his interests.

Mr. Fall. I think that was pretty well known, or else these inquiries as to the contract, where it was and what was being done about it, causing a Cabinet meeting during my absence, as I understand it, would not have occurred.

Senator Walsh. But that information was given on April 21 by Mr. Finney.

Mr. Fall. After a consultation and after he had wired me. The Secretary of the Navy had stated that after a Cabinet meeting it had been decided, in view of the talk about it, to give out the contract. I wired to Secretary Finney that we had no objection. It was the Navy's business.

Senator Walsh. Well, you, of course, would anticipate, Mr. Secretary, that all sorts of rumors concerning the existence or the nonexistence of a contract of that importance would be floating around immediately after its execution?

Mr. Fall. I do not know that I had anticipated it. Possibly I should have done so.

Senator Walsh. Well, I am told, and possibly we will have some evidence upon that point, that during the time between April 7, when it was executed, and April 21, when it was made public, transactions in Sinclair oil stock on the New York market amounted to thirty million.

Mr. Fall. I do not know. I have heard that rumor and it was so stated in the records of the United States Senate. I immediately caused an investigation to be made and I found that practically all oil stocks had gone up at that time, many of them much more than the Sinclair stocks.

The Chairman. None of them has dropped so rapidly, though?

Mr. Fall. No; I think not. A short time ago through a friend of mine, who repeated it to me, I heard of a party who came from Mexico, a straightforward, honest man, my friend told me, who stated that, as a matter of information, he thought he would enjoy it because it affected my good fortune in that I had made a great deal of money in this oil stock. I want to say that I never bought or owned one dollar of oil stock in my life, directly or indirectly. I never owned an interest in an oil well in my life, and I was never in the employ of an oil company in my life as a lawyer. Now, I had not intended giving way to anything.

Senator Walsh. I intended speaking about that a little later, Senator. The newspapers say you have been during the past summer in Russia with Mr. Sinclair.

Mr. Fall. Yes, sir.

Senator Walsh. How long did you travel with him?

Mr. Fall. I was in Russia and in Europe approximately two or three months.

Senator Walsh. Did you start from this country together, or did you meet on the other side?

Mr. Fall. We met on the other side.

Senator Walsh. Where?

Mr. Fall. In London.

Senator Walsh. And were there any business relations existing between you and Mr. Sinclair in connection with the trip?

Mr. Fall. None, except of this character: Mr. Sinclair informed me about the time that I left Washington at the close of my administration in the department that he had a contract with the Chita Government in Russia for the development of oil on the island of Sakhalin; that he regarded it as a very important matter, and that if I had time after I went out of office he would like to consult me about it. I said "Very well." He said it might possibly mean a trip to Japan. I said, "Well, I am going to be out of any kind of office and I am not going to make any business connections of any kind until I attend to my own private business, and I might enjoy a trip to Japan." I was at my ranch in the latter part of May, and very busily engaged when I had a telegram from Mr. Sinclair, asking me if I could come to New York immediately prepared possibly to go to Europe. I wired him at once that I could not, and I said, "What are you talking about? What do you want? Wire me fully." Instead of wiring me fully, he said it was with reference to the country we had discussed, this contract with the Chita Government. I know something about foreign affairs and keep pretty thoroughly posted, and I had been very much interested in oil development before I went out of office. I was very anxious, pursuant to what I understood to be the policy of this Government, to see American citizens secure oil supplies abroad for the future use of the Navy and the shipping of the United States, and I was more than glad to be of any assistance, if possible, in the matter of securing or assisting in securing contracts for American investors for oil abroad.

So I then cheerfully said I would go. When I received that telegram I wired him that I could leave for a consultation with him within a few days. He replied by wire—I am just repeating the substance; I do not remember the text of the telegram, which was open and uncoded, that he was going to be compelled to leave for London and that after I reached New York the documents would be submitted to me and he hoped I could come at least as far as London. When I reached New York I found two telegrams, one to and one from Mr. Krassin, the commercial agent of the Russian Government. They were not signed by Mr. Sinclair. The telegrams were not to or from Mr. Sinclair, but one of the signers was one of the very prominent bankers of New York. I was informed that in addition to the discussion of the Sakhalin matter a new proposition, such as was incidentally referred to in both telegrams from Krassin and to Krassin was under consideration, and that certain parties were along with Mr. Sinclair and were very anxious to have a consultation with me, but upon some subject of the prospects of securing contracts for the development of vastly larger oil fields in Russia. Now, this a private business matter that I do not think should be of material interest in this investigation, but to clear up the situation, as you suggested, I am giving it to you as far as I can without betraying any confidence as an attorney. When I arrived there I found they were the presidents of two very important banks—

The Chairman. That was at London?

Mr. Fall. At London—and the general attorney and the president of another large independent oil company of the United States which had a contract in the Baku fields with the Russian Government. Mr. Sinclair and his attorney, Mr. Stanford, I think his name was, discussed the matter with me generally as to what they proposed to do. The Russian Government had made certain propositions to some one who had gotten in communication with Sinclair and these bankers or with the bankers and through the bankers with Sinclair with reference to the handling of certain oil business for the Russian Soviet Government. The matter was discussed with me, and I was asked for my advice concerning it. I gave it. Now, do you want to know what that advice was? If so, I have no hesitation in giving it, although I am not going to mention names of parties, but my advice was that they should under no circumstances take possession of or utilize, no matter under what favorable conditions, any property in Russia which had been confiscated from any foreign holder, and that no American company with my advice would secure any advantage by a contract with the Soviet Government in the handling of property the investment to develop which had been made in good faith during former administration by Swedish or other citizens. That was my advice to him.

Mr. Krassin thought that possibly the matter could be arranged in a satisfactory way. This government, as I understand, has been demanding of the Russian Government that it recognize its responsibility for the recompensing to our citizens and to others for property which has been nationalized or confiscated. They have declined to do so. They have declined as I understand to recognize their foreign debts. That has been the cause of the failure of other Governments to recognize the Soviet Government of Russia, or is at least very largely the reason. I was informed that that was the attitude of this Government; I knew it was the attitude of this Government. I made the statement just as I have made it to you, to Mr. Tcherin, Minister of Foreign Affairs of Russia, and I made it to Mr. Barakof, Chairman of Concessions of Russia, that any people acting under my advice or with whom I might be in any way connected should never get into a contract as they were proposing because it would involve the turning over of large amounts of property which had been developed under the laws of Russia at the time of development by Swedish and other nationals, but largely Swedish. And I thought no American ought to do that.

So, gentlemen, when the proposed contract was drafted I myself wrote into it "The Russian Government recognizes its responsibility for the recompensing of all former owners in properties which might be involved in this contract." But that was not signed.

Now, Senator Walsh, as to my being in Mr. Sinclair's employ. I went there, as I say, to consult with him about the Sakhalin contract, and then this other matter was brought up. This was a syndicate matter and not Mr. Sinclair's personal matter. He was called into it as I understood by some bankers because he was an oil man, and I suppose considered informed, and would have been the operating man, as I was told later if the contract had been made.

I do not know what the business end of it would have been, but that was as far as Mr. Sinclair was connected with it. My understanding was—and it was stated to me by all parties—that Mr. Sinclair and his associates would have a one-sixth interest in the syndicate. I went there and advised Mr. Sinclair, but, contrary to my advice, he authorized the signing of the Sakhalin contract. I advised him not to do it. My reason for that I will state to you.

Senator Walsh. I have no objection.

Mr. Fall. The Sakhalin contract provided, among other things—well, you understand that it did not involve the use of confiscated property. It was raw territory. They had a perfect right to make it. But it involved a clause to this effect: That in event—these are business matters; under no other circumstances, of course, would I give publicity to such a matter, but this, I think, can not do any harm—that in event that the Government was not recognized by this Government within five years from the date of the contract that they would forfeit the contract entirely. I advised Mr. Sinclair not to sign any such contract at all, to have nothing to do with it; that it would embarrass any administration of this Government, because if they were later recognized in any way some one who happened to be an enemy of the then administration would say they had done it because Sinclair or some other American had a favorable contract.

Senator Walsh. Senator, the only thing I am interested in and the only thing I inquired about was, Under whose employment did you go to Europe?

Mr. Fall. Not under any terms of employment at all. My expenses were paid by the syndicate—$10,000.

Senator Walsh. Did you get any compensation at all?

Mr. Fall. I have never even suggested any compensation and have received none.

Senator Walsh. You went at the instance of Mr. Sinclair.

Mr. Fall. Oh, yes. I went to New York at his instance, and then this matter was presented to me there and I went to London at his expense. And then I went farther—to Russia—not at his expense, but at the request of the other gentlemen who accompanied us and at the very pressing request of an official of the Russian Government.

Senator Walsh. You had no personal pecuniary interest in the transaction?

Mr. Fall. No.

Senator Walsh. Would you have us to understand that this was a service which took you some months and yet was perfectly gratuitous on your part?

Mr. Fall. In event they had gone ahead successfully I would then have undoubtedly suggested to these gentlemen that I receive some compensation.

Senator Walsh. I would naturally have thought so.

Mr. Fall. And I should have placed it at a figure that would have recompensed me.

Senator Lenroot. You have had no other business relations with Mr. Sinclair since that time other than that?

Mr. Fall. No.

Senator Walsh. While we are on that subject, Senator Fall, and just to clear it up, let me ask: It has also been stated that you were under some employment, or have been, from the Doheny interests.

Mr. Fall. That is incorrect. I have been advising Mr. Doheny recently in California with reference to some other important matter, of which I think our Government is informed, but without any compensation at all.

Senator Walsh, I am going into business. I am going to capitalize as well as I can my limited ability during the remaining years of my life. I reserve to myself the right to seek or to accept employment from Mr. Doheny or Mr. Sinclair or anyone else. I have absolutely declined to make any connection with anyone at this time. I so stated when I went out of office, that for at least six months I would not consider any character of employment; that I would need that time to take care of my own private business at my home, to get it in order. You must know from your own experience that it becomes disorganized after a good many years in the public service.

Senator Walsh. I have no doubt of it.

Mr. Fall. That was my purpose. This matter of Mr. Doheny's is a matter in which I am supposed to be peculiarly well informed. It was almost in the nature—not of negotiations with a foreign Government, but of assisting in arranging certain difficulties which are coming up, through my knowledge of the laws of that country and its people. And it was most cheerfully given my assistance.

Now, I want to say to you that I may later on form some connection with the Doheny interests, the Sinclair interests, some of the coal interests of the United States, or the transport interests of some large municipality in the

United States, with some syndicate which owns railroads and is proposing to operate very largely in certain countries on this continent.

Offers of that kind have been made, but none of them has been accepted, and I have declined to even consider them at the present time. . . .

"THE TALE OF THE TEAPOT"
BY WILLIAM HARD
NOVEMBER 21, 1923

The Nation, Vol. 117, No. 3046 (November 21, 1923), 575–77.

Now that the first senatorial hearings on the Teapot Dome Naval Oil Reserve affair have been completed, and now that all the star witnesses have shed their full if not their final rays upon the subject, it becomes possible for the first time to tell in assured detail and in coherent sequence the total story of the policy and behavior of the United States Government in the management of its naval oil estate, called the Teapot Dome, in Wyoming.

The first character in the story is President Roosevelt. He gave support and prestige to the policy of the conservation of oil in the ground for the use of the government at some future time when the customary commercial supplies of oil might be insufficient and when some great impending national emergency might demand a governmentally reserved and controlled abundant source of fuel for our fighting ships.

The second character in the story is President Wilson. Out of the Federal public domain in Wyoming he set aside for exclusively naval purposes a reserve called commonly the Teapot Dome and called technically Naval Oil Reserve Number Three.

The third character is Secretary of the Navy Josephus Daniels. He stood resolutely on the rights of the United States Government in Naval Oil Reserve Number Three and also in all of our other naval oil reserves, totaling five; and he refused to budge from those rights, when attacked by private citizens urging private claims upon naval oil-reserve lands. Under him the policy of the Navy Department was to resist private claims by every possible resource of administrative action in the government departments and by every possible resource of legal defense in the courts. Under him, at one time, when a certain other member of the Cabinet proposed to make a surrender of naval oil land to a private claimant without a fight, President Wilson told that other Cabinet member that any such behavior on his part would mean his resignation.

The stage thus having been set and the preliminary dialogue having thus been delivered, the fourth and final great character of the play was ready to make his entrance. This character is Albert B. Fall. Mr. Fall, as a Senator of the United States, had evidenced a great interest in conservation. His interest in it was that he disapproved of it. It was his view that the public domain of the United States should go as rapidly as possible into private hands.

Mr. Fall's first feat as Secretary of the Interior was to provide the State Department and the chairman of the Foreign Relations Committee of the United States Senate with the oil-exploitation motives and arguments which led to the ratification of our $25,000,000 treaty with Colombia. Mr. Fall, as a Senator of the United States, had taken the position that the United States owed nothing to Colombia for any alleged violation of the national rights of Colombia in the matter of the setting up of the Republic of Panama in the days of President Roosevelt. Mr. Fall, as a Senator of the United States, had sided with the memory of Theodore Roosevelt against the claim of Colombia. As Secretary of the Interior, however, he perceived before him a divided duty. On the one hand there was the memory of Theodore Roosevelt which he had defended. On the other hand there was the opportunity on behalf of American oil interests to get from Colombia a new and open era of oil concessions. Mr. Fall chose oil.

He sent to the United States Senate a document in which the oil holdings of British oil companies in Colombia were listed; and in this document it was erroneously alleged that these holdings were holdings of the British Government; and on that argument, and in the openly admitted hope that for $25,000,000 out of the public treasury of the United States the Colombian Government would give oil concessions to the oil companies of the United States, the Colombia Treaty was passed.

Having thus demonstrated his willingness, at any cost to what he had once regarded as national honor, to secure oil concessions for oil companies, Mr. Fall was then picked out by Secretary of the Navy Denby to be made the managing master of the navy's oil reserves with this country. Known to be an anti-conservationist, and known to have been willing to take $25,000,000 out of the United States treasury to buy an entrance for American oil companies into the public domain of Colombia, he was made the supervisor of the navy's public domain in the United States.

This honor, however, was not heaped upon him by its own spontaneous gravitation toward him. He sought it. He wrote the order transferring the control of the naval oil reserves from the Navy Department to the Department of the Interior. He composed a letter for the Secretary of the Navy to sign, transmitting that order to the President to be signed.

Admiral Griffin, chief of the Navy Department's Bureau of Engineering, in charge of the naval oil reserves, objected to the transfer. Commander Stewart, in immediate management of the reserves, objected. No naval officer technically familiar with the naval oil-reserve situation is reported to have concurred in the transfer. Nevertheless Mr. Denby, choosing between the proved advice of his technically experienced officers and the proved passion of Mr. Fall for getting public lands into private hands, transmitted the order for the transfer on Mr. Fall's behalf to President Harding, who signed it on May 3, 1921.

Approximately one year later, on April 7, 1922, Mr. Fall leased the Teapot Dome Naval Oil Reserve to Mr. Harry Sinclair. For two weeks thereafter he made no announcement of his action. He then announced it only in reply to an urgent communication to him from Senator Kendrick of Wyoming who had heard rumors of such an action and who wished to know if those rumors were correct.

Mr. Fall, admitting that they were correct, lifted for the first time the curtain of secrecy behind which his action had been consummated. It then simultaneously appeared that the lease, besides being secret, had been non-competitive. No bids by others than Mr. Sinclair were disclosed. *Mr. Sinclair, by himself, and in the dark, on his merits as oil man, as campaign contributor, as friend, and as hospitable owner of a private car suitable for personal conferences, had become the sudden owner of the total right to drill oil-wells over the whole of the Teapot Dome.*

Then, after the event, came the setting forward of the alleged reason for it. This reason was, and is, that oil is said to be leaking out of the Teapot Dome Naval Oil Reserve into wells located on other federally owned public land just outside the Reserve. The Department of the Interior had granted the permits for the drilling of those wells. It itself had permitted and procured the activities responsible for the draining of oil out of the navy's reserved oil supply. It itself had authorized this indirect and partial loss of that supply. Its contention thereupon was, and is, that the loss should become direct and total.

Geological testimony adduced before the Public Lands Committee of the Senate in the course of its Teapot Dome hearings has been strongly to the effect that straight across the Teapot Dome there is a "fault" which protects a certain considerable part of it from leakage. The leakage from the remaining part of it was alleged by geological testimony to be likely to be perhaps not more than 25 per cent. It was convincingly demonstrated that there was a strong technical possibility that if the total oil content of the Teapot Dome is 25,000,000 barrels, then not more than 4,000,000 barrels of it was in danger of flowing away into the private wells on the adjoining public domain.

It now appears that from the wells which on adjacent public domain are draining oil out of the Teapot Dome the government gets royalties averaging from 25 to 50 per cent of the flow, whereas from the wells which Mr. Sinclair has sunk in the Teapot Dome itself the government is getting royalties averaging less than 20 per cent. From the standpoint of income in oil for the government it thus appears that the government was better off when the oil was coming to the surface in the wells which were called a "menace" to the Teapot Dome than it is now when the oil is coming to the surface within the Teapot Dome in Mr. Sinclair's wells.

It further appears that perhaps two-thirds of the oil which Mr. Sinclair will pay to the government in royalties will not remain in the possession of the navy in the form of oil. Perhaps two-thirds of it will be paid back to Mr. Sinclair by the navy for some tanks in which to keep the remaining one-third of it.

It has been customary for the Navy Department, when it feels in need of tanks or of guns or of battleships or of money with which to pay its employees, to ask Congress for it. It has also been customary to believe that when the people of the United States gave the Navy Department a lot of oil in the ground of the public domain, it gave it to the Navy Department to be a supply of oil and not to be a means by which it could purchase other supplies without going to Congress for authorization.

Under Mr. Fall's influence, however, the Navy Department proceeded to sign contracts for the building not only of tanks but also of docks and of channels leading to the docks on the basis of paying for these things with oil out of naval oil reserves. Thus not only was this oil taken out of the ground, where President Roosevelt had wished it to be left, but, having been taken out, a large part of it was spent, or will be spent, in acquiring things other than oil and in escaping the customary legalistic squeamish necessity of going to Congress for the people's consent to naval expenditures.

If in the Teapot Dome there were originally 25,000,000 barrels of oil, and if Mr. Sinclair now gets all of it out, the government, at the present running rate of royalties, will get—at the most—5,000,000 barrels. Of this 5,000,000 barrels, at the present running cost of materials, it will pay back to Mr. Sinclair some 3,333,000 barrels for tanks. It then in those tanks will have the residuum of its Teapot Dome inheritance—namely, some 1,666,000 barrels of oil out of an original total of 25,000,000; and it will have it not in the ground, where it would be totally safe to be used at some future time in the forms which that future time with new technical developments might unfold and require, but in metal containers in seashore positions and in manufactured forms and qualities which the technique of this passing and changing moment has fixed.

Either this result is an absurdity or else President Roosevelt, with his policy of naval oil conservation, was an idiot.

Theodore Roosevelt, Jr., Assistant Secretary of the Navy, did not make the decisions which have brought his father's naval oil policy to frustration, nor did he have knowledge of them while they were being made.

The Roosevelt naval oil conservation policy is dead, and the final stab given to it was by the same man who stabbed the Roosevelt justification of the Roosevelt Panama policy to the heart in the Colombian Treaty.

Senator Walsh of Montana, a member of the Senate's Public Lands Committee, a man of the deepest learning: a man of the highest personal probity, a man who morally is not capable of deception and who mentally is not capable of self-deception, has taken the leading part in the toilsome task of eliciting the pivotal facts from the chaos of the bewildering situation presented in testimony to the committee; and he has seemed to be moved toward entertaining the belief that possibly the contract leasing the Teapot Dome to Mr. Sinclair is illegal in that there was no competitor bidding for it and in that it includes provisions for the purchase of naval supplies—namely, tanks—not with money from Congress but with oil which already was naval property and which was not negotiable.

Meanwhile, however, Mr. Sinclair has long been at work drilling the Teapot Dome and draining oil from it; and Mr. Fall, having retired from office, has entered the employ of Mr. Sinclair and has visited Russia to induce the Russian Government to allow Mr. Sinclair to drain oil from the Russian public domain in Sakhalin.

Thus Mr. Fall departs from the story, carrying with him his well-known fear of a British world-wide monopoly in oil and having done something to exhaust our government's reserved supply of oil in its own country and having done nothing to acquire for it any other reserved supply; and if ever this country comes to be without oil while in Latin America north or south of Panama there still are undrained reservoirs of it, the ultimate chapter of our abandonment of our naval oil conservation policy will be written.

It will be written in intrigues and aggressions, diplomatic or military or both, to acquire abroad the naval fuel security which was ours for the keeping at home.

TESTIMONY OF CARL C. MAGEE
NOVEMBER 30, 1923

U.S. Senate, Leases Upon Naval Oil Reserves, Hearings Before the
Committee on Public Lands and Surveys, 68th Congress, 1st Session, Vol. 1, 830–35; 840–41.

Senator Walsh. Give us your full name.

Mr. Magee. Carl C. Magee, Albuquerque, N. Mex.

Senator Walsh. Are you in business there, Mr. Magee?

Mr. Magee. Yes, sir; I am editor of a newspaper.

Senator Walsh. What is it called?

Mr. Magee. New Mexico State Tribune.

Senator Walsh. How long have you been in the newspaper business in New Mexico?

Mr. Magee. About four years, nearly.

Senator Walsh. Where had you resided prior to that time?

Mr. Magee. Tulsa, Okla.

Senator Walsh. And what business did you follow there?

Mr. Magee. I was an attorney.

Senator Walsh. How long have you lived in Tulsa?

Mr. Magee. Seventeen years.

Senator Walsh. How did you come to go to New Mexico, Mr. Magee?

Mr. Magee. Because of my wife's health. She became tuberculous.

Senator Walsh. And going to New Mexico did you engage in the newspaper business?

Mr. Magee. At once; yes, sir.

Senator Walsh. What property did you acquire?

Mr. Magee. The Albuquerque Morning Journal.

Senator Walsh. I wish you would tell the committee about the circumstances attending your acquisition of that property, and with whom you dealt.

Mr. Magee. I had always said that at some time I was going into the newspaper business, and the necessity of change of location led me to desire to get the Morning Journal, which was and is the only morning newspaper in the State. I made some inquiries in August, 1919, as to the ownership, and all that I could ascertain was that George E. Roberts, vice president of the National City Bank of New York, had paid over the purchase money and taken over the securities just prior to the election of 1918, when Senator A. B. Fall was a candidate for reelection.

About a month later I went to New York and went to Mr. Roberts, who came from my native State of Iowa and was a friend of my father's, and asked him for information. He told me that Thomas Schumacher, the president of the El Paso & Southwestern Railway Co. had brought him the purchase price and asked him upon the delivery of securities to turn over the money. And he gave me a letter of introduction to Mr. Schumacher at 99 John Street. I went to Mr.

Schumacher, and he told me that he was opposed to his railroad company continuing an interest in the ownership, and would try to help bring about a sale, and informed me that the El Paso & Southwestern, Senator John W. Weeks, a firm of Coolidge and somebody at Boston—not the President, however—and Price Kinney, a steel manufacturing company at Cleveland, and the Chino Copper Co., were the owners of the Morning Journal, giving me the proportions in which they owned it. He said he would see them and try to buy it. He reported to me two weeks later—I stayed in New York—that they all refused to sell, because Senator Fall was opposed to the sale of the paper, although he had informed me that Senator Fall had no interest.

I continued those negotiations on three different trips to New York from then till December, at which time Mr. Schumacher told me that he had pressed hard on the proposition, and that Senator Fall had become irritated, and had offered the water rights in perpetuity at Three Rivers, N. Mex., to the El Paso & Southwestern Railroad Co., in return for the $25,000 of stock and bonds they had in the Journal.

It might be well to add that both Senator Fall and Mr. Schumacher informed me that Senator Fall had been receiving an annual stipend to supply them with water from the stream which comes down out of his ranch, and that it was then given in perpetuity for the $25,000 interest. And he said. "I have got no further interest in the matter, and the deal is off."

I then abandoned the idea of purchasing the paper until about the 8th of February, 1920, at which time some one in Tulsa called me over the telephone and said that he believed that if I would communicate with Senator Fall at El Paso that I could buy the Journal. I was then in Tulsa. The voice refused to give a name when I asked who it was. However, I wired Senator Fall at El Paso, and a wire from Senator Fall crossed my wire, and in a few minutes I received a wire, although he had not received mine, saying that if I would come to El Paso he believed we could deal.

I went to El Paso and found that he was at Three Rivers sick, and had left word for me to come with a secretary to Three Rivers—one of his congressional secretaries. I went to Three Rivers at noon, about the 10th or 11th or 12th of February, 1920. He then informed me that—we had a long conversation about New Mexico politics that day, and I stayed all night at his home—the next morning he informed me his financial situation was so straitened, and he was in such a dilemma financially that he had decided to sell the Journal, he having acquired a $25,000 interest in it, and explained how, provided he could get the payment in cash. I told him that I would be prepared to pay the cash upon the assembling of the securities.

Senator Walsh. What was the amount asked for the paper?

Mr. Magee. $115,000, sir. I left Mr. Fall a check for $10,000 to be used whenever a binding contract had been signed. He gave me a letter of introduction to Mr. W. A. Hawkins, the attorney for the El Paso & Southwestern Railroad Co., and Mr. Sully of the Chino Copper Co., who were at Santa Fe attending a special session of the legislature, that is, present at a special session of the legislature, which was an authority for Mr. Hawkins to deal in his behalf and in behalf of Mr. Kinney and the others, sending by me telegrams from them which authorized Senator Fall to deal for them. I went to Santa Fe and entered into a contract with Mr. Hawkins.

The Chairman. This was in 1920?

Mr. Magee. This was in February of 1920; yes, sir.

Senator Walsh. Now, Mr. Magee, what did Senator Fall say at that time concerning his then financial condition?

Mr. Magee. He told me that he was going to resign shortly from the United States Senate because of his financial condition, and attempt to rehabilitate it. That it had broke him. That he couldn't pay taxes on his property. That his ranch was in a dilapidated condition, and it showed it, and that he must rehabilitate himself financially, and dwelt quite at length upon the personal private financial problem he had on his hands.

Senator Norris. What was his interest in the paper—$25,000?

Mr. Magee. $25,000 out of $115,000. It was a hundred and seventeen thousand and something, because I agreed to pay accumulated interest since the last payment of bond interest, and there was some two thousand or twenty-five hundred dollars of accumulated interest which I also paid.

The Chairman. This was for the Morning Journal?

Mr. Magee. Yes, sir.

Senator Lenroot. And this was February, 1920, did you say?

Mr. Magee. Yes, sir.

Senator Norris. Now I understood you earlier that Senator Fall had disposed of his interest in there?

Mr. Magee. No, sir, he had acquired it. He had had no interest: he simply dominated the situation for political reasons among his friends, and he sold the perpetual water rights to the El Paso & Southwestern Railroad Co. on water coming out of his ranch, in return for their holdings in the Morning Journal, and he thereby acquired—

Senator Norris. That was $25,000?

Mr. Magee. Yes.

The Chairman. Was the Morning Journal a Republican paper at that time?

Mr. Magee. Well, it was an independent newspaper, but it was strictly Republican in its policy.

The Chairman. Is it an independent paper now?

Mr. Magee. It still carries the same title. I am not connected with it. It still carries the same title of independent newspaper, but it is a supporter of Republican policies.

The Chairman. You are not owner of the Journal now?

Mr. Magee. No, sir; I sold the Journal June 1, 1922, and started another newspaper, a weekly paper, under the name of "Magee's Independent," and on the 5th of last April converted it into the New Mexico State Tribune, an afternoon paper.

Senator Walsh. Those things would come in regular order, gentlemen.

Senator Kendrick. Mr. Magee, in speaking of the water rights, have you any information as to the value of the water rights that were traded for this stock?

Mr. Magee. No, sir; only I know he sold it too cheap.

Senator Walsh. I offer in this connection, Mr. Chairman, a certified copy of deed by Senator Fall and his wife to the El Paso & Northeastern Railway Co., under date of January 20, 1920, reciting the consideration of $45,000 for the conveyance of a daily flow of 75,000 gallons of water.

Mr. Magee. I didn't know of the existence of that. There may have been some additional cash consideration. . . .

Senator Walsh. You spoke about the condition of and the appearance of the ranch at the time you were there, Mr. Magee. What can you tell us about that?

Mr. Magee. Well, Senator Fall met me at the railway station at Three Rivers. There is nothing but a station there. There is no town there. And I was impressed with the character of the car he was driving. He had a Franklin that we had to get out and fix three or four times to get 3 or 4 miles up to his house, in a very dilapidated condition, and I was impressed before he told me about his financial situation, with the very dilapidated condition of the house, both inside and outside, and the general run-down condition of the place. I at first attributed it to the fact that his son had died in 1918—he had had charge of the ranch—and I thought it was neglect. He informed me that it was poverty, in the course of a conversation; that he needed the money.

Senator Walsh. How far is the ranch house from the station?

Mr. Magee. Well, I would have to guess, Senator. I have never been there right at the house but the one time, and it would be my guess that it was 3 or 3½ miles, but it might be somewhat farther. I only have a 4-year-old recollection as to the distance from the station.

Senator Walsh. And what was the character of the road which you traveled over?

Mr. Magee. It was a very inferior, winding road, unmade road, and very rough.

Senator Walsh. And I ask you now, have you been there more recently?

Mr. Magee. Returning from a speech-making trip over the State the latter part of August, 1923, I came down the main road and passed the Three Rivers railroad station, passed the entrance to this road going up to the Senator's ranch, but I didn't go up to the ranch. I couldn't see it from the road, and I didn't go up there. I simply passed the road. . . .

Senator Walsh. Now, Mr. Magee, we had got to the point where I wanted to inquire of you about what change, if any, there was in the road leading up to the ranch at your recent visit; and when did you say that was?

Mr. Magee. The latter part of August—just the last days of August, 1923.

Senator Walsh. Of this present year?

Mr. Magee. Yes; I was going from Carrizozo to Alamogordo, and when I came in sight of Three Rivers I was lost; that is, I knew I was on the right road, but I couldn't locate myself. And I was puzzled, and I discovered when I came down there that a change had been made in the road going to Mr. Fall's place, was the cause of my confusion. There had been pillars built up to this road, and beautiful woven wire fence put along, and trees planted, and beautifully concreted gutters, and a very expensive road, as far as I could see, up to the ranch house. I couldn't see all the way. The conditions were so changed I couldn't recognize it.

Senator Walsh. Were you able to observe any changes in the conditions of the ranch itself?

Mr. Magee. No, sir; I couldn't see the ranch.

Senator Walsh. Did you learn of any other improvements in the place?

Mr. Magee. I have heard quite a bit, but I have not been at the place.

Senator Walsh. How did you learn of it?

Mr. Magee. At Carrizozo there was an electrician who seemed to be acquainted with me, who came and talked to me, and told me what his business was. I asked him what he was doing in that part of the country, and he said he was making about a $40,000 electrical installation on Senator Fall's ranch.

Senator Walsh. That is all.

Senator Norris. Do you know anything about the difference in the consideration named in this deed and the amount that Senator Fall told you that he had for his interest in the paper?

Mr. Magee. No, sir; I never heard of this deed until it was read here this morning.

Senator Norris. You noticed it was $45,000?

Mr. Magee. Yes; I noticed it was. There may have been an additional consideration of which I knew nothing. I hadn't heard of it until I heard it read here.

Senator Norris. Then there may have been other considerations?

Mr. Magee. There certainly might. The only consideration I knew was in the interest in the Journal. That had changed, and I was informed about that.

Senator Lenroot. What are your politics, Mr. Magee?

Mr. Magee. I went to New Mexico a Republican. I am running an independently Democratic newspaper at the time.

The Chairman. You know nothing about Senator Fall's financial condition, do you, except by hearsay?

Mr. Magee. No, sir; I know nothing at all about it.

The Chairman. You do not know what his financial condition is, or his resources?

Mr. Magee. Not in any competent way. I know by rumors, but nothing competent.

The Chairman. I have heard so many Senators say that they are going to resign to recuperate lost fortunes, and I thought maybe Senator Fall was going to do the same thing. . . .

TESTIMONY OF HARRY F. SINCLAIR
DECEMBER 4, 1923

U.S. Senate, Leases Upon Naval Oil Reserves, Hearings Before the Committee on Public Lands and Surveys, 68th Congress, 1st Session, Vol. 2, 1017; 1032–37.

. . . Senator Walsh. Mr. Sinclair, our attention has been called to a shipment of some Holstein cattle, consisting of eight cows, or seven cows and two bulls, from the Rancocas Stock Farm at Rancocas, N.J., to Senator Fall, about the month of February, 1922. Are you interested in any way in the Rancocas Stock Farm?

Mr. Sinclair. Yes, sir.

Senator Walsh. How?

Mr. Sinclair. I own it.

Senator Walsh. And did you at that time?

Mr. Sinclair. Yes, sir.

Senator Walsh. And how long prior thereto?

Mr. Sinclair. Several years. . . .

Mr. Sinclair. . . . I think I can straighten out this matter that has been talked about.

Senator Walsh. I would be glad to have you do so.

Mr. Sinclair. I visited Secretary Fall's ranch in January, the first of the year. In going over his ranch and discussing the situation with him I found he did not have any milch cows, and I was telling him about my herd of Holstein cattle, and suggested to him he better let me send him some milch cows. He thought they would be too expensive. I told him no, they were not expensive unless he wanted some particularly showy cattle.

After some discussion, more or less earnestly but with some kidding, he said all right, if I would send him some cattle he would be very glad to buy them if I would sell them at prices we usually received. I said "all right," and I did. I sent these cattle along with the horse that I gave Mr. Johnson. Mr. Johnson is his manager there who has charge of the cowboys. He at that time had a studhorse that was given to him by Mr. McLean. He was very proud of it and was showing it to me, and I told him I would send him a real studhorse if would allow me to do it. He said he would be very glad to have it. So in sending the horse to Mr. Johnson I sent the cattle along with him. I told my man on the farm to get together a bull and half a dozen heifers and a few pigs and send them down. I told him over the telephone, and he did so. I told him to send something that would be all right for milch cows. He did that. Afterwards I saw him and I told him to make up some sort of bill, to make up a bill for these cattle. There was no price decided on them but I wanted the bill to be fair. I think that is what caused the delay in sending this thing in.

It is my recollection that Mr. Everhart was in New York, or came to New York, and asked for this bill. I was not there. That is the way he got it. Now, if he had not asked for the bill at that time I imagine I would still be carrying that shipment on my mind. I did not think it was absolutely necessary to be very prompt about a shipment of that sort. I sent a shipment of cattle to Mr. Whitney not long ago, somewhat about the same matter, to his hunting farm down in Georgia. I do not think he has paid me for them; in fact, I do not think that a bill is in the office.

Senator Walsh. As I understand you the exact number of cattle in your talk with Senator Fall was not arrived at. You told your foreman to fix up, perhaps, half a dozen or so.

Mr. Sinclair. Yes; those cattle were sent in the car with the horse, which car only held so many cattle, but, I think, seven is correct.

Senator Walsh. And the price was not agreed on with Senator Fall, either?

Mr. Sinclair. No, sir. I think I am to blame if this price or memorandum was not in the office in the regular form.

Senator Walsh. Do you know, Mr. Sinclair, how many head of cattle were actually shipped?

Mr. Sinclair. I understand, seven.

Senator Walsh. Seven cows?

Mr. Sinclair. No; six heifers and, I understand, one bull.

Senator Walsh. But the certificate before us recites seven cows, or heifers, and two bulls.

Mr. Sinclair. I think there is a mistake in the certificate, although I might be wrong.

Senator Walsh. Were those registered cattle?

Mr. Sinclair. Yes.

Senator Walsh. Registered where?

Mr. Sinclair. Registered in New Jersey.

Senator Walsh. Have you a New Jersey Holstein-Friesian association?

Mr. Sinclair. Yes, sir; I think so.

Senator Walsh. Where are its headquarters?

Mr. Sinclair. Well, I do not know. I will have to get that information. Mr. Wahlberg can get that. I think at Trenton, though. Mr. Wahlberg, where are their headquarters?

Mr. Wahlberg. I do not know; but I believe in Camden, N. J.

Senator Walsh. Where?

Mr. Wahlberg. I believe in Camden, N.J.; but I do not know.

Senator Walsh. How large a herd have you, Mr. Sinclair?

Mr. Sinclair. About 125.

Senator Walsh. And those were intended for milch cows?

Mr. Sinclair. Yes, sir.

Senator Walsh. Have you ever made a shipment other than this one as far west as New Mexico?

Mr. Sinclair. Well, I have made a shipment to Georgia—to Thomasville.

Senator Walsh. To whom?

Mr. Sinclair. To Mr. H. B. Witney.

Senator Walsh. Is that the farthest you have ever shipped?

Mr. Sinclair. Yes, sir.

Senator Walsh. Evidently you are something of a fancier of that breed of cattle. Where are they found in most abundance in this country?

Mr. Sinclair. Where are the cattle found?

Senator Walsh. Yes; these Holstein-Friesian blooded cattle.

Mr. Sinclair. Well, there are a number of herds in New Jersey. There are quite a number of herds in Pennsylvania and in New York State.

Senator Walsh. Do you know anything about them farther west?

Mr. Sinclair. I do not. In fact, I do not know a great deal about the matter. I attempted to put my herd on what they call the accredited herd list, taking away the tubercular cattle, and I think I lost about half of them. I have a man on my farm who seems to be an expert. I do not spend a great deal of my time about it. He breeds the cattle. He knows all about the matter. If you would like to have him come as an expert to tell you about it, he would be very glad to do it.

Senator Walsh. We would like to have your farm manager, who actually made the shipment or the transaction, to come.

Mr. Sinclair. All right.

Senator Walsh. Did you inquire about the freight rate about making the shipment?

Mr. Sinclair. I did.

Senator Walsh. You gave the order personally to the farm manager in the manner you have indicated?

Mr. Sinclair. Yes, sir.

Senator Walsh. And he looked after the rest of it?

Mr. Sinclair. The freight rate would naturally be more expensive on account of sending the horse along with them, or sending them with the horse. We do not ship horses in regular cattle cars, you understand; horses are shipped in express cars.

Senator Jones. Who paid the freight?

Senator Walsh. Yes; did you pay the freight on the horse?

Mr. Sinclair. I paid the freight on the whole car.

Senator Walsh. Can you tell us what it amounted to?

Mr. Sinclair. I can not. My manager paid it, but I will find out for you. I think perhaps it was in the neighborhood of $800 or $900; but I do not know.

Senator Walsh. Is that included in the $1,100?

Mr. Sinclair. No, sir. It was not charged at all. There was nothing charged for freight.

Senator Walsh. So that the net to you out of the transaction was something like $200 or $300?

Mr. Sinclair. I would say so.

Senator Walsh. That is all.

Senator Lenroot. Mr. Sinclair, when did you first become acquainted with Mr. Fall?

Mr. Sinclair. Well, I could not give you the date, Senator Lenroot, but it was several years ago.

Senator Lenroot. How often had you seen him prior to this visit in January, 1922?

Mr. Sinclair. Not a great many times.

Senator Lenroot. Had you ever had any business with him?

Mr. Sinclair. No, sir.

Senator Lenroot. Of any kind?

Mr. Sinclair. No, sir.

Senator Lenroot. On this visit to his farm in January, 1922, when this question came up what was the object of your visit at that time?

Mr. Sinclair. I went to Three Rivers to discuss with Senator Fall the leasing of Teapot Dome.

Senator Lenroot. So far as you know, Mr. Sinclair, is there any profit to be received in this transaction that Mr. Fall received, any benefits or profits, directly or indirectly, in any manner whatsoever, in connection with you?

Mr. Sinclair. No, sir; none, unless he had received some benefits from the cattle.

Senator Lenroot. Of course, I meant with the exception of the cattle.

Mr. Sinclair. No, sir.

Senator Lenroot. That is all.

Senator Walsh. Mr. Sinclair, did not you have any other business that called you to Three Rivers on that occasion?

Mr. Sinclair. Yes.

Senator Walsh. What was it?

Mr. Sinclair. We were discussing some matters with Mr. Fall's department in reference to some royalties on some purchases of some leases in
Oklahoma. It was business we had before the Interior Department, regular
business.

Senator Walsh. Just what was the nature of that transaction?

Mr. Sinclair. I think, if I remember correctly, Senator Walsh, it was in the
nature of payments on some leases which we purchased by sale from the
Osage Tribe.

Senator Walsh. That is to say, prior to this time, leases on the Osage
Reservation had been offered to the public at competitive bidding and you
had secured some of these leases?

Mr. Sinclair. Yes; they had been offered along for a number of years.

Senator Walsh. When had you secured those particular leases?

Mr. Sinclair. I could not say, but sometime before that time.

Senator Walsh. How long before?

Mr. Sinclair. I do not know, but perhaps six weeks or a month or two
months, whenever the sale might have happened.

Senator Walsh. What was the particular matter that seemed to make it
necessary for you to have a conference with Secretary Fall out at Three Rivers
on that subject just at that particular time?

Mr. Sinclair. Well, that was not altogether necessary, I do not think.

Senator Walsh. Really your business out there was to take up this Teapot
Dome matter?

Mr. Sinclair. Both matters, yes. . . .

ALBERT B. FALL TO THOMAS B. WALSH
JANUARY 11, 1924

U.S. Senate, Leases Upon Naval Oil Reserves, Hearings Before the
Committee on Public Lands and Surveys, 68th Congress, 1st Session, Vol. 2, 1699.

Palm Beach, Fla.
January 11, 1924

Senator Thomas F. Walsh
Breakers Hotel, Palm Beach, Fla.
Dear Sir:

I am in receipt of your communication of this date, advising me that after
the taking of Mr. McLean's deposition to-day you are ready, under the authority granted you by the committee, to take any statement that I might desire to
make or to accept from me any subsequent written statement from me to the
committee.

I desire to advise you that I have carefully read the testimony which Mr. McLean gave to-day and that I endorse the accuracy of same. I will also say that before giving his testimony Mr. McLean had a conference with me and I told him that, so far as I was concerned, it was my wish that he answer freely, and, in this connection, I will say that it is absolutely true that—I did not finally use the money from Mr. McLean, which he expressed himself willing to give me, because I found that I could readily obtain it from other sources. I wish it thoroughly understood that the source from which I obtained the money which I used was in no way connected with Mr. Sinclair or in any way involved in any concession regarding the Teapot Dome, or any other oil concession.

Further than this, I would not care to go at the present time, inasmuch as I am not in anything like the physical condition to stand the ordeal of an examination. It may be, though, that I will desire to amplify this statement to you for the committee at a later date.

Very truly yours,

Albert B. Fall

TESTIMONY OF EDWARD B. McLEAN
JANUARY 11, 1924

U.S. Senate, Leases Upon Naval Oil Reserves, Hearings Before the Committee on Public Lands and Surveys, 68th Congress, 1st Session, Vol. 2, 1694–97.

In the matter of the investigation of the leasing of the naval oil reserves before the Committee on Public Lands and Surveys of the United States Senate. Proceeding, before the Hon. Thomas J. Walsh as a subcommittee of the said committee at Palm Beach, Fla., January 11, 1924, Edward B. McLean, [Editor-President of *The Washington Post*] being present and represented by his counsel, Wilton J. Lambert, and being duly sworn said:

"I am now to testify under oath, am I not?"

Senator Walsh. You are. That I may be understood, I incorporate in the report the following order made by the Committee on Public Lands and Surveys of the United States Senate:

That Senator Thomas J. Walsh be, and he is hereby, appointed a subcommittee to take the testimony of Edward B. McLean, at Palm Beach, State of Florida, or elsewhere, and any other witnesses as the said subcommittee may require to attend before him by subpoena; and authority is hereby given to said subcommittee to issue subpoenas in the name of the committee that require the attendance before him of said Edward B. McLean or any other witnesses; that if said Edward B. McLean so desires he may be represented by counsel and he may participate in the proceedings.

I. L. Lenroot
Chairman Committee on Lands
and Surveys

Now, Mr. McLean, in a letter dated December 26, 1923, addressed by Senator Albert B. Fall to the chairman and members of the Committee on Public Lands and Surveys of the United States Senate, after setting forth some negotiations he had had for the purchase of a ranch in New Mexico during the latter part of the year 1921, he stated as follows:

> I came to Washington and approached a friend of mine here who had spoken to me about acquiring a ranch in New Mexico and particularly about the raising of thoroughbred horses in that State. I placed before him the Brownfield-Harris proposition at the prices which they had given me, that is to say, immediate purchase of real estate and cattle of the Harris estate would require $91,500. I stated to him also that other lands should be acquired in connection with these and that ultimately the total amount would approximate $125,000. I suggested to him that he should make this purchase outright in his own name and own the ranch and stock it as he pleased or that the cattle might be sold and the real estate retained for horse ranch purposes. I also proposed that in the event he preferred to do so if he would advance the money and make the purchase, take title in his own name I would agree with him upon an equal amount in value of my own adjoining properties and form a copartnership on a 50–50 basis. The matter was considered for several days and this gentleman decided that at the time he was not ready to make this investment outright. He stated, however, he would advance me the money or advance me $100,000 in event I needed it, simply upon my own note without security or indorsement. I told him that I had the other two sources from which I could obtain the money or from which I could obtain the money to repay him in event I accepted his loan. It was finally agreed that he would loan me $100,000—and I gave him my note for that amount due on demand with a memorandum which I think he attached to the note, to the effect that if at any time within three years he desired to call the loan, I would pay it immediately or if he, after further consideration desired to acquire the title to the Harris property he should do so at the actual cost, or if he desired to go in partnership with me I would agree to put in an equal amount and we would jointly own the combined property. The arrangement was made on this basis. The gentlemen from whom I obtained it, that is, the money, and who furnished me the cash was the Hon. Edward B. McLean of Washington, D. C.

Senator Walsh. Mr. McLean, did you loan $100,000 to Mr. Fall?
Mr. McLean. I did, yes, sir, in checks.

Senator Walsh of Montana. Whose checks?

Mr. McLean. My own checks.

Senator Walsh of Montana. Drawn on what bank?

Mr. McLean. Drawn, to the best of my recollection, on the Federal, the Commercial—and there might have been a smaller one drawn on one other third bank which was a very small amount.

Senator Walsh of Montana. Have you got the checks?

Mr. McLean. I do not think so—I am not positive.

Senator Walsh of Montana. Were they returned? What became of them?

Mr. McLean. Senator Fall returned them to me.

Senator Walsh of Montana. When?

Mr. McLean. In the last part of December 1921, sir—the last week—I am not positive as to date.

Senator Walsh of Montana. They never did go through the bank?

Mr. McLean. No, sir.

Senator Walsh of Montana. So that so far as you are concerned you did not give him any cash?

Mr. McLean. Cash? No, sir.

Senator Walsh of Montana. Now, Mr. McLean, I wish you would just tell me about the transaction.

Mr. McLean. I will tell you, sir, to the best of my recollection.

Sometime in November, 1920, I was a member of a party invited by ex-President Harding to go on a fishing trip, or a trip of general recreation. We went from Brownsville to a town called Point Isabel, Tex. I came back to Brownsville in the morning, and the rest of the party coming back in the afternoon, and I met the Honorable Albert B. Fall in a hotel—the main hotel in Brownsville—I don't remember the name of it—and during that day, to the best of my recollection, and especially going back on the trip, he touched on the subject of his ranch and the possibilities of a profitable venture if anyone cared to put up the amount of money which it would entail to go into the business of raising thoroughbred horses. He explained to me about the ranch being 100 miles from Juarez, where there is a big race track, it would be a profitable venture, in his opinion. I told him at that time that I had a farm in Virginia which was getting overstocked and asked him in an off-hand way what, without serious intentions, the Harris ranch was worth. My recollection is that either he did not tell me the price or his answer was so vague it made no impression on my mind. That was the first mention that Senator Fall had ever made to me.

In the early part of November, 1921, I received a letter from him describing the Harris ranch—a rather bulky letter—I should think about 14 pages, approximately that anyhow, asking me if I would care to buy it or go into partnership with him. I replied that it was impossible at that time. There was then a lapse of possibly two weeks. He then came to my house one day and asked me if I could loan him $100,000 on his personal note, as the Harris ranch was to be sold and there were seven or eight heirs, the exact number of whom I am not sure, and that the purchase had to be arranged at once. After a long conversation, I do not know how long it was, but I told him I could do it. I gave him two or three checks, made out on different banks. I am positive that it was two, but it may have been three. In two or three days from then Senator Fall dropped in and gave me a note with a memorandum attached for $100,000. Within two or three days after that he came to see me at my house in Washington in the evening and returned me the checks in the same condition I had given them to him. In other words, they had not gone through the paying tellers at the banks.

Senator Walsh of Montana. What became of the note?

Mr. McLean. He took the note.

Senator Walsh of Montana. Do you still retain the memorandum?

Mr. McLean. I don't believe so. Though there is a possibility that I may. As far as I was concerned, I believed the transaction concluded and, I believe I destroyed the memorandum.

Senator Walsh of Montana. You haven't the note?

Mr. McLean. No.

Senator Walsh of Montana. You have not got it as far as you know?

Mr. McLean. Not as far as I know; no, sir.

Senator Walsh of Montana. What explanation did he make at that time?

Mr. McLean. That he had made arrangements through other sources. He did not say through what other sources.

Senator Walsh of Montana. There was no further talk about the matter at that time, nor at the time the checks were given or at the time he applied to you for loan of $100,000?

Mr. McLean. Yes, sir.

Senator Walsh of Montana. What representation did he make concerning the payment of note?

Mr. McLean. He would either give me option on the Harris ranch or he would put an equal part in of his own ranch. There was never any mention whether the Harris ranch was worth $100,000. And I didn't know the value of his ranch. I have never been to his ranch—I do not know anything about it; I am as ignorant as you are about it.

Senator Walsh of Montana. Did you at that time know anything about Mr. Fall's financial condition?

Mr. McLean. No, sir; except I knew he had a lot of land and a lot of cattle.

Senator Walsh of Montana. In detail, you did not know anything about it?

Mr. McLean. No, sir.

Senator Walsh of Montana. When did you see Senator Fall last?

Mr. McLean. Fifteen minutes ago.

Senator Walsh of Montana. Is he here in the city?

Mr. McLean. To the best of my knowledge he is, sir.

Senator Walsh of Montana. How long has he been here, as far as you know?

Mr. McLean. I think about a week or 10 days—I am not trying to evade the question, but that is as far as I know.

Senator Walsh of Montana. Have you and he conferred about this matter during that period?

Mr. McLean. This morning, sir.

Senator Walsh of Montana. Is that the first time you talked about it?

Mr. McLean. I have talked to him two or three times.

Senator Walsh of Montana. You do not know whether the note is in existence still or not?

Mr. McLean. I could not answer that question.

Senator Walsh of Montana. Have you a confidential secretary?

Mr. McLean. Yes; Mr. Major.

Senator Walsh of Montana. Then you do not know where the note is?

Mr. McLean. The note must have been torn up, as the transaction was finished, in my opinion. The way I look at it, Senator, is this: I loaned him the money, but it had not been made use of.

Senator Walsh of Montana. Do you remember if there was any notation made on the stubs of the checks showing the checks had never been used?

Mr. McLean. No, sir; I handled that transaction myself.

Senator Walsh of Montana. You would have, of course, the stubs in your check book.

Mr. McLean. I think that is very doubtful. I burn all my checks every two years.

Senator Walsh of Montana. But don't you keep your stubs for reference?

Mr. McLean. No, sir.

Senator Walsh of Montana. If the stubs are still in existence, where would they be? In Washington?

Mr. McLean. They might be in my office in Washington. I could find out by telegraph.

Senator Walsh of Montana. I would like you to do so, Mr. McLean.

Mr. McLean. May I put something in that I would like to say? I conferred this morning with the Hon. A. B. Fall and my attorney, Wilton J. Lambert. Mr. Fall suggested that I make the statement which I have made before Senator Walsh to-day.

Senator Walsh of Montana. Is there anything further?

Mr. McLean. No, sir.

Senator Walsh of Montana. That is all.

TESTIMONY OF EDWARD L. DOHENY
JANUARY 24, 1924

U.S. Senate, Leases Upon Naval Oil Reserves, Hearings Before the Committee on Public Lands and Surveys, 68th Congress, 1st Session, Vol. 2, 1771–75; 1778–79; 1795–97; 1800; 1817.

Mr. Doheny [President, Pan-American Petroleum and Transport Co.]. I have been following the reports of the proceedings before your committee and have concluded that notwithstanding my authorization to ex-Secretary Fall early in December to state the full and complete facts in connection with a personal transaction had in 1921 between Mr. Fall and myself, Mr. Fall has been making an effort to keep my name out of the discussion for the reason that a full statement might be misunderstood. Whether there is a possibility of such misunderstanding or not, I wish to state to the committee and to the public the full facts, and I may say here that I regret that when I was before your committee I did not tell you what I am now telling you. I did not do so for the reason that such statement was not pertinent in answer to any of the questions asked me by members of the committee, and to have done so would have been volunteering something in no way connected with the contracts made with the Pan American Petroleum & Transport Co. When asked by your chairman whether Mr. Fall had profited by the contract, directly or indirectly, I answered in the negative. That answer I now reiterate.

I wish first to inform the committee that on the 30th of November, 1921, I loaned to Albert B. Fall $100,000 upon his promissory note to enable him to purchase a ranch in New Mexico. This sum was loaned to Mr. Fall by me personally. It was my own money and did not belong in whole or in part to any oil company with which I am or have been connected. In connection with this loan there was no discussion between Mr. Fall and myself as to any contract whatever. This loan had no relation to any of the subsequent transactions. The transactions themselves, in the order in which they occurred, dispose of any contention that they were influenced by my making a personal loan to a lifelong friend.

The reason for my making and Mr. Fall's accepting the loan was that we had been friends for more than 30 years. He had invested his savings for those years in his home ranch in New Mexico, which I understood was all that remained to him after the failure of mining investments in Mexico and nine years of public service in Washington, during which he could not properly attend to the management of his ranch. His troubles had been increased in 1918 by the death of his daughter and his son, who up to then had taken his place in the management of his ranch. In our frequent talks it was clear that the acquisition of a neighboring property controlling the water that flows through his home ranch was a hope of his amounting to an obsession. His failure to raise the necessary funds by realizing on his extensive and once valuable Mexican mine holdings had made him feel that he was a victim of an untoward fate. In one of these talks I indicated to him that I would be willing to make him the loan, and this seemed to relieve his mind greatly. In the autumn of 1921 he told me that the purchase had become possible by reason of the willingness of the then owners of the Harris ranch to sell and that the time had arrived when he was ready to take advantage of my offer to make the loan.

The lease on naval reserve No. 1 was the direct outgrowth of the contract which the Pan American Petroleum & Transport Co. made with the Navy as a result of competitive bids, in which that company was the lowest bidder, for the construction of certain storage facilities and the furnishing of fuel oil at Pearl Harbor, Hawaii, and in the absence of that contract the lease would never have been executed. The Navy Department, through its representative, took up with us the question of constructing the improvements and facilities at Pearl Harbor, and of paying for them with the royalty oil which the Navy was then obtaining from the various leases in naval reserves Nos. 1 and 2, and of filling the tankage constructed with a large quantity of fuel oil. I was entirely in sympathy with the purpose of the Navy, the reasons for which have perhaps been better explained to your committee by the Navy's representative, Admiral Robison, than I could hope to do. I promised Admiral Robison that our company would at least submit a bid to perform the work under those conditions; that is, furnish the money to pay for the work of construction at the harbor and of filling the tanks with oil and receive in return royalty oil at the posted field price to the value of the money so expended. The incidents up to the date of the contract, and the fact that the contract was let on competitive bidding eliminate any possibility of favor to the company by either the Navy Department or the Interior Department.

The negotiations for the contract between the Navy Department and the company were conducted by our local Washington attorney who was assisted in determining the necessary calculations by our California general manager, who is president of the California company. As a result of their exchange of ideas, our California general manager decided that the terms of the proposed contract were not such as to be of any advantage to the company and that the company could not afford to take the risks attached to the performance of the contract for the conjectural profit that might result therefrom, and he so stated in a letter which he wrote to our Washington attorney.

Neither our Washington attorney nor our California general manager nor any other officer or attorney of the company had any knowledge of the loan which I made to Mr. Fall, that being an entirely private matter, involving in no way the company's funds. . . .

Later in the year 1922, and nearly a year after I had made the loan to Mr. Fall, the Navy Department, desiring additional storage facilities and petroleum products at Pearl Harbor, requested that the original contract of the Pan American Petroleum & Transport Co. be supplemented or that a new contract be made providing for the additional work and supplies, . . . For some time negotiations were carried on in which the president of our California company, who came on to Washington for that purpose, together with our Washington attorney, discussed all phases of the proposed supplemental agreement with the representatives of the Navy and the Interior Department. . . .

On the last day before the contract was signed, the president of the California company absolutely turned down the contract, stating that he believed there were not adequate benefits commensurate with the great risks assumed by the advancement on the part of the company of the necessary millions to pay the contractors who were to perform the construction work at Pearl Harbor and to furnish the petroleum products required. The estimated expenditure to be made under this supplemental contract for tankage facilities and petroleum products is $9,017,000, about one-half for petroleum supplies and one-half for storage facilities. The work is well under way and about $1,000,000 has been expended by the company on it.

This contract gave to the Navy just that service from the naval reserves that the Navy Department through its active engineering head desired, which was immediate availability of its anticipated production, delivered where the Navy wanted it, at the time it wanted it, in such quantities as were needed, and of the character and quality which the Navy's requirements called for.

In addition, a burden, the advantage of which to the Navy can scarcely be measured, was assumed by the company; that of providing for the Navy in southern California 1,000,000 barrels of free oil storage, and of devoting 3,000,000 barrels of the company's Atlantic seaboard storage to the holding of that quantity of fuel oil subject to the Navy's call at any time for a period of 15 years.

The contract also gave the option to the Navy of purchasing at the company's terminal station at San Pedro such petroleum supplies as the Navy may require at 10 per cent below the market price.

I want to say right here that that is in answer to an article I saw in a newspaper this morning to the effect that there was no chance for the Navy to get petroleum supplies. Our contract provided that the Navy could get anything it wanted at 10 per cent below the market price.

In closing, I wish to state that I left Los Angeles on January 19 to come to Washington to present a statement of all the facts to the committee, and having been informed that Mr. Fall was in New Orleans, took that route in order to apprise him of my intention and found him already in entire accord with my purpose. . . .

Mr. Doheny. I had known Senator Fall for about 30 years or more. We had been old-time friends. We both worked in the same mining district in New Mexico in 1885. In those days the Indian troubles were still on the country, and we were bound together by the same ties that men usually are, especially after they leave camp where they have lived under trying circumstances and conditions. Sometimes when men are in camp where their conditions are hard, and where the struggle for a living is precarious and the danger from Indians is bad, they do not have such a very great feeling for each other; but after they leave there they become warmer friends by reason of having associated under the same conditions.

Furthermore, I studied law at the same time that Senator Fall did. I practiced for a short time in the same district that he did. I watched his career all through the development of it, as district attorney, United States judge, and United States Senator. I was very much interested in him on account of our old associations. I, myself, followed prospecting. I was fortunate and accumulated quite a large amount of money. Senator Fall was unfortunate, and when he was telling me about his misfortunes, and at a time when it was coupled with his misfortune of having to bear the loss of his two children—two grown children—I felt greatly in sympathy with him. He was telling me about his hope of acquiring this ranch, and being of an impulsive nature I said to him, "Whenever you need some money to pay for that ranch I will lend it to you."

He spoke to me at that time about possibly borrowing it from Ned McLean. And he said something at that time about giving the ranch as security. I said, "I will lend it to you on your note. You do not need to give the ranch as security."

That relieved Senator Fall greatly. Later on he telephoned to me that the time had come when the ranch could be purchased. When he telephoned to me about it I sent him the money. Whether he asked for the money in the form that I sent it, or whether I sent it in that form of my own election, I do not know. But I sent it in cash.

Senator Walsh of Montana. This conversation was some three or four weeks before that?

Mr. Doheny. Yes, sir; I think so; at least three or four weeks prior to that time. It may not have been quite that long before, but it was about that time.

Senator Walsh of Montana. How soon after the telephone talk in which it was agreed between you that you should loan him the money did you actually send it to him?

Mr. Doheny. I sent it to him right away, I think the next day, or within a couple of days.

Senator Walsh of Montana. From New York to Washington?

Mr. Doheny. Yes, sir.

Senator Walsh of Montana. And the note then went back to you?

Mr. Doheny. Yes, sir; the note was brought back to me.

Senator Walsh of Montana. How did you transmit the money to him?

Mr. Doheny. In cash.

Senator Walsh of Montana. How did you transport the cash?

Mr. Doheny. In a satchel. The cash was put up in a regular bank bundle, and taken over and delivered to him.

Senator Walsh of Montana. Who acted as your messenger in the matter?

Mr. Doheny. My son. . . .

The Chairman. Now, your contract of December 12, as a matter of fact, gave you a lease of the entire reserve?

Mr. Doheny. Yes, sir.

The Chairman. At fixed royalties?

Mr. Doheny. Yes, sir.

The Chairman. And it is that contract out of which you testified that you expect to make $100,000,000?

Mr. Doheny. Yes, sir.

The Chairman. Now, Mr. Doheny—

Mr. Doheny. But pardon me for a moment, Mr. Senator. For fear that that statement may seem to you as wild as it seems to a great many of my friends. If anybody had spoken to the gentleman who invented the telephone, or to Mr. Ford in the early days of his business—if he had said to them, that he expected to make two or three hundred million dollars out of his machine he would have been regarded by his own associates as crazy. And the oil people in California, the oil men who have a knowledge of the business were satisfied in their own minds that I had gotten a lemon from the Government when I took that contract of April 25, 1922.

The Chairman. Yes; the one of April.

Mr. Doheny. Yes; and they didn't regard the other one highly; nobody regarded the other one highly. They said that with the responsibility which I assumed for my company, which meant that I had to expend over $14,000,000, that there was nothing known about the territory that justified advancing that amount of royalty. That is what they all thought. My thoughts about that I gave to you honestly, and I expect to make $100,000,000 out of that contract.

The Chairman. Under your own statement on the 25th of April you yourself did not enter into it for profit.

Mr. Doheny. Yes; that is right.

The Chairman. But the contract of December you certainly did enter into for profit?

Mr. Doheny. Yes, sir.

The Chairman. And you testified before this committee that you expected to make $100,000,000 of profit?

Mr. Doheny. Yes, sir.

The Chairman. Now, if Secretary Fall did in fact exercise his judgment about the granting of that contract in December, in view of your own statement that you think he might be influenced in your favor by reason of the loan by you, wouldn't you be willing, Mr. Doheny, in view of those facts, to turn back that contract to the Government?

Mr. Doheny. I would be willing to do just what I have offered, Mr. Chairman. . . .

The Chairman. You have offered to do it upon a basis of experts examining the question. I am asking you now: In view of that situation, of your possibly having secured an advantage, whether you are not willing to turn the contract back to the Government as it stands?

Mr. Doheny. If that will clear Mr. Fall of any suspicion of collusion, I will be very glad, indeed, to suggest that to our company. Now, recollect, I am not our company. While I exercise a great deal of influence on it, we have 9,000 stockholders and we have a board of directors.

The Chairman. It would clear you of any suspicion of profit, of course, out of the Government.

Mr. Doheny. What is that?

The Chairman. It would clear you of any suspicion of profit out of the Government. I am not speaking of collusion.

Mr. Doheny. Well, if it will clear Senator Fall from any suspicion of being in collusion, I am perfectly willing to do it.

The Chairman. At the time you made this loan, Mr. Doheny, you had had relations with the Interior Department with reference to this very naval reserve, and had a certain lease?

Mr. Doheny. Our company had, Mr. Chairman.

The Chairman. I say your company, and you expected to have other relations, did you not?

Mr. Doheny. I didn't know whether we would or not. There was nothing in sight at that time.

The Chairman. Well, so far as offset wells were necessary from time to time your company had got into that field, hadn't it?

Mr. Doheny. Yes.

The Chairman. You expected, of course, did you not, to continue?

Mr. Doheny. Well, we expected, of course, to be always in the field to bid on any contracts that the Government had to let.

The Chairman. Yes.

Mr. Doheny. Yes, sir.

The Chairman. Well, did it occur to you at all, Mr. Doheny, that to get a contract from the department under those circumstances, other than by competitive bidding, would be a matter of embarrassment?

Mr. Doheny. Oh, I don't think we did, Mr. Chairman.

The Chairman. You didn't?

Mr. Doheny. No, sir.

The Chairman. Why, this contract was not by competitive bidding, was it?

Mr. Doheny. I think it was.

The Chairman. Well, let us see. Bids were called for, were they not?

Mr. Doheny. Yes, sir.

The Chairman. And you made two bids?

Mr. Doheny. Yes.

The Chairman. One of them strictly under the proposal?

Mr. Doheny. Yes, sir.

The Chairman. And another in which you made a proposition that no other bidder was permitted to make; that you would make a price—$235,000, I think was the sum?

Mr. Doheny. Yes.

The Chairman. Less, provided you could have a percentage rate to lease certain lands?

Mr. Doheny. Yes.

The Chairman. No other bidder had that opportunity?

Mr. Doheny. They did. Any bidder that wanted to could have made an alternative bid.

The Chairman. You mean they could have made a conditional bid?

Mr. Doheny. Yes.

The Chairman. But that was not a part of the proposal, was it?

Mr. Doheny. No. . . .

Senator Dill. You said you would be willing, in this statement, to turn back the leases if a board of experts would decide that something better could be gotten.

Mr. Doheny. No, if a board of experts would decide that the lease at the time it was made was not fair and reasonable, and a good lease for the Government, and as good as they could have obtained at that time.

Senator Dill. But you do not stand willing to turn the lease back on payment of the money expended, in the light of what has developed?

Mr. Doheny. Well, I have not decided to do that. I might, but the point is that I am not here to confess that there was anything wrong in connection with this matter. To turn this back would be a confession of wrong-doing. I am here, though, under a charge of doing something unfair, of obtaining unfair advantage of the Government. I do not want it to be decided by the public opinion on this testimony, I want it to be decided by a board of experts appointed by some responsible party who is unprejudiced, and who will examine into the matter impartially, and decide the matter, just what the terms of the lease amounted to for the Government at that time, and I would think this, that the board of experts ought to take witnesses from either side, to get the testimony, because I don't believe there is any board of unprejudiced experts who could be gotten to-day in the United States to pass upon that. They would have to take the testimony, and it would have to be based upon the testimony of various people. . . .

Senator Stanfield. Mr. Doheny, did it not occur to you at the time you were making this loan to Mr. Fall that if the public should become cognizant of the fact that you were making such a loan you might be misjudged, or Mr. Fall might be misjudged? And did not that prompt you to send money to Mr. Fall in cash rather than transmit it through the banks, as in the ordinary course of business?

Mr. Doheny. I am not quite certain whether I was prompted by any opinion of my own, or whether I did it at the request of Senator Fall. Of course, I might have been influenced by some such thought.

Senator Stanfield. Does it not seem to you that it should occur to a man whose relations to the Government were such as yours were, that you would be so discreet that you would not want that to become public, being a friendly act on your part, and a personal act as between you and Mr. Fall, and that you would not want to take the chance?

Mr. Doheny. Usually I am not very discreet. I do things offhand without thinking of the consequences.

Senator Stanfield. Well, it does seem to me, and I dare say it does to many others, that it was an unusual procedure for you to send that in money rather than to transmit it in a draft in the ordinary course of business, and I am trying to get it clear in my mind if you did it that way because it was a matter of discretion and you did not want any reflection on Mr. Fall.

Mr. Doheny. I don't know whether I was influenced by any matter of discretion or whether I was influenced by a request from Mr. Fall to send it in cash. . . .

TESTIMONY OF ARCHIE ROOSEVELT
JANUARY 26, 1924

U.S. Senate, Leases Upon Naval Oil Reserves, Hearings Before the Committee on Public Lands and Surveys, 68th Congress, 1st Session, Vol. 2, 1870–75.

. . . Senator Smoot. How long have you been in the service of Mr. Sinclair?

Mr. Roosevelt. August 1, 1919, I think it was, sir; right after the year of the armistice.

Senator Smoot. What positions have you held?

Mr. Roosevelt. I was just employed in learning the oil business out in Chicago at first. And then I went to—let me see—then I traveled around through the oil countries. Then I went to Costa Rica and Panama for certain interests of the Sinclair Consolidated Oil Corporation there. Then I was sent to Europe in connection with the French interests of Mr. Sinclair. Then I was transferred to the Union Petroleum Co., which was a marketing subsidiary of the Sinclair company, and I was with them in connection with their European affairs.

Senator Smoot. What year was that?

Mr. Roosevelt. Let me see—this is 1923; no, it is 1924. I think, Senator, that was in 1922, but I could not tell you for certain. It must have been around Christmas, 1921, or New Year's, 1922; I think it was New Year's, 1922.

Senator Smoot. In the last year what have you been doing?

Mr. Roosevelt. Then I was with the Union Petroleum Co., until the Union

Petroleum Co. was absorbed in some sort of combination or other with the rest of the Sinclair companies. I do not know how it was, but there was some rechanging of them. Then I went with Mr. Sinclair to Russia—while Mr. Sinclair was in Moscow and those places I was down in the oil fields in a technical capacity to examine their worth, you know, of Russian things; not as to Mr. Sinclair's things but Russian things generally.

Senator Smoot. The Russian situation as affecting oil?

Mr. Roosevelt. Yes.

Senator Smoot. Have you discussed this subject that is before this committee with any other employee of the Sinclair Consolidated Oil Co. with the exception of Mr. Wahlberg?

Mr. Roosevelt. Do you mean—

Senator Smoot (interposing). I mean the subject that is under discussion here, the lease to the Sinclair Consolidated Oil Corporation.

Mr. Roosevelt. Oh, yes, sir. I read the lease when it came out in the newspapers, and, naturally, it was a topic of interest all over the office. I have discussed it with a great many.

Senator Smoot. Have you heard any other employee outside of Mr. Wahlberg state that they thought there were payments made by Mr. Sinclair to Albert B. Fall?

Mr. Roosevelt. Yes; I have, sir. I have asked—I have done it this way: I have asked them if they thought it could be possible that such things would happen. I have been worried about the thing, you know, for quite awhile.

Senator Smoot. Well, it is quite natural you should be.

Mr. Roosevelt. I do not want to get any more people in wrong, really. I am in wrong, you know.

Senator Cameron. Speak a little louder, please.

The Chairman. Speak a little louder, Mr. Roosevelt, so that the members of the committee over here may hear.

Mr. Roosevelt. Yes, sir.

Senator Smoot. What the committee wants are the facts in the case, and we are not so much concerned as to whom we should call.

Mr. Roosevelt. Well, there is nobody that I have discussed this thing with who could in the slightest way give the committee any more information. I have simply confided to them my suspicions, and asked them if they thought there was any thing that warranted me—well, I was particularly anxious to know whether I should resign from the company. That is the truth of it.

Senator Smoot. When did you first think of resigning from the company?

Mr. Roosevelt. Well, I thought—not in connection with this exact fact, but I have considered resigning from the company before this. Do you mean just in connection with this exact fact?

Senator Smoot. No; when did you first contemplate resigning?

Mr. Roosevelt. Well, I have always wanted to leave the corporation simply because I thought I could make more money if I worked for myself some day.

Senator Smoot. Why did not you do it?

Mr. Roosevelt. Because I was unable to make the combination.

Senator Smoot. It was a financial matter, do you mean?

Mr. Roosevelt. Yes, sir; I did not have money enough.

Senator Smoot. You have spoken to virtually no one who knew of or thought there was any fraud in connection with this lease?

Mr. Roosevelt. Nobody; no, sir. I can definitely state that, sir.

Senator Smoot. It was January 18 that you called on Mr. Wahlberg?

Mr. Roosevelt. Let me see; the 13th was Sunday—

Senator Smoot (interposing). January 13 was Friday.

Mr. Roosevelt. Yes, sir.

Senator Smoot. Won't you state to the committee just what was said at that meeting, and why you went there, and all the facts connected with the conference?

Mr. Roosevelt. Of course, I want to again say it is a sort of hearsay evidence, is it not? I do not want to get anybody thinking I accuse them, or anything like that, or of any wrong, but I will tell you absolutely what I remember.

Senator Smoot. Well, I do not think telling the truth is an accusation.

Mr. Roosevelt. No, sir.

Senator Smoot. What we want here are the absolute facts in this case.

Mr. Roosevelt. Mr. Wahlberg—well, I have been worried about this thing for quite a while for several reasons. You can see that with my family connected with the Government, and in the Navy Department, I was anxious about it all the way through. As to Mr. Wahlberg, I either met him or he called me up, and I don't remember which, sir, and said he would like to see me. I said, "Fine," and he said, "Come up toward the end of the afternoon." I said, "All right." I went up there, and we had a long and rather rambling conversation, lasting, I should say, until around 6 o'clock. I asked him, and I think it was I who asked him, why Mr. Sinclair had left, why he thought Mr. Sinclair had left so suddenly for Europe. He said that he thought it must have been on account of the evidence that Mr. Walsh, that Senator Walsh, collected in Palm Beach.

The conversation went on, you know, and Mr. Wahlberg then—and I think at my request, I think I asked him if he would advise me to resign, and he said, yes—he did advise me to resign. We then talked about his situation. He said that he was very much worried; that he was unhappy; seemed to feel that he would be called up before the committee and asked to explain things and answer questions, and he wanted to know how far his loyalty to his employer went. And I—then I think he brought in the fact that he was frightened as to a great many questions, and did not know how far his loyalty to his employer went, because he had $68,000 of canceled checks of the foreman of the Fall ranch—not of the foreman, but $68,000 worth of checks, canceled, which had been made out to the foreman of the Fall ranch.

Then Mr. Wahlberg asked me how much he thought his loyalty to his employer went. I, of course, was thinking of that last thing. I said, "Well, of course, it would be absolutely my opinion that in anything like that, if you are called upon, you should tell the whole truth for the benefit of the country."

Then after that we left, and I got to thinking of this whole thing, got to thinking this whole thing over, and I talked to my brother about it, and the rest of the thing you know.

Senator Smoot. Did Wahlberg make any complaint to you about Sinclair not increasing his salary?

Mr. Roosevelt. He spoke to me of his general hard times that he was having.

Senator Smoot. Did he say anything to you that he had helped others but he had not helped him?

Mr. Roosevelt. I do not think he did, sir; no, sir; I do not think so.

Senator Smoot. You are not sure that he said those canceled checks were checks sent to the foreman or the manager of the Fall ranch?

Mr. Roosevelt. That is absolutely what I understood, sir.

Senator Smoot. You do not think you could be mistaken about that?

Mr. Roosevelt. I do not see how I could.

Senator Smoot. He did not mention the farm of Mr. Sinclair, the Sinclair ranch, did he?

Mr. Roosevelt. No, sir; I do not think he mentioned that.

Senator Smoot. He did not mention the foreman of the Sinclair ranch?

Mr. Roosevelt. No, sir; I do not think he mentioned him at all.

Senator Smoot. Well, did he show you those checks?

Mr. Roosevelt. No, sir.

Senator Smoot. What kind of table were you sitting at?

Mr. Roosevelt. We were not sitting. We were standing at the window looking out over the city, up at the top. The lights were lit, I remember, in the city.

Senator Smoot. So you did not see any checks at all?

Mr. Roosevelt. No, sir.

Senator Smoot. I did not know whether you did or not.

Mr. Roosevelt. No, sir.

Senator Smoot. The second conversation you had with him was over the telephone, was it not?

Mr. Roosevelt. Yes, sir.

Senator Smoot. That was on Sunday evening?

Mr. Roosevelt. Sunday around 1 o'clock in the morning.

Senator Smoot. One thirty o'clock in the morning?

Mr. Roosevelt. One thirty.

Senator Smoot. Did he telephone to you?

Mr. Roosevelt. Yes, sir.

Senator Smoot. Was it at your request?

Mr. Roosevelt. Yes, sir. I had asked a man that I know in New York—I said it was important business for me to get hold of Mr. Wahlberg, and he asked Mr. Wahlberg to call me up. And Mr. Wahlberg called me. I did not know Mr. Wahlberg's number; I had forgotten it. Mr. Wahlberg called me up, I should say, around 1 o'clock, or half past 1; somewhere around that hour. And that time, of course, my brother listened in. We had a double connection, you know. . . .

Senator Smoot. It was Mr. Crandall, was it not?

Mr. Roosevelt. Yes, sir.

Senator Smoot. You telephoned to him?

Mr. Roosevelt. Yes, sir.

Senator Smoot. Down to Port Washington, Long Island?

Mr. Roosevelt. Yes, sir.

Senator Smoot. And he came from Port Washington, Long Island, after you telephoned to him from New York?

Mr. Roosevelt. Yes, sir.

Senator Smoot. And went to the room of Mr. Wahlberg?

Mr. Roosevelt. Well, I asked him to do it anyhow, and I judge that he did.

Senator Smoot. You evidently think he did because Wahlberg telephoned you?

Mr. Roosevelt. Yes, sir; I am sure that he did.

Senator Smoot. And Wahlberg would not have known anything about it unless he had gone to his room?

Mr. Roosevelt. No, sir.

Senator Smoot. Evidently he did go there?

Mr. Roosevelt. Yes, sir.

Senator Smoot. Did you have any conversation with Mr. Crandall?

Mr. Roosevelt. Yes, sir.

Senator Smoot. Tell us what conversation you and Mr. Crandall had, I mean in substance. I know that you can not give it in detail.

Mr. Roosevelt. I told him it was awfully important for me to get hold of Mr. Wahlberg, and that—I think I told him I had to testify the next morning on the Teapot Dome thing.

Senator Smoot. Did Crandall know anything about the position held by Mr. Wahlberg in the Sinclair Consolidated Oil Co.?

Mr. Roosevelt. Oh, I guess everybody does.

Senator Smoot. He did not discuss the question with you at all, did he?

Mr. Roosevelt. Over the telephone?

Senator Smoot. Yes; over the telephone, when you telephoned to Port Washington?

Mr. Roosevelt. Mr. Chairman, I have discussed the question with Mr. Crandall. Mr. Crandall is a very good friend of mine, and I have asked him—well, I might just as well tell you about it even if it does get him in a little wrong. I asked him whether he thought I ought not to resign, and I said to him, "I am going to write my brother about this." And I told him I was worried to death about it, and worried to death how it connected me up with it, worried to death how it connected my brother up with it, and that I was going to telephone my brother, and probably write to him about it, and probably go to Washington, and if I had anything I wanted to look up I expected him as a friend of mine to do it for me.

Senator Smoot. The third call was on the morning of the 21st, Monday?

Mr. Roosevelt. Yes, sir.

Senator Smoot. About 7 or 8 o'clock. Will you state just what was said over the telephone at that time?

Mr. Roosevelt. He called me up and he said—let me see now how it started out. My brother was on the other end of that, too, both of us were there.

Senator Smoot. Then you were here in Washington?

Mr. Roosevelt. Yes, sir; in my brother's house.

Senator Smoot. He had to telephone from New York to Washington?

Mr. Roosevelt. Yes, sir. And my brother had an extension phone. He was up in his room and I was down in the downstairs part of the house. Mr. Wahlberg said he thought I was laboring under a false apprehension, that he had no facts, that he had only suspicions—

Senator Smoot (interposing). I did not hear the last of that answer.

Mr. Roosevelt. That he had no facts, that he had only suspicions. "But" I said, "Mr. Wahlberg, you told me this." He said "Oh, I could not." Now I am giving you direct quotations when I should not do that. I mean he stated to that effect, that he could not have said that because it was not the case, and that I must have been mistaken. I said "Mr. Wahlberg, I am sure you said that." And my brother cut in from up above. He said "Yes, I know, because Archie told me that you had said that." That was what the whole excitement was about. I said "Are you willing to go through with it?" He said "I will come down and tell the—" I said "Whatever you do, tell the truth." And he said "You bet I will do that." I said "Are you scared?" He said "Yes; I am awfully scared." And I said I was too. I think that was it.

Senator Smoot. You are convinced, are you not, that there were those two checks amounting to $68,000, or did you say the number of checks? He just said checks, did he?

Mr. Roosevelt. I think he said checks. I have been trying to go over this so much all the time, you know, that now I can not remember whether he said two or three checks.

Senator Smoot. You feel quite sure that he said that checks amounting to $68,000—

Mr. Roosevelt (interposing). Yes, sir.

Senator Smoot (continuing). Were canceled checks and that they were made payable to the foreman of Fall's ranch?

Mr. Roosevelt. I am sure that he said that. . . .

REFUSAL BY SENATOR ALBERT FALL
TO TESTIFY AND COMMITTEE
DEBATE
FEBRUARY 2 AND 7, 1924

U.S. Senate, Leases Upon Naval Oil Reserves, Hearings Before the Committee on Public Lands and Surveys, 68th Congress, 1st Session, Vol. 2, 1961–63; 1967–68.

. . . Senator Walsh of Montana. Senator Fall, do you care to make any further statement about the matters under consideration by the committee?

Mr. Fall. Mr. Chairman and gentlemen of the committee, I decline to answer the question for the following reasons and on the following grounds:

The committee is conducting an investigation under Senate Resolution 282, agreed to April 21, 1922, in the Sixty-seventh Congress, and Senate Resolution 294, agreed to May 15, 1922, in the same Congress; and further by virtue of Senate Resolution 434, agreed to by the Senate on February 5, 1923, during the same Congress; and I do not consider that, acting under those resolutions or under the last-mentioned resolution, which authorizes the committee to sit after the expiration of the Sixty-seventh Congress "until the assembling of the Sixty-eighth Congress, and until otherwise ordered by the Senate," this committee has any authority to conduct the investigation now attempted to be conducted by the addressing of this question to me.

I decline to answer on the further ground that on January 7, 1924, Senator Caraway introduced in the Senate of the United States, in this Congress, Senate Joint Resolution 54, attempting to deal with the lease of the Mammoth Oil Co.; that that resolution was referred to this committee and in due course the Senate discharged this committee as of January 24, 1924, and the Senate thereafter, on January 31, 1924, agreed to that resolution and completed its consideration thereof, the resolution being so amended as to deal in the Senate in a plenary way with the leases upon naval oil reserves which were before this committee under Senate Resolution 282 and Senate Resolution 294; and that this committee has no further authority to deal with Senate Joint Resolution 54, since it has been discharged by the Senate and the Senate itself has finally acted upon the resolution.

I decline to answer on the further ground that Senate Joint Resolution 54, as passed unanimously by the Senate, recites that it appears from evidence taken by this committee that certain lease of naval reserve No. 3 in the State of Wyoming, bearing date April 7, 1922, made in form by the Government of the United States through myself, Albert D. Fall, Secretary of the Interior, and Edwin Denby, Secretary of the Navy, as lessor, and certain lease of naval reserve No. 1 in the State of California, bearing date December 11, 1922, made in form by the Government of the United States through myself, Albert B. Fall, Secretary of the Interior, and Edwin Denby, Secretary of the Navy, as lessor, "were executed under circumstances indicating fraud and corruption"; that said leases were entered into without authority on the part of the officers purporting to act in the execution of the same for the United States and in violation of the laws of Congress; and that in the same resolution it is resolved that the President of the United States be authorized and directed immediately to cause suit to be instituted and prosecuted for the annulment and cancellation of the leases, and to prosecute such other actions and proceedings, civil and criminal, as may be warranted by the facts in relation to the making of said leases, and the President is further authorized and directed to appoint special counsel to have charge and control of the prosecution of such litigation, and I decline to answer on the ground that my answer may tend to incriminate me.

In declining to answer and in stating these reasons I wish to express full respect for the committee and for the Senate, but to remind the committee that on October 23d and 24th last, while this committee was sitting in recess of Congress and dealing with Senate Resolution 282, and Senate Resolution 294, I appeared before the committee and discussed at length the negotiations of the leases, including the lease of April 25, 1922, signed by Edwin C. Finney, Acting Secretary of the Interior, and Edwin Denby, Secretary of the Navy, relating to construction of oil tanks at Pearl Harbor, Hawaii; and thereafter was prepared to appear again before the committee; but since the Senate of the United States has passed the Senate Resolution 54, that action being concurred in by the House of Representatives, and the Congress of the United States has adjudicated, by the resolution, its finding that the leases were executed under circumstances indicating fraud and corruption, and has directed the President of the United States to prosecute such proceedings, civil and criminal, as may be warranted by the facts in the making of the said leases, I decline further to answer any question of this committee, on the ground that it may tend to incriminate me, and on the further ground first above stated.

The Chairman. The committee will go into executive session, and the room will be cleared. Mr. Fall, you may retire to another room.

Mr. Fall. Shall I remain outside?

The Chairman. If you please.

Mr. Fall. In any particular place?

The Chairman. No; so that you may be within call.

(The room was cleared at 10.45 a. m. of everybody except the members of the committee heretofore noted as present. At 10.55 a. m. the reporter was called into the room, and the following proceedings were had:)

The Chairman. The committee will be in order.

Senator Walsh of Montana. On February 5, 1923, the Senate adopted Senate Resolution 434, which authorized this committee to proceed, as it had proceeded, under Senate Resolution 282 and Senate Resolution 294, "which by the express terms of Senate Resolution 434 were continued in full force and effect until the end of the Sixty-eighth Congress," which resolutions authorized the committee "to sit during the sessions or the recesses of the Senate and after the expiration of the present (67th) Congress, until the assembling of the Sixty-eighth Congress and until otherwise ordered by the Senate."

While this resolution would clearly seem to warrant the proceedings heretofore had since the adjournment of the Sixty-seventh Congress, yet our right to do so having been challenged by Mr. Albert B. Fall in the statement read by him to the committee this morning, I move that when the committee adjourns it adjourn to meet at 10 o'clock Tuesday morning, February 5, 1924, and that the committee present to the Senate on Monday next, February 4, and ask the immediate adoption of a resolution in substance identical with Senate Resolution 282 and Senate Resolution 294 (67th Cong.) in order that the question raised by the statement of Mr. Fall may be eliminated.

The Chairman. You have heard the motion. Those in favor will say "aye." Those opposed say "no." The motion prevails. . . .

Senator Walsh of Montana. The witness, Albert B. Fall, having refused to answer any questions that might be put to him touching the matters under investigation by the committee, on the ground that his evidence might tend to incriminate him, and the committee being advised by counsel that the statute providing that a witness should not be excused from testifying before a congressional committee on such ground being less broad in its scope than the constitutional guaranty, so that proceedings for contempt or by indictment against the witness for contumacy would probably fail; and that if the witness proceeded to testify before the committee under protest he might gain immunity from prosecution, and the committee being advised by the attorney for the witness that his purpose to stand on his constitutional right is irrevocable, I move that the subpoena issued for the witness. Albert B. Fall, be vacated, and that he be released from further attendance on the committee.

The Chairman. You have heard the motion. All in favor of the motion say "aye." Those opposed say "no." The ayes have it and the motion prevails.

There will also be made a part of the record the opinion of counsel, Messrs. Pomerone and Strawn, furnished to the committee and referred to by Senator Walsh in his motion just made.

(The opinion is here made a part of the record, as follows:)

If the committee should undertake to compel a witness to answer under duress, either by contempt proceedings in the Senate or through the criminal process provided in section 104 of the Revised Statutes, necessarily the Government would be forced to take the position that section 859 is coextensive with the immunity provision of the fifth amendment to the Constitution.

If the witness is menaced by a threat, either of punishment for contempt or proceedings in the District court of the District of Columbia, he may acquiesce and testify, claiming that he is testifying under compulsion.

Such a witness might assert that under the Constitution he can not be compelled to be a witness against himself, and that if indicted for an offense relating to the subject matter about which he is compelled to testify he would be immune against the use of such testimony.

The Government, being forced to take the position as above indicated, that section 859 is coextensive with the immunity of the fifth amendment, the witness would doubtless insist that the position taken by the Government above referred to would work his complete immunity.

The decision in Counselman v. Hitchcock (142 U.S.) held that the scope of section 860 was not coextensive with the fifth amendment and that Counselman was within his rights in refusing to testify on the ground that he might incriminate himself.

In the Counselman case the court also said that while any testimony given by the witness could not be used against him in a criminal proceeding, yet the Government might avail itself of any leads or information derived from that testimony which would enable it to procure and use other evidence against the witness. The danger of proceeding along those lines is that, in the prosecution of a witness who might subsequently be indicted for the offense about which he is compelled to testify, the line of distinction between the evidence which the defendant was compelled to give and the other evidence obtained as the result of his testimony might be so indefinite as to make it practically impossible to distinguish, and therefore the probability of error would be great. Indeed, the testimony of the witness and the other evidence might be so commingled as to preclude the acceptance of any evidence concerning the subject matter. In view of the provisions of the fifth amendment we advise against permitting Mr. Fall to testify, unless he waives his constitutional privilege.

Note—Section 859 of the Judicial Code above referred to is to the same legal effect as section 860. . . .

WILLIAM G. McADOO TO IRVINE L. LENROOT
FEBRUARY 7, 1924

U.S. Senate, Leases Upon Naval Oil Reserves, Hearings Before the
Committee on Public Lands and Surveys, 68th Congress, 1st Session, Vol. 2, 1970–72.

Hotel Hamilton
Washington, D. C., February 7, 1924

Hon. Irvine L. Lenroot
Chairman Public Lands Committee
United States Senate, Washington, D. C.

My Dear Senator:

Since my arrival here yesterday a copy of the letter to you from Mr. E. L. Doheny has been shown me correcting his testimony before your committee with respect to the aggregate counsel fees paid to my former law firms, Messrs. McAdoo, Cotton & Franklin, and the annual retainer to myself. Mr. Doheny's letter confirms my statement issued recently in Los Angeles, namely, that my said firm received $100,000 in fees and that I have received as special counsel at Los Angeles $25,000 per annum for the past two years, and that Mr. Doheny's previous statement that there had been paid to me or to my firm and myself $250,000 was incorrect. Despite this correction, I desire to appear and testify before your committee immediately. I conceive (notwithstanding that Mr. Doheny's letter emphasizes his testimony to the effect that neither I nor my firm were ever employed in any way in connection with any matter relating to the contracts and leases which have been under investigation by your committee) that it is my right to submit to your committee and to the American people a complete statement of my professional association to Mr. Doheny's companies in order to show conclusively and succinctly that neither as counsel, nor in any other capacity, have I had any relation near or remote, to the contracts and leases which have been the subject of investigation before your committee.

It is also important that I appear promptly because the newspapers throughout the land have blazoned my name on the front page in glaring type in the most unfair and libelous manner as though I were involved in some way in this nauseating scandal. This has had the wholly unfair effect of diverting attention, temporarily at least, from the real culprit—an ex-member of the Cabinet of this administration who appears to have acted corruptly and to have grossly betrayed a public trust. I am not willing that the innocent shall be made to suffer in order that the guilty may be protected or shielded by this transparent effort to bring odium upon innocent men connected with a former administration.

In the several capacities in which I served the Government during the administration of the late President Wilson my record is an open book. I invite the most searching investigation of my official conduct while in public office, if it has not already been made. I betrayed no trust while I was in office, neither did I enrich myself at the expense of my country or its people, nor permit any other man to do so. As Secretary of the Treasury I received a salary of $12,000 per annum only, and as director general of all of the railroads of the United States I served without additional compensation. After the armistice was signed in 1918 I resigned as Secretary of the Treasury, because after six years in office I was in reduced circumstances and my health was seriously impaired. I had a large number of people depending on me for their living and their future and I was obliged, upon my return to private life, to take up the practice of my profession in order to make provision for them and for their future. To resume the practice of my profession was obviously the proper and necessary thing for me to do.

Early in 1919 I entered an active law firm in New York with a wide general practice as its senior member and until January 1, 1922, continued in the active practice of law in New York City. Since that time I have been actively engaged in the practice of law in Los Angeles.

With the growth of governmental instruments, the contacts of modern business of all kinds with the Government have become more frequent and necessary, and no lawyer can enjoy a remunerative practice without appearing in behalf of his clients before the courts, governmental agencies, commissions, and departments. If public opinion debarred a lawyer who had held public office from such work, his opportunity to make a living or acquire a competence for his family would be at an end. In my work, both in New York and Los Angeles, I have accepted such law business as has been offered to me and which I was legally entitled to take, provided the business was honorable and proper. In addition to arguing cases in the courts, I have argued matters before some of the Federal departments and have filed briefs and memoranda in these departments, among others, the State and Treasury Departments and the Shipping Board.

I never knew Mr. Doheny until after I resigned as Secretary of the Treasury. About a year after my resignation he called on me in my office in New York City and expressed a desire to retain me in his companies' Mexican difficulties, growing out of article 27 in the Mexican constitution, adopted some years before, under which the Mexican Government was attempting to confiscate property of American citizens by giving retroactive effect to said article. I knew that our Government, early in 1918, while I was a member of the Cabinet, had solemnly protested against the unfairness of the retroactive effect of this article of the Mexican constitution and that to represent a client whose property in Mexico was jeopardized thereby was in harmony. I was willing to accept the employment and my firm was paid a fee of $100,000.

At that time Mr. Doheny stated that the properties of the Doheny companies then threatened with confiscation were worth several hundred million dollars, so that the question was vital to his companies and he would be willing to pay ten times the fee if we got for his companies a satisfactory settlement in the Mexican question. No additional fee was ever paid.

Thereafter for a period of over two years I and members of my firm conferred frequently with Mr. Doheny and his officers and joined with other counsel representing American oil interests in Mexico in filing briefs and memoranda and representations to the State Department in an attempt to get such diplomatic action as the rights of the oil companies were entitled to under the various notes of the State Department. My connection with the Doheny companies was, I think, known to all those officially connected with Mexican oil interests. In that period also my firm worked on matters concerning a commandeered tanker which the Government had agreed to return to the Doheny companies.

During the year 1921 I made a trip to Mexico and interviewed Mexican authorities, among others President Obregon, in an effort to have the retroactive effect of the clause in the Mexican Constitution, to which I have referred, modified or changed. On my return I advised Mr. Doheny that the oil companies having interests in Mexico would, in my opinion, do well to have representatives confer with the Mexican officials with a view to effecting an adjustment.

In January, 1922, my firm dissolved and I then informed Mr. Doheny that it was my intention to take up my residence and practice law in California, whereupon he said to me that he would like to retain me as special counsel in connection with his companies at an annual compensation of $25,000 and proposed the duration of such employment to be for a term of four years. To this I suggested a modification so that at the end of three years, at the will of either party, my services could be terminated. During my professional employment since moving to California, Mr. Doheny has conferred with me from time to time upon questions concerned exclusively with his Mexican interests.

When I read in the newspapers Mr. Doheny's amazing disclosures about his transactions with ex-Secretary Fall I refrained from immediately terminating my professional services with him, as was my first impulse, although I have now done so, fearing that the newspaper accounts might be as vicious and unfair to him as Charles P. Taft's partisan organ, the Times-Star, of Cincinnati, has been to me when in its issue of February 1 it set out in flash headlines on its front page the following malicious, and I charge purposely malicious, libel and lie: "McAdoo received $250,000 from the Doheny interests—was paid $50,000 a year 'on outside' while he was Secretary of the Treasury."

I indignantly protest against the widespread suggestion that I—and others, lawyers and laymen, who helped in the Mexican enterprises, of which

Mr. Doheny is the head—share any taint of any kind. I deny that insinuation as monstrously unfair. For those who, like myself, can stand up and make good this denial, it is not so important, but particularly do I resent the insinuation that because the late Franklin K. Lane, after his service as Secretary of the Interior, resigned and became, quite openly, an officer of the Doheny companies, he thereby shares the taint of corruption. It would be ridiculous if not so vicious.

What I have done was within my rights as a lawyer. In my representation of the Doheny companies in Mexican matters I never dealt in political influence, nor did I ask, or promise, or give, or receive political favors or other favors. If my conduct in acting professionally in these matters is open to criticism, then no lawyer can take a Cabinet office unless he be rich enough to give up all professional employment in business when he comes out of office. I do not believe that any such standard is wise or proper. I believe that the spirit of fair play of the honest-minded American people will not misunderstand my course in this matter, nor take their minds off of those who are guilty of betraying their trust as disclosed in this investigation.

Yours very truly,

W. G. McAdoo

TESTIMONY OF WILLIAM G. McADOO
FEBRUARY 11, 1924

U.S. Senate, Leases Upon Naval Oil Reserves, Hearings Before the Committee on Public Lands and Surveys, 68th Congress, 1st Session, Vol. 2, 2059–68.

The Chairman. Do you desire to make a statement, Mr. McAdoo?
Mr. McAdoo. Yes, sir.
Gentlemen of the committee, I am informed by your chairman that already there has been inserted in the record the letter I addressed to him on February 7, 1924, setting forth in detail the facts concerning the professional services rendered by my former law firm in New York, Messrs. McAdoo, Cotton & Franklin, and subsequently by myself in Los Angeles, in connection with the Mexican properties of Mr. Doheny's companies. It is clearly shown in my letter and in the testimony before the committee that neither they nor I have had any relation whatever to the leases made of the Teapot Dome and naval reserve. There is, therefore, nothing more to be said on that score. But I have sought the privilege of appearing before you in person for the purpose of contributing in any way in my power as a private citizen to the objects of this inquiry.

It has been assumed that honorably conducted law practice of a citizen holding no public office is not ordinarily a subject of congressional inquiry. I think it may fairly be presumed that if my name was not prominently mentioned in connection with high office my private practice as a lawyer would be of no interest to this committee or to the public. Whether or not it has been drawn into this inquiry to serve a partisan political purpose the country will judge.

It would be a crime against the public if the dragging of innocent people into this affair should divert attention from the guilty or prevent the discovery of those who have betrayed the public interest. The whole country is shocked and appalled by what has been revealed in this investigation. The fact that a former Cabinet office of this administration is already gravely involved has raised a strong suspicion in the public mind that others may be guilty. The faith of the people in their own Government is shaken, and the damaging effects upon public morale are so grave that the security of democratic institutions is seriously imperiled. The first duty, the imperative duty of the hour, is mercilessly to uncover and to bring to public view and scorn and punishment everyone who has betrayed the public trust or who has been guilty of wrongdoing in this humiliating and dangerous affair.

This question transcends political parties and partisan consideration. Clean and incorruptible government is vital not alone to Republicans and Democrats but to every citizen. For my part, I am eager to see partisanship stilled in the face of so grave a danger to our common country. It would be an inspiration to see men and women in private life and partisans of all parties in public life united as they were in the Great War in the common effort to destroy corruption and bring the Government back to honesty.

I should like to supplement my letter of February 7 with some of the reasons that prevailed upon me to represent Mr. Doheny's companies professionally in his Mexican difficulties.

Article 27 of the Mexican constitution of May 1, 1917, was an attempt to assert ownership by the Mexican Government in the mineral deposits of the subsurface land in Mexico. If this article should be given retroactive effect, it would result in the confiscation of properties of American citizens lawfully acquired prior to the adoption of that constitution. This presented a grave situation for American property rights in Mexico; so grave, in fact, that the Wilson administration on April 2, 1918, through Ambassador Fletcher, at Mexico City, filed a solemn protest against it. . . .

. . . This attitude was consistently maintained by the Wilson administration throughout its life. When the Harding administration came in Secretary Hughes adopted the same policy. This policy was insisted upon by the American commissioners to Mexico, Messrs. Warren and Payne, and, as I understand it, was practically made a condition of recognition of Mexico by the United States.

During the year 1918 I was Director General of Railroads of the United States. The fuel problem was one of the most serious with which we had to deal. I was then made to realize keenly the tremendous importance of fuel oil from Mexico. A great number of American industries along the Atlantic seaboard were dependent upon Mexican fuel oil. The preservation of this fuel oil supply was then and is now essential to our internal economy. Not alone is this true, but the question of an adequate oil supply and of an adequate oil reserve is one of the most important for any nation under conditions of modern warfare. In fact the crucial test, in the next war if one should come, is going to be not alone war machinery and appliances but control of an adequate supply of petroleum to meet the needs of national defense and offense. It is no exaggeration to say that the strongest nation in petroleum resources will be the most likely victor in such a contest. For all of these reasons, therefore, the American Government and the American people were interested in preserving the Mexican oil supply which was lawfully owned or controlled by American citizens.

In 1915 I called the First Pan American Financial Conference in Washington. It was attended by all the South and Central American republics except Mexico, which was then in a state of revolution. The following year, 1916, I attended the first session of the International High Commission of all the South and Central American Republics at Buenos Aires in Argentina. At this session were discussed economic, financial, and other problems of great consequence to the whole of Latin America, and I gained a familiarity with conditions prevailing throughout South and Central America which could not have been secured in any other way. I was deeply interested not alone in these economic and financial problems but in promoting closer and better relations between the United States and all of these Republics.

Mr. Doheny's companies as well as Mr. Doheny enjoyed an enviable reputation when he called on me in 1919. His companies were the outstanding independent oil companies furnishing the required supply of Mexican fuel oil to our industries along the Atlantic seaboard. They were also the only strong companies offering competition with the so-called Oil Trust in the United States. For the purpose of preserving competition and securing the essential supplies of fuel oil for our industries along the Atlantic seaboard, it was highly desirable to protect, by every legitimate and proper means, the oil-bearing properties of American citizens in Mexico.

When Mr. Doheny, therefore, asked my firm to act for him professionally in trying to prevent the confiscation of his valuable petroleum properties in Mexico, representing several hundred millions of dollars, it appealed to me because of my general knowledge of the oil industry and of Mexican and Latin-American relations gained in the manner I have described and because it was in line with the declared policy of the administration to protect American properties against confiscation in Mexico.

I believed that an opportunity was presented to render a genuine service, outside of my professional work, in promoting Latin American commerce, and more particularly in contributing to the protection of all American rights in Mexico, if retroactive and confiscatory effect to article 27 of the Mexican constitution could be prevented.

This, with my letter of February 7, 1924, gives the history of my professional connection with the Doheny companies. The service I have rendered to them was in good faith and in full satisfaction for the fees that have been paid. I owe them nothing and they owe me nothing.

I conceive that this matter is wholly irrelevant to the subject matter of your inquiry, but I have been willing to come here and give these facts for such use and for such value as they may have in the pursuit of your investigation.

The Chairman. Are there any questions?

Senator Walsh of Montana. I want to ask a few questions. Mr. McAdoo, when did you quit the Treasury?

Mr. McAdoo. December 16, 1918.

Senator Walsh of Montana. And the position of Director General of Railroads?

Mr. McAdoo. The 11th of January, 1919.

Senator Walsh of Montana. When did you start up your law business?

Mr. McAdoo. The firm was organized—there was already an existing firm of Cotton & Franklin, or they had an existing practice. They both had served during the war; and agreement was made for my entry into that firm in the early part of 1919. I took three months' rest after leaving the Treasury, in California, and on my return to New York, in April, 1919, I undertook the practice of my profession as a member of that firm.

Senator Walsh of Montana. And when did you first go into the service of Mr. Doheny?

Mr. McAdoo. I think it was November 30, 1919.

Senator Walsh of Montana. Had you had any business relations of any kind prior to that time with him, or with any of his companies?

Mr. McAdoo. None whatever. I had never known Mr. Doheny until I met him—he was on a citizens' committee of reception which met me when I arrived in Los Angeles, in January, 1919. I had not met him before, nor had I seen him from that time until he called at my office about this matter.

Senator Walsh of Montana. What have you to say as to the existence of any arrangement between you and Mr. Doheny as to your going into his service, prior to the time that you severed your official connection with the Government?

Mr. McAdoo. Why, there was never any such suggestion or thought. As I say, I never had met him until after I left the Cabinet.

Senator Walsh of Montana. It is in evidence here, Mr. McAdoo, that you made a trip to Mexico at one time?

Mr. McAdoo. Yes, sir.

Senator Walsh of Montana. What was the nature of your business in Mexico at that time?

Mr. McAdoo. Well, I went there—

Senator Walsh of Montana (interposing). First, when did you go there?

Mr. McAdoo. I went to Mexico in January, 1921, and one of the purposes was to discuss with the Mexican Government, or the Mexican authorities, these matters concerning article 27 of the Constitution. I had a conference with President Obregon, in which I sought to impress upon him the genuine disaster that would result to Mexico if an attempt were made to give article 27 retroactive effect. I not only outlined to him that any such attempt would prevent all American enterprise in Mexico, destroy all confidence in the Government, but that the credit which Mexico needed imperatively to rehabilitate her finances and to develop the country, could not be had if any such thing should be undertaken. I explained to him at that time that the American market was the only available market where there was any large supply of credit in the world, and that Mexico had no other resort except to the American market for such credit. Therefore, it was essential that the Government should make it explicit and definite that no retroactive effect would be given to this article, and that no confiscation of American properties would be attempted. President Obregon expressed himself as being entirely in accord with that view, and said that his Government did not intend to give retroactive effect to this article, and that certainly there was no intention to confiscate American properties in Mexico. I told him there was a general feeling of insecurity as to that matter, and would be until some definite and decided action had been taken by the Government with respect to it, which would satisfy the doubts which had been raised.

Senator Walsh of Montana. That is all.

The Chairman. Are there other questions by members of the committee?

Mr. McAdoo, in order that the record may be complete, I would like to state to you that on January 31 Senator Reed of Missouri, on the floor of the Senate, made this statement:

> I understand that Mr. Doheny is still in town and that he is about to leave. Before he leaves this city I want to ask the committee to give him a thorough examination. I want to ask the committee, by direct and pointed questions, to inquire from Mr. Doheny whether he has ever at any time, either by himself directly, through his agents, or through his corporation, given or contributed any money to any person at the time holding a public position, and who the person is, or whether he has, immediately or shortly after discontinuance in office of any such public official in the manner I have already specified, contributed or given any money to him.

It was upon that request, Mr. McAdoo, that Mr. Doheny was asked the question in which your name was drawn out as one of that counsel. Do you think this committee would have been justified in refusing that request of Senator Reed?

Mr. McAdoo. No, sir. I am glad you brought it out. I hope this committee will not think that I am criticizing them in any way for bringing out these facts. On the contrary, I think nothing was left to you, in the face of that statement, except to bring it out. And I repeat, I am glad it was brought out. I think the matter is wholly immaterial and irrelevant to this inquiry, I am frank to say, and I do not see that it has any concern with it. But, nevertheless, if it has any concern with it, and if it will contribute in any way in discovering or revealing the people who have been guilty of wrongdoing, I am very glad indeed to have it brought out.

The Chairman. You have now severed your connection with Mr. Doheny?

Mr. McAdoo. I have, sir.

The Chairman. When did you do that?

Mr. McAdoo. I did it February 2.

The Chairman. The day after he testified?

Mr. McAdoo. The day after he testified. I have explained in my letter why I did not do it sooner. I am not misled generally by newspaper headlines. He had been a client, and he had acted in the most honest and scrupulous way always with me. There was never any suggestion of anything else in the matter that he consulted me about. And I was unwilling, in reading the headlines about his testimony, which grieved me very much, to discontinue the connection. I wanted to see all there was in that connection. Otherwise I should have acted immediately.

The Chairman. When did your retainer—yours, individually—with Mr. Doheny begin?

Mr. McAdoo. When I went to Los Angeles.

The Chairman. About what time?

Mr. McAdoo. About January, 1922.

The Chairman. About the first of the year?

Mr. McAdoo. Yes, sir.

The Chairman. And what services have you performed for Mr. Doheny since that time?

Mr. McAdoo. Well, I have been simply his special counsel, acting in an advisory capacity from time to time.

The Chairman. As he chose to advise with you about matters?

Mr. McAdoo. As he chose to advise with me about matters.

The Chairman. But he has not advised with you with respect to any matters other than Mexican matters?

Mr. McAdoo. No, sir. The professional relationship began in that connection, and it continued in that connection. I have never been consulted about any of his oil leases. He has his regular attorneys. I am not one of them. I have simply been acting in the capacity of special counsel to pass upon such matters and to give advice upon such matters as he presented to me. He was free to ask me, but he never did.

The Chairman. You would have advised him if he had asked you?

Mr. McAdoo. I would have advised him if he had asked me. I am free to say if he had advised with me about this matter he never would have gotten into this difficulty.

The Chairman. Now, in your letter you state, Mr. McAdoo, with reference to your employment here—

> Thereafter for a period of over two years I and members of my firm conferred frequently with Mr. Doheny and his officers and joined with other counsel representing American oil interests in Mexico in filing briefs and memoranda and representations to the State Department in an attempt to get such diplomatic action as the rights of the oil companies were entitled to under the various notes of the State Department.

Did you appear personally before the departments here in that matter?

Mr. McAdoo. I did not, sir. My partner, Mr. Cotton, appeared before the State Department on occasions. I purposely refrained from going in person, merely because I wanted to scrupulously observe every possible propriety in this matter. There was no question of political influence, because the policy of the administration was to protect American properties in Mexico. All we were seeking to do was to follow the declared policy of the administration. That is the policy of this administration, and it was of the Wilson administration.

The Chairman. There had been no change in the policy from the Wilson administration and this one?

Mr. McAdoo. No, sir. I do not believe any American administration could survive if they did not stand for the protection of American life and property, not only in Mexico but in every nation in the world.

The Chairman. Mr. Doheny testified that the employment of your firm here ceased with the incoming of the new administration.

Mr. McAdoo. He is in error about that. Mr. Doheny made several errors—unconsciously, I am sure—

The Chairman (interposing). You still think unconsciously, Mr. McAdoo?

Mr. McAdoo. I do not believe, for instance, that Mr. Doheny deliberately intended to create a wrong impression about the amount of fees paid to my firm and myself. But he did misstate the amount. He missed is very widely. But my firm remained as counsel under that retainer for the 15 months of the Wilson administration; it began about November 30, 1919, and continued throughout that term until March 4, 1921, and continued throughout the Harding administration until 1922, when the firm of McAdoo, Cotton & Franklin was dissolved. We were subject to consultation about any matters during that time.

The Chairman. What did your firm do after the new administration came in, if anything, with reference to briefs, appearances, or otherwise, under the new administration?

Mr. McAdoo. I made only one appearance. I felt that certainly no one could claim—although it was an unconscious feeling—that no one could claim that there was any attempt on the part of a Democrat to exercise influence on a Republican administration. So I appeared before Undersecretary Fletcher, who has been ambassador to Mexico, and expressed the hope that the new administration would be as vigorous in its assertions of the right of Americans as the other administration had been. I knew Mr. Fletcher very well. He had been ambassador to Mexico, and had been highly honored, and I knew his familiarity with the Mexican problem. I made no other appearance before the State Department.

The Chairman. Is that the extent of your appearance before the official of the new administration in behalf of Mr. Doheny? I am confining it to that.

Mr. McAdoo. I think it was, because as a result of the trip I made to Mexico in 1921 I suggested to Mr. Doheny that I thought the time had arrived for him and other Americans similarly situated to visit Mexico and take up in person the difficulties with the authorities that had so long been there. They made that trip in 1921. I do not remember what month. And they arrived at some sort of understanding with the Mexican Government. The result was that the acute stages were relieved shortly after the Harding administration came into existence.

The Chairman. When was it you went to Mexico?

Mr. McAdoo. In January, 1921.

The Chairman. And when was it you concluded your visit and returned? How long were you there, in other words?

Mr. McAdoo. I was there 10 days to 2 weeks in Mexico City, as I recall it.

The Chairman. Then that was done during the last administration?

Mr. McAdoo. During the last administration; yes—no; 1921—the Harding administration came in on March 4, 1921.

The Chairman. You said you went in January?

Mr. McAdoo. Yes, sir.

The Chairman. And you said the last administration.

Mr. McAdoo. Yes.

The Chairman. So the trip to Mexico was not during this administration?

Mr. McAdoo. No, sir; it was just prior to the incoming of this administration.

The Chairman. Then since this administration has come in your service has been confined to such matters as Mr. Doheny chose to advise with you about?

Mr. McAdoo. With respect to these matters.

The Chairman. I say as he chose to advise with you about, and you say he only advised with you about this matter?

Mr. McAdoo. Precisely.

The Chairman. You referred to a contract you had with Mr. Doheny, extending over a certain period of time, in your letter to us, I mean.

Mr. McAdoo. This last retainer, do you mean?

The Chairman. Yes.

Mr. McAdoo. Yes, sir.

The Chairman. He desired a four-year contract and you agreed on a three-year contract?

Mr. McAdoo. He suggested he would be glad to retain me; yes.

The Chairman. You say in your letter requesting appearance before the committee:

> It is also important that I appear promptly, because the newspapers throughout the land have blazoned my name on the front page in glaring type in the most unfair and libelous manner, as though I were involved in some way in this nauseating scandal. This has had the wholly unfair effect of diverting attention, temporarily at least, from the real culprit—an ex-member of the Cabinet of this administration, who appears to have acted corruptly and to have grossly betrayed a public trust.

If it be true that that ex-Cabinet member has so acted, and that the other party to the transaction was Mr. Doheny, do you consider Mr. Doheny equally guilty with the ex-Cabinet official?

Mr. McAdoo. Not equally; but I think he is guilty of a very serious matter. Of course, gentlemen of the committee, I do not undertake to express judgment before you have your testimony completed. I say it appears.

The Chairman. Yes.

Mr. McAdoo. I do not think anything about these facts except what have been revealed before this committee.

The Chairman. I understand.

Mr. McAdoo. And I think it would be uncharitable really, to seek to render premature judgment about anything. In my feeling, and I think justified, of indignation—in my feeling, quite keenly, of the way in which my name has been presented to the country as involved in some way in this affair, when I have had no more to do with it than the planet Mars, I have, perhaps, expressed myself with some indignation. I think any righteous—I think any honest man would feel the same way.

I called attention in my letter to the headlines in the Times-Star of Cincinnati, a paper owned by Mr. Charles P. Taft, a partisan paper, in which it is represented, in the headlines, that I was getting a retainer from Mr. Doheny on the side while I was Secretary of the Treasury. Now, gentlemen, a frightful wrong is done to any decent citizen when such things are made possible in this country. Under our Anglo-Saxon system of jurisprudence we console ourselves with the axiom that every wrong has a remedy. Well, we know that is not true. Here is a wrong for which it is very difficult to find a remedy. Libel suits do not offer a satisfactory remedy.

The Chairman. Mr. McAdoo, that statement was not justified by anything which came before this committee.

Mr. McAdoo. No; and I do not accuse the committee, Mr. Chairman, of any responsibility for that. Of course, the fact that irrelevant testimony was introduced here—and you have explained the conditions under which it was introduced, and I have stated already I do not think the committee could have avoided acting as it did—nevertheless, it has given the newspapers, or such newspapers, an opportunity of making these gross misrepresentations and publishing these hideous libels.

SENATE DEBATE OVER DEMANDS FOR DENBY RESIGNATION FEBRUARY 11, 1924

Congressional Record, 68th Congress, 1st Session, 2223–26; 2230–45.

Mr. Spencer. Mr. President, we are called upon to-day to vote upon a resolution expressing as the sense of the United States Senate that the President of the United States immediately request the resignation of Edwin Denby as Secretary of the Navy. There are one or two observations which it seems to me, in fairness in considering the question, we ought to bear carefully in mind.

The first one is that we are called upon in a quasi judicial capacity to give our judgment in a matter which is at the present time pending, at least the subject matter out of which it grew is pending, before a committee of the Senate who have not yet made their final report or completed their examination. We are asked to take an action which in the very necessity of the case places the brand of shame upon a man certainly whose career is during years of services untainted with dishonor because in the judgment of some he was mistaken in his interpretation, as I shall show in a moment, of a law which we ourselves passed. We are called upon to take that action while the very subject matter out of which it grew is still pending and the evidence in which is not yet completely received, nor have the committee yet made their report.

The second observation that I care to make is that the Cabinet of the

President of the United States is his official family. There is no constitutional provision for a Cabinet by that name. Every member of the Cabinet is provided for by legislation and the combined membership make up the official family of the President. When the President is considering the make-up of his official family, I take it, there are few Senators in this Chamber who would think it either proper or desirable for the Senate to pass any resolution either advocating or disapproving of any proposed member of the Cabinet. We have one function in the selection of Cabinet members and only one, and that is when the appointment is made and comes before the Senate we can then, if in the judgment of the Senate that man is either incapable or unworthy of the office, fail to confirm him and the matter there ends.

Our function is somewhat similar in connection with the removal of a Cabinet officer. We have only one method by which we can properly participate in the removal of a Cabinet officer. We can not impeach him. If the House of Representatives, in its judgment, impeaches a Cabinet officer we can try that impeachment, and except for that we have no official function in connection with his continuance in office. It is the President's official family, and neither in the selection of it, except the power of confirmation, nor in the removal of a Cabinet officer, except by way of impeachment instituted by the House of Representatives, have we any proper mode of procedure.

The third observation I desire to make, Mr. President, is this: On neither side of the Chamber, either in the judgment or from the speech of those who believe Secretary Denby ought not to remain a member of the Cabinet, or in the judgment or from the speech of those who think he ought to remain as a member of the Cabinet has there been the slightest intimation of anything that has been dishonorable or corrupt on his part or that he had any knowledge of anything that was dishonorable or corrupt. The basis of this resolution lies in the fact that he misinterpreted, if he did, the construction of an existing law.

I call attention to the consideration of the provisions of that law. In 1920 Congress passed this law to which I shall refer. It was in the administration of President Wilson. That law certainly had the entire approval of, if it did not originate with, the Secretary of the Navy in the Wilson Cabinet, Mr. Daniels. Congress said when they passed that law—and I call my colleagues' attention particularly to the language which we used in that law. We provided:

> That the Secretary of the Navy is directed to take possession of all properties within the naval petroleum reserves as are or may become subject to the control and use by the United States for naval purposes and on which there are no pending claims or applications for permits or leases—

What was the purpose of placing in the hands of the Secretary of the Navy these oil reserves, and how broad was the power which we conferred upon him? We said that when the Secretary of the Navy should come into the possession of those oil reserves which we had directed him to take possession of—here I digress for a moment to emphasize the language—that the Secretary of the Navy in taking possession of the oil reserves of the Nation should "conserve, develop, use, and operate the same."

An oil field can not be developed except by taking the oil out of the ground; the oil in an oil field can not be used except by removing it to the surface of the earth. We followed the grant of power over the naval oil reserves by saying to the Secretary of the Navy—and notice the broadness of the power conferred—that in his discretion he should "conserve, develop, use, and operate those oil fields," "directly," if he liked, "or by contract, lease, or otherwise." We gave him the power to lease those lands when we passed that law. Approved June 4, 1920.

More than that, when we gave him the power to "develop, use, and operate" those lands, and said to him, "You can do it yourself or you can lease or contract the doing of it," we also said to him—and, Mr. President, I call attention to these words—you can "use, store, exchange, or sell the oil and gas products thereof.". . .

Mr. Robinson. In view of the controversy that was in progress about the matter, does the Senator think that the transaction should have been conducted in secret, or does he think that the public should have been given an opportunity to know that a plan had been formed to transfer control over the naval oil reserves from the Navy Department to the Interior Department, and to lease them, so that the entire quantity of oil stored in the reserves might be exhausted?

Mr. Spencer. I think publicity is always most desirable, and anything done in secret is not only an undesirable but a most unwise policy.

The main proposition is, Did the Secretary of the Navy, first, have the legal right to transfer the power to make those leases from himself to the Secretary of the Interior, or did the President have the right to designate any such removal? I do not think he did; but that is a judicial question about which there is doubt.

Mr. Robinson. Will the Senator yield to one further question?

Mr. Spencer. If it is one further question, I will do so with pleasure.

Mr. Robinson. It is one further question, and I would like to have the Senator answer it. Why, why, why was this transaction conducted in secret?

Mr. Spencer. I do not know; perhaps the Senator does.

Mr. Robinson. Does not the Senator think it would be interesting to find out, if possible?

Mr. Spencer. It might be. I think the Senator has struck the nail on the head. It would be interesting and fair to find out something more about this matter before, like a mob, we rush into the Executive office with our resolution saying that it is our "sense," and before we ourselves know all the facts, that the President immediately request the resignation of the Secretary of the Navy—

Mr. Robinson. Now, will the Senator yield for a question?

Mr. Spencer. Just wait a moment. When, as I said a moment ago, the very committee out of which these things grew have not yet finished their examination of the question; but the Senate, not waiting for the completion of that examination, nor waiting until all the evidence is in, while the proceeding is still pending, does what a justice of the peace would not do, jumps to a conclusion and, as far as it can, decides that question for one side while the evidence is still being introduced.

Mr. Robinson. Will the Senator yield now for a question?

Mr. Spencer. I thought awhile ago it was "one further question." I yield with pleasure.

Mr. Robinson. This is one further still. The Senator knows that Secretary

Denby has been upon the witness stand three times in the hearings before the Committee on Public Lands and Surveys. Does he not know that the Secretary has been repeatedly asked why the transaction was carried on in secret, and that he has failed to give any reason whatever?

Mr. Spencer. If the Senator from Arkansas says so, I have no doubt about it. That does not change the fact that the Senate of the United States, in whose history the Senator from Arkansas has had a great part, should not be so precipitate in interfering with executive matters as to demand, during the pending hearing, the immediate resignation of the Secretary of the Navy. . . .

Mr. Fletcher. I wanted to ask the Senator this question: Conceding, for the sake of the argument, that the transfer of authority from the Secretary of the Navy to the Secretary of the Interior, which the Senator himself does not approve, is a judicial question, the fact is that the Secretary of the Navy joined in these leases with the Secretary of the Interior. What will the Senator do with the question of the poison of fraud which permeates those leases from beginning to end?

Mr. Spencer. The authority to transfer we have already discussed. Undoubtedly there must have been doubts in the minds even of those to whom the leases were given, because they were not content, as the Senator from Florida has suggested, that the signature of the Secretary of the Interior, to whom the authority had been transferred, would alone suffice. The signature of the Secretary of the Navy was added. But, I say to the Senator from Florida, and I am sure he will agree with me in this, that if there was any fraud in the action of the Secretary of the Interior, or in connection with these leases; if there was bribery or corruption, it has not yet been suggested upon the floor of the Senate, from either side of the Chamber, that the Secretary of the Navy either himself participated in it, or that he had the faintest suspicion or the slightest knowledge of any such fraud or corruption. Therefore, where is the basis, so far as the Secretary of the Navy is concerned, for requesting his immediate resignation? . . .

Mr. La Follette. Mr. President, I observe that there remains for general discussion but an hour and 10 minutes. I will make all possible haste, in order that I may leave, as I hope to, some portion of the time for my colleagues, many of whom I know are anxious to speak upon this important subject, before the time fixed for the termination of general discussion shall be reached.

In order that I might keep within compass upon a subject which tempts me to extended discussion, I have reduced to manuscript all that I hope to say, and shall follow my prepared remarks unless in a way compelled to make digressions.

Mr. President, before I discuss the pending resolution I wish to say a word in commendation of the senior Senator from Montana [Mr. Walsh] for the great public service he has performed in conducting the investigation into the entire subject of the leasing of our naval oil reserves.

This investigation has taken a full year of time and of his energy. He has conducted it under conditions of great difficulty and against obstacles which must at times have seemed almost insuperable. It has made heavy inroads upon his strength and health and has demanded the sacrifice of all other interests.

It may well be that the widespread ramifications of the scandal which has been recently unearthed largely through the efforts of the senior Senator from Montana may impose upon him too heavy a burden. He must not be hampered by lack of capable and trustworthy assistance. This investigation is not yet concluded, and I venture to say therefore to the Senate and to the members of the Public Lands Committee that he should be given the strongest support in directing this investigation to its conclusion and absolute freedom to select and employ whatever assistance he may need.

Throughout all the weary months of this investigation he has driven straight ahead, turning neither to the right nor to the left; often no doubt discouraged but never permitting discouragement to dull his determination to go to the very bottom of this affair.

I believe also that the Senate should in a proper manner express its appreciation of the faithful and loyal services to the best interests of the Nation and the highest traditions of the Navy of those naval officers who have resisted in every honorable manner the surrender of the naval oil reserves. Among those who have rendered this high service are Admiral Griffin, retired; the late Admiral Schroeder, Admiral McGowan, retired; Captain Halligan, Commanders Richardson, Stuart, Landis, and Wright, and Lieutenant Commander Shafroth. I do not know these gentlemen personally, except Admiral Griffin, whom I have not seen in probably 8 or 10 years. There may be others who are equally entitled to recognition, but I feel that it is as important to award honor to those to whom honor is due as it is to fix responsibility for every breach of trust.

Nor can I pass on to the body of my address without saying a word about the splendid services of a private citizen, Harry A. Slattery, of Washington, D.C., who I know has contributed in no small measure to the development of this case. For many years as secretary of the National Conservation Association and later as a practicing attorney, Mr. Slattery has been a veritable watchdog of the Nation's resources. In every contest over these resources he has been on the people's side, ready to give his time without compensation and devote his knowledge of these questions to the public service. On more than one occasion during the long fight that has been made on this floor to protect the Nation's waterpower, its timber, its ores, and its oil from ruthless exploitation I have called for Mr. Slattery's assistance and I never found him wanting.

I feel that we are too often unappreciative of the splendid services that are performed both by those who are in public office and by the numbers of private citizens who are giving constantly of their time and energy to preserve this as a government of the people and for their benefit. So I take this occasion to express my own personal appreciation of the splendid services which these, as well as many others whom I have not named, have performed.

Mr. President, the question before the Senate is really a very plain one. Shall the Senate pass the pending resolution which, after reciting the provisions of a resolution already passed by the Senate, provides:

> *Resolved,* That it is the sense of the United States Senate that the President of the United States immediately request the resignation of Edwin Denby as Secretary of the Navy.

That is the question, and the only one before the Senate. . . .

No Senator participating in this debate has contended that it is in the public interest to continue Mr. Denby as Secretary of the Navy. None, so far as I am advised, have denied that it would be vastly to the public interest to remove him from the position of great power and responsibility he now occupies. Indeed, the most elaborate speeches made in opposition to the pending resolution rest in the last analysis upon the contention that he should be impeached rather than removed by the President.

The farthest that any Senator has gone in defending Mr. Denby, so far as I have heard, is to contend that it is open to question whether he is or is not guilty of those "high crimes and misdeameanors" which must be established under the Constitution before he can be impeached. Yet, sir, we are told that in this condition of our naval service—a service upon the intelligence and integrity of which the safety of the Nation is absolutely dependent—the Senate must remain silent and impotent no matter what the consequences of its inaction may be to the country.

Mr. President, I subscribe to no such doctrine, and I assert that such doctrine is without support in our Constitution, or in the laws of the land, or in any of the precedents of this body. On the contrary, it is the plain constitutional duty of the Senate, under the admitted facts, the undoubted facts, the undisputed facts, the statement of Secretary Denby himself, to adopt this resolution.

I shall take only a few minutes of the Senate's time to demonstrate this proposition, but I hope to demonstrate it so completely that it can never be fairly questioned again in the Senate or elsewhere.

What are the facts?

First, the President nominated and the Senate advised and consented to the appointment of Mr. Denby as Secretary of the Navy.

Second, the Senate must therefore share with the President the responsibility for Mr. Denby's official position and power and every act which he commits.

Third, by the joint action of the President and the Senate, Mr. Denby under the law, by virtue of his office, became trustee for the people of this country of great property interests, including (1) the entire Navy of the United States, its docks, navy yards, arsenals, etc.; and (2) three great naval oil reserves, Nos. 1 and 2 in California, and No. 3, known as Teapot Dome, in Wyoming. These naval oil reserves were created for, and were vital to, the operation of the Navy, which had been made as required by modern navy construction an oil-burning navy. It is common knowledge, and nowhere questioned, that oil is safest in the ground, where it can not be evaporated, or burned, or otherwise lost or destroyed.

The Navy rider amendment of June, 1920, gave to the Secretary of the Navy the power, and imposed upon him the duty, to preserve and protect the Government's oil supply contained in these great naval oil reserves. Mr. Denby could no more divest himself of his duties as the trustee of the naval oil reserves than he could divest himself of his duty to preserve and protect the ships of the Navy, the docks, the navy yards, and the arsenals. The statute which imposed upon him the duty of preserving these naval oil reserves gave him power equally to protect and preserve all the classes of property for which he was a trustee. He could no more divest himself of responsibility for one than he could divest himself of responsibility for the other. No Executive order could override the statute, which in this matter was the supreme law of the land. Under the power conferred upon the Secretary of the Navy by the rider amendment to the naval appropriation bill, adopted on June 20, he was invested, as was Secretary Daniels, with all the power necessary to protect the oil in the ground.

Fourth, Denby, almost immediately following his appointment as Secretary of the Navy, entered into a scheme with Albert B. Fall, Secretary of the Interior, whereby he proposed to turn over to Fall all power and responsibility for the naval oil reserves. His testimony and public statements show that he claims to have taken the initiative in thus surrendering his exclusive custody and trusteeship of the naval oil reserves to Fall, and in attempting to transfer to the Secretary of the Interior the most important powers and duties of his office.

It is obvious that Edwin Denby, Secretary of the Navy, could not lawfully divest himself of the trust which his great office imposed exclusively upon him. If he could delegate to Fall the powers and obligations of his office in part—of those relating to the naval oil reserves—he could delegate to Fall all the duties and all the powers of his office, and the position of Secretary of the Navy would, in effect, have been abolished. That Denby knew his action in this respect was unlawful is shown by the fact that after the lease of Teapot Dome was made by Fall, many days after, he subsequently signed the leases in an attempt to make it lawful. But Denby testified before the Public Lands Committee of the Senate in effect that it was the mind of Fall and not the mind of Denby which made the leases. The negotiations were conducted by Fall, the ranch of Fall, not the home of Denby, was the place of rendezvous with Sinclair. The hundred thousand dollars in bills so far proven to have been loaned was turned over by Doheny to Fall and not to Denby. But this does not absolve Denby.

Let me put to you a very simple illustration of the situation. Suppose a private individual is a trustee and has the possession of a great fund, which as trustee he is bound in the most solemn manner to preserve and protect for the benefit of the cestui que trust. And suppose, sir, under certain circumstances the trustee turns over to a third party the entire management and control and disposition of the trust fund, and merely signs without question and without investigation whatever documents are presented to him by the third person for the purpose of disposing of the trust fund. And suppose that this third person to whom the trustee has turned over the trust funds unlawfully dissipates and misapplies the funds for his own personal gain and profit. There may have been nothing criminal on the part of the trustee in thus turning over the trust funds to another, although his action was certainly unlawful, yet would any court absolve the trustee from responsibility for the misapplication and loss of the trust funds? Of course not. The question answers itself. But that is not all. Any court would immediately remove from office such unfaithful trustee just as quickly as it would remove him if he had profited personally by the misapplication of the trust funds.

Now, sir, no court can remove Denby from office except a court of impeachment, and then only upon proof of high crimes and misdemeanors —and upon proof so clear and explicit that it would compel a two-thirds vote of the Senate in favor of conviction.

As a practical matter, every Senator here knows that on the evidence as it now stands Denby can not be thus convicted, and an argument that the people of this country should be relegated to the slow and uncertain and probably unsuccessful procedure by impeachment, is merely an argument for the continuance of Denby in office.

The only other method by which he can be removed, and the only practicable method by which he can be ousted, is by action of the President. And just here, sir, is where the right and the duty of the Senate arises. The Senate, by its confirmation of Edwin Denby's appointment as Secretary of the Navy, advised the President in the most solemn manner, and by the deliberate and formal action of the Senate, that it approved Denby as a fit man for the office of the Secretary of the Navy. Since that time information has come to the Senate which shows Denby, even by his own admissions, not to be a fit and trustworthy man for the office, for, mind you, Mr. President, in the very face of the shocking testimony of the payment of money to Fall by Sinclair and Doheny, Denby—intellectually and morally abnormal, as it seems to me —publicly declared that if the opportunity were offered to repeat this monstrous proceeding, that he would do the same thing again. That deliberate and shocking statement made by Edwin Denby is found in the Congressional Record of January 29, and also in a more elaborate statement given by him personally to the press a few days ago.

Now, of course, Senators who wish to do so may argue that in this situation they have no duty to perform relative to Secretary Denby's further continuance in this responsible office. They may argue, if they choose, that it is an invasion of the President's prerogatives for the Senate to advise the President that it no longer believes Denby to be a fit man for the office to which the Senate confirmed him, and therefore that it has become the sense of the Senate that the resignation of Secretary Denby should be requested.

But, sir, so far from being an invasion of the President's prerogatives, I submit that common honesty and the purpose of the Senate to keep its own hands clean requires that it should certify to the President its conviction that Edwin Denby is unfit to hold the office of Secretary of the Navy and to urge that his resignation be requested. . . .

Mr. President, if we were here dealing with an exceptional case of official corruption, or discussing the fate of a single Cabinet officer, I should not trespass for another moment on the time of the Senate. But this case does not stand alone, and every Senator knows it.

This is but the latest of a series of organized raids upon the Public Treasury and the public domain carried out with the connivance of public officers. The distinguishing characteristic of the transaction now before us is that in this case a part of the corrupt consideration has been publicly confessed. I do not mean that in every case a man with a fat bag full of cash visited the public officials and in cash paid the price for the bartering of a public trust. But every man knows that public officials have not permitted the enormous frauds of recent years to be perpetrated either with their aid or without their opposition and not have received compensation for the betrayal of the public interest through some of the many indirect ways in which men can be bribed as effectively as if the cash were placed in their hands. . . .

You all know, as I do, that Albert B. Fall is not the only man who has profited by his betrayal of the public trust. We all know that Doheny and Sinclair are not the only captains of industry ready and eager to reward old friends with loans or other favors. We all know and the public knows that this Denby-Fall case is only one of a large number of public betrayals—that it is merely a putrid eruption on the body politic and important largely because it indicates a generally diseased condition.

You ask what I propose to do about it? I will tell you, in part. I propose in the first place that we have a thorough house cleaning; that those public officials whose hands are not clean shall be removed from office; that offenses such as those revealed in the present investigation of naval oil reserves shall not be condoned, and no official involved in scandal shall successfully hide behind legal technicalities or unsound constitutional contentions. There must be a public sentiment in office and out of it which will demand and exact from every public official the highest degree of diligence and integrity in public service. And there must be such drastic amendments of existing law and, if need be, new ones enacted which will properly punish such crimes as have recently been committed in the leasing of the naval oil reserves.

I pause at this point, Mr. President, to say that while no language is strong enough to properly condemn the dishonesty involved in these leases, the real wrong and the great wrong to the people of this country consists not in the individual dishonesty in this single transaction, but in the general policy which barters to private interests the great oil and coal deposits and the other natural resources belonging to the Government, and which should be held for all time for the benefit of all the people. The policy which permits officials to bargain away to private individuals these great resources of the Government is sure to result in just such scandals as the present. The only way to prevent such scandals and such crimes is to change the policy. . . .

. . . Not only must the individual, whether in office or out of office, be made answerable for his acts, but the political party, the managers of which connive at the looting of the public and seek to excuse the misconduct of the members of its party in high official position, also be held to strict account-ability. I say it with shame and mortification, but it is unfortunately true, that the political party of which I am a member, as represented by those in control of the machinery of the party, has played as sorry a part in this investigation as it did in the Ballinger investigation. The action of the leaders of the Repub-lican Party in the Ballinger case as much as any other one thing discredited the Taft administration and drove the Republican Party from power. So in the present investigation it has been reserved for a member of the opposing party to take the lead in the investigation, and without his persistance and insistence upon getting after the facts the investigation would have resulted in whitewashing public officials guilty of the gravest wrongdoing, as I believe.

It would seem as though the Ballinger case should have taught us a lesson, but apparently it has not done so, for the administration of President Coolidge is employing the same tactics in this case that the administration of President Taft employed in the Ballinger case. And I say to the leaders of the Republican Party to-day that the result of the policy they are adopting will be just as fatal to the administration of President Coolidge as their policy in the Ballinger case was fatal to the administration of President Taft. The policy of evading so long as evasion is possible, of excusing so long as there is the least possibility of having the public accept the excuse, and of hiding behind a paper barricade of legal technicalities can only spell defeat and possibly ruin for the Republican Party.

But it must be said that Democratic administrations are not by any means free from like offenses. The records of the Interior Department and the Department of Justice as well as other departments have their dark pages written under Democratic rule since I have been in public life in Washington. You will not have to search your memories or go far to find a fit companion in your own party, in the same office, for Harry M. Daugherty; and I venture to say—and I refer to it with some reluctance because of the death of the incumbent—that the Interior Department under the Democratic administration crowded close, with respect to some of these oil transactions, upon the disclosures that have caused such appalling shock to the country.

Mr. President, I still hope that the Republicans in the Senate will act in this case with due appreciation of the practical needs of the hour. There should be no politics on an issue like the present one. Do not attempt to throw dust in the eyes of the people. They see clearly what the issue is even if "great constitutional lawyers" are unable to discern it. The real issue here is whether the Senate shall go on record as being in favor of Denby's continuance in office or in favor of removing him from that office by the quickest and most practical legal means available. That is the real question here, and the people know that is the question; and the position upon that question of Senators voting here to-day will be determined in the public mind and properly so, according as they vote aye or nay upon that question. . . .

Mr. Howell. Mr. President, the purpose of our Constitution and our laws, unwritten and statutory, is to define, establish, and maintain the rights of our people. These rights fall into two general classes, first, property rights, alienable rights; and second, what I shall term human rights, which are primary and inalienable rights, such as the right to life, liberty, reputation, and the pursuit of happiness.

From time immemorial property rights have been the cause of encroachments on human rights by virtue of the power of wealth and its assumed privileges. The most glorious pages of history recount the struggles of mankind against such encroachments. It was the burden of these encroachments and an exalted ideal of human rights that led the Pilgrm Fathers to Plymouth, that sustained the Colonies throughout the stormy period of their infancy. It was this ideal that wrote the Declaration of Independence and laid the foundations of this Government. And yet notwithstanding this great dominating note in our history, the power of great wealth and its encroachments upon our institutions is the chief menace that confronts us to-day. Is it not lawless wealth—the insolence of wealth—that is responsible for these deplorable oil-lease scandals?

Mr. President, in view of these facts is this not an auspicious time to reassert the spirit of the Declaration of Independence, to announce anew our adherence to the exaltation of human rights above property rights? If this is so, Mr. President, the resolution now before the Senate should not be adopted, for if it is the Senate will go on record because of its action last week respecting these oil leases as placing property rights above human rights.

For days Secretary Denby has been on trial before this body, prosecuted by a score of most able pleaders. Has he been here, so that he might be confronted with his accusers, with the right of counsel and defense? No; he could not be here. It has been impossible for him to enjoy the constitutional privileges guaranteed to every accused person in this country. Nevertheless, last week, after declaring in effect the naval oil leases void from the beginning, the Senate afforded Sinclair and Doheny the privilege of maintaining in the courts their alleged property rights as defendants. But consider if the resolution is adopted in its present form Secretary Denby will receive no such consideration. He will be convicted and sentenced by this body as effectually as if it were sitting as a court of impeachment, and moreover, he will have no right of appeal. Yet Sinclair and Doheny will be haled into the district court, and may submit any verdict obtained therein to the court of appeals, and then there is the United States Supreme Court. This litigation may take 5 years, 10 years. By such action and the adoption of this resolution, would not the Senate be putting itself upon record as placing property rights above human rights? Can such a course be justified?

Let us consider the record as it stands. The Senator from Arkansas introduced a resolution that reads, omitting the preamble, as follows:

> That said lease of said date, and all modifications and contracts made thereunder, and all rights and immunities thereunder granted, is and are hereby canceled; that all of the resources therein sought to be conveyed, are hereby restored to the possession of the United States, and shall be held and retained for the use and benefits for which they were dedicated by Executive order prior to the execution of said lease; that there shall be an accounting had by the said lessee and assignees with the United States for all oils, gases, and minerals by it taken from said lands.

Had this resolution been adopted it would have placed in jeopardy the property rights of Sinclair and Doheny under these leases, because their only redress would have been as plaintiffs and not as defendants. The full meaning of this is not evident until it is remembered that should a judgment be secured by either of them, they would then have to come to Congress and secure an appropriation for its payment.

A substitute for this resolution was offered by the Senator from Montana, the original resolution being abandoned. The second preamble of this substitute resolution reads as follows:

> Whereas the said leases and contracts were entered into without authority on the part of the officers purporting to act in the execution of the same for the United States Senate and in violation of the laws of Congress.

This preamble was approved by the Senate prior to the adoption of the substitute resolution, of which it formed a part. The Senate thus being on record in a positive opinion that the leases were granted without authority, it necessarily followed that in the view of the Senate the leases were void from the beginning—that is, that there never had been a lease—and hence Sinclair and Doheny were merely trespassers. Therefore, the logic of the situation demanded that they should be treated as trespassers and ejected from the properties. In this manner only could they be forced into the position of plaintiffs in any litigation that might follow. At the same time, the Government in possession of the oil lands, would be in the best possible position to protect its interest by preventing the drainage of these oil lands through adjacent wells. It could do this untrammeled, and as it might deem necessary in the public interest.

Such a course has been followed by the Government time and time again in connection with the public lands. Thomas Jefferson, when President, proceeded in this manner. In 1807 Congress enacted a law authorizing the President to proceed in the same way in connection with trespassers upon certain public lands. During President Harding's incumbency a similar course was pursued in connection with this same Teapot Dome oil reserve, and for the ultimate benefit of Sinclair.

Why should the Senate have afforded Sinclair and Doheny special or greater consideration in view of all the circumstances?

To the end of carrying the Senate's attitude respecting the validity of these leases to this logical conclusion, I offered an amendment to this substitute resolution, which reads as follows:

> *Resolved, etc.,* That the said leases and contract are against the public interest, and the same were and are hereby declared null and void from the beginning.
>
> *Resolved further,* That the President of the United States be, and he hereby is, authorized and directed immediately to seize and take possession of the lands included in said leases and to cause suit or suits to be instituted and prosecuted for the annulment and cancellation of said contract, and all contracts incidental or supplemental thereto, and to recover the value of the oil thus far extracted under the provisions of said leases, and to prosecute such other actions or proceedings, civil or criminal, as may be warranted by the facts in relation to the making of the said leases and contract.

I regret to be compelled to add that this amendment was rejected.

In view of the foregoing facts, Mr. President, Secretary Denby's reputation is certainly entitled, at the hands of the Senate, to as much consideration as the property rights of Sinclair and Doheny. Therefore, I am not willing to vote for the resolution now before the Senate in its present form. However, I am willing to vote for the resolution if the following words are added thereto:

> If guilty of malfeasance or misfeasance in office.

I sincerely trust that this amendment will be adopted, thus placing human rights, so far as the Senate is concerned, at least upon the same plane as property rights, leaving the guilt or innocence of the accused to be determined by a court of impeachment or other constitutional tribunal, a proceeding wholly within the power of Congress to compel. . . .

Mr. Reed of Missouri. Mr. President, the argument is made that Mr. Denby has not had his day in court. We are not trying a lawsuit, prosecuting a man as a criminal, or foreclosing any rights of property. This resolution is before the Senate to be acted upon in view of the evidence that has been brought before the Senate. An office is not a property right. The sole question to be determined is whether, in view of the facts now before the Senate, the Senate ought to express an opinion to the President with reference to the continuance of Mr. Denby in office.

No one ought to desire to deny Mr. Denby a fair hearing with reference to the facts upon which we are about to act, and if he were denied that hearing I would be among those who would vote against this resolution. Three times he has been called before the committee, and has been permitted to make any statement he desired to make, and has been allowed to present fully and absolutely his explanation regarding every question involved in that investigation which concerned him personally, and acting upon his own statements, without any evidence outside of his own statements, we are confronted by the fact that he connived at a violation of the law by assisting in, if not instigating, the transfer of the properties of the Government, placed by law in his hands, into the hands of Mr. Fall.

We further know from his testimony, or undisputed facts which he in no manner denied, that while the transactions were being carried on between Denby and Sinclair, they were carried on secretly.

We know the further fact that he now reaffirms all that has been done, and declares that he would repeat the same performance if given the opportunity.

In the light of that undisputed situation, the Senate is simply called upon to say whether it desires to advise the President that the Senate thinks Mr. Denby should be no longer retained in office. Our action will not oust him from office; the President can still retain him, but we, as representatives of 48 States, can express an opinion to the President, and if he shall see fit to disregard it, then the onus will be upon the President. . . .

Mr. Brandegee. Mr. President, I do not intend to discuss the various phases of this transaction or their merits. I do not intend to discuss the question whether the President of the United States had a right to issue an executive order transferring the development of the oil fields from the Secretary of the Navy to the Secretary of the Interior. I do not intend to discuss whether the Secretary of the Navy or any other Government official violated the statute which I have just had incorporated as a part of my remarks, or whether he violated it, if he did, with honest intent or criminal intent. Those are all questions of law. I am not able to decide them. We as individuals may have our opinions about them, but they simply go for what they are worth as individual opinions.

On the 31st of January last, Congress passed Senate Joint Resolution 54, which authorized the President to retain special counsel in the case, and, without reciting the language of the resolution verbatim, it in substance directed the President to take all measures, legal or otherwise, for the protection of the public interest in this matter. That I think was appropriate for Congress to do as the custodian under the law of the public domain of the United States; because the Constitution gives Congress that authority.

At the time of the passage of that joint resolution, as to the preamble to it, containing the several whereases which recited as facts that the leases and the contract were entered into without authority on the part of the officers purporting to act in the execution of the same for the United States and in violation of the laws of Congress, and that the contract and leases were made in defiance of the settled policy of the Government, and so forth, I took occasion to state that I thought it was without the jurisdiction of Congress to express any authoritative opinion upon those matters whatever. I stated that I thought they were judicial questions which were to be determined in the legal proceedings which we had authorized to be taken under the joint resolution, but that I should vote for the resolution, the resolving part of it, withholding my approval from the whereases, because I was unwilling to vote against the joint resolution authorizing the President to bring the proceedings, and I could not get rid of the preamble to which I objected.

Mr. President, my opposition to the pending resolution, or to any resolution attempting to express the opinion of the Senate on the question of the dismissal or resignation of public officers of the United States, is based simply and solely upon my respect for what I consider to be the proper division of the governmental authority under the Constitution into the three coordinate departments of the Government. I do not think that the Senate has any jurisdiction of the question. I know that we all have our individual opinions. Mr. Denby, the Secretary of the Navy, was appointed by the President of the United States under the Constitution. The Constitution provides that the President may appoint, subject to the advice and consent of the Senate. We gave that advice and consent. We were functus officio when we had done that. The man had a complete title to his office. For the Senate of the United States to attempt to advise the head of the executive department of the Government that he ought to dismiss one of the officers whom he has appointed to office is, in my opinion, without authority on the part of this body and comes very nearly to being a piece of impertinence, if I may use the word without being offensive.

What would we say if the President of the United States, in whom the Constitution reposes the sole executive authority of the Government, should send his messenger over here with a communication to the United States Senate that in his opinion we ought to proceed to eject the President pro tempore of the Senate from his office? We would not even receive the messenger at the door. We would say to the President, practically, "This is no business of yours; this is a legislative matter; you attend to your executive business and we will attend to our legislative matters." What would be said of a Senator who would stand up here and advocate the passage by the Senate of a resolution resolving that a certain judge, who might have rendered an opinion that was unpopular in the country, should resign his office, or that the President of the United States should request him to resign because he had construed a statute in some way different from what our individual conception of it might be? . . .

Mr. Trammell. Mr. President, the defense offered on behalf of those presenting the case of Mr. Denby to the Senate seems to be principally based upon the alleged ground that he has not had a hearing, and also upon the further contention of some imaginary constitutional inhibition against Congress expressing itself upon a subject of this character. It has been stated, iterated and reiterated, that Mr. Denby has repeatedly had an opportunity of hearing before an authorized committee of the Senate, and the Record discloses that he was before that committee three times. How much more of a hearing could be desired? This resolution has been pending for two or three weeks, but neither the Senate nor the committee have received any communication from Mr. Denby asking for a further hearing; yet some Senators, in an effort to elicit sympathy for Mr. Denby, try to muddy the water and confuse the issue by saying he has not had "fair play." I would like for some of these Senators to suggest what they mean by "fair play." If calling him before the committee, if permitting him to testify three times before the committee is not "fair play," I would like to know what the Senators consider "fair play." He has had a hearing; he has had ample opportunity to present his case, and I do not see how Senators can contend otherwise, nor do I think the country, at least, will take seriously their position upon this question. No snap judgment is being taken against Mr. Denby. It might as well be said that we should not have passed any resolution with regard to Mr. Fall; it might as well be said that we should not have adopted any resolution looking to the recovery of these lands, because there had not been fair play with regard to Mr. Fall; there had not been fair play with regard to Mr. Sinclair and Mr. Doheny, because they had had only the same opportunity to present their side of the case that Mr. Denby has had to present his case. They were not on trial. No indictments had been placed against them. No resolution was pending here against them. So Mr. Denby has had the same opportunity, the same privilege of a hearing, that Mr. Fall had, or that Doheny had, or that Sinclair had; and I did not hear anybody raise his voice in defense of these gentlemen or attempt to excite sympathy for them. . . .

In my opinion, there is nothing in the Constitution that in any wise makes such an expression on the part of the Senate improper, and certainly the precedents of the Senate, in expressing itself on other questions, justify the Senate in taking such action, just as much as the Senate was justified and authorized in expressing its views upon other features of the inquiry. There is lodged in the President under the Constitution the duty of seeing to the enforcement and the execution of the laws, yet nobody said that we should not pass a resolution providing that this land should be recovered, and that appropriate action should be taken. Nobody questioned that, at least.

Mr. President, I think that Secretary Denby in his important office has failed utterly to conserve the interest of his country, that he has proven unworthy of his trust. This being true, he should be put upon notice that, as far as the United States Senate is concerned, it is the sense of this body that the President should request his resignation. . . .

The President pro tempore. . . . The Secretary will report the amendment proposed by the Senator from Nebraska [Mr. Howell]. . . .

The President pro tempore. The question is upon agreeing to the resolution.

Mr. Harrison and Mr. Robinson called for the yeas and nays, and they were ordered.

The result was announced—yeas 47, nays 34, . . .

So the resolution was agreed to.

The President pro tempore. The question now is upon agreeing to the preamble to the resolution. Without objection, it will be agreed to.

The resolution as agreed to is as follows:

Whereas the United States Senate did on January 31, 1924, by a unanimous vote adopt Senate Joint Resolution No. 54 to procure the annulment of certain leases in the naval oil reserves of the United States; and

Whereas the said resolution, among other things, declared as follows:

"Whereas it appears from evidence taken by the Committee on Public Lands and Surveys of the United States Senate that certain lease of naval reserve No. 3, in the State of Wyoming, bearing date April 7, 1922, made in form by the Government of the United States, through Albert B. Fall, Secretary of the Interior, and Edwin Denby, Secretary of the Navy, as lessor, to the Mammoth Oil Co., as lessee, and that certain contract between the Government of the United States and the Pan American Petroleum & Transport Co., dated April 25, 1922, signed by Edward C. Finney, Acting Secretary of the Interior, and Edwin Denby, Secretary of the Navy, relating, among other things, to the construction of oil tanks at Pearl Harbor, Territory of Hawaii, and that certain lease of naval reserve No. 1, in the State of California, bearing date December 11, 1922, made in form by the Government of the United States through Albert B. Fall, Secretary of the Interior, and Edwin Denby, Secretary of the Navy, as lessor, to the Pan American Petroleum Co., as lessee, were executed under circumstances indicating fraud and corruption; and

"Whereas the said leases and contract were entered into without authority on the part of the officers purporting to act in the execution of the same for the United States and in violation of the laws of Congress; and

"Whereas such leases and contract were made in defiance of the settled policy of the Government, adhered to through three successive administrations, to maintain in the ground a great reserve supply of oil adequate to the needs of the Navy in any emergency threatening the national security."

The result was announced—yeas 11, nays 70. . . .

Therefore be it

Resolved, That it is the sense of the United States Senate that the President of the United States immediately request the resignation of Edwin Denby as Secretary of the Navy. . . .

The result was announced—yeas 51, nays 25, . . .
So Mr. Robinson's motion was agreed to. . . .

TESTIMONY OF EDWARD McLEAN
MARCH 12, 1924

U.S. Senate, Leases Upon Naval Oil Reserves, Hearings Before the
Committee on Public Lands and Surveys, 68th Congress, 1st Session, Vol. 3, 2679–85; 2712–17.

. . . Mr. McLean. Senator Walsh, may I have the privilege of reading a
statement before cross-examination?

Senator Walsh of Montana. Yes.

Mr. McLean (reading):

My attention has been called to the fact that the authority of this committee in conducting this investigation is based on Senate Resolution No. 282 as
amended by Senate Resolution No. 294, both of which were adopted during
the last session of Congress.

In substance this committee is authorized to conduct an investigation of
the entire subject of leases upon naval oil reserves. Nothing that is not
connected with the leases by the United States Government to individuals,
persons, or corporations of lands included within the Government's naval oil
reserves, is pertinent or relevant to your investigation. I am advised that that
proposition can not be successfully or truthfully questioned.

Having in mind, therefore, the subject of this investigation and having
also in mind the widespread use in the public press of my name as one who
might have had some connection with the naval oil leases, or with the companies, individuals, Government departments, or public officials who did
have connection with the leases of the naval oil reserves, I want to make now
the following detailed and emphatic statement of facts:

I have absolutely no knowledge regarding any leases upon naval oil
reserves made at any time to any person or any company except such knowledge as I, in common with all the rest of the American public, have received
from newspaper reports or casual conversation.

As to the so-called Sinclair leases and companies; I never have known
anything about any lease of any oil land to the Sinclair company and know
nothing to-day about this except what I have learned in the newspapers and
from casual conversation. I do not know Mr. Harry F. Sinclair and have no
recollection of ever having met him even in a casual way. I have never had any
interest of any kind, directly or indirectly, for myself or any other person, in any
of the so-called Sinclair companies. I did not even know there was such a thing
as the Mammoth Oil Co. until I saw it mentioned in the press reports in
connection with this investigation. I did know, as any one who reads the
newspapers would have known, that there was a company known as the
Sinclair Consolidated Oil Co., but I have never had any connection with it or
any interest in it and have never owned or had any interest in a single share of
the stock of that company or any company connected in any way with it.

In a word, I had no knowledge of or connection with Mr. Sinclair's oil leases or his companies or his business or his transactions.

I do not know Mr. Edward L. Doheny, and as far as I am aware I have never seen him in my life. I did not know that he had any connection with any leases upon naval oil reserves until I read of them in the newspapers.

I do not know the names of Mr. Doheny's companies, but I am informed that he is president of the Mexican Petroleum Co. and of the Pan American Petroleum Co., and that those companies, like most large oil companies, have branches.

I have never owned, directly or indirectly, for myself or in connection with any other person whatever, a single share of stock in the Mexican Petroleum Co., the Pan American Petroleum Co., or any of their dependent companies, or, so far as I know, any company that Mr. Doheny had any interest in or connection with.

I know nothing about the contracts or leases between the Government and the Doheny companies.

Again, in brief, I have had no connection with, interest in, or transaction with Mr. Edward L. Doheny, or any company or business of his at any time in my life.

Former Secretary of the Interior Albert B. Fall has for several years been a personal friend of mine. My relations with him have, however, been personal and never official. I have never at any time had any official transactions with the Interior Department of the United States Government.

As regards the Navy Department and Secretary Denby, I can say the same as I have already said about the Interior Department. My personal acquaintance with Secretary Denby has been a very slight one. I have had no business relations whatever with the Navy Department and have never been interested in or connected with any contracts of any kind made by or with that department. The newspapers which I am connected with may have carried some Government advertising, but of course it will be recognized that this is a matter not handled by me personally.

Because there have been published indefinite and unfounded rumors from which the inference might be drawn that I had participated in the purchase of oil stocks, although any stock transactions I have ever had are my own personal affair and have no relation to the subject which your committee is authorized to investigate, to the end that the utter lack of foundation for many of the reports which have been sent out of this city may be shown, I desire to tell you just what stock transactions I have had. Only twice in my life have I bought New York Stock Exchange stocks and here are the facts about those two transactions:

In November, 1922, I bought 2,000 shares of Pure Oil Stock through Hibbs & Co., Washington, D. C. I sold this stock February, 1923, through Hutton & Co., Palm Beach, Fla., at a profit of about $5,500. This profit was entirely mine. My understanding is the the Pure Oil Co. is a company that has never had any connection with any Government leases and is in no wise concerned in this investigation.

In March, 1923, I bought 2,000 shares of Bethlehem Steel through Hutton & Co., Palm Beach, Fla. I sold it through Hibbs & Co., Washington, D. C., in

December, 1923, at a loss of approximately $30,000. This loss was entirely mine.

This is the entire story of any New York Stock Exchange stocks ever purchased or sold by me. I have never traded in any of the so-called curb stocks, nor have I bought or sold any stocks except those mentioned, with the exception of such local bank and trust company stocks as I am interested in.

I have never been interested in the purchase of any Sinclair or Doheny oil stocks, directly or indirectly, by which I mean that I have never made any such purchase nor have I had any interest in any such purchases made by anyone at any time.

The public press has repeatedly carried reports that an important witness was negotiating for immunity from prosecution in consideration of the disclosure by him of sensational facts. The press reports have too clearly indicated that I was that important witness for me not to be sensitive to that imputation.

The facts are:

First. I have no knowledge of any such facts and therefore could not disclose any to this committee or to any Senator or any other committee or person whatever.

Second. I have no need of immunity of any kind and I have neither asked for it nor authorized any person to do so.

The only consideration I have sought was that which would excuse me from appearing on the witness stand.

You have examined with considerable fullness telegraphic correspondence between my employees, my counsel, several of my friends, and myself. I believe that you will agree that those telegrams may be divided into three classes:

First. Those that brought me information.

Second. Those that show my desire to avoid appearance as a witness.

Third. Those that relate to my personal and business affairs.

Certainly, none of them indicate that I had any connection with the oil leases which you are investigating, and none of them could so indicate.

I am now ready, gentlemen, to answer any relevant questions relating to the subject of this investigation that you may have to ask, upon the assurance and confidence, of course, that I will not be called upon to answer any question which the law protects as privileged between my counsel and myself.

Senator Walsh of Montana. Mr. McLean, you were interrogated about some features of this at Palm Beach on January 11 last?

Mr. McLean. Yes, sir.

Senator Walsh of Montana. The committee has not failed to observe that in the statement which you have just read you have not adverted at all to the subject matter of that investigation. That is correct, is it not?

Mr. McLean. Yes, sir.

Senator Walsh of Montana. Well, considerable water has gone by the mill since that time, Mr. McLean. Do you care to make any statement with relation to that particular subject?

Mr. McLean. I don't quite understand your question, Senator.

Senator Walsh of Montana. You were interrogated at Palm Beach concerning an alleged loan of $100,000 to Mr. Fall?

Mr. McLean. Yes, sir.

Senator Walsh of Montana. Do you care to make any further statement in relation to that subject?

Mr. McLean. No, sir.

Senator Walsh of Montana. Have you made search for the stub checks that you were interrogated about at that time?

Mr. McLean. I have searched for everything, Senator.

Senator Walsh of Montana. Are you able to produce them?

Mr. McLean. No, sir.

Senator Walsh of Montana. There are not any, are there, Mr. McLean?

Mr. McLean. Not as far as I know, no sir.

Senator Walsh of Montana. And never were?

Mr. McLean. You mean never were?

Senator Walsh of Montana. Never were, yes.

Mr. McLean. Why yes, there were, Senator, to the best of my recollection, as I told you.

Senator Walsh of Montana. You told us down there that in the fall of 1921 there were certain negotiations between you and Senator Fall concerning the purchase of lands down in New Mexico by you, or your going into partnership with him in ranch enterprises down there?

Mr. McLean. Yes, sir.

Senator Walsh of Montana. And that you stated to him at that time that you did not care to go in, and that you were not in a position to go in?

Mr. McLean. Yes, sir.

Senator Walsh of Montana. After he had sent you a rather elaborate statement of the proposition?

Mr. McLean. Yes, sir.

Senator Walsh of Montana. Do you recall just about what time in 1921 that was?

Mr. McLean. November, sir. It all happened in November.

Senator Walsh of Montana. November, 1921?

Mr. McLean. Yes, sir.

Senator Walsh of Montana. Where and when did you last see Secretary Fall before going to Palm Beach last December?

Mr. McLean. In Atlantic City, Senator.

Senator Walsh of Montana. When was that?

Mr. McLean. It was the latter part—it was very shortly before I went to Atlantic City—I mean very shortly before I went to Palm Beach, Senator.

Senator Walsh of Montana. How did you come to go to Atlantic City on that occasion?

Mr. McLean. At the request of Mrs. Fall; I think by telegram and two or three telephone conversations.

Senator Walsh of Montana. What was the nature of these conversations?

Mr. McLean. Why, she called me up and said that I was—first I got a telegram, I think, Senator. I would not want to swear to that. You have the telegrams so you probably know more about that than I do—I have forgotten it—but I have a recollection that I received a telegram from Secretary Fall, either from Chicago or Cleveland, saying "Want to see you on important business." Then there was a lapse that I didn't know where he was. Then Mrs. Fall called up—I know she called up, and she might have telegraphed—I doubt the telegraph part of it—called up from Atlantic City saying that Mr. Fall wanted to see me very much, and he was knocked out and in a very nervous condition, and I told her that it was nearly impossible for me to come down. I said, "I am going away in a day or so to Palm Beach, and I have got some meetings on, and it is going to be very hard for me to leave the city, but if Albert is sick and wants to see me I will come, if it is absolutely necessary." Then she called up again, to the best of my recollection in about an hour or an hour and a half—I know it was at 7 o'clock, because I was having supper—and she said, "Yes, he wants you to come down, and he can't come up." Then my recollection is that I told her I would come, and I think I sent her a telegram that unless I had contradiction to our understanding over the telephone I would leave the next day for Atlantic City.

Senator Walsh of Montana. Well, where did you understand Senator Fall was at that time?

Mr. McLean. Oh, I knew where he was, Senator. He was at Atlantic City.

Senator Walsh of Montana. At Atlantic City?

Mr. McLean. At the Ritz-Carlton.

Senator Walsh of Montana. Well, what explanation was made as to why he did not come down here to Washington to see you?

Mr. McLean. I said that—I thought I said it, Senator, that it was impossible for him to come; that he was sick, and in too nervous a condition.

Senator Walsh of Montana. Well, you were not in very good health yourself, Mr. McLean?

Mr. McLean. Not now; just my nose, that is all.

Senator Walsh of Montana. Well, I am speaking about December last?

Mr. McLean. No; I was not, sir.

Senator Walsh of Montana. Well, you went to Atlantic City?

Mr. McLean. I did, sir.

Senator Walsh of Montana. And had a conversation there with Fall?

Mr. McLean. I did, sir.

Senator Walsh of Montana. Please tell us about that.

Mr. McLean. I went in a private car—not that that has anything to do with it, Senator, but I just want to assure you there was no secrecy about the trip—and I was let in the door by Mrs. Fall. They had three or four rooms, and a very big parlor. It struck me as a very big parlor; it was the biggest I have ever seen in a hotel. And she said, "The Secretary is asleep; and you can't wake him." She said, "He had a dreadful night." "Well," I said. "Mrs. Fall, I have to go back in an hour and a half from now to catch the train; it is the only decent connection I can get; and I will wait as long as I can possibly."

I think I stood there in the room for at least 20 minutes, Senator, before Mr. Fall finally came in. He was in a sort of a dark red wrapper, or smoking gown, and he had been asleep, and he was in a very nervous, bad physical condition. It didn't need a doctor to tell me that, or anything. And he talked to me for a couple of minutes, and he was awfully upset. He seemed to be in a very bad condition, as I have said.

But what you want to hear I will tell you now, Senator. He said, "Ned, you remember our check transactions of two or three years ago." I said, "I do." He said, "Will you say"—or "do you mind saying"—I don't know the exact phraseology used—"that you loaned me that in cash?" And he said one thing, he said, "It has nothing to do with Harry Sinclair or Teapot Dome." And now these are his exact words: He said, "They are barking up the wrong tree." I remember that most distinctly, because I hadn't heard that expression before. He said, "They are barking up the wrong tree," and he said, "Will you do this? I am in an embarrassing position here. Some of my enemies are just trying to make it look as if it was something which it is not, and it has nothing to do with Harry Sinclair or Teapot Dome; not a cent of it came from them."

Then the result of that was I said. "Yes, I will, Senator."

Senator Walsh of Montana. And your telegrams to the committee were sent pursuant to that arrangement with Mr. Fall?

Mr. McLean. They were, sir; as long as I believed my friend, that he had never received a cent of that money from Harry Sinclair, and it had nothing to do with Teapot Dome.

Senator Walsh of Montana. Well, going back to the check transaction, Mr. McLean. You told us those checks were drawn upon a couple of banks here, but apparently you did not have any funds there to meet such checks, or checks for any such amounts as you told us at Palm Beach.

Mr. McLean. Do you want me to explain that, Senator?

Senator Walsh of Montana. Yes; whatever you care to say about it.

Mr. McLean. Why, Senator, in the first place there was no trouble about me raising $100,000 or $200,000. I am not saying that in a bragging way, but I mean my credit was good for that. I had $140,000, about, collateral in a safe deposit vault, and I am sure that the banks would have honored my checks for $50,000 or $60,000 apiece.

Senator Walsh of Montana. But you made no arrangement to do so, did you?

Mr. McLean. No, sir; none whatever.

Senator Walsh of Montana. And Mr. Fall had the checks?

Mr. McLean. Yes, sir.

Senator Walsh of Montana. For several days before he returned them to you?

Mr. McLean. Yes, sir.

Senator Walsh of Montana. Meanwhile you had made no provision to take care of the overdraft?

Mr. McLean. No, sir; he was going to tell me if he was going to cash them; I mean that was I understood that he would have called me up if he was going to cash them.

Senator Walsh of Montana. Well, I do not remember that you said anything about that at Palm Beach, Mr. McLean.

Mr. McLean. Well then, it is my fault, Senator.

Senator Walsh of Montana. Well, please tell us what that arrangement was.

Mr. McLean. Well, the arrangement was that if he was going to use the checks that he would—he didn't say that he wouldn't use them; he said, "I will call up before I will present them for payment." The Washington Post also had a fund, Senator, in the Federal Bank.

Senator Walsh of Montana. How were drafts made upon that fund?

Mr. McLean. They could have been made technically by me. There never has been any occasion to.

Senator Walsh of Montana. What was the usual way?

Mr. McLean. Well, I would call a directors' meeting if I wanted any money, and draw it out.

Senator Walsh of Montana. Yes; but you did not call any directors' meeting?

Mr. McLean. No, sir.

Senator Walsh of Montana. Upon what kind of a signature were checks drawn upon the Washington Post account in the bank?

Mr. McLean. By Edward McLean as president, or Arthur D. Marks.

Senator Walsh of Montana. That was not your private account at all?

Mr. McLean. No, sir; had nothing to do with my private account.

Senator Walsh of Montana. But of course you could have called a meeting of the board of directors and transferred it from the Washington Post account to your own account?

Mr. McLean. If it had become necessary, but there was no necessity of that sort.

Senator Walsh of Montana. Well, anyway at the time that these checks were made Fall said that he would call you up before he presented them?

Mr. McLean. Yes, sir.

Senator Walsh of Montana. Well, that is a rather extraordinary thing, is it not, Mr. McLean?

Mr. McLean. I don't think so, Senator.

Senator Walsh of Montana. What did he want with the checks then?

Mr. McLean. Now, Senator, you are trying to get me to think what he wanted. I am having trouble enough to think about my own things. I don't know what on earth the whole thing is about, in a way, about Mr. Fall.

Senator Walsh of Montana. Well, had you suggested to Senator Fall at the time these checks were made that you did not have the funds in the bank with which to meet them?

Mr. McLean. No, sir.

Senator Walsh of Montana. Well, why should he have said, then, that he would not present them until he called you up?

Mr. McLean. Because it was a very big loan. It was not a casual one, Senator. I don't know why he should have said that, or whether—I wouldn't say even that I didn't ask him to now, Senator. I am just giving you the best of my recollection. . . .

Senator Bursum. Did Mr. Fall at any time tell you about a loan from Mr. Doheny?

Mr. McLean. Yes, sir; after Mr. Walsh examined me in Palm Beach, this year.

Senator Bursum. Was it your purpose in stating that you had loaned Fall $100,000, and was it intended to relieve Mr. Fall from the embarrassment of disclosing the loan of $100,000 made by Mr. Doheny to Mr. Fall?

Mr. McLean. No; I just told you, Senator, I did not know at the time that he ever had gotten a loan from Mr. Doheny.

Senator Bursum. Well, you saw Mr. Fall at Atlantic City in 1923?

Mr. McLean. Yes, sir.

Senator Bursum. And when did Mr. Fall tell you about the $100,000 loan?

Mr. McLean. After Senator Walsh's examination of me, Senator, at Palm Beach.

Senator Bursum. Well, you did know that the purpose of making the statement that you had loaned Mr. Fall $100,000 in cash was intended to relieve him in some way, to help him out, on account of some embarrassment or some charges, is that true?

Mr. McLean. Yes, sir.

Senator Bursum. That is, you wanted to help Mr. Fall out?

Mr. McLean. I wanted to help Mr. Fall out as far as I could as long as he told me, Senator, that he never had received a nickel from Harry Sinclair or Teapot Dome. He said "They are barking up the wrong tree." If he had told me it had been Mr. Doheny or Mr. Sinclair, I naturally would not have done it, sir, for anybody. . . .

Senator Walsh of Montana. . . . he told you he had arranged to get the money elsewhere?

Mr. McLean. Yes, sir.

Senator Walsh of Montana. But he did not tell you where?

Mr. McLean. No, sir.

Senator Walsh of Montana. Well, now, Mr. McLean, I want to get back to this meeting at Atlantic City.

Mr. McLean. Yes, sir.

Senator Walsh of Montana. When this extraordinary request was made of you by Senator Fall.

Mr. McLean. Yes, sir.

Senator Walsh of Montana. That, in substance, you should deceive the committee.

Mr. McLean. Yes, sir.

Senator Walsh of Montana. Concerning the source from which he got this money. Now, what did he tell you as to his situation which impelled him to make such an enormous draft as that on the friendship which you had entertained theretofore for him?

Mr. McLean. Senator, just what I told you before. He said that he was being bedeviled by his political enemies. Whether he said New Mexico politicians or not I am not positive, but the impression is that he did. And he said:

Ned, this has nothing to do with Harry Sinclair or Teapot Dome whatever. They are barking up the wrong tree.

That is the best of my recollection what he said, sir.

Senator Walsh of Montana. Well, yes; but what did he say as to why he did not go on and tell the plain truth about it, instead of asking you to tell a lie about it?

Mr. McLean. I don't know, sir. He didn't say anything. If he had brought it up as clearly as that I never would have done it.

Senator Walsh of Montana. Well, that was the plain situation, was it not?

Mr. McLean. Unfortunately it was, sir.

Senator Walsh of Montana. And without inquiring of him what the embarrassing feature was which induced him to withhold the true source of it and to endeavor to get you to join with him to impose upon the committee, he did not make any explanation?

Mr. McLean. Only about his political enemies, and assuring me that it had nothing to do with Harry Sinclair or Teapot Dome, Senator. Those are the very words he used.

Senator Walsh of Montana. Yes; but the political enemies were pressing the inquiry as to where he got the money. We understand that. His political enemies were just bedeviling him and trying to find out where this money came from?

Mr. McLean. Yes, sir.

Senator Walsh of Montana. Yes. Did you not say to him:

> Well, why don't you tell the truth about it; where you got the money?

Mr. McLean. No, sir; I did not.

Senator Walsh of Montana. It would be a good deal easier for him to tell the truth than for you to tell a falsehood about it, Mr. McLean.

Mr. McLean. It would have, and for me too; both of us; yes, sir.

Senator Walsh of Montana. You had a conference with Mr. Fall at Palm Beach, did you not, prior to the time that you were investigated concerning the general subject matter?

Mr. McLean. You mean I had—yes, sir; I had a conference with him. Not on this particularly. He was an awfully ill man when he got there, Senator. You didn't see him, Senator, but he really was shot to pieces. If you have ever seen a man shot to pieces physically he was.

Senator Walsh of Montana. Well, you were examined about 2 o'clock in the afternoon?

Mr. McLean. Yes, sir.

Senator Walsh of Montana. Yes. And you had a conference evidently with Mr. Fall prior to the time that you testified?

Mr. McLean. Yes, sir.

Senator Walsh of Montana. As to what you were to say?

Mr. McLean. No, sir.

Senator Walsh of Montana. No; as to what you were going to say?

Mr. McLean. Yes, sir; that is correct.

Senator Walsh of Montana. Now, tell us about that conversation. What was that?

Mr. McLean. I just told him, I said:

> Albert, this thing has gone as far as it can go. I have gone down the line for you, I have done everything, but it has come to the point where I have got to tell the truth.

And then, Senator, after I said that it wasn't until, I think, I met you on the porch of the Breakers—yes, I am sure I did, you and Mr. Lambert—it was after that that I knew that Doheny was the man who loaned him the money.

Senator Walsh of Montana. That was before you testified?

Mr. McLean. No, sir; it was after I saw you on the porch. You remember you were sitting—you asked me to deliver a letter, wasn't it, to Mr. Fall?

Senator Walsh of Montana. Yes.

Mr. McLean. Well, it was after that. You were sitting on the porch with General—you know, that tall man.

Senator Walsh of Montana. Yes; I remember.

Mr. McLean. And Mr. Lambert. It was after that that he told me, and it was for the first time then that I knew that Doheny had anything more to do with it than I did or you did, Senator. It was my first knowledge of it.

Senator Walsh of Montana. And what did he tell you then?

Mr. McLean. He said that Mr. Doheny had loaned him the money.

Senator Walsh of Montana. Well, what did you say?

Mr. McLean. I said, "I be damned.". . .

Senator Stanfield. That is all.

Mr. McLean. May I be excused, Senator Walsh?

Senator Walsh of Montana. Yes.

(Thereupon a short recess was taken, after which the following proceedings were had:)

Senator Stanfield. Do you wish to ask a question, Mr. Lambert?

Mr. Lambert. Yes; I do, but after you, Senator.

Senator Stanfield. You may proceed.

Mr. Lambert. Mr. McLean, I noticed in connection with the question that Senator Walsh asked you about the safe deposit box, that you spoke of Mr. Duckstein having procured it. The Senator's question assumed that you took the papers out of that box, or had them taken out after the deposition was taken in Palm Beach in which Senator Walsh participated. I ask you whether that is a fact, or were they taken out after that?

Mr. McLean. They were taken out, Mr. Lambert, when you sent them down to me at Palm Beach.

Mr. Lambert. That was after the deposition?

Mr. McLean. Yes.

Mr. Lambert. And after my return from Palm Beach?

Mr. McLean. Yes.

Mr. Lambert. Now, another question that was asked you was as to Secretary Fall asking you to deceive the committee. I did not recall in your testimony that you stated anything about his asking you to deceive the committee.

Mr. McLean. Well, I think that was an implied thing rather than the question. He never mentioned the committee.

Mr. Lambert. That is what I thought. Now you say that it was not until after the deposition had been taken at Palm Beach that you were apprised by Secretary Fall that the money that he actually received had come from Mr. Doheny. Can you tell us in what way or how you were informed of that?

Mr. McLean. I think I was informed of it the same time you were, or a second or two afterwards. He was writing out a telegram—Senator, I think you have the telegram—to Doheny, that he was going to testify about it.

Mr. Lambert. Wasn't it that he showed us a copy of a telegram that he had sent to Mr. Doheny that afternoon?

Mr. McLean. To Edward Doheny; yes.

Mr. Lambert. In which he stated something to the effect to Mr. Doheny that he was going to tell the facts?

Mr. McLean. Yes.

Mr. Lambert. And that was the first knowledge you had?

Mr. McLean. Yes, absolutely; and I told Senator Walsh that, didn't I, Senator?

Mr. Lambert. You didn't mention the telegram.

Mr. McLean. Well, I remember the telegram.

Mr. Lambert. You corrected the inaccuracy, I believe, with reference to your testimony at Palm Beach relative to the month of November instead of the month of December?

Mr. McLean. I think I did; yes.

Mr. Lambert. You did?

Mr. McLean. Yes, sir.

TESTIMONY OF HARRY F. SINCLAIR
MARCH 22, 1924

U.S. Senate, Leases Upon Naval Oil Reserves, Hearings Before the Committee on Public Lands and Surveys, 68th Congress, 1st Session, Vol. 3, 2894–99.

. . . Mr. Sinclair. Mr. Chairman, I do not decline to answer any question upon the ground that my answers may tend to incriminate me, because there is nothing in any of the facts or circumstances of the lease of Teapot Dome which does or can incriminate me.

In January of last year I was called before the Manufacturers Committee of the Senate and produced all books and papers called for and testified fully regarding the lease of Teapot Dome and the organization of Mammoth Oil Co., which holds that lease. On October 28 last past, I came before your committee and answered all questions put to me by your committee in respect to the lease of Teapot Dome and the organization of Mammoth Oil Co. and was excused. In the afternoon of the same day I was recalled and answered all questions put to me by your committee and was again excused. On December 4 last past I was called again before your committee and answered all questions put to me and had my auditor present, who also testified. I was requested to furnish the committee with certain papers and memoranda, which was promptly done. On December 27 last past I was again called before your committee and answered all questions put to me and produced all books and papers asked for by the committee. I was then excused until the 4th of January, on which date I again appeared and answered all questions put to me by the committee and produced all books and papers asked for, and I was finally excused from further attendance.

Thus, it appears that I have been before your committee at five different sessions and answered all questions and produced all books and papers called for, and I was finally excused from further attendance. I went abroad on business which had been delayed owing to the necessity of my attendance on your hearings, as I had a perfect right to do, without secrecy and without evasion.

When I appeared before your committee at these dates and answered your questions and produced all books and papers asked for, your committee was acting under Senate Resolution 282 of the Sixty-seventh Congress, which authorized you:

> To investigate the entire subject of leases upon naval oil reserves, with particular reference to the protection of the rights and equities of the United States and the preservation of its natural resources.

Since the date of my last appearance before your committee, and at the instance of your committee, the Senate and House passed Senate Joint Resolution 54, which has been signed by the President. I make that resolution a part of this statement:

> Whereas it appears from evidence taken by the Committee on Public Lands and Surveys of the United States that certain lease of naval reserve No. 3, in the State of Wyoming, bearing date April 7, 1922, made in form by the Government of the United States, through Albert B. Fall, Secretary of the Interior, and Edwin Denby, Secretary of the Navy, as lessor, to the Mammoth Oil Co., as lessee, and that certain contract between the Government of the United States and the Pan American Petroleum & Transport Co., dated April 25, 1922, signed by Edward C. Finney, Acting Secretary of the Interior, and Edwin Denby, Secretary of the Navy, relating among other things to the construction of oil tanks at Pearl Harbor, Hawaii, and that certain lease of naval reserve No. 1, in the State of California, bearing date December 11, 1922, made in form by the Government of the United States through Albert B. Fall, Secretary of the Interior, and Edwin Denby, Secretary of the Navy, as lessor, to the Pan American Petroleum Co., as lessee, were executed under circumstances indicating fraud and corruption; and
>
> Whereas the said leases and contract were entered into without authority on the part of the officers purporting to act in the execution of the same for the United States and in violation of the laws of Congress; and
>
> Whereas such leases and contract were made in defiance of the settled policy of the Government, adhered to through three successive administrations, to maintain in the ground a great reserve supply of oil adequate to the needs of the Navy in any emergency threatening the national security:
>
> Resolved, etc., That the said leases and contract are against the public interest, and that the lands embraced therein should be recovered and held for the purpose to which they were dedicated; and
>
> Resolved further, That the President of the United States be, and he hereby is, authorized and directed immediately to cause suit to be instituted and prosecuted for the annulment and cancellation of

the said leases and contract and all contracts incidental or supplemental thereto; to enjoin the further extraction of oil from the said
reserves under said leases or from the territory covered by the same;
to secure any further appropriate incidental relief; and to prosecute
such other actions or proceedings, civil and criminal, as may be
warranted by the facts in relation to the making of the said leases
and contract.

And the President is further authorized and directed to appoint,
by and with the advice and consent of the Senate, special counsel
who shall have charge and control of the prosecution of such litigation, anything in the statutes touching the powers of the Attorney
General of the Department of Justice to the contrary notwithstanding.

This resolution in effect denounces the lease between the Government
and the Mammoth Oil Co., of which I am president, as void because of fraud
and corruption and for want of lawful authority on the part of the Secretary of
the Navy and the Secretary of the Interior to execute it. This is an assertion that
under the "rights and equities" of the United States the land covered by the
lease of Teapot Dome belongs to the United States. The resolution further
asserts that the lease was made "in defiance of the settled policy of the
Government, adhered to through three successive administrations, to maintain in the ground a great reserve supply of oil, adequate to the needs of the
Navy in any emergency threatening the national security." This is a definite
outline of the policy of the Government with respect to the "preservation of its
natural resources." The resolution further declares said lease is "against the
public interest and the lands embraced therein should be recovered and held
for the purpose to which they were dedicated." This is a further definite
declaration of the policy of the Government for the "preservation of its natural
resources." It further provides:

That the President of the United States be, and he hereby is,
authorized and directed immediately to cause suit to be instituted
and prosecuted for the annulment and cancellation of the said
leases and contract and all contracts incidental or supplemental
thereto; to enjoin the further extraction of oil from the said reserves
under said leases or from the territory covered by the same, to
secure any further appropriate incidental relief and to prosecute
such other actions or proceedings, civil and criminal, as may be
warranted by the facts in relation to the making of said leases and
contract.

The President was further authorized to employ special counsel to prosecute such litigation, and in a further resolution instituted in the House,
$100,000 was appropriated to cover the expenses incurred in such litigation.

Thereafter the President, by and with the advice and consent of the
Senate, did appoint counsel, who were duly sworn and took their office as
special counsel to the Government authorized by said Senate Joint Resolution
54, and the said counsel by bill of complaint in the District Court of the United
States for the District of Wyoming, sued the Mammoth Oil Co., the holder of
the lease, the Sinclair Crude Oil Purchasing Co., and the Sinclair Pipe Line

Co., and applied for relief by temporary injunction and receivers, which was granted. In said bill of complaint it is charged in paragraph 28:

> In negotiating and concluding said agreement said Albert B. Fall and said Harry F. Sinclair, acting for and on behalf of the defendant Mammoth Oil Co., did fraudulently and covinously combine, confederate, and conspire, in the manner and in the acts hereinbefore set forth and other matters and things, to defraud the United States of America:
>
> (a) By granting said lease upon said naval petroleum lands in violation of law.
>
> (b) To favor and prefer said defendant Mammoth Oil Co. over and above other persons desirous of taking lease upon said lands.
>
> (c) To insure to said defendant Mammoth Oil Co. the valuable right to receive and take to exhaustion all of the oil and gas which might be obtained from said lands in said agreement mentioned.
>
> (d) To lease the said lands to said defendant Mammoth Oil Co. by said agreement at an inadequate, improper, and fraudulent consideration.

And thereafter the said special counsel, acting for the Government, made an official announcement that application had been made for the organization of a special grand jury in the District of Columbia, for the purpose of inquiring into offenses and crimes growing out of the circumstances attending the execution of this lease.

It is perfectly clear, therefore, from the language of the resolution that your committee, by reason of any constitutional power which it may possess or by virtue of the resolution under which it is acting, is not now engaged, nor could it be engaged in an investigation "with particular reference to the protection of the rights and equities of the United States and the preservation of its natural resources"; because the Senate, from whom you derive your authority, has unanimously passed upon all questions embraced within that authorization and exhausted whatever power or authority it had in the premises. It is further perfectly clear that the Congress and the President have made of the whole matter a judicial question, determinable solely by the courts of the country, and such question is now actually pending in the District Court of the United States for the District of Wyoming, and whatever criminal act is claimed is about to be investigated by a special grand jury of the District of Columbia. With due respect to your committee, I claim that you are without any jurisdiction to question me further regarding the procurement of the lease or the validity thereof or any fact or circumstance pertaining thereto; that such an examination of me by your committee would not only be clearly outside of your jurisdiction but would be, in effect, an examination before trial in a civil action between the Government and the company I represent, by a body of men wholly unauthorized by law and in a wholly unauthorized manner. Or, if your examination should be directed toward eliciting facts concerning fraud or corruption, your committee in effect would have constituted itself a grand jury as to a matter which Congress and the President, by Joint Resolution 54 have directed should be presented to the constitutional authorities of the country.

I am the president of the Mammoth Oil Co. and as such represent all others interested in that company. I negotiated the lease of Teapot Dome and am responsible for those negotiations. Any pertinent question which your committee could ask would necessarily relate to the procurement of that lease and its validity. You and the body from which you derive your authority have already sat in judgment on these questions and remitted them to courts of proper jurisdiction. I shall reserve any evidence I may be able to give for those courts to which you and your colleagues have deliberately referred all questions of which you had any jurisdiction, and shall respectfully decline to answer any questions propounded by your committee.

Senator Walsh of Montana. Mr. Sinclair, I desire to interrogate you about a matter concerning which the committee had no knowledge or reliable information at any time when you had heretofore appeared before the committee and with respect to which you must then have had knowledge. I refer to the testimony given by Mr. Bonfils concerning a contract that you made with him touching the Teapot Dome. I wish you would tell us about that.

Mr. Sinclair. I decline to answer on advice of counsel on the same ground.

Senator Walsh of Montana. Since you were last upon the stand we had, Mr. Sinclair, before us a copy of a contract entered into between the Mammoth Oil Co. and the Pioneer Oil Co. and the Belgo Co., under which, or as a consequence of which, the Pioneer Oil Co. ceased to be a competitor of yours in this lease of the Teapot Dome. Will you tell us about that matter?

Mr. Sinclair. I decline to answer on advice of counsel on the same ground.

Mr. Walsh of Montana. When your private confidential secretary, Mr. Wahlberg, was before the committee he told us about the loan of some stock of the Sinclair Consolidated Co. to one Hays. Will you tell us about that transaction?

Mr. Sinclair. I decline to answer by advice of counsel on the same ground.

Senator Walsh of Montana. Since you were on the stand last, Mr. John C. Shaffer told us about an agreement between yourself and Secretary Fall, under which Mr. Shaffer was to receive from you a certain portion of the territory covered by the lease which you secured for the Mammoth Oil Co. Will you tell us about that matter?

Mr. Sinclair. I decline to answer on the advice of counsel on the same ground.

Senator Walsh of Montana. Mr. Sinclair, will you tell the committee where and when you met Secretary Fall during the months of November and December last?

Mr. Sinclair. I decline to answer on the advice of counsel on the same ground.

Senator Walsh of Montana. On the 3d day of February, 1923, Mr. Sinclair, as my information is, you caused to be transmitted to the National Metropolitan Bank of this city from the National Park Bank of New York the sum of $100,000 payable to your order, which, on the 7th day of February, 1923, you transmitted to the Chase National Bank upon your direction. Will you tell us about that transaction?

Mr. Sinclair. On advice of counsel I decline to answer on the same ground.

Senator Walsh of Montana. Information has come to the committee to the effect that you contributed 75,000 shares of the stock of the Sinclair Consolidated Co. to Mr. Hays, or to some one representing the Republican National Committee, for the purpose of making up the deficit in the account of that committee. Will you tell us about that matter?

Mr. Sinclair. On advice of counsel I decline to answer on the same ground.

Senator Walsh of Montana. The committee is still desirous, Mr. Sinclair, of examining the books of the Hyvas Corporation. Are your prepared to produce those books?

Mr. Sinclair. On advice of counsel I decline to bring the books before this committee, upon the same ground.

Senator Walsh of Montana. Then, Mr. Chairman, I offer to prove by the witness, if the would answer, that, among other things—

Senator Spencer (interposing). Do I understand, Senator Walsh, that what you propose to put into the record is what you think the witness would testify if he did not claim exemption?

Senator Walsh of Montana. Yes, sir. I propose to prove certain facts by this witness.

Mr. Littleton. If I have any rights at all here—I am counsel for the witness—I certainly object to your putting into this record what you imagine the witness would have answered when he has claimed his rights here under the law.

Senator Walsh of Montana. All right, Mr. Littleton.

Mr. Littleton. I protest most earnestly against it as an outrage.

Senator Walsh of Montana. I protest, Mr. Chairman, against any such remark from counsel as an abuse of his privilege. Counsel yesterday, here by the courtesy of this committee, said that certain things that this committee propose to do were monstrous, and now we are told this morning that what I offered to do, with the privilege of the committee, is an outrage. That is an abuse of the privilege of counsel, and I desire the chairman to admonish counsel to that effect.

The Chairman. It is the opinion of the chairman that counsel went beyond his rights, both yesterday and to-day, in his statements.

Senator Walsh of Montana. Now, Mr. Chairman, inasmuch as the witness, through his counsel, has objected and protested against the proposal which I make to set out what I expect to prove by the witness, I do not press my purpose to state the facts to the committee. That is all, Mr. Chairman.

The Chairman. Any further questions?

Senator Dill. I wanted to ask Mr. Sinclair whether he was willing to answer any questions about the services that Mr. Archie Roosevelt performed for his organization in reference to testimony given here since he was last before us.

Mr. Sinclair. I decline to answer by advice of counsel on the same ground.

Senator Adams. Mr. Sinclair, I believe in an earlier hearing you testified, in answer to a question, that you had in no way, and none of your companies had in any way, given or loaned anything to Secretary Fall. Is that correct?

Mr. Sinclair. I decline to answer on advice of counsel on the same ground.

The Chairman. Are there any further questions on the part of any member of the committee? Senator Adams, have you any further questions?

[No response.]

Mr. Sinclair, you are excused. . . .

"HANDS OFF THE INVESTIGATIONS" BY FELIX FRANKFURTER MAY 21, 1924

The New Republic, May 21, 1924, 329–31.

So grave were the first disclosures made by the Walsh and Wheeler investigations that the immediate response of the country was profound humiliation. Only the recently disavowed organ of the Republican National Committee ventured brazenly to attack the exposers and minimize the exposure. But, as the effect of the impact of these disclosures wore off, partly because of the very extent of the revelations, public preoccupation with private worries and bewilderment over the variety of complicated issues were exploited by various powerful forces, from a variety of motives ranging from the lowest to moral confusion, all with a view to discrediting investigation and arresting its further progress. The gathering forces against the investigations and the investigators reached their culminating reinforcement in the support of a President who, while professing a desire to vindicate the law, assumes that law and order are bounded by the Penal Code, and helped to create an atmosphere in which necessary investigation could not thrive. The President's lead was promptly followed by such guardians of the public interest as Judge Gary. The most disheartening experience of the Ballinger investigation repeats itself: the condemnation of the most powerful is reserved for the exposers and not for the exposed.

Emboldened by the successful offensive against the pending investigations in Washington, various suggestions are afloat with a view to curbing future Walsh and Wheeler investigations. Professing, of course, that wrongdoing, impropriety and unwholesome standards in public life should be exposed, critics, who have nothing to say for the astounding corruption and corrupting soil which have been brought to light, seek to divert attention and shackle the future by suggesting restrictions in the procedure of future congressional investigations. Not only do members of the Bar thus propose to hamper a power which has been exercised since 1789, but even one of our financiers, who is a self-appointed mentor for all our national ills, urges curbs upon Congress drawn from his deep study of comparative parliamentary procedure.

A proper judgment of the Walsh and Wheeler investigations involves a consideration of (1) the situation which confront them, (2) their accomplishments, (3) their alleged abuses. Only after such consideration can we properly assess (4) the pertinence of any formal change in the procedure of congressional investigation.

(1) *Situation confronting Walsh and Wheeler.*

When the Harding administration began—in fact preceding it—the air was full of indications of the sinister influences that were to prevail and were prevailing in the conduct of some of the vital departments of the government. Around Fall and Daugherty suspicions steadily clustered. Washington was thick with talk, and not the talk of irresponsibles. As time went on the intimations became more and more outspoken; but every influence of authority, of powerful social connections, of the press, the whole milieu of officialdom in Washington was on the side of those in power and against disclosure and truth-telling. More than that, when things could no longer be stemmed and an investigation of Daugherty's administration was entered upon by a House Committee, the forces of wrong-doing rendered such an investigation abortive and futile, and thereby served to discredit further accusations and their investigation.

For nearly two years the efforts to uncover wrong-doing in the disposal of our public domain were hampered by every conceivable obstruction on the part of those in office and those influential out of office; involving members of the President's official entourage, and including perjury before a Senate committee on the part of one of the closest friends of the late President and one on close terms with the present Executive. The vast investigatorial agencies of the government not only failed to coöperate with the efforts to unearth wrong-doing; they positively sought to frustrate congressional activity.

Governmental machinery, prestige, wealth, agencies of publicity—all were for covering up things. No one who has not had some experience of the power the government *can* exert is able to realize the tremendous pressure against which Walsh and Wheeler were contending. Both the hostile resources and the inertia which they had to overcome were incredible. The odds which they thus encountered must be felt and not merely intellectually admitted and lightly dismissed.

(2) *Accomplishments of Walsh and Wheeler*

These are beyond question: the bills filed by the government against the Sinclair and Doheny leases are based upon the findings of the Walsh committee, namely, corruption and conspiracy rendered possible through Secretary Fall's corruption and Secretary Denby's guileless incompetence; the disgrace of, and pending grand jury inquiry into, a recent member of the Cabinet —Fall; the resignation of another member through incompetence—Denby; the dismissal of a third member—the Attorney-General—because of an enveloping, malodorous atmosphere.

It is safe to say that never in the history of this country have congressional investigations had to contend with such powerful odds, never have they so quickly revealed wrong-doing, incompetence, and low public standards on such a wide scale, and never have such investigations resulted so effectively in compelling correction through the dismissal of derelict officials. All this, it must be remembered again and again, was done by Congress against obstructing executive departments and, to put it mildly, unassisted by a President, who, unlike Roosevelt, is not a crusader against wrong-doing.

(3) *Alleged Abuses.*

One would like to have a bill of particulars of these alleged abuses. Objection is frequently taken against irrelevant, unfair, and unsubstantial charges and to the character of some of the witnesses. It is not easy to be patient with such an attitude. What were the irrelevant charges before the Walsh committee, and what were the improprieties in pursuing those charges? Certainly Senator Walsh has established all the charges surrounding the oil leases up to the hilt. Objections are made to the testimony centring around alleged prenomination and preëlection affairs in 1920. Surely it was relevant to ascertain whether interests were on the lookout to put into the Department of the Interior a man who, honestly or dishonestly, held one attitude rather than another towards our natural resources. Necessarily much of this was hearsay and gossip. Nevertheless there emerged definitely the fact that Hamon spent a huge sum of money for campaign purposes. If these aren't "leads" properly to be pursued, then we had better frankly admit that the power of congressional investigation is a sham, and not an effective instrument for ventilating issues for the information of Congress and of the public.

What are the specific objections to be made against the hearings conducted by Senator Wheeler? Of course the character of the witnesses in many instances was disreputable. It is of the essence of the whole Daugherty affair that the Attorney-General of the United States was involved in questionable association with disreputable characters. It is naïvely suggested as to these individuals, that "they are not competent witnesses. But they are exhibits." But in order to be exhibits, they had to be witnesses. This is the kind of hair-splitting that has for decades been attacked as a disgrace to American criminal procedure. In suggesting that Wheeler's witnesses were not competent witnesses but merely "exhibits," perhaps all that was intended was that Senator Wheeler should have preceded the calling of each one of his disreputable witnesses by a speech stating that they were disreputable. Surely this is a naïve suggestion. It is difficult, at best, to get witnesses to talk. This criticism is familiar to everyone who has ever had anything to do with criminal prosecutions, namely, an attempt to divert attention from the misconduct of the defendant to the character of the witnesses against him. Of course the character of a witness is a relevant item. As to Daugherty, it was a damning item. But the testimony of such people is not at all incompetent, and their character, as the New York World pointed out in an editorial on April 24, may be conclusive testimony on the issue of the fitness of a man to be Attorney-General of the United States. If by the witnesses which Senator Wheeler produced he was able to furnish a "living demonstration of the atmosphere which prevailed in and around the Attorney-General of the United States," how possibly could that conclusion have been demonstrated except in the way in which Senator Wheeler demonstrated it? Eminent lawyers might have done it a little differently—but the chances are very strong that they wouldn't have done it at all. It requires pertinacity and high indifference to the winds that blow to drive through the obstacles which faced Senator Wheeler. The performance of such a man in such a situation cannot be finely weighed, by a distant onlooker after the event, on an apothecary's scale. We have clear indications as to how a "better lawyer than Senator Wheeler" would have dealt with the situation. The indications are furnished by the attitude of Senator Pepper; they are furnished by the supine silence of the Bar before Senator Wheeler began, for from the time of his appointment as Attorney-General lawyers widely knew Daugherty's unfitness for the post; they are revealed in the criticisms by the

Bar not of Daugherty but of his exposer, after the first flicker of indignation over the disclosures had subsided.

(4) *Revision of Procedure of Congressional Investigations*

Nothing in the experience of the Walsh and Wheeler investigations reveals the need of changing the process or confining the limits of congressional investigations. The proper scope and methods of procedure appropriate to congressional investigations depend on the conception of the part they play in enabling Congress to discharge its basic duties. This has been nowhere better expressed than by Woodrow Wilson in his Congressional Government:

> It is the proper duty of a representative body to look diligently into every affair of government and to talk much about what it sees. It is meant to be the eyes and the voice, and to embody the wisdom and will of its constituents. Unless Congress have and use every means of acquainting itself with the acts and the disposition of the administrative agents of the government, the country must be helpless to learn how it is being served; and unless Congress both scrutinize these things and sift them by every form of discussion, the country must remain in embarrassing, crippling ignorance of the very affairs which it is most important that it should understand and direct. The informing function of Congress should be preferred even to its legislative function.

Undoubtedly, the names of people who have done nothing criminal or wrong, or nothing even offending taste perhaps, have been mentioned in connection with these investigations. A number of such instances appeared in connection with "Ned" McLean's name. All those references are pertinent in showing the ramifications of McLean's influence in official Washington. Also, the names of counsel were mentioned who have had dealings with the Department of Jusice which were wholly proper. But where so much that the Department of Justice was doing under Daugherty was not innocent, it is highly important that even innocent transactions in the general field of fraud and suspicion be explained in order to separate the sheep from the goats. The question is not whether people's feelings here and there may be hurt, or names "dragged through the mud," as it is called. The real issue is whether the danger of abuses and the actual harm done are so clear and substantial that the grave risks of fettering free congressional inquiry are to be incurred by artificial and technical limitations upon inquiry. Any quantitative and qualitative judgment of what Walsh and Wheeler were up against, what they produced and how they produced it, leaves the experienced and disinterested mind, duly regardful of the investigating duties of Congress, wholly without justification for changing congressional procedure.

It must be remembered that our rules of evidence are but tools for ascertaining the truth, and that these tools vary with the nature of the issues and the nature of the tribunal seeking facts. Specifically, the system of rules of evidence used in trials before juries "are mainly aimed at guarding the jury from the over-weening effect of certain kinds of evidence." That system, as pointed out by Wigmore, "is not applicable by historical precedent, or by sound practical policy" to "inquiries of fact determinable by administrative tribunals." Still less is it applicable to inquiries by congressional committees. Of course the essential decencies must be observed, namely opportunity for cross-examination must be afforded to those who are investigated or to those representing issues under investigation. Despite Daugherty's statement to the contrary, that opportunity has been scrupulously given by the Brookhart committee.

It must be remembered that in various fields there is no legal protection against harm due to unfettered speech. The only safeguards are those secured by social and moral pressure. Thus the immunities enjoyed by judges and legislators for anything said by them as judges and as legislators are founded on deep experience. So also, the abuses of the printing press are not sought to be corrected by legal restriction or censorship in advance because the remedy is worse than the disease. For the same reason, congressional inquiry ought not to be fettered by advance rigidities, because in the light of experience there can be no reasonable doubt that such curtailment would make effective investigation almost impossible.

Our criminal procedure has been constantly under fire by the legal profession, from Chief Justice Taft down, because of its self-defeating technicalities. In a report to the American Bar Association, vigorous demand has recently been made for the liberalization of rules of evidence and procedure in criminal cases. Taken in connection with the proposal to curb the investigating powers of Congress, what is urged, in effect, is that we abandon the technical limitations which have been established to protect men from being sent to jail too readily, but introduce them into a field where they have never been resorted to and where they are wholly out of place, namely, in the exercise of the informing function of Congress.

A good deal must be left to the standards which Congress imposes upon itself and its committees; a good deal must be left to the duty of newspapers to report fairly and not sensationally, and to interpret wisely; a good deal must be left to the good sense of people.

In conclusion, there is no substantial basis for criticism of the investigations conducted by Senator Walsh and Senator Wheeler. Whatever inconveniences may have resulted are inseparable incidents of an essential exertion of governmental power, and to talk about these incidents is to deflect attention from wrong-doing and its sources.

The procedure of congressional investigation should remain as it is. No limitations should be imposed by congressional legislation or standing rules. The power of investigation should be left untrammelled, and the methods and forms of each investigation should be left for determination of Congress and its committees, as each situation arises. The safeguards against abuse and folly are to be looked for in the forces of responsibility which are operating from within Congress, and are generated from without.

Felix Frankfurter

"WHAT THE OIL INQUIRY DEVELOPED" BY THOMAS WALSH MAY 21, 1924

The Outlook, May 21, 1924, 96–98.

At the request of The Outlook, the following summary is submitted of what was disclosed by the inquiry authorized by the Senate into the leasing of the naval oil reserves:

1. In the first place, the outstanding item is that in the very midst of the negotiations culminating in the contract under which, without competitive bidding, E. L. Doheny secured a preference right to a lease of a considerable portion of Naval Reserve No. 1, approximately one-half of its entire area of 32,000 acres, he delivered to Fall in cash $100,000, transported in a satchel from New York to Washington, which Fall afterwards carried in a tin box to El Paso, Texas, making from it in bills an initial payment of $10,000 on a purchase of a ranch for which, with cattle and equipment appurtenant, he paid $91,500, though he had theretofore been so financially embarrassed that he had not paid his taxes for ten years, and admitted that he was "broke."

To elaborate for a more complete understanding. Doheny, in June, 1921, by open competitive bidding, secured a lease authorizing him to drill in the remote southeastern part of Naval Reserve No. 1 twenty-two line wells to arrest drainage through wells on adjacent territory held in private ownership outside the reserves. On April 25, 1922, he secured the contract above referred to for the construction at Pearl Harbor, H. T., of steel storage tanks adequate to hold 1,500,000 barrels of fuel oil, the construction cost to be paid for in oil accruing to the Government as royalty from leases or otherwise. It has been represented that this contract was secured by competitive bidding, but it was not. Bids were called for in accordance with proposals submitted, and a number were received, though some large companies declined to bid, believing, as the Government now contends, that there was no authority to pay for such work in oil. Doheny submitted two bids, one in conformity with the proposals, the other departing from them, the essential difference being that the bid accepted proposed that he be given a preference right, as heretofore recited. No other bidder was given an opportunity to bid on that basis. The money was delivered to Fall on November 30, 1921. Two days theretofore Doheny had written him a letter discussing the Pearl Harbor work and indicating his desire and purpose to bid on it. He says the money was advanced to Fall as a loan in consideration of old friendship and association and in commiseration of the business reverses that had been the lot of Fall. Neither time nor space will permit of a review of the evidence supporting or discrediting the story of a loan. Even a loan under the circumstances is in the last degree reprehensible on the part of every one concerned in it.

2. In addition to the Harris ranch, Fall, at or about the time he was

carrying on negotiations culminating in the lease of Naval Reserve No. 3, the Teapot Dome, to the Mammoth Oil Company, organized by Sinclair, which negotiations were initiated while Sinclair was visiting Fall at the ranch of the latter in New Mexico in December, 1921, purchased additional lands at a cost of $33,000, paid his delinquent taxes covering a period of ten years, to the amount of $8,000 odd, and made other expenditures aggregating at least $50,000, the source from which the funds came being undisclosed. He expended about as much more in the installation of a hydroelectric plant on his ranch, the funds being borrowed from his regular banker, who was unable to shed any light on the origin of the remainder. In 1923, however, upon his leaving the office of Secretary of the Interior, Sinclair delivered to him Liberty Bonds to the amount of $25,000, said to have been loaned, though no note or evidence of indebtedness ever passed.

3. The Naval Reserves have all passed into private hands, after a struggle to maintain them intact dating from the time the areas comprising them were set aside by President Taft in 1909, upon a study theretofore instituted by President Roosevelt—the policy advocated by all conservationists and adhered to through three Administrations. The initial step in this process was the promulgation of the Executive Order of May 31, 1921, transferring the administration of the Naval Reserves from the Navy Department, to which it was confided by Congress, to the Department of the Interior, at the head of which was Secretary Fall, an avowed opponent of the whole conservation policy.

The effort to secure the right to exploit the Naval Reserves gave rise to one of the historic controversies of the Wilson Administration, leading ultimately to the resignation of Secretary Lane, believed by many to have been unduly friendly to the private claimants. The Secretary of the Navy, on the other hand, was charged with being too rigidly insistent upon keeping the reserves intact despite the legal rights and equities of the claimants. The contest went on both in the Department and before Congress, President Wilson supporting Secretary Daniels. Out of this contest grew the acts of February 25, 1920, and June 4, 1920. By the former Congress declared its purpose to repose no power in the Secretary of the Interior as to the disposition of lands within the Naval Reserves except the power to lease wells that were actually producing. But, some drainage even then taking place or to be apprehended in Naval Reserve No. 2, the Secretary of the Navy was authorized to meet the situation by making the necessary leases—in fact, was invested with authority, at his discretion, to lease the whole or any portion of the reserves, the general authority being given for exercise whenever the contingency to meet which the reserves were set apart should arise.

Notwithstanding the purpose of Congress thus plainly expressed to exclude the Interior Department from the control of the Naval Reserves, within thirty days after Secretary Denby was installed he announced to Admiral Griffin, the Chief of the Bureau of Engineering, to whose immediate charge the care of the reserves had been confided, that he intended turning them over to Fall. Bear in mind, he did not ask Griffin, or any other naval officer, for that matter, for his advice; he apprised him of his purpose, asserting on the witness stand that he had been told that the reserves were being drained. He was unable to remember who told him, but it was no officer of the Navy. No one now pretends that this order can be defended—that is, that the President had any power thus to transfer to one Cabinet officer powers which Congress designed and provided should be exercised by another. In two letters to the President, upon inquiries from Senators, Fall sought to justify it under the Overman Act and the two acts above referred to, but when he was confronted with these statutes on the stand he was forced to admit that none of them afforded even a color of authority for the order.

4. Sinclair declared that he expected to make $100,000,000 out of the Teapot Dome lease and Doheny a like amount of his lease of Reserve No. 1, which, when it was awarded, embraced not only the area to which he had secured a perference right by his contract of April 25, 1922, but the whole reserve. Under that lease the western portion can be drilled only when the Navy so directs. Accordingly, if it should be thought wise to hold that part intact for an indefinite period, say twenty-five, fifty, or one hundred years, the Government may not take out the oil; Doheny must be directed to do it, the Government getting only the share prescribed in the lease as royalty, which may be fair now, but utterly unfair when in the possibly distant future that source of supply must be resorted to.

5. The leases contemplate taking the oil out of the ground and storing it in steel tanks at the seaboard—that is, keeping it in artificial instead of the natural storage. Storage of that character is expensive. No funds were available through any appropriation by Congress for the construction of any storage, except that of relatively inconsequential capacity, to hold the supply needed for current use. The idea was evolved of having the tanks constructed by the lessee, the cost to be met from the royalty oil coming to the Government under the lease.

A programme of tank construction to cost approximately $102,000,000 has been outlined by the Navy, the whole to be paid for in oil, not from funds in the Treasury—two-thirds of our reserve supply of oil is to be devoted to the construction of tanks; oil, it was contemplated, should be held until commercial sources of supply should be exhausted. But, worse, on any reasonable estimate of the contents of the reserves, there is not in them sufficient to meet the demands of a war under the plan being followed, yielding, as elsewhere explained, only six per cent of the recoverable content of the reserves for the use of the Navy.

6. It is asserted by Fall and his apologists and defenders, as well, of course, as by the beneficiaries of the leases and their representatives, that they were rendered necessary because the oil within the reserves was being drained by wells in adjacent territory. It is conceded that some drainage was taking and would take place; the difference of opinion arises as to how serious was the drainage and how the condition should be met. As to the Teapot Dome, it is contended by the experts of the Geological Survey that the loss was inconsequential and that the drilling of a few line wells along the common boundary would take care of the situation. But the good faith of the claim put forth in that respect may be judged from the fact, as testified to by Admiral Robison, who acted for the Navy in the transaction, that the great Doheny lease was not induced by any reason of drainage, present or prospective. The great works being carried on at Pearl Harbor, involving an expenditure to be paid for in oil, called for more oil than was accruing to the Government as royalty from the

defensive wells for which leases were awarded in the two Naval Reserves in California, and the whole No. 1 Reserve was leased in order that the Government might have the royalty oil to pay for the tanks. He frankly admitted that the Navy developed a new policy, namely, to keep the oil in storage in tanks at the seaboard instead of in the ground.

Space will not permit an analysis of the testimony as to drainage. The more reliable of the two experts employed by the committee testified that the Teapot Dome reserve contained 26,000,000 barrels of recoverable oil, 16,000,000 north of a great fault and subject to drainage and 10,000,000 south and safe, and that if nothing was done, if no line wells were drilled, the loss from actual drainage and reduction of the gas pressure might amount to twenty-five per cent of the oil north of the fault or 4,000,000 barrels, leaving 22,000,000 in the ground. Now the average royalty being paid by Sinclair is between 16 and 17 per cent. For ease of computation, say 20 per cent, and that the total content of the reserve is 25,000,000 barrels. The Government would then be entitled to 20 per cent of 25,000,000 barrels, or 5,000,000 barrels. But it must utilize two-thirds of that to pay for the construction of the storage tanks, about two barrels of crude oil being required to pay for one barrel of storage; that is to say, the Government will have available for the use of the Navy in the tanks only one-third of 5,000,000 barrels, or 1,666,666 barrels—6 per cent of the total content of the reserve. Those who care to consider whether the lease is a good bargain for the Government or a bad bargain must determine whether it is better to have 22,000,000 barrels in the ground (assuming that the whole 4,000,000 are lost) or to have 1,666,666 barrels in the tanks.

It has been said that Doheny pays the Government, not 6 per cent, but 31 per cent. More than two-thirds of his 31 per cent goes to pay for tank construction, the works at Pearl Harbor, including docks, wharves, loading equipment, and dredging, making the charge there abnormally high. But it is an error to assume and a misrepresentation to assert that his great lease will produce a 30 per cent royalty. He first secured a contract to drill twenty-two offset wells in territory of bonanza character, as proved by wells immediately outside the reserve, on which he pays a royalty of 55 per cent, the wells, at least the outside wells, producing in the neighborhood of 5,000 barrels per day. Leases of relatively small tracts adjacent bring down the average royalty to 31 per cent, but the area drilled is relatively of very limited area. No estimate of a like average royalty for the whole reserve is at all justified, and it is unlikely that it will be higher than the average for the Teapot Dome.

The "loans" made by Doheny and Sinclair to Fall may quite properly be considered in arriving at a conclusion as to whether the leases made by him to them in secret and without competitive bidding were or were not fair to the Government, and some people will think that the fact that Sinclair contributed $75,000 to make up the deficit of the Republican National Committee after the election of 1920 is not without significance.

So likewise may the proof be considered showing that he gave up or agreed to give up $1,000,000 to the proprietors of a newspaper and their associates, on account of some shadowy rights claimed to the greater portion of the reserve. The paper, having virulently assailed the lease as corrupt, desisted, after being satisfied, from unfavorable comment.

The whole case, as to that unsavory transaction, is not stated above.

Sinclair had already paid or agreed to pay $1,000,000 to another outfit for those same claims ostensibly, but in reality, as the evidence leaves little room to doubt, to remove from the field a powerful potential competitor for the lease.

7. It appears that on so much of the oil as was or would be drained by the wells in the Salt Creek field from the Teapot Dome the Government would get a higher royalty than Sinclair pays.

8. It also plainly appears that the pipe line which, upon certain conditions, was to be constructed by Sinclair under his lease, is not being installed because of any obligation therein, but because he and the Standard Oil, owning equal undivided interests in it, control the output of the Salt Creek field, which can produce 190,000 barrels a day, the line carrying only 40,000 barrels. He contracted to construct it only when and if the yield of the Teapot Dome should be at least 20,000 barrels per day, and it has never even approached that figure.

9. Incidentally, it was established that Jake Hamon, an Oklahoma oil operator of unsavory reputation, who, with Sinclair, was a prominent figure at the Republican National Convention at Chicago, spent $105,000 to elect a delegation from that State favorable to him for National committeeman and afterwards $100,000 more to carry the State for the National ticket—as sinister a revelation as any made by the committee.

The foregoing is merely in outline, and the full significance of the disclosures is not appreciated unless they are considered in connection with those relating to the administration of the Veterans' Bureau and the Department of Justice.

MAJORITY REPORT AND VIEWS OF
THE MINORITY
JUNE 6, 1924

Congressional Record, 68th Congress, 1st Session, 10940–45; 10948–49.

Execution of the Teapot Dome Lease

In the spring of the year 1922 rumors were current that a lease of the naval reserve No. 3 had been executed. Early in April of that year, importunate requests for information being sent to Senator Kendrick by citizens of his State deeply interested in the future of the reserves, he caused inquiry to be made at the department without being able to secure any satisfactory answer, though his efforts continued until he introduced in the Senate on April 16, 1922, a resolution, forthwith passed, calling upon the Secretary of the Interior for information as to whether a lease of naval reserve No. 3 had been executed or whether the leasing of the same was in contemplation. Inquiry by representatives of the public press had likewise been diligently prosecuted along the same line without eliciting any definite information. On April 21, 1922, the Assistant Secretary of the Interior transmitted to the Senate in response to the resolution referred to a letter apprising it of the fact that a lease of the entire reserve had been, under date of April 7, 1922, executed to the Mammoth Oil Co. A definite statement to the effect that the lease had been made emanated from the Interior Department, however, on April 18, and the Wall Street Journal of the 14th of the same month gave to its readers notice of the same facts. The resolution of inquiry of April 20, 1922, introduced by Senator La Follette, followed. Pursuant to this resolution the Secretary of the Interior, under date of June 3, 1922, transmitted to the President a letter which was, by the latter, sent to the Senate, in which were set out at length the conditions deemed by him to require or justify the execution of the lease in question with a recital of some of the circumstances attending its execution and other matters believed to be important in connection with the same. At the same time he submitted to the committee photostatic copies of a vast number of documents relating more or less directly to the subject of inquiry and asserted to be in response to one of the paragraphs of the resolution of April 29.

In the letter of Secretary Fall referred to the view is advanced with fullness of argument that the leasing of the reserve was rendered necessary by reason of the fact that it was being drained by the wells in the adjacent Salt Creek field. This contention, advanced in statements made public at or near the time information concerning the lease became rife, being stoutly controverted by public men of the State of Wyoming and others more or less qualified to speak, the committee selected and appointed two geologists to make a survey of the ground with a view to acquaint it with the facts in relation thereto and to its further information concerning geological conditions having more or less importance in connection with the execution of the lease. The reports of the geologists confirmed the view that drainage was actually taking place and that loss was being suffered not only by the actual migration of the oil but by the reduction of the gas pressure within the reserve area, affecting the amount of oil which could eventually be recovered. There seems never to have been any very sound reason for the contention that it was geologically impossible to drain the reserve, to some extent at least, through the wells in the Salt Creek field. From the beginning the relation between the Salt Creek structure and the Teapot Dome structure, if they can be considered as separate, was regarded as so intimate that in setting apart the reserve an area in what was believed to be the Salt Creek structure was included within the reserve in order to forestall any likelihood of drainage of the area of oil contained in the adjacent region which it was proposed should be preserved for the Navy. Reference will hereafter be made to this subject.

The Executive Order

A study of the attendant circumstances revealed, and the hearings which were begun October 22, 1923, early disclosed, that on May 31, 1921, an order was signed by President Harding transferring the administration of the reserves from theNavy Department to the Interior Department, the order being as follows:

Executive Order

Under the provisions of the act of Congress approved February 25, 1920 (41 Stat. 437), authorizing the Secretary of the Interior to lease producing oil wells within any naval petroleum reserve; authorizing the President to permit the drilling of additional wells or to lease the remainder or any part of a claim upon which such wells have been drilled, and under authority of the act of Congress approved June 2, 1920 (41 Stat. 912), directing the Secretary of the Navy to conserve, develop, use, and operate, directly or by contract, lease, or otherwise, unappropriated lands in naval reserves, the administration, and conservation of all oil and gas bearing lands in naval petroleum reserves Nos. 1 and 2, California, and naval petroleum reserve No. 3, in Wyoming, and naval shale reserves in Colorado and Utah are hereby committed to the Secretary of the Interior, subject to the supervision of the President, but no general policy as to drilling or reserving lands located in a naval reserve shall be changed or adopted except upon consultation and in cooperation with the Secretary or Acting Secretary of the Navy. The Secretary of the Interior is authorized and directed to perform any and all acts necessary for the protection, conservation, and administration of the said reserves, subject to the conditions and limitations contained in this order and the existing laws or such laws as may hereafter be enacted by Congress pertaining thereto.

Warren G. Harding

The White House, May 31, 1921
Copy sent: Mr. Mendenhall, Survey. Comr. G.L.O.
Director Mines. (Rec. pt. 2, p. 177.)

This order, running counter as it did to the well-understood policy of Congress as manifested in the legislation referred to, merits more than a passing notice. Its illegality ought to have been recognized by everyone concerned in its promulgation. The idea that the President may, by his fiat, transfer powers reposed in or duties imposed upon one Cabinet officer to another is intolerable and indefensible. Doubts having been expressed concerning the validity of this order in communications addressed to the President by two Senators. Secretary Fall undertook to justify it upon the so-called Overman Act and the acts of February 25, 1920, and June 4, 1920, above referred to, but upon the hearings which began with the examination of Secretary Fall, he admitted that by its plain language the Overman Act was restricted in its operation to legislation enacted during the war for its progress and that there was nothing in the other acts referred to which in any wise justified the order. He then attempted to defend it upon some vague power springing from the presidential office and the general scheme of our Government. No information was sought from any of the law officers of the Government on the power of the President to make this extraordinary order. It was resolved upon as early as the 1st of April, 1921.

About that time the Secretary of the Navy announced to Admiral Griffin his purpose to surrender control of the reserves. Griffin was Chief of the Bureau of Engineering, to which had been committed the important custody of these properties. His advice as to the wisdom of making the transfer was not sought. He was told that the policy had been determined upon. None of the officers of the Navy, nor even those who, by virtue of their service, had become familiar with the subject, were consulted. Secretary Denby told the committee that he had been advised that the reserves were being drained. He was unable to recall who told him so; but maps, he said, were laid before him in connection with the imparting of the information. He assumed full responsibility for the policy, saying that the idea originated with him and that he resolved upon the course which was followed because the Navy Department was not equipped to handle the situation, while the Department of the Interior with its Bureau of Mines and the Geological Survey was able to do so. Prior thereto these two bureaus had worked in conjunction with the Navy Department in its handling of the reserves without friction or embarrassment. About the time that Denby announced to Griffin his purpose he also communicated it to Assistant Secretary Roosevelt, the latter saying that the Secretary had just come from a Cabinet meeting.

The original draft of the Executive order was made by Secretary Fall, who transmitted it to Secretary Denby with a draft of a letter to be signed by the latter and transmitted to the President explaining the occasion and necessity for the order. Amendments to it, drafted by Admiral Griffin, intended to necessitate the sanction of the Navy Department of any lease which might be made were taken by Colonel Roosevelt to Secretary Fall, who declined to adopt them, but some alterations were made in the draft which did not materially change its significance. Colonel Roosevelt explaining to Admiral Griffin upon his return that he had done the best he could with Fall. The draft thus being perfected it was taken to the Executive Office by Colonel Roosevelt and subsequently signed by the President. The original draft of the letter of transmittal prepared by Fall also went to the White House unsigned. Testifying before the committee Secretary Denby read a letter purporting to have been signed by him and which he said he transmitted to the President, explaining at some considerable length the reasons which made the order desirable in his opinion. In this letter it was stated that the policy represented by the order was not approved by all the officers of the Navy conversant with the subject, and that in particular Admiral Griffin was opposed to it, his views being expressed in a formal protest which the letter recited would be found accompanying it. As a matter of fact, neither the letter nor the protest of Admiral Griffin ever was sent to the President, and the order was signed without documentary support of any kind.

Negotiations for the Teapot Dome Lease

Near the close of the year 1921, Harry F. Sinclair traveled in his private car to Three Rivers, N. Mex., a railroad station adjacent to the ranch of Secretary Fall, where he remained for some days, visits being exchanged between the family of Secretary Fall at the ranch and that of Mr. Sinclair at his private car. In the letter of Secretary Fall to the President of June 3, 1922, it is stated that

Sinclair having come to see him in connection with certain leases of Indian lands in Oklahoma, and that that business being discharged, he took up with him the subject of leasing the Teapot Dome. From Sinclair's testimony it seems quite apparent that the trip was made for the express purpose of opening up negotiations for a lease of that property. Such negotiations were entered upon, culminating in the lease which was signed by Secretary Fall on April 7, 1922, as heretofore stated.

While at the ranch arrangements were made for the shipment from the farm of Sinclair in the State of New Jersey to the foreman of the ranch of a blooded horse and to Secretary Fall of a few head of blooded Holstein cattle. These were shipped some time in February or early in March at an expense to Sinclair of $1,105. There was no discussion of any price to be paid for the animals, but about the 1st of May some one, believed to be the son-in-law of Fall, appeared at the office of Sinclair in New York to make payment. The auditor thereupon called up the foreman of the Sinclair ranch, from whom he procured a bill for the cattle and some hogs shipped with them amounting to $1,100, which sum was paid by the stranger.

The negotiations leading to the lease were conducted in secret. There was no competition. Secretary Fall stated in his letter to the President and on the witness stand that he had consulted, before executing the lease, with leading oil men, but he omitted to specify in the letter, and declined to disclose on the stand, with whom he had talked on the subject. It appeared, however, that rumors of an impending lease reached a representative of the Texas Co., who sought out Secretary Fall with a view to offering a proposal, but was deterred by a rather unsatisfactory interview. He encountered what seemed an insuperable difficulty, the nature of which requires a somewhat extended explanation.

It will be recalled that the authority of the Secretary of the Navy by the act of June 4, 1920, was not to extend to any portion of the reserves on which there should be "pending claims or applications for permits or leases under" the so-called leasing law. Now the entire naval reserve No. 3, save about 400 acres, was covered by "claims" more or less shadowy, to be sure, but claims nevertheless, evidenced by notices of placer locations on file in the appropriate local recording office. On three of these claims wells had been drilled to the first shallow Shannon sands, yielding, it was claimed at the time they were first brought in, from 3 to 8 barrels of oil per day. One of these wells was begun December 4, 1917, and reached the oil sands December 20, 1917, at a cost of $960. The second was begun December 22, 1917, and finished January 7, 1918, at a cost of $962.50. And the third was begun January, 1918, and finished January 17, 1918, at a cost of $1,176.68. Applications had been made for leases of these wells as "producing wells" under the provisions of the act of February 25, 1920, and had been denied by Secretary of the Interior Payne on March 1, 1921, who held that the proof did not show that the wells were commercially producing wells, as he insisted the statute contemplated.

A motion for a rehearing was then filed and denied by Assistant Secretary Finney on April 28, 1921. Under the practice of the Department of the Interior in relation to these matters this decision was final and became a conclusive determination that the applicants were not entitled to the lease. Their application for a lease was undeniably an admission that they were not entitled to patents for the land for, obviously, they would not have contented themselves with a lease of one well if, under the facts of the case, they were entitled to a patent for the entire 160 acres embraced in the claim. Indisputably, they were not entitled to patents because, as heretofore stated, the right of placer mining claims depends upon a discovery within lands open to appropriation, and these lands had been withdrawn from appropriation since the year 1909. The only basis upon which a right to any of the land could be founded is a discovery; that is, a discovery of oil antedating the withdrawal order of 1909. None of the claims were so supported. The drilling of the wells referred to was carried on in defiance of the withdrawal order, the parties prosecuting it being mere trespassers. Notwithstanding the final disposition of the applications for leases referred to, the applicants filed an application for the exercise of supervisory control of the Secretary of the Interior over the officers charged with the disposition of public lands. Secretary Fall, in his letter to the President, treats this action seriously, but Assistant Secretary Finney, intimately familiar with the practice of the department and with all of the laws in relation to the disposition of the public domain from an experience of over 20 years in the department, asserts that no such proceeding is recognized by the rules of practice of the department. A careful study of all the so-called claims within naval reserve No. 3 had been made by the Department of the Interior by an experienced investigator of legal attainments, who reported that they were, as obviously they were, utterly baseless.

Under some arrangement or understanding between Sinclair and Fall the former acquired all of the so-called claims within naval reserve No. 3, which, as a condition of his securing the lease, were to be conveyed to the United States. In his consultation with the oil men he named, and with the representative of the Texas Co., Secretary Fall "particularly stressed the fact that Mr. Sinclair stated that if his proposition was considered favorably he would deliver the outstanding titles to the Government of the United States," and that if they "were not able to make better bids" than Sinclair "equitable consideration would be given to him."

Thus even those to whom in one way or another an opportunity had come to bid, if there were any such outside of the Texas Co., were at a disadvantage in the competition.

The facts are that all of the claims were held or controlled by the Pioneer Oil Co., a subsidiary of the Midwest Co., which in turn is a subsidiary of the Standard Oil. One or more of these companies had, at least since 1919, been endeavoring to secure a lease of naval reserve No. 3, or some portion of it. They were all amply able to undertake the development of the territory and were potential competitors for the lease. Sinclair paid, or agreed to pay, to the Pioneer Oil Co. some short time before the execution of the lease a million dollars nominally for the claims so reported, as above stated, to be worthless. Though that construction of the transaction is denied by Sinclair, your committee is of the opinion that the payment was not made in fact for the transfer of the title of these claims, but to remove from the field a formidable competitor for the lease and that the true nature of the transaction was thoroughly understood by Secretary Fall.

Another feature of it may as well be told in this connection. One Leo Stack, toward the close of the year 1920, associated himself with E. L. Doheny in an effort to secure from Secretary Daniels a lease of a double row of offset wells along the boundary line between naval reserve No. 3 and the Salt Creek field. The effort was fruitless, and an arrangement was entered into under which the Pioneer Oil Co. became substituted for Doheny. It thereupon entered into some kind of an agreement with Stack under which he was to assist, presumably in Washington, in securing a lease of the reserve or some portion of it for the Pioneer Oil Co., Stack having been active at the Capital in some form of lobbying, in return for which service so to be rendered by Stack he was to have an interest in any lease which might be secured by the Pioneer Oil Co. Notwithstanding this, Stack was not called upon for assistance. The Pioneer Oil Co. entered into the agreement referred to with Sinclair and retired from the field as a suitor for the lease. Stack then enlisted the interest of the owners of a newspaper in Denver, Colo., which immediately upon the execution of the lease began the publication of articles denouncing it as corrupt and contrary to public policy. They caused an investigation to be made in the State of New Mexico touching the matter of Fall's finances, hereafter to be referred to, and secured a report of a damaging character, detailing facts also to be referred to later. Stack and the newspaper proprietors entered into an agreement by which the latter acquired an interest in his claim against the Pioneer Oil Co. Suit was started in the State court of the State of Colorado in the name of Stack against that company and Sinclair, alleging a conspiracy against Stack.

The complaint was never filed, but summons was issued pursuant to the procedure of that State. After some negotiations in New York and Kansas City, Sinclair settled this suit by an agreement under which he paid $250,000 and agreed to pay $750,000 more. The attacks of the newspaper thereupon ceased. The proprietor of a rival newspaper, upon a claim even more shadowy, if, indeed, it can be called a claim at all, got $92,500 out of the Pioneer Oil Co. as his share of the moneys yielded up by Sinclair. These sums are less staggering when it is borne in mind that Sinclair testified before another committee of the Senate that he expected to make $100,000,000 from the lease, though in the hearing he expressed the view that he has erred on his estimate.

To recur to the claims asserted to the lands within the reserve. As intimated above, there were but about 400 acres over which, by virtue of the act of June 4, 1920, the Secretary of the Navy or the Secretary of the Interior, by his delegated authority, could exercise any sway. In order to carry out the plan of leasing the entire reserve it became necessary in some way to extend the field of operations open under the act referred to by the extinction of these claims. Undoubtedly the statute contemplated that as their validity should be determined one by one before the Interior Department in favor of the Government the authority of the Secretary of the Navy over the area embraced in each should be to that extent enlarged. The alleged title was not extinguished, however, in any such way. In effect, the Secretary of the Interior compromised and settled these outstanding claims by the payment or the agreement to pay a million dollars for them. This was not done by him directly, of course, but through Sinclair, the result, so far as the Government is concerned, being exactly the same. The Government, in effect, paid a million dollars for these worthless claims; that is, Sinclair could without loss to himself have offered a bonus of a million dollars for the lease if the "claims" had been extinguished in the regular way or wholly disregarded.

The execution of the lease without competitive bidding was effected in apparent disregard of statutes applicable to contracts let by the Navy Department enacted for the purpose of forestalling collusion with the officers of the Navy and securing to the Government the advantage of competitive bids. Consideration of that feature requires attention to the general provisions of the lease contract.

The Lease Analyzed

It gave to the Mammoth Oil Co. the right to occupy the territory embraced in it for the period of 20 years and so much longer as oil should be produced from it in commercial quantities; that is, it was leased for as long as there remained within the ground oil in recoverable quantities. The lessee agreed to pay to the Government royalty depending upon the productivity of the wells ranging from 12½ percent in the case of wells producing less than 50 barrels per day to 50 per cent in the case of wells producing more than 1,000 barrels per day. The average royalty from the operations thus far is between 16 and 17 per cent. The Government did not become entitled, however, to the royalty mentioned in the lease in kind. It sold its royalty oil by another provision to the lessee under an arrangement by which it was to receive oil certificates reciting the amount of oil sold and the value of the same, calculated on the basis of the "highest posted market price offered or paid" either "(1) in the Salt Creek oil field in Wyoming for a majority of the oil purchased in said field, or (2) in the mid-continent oil field by the Sinclair Crude Oil Purchasing Co., or (3) . . . by the Prairie Oil & Gas Co."

It might be here explained that the Sinclair Crude Oil Purchasing Co. is owned in equal undivided interests by the Sinclair Consolidated Co., controlled by Sinclair, and the Standard Oil Co., or one of its subsidiaries, and that the Prarie Oil & Gas Co. is a Standard company, and that the Midwest, as heretofore stated, a subsidiary of the Standard, controls the output of the Salt Creek field.

The certificates above referred to might be utilized by the Government: (1) In the purchase of fuel oil from the Mammoth Oil Co. on the basis of one barrel of fuel oil for each barrel of crude oil represented by the certificate, if such oil should register 34° Baumé or higher, or 63 per cent of one barrel of fuel oil should it fall below 34° Baumé, the fuel oil to be delivered at the seaboard; (2) in the purchase from the lessee of gasoline, kerosene, lubricating oil, and other petroleum products at a price to be agreed upon between the parties; (3) the lessee might redeem in cash; (4) the Government might tender certificates in payment for oil-storage tanks to be constructed by the lessee at the direction of the Government in which to hold the fuel oil acquired by it on the surrender of the certificates to the amount of the cost of construction.

Your committee is of the opinion in the first place that the law provides that the lease itself could not be legally executed except upon competitive bidding. . . .

Competitive bidding is excused in the case of certain supplies for the Navy by the provisions of section 3721 of the Revised Statutes, but not supplies of the character indicated above. These supplies are to be secured from the lessee at the market price, but it is quite likely that many corporations would be delighted to be able to secure a contract to provide the Government with all supplies needed by it at the market price. The Assistant Secretary of the Interior advised the committee that under the system of competitive bidding the Government secures a large part at least of what it requires in the nature of supplies at a price at least 10 per cent below the market. . . .

But there is another and more serious infirmity in this contract. Though the contract itself provides for the sale of the royalty oil to the lessee and the subsequent purchase from it by the Government of fuel oil and other supplies, the transaction may be viewed as an exchange, as indeed it is claimed it is, the contention being made that it is justified by the use of the word "exchange" in the act of June 4, 1920. It may well be admitted that the act authorizes, as undoubtedly it does authorize, the exchange of crude oil for fuel oil or for oil products, but in order to justify this contract it is necessary to go further and maintain the the word "exchange" authorizes that essential part of the contract under which the oil certificates may be utilized to pay for the cost of construction of the tanks, or as it is expressed by those upholding the contract that crude oil may be exchanged for tanks. The soundness of this view may be tested by what has actually transpired in connection with the disposition of these great properties of the Government. Contemporaneously with the negotiations resulting in the leasing of the Teapot Dome, others were carried on, culminating in the contract with the Pan American Petroleum & Transport Co., of which E. L. Doheny, heretofore mentioned, is the controlling spirit, for the construction of tanks at Pearl Harbor, Hawaii, to hold 1,500,000 barrels of fuel oil, payment for the construction to be made in oil under the authority of the statute giving to the word "exchange" the liberal construction referred to. The contract in question contemplated not only the construction of the tanks themselves but of docks and wharves at which ships loading and unloading might moor; of the installation of contrivances for loading and unloading, and for the dredging of a somewhat lengthy channel to permit ships of considerable draft to approach the tanks, all these appurtenant improvements to cost in the neighborhood of $400,000. Furthermore, the Navy Department has elaborated a program of tank construction involving subsidiary works such as those last above referred to, the whole to cost, if paid for in cash, approximately $102,000,000, the expense to be met by the delivery of royalty oil accruing to the Government under its leases of the various oil reserves.

Though no one having an intimate knowledge of the transaction seems to have been troubled with any doubts concerning the validity of the Executive order, some misgivings were felt in regard to stretching the word "exchange" so as to embrace transactions such as that evidenced by the lease under consideration. In the letter of Secretary Fall of June 3, 1922, to the President it is said that that subject was referred to in a casual way in a number of meetings of the Cabinet, and that the authority to enter into a contract of that character had been vindicated in an opinion of the Judge Advocate General of the Navy. The Judge Advocate General of the Navy is a line officer. He is not a lawyer, and did not write the opinion. It was prepared by a clerk in his office who commands a salary of $2,640 a year. He ventured the opinion on the witness stand that Congress never intended to grant powers so extensive to the Secretary of the Navy, but that it had actually done so, the substance of the opinion being that inasmuch as the word "exchange" was in nowise limited, the Secretary was authorized to exchange oil for anything—a battleship, ordnance, or an addition to the State, War, and Navy Building. He took no notice whatever of the provision of the statute to the effect that for the purpose, among other things, of providing storage for the oil issuing from the reserves as royalty or otherwise, prior to July 1, 1921, the Secretary of the Navy was authorized to use until July 1, 1922, not to exceed $500,000. It was contemplated that it would be necessary to provide storage for the oil accruing to the Government, and provision was made to meet the expense of such storage as well as other expenses which might be incurred by the Secretary in carrying out the act.

Some of the strongest companies in the country declined to bid on the contract for the construction of the storage at Pearl Harbor upon the ground that the statute did not authorize payment of work of that character in oil. Notwithstanding their reluctance upon the advice of counsel and of an intimation to Secretary Fall that it would be wise on his part to do so, no opinion concerning the validity of such a contract was sought from the Department of Justice, nor from the Solicitor of the Interior Department, nor any of the law officers of the Government except as above stated. . . .

The Doheny Leases

The fact that drainage to an appreciable extent and, indeed, to a serious extent, was taking place in naval reserve No. 1 and naval reserve No. 2 was recognized by Secretary Daniels, who resolutely, and perhaps obdurately, resisted every suggestion of drilling within the reserves, even to protect them from drainage, until the seriousness of the situation was realized even by him. It is represented by the Bureau of Mines that the failure to drill all necessary offset wells prior to March 4, 1921, resulted in the loss to the Government of 6,800,000 barrels of royalty of the value of $8,800,000. The accuracy of this contention is disputed, and it is conceded at the drainage which had actually taken place and the damage done in naval reserve No. 3 prior to the execution of the lease thereof was inconsequential. However, in 1920 highly productive wells were brought in in territory immediately outside the southeasternmost extremity of naval reserve No. 1, and Secretary Daniels, prior to his retirement on March 4, 1921, had called for bids for the drilling of 22 offset wells within that reserve. The proposals were not submitted, however, until after the new administration came in, and the contract was awarded to Doheny by Fall on July 12, 1921, acting under the pretended authority of the Executive order of May 21, 1921. This contract appears to have been otherwise unexceptionable. It was awarded upon open competitive bidding to the highest and best bidder.

The policy thus having been evolved of utilizing a part—and, as it transpired, the larger part—of the royalty oil accruing to the Government for the construction of tanks, bids were solicited for the construction of tanks at Pearl Harbor, as heretofore stated, payment to be made in oil. A number of companies, including the Pan American Petroleum & Transport Co., a Doheny organization, bid upon the contract, others being deterred, as heretofore stated, by doubt as to the legality of a contract of that character. Doheny submitted two bids, one of which was in strict conformity with the proposals and the other offering to do the work at a less cost, but securing to him a preference right to a lease of practically the eastern half of the reserve. His alternate proposal was accepted and the contract entered into accordingly under date of April 25, 1922. The negotiations for this contract were carried on simultaneously with those culminating in the lease of naval reserve No. 3. Some of the reluctance to give to the public information concerning the execution of that lease was attributed to a desire to make it and the Doheny contract above referred to public at the same time. Whether this was due to an appreciation that disapproval of the new policy might make it impracticable to complete the Doheny contract is a matter of speculation. On December 11, 1922, in the same secret manner as characterized the execution of the lease of naval reserve No. 3, a lease of the entire naval reserve No. 1 was executed to the Pan American Petroleum Co., another Doheny organization, under which it agreed to pay royalties ranging from 12½ to 35 per cent. A supplemental contract provided for the construction of tankage by the lessee company, to be paid for out of the royalty oil accruing under the Doheny lease, identical in its essential features in that respect with the provisions of the Sinclair lease. . . .

The conditions giving rise to this lease are of such supreme importance as to require detailed attention. There was here no impending loss from drainage. That situation had been taken care of by the lease of July 12, 1921, under which the 22 offset wells had been drilled, and by other leases of relatively small tracts upon which offset wells had been or would be drilled to meet operations that had been conducted or were being conducted outside the reserve and by an agreement which had been entered into with parties owning lands within the exterior boundaries of the reserve for a suspension of drilling operations to be renewed only upon six months' notice. It is frankly admitted that the lease in question was executed because the Navy Department had evolved an entirely new policy, concluding that the wiser plan would be to take the oil out of the ground and store it in tanks at the seaboard. Carrying out this plan, which included the construction of the storage works at Pearl Harbor, it transpired that the royalty oil coming to the Government was not sufficient to meet the current expenditures incident to the prosecution of the construction program, and the Doheny lease was executed, the committee was told by Admiral Robison, in order that there might be available a more abundant quantity of royalty oil with which to meet the accruing obligations. Two circumstances disclosed by the testimony have an important bearing upon the good faith back of the reason thus assigned:

First. During the war Robison was in command of a ship at Pensacola, Fla., of which the son of Doheny was a junior officer. The elder Doheny visited his son while the ship was at that port and in that connection he became acquainted with Robison. In the intimacy bred by this association, the naval oil reserves became the subject of conversation, in the course of which Doheny expatiated upon the unwisdom of the policy which had been pursued by Secretary Daniels with such effect that Robison, who theretofore had no connection whatever with the reserves nor any special information about oil matters, entered upon the discharge of his duties as Chief of the Bureau of Engineering with a settled conviction that the policy which had been pursued was unwise and that the oil should be taken out of the ground as speedily as possible and stored in tanks at the seaboard.

Second. There has been no substantial production under the lease of

December 11, 1922, and only three wells have been drilled within the territory covered by it, all of the production under any of the Doheny leases coming from the territory covered by the relatively small leases. The wells which are drilled penetrate the ground in the remote southeastern part of the reserve, the rich character of which was demonstrated by wells immediately beyond. The first of these leases, that of July 12, 1921, pays a royalty of 55 per cent, the average royalty under these leases covering an area of 1,108 acres, being about 28 per cent. In view of the lack of development of the area covered by the lease of December 11, 1922, embracing the greater portion of the reserve, it is impossible to estimate with any degree of accuracy the average royalty which would be yielded by the entire reserve under the lease.

It should be stated in this connection that neither the Secretary of the Navy nor the Assistant Secretary had any part whatever in the negotiations resulting in the execution of the leases here being canvassed, or, for that matter, in those culminating in the Sinclair lease. Neither of them, when on the stand, was able to give the committee any information concerning the leases of naval reserve No. 1 or of the conditions leading up to the execution of them or of the circumstances and conditions inducing them. The Secretary had no knowledge, when on the stand, that any lease of naval reserve No. 1 had been executed, though the instrument itself bears his signature.

Fall's Financial Transactions

The taking of testimony began with the examination of Secretary Fall, who was subjected to a somewhat searching inquiry extending over a period of two days. It was disclosed in his examination that shortly after quitting the office of Secretary of the Interior on March 4, 1923, he made a trip to Europe with Sinclair as counsel for him and associates interested in securing oil concessions from the Russian Government and that he had also, after leaving office, acted in an advisory capacity for Doheny. (Rec. pt. 2, p. 274.) The circumstances of the employment of Fall for the European trip were peculiar. One J. W. Zevely, an attorney with offices in Washington, D. C., and a home on Long Island, N. Y., costing in the neighborhood of $100,000, acquired through funds loaned to him by Sinclair, had acted for some years as a kind of confidential man and attorney for Sinclair and had been associated with him as such in all of the transactions here narrated. Zevely made a trip from New York to Three Rivers, N. Mex., to convey to Fall Sinclair's desire that the late Secretary should accompany him on his Russian quest as counsel. Fall acceded and was paid $10,000 to cover his expenses on the trip. While at Three Rivers he confided to Zevely that he needed $25,000 or $30,000 for some purpose not disclosed, and on his return to New York, the fact being communicated to Sinclair, he directed that Liberty bonds or the proceeds of them to the amount of $25,000 should be loaned to Fall. They were, accordingly, sent by express, the loan being evidenced by a note to Zevely.

Fall left the stand without having disclosed that after his letter of June 3, 1922, had been written the whole of naval reserve No. 1 had been leased to E. L. Doheny as heretofore stated. The facts came to the attention of the committee quite accidentally upon its request of the Interior Department for maps of the reserves in question showing the leases which had been executed of the areas within them. About the same time there came to the knowledge of one of the members of the committee the fact that an enterprising newspaper had, in the summer of 1922, sent to New Mexico a reporter to investigate the alleged rise of Secretary Fall from a condition of financial embarrassment to relative affluence. The investigator came to Washington at the invitation of the committee and brought with him the report of his investigation made to his paper at the time but which, for some reason, was never published.

In consequence of information secured through him and the report, witnesses were brought before the committee from New Mexico who, with official documents, brought to light that, whereas Senator Fall, who was engaged in the ranching and cattle business, had been in straitened circumstances and had not paid his local taxes for 10 years, he had during the latter part of the year 1921 and the early part of 1922 purchased property in his neighborhood and made improvements in his holdings involving an expenditure of from $175,000 to $200,000, and that in particular he had purchased the property adjacent to his own, known as the Harris Ranch, for which, with the cattle and equipment appurtenant thereto, he had paid $91,500, the initial payment of $10,000 taking place in El Paso, Tex., having been made in bills taken by him from a tin box in which there was other currency.

This testimony was presented to the committee on the 3d day of November, 1923, at which time Fall was in New Mexico. He sent word to the committee that his son-in-law, one C. C. Chase, who was entirely familiar with his business affairs, would shortly appear and explain the transaction satisfactorily. Chase did not present himself, and Fall reached Washington some time after the middle of December, coming by way of Chicago, New York, and Atlantic City, explaining his delay in appearing by the representation that he was ill. On December 27 he sent a communication to the committee pleading illness as an excuse for not appearing in person, in which communication he informed the committee that the money with which he purchased the Harris Ranch had been loaned to him to the extent of $100,000 by one Edward B. McLean, of Washington, D. C., and referring to banking connections at Pueblo, Colo., intimating, without definitely asserting, that he had secured further funds to meet the additional expenditures proven to have been by him made from that source. Thereupon Mr. McLean, who was at that time in Palm Beach, Fla., made repeated requests to the committee to be excused from appearing as a witness on account of his ill health and illness in his family, and asserted that he had, in the latter part of November, 1921, loaned Fall $100,000. His testimony was taken by a member of the committee at Palm Beach on the 11th of January, 1924, when he repudiated his former statement and admitted that he had not made the loan or any loan to Fall, asserting in that connection that Fall having applied to him for a loan he gave to Fall his checks for the sum named, but that the latter a few days later returned them, saying that he had arranged to secure the money elsewhere. Fall, who was at that time himself in Palm Beach, a guest of McLean's, in a letter to the examining member of the committee, confirmed the testimony given by Mr. McLean.

Thereafter, on the 24th day of January, 1924, E. L. Doheny appeared before the committee and testified that he had, on November 30, 1921, loaned to Fall $100,000. Your committee ventures no opinion as to whether the transaction was in fact a loan or whether it might more appropriately be otherwise denominated. Fall and Doheny were friends, or at least acquaintances, in the mining camps of the Southwest many years ago. The latter had prospered to such an extent that he was able to say, and perhaps truthfully, that such a sum as $100,000 was in the nature of a bagatelle to him. He insisted that he let Fall have the money in consideration of old associations and commiseration for the reverses financially which had befallen his friend of other days. The money was delivered to Fall in cash by the son of Doheny, who brought it from New York, where is the main office of Doheny's companies, to Washington in a satchel, the money having been secured from the bank upon the check of the younger Doheny under an arrangement with his father.

It appeared that two days before the money was delivered Doheny had written a letter to Fall in which the contract for the construction of the tanks at Pearl Harbor was discussed, and Doheny signified his desire and purpose to bid on the contract. Doheny stated that he expected the loan to Fall would eventually be paid by legal services.

Though the committee refrains, as indicated, from characterizing the transactions referred to, it does not hesitate to condemn it as, in the last degree, reprehensible on the part of all concerned in it. The essentially corrupt character of a loan made under such circumstances requires no comment. It would be impossible for an officer to accept a loan of such an amount, or perhaps of any amount, under the circumstances without a sense of obligation to the lender, which, unless his character was cast in heroic mold, would be revealed in subsequent official transactions with him. Its sinister import is appreciated when it is borne in mind that, without competitive bidding, as heretofore explained, Doheny got from Fall, in the month of April following, the contract for the construction of the tanks at Pearl Harbor, and with it a preference right to a lease of a large share of naval reserve No. 1, to be followed, without competitive bidding, by a lease of the entire reserve, comprising over 30,000 acres, estimated to contain 250,000,000 barrels of oil, out of which, Doheny told the committee, he would be in bad luck if he did not make $100,000,000 profit. It should be added here that Fall's son-in-law, C. C. Chase, then collector of customs at the port of El Paso, Tex., did come to Washington, as Fall said he would, stopping on the way at Cleveland, Ohio, to persuade another old friend of Fall to testify before the committee to the effect that he had loaned to the latter the money with which to buy the Harris ranch, comformably to a request made in a letter by Fall to the gentleman in question, with which the latter promptly declined to comply, as he told the committee on the stand. It was further disclosed that on the invitation of Fall, Mr. McLean, above referred to, met him at Atlantic City, and that it was there agreed upon between them, at the instigation of Fall, that McLean and he should both advise the committee as they did, that McLean had made the loan which enabled Fall to buy the Harris ranch.

Having heard the testimony of Mr. Doheny concerning the alleged loan of $100,000 to Fall, the latter was again called by the committee. Pleading illness, he sent his physicians to inform the committee of his inability to attend, whereupon it sent three others of its own choice to inquire into his condition. These reporting that he was physically able to appear, he was required to attend and, appearing, challenged the right of the committee to proceed because, among other reasons assigned, its authority was derived from a Congress which had expired, and at the same time he claimed immunity from testifying upon the ground that any evidence he might give might tend to incriminate him. The confirmatory resolution of the Senate before referred to was then adopted, and upon the witness being recalled he stood upon his constitutional right and was excused. . . .

The Leases as Good Bargains

A disposition is evinced in some quarters to dismiss or overlook the very suggestive circumstances shown in the hearings indicating corruption in connection with the Sinclair and Doheny leases, the flagrant disregard of the law and the unwarranted assumption of authority that attended their execution, the abandonment of the settled policy of the Government evidenced by them, to inquire as to whether they are or are not excellent bargains viewed from the standpoint of the Government. These efforts invariably arriving at or pointing to the conclusion that they are such are obviously designed to divert attention from or to overcome the effect upon the public mind of the features of the transactions above referred to.

Your committee can not believe that a lease under which the Government receives 6 per cent of the oil in the ground and the lessee gets 94 including what it receives on account of the construction of tankage can possibly be in the interest of or just to the former. Had the leases been awarded upon competitive bidding, there would have been no occasion to inquire whether they are or are not fair or just to the Government. Such a test would have conclusively established the fact. That omission to invite competition casts a suspicion on the transaction as being in the interest of the Government. Even if the law does not require that such a contract be let upon competitive bids, business prudence would dictate that such a course be followed, as it was followed in the case of some of the minor leases of areas within the two California reserves.

If the Secretary of the Interior consulted with anyone competent from experience in affairs of such magnitude to advise him concerning the terms of the lease, viewed as a business proposition, the fact was not divulged. Evidently he conceived himself quite competent unaided to negotiate with such veterans in the oil business as Sinclair and Doheny. It is true he conferred with officials of the Bureau of Mines, technical men not chosen by reason of their skill or success in business.

Not only was the Teapot Dome lease awarded to Sinclair without competition, but he paid a fabulous price to procure the elimination of a potential rival. One seeking only a fair contract from the Government does not buy off his competitors; neither does he, when he secures it ordinarily, submit to blackmail in connection with it; nor does he, while negotiations are pending, accommodate the awarding officer with loans or gifts.

It is of little consequence that the royalty mentioned in the leases is approximately or even that it may be higher than that stipulated in leases between private individuals or companies. Not to mention other considerations under the Sinclair lease, he purchases without competition the royalty oil of the Government, paying the current price. Upon competitive bidding the royalty oil accruing to the Government from leases of areas in the adjacent Salt Creek field was sold at a price greatly in excess of the current market price. Sinclair likewise secures the opportunity, should the Secretary of the Navy choose to exercise an option accorded him by the contract, to supply the Navy with oil products, of which it requires great quantities, at the market price. Considering the reasonableness of the royalties in his lease stipulated, it is just to institute a comparison with those paid to the Government under leases covering the immediately adjacent territory in the Salt Creek field. They were awarded June 15, 1921, upon competitive bidding, the royalty being fixed at either 25 per cent of 33-⅓ per cent flat, the bidders offering bonuses, in one instance as high as $1,412.50 per acre and bringing the Government an aggregate above the royalty of $1,687,000 for 6,400 acres in all. (Rec., pt. 4, p. 1112).

There were, furthermore, 22 of such leases, embracing 40 tracts of limited areas, not permitting the economies resulting from unified control and mass production capable of being exercised under the Sinclair lease. It is doubtful whether a lease of an area of proven territory equal to that covered thereby or by the Doheny lease is known in the history of oil production, and comparison with the terms of leases of relatively small tracts is likely to be deceptive.

Notwithstanding better terms can ordinarily be secured for leases of larger areas, Congress has deemed it wise to limit the acreage of oil land which may be leased to any individual or corporation at least as one transaction, fixing 4,800 acres in the case of Indian lands and 640 acres under the act of February 25, 1920.

The act of June 4, 1920, placed no limitation upon the area that might be embraced in a lease or upon the area that might be leased to a single individual, but the policy of Congress was clearly evinced in the acts referred to.

It is pertinent to remark in this connection that whatever drainage might take place from naval reserve No. 3, had it not been leased or protected by offset wells, would have swelled the production of the wells on the tracts to the north so leased. In other words, the Government would be entitled to, and would have received, a royalty of 25 or 33⅓ per cent instead of 16-odd, which either 25 per cent of 33⅓ per cent flat, the bidders offering bonuses, in one to the benefit of the Navy but would be deposited in the fund established by the act of February 25, 1920, to be distributed as therein provided, in part to the General Treasury, the reclamation fund, and the State of Wyoming, but Congress would have full power at any time to provide that an equitable portion of the royalty paid on leases, the production of which was enhanced by drainage, should inure to the benefit of the Navy. . . .

Your committee is of the opinion that to utilize two-thirds of the royalty oil received by the Government from leases it may find it advisable to make of portions of the reserves is not only indefensibly wasteful but would leave it without an adequate supply of fuel oil to meet such an emergency as was contemplated in the creation of them. The policy which was followed in that regard was entered upon without any serious consideration of the question as to whether thus utilizing two-thirds of the royalty oil to pay for tankage there would be secured enough fuel oil to meet the needs of the Navy should occasion arise to resort to the reserves. No one concerned in the transaction or in the adoption of the policy pursued was able to give the committee an approximate estimate of the quantity which the reserves would produce or the quantity reasonably necessary as a reserve.

Incidental Inquiries

In the prosecution of the investigation with which it was charged by the Senate your committee felt called upon to follow some lines of inquiry that yielded nothing.

The rumor was current, particularly after evidence that the transactions to which attention had been given were tainted, that public officers had been concerned in dealings in the stocks of the companies to which the leases had been awarded or of companies bearing close relation to them, presumably upon information referable to official sources. Diligent inquiry into the foundation of the rumor revealed no facts of sufficient importance to report. In like manner the rumor persisted that the appointment of Secretary Fall was brought about or was made pursuant to a conspiracy which was entered into between certain prominent oil opeators and others at or prior to the Republican National Convention of 1920 which, in its general scope, contemplated the exploitation of the public-land resources by those concerned in it.

The remarkable circumstances attending the promulgation of the Executive order of May 31, 1921, and the leases of the naval reserves gave color to the rumor and a searching inquiry seemed warranted. The committee was appointed to investigate and it proceeded to investigate. The evidence failed to establish the existence of any such conspiracy. It was revealed, however, that Mr. Sinclair contributed $10,000 to the campaign fund raised by the Republican National Committee in connection with the election of 1920, and that he subsequently contributed $75,000 to make up the deficit carried over that election by it; and further that E. L. Doheny contributed $75,000, as he testified, or $32,500, as testified by the chairman thereof, to the Democratic National Committee in the same contest, and that he likewise contributed $25,000 to the Republican committee.

Conclusion

As the Senate has heretofore been advised, H. F. Sinclair being recalled before the committee to testify, among other things, concerning features of the transactions under investigation developed since he was last on the stand, declined to testify upon various grounds, among others, that the Senate has no power, under the Constitution, to require an unwilling witness either to attend or testify before it or any of its committees. Proceedings are now pending in the courts to secure an adjudication of the right to the immunity so claimed. Should the authority of the committee, as the representative of the Senate, be vindicated, it will desire further to interrogate Mr. Sinclair. It accordingly reports that it has not finished its labors under the resolutions of the Senate and will resume them at some appropriate and convenient season unless otherwise ordered.

It is unnecessary to say that pursuant to the directions of Congress the validity of the leases canvassed of naval reserves No. 1 and No. 3 is under inquiry by the courts in suits to recover the lands involved. The committee accordingly reserves to a later date such recommendations as it may deem advisable to make touching legislation affecting the reserves.

Respectfully submitted. By the
committee:

E. F. Ladd
Chairman
Peter Norbeck
A. A. Jones
Alva B. Adams
John B. Kendrick
C. C. Dill
T. J. Walsh
Key Pittman

Mr. Spencer, from the Committee on Public Lands and Surveys, submitted the views of the minority pursuant to sundry Senate resolutions relative to investigations of leases upon naval oil lands: The undersigned members of the Committee on Public Lands and Surveys submit to the Senate the following statement with regard to the report on the lease upon naval oil reserves as presented by the committee:

No adequate opportunity has been given them to examine the report which has been submitted. The final hearings are not yet returned from the printer.

A casual reading of the report indicates many mistakes and conclusions and inferences of facts and law which, in the judgment of the undersigned, are unwarranted by the testimony.

On May 14, when the hearings were discontinued for this session, request was made, of record, that an opportunity of at least a few days be afforded in order to examine the report which the senior Senator from Montana [Mr. Walsh] indicated he intended to prepare, and that such opportunity be given before the report was submitted to the committee for final action. No such opportunity was afforded.

The report was printed and presented June 4 to the committee for immediate consideration and action. It was on that date first presented to the undersigned. It has been physically impossible to examine, in any fair or adequate manner, the statements of the report which deals with such voluminous testimony and which attempts to pass judgment on disputed questions of law and upon controverted facts.

The report indicates that the hearings before the committee are not yet concluded, and are to be resumed in case "the authority of the committee as the representative of the Senate be vindicated" in its attempt to further interrogate Mr. H. F. Sinclair.

The undersigned will prepare and submit to the Senate such matters as may, in their judgment, have been overlooked by the report as presented, and such corrections and changes as, in their judgment, should be brought to the attention of the Senate before any final action is taken.

Selden P. Spencer
Reed Smoot
Robt. N. Stanfield
Ralph H. Cameron
H. O. Bursum

OPINION IN *McGRAIN* v. *DAUGHERTY*
JANUARY 17, 1927

McGrain v. *Daugherty*, 273 U.S. 135 (1927).

Mr. Justice Van Devanter delivered the opinion of the court.

This is an appeal from the final order in a proceeding in *habeas corpus* discharging a recusant witness held in custody under process of attachment issued from the United States Senate in the course of an investigation which it was making of the administration of the Department of Justice. A full statement of the case is necessary.

The Department of Justice is one of the great executive departments established by congressional enactment and has charge, among other things, of the initiation and prosecution of all suits, civil and criminal, which may be brought in the right and name of the United States to compel obedience or punish disobedience to its laws, to recover property obtained from it by unlawful or fraudulent means, or to safeguard its rights in other respects; and also of the assertion and protection of its interests when it or its officers are sued by others. The Attorney General is the head of the department, and its functions are all to be exercised under his supervision and direction.

Harry M. Daugherty became the Attorney General March 5, 1921, and held that office until March 28, 1924, when he resigned. Late in that period various charges of misfeasance and nonfeasance in the Department of Justice after he became its supervising head were brought to the attention of the Senate by individual senators and made the basis of an insistent demand that the department be investigated to the end that the practices and deficiencies which, according to the charges, were operating to prevent or impair its right administration might be definitely ascertained and that appropriate and effective measues might be taken to remedy or eliminate the evil. The Senate regarded the charges as grave and requiring legislative attention and action. Accordingly it formulated, passed and invited the House of Representatives to pass (and that body did pass) two measures taking important litigation then in immediate contemplation out of the control of the Department of Justice and placing the same in charge of special counsel to be appointed by the President; and also adopted a resolution authorizing and directing a select committee of five senators—

"to investigate circumstances and facts, and report the same to the Senate, concerning the alleged failure of Harry M. Daugherty, Attorney General of the United States, to prosecute properly violators of the Sherman Anti-trust Act and the Clayton Act against monopolies and unlawful restraint of trade; the alleged neglect and failure of the said Harry M. Daugherty, Attorney General of the United States, to arrest and prosecute Albert B. Fall, Harry F. Sinclair, E. L. Doheny, C. R. Forbes, and their co-conspirators in defrauding the Government, as well as the alleged neglect and failure of the said Attorney General to arrest and prosecute many others for violations of Federal statutes, and his alleged failure to prosecute properly, efficiently, and promptly, and to defend, all manner of civil and criminal actions wherein the Government of the United States is interested as a party plaintiff or defendant. And said committee is further directed to inquire into, investigate and report to the Senate the activities of the said Harry M. Daugherty, Attorney General, and any of his assistants in the Department of Justice which would in any manner tend to impair their efficiency or influence as representatives of the Government of the United States."

The resolution also authorized the committee to send for books and papers, to subpoena witnesses, to administer oaths, and to sit at such times and places as it might deem advisable.

In the course of the investigation the committee issued and caused to be duly served on Mally S. Daugherty—who was a brother of Harry M. Daugherty and president of the Midland National Bank of Washington Court House, Ohio,—a subpoena commanding him to appear before the committee for the purpose of giving testimony bearing on the subject under investigation, and to bring with him the "deposit ledgers of the Midland National Bank since November 1, 1920; also note files and transcript of owners of every safety vault; also records of income drafts; also records of any individual account or accounts showing withdrawals of amounts of $25,000 or over during above period." The witness failed to appear.

A little later in the course of the investigation the committee issued and caused to be duly served on the same witness another subpoena commanding him to appear before it for the purpose of giving testimony relating to the subject under consideration—nothing being said in this subpoena about bringing records, books or papers. The witness again failed to appear; and no excuse was offered by him for either failure.

The committee then made a report to the Senate stating that the subpoenas had been issued, that according to the officer's returns—copies of which accompanied the report—the witness was personally served; and that he had failed and refused to appear. After a reading of the report, the Senate adopted a resolution reciting these facts and proceeding as follows.

> Whereas the appearance and testimony of the said M. S. Daugherty is material and necessary in order that the committee may properly execute the functions imposed upon it and may obtain information necessary as a basis for such legislative and

other action as the Senate may deem necessary and proper: Therefore be it

Resolved, That the President of the Senate pro tempore issue his warrant commanding the Sergeant at Arms or his deputy to take into custody the body of the said M. S. Daugherty wherever found, and to bring the said M. S. Daugherty before the bar of the Senate, then and there to answer such questions pertinent to the matter under inquiry as the Senate may order the President of the Senate pro tempore to propound; and to keep the said M. S. Daugherty in custody to await the further order of the Senate.

It will be observed from the terms of the resolution that the warrant was to be issued in furtherance of the effort to obtain the personal testimony of the witness and, like the second subpoena, was not intended to exact from him the production of the various records, books and papers named in the first subpoena.

The warrant was issued agreeably to the resolution and was addressed simply to the Sergeant at Arms. That officer on receiving the warrant endorsed thereon a direction that it be executed by John J. McGrain, already his deputy, and delivered it to him for execution.

The deputy, proceeding under the warrant, took the witness into custody at Cincinnati, Ohio, with the purpose of bringing him before the bar of the Senate as commanded; whereupon the witness petitioned the federal district court in Cincinnati for a writ of *habeas corpus*. The writ was granted and the deputy made due return setting forth the warrant and the cause of the detention. After a hearing the court held the attachment and detention unlawful and discharged the witness, the decision being put on the ground that the Senate in directing the investigation and in ordering the attachment exceeded its powers under the Constitution, 299 Fed. 620. The deputy prayed and was allowed a direct appeal to this Court under § 238 of the Judicial Code as then existing.

We have given the case earnest and prolonged consideration because the principal questions involved are of unusual importance and delicacy. They are (a) whether the Senate—or the House of Representatives, both being on the same plane in this regard—has power, through its own process, to compel a private individual to appear before it or one of its committees and give testimony needed to enable it efficiently to exercise a legislative function belonging to it under the Constitution, and (b) whether it sufficiently appears that the process was being employed in this instance to obtain testimony for that purpose.

Other questions are presented which in regular course should be taken up first.

The witness challenges the authority of the deputy to execute the warrant on two grounds—that there was no provision of law for a deputy, and that, even if there were such a provision, a deputy could not execute the warrant because it was addressed simply to the Sergeant at Arms. We are of opinion that neither ground is tenable.

The Senate adopted in 1889 and has retained ever since a standing order declaring that the Sergeant at Arms may appoint deputies "to serve process or perform other duties" in his stead, that they shall be "officers of the Senate," and that acts done and returns made by them "shall have like effect and be of the same validity as if performed or made by the Sergeant at Arms in person." In actual practice the Senate has given full effect to the order; and Congress has sanctioned the practice under it by recognizing the deputies—sometimes called assistants—as officers of the Senate, by fixing their compensation and by making appropriations to pay them. Thus there was ample provision of law for a deputy.

The fact that the warrant was addressed simply to the Sergeant at Arms is not of special significance. His authority was not to be tested by the warrant alone. Other criteria were to be considered. The standing order and the resolution under which the warrant was issued plainly contemplated that he was to be free to execute the warrant in person or to direct a deputy to execute it. They expressed the intention of the Senate; and the words of the warrant were to be taken, as they well could be, in a sense which would give effect to that intention. Thus understood, the warrant admissibly could be executed by a deputy if the Sergeant at Arms so directed, which he did.

The case of *Sanborn* v. *Carleton,* 15 Gray 399, on which the witness relies, related to a warrant issued to the Sergeant at Arms in 1860, which he deputed another to execute. At that time there was no standing rule or statute permitting him to act through a deputy; nor was there anything in the resolution under which the warrant was issued indicative of a purpose to permit him to do so. All that was decided was that in the absence of a permissive provision, in the warrant or elsewhere, he could not commit its execution to another. The provision which was absent in that case and deemed essential is present in this.

The witness points to the provision in the Fourth Amendment to the Constitution declaring "no warrants shall issue but upon probable cause supported by oath or affirmation" and contends that the warrant was void because the report of the committee on which it was based was unsworn. We think the contention overlooks the relation of the committee to the Senate and to the matters reported, and puts aside the accepted interpretation of the constitutional provision.

The committee was a part of the Senate, and its members were acting under their oath of office as senators. The matters reported pertained to their proceedings and were within their own knowledge. They had issued the subpoenas, had received and examined the officer's returns thereon (copies of which accompanied the report), and knew the witness had not obeyed either subpoena or offered any excuse for his failure to do so.

The constitutional provision was not intended to establish a new principle but to affirm and preserve a cherished rule of the common law designed to prevent the issue of groundless warrants. In legislative practice committee reports are regarded as made under the sanction of the oath of office of its members; and where the matters reported are within the committee's knowledge and constitute probable cause for an attachment such reports are acted on and given effect without requiring that they be supported by further oath or affirmation. This is not a new practice but one which has come down from an early period. It was well recognized before the constitutional provision was adopted, has been followed ever since, and appears never to have been challenged until now. Thus it amounts to a practical interpretation, long continued, of both the original common law rule and the affirming constitutional provision, and should be given effect accordingly.

The principle underlying the legislative practice has also been recognized and applied in judicial proceedings. This is illustrated by the settled rulings that courts in dealing with contempts committed in their presence may order commitments without other proof than their own knowledge of the occurrence, and that they may issue attachments, based on their own knowledge of the default, where intended witnesses or jurors fail to appear in obedience to process shown by the officer's return to have been duly served. A further illustration is found in the rulings that grand jurors, acting under the sanction of their oaths as such, may find and return indictments based solely on their own knowledge of the particular offenses, and that warrants may be issued on such indictments without further oath or affirmation, and still another is found in the practice which recognizes that where grand jurors, under their oath as such, report to the court that a witness brought before them has refused to testify, the court may act on that report, although otherwise unsworn, and order the witness brought before it by attachment.

We think the legislative practice, fortified as it is by the judicial practice, shows that the report of the committee—which was based on the committee's own knowledge and made under the sanction of the oath of office of its members—was sufficiently supported by oath to satisfy the constitutional requirement.

The witness also points to the provision in the warrant and in the resolution under which it was issued requiring that he be "brought before the bar of the Senate, then and there" to give testimony "pertinent to the subject under inquiry," and contends that an essential prerequisite to such an attachment was wanting, because he neither had been subpoenaed to appear and testify before the Senate nor had refused to do so. The argument in support of the contention proceeds on the assumption that the warrant of attachment "is to be treated precisely the same as if no subpoena had been issued by the committee, and the same as if the witness had not refused to testify before the committee." In our opinion the contention and the assumption are both untenable. The committee was acting for the Senate and under its authorization; and therefore the subpoenas which the committee issued and the witness refused to obey are to be treated as if issued by the Senate. The warrant was issued as an auxiliary process to compel him to give the testimony sought by the subpoenas; and its nature in this respect is not affected by the direction that his testimony be given at the bar of the Senate instead of before the committee. If the Senate deemed it proper, in view of his contumacy, to give that direction it was at liberty to do so.

The witness sets up an interlocutory injunction granted by a state court at Washington Court House, Ohio, in a suit brought by the Midland National Bank against two members of the investigating committee, and contends that the attachment was in violation of that injunction and therefore unlawful. The contention is plainly ill-founded. The injunction was granted the same day the second subpoena was served, but whether earlier or later in the day does not appear. All that the record discloses about the injunction is comprised in the paragraph copied in the margin from the witness's petition for *habeas corpus*.

But it is apparent from what is disclosed that the injunction did not purport to place any restraint on the witness, nor to restrain the committee from demanding that he appear and testify personally to what he knew respecting the subject under investigation; and also that what the injunction did purport to restrain has no bearing on the power of the Senate to enforce that demand by attachment.

In approaching the principal questions, which remain to be considered, two observations are in order. One is that we are not now concerned with the direction in the first subpoena that the witness produce various records, books and papers of the Midland National Bank. That direction was not repeated in the second subpoena; and is not sought to be enforced by the attachment. This was recognized by the court below, 299 Fed. 623, and is conceded by counsel for the appellant. The other is that we are not now concerned with the right of the Senate to propound or the duty of the witness to answer specific questions, for as yet no questions have been propounded to him. He is asserting—and is standing on his assertion—that the Senate is without power to interrogate him, even if the questions propounded be pertinent and otherwise legitimate—which for present purposes must be assumed.

The first of the principal questions—the one which the witness particularly presses on our attention—is, as before shown, whether the Senate—or the House of Representatives, both being on the same plane in this regard —has power, through its own process, to compel a private individual to appear before it or one of its committees and give testimony needed to enable it efficiently to exercise a legislative function belonging to it under the Constitution.

The Constitution provides for a Congress consisting of a Senate and House of Representatives and invests it with "all legislative powers" granted to the United States, and with power "to make all laws which shall be necessary and proper" for carrying into execution these powers and "all other powers" vested by the Constitution in the United States or in any department or officer thereof. Art. I, secs 1, 8. Other provisions show that, while bills can become laws only after being considered and passed by both houses of Congress, each house is to be distinct from the other, to have its own officers and rules, and to exercise its legislative function independently. Art. I, secs. 2, 3, 5, 7. But there is no provision expressly investing either house with power to make investigations and exact testimony to the end that it may exercise its legislative function advisedly and effectively. So the question arises whether this power is so far incidental to the legislative function as to be implied.

In actual legislative practice power to secure needed information by such means has long been treated as an attribute of the power to legislate. It was so regarded in the British Parliament and in the Colonial legislatures before the American Revolution; and a like view has prevailed and been carried into effect in both houses of Congress and in most of the state legislatures.

This power was both asserted and exerted by the House of Representatives in 1792, when it appointed a select committee to inquire into the St. Clair expedition and authorized the committee to send for necessary persons, papers and records. Mr. Madison, who had taken an important part in framing the Constitution only five years before, and four of his associates in that work, were members of the House of Representatives at the time, and all voted for the inquiry. 3 Cong. Ann. 494. Other exertions of the power by the House of Representatives, as also by the Senate, are shown in the citations already made. Among those by the Senate, the inquiry ordered in 1859 respecting the raid by John Brown and his adherents on the armory and arsenal of the United States at Harper's Ferry is of special significance. The resolution directing the inquiry authorized the committee to send for persons and papers, to inquire into the facts pertaining to the raid and the means by which it was organized and supported, and to report what legislation, if any, was necessary to preserve the peace of the country and protect the public property. The resolution was briefly discussed and adopted without opposition. Cong. Globe, 36th Cong., 1st Sess., pp. 141, 152. Later on the committee reported that Thaddeus Hyatt, although subpoenaed to appear as a witness, had refused to do so; whereupon the Senate ordered that he be attached and brought before it to answer for his refusal. When he was brought in he answered by challenging the power of the Senate to direct the inquiry and exact testimony to aid it in exercising its legislative function. The question of power thus presented was thoroughly discussed by several senators—Mr. Sumner of Massachusetts taking the lead in denying the power and Mr. Fessenden of Maine in supporting it. Sectional and party lines were put aside and the question was debated and determined with special regard to principle and precedent. The vote was taken on a resolution pronouncing the witness's answer insufficient and directing that he be committed until he should signify that he was ready and willing to testify. The resolution was adopted—44 senators voting for it and 10 against. The arguments advanced in support of the power are fairly reflected by the following excerpts from the debate:

Mr. Fessenden of Maine. "Where will you stop? Stop, I say, just at that point where we have gone far enough to accomplish the purposes for which we were created; and these purposes are defined in the Constitution. What are they? The great purpose is legislation. There are some other things, but I speak of legislation as the principal purpose. Now, what do we propose to do here? We propose to legislate upon a given state of facts, perhaps, or under a given necessity. Well, sir, proposing to legislate, we want information. We have it not ourselves. It is not to be presumed that we know everything; and if any body does presume it, it is a very great mistake, as we know by experience. We want information on certain subjects. How are we to get it? The Senator says, ask for it. I am ready to ask for it; but suppose the person whom we ask will not give it to us: what then? Have we not power to compel him to come before us? Is this power, which has been exercised by Parliament, and by all legislative bodies down to the present day without dispute—the power to inquire into subjects upon which they are disposed to legislate—lost to us? Are we not in the possession of it? Are we deprived of it simply because we hold our power here under a Constitution which defines what our duties are, and what we are called upon to do?

Congress have appointed committees after committees, time

after time, to make inquiries on subjects of legislation. Had we not power to do it? Nobody questioned our authority to do it. We have given them authority to send for persons and papers during the recess. Nobody questioned our authority. We appoint committees during the session, with power to send for persons and papers. Have we not that authority, if necessary to legislation? . . .

Sir, with regard to myself, all I have to inquire into is: is this a legitimate and proper object, committed to me under the Constitution; and then, as to the mode of accomplishing it, I am ready to use judiciously, calmly, moderately, all the power which I believe is necessary and inherent, in order to do that which I am appointed to do; and, I take it, I violate no rights, either of the people generally or of the individual, by that course.

Mr. Crittenden of Kentucky. I come now to a question where the coöperation of the two branches is not necessary. There are some things that the Senate may do. How? According to a mode of its own. Are we to ask the other branch of the Legislature to concede by law to us the power of making such an inquiry as we are now making? Has not each branch the right to make what inquiries and investigation it thinks proper to make for its own action? Undoubtedly. You say we must have a law for it. Can we have a law? Is it not, from the very nature of the case, incidental to you as a Senate, if you, as a Senate, have the power of instituting an inquiry and of proceeding with that inquiry? I have endeavored to show that we have that power. We have a right, in consequence of it, a necessary incidental power, to summon witnesses, if witnesses are necessary. Do we require the concurrence of the other House to that? It is a power of our own. If you have a right to do the thing of your own motion, you must have all powers that are necessary to do it.

The means of carrying into effect by law all the granted powers, is given where legislation is applicable and necessary; but there are subordinate matters, not amounting to laws; there are inquiries of the one House or the other House, which each House has a right to conduct; which each has, from the beginning, exercised the power to conduct; and each has, from the beginning, summoned witnesses. This has been the practice of the Government from the beginning; and if we have a right to summon the witness, all the rest follows as a matter of course.

The deliberate solution of the question on that occasion has been accepted and followed on other occasions by both houses of Congress, and never has been rejected or questioned by either.

The state courts quite generally have held that the power to legislate carries with it by necessary implication ample authority to obtain information needed in the rightful exercise of that power, and to employ compulsory process for the purpose.

In *Burnham* v. *Morrisey,* 14 Gray 226, 239, the Supreme Judicial Court of Massachusetts, in sustaining an exertion of this power by one branch of the legislature of that Commonwealth, said:

The house of representatives has many duties to perform, which necessarily require it to receive evidence and examine witnesses. . . . It has often occasion to acquire certain knowledge of facts, in order to the proper performance of legislative duties. We therefore think it clear that it has the constitutional right to take evidence, to summon witnesses, and to compel them to appear and testify. This power to summon and examine witnesses it may exercise by means of committees.

In *Wilckens* v. *Willet,* 1 Keyes 521, 525, a case which presented the question whether the House of Representatives of the United States possesses this power, the Court of Appeals of New York said:

That the power exists there admits of no doubt whatever. It is a necessary incident to the sovereign power of making laws; and its exercise is often indispensable to the great end of enlightened, judicious and wholesome legislation.

In *People* v. *Keeler,* 99 N.Y. 463, 482, 483, where the validity of a statute of New York recognizing and giving effect to this power was drawn in question, the Court of Appeals approvingly quoted what it had said in *Wilckens* v. *Willet,* and added:

It is difficult to conceive any constitutional objection which can be raised to the provision authorizing legislative committees to take testimony and to summon witnesses. In many cases it may be indispensable to intelligent and effectual legislation to ascertain the facts which are claimed to give rise to the necessity for such legisla- tion, and the remedy required, and, irrespective of the question whether in the absence of a statute to that effect either house would have the power to imprison a recusant witness, I cannot yield to the claim that a statute authorizing it to enforce its process in that manner is in excess of the legislative power. To await the slow process of indictment and prosecution for a misdemeanor, might prove quite ineffectual, and necessary legislation might be ob- structed, and perhaps defeated, if the legislative body had no other and more summary means of enforcing its right to obtain the required information. That the power may be abused, is no ground for denying its existence. It is a limited power, and should be kept within its proper bounds; and, when these are exceeded, a jurisdic- tional question is presented which is cognizable in the courts. . . . Throughout this Union the practice of legislative bodies, and in this State, the statutes existing at the time the present Constitution was adopted, and whose validity has never before been questioned by our courts, afford strong arguments in favor of the recognition of the right of either house to compel the attendance of witnesses for legislative purposes, as one which has been generally conceded to be an appropriate adjunct to the power of legislation, and one which, to say the least, the State legislature has constitutional authority to regulate and enforce by statute.

Other decisions by state courts recognizing and sustaining the legislative practice are found in *Falvey* v. *Massing,* 7 Wis. 630, 635–638; *State* v. *Frear,* 138

Wis. 173; *Ex parte Parker,* 74 S. C. 466, 470; *Sullivan* v. *Hill,* 73 W. Va. 49, 53; *Lowe* v. *Summers,* 69 Mo. App. 637, 649–650. An instructive decision on the question is also found in *Ex parte Dansereau* (1875), 19 L. C. Jur. 210, where the legislative assembly of the Province of Quebec was held to possess this power as a necessary incident of its power to legislate.

We have referred to the practice of the two houses of Congress; and we now shall notice some significant congressional enactments. May 3, 1798, c. 36, 1 Stat. 554, Congress provided that oaths or affirmations might be adminis- tered to witnesses by the President of the Senate, the Speaker of the House of Representatives, the chairman of a committee of the whole, or the chairman of a select committee, "in any case under their examination." February 8, 1817, c. 10, 3 Stat. 345, it enlarged that provision so as to include the chairman of a standing committee. January 24, 1857, c. 19, 11 Stat. 155, it passed "An Act more effectually to enforce the attendance of witnesses on the summons of either house of Congress, and to compel them to discover testimony." This act provided, first, that any person summoned as a witness to give testimony or produce papers in any matter under inquiry before either house of Congress, or any committee of either house, who should wilfully make default, or, if appearing, should refuse to answer any question pertinent to the inquiry, should, in addition to the pains and penalties then existing, be deemed guilty of a misdemeanor and be subject to indictment and punishment as there prescribed; and secondly, that no person should be excused from giving evidence in such an inquiry on the ground that it might tend to incriminate or disgrace him, nor be held to answer criminally, or be subjected to any penalty or forfeiture, for any fact or act as to which he was required to testify, excepting that he might be subjected to prosecution for perjury committed while so testifying. January 24, 1862, c. 11, 12 Stat. 333, Congress modified the immun- ity provision in particulars not material here. These enactments are now embodied in §§ 101–104 and 859 of Revised Statutes. They show very plainly that Congress intended thereby (a) to recognize the power of either house to institute inquiries and exact evidence touching subjects within its jurisdiction and on which it was disposed to act; (b) to recognize that such inquiries may be conducted through committees; (c) to subject defaulting and contumacious witnesses to indictment and punishment in the courts, and thereby to enable either house to exert the power of inquiry "more effectually" ; and (d) to open the way for obtaining evidence in such an inquiry, which otherwise could not be obtained, by exempting witnesses required to give evidence therein from criminal and penal prosecutions in respect of matters disclosed by their evidence.

Four decisions of this Court are cited and more or less relied on, and we now turn to them.

The first decision was in *Anderson* v. *Dunn,* 6 Wheat. 204. The question there was whether, under the Constitution, the House of Representatives has power to attach and punish a person other than a member for contempt of its authority—in fact, an attempt to bribe one of its members. The Court regarded the power as essential to the effective exertion of other powers expressly granted, and therefore as implied. The argument advanced to the contrary was that as the Constitution expressly grants to each house power to punish or expel its own members and says nothing about punishing others, the implication or inference, if any, is that power to punish one who is not a member is neither given nor intended. The Court answered this by saying:

> (p. 225) There is not in the whole of that admirable instrument, a grant of powers which does not draw after it others, not expressed, but vital to their exercise; not substantive and independent, indeed, but auxiliary and subordinate.
>
> (p. 233) This argument proves too much; for its direct application would lead to annihilation of almost every power of Congress. To enforce its laws upon any subject without the sanction of punishment is obviously impossible. Yet there is an express grant of power to punish in one class of cases and one only, and all the punishing power exercised by Congress in any cases, except those which relate to piracy and offenses against the laws of nations, is derived from implication. Nor did the idea ever occur to any one, that the express grant in one class of cases repelled the assumption of the punishing power in any other. The truth is, that the exercise of the powers given over their own members, was of such a delicate nature, that a constitutional provision became necessary to assert or communicate it. Constituted, as that body is, of the delegates of confederated States, some such provision was necessary to guard against their mutual jealousy, since every proceeding against a representative would indirectly affect the honour or interests of the state which sent him.

The next decision was in *Kilbourn* v. *Thompson*, 103 U.S. 168. The question there was whether the House of Representatives had exceeded its power in directing one of its committees to make a particular investigation. The decision was that it had. The principles announced and applied in the case are—that neither house of Congress possesses a "general power of making inquiry into the private affairs of the citizen"; that the power actually possessed is limited to inquiries relating to matters of which the particular house "has jurisdiction" and in respect of which it rightfully may take other action; that if the inquiry relates to "a matter wherein relief or redress could be had only by a judicial proceeding" it is not within the range of this power, but must be left to the courts, conformably to the constitutional separation of governmental powers; and that for the purpose of determining the essential character of the inquiry recourse may be had to the resolution or order under which it is made. The court examined the resolution which was the basis of the particular inquiry, and ascertained therefrom that the inquiry related to a private real-estate pool or partnership in the District of Columbia. Jay Cooke & Co. had had an interest in the pool, but had become bankrupts, and their estate was in course of administration in a federal bankruptcy court in Pennsylvania. The United States was one of their creditors. The trustee in the bankruptcy proceeding had effected a settlement of the bankrupts' interest in the pool, and of course his action was subject to examination and approval or disapproval by the bankruptcy court. Some of the creditors, including the United States, were dissatisfied with the settlement. In these circumstances, disclosed in the preamble, the resolution directed the committee "to inquire into the matter and history of said real-estate pool and the character of said settlement, with the amount of property involved in which Jay Cooke & Co. were interested, and the amount paid or to be paid in said settlement, with power to send for persons and papers and report to the House." The Court pointed out that the resolution contained no suggestion of contemplated legislation; that the matter was one in respect to which no valid legislation could be had; that the bankrupts' estate and the trustee's settlement were still pending in the bankruptcy court; and that the United States and other creditors were free to press their claims in that proceeding. And on these grounds the Court held that in undertaking the investigation "the House of Representatives not only exceeded the limit of its own authority, but assumed power which could only be properly exercised by another branch of the government, because it was in its nature clearly judicial."

The case has been cited at times, and is cited to us now, as strongly intimating, if not holding, that neither house of Congress has power to make inquiries and exact evidence in aid of contemplated legislation. There are expressions in the opinion which, separately considered, might bear such an interpretation; but that this was not intended is shown by the immediately succeeding statement (p. 189) that "This latter proposition is one which we do not propose to decide in the present case because we are able to decide the case without passing upon the existence or non-existence of such a power in aid of the legislative function."

Next in order is *In re Chapman*, 166 U.S. 661. The inquiry there in question was conducted under a resolution of the Senate and related to charges, published in the press, that senators were yielding to corrupt influences in considering a tariff bill then before the Senate and were speculating in stocks the value of which would be affected by pending amendments to the bill. Chapman appeared before the committee in response to a subpoena, but refused to answer questions pertinent to the inquiry, and was indicted and convicted under the act of 1857 for his refusal. The Court sustained the constitutional validity of the act of 1857, and, after referring to the constitutional provision empowering either house to punish its members for disorderly behavior and by a vote of two-thirds to expel a member, held that the inquiry related to the integrity and fidelity of senators in the discharge of their duties, and therefore to a matter "within the range of the constitutional powers of the Senate" and in respect of which it could compel witnesses to appear and testify. In overruling an objection that the inquiry was without any defined or admissible purpose, in that the preamble and resolution made no reference to any contemplated expulsion, censure, or other action by the Senate, the Court held that they adequately disclosed a subject-matter of which the Senate had jurisdiction, that it was not essential that the Senate declare in advance what it meditated doing, and that the assumption could not be indulged that the Senate was making the inquiry without a legitimate object.

The case is relied on here as fully sustaining the power of either house to conduct investigations and exact testimony from witnesses for legislative purposes. In the course of the opinion (p. 671) it is said that disclosures by witnesses may be compelled constitutionally "to enable the respective bodies to discharge their legitimate functions, and that it was to effect this that the act of 1857 was passed"; and also "We grant that Congress could not divest itself, or either of its houses, of the essential and inherent power to punish for contempt, in cases to which the power of either house properly extended; but, because Congress, by the act of 1857, sought to aid each of the houses in the discharge of its constitutional functions, it does not follow that any delegation of the power in each to punish for contempt was involved." The terms "legitimate functions" and "constitutional functions" are broad and might well be regarded as including the legislative function, but as the case in hand did not call for any expression respecting that function, it hardly can be said that these terms were purposely used as including it.

The latest case is *Marshall* v. *Gordon*, 243 U.S. 521. The question there was whether the House of Representatives exceeded its power in punishing, as for a contempt of its authority, a person—not a member—who had written, published and sent to the chairman of one of its committees an ill-tempered and irritating letter respecting the action and purposes of the committee. Power to make inquiries and obtain evidence by compulsory process was not involved. The Court recognized distinctly that the House of Representatives has implied power to punish a person not a member for contempt, as was ruled in *Anderson* v. *Dunn, supra,* but held that its action in this instance was without constitutional justification. The decision was put on the ground that the letter, while offensive and vexatious, was not calculated or likely to affect the House in any of its proceedings or in the exercise of any of its functions— in short, that the act which was punished as a contempt was not of such a character as to bring it within the rule that an express power draws after it others which are necessary and appropriate to give effect to it.

While these cases are not decisive of the question we are considering, they definitely settle two propositions which we recognize as entirely sound and having a bearing on its solution: One, that the two houses of Congress, in their separate relations, possess not only such powers as are expressly granted to them by the Constitution, but such auxiliary powers as are necessary and appropriate to make the express powers effective; and, the other, that neither house is invested with "general" power to inquire into private affairs and compel disclosures, but only with such limited power of inquiry as is shown to exist when the rule of constitutional interpretation just stated is rightly applied. The latter proposition has further support in *Harriman* v. *Interstate Commerce Commission*, 211 U.S. 407, 417–419, and *Federal Trade Commission* v. *American Tobacco Company*, 264 U. S. 298, 305–306.

With this review of the legislative practice, congressional enactments and court decisions, we proceed to a statement of our conclusions on the question.

We are of opinion that the power of inquiry—with process to enforce it—is an essential and appropriate auxiliary to the legislative function. It was so regarded and employed in American legislatures before the Constitution was framed and ratified. Both houses of Congress took this view of it early in their history—the House of Representatives with the approving votes of Mr. Madison and other members whose service in the convention which framed the Constitution gives special significance to their action—and both houses have employed the power accordingly up to the present time. The acts of 1798 and 1857, judged by their comprehensive terms, were intended to recognize the existence of this power in both houses and to enable them to employ it "more effectually" than before. So, when their practice in the matter is appraised according to the circumstances in which it was begun and to those in which it has been continued, it falls nothing short of a practical construction, long continued, of the constitutional provisions respecting their powers, and therefore should be taken as fixing the meaning of those provisions, if otherwise doubtful.

We are further of opinion that the provisions are not of doubtful meaning, but, as was held by this Court in the cases we have reviewed, are intended to be effectively exercised, and therefore to carry with them such auxiliary powers as are necessary and appropriate to that end. While the power to exact information in aid of the legislative function was not involved in those cases, the rule of interpretation applied there is applicable here. A legislative body cannot legislatve wisely or effectively in the absence of information respecting the conditions which the legislation is intended to affect or change; and where the legislative body does not itself possess the requisite information—which not infrequently is true—recourse must be had to others who do possess it. Experience has taught that mere requests for such information often are unavailing, and also that information which is volunteered is not always accurate or complete; so some means of compulsion are essential to obtain what is needed. All this was true before and when the Constitution was framed and adopted. In that period the power of inquiry—with enforcing process—was regarded and employed as a necessary and appropriate attribute of the power to legislate—indeed, was treated as inhering in it. Thus there is ample warrant for thinking, as we do, that the constitutional provisions which commit the legislative function to the two houses are intended to include this attribute to the end that the function may be effectively exercised.

The contention is earnestly made on behalf of the witness that this power of inquiry, if sustained, may be abusively and oppressively exerted. If this be so, it affords no ground for denying the power. The same contention might be directed against the power to legislate, and of course would be unavailing. We must assume, for present purposes, that neither house will be disposed to exert the power beyond its proper bounds, or without due regard to the rights of witnesses. But if, contrary to this assumption, controlling limitations or restrictions are disregarded, the decisions in Kilbourn v. Thompson and Marshall v. Gordon point to admissible measures of relief. And it is a necessary deduction from the decisions in Kilbourn v. Thompson and In re Chapman that a witness rightfully may refuse to answer where the bounds of the power are exceeded or the questions are not pertinent to the matter under inquiry.

We come now to the question whether it sufficiently appears that the purpose for which the witness's testimony was sought was to obtain information in aid of the legislative function. The court below answered the question in the negative and put its decision largely on this ground, as is shown by the following excerpts from its opinion (299 Fed. 638, 639, 640):

> It will be noted that in the second resolution the Senate has expressly avowed that the investigation is in aid of other action than legislation. Its purpose is to 'obtain information necessary as a basis for such legislative and other action as the Senate may deem necessary and proper.' This indicates that the Senate is contemplat-

ing the taking of action other than legislative, as the outcome of the investigation, at least the possibility of so doing. The extreme personal cast of the original resolutions; the spirit of hostility towards the then Attorney General which they breathe; that it was not avowed that legislative action was had in view until after the action of the Senate had been challenged; and that the avowal then was coupled with an avowal that other action was had in view—are calculated to create the impression that the idea of legislative action being in contemplation was an afterthought.

That the Senate has in contemplation the possibility of taking action other than legislation as an outcome of the investigation, as thus expressly avowed, would seem of itself to invalidate the entire proceeding. But, whether so or not, the Senate's action is invalid and absolutely void, in that, in ordering and conducting the investigation, it is exercising the judicial function, and power to exercise that function, in such a case as we have here, has not been conferred upon it expressly or by fair implication. What it is proposing to do is to determine the guilt of the Attorney General of the shortcomings and wrongdoings set forth in the resolutions. It is 'to hear, adjudge, and condemn.' In so doing it is exercising the judicial function.

What the Senate is engaged in doing is not investigating the Attorney General's office; it is investigating the former Attorney General. What it has done is to put him on trial before it. In so doing it is exercising the judicial function. This it has no power to do.

We are of opinion that the court's ruling on this question was wrong, and that it sufficiently appears, when the proceedings are rightly interpreted, that the object of the investigation and of the effort to secure the witness's testimony was to obtain information for legislative purposes.

It is quite true that the resolution directing the investigation does not in terms avow that it is intended to be in aid of legislation; but it does show that the subject to be investigated was the administration of the Department of Justice—whether its functions were being properly discharged or were being neglected or misdirected, and particularly whether the Attorney General and his assistants were performing or neglecting their duties in respect of the institution and prosecution of proceedings to punish crimes and enforce appropriate remedies against the wrongdoers—specific instances of alleged neglect being recited. Plainly the subject was one on which legislation could be had and would be materially aided by the information which the investigation was calculated to elicit. This becomes manifest when it is reflected that the functions of the Department of Justice, the powers and duties of the Attorney General and the duties of his assistants, are all subject to regulation by congressional legislation, and that the department is maintained and its activities are carried on under such appropriations as in the judgment of Congress are needed from year to year.

The only legitimate object the Senate could have in ordering the investigation was to aid it in legislating; and we think the subject-matter was such that the presumption should be indulged that this was the real object. An express avowal of the object would have been better; but in view of the particular subject-matter was not indispensable. In the *Chapman* case, where the resolution contained no avowal, this Court pointed out that it plainly related to a subject-matter of which the Senate had jurisdiction, and said "We cannot assume on this record that the action of the Senate was without a legitimate object"; and also that "it was certainly not necessary that the resolutions should declare in advance what the Senate meditated doing when the investigation was concluded." (166 U.S. 669–670.) In *People v. Keeler,* 99 N.Y. 463, where the Court of Appeals of New York sustained an investigation ordered by the Senate of that state where the resolution contained no avowal, but disclosed that it definitely related to the administration of a public office the duties of which were subject to legislative regulation, the court said (pp. 485, 487): "Where public institutions under the control of the State are ordered to be investigated it is generally with the view of some legislative action respecting them, and the same may be said in respect of public officers." And again: "We are bound to presume that the action of the legislative body was with a legitimate object if it is capable of being so construed, and we have no right to assume that the contrary was intended."

While we rest our conclusion respecting the object of the investigation on the grounds just stated, it is well to observe that this view of what was intended is not new, but was shown in the debate on the resolution.

Of course, our concern is with the substance of the resolution and not with any nice questions of propriety respecting its direct reference to the then Attorney General by name. The resolution, like the charges which prompted its adoption, related to the activities of the department while he was its supervising officer; and the reference to him by name served to designate the period to which the investigation was directed.

We think the resolution and proceedings give no warrant for thinking the Senate was attempting or intending to try the Attorney General at its bar or before its committee for any crime or wrongdoing. Nor do we think it is a valid objection to the investigation that it might possibly disclose crime or wrongdoing on his part.

The second resolution—the one directing that the witness be attached —declares that his testimony is sought with the purpose of obtaining "information necessary as a basis for such legislative and other action as the Senate may deem necessary and proper." This avowal of contemplated legislation is in accord with what we think is the right interpretation of the earlier resolution directing the investigation. The suggested possibility of "other action" if deemed "necessary or proper" is of course open to criticism in that there is no other action in the matter which would be within the power of the Senate. But we do not assent to the view that this indefinite and untenable suggestion invalidates the entire proceeding. The right view in our opinion is that it takes nothing from the lawful object avowed in the same resolution and rightly inferable from the earlier one. It is not as if an inadmissible or unlawful object were affirmatively and definitely avowed.

We conclude that the investigation was ordered for a legitimate object; that the witness wrongfully refused to appear and testify before the committee and was lawfully attached; that the Senate is entitled to have him give testimony pertinent to the inquiry, either at its bar or before the committee; and that the district court erred in discharging him from custody under the attachment.

Another question has arisen which should be noticed. It is whether the case has become moot. The investigation was ordered and the committee appointed during the Sixty-eighth Congress. That Congress expired March 4, 1925. The resolution ordering the investigation in terms limited the committee's authority to the period of the Sixty-eighth Congress; but this apparently was changed by a later and amendatory resolution authorizing the committee to sit at such times and places as it might deem advisable or necessary. It is said in Jefferson's Manual: "Neither House can continue any portion of itself in any parliamentary function beyond the end of the session without the consent of the other two branches. When done, it is by a bill constituting them commissioners for the particular purpose." But the context shows that the reference is to the two houses of Parliament when adjourned by prorogation or dissolution by the King. The rule may be the same with the House of Representatives whose members are all elected for the period of a single Congress; but it cannot well be the same with the Senate, which is a continuing body whose members are elected for a term of six years and so divided into classes that the seats of one-third only become vacant at the end of each Congress, two-thirds always continuing into the next Congress, save as vacancies may occur through death or resignation.

Mr. Hinds in his collection of precedents says: "The Senate, as a continuing body, may continue its committees through the recess following the expiration of a Congress"; and, after quoting the above statement from Jefferson's Manual, he says: "The Senate, however, being a continuing body, gives authority to its committees during the recess after the expiration of a Congress." So far as we are advised the select committee having this investigation in charge has neither made a final report nor been discharged; nor has it been continued by an affirmative order. Apparently its activities have been suspended pending the decision of this case. But, be this as it may, it is certain that the committee may be continued or revived now by motion to that effect, and, if continued or revived, will have all its original powers.

OPINION IN *SINCLAIR* V. *UNITED STATES*
APRIL 8, 1929

Sinclair v. *United States* 279 U.S. 263 (1929).

Mr. Justice Butler delivered the opinion of the Court.

Appellant was found guilty of violating R. S., § 102; U.S.C., Tit. 2, § 192. He was sentenced to jail for three months and to pay a fine of $500. The case was taken to the Court of Appeals of the District of Columbia; that court certified to this court certain questions of law upon which it desired instruction for the proper decision of the case. We directed the entire record to be sent up. Judicial Code, § 239, U.S.C., Tit. 28, § 346.

Section 102 follows: "Every person who having been summoned as a witness by the authority of either House of Congress, to give testimony or to produce papers upon any matter under inquiry before either House, or any committee of either House of Congress, willfully makes default, or who, having appeared, refuses to answer any question pertinent to the question under inquiry, shall be deemed guilty of a misdemeanor, punishable by a fine of not more than $1,000 nor less than $100, and imprisonment in a common jail for not less than one month nor more than twelve months."

By way of inducement the indictment set forth the circumstances leading up to the offense, which in brief substance are as follows:

For many years, there had been progressive diminution of petroleum necessary for the operation of naval vessels; consequently the Government was interested to conserve the supply and especially that in the public domain.

Pursuant to the Act of June 25, 1910, 36 Stat. 847, the President, by executive orders dated September 2, 1912, December 13, 1912, and April 30, 1915, ordered that certain oil and gas bearing lands in California and Wyoming be held for the exclusive use of the navy. These areas were designated Naval Petroleum Reserves 1, 2 and 3, respectively.

The Act of February 25, 1920, 41 Stat. 437, provided for the leasing of public lands containing oil and other minerals. And the Act of June 4, 1920, 41 Stat. 812, directed the Secretary of the Navy to take possession of all properties in the naval reserves "on which there are no pending claims or applications for permits or leases under the" Leasing Act of February 25, 1920, "or pending applications for United States patent under any law," to conserve, develop, use and operate the same by contract, lease or otherwise, and to use, store, exchange or sell the oil and gas products thereof for the benefit of the United States. And it was declared that the rights of any claimants under the Leasing Act were not thereby adversely affected.

May 31, 1921, the President promulgated an executive order purporting to give the administration and conservation of all oil and gas bearing lands in the naval reserves to the Secretary of the Interior subject to supervision by the President.

April 7, 1922, the Secretary of the Navy and the Secretary of the Interior made a lease of lands in Reserve No. 3 to the Mammoth Oil Company. This was done by the procurement of the appellant acting as the president of the company. The lease purported to grant to the company the right to take oil and gas and contained a provision selling royalty oils to the company. And February 9, 1923, a supplemental contract was made by which the company agreed to furnish storage facilities for the Navy. [*Mammoth Oil Company* v. *United States*, 275 U.S. 313.]

April 25, 1922, the same Secretaries made a contract with the Pan American Petroleum and Transport Company for the sale to it of royalty oils from Reserves 1 and 2. December 11, 1922, another contract was made by them. The purpose of these agreements was to arrange that the company furnish storage facilities for the Navy in exchange for royalty oils to be received by the United States under leases then in force and thereafter to be made. December 11, 1922, the same Secretaries made a lease to the Pan American Petroleum Company purporting to grant to it the right to take oil and gas from Reserve No. 1. [*Pan American Co.* v. *United States*, 273 U.S. 456.]

The lease to the Mammoth Company and the contract with the Transport Company came to the attention of the Senate, and it was charged that there had been fraud and bad faith in the making of them. Questions arose as to their legality, the future policy of the Government as to them and similar leases and contracts, and as to the necessity and desirability of legislation upon the subject.

April 29, 1922, the Senate adopted Resolution 282, calling upon the Secretary of the Interior for information and containing the following: "That the Committee on Public Lands and Surveys be authorized to investigate this entire subject of leases upon naval oil reserves with particular reference to the protection of the rights and equities of the Government of the United States and the preservation of its natural resources, and to report its fundings and recommendations to the Senate."

June 5, 1922, Resolution 282 was amended by Resolution 294 by adding a provision that the committee "is hereby authorized . . . to require the attendance of witnesses by subpoenas or otherwise; to require the production of books, papers and documents . . . The chairman of the committee, or any member thereof, may administer oaths to witnesses and sign subpoenas for witnesses."

February 5, 1923, the Senate passed Resolution 434, which continued in force and effect until the end of the Sixty-eighth Congress and until otherwise ordered, "Senate Resolution 282 agreed to April 21 [29], 1922, and Senate Resolution 292, agreed to May 15, 1922." [The Government suggests that, instead of the resolution last mentioned there was meant Resolution 294 adopted June 5, 1922.]

February 7, 1924, the Senate passed Resolution 147, directing in substance the same as it had theretofore done by the two resolutions first above mentioned and also that the committee "ascertain what, if any, other or additional legislation may be advisable, and to report its findings and recommendations to the Senate."

The committee proceeded to exercise the authority conferred upon it and for that purpose held hearings at which witnesses were examined and documents produced. Appellant was summoned, appeared and was sworn December 4, 1923.

And the indictment charges that, on March 22, 1924, the matters referred to in these resolutions being under inquiry, and appellant having been summoned to give testimony and having been sworn as aforesaid did appear before the committee as a witness. The first count alleges that Senator Walsh, a member of the committee, propounded to him a question which appellant knew was pertinent to the matters under inquiry: "Mr. Sinclair, I desire to interrogate you about a matter concerning which the committee had no knowledge or reliable information at any time when you had theretofore appeared before the committee and with respect to which you must then have had knowledge. I refer to the testimony given by Mr. Bonfils concerning a contract that you made with him touching the Teapot Dome. I wish you would tell us about that."

And, to explain that question, the indictment states: "said Hon. Thomas J. Walsh thereby meaning and intending, as said Harry F. Sinclair then and there well knew and understood, to elicit from him the said Harry F. Sinclair, facts, which then were within his knowledge, touching the execution and delivery of a certain contract bearing date September 25, 1922, made and executed by and between said Mammoth Oil Company, one F. G. Bonfils and one John Leo Stack, which was executed on behalf of said Mammoth Oil Company by said Harry F. Sinclair as President of said Mammoth Oil Company, and which, among other things, provided for the payment, by said Mammoth Oil Company, unto said F. G. Bonfils and said John Leo Stack, of the sum of $250,000.00, on or before October 15, 1922, in consideration of the release by said F. G. Bonfils and said John Leo Stack, of rights to lands described in said Executive Order of April 30, 1915, and embraced in the aforesaid lease of April 7, 1922." And that count concluded: "and that said Harry F. Sinclair then and there unlawfully did refuse to answer said question . . ."

Senate Joint Resolution 54 was approved February 8, 1924. 43 Stat. 5. It recited that the leases and contracts above mentioned were executed under circumstances indicating fraud and corruption, that they were without authority, contrary to law, and in defiance of the settled policy of the Government; and the resolution declared that the lands embraced therein should be recovered and held for the purposes to which they were dedicated. It directed the President to cause suit to be instituted for the cancellation of the leases and contracts, to prosecute such other actions or proceedings, civil and criminal, as were warranted by the facts, and authorized the appointment of special counsel to have charge of the matter.

Prior to March 22, 1924, appellant, at the request of the committee, appeared five times before it, and was sworn as alleged. March 19, 1924, a United States marshal at New York served upon him a telegram, which was in form a subpoena signed by the chairman of the committee, requiring him to appear as a witness; and he did appear on March 22. Before any questions were put, he submitted a statement.

He disclaimed any purpose to invoke protection against self-incrimination and asserted there was nothing in the transaction which could incriminate him. He emphasized his earlier appearances, testimony, production of papers and discharge from further attendance. He called attention to Joint Resolution 54, discussed its provisions, and stated that a suit charging conspiracy and fraud had been commenced against the Mammoth Company and others and that the Government's motion for injunction and receivers had been granted, and that application had been made for a special grand jury to investigate the making of the lease. He asserted that the committee could not then investigate the matters covered by the authorization because the Senate by the adoption of the joint resolution had exhausted its power and Congress and the President had made the whole matter a judicial question which was determinable only in the courts. The statement concluded: "I shall reserve any evidence I may be able to give for those courts to which you and your colleagues have deliberately referred all questions of which you had any jurisdiction and shall respectfully decline to answer any questions propounded by your committee."

After appellant's statement, his counsel asked the privilege of presenting to the committee reasons why it did not have authority further to take testimony of appellant. In the course of his remarks he said: "Mr. Sinclair is already under oath before the committee. . . . He is on the stand now in every sense of the word, and the objection really is to any further examination of him on the subjects involved in this resolution." Discussion followed, and a motion was made: "That in the examination the inquiry shall not relate to pending controversies before any of the Federal courts in which Mr. Sinclair is a defendant, and which questions would involve his defense." During a colloquy that followed, one of the members said: "Of course we will vote it [the motion] down. . . . If we do not examine Mr. Sinclair about those matters, there is not anything else to examine him about." The motion was voted down. Then the appellant was asked the question set forth in the first count, and he said: "I decline to answer on the advice of counsel on the same ground."

Appellant contends that his demurrer to the several counts of the indictment should have been sustained and that a verdict of not guilty should have been directed. To support that contention he argues that the questions related to his private affairs and to matters cognizable only in the courts wherein they were pending, and that the committee avowedly had departed from any inquiry in aid of legislation.

He maintains that there was no proof of any authorized inquiry by the committee or that he was legally summoned or sworn or that the questions propounded were pertinent to any inquiry it was authorized to make, and that because of such failure he was entitled to have a verdict directed in his favor.

He insists that the court erred in holding that the question of pertinency was one of law for the court and in not submitting it to the jury and also erred in excluding evidence offered to sustain his refusal to answer.

1. The Committee on Public Lands and Surveys is one of the standing committees of the Senate. No question is raised as to the validity of its organization and existence. Under § 101 of the Revised Statutes, U.S.C., Tit. 2, § 191, its chairman and any of its members are empowered to administer oaths to witnesses before it. Section 102 plainly extends to a case where a person voluntarily appears as a witness without being summoned as well as to the case of one required to attend.

By our opinion in *McGrain* v. *Daugherty*, 273 U. S. 135, 173, decided since the indictment now before us was found, two propositions are definitely laid down: "One, that the two houses of Congress, in their separate relations, possess not only such powers as are expressly granted to them by the Constitution, but such auxiliary powers as are necessary and appropriate to make the express powers effective; and, the other, that neither house is invested with 'general' power to inquire into private affairs and compel disclosures, but only with such limited power of inquiry as is shown to exist when the rule of constitutional interpretation just stated is rightly applied." And that case shows that, while the power of inquiry is an essential and appropriate auxiliary to the legislative function, it must be exerted with due regard for the rights of witnesses, and that a witness rightfully may refuse to answer where the bounds of the power are exceeded or where the questions asked are not pertinent to the matter under inquiry.

It has always been recognized in this country, and it is well to remember, that few if any of the rights of the people guarded by fundamental law are of greater importance to their happiness and safety than the right to be exempt from all unauthorized, arbitrary or unreasonable inquiries and disclosures in respect of their personal and private affairs. In order to illustrate the purpose of the courts well to uphold the right of privacy, we quote from some of their decisions.

In *Kilbourn* v. *Thompson,* 103 U.S. 168, this court, speaking through Mr. Justice Miller, said (p. 190): ". . . we are sure that no person can be punished for contumacy as a witness before either House, unless his testimony is required in a matter into which that House has jurisdiction to inquire, and we feel equally sure that neither of these bodies possesses the general power of making inquiry into the private affairs of the citizen." And referring to the failure of the authorizing resolution there under consideration to state the purpose of the inquiry (p. 195): "Was it to be simply a fruitless investigation into the personal affairs of individuals? If so, the House of Representatives had no power or authority in the matter more than any other equal number of gentlemen interested for the government of their country. By 'fruitless' we mean that it could result in no valid legislation on the subject to which the inquiry referred."

In *Re Pacific Railway Commission,* (Circuit Court, N. D., California) 32 Fed. 241, Mr. Justice Field, announcing the opinion of the court, said (p. 250): "Of all the rights of the citizen, few are of greater importance or more essential to his peace and happiness than the right of personal security, and that involves, not merely protection of his person from assault, but exemption of his private affairs, books, and papers from the inspection and scrutiny of others. Without the enjoyment of this right, all other rights would lose half their value." And the learned Justice, referring to *Kilbourn* v. *Thompson, supra,* said (p. 253): "This case will stand for all time as a bulwark against the invasion of the right of the citizen to protection in his private affairs against the unlimited scrutiny of investigation by a congressional committee." And see concurring opinions of Circuit Judge Sawyer, p. 259 at p. 263, and of District Judge Sabin, p. 268 at p. 269.

In *Interstate Commerce Commission* v. *Brimson,* 154 U.S. 447, Mr. Justice Harlan, speaking for the court said (p. 478): "We do not overlook these constitutional limitations which, for the protection of personal rights, must necessarily attend all investigations conducted under the authority of Congress. Neither branch of the legislative department, still less any merely administrative body, established by Congress, possesses, or can be invested with, a general power of making inquiry into the private affairs of the citizen. . . . We said in *Boyd* v. *United States,* 116 U.S. 616, 630,—and it cannot be too often repeated,—that the principles that embody the essence of constitutional liberty and security forbid all invasions on the part of the government and its employés of the sanctity of a man's home and the privacies of his life."

Harriman v. *Interstate Commerce Commission,* 211 U.S. 407, illustrates the unwillingness of this court to construe an Act of Congress to authorize any examination of witnesses in respect of their personal affairs. And see *United States* v. *Louisville & Nashville R.R.,* 236 U.S. 318, 335.

In *Federal Trade Commission* v. *American Tobacco Co.,* 264 U.S. 298, this court said (pp. 305–306): "Anyone who respects the spirit as well as the letter of the Fourth Amendment would be loath to believe that Congress intended to authorize one of its subordinate agencies to sweep all our traditions into the fire (*Interstate Commerce Commission* v. *Brimson*, 154 U.S. 447, 479), and to direct fishing expeditions into private papers on the possibility that they may disclose evidence of crime. We do not discuss the question whether it could do so if it tried, as nothing short of the most explicit language would induce us to attribute to Congress that intent. . . . It is contrary to the first principles of justice to allow a search through all the respondents' records, relevant or irrelevant, in the hope that something will turn up."

2. But it is clear that neither the investigation authorized by the Senate resolutions above mentioned nor the question under consideration related merely to appellant's private or personal affairs. Under the Constitution (Art. IV, § 3) Congress has plenary power to dispose of and to make all needful rules and regulations respecting the naval oil reserves, other public lands and property of the United States. And undoubtedly the Senate had power to delegate authority to its committee to investigate and report what had been and was being done by executive departments under the Leasing Act, the Naval Oil Reserve Act, and the President's order in respect of the reserves, and to make any other inquiry concerning the public domain.

While appellant caused the Mammoth Oil Company to be organized and owned all its shares, the transaction purporting to lease to it the lands within the reserve can not be said to be merely or principally the personal or private affair of appellant. It was a matter of concern to the United States. The title to valuable government lands was involved. The validity of the lease and the means by which it had been obtained under existing law were subjects that properly might be investigated in order to determine what if any legislation was necessary or desirable in order to recover the leased lands or to safeguard other parts of the public domain.

Neither Senate Joint Resolution 54 nor the action taken under it operated to divest the Senate, or the committee, of power further to investigate the actual administration of the land laws. It may be conceded that Congress is without authority to compel disclosures for the purpose of aiding the prosecution of pending suits; but the authority of that body, directly or through its committees, to require pertinent disclosures in aid of its own constitutional power is not abridged because the information sought to be elicited may also be of use in such suits.

The record does not sustain appellant's contention that the investigation was avowedly not in aid of legislation. He relies on the refusal of the committee to pass the motion directing that the inquiry should not relate to controversies pending in court, and the statement of one of the members that there was nothing else to examine appellant about. But these are not enough to show that the committee intended to depart from the purpose to ascertain whether additional legislation might be advisable. It is plain that investigation of the matters involved in suits brought or to be commenced under Senate Joint Resolution 54 might directly aid in respect of legislative action.

3. There is no merit in appellant's contention that a verdict should have been directed for him because the evidence failed to show that the committee was authorized to make the inquiry, summon witnesses and administer oaths. Resolutions 282 and 294 were sufficient until the expiration of the Sixty-seventh Congress during which they were adopted, but it is argued that

Resolution 434 was not effective to extend the power of the committee. As set out in the indictment and shown by the record, Resolution 434 does not mention 294 or refer to the date of its adoption. The former so far as material follows: "Resolved, That Senate Resolution 282, agreed to April 21, 1922, and Senate Resolution 292, agreed to May 15, 1922, authorizing and directing the Committee on Public Lands and Surveys to investigate the entire subject of leases upon naval oil reserves, with particular reference to the protection of the rights and equities of the Government of the United States and the preservation of its natural resources, and to report its findings and recommendations to the Senate . . . be . . . continued in full force and effect until the end of the Sixty-eighth Congress. The committee . . . is authorized to sit . . . after the expiration of the present Congress until the assembling of the Sixty-eighth Congress and until otherwise ordered by the Senate.

There is enough in that resolution to show that where "292" appears 294 was meant. The subject of the investigation is specifically mentioned. That is the only matter dealt with. The sole purpose was to authorize the committee to carry on the inquiry. It would be quite unreasonable, if not indeed absurd, for the Senate to direct investigation by the committee and to allow its power to summon and swear witnesses to lapse. The context and circumstances show that Resolution 294 was intended to be kept in force. See *School District No. 11* v. *Chapman*, 152 Fed. 887, 893–894.

4. Appellant earnestly maintains that the question was not shown to be pertinent to any inquiry the committee was authorized to make. The United States suggests that the presumption of regularity is sufficient without proof. But, without determining whether that presumption is applicable to such a matter, it is enough to say that the stronger presumption of innocence attended the accused at the trial. It was therefore incumbent upon the United States to plead and show that the question pertained to some matter under investigation. Appellant makes no claim that the evidence was not sufficient to establish the innuendo alleged in respect of the question; the record discloses that the proof on that point was ample.

Congress, in addition to its general legislative power over the public domain, had all the powers of a proprietor and was authorized to deal with it as a private individual may deal with lands owned by him. *United States* v. *Midwest Oil Co.*, 236 U.S. 459, 474. The committee's authority to investigate extended to matters affecting the interest of the United States as owner as well as to those having relation to the legislative function.

Before the hearing at which appellant refused to answer, the committee had discovered and reported facts tending to warrant the passage of Senate Joint Resolution 54 and the institution of suits for the cancellation of the naval oil reserve leases. Undoubtedly it had authority further to investigate concerning the validity of such leases, and to discover whether persons, other than those who had been made defendants in the suit against the Mammoth Oil Company, had or might assert a right or claim in respect of the lands covered by the lease to that company.

The contract and release made and given by Bonfils and Stack related directly to the title to the lands covered by the lease which had been reported by the committee as unauthorized and fraudulent. The United States proposed to recover and hold such lands as a source of supply of oil for the Navy. S.

J. Res. 54. It is clear that the question so propounded to appellant was pertinent to the committee's investigation touching the rights and equities of the
United States as owner.

Moreover, it was pertinent for the Senate to ascertain the practical effect of
recent changes that had been made in the laws relating to oil and other mineral
lands in the public domain. The leases and contracts charged to have been
unauthorized and fraudulent were made soon after the executive order of May
31, 1921. The title to the lands in the reserves could not be cleared without
ascertaining whether there were outstanding any claims or applications for
permits, leases or patents under the Leasing Act or other laws. It was necessary
for the Government to take into account the rights, if any there were, of such
claimants. The reference in the testimony of Bonfils to the contract referred to
in the question propounded was sufficient to put the committee on inquiry
concerning outstanding claims possibly adverse and superior to the Mammoth Oil Company's lease. The question propounded was within the authorization of the committee and the legitimate scope of investigation to enable the
Senate to determine whether the powers granted to or assumed by the Secretary of the Interior and the Secretary of the Navy should be withdrawn, limited, or allowed to remain unchanged.

5. The question of pertinency under § 102 was rightly decided by the
court as one of law. It did not depend upon the probative value of evidence.
That question may be likened to those concerning relevancy at the trial of
issues in court, and it is not essentially different from the question as to
materiality of false testimony charged as perjury in prosecutions for that
crime. Upon reasons so well known that their repetition is unnecessary it is
uniformly held that relevancy is a question of law. Greenleaf on Evidence (13th
ed.) § 49. Wigmore on Evidence, §§ 2549, 2550. And the materiality of what is
falsely sworn, when an element in the crime of perjury, is one for the court.
Carroll v. *United States*, 16 F. (2d) 948, 950. *United States* v. *Singleton*, 54 Fed.
488. *Cothran* v. *State*, 39 Miss. 541, 547.

The reasons for holding relevancy and materiality to be questions of law
in cases such as those above referred to apply with equal force to the determination of pertinency arising under § 102. The matter for determination in this
case was whether the facts called for by the question were so related to the
subjects covered by the Senate's resolutions that such facts reasonably could
be said to be "pertinent to the question under inquiry." It would be incon-
gruous and contrary to well-established principles to leave the determination of such a matter to a jury. *Interstate Commerce Commission* v. *Brimson*,
supra, 489. *Horning* v. *District of Columbia*, 254, U.S. 135.

6. There is no merit in appellant's contention that he is entitled to a new
trial because the court excluded evidence that in refusing to answer he acted in
good faith on the advice of competent counsel. The gist of the offense is refusal
to answer pertinent questions. No moral turpitude is involved. Intentional
violation is sufficient to constitute guilt. There was no misapprehension as to
what was called for. The refusal to answer was deliberate. The facts sought
were pertinent as a matter of law, and § 102 made it appellant's duty to answer.
He was bound rightly to construe the statute. His mistaken view of the law is
no defense. *Armour Packing Co.* v. *United States*, 209 U.S. 56, 85. *Standard
Sanitary Mfg. Co.* v. *United States*, 226 U.S. 20, 49.

7. The conviction on the first count must be affirmed. There were ten counts, demurrer was sustained as to four, *nolle prosequi* was entered in respect of two, and conviction was had on the first, fourth, fifth and ninth counts. As the sentence does not exceed the maximum authorized as punishment for the offense charged in the first count, we need not consider any other count. *Abrams* v. *United States,* 250 U.S. 616, 619.

Judgment affirmed.

BIBLIOGRAPHY

Congressional Record. 67th Cong., 2nd sess., 68th Cong., 1st sess.

Frankfurter, Felix. "Hands Off the Investigations." *The New Republic,* (May 21, 1924).

Hard, William. "The Tale of the Teapot." The Nation, November 21, 1923.

McGrain v. *Daugherty* 273 U.S. 135 (1927).

Noggle, Burl. *Teapot Dome: Oil and Politics in the 1920's.* (Baton Rouge, 1962).

Sinclair v. *United States* 279 U.S. 263 (1929).

U.S. Congress. Senate hearings. 68th Cong., 1st sess.

Walsh, Thomas. "What the Oil Inquiry Developed." *The Outlook,* (May 21, 1924).

Werner, Morris R. and Starr, John. *Teapot Dome.* (New York, 1959).

The Pecora Wall Street Exposé
1934

The Pecora Wall Street Exposé 1934

by Donald A. Ritchie

Suspicious, fearful, and frustrated, the Depression Congress of 1932 filled its hampers with a record number of resolutions for investigation. Most sought some explanation for the stock market crash, business liquidations, and bank failures. Unemployment paralyzed the nation, demanding exposure of the conditions and persons responsible. Few of these investigations ever materialized—only the Senate Banking and Currency Committee's examination of Wall Street captured the public's attention. After the committee had stumbled aimlessly through a maze of incomprehensible financial data under a series of inept counsels, the investigation at last succeeded when it gained the leadership of Ferdinand Pecora and his staff. So thoroughly did Counsel Pecora dominate the proceedings that *his* name, rather than the committee chairman's, became irrevocably identified with the hearings. The Pecora probe, with its careful documentation of banker and broker misdeeds, and its contributions to corrective legislation, set a worthy model for future congressional investigations.

In the twenty years since the Pujo Committee hearings on the "Money Trust," the American economic structure had grown disastrously worse. Of fifty billion dollars' worth of stocks sold in the United States during the 1920s the House Commerce Committee estimated, half had been "undesirable or worthless." Securities houses of the most reputable banks manifoldly increased their profits at the expense of their own clients. Powerful investment bankers continued to fill key corporations' boards of directors. Overly-optimistic loan programs threatened vast banking chains with domino-like collapse. Utility holding companies teetered precariously upon an intricate system of interlocking directorates with little regard for corporate efficiency or local requirements. Concurrently, the federal government remained willfully ignorant of stock exchange and private banking operations. "The business of America is business," Calvin Coolidge had noted with satisfaction during the 1920s; by 1932 that business verged on bankruptcy.

To a generation of liberals, the market crash and the subsequent Depression verified the prophesies of Louis Brandeis's economic tract, *Other People's Money*. Drawing from the Pujo Committee findings, first in a series of articles for *Harper's Weekly* and then in his book, Brandeis had warned that an amalgamation of investment bankers and insurance companies was using its control of "other people's money" to infiltrate American industry. These "banker-barons" were more concerned about the market value of a corporation's securities than for the value of its product. Worried that their combination of wealth and power had slowly stifled the competitive free market system, Brandeis sounded the alarm: "We must break the Money Trust or the Money Trust will break us." The government, he declared, must demand full publicity on all stock dealings, including bankers' commissions and the extent of the bankers' control over the issuing corporation. "Sunlight is said to be the best of disinfectants; electric light the most effective policeman," he concluded, so full financial disclosure would purify imperfections within the economic system.

Armed with the first new reprinting of the book in twenty years, old and young liberals alike carried its message to Washington with the new Roosevelt Administration. In congressional committee rooms the book became a familiar sight—many witnesses introduced it as proof of their arguments. Legislative drafts emerged verbatim from its pages. The book also provided a historical link between the two great financial investigations, for Brandeis and his followers viewed Pecora's work as the fulfillment of the Pujo investigation.

Economic conditions, political support, and public interest all gave Pecora advantages denied to his predecessor, Samuel Untermyer, counsel for Pujo. Where the Pujo hearings had commenced in a relatively prosperous period, Pecora began his hearings at the nadir of the Depression. Where President William Howard Taft had withheld cooperation from Untermyer, President Franklin D. Roosevelt personally encouraged Pecora, endorsed the hearings, and incorporated their recommendations into his legislative program. The press, hostile to the earlier inquiry, lavished extensive coverage on Pecora, filling columns with his photographs and accounts of his activities. Pecora also benefited from Untermyer's mistakes. Recalling his unsuccessful attempts to gain sufficient evidence, Pecora acquired far stronger subpoena powers than his predecessor. He marched his staff directly into the banks and brokerage houses rather than depend upon his witnesses to produce material voluntarily.

For more than a year Pecora called many of the nation's most prestigious financiers before the public. Repeatedly, he elicited from them such startling admissions of wrongdoing that he stole headlines from even the masterful Franklin Roosevelt. Nevertheless, Roosevelt cheerfully supported the hearings, for their publicity helped counteract business opposition to his financial reforms and aided passage of such controversial measures as the Securities Act of 1933, the Securities and Exchange Act of 1934, and the Public Utilities Holding Company Act of 1935. Constant revelations from the witness stand and revulsion against them distracted the attention of liberal elements within Roosevelt's loose political coalition. At the same time FDR more actively courted the business community through the National Recovery Administration.

In a small part, the Pecora investigations contributed to a reforming rather than a revolutionary spirit in the New Deal's program. At a time of considerable questioning of the capitalist system, the hearings personalized the causes of the Depression. By producing a string of villains, they translated complicated economic problems into moral terms. Bankers, Pecora demonstrated, had abandoned their fiduciary responsibilities. He expended his greatest wrath on the "incompetence, negligence, irresponsibility, or cupidity in the profession." The banking and securities systems, it followed, needed only a change in personnel and stricter governmental supervision so that such abuses might not reoccur. Government regulation of private finance, rather than nationalization or centralization, was the investigation's message and its legislative legacy.

The Banking Committee hearings could claim both the Hoover and Roosevelt Administrations as patrons, and as a result enjoyed unusual bipartisan support. Herbert Hoover, despite his philosophical aversion to government interference with the stock exchanges and other market machinery, took credit for initiating the investigation. These claims, however, deserved some qualification. Early in his presidential term, Hoover had summoned various stock exchange officials for talks on the economy. Worried over the dangers of unrestrained speculation and unrealistically high market prices, but also convinced he had no constitutional right or power to intervene, Hoover urged the exchange leaders to assume more self-discipline over the stock markets. For his efforts he received "profuse promises" but no action. Within months the market crashed, but Hoover clung to his narrow interpretation of government responsibility. To quiet congressional murmurs, the White House issued assurances that "in the long run the system of free selling is better." When a flurry of resolutions from both Republicans and Democrats made some action imminent, the President stepped up his campaign for stock exchange self-reform.

Continually declining markets in 1930 and 1931 led Hoover to lay blame for the economic collapse on the "bear raiding" tactics of professional stock manipulators. These "bears" made commitments to sell stock which they did not own, on the assumption that the stock's price would soon drop. Borrowing equal amounts of stock from cooperative underwriters to cover their sales, they waited until the market sank far enough to buy shares at a lower price than that at which they had agreed to sell. The difference, less a percentage for the underwriters, was pure profit. Frequently short sales like these first involved boosting the stock's price through calculated purchases on different exchanges, and then a sudden burst of sales to bring the price down: the bear raid. When organized pools of speculators abruptly unloaded stock, they often created panic selling among smaller investors, further depressing the market to the bears' financial advantage. Such profiteering on the Depression appeared particularly reprehensible to the Congress. Yet despite their threats of investigation and urgent presidential pleas, the governing boards of the major exchanges refused to outlaw short selling.

Richard Whitney, speaking for the New York Stock Exchange, which handled more than half the nation's stock transactions, expressed the belief that short selling provided badly needed liquidity in times of crisis. Short sellers eventually had to buy stocks to settle their sales, the exchange argued, and thereby provided purchasers during periods of heavy selling. The exchange preferred to retain the practice under limited controls and threaten its temporary suspension as a weapon in cases of emergency. As a concession, the New York Stock Exchange agreed only to prohibit its member firms from lending stocks to short sellers without the original stockholder's written consent, a rule which they predicted would reduce short selling by fifty percent. Hoover, however, considered this action totally insufficient. On February 19, 1932, the day after the exchange announced its new rules, the President met with Republican Senators Frederic Walcott and Peter Norbeck of the Senate Banking and Currency Committee, endorsed an investigation of short selling, and encouraged them to proceed vigorously.

Hoover's fears extended to his political future. Facing a hard reelection campaign that year, he imagined that the bear raiding represented secret Democratic attempts to embarrass his Administration. He reserved his deepest suspicions for such prominent Democratic financiers as Bernard Baruch and John J. Raskob, then chairman of the Democratic National Committee, and he hoped the investigation would reveal their stock dealings. Ironically, while none of these men was engaged in bear raiding, some of the most active bears, like "Sell 'Em" Ben Smith, did time their larger sales to correspond with Hoover's optimistic speeches. They had learned that whenever the President predicted recovery, the market invariably declined.

Acting for Hoover, Senator Walcott had already introduced a resolution allotting $3,000 for an investigation into the specific practice of short selling. Walcott made it clear he wanted no federal legislation to reform the exchanges. Instead, he planned to force the exchanges, through adverse publicity, to adopt stronger rules on their own. This measure proved too tepid for the majority in Congress. Sentiments against the exchanges had grown too powerful, and on March 4 the Senate endorsed an investigation into all stock market practices. To support this investigation they appropriated $50,000, an unexpectedly large sum, considering that the hearings were scheduled to end with the adjournment of Congress in June.

Even after the resolution passed, the Banking Committee made little effort to implement it. The committee had already voted to make Senator Carter Glass's banking reform bill its pending business, and unforeseen altercations and lengthy deliberations on that bill delayed any investigation planning for another month. Its sponsors soon began to fear that the session would close without having opened hearings into stock exchange abuses.

Then, on Friday, April 8, 1932, Hoover received private warnings that bear raiders planned heavy stock sales for the next day, to sabotage his recovery program. Senator Walcott rushed to the Republican cloakroom to gather majority members of the Banking Committee. Since Chairman Norbeck was absent, campaigning for reelection in South Dakota, Senator Smith W. Brookhart, an insurgent Republican from Iowa, stood as the acting chairman. But Brookhart allowed the conservative Walcott to take command in spreading word of the "great bear raid." From the cloakroom Walcott telephoned New York Stock Exchange President Richard Whitney and demanded that he provide the committee with a list of all short sellers on the exchange. When Whitney refused to comply voluntarily, Walcott won committee approval to subpoena him. The committee ordered the exchange president to appear on Monday with lists of all stocks sold short in excess of ten thousand shares, and all those who traded in the stocks. Senator Brookhart, long a supporter of a Wall Street investigation, rejoiced in the move. "We are going to look into Mr. Whitney's machine," he promised. "We are going to get the real facts, and we think he knows them."

Chairman Peter Norbeck hurried back from South Dakota to be present when Richard Whitney appeared before the committee's Monday morning session. The hastily called hearings quickly developed into a complete debacle for the committee. Walcott had appointed Claude R. Branch, a soft-spoken and unimpressive lawyer from Rhode Island, as the tentative counsel, but Branch pursued an ill-prepared and fruitless examination of Whitney. The stock exchange president had appeared without the data which the committee had requested, explaining that 175 exchange employees were busily compiling the voluminous records. Deprived of any hard evidence, neither Branch nor the committee could follow any intensive line of inquiry. Innocently, Whitney pleaded no knowledge of any bear raid, nor any widespread short selling. He could not explain "rigging" stock to them, and begged ignorance of "floor pools." The hearings that promised sensational disclosures produced nothing at all, and no bear raid took place that Saturday. Public interest in the hearings faded, the *New York Times* noted editorially, "because of the somewhat foolish anticlimax that has been reached."

Much chagrined at Whitney's easy success, Chairman Norbeck dismissed Branch and hired Philadelphia attorney William A. Gray to continue the examination. Gray had the added advantage of the lengthy short selling reports which the New York Stock Exchange had finally submitted. Since this material consisted entirely of raw data, and Gray had the aid of only one secretary and one financial advisor, he decided not to examine the report. "The exchange furnished information from which you could not get anything unless you studied it for a week," he explained as he reconvened the hearings. Relying on his skillful courtroom tactics to draw out information, Gray immediately recalled Whitney to the stand and led him through a repetition of much of the same questioning that Branch had already conducted. Again, Whitney easily avoided or deflated the questions.

Eventually, Gray realized the futility of his approach and adjourned the hearings to collect and analyze his data. The Banking Committee subpoenaed the general records of ten brokerage firms, and after reading through the material, published the names of 350 bear traders. To Hoover's disappointment, no leading Democrats appeared on the list. "These obviously are dummy names in many cases," Senator Walcott explained bitterly. Again

Gray called Whitney to testify on the exchange's attitude toward short selling, and Whitney continued to profess ignorance of any wrongdoing. "You make rules that are just paper rules,"Chairman Norbeck exploded in exasperation."I ask for proof of that," Whitney countered. "You attend these hearings for a while and you will see," Norbeck assured him. "I have been," Whitney responded wearily. "Yes," Norbeck thundered back, "but up to now you have been running them!" (Reported in the press, Norbeck's last statement does not appear in the official committee transcripts.)

Opponents of the hearings charged that they had done nothing to restore public confidence in the exchanges nor to drive out the bear raiders. Even the once militant Walcott hedged his support. "I am not sure now that short sales depress the market," he admitted. For the more progressive Norbeck, the humiliating hearings and growing public disenchantment with the investigation were infuriating. Storming out of an executive session of the committee, he shouted to reporters: "We are going to carry this investigation through to the end."

Seizing full control of the investigation, Norbeck established a five member steering committee, which he headed, and which noticeably omitted Walcott. The subcommittee then hired four special investigators and an accounting firm to assist Gray in sifting through the mountains of financial records they had accumulated. These new directions produced new witnesses. Percy Rockefeller, nephew of John D. Rockefeller, sr., appeared and confessed that he sold short to cover his losses of "many, many millions of dollars" in the stock market crash. One of his partners in these transactions, Ben Smith, also testified, admitting that he participated in a pooling of R.C.A. stock, along with John J. Raskob and Michael J. Meehan, a heavy contributor to the campaigns of Alfred E. Smith.

In early June, the committee called Raskob to testify. Prodding the Democratic national chairman on his trading of General Motors stocks, Counsel Gray attempted to paint him as a short seller deliberately undermining Hoover's programs. Raskob urbanely parried each question, maintaining that he had "always been a bull on America." Bluntly, Senator Carter Glass interjected that "it has been whispered for weeks around the Capitol that this investigation was initiated to involve several prominent Democrats." Gray's badgering of Raskob irritated even Republican Senator James Couzens, who complained, "I don't see where we are drifting." But Gray persisted. Excusing Raskob he subpoenaed Charles E. Mitchell, chairman of the National City Bank, to explain that bank's dealings in speculative Anaconda Copper stocks. Soon after, he launched into a brief examination of the Radio-Keith-Orpheum transactions. When Congress adjourned on July 16, the hearings had produced no significant revelations nor any report on possible further action. Despite rising criticism, Chairman Norbeck vowed to continue, "The bigger things are still to be done."

November's elections brought major political changes. Depression politics swept Hoover out of the White House and obliterated the tenuous Republican majority in the Senate. The Seventy-Third Congress would contain fifty-nine Democratic and thirty-six Republican senators. Florida Senator Duncan U. Fletcher would move to the chairmanship of the Banking Committee. However, the new President and Congress would not arrive until the following March and the Seventy-Second Congress which returned to Washington in December contained an unusually large flock of lame ducks. At first the Banking Committee busied itself with new banking legislation, revisions in the Reconstruction Finance Corporation Act, and numerous monetary proposals, but Norbeck had won a new resolution, increasing the investigation's appropriation and granting it power to examine income tax records in executive sessions. At the same time, he dismissed Gray and began the search for a Democratic counsel.

Early in January, the committee selected Irving Ben Cooper as its new counsel. Fresh from a successful investigation of corruption in New York City as Samuel Seabury's chief assistant, Cooper promised a burst of new enthusiasm. Unexpectedly, though, he demanded complete freedom to conduct his investigation, plus fifty blank subpoenas, and announced he would conduct most of his work in New York. Jealous of their prerogatives, and still sensitive over Gray's misguided tactics, the committee balked at losing control and refused this blank check request. Insulted, Cooper promptly resigned.

Since Norbeck had failed with three counsels, Senator Fletcher approached his longtime friend, former Secretary of State Bainbridge Colby, to offer the position. Colby declined but recommended an associate from the old Bull Moose Progressive party of 1912, who like himself had jointed the Democrats in 1916. His choice was Ferdinand Pecora.

Then fifty-one, Pecora had been born in Nicosia, Sicily, and came to the United States at the age of five, where he grew up in the Chelsea area of New York City. At first studying for the Episcopal ministry, Pecora had quit to help support his family. Working in a law office, he financed his own way through New York University Law School. From 1918 until 1930 he served as chief assistant district attorney for New York County. His former boss, District Attorney Jacob Banton, assured the senators that Pecora would conduct the hearings with a "lawyer-like, scholarly manner, without playing up to publicity." During Banton's long illnesses, Pecora had directed much of his office's work. He established an impressive record of convictions in eighty percent of the one thousand cases he handled. His investigations into small "bucketshop" stock selling operations had introduced him to the murky practices of securities fraud, and he had helped to close 150 such shops through numerous prosecutions. He had also won the conviction of the New York State banking superintendent on bribery charges. Honest and diligent, with a sharp and retentive mind, Pecora would provide the shrewd stewardship missing so long from the investigation.

Offer of the job came as a surprise to Pecora, who thought the committee had already concluded its work. Senator Norbeck assured him that little business remained other than preparing the final report to the Senate, due before Congress adjourned on March 4. When Pecora arrived in Washington, he found the committee's records stuffed into a large file cabinet in Norbeck's office. As he sifted through the material, he was struck by its limited nature and lack of conclusive evidence. The original resolution, he decided, had called for a much broader investigation. Norbeck, who had always shared these opinions, gladly threw his support behind a resumption of the hearings during the few short weeks that remained.

Fully aware of the difficulties of his assignment, Pecora stopped first to build a staff that he could trust. He drew primarily from the bright and industrious young men who had worked with him in the D.A.'s office. Two young lawyers, David Saperstein and Julius Silver, became his chief assistants, while Frank J. Meehan, an accountant who had worked on the bucket-shop investigations, joined the team as chief statistician. Pecora added other lawyers and accountants, but the committee's tight budget limited his selection. The highest salary he could offer, and take himself, was $3,000 a year, much less than any earned in private practice, even during the Depression. Two old anti-Wall Street warhorses volunteered their services without compensation: Max Lowenthal, a former Harvard Law School student of Felix Frankfurter, who had made a fortune handling stockholder suits against corporations and had written a muckraking account of corporation reorganization in *The Investor Pays;* and John T. Flynn, a highly successful freelance writer, financial editor of *The New Republic,* and lecturer on contemporary economics at the New School. Both men eagerly sought the opportunity to expose business practices they abhorred. Fiery financial iconoclasts, they added a measure of experience and fearless disapproval of the bankers that the younger men might have lacked.

Pecora officially opened his probe in February 1933, a week after the governor of Michigan had declared a "bank holiday" to salvage his state's banking system. Nationwide, more than five thousand banks had suspended operations since the 1929 stock market crash. Now, state after state followed Michigan's example. For the bewildered thousands of depositors who waited in line to withdraw their savings, if possible, the Banking Committee hearings provided a timely financial education.

Aiming for the March 4 deadline, Pecora had hurriedly planned a tentative schedule of witnesses. By chance, Charles E. Mitchell, flamboyant chairman of the National City Bank, became the first target when Pecora read of his impending trip to Europe to discuss stabilization of the lira with Mussolini. Tracking down the banker to his Bermuda retreat, Pecora issued subpoenas for his appearance and for all minutes and records of the National City Bank and its investment affiliate, the National City Company, for the five years prior to October 1929. On Thursday, February 9, Pecora and his staff arrived at the bank's Wall Street headquarters. As they waited, a parade of bank clerks carried in massive volumes of records and piled them into high stacks. Privately, the counsel admitted he felt "appalled by their magnitude." From Thursday night until Saturday night, working almost around-the-clock, he and a corps of accountants combed through the records, photostating all documents they thought useful for the hearings. On Monday, Pecora returned to Washington to conduct a brief inquiry into the Samuel Insull utility company system, while his staff continued to collect and analyze National City data.

By February 21, when the National City hearings began, Pecora had acquired far more damaging information than the unsuspecting Mitchell imagined. With an air of obvious self-confidence, Mitchell swept into the Senate caucus room, with a crowd of lawyers and bank officials surrounding him. No stranger to Washington, the tall, well-tanned, gray-haired Mitchell had advised every Republican President since Warren Harding. A year before he had sat through Counsel Gray's quizzing with no damage to his reputation as a responsible banker. Pecora, the short, cigar-smoking Italian immigrant, did not worry him. Yet, within a day under Pecora's persistent questioning, Mitchell's self-confidence waned. He seemed perplexed at Pecora's detailed knowledge of his doings, and the counsel wondered if Mitchell understood how completely they had examined the bank's records. On his first day as a witness, Mitchell admitted he paid no income taxes in 1929 after selling 18,000 shares of stock to his wife to establish a $2,800,000 loss. "That sale was really just a sale of convenience to reduce your taxes?" asked Senator Brookhart. "Yes," Mitchell replied frankly. From 1927 until 1929, he confirmed, he had received bonuses of $3,500,000 from the National City Bank and its investment company, in addition to his annual salary of $25,000.

A large portion of these bountiful profits came from the speculative successes of the National City Company, which had distributed more stocks than any other investment firm during the 1920s. Mitchell, who originally rose to prominence as president of the National City Company and was the firm's greatest salesman, tried to rationalize its more questionable dealings with the bank. Early in the 1920s, for example, the bank had made several large loans to the Cuban sugar industry. In 1927, when these loans were in default, National City Bank issued $50,000,000 in new bank stocks. Without informing the stock purchasers, the bank then transferred this additional capital to the National City Company, which purchased controlling interest in the sugar industry, recently consolidated into the General Sugar Corporation. With this windfall, the sugar industry promptly repaid its debt to the National City Bank. Unweaving the story, Pecora asked: "Is this what is known in the vernacular as 'bailing out' of the bank of a bad loan?" Mitchell protested this implication, but did admit that the stockholders had no idea their money had enabled the investment company to assume the bank's "slow and doubtful" sugar loans. Such conflicting banking and investment interests had troubled the government as early as 1911 when Solicitor General Frederick Lehmann found the National City Company clearly in violation of federal laws for holding the stocks of its parent bank and for engaging in illegal investments. Lehmann's opinion, however, had gathered dust in government files, wholly ignored for the next twenty years.

When Mitchell stepped down, an investor who had placed his fortune in the trust of the National City Company succeeded him to the stand. Edgar Brown of Pottsville, Pennsylvania, explained to the committee how the National City Bank had recommended that he allow the investment company to convert his $225,000 savings in U.S. bonds into a portfolio of stocks. He accepted their advice. When the stocks did poorly, Brown nervously tried to sell, but the agents of the company talked him out of it. "I was placed in the position of one who was about to put his own mother out of the house," he recalled. As a final insult, when Brown's investments collapsed, leaving him bankrupt, the National City Bank refused his application for a loan. Yet, simultaneously, as Pecora's documentation revealed, the bank freely advanced loans on insufficient collateral to its own officers to meet their market commitments.

The National City investigations shocked Wall Street and made headlines across the country. President-elect Roosevelt congratulated Pecora and urged him to carry on the hearings into the next Congress. Chairman-designate

Fletcher introduced the resolution to make this possible. On February 27, Charles Mitchell offered his resignation as chairman of the National City Bank, which its board of directors hastily accepted. A week later, the bank's new chairman announced the severing of all connections between the bank and the investment company. The New York district attorney then filed a suit against Mitchell for tax evasion. On March 2, as the committee recessed for the inauguration, Pecora conferred with Senator Norbeck at his office. As the two men looked out of the window towards Union Station, they spied Mitchell, with shoulders stooped, carrying his own luggage across the plaza from his hotel to the railway station. The retinue of bank officials who had accompanied him at the start of the hearings were now nowhere in sight. Mitchell left quietly and alone.

"The money changers have fled from their high seats in the temple of our culture," Franklin Roosevelt proclaimed in his inaugural address two days later. Roosevelt's Administration took office in the midst of a nationwide banking chaos. When the President declared a national bank holiday, the Senate Banking Committee moved to devote its entire energies to banking reform legislation. A week later, when the banks reopened, one of those that remained closed was Joseph Harriman's National Bank and Trust Company. A year before, when the Banking Committee hearings had first begun, Harriman had taken out a newspaper advertisement to warn against them. "Washington is ill equipped to investigate important matters of commerce and finance affecting the public welfare," he warned ominously, "and in the present instance there is no certainty that it will not uncover things much better left sealed." Now, Harriman fled from federal agents before his eventual arrest and imprisonment for misappropriating funds and tampering with his bank's records.

As the senators rushed through the "first hundred days" of Roosevelt's legislative program, Pecora returned to New York and planned new strategy for the investigations. Having finished with the commercial National City Bank, he turned to the practices of the great private banks, and chose their most impressive figure, J. P. Morgan, jr., as his next subject for examination. Arriving in New York, Pecora telephoned Morgan to arrange a preliminary meeting before issuing the banker a subpoena. "Yes, I think I've heard of you, Mr. Pecora," Morgan acknowledged, and invited him down to his office at 23 Wall Street. But Pecora refused his request and insisted that Morgan come uptown and meet him at his own offices. He wanted to make it dramatically clear that the banker faced a representative of the United States government rather than Ferdinand Pecora, the individual.

Pecora's New York office was a small suite of rooms, rented on a monthly basis, in the same building as his private law firm. Filled with second-hand furniture, without rugs, draperies or any other ornamentation, it presented a starkly functional appearance. Morgan arrived with his silver-maned and stately lawyer, John W. Davis, the 1924 Democratic presidential nominee. As Pecora had hoped, the two seemed "impressed by the shabbiness of the room." Without excessive formalities, he proceeded forthrightly to tell them he wanted complete access to the files of J. P. Morgan & Company and any subsidiaries. Morgan, taken out of his baronial surroundings, cut a rather shy and deferential figure. Pecora found him exceedingly courteous and cooperative. Morgan's lawyer, on the other hand, strenuously objected to all his requests as an unconstitutional intrusion into a private citizen's business. A rigid conservative, John W. Davis held sacred the rights of privacy, economic liberty, and the sanctity of private banking. He dismissed most congressional investigations as publicity-seeking, and distrusted all sweeping reforms. Davis insisted that Pecora specify exactly what material the bank should prepare for the committee; he wanted no invasion of the bank's records by Pecora's staff of accountants. In response, Pecora submitted twenty-three specific requests for materials. Morgan & Company agreed to fifteen, took seven under consideration, and rejected one, a request to see the bank's articles of co-partnership and distribution of profits.

Pecora would stand for no recalcitrance. Together with Senator Fletcher he prepared a new resolution to broaden his mandate to cover all phases of banking beyond the original securities objective. The resolution passed unanimously, and the Senate granted an additional $25,000 for further hearings.

Throughout April, Pecora's investigators sorted through the voluminous records at the Morgan bank on Wall Street. Davis and Pecora sparred frequently over the confidentiality of the bank's depositors and borrowers. Not quite as obliging as the National City Bank's counsel, Davis denied Pecora the right to work nights in the bank after closing hour. But by the end of May, Pecora had accumulated enough material to call J. P. Morgan, jr., as a witness.

Long lines of curiosity-seekers filled the corridors of the Senate Office Building as the Banking Committee inquiry resumed on May 23. A squad of telegraph operators stood ready to relay reporters' stories to newspapers across the country. Press photographers stationed themselves in the caucus room. All waited to see the head of the famed House of Morgan testify before Congress for the first time since 1912, when the elder J. P. Morgan faced the Pujo Committee; and many wondered if Pecora would again score as heavily as he had against Mitchell. Entering the great marble chamber, the ponderous Morgan perfectly fit his austere public image. On the stand, however, he palled in comparison with his father. Gone were the arrogant, self-assured responses with floor-thumping emphasis. Morgan, jr. was an affable, quiet-spoken witness. His voice, with its distinct British accent, fell so low that few spectators could hear him. Although he and his firm's other partners had studiously undergone Davis's coaching sessions before the hearings, Morgan still stumbled over names and events and frequently conferred with his counsel before answering.

After the sordid revelations on the National City Bank, Pecora found J. P. Morgan & Company a relatively conservative institution. Even so, he unveiled enough surprising evidence to fill headlines for the next two weeks, exposing the private dealings of a very private banker. In every instance, Morgan & Company could claim the technical legality of their policies, while Pecora could demonstrate how far they had gone to stretch their legal and ethical standards. Most shocking to the Depression-ridden public was the initial disclosure that the fabulously wealthy Morgan and his partners paid no income taxes during the years 1931 and 1932 in the United States, although Morgan had paid taxes in England during those years. This deficiency had resulted from the firm's net loss of twenty-one million dollars during 1930; and

Morgan put his office manager, Leonard Keyes, on the stand to verify the bank's substantial decline. Pecora rebutted these contentions by revealing that the bank had added a new partner two days after the New Year in 1931 in an intricate maneuver to extend their losses of 1930 for another year. "That sort of parlor magic may satisfy the courts and the moronic sycophants of big business," a columnist for *The Nation* wrote in undisguised anger, ". . . but it will neither soothe nor deceive any honest person of adult intelligence."

Bringing Morgan back to the stand on the second day, Pecora moved from taxes to stock distribution and created an even greater shock wave by disclosing a long list of dignitaries who had accepted favors from the Morgan bank. In 1929 these favors had taken the form of preferential invitations to buy stock in the Allegheny Corporation, a railroad holding company venture which the Morgan firm was handling. Since Morgan & Company generally dealt in bonds and did not sell common stock to the public, it decided to permit certain individuals to privately purchase the stock, offering it to them at twenty dollars a share, while the market value averaged thirty-five dollars a share. Invited purchasers included officials from banks, insurance companies, industry, railroads, and utilities, as well as editors, lawyers, and politicians. The names of Roosevelt's Secretary of the Treasury, William H. Woodin, Ambassador-at-Large Norman H. Davis, Senator William G. McAdoo, Charles A. Lindbergh, John W. Davis, former Vice President Charles G. Dawes, and Democratic National Chairman John J. Raskob peppered the Allegheny list. While the bank disclaimed any desires for favors in return, Pecora was able to produce an embarrassing note from Raskob, who assured the bank of his deep appreciation and sincerely hoped that "the future holds opportunities for me to reciprocate." Finding public officials from both parties on the list seriously damaged the bank's credibility. Few observers accepted it as a strictly business arrangement. Such conservative journals as the *New York Times* and *Business Week* editorially criticized the House of Morgan, while columnist Walter Lippmann denounced such practices as preferential lists as evidence "that no set of men, however honorable they may be and however good their traditions, can be trusted with so much power and the opportunity for personal gain which it carried with it."

Twenty years earlier, Brandeis had warned in *Other People's Money* that "the dominant element in our financial oligarchy is the investment banker." These bankers used their depositors' funds and their own profits from stock underwriting to move onto innumerable boards of directors, where they could heavily influence the course of American industry. In 1933, Pecora revealed that Morgan partners held 126 directorships in 89 different corporations, with total resources of nineteen billion dollars. Morgan's influence further spread through the loans his bank had made to select individuals, including many prominent bankers. "They are friends of ours, and we know that they are good, sound, straight fellows," Morgan insisted, denying any improprieties.

The banker objected most strenuously to Pecora's plans to make public J. P. Morgan & Company's articles of copartnership. These impressively engrossed parchments, hung from a metal bar with a new sheet for each partner, pinpointed Morgan as the exceedingly powerful lord of his own financial empire. Final decisions in all banking matters lay with Morgan. He approved all new partners and could fire any one of them at any time. Further, Morgan retained complete discretion over the distribution of half of the firm's annual profits. None of this information had been public knowledge. No bank examiner ever went through the bank's books. Morgan insisted that he would not have had the "slightest objection" to releasing the information, but that no one had ever asked, except for the Pujo Committee. "That investigation was the one held about twenty years ago?" Pecora asked. "That is the only public statement we have ever made about anything," Morgan responded.

On May 25, while Morgan was still on the stand, the Senate passed the Glass-Steagall banking reform bill. In the light of the Pecora inquiry, Congress had amended the bill to cut from two years to one the time in which all commercial banks, like National City, must divorce their investment affiliates, and private banks, like Morgan & Company, must abandon either their banking or investment functions. Passage of the bill also freed its sponsor, Senator Carter Glass of Virginia, to devote more time to the Wall Street hearings. Alternately ill and busy with his own bill, Glass had rarely attended the early committee meetings when Pecora had outlined the broad scope of his plans. Now, the senator insisted that the counsel should give preliminary briefings to the committee before each session. Beyond his concern for senatorial prerogatives, Glass felt personally involved in the Morgan inquiry. Two of Morgan's partners, Russell C. Leffingwell and S. Parker Gilbert, had served as Glass's assistants when he was secretary of the treasury in the Wilson Administration. Both now complained to him of the injustices in the committee's proceedings. At closed-door executive sessions Glass supported the Morgan contention that the committee should not make public such information as the preferential stock lists or the names of borrowers from the bank.

Glass's impatience finally burst into the public hearings during Pecora's examination of another Morgan-sponsored holding company, the United Corporation, and its preferential stock lists. Peevishly, the senator questioned the whole point of the hearing. Pecora responded by reading aloud the text of the resolution authorizing the hearings, but Glass remained unsatisfied. Pecora was wasting the committee's time, he argued, with highly technical questions of "no significance to a man of ordinary intelligence." Obviously irritated over Glass's heckling, Pecora described his plans to the committee, plans which had already been outlined during Glass's absence, and remarked that not a single committee member had requested further information. "I want to assure Senator Glass that the compensation of $255 a month which I am receiving for these services is no incentive to me to render these services or continue to render them," Pecora said heatedly. With these words, spectators in the chamber suddenly broke into loud and prolonged applause for the counsel, visibly startling many of the senators. "Oh yes," Glass grumbled as the cheering died down, "this is what it is all about. We are having a circus and the only thing lacking now are peanuts and colored lemonade."

Throughout these clashes, the committee's chairman, Duncan Fletcher, consistently came to Pecora's defense. A small, frail man of seventy-five, with a thin, quavering voice, Fletcher generally played a passive role in the hearings, rarely interrupting Pecora's questioning. When Senator Glass demanded a special executive session to discuss the counsel's techniques, Fletcher invited Pecora to attend and defend himself. "Our members have been drawn around a long table for nearly a week without one particle of knowledge beforehand about what counsel for the committee proposed to disclose," Glass complained. At the session on Thursday morning, June 1, Glass proposed that counsel should not introduce any testimony that he had not already explained in advance to the committee. Senators James Couzens and Fred Steiwer, both Republicans, and Democrat Edward Costigan, all spoke out against the proposal. Pecora, at Fletcher's request, added that the proposal would destroy the investigation's effectiveness by increasing chances of premature leaks to the press. "How dare you tell this committee what to do?" Glass interrupted indignantly. If the motion passed, Pecora continued, he would resign and tell the press the reasons why. "Now you're trying to intimidate us!" Glass stood up shouting. Fletcher and the majority of the committee, however, rallied to Pecora's support and solidly defeated the Glass proposal. On their way back to the hearings, Fletcher pointedly took hold of Pecora's arm as a physical gesture of support.

Passing through the crowd of reporters at the caucus room doorway, the senators sensed from the commotion that something unusual had happened in their absence. While the committee had met in executive session, an enterprising press agent had slipped into the hearing room and placed a circus midget in the lap of an unsuspecting J. P. Morgan. Thinking at first it was a child, Morgan put his arm protectively around her. "I've got a grandson bigger than you," he said. "But I'm older," replied the midget. "She's thirty-two," the press agent informed him, and Morgan slid the little woman off his lap while press photographers clamored around taking pictures. Thoroughly angered, Chairman Fletcher denounced the incident as a discourtesy and requested that newspapers refrain from printing any photos. But the next morning pictures of Morgan with the midget in his lap spread across the nation—ironically symbolizing the congressional humbling of the once Olympian bankers.

"Public opinion unquestionably is behind me," Pecora told the press after his confrontation with Glass, "and I will bring out all the facts regardless of whence they hit." Even Glass recognized the political liability in defending Morgan, and at the next week's session he pressed for a new resolution to give Pecora more power to delve into Morgan's taxes. The Internal Revenue Service, the committee felt, had treated such prominent bankers as Mitchell and Morgan far too gently. It had spent merely one day in examining tax returns from J. P. Morgan & Company and its investment house, Drexel & Company, for 1930; and a revenue agent had approved one statement with the notation: "Returned without examination for the reason that the return was prepared in the office of J. P. Morgan and Company and it has been our experience that any schedule made by that office is correct." J. P. Morgan, however, believed that Pecora had distorted his tax situation. He reminded the committee during his final day of testimony that his firm paid heavy taxes all during the 1920s until the stock market crash. "Income taxes are, after all, paid upon income and not upon deficits," he concluded. Not all of his partners could afford such indignation. Two Morgan associates, Thomas W. Lamont and his son, Thomas S. Lamont, paid back taxes and stiff delinquency fines as a result of Pecora's disclosures.

Additional power to examine and use income tax records assured an inescapably tight legal and financial web against any witness. The great success of Pecora's investigations came primarily from his skill at collecting, analyzing, and assimilating large quantities of data concerning his witnesses' activities. With the power of subpoena, his staff would descend upon a banker or broker and go through his records, file drawer after file drawer, page by page, selecting and photostating documents. Staff lawyers and accountants would assemble this material to reconstruct the motivations, discrepancies, delinquencies, and frauds involved. They drew a multitude of charts, tracing every event and statistic. After narrowing down the documentation, they outlined the subject's transactions in chronological narrative on letter-sized sheets, with citations in the margins to specific documents which could prove each assertion. The corresponding records filled two large trunks, which Pecora entrusted to his nephew, Louis Stephens, who made sure that the appropriate item was ready at each stage of the hearings. Armed FBI agents guarded these trunks day and night.

Such a mass of documentation, covering long and obscure financial dealings, presented a formidable challenge for any attorney to keep straight during his cross-examination. Here Pecora's photographic memory amazed even his own staff. Each night he would read rapidly through the thirty- or forty-page memorandum they had prepared for the next day, stopping to question only an occasional reference. After that he would rarely refer to the memorandum again. Yet he covered the material coherently and correctly during the next day's proceedings. "I looked with astonishment," wrote John T. Flynn," at this man who, through the intricate maze of banking syndicates, market deals, chicanery of all sorts, and in a field new to him, never forgot a name, never made an error in a figure, and never lost his temper."

Since Pecora already knew the answers he expected to elicit during testimony, and had the proof to challenge any witness who lied, he could proceed in a genial fashion, without badgering his witnesses. Politely, he would allow them to go off on their own stories until he felt they had registered a point, then he would return to his own line of questioning. He worked around the periphery of each problem. When a witness began to suspect his intentions and balked at answering, Pecora would start at another point on the periphery and work inwards from that direction, until finally his central objective became obvious to everyone. At the crucial moment in the testimony, Pecora's whole demeanor would change. Leaning forward in his chair he would rapidly recall all of the earlier admissions he had led the witness to make, pointing inexorably toward his guilt or complicity. Attuned to public relations, he also geared his questioning towards the daily press deadlines. As the hearings progressed he learned to make his most important points early at each session to ensure press attention and headlines in the afternoon papers. He saved some entirely new material for late in the day for the next morning's papers. Public dissemination of information always remained one of his fixed goals, as important as establishing corrective legislation.

Throughout the long hearings, Pecora depended heavily upon his staff and maintained a close working relationship with them. From Monday through Friday he shared a suite of rooms with them at the Mayflower Hotel, which the nearly bankrupt hotel provided at a reduced rate for them and other luminaries, in an attempt to attract more guests. At night, Pecora would return to the Mayflower, look over new material for the next day, and then relax with the staff, usually in long card-playing sessions. For the most part, the staff worked together smoothly. As the hearings wore on and pressures mounted, tensions did rise, but Pecora, an excellent raconteur, could lean back, light his cigar, and tell another long story to ease the situation. The staff of younger men called him "Chief," a moniker from his days as chief assistant D.A. He in turn called them "Boys." This paternalistic relationship brought him complete devotion from them, although he demanded the last word on all decisions and could summarily dismiss a subordinate whose loyalty he doubted.

The Congress of the New Deal's "first hundred days" recessed on June 16, 1933, but the Pecora hearings continued on into the summer. Oppressive heat and humidity, perennial afflictions of Washington summers, soon had an impact. By the end of the Morgan hearings, Fletcher had permitted gentlemen in the room to remove their jackets, J. P. Morgan dozed in his chair, and other witnesses appeared dazed and tired on the stand. Before adjourning, however, Pecora wanted to examine the second most prominent private banking house in the United States, Kuhn, Loeb & Company. Otto Kahn, senior partner in the firm, had already informed Pecora of his deep distress over the National City Bank revelations and his desire to cooperate fully with the committee to help end "improper practices." As a witness, the elderly banker, dapper and cosmopolitan, with a large handlebar mustache, condemned the "cutthroat competition of bankers in the 1920s," and he recounted tales of American bankers fighting each other for control over European and South American bonds. Kahn denounced the profit-and-loss provisions of tax laws which created artificial depressions each December when investors sold stocks to establish losses, and he called for government control of every organization that dealt with money. "I know a great deal must be changed," he admitted. "And I know the time is ripe to have it changed."

Out of deference to other members of the financial community, however, Kahn was less than candid, and reneged on his promise of complete honesty. Annoyed over Kahn's increasing hesitancy, Pecora pointed out that Kuhn, Loeb & Company had not been free from transgressions themselves. When he brought up the issue of ninety million dollars in loans that the company had arranged in Chile, Kahn winced. "You have touched on a sore spot," he admitted. "It is the only issue which my firm has made, the only foreign issue, which is in default." Kahn himself, Pecora revealed, had paid no income taxes for 1930, 1931, and 1932, although his firm reaped profits of more than twenty million dollars from pool operations between 1927 and 1931. For distributing the stocks of the Pennroad Corporation, a railroad holding company, Kuhn, Loeb & Company had earned a profit of $5,840,000, although investors in the stock had lost over $106,000,000 collectively when its price plunged in the crash. "We were all sinners," Kahn now repented. "If we indulge again in practices that are socially, economically and from the point of view of the country undesirable, I think the policeman ought to be ready to step in."

As Kahn stepped down, Pecora conceded to the heat and senatorial pressures to recess his investigation for the summer. During their vacation, he set his staff at examining the records of two other well-known banks: Dillon, Read & Company, a private bank influential in the stock markets; and the Chase National Bank, reputedly the largest commercial bank in the world.

Concentrating first on Dillon, Read, Pecora subpoenaed its officers to testify in early October. The bank actually specialized in selling securities and did a relatively small business in accepting deposits, but Dillon, Read & Company had shown much ingenuity in raising funds from other sources.

During the "Great Bull Market" of the 1920s, Dillon, Read had pioneered in developing the highly popular investment trust. Through this device they offered average investors an opportunity to buy shares of a corporation which did nothing but invest in stocks itself. Presumably, with its experienced management and skilled analysts, the investment trust would purchase only the most sound and productive stocks available. At the height of the speculative heyday of 1929, an average of one new investment trust appeared every day. Dillon, Read exhibited particular skill in organizing such trusts and managed to maintain control over them through the use of "nonvoting" stocks. Only a small portion of the investment trust's stocks which Dillon, Read retained carried voting privileges. The far greater number of stocks earned dividends, but their holders had no say in the trust's management.

In 1924 they formed the Foreign Securities Corporation, capitalized at $30,000,000, of which Dillon, Read purchased $5,000,000 in voting stocks, enough to totally control the organization. Later that same year, they formed the even larger United States and International Securities Corporation, capitalized at $60,000,000, of which Dillon, Read purchased $10,000,000 worth of controlling voting stock. This latter ten million, however, came not from Dillon, Read, but from the earnings of the Foreign Securities Corporation. The bank had thus used its voting privileges in one investment trust to divert its surplus funds into another, rather than distribute the money as dividends to the common stock holders. Furiously, Senator James Couzens called it "rotten ethics to take $10,000,000 out of an investment trust you own, or which you control . . . and put it into another investment to further augment your own profits. I think that is reprehensible." Furthermore, Pecora noted that eleven members of Dillon, Read & Company had made almost seven million dollars in profits on the common stock of these trusts, after an initial investment of only $24,110.

Greed and excessive profits also characterized the activities of the giant Chase National Bank, as Pecora unraveled that story. Earlier that year Chase had deflected public attention by adopting his own sweeping reforms. President Winthrop Aldrich endorsed the National City Bank plan to divorce banking and investment facilities, and Chase cut loose its own Chase Securities Corporation. At the same time, Aldrich called for stronger federal laws to regulate commercial and private banking. But Pecora was less interested in Aldrich than he was in the bank's recently retired chairman, Albert H. Wiggin, known as "the most popular banker in Wall Street." Wiggin had stepped down from the bank in December 1932 after twenty-eight years of service, shortly after Chase had merged with the Rockefeller-dominated Equitable Trust Company.

Still held in high esteem on Wall Street, Wiggin was a member of fifty-nine boards of directors and served on the executive committee of the Federal Reserve Bank of New York. In fact, stockholders of Chase National Bank had little idea of the complete extent of Wiggin's popularity until the investigations disclosed how the bank's executive board had secretly granted Wiggin a yearly retirement salary of $100,000 for life. During the last four years of his active service, the banker had also received $1,500,000 in salaries and bonuses from the bank and securities company. Wiggin protested that his associates from the bank had determined these generous emoluments. "And I helped to fix theirs," he added. "You helped to fix theirs and they helped to fix yours?" Pecora asked incredulously. "Yes," said Wiggin, "we all sat together." As a result of the hearings, an intensely negative reaction from Chase stockholders forced Wiggin to relinquish his $100,000 annual salary.

Unlike many of his predecessors on the stand, Wiggin had dutifully paid his income taxes throughout the panic and Depression. Indeed, Pecora found it interesting that Wiggin and his family paid $4,625,000 in taxes from 1928 to 1932, surprisingly excessive even considering Chase's bonus system. This evidence led Pecora into an examination of three Wiggin family corporations, the Shermar, Murlyn, and Clingston, named for Wiggin's daughters and their husbands, and three other family corporations in Canada. He discovered, as he had anticipated, that the banker had used these corporations for speculative purposes, engaging in a number of pool operations. But even Pecora had not suspected the chairman of the Chase National Bank of speculating in his own bank's stocks. From 1927 until 1931 the Chase Securities Corporation, with Wiggin's full knowledge, had manipulated Chase stocks by purchasing and selling over $860,000,000 in shares to exercise a "steadying effect" on its market value. Despite these efforts, the stock had fallen from a high of 575 in 1927 to 17¾ in 1933. During these same years the Wiggin corporations realized a net profit of $10,425,000, largely by selling short the bank's stocks.

Wiggin admitted his transgressions in a quiet voice, in short, simple answers, without the lengthy attempts at explanations that had so ensnared other bankers on the stand. He made no attempt to accept personal blame for any actions, but attributed the banking abuses of the 1920s to simply "the time." During one discussion of pool operations, Pecora inquired: "Is that not a scheme for 'churning the market' and producing an activity that would stimulate prices?" "I think the market was a 'God-given' market," Wiggin replied. "Are you sure of the source?" one committee member interrupted.

In the audience, Chase President Winthrop Aldrich sat mortified over Wiggin's confessions. When Wiggin concluded his testimony, Aldrich stepped forward and asked permission to address the committee. "As long as I have anything to do with the management. the market in Chase stocks shall not be affected by the operation of trading accounts by affiliates of the bank," he swore. Later Aldrich approached Pecora privately. He had learned more about the operations of the Chase Bank during Pecora's interrogation, he admitted, than during his four years as the bank's president. The record of Wiggin's transactions, the New York Times bemoaned, "brought astonishment and pain to all his friends and former admirers. But this personal consequence is as nothing compared to the great shock to public confidence in our banking system."

On Wall Street, feelings ran contrary to these fears. Bankers and brokers at the securities exchanges questioned Pecora's purposes and his tactics. Although they had reached a consensus that some form of federal regulation would undoubtedly follow the investigation, many asked how the exposure of individual bankers' indiscretions could produce legislation for the stock mar-

kets. Some members of the Banking Committee agreed and anxiously coun-
seled that the hearings return to a focus on stock manipulation. Pecora, too,
was ready to shift emphasis. He had used the banking probe to examine
banks' roles in stock distribution, syndicates, and the granting of loans for
buying stocks on margin. Having boldly publicized the machinations of
Mitchell, Morgan, and Wiggin, he turned his attention to the manipulative
practices of brokers and floor traders at the mammoth New York Stock
Exchange.

In this pursuit, Pecora had plenty of company. The Roosevelt Administration considered stock exchange reform among its first priorities. Because of his
experiences with the Pujo Committee, the assignment for drafting an exchange reform bill fell to seventy-five-year-old Samuel Untermyer. Unfortunately, Untermyer devoted himself less to the bill than to his dream of returning to the spotlight as chief counsel for the Banking Committee. Months earlier
he had rejected Senator Norbeck's pleas to accept the post under the then
valid assumption that the original resolution granted insufficient powers for a
complete investigation. Since then, Pecora had won new powers and considerable glory, and Untermyer realized his error. As a result of his preoccupation, he submitted a bill rehashing his earlier proposals that the Post Office
Department regulate stock exchanges through control of their use of the mails.
Roosevelt's advisors scoffed at this idea; it was twenty years out of date.

To ease Untermyer's disappointment, Roosevelt divided the responsibilities of the job in half. He granted Untermyer another year to devise a new
exchange regulation formula, and he assigned former Federal Trade Commissioner Huston Thompson to prepare legislation for the more immediate problem of preventing fraudulent stock sales. The Senate Banking Committee,
busy with the Glass bill and the Morgan inquiry, readily accepted Thompson's
draft for securities regulation. But the House Interstate and Foreign Commerce
Committee, under Chairman Sam Rayburn, found his version hopelessly
inadequate and secured a more sophisticated bill from three young proteges of
Felix Frankfurter: Thomas Corcoran, Benjamin Cohen, and James Landis. At
the joint Senate-House conference committee, the wily Rayburn outmaneu-
vered Senator Fletcher to win adoption of the House bill. Since the Securities
Act of 1933 contained no provisions for general exchange regulation, Pecora
was determined to impress the findings of his investigation more fully upon
the eventual exchange bill.

During the summer recess, Pecora informed Chairman Fletcher of his
planned study of the New York Stock Exchange to see "the way the wheels
turn around." Unexpectedly, the market mechanism gave him a spectacular
show in mid-July when the "New Deal Market," a brief boom that had
followed the creation of the NRA, suddenly burst. In one week thirty million
shares changed hands in a downward spiral sickeningly reminiscent of 1929.
Dragging the market down were the "wet" stocks of breweries and other
post-Prohibition businesses that had soared in anticipation of final ratification of the Twenty-First Amendment. The pattern of short selling accompanying the decline convinced Pecora that manipulative pools were at work. Staff
investigator John T. Flynn charged in his regular *New Republic* column that
many of the stocks had obviously been "rigged." Commercial solvents stood
at 16½ in May 1933, but during nineteen days in July almost all of its two and a

half million shares were traded, running the price up to 57¼. Just as abruptly, the pool behind it unloaded the stock, which then slid to 36. Similarly, a pool had pushed National Distiller's Products up from 9 in May to 124¾ in July. During the week of July 17 the stock plunged 68 points.

Keenly interested in these developments, Pecora called upon President Richard Whitney of the New York Stock Exchange. Despite Whitney's assurances that the exchange would carefully investigate all pool operations, Pecora doubted the effectiveness or sincerity of exchange self-regulation. He intended to pursue public hearings on exchange practices, but found he faced an entirely different situation than with the banks. Rather than a single organization with a single set of books, the exchange actually performed as a trading post for thousands of brokers dealing with millions of corporate stocks. Finding it impossible to subpoena all these records, Pecora chose the method of a questionnaire centered on pool activities for the exchange and all of its members.

On September 30, 1933, Pecora sent two of his staff members, young David Schenker and the more experienced John T. Flynn, to present Whitney with the questionnaires. Whitney immediately recognized Flynn, whom he loathed for his caustic books and anti-Wall Street columns. Flushed with anger, the stock exchange president rushed from the room to compose himself before he could begin any conversation with them. When he returned, the two men requested that the exchange distribute their questionnaires. "You gentlemen are making a great mistake," Whitney said of their investigation. "The Exchange is a perfect institution." Two weeks later, he wrote to Pecora rejecting the request to send out the questionnaires. The cost of time and accountants to prepare answers would run into the millions of dollars, Whitney complained, and he did not feel he had the authority to make exchange members comply.

Pecora responded by subpoenaing records from the most active floor traders on the exchange. With this information, and the advice of the commission houses' brokers who generally opposed Whitney's domination of the exchange, Pecora fashioned a new questionnaire which he sent directly to the 1,375 exchange members, and a special questionnaire for the exchange itself. It then took months for the recipients to complete and return these questionnaires, and for Pecora's staff to wade through the accumulated data.

In the interim, the Banking Committee's hearings continued at a hectic pace and with a wide variety of witnesses. John J. Raskob appeared again to explain a large speculative loan that he and former Governor Alfred E. Smith had received from the Chase National Bank. Reconstruction Finance Corporation chief Jesse H. Jones testified on loans his agency had made to Texas banks with which he was associated. Harry Sinclair of Teapot Dome fame came under subpoena to discuss syndicate dealings in Sinclair Oil stock. The seeming unwieldiness of the hearings caused some dissension. "Pecora was like a police chief who rounds up all the suspicious characters in town to solve a jewel robbery," presidential-advisor Raymond Moley sniffed. But Pecora also bore much pressure not to miss any opportunities to expose financial ills. Banking Committee members each had areas of special concern they urged upon him. Michigan Senator James Couzens directed him towards the Detroit bank crisis. Ohio Senator Robert Bulkley was interested in the Cleveland bank situation. New Jersey Senator Hamilton Kean asked for an investigation of short selling in airline stocks. Eventually the long length and diversification of the hearings began to weigh upon their effectiveness. The three-ring-atmosphere of New Deal Washington came to dwarf Pecora's side show. His additional evidence disappeared into the financial pages, and only occasionally could he grab new headlines. Senator Fletcher finally concluded that the hearings had lasted long enough. He asked for completion by January 1, 1934, in time for the committee to draft legislative recommendations.

Competition from other quarters also hastened the committee's concern for a stock exchange bill. Although Untermyer had made little progress with his bill, a special committee under the chairmanship of Assistant Secretary of Commerce John Dickinson was also examining stock exchange regulation. Roosevelt had appointed the Dickinson Committee in response to both the July market crash and the growing hostility on Wall Street to the strict Securities Act. Characteristically, the President had filled the committee with a mixture of liberal reformers and arch-conservatives. As a result, they had produced a blandly moderate report. Racing against the Dickinson Committee, one of Pecora's staff investigators, Max Lowenthal, approached Securities Act drafters Corcoran, Cohen, and Landis and asked them to assist in preparing an exchange bill for the Banking Committee. Lowenthal, like the three young men, was a representative of Felix Frankfurter's large contingency of former law students working in the New Deal, and he knew he could count on their help. Landis, then an FTC commissioner, sent two young aides, I.N.P. Stokes and Telford Taylor, to draft the initial versions of the bill. Cohen and Corcoran revised their draft, working nights, weekends, and vacations, while holding other government positions. By January when the Dickinson report went to the White House and when Senator Fletcher was ready to ask Pecora for a bill, they had almost finished.

Fletcher's request caught Pecora in the middle of his investigation into the complicated Detroit banking collapse. Unwilling to break off the hearings, he accepted the Cohen and Corcoran draft and assigned several of his aides, including Schenker, Saperstein, Meehan, Lowenthal, and Flynn to help shape the bill into final form. After so many months of delving into Wall Street malpractice, these staff members found the Cohen-Corcoran draft far too lenient to suit their tastes. Rather than grant broad discretionary powers to any regulatory agency, they wanted the bill to specifically prohibit all forms of stock manipulation, such as short selling, pools, and wash sales. Furthermore, they insisted that the bill forbid brokers from buying and selling for their own accounts at the same time they transacted business for their clients. To prevent conflict of interest, they wanted brokers to choose either one function or the other, but not to practice both. John Flynn, who passionately distrusted all bankers and brokers, warned that any vague sections in the bill would permit shrewd Wall Street lawyers to circumvent its basic intent. Flynn's strong arguments accounted for much of the stringency in the final draft. Both Cohen and Corcoran recognized they were working for Pecora and must adhere to the wishes of his staff. In a final forty-eight hour session of continuous work, the combined group produced a bill which Pecora could wholeheartedly endorse.

As the legislative process took up the exchange bill, Pecora's role diminished. He concluded his investigations into the Detroit and Cleveland banking structures as the Senate Banking Committee prepared to open hearings on the bill. The whole focus of committee procedures shifted, with the center of attention moving from the counsel as prosecutor questioning unsuspecting witnesses to the witnesses as advocates, arriving with prepared speeches for or against the bill. Where the senators had previously permitted Pecora to conduct the questioning relatively unhindered, they now took the lead in quizzing the witnesses themselves. When Thomas Corcoran appeared to defend the exchange bill, the committee even permitted Roland Redmond, counsel for the New York Stock Exchange, to cross-examine him. Pecora fell increasingly into the background.

The New York Stock Exchange and its allies conducted a bitter lobbying and publicity campaign against the bill, convincing many congressmen of the need for compromises in the stern first draft. Whitney testified that the bill, by tampering with margin trading, might disrupt the nation's credit system, that its requirements for regular financial reports would be "absolutely prohibitive," and that it might drive stocks and investors to foreign exchanges. Instead, he proposed a program of exchange self-regulation through participation on a federal regulatory panel, similar to the Dickinson Committee recommendations. Conservative opposition in Congress, small but intense, followed this line. Republican representatives also attacked Cohen and Corcoran personally as the boys from "the little red house in Georgetown" who had prepared the bill to "Russianize everything worthwhile."

By the time the conference committee met to settle differences between House and Senate versions of the exchange bill, the original draft had undergone serious revision. The congressmen had reduced margin requirements and made them more flexible, authorized a new Securities and Exchange Commission, and delegated to it powers to oversee the activities of the nation's stock exchanges. Congress also avoided prohibiting several controversial practices and, instead, authorized the SEC to carry out further studies on segregation of broker-dealer functions, regulation of the vast "over-the-counter" market of unlisted securities, and revising exchange rules for more self-regulation. After it passed overwhelmingly in both houses, Cohen and Corcoran found genuine pleasure with the compromise bill. Both suspected that they would never have gained so much if the original draft had not been so demanding. But many of the Pecora staffers were bitterly disappointed with the enacted law. They especially blamed Treasury Department and Federal Reserve Board conservatives for weakening the measure and scorned the President for not endorsing their draft more vigorously. "One word from Franklin D. Roosevelt, and the dramatic first bill would have been passed with a whoop," Flynn concluded in disgust.

Passage of the Securities and Exchange Act of 1934 brought the Pecora investigations to a close, an event not entirely satisfying to the chief counsel. He still had numerous topics left which he had hoped to cover. Max Lowenthal and others begged him to reconsider demobilizing his staff and reminded him of the work remaining. Pecora himself had hoped to conduct an extensive survey into the abuses of protective committees which reorganized bankrupt corporations. But time had run out. Many of these unfinished examinations became the responsibility of the new SEC, including the protective committee study which two young Yale faculty members, William O. Douglas and Abe Fortas, ably conducted for the agency.

In his final report, drawn from the twenty-two volumes of committee transcripts and still unused evidence, Pecora strongly indicated the need for further study and additional legislation. The Glass-Steagall Banking Act, for instance, had made a first step in detaching investment houses from the powerful banks, but too often these divisions were more real on paper than in practice. J. P. Morgan & Company gave up its securities business to the newly created firm of Morgan, Stanley & Company, and Morgan placed his son Henry in charge of this "independent" house. Brown Brothers, Harriman & Company continued as a commercial bank, while it created Brown, Harriman & Company to assume its investment business; W. Averell Harriman and his family remained as major stockholders in both. The income tax laws also needed revision. Attorney General Homer Cummings was already conducting further investigations into tax evasions on the part of bankers and brokers, even delving into the tax returns of former Treasury Secretary Andrew Mellon. Pecora was especially pleased to note that the Internal Revenue Service had recovered several million dollars in back taxes as a result of the hearings, far more than the $225,000 which the investigation had cost the government.

Whatever Pecora's admiration for the frugality of the hearings, their low budget had placed serious financial burdens upon him. He had dropped his own private law practice and felt uneasy about resuming it. Fundamentally, he could not envision serving as counsel for the banking and brokerage houses he had so recently exposed, and yet he knew the pressures he would feel to take their cases. Nor had the meager $255-a-month salary he collected during the hearings helped his financial independence. When the hearings came to a close, the Banking Committee met in executive session with Pecora to discuss that very question. His persistent nemesis, Carter Glass, introduced a resolution to compensate Pecora for the true worth of his time and energy. Glass proposed that the Senate pass a special appropriation of not less than $125,000 for his services, "a drop in the bucket" compared with the retainers of the Wall Street lawyers appearing in adversary during the hearings. The full committee unanimously approved Glass's resolution, but Pecora asked them not to pass it. He had acted strictly out of public service, he explained. Furthermore, having received an outpouring of mail from across the country commending him for working on a small salary, he could not accept such a large reward now.

His refusal was altruistic, but Pecora also had political ambitions. In October 1933, for example, he had acquiesced to the urgings of James Farley and President Roosevelt to accept the reform Democratic nomination for New York district attorney, although he could campaign only on weekends so as not to interrupt his hearings. In the LaGuardia fusion sweep in that municipal election, Pecora lost badly. Many observers, however, felt that the President owed him a favor. Pecora dropped a hint to that effect at the White House ceremony when Roosevelt signed the Securities and Exchange Act. "Ferd, now that I have signed this bill and it has become law, what kind of a law will it be?" the President asked as he handed him one of the pens. "It will be a good bill or a bad bill, Mr. President," Pecora replied, "depending upon the men who administer it." Afterwards, Pecora let it become widely known in Washington that he expected the chairmanship of the new SEC.

It came as a definite shock to Pecora, therefore, when Roosevelt nominated him for a one-year post on the commission and gave the five-year post, with his implicit approval for chairman, to financier Joseph P. Kennedy. Only a few months earlier, Pecora had uncovered Kennedy's name as a participant in a pool of Libby-Owens-Ford Glass Company stocks during the July crash. Neither he nor his staff could believe that such a stock market operator could lead the commission they had helped create. "I did not in my wildest dreams imagine he would appoint a speculator as chairman of that body," John T. Flynn exclaimed. "I say it isn't true. It is impossible. It could not happen." Pecora thought first of refusing the appointment, but then he appeared for the swearing-in ceremony and delayed it for two hours while he privately negotiated with Kennedy over commission policies and personnel. Several of his assistants from the hearings, including Saperstein, Schenker, and Stephens, eventually followed him to the SEC. But after so long in the spotlight as the leader of the hearings, Pecora could not adjust to the bureaucratic routines of the new regulatory commissions. Within six months he resigned the post to take a seat on the New York Supreme Court, where he remained for the rest of his career, with the exception of an unsuccessful campaign for mayor of New York in 1950.

Nor were the years of aftermath totally rewarding for other participants in the Pecora hearings. Albert Wiggin returned to his retirement still wealthy, but with his reputation shattered. J. P. Morgan left the Pecora hearings only to face more congressional scrutiny before the Nye Committee. Increasingly, Morgan withdrew from his banking firm and spent his last ten years as far away from press photographers as he could. In 1940 the Morgan bank finally incorporated, and in 1942 it joined the Federal Reserve System, ending its aloof and private status. Richard Whitney, the aristocratic president of the New York Stock Exchange, lost his position with the help of new SEC-sponsored exchange rules. In 1938 he confessed to insolvency and admitted to embezzling funds entrusted to his investment company. As his property went on the auction block to pay his debts, Whitney left for imprisonment at Sing Sing. Of all the discredited witnesses, Charles E. Mitchell emerged the most honorably in later years. In 1938 the Supreme Court ruled he owed the government $1,100,000 in taxes and penalties. Refusing to declare bankruptcy because it was not the "square" thing to do, Mitchell worked for years to repay his taxes and debts.

The Pecora investigations and the creation of the Securities and Exchange Commission profoundly affected Wall Street. They transformed the New York Stock Exchange from an almost private club into a semi-public institution, and they made the federal government responsible for overseeing nationally vital banking and brokerage activities. The flagrant financial abuses that characterized the 1920s became less pronounced, although they did not disappear. Five years later, while writing his memoirs of the hearings, *Wall Street Under Oath,* Pecora predicted possible regression. "These laws are no panacea; nor are they self-executing," he warned. "More than ever we must maintain our vigilance. If we do not, Wall Street may yet prove to be not unlike that land, of which it has been said that no country is easier to overrun or harder to subdue."

LOUIS D. BRANDEIS ON *OTHER PEOPLE'S MONEY* 1914

Louis D. Brandeis, *Other People's Money, And How the Bankers Use It* (New York, 1914), reprinted, 1971, 4–28.

The dominant element in our financial oligarchy is the investment banker. Associated banks, trust companies and life insurance companies are his tools. Controlled railroads, public service and industrial corporations are his subjects. Though properly but middlemen, these bankers bestride as masters America's business world, so that practically no large enterprise can be undertaken successfully without their participation or approval. These bankers are, of course, able men possessed of large fortunes; but the most potent factor in their control of business is not the possession of extraordinary ability or huge wealth. The key to their power is Combination—concentration intensive and comprehensive—advancing on three distinct lines:

First:
There is the obvious consolidation of banks and trust companies; the less obvious affiliations—through stockholdings, voting trusts and interlocking directorates—of banking institutions which are not legally connected; and the joint transactions, gentlemen's agreements, and "banking ethics" which eliminate competition among the investment bankers.

Second:
There is the consolidation of railroads into huge systems, the large combinations of public service corporations and the formation of industrial trusts, which, by making business so "big" that local, independent banking concerns cannot alone supply the necessary funds, has created dependence upon the associated New York bankers.

But combination, however intensive, along these lines only, could not have produced the Money Trust—another and more potent factor of combination was added.

Third:
Investment bankers, like J. P. Morgan & Co., dealers in bonds, stocks and notes, encroached upon the functions of the three other classes of corporations with which their business brought them into contact. They became the directing power in railroads, public service and industrial companies through which our great business operations are conducted—the makers of bonds and stocks. They became the directing power in the life insurance companies, and other corporate reservoirs of the people's savings—the buyers of bonds and stocks. They became the directing power also in banks and trust companies

—the depositaries of the quick capital of the country—the life blood of business, with which they and others carried on their operations. Thus four distinct functions, each essential to business, and each exercised, originally, by a distinct set of men, became united in the investment banker. It is to this union of business functions that the existence of the Money Trust is mainly due.[1]

The development of our financial oligarchy followed, in this respect, lines with which the history of political despotism has familiarized us:—usurpation, proceeding by gradual encroachment rather than by violent acts; subtle and often long-concealed concentration of distinct functions, which are beneficent when separately administered, and dangerous only when combined in the same persons. It was by processes such as these that Caesar Augustus became master of Rome. The makers of our own Constitution had in mind like dangers to our political liberty when they provided so carefully for the separation of governmental powers.

The Proper Sphere of the Investment Banker

The original function of the investment banker was that of dealer in bonds, stocks and notes; buying mainly at wholesale from corporations, municipalities, states and governments which need money, and selling to those seeking investments. The banker performs, in this respect, the function of a merchant; and the function is a very useful one. Large business enterprises are conducted generally by corporations. The permanent capital of corporations is represented by bonds and stocks. The bonds and stocks of the more important corporations are owned, in large part, by small investors, who do not participate in the management of the company. Corporations require the aid of a banker-middleman, for they lack generally the reputation and clientele essential to selling their own bonds and stocks direct to the investor. Investors in corporate securities, also, require the services of a banker-middleman. The number of securities upon the market is very large. Only a part of these securities is listed on the New York Stock Exchange; but its listings alone comprise about sixteen hundred different issues aggregating about $26,500,000,000, and each year new listings are made averaging about two hundred and thirty-three to an amount of $1,500,000,000. For a small investor to make an intelligent selection from these many corporate securities—indeed, to pass an intelligent judgment upon a single one—is ordinarily impossible. He lacks the ability, the facilities, the training and the time essential to a proper investigation. Unless his purchase is to be little better than a gamble, he needs the advice of an expert, who, combining special knowledge with judgment, has the facilities and incentive to make a thorough investigation. This dependence, both of corporations and of investors, upon the banker has grown in recent years, since women and others who do not participate in the management, have become the owners of so large a part of the stocks and bonds of our great corporations. Over half of the stockholders of the American Sugar Refining Company and nearly half of the stockholders of

[1] Obviously only a few of the investment bankers exercise this great power; but many others perform important functions in the system, as hereinafter described.

the Pennsylvania Railroad and of the New York, New Haven & Hartford Railroad are women.

Good-will—the possession by a dealer of numerous and valuable regular customers—is always an important element in merchandising. But in the business of selling bonds and stocks, it is of exceptional value, for the very reason that the small investor relies so largely upon the banker's judgment. This confidential relation of the banker to customers and the knowledge of the customers' private affairs acquired incidentally—is often a determining factor in the marketing of securities. With the advent of Big Business such good-will possessed by the older banking houses, preëminently J. P. Morgan & Co. and their Philadelphia House called Drexel & Co., by Lee, Higginson & Co. and Kidder, Peabody, & Co. of Boston, and by Kuhn, Loeb & Co. of New York, became of enhanced importance. The volume of new security issues was greatly increased by huge railroad consolidations, the development of the holding companies, and particularly by the formation of industrial trusts. The rapidly accumulating savings of our people sought investment. The field of operations for the dealer in securities was thus much enlarged. And, as the securities were new and untried, the services of the investment banker were in great demand, and his powers and profits increased accordingly.

Controlling the Security Makers

But this enlargement of their legitimate field of operations did not satisfy investment bankers. They were not content merely to deal in securities. They desired to manufacture them also. They became promoters, or allied themselves with promoters. Thus it was that J. P. Morgan & Company formed the Steel Trust, the Harvester Trust and the Shipping Trust. And, adding the duties of undertaker to those of midwife, the investment bankers became, in times of corporate disaster, members of security-holders' "Protective Committees"; then they participated as "Reorganization Managers" in the reincarnation of the unsuccessful corporations and ultimately became directors. It was in this way that the Morgan associates acquired their hold upon the Southern Railway, the Northern Pacific, the Reading, the Erie, the Pere Marquette, the Chicago and Great Western, and the Cincinnati, Hamilton & Dayton. Often they insured the continuance of such control by the device of the voting trust; but even where no voting trust was created, a secure hold was acquired upon reorganization. It was in this way also that Kuhn, Loeb & Co. became potent in the Union Pacific and in the Baltimore & Ohio.

But the banker's participation in the management of corporations was not limited to cases of promotion or reorganization. An urgent or extensive need of new money was considered a sufficient reason for the banker's entering a board of directors. Often without even such excuse the investment banker has secured a place upon the Board of Directors, through his powerful influence or the control of his customers' proxies. Such seems to have been the fatal entrance of Mr. Morgan into the management of the then prosperous New York, New Haven & Hartford Railroad, in 1892. When once a banker has entered the Board—whatever may have been the occasion—his grip proves tenacious and his influence usually supreme; for he controls the supply of new money.

The investment banker is naturally on the lookout for good bargains in bonds and stocks. Like other merchants he wants to buy his merchandise cheap. But when he becomes director of a corporation, he occupies a position which prevents the transaction by which he acquires its corporate securities from being properly called a bargain. Can there be real bargaining where the same man is on both sides of a trade? The investment banker, through his controlling influence on the Board of Directors, decides that the corporation shall issue and sell the securities, decides the price at which it shall sell them, and decides that it shall sell the securities to himself. The fact that there are other directors besides the banker on the Board does not, in practice, prevent this being the result. The banker, who holds the purse-strings, becomes usually the dominant spirit. Through voting-trusteeships, exclusive financial agencies, membership on executive or finance committees, or by mere directorships, J. P. Morgan & Co., and their associates, held such financial power in at least thirty-two transportation systems, public utility corporations and industrial companies—companies with an aggregate capitalization of $17,273,000,000. Mainly for corporations so controlled, J. P. Morgan & Co. procured the public marketing in ten years of security issues aggregating $1,950,000,000. This huge sum does not include any issues marketed privately, nor any issues, however, marketed, of intra-state corporations. Kuhn, Loeb & Co. and a few other investment bankers exercise similar control over many other corporations.

Controlling Security Buyers

Such control of railroads, public service and industrial corporations assures to the investment bankers an ample supply of securities at attractive prices; and merchandise well bought is half sold. But these bond and stock merchants are not disposed to take even a slight risk as to their ability to market their goods. They saw that if they could control the security-buyers, as well as the security-makers, investment banking would, indeed, be "a happy hunting ground"; and they have made it so.

The numerous small investors cannot, in the strict sense, be controlled; but their dependence upon the banker insures their being duly influenced. A large part, however, of all bonds issued and of many stocks are bought by the prominent corporate investors; and most prominent among these are the life insurance companies, the trust companies, and the banks. The purchase of a security by these institutions not only relieves the banker of the merchandise, but recommends it strongly to the small investor, who believes that these institutions are wisely managed. These controlled corporate investors are not only large customers, but may be particularly accommodating ones. Individual investors are moody. They buy only when they want to do so. They are sometimes inconveniently reluctant. Corporate investors, if controlled, may be made to buy when the bankers need a market. It was natural that the investment bankers proceeded to get control of the great life insurance companies, as well as of the trust companies and the banks.

The field thus occupied is uncommonly rich. The life insurance companies are our leading institutions for savings. Their huge surplus and reserves, augmented daily, are always clamoring for investment. No panic or money shortage stops the inflow of new money from the perennial stream of premiums on existing policies and interest on existing investments. The three great companies—the New York Life, the Mutual of New York, and the Equitable—would have over $55,000,000 of *new* money to invest annually, even if they did not issue a single new policy. In 1904—just before the Armstrong investigation—these three companies had together $1,247,331,738.18 of assets. They had issued in that year $1,025,671,126 of new policies. The New York legislature placed in 1906 certain restrictions upon their growth; so that their new business since has averaged $547,384,212, or only fifty-three per cent. of what it was in 1904. But the aggregate assets of these companies increased in the last eight years to $1,817,052,260.36. At the time of the Armstrong investigation the average age of these three companies was fifty-six years. *The growth of assets in the last eight years was about half as large as the total growth in the preceding fifty-six years.* These three companies must invest annually about $70,000,000 of new money; and besides, many old investments expire or are changed and the proceeds must be reinvested. A large part of all life insurance surplus and reserves are invested in bonds. The aggregate bond investments of these three companies on January 1, 1913, was $1,019,153,268.93.

It was natural that the investment bankers should seek to control these never-failing reservoirs of capital. George W. Perkins was Vice-President of the New York Life, the largest of the companies. While remaining such he was made a partner in J. P. Morgan & Co., and in the four years preceding the Armstrong investigation, his firm sold the New York Life $38,804,918.51 in securities. The New York Life is a mutual company, supposed to be controlled by its policy holders. But as the Pujo Committee finds "the so-called control of life insurance companies by policy-holders through mutualization is a farce" and "its only result is to keep in office a self-constituted, self-perpetuating management."

The Equitable Life Assurance Society is a stock company and is controlled by $100,000 of stock. The dividend on this stock is limited by law to seven percent.; but in 1910 Mr. Morgan paid about $3,000,000 for $51,000, par value of this stock, or $5,882.35 a share. The dividend return on the stock investment is less than one-eighth of one per cent.; but the assets controlled amount now to over $500,000,000. And certain of these assets had an especial value for investment bankers;—namely, the large holdings of stock in banks and trust companies.

The Armstrong investigation disclosed the extent of financial power exerted through the insurance company holdings of bank and trust company stock. The Committee recommended legislation compelling the insurance companies to dispose of the stock within five years. A law to that effect was enacted, but the time was later extended. The companies then disposed of a part of their bank and trust company stocks; but, as the insurance companies were controlled by the investment bankers, these gentlemen sold the bank and trust company stocks to themselves.

Referring to such purchases from the Mutual Life, as well as from the Equitable, the Pujo Committee found:

Here, then, were stocks of five important trust companies and one of our largest national banks in New York City that had been held by these two life insurance companies. Within five years all of these stocks, so far as distributed by the insurance companies, have found their way into the hands of the men who virtually controlled or were identified with the management of the insurance companies or of their close allies and associates, to that extent thus further entrenching them.

The banks and trust companies are depositaries, in the main, not of the people's savings, but of the business man's quick capital. Yet, since the investment banker acquired control of banks and trust companies, these institutions also have become, like the life companies, large purchasers of bonds and stocks. Many of our national banks have invested in this manner a large part of all their resources, including capital, surplus and deposits. The bond investments of some banks exceed by far the aggregate of their capital and surplus, and nearly equal their loanable deposits.

Controlling Other People's Quick Capital

The goose that lays golden eggs has been considered a most valuable possession. But even more profitable is the privilege of taking the golden eggs laid by somebody else's goose. The investment bankers and their associates now enjoy that privilege. They control the people through the people's own money. If the bankers' power were commensurate only with their wealth, they would have relatively little influence on American business. Vast fortunes like those of the Astors are no doubt regrettable. They are inconsistent with democracy. They are unsocial. And they seem peculiarly unjust when they represent largely unearned increment. But the wealth of the Astors does not endanger political or industrial liberty. It is insignificant in amount as compared with the aggregate wealth of America, or even of New York City. It lacks significance largely because its owners have only the income from their own wealth. The Astor wealth is static. The wealth of the Morgan associates is dynamic. The power and the growth of power of our financial oligarchs comes from wielding the savings and quick capital of others. In two of the three great life insurance companies the influence of J. P. Morgan & Co. and their associates is exerted without any individual investment by them whatsoever. Even in the Equitable, where Mr. Morgan bought an actual majority of all the outstanding stock, his investment amounts to little more than one-half of one per cent. of the assets of the company. The fetters which bind the people are forged from the people's own gold.

But the reservoir of other people's money, from which the investment bankers now draw their greatest power, is not the life insurance companies, but the banks and the trust companies. Bank deposits represent the really quick capital of the nation. They are the life blood of businesses. Their effective force is much greater than that of an equal amount of wealth permanently invested. The 34 banks and trust companies, which the Pujo Committee declared to be directly controlled by the Morgan associates, held $1,983,000,000 in deposits. Control of these institutions means the ability to lend a large part of these funds, directly and indirectly, to themselves; and what is often even more important, the power to prevent the funds being lent to any rival interests. These huge deposits can, in the discretion of those in control, be used to meet the temporary needs of their subject corporations. When bonds and stocks are issued to finance permanently these corporations, the bank deposits can, in large part, be loaned by the investment bankers in control to themselves and their associates; so that securities bought may be carried by them, until sold to investors. Or these bank deposits may be loaned to allied bankers, or jobbers in securities, or to speculators, to enable them to carry the bonds or stocks. Easy money tends to make securities rise in the market. Tight money nearly always makes them fall. The control by the leading investment bankers over the banks and trust companies is so great, that they can often determine, for a time, the market for money by lending or refusing to lend on the Stock Exchange. In this way, among others, they have power to affect the general trend of prices in bonds and stocks. Their power over a particular security is even greater. Its sale on the market may depend upon whether the security is favored or discriminated against when offered to the banks and trust companies, as collateral for loans.

Furthermore, it is the investment banker's access to other people's money in controlled banks and trust companies which alone enables any individual banking concern to take so large part of the annual output of bonds and stocks. The banker's own capital, however large, would soon be exhausted. And even the loanable funds of the banks would often be exhausted, but for the large deposits made in those banks by the life insurance, railroad, public service, and industrial corporations which the bankers also control. On December 31, 1912, the three leading life insurance companies had deposits in banks and trust companies aggregating $13,839,189.08. As the Pujo Committee finds:

> The men who through their control over the funds of our railroads and industrial companies are able to direct where such funds shall be kept and thus to create these great reservoirs of the people's money, are the ones who are in position to tap those reservoirs for the ventures in which they are interested and to prevent their being tapped for purposes of which they do not approve. The latter is quite as important a factor as the former. It is the controlling consideration in its effect on competition in the railroad and industrial world.

Having Your Cake and Eating It Too

But the power of the investment banker over other people's money is often more direct and effective than that exerted through controlled banks and trust companies. J. P. Morgan & Co. achieve the supposedly impossible feat of having their cake and eating it too. They buy the bonds and stocks of controlled railroads and industrial concerns, and pay the purchase price; and still do not part with their money. This is accomplished by the simple device of becoming the bank of deposit of the controlled corporations, instead of having the company deposit in some merely controlled bank in whose operation others have at least some share. When J. P. Morgan & Co. buy an issue of securities the purchase money, instead of being paid over to the corporation, is retained by the banker for the corporation, to be drawn upon only as the funds are needed by the corporation. And as the securities are issued in large blocks, and the money raised is often not all spent until long thereafter, the aggregate of the balances remaining in the bankers' hands are huge. Thus J. P. Morgan & Co. (including their Philadelphia house, called Drexel & Co.) held on November 1, 1912, deposits aggregating $162,491,819.65.

Power and Pelf

The operations of so comprehensive a system of concentration necessarily developed in the bankers overweening power. And the bankers' power grows by what it feeds on. Power begets wealth; and added wealth opens ever new opportunities for the acquisition of wealth and power. The operations of these bankers are so vast and numerous that even a very reasonable compensation for the service performed by the bankers, would, in the aggregate, produce for them incomes so large as to result in huge accumulations of capital. But the compensation taken by the bankers as commissions or profits is often far from reasonable. Occupying, as they so frequently do, the inconsistent position of being at the same time seller and buyer, the standard for so-called compensation actually applied, is not the "Rule of reason," but "All the traffic will bear." And this is true even where there is no sinister motive. The weakness of human nature prevents men from being good judges of their own deservings.

The syndicate formed by J. P. Morgan & Co. to underwrite the United States Steel Corporation took for its services securities which netted $62,500,000 in cash. Of this huge sum J. P. Morgan & Co. received, as syndicate managers, $12,500,000 in addition to the share which they were entitled to receive as syndicate members. This sum of $62,500,000 was only a part of the fees paid for the service of monopolizing the steel industry. In addition to the commissions taken specifically for organizing the United States Steel Corporation, large sums were paid for organizing the several companies of which it is composed. For instance, the National Tube Company was capitalized at $80,000,000 of stock; $40,000,000 of which was common stock. Half of this $40,000,000 was taken by J. P. Morgan & Co. and their associates for promotion services; and the $20,000,000 stock so taken became later exchangeable for $25,000,000 of Steel Common. Commissioner of Corporations Herbert Knox Smith found that:

> More than $150,000,000 of the stock of the Steel Corporation was issued directly or indirectly (through exchange) for mere promotion or underwriting services. In other words, nearly one-seventh of the total capital stock of the Steel Corporation appears to have been issued directly or indirectly to promoters' services.

The so-called fees and commissions taken by the bankers and associates upon the organization of the trusts have been exceptionally large. But even after the trusts are successfully launched the exactions of the bankers are often extortionate. The syndicate which underwrote, in 1901, the Steel Corporation's preferred stock conversion plan, advanced only $20,000,000 in cash and received an underwriting commission of $6,800,000.

The exaction of huge commissions is not confined to trust and other industrial concerns. The Interborough Railway is a most prosperous corporation. It earned last year nearly 21 per cent. on its capital stock, and secured from New York City, in connection with the subway extension, a very favorable contract. But when it financed its $170,000,000 bond issue it was agreed that J. P. Morgan & Co. should receive three per cent., that is, $5,100,000, for merely forming this syndicate. More recently, the New York, New Haven & Hartford Railroad agreed to pay J. P. Morgan & Co. a commission of $1,680,000; that is, 2½ per cent., to form a syndicate to underwrite an issue at par of $67,000,000 20-year 6 per cent. convertible debentures. That means: The bankers bound themselves to take at 97½ any of these six per cent. convertible bonds which stockholders might be unwilling to buy at 100. When the contract was made the New Haven's then outstanding six per cent. convertible bonds were selling at 114. And the new issue, as soon as announced, was in such demand that the public offered and was for months willing to buy at 106 bonds which the Company were to pay J. P. Morgan & Co. $1,680,000 to be willing to take at par.

Why the Banks Became Investment Bankers

These large profits from promotions, underwritings and security purchases led to a revolutionary change in the conduct of our leading banking institutions. It was obvious that control by the investment bankers of the deposits in banks and trust companies was an essential element in their securing these huge profits. And the bank officers naturally asked, "Why then should not the banks and trust companies share in so profitable a field? Why should not they themselves become investment bankers too, with all the new functions incident to 'Big Business'?" To do so would involve a departure from the legitimate sphere of the banking business, which is the making of temporary loans to business concerns. But the temptation was irresistible. The invasion of the investment banker into the banks' field of operation was followed by a counter invasion by the banks into the realm of the investment banker. Most prominent among the banks were the National City and the First National of New York. But theirs was not a hostile invasion. The contending forces met as allies, joined forces to control the business of the country, and to "divide the spoils." The alliance was cemented by voting trusts, by interlocking directorates and by joint ownerships. There resulted the fullest "cooperation"; and ever more railroads, public service corporations, and industrial concerns were brought into complete subjection.

HOW THE COMBINERS COMBINE

Among the allies, two New York banks—the National City and the First National—stand preëminent. They constitute, with the Morgan firm, the inner group of the Money Trust. Each of the two banks, like J. P. Morgan & Co., has huge resources. Each of the two banks, like the firm of J. P. Morgan & Co., has been dominated by a genius in combination. In the National City it is James Stillman; in the First National, George F. Baker. Each of these gentlemen was formerly President, and is now Chairman of the Board of Directors. The resources of the National City Bank (including its Siamese-twin security company) are about $300,000,000; those of the First National Bank (including its Siamese-twin security company) are about $200,000,000. The resources of the Morgan firm have not been disclosed. But it appears that they have available for their operations, also, huge deposits from their subjects; deposits reported as $162,500,000.

The private fortunes of the chief actors in the combination have not been ascertained. But sporadic evidence indicates how great are the possibilities of accumulation when one has the use of "other people's money." Mr. Morgan's wealth became proverbial. Of Mr. Stillman's many investments, only one was specifically referred to, as he was in Europe during the investigation, and did not testify. But that one is significant. His 47,498 shares in the National City Bank are worth about $18,000,000. Mr. Jacob H. Schiff [2] aptly described this as "a very nice investment."

Of Mr. Baker's investments we know more, as he testified on many subjects. His 20,000 shares in the First National Bank are worth at least $20,000,000. His stocks in six other New York banks and trust companies are together worth about $3,000,000. The scale of his investment in railroads may be inferred from his former holdings in the Central Railroad of New Jersey. He was its largest stockholder—so large that with a few friends he held a majority of the $27,436,800 par value of outstanding stock, which the Reading bought at $160 a share. He is a director in 28 other railroad companies; and presumably a stockholder in, at least, as many. The full extent of his fortune was not inquired into, for that was not an issue in the investigation. But it is not surprising that Mr. Baker saw little need on new laws. When asked:

"You think everything is all right as it is in this world, do you not?"
He answered:
"Pretty nearly."

Ramifications of Power

But wealth expressed in figures gives a wholly inadequate picture of the allies' power. Their wealth is dynamic. It is wielded by geniuses in combination. It finds its proper expression in means of control. To comprehend the power of the allies we must try to visualize the ramifications through which the forces operate.

Mr. Baker is a director in 22 corporations having, with their many subsidiaries, aggregate resources or capitalization of $7,272,000,000. But the direct and visible power of the First National Bank, which Mr. Baker dominates, extends further. The Pujo report shows that its directors (including Mr. Baker's son) are directors in at least 27 other corporations with resources of $4,270,000,000. That is, the First National is represented in 49 corporations, with aggregate resources or capitalization of $11,542,000,000.

It may help to an appreciation of the allies' power to name a few of the more prominent corporations in which, for instance, Mr. Baker's influence is

[2] Jacob Henry Schiff, 1847–1920, head of Kuhn, Loeb & Company from 1885 virtually until his death.

exerted—visibly and directly—as voting trustee, executive committee man or simple director.

1. *Banks, Trust, and Life Insurance Companies:* First National Bank of New York; National Bank of Commerce; Farmers' Loan and Trust Company; Mutual Life Insurance Company.
2. *Railroad Companies:* New York Central Lines; New Haven, Reading, Erie, Lackawanna, Lehigh Valley, Southern, Northern Pacific, Chicago, Burlington & Quincy.
3. *Public Service Corporations:* American Telegraph & Telephone Company, Adams Express Company.
4. *Industrial Corporations:* United States Steel Corporation, Pullman Company.

Mr. Stillman is a director in only 7 corporations, with aggregate assets of $2,476,000,000; but the directors in the National City Bank, which he dominates, are directors in at least 41 other corporations which, with their subsidiaries, have an aggregate capitalization or resources of $10,564,000,000. The members of the firm of J. P. Morgan & Co., the acknowledged leader of the allied forces, hold 72 directorships in 47 of the largest corporations of the country.

The Pujo Committee finds that the members of J. P. Morgan & Co. and the directors of their controlled trust companies and of the First National and the National City Bank together hold:

> One hundred and eighteen directorships in 34 banks and trust companies having total resources of $2,679,000,000 and total deposits of $1,983,000,000.
> Thirty directorships in 10 insurance companies having total assets of $2,293,000,000.
> One hundred and five directorships in 32 transportation systems having a total capitalization of $11,784,000,000 and a total mileage (excluding express companies and steamship lines) of 150,200.
> Sixty-three directorships in 24 producing and trading corporations having a total capitalization of $3,339,000,000.
> Twenty-five directorships in 12 public-utility corporations having a total capitalization of $2,150,000,000.
> In all, 341 directorships in 112 corporations having aggregate resources or capitalization of $22,245,000,000.

Twenty-Two Billion Dollars

Twenty-two billion dollars is a large sum—so large that we have difficulty in grasping its significance. The mind realizes size only through comparisons. With what can we compare twenty-two billions of dollars? Twenty-two billions of dollars is more than three times the assessed value of all the property, real and personal, in all New England. It is nearly three times the assessed value of all the real estate in the City of New York. It is more than twice the assessed value of all the property in the thirteen Southern states. It is more than assessed value of all the property in the twenty-two states, north and south, lying west of the Mississippi River.

But the huge sum of twenty-two billion dollars is not large enough to include all the corporations to which the "influence" of the three allies, directly and visibly, extends, for

First:

There are 56 other corporations (not included in the Pujo schedule) each with capital or resources of over $5,000,000, and aggregating nearly $1,350,000,000, in which the Morgan allies are represented according to the directories of directors.

Second:

The Pujo schedule does not include any corporation with resources of less than $5,000,000. But these financial giants have shown their humility by becoming directors in many such. For instance, members of J. P. Morgan & Co., and directors in the National City Bank and the First National Bank are also directors in 158 such corporations. Available publications disclose the capitalization of only 38 of these, but those 38 aggregate $78,669,375.

Third:

The Pujo schedule includes only the corporations in which the Morgan associates actually appear by name as directors. It does not include those in which they are represented by dummies, or otherwise. For instance, the Morgan influence certainly extends to the Kansas City Terminal Railway Company, for which they have marketed since 1910 (in connection with others) four issues aggregating $41,761,000. But no members of J. P. Morgan & Co., of the National City Bank, or of the First National Bank appears on the Kansas City Terminal directorate.

Fourth:

The Pujo schedule does not include all the subsidiaries of the corporations scheduled. For instance, the capitalization of the New Haven System is given as $385,000,000. That sum represents the bond and stock capital of the New Haven *Railroad*. But the New Haven *System* comprises many controlled corporations whose capitalization is only to a slight extent included directly or indirectly in the New Haven Railroad balance sheet. The New Haven, like most large corporations, is a holding company also; and a holding company may control subsidiaries, while owning but a small part of the latters' outstanding securities. Only the small part so held will be represented in the holding company's balance sheet. Thus, while the New Haven Railroad's capitalization is only $385,000,000—and that sum only appears in the Pujo schedule—the capitalization of the New Haven System, as shown by a chart submitted to the Committee, is over twice as great; namely, $849,000,000.

It is clear, therefore, that the $22,000,000,000, referred to by the Pujo Committee, understates the extent of concentration effected by the inner group of the Money Trust.

Cementing the Triple Alliance

Care was taken by these builders of imperial power that their structure should be enduring. It has been buttressed on every side by joint ownerships and mutual stockholdings, as well as by close personal relationships; for directorships are ephemeral and may end with a new election. Mr. Morgan and his partners acquired one-sixth of the stock of the First National Bank, and made a $6,000,000 investment in the stock of the National City Bank. Then J. P. Morgan & Co., the National City, and the First National (or their dominant officers—Mr. Stillman and Mr. Baker) acquired together, by stock purchases and voting trusts, control of the National Bank of Commerce, with its $190,000,000 of resources; of the Chase National, with $125,000,000; of the Guaranty Trust Company, with $232,000,000; of the Bankers' Trust Company, with $205,000,000; and of a number of smaller, but important, financial institutions. They became joint voting trustees in great railroad systems; and finally (as if the allies were united into a single concern) loyal and efficient service in the banks—like that rendered by Mr. Davison and Mr. Lamont in the First National—was rewarded by promotion to membership in the firm of J. P. Morgan & Co.

The Provincial Allies

Thus equipped and bound together, J. P. Morgan & Co., the National City and the First National easily dominated America's financial center, New York; for certain other important bankers, to be hereafter mentioned, were held in restraint by "gentlemen's" agreements. The three allies dominated Philadelphia too; for the firm of Drexel & Co. is J. P. Morgan & Co. under another name. But there are two other important money centers in America, Boston and Chicago.

In Boston there are two large international banking houses—Lee, Higginson & Co., and Kidder, Peabody & Co.—both long established and rich, and each possessing an extensive, wealthy clientele of eager investors in bonds and stocks. Since 1907 each of these firms has purchased or underwritten (principally in conjunction with other bankers) about 100 different security issues of the greater interstate corporations, the issues of each banker amounting in the aggregate to over $1,000,000,000. Concentration of banking capital has proceeded even further in Boston than in New York. By successive consolidations the number of national banks has been reduced from 58 in 1898 to 19 in 1913. There are in Boston now also 23 trust companies.

The National Shawmut Bank, the First National Bank of Boston and the Old Colony Trust Co., which these two Boston banking houses and their associates control, alone have aggregate resources of $288,386,294, constituting about one-half of the banking resources of the city. These great banking institutions, which are themselves the result of many consolidations, and the 21 other banks and trust companies, in which their directors are also directors, hold together 90 per cent. of the total banking resources of Boston. And linked to them by interlocking directorates are 9 other banks and trust companies whose aggregate resources are about 2 ½ per cent. of Boston's total. Thus of 42 banking institutions, 33, with aggregate resources of $560,516,239, holding about 92½ per cent. of the aggregate banking resources of Boston, are interlocked. But even the remaining 9 banks and trust companies, which together hold but 7½ per cent. of Boston banking resources, are not all independent of one another. Three are linked together; so that there appear to be only six banks in all Boston that are free from interlocking directorate relations. They together represent but 5 per cent. of Boston's banking resources. And it may well be doubted whether all of even those 6 are entirely free from affiliation with the other groups.

Boston's banking concentration is not limited to the legal confines of the city. Around Boston proper are over thirty suburbs, which with it form what is popularly known as "Greater Boston." These suburban municipalities, and also other important cities like Worcester and Springfield, are, in many respects, within Boston's "sphere of influence." Boston's inner banking group has interlocked, not only 33 of the 42 banks of Boston proper, as above shown, but has linked with them, by interlocking directorships, at least 42 other banks and trust companies in 35 other municipalities.

Once Lee, Higginson & Co. and Kidder, Peabody & Co. were active competitors. They are so still in some small, or purely local matters; but both are devoted co-operators with the Morgan associates in larger and interstate transactions; and the alliance with these great Boston banking houses has been cemented by mutual stockholdings and co-directorships. Financial concentration seems to have found its highest expression in Boston.

Somewhat similar relations exist between the triple alliance and Chicago's great financial institutions—its First National Bank, the Illinois Trust and Savings Bank, and the Continental & Commercial National Bank—which together control resources of $561,000,000. And similar relations would doubtless be found to exist with the leading bankers of the other important financial centers of America, as to which the Pujo Committee was prevented by lack of time from making investigation. . . .

SENATE RESOLUTION 84
MARCH 4, 1932

U.S. Senate, Stock Exchange Practices, *Hearings Before the Committee on Banking and Currency*, 72nd Congress, 1st Session, Part I, 1.

Resolved, That the Committee on Banking and Currency, or any duly authorized subcommittee thereof, is authorized and directed (1) to make a thorough and complete investigation of the practices with respect to the buying and selling and the borrowing and lending of listed securities upon the various stock exchanges, the values of such securities, and the effect of such practices upon interstate and foreign commerce, upon the operation of the national banking system and the Federal reserve system, and upon the market for securities of the United States Government, and the desirability of the exercise of the taxing power of the United States with respect to any such securities; and (2) to report to the Senate as soon as practicable the results of such investigation and, if in its judgment such practices should be regulated, to submit with such report its recommendations for the necessary remedial legislation.

For the purposes of this resolution the committee, or any duly authorized subcommittee thereof, is authorized to hold such hearings, to sit and act at such times and places during the first session of the Seventy-second Congress, to employ such experts, and clerical, stenographic, and other assistants, to require by subpoena or otherwise the attendance of such witnesses and the production of such books, papers, and documents, to administer such oaths, and to take such testimony and to make such expenditures, as it deems advisable. The cost of stenographic services to report such hearings shall not be in excess of 25 cents per hundred words. The expenses of the committee, which shall not exceed $50,000, shall be paid from the contingent fund of the Senate upon vouchers approved by the chairman of the committee.

TESTIMONY OF RICHARD WHITNEY
APRIL 21, 1832

U.S. Senate, Stock Exchange Practices, *Hearings Before the Committee on Banking and Currency*, 72nd Congress, 1st Session, Part I, 276–81.

Mr. Branch. I should like to make a statement as to my idea of the future conduct of this matter. If the committee does not agree with this I suppose they will let me know. I have very few more questions which I contemplate asking this morning.

Mr. Whitney's statement was that it would take him several days to get the information which the subpoena calls for, and it seems to me it would be better to defer the most of the examination until those figures and statistics are forth coming. There will undoubtedly be other statistics that we will require in the future and which were not mentioned in the subpoena.

Mr. Redmond, it may interest you to have an answer to those questions which Mr. Whitney suggested in his written statement and, of course, I am giving merely my ideas and I assume that if the committee disagrees with me about the matter they will so state at the present time.

Mr. Whitney said in regard to the third section that if the information sought is a list of the members of the exchange who originally executed the selling orders of the stock now held in short account he was afraid it would be almost impossible to answer the question. It does not seem to me that at the present time it is worth while going into that. Unless the committee dissents I think you may assume that that information will not be required at the present time.

Mr. Whitney. And that you merely desire to know in what firms the short accounts now reside.

Mr. Branch. That is, we do not need to go back to the previous accounts at the present time. That was the point you made, was it not, Mr. Whitney?

Senator Gore. Now, on the other hand, the speculator is figuring the prices are too high, that they are fabulously high and can not stay up, and he goes in and sells, figuring they are going down, and they do go down, and he makes a profit. That is a bear raid. He has broken the price of the stock. If, on the other hand, he figures the price is going down and sells short and makes a mistake and the prices go up, he gets stung and takes a loss. He is just as fool- ish to start with, and it serves him right. [Laughter and applause.] Is not that the mental process of people of that sort?

Mr. Whitney. That, I think, is the way the people of the country are thinking.

Senator Gore. That is all, Mr. Chairman.

The Chairman. I want you to get through, Senator Gore. I do not want to interrupt you.

Senator Gore. I am through, Mr. Chairman. I am just trying to get the lamb in the fold, if I can. I would let the bulls and bears fight it out. [Laughter.]

The Chairman. Vanadium earned $1.50 in 1930 and pays no dividend now, but in 1930 hit a new high at 134. Was that the result of a pool operation?

Mr. Whitney. I do not know it, Mr. Chairman. All the steel stocks were selling at tremendous prices in that period. You say 1929?

The Chairman. No; in 1930. It hit the high price in 1930. What action would be taken if it was found that there was a group of brokers whose own records would show they had optioned large amounts of stock for the benefit of pool operators; would that be in violation of the rules?

Mr. Whitney. If they had options to buy stock for pool operators?

The Chairman. If they had optioned large amounts of stock for the benefit of pool operators, if they had gone in with the pool operators to buy the necessary stocks for them?

Mr. Whitney. It would all depend, Mr. Chairman, on what the operation was with reference to the conduct of the pool. There is no objection, certainly, to a man giving an option to another man in a legitimate way. Each and every case would have to stand on its own bottom.

The Chairman. I intended to go into that pool matter quite fully, but it is getting so late that I will just ask a few questions. Is it not a fact that such options are often secured without the payment of cash?

Mr. Whitney. I can not answer that, Mr. Chairman. I do not know.

The Chairman. Is it not a fact that in rigging the market they go out and take options for a certain time, at a certain price, and then later at another price, and then often it is done even without the investment of cash and without a single question being asked?

Mr. Whitney. I will try to answer that question in connection with Senator Brookhart's.

The Chairman. All right.

Mr. Whitney. I don't know what you mean. I would like you to explain what you mean by rigging a market.

The Chairman. Oh, every person in this room knows what rigging a market is. I am not going to try to explain that to the best informed man on the stock market present. [Laughter.] Market letters have gone out indicating rises. Pools have been formed for the purpose of effecting them. Even houses of good reputation have aided in advancing the prices of stocks which sold for ten times what they are worth now.

Mr. Whitney. That may be, but is that proof that the prices were not realistic and proper?

The Chairman. There will be a good deal of proof brought out to show they were not realistic; yes. I will admit it is hard to demonstrate between what is realistic and what is artificial in a market of this kind. The artificial element is introduced so often and the blame is placed on the natural trend. Have you any knowledge of financial writers who prognosticate great increases in prices and hold options on shares of stock that they are trying to boost?

Mr. Whitney. I have not, sir.

The Chairman. All right. We just want to get you on record on some of these. Is there such a thing as a floor pool?

Mr. Whitney. I have answered that. I never heard of it before.

The Chairman. Is it not really a well-known fact that pools are sometimes formed on the floor, together with the specialist, to hold the price up at a certain point for a certain length of time? You are not going to admit that?

Mr. Whitney. No. I will admit that people may get together and try to buy stock in a particular security, but I can not understand——

The Chairman. The specialist has his book before him and he knows the exact status of the whole matter, and sometimes brokers on the floor get together with him or get together among themselves and form pools for the purpose of holding the market up a certain length of time.

Mr. Whitney. But to whose detriment is that?

The Chairman. That is the way you have been answering us for five days.

Mr. Whitney. But I don't see, Mr. Chairman——

The Chairman. I ask you whether it is a fact and you ask to whose detriment is it.

Mr. Whitney. I just said it could be done, but I don't think that anybody is being hurt, that any rigging of the market is taking place.

The Chairman. You admit it is done?

Mr. Whitney. I say it may be done.

The Chairman. Referring to wash sales, you say they are not permitted, I understand.

Mr. Whitney. They are not permitted.

Senator Gore. May I ask one question there, Mr. Chairman?

The Chairman. Certainly.

Senator Gore. I wish you would put in there in connection with Mr. Gray's question, as to what is the definition of a wash sale, what is a matched order.

Mr. Whitney. I should consider a matched order a wash sale. They are both of the same nature.

The Chairman. What is churning, according to your ideas?

Mr. Whitney. We have no such thing.

The Chairman. Is not the effect just the same as a wash sale?

Mr. Whitney. Mr. Chairman, I don't understand you. Churning, by its name, would seem to be buying and selling stock actively.

The Chairman. You know that the papers have carried that churning story all the way from 1929, and yet the managers of the exchange don't know anything about it. You don't read the papers, evidently.

Mr. Whitney. I don't agree with everything the press says, not always. I don't always agree with them.

The Chairman. Is it not a fact that churning is a wash sale?

Mr. Whitney. No, sir.

The Chairman. Is it not a fact that the same time that they buy they also sell?

Mr. Whitney. If they sell——

The Chairman. That the operations are in connection with the specialist, who has the books there and knows everything?

Mr. Whitney. If a purchase is made at one price and a sale is made at another by the same individual, that is not in any way a wash sale.

The Chairman. In other words, to sell for the purpose of creating action, where nobody gains anything and nobody loses anything, is not a wash sale, unless it is called a wash sale; if it is called churning, it is not a wash sale, is that it?

Mr. Whitney. No; it is not a wash sale in either case, as I understand you.

The Chairman. But it washes, doesn't it?

Mr. Whitney. No, sir.

The Chairman. It washes out.

Mr. Whitney. Some one must lose on such a transaction.

The Chairman. Yet if they are on both sides of the market they don't need to lose, do they?

Mr. Whitney. I said if they traded, sir, at the same price, that is a wash sale. If they trade at different prices, the same individual, that is not a wash sale, and he must lose the difference.

The Chairman. What is the object of churning then, if your statement is correct?

Mr. Whitney. The object of churning, as you interpret the word, is activity in the market.

The Chairman. Is activity in the market for the purpose of fooling the public? Won't you admit that it has no other purpose?

Mr. Whitney. I do not think you have asked me a specific question as to what you want me to answer, Mr. Chairman.

The Chairman. I just asked you whether that was not the whole purpose of it.

Mr. Whitney. But aren't we assuming that something illegal or improper has been done; and that I do not grant.

The Chairman. You don't grant that anything on the street is improper or anything is illegal?

Mr. Whitney. Oh, yes, I do.

The Chairman. We are thoroughly convinced of that.

Mr. Whitney. Yes; I do.

The Chairman. We are not going to argue that with you. We can not convince you. You are hopeless. [Laughter.]

Mr. Whitney. I grant that lots of things are improper and illegal, sir. I have only tried to tell you that I thought the New York Stock Exchange was doing its utmost as a body of men to prevent illegal practices.

The Chairman. I notice in several cases that I called your attention to that there was not one where the New York State legislature had not forced the hand of the exchange. My attention has been called to other matters since. The rules against improper practices on the exchange can be traced right back to the State law that forced them. I notice that.

Mr. Whitney. And we have gone further than the State law in many cases.

The Chairman. And sometimes the rule you make is a paper rule and is not observed.

Mr. Whitney. That I do not agree with, sir.

The Chairman. No; of course not.

Mr. Whitney. Well, I ask for proof. I think that is but fair.

The Chairman. You attend these hearings for a while and we will give you some proof.

Mr. Whitney. I have. [Laughter.]

The Chairman. After a while we will have some other witnesses. Does the pool operator know the condition of the stock from the speculator?

Mr. Whitney. He may.

The Chairman. He may?

Mr. Whitney. As I have answered you, sir.

The Chairman. You will also admit that the public knows nothing about it, won't you?

Mr. Whitney. I will not.

The Chairman. Of course, we should not expect you to admit it.

Mr. Whitney. Mr. Chairman, if an investor came to me and asked me to find out about a specific stock, as to how he could buy a thousand shares, I would go to the specialist and ask him, and find out, and tell that investor, he being a part of the public.

The Chairman. He is a very small part of the public that deals on the market though, is he not? You tell one man, and he is part of the public, but the public itself would not know, would it?

Mr. Whitney. If they were interested, I see no reason not to tell them.

The Chairman. Of course, that is getting outside of the question.

Mr. Whitney. No; it is not getting outside of the question.

The Chairman. The specialist has information the public can not have, and therefore the public gets soaked, isn't that true?

Mr. Whitney. No, sir; I don't agree with that.

The Chairman. You and I don't agree on many things. Therefore, we will have to leave it there. Is it not a fact also that rigging the market and sending the values up to a high point works pretty good, but as soon as the support is withdrawn, then down it goes?

Mr. Whitney. I don't know, Mr. Chairman. The market went up and sustained itself on an upward curve with respect to almost every share, until the panic came.

The Chairman. There is a great difference in shares. The pool operations are quite evident.

Mr. Whitney. I do not know of pool operations in September and October of 1929.

The Chairman. Sir?

Mr. Whitney. I do not know of pool operations at that time.

The Chairman. We don't expect to prove that by you; not at all. But I thought you would admit that one stock that did not pay a dividend, but still getting way up, and maybe going up while the general trend of the market was high, would almost in itself be proof of a pool support; but you won't admit that.

Mr. Whitney. Supposing that particular company discovered some very valuable oil on its property or discovered a gold mine or one thing and another; those things happen.

The Chairman. Supposing in two weeks it all went to the dickens, after the support is withdrawn.

Mr. Whitney. Yes.

The Chairman. And supposing the report of the discovery of oil was just a paper report, one of these letters we talk about, that is, to fool the public. Now, you won't admit wash sales, of course.

Mr. Whitney. No, sir.

The Chairman. But don't you think we can prove that from the market tape?

Mr. Whitney. No, sir.

The Chairman. You don't think we can?

Mr. Whitney. No, sir.

The Chairman. Well, we will try to.

Mr. Whitney. I will be glad to have you do it.

The Chairman. We think we are going to prove some of these things by your own records.

Mr. Whitney. There are a great many things, Mr. Chairman, that I would like the opportunity to put in the record, too.

The Chairman. We have quite a record already and we will give you some more chance. But we will go on. Is there any stock exchange rule that prevents any trader on the floor from selling 10,000 shares of stock to the specialist and then buying it from him at an eighth of a cent or a quarter of a point higher?

Mr. Whitney. Yes.

The Chairman. There is such a rule?

Mr. Whitney. Yes.

The Chairman. Have you any knowledge of the fact that it is done?

Mr. Whitney. I have not, sir, nor do we know of its having been done of late. That is not an actual rule of the exchange. It is an interpretation of exchange rules. I myself stated that to the specialists and other members of the exchange some time in the past.

The Chairman. What is meant, for instance, by a strong opening of a stock?

Mr. Whitney. More buyers than sellers as it opens up.

The Chairman. Is it not also a fact that a great deal of stock may be offered and some interested in boosting the market will buy a few shares just before the close of the day, and that goes out as a high quotation, showing a strong market in the stock. The stock may be bought at a relatively high price and it may make it look as though it is a good market for the public to get into. Do not those things happen?

Mr. Whitney. That is not going to affect the price at the close if there are a lot of shares offered at a price and they take two or three hundred of them.

The Chairman. Is it not a fact that the sale is reported at a higher price and goes out at that price and is an invitation?

Mr. Whitney. It is perfectly proper for an individual, if the market is 15½—16, to pay 16 at the close.

The Chairman. Isn't that one of the methods used to boost the stock?

Mr. Whitney. It may be, Mr. Chairman. You have not cited to me any pool operation on which I can give you a proper answer. These are hypothetical questions.

The Chairman. They are hypothetical questions asked of a man who is a perfect encyclopedia of information in this matter and whose business, as Senator Brookhart has said, is not to know anything. I agree with the Senator on that. We have not had frank answers to many of the questions we have asked you.

Mr. Whitney. I am sorry, Mr. Chairman, but I have endeavored to do my best.

The Chairman. We will see if we can develop our case anyway.

SPEECH OF SENATOR PETER NORBECK
MAY 9, 1932

Congressional Record, 72nd Congress, 1st Session, 15703–34.

Every man, woman, and child in the United States has been stung by the bad practices of the stock exchange, which have now taken the form of short selling and bear raiding. The stock-exchange boom burst in the fall of 1929, a couple of years ago. Prior to that there was a steady rise and wild speculation such as was unknown in all history of mankind. The speculators were rigging the market by all sorts of misleading reports, and they were making big profits. They were bulls then; they are bears now. They took large profits while the market was rising; now they are taking large profits while the market is falling.

When they could think of nothing else to sell they would go out and sell shares in themselves. Some of our large bankers would sell shares in their own banks and recommend them highly, at ten times their actual value. Now they are getting the shares back at their own price. The Great War cost us $20,000,000. The boys who saw service will be old men before the war debt is paid, but the loss to the American public through the shrinkage of stocks and bonds is many times as large.

Why did you buy stocks and bonds on the market? You did it upon the advice of those in whom you had confidence. They kept going up. By that time you began to feel certain the advice was good, and more advice was freely given. You got it from newspapers, you got it from magazines, and you got it from books. You got it from promoters and got it from professors of political economy. You got it from everywhere. The country was full of people who were willing to misrepresent things to you in order that they might line their own pockets. Some, of course, were simply mistaken. But how easy it is to give the wrong advice when there is a gain connected with the advice.

Anyone who examines the tons of literature, dealing with investments, which appeared in books, magazines, and the daily press during the period between 1924 and 1929 can not escape the conclusion that there was a large measure of direction given to the publicity of speculative security markets. First, they played up common stocks instead of bonds. Then, when the public had digested all the common stock it would take, they changed the tune and started a systematic publicity campaign for investment trust shares. They not only employed high-pressure publicity writers, but men of learning occupying distinguished positions in eastern universities prepared articles which curiously fitted well into the general program of the stock promoters. The committee in investigating has already found where one man, a Mr. Plummer, of New York, paid out over a quarter of a million dollars for ballyhoo articles sent through the public press for you to read and bet your money on. The evidence was undisputed. Canceled checks were brought before the committee, and in some cases the actual contracts for publicity work. This sum he paid out mostly in one year—1924—before the boom had fairly started. Financial writers were not making any big profit in 1924. That is before they bought Ford cars. Later they had Buicks, Cadillacs, and Packards. But the real display of luxury among them did not come until 1928 and '29. The boom burst in the fall of '29.

The present severe depression is largely the result of stock-market operations. The cash flowed into New York from every community. There had never been such a centralization of wealth as that which flowed so freely into Wall Street in 1927, 1928, and 1929. The results, however, are severe. Families are destitute. Suicides are common. Widows and orphans are the harvest. Should we stand idly by? It is admitted that more than 20,000,000 people, most of them heads of families, lost their savings when the boom burst in 1929. Just think of it—20,000,000 families in the United States were affected by these losses! That is, only one-third of the population of this country escaped the direct effect, and they suffered indirectly. In the spring of 1928, a year and a half before the boom burst in Wall Street, the Senate Banking Committee recommended remedial measures, but it was impossible to get the approval of Congress. Even at that time stocks sold at fictitious values, but the public enjoyed the situation. Stocks were going up from day to day, they said. Why disturb such prosperity as that? Technical lawyers argued then as now that Congress had no control over the stock exchanges. We got no support. All we could do was to make a report predicting disaster, and nobody wanted to read that. Bad news was not wanted. Our committee implored members of the Federal Reserve Board to prevent the use of that banking system for speculation. Such a wild orgy might have been prevented, but the board sat with their hands folded and drew their salaries.

The American people had forgotten that what goes up must come down.

They knew these shares were not earning much dividend. Many were paying only 1 or 2 per cent, but selling at more than $100. The stock-market operators knew the break was sure to come. The public also should have known that much, but they did not.

One of the large bankers in Chicago referred to the stock market as the worst crap game in the country.

The road to prosperity must be built upon confidence; the confidence is lacking. The Street sold it out for cash. The lambs have been sheared and it takes time to grow more wool.

If you ask me again what is the major cause of the present depression, I again answer you—it was due to the manipulation of the stock market, the booming of the market, and the bursting of the market.

The vicious practices of the market are well known, but they are hard to prove. Mr. Whitney, the president of the stock exchange, was amazingly ignorant of manipulations and pools. For some time he even denied their existence, though there are dozens of books in the library which devote long discussions on the manipulations of a pool. Mr. Whitney drove the committee to seek information from other quarters.

The committee has to get actual proof. Many men come to me who know the New York Stock Market, its ins and outs, its ups and downs, and who are familiar with the methods of robbing the public, but are not willing to testify before the committee. They insist their names must be withheld. They say the system will get them. They will be ostracized; their credit will be curtailed. They will be driven out of business. They will be made bankrupt, and some actually go so far as to express fear of their lives. They tell me the system has so many ramifications. It is even claimed the Chicago gangsters are interested in certain manipulations. It has a string on so many people that it has friends in every place, high or low. The number of manipulators is small. The lambs are many. In this game, the ninety-nine have no chance against the one—the wolf.

One of the leading operators, who was compelled to testify under oath before the Banking Committee as to stock-market manipulations, frankly expressed fear of his safety and said Capone was a piker compared to these people.

There has been much division of opinion in the committee as to the advisability of proceeding with this investigation and as to what remedy might be applied. One Senator frankly stated in print that Congress should not interfere with this institution or its practices. He shares the views of the exchange—that all the regulating they need is to regulate themselves.

I am happy to say, however, that I believe a majority of the committee are for a real investigation, both of the bulls and the bears, no matter who gets hurt by it, for they believe in the end it will help to restore a better condition throughout the country. I believe a majority of the Senators consider it just as wrong to misrepresent the value of a stock or bond as to sell rotten eggs for fresh eggs.

A generation ago only a few stocks were listed on the market. Property was owned by individuals, not by corporations. To-day the reverse is true. The average man or woman in the eastern section of the United States now owns very little property, except as shares in some big corporation, or bonds on same, and these shares and bonds are being manipulated up and down to the great loss of those who actually own same. I believe that owners of shares should be protected by law, the same as the owners of a home, a farm, or a town lot; they are not so protected now. If your property is in the form of stock or bond, a manipulation of the market may make you poor in a day, even though you are not a speculator. If the market practices had been more fair and the investor had been protected there would not have been such a severe depression; there would not have been so much unemployment. But the manipulators are powerful and they don't intend that anybody shall interfere with their game.

One of the witnesses before the committee declared that the violence of speculation was caused by stupid money in the hands of stupid people.

Some of this stupid money found its way into membership on the New York Stock Exchange. One member, who was a theater ticket agent in 1918, found his way into the exchange in 1920 and at the peak of the bull market had eight memberships among his partners.

The management of one newspaper which has called the investigation "one of the most fantastic affairs that unreason could create" is closely associated with a great bank and a large oil-producing concern, neither one of which would enjoy public examination of its affairs.

Another critical journal has a president who was in the midst of the investment trust movement. One of his pet trusts enjoyed a price range for its shares between $190 and 5 cents.

Testimony before this committee regarding the radio pool showed that brokers participated in the pools and pool manipulations. One of these brokers was the specialist of the stock in which the pool dealt. At least he operated through use of his wife's name. There was no regard for anything except profits. The public was not considered.

This is even a violation of the rules of the New York Stock Exchange—this stock exchange that insists that they should be allowed to govern themselves and that Congress should not undertake their regulation.

A year ago we had one of the largest bankers in the country before the Committee on Banking and Currency. He admitted in his testimony that he had recommended the purchase of Anaconda Copper mining stock to the general public at $140 per share. It is now down to $5 or $10 per share, and this man wonders now why there isn't confidence—confidence in him, confidence in his bank, confidence in Wall Street, confidence in New York.

Can the public be blamed for the lack of confidence in our markets, lack of confidence in our institutions, lack of confidence in our Government, and lack of confidence in themselves?

A method must be found to prevent a repetition of this. Congress does not want to interfere with private business, but Congress may have to do that very thing.

The New York market boasts of its reform rules, and there are some that can fairly be called so, but often they are traceable to laws enacted by the State of New York to make certain practices criminal. The stock-market reform rules come late and are observed poorly after they have been adopted.

I maintain, however, that the New York Stock Exchange does not and can not reflect the true values of the securities which are traded thereon. As long as the natural and normal laws of supply and demand are denied and while a selected group of powerful individuals can influence values to their own advantage, an honest and equitable exchange for the purchase and sale of securities can not exist.

For a generation, at least, a big cloud has hung over the land—the threat of centralized wealth. The bulk of the national income falls in a very few hands. Their income is so enormous that it gains additional velocity every year, but no force has been so potent in the concentration of wealth as the extreme fluctuations in the stock and bond market—the boom and the bursting of the boom.

It is not only the stock market and the bond market but similar bad practices exist in the commodity market. Wheat and cotton often go up or down without much regard to supply or demand. It fluctuates according to the will of the powerful operators. Traders prefer this kind of a market; they call it an active market, but it is sometimes so active that the farmer goes without pay for his labor and the workingman pays "what the traffic will bear." The middleman gets the bulk of it, but the present investigation is of the stock exchange. If better market conditions can be brought about, it will point the way to certain changes in the farmer's market also.

I feel the need of drastic revision of the stock-exchange practices; the buying public are entitled to full information. They do not have it now.

A pool is formed and a stock issue is taken on. Various methods are used in boosting such stock. It is misrepresented in many ways. You are advised that it has large earnings. You read the recommendation of well-known investment firms. You are even told by your bankers that it is good stock to buy. You receive market letters from New York brokers recommending it highly. It rises steadily and the manipulators profit greatly, but when they have sold it to the public they have no more interest in it. Their support is withdrawn, the publicity ceases, the buying end of the slump starts.

It is a common practice for the buyer to leave his stock with the broker. The broker is called upon by a bear raider who wants to break the market. For a consideration he lends your stock to the raider, who sells short—that is, he sells what he has not got, but he has borrowed some of it. He has options on more of it. He is fairly well protected. He starts out to destroy public confidence and to break its value. He succeeds, and he profits immensely by that.

You will recall the recent Swedish Match Co. debacle. The firm name was Kreuger & Toll. It was after Kreuger committed suicide that the irregularities of the firm were discovered, among which were forged bonds on which they had secured credit.

Is it conceivable that all the selling that took place just before Kreuger's suicide was done by those who knew a great deal more about the situation than the buyer did?

Did they know what was coming?

Did they take advantage of the unsuspecting public and sell them that which they knew to be worthless?

The bear raiders are especially active now. They depress a weak market and ruin the value of other people's property. One witness before our committee admitted frankly that it was "pathetic" the way the public put their money into the stock market—and "pathetic" is the right word.

Many obstacles are thrown in the way of investigation. We are dealing with men who are powerful and high-handed. They are in the habit of having their own way. They don't intend to be interfered with. But Congress has a duty to perform; at least, the duty to put the searchlight on and show the public the real situation. It is a debt we owe to every taxpayer, property owner in the land—yes, to every citizen of the Republic.

President Whitney of the stock exchange wanted to give the exchange credit for saving the country when England went off the gold standard. He said if it had not been for the exchange a moratorium would have been precipitated—in other words, the panic would have been brought on.

It follows that any critical time the New York Stock Exchange can bring on a panic.

Is it possible that so much power is lodged in a voluntary association for profit—operating entirely outside governmental regulations?

It is a century since powerful financial interests of the land, the bank profiteers of this land, said to President Jackson that if they could not have their way a panic would result. He told them if they brought on a panic they would be hung. But Jackson stood his ground and no panic followed.

ARTICLE BY PAUL Y. ANDERSON, "SACRED BULLS AND SINISTER BEARS" MAY 11, 1932

Paul Y. Anderson, "Sacred Bulls and Sinister Bears," *The Nation*, CXXXIV (May 11, 1932), 538–39.

The captain of finance who descends on Washington determined to make a monkey of a Senate investigating committee nearly always comes to grief, and President Whitney of the New York Stock Exchange may be listed as the latest casualty. Yet so beautifully did he get away with it during the first few days that I, who ought to know better, pitied the Banking and Currency Committee for its amateurishness and was resigned to a fiasco. The patois of the financial district rippled from President Whitney's tongue with soporific suavity. In dulcet tones he explained that short selling is not gambling, "but an integral part of speculation, the other part being marginal buying, both of which are essential to keep the market liquid." He murmured of "cushioning" and "stabilizing" influences. He was not sure what a bear raid might be, except that it was an impossibility. He had heard some talk of pools but was not certain how they were operated, if at all. About all that he was positive of was that the Stock Exchange is a splendid and indispensable institution and that the chastity of its practices is above suspicion. If he had not claimed most of the known virtues for it, the subsequent disclosures of market rigging and blue-sky promotion might seem less criminal in contrast. He took several days to describe the market as a benevolent institution. Matt Brush took two hours to prove that it is largely a craps game, and in thirty minutes Representative La Guardia showed that it sometimes operates with loaded dice. In retrospect Mr. Whitney's performance sounds like that of a piano-player sitting all alone in the parlor of a certain kind of establishment and playing "Home, Sweet Home" while business proceeds as usual in the upper rooms. I cannot be positive whether Whitney is the babe in the woods that his testimony makes him out or whether he is the wilful deceiver that La Guardia pronounced him, although thus far the weight of evidence is heavily on the side of Brush and La Guardia. In either instance one marvels that he remains at the head of the Stock Exchange.

Some inspired hand wrote in the New York *Herald Tribune* that the investigation might result in unfortunate consequences. Sure enough, one of the first consequences was the discovery that several New York financial writers, including one then employed by the *Herald Tribune*, had taken money for puffing certain stocks through the columns of their papers. We may acquit the editors of guilty knowledge and still be warranted in asking how that sort of thing could go on under their noses for any length of time without being detected. Editors should know their business, and systematic puffing is easily recognized. The truth is, as all newspapermen know, that financial writers are allowed to become entirely too much attached to the market and too much detached from their own offices. To those of us here who are familiar with the stern moral lectures which certain types of editors and financiers are constantly delivering to Congress, there is excruciating irony in the revelation that these financiers rigged the market for certain stocks, that the public was induced to buy them by stories written for these newspapers by bribe-taking reporters—and that when the inevitable collapse followed, these financiers and newspapers blamed it on Congress! Marvelous! It could only happen in the good old U. S. A. For the assurance of those who might have doubts, let me state that a great majority of reporters undoubtedly are honest. But don't place too much confidence in the editor or financier who makes a habit of blaming Congress.

As for the Senate inquiry, two things may be stated. First, information already in the possession of Chairman Norbeck shows that the committee has not scratched the surface and that disclosures of the utmost significance are inevitable unless someone puts the lid on; and, second, that terrific efforts are being made to put it on. Among the most anxious are men who have contributed heavily to the campaign funds of both political parties, and the pressure they will be able to apply can be estimated. Their anxiety is easy to understand when one knows the methods they employed and the type of characters with whom they associated in their schemes to unload inflated securities on the public. Brush was not overstating the situation when he said that Al Capone was a piker. Of course, none of these gentlemen—or only a few of the indiscreet—took any chance on going to jail. Whether the investigation can be smothered will soon be seen. It started in a curious fashion. Senator Walcott of Connecticut, President Hoover's spokesman on the committee, received an alarming telegram from George Barr Baker, the Administration's New York sentry, stating that a terrible bear raid was being hatched. It was inevitable that such a report from such a source would throw a scare into the Administration. Poor Mr. Hoover labors under the delusion that the return of prosperity is dependent on the return of a bull market and that forces mysterious and hostile to him are conspiring to keep the market down. In the absence of Chairman Norbeck, Walcott summoned the committee and launched the inquiry. A week later, when it became evident that the sacred bulls no less than the sinister bears were becoming unfavorably involved, the Connecticut statesman made a rather inglorious attempt to stop what he had started, but his colleagues simply brushed him aside and further humiliated him by leaving him off the steering subcommittee which it designated to plan future procedure. From this angle it appears that the thing has gone too far to be stopped, even by the Rockefellers, Raskobs, and Whitneys. But events will bear close watching, because the heat really is being turned on.

The Senate Finance Committee has by no means immortalized itself by its revision of the tax bill. A combination of Democrats and Progressive Republicans succeeded in making mild increases in the surtaxes, estate taxes, and corporation taxes, but this achievement was immediately nullified by the elimination of the House provision which applied the normal income rate to dividends, and the whole procedure became definitely ridiculous when a group of log-rollers first voted to include tariffs on oil, gasoline, coal, and copper, and then quarreled among themselves and voted them all out. The effect of such tariffs probably would be the destruction of the remaining vestiges of our trade with Canada and South America. To make up the revenue that would be lost by failing to apply the normal income rate to dividends, the committee proposes drastic increases in the normal rates on income from other sources. If that policy prevails, the Treasury deficit will be paid mainly by persons making between $3,500 and $25,000 a year. It must be admitted that the hearings did not serve greatly to illuminate the committee. Not even the carefully staged forensic gestures of Secretary Mills shed much light. Once more we heard the two familiar arguments against high taxes on large incomes, to wit: that they wouldn't produce any revenue; and that they would produce an exorbitant and cruel amount of revenue. Once again we were told that a man would become discouraged and refuse to work any longer upon hearing that he would not be allowed to keep more than 53 per cent of his earnings after the first $5,000,000 a year, and would absolutely throw everything over and resign himself to despair if told that he could not leave his heirs more than 75 per cent of his fortune in excess of the first $10,000,000. All the arguments rested, as usual, on the premise that the thing which has made this nation great and prosperous is the unparalleled rapacity of its citizens. Individual avarice may be an important factor in the national economy, but I am not prepared to agree with Secretary Mills that the national destiny depends on pandering to it. If it is true that the rich are confessed and incorrigible tax-dodgers, so much more reason for soaking them!

Several months ago the United States Chamber of Commerce initiated a general 10 per cent cut in the wages of its employees and ever since then it has been urging the government to do likewise. The force of the government's example would be tremendous and the number of "patriotic" employers to follow it would be legion. Nevertheless, the movement is encountering difficulties in the House, which under its liberalized rules seems bent on demonstrating that it has become a more democratic body than the Senate. President Hoover's generous proposal to bestow longer vacations (without pay) on government clerks already has been rejected, and the Administration's whole picayunish program of "economy" is in a fair way to be ditched. It should be. Government employees always have been notoriously underpaid. In Washington, where an army of them reside, commodity prices have remained comparatively high, and most of them are just now catching up on the instalment purchases made when their pay checks looked like cigar coupons. But if the Chamber of Commerce is disappointed by Congress, it can still "look to the press for leadership." I am proud to report that a 10 per cent reduction in salaries has been initiated by the newspapers owned by Cyrus H. K. Curtis (Philadelphia *Public Ledger, Evening Ledger,* and New York *Evening Post*), and that a similar reduction has been ordered by the New York *Times* to take effect May 1. In the case of Mr. Curtis (who also publishes the *Saturday Evening Post,* the *Ladies' Home Journal,* and the *Country Gentleman*) this regrettable necessity may be explained. In fact, it has been explained. Writing from aboard Mr. Curtis's magnificent yacht, Lyndonia, at Miami Beach, Arthur Brisbane recently reported that Mr. Curtis's net profits fell from $20,000,000 in 1930 to $8,000,000 in 1931. By making this cut in salaries Mr. Curtis will be able to keep the Lyndonia in commission. When the excellent reporters in the Washington bureau of the *Evening Post* and *Public Ledger* sit in their office on the twelfth floor of the Press Club Building here and watch the Lyndonia steam gallantly into harbor bearing its venerable owner to a dinner engagement at the White House—as it does once a year—they certainly must thrill to think of what their contributions meant. In the case of the *Times,* alas, no such comforting explanation is available. Its owners are filthy with cash and have been for years. Just think of writing that tripe *for less pay!*

Humbled by events of the last two years, the Administration is edging nearer to recognition of Soviet Russia. Obviously this development is prompted more by necessity than desire. The bureaucrats in the State Department are no fonder of the despised Bolsheviks now than they were in 1922 when they succeeded in confusing Mr. Hughes. But finally they have reasoned around to the point of recognizing that if we are to have war with Japan, Russia is our natural—and indispensable—ally. But before the white-spatted and side-whiskered young-old blades in the State Department had arrived at this somewhat belated discovery, their brisker colleagues in the Department of Commerce had found that Russia offered the lone hope of nourishing our emaciated export trade. The idea, which has been common property among thinking persons in the capital for four or five years, threatens now to make a real impression on those who direct our foreign relations. The pressure of necessity may yet compel the Administration to do the thing which is both right and sensible.

MEMOIRS OF HERBERT HOOVER
1929

Herbert Hoover, *The Memoirs of Herbert Hoover, The Great Depression, 1929–1941*, (New York, 1952), 16–20; 125–30.

WE ATTEMPT TO STOP THE ORGY
OF SPECULATION

By the last months of 1928, Benjamin Strong of the Federal Reserve Bank of New York had died and Daniel Crissinger of the Federal Reserve Board had resigned. Roy Young had been appointed by President Coolidge to the Governorship of the Reserve Board. Young was an able, courageous, and cooperative man. Prior to my inauguration as President I conferred several times with him and found him fully alive to the situation. He agreed to use the full powers of the Board to strangle the speculative movement.

On February 7, 1929, the Board issued public notice of drastic "direct action" to the banks to restrain indirect use of Federal Reserve credits for speculative loans. But the stimulant had been too successful. The fever was beyond control.

Moreover, the effect of the Board's action was greatly minimized by an unfortunate press statement by President Coolidge, a few days before he left office, in which he assured the country that its prosperity was "absolutely sound," and that stocks were "cheap at current prices."

The stock boom was blowing great guns when I came into the White House. Being fully alive to the danger inherent in this South Sea Bubble and its inevitable reaction, my first interest was to get it under restraint. It was obvious that there had to be vast liquidation of paper values, and especially a liquidation of the mental attitude of people mesmerized by the idea of speculation as a basis of living and of national progress.

The initial difficulty was a lack of government authority, except such as could be exerted by the Federal Reserve System. To ask Congress for powers to interfere in the stock market was futile and, in any event, for the President to dictate the price of stocks was an expansion of Presidential power without any established constitutional basis.

I, therefore, resolved to attack the problem from several directions in addition to securing cooperation from the Federal Reserve System.

To create a spirit of caution in the public, I sent individually for the editors and publishers of major newspapers and magazines and requested them systematically to warn the country against speculation and the unduly high price of stocks. Most of them responded with strong editorials. This had no appreciable effect, however.

Secretary of the Treasury Mellon and others, at my request, issued repeated statements urging the public to convert their stocks into bonds and advising other forms of caution. This also had no effect.

My second line of attack, six weeks after my inauguration, was to request Henry M. Robinson, President of the First Security National Bank of Los Angeles, to go to New York and to talk in my name to the promoters and bankers behind the market. He fully agreed with me as to the dangers of the situation. But the New York bankers all scoffed at the idea that the market was not "sound." They were certain this was a "New Era," to which old economic experience did not apply. To prove it, Thomas Lamont of Morgan's wrote me a long memorandum which makes curious reading today.

My third effort was to send for Richard Whitney, the President of the New York Stock Exchange, and urge that the Exchange itself curb the manipulation of stocks. I informed him that I had no desire to stretch the powers of the Federal government by legislation to regulate the Stock Exchange—that authority rested only in the Governor of New York, Franklin D. Roosevelt. I stated that I preferred to let American institutions and the states govern themselves, and that the Exchange had full power under its charter to control its own members and to prevent it from being used for manipulation against the public interest. Mr. Whitney made profuse promises, but did nothing.[1]

Through the use of some Federal powers in post-office fraud matters we did stop a flock of bucket-shop operators.

A dispute arose between Governor Young of the Federal Reserve Board and important banks as to whether or not the discount rates should be raised as a brake on speculation. Governor Young contended that to raise the rate simply gave the banks larger returns by penalizing commercial business. He contended that the banks could curb loans for speculation, just by simply refusing to make such loans.

I held with the Governor, who now proceeded by direct action. He issued orders to the Reserve Banks to refuse rediscounts to banks which were lending largely on stocks. Their practice was to rediscount their commercial bills at the Reserve Banks, then loan the proceeds to the market.

At one moment the Federal Reserve Board's action forced money rates for speculative purposes up to 20 per cent per annum. But people who dreamed of 100 per cent profit in a week were not deterred by an interest rate of 20 per cent a year. Mr. Young fully demonstrated the futility of the idea upon which the Reserve System had been founded that it could control booms. Control of interest rates could not stop them. When the public becomes mad with greed and is rubbing the Aladdin's lamp of sudden fortune, no little matter of interest rates is effective.

We did at one time almost secure a stranglehold on the stock market when the Reserve Banks had so tightened the call-loan situation that a moment arrived when there was no money available to the market. A break seemed inevitable. But Charles E. Mitchell, President of the National City Bank of New York, announced that in this emergency his bank would furnish the deficient credit.

Senator Glass expressed my feelings when he said of Mr. Mitchell:

[1] He was subsequently sent to the penitentiary for mishandling trust funds.

He avows his superior obligation to a frantic stock market over against the obligations of his oath as a director of the New York Federal Reserve Bank. . . .

Mr. Mitchell's proclamation is a challenge to the authority and the announced policy of the Federal Reserve Board. The challenge ought to be promptly met and courageously dealt with.

The Board should ask for the immediate resignation of Mr. Mitchell as a Class A director of the New York Federal Reserve Bank. . . .

The whole country has been aghast for months and months at the menacing spectacle of excessive stock gambling, and when the Federal Reserve Board mildly seeks to abate the danger by an administrative policy, fully sanctioned by law, rather than by a prohibitive advance in rediscount rates, which might penalize the legitimate business of the entire country, an officer of the System issues a defiance and engages in an attempt to vitiate the policy of the Federal Reserve Board.[2]

The Federal Reserve Board on August 6th finally increased the discount rate to 6 per cent. It had no effect whatsoever on this Mississippi Bubble.

All our efforts to secure an orderly readjustment covered six months and perhaps served somewhat to slow up the orgy. The real trouble was that the bellboys, the waiters, and the host of unknowing people, as well as the financial community, had become so obsessed with the constant press reports of great winnings that the movement was uncontrollable.

The stock-market slump on October 29, 1929, came seven months after I entered the White House.

When the inevitable black morning of their dream dawned, the exponents of the "New Era" were surprised. Promptly we had a flood of reassuring statements to the anxious speculators from economists, bankers, the press, and labor leaders. Professor Irving Fisher of Yale said that stocks had not even reached their full values. Charles E. Mitchell of the National City Bank announced that "the reaction had outrun itself." The New York Times praised the soundness of the financial structure. Mr. Rockefeller, Mr. Morgan, Mr. Raskob all announced that they were buying stocks. William Green of the American Federation of Labor declared, "In a few months we will be back to normal." A left-wing economist, Stuart Chase, said, "The stock market will not affect general prosperity."

I am not a pessimistic soul, but I was not impressed by any of this optimism. The press insistently urged that I make a statement. Obviously, as President, I had no business to make things worse in the middle of a crash. Loath to speak of the stock market, I offered as encouragement a short statement on our progress in the productive system and the long-view strength of the country.

The normal business cycle periodically must readjust disequilibriums which are a part of the rhythm of any growing free economy. But this was more than rhythms. Our overpriced stocks and real estate were bound to come down; and the degree of down is influenced by the degree of up—which means a descent from overvalue to undervalue. The boom had lifted securities

[2] New York Times, March 29, 1929.

and real estate far up and, to this degree, was to deepen further the slump by the downward swing.

Within a few weeks the slump began seriously to affect industrial employment and farm prices, confronting us with problems of the first order. . . .

Reforming the Stock Exchanges (By Exposure)

A contributing factor to public fear was the continuous misuse of the New York and other stock exchanges. Early in the administration in 1929 I had tried to persuade the officials of the New York Stock Exchange to restrain the use of the Exchange for manipulation, destructive speculation and distribution of doubtful securities. Conscientious and leading members had informed me that the Exchange could do all this itself by changing its own rules. I had made no progress. They were in the "New Economic Era."

After the slump came, in October, 1929, the misuse of the machinery of the Exchange appeared in another sinister aspect. Insiders "sold short" and then by propaganda and manipulation which lowered stock prices caught investors who could no longer support loans they had obtained on stocks and were obliged to sell. The "shorts" bought them in.

I deplored the idea of extending Federal power over organizations which had the power to remedy their own evils. The Stock Exchange properly conducted is a vital part of the free-enterprise system. In any event, the primary responsibility for initiation of official action lay on Governor Franklin Roosevelt of New York. That state had power to reform Exchange methods. Charles Evans Hughes, in the case of the dishonest management of the insurance companies, had not hesitated to clean them up in the public interest, and for the reputation of New York business.

In the summer and fall of 1931, during the European collapse, there were again systematic bear raids on the Exchange, and again I urged reforms on its directors. These actions appreciably deepened the depression.

In January and February, 1932, I twice again called Exchange directors to the White House and urged that they amend their rules so as to stop manipulation. I pointed out that new bear raids had again taken place in anticipation of every periodic crisis, and, in addition, there were other large pool operations against investors' interests, the information as to which was supplied me by responsible members of the Exchange. These responsible members formulated for me some curative amendments to their rules. The directors repeatedly promised they would adopt these amendments, but made only minor changes. I finally warned Richard Whitney and other directors that unless they took measures to clean their own house I would ask Congress to investigate the Stock Exchange with a view to Federal control legislation.

These discussions with Stock Exchange representatives having leaked out, I made a public statement on the 19th of February—in restrained terms —since I did not wish to add to public discouragement by denunciation, even though it would have been just:

> There have been discussions, as is reported, between myself and
> other officials of the Administration with officials of the New York
> Stock Exchange. . . . I, and other Administration officials, again

expressed our views to the managers of the Exchange that they should take adequate measures to protect investors from artificial depression of the price of securities for speculative profit. Individuals who use the facilities of the Exchange for such purposes are not contributing to recovery of the United States.

Despite these urgings I received still more depressing information that vicious pools were continuing in which corporation and even bank directors were manipulating their own stocks. I, therefore, called in Senator Frederic Walcott, strongest Republican member of the Senate Banking and Currency Committee, who, having been an honest investment banker, was familiar with Exchange practices, and Senator Peter Norbeck, chairman of the committee. Norbeck was a well-intentioned well-driller from South Dakota. I urged that the committee launch an investigation of practices of the Exchange, with a view to legislation and I gave them much information to start on. I was extremely loath to take this step, as we had enough burdens to carry, without all the discouraging filth such exposure entailed. But the truth could be brought out only under the compulsion which a Senate committee would exert. The Senate authorized the investigtion on March, 4, 1932. There was some doubt as to the constitutionality of Federal control of the stock exchanges but I hoped that at least, when we had exposed the situation, the Governor of New York would recognize his fundamental responsibility and act accordingly. That hope, however, proved to be little more than wishful thinking.

On April 2nd a group of New York bankers, headed by Thomas Lamont of Morgan & Company, protested my actions in a memorandum explaining the virtues of the Exchange. A few sentences from my reply are as follows:

My dear Mr. Lamont:

. . . Prices today [of securities] do not truly represent the values of American enterprise and property . . . [and the] pounding down of prices . . . by obvious manipulation of the market . . . is an injury to the country and to the investing public. . . .

. . . These operations destroy public confidence and induce a slowing down of business and a fall in prices.

. . . Men are not justified in deliberately making a profit from the losses of other people.

I recognize that these points of view are irreconcilable, but I hope you will agree with me that there is here an element of public interest.

Yours faithfully,   *Herbert Hoover*

In the meantime, a committee had been organized among New York bankers, chiefly through the efforts of Secretary Mills, to support the bond market, which was thoroughly demoralized. On April 3rd I received word from this committee that they could not get important financial houses to join them unless I agreed to call off the Senate investigation and halt my own activities in their direction. When I asked Secretary Mills if this were true, he made an unprintable reply amply in the negative.

It soon became evident that efforts were being made to smother the Senate inquiry. Republican Senate Leader Watson visited me with a strong appeal to quash this "dangerous activity." But Walcott's courage was equal to the mission. He undertook to build a fire under the Senate committee and finally got the inquiry under way. Quickly the committee exposed a rottenness far worse than even I had anticipated. Testimony confirmed to the public that directors of great corporations and banks had been manipulating and speculating in their own stocks. Huge pools had been organized for pushing stocks on to the public at prices far beyond their worth, and for manipulating prices upward and downward. Great figures in the industrial, financial, and political world had engaged in these operations. With the exposures over, such men as Albert Wiggin, chairman of the Chase National Bank, and Charles E. Mitchell,[3] chairman of the National City Bank of New York, resigned their positions. Among those brought before the committee to explain many very sorry things were Percy Rockefeller, John Raskob, chairman of the Democratic National Committee, Matthew Brush, Ben Smith, W. F. Kenny, M. J. Meehan, and others.

The shock to our people and their loss of confidence in the integrity of men high in business and finance was great indeed. Such exposures take no account of the thousands of honest, constructive men in the same walks of life.

To Senator Walcott and his Republican colleagues, we outlined our views of the character of the corrective legislation needed. I assumed that the Constitutional difficulty as to whether or not security trading was inter-state commerce could be overcome. I did not consider it necessary to set up a special commission of so-called administrative law, but to follow the British experience which had been reasonably successful over many years. Copies of the British laws adapted to our scene were furnished to the Senators. The ideas which we advanced were:

(a) A prospectus should be filed with the Department of Justice on every stock offering for interstate sale to the public, stating all the essential facts, including the direct and indirect beneficiaries.

(b) All promoters or other persons appearing upon the prospectus should be liable in damages to any persons injured through misstatement or incomplete disclosure, with the Department of Justice authorized to act in cases of malfeasance coming to their attention.

(c) Congress should enact definite statutory rules governing interstate purchase and sale of securities on the exchanges, again providing for damages to injured persons.

The essence of these proposals was to accomplish our ends through the courts.

The Senate committee had no time before the end of the 1932 session to formulate legislation; and, having lost the election, we could go no further with the matter.

---

[3] We subsequently obtained the indictment of Charles E. Mitchell of the National City Bank for malfeasance.

The reaction from these exposures, of course, paved the way for drastic legislation in the Roosevelt administration. That legislation has perhaps hampered honest business. But when representative government becomes angered, it will burn down the barn to get a rat out of it.

Some statements having been made later in respect to the origin of the Senate inquiry, Senator Walcott wrote to me as follows:

> I recall vividly the events which led up to our meetings at the White House, when you urged me, . . . to persuade the Banking and Currency Committee of the Senate to use every effort to determine the facts connected with . . . the New York Stock Exchange.
>
> You explained very definitely to Senator Norbeck and me your reasons. . . . I then talked the matter over fully with several of the more active members of the Banking and Currency Committee, who were eager to get at the facts.
>
> The situation was critical. You, as President, were urging haste and definite action. . . . Previous to these events, you had talked with me several times at the White House about the danger. . . . You gave me definite instructions to proceed without delay. . . . You were determined to get at some evil practices. . . .
>
> . . . The complete study was made by public hearings and expert investigations, of the operations and ramifications of certain investment companies that were affiliates of some of the large national banks. . . .
>
> You were backing courageously and without fear or favor all of these endeavors to get at the facts and correct the evils, and you, more than any one else, were responsible for the constructive reforms that were eventually adopted in connection with the correction of the abuses among the banks and bankers. . . .

TESTIMONY OF CHARLES E. MITCHELL AND LETTER OF SOLICITOR GENERAL FREDERICK W. LEHMANN FEBRUARY 21, 1933

U.S. Senate, Stock Exchange Practices, *Hearings Before the Committee on Banking and Currency*, 72nd Congress, 2nd Session, Part 6, 2026–42.

Senator Fletcher. Mr. Mitchell, while they are conferring about another matter I want to ask you, based on your experience and from your knowledge of the public and of conditions, could you offer any suggestion respecting legislation by Congress that might tend to protect and safeguard the interests of the public, either as to banks, investment companies, or stock-exchange operations?

Mr. Mitchell. I think there should very definitely be legislation enacted; yes, sir.

Senator Fletcher. Of what character? Now can you give us an idea about what should be done?

Mr. Mitchell. Well, take for instance, this matter of investment affiliates of banks: I have a feeling that the whole system should be revamped, that there should be in an institution some portion of it dealing with the long-term credit market. I subscribe to that. I think there must be that.

But it is this contact with the public that disturbs me, coming as it does through the investment affiliate, and I think we have got to find some different means of distribution.

Furthermore, I think there should be added controls with respect to the character of securities handled. The investment affiliate is an established thing. It is handling apparently something over 50 per cent of the total volume of the long-term credit business. I do not think that you can eliminate it, certainly carelessly, without very definitely retarding any period of recovery, because there is a great deal of financing to be done and the machinery is there.

I think the investment affiliate should be put under regulation and control, because that after all is the one place where the Government has got a chance to regulate and control. If you take the investment affiliate and throw it out completely and say, "Let all of this business develop through private agencies," you have taken the long-term credit machinery away from the place where you can control it and put it in a place where you can not control it.

Therefore, I think we ought to look for legislation and control of the long-term credit market, which is handled so largely by the investment affiliate, under stronger regulation.

Senator Fletcher. Do you think the investment affiliate should be separated from a commercial bank?

Mr. Mitchell. No; I think that its methods of doing business should be regulated and controlled.

Senator Fletcher. As distinguished from the bank itself?

Mr. Mitchell. The control and regulation should be separate from the control and regulation of the bank itself, because they constitute two different problems. But there is a vast amount of financing that must be done over such a period as we have been through. You take, for instance, the Insull properties that have been a matter for your study here. Those properties come into a period like this, where they have got to be financed on new lines. The banks who handle short credits for them and who have handled them in quantity are going to get rid of those credits by putting them into perfectly sound long-term securities. Those banks really are the ones to do that. It means, perhaps, as it did in that case, actually carrying a considerable quantity of new perfectly sound securities for some time awaiting a market, and it was largely the affiliates of banks who found the long-term market for those securities.

We are trying in our company to-day, Senator, as a result of all these things that we have learned to be along the path of error, to find regulation for ourself, and I think we will find it little by little, and as a matter of fact, I think we have got to go a long way further than we have.

Answering your question directly, I do not believe in the elimination of the investment affiliate, but I do believe in legislation by Congress to put such companies under very definite regulation and control, which would be exactly the kind of regulation and control that we are trying to build up for ourselves at the present moment.

Mr. Pecora. Mr. Mitchell, I have come right to a subject collateral to that. Are you familiar with the opinion that was rendered to the Attorney General of the United States in November, 1911, by Frederick W. Lehmann, at that time Solicitor General of the United States?

Mr. Mitchell. I am not; no, sir.

Mr. Pecora. Did you ever hear of that?

Mr. Mitchell. I have heard of that, and at one time I read it, but I don't recall it now. It has been many, many years since I saw it.

Mr. Pecora. Well, I happen to have a copy of it before me.

Mr. Mitchell. Yes.

Mr. Pecora. Let us see how far we can recall it. It is dated November 6, 1911, addressed to the Attorney General, and I will just read a few excerpts from it, Mr. Mitchell, and then, Mr. Chairman, I propose to have the entire opinion spread in full on the record here [reading]:

November 6, 1911

The Attorney General
Sir:

You advise me that the President desires that there shall be submitted to him upon his return to Washington a fuller discussion of the question of the legality of the agreements and arrangements existing between the National City Bank of New York and the National City Co., a corporation of the State of New York.

On August 1, 1911, I submitted to you an opinion, in which you concurred, that the agreements and arrangements in question were means of enabling the bank to carry on business and exercise powers prohibited to it by the national banking act.

I have reconsidered the question with the care demanded by its importance, and have reached the conclusion that both the bank and the company, whether considered as affiliated or as unrelated, are in violation of the law.

Now, there follows considerable matter after that which I have not the time to read but which relates to certain provisions of the national banking act and the United States Statutes. We come to this statement [reading]:

In Logan County National Bank v. Townsend (139 U.S. 67, l. c. 73), the court, speaking through Mr. Justice Harlan, said:

"It is undoubtedly true, as contended by the defendant, that the national banking act is an enabling act for all associations organized under it, and that a national bank can not rightfully exercise any powers except those expressly granted by that act, or such incidental powers as are necessary to carry on the business of banking for which it was established."

Then follows other matter. Then I want to read this excerpt [reading]:

It follows that while a bank may take the stocks of another corporation as collateral to a loan, or take them in payment of a debt
previously incurred, it can not deal in stocks. The limit of its powers
in this respect is stated by Chief Justice Waite in First National Bank
v. National Exchange Bank (92 U.S. 122, 128).

Then follows other matter, and I come to this excerpt [reading]:

The investment by national banks of their surplus funds in other
national banks, situated, perhaps, in distant States, as in the present case, is plainly against the meaning and policy of the statutes
from which they derive their powers, and evil consequences would
be certain to ensue if such a course of conduct were countenanced as
lawful.

Then follows other matter and I now come to this excerpt [reading]:

Another evil that might result, if large and wealthy banks were
permitted to buy and hold the capital stock of other banks, would
be that, in that way, the banking capital of a community might be
concentrated in one concern, and business men be deprived of the
advantages that attend competition between banks. Such accumulation of capital would be in disregard of the policy of the national
banking law, as seen in its numerous provisions regulating the
amount of the capital stock and the methods to be pursued in
increasing or reducing it. The smaller banks, in such a case, would
be in fact, though not in form, branches of the larger one.

Then there is other matter and I come to this excerpt [reading]:

Section 5201 may also be referred to as indicating the policy of
this legislation. This provision, forbidding a national bank to own
and hold shares of its own capital stock, would, in effect, be defeated if one national bank were permitted to own and hold a
controlling interest in the capital stock of another.

Then comes much other matter, and I reach this excerpt [reading]:

From the history of the national banking act, from its terms and
provisions, and from the decisions of the Supreme Court construing it, these propositions are derived:
I. The banks are local institutions and independent of each other,
none the less that they are creatures of Federal power and subject to
Federal supervision and control.
II. A bank may in its by-laws regulate the manner in which its
shares may be transferred, but it can not impair or limit the right of
transfer.
III. As to business operations, the bank has such powers as are
expressly granted by the act and such as are properly incidental to
those expressly granted, and none other, and so can engage only in
the business of banking as that business is defined by the act.

IV. It is neither banking nor an incident of banking to invest the funds of the bank in another business, in any manner or to any extent; and the bank has therefore no right to invest its funds in the stocks of another corporation, and especially not in the stocks of another national bank.

V. The powers of a national banking association are and can be granted only by the United States, and as no grant of such powers is made by the act to any State corporation, they may not be exercised by such a corporation.

These propositions relate to matters of substance, and so may be no more evaded than violated. Indirection, if it accomplishes the same purpose, stands upon the same footing with direction.

Then I come, after much other matter that follows, to this excerpt [reading]:

This, then, is the situation: The company was not independently organized, but was organized by the bank, its officers and shareholders acting as such.

This, of course, refers to the National City Co.

Only shareholders of the bank were permitted an interest in the company and these only in the proportion of their holdings in the bank. This constitution of the interests of the company must continue to end, for no one can ever come into the company without coming into the bank, and no one can ever go out of the company without going out of the bank. The bank, by declaration of a dividend, furnished the entire capital of the company. No person can be an officer or director of the company unless he is an officer or director of the bank.

This is not all. The company has no independence of action. It has no control or authority over its own affairs. It is to be remembered that all its stock is to be held by the trustees, and of course is to be voted by them. Plenary power over the company is therefore held by these trustees. Now, these trustees were not elected by the incorporators of the company, nor by its stockholders. They were nominated by the agreement between the bank, its officers and shareholders, made before the company was in existence. They can not be removed, nor can their successors be elected or determined by any power or interest of the company. The trustees, nominated by the agreement, perpetuate themselves. They appoint their own successors. The only power outside themselves which can make a change in their membership is the shareholding body of the bank. The shareholders by not continuing a trustee as an officer or director of the bank eliminate him as a trustee. The official organization of the company and the vesting of its powers are determined and can be determined only by the corporate action of the bank.

Then follows, after much other matter, the following excerpt [reading]:

And the National City Co., considered by itself and apart from its relations to the National City Bank, is also in violation of law. Its charter from the State of New York expressly prohibits it from the business of banking. And that charter could not confer the power to engage in the business of national banking. Such power could be conferred only by the laws of the United States.

Then follows much other matter, and I come to this concluding paragraph [reading]:

Here the National City Co. is not simply to control banks, but it may engage in any business whatever, even that forbidden by its charter, if, despite its charter prohibition as to certain kinds of business, it may invest in the stocks of companies conducting such business. The other enterprise in which the company is engaged may stand in need of credit and of funds, and it is too much to expect that the company's banks will deal simply as banks, equitably and impartially as between its own subsidiaries, and persons and corporations with whom it is not affiliated. The temptation to the speculative use of the funds of the banks at opportune times will prove to be irresistible. Examples are recent and significant of the peril to a bank, incident to the dual and diverse interests of its officers and directors. If many enterprises and many banks are brought and bound together in the nexus of a great holding corporation, the failure of one may involve all in a common disaster. And if the plan should prosper, it would mean a union of power in the same hands over industry, commerce, and finance, with a resulting power over public affairs, which was the gravamen of objection to the United States Bank.

I conclude the National City Co. in its holding of national-bank stocks is in usurpation of Federal authority and in violation of Federal law.

Respectfully submitted.

Frederick W. Lehmann
Solicitor General

Now, I may say, Mr. Chairman, that the Attorney General of the United States at the time when the Solicitor General rendered this opinion was the Hon. Charles W. Wickersham, and upon communication with his office, which communication I had for the purpose of requesting him or subpoenaing him to appear before this committee, I learned that he is now in Europe.

I ask that this opinion be spread in full upon the record.

The Chairman. There being no objection, it is so ordered.

Mr. Pecora. What I am submitting is a carbon copy produced from the files of the Department of Justice.

(The opinion is as follows:)

Department of Justice
November 6, 1911

The Attorney General
Sir:

You advise me that the President desires that there shall be submitted to him upon his return to Washington a fuller discussion of the question of the legality of the agreements and arrangements existing between the National City Bank of New York and the National City Co., a corporation of the State of New York.

On August 1, 1911, I submitted to you an opinion, in which you concurred, that the agreements and arrangements in question were means of enabling the bank to carry on business and exercise powers prohibited to it by the national banking act.

I have reconsidered the question with the care demanded by its importance, and have reached the conclusion that both the bank and the company, whether considered as affiliated or as unrelated, are in violation of the law.

At the outset it is well to consider the purposes which the framers of the national banking act had in view. The first, the paramount purpose was to secure a uniform national system of currency, and to do this without the creation of a great central institution like the old United States Bank.

The opposition to such an institution was deep seated and widespread and the sponsors of the various plans which took final shape in the national banking act were careful to point out that the objections to the United States Bank had been duly considered and had been avoided by them.

In August 1861 O. B. Potter of New York submitted to the Secretary of the Treasury a scheme to permit State banks and bankers to issue notes secured by United States bonds, saying, "None of the objections justly urged against a United States bank lie against this plan. It gives to the Government no power to bestow favors and does not place a dollar in its hands to lend. . . . It is impossible to see how such a system can be made use of for political ends." (The origin of the national banking system, S. Doc. No. 582, pp. 46–48, 61st Cong., 2d sess.)

Samuel Hooper, a member of the House from Massachusetts, was an active agent in the attainment of the end sought. In support of one of the early measures proposed, which, while it did not become a law, was a step in that direction, he said:

"Thus are secured all the benefits of the old United States Bank without many of those objectionable features which aroused opposition. It was affirmed that, by its favors, the Government enabled that bank to monopolize the business of the country. Here no such system of favoritism exists. . . . It was affirmed that frequently great inconvenience and sometimes terrible disaster resulted to the trade and commerce of different localities by the mother bank of the United States arbitrarily interfering with the management of the branches by reducing suddenly their loans and sometimes withdrawing large amounts of their specie, for political effect. Here each bank transacts its own business upon its own capital, and is subject to no demands except those of its own customers and its own business. It will be as if the Bank of the United States had been divided into many parts, and each part endowed with the life, motion, and similitude of the whole, revolving in its own orbit, managed by its own board of directors, attending to the business interests of its own locality and yet to the bills of each will be given as wide a circulation and as fixed a value as were given to those of the Bank of the United States in its palmiest days." (Cong. Globe, 37th Cong., 2d sess., part 1, p. 616.)

In the national banking act as passed in 1863 it was believed that the desired result had been obtained.

Mr. Hugh McCulloch, president of a leading bank at Indianapolis, and distinguished as a financier, was induced, at great sacrifice to himself, to accept the office of Comptroller of the Currency and inaugurate the new system. In a letter to a friend published in the Banker's Magazine, Vol. XVIII, pages 8 and 9, he said:

"The national system of banking has been devised with a wisdom that reflects the highest credit upon its author, to furnish to the people of the United States a national-bank-note circulation without the agency of a national bank. It is not to be a mammoth corporation, with power to increase and diminish its discounts and circulation, at the will of its managers, thus enabling a board of directors to control the business and politics of the country. It can have no concentrated political power. Nor do I see how it can be diverted from its proper and legitimate objects for partisan purposes. It will concentrate in the hands of no privileged persons a monopoly of banking. It simply authorizes, under suitable and necessary restrictions, any number of persons, not less than five in number, in any of the States or Territories of the Union, to engage in the business of banking, while it prevents them from issuing a single dollar to circulate as money which is not secured by the stocks and resources of the Government. It is, therefore, in my judgment (as far as calculation is regarded), not only a perfectly safe system of banking, but it is one that is eminently adapted to the nature of our political institutions."

In his first report as Comptroller of the Currency, made November 28, 1863, he says:

"By the national currency act the principle is for the first time recognized and established, that the redemption of bank notes should be guaranteed by the Government authorizing their issue. The national currency will be as solvent as the Nation of which it represents the unity. The country has at last secured to it a permanent paper circulating medium of a uniform value, without the aid of a national bank. This national system confers no monopoly of banking, but opens its advantages equally to all. It interferes with no State rights. It meets both the necessities of the Government and the wants of the people. It needs modifications and may require others than those which are suggested in this report; but it is right in principle, and of its success there can, I think, be no reasonable doubt."

And again in his second report, made November 25, 1864:

"This examination of the act, and the observation of the manner in which it is being administered, have resulted in the entering up of a popular judgment in favor of the national banking system; a judgment, not that the system is a perfect one, nor free from danger of abuse, but that it is a safer system, better adapted to the nature of our political institutions and to our commercial necessities, giving more strength to the Government, with less risk of its being used by the Government against the just rights of the States or the rights of the people than any system which has yet been devised, and that by such amendments of the act as experience may show to be needful, it may be made as little objectionable, and as beneficial to the Government and the people, as any paper money banking system that wisdom and experience are likely to invent. It promises to give to the people that long-existing "desideratum," a national currency without a national bank, a bank-note circulation of uniform value without the creation of a moneyed power in a few hands over the politics and business of the country."

When in his letter and reports Mr. McCulloch speaks of "a national bank note circulation without the agency of a national bank," etc., he manifestly has reference to an institution national in the sense of being a central institution like the old United States Bank, operating throughout the country by means of branches.

The banks created by the national banking act were, and were designed to be, local institutions and independent of each other, but under national control and supervision. Nationalization without centralization was the keynote of the law. This is demonstrated by the structure of the banks provided for.

Reference will be made to the national banking act as contained in the United States Compiled Statutes, 1901. It is title 62, and consists of four chapters. The first chapter deals with "organization and powers," the second with "obtaining and issuing circulating notes," the third with "regulation of the banking business," and the fourth with "dissolution and receivership." The entire act is too long for reproduction here, but pertinent sections will be set out in full, or in their substance.

Section 5133—"formation of national banking associations"—provides:

"Associations for carrying on the business of banking under this title may be formed by any number of natural persons, not less in any case than five. They shall enter into articles of association, which shall specify in general terms the object for which the association is formed, and may contain any other provisions, not inconsistent with law, which the association may see fit to adopt for the regulation of its business and the conduct of its affairs. These articles shall be signed by the persons uniting to form the association, and a copy of them shall be forwarded to the Comptroller of the Currency, to be filed and preserved in his office."

It should be noted in passing that only "natural persons" may engage in the formation of a bank.

Section 5134—"requisites of organization certificate"—provides:

"The persons uniting to form such an association shall, under their hands, make an organization certificate, which shall specifically state:

"First. The name assumed by such association; which name shall be subject to the approval of the Comptroller of the Currency.

"Second. The place where its operations of discount and deposit are to be carried on, designating the State, Territory, or District, and the particuar county and city, town, or village.

"Third. The amount of capital stock and the number of shares into which the same is to be divided.

"Fourth. The names and places of residence of the shareholders and the number of shares held by each of them.

"Fifth. The fact that the certificate is made to enable such persons to avail themselves of the advantages of this title."

By this section the bank is distinctly localized, for it requires that "the place where its operations of discount and deposit are to be carried on" shall be designated as to State, county, and city, town, or village; and it allows but one place.

This is repeated in section 5190—"place of business"—which provides:

"The usual business of each national banking association shall be transacted at an office or banking house located in the place specified in its organization certificate."

By an act of May 1, 1886 (ch. 73, 24 Stat. 18), a bank was authorized to change its location, but not to a place more than 30 miles distant, and the new location must be within the same State. No provision has ever been made for increasing the number of cities, towns, or villages in which a bank may do business.

Section 5138—"requisite amount of capital"—provides:

"No association shall be organized with a less capital than $100,000, except that banks with a capital of not less than $50,000 may, with the approval of the Secretary of the Treasury, be organized in any place the population of which does not exceed 6,000 inhabitants, and except that banks with a capital of not less than $25,000 may, with the sanction of the Secretary of the Treasury, be organized in any place the population of which does not exceed 3,000 inhabitants. No association shall be organized in a city the population of which exceeds 50,000 persons with a capital of less than $200,000."

This, because of the small amount of capital required in such case, extends the facilities of national banking to the smallest communities.

Section 5146—"requisite qualifications of directors"—provides:

"Every director must, during his whole term of service, be a citizen of the United States, and at least three-fourths of the directors must have resided in the State, Territory, or District in which the association is located, for at least one year immediately preceding their election, and must be residents therein during their continuance in office. Every director must own, in his own right, at least 10 shares of the capital stock of the association of which he is a director. Any director who ceases to be the owner of 10 shares of the stock, or who becomes in any other manner disqualified, shall thereby vacate his place."

Here the local character of the bank is secured. The directors must all be shareholders, they must all be citizens of the United States, and three-fourths of them must be residents of the State.

The powers of the bank are conferred in general terms by section 5136, and they are: to have a seal, and perpetual succession, to make contracts, sue and be sued, elect officers and define their duties, and further——

"Sixth. To prescribe, by its board of directors, by-laws not inconsistent with law, regulating the manner in which its stock shall be transferred, its directors elected or appointed, its officers appointed, its property transferred, its general business conducted, and the privileges granted to it by law exercised and enjoyed.

"Seventh. To exercise by its board of directors, or duly authorized officers or agents, subject to law, all such incidental powers as shall be necessary to carry on the business of banking; by discounting and negotiating promissory notes, drafts, bills of exchange, and other evidences of debt; by receiving deposits; by buying and selling exchange, coin, and bullion; by loaning money on personal security; and by obtaining, issuing, and circulating notes according to the provisions of this title.

"But no association shall transact any business except such as is incidental and necessarily preliminary to its organization, until it has been authorized by the Comptroller of the Currency to commence the business of banking."

Section 5137 confers power to hold real property and limits it to such as may be necessary for "its immediate accommodation in the transaction of its business," and such as it may acquire in the way of securing payment of debts previously contracted, but real estate so acquired can not be held for a longer period than five years.

Section 5197 limits the rate of interest which may be taken to that "allowed by the laws of the State, Territory, or District where the bank is located."

This again emphasizes the local character of the institution.

Section 5201 prohibits a bank from loaning upon or purchasing its own shares.

It has been repeatedly held that the powers of a national bank are limited to those expressly granted by the act and such as are properly incidental to those granted.

In Logan County National Bank v. Townsend (139 U.S. 67, l. c. 73), the court, speaking through Mr. Justice Harlan, said:

"It is undoubtedly true, as contended by the defendant, that the national banking act is an enabling act for all associations organized under it, and that a national bank can not rightfully exercise any powers except those expressly granted by that act, or such incidental powers as are necessary to carry on the business of banking for which it was established. The statute declares that a national banking institution shall have power to 'exercise, by its board of directors, or duly authorized officers or agents, subject to law, all such incidental powers as shall be necessary to carry on the business of banking; by discounting and negotiating promissory notes, drafts, bills of exchange, and other evidences of debt; by receiving deposits; by buying and selling exchange, coin and bullion; by loaning money on personal security; and by obtaining, issuing, and circulating notes according to the provisions' of title 62 of the Revised Statutes."

And in California Bank v. Kennedy (167 U.S. 362, l. c. 366), the court, through Mr. Justice White, said:

"It is settled that the United States statutes relative to national banks constitute the measure of the authority of such corporations, and that they can not rightfully exercise any powers except those expressly granted, or which are incidental to carrying on the business for which they are established. Logan County Bank v. Townsend (139 U.S. 67, 73). No express power to acquire the stock of another corporation is conferred upon a national bank, but it has been held that, as incidental to the power to loan money on personal security, a bank may in the usual course of doing such business accept stock of another corporation as collateral, and by the enforcement of its rights as pledges it may become the owner of the collateral and be subject to liability as other stockholders. (National Bank v. Case, 99 U.S. 628). So, also, a national bank may be conceded to possess the incidental power to accept in good faith stock of another corporation as security for a previous indebtedness. It is clear, however, that a national bank does not possess the power to deal in stocks. The prohibition is implied from the failure to grant the power." (First National Bank v. National Exchange Bank, 92 U.S. 122, 128.)

The proposition is an elementary one in corporation law and needs no elaboration.

It follows that while a bank may take the stocks of another corporation as collateral to a loan, or take them in payment of a debt previously incurred, it can not deal in stocks. The limit of its power in this respect is stated by Chief Justice Waite in First National Bank v. National Exchange Bank (92 U.S. 122, 128):

". . . In the honest exercise of the power to compromise a doubtful debt owing to a bank, it can hardly be doubted that stocks may be accepted in payment and satisfaction, with a view to their subsequent sale or conversion into money so as to make good or reduce an anticipated loss. Such a transaction would not amount to a dealing in stocks."

In First National Bank v. Converse (200 U.S. 425), a manufacturing company had failed, and the creditors, among whom was the bank, organized a new corporation to purchase the stocks, evidences of debt, and assets of the old, and to continue in the manufacture of the same articles that had been manufactured by the old company. This transaction was held to be without the powers of the bank. The court, p. 439, said:

". . . To concede that a national bank has ordinarily the right to take stock in another corporation as collateral for a present loan or as security for a preexisting debt does not imply that because a national bank has lent money to a corporation it may become an organizer and take stock in a new and speculative venture; in other words, do the very thing which the previous decisions of this court have held can not be done."

As to acquiring the stocks of other national banks, the ruling of the court is very explicit.

In Concord First National Bank *v*. Hawkins (174 U.S. 364), the Bank of Concord, N.H., had bought and held as an investment 100 shares of the stock of the Indianapolis National Bank. The last-named bank failed and Hawkins as receiver sued the Concord bank to recover the assessment which had been made upon the stock of the Indianapolis bank. The Concord bank denied liability upon the ground that it had no right to hold the stock. The court refused so much as to apply the doctrine of estoppel in favor of creditors. Referring to previous decisions of the court and to the distinction made by the Circuit Court between the acquisition of stocks in national banks and of stocks in other corporations, the court, p. 368, said:

"No reason is given by the learned judge in support of the solidity of such a distinction, and none occurs to us. Indeed, we think that the reasons which disqualify a national bank from investing its money in the stock of another corporation are quite as obvious when that other corporation is a national banks as in the case of other corporations. The investment by national banks of their surplus funds in other national banks, situated, perhaps, in distant States, as in the present case, is plainly against the meaning and policy of the statutes from which they derive their powers, and evil consequences would be certain to ensue if such a course of conduct were countenanced as lawful. Thus, it is enacted, in section 5146, that 'every director must, during his whole term of service, be a citizen of the United States, and at least three-fourths of the directors must have resided in the State, Territory, or district in which the association is located for at least one year immediately preceding their election, and must be residents therein during their continuance in office.' "

One of the evident purposes of this enactment is to confine the management of each bank to persons who live in the neighborhood, and who may, for that reason, be supposed to know the trustworthiness of those who are to be appointed officers of the bank, and the character and financial ability of those who may seek to borrow its money. But if the funds of a bank in New Hampshire, instead of being retained in the custody and management of its directors are invested in the stock of a bank in Indiana, the policy of this wholesome provision of the statute would be frustrated. The property of the local stockholders, so far as thus invested, would not be managed by directors of their own selection, but by distant and unknown persons. Another evil that might result, if large and wealthy banks were permitted to buy and hold the capital stock of other banks, would be that, in that way, the banking capital of a community might be concentrated in one concern, and business men be deprived of the advantages that attend competition between banks. Such accumulation of capital would be in disregard of the policy of the national banking law, as seen in its numerous provisions regulating the amount of the capital stock and the methods to be pursued in increasing or reducing it. The smaller banks, in such a case, would be in fact, though not in form, branches of the larger one.

Section 5201 may also be referred to as indicating the policy of this legislation. It is in the following terms:

"No association shall make any loan or discount on the security of the shares of its own capital stock, nor be the purchaser or holder of any such shares, unless such security or purchase shall be necessary to prevent loss upon a debt previously contracted in good faith; and stock so purchased or acquired shall, within six months from the time of its purchase, be sold or disposed of at public or private sale; or, in default thereof, a receiver may be appointed to close up the business of the association."

This provision, forbidding a national bank to own and hold shares of its own capital stock, would, in effect, be defeated if one national bank were permitted to own and hold a controlling interest in the capital stock of another.

Here is an express recognition and assertion of the local and independent character of our national banks and the denial of any power which would tend to create what is in effect a central bank with branches.

As to the transfer of its shares, a national bank has power only "to prescribe, by its board of directors, by-laws not inconsistent with law, regulating the manner in which its stock shall be transferred." Manner relates to method or form and not to substance. So the by-laws may require a formal indorsement of the outstanding certificates, the issuance of a new one, and a register of the transfer upon the books of the bank. But no condition can be imposed which limits or impairs the right of transfer.

The national banking act as originally passed in 1863, by section 36, denied to the stockholder "power to sell or transfer any share held in his own right so long as he shall be liable, either as principal debtor, surety, or otherwise, to the association for any debt which shall have become due and remains unpaid," etc.; but this provision was repealed by the act of 1864, which, with amendments, is the act now upon the books. The purpose of the repeal was to make the shares more readily transferable. Banks thereafter, however, attempted to enforce the restrictions of the original act by means of by-laws, but these have been held always to be invalid. Speaking to this subject in Bank v. Lanier (11 Wall. 369, 1, c. 377–378), the court said:

"The power to transfer their stock is one of the most valuable franchises conferred by Congress on banking associations. Without this power it can readily be seen the value of the stock would be greatly lessened, and, obviously, whatever contributes to make the shares of the stock a safe mode of investment, and easily convertible, tends to enhance their value. It is no less the interest of the shareholder, than the public, that the certificate representing his stock should be in a form to secure public confidence, for without this he could not negotiate it to any advantage.

"It is in obedience to this requirement, that stock certificates of all kinds have been constructed in a way to invite the confidence of business men, so that they have become the basis of commercial transactions in all the large cities of the country, and are sold in open market the same as other securities. Although neither in form or character negotiable paper, they approximate to it as nearly as practicable. If we assume that the certificates in question are not different from those in general use by corporations, and the assumption is a safe one, it is easy to see why investments of this character are sought after and relied upon. No better form could be adopted to assure the purchaser that he can buy with safety. He is told, under the seal of the corporation, that the shareholder is entitled to so much stock, which can be transferred on the books of the corporation, in person or by attorney, when the certificates are surrendered, but not otherwise. This is a notification to all persons interested to know, that whoever in good faith buys the stock, and produces to the corporation the certificates, regularly assigned, with power to transfer, is entitled to have the stock transferred to him. And the notification goes further, for it assures the holder that the corporation will not transfer the stock to any one not in possession of the certificates."

This ruling holding the restrictive by-law to be invalid was repeated in Bullard v. National Eagle Bank (18 Wall. 594), Third National Bank v. Buffalo German Ins. Co. (193 U.S. 581); and in many cases on the circuit and in the State courts.

If the law was changed to permit a transfer, when to deny it was in the immediate interest of the bank, it surely never was the purpose to authorize a restriction upon transfer in behalf of any interest foreign to the bank, and with which it is forbidden that the bank as a bank may be identified.

From the history of the national banking act, from its terms and provisions, and from the decisions of the Supreme Court construing it, these propositions are derived:

I. The banks are local institutions and independent of each other, none the less that they are creatures of Federal power and subject to Federal supervision and control.

II. A bank may in its by laws regulate the manner in which its shares may be transferred, but it cannot impair or limit the right of transfer.

III. As to business operations, the bank has such powers as are expressly granted by the act, and such as are properly incidental to those expressly granted, and none other, and so can engage only in the business of banking as that business is defined by the act.

IV. It is neither banking nor an incident of banking to invest the funds of the bank in another business, in any manner or to any extent; and the bank has therfore no right to invest its funds in the stocks of another corporation, and especially not in the stocks of another national bank.

V. The powers of a national banking association are and can be granted only by the United States, and as no grant of such powers is made by the act to any State corporation, they may not be exercised by such a corporation.

These propositions relate to matters of substances, and so may be no more evaded than violated. Indirection, if it accomplishes the same purpose, stands upon the same footing with direction.

Coming now to the case in hand, we have to consider what is the practical effect of the creation of the National City Co. and its affiliation with the National City Bank of New York.

So far as concerns matters of form, it may be conceded that the National City Co. was incorporated as an independent institution. Still, its certificate of incorporation while not compelling dependence upon or interrelation with any other institution, does provide for it. Its business powers and capacities are very extensive. They authorize the acquisition of any kind of property and the conduct of any kind of business, and the doing of whatever may be incident thereto. (See article second of the certificate of association.) The only limitation upon its business activities is to be found in paragraph VIII of article II, and this is:

". . . but nothing herein contained shall be construed as authorizing the business of banking nor as including the business purpose or purposes of a money corporation or a corporation provided for by the banking, insurance, railroad, and the transportation corporations laws, or an educational institution or corporation which may be incorporated as provided in the education law, nor as authorizing or intending to authorize the performance at any time of any act or acts then unlawful."

As the business of banking, which must be taken to include the business of banking under the national banking laws, is expressly prohibited, the powers of the company as granted by its charter do not offend the Federal laws.

The tenth article provides in its first paragraph that "the directors of the company need not be stockholders," and in the second paragraph that—

"No transaction entered into by the company shall be affected by the fact that the directors of the company were personally interested in it, and every director of the company is hereby relieved from any disability that might otherwise prevent his contracting with the company for the benefit of himself or any firm, association, or corporation in which he may be in anywise interested."

These provisions in and of themselves violate no Federal statutes, but they give a facility for serving two masters, which is, to say the least, unusual; and they do permit the use of the company as a mere instrumentality or convenience of some other institution.

The capital stock of the company is by the third article fixed at $10,000,000, but it is provided by paragraph 5 of article 10 that—

"The board of directors shall have absolute discretion in the declaration of dividends out of the surplus profits of the company, and they may accumulate such profits to such extent as they may deem advisable instead of distributing them among the stockholders, and may invest and reinvest the same in such manner as in their absolute discretion they may deem advisable."

Thus, while there is a limit placed upon the capital stock of the company, there is none upon the actual capital it may accumulate, and so none upon its possible financial power.

These various provisions of the certificate of incorporation are important to be considered in view of the use which has been made of the company.

The certificate is dated July 5, 1911, but prior to that date, on June 1, 1911, an agreement was entered into between the National City Bank of New York as the first party, James Stillman, Frank A. Vanderlip, and Stephen S. Palmer, trustees, as the second party, and Henry A. C. Taylor, Cleveland H. Dodge, William Rockefeller, Moses Taylor Pyne, J. Pierpont Morgan, and other sub-scribers, "who are shareholders of the said bank," as parties of the third part. In the agreement these parties are designated, respectively, as "the bank," "the trustees," and "the subscribers."

The trustees are all of them officers of the bank. Mr. Stillman is the chairman of the board of directors, Mr. Vanderlip is its president, and Mr. Palmer is a director.

The agreement, then, is one between the bank, its officers, and its shareholders, and, as will be seen, the officers and shareholders are dealt with not as individuals, but as officers and shareholders.

The preamble recites that—

"Opportunities and facilities for making desirable investments, other than those which are possible in the ordinary course of the banking business, are, from time to time, presented to the officers of the bank, which they desire to make available to the shareholders of the bank."

Here is the declared purpose to do something, make investments, not within the scope of the bank's powers. That the officers and shareholders of the bank as individuals may make such investments is conceded, but that the bank, or its officers or shareholders, as officers and shareholders, may do so, in other words, that the powers and facilities granted by the national banking act may be used for purposes outside the ordinary course of banking business, is denied.

The first article of the agreement provides for the organization of an investing company. It is here called the United States Investing Co. It is, however, the National City Co. under a provisional name.

It is not within the scope of the bank's powers to have part or lot in such an agreement, for the simple reason that the formation of an investing company under State corporation laws is not the conduct of banking under national laws. And what is true of the bank is true of its officers and shareholders acting as such.

The second article accords to each shareholder of the bank, as a right, a beneficial interest, through the trustees, in the capital stock of the investing company, to the extent of two-fifths of the par value of his capital stock in the bank, provided he exercises his right by executing the agreement or by having his bank stock stamped as thereafter provided in the agreement. If the shareholder does not exercise his right in time, the trustees may determine the conditions upon which he may do so thereafter.

The par value of the capital stock of the bank is $25,000,000, and two-fifths of this is ten millions, which is the par value of the stock of the investment company. Every shareholder of the bank exercising his right, the stock of the company is fully provided for.

It is contended that the shareholder of the bank is not required to take his allotted beneficial interest in the company, but manifestly he is under strong compulsion. The bank and the compay, as will be seen from later provisions of the agreement, are so closely bound together that the welfare of the company will always be the serious concern of the bank. For better or for worse the bank and the company are united. The shareholder, if he is not in the arrangement, must none the less hazard the worse and get none of the better, and so, inasmuch as against his will he is in for the worse, he will in self-protection go in further and entitle himself to the better.

The third article provides that in order to facilitate participation by the shareholders of the bank in the beneficial interests in the company, the trustees will recommend to the directors of the bank the declaration of a special dividend of 40 per cent on the capital stock of the bank, which will amount to $10,000,000, or the exact amount of the capital stock of the company. The subscribers, shareholders of the bank, agree to apply the dividend to the payment of the stock of the company.

The recommendation of the trustees, officers of the bank, assented to by the bank and by two-thirds of its shareholders, are sure to be adopted, but not even as against a dissenting or nonassenting minority, no matter how small that minority might be, was there a right to declare a dividend except as such declaration was made in the interest of the bank and its shareholders as such. And there is a larger interest, that of depositors and of the Naional Government, which requires that the bank shall be conducted as a bank pure and simple and not as a promoting agency of speculative investment companies.

The fourth article requires that the subscribers at once assign the special dividend to the trustees in order to enable the trustees to organize the investing company.

This only emphasizes the fact that the resources and facilities of the bank were utilized to create the investing company.

The fifth article provides (1) that the stock of the investing company shall be issued to the trustees and shall be held by them and their successors in trust, and (2) that the beneficial interest of the subscribers in this stock "Shall not be transferable separately, but only by the transfer of the shares of stock of the bank held by them respectively; and every sale or transfer of stock of the bank by a subscriber or his successor shall include the beneficial interest of such subscriber or his successor in the capital stock of the investing company attaching to the shares of the bank so sold or transferred."

The first clause of this article limits the number of stockholders in the company to three, the three being the trustees and their successors in trust.

Article 9 of the agreement provides:

"The number of trustees hereunder shall not be less than three. Any trustee may, at any time, resign. In case of any vacancy in the number of trustees, it shall be filled by the remaining trustees by the selection of someone who is an officer or a director of the bank; and any trustee who shall cease to be an officer or a director of the bank shall thereupon also cease to be a trustee hereunder; it being intended that only officers or directors of the bank shall act as trustees.

"No trustee shall be liable for the acts of any other trustee, but shall be liable only for his own willful misconduct.

"The trustees may act by a majority, either at a meeting or by writing with or without a meeting; and they may vote in person or by proxy."

Thus only officers or directors of the bank can ever be stockholders in the company, for the trustees held the stock and only officers and directors of the bank can be trustees. And the trustees are a self-perpetuating body. Any vacancy is to be filled by the remaining trustees.

By article 8 it is provided that the trustees and such other persons as they may designate, who shall be officers or directors of the bank, shall constitute the first board of directors of the company, and that no one shall ever be a director of the company who is not also an officer or director of the bank.

The certificate of incorporation of the company provides for five directors, but it has only three stockholders; therefore, it was provided in the certificate that directors need not be stockholders.

The second clause of article 5 prohibits transfer of beneficial interests in the company without a transfer of the corresponding shares of the bank, and, conversely, prohibits transfer of shares in the bank without a transfer of the corresponding beneficial interest in the company.

Article 6 provides for certain indorsements upon the certificate of bank shares and upon the certificates of beneficial interest in the company. These indorsements are in aid of the plan and purpose of the agreement.

Article 7 requires payment of company dividends to be made to shareholders of the bank, whose certificates of bank shares are stamped or indorsed as provided in article 5. Payments of these dividends may be made by the trustees to the bank, and such payment will relieve the trustees from further liability on their account.

Article 10 provides for the amendment, modification, or termination of the agreement. Any of these can be accomplished only "with the written consent of the trustees and of two-thirds in interest of those for whom the capital stock of the investing company is then held by the trustees."

This, then is the situation. The company was not independently organized, but was organized by the bank, its officers and shareholders acting as such. Only shareholders of the bank were permitted an interest in the company and these only in the proportion of their holdings in the bank. This constitution of the interests of the company must continue to the end, for no one can ever come into the company without coming into the bank, and no one can ever go out of the company without going out of the bank. The bank, by declaration of a dividend, furnished the entire capital of the company. No person can be an officer or director of the company unless he is an officer or director of the bank.

This is not all. The company has no independence of action. It has no control or authority over its own affairs. It is to be remembered that all its stock is to be held by the trustees and, of course, is to be voted by them. Plenary power over the company is therefore held by these trustees. Now, these trustees were not elected by the incorporators of the company nor by its stockholders. They were nominated by the agreement between the bank, its officers, and shareholders, made before the company was in existence. They can not be removed, nor can their successors be elected or determined by any power or interest of the company. The trustees, nominated by the agreement, perpetuate themselves. They appoint their own successors. The only power outside themselves which can make a change in their membership is the shareholding body of the bank. The shareholders by not continuing a trustee as an officer or director of the bank eliminate him as a trustee. The official organization of the company and the vesting of its powers are determined and can be determined only by the corporate action of the bank.

And the agreement which accomplishes all these things is beyond the scope of the legitimate action of the bank to change or terminate. Two-thirds of the shareholders of the bank and the trustees must agree before there can be a change in it or an end of it. In this matter, so material to the welfare of the bank, the shareholders and the directors have abdicated their powers and duties and abandoned them to a minority of their number and the three trustees.

To facilitate the conduct of the business of the company by the officers of the bank, article 10 of the certificate of incorporation of the company provides that no transaction entered into by the company shall be affected by the fact that its officers or directors are contracting for their own benefit, or for the benefit of any firm, association, or corporation in which they may be interested in any wise.

This arrangement between the bank and the company virtually consolidates them, unifies their every interest, and requires that all the powers and capacities of both shall always be exerted in unison—or it does not.

If we have two institutions, and not one, chartered as each one of them is by public authority, and by different sovereignties, then each has its own peculiar mission and its own distinctive rights and duties, powers, and obligations. The bank is not concerned with the company, except as it might be with any other possible borrower of its funds, and the company is not concerned with the bank except as it might be with any other institution whose funds it might wish to borrow. The bank will not be influenced to lend money in aid of any enterprise in which the company may be engaged, because of that fact, and the company will not, because of its relations with the bank, look to it the more readily for financial support. The business of each will be conducted with regard to its own distinctive advantage.

If these institutions are twain in the substantial sense indicated, then the arrangement which places the control of the company so absolutely and irrevocably under trustees appointed by the bank, and subject to change only by the corporate action of the bank, offends the fundamental law that "no servant can serve two masters; for either he will hate the one and love the other or else he will hold to the one and despise the other." This law is implied in every line of the charter of the bank, and the attempt to repeal it in the tenth article of incorporation of the company is vain and nugatory.

If, however, the mission of the bank and the mission of the company are alike and linked always in interest and welfare, if the rights and duties of the two are necessarily harmonious and reciprocal, if the bank at all times must cooperate with the company and the company with the bank, if the officers and directors of the bank who are also the officers and directors of the company can not come into the predicament of divided allegiance, and, indeed, are in the service of but one master, then the bank is involved; engaged, participating in, and conducting the business of the company, business beyond its chartered powers, business that is not national banking.

Only the absolute unity and identity of interest between the two institutions would afford moral excuse for the fusion of their powers under one control, but that excuse can not justify transgression of the positive mandate of the national banking act, which, from considerations of public interest, has determined that national banking shall be a business apart to be conducted by institutions organized for that purpose and for no other.

I am constrained to conclude that as to the bank the agreement violates the law, in its details, because it impairs and limits the right of transfer of shares, and because it assumes to bind the bank beyond the possibility of release by the majority action of its shareholders and directors, and in its general plan and scope, because it embarks the bank in business and ventures beyond its corporate powers.

The operations under this agreement are proper to be considered, and what is said in this connection is based upon a letter of date July 26, 1911, from President Vanderlip to United States Attorney Wise.

At that date $9,679,000 of the capital stock of the company had been paid up, showing that more than 96 per cent of the shareholders of the bank had come into the arrangement.

The company had made investments in the shares of 16 different banks and trust companies, the aggregate number of shares being 29,178. The market value of these was not shown. In addition, approximately $3,200,000 had been invested in other companies of different character.

Of the banks, nine were national banks. The number of shares held by the company and the total number of shares of the capital stock of the banks is as follows:

Bank	Company's holdings	Total number of shares of capital stock of bank
Second National Bank of New York	10	10,000
Fletcher American National Bank of Indianapolis	167	20,000
American National Bank of Indianapolis[1]	250	....
Fourth Street National Bank of Philadelphia	500	30,000
National Shawmut Bank of Boston	1,000	35,000
Riggs National Bank of Washington	2,240	10,000
National Butchers & Drovers Bank of New York	3,000	3,000
Lincoln National Bank of New York	4,324	10,000
National Bank of Commerce of New York	9,800	250,000

[1] No such bank shown in the American Bank Reporter.

Thus the company holds the entire capital stock of the National Butchers & Drovers Bank, not even deducting the shares, 10 each, which its 9 directors are by the law required to hold in their own right. This bank surely is not independent of the National City Bank in view of the relations of each to the company.

The company wants but 677 shares to hold a majority of the capital stock of the Lincoln National Bank, and practically it may be said that when 4,324 out of 10,000 shares are held in one ownership the control of the corporation has been secured.

If the National City Bank may extend its powers to the control of two other national banks, there is no limit to what it may do in that way. If the power exists, there is no restraint upon its exercise. By different methods and under other forms the National City Bank is doing, and in larger measure, what the Supreme Court in Concord National Bank v. Hawkins, supra, declared to be in contravention of the national banking act.

And the National City Co., considered by itself and apart from its relations to the National City Bank, is also in violation of law. Its charter from the State of New York expressly prohibits it from the business of banking. And that charter could not confer the power to engage in the business of national banking. Such power could be conferred only by the laws of the United States.

Section 5133, quoted above, confers the power to form a national banking association only upon "natural persons." Other sections of the law restrict the place of operations of the association to a single city, town, or village and require that the directors shall be natural persons, all of whom have a substantial interest in the bank and three-fourths of whom must be citizens and residents of the State in which the association operates. Then, too, as we have seen, the bank may not as an investment acquire the shares of another bank, or, indeed, of any other corporation. The purpose and the result are that each national bank must be a local, independent, institution, managed by natural persons, and not linked by proprietary interest with any other business than that of national banking.

It is not necessary to consider whether the national banking act absolutely prohibits the holding of shares in a national bank by a State corporation to any extent or for any purpose, and it may be conceded that a State corporation may acquire such shares as an incident to securing payment of a debt and hold them to a convenient time for sale, or that an institution like a trust company may hold them in a fiduciary capacity, but certainly there can be no holding of such shares by any corporation when the result is to defeat the policy of the national banking act; that is, to destroy the local character of the bank, break down its independence, vest its control in another corporation, and link it in substantial proprietary interest with some other business than national banking.

The National City Co. may embark in almost any business whatever, and in fact has made large investments in other enterprises than banking. It has acquired ownership of all the stock of the National Butchers & Drovers Bank, a virtually controlling interest in the Lincoln National Bank, and interests of magnitude in other national banks.

The ownership of property implies duties as well as rights. As the company owns all the shares of the Butchers & Drovers Bank, it has a duty with respect to them. It must vote them at shoreholders' meetings, it must elect the directors of the bank, and decide important questions of policy. If this is not conducting the business of a national bank how shall it be characterized?

In *Anglo-American Land Co.* v. *Lombard* (132 Fed. Rep. 721, l. c. 736), the Court of Appeals for the Eighth Circuit, in an opinion by Judge Van Devanter, now a justice of the Supreme Court, held that the acquisition by a Missouri company of the stock and control of a Kansas company was illegal. He said:

". . . Where it is not otherwise provided, the implication in a grant of corporate power and life is that the corporation shall exercise its powers and carry on its business through its own officers and employees, and not indirectly, through another corporation operated under its control, and that it shall maintain an independent corporate existence, and not surrender the control of its affairs or the exercise of its powers in another corporation. Conceding that a corporation of a private character, not charged with any public duties, may, in pursuance of appropriate action on the part of its stockholders, sell all of its property, wind up its affairs, and permanently retire from business, still, in the absence of express authorization, neither the corporation nor its stockholders can, incidental to the sale of its property or otherwise, clothe another corporation with the right to maintain the corporate life or exercise the corporate powers. These views are sustained, and the reasons therefor are fully set forth in *De La Vergne Co.* v. *German Savings Institution* (175 U. S. 40, 54, 20 Sup. Ct. 20, 44 L. Ed. 66), *Buckeye Marble & Freestone Co.* v. *Harvey (Tenn.)* (20 S. W. 427, 18 L. R. A. 252, 36 Am. St. Rep. 71), *Easum* v. *Buckeye Brewing Co.* (C. C. 51 Fed. 156), and in the cases there cited.

We are dealing with corporations of a public character, with national banks, which have public duties to perform, and of these it is a peculiar obligation "to maintain independent corporate existence and not surrender control of their affairs or the exercise of their powers to another corporation."

No authority is given by the Federal statutes to the national banking associations for assigning their powers and delegating their duties to a corporation created by a State, and which, under its charter from the State, may engage in a business and exercise powers denied to the banking association by the law of its creation.

Here again it is to be observed that if the power in question exists, it exists without limit. The company may extend its power to the full control of all the banks into which it has made entrance. Nor need it stop with these. As it grows by what it feeds upon it may expand into a great central bank, with branches in every section of the country. It is, in incipient stage, a holding company of banks, with added power to hold whatever else it may find to be to its advantage.

Where public law and public policy are involved, forms and fictions are disregarded and the facts are dealt with as facts. In the Northern Securities Case (193 U.S. 197), the Securities Co. had acquired the majority of the shares of two great competing railway companies, and this was dealt with in effect as a consolidation of the railway companies. Judge Harlin, affirming the decree of the circuit court, said (p. 326):

The stockholders of these two competing companies disappeared, as such, for the moment, but immediately reappeared as stockholders for the holding company which was thereafter to guard the interests of both sets of stockholders as a unit, and to manage, or cause to be managed, both lines of railroad as if held in one ownership. Necessarily by this combination or arrangement the holding company in the fullest sense dominates the situation in the interest of those who were stockholders of the constituent companies; as much so, for every practical purpose, as if it had been itself a railroad corporation which had built, owned, and operated both lines for the exclusive benefit of its stockholders. Necessarily, also, the constituent companies ceased, under such a combination, to be in active competition for trade and commerce along their respective lines, and have become, practically, one powerful consolidated corporation, by the name of a holding corporation the principal, if not the sole, object for the formation of which was to carry out the purpose of the original combination under which competition between the constituent companies would cease.

So in the Standard Oil case (221 U. S. 1), and in the Tobacco case (221 U. S. 106), the holding of stocks by the principal companies in the various subsidiary companies was recognized and dealt with as engaging in, directing and controlling the business of the subsidiary companies.

Here the National City Co. is not simply to control banks, but it may engage in any business whatever, even that forbidden by its charter, if, despite its charter prohibition as to certain kinds of business, it may invest in the stocks of companies conducting such business. The other enterprises in which the company is engaged may stand in need of credit and of funds, and it is too much to expect that the company's banks will deal simply as banks, equitably and impartially as between its own subsidiaries, and persons and corporations with whom it is not affiliated. The temptation to the speculative use of the funds of the banks at opportune times will prove to be irresistible. Examples are recent and significant of the peril to a bank, incident to the dual and diverse interests of its officers and directors. If many enterprises and many banks are brought and bound together in the nexus of a great holding corporation, the failure of one may involve all in a common disaster. And if the plan should prosper it would mean a union of power in the same hands over industry, commerce, and finance, with a resulting power over public affairs, which was the gravamen of objection to the United States Bank.

I conclude the National City Co. in its holding of national bank stocks is in usurpation of Federal authority and in violation of Federal law.

Respectfully submitted.

_____ _____

Solicitor General

SENATE RESOLUTION 56 AND DEBATE
APRIL 3, 1933

Congressional Record, 73rd Congress, 1st Session, 1101–02.

Mr. Fletcher. Mr. President, from the Committee on Banking and Currency, I report back favorably, with an amendment, Senate Resolution 56, to enlarge the authority of that committee, and I ask unanimous consent for its immediate consideration.

The Vice President. The resolution will be read.

The Chief Clerk read Senate Resolution 56, submitted by Mr. Fletcher March 31, 1933, as follows:

Resolved, That the Committee on Banking and Currency, or any duly authorized subcommittee thereof, in addition to the authority granted under Senate Resolution 84, Seventy-second Congress, agreed to March 4, 1932, and continued in force by Senate Resolution 239, Seventy-second Congress, agreed to June 21, 1932, and further continued by Senate Resolution 371, Seventy-second Congress, agreed to February 28, 1933, shall have authority and hereby is directed—

1. To make a thorough and complete investigation of the operation by any person, firm, copartnership, company, association,

corporation, or other entity, of the business of banking, financing, and extending credit; and of the business of issuing, offering, or selling securities;

2. To make a thorough and complete investigation of the business conduct and practices of security exchanges and of the members thereof;

3. To make a thorough and complete investigation of the practices with respect to the buying and selling and the borrowing and lending of securities which are traded in upon the various security exchanges, or on the over-the-counter markets, or on any other market, and of the values of such securities; and

4. To make a thorough and complete investigation of the effect of all such business operations and practices upon interstate and foreign commerce, upon the industrial and commercial credit structure of the United States, upon the operation of the national banking system and the Federal Reserve System, and upon the market for securities of the United States Government, and the desirability of the exercise of the taxing power of the United States with respect to any such business and any such securities, and the desirability of limiting or prohibiting the use of the mails, the telegraph, the telephone, and any other facilities of interstate commerce or communication with respect to any such operations and practices deemed fraudulent or contrary to the public interest.

For the purpose of this resolution the committee, or any duly authorized subcommittee thereof, is authorized to hold such hearings, to sit and act at such times and places, either in the District of Columbia or elsewhere, during the first session of the Seventy-third Congress or any recess thereof, and until the beginning of the second session thereof; to employ such experts and clerical, stenographic, and other assistants; to require by subpena or otherwise the attendance of such witnesses and the production and impounding of such books, papers, and documents; to administer such oaths and to take such testimony and to make such expenditures as it deems advisable. The cost of stenographic services to report such hearings shall not be in excess of 25 cents per hundred words.

The Vice President. The amendment of the committee will be stated.

The Chief Clerk. After the word "telephone" in line 20 it is proposed to insert the word "radio."

The Vice President. The Senator from Florida requests unanimous consent for the present consideration of the resolution.

Mr. McNary. Mr. President, under the rule and practice of the Senate, a resolution of this character must necessarily go to the Committee to Audit and Control the Contingent Expenses of the Senate. I ask that the resolution be so referred.

The Vice President. That is the rule of the Senate.

Mr. Couzens. Mr. President, before the Senator objects, let me say to him that this is not a new appropriation of money. The committee will carry on the investigation under an appropriation already approved by the Committee to Audit and Control the Contingent Expenses of the Senate.

Mr. Robinson of Arkansas. May I inquire if the resolution contemplates any additional expense?

Mr. Couzens. It does not contemplate any additional expense over and above what has already been approved by the Committee to Audit and Control the Contingent Expenses of the Senate.

Mr. Robinson of Arkansas. Then the rule referred to by the Senator from Oregon does not apply.

Mr. Fletcher. Mr. President, I will say to the Senator that this resolution is supplementary to a resolution already adopted by the Senate. It is in the nature of an amendment to a resolution which has already been adopted.

Mr. McNary. It is my conviction that it does imply an additional expenditure of public funds, and I shall ask that it go to the Committee to Audit and Control the Contingent Expenses of the Senate.

Mr. Fletcher. I think that is wholly unnecessary. The Senator from Michigan has pointed out that the appropriation has already been made, and it does not call for any new appropriation.

Mr. Couzens. Mr. President, a parliamentary inquiry.

The Vice President. The Senator will state it.

Mr. Couzens. Under the rule, is an amendment to a resolution heretofore adopted by the Senate and carrying no additional appropriation required to go to the Committee to Audit and Control the Contingent Expenses of the Senate?

The Vice President. The parliamentary clerk advises the Chair that the precedents are that it is subject to the rule in that it makes a charge on the contingent fund.

Mr. Robinson of Arkansas. Mr. President, it should not be subject to the rule unless it imposes an additional expenditure, a cost in addition to that which has already been authorized. If the resolution does not impose a charge, it would not necessarily go to the Committee to Audit and Control the Contingent Expenses of the Senate. Of course, any report from a committee, if objection is made, must lie over; but the objection which has been made that this amendment to a resolution heretofore adopted must go over because it must be referred to the Committee to Audit and Control the Contingent Expenses of the Senate is apparently incorrect.

Mr. Fess. Mr. President——

Mr. Robinson of Arkansas. I yield to the Senator from Ohio.

Mr. Fess. There is a provision in the resolution which imposes the usual limitation we always write in original resolutions limiting the amount that may be paid to stenographers, and so on. I think that, under a strict interpretation of the rule, it would have to go to the Committee to Audit and Control the Contingent Expenses of the Senate.

Mr. Robinson of Arkansas. If the resolution does not contemplate any additional expenditure, there is no reason for referring it to the Committee to Audit and Control the Contingent Expenses of the Senate. The object of that committee and of referring resolutions to it is to keep the expenditures of the Senate within proper limits. If the resolution does not add any additional expense, it ought not of necessity to go to the Committee to Audit and Control the Contingent Expenses of the Senate. Of course, as I have already said, an objection would carry over the report on other grounds and under other provisions of the rule; but why should anyone insist on sending this resolution to the Committee to Audit and Control the Contingent Expenses of the Senate if it does not involve an additional expenditure? Let any Senator answer me that question, and I shall have nothing further to say.

Mr. Borah. Mr. President——

Mr. Robinson of Arkansas. I yield.

Mr. Borah. May I ask what change the amendment makes in the original resolution in the way of an additional authority? What is the purport of the amendment?

Mr. Fletcher. It gives the committee somewhat larger jurisdiction. It extends that jurisdiction so as to enable the committee to make some inquiries it is desirous of making. The resolution is broadened so that there can be no objection to our making the investigation which we have been directed to make.

Mr. Borah. I know it broadens it, but what is undertaken to be covered by broadening it?

Mr. Couzens. Mr. President, may I answer the Senator's question?

Mr. Fletcher. I yield to the Senator from Michigan.

Mr. Couzens. May I point out that Mr. Pecora, the counsel for the Committee on Banking and Currency, asked the Morgan house to answer 23 questions? The Morgan house agreed to answer 17 of them; they distinctly refused to answer 1; and as to the other questions, they said they would take them under consideration. One of the questions, as I recall, that the counsel asked Morgan & Co. was how much they divided among the partners, and, as I understood, Mr. John W. Davis advised the Morgan house that they need not answer that question. This resolution extends the power of the Banking and Currency Committee so that they may require an answer to that question. That is just one of the elements which we thought necessitated the reporting of this resolution.

Mr. Borah. What I should like to know is, by what language or terms is it undertaken to compel them to answer that question? It presents a rather interesting point.

Mr. Fletcher. In large part this resolution is simply a repetition of the resolution heretofore adopted.

Mr. Borah. I understand that.

Mr. Fletcher. It enlarges the previous resolution so as to go into private banking or investment security concerns which raise some question about our authority to inquire into their affairs.

Mr. Borah. The resolution, then, includes private banking, and so forth?

Mr. Fletcher. I will say to the Senator that there are private bankers, for instance, in the city of New York—and there may be others elsewhere; but in New York, we will say—who are exempt from any supervision or control or suggestion from the bank commissioner of the State; they operate without any sort of supervision or regulation on the part of any State or National authority.

Mr. Borah. Have the committee been advised that they have the legal authority or right to make this additional inquiry?

Mr. Fletcher. Yes; we think beyond any doubt we have that authority. I will say, Mr. President, that this resolution was submitted last Friday; it has been printed, so that the substance of it is not entirely new. It was considered by the Banking and Currency Committee on Saturday and was reported out unanimously with only one amendment, and that was adding the word "radio" after the word "telephone." The resolution is here with the unanimous report of the committee. We feel that we ought to have this authority in order to proceed with the investigation.

The Vice President. The Senator from Oregon objects and the resolution will go over under the rule. However, may the Chair say with reference to the point of order made by the Senator from Oregon that the reasoning of the rule seems to be this: That any resolution making an original charge or an additional charge on the contingent fund of the Senate must go to the Committee to Audit and Control the Contingent Expenses of the Senate. This resolution requires additional labors on the part of the Committee on Banking and Currency, and it seems logical that if it does require additional labors, the Banking and Currency Committee might incur additional expenses to come from the contingent fund of the Senate. However, it is not necessary for the Chair to pass upon that question, for the reason that the Senator from Oregon has objected to the consideration of the resolution today.

Mr. Fletcher. May I ask the Senator from Oregon if he will not now have the resolution referred to the committee, so that there will be no delay?

Mr. McNary. I think the Chair misunderstands my attitude. I believe, from the knowledge that I have of the rules and precedents, that this resolution should go to the Committee to Audit and Control the Contingent Expenses of the Senate. It certainly enlarges the authority of the committee.

The Vice President. The Chair so held in the beginning.

Mr. McNary. The Chair holds that it goes to the Committee to Audit and Control the Contingent Expenses of the Senate. Otherwise, I should invoke the rule. I am content to have it go to the Committee to Audit and Control the Contingent Expenses of the Senate.

Mr. Fletcher. That is what I am asking; that the Senator from Oregon now permit the resolution to go to the Committee to Audit and Control the Contingent Expenses of the Senate.

Mr. Robinson of Arkansas. It goes automatically to that committee.

Mr. McNary. I said that I thought it should go to the Committee to Audit and Control the Contingent Expenses of the Senate. I insist on that disposition, and that is what was ruled by the Chair, and so it goes there.

The Vice President. The resolution will be referred to the Committee to Audit and Control the Contingent Expenses of the Senate.

LITERARY DIGEST ARTICLE, "ROOSEVELT'S DRIVE AGAINST THE BANKERS" APRIL 8, 1933

"Roosevelt's Drive Against the Bankers," *The Literary Digest*, CXV
(April 8, 1933), 4–5.

"The government is on the war-path against the financial world."

This statement by David Lawrence of the Consolidated Press Association is based on recent developments which have tagged several prominent bankers with criminal charges.

And that others will be forced to fight to stay out of prison is taken for granted by Washington correspondents as they see Attorney-General Cummings and a Senate investigating committee turning to new financial trails.

And this is as it should be, assert many papers, agreeing with the Memphis *Commercial Appeal* that "bankers should surely be held to as strict morality as gangsters."

"Investment banking and commercial banking," explains Mr. Lawrence, "having dealt in billions of dollars of the funds of the people and much of the same having been lost through a combination of bad judgment, irresponsibility, and betrayal of trust, the Roosevelt Administration is feeling the impact of an intense indignation."

And the result is that "the safety-valve of prosecution of the offenders, whether they come from high places or low, has begun to function." "Naturally," Mr. Lawrence adds—

Chicago and New York financial districts are apprehensive, for every day come rumors of this or that celebrity or noted institution which is to have its affairs pried into and indictments sought of individuals irrespective of their station.

This development is not uncharacteristic of what has happened after other depressions in the past. Feeling always runs high in periods of deflation. Mr. Roosevelt has issued orders that nobody be spared if he is guilty.

The first big jolt of the campaign against bankers came with the arrest of Joseph W. Harriman, chairman of the board of the Harriman National Bank and Trust Company of New York City. Arrested and arraigned in his bed where he lay ill of a complication of diseases, he was accused, according to the press, of causing the books of his bank to be falsified. There had been in all a $1,393,000 misuse of the bank's funds, "undertaken to finance purchases of the bank's stock and covered by various false entries," according to United States Attorney Medalie as quoted by the New York *Times*.

Later, Mr. Medalie announced that he had withheld action in the Harriman case for three months at the direction of the Department of Justice after counsel for the New York Clearing House Association and the Controller of the Currency had asked delay in the hope that the bank's affairs could be straightened out.

This caused repercussions in Congress and the result is that the Senate Banking Committee has ordered its counsel to investigate the matter.

On the same day that Mr. Harriman was arrested, altho this case had no connection with the Government's campaign, Bernard K. Marcus and Saul Singer, chief officers of the defunct Bank of United States, in New York City, lost their fight to escape serving sentences of three to six years for misapplication of the bank's funds. The $240,000,000 collapse of their bank, affecting 400,000 depositors, was, we read, the greatest bank failure in American history.

On the day that Marcus and Singer landed in Sing Sing, developments came fast in the Government's campaign. A few hours after they had had their first prison meal—corned-beef hash, cheese, corn and cake, bread, tea, and milk—a United States marshal went at night to the Fifth Avenue home of Charles E. Mitchell, who recently had resigned as head of the National City Bank, New York, and arrested him on a charge of wilfully attempting to evade a $573,312 income tax in 1929.

Shortly before, Horace C. Sylvester, Jr., until recently a vice-president of the National City Company, an affiliate of the National City Bank, was arrested and arraigned on an indictment charging third-degree forgery.

"The indictment alleges," we read in the New York *Herald Tribune*, "that Sylvester directed the treasurer of the company to take $10,020 out of the account of a syndicate formed to float a Port of New York Authority bond issue as an expense of the syndicate when it was really used for a loan to John E. Ramsey, general manager of the Port of New York Authority."

Mr. Sylvester was freed in $2,500 bail while Mr. Mitchell's bond was fixt at $10,000. Next came Mr. Mitchell's indictment. Wearing a gray suit and topcoat, the banker appeared in Federal Court and pleaded "not guilty" in a loud, clear voice. The maximum penalty, if the trial jury convicts and the verdict is upheld, is five years' imprisonment and a $10,000 fine.

The indictment, explains the New York *Times*, "charges that Mr. Mitchell received a net income of $2,823,405.95 in 1929, whereas he reported on his income-tax return for that year a net loss of $48,000, paying no tax." Furthermore:

> According to the indictment, Mr. Mitchell's income-tax return was erroneous in that it reported a loss of $1,484,067.53 from the sale of stocks instead of a profit of $1,388,237.97. The difference is represented by a loss of $2,872,305.50 taken from the sale of 18,300 shares of National City Bank stock by Mr. Mitchell to his wife. The Government contends that this was not a bona fide sale.

The actions against both Mr. Mitchell and Mr. Sylvester, we read, resulted from their testimony before the Senate Banking Committee shortly before President Roosevelt's inauguration. At the hearing Senator Brookhart asked Mr. Mitchell about the sale of stock whereby he established a loss in 1929. The reply was freely given, altho Mr. Mitchell identified the buyer simply as a member of his family.

It was not long after he gave this testimony that Mr. Mitchell resigned from the bank, and, according to Washington correspondents, Mr. Roosevelt advised him to take that action.

In the editorial comment on these cases, particularly that of Mr. Mitchell, one finds some pretty harsh language. However, most editors deal with the situation in its broader outlines, and, if they attack an individual, it is generally because he symbolizes a situation which, admittedly, led to abuses. But it is only fair to remind the reader that every man must be considered innocent until he is proved guilty.

Mr. Mitchell, "like Mr. Capone, formerly of Chicago," says the Chicago *Daily News*, "committed the tactical error of writing down the name of Uncle Sam on his sucker list."

"The irony of this case," asserts the Washington *News*, "is that Mr. Mitchell is to be tried for the relatively unimportant offense of an evasion and not for the larger offense of high-finance racketeering as head of the National City Bank." And again:

> It is important that Mr. Mitchell be punished under any law that can be found which he was not clever enough to evade technically. It is also important that Mr. Mitchell not become the scapegoat by which others escape their share of responsibility.
>
> But far more important than the punishment of any guilty person is basic reform of the banking system which not only protected but encouraged financial racketeering. An emotional campaign of personal villification against the Mitchells and the Insulls may make us feel better for the moment, but it will not get us anywhere.
>
> The New Deal in finance involves far more than the arrest or conviction of Mr. Mitchell or any other individual.

But read this statement by the New York *Daily Investment News:*

> If the Government is seeking to punish Mr. Mitchell for banking mistakes or legal encroachments, it would seem meet to try Mr. Mitchell on evidence based on his conduct of the National City Bank and National City Company, rather than to hop off on a by-way to fasten ignominy upon him.
>
> This particular income-tax charge is no charge at all. Payment of income taxes is as honored in the breach as in the observance —something like fealty to the Eighteenth Amendment. By that is not meant that wilful avoidance of income tax payments is pardonable. But to try to inflate such a charge to the heights of dastardliness is overdoing things in a fanatical sense.
>
> Furthermore, what Mr. Mitchell did is common practise. Good counsel agree that it is legitimate practise. And when the case comes up for trial it is probable that Mr. Mitchell will show that he acted upon advice of counsel. Lawyers will undoubtedly testify that they so advised him. Certainly that would not constitute wilful evasion of taxes. At most, it would be an honest mistake.

Agreeing that breaches of trust should be punished, the New Orleans *Item* says that "it is quite easy, on the other hand, to go much too far in condemnation of bankers as a class." When the present investigation is over, this paper adds—

> It will be found that most of our bankers have been just about as honest and well-meaning as grocers and college professors and that many of them have themselves been victims of the passing storm.

NEW YORK TIMES REPORT OF WINTHROP ALDRICH STATEMENT MARCH 9, 1933

A reform program, designed to purge the commercial banking business of all taint of speculative leadership and calculated to reduce the present overlords of the New York money market to a position of relative impotence, was proposed last night by Winthrop W. Aldrich, chairman of the governing board of the Chase National Bank, in connection with an announcement that the bank had decided to divorce its security affiliate, the Chase Securities Corporation. The plan involves inclusion of all commercial banks in the Federal Reserve System.

Calling for the complete separation of deposit banking and investment banking, even to the extent of forbidding private bankers to take deposits or to be directors of banks of deposit, the program strikes directly at the position of J. P. Morgan & Co., the members of which are directors of some of the largest commercial banks of the city and who hold important foreign and domestic deposits.

In his statement Mr. Aldrich, who is a representative of the John D. Rockefeller interests, largest stockholders of the Chase, and who succeeded Albert H. Wiggin as executive head of the Chase organization last January, not only condemned the policies of his predecessor, but, in effect, declared his opposition to some of Wall Street's most powerful figures and their particular interests.

Criticism Hits at Own Bank

In so doing, Mr. Aldrich did not spare his own bank, for the Chase National organization, as it is at present constituted, violates almost every one of the principles he advocated. Coming at a moment when the financial community is shaken by the nation-wide bank closing, the declaration is calculated to strike down what little opposition remains to a drastic reform of the entire banking system. It was looked upon last night as convincing proof of the readiness of Wall Street leaders to scrap old ways and begin anew. One phrase alone, "I do not think, however, that the Glass bill goes sufficiently far," illustrates how far the change of opinion among the banking leaders has gone. It contrasts with the valedictory of Mr. Wiggin, delivered only on Jan. 10, which expressed the conviction that abolition of security affiliates would be "very ill-advised."

In addition to declaring for a complete divorce between the security business and the business of commercial deposit banking, Mr. Aldrich asserted that no corporation or partnership should be permitted to take deposits unless it is subjected to the same regulations as commercial banks and is required to publish a statement of its condition. Such a ruling would force the private banking houses of Morgan's, Kuhn, Loeb & Co. and others to disclose for the first time the extent of their capital and resources.

The reforms suggested by Mr. Aldrich would curb the power of the large private investment banking firms in three respects. First, by depriving these firms of the right to accept deposits, they would make it necessary for the private banks to obtain credit from the commercial banks in financing their security flotations. Second, by doing away with the security affiliates of the commercial banks, the proposed regulations would take from the private banks outlets for the syndicating of their securities which have in the past been of great importance. Third, by removing all private bankers from their positions as directors of the commercial banks, the changes would greatly reduce the prestige, influence and "inside information" available to the partners of investment houses at present.

STATEMENT OF ALDRICH

Mr. Aldrich's statement follows:

I heartily commend the action of the National City Bank in taking steps to divorce its security affiliate, the National City Company. It is impossible to consider the events which took place during the past ten years without being forced to the conclusion that intimate connection between commercial banking and investment banking almost inevitably leads to abuses.

For some time past the Chase National Bank has been giving serious consideration to the question of severing the connection between itself and its security affiliate. The matter was discussed at the last meeting of the directors and a subcommittee has been appointed by the executive committee to report as soon as possible upon ways and means of bringing about this result.

I am entirely in sympathy with the divorcing by law of security affiliates from commercial banks. I do not think, however, that the Glass bill goes sufficiently far in separating the business of commercial banking from that of dealing in securities. To separate commercial banks from their security affiliates is only half the problem. The following additional steps should ultimately be taken:

1. No corporation or partnership should be permitted to take deposits unless such corporation or partnership is subjected to the same regulations and required to publish the same statements as are commercial banks.

2. No corporation or partnership dealing in securities should be permitted to take deposits even under regulation.

3. No officer or director nor any member of any partnership dealing in securities should be permitted to be an officer or director of any commercial bank or bank taking deposits, and no officer or director of any commercial

bank or bank taking deposits should be permitted to be an officer or director of any corporation, or a partner in any partnership, engaged in the business of dealing in securities.

4. Boards of directors of commercial banks should be limited in number by statute so as to be sufficiently small to enable the members to be actually cognizant of the affairs of their banks and in a position really to discharge their responsibility to stockholders, depositors and the business community.

The spirit of speculation should be eradicated from the management of commercial banks, and commercial banks should not be permitted to underwrite securities except securities of the United States Government and of States, Territories, municipalities, and certain other public bodies in the United States.

The Federal Reserve System was founded for the purpose of serving the governmental and commercial life of the country. I think that all commercial banks should be members of the system and that their management should be actuated solely by the desire to carry out such purposes in a sound and conservative manner. In my opinion, not until the reforms above mentioned have been put into effect will this result be obtained.

To what extent Mr. Aldrich's program of banking reform represents a change in view by the officers and directors of the Chase, and to what extent it reflects views which Mr. Aldrich and his group have held, but which they have not hitherto expressed, it is impossible to judge. As one prominent banker, not connected with the Chase, remarked after hearing of the statement, Mr. Aldrich is a comparative new-comer to the banking field. He assumed the executive direction of the largest bank in the world less than two months ago, after a banking career of only three years. Prior to taking charge of the Rockefeller-controlled Equitable Trust Company in December, 1929, he had been a lawyer, but since the merger of the Equitable with the Chase in June, 1930, he has taken an increasingly important part in the affairs of the bank and in banking generally.

Comments on his plan by other bankers were cautions, as was to be expected in view of the fact that the reforms he suggested would involve changes in the structure or personnel of the most important banks of the city. Several of the points made by Mr. Aldrich would involve changes in the board of directors of the Chase National Bank itself. The bank has at present seventy-eight directors, one of the largest directorates of any bank, and among them are several members of private banking houses.

Among the partners of private banking houses which deal in securities, who are also directors of the Chase, are Frank Altschul of Lazard Freres, Frederic W. Allen of Lee, Higginson & Co.; Clarence Dillon of Dillon, Read & Co., and Charles Hayden of Hayden, Stone & Co.

Morgan Partners Affected

Mr. Aldrich's program, if it were carried out, would bring wholesale realignments of the directorates of some of the most important banks in the country and would affect every private banking house. Of the twenty partners of J. P. Morgan & Co. ten are directors of one or more commercial banks.

Among the important local banks of which Morgan partners are directors are the Guaranty Trust Company, the Bankers Trust Company, the Corn Exchange Bank Trust Company, the New York Trust Company and the City Bank Farmers Trust Company. In addition J. P. Morgan and Thomas W. Lamont are directors of the First Security Company, affiliate of the First National Bank. In the case of the Guaranty, the Bankers, the First National Bank and the New York Trust Company, the influence of the Morgan firm is popularly supposed to be dominant.

According to testimony given by John P. Frey, secretary-treasurer of the Metal Trades Division of the American Federation of Labor, before a subcommittee of the Senate Judiciary Committee in January, private banks dominate the large commercial banks of the country and these in turn dominate the smaller commercial banks and the industries of the country.

Mr. Aldrich's proposal that all banks in the country should be brought into the Federal Reserve System found quick endorsement among other bankers. The opinion has been growing since the banking crisis that a unified national system of banking is imperative, and most bankers think that the first step should be universal bank membership in the Federal Reserve.

The belief that the security business should be separated from commercial banking has been growing in force ever since the stock market crash of 1929, but the first definite move in that direction, taken by Senator Carter Glass in his bill introduced a year ago, aroused strong opposition in Wall Street.

It has only been since the recent disclosures of the practices of the National City Company during the boom years, before the Senate committee investigating stock market practices, aroused widespread popular feeling that the Wall Street community has gone over in large numbers to the side of the reformers.

The National City testimony was followed by the resignation of Charles E. Mitchell, chairman of the bank and its affiliates, and of Hugh B. Baker, president of the National City Company. On Tuesday night James H. Perkins, newly elected chairman of the board of the National City, announced that the bank had decided to divorce its affiliate. . . .

TESTIMONY OF J. PIERPONT MORGAN
MAY 23, 1933

U.S. Senate, Stock Exchange Practices, *Hearings Before the Committee on Banking and Currency*, 73rd Congress, 1st Session, Part I, 36–49; 53; 131.

Mr. Pecora. In the balance sheet furnished to me and which has been read into the record, Mr. Morgan, it appears that at the end of the last fiscal year the firms of J. P. Morgan & Co. and Drexel & Co. had among its assets corporate bonds of a figure of $15,073,885.29.

Mr. Morgan. Yes.

Mr. Pecora. Does that value represent market value or cost as of the end of the fiscal year?

Mr. Morgan. Market value.

Mr. Pecora. Is that true of all the other items shown on this balance sheet relating to securities on hand?

Mr. Morgan. Yes.

Mr. Pecora. Such as the item of corporate stocks and other investments?

Mr. Morgan. That is true of them all.

Mr. Pecora. Now, in looking over this consolidated balance sheet, Mr. Morgan, I notice that there is no statement of condition as of the end of the fiscal year 1930, the calendar year which corresponds to your fiscal year 1930. Can you account for that?

Mr. Morgan. I don't know about that. A new partner came in on the 2d of January, and I don't suppose he gave the 31st—we did not figure it in there because it was practically the same as the 2d of January. But a new partner came in on January 2, 1931. The two days we did not bother about. I think that that is the reason why it was not put in there. We did figure our accounts on the 31st of December.

Mr. Whitney. A new partner came in on January 2. We put it up the same way as we did to the Federal Reserve bank. We took that as a real valuation, so we took that date, and that was set forth in the statement given to the Federal Reserve banks. That question came up, and it is the same date and approximate figures.

Mr. Pecora. Now, Mr. Morgan, was a statement of financial condition made up by your firm as of the end of the calendar year 1930?

Mr. Morgan. Yes; I think so.

Mr. Pecora. Is that here?

Mr. Morgan. How?

Mr. Pecora. Can a copy of that be introduced?

Mr. Morgan. Then I am wrong about it. There was not one.

Mr. Pecora. There was not one?

Mr. Morgan. No. Do you want that matter explained—because Mr. Keyes can do it much better than I can.

Mr. Pecora. What is the relationship of Mr. Keyes to your firm?

Mr. Morgan. Mr. Keyes is a sort of general office manager and most confidential clerk.

Mr. Pecora. To your knowledge was a statement of the financial condition of the firm prepared as of December 31, 1930?

Mr. Morgan. I do not have any knowledge about it, no recollection.

Mr. Pecora. Was one prepared as of the 2d day of January 1931?

Mr. Morgan. There was.

Mr. Pecora. Do you know the reason why that date was adopted for the balance sheet or statement of condition——

Mr. Morgan (interposing). Because a new partner——

Mr. Pecora (interposing). And embraced the calendar year 1930 instead of the date of December 31, 1930?

Mr. Morgan. Simply because there was a new partner coming in, I believe. I don't know any other reason.

Mr. Pecora. Is that the only reason?

Mr. Morgan. So far as I know.

Mr. Pecora. Who was the new partner that came in there?

Mr. Morgan. Mr. Parker Gilbert.

Mr. Pecora. Was the statement of financial condition as of January 2, 1931, about the same as would have been as of December 31, 1930, had a statement been drawn as of that date?

Mr. Morgan. I am informed that it would have been about the same.

Mr. Pecora. Mr. Morgan, did your firm make a tax return, a return for income-tax purposes, for the fiscal year of 1930?

Mr. Morgan. I presume we did; the calendar year 1930.

Mr. Pecora. For the calendar year 1930?

Mr. Morgan. Yes. We do not make a firm return on income tax, do we [addressing an associate]? Oh, we do.

Mr. Pecora. Do you know whether the firm of J. P. Morgan & Co. made out another return for income-tax purposes as of the 2d day of January 1931, which was only 2 days after the end of the calendar year 1930?

Mr. Morgan (addressing an associate). Did we? Yes, we did.

Senator Barkley. How could you include those 2 days in January in your income-tax report for 1930?

Mr. Morgan. We did not include them in the income-tax report for 1930.

Mr. Pecora. What would be the object of making it for that date?

Mr. Morgan. Huh?

Senator Barkley. Regardless of any new partnership, your income tax report would have been the same for 1930, and it did not have to be made out until the middle of March?

Mr. Morgan. But it was made out as of December 31, 1930. We had two accounting periods.

Senator Barkley. I don't know just how important that is, but it does not seem to me a few days amounted to much.

Mr. Morgan. I do not think it did amount to much.

Senator Glass. Mr. Morgan——

Mr. Morgan. Yes.

Senator Glass. Does the Internal Revenue Bureau, through its expert examiners, inquire into your income-tax returns?

Mr. Morgan. Oh, yes, sir. He has done it for the last 20 years, I think, ever since there was an income tax.

Senator Glass. Did he express any suspicion or institute any investigation of this 2 days' variation in your report?

Mr. Morgan. I think he received an explanation of the reason why it was done from Mr. Keyes, which I think he accepted as being correct and in order. That is what I understand. They are all there through 1930 [addressing an associate], aren't they? Yes.

Senator Glass. I do not know just where we are headed, how we are going there. I have just had the privilege of reading your statement to the committee before I got in; with some of the things I do not agree at all. But whether your statement or my disagreement has any pertinent relation to this inquiry I suppose I shall find out in time. You say that in the first place you risk your own money. Is that especially accurate?

Mr. Morgan. I say that we do what?

Senator Glass. That your firm risks its own money. I understood that you received deposits to the extent of——

Mr. Morgan (interposing). We do.

Senator Glass (continuing). Three hundred millions of dollars plus.

Mr. Morgan. We do.

Senator Glass. Well, somebody else's money you risk too, isn't it?

Mr. Morgan. Well, we keep that in the banking fund. We do not risk our depositors' money in speculative investments.

Senator Glass. Well, you loan it, don't you?

Mr. Morgan. Only——

Senator Glass (interposing). You don't keep it there as dead lumber; you loan your deposits just as an association does?

Mr. Morgan. We loan it with a great deal more care. That is it.

Senator Glass. Oh, I am not questioning that, but I think that is an inaccurate expression of your activity there. You do not simply risk your own money; you loan your depositors' money. You risk that to the extent that any risk is involved?

Mr. Morgan. To the extent that that risk is involved; yes.

Senator Glass. Now, you say here on page 2 that you are compelled to keep a strong position and that the private banker is compelled to keep a strong position, knowing, as he does, that none of the aids provided by the Government for incorporated banks, such as the Federal Reserve System or the Reconstruction Finance Corporation, are at its disposal. Do you think that is exactly right?

Mr. Morgan. I have not intended that they are at our disposal in any way.

Senator Glass. Have you any idea, can you approximate the volume of bills sold by your concern to the Federal Reserve banks?

Mr. Morgan. Well, I don't know how much it would run to over a period of years. It is something like—it is probably fifteen or twenty millions outstanding, on an average, of acceptances.

Senator Glass. Isn't that availing yourself of the privileges of the Federal Reserve System?

Mr. Morgan. It does go up to 30. No, because after all, you can sell them to the banks quite well.

Senator Glass. Yes, I know, but that is availing yourself of the——

Mr. Morgan (interposing). Oh, we never have sold—we have only once sold them, I am informed, directly to the Federal Reserve bank.

Senator Barkley. Did they buy them as an investment?

Mr. Morgan. They bought them as an investment.

Senator Glass. Yes, but that is availing of the facilities of the Federal Reserve bank. But the point I want to arrive at is to dissipate a popular error, and that is that the Government of the United States neither owns a dollar of proprietary interest in the Federal Reserve Banking System nor does it provide the Federal Reserve Banking System any aid. What aid do you think it provides them?

Mr. Morgan. The Government is an aid provided—the Government provides an aid to the incorporated banks of the Federal Reserve System.

Senator Glass. Oh, no; the Government does not provide that; the banks themselves provide that. The Government does not own a dollar of the stock under the Federal Reserve Banking Act.

Mr. Morgan. But under that very admirable law, the Federal Reserve law, the banks are incorporated by the United States.

Senator Glass. Yes. But so far as the Government aiding it, the only aid that the Government does is to institute a system of espionage in them.

Mr. Morgan. Yes; but the provision of the Federal Reserve bank is a very great aid by the Government to the national bank, a very great aid, and it was devised for that purpose, Senator.

Sentor Glass. It is an aid not extended by the Government of the United States; it is an aid by the banks to themselves. They own the Federal Reserve System. The Government simply has a supervisory control over it.

Mr. Morgan. I know, but when the Government has complete control over it I think that——

Senator Glass (interposing). It has not complete control; it has supervisory control.

Mr. Morgan. Very nearly so.

Senator Glass. It has supervisory control. But how does the Government aid it?

Mr. Morgan. I do not say the Government aids the Federal Reserve bank itself. I say that the Government provides the Federal Reserve banks, gives authority to make them Federal Reserve banks. It is a great aid to the Federal Reserve System. I still think so.

Senator Glass. The Government gives authority to the banks themselves to organize a Federal Reserve bank.

Mr. Morgan. Yes; that is a great help.

Senator Glass. And avail themselves of the facilities.

Mr. Morgan. Yes.

Senator Glass. That is not any financial aid by the Government.

Now, some people talk about the right of issue. Federal Reserve banks have not the right to issue. The Government has the right of issue upon the request of the Federal Reserve bank, and you know perfectly well that the member banks of the system did not want that done, don't you?

Mr. Morgan. No; I did not know about that at all, sir.

Senator Glass. In other words, the responsibility of the Government for a Federal Reserve bank note is so absolutely remote as to scarcely be detected. In other words, the Government issues a note and it interposes all of the assets and facilities of the 12 Federal Reserve banks to liquidate that note before the Government assumes any responsibility whatsoever—isn't that so?

Mr. Morgan. Yes.

Does that mean—I do not quite understand the thing in that way—but does that mean that the Government is really the endorser of the note?

Senator Glass. Does that what?

Mr. Morgan. Does that mean that the Government is really an endorser of the note?

Senator Glass. Yes. But this endorsement is not worth a flip of the hand for it has to be paid 20 times over before it reaches Government responsibility.

Mr. Morgan. That is not an endorsement?

Senator Glass. It was just an idle theory that was put there. It was the only scientific mar upon the then Federal Reserve Bank Act. There have been a devil of a lot of mars put on it since, I can tell you that.

Mr. Morgan. Well, I am sorry that I started this mare's nest.

Senator Glass. And do you say that private bankers have not access to the Reconstruction Finance Corporation?

Mr. Morgan. I have not known that they have.

Senator Glass. May be you have never availed yourself of it. But everything on the face of God's green earth has access to the Reconstruction Finance Corporation, I should say. [Laughter.]

Mr. Morgan. I am sorry I am the only exception, then.

Senator Glass. All that you would have to do would be to come down here and tell them your tale of woe in order to borrow the Government money at the expense of the taxpayers of the United States.

Senator Couzens. And I might point out that in the case of the railroads J. P. Morgan & Co. have received the benefit of the Reconstruction Finance Corporation. They have received loans, the railroads have, from the Reconstruction Finance Corporation.

Mr. Morgan. But we did not.

Senator Couzens. They paid you off with the money that they got from the Reconstruction Finance Corporation.

Mr. Morgan. When the money was due.

Senator Couzens. In no way else could you have got it.

Mr. Morgan. Well, we could have foreclosed.

Senator Couzens. But you could not have got the money by foreclosing, because they did not have any money to pay you with.

Senator Glass. I should like to say that I included the railroads in my very comprehensive question.

Senator Couzens. I simply want the record to show that the house of Morgan has gotten money because the railroads came down here and got money.

Mr. Morgan. I beg your pardon, but doing what?

Senator Couzens. The railroads came down here and got money from the Reconstruction Finance Corporation.

Mr. Morgan. You said something about controlled the railroads, I thought.

Senator Couzens. I should like to have that point brought out.

Mr. Pecora. We will probably bring it out before the hearings are over.

The Chairman. Mr. Morgan, do I understand it to be your theory that the better system would be a system of private banks rather than the system that we now have?

Mr. Morgan. Oh, I think both have their places.

The Chairman. Do you think we ought to have both?

Mr. Morgan. I hope we will have both, will continue to do so.

The Chairman. I did not know but what your line of thought was that really the better system would be a private banking system and take the Government out of the matter.

Mr. Morgan. Oh, I was not suggesting that.

Senator Barkley. I understand that your position is one of justifying private bankers without attacking public bankers, is that it?

Mr. Morgan. That is exactly what I am doing.

Mr. Pecora. Mr. Morgan, you know that your firm filed an income tax statement or return for a portion of the calendar year 1930, embraced between the dates January 1 and June 30, both inclusive; and also filed a separate return for the balance of that calendar year, that is to say, for the period between July 1, 1930, and December 31, 1930, both inclusive, do you not?

Senator Gore. State those dates again?

Mr. Morgan. I do not know anything about income tax questions at all, sir, I am sorry to tell you.

Mr. Pecora. Well, you stated a few moments ago when I was questioning you about the making of these returns, that a balance sheet was not taken as of the end of the calendar year 1930 because a new partner came into the firm on the 2d of January, 1931, and that hence a balance sheet was taken as of that date. Do you recall that testimony?

Mr. Morgan. I recall that testimony. I made that on statements that were made to me, and perhaps I was not entirely correct, but I think I was. That is correct, sir, I find.

Mr. Pecora. Do you know that your firm made a return for income-tax purposes for the 2-day period between January 1 and January 2, 1931?

Mr. Morgan. I think it is very probable but I do not know it.

Mr. Pecora. You stated before that the condition which would be shown as of January 2, 1931, would be about the same as the condition that would be shown as of December 31, 1930; do you recall that?

Mr. Morgan. No.

Mr. Pecora. Do you know that in the income-tax return filed by your firm for the 2-day period of January 1 and January 2, 1931, deductions were claimed by way of losses for that 2-day period amounting to $21,071,862.94?

Mr. Morgan. I do not know about the thing at all.

Mr. Pecora. Well, that isn't an item of such small consequence that the partners would not know of it, is it Mr. Morgan?

Mr. Morgan. I really do not know anything whatever about the income-tax statements of the office. They are all made up apart from me and I cannot base an examination on them.

Mr. Pecora. Do you know of any loss that accrued to the firm of J. P. Morgan & Co. for the two days of January 1 and January 2, 1931; do you?

Mr. Morgan. Well, do I know of that loss?

Mr. Pecora. Of any loss which accrued to the firm on account of the business it transacted in those two days?

Mr. Davis. Mr. Chairman, may I suggest that, if the committee thinks it important to go into these income-tax matters, and that it is relevant, and inasmuch as Mr. Morgan has said it was all done by Mr. Keyes, the office manager, who is here and is prepared to respond to any questions Mr. Pecora may want to inquire of him.

The Chairman. He might state any losses that occurred.

Senator Glass. Mr. Chairman, Mr. Morgan has stated distinctly that he does not know anything about it. It seems to me we ought to have the man before the committee who knows about the matter.

Mr. Morgan. And the man is here.

Mr. Davis. The man is here, and is quite ready for it if you want to go into it with him.

Mr. Pecora. Mr. Morgan, did the firm of J. P. Morgan & Co. do business for the 2 days of January 1 and January 2, 1931, which resulted in any considerable loss to them, to your knowledge?

Mr. Morgan. No, sir.

Mr. Pecora. It did not?

Mr. Morgan. The loss did not result at that time. The loss was taken at that time. But I do not want to discuss this because I have not the books before me and I cannot talk about it. I do not know anything about it. But if you will inquire of Mr. Keyes, and he has all of the records, you can get all of the information about the thing from him. He can give it to you perfectly easily.

Mr. Pecora. Mr. Keyes is an employee of the firm and not a partner, is he not?

Mr. Morgan. Yes, sir.

Mr. Pecora. And his position is that of general manager?

Mr. Morgan. Yes.

Mr. Pecora. And as general manager he carries out the decisions and policies of the partners, does he not?

Mr. Morgan. Yes.

Mr. Pecora. As a partner, did the firm of J. P. Morgan & Co. transact any business on January 1 and January 2, 1931, that you have any knowledge of?

Mr. Morgan. I want to get the answer to this right: We revalued the securities, didn't we? (Inquiring of some of his own people.)

The Chairman. Those were not holidays if they did business.

Mr. Pecora. One day was a holiday.

Mr. Morgan. I cannot say.

Mr. Pecora. Was any decision arrived at in a conference of the partners of J. P. Morgan & Co. which led to the filing of an income-tax return in behalf of that firm for that 2-day period?

Mr. Morgan. I was probably not present at the time it was not taken. I don't know.

Mr. Pecora. Have you any knowledge at all of any such decision having been reached by the members of the firm?

Mr. Morgan. I assume it was reached, because it was there.

Mr. Pecora. Have you any knowledge of making such a thing?

Mr. Morgan. I have not.

Senator Glass. Mr. Chairman, I respectfully submit that Mr. Morgan has stated over and over again that he has no knowledge of this income-tax business, but that the general manager of the firm, who is here, has complete knowledge of it. I do not see any use in the world, or anything to be gained by badgering Mr. Morgan about his knowledge or lack of knowledge of that particular item.

Mr. Pecora. Mr. Chairman, I certainly have no desire to badger Mr. Morgan or any other witness. I am simply asking him questions as a witness.

Senator Glass. Yes; but you are repeating the questions over and over again, questions that have already been answered.

Mr. Pecora. I beg pardon, Senator Glass, but——

Senator Glass (continuing). He has repeatedly answered that question.

Mr. Pecora. I do not recall asking Mr. Morgan any question twice. A succeeding question may have related to the former subject, or to a question previously propounded.

Senator Glass. They are questions with the same background.

Senator Gore. I should like to know what the background is of the figure $20,000,000 loss. I should like to have some information about that subject. I do not see how an income-tax return can be made for two days.

Senator Barkley. Was an income tax return for those two days made separately because you could not include them in your 1930 report because the law fixes it for the calendar year, and for those two days the firm was the same as it had been in 1930, but you could not include those two days in your 1931 report because it was a different firm after the second of January?

Mr. Morgan. That is exactly what I understand to be the case.

Senator Barkley. And you included those two days because you had to make a separate report for the reason that they were the only two days in 1931 when the firm as it existed in the year 1930 was the same, is that correct?

Mr. Morgan. That is correct.

Senator Couzens. But you revalued your securities during that time?

Mr. Morgan. Yes; we revalued the securities.

Senator Couzens. And that created a loss. That did not have anything to do with the new partnership?

Mr. Morgan. We had to revalue the securities at that time because a new partner came in.

Senator Couzens. Then Mr. Morgan did understand about that. Now he states that he knows something about that.

Mr. Morgan. I do not understand what the difficulty was.

Senator Glass. He was asked that question and has answered.

Senator Adams. Mr. Chairman, might I ask a question of Mr. Pecora? As I understand, the partnership itself makes reports not for the purpose of paying a tax as a partnership but for the purpose of furnishing information, and the tax is paid by the individual partners?

Mr. Pecora. Yes, sir.

Senator McAdoo. On their distributary shares.

Mr. Pecora. Yes, sir. Apparently now, Mr. Chairman, the witness has some knowledge of the revaluation of securities composing the assets of the partnership as of January 2, 1931. Is that correct, Mr. Morgan; have you any such knowledge?

Mr. Morgan. I have no knowledge that I could go back to and cite to you; no.

Senator Barkley. Could Mr. Keyes give full information as to that loss and the revaluation?

Mr. Morgan. Perfectly.

Mr. Pecora. Do you know at what figure the securities owned by the firm were valued as of the end of the calendar year 1930?

Mr. Morgan. No.

Mr. Pecora. Were they valued at the market or at cost on that date?

Mr. Morgan. They were not valued on that date. They were not valued at that date.

Mr. Pecora. Was there a write-off due to depreciation of the value of the securities that J. P. Morgan & Co. owned as assets as of the end of the calendar year 1930?

Mr. Morgan. I do not know.

Mr. Pecora. Do you know who signed the partnership income-tax return?

Mr. Morgan. I have no doubt that I did.

Mr. Pecora. For the calendar year 1930?

Mr. Morgan. Yes. But I have not the slightest recollection of it.

Mr. Pecora. Did you sign it for the 2-day period January 1 and 2, 1931?

Mr. Morgan. I do not remember.

Mr. Pecora. Sir?

Mr. Morgan. I do not remember.

Mr. Pecora. Do you know who prepared those returns?

Mr. Morgan. Yes.

Mr. Pecora. Who?

Mr. Morgan. Mr. Keyes.

Senator Glass. Again I should like to ask you, Mr. Morgan: Do not the expert examiners of the Internal Revenue Bureau review all these matters?

Mr. Morgan. I understand so.

Senator Glass. In examining your income-tax return?

Mr. Morgan. Yes. I understand they have done so. I was told the other day that we were clear up to 1931, was it?

Mr. Keyes. 1930.

Mr. Morgan. 1931 is now being examined.

Senator Couzens. I might point out that they also examined Mr. Charles Mitchell's income-tax return.

Senator Glass. Well, that is an implication that I am not participating in.

Senator Couzens. No, and I am not participating in it either, but I do object to the fact that this examination is to be curtailed any more than the examination of Mr. Charles Mitchell was curtailed. I want the testimony to go through.

Senator Glass. I won't curtail the examination, but as a member of the subcommittee I claim the right to know something in advance of what would be proven here, and I was not given any information whatsoever.

Senator Couzens. And I do not wish the examination to be stopped. And I will say that I, too, did not get any information, and I relied upon the chairman of the committee for it.

The Chairman. I will say that I tried to get the members of the subcommittee together time and again, and could not find them every time by any means.

Mr. Pecora. I wish to say that whenever I received a request from any member of the committee, that information I gladly furnished.

Senator Glass. And how could a member of the subcommittee ask you for information when he has no conception of what is to be found out?

The Chairman. Well, let us go on with the examination of the witness.

Senator Glass. We will go on with the examination, but a member of the subcommittee has a right to interrupt with questions to find out what it is all about, and as long as I am a member of the subcommittee I will do it.

Senator Couzens. And so will I.

Mr. Pecora. Mr. Morgan, do you know how much time was devoted by any member of the Internal Revenue Department on the income-tax returns filed by your concern?

Mr. Morgan. No; I have no knowledge whatever of what goes on about the income-tax matters, as I told you before. That is all done without my intervention at all.

Senator Glass. I will say to Mr. Pecora and to the Senator from Michigan (Mr. Couzens) that if they want to do so they can indict me. I do not know anything more about my income tax than the man in the moon. I employ an expert accountant, an accredited and attested accountant, certified by the State of Virginia, to make out my income-tax return, and then I sign on the dotted line.

Senator Couzens. And I assume that Mr. Mitchell did the same thing.

Senator Glass. And if you think that is dishonest, then go ahead with it.

Senator Couzens. I resent the inclusion of that insinuation in that remark, because I have charged nothing wrong to Mr. Lamont or to Mr. Morgan. I have known Mr. Lamont for years. But I resent any one witness being treated differently than any other witness, whether it happens to be Mr. Morgan or anyone else.

Senator Glass. I do not care anything about Mr. Morgan. I never saw him but once before in my life. My whole contention is as to the matter of procedure.

Senator Barkley. Mr. Chairman, I suggest that these personal differences be referred for consideration in an executive session.

Senator Couzens. So do I.

Senator Glass. And I am not dissenting.

Mr. Davis. Mr. Chairman, I should like to submit that as to all these income-tax questions, the expert who made out the returns, who is the manager of the firm, who knows the business in detail, is here ready to respond; I offer him to the committee.

Mr. Pecora. I submit that we are entitled to find out whether the senior member of the firm knows anything about the negotiations or the business of the firm which resulted in a $21,000,000 loss plus for two days' business transactions of a banking firm accepting deposits from the public and from public corporations.

Mr. Davis. That statement, with great respect to the distinguished counsel, is a pure figment of the imagination. The man who made the figures is here and knows how it was done, while Mr. Morgan has told you that he does not know.

Mr. Pecora. It is not a figment of my imagination when I refer to the file of the records.

Mr. Davis. Oh, all right.

Senator Gore. Let us get the facts in the records, and the background, and then we can reason on it and quarrel on it, too, if you want to.

The Chairman. Go ahead with the examination.

Mr. Pecora. Mr. Morgan, I want to ask you definitely: Do you know of any business transactions of operations that resulted in a loss of—$21,071,862.94 to the firm of J. P. Morgan & Co. for the two days of January 1 and January 2, 1931?

Mr. Morgan. I have already told you, sir, that I do not know.

Mr. Pecora. You do not know?

Mr. Morgan. No.

Senator Gore. Mr. Pecora, is it a fact that such a loss occurred? I am trying to get into the record the facts and background. I can appreciate the importance and the priority of bringing it out. Are you trying to elicit the facts, or do you have the facts already?

Mr. Pecora. I have the fact only as indicated by the income-tax return filed in behalf of J. P. Morgan & Co. for the 2-day period, January 1 and January 2, 1931, and a comparison of that return with one filed in behalf of that firm for the last 6 months of the preceding calendar year, terminating December 31, 1930.

Senator Gore. And it shows that discrepancy or difference?

Mr. Pecora. Yes, sir.

Senator Gore. Does anybody have that information except Mr. Keyes?

The Chairman. He is asking Mr. Morgan if he knows about it, and he can say yes or no.

Senator Byrnes. Mr. Chairman, I want to submit that that is perfectly proper. Counsel may ask the witness and if the witness answers "no", then if counsel wants the information from the gentleman who has it, he can let him answer.

Senator Glass. Now, you can go into executive session if you want to make suggestions of that sort, Senator Byrnes.

The Chairman. Mr. Pecora has a perfect right to ask Mr. Morgan what he knows about it, and that is all that he has done.

Senator Glass. And when Mr. Morgan answers over and over again that he does not know anything about it, what is the use of asking him again?

The Chairman. He asked Mr. Morgan if he knows about it.

Senator Glass. He asked him over and over again if he did not know about it.

Mr. Pecora. At one time, when Senator Couzens asked Mr. Morgan a question, the answer indicated some knowledge of the general subject, and then I followed that up.

The Chairman. Go ahead, Mr. Pecora.

Mr. Pecora. Mr. Morgan, do you know that returns made in behalf of the individual members of your firm, income-tax returns, have been accepted without examination on various occasions?

Mr. Morgan. I do not know anything about it.

Mr. Pecora. Have you ever heard of the making of this statement on the record of the income-tax return filed in behalf of Mrs. Margaret Y. Newbold, care J. P. Morgan & Co., 23 Wall Street, which I will read:

> Returned without examination for the reason that the return was prepared in the office of J. P. Morgan & Co., and it has been our experience that any schedule made by that office is correct. The books of the taxpayer are located in Philadelphia, and if necessary Schedule C may be verified in that city. This office, however, recommends that the return be accepted as filed.
>
> C. M. *Sheppard*
> Internal Revenue Agent

Did you ever know of that?

Mr. Morgan. No.

Mr. Pecora. Do you know that the records of the Income Tax Department——

Senator Couzens (interposing). What year was that?

Mr. Pecora. 1928.

Senator Gore. Where does Mr. Sheppard hold out?

Mr. Pecora. I do not know, sir. I am simply reading from a photostatic copy of the record.

Senator Gore. In New York, I suppose, or for that district?

Mr. Pecora. I imagine he is a revenue agent either in New York or Washington.

Senator Gore. And you do not know whether he is still in office or not?

Mr. Pecora. I did not. And this statement bears date August 15, 1930.

Senator Glass. Have you had any contact with Mr. Sheppard, Mr. Pecora?

Mr. Pecora. No, sir.

Senator Glass. Have you made any effort to have contact with him?

Mr. Pecora. No, sir.

Senator Glass. To ascertain the meaning of it?

Mr. Pecora. The meaning seems to me to be plain. The language used by him seems quite plain, and I have not asked him to explain anything about it, because I do not consider it is ambiguous. Furthermore, the return bears the stamp on its face:

> No field examination necessary.

Senator Barkley. These notations are all made by agents of the Government after the income-tax return has been made out by the taxpayer?

Mr. Pecora. Yes, sir.

Senator Barkley. And has left his hands?

Mr. Pecora. Yes, sir. Furthermore, may I state, Senator, that the records of the Income Tax Bureau show that only 1 day was spent on the partnership return of J. P. Morgan & Co. and of Drexel & Co., of Philadelphia, filed for the year 1930.

Mr. Davis. Is it unfair to ask distinguished counsel if he is testifying as a witness?

Mr. Pecora. I am giving the results of the examination of official reports and data in the bureau.

Mr. Davis. Are you testifying as a witness?

Mr. Pecora. I am putting this statement in the record, and stating where it came from, Mr. Davis.

Senator Couzens. And the committee will decide that question, not counsel for the house of Morgan.

The Chairman. Yes. You may proceed, Mr. Pecora.

Mr. Pecora. Mr. Morgan, don't you know as a matter of fact one of the reasons for the filing of this income-tax return in behalf of the firm for the 2-day period of January 1 to January 2, 1931, showing losses of over $21,000,000, enabled your firm, or would enable your firm under the income-tax law in effect at the time this return was made and filed, to carry forward those losses of over $21,000,000 against the taxable income for the ensuing two years, that is, for the years 1932 and 1933?

Mr. Morgan. No; I do not know that of my own knowledge. . . .

Mr. Pecora. Mr. Morgan, as the senior partner of the firms of J. P. Morgan & Co. and Drexel & Co. am I justified in assuming that you have a substantial participation in the income and profits of those firms?

Mr. Morgan. I have, sir.

Mr. Pecora. Now, according to the income-tax returns personally made by you for the calendar year 1930, were you taxed upon any taxable income?

Mr. Morgan. I do not remember my income-tax return for 1930, sir.

Mr. Pecora. You recall that according to your return you had no net taxable income for that year?

Mr. Morgan. In that case—that is made up on a mathematical basis out of the figures in the books. I do not know anything about it.

Mr. Pecora. Well, do you know whether or not you paid an income tax for the calendar year 1930?

Mr. Morgan. I cannot remember, but I can find out.

Mr. Pecora. Can you remember whether or not you paid one for the calendar year 1931?

Mr. Morgan. I did not, I know, that year.

Mr. Pecora. And do you know whether or not you paid an income tax for the calendar year 1932?

Mr. Morgan. No.

Senator Couzens. Does your "No" mean that you did not, or that you do not know whether you did?

Mr. Morgan. My "No" means that I did not pay any income tax. I might remind you, Mr. Pecora, that if I have a substantial interest in the profits of the concern I also have a substantial interest in the losses. Which might account for some of my troubles.

Mr. Pecora. Is it within your knowledge that the aggregate amount of income taxes paid by the members of the firms of J. P. Morgan & Co. and Drexel & Co. for the calendar year 1930 was about $47,000 or $48,000?

Mr. Morgan. Not within my knowledge. I do not know about the other men's returns.

Mr. Pecora. Is it within your knowledge that the aggregate amount of income taxes paid for the calendar year 1931 by the members of the firms of J. P. Morgan & Co. and Drexel & Co. was zero?

Mr. Morgan. I believe it to be true, but I do not know. I don't see their income-tax returns. . . .

Mr. Pecora. Mr. Morgan, you have already testified that for the calendar years 1931 and 1932 you paid no income tax to the United States Government. I wish to ask you if during either one of those calendar years you paid an income tax to any other government for any income received by you from within the jurisdiction of any such government?

Mr. Morgan. I think so. In England.

Mr. Pecora. For what years? For each of those 2 years?

Mr. Morgan. Each of them, I should think.

Mr. Pecora. That is for each of the years 1931 and 1932?

Mr. Morgan. Yes.

Mr. Pecora. Are you familiar with a corporation called the Alleghany Corporation?

Mr. Morgan. No.

Mr. Pecora. Haven't you ever heard of that corporation?

Mr. Morgan. I have heard of that corporation.

Mr. Pecora. Did your firm have anything to do with the financing of that corporation.

Mr. Morgan. It did, sir. Yes; it did.

Mr. Pecora. Would you call that a major financing operation on the part of your firm?

Mr. Morgan. It was certainly a very large one; yes.

Mr. Pecora. It was a large one. Are you familiar with any of the details of it?

Mr. Morgan. None whatever.

Mr. Pecora. None whatever? If I were to ask you any questions concerning the issue of stock by that corporation in connection with the financing of it by your firm would you be able to answer any of the questions?

Mr. Morgan. No.

TESTIMONY OF LEONARD KEYES
MAY 23, 1933

Stock Exchange Practices, *Hearings Before the Committee on Banking and Currency*, U.S. Senate, 73rd Congress, 1st Session, Part I, 76–87.

Senator Glass. Mr. Keyes, the impression, as indicated by Mr. Morgan, has been made that in some mysterious way between the 31st day of December 1930 and the 2d day of January 1931, a loss in excess of $21,000,000 had occurred. That income statement was in strict accord with the revenue laws and requirements?

Mr. Keyes. Yes, sir.

Senator Glass. Did the Internal Revenue Bureau examiners take note of that and make inquiry about it?

Mr. Keyes. There are making inquiry now, Senator. The 1931 in the normal course of events would have been made along late in the summer or in the fall, but they started making their examination about a month ago. Prior to 1931, the year 1930 was very thoroughly checked up and gone over very carefully, and that double closing or double accounting period, as we call it in the bureau, has been passed and approved. We again had a double accounting period and a double closing in 1926 on account of the death of Mr. Porter.

Senator Byrnes. Will you talk louder? I know these gentlemen over here cannot hear you.

Mr. Keyes. We had a double closing or a double accounting period in 1926, when the period included the income that accrued up to November 30, the day that Mr. Porter died. We had a double accounting period or a double closing in 1925, when Mr. Stettinius died. We had a double accounting period the year before that, when Mr. Baker died. In fact, the present articles began on March 11, 1916, when the first one came up about a double accounting period, and that period and that method has been very consistently adhered to ever since.

Senator Gore. And that double accounting had no effect on the income-tax payment in the long run by the members of the firm?

Mr. Keyes. No, sir; none at all, sir.

Senator Glass. Have the examiners of the Internal Revenue Bureau raised any objection to that procedure?

Mr. Keyes. They are questioning us as to whether we had any right, so to speak, to even include things by way of revaluation now when the partnership changes, but they say positively that the loss could not be deducted on December 31, 1930, by way of revaluation between the two partners.

Senator Gore. Have you had any information from the Internal Revenue Bureau that it suspects your concern of having manipulated its figures so as to show a loss in excess of $21,000,000.

Mr. Keyes. No, sir; none at all, and the very purpose of filing two returns as we have—we keep a separate accounting period—is to lay the full facts before the Bureau of Internal Revenue.

Mr. Pecora. Now, Mr. Keyes, if the securities composed of the capital assets of the firm had been valued as of the 31st day of December 1930 at market value, would not the loss have been some $21,000,000 greater than the loss of $817,000 that was reported in the return for the period of July 1, 1930, to December 31, 1930?

Mr. Keyes. We had no right to revalue it.

Mr. Pecora. I did not ask you that; I asked you if the loss would not have been reported as some $21,000,000 in excess of this figure of $817,000 plus.

Mr. Keyes. It would not have been reported, but I will grant you that the loss is there on the books on December 31, 1930.

Mr. Pecora. Now, the reason why that loss was not reported on a basis of a revaluation of the securities at the market price of December 31, 1930, if I correctly understood your previous testimony, was because of the change of partnership that took effect on January 2, 1931?

Mr. Keyes. Plus the fact that there is nothing in regulation 72 that would justify putting that loss in in December 1930.

Mr. Pecora. All right; but that factor of the change of personnel of the partnership played a part in it, didn't it?

Mr. Keyes. No; I don't agree with you.

Mr. Pecora. No?

Mr. Keyes. No.

Mr. Pecora. Well, you said in answer to my previous question that that was the fact, plus regulation 72?

Mr. Keyes. That is right.

Mr. Pecora. What change actually took place in the personnel of the firm on January 2, 1931?

Mr. Keyes. The admission—on January 2, 1931, there was a new partner admitted.

Mr. Pecora. Who was it?

Mr. Keyes. Mr. Charles D. Dickey—I beg your pardon, Mr. S. Parker Gilbert.

Mr. Pecora. And have you any knowledge as to when the decision was reached to admit him into the partnership?

Mr. Keyes. No, sir; I have not.

Mr. Pecora. Had you heard as manager of the firm at any time prior to the second day of July, 1931, that Mr. Gilbert was coming into the firm on that date?

Mr. Keyes. Yes; I heard that.

Mr. Davis. July or January?

Mr. Pecora. Yes; I meant January, not July. How long before January 2, 1931, had you heard that?

Mr. Keyes. I don't remember.

Mr. Pecora. Was it prior to December 31, 1930, that you heard it?

Mr. Keyes. Yes.

Mr. Pecora. Is that the only change in the personnel of the firm that took place at that time?

Mr. Keyes. That is all.

Mr. Pecora. Now, January 1, 1931, was a legal holiday in the State of New York, as you know, isn't it?

Mr. Keyes. Yes; that is right.

Mr. Pecora. New Year's?

Mr. Keyes. Yes.

Mr. Pecora. Did the firm of J. P. Morgan & Co. and of Drexel & Co. transact any business on that holiday?

Mr. Keyes. No, sir; none of them.

Mr. Pecora. Well now, on January 2, 1931, the change in the personnel of the firm that has already been referred to by you took effect?

Mr. Keyes. At the close of business.

Mr. Pecora. At the close of business. Now, what business was transacted on the 2d day of January 1931, by the firm of J. P. Morgan & Co. prior to the admission of Mr. Gilbert as a partner at the close of business on that day?

Mr. Keyes. I could not tell you, Mr. Pecora, what was done that day.

Mr. Pecora. Well, you prepared the income tax return for the firm?

Mr. Keyes. Yes, sir.

Mr. Pecora. That was filed for the period of time represented by January 1 and 2, 1931—didn't you?

Mr. Keyes. Yes, sir.

Mr. Pecora. And in that return you include in the income an item of profits, commissions, brokerage, et cetera, of $2,249,632.97?

Mr. Keyes. Yes.

Senator Gore. What is that? What does that represent?

Mr. Pecora. Profits, commissions, brokerage, et cetera, of the firm for January 1 and 2, 1931.

Now, in view of the fact that January 1, 1931, was a legal holiday on which, as you said, the firm transacted no business, are you still unable to tell us what business was transacted by the firm on the 2d day of January 1931 that enabled it to receive an income consisting of profits, commissions, brokerage, et cetera, of nearly $2,250,000?

Mr. Keyes. On January 2, 1931, without referring to the books, I would say that they transacted the normal routine banking business. January 2, 1931, is a very large interest and coupon payment date. Some of those amounts represent commissions that were entered into. The bulk of that represents increase in revaluation, coupled with the change in partnership.

Senator Barkley. Do you mean to say that on the 2d of January you had both a decline and an increase in the value of your assets?

Mr. Keyes. Yes, sir; undoubtedly. There were no doubt some assets that had shown an increase and those were included and shown on the income side.

Senator Barkley. I know, but the same assets that had come over from the previous day from the old firm to the new one?

Mr. Keyes. No; the previous firm, Senator, was June 1930, on the revaluation.

Senator Barkley. Then as I understand, you took those that had declined and charged that loss of $21,000,000?

Mr. Keyes. Yes, sir.

Senator Barkley. Against the old firm, and those that had gone up you credited that to the new firm?

Mr. Keyes. No, sir. No, Senator. The old firm. Both ways.

Senator Barkley. Was the $21,000,000 the net loss after considering increases since the previous June?

Mr. Keyes. I have not my figures here, but I am not sure whether that was net or not. I think Mr. Pecora has our return.

Mr. Pecora. Well, these profits, commissions, brokerage, et cetera, amounted to nearly two and a quarter million dollars estimated and reported on a payment basis or on an accrual basis on this income tax return for January 1 and 2, 1931?

Mr. Keyes. On a payment basis, but there was very little that would be included by way of accrual on commissions.

Mr. Pecora. Now, what transaction or operation that took place on January 2, 1931, resulted in the loss of $21,071,862.95 that I understand was reported by the firm in the income-tax return which is filed for those 2 days?

Mr. Keyes. That again represents the decline in assets from the prior closing period of June 30, 1930, when Mr. Gates was admitted, and the assets were revalued—when Mr. Gates retired from the firm, on January 2, 1931, when Mr. Gilbert was admitted to the firm.

Mr. Pecora. Had Mr. Gilbert been admitted into the firm on the 31st of December 1930, this revaluation at market would have likewise shown a loss of some $21,000,000, would it not?

Mr. Keyes. Yes.

Mr. Pecora. And had the admission of Mr. Gilbert to the firm taken place 2 days prior to January 2, 1931, this resultant loss by the revaluation at market of the securities of over $21,000,000 would have had to be included in the income-tax return for the firm for the latter part of the calendar year 1930, would it not?

Mr. Keyes. Would have been any day prior to 1931, the closing as of that day.

Mr. Pecora. Yes. And under the income-tax law as existed at that time, namely, December 31, 1930, the firm would only have been allowed the right to carry forward these losses of $21,000,000 plus for the succeeding two calendar years?

Mr. Keyes. Yes, sir.

Mr. Pecora. That is, the year 1931 and 1932?

Mr. Keyes. That is right.

Mr. Pecora. And consequently because Mr. Gilbert's admission into the firm took place on January 2, 1931, instead of December 31, 1930, your firm, by the filing of this return, was in the position of having the right to carry forward against possible taxable income for the years 1932 and 1933 this loss of over $21,000,000; is not that right?

Mr. Keyes. Mr. Gilbert being admitted January 2, that is the date that you would take for the establishment of that loss.

Mr. Pecora. Exactly. If the admission had been on December 31 instead of 2 days later, the firm would not have the right to offset against possible taxable income for the year 1933 any part of this loss of $21,000,000 or more?

Mr. Keyes. That would have been true if Mr. Gilbert had been admitted any day prior to December 31. But they had the right to carry it forward 2 years.

Senator Barkley. In other words, you got 1 year's extension in the period of which it might be carried forward by this January the 2d transaction instead of December 31?

Mr. Keyes. Yes; by his admission January 2.

Senator Barkley. Yes.

The Chairman. You made a deduction on account of loss in your income tax of this $21,000,000?

Mr. Keyes. Yes, sir.

The Chairman. When?

Mr. Keyes. In 1931.

The Chairman. What time in 1931?

Mr. Keyes. We filed two returns for the partnership, one at the close of business January 2, 1931, and the second covering the period of January 3 to December 31, and both of those returns followed through into the individual partnership returns, as required under the revenue act.

Senator Glass. As far as you know and have been advised up to date, you filed your return in strict accordance with the revenue act?

Mr. Keyes. Yes, sir; and we have taken the best advice, I am sure. We have been advised that our return is in strict accordance with the revenue act and proper and correct.

Senator Glass. And up to this time there has been no criticism of the transaction by the Internal Revenue Bureau?

Mr. Keyes. No, sir; none at all, Senator.

Senator Couzens. I thought you testified a while ago that they did question your method of changing the values.

Mr. Keyes. No. They questioned, Senator Couzens, whether under the new revenue act as it was passed after January 6, 1932—whether under the new revenue act we could continue to make any deduction for a revaluation based upon a change of partnership.

Senator Barkley. But that would not affect the law in 1931?

Mr. Keyes. No, sir.

Senator Glass. Do you know any large taxpayer, or small taxpayer, either, who does not avail himself of any permissibility of the law which enables him to reduce his income tax?

Mr. Keyes. In my tax practice I do not, Senator. The taxpayer is always ready to take good advice as to any proper and lawful methods that he may take to reduce taxes.

Senator Glass. Did you ever know the Government to collect a dollar that it did not take the citizen $2 to get it back from it if it was not right?

Mr. Keyes. That I have not quite checked up yet.

Senator Couzens. I can state that that is not a fact.

Mr. Pecora. I understood you to say before in answer to a question that the Income Tax Bureau is now engaged in some kind of inquiry into these returns that have been the subject of this examination. Is that so, Mr. Keyes, or did I misunderstand you?

Mr. Keyes. They are engaged in the same kind of an inquiry that they have made every year. We have had an income-tax inspector come into our office annually ever since 1916.

Mr. Pecora. Well, are they now engaged in making an inquiry, so far as you know, into the income-tax return filed in behalf of the firm for the calendar year 1930 and for these two days of January 1 and 2 of the year 1931?

Mr. Keyes. The internal-revenue agent was in our office checking up the partnership returns and the individual returns, the same as they had done in prior years. I know nothing of any special inquiry.

Mr. Pecora. Didn't you say in the course of your earlier testimony that within the past month some such inquiry had been instituted?

Mr. Keyes. Yes; it is bound to be. Our partnership return is the subject of inspection.

Mr. Pecora. Was an investigation made or examination made by any of the field agents of this return prior to this year?

Mr. Keyes. No, sir. And normally the examination would not be made prior to this year.

Mr. Pecora. You mean the period of 2 years as a rule elapsed——

Mr. Keyes (interposing). Yes, sir; I mean exactly——

Mr. Pecora (continuing). Before the making of an examination by a field agent?

Mr. Keyes. It is not 2 years; it is only—it is a year and a half, and that has been the period right through from the start.

Mr. Pecora. Is it a year and a half?

Mr. Keyes. Yes, sir.

Mr. Pecora. January 1931 to April or May 1933 is a year and a half?

Mr. Keyes. The return is to be filed in March. The return for 1931 is filed in March 1932, and the 2-year period in the act that you probably have in mind commences to operate on March 15, 1932.

Senator Byrnes. Well, one minute; let me get that right. This return in question was January 2, 1931?

Mr. Keyes. Yes, sir.

Senator Byrnes. And because of this provision in the law, any loss then ascertained could be deducted from any profit for the next calendar year, 1932 or 1933?

Mr. Keyes. Yes; by the carry-forward provision of the act.

Senator Byrnes. By the carry-forward?

Mr. Keyes. Yes, sir.

Senator Byrnes. Now, if the question has not been asked, what income tax, if any, did you pay in 1932?

Mr. Keyes. There were not any taxes paid in 1932.

Senator Byrnes. Then if no taxes were paid, the carrying forward of the loss of 21 million to the calendar year 1932 did not affect you because you had no profit?

Mr. Keyes. That is right.

Senator Byrnes. And the question as to whether by that procedure you profited will depend upon whether you have profits under the income-tax law for the calendar year 1933?

Mr. Keyes. Yes, sir.

Senator Byrnes. If you had profits and you could deduct 21 million from those profits, it would affect your income tax for the calendar year 1933?

Mr. Keyes. Yes, sir.

Senator Byrnes. That is the situation.

Senator Adams. Was part of this $21,000,000 deducted in 1932? Did you make up a part of that?

Mr. Keyes. No, sir.

Senator Adams. You did not need that?

Mr. Keyes, No, sir.

Senator Adams. You had loss enough?

Mr. Keyes. Yes.

Senator Barkley. You mean you had no profits at all after deducting nothing?

Mr. Keyes. No, sir; after deducting nothing, and there was none of that carried forward.

Senator Gore. You were lucky.

Mr. Pecora. You did not need this loss as an offset to taxable income in the year 1930, did you, in order to avoid a liability for payment of income taxes?

Mr. Keyes. No, sir.

Senator Barkley. You mean 1930?

Mr. Pecora. 1930. Didn't need it that year. The losses were there—that is right, isn't it, Mr. Keyes?

Mr. Keyes. Beg pardon? Well, we paid, some of the partners did pay, a tax in 1930.

Mr. Pecora. Yes; but they paid those not on account of income of the firm, firm transactions, isn't that so?

Mr. Keyes. Well, a partner's return covers all of his income, including the firm. It is all combined under one individual return.

Senator Byrnes. May I interrupt you one moment? Whether or not you profited by this revaluation as a partner went out of the firm and there was a dissolution would depend upon whether or not upon that date of the dissolution of the partnership there was an increase in the value of the capital assets; is that right?

Mr. Keyes. Yes, sir.

Senator Byrnes. Now, in these very changes in 1927, for instance, when, by reason of the dissolution June the 30th, you filed an income-tax return, did it affect you so as to cause you to pay less or more taxes?

Mr. Keyes. No, sir; it affected us very adversely and caused us to pay very much more taxes by being required to mark up the securities.

Senator Byrnes. Well, how about the next time, 1928? I would like to know whether by reason of these dissolutions and these returns being filed on each occasion you profited or lost.

Mr. Keyes. The same in 1928, Senator. The increase in market value was greater.

Senator Byrnes. Was greater?

Mr. Keyes. Yes, sir.

Senator Byrnes. In 1928?

Mr. Keyes. In 1928, and also in 1929.

Senator Byrnes. Then the next time, was that June the 30th? Did you have——

Mr. Keyes. June the 30th——

Senator Byrnes. In 1930.

Mr. Keyes. June the 30th was about even over the values as it had existed on December 31, 1929.

Senator Byrnes. Then we have referred to the 1931 without it.

Mr. Keyes. Yes, sir.

Senator Byrnes. January the 2d.

Mr. Keyes. May I also add to that that there was taxable income that was realized on that second period in 1931 going from January 3d to December 31, which was quite a substantial set-off to that 21 million?

Senator Byrnes. I did not get that. How is that?

Mr. Keyes. The period of January 3——

Senator Byrnes. Yes.

Mr. Keyes. To December 31, 1931——

Senator Byrnes. Yes.

Mr. Keyes. Showed an increase in income that was quite a set-off to the 21 million.

Senator Gore. That is, the 21 million absorbed the profits?

Senator Byrnes. What you mean is that the 21 billion absorbed some of the profits, as Senator Gore said, for that year?

Mr. Keyes. For the later period of the year; yes, sir.

Senator Barkley. It is just the other way around, isn't it, that you had a profit but it was not sufficient to absorb the $21,000,000 loss?

Mr. Keyes. That is it.

Senator Barkley. And the question whether you actually gained anything by this 2-day period will depend a good deal on whether you have enough income in 1933 from which you can deduct this $21,000,000?

Mr. Keyes. Yes, sir.

Senator Byrnes. That is the whole question on that.

Senator Gore. Do you know how much of the $21,000,000 was absorbed by your profits in 1931?

Mr. Keyes. I did not get that.

Senator Gore. Do you know how much of the $21,000,000 losses taken on January 2, 1931, were absorbed by your profits during the remainder of that year till December 31, 1931?

Mr. Keyes. I do not recall the exact figure, but I think it some three or four million dollars.

Senator Byrnes. Which would leave it about $18,000,000 to carry forward to 1933 there?

Mr. Keyes. Before it is carried forward it has to go through a distribution into the partners' individual returns. It is a very complicated picture to compute as to the amount that could be carried forward.

Senator Glass. Mr. Keyes, Mr. Parker Gilbert is a man of some reputation, isn't he?

Mr. Keyes. Yes, sir.

Senator Glass. He was formerly an Under Secretary of the Treasury, was he not?

Mr. Keyes. Yes, sir.

Senator Glass. And he afterward was put in charge of this foreign financing of the Young plan, was he not, and he is still a member of the firm?

Mr. Keyes. Yes, sir.

Senator Glass. He was not a dummy member of the firm then?

Mr. Keyes. No, sir; quite the contrary.

Senator Glass. Not put in for the purpose of affecting the income account?

Mr. Keyes. No, sir.

Senator Barkley. Still in the firm, is he?

Mr. Keyes. Yes, sir; still in the firm.

Mr. Pecora. Mr. Keyes, are you familiar with the report made by Revenue Agent Newell C. Shields under date of October 15, 1932, in which he makes the following comment or statement with respect to the income-tax returns that have been the subject of your testimony this afternoon:

Since the inception of the income tax law taxpayer——

By taxpayer is meant J. P. Morgan & Co.—

has terminated the partnership on December 31st of each year, and each year the old partnership has sold all of its assets to the new partnership at the market values of December 31. Following this theory the tax returns have reflected the profits based on the market valuation placed on the assets at the end of each year. This procedure has had the effect of inventorying at market, although taxpayer contends that they are on a strictly cost basis.

The year 1930 produced the first deviation from this procedure, as the partnership in existence January 1, 1930 was dissolved on June 30, 1930, and a new partnership found on July 1, 1930. This new partnership was not dissolved until January 2, 1931. The tax returns for the first six months' partnership includes the losses and gains sustained through the sale of all of the assets at market values of June 30 to the new partnership. On the other hand, the return of the partnership in existence from July 1, 1930, to January 2, 1931, has carried its assets at cost (since no sale was made to a new firm on December 31, 1930), such cost being the values of July first at which assets were taken over from the old firm with subsequent purchases at cost.

The importance to taxpayer of the correctness of their basis of reporting lies in the fact that there was a tremendous shrinkage in the value of their assets on December 31, 1930. If a new firm had been organized at that time the loss for 1930 would have been so large that it would have been improbable that the statutory could have been absorbed by the income of the two succeeding years. By forming a new firm on January 2, 1931, and recording the losses based on the sale of the assets to the new firm, the loss became a 1931 loss, which, under the then existing law could have been carried forward to apply against 1933 income.

Do you agree with the statements embodied in that portion of this report?

Mr. Keyes. Mr. Pecora, I never saw that report, and I would like to know to whom that report is made.

Mr. Pecora. By Mr. Newell C. Shields.

Mr. Keyes. To whom?

Mr. Pecora. Apparently to his bureau.

Mr. Keyes. Well, we never saw the report.

Mr. Pecora. Well, do you agree with the statements and comments and conclusions that are set forth——

Mr. Keyes. I do not agree with them.

Mr. Pecora (continuing). In this report, as I have read them to you?

Mr. Keyes. Taking them item by item I do not agree with the statement that he makes about our having established an accounting method for December 31 without mentioning in there that that is coupled with a change of copartnership. That is not mentioned in there. Mr. Shields has not examined our returns rightly.

Mr. Pecora. There was nothing to prevent your firm from making a return for the 6 months' period terminating on December 31, 1930, which would have included a revaluation of the securities among its assets on that date, was there?

Mr. Keyes. Without the admission of a partner?

Mr. Pecora. Without the admission of a partner.

Mr. Keyes. There certainly was. Regulation 72.

Mr. Pecora. Have you got that Regulation 72 with you?

Mr. Keyes. No; I have not. No.

Senator Couzens. That in effect prevents the taking of a loss until it occurs, does it not?

Mr. Keyes. Exactly. And no individual who might have some bonds and stock in his pocket has any right to say that he is going to mark them down in his tax return. And they have not qualified as dealers in securities so that they can inventory the cost or market, which ever was lower.

Mr. Pecora. What?

Mr. Keyes. We have not qualified under the tax laws as a dealer in securities who can inventory the cost or market, whichever is the lower.

Mr. Pecora. Are you not dealers in securities?

Mr. Keyes. No; not within the meaning of the tax law. We have never qualified as such. That is a very narrow and limited definition, that "dealer in securities", and we could not qualify if we wanted to, because that is limited primarily to securities sold to customers.

Mr. Pecora. Do you know whether any of the individual partners have qualified as dealers in securities within the meaning and intent of the provisions of the tax law?

Mr. Keyes. I know they have not.

Senator Byrnes. In other words, the only way you can get a loss is that the loss must be ascertained by the actual sale, unless there is a dissolution of the partnership?

Mr. Keyes. Yes, sir.

Senator Byrnes. When you can file a statement based upon the valuation of your assets, is that right?

Mr. Keyes. Exactly, Senator. That is correct.

Senator Couzens. Well, is not the inference there, as I understood the reading by Mr. Pecora, that they changed corporations every few years regardless of whether there were new partners taken in? Is that true?

Mr. Keyes. That they changed corporations?

Senator Couzens. That is, that they sold out to a new partnership?

Mr. Keyes. To a partnership; yes, sir. That the valuation of the partnership interest as it existed before the change constituted a closed transaction.

Senator Couzens. Yes. But what I am trying to get at——

Mr. Keyes. But not every December 31, sir.

Senator Couzens. No; I am not speaking of any date. If I remember correctly what Mr. Pecora read, the inference was that a new partnership was created every year or so, regardless of whether there were any new partners taken in, so as to create a new status for income tax.

Mr. Keyes. No, sir. I understood the inference merely to be that we had revalued on December 31, whether a new partner was taken in or not, or whether there was any change in partnership.

Senator Byrnes. No; I agree with Senator Couzens. The question is, Whether the change of partnership occurring every year was done with the intent on June 30 or on December 31 of permitting this revaluation and thereby taking a loss?

Senator Couzens. Well, it is perfectly practicable and perfectly easily done to create a new partnership every year when it is advantageous to do so, and sell out to the new partnership if it creates a loss in the interest of the partners. I am not charging that is done, but that is a very simple procedure.

Senator Byrnes. We are just asking for the facts.

Senator Couzens. Yes.

Mr. Pecora. So, whether or not it was done with any such intent, as was indicated by Senator Byrnes' question, the actual result was that it enabled the firm to carry forward through the calendar years of 1932 and 1933 these losses of $21,000,000?

Mr. Keyes. We did not carry them forward, Mr. Pecora.

Mr. Pecora. What is that?

Mr. Keyes. We did not carry them forward. Our income-tax returns——

Mr. Pecora. You did not have to, but you could have if the income of the firm during the calendar years of 1932 and 1933 were to yield profits or income in excess of $21,000,000.

Mr. Keyes. Or, perhaps, that remaining period in 1931.

Mr. Pecora. Yes.

Mr. Keyes. Which happened to an extent.

Senator Glass. Well, if that could have been done, and should it have been done, and the law permitted it to be done, the fault, if any, is in the law and not in any intent on the part of your firm to cheat the Government; is that not so?

Mr. Keyes. Well, Senator Glass, I think that the selection of partners is covered by partnership law, and electus personorum goes as to time as well as to persons. So that the partnership would have the right to admit the partners on the dates that they select. And, following your question through, that if, on the change of copartnership, we would have to have a revaluation, then the fault would be in the law if on the following December 31 the law did not compel us to have another revaluation whether you had a change in the partnership or not.

Mr. Pecora. Mr. Keyes, let me ask you this. Do you know of any time prior to the year 1931 when the firm of J. P. Morgan & Co. took in a new partner——

Mr. Keyes. Yes, sir.

Mr. Pecora (continuing).—On the 2d of January of any year?

Mr. Keyes. Not on the 2d of January. It was on March 31, 1916. The present articles are dated that date. It is not tradition entirely that it is done on December 31.

Senator Byrnes. Let me ask you this: Several times during this period you say one of the partners died?

Mr. Keyes. Yes, sir.

Senator Byrnes. On each of those occasions a return was filed as the result of the dissolution resulting from the death, is that right?

Mr. Keyes. Yes, sir; that is right.

Senator Glass. He did not die on purpose?

Senator Byrnes. How many times was there a reorganization by reason of death?

Mr. Keyes. There were two separate accounting periods in 1926 by the death of Mr. Porter; in 1925 by the death of Mr. Stettinius; in 1924 by the death of Mr. Bacon; in 1922 by the death of Mr. Davison; in 1920 by the death of Mr. Newbold. We had a change in 1927 by the retirement of the late Mr. Dwight W. Morrow, which occurred in September 1927. And that return was a substantial write-up and an increase in value which had to be included because of the dissolution of the partnership.

Senator Couzens. What tax did you have to pay that year?

Mr. Keyes. Well, we would have to figure it out, Senator, because the tax is commuted right into the final return, but the total was quite a substantial sum. Some six or seven million dollars, the total.

Mr. Pecora. Mr. Keyes, I understand that no deceased partner died purposely on any particular date. But the date of January 2, 1931, was advisedly fixed as the date of the admission of Mr. Gilbert into the firm, was it not?

Mr. Keyes. I think it is the partners' privilege to fix the date of the admission into the firm.

Mr. Pecora. I say it was fixed for that date, was it not? That was not a mere accident; it was the result of deliberation and decision, was it not?

Mr. Keyes. Yes, sir.

Senator Couzens. Is that all?

Mr. Pecora. That is all on this subject with this witness; yes, sir.

CARTER GLASS–FERDINAND PECORA EXCHANGE
MAY 26, 1933

U.S. Senate, Stock Exchange Practices, *Hearings Before the Committee on Banking and Currency,* 73rd Congress, 1st Session, Part 2, 228–45.

Senator Glass. . . . I say that in compliance with this resolution Mr. Pecora and his numerous investigators went to New York and made this preliminary investigation, having had access to all of the books of this and perhaps other concerns—we do not know how many other concerns; he obtained apparently complete information as to those things—and I have said and I insist now that it was his duty to have come here to Washington and have appeared before the subcommittee of which I am a member and to have told us what he found, what significance he attached to what he found, and what he proposed to establish by the investigation before this committee, and not have to have brought the members of the committee here before a crowded assembly room without knowing one solitary thing about the meaning of all this. And I say that is so, and other members of the committee agree with me.

Mr. Pecora. May I remind Senator Glass that after the enactment——

Senator Glass. So far as that is concerned, now, since the Senator from Michigan raises the issue, I have examined the minutes of the various meetings of the subcommittee, and I do not find that at any meeting of the subcommittee the employment of Mr. Pecora was authorized.

The Chairman. The minutes have not been written up, then. That is all I can say about that. I know he was employed, and the subcommittee did it unanimously.

Senator Costigan. I agree with what the chairman says, as a member of the subcommittee. There can be no question, in my judgment, about the employment of Mr. Pecora.

Senator Glass. I have within the three last hours examined the minutes in detail. It may have been that the employment was authorized, but there is no record of it. That is immaterial, because I think the committee is satisfied with Mr. Pecora's employment. But the Senator from Michigan seems always willing to dig me——

Senator Couzens. I deny that.

Senator Glass (continuing). And has undertaken to challenge my right here to insist upon some knowledge beforehand of what we are to sit around this table all day long to listen to.

Senator Byrnes. May I suggest this? Mr. Pecora, having read the resolution, would it accomplish the purpose of the examination if he could make a statement instead of propounding all these questions?

The Chairman. I think he has stated the new resolution and what he has directed to be done.

Mr. Pecora. I was coming to that when I was interrupted——

Senator Costigan (interposing). Mr. Chairman, before Mr. Pecora proceeds further I desire to say that I have just entered the room, and I do not want to be recorded as committed to any of the statements which have preceded my entrance. It was my understanding that one statement was made to the effect that all members of the committee were agreed on some course of procedure or on some view of the evidence——

Senator Byrnes (interposing). Oh, no; Senator Costigan.

Senator Costigan. I did not hear precisely the purport of that statement, and I speak now solely in order that I may have a chance to examine the record before I appear to be committed.

Senator Byrnes. Senator Costigan, I do not think any such statement was made.

Senator Barkley. I suggest that in executive session this morning we agreed to recess at 1 o'clock today until next Wednesday. That hour having arrived I wish to make a motion——

The Chairman (interposing). Let Mr. Pecora make a statement first.

Senator Barkley. I have no objection to his doing that.

Mr. Pecora. This particular line of examination, into the activities and operations of the issuance of securities of the United Corporation, is being conducted under that clause of the resolution which empowers and directs the committee to make a thorough and complete investigation, among other things, of the business of banking, financing, and extending credit, and of the business of issuing, floating or selling securities. This United Corporation it has already been shown, to the extent that I have been permitted to proceed up to the present moment, is a corporation that has issued hundreds of millions of dollars of securities to the investing public. And certainly its size and the area of its operations were deemed to be of sufficient importance to merit the attention of this committee under this resolution. It has already further been shown by the evidence presented at this hearing, that 1,000,000 option warrants were issued to J. P. Morgan & Co. for an allocated value or consideration of $1 each, and a similar amount for a similar valuation to the banking house of

Bonbright & Co.; that those option warrants are unlimited as to time, and entitled the holders thereof to purchase for each warrant a share of the common stock of the United Corporation at $27.50. It has already been shown at this hearing that within a few days after the issuance of those option warrants for that consideration of $1 each, the common stock of this company was traded in on the public exchange in Philadelphia at prices doubling or more the sum of $27.50.

Now, there was proof, and the proof on that has not yet been completed, gentlemen of the committee, that the securities of the United Corporation were issued under circumstances and upon terms that enabled a very small number or group of individuals to acquire, at terms certainly against the interests of the corporation, those of its securities that are called option warrants. Now, I want to pursue the inquiry further, and I think the developments will throw considerable light on a certain phase of the business of issuing and floating and selling securities.

Senator Glass. Now, let me ask Mr. Pecora if he did not ascertain all these things by reason of his investigation in New York, and if he could not have made to the subcommittee, prior to the meeting of the general committee, just the statement that he has made here, that he expected to develop those facts.

Mr. Pecora. Senator Glass, if I had to come to Washington to consult the members of the subcommittee every time I had any development to report——

Senator Glass (interposing). I did not ask you that.

Mr. Pecora (continuing). I would have been busy taking every train between New York and Washington.

Senator Glass. I did not ask you about every time you discovered anything or had any development. What I wanted you to do was to come here at some time after you completed your investigation and give to us some idea of what you proposed to develop here, in order that we might not waste our valuable time sitting around a table here listening to questions propounded and answers given which were of no significance to a man of ordinary intelligence, if I have ordinary intelligence.

Mr. Pecora. Senator Glass will probably recall that in the latter part of March, or shortly after the adoption of Senate Resolution 56, under which this committee is functioning, I appeared before a meeting of the Senate Banking and Currency Committee and outlined to the members thereof the general scope, the lines of inquiry that I was about to undertake as counsel for the committee. I specifically read to the members of the committee at that meeting the draft of the "questionnaire", so-called, that has been alluded to in the evidence here in the past few days, which I had sent to J. P. Morgan & Co. and other private banking firms doing business in the city of New York.

Now, that questionnaire to a definite extent suggested quite fully I think the lines and scope of the inquiry that I was undertaking to pursue as counsel for the committee. Since that time I have received not a single request from any Senator on the committee for any further or more specific advices or information concerning what I was doing. In view of that I have been, with the exception of one visit to Washington that I made about 3 weeks ago, spending my time in the city of New York, from early morn until late at night, engaged on this preliminary investigative work.

And I want to add that I did not seek this assignment as counsel to the committee. I appreciated and I still appreciate the honor and the dignity and opportunity for service in having been asked to serve as committee counsel. I have been happy to render whatever service, modestly I could render as counsel to the committee; and I want to assure Senator Glass that the compensation of $255 a month which I am receiving for these services certainly is no incentive to me to render these services or to continue to render them. [Applause in the room, on the part of spectators, loud and long continued.]

Senator Glass. I will say to the counsel to the committee that——

The Chairman (interposing). Let us have order in the room. Order, please.

Senator Glass. Oh, yes; that is what it is all about. We are having a circus, and the only things lacking now are peanuts and colored lemonade. [Laughter, and applause.]

The Chairman. Let us have order.

Senator Glass. I want to say to the counsel to the committee that the mere sending out of interrogations to bankers did not constitute for the purpose of the committee evidence of data which should have been submitted to the subcommittee.

As I have said and as I insist, so far as the compensation of counsel to the committee is concerned, and I want to say this to the counsel and to the committee, I was utterly opposed to an arrangement of that sort. I do not think that this counsel or any other counsel ought to be required to come here to Washington or to go to New York or anywhere else and work for the United States Senate without adequate compensation. And I was in favor of giving whatever counsel might be employed adequate compensation.

The Chairman. Senator Glass realizes, I am sure, that——

Senator Glass (continuing). And I do not imagine that counsel for the committee is working just for the $255 a month. Far from it.

The Chairman. I am sure the Senator realizes that the statute on that subject limits the amount which a Senate committee can pay.

Senator Glass. And I realize that we could have passed a resolution through the United States Senate authorizing the employment of counsel for this work. Now, I think counsel to the committee wants to make a further statement before we adjourn.

Senator Byrnes. Mr. Chairman.

Senator Kean. Mr. Chairman, I should like to ask the witness a couple of questions before he leaves the committee table.

Senator Couzens. Mr. Chairman, we agreed to adjourn at 1 o'clock today.

The Chairman. I know, but Senator Kean wants to ask a couple of questions, and he may now do it.

Senator Costigan. Mr. Chairman, before the questioning proceeds I desire to say one word.

The Chairman. Very well, Senator Costigan.

Senator Costigan. As a member of the committee I wish to express at this time my appreciation of the ability and the efficiency of counsel for the committee. Also to state that in my judgment the investigation thus far conducted has been relevant and material.

The Chairman. Senator Kean, do you want to ask a question?

Senator Kean. Mr. Howard, I should like to know at what price the stock of your company is selling at the present time.

Mr. Howard. I think about $8 or $9 a share. I do not know the quotation today.

Senator Kean. Then the people who had those options and have exercised them at $27 and what was the price?

Mr. Howard. It was $27.50.

Senator Kean. At the price of $27.50 a share, at the present time they have made a real contribution to the company's capital, haven't they?

Mr. Howard. They did.

The Chairman. If they held them?

Mr. Howard. Yes.

Senator Byrnes. Mr. Chairman, I should like to ask: Is it the desire of counsel to the committee to ask Mr. Whitney to return to the stand for any specific purpose before this session is adjourned?

Mr. Pecora. I think in view of the hour, if it be the pleasure of the committee, that we might suspend the examination of witnesses at this point.

Senator Byrnes. Is there anything more?

Mr. Pecora. I think I have reached the stage in this particular line of examination that——

Senator Costigan (interposing). I hope the witness will not be excused without an opportunity being afforded to members of the committee to ask further questions.

Senator Byrnes. Counsel to the committee has called Mr. Whitney to the stand for some purpose.

Senator Costigan. And Mr. Howard will return?

Mr. Howard. That is what I want to know.

The Chairman. Mr. Pecora has another statement to make.

Mr. Howard. That will be next Wednesday?

Mr. Pecora. I believe so.

The Chairman. We will decide that, but I think it will be next Wednesday.

Mr. Pecora. Mr. Chairman and Senators, my attention has been called to certain publications in the press of today to the effect that I had threatened to resign on last Tuesday and make a public statement unless the committee rendered a decision with regard to certain matters that it considered in its executive session on the afternoon of last Tuesday, which I thought was proper. I want to say that I never made any threat of any such character. The members of the committee I am satisfied did not hear me make any such threat, and I never made any statement to anybody, in or out of the committee room, or anywhere else on this green earth, that I had made any such threat to resign. Is that satisfactory, Senator Glass?

Senator Glass. Entirely satisfactory, except that the statement contains the vote in executive session.

Senator Byrnes. Well, Mr. Pecora has stated that he did not make that statement.

Senator Glass. I never cast a vote in my life in executive session or anywhere else in the Congress of the United States in 32 years that I objected to having published. When this committee has an executive session the supposition is that it is a confidential meeting of the committee, and that what occurs should not be revealed. And in connection with the statement that Mr. Pecora threatened to resign, which was absolutely untrue because I sat right beside him in the committee and he made no such threat, we have published accurately the vote that took place in the subcommittee. That may go for what it is worth.

Mr. Pecora. As to that may I also disclaim any measure of responsibility, for the publication of the vote.

The Chairman. And as chairman of the committee I say the same thing. I never gave any such information to anybody.

Senator Barkley. Mr. Chairman, I should like to make just this observation: I think it ought to be said that so far as the subcommittee or the general committee are concerned, according to my view at least, Mr. Pecora's services in connection with this investigation have been efficient and of value. And I frankly say that I was amazed when I saw in a paper a day or two ago that he is only receiving the compensation which he has this morning stated he is receiving. As a matter of orderly procedure, however, I think it would have been better if the subcommittee had been called and Mr. Pecora had been asked to briefly outline what he proposed to prove. Whose fault it was that the subcommittee did not meet, and that such preliminary report was not made, I do not know. But I do not think the fact that it was not called and that he did not make such report is to be blamed upon anybody particularly, or that it ought to interfere with the orderly procedure of this committee in continuing this investigation.

Senator Byrnes. Mr. Chairman, we will continue on next Wednesday morning at 10 o'clock, I believe?

The Chairman. I want to say as chairman of the subcommittee that I became chairman when this extra session was called on March 4. Prior to that time Senator Norbeck was the chairman of the committee. And the subcommittee has continued the same as it was under him. Senator Norbeck has not been a well man. He has not been able to get together his own committee from time to time to hold sessions if he desired to do so. When I became chairman, as Mr. Pecora has stated, he came here at our instance and made his statement; in fact, we asked him to prepare this resolution. He prepared the resolution, and I introduced it after the committee had seen it and knew of it.

Senator Glass. Why, I voted for it.

The Chairman. Absolutely. And this resolution was passed unanimously. That is the authority under which we are acting, is the direction under which we are acting. After that, as Mr. Pecora has stated, he came here before the committee, outlined the plan and purposes he had in view, and submitted the interrogatories he was going to propose. That was all explained before the full committee, not merely the subcommittee but the whole committee. They all told him to go on. I have not asked him to come down here and report to me from time to time because I knew he was busy with his work. I have been in communication with him. He has told me from time to time that he was going along with the work, that he had so many people for this, that, and the other thing, and that he was carrying out the purposes of the resolution. I have trusted him. He was selected by the committee and I had no reason to doubt but what he was acting in thorough good faith in carrying out this resolution, none in the world.

I have been very proud of the work that Mr. Pecora has done. I think it has been quite efficient and thorough, so far as I have been able to keep up with it. He has not been called down here to report to us from time to time what he was doing in detail. The fact is——[Applause.] The fact is that he has been in touch with our office here. He has had Mr. Marrinan here in connection with his work. He has had him to come to New York to report from time to time, and has instructed him what to do here, and how to do it. And they have been in communication, not only as respects themselves but with regard to going into details in a general way with me. I have not asked the committee to meet together to ask Mr. Pecora to come down here and lay before them what he was doing, and how he was doing it, and what it all meant or would lead to or what he supposed it would mean. But he has been busy, and we have all been busy. He set this date, May 23, himself, for the hearing. I have followed his request about that, and the comittee has, and we set that date for the hearing. I supposed he would be here on Saturday before the Tuesday, and I wanted to get the committe together to confer with him before the meeting, but he was occupied and he could not get here before the time set for the meeting. So that there has been nothing that the subcommittee could do except to tell him as counsel for the committee to proceed with this work and do it as the law requires and as we expected it to be done.

Senator Byrnes. Mr. Chairman, I am not on the subcommittee, but——

Senator Glass (interposing). Now, Mr. Chairman——

Senator Byrnes (continuing). Mr. Chairman, there is no motion before the whole committee with reference to the services of counsel. We were to adjourn at 1 o'clock to meet next Wednesday, at which time we expect Mr. Pecora to proceed with the investigation. And in accordance with the agreement, I move that the committee do now adjourn.

Senator Glass. Mr. Chairman, I hope the Senator won't make that motion. I do not intend to be put in an unreasonable attitude.

Senator Byrnes. Then I withhold my motion.

Senator Glass. And I am perfectly indifferent to clamor or applause. I want that understood. I still say that it would have facilitated the operations of this hearing, and would have enabled the members of this committee to have come in session with some comprehension of what has been discovered by Mr. Pecora, and what he expected to develop here, had he come to Washington and laid before the subcommittee, briefly, the results of his examinations in New York. I say that again. And member after member of the committee have agreed that that would have been the better course to pursue. Now, I do not care anything about the house of Morgan. The house of Morgan never loaned me a dollar in their lives and very likely never would, in any way, shape or form——

Senator Couzens. Unless you were properly introduced.

Senator Adams. And they told Senator Fletcher that they would not take a deposit from him.

Senator Glass. I am not careful of the house of Morgan except that I am careful of the dignity and orderly procedure of this committee. And as one member of this committee I do not intend to see any injustice done to the house of Morgan or any other house, whether it be of large consequence or of little consequence or of no consequence. That is my attitude, and it is the attitude I intend to maintain to the end of these hearings. I am not afraid to do J. P. Morgan & Co. justice, and if they have done anything they ought not to have done I am not afraid to legislate accordingly. And I want to call to the attention of this committee that the only sentence of statutory legislation that has been put upon the books, that has been offered in either branch of Congress, was framed by me; the only solitary sentence of statutary law that would have corrected the things that we have here talked about was framed by me and passed under my management on the floor of the United States Senate.

Senator Adams. Mr. Chairman, might I make a suggestion?

The Chairman. Certainly, Senator Adams.

Senator Adams. These things that have transpired are things of the past. I am not a member of the subcommittee, like Senator Byrnes, but if the committee or the subcommittee feel that counsel should make some statement to them in advance, I am satisfied that in the future they would have no difficulty with counsel as to advice in advance as to the prospects. But I do not believe we are getting very far in going back over these things of the past. I am not a member of the subcommittee but I would suggest——

Senator Byrnes (interposing). Mr. Chairman, I renew my motion to adjourn.

Senator Glass. That does not alter my contention that it ought to have been done in the past.

TESTIMONY OF OTTO H. KAHN, KUHN, LOEB & CO. JUNE 30, 1933

U.S. Senate, Stock Exchange Practices, *Hearings Before the Committee on Banking and Currency,* 73rd Congress, 1st Session, Part 3, 1305–17.

Mr. Pecora. Now, Mr. Kahn, are you familiar with the transaction that involved the acquisition by the Pennroad Corporation of 402,119 shares of the Seaboard Airline Railway for $4,529,838.75?

Mr. Kahn. No, Mr. Pecora; I knew nothing about that.

Mr. Pecora. Your firm was not consulted in any way by the officers or directors of the Pennroad Corporation with regard to this purchase?

Mr. Kahn. In no way, to the best of my knowledge.

Mr. Pecora. Did your firm handle any other transactions in behalf of the Pennroad Corporation, or did it have any other transactions with the Pennroad Corporation?

Mr. Kahn. The only other transactions we handled were purchases in the market, for which we got the regular broker's commission, amounting to approximately the figure which I gave you this morning, in the way of brokerages; but we suggested nothing; we had a hand in nothing, except the Canton transaction.

Mr. Pecora. Was the transaction to which you have just referred one involving the acquisition of shares of the New York, New Haven & Hartford Railroad?

Mr. Kahn. Yes, That was one of them.

Mr. Pecora. And how many shares of that road were acquired by the Pennroad Corporation through your firm?

Mr. Kahn. One hundred and forty-eight thousand eight hundred shares of common stock and 1,200 shares of preferred stock.

Mr. Pecora. Were those purchases made in the open market by your firm?

Mr. Kahn. To the best of my knowledge, yes. I do not know of any other way in which they could have been made by us. Yes.

Mr. Pecora. That is, they were not made in the way that the Canton Co. stock was acquired?

Mr. Kahn. Oh, no.

Mr. Pecora. And over what period of time were the market operations?

Mr. Kahn. That was between July 31, 1929, and June 15, 1930.

Mr. Pecora. That was found to be a convenient method for the Pennroad Corporation in acquiring this stock of the New Haven road, wasn't it?

Mr. Kahn. I do not know of any other way in which they could have done it.

Mr. Pecora. In your testimony this forenoon reference was made to the fact that the stock of the Pennroad Corporation was offered on the date of its incorporation, namely, April 24, 1929, to the stockholders of the Pennsylvania Railroad Co. at $15 a share.

Mr. Kahn. Yes.

Mr. Pecora. And reference also was made, as I recall it, to the fact that the following day, April 25, the stock was traded in in the open market, I suppose, on a when-issued basis?

Mr. Kahn. Yes.

Mr. Pecora. At something like $25 or $26; was that the figure you mentioned this morning?

Mr. Kahn. A few hundred shares, as I recall it; yes.

Mr. Pecora. There was a considerable variance between the offering price and the price at which the opening trades were made?

Mr. Kahn. Yes.

Mr. Pecora. At practically the same time?

Mr. Kahn. Yes.

Mr. Pecora. Do you know who made that market on the open trades?

Mr. Kahn. To the best of my knowledge the people who are buying and selling. I know of no one who instigated the buying and selling.

Mr. Pecora. Could you tell this committee, out of your experience, how these markets are made under similar circumstances?

(Mr. Kahn conferred with Mr. Stewart.)

Mr. Pecora. Let us rehearse briefly the circumstances.

Mr. Kahn. Yes.

Mr. Pecora. On April 24, 1929, the Pennroad Corporation was organized.

Mr. Kahn. Yes.

Mr. Pecora. Certificate of incorporation was filed. And on the same date its stock, or rather 5,800,000 shares of its total authorized issue of 10,000,000 shares, was offered by letter.

Mr. Kahn. Yes.

Mr. Pecora. Sent by General Atterbury, head of the Pennsylvania Railroad Co., to the shareholders of the Pennsylvania Railroad Co.

Mr. Kahn. Yes.

Mr. Pecora. At $15 a share.

Mr. Kahn. Yes.

Mr. Pecora. The only other persons that had any interest or right to subscribe for the stock or were given the opportunity at that time were Kuhn, Loeb & Co.—

Mr. Kahn. Yes.

Mr. Pecora. Which had agreed to purchase up to 250,000 shares, any shares of the original allotment of 5,800,000 that were not subscribed for by the shareholders of the Pennsylvania Railroad Co.

Mr. Kahn. Yes.

Mr. Pecora. Now, no business had been transacted by the Pennroad Corporation which gave any value to its stock between April 24 and April 25?

Mr. Kahn. I suppose not.

Mr. Pecora. What were the circumstances that you could point to that tended to make the opening price for this stock in the public trading on April 25 something like $25 a share?

Mr. Kahn. 1929, Mr. Pecora——

Mr. Pecora (interposing). Or, in other words, 66⅔ percent in excess of the price at which it was offered to the stockholders of the Pennsylvania Railroad?

Mr. Kahn. I put the responsibility of all these things—and I can give you much more striking examples than this one—I put the responsibility for that upon 1929 in the first instance. People were wild to buy pieces of paper, and they were sure that the next day they would be worth more and the second day still more, and so on, and so on.

I do not mean to say—I am not as innocent as that—I do not mean to say that that is always the fact. Occasions do occur—I suppose legitimate occasions do occur—where a market is made in the sense that stocks are offered, stocks are bought perfectly innocently, simply for the purpose of establishing a market. A market has usually got to have some kind of trading activity in order to be a market.

I said yesterday usually stocks spring up like weeds as compared with bonds, which have to be carefully nursed, and I used the word "watered." But quite normally it may be a perfectly legitimate and innocent thing to provide material out of which a legitimate market can be made, but it is not always, Mr. Pecora, a legitimate and innocent thing. I say I am not as innocent in saying that, and I know you are not as innocent in believing me if I did say it.

There are activities which are made for the deliberate purpose of agitating the market. I believe the exchange is doing all that it can to discourage that, to control it, and to stop it. But it is a difficult thing to stop. I know that of late there has been enormous activity in silver mines and in gold mines that were introduced in the market perhaps quite legitimately. The enormous profits which have been made in that connection—and they were huge profits—are due to the change in our governmental policy. To what extent the people who bought these bonds in the market acted in perfect good faith—because they believed that they would be worth more—to what extent they took advantage of the gullibility of the public is very difficult to say. But if I had to draw a line it would vary between innocence, between legitimacy, and between taking advantage of the gullibility of the public. I think all three elements enter.

Mr. Pecora. Well, you have observed, and doubtless soundly, that in many instances opening trades in a new issue of common stock were made at prices that are excessive. In saying "excessive" I am using my own term as defining what I believe you had in mind.

Mr. Kahn. Yes; I have seen such cases.

Mr. Pecora. How could that be stopped, in your opinion?

Mr. Kahn. I said before, and I repeat it, that I have the utmost confidence in public opinion being guided so as to assert itself in what would be an irresistible way. If a thing by public opinion is condemned as something which no decent person ought to do, ultimately no decent person will do it. It requires education. It requires a very definite guidance and expression of public opinion. But I believe the greatest guardian and the greatest educator against things which ought to be prevented is public opinion under suitable guidance.

I also believe that the watchfulness of the stock exchange ought to be most carefully concentrated against any attempt to take advantage of the one function for which it exists, namely, to offer a fair and free market for securities, and that anything which tends artificially to interfere with that market ought to be punished not merely by the stock exchange but otherwise. It ought not to be permitted. The only legitimate function of the stock exchange is to be a fair and free market. If they cannot control it themselves—I believe so far, of late particularly, they have made a very great effort to control it; I think they are doing everything now that I could think of if I were a Mussolini of the stock exchange, to prevent these artificial, antisocial, illegitimate practices which thrive on the gullibility of the public.

But if it should be found that they are not capable of handling that situation, then some other means, I think, should be found to deal with it.

Mr. Pecora. What means have been adopted or devised by the stock exchange, say, since last February, along those lines?

Mr. Kahn. As far as I know, they are exceedingly watchful as far as it is possible, and they have introduced such regulations as their wisdom dictated to prevent pool activities of an illegitimate or of an artificial character. I do not claim that they have wholly succeeded. I know that the activities in the New York market in the last 3 or 4 months have been somewhat comparable to the activities in 1929. Buy—buy—buy—you will make money.

Mr. Pecora. Do you suspect that the activities of the present market or market within recent months contain any evidences or signs that you would interpret as evidences of pool operations?

Mr. Kahn. I ought not give an opinion on something which I have not investigated.

Mr. Pecora. Still your opinion would be valuable, I think.

Mr. Kahn (after conferring with Mr. Buttenwieser). My partner calls my attention to the fact that the stock exchange has made short selling something as to which you have got to give to the stock exchange public notice and mark your sales "short sales." They have also regulated the activities of the specialists, which in the past have given ground for complaint and objection.

It is something as to which I suppose I ought not to express myself without having had much access to the facts as to whether in this particular year since the month of March pool activities of an illegitimate character have been in evidence. But if, as appears to my knowledge this year, a number of people reach the conclusion simultaneously that people ought to buy gold-mining shares, so they are safe against inflation, or they ought to buy silver-mining shares because silver will form part of the Nation's official currency, I do not suppose that is a pool activity in the sense in which I mean it.

I think, perhaps, I can best define my conception of a pool activity by saying that it is an activity which is based upon a definite purpose to affect the market, irrespective of the opinions of the people concerned as to intrinsic value or nonvalue of the security they are dealing with. I believe in this year most people that display an active part in the market did believe that buying shares—the kind of swaps which they had to offer, pretty nearly any kind of shares—was a wise and legitimate thing to do. In 1929 our guide was greed.

At the end of 1929 our guide was fear. I think they are the two worst guides in the world, greed and fear. I think at this time our guide was a desire for self-protection to a large extent, and if that is so, if my analysis is correct, then it is very difficult, in fact for me impossible, to determine in what instance those who were seeking self-protection were right, were justified, in commending their goods to the public. They were wrong, unquestionably wrong, in 1929, because greed was their guide. I think they were frequently wrong in 1931, because they had been made by fear incapable of judging, or permitted their own fear to affect their judgment and to act upon the judgment of others.

I am not prepared at this time to say in what way this at times undoubted evil can be dealt with. If you would like me to I will give it some further thought, especially in the light of the securities bill, which ought to help a good deal—I think in some respects, as I said yesterday, it is unworkable. In some respects I think it defeats its own purpose. But the effect of it, even with its existing shortcomings, ought to be good, and I think some of the things which have been done with impunity heretofore cannot be done any longer, and to that extent they ought also to have a beneficial effect upon the activities inside of the stock exchange.

Mr. Pecora. Now, do you recognize that the activities or operations of pools in the stock market gave that artificial stimulation to the market?

Mr. Kahn. Frequently; yes.

Mr. Pecora. And such artificial stimulation is misleading and deceptive to the average investor, isn't it?

Mr. Kahn. Yes.

Mr. Pecora. And to that extent such pool activities should be restrained or curbed, some way found for eliminating them, on account of their baneful influences?

Mr. Kahn. Yes. I would like—no; I think you are absolutely right. "Restraint" I think is the right word. Precisely in what way, I am not prepared to say.

Mr. Pecora. You are anticipating my next question now.

Mr. Kahn. But I agree with you that these things which in my opinion are antisocial activities and which deal with what I think is one of the most solemn obligations, to indicate to people how they ought to invest their savings. What is the right and the desirable and the responsible way so to indicate I think is a very great responsibility; and if you see that that responsibility is not properly fulfilled, it ought to be guided by some agency in some way. I agree with you. But I also say that I have not found the way yet; and whether regulation is the way I do not know yet.

Mr. Pecora. Are you prepared to say whether or not such restraint should be applied by governmental agencies or by the application of governmental power and authority, or should it be left to the governing authorities of the stock exchange?

Mr. Kahn. I should hope it could safely be left to regulation which, under the spur of public opinion and with the fear of government in the offing, I think is the best kind of regulation.

Mr. Pecora. There has been agitation now over a period of many years for some kind of Government or State regulation of the stock exchange, and yet that fear has not yet been strong enough to bring about the necessary reformative, corrective measures by the authorities of the exchange. Is not that true?

Mr. Kahn. Mr. Pecora, I think that a great many corrective and wise and effective measures have been brought about by that assertion of public opinion and by that agitation.

Mr. Pecora. You may or may not be familiar with the fact, but last February before this committee Mr. Richard Whitney, then and still the president of the New York Stock Exchange, appeared as a witness and testified that the New York Stock Exchange did not then and never had considered itself as having any right to evaluate securities traded in on its floor. If that attitude be persisted in or that opinion be maintained consistently by the officials of the exchange, what reasonable hope is there that they will apply the necessary corrective measures to those conditions?

Mr. Kahn. You say "devaluate"?

Mr. Pecora. Evaluate.

Mr. Kahn. Can there be more than a fair and free market, with every possible precaution taken that no advantage is taken of the forum which is given to the public to buy and to sell?

Mr. Pecora. Should they not be alert to see to it that that forum is not used in a manner that deceives or misleads the investing public?

Mr. Kahn. Decidedly.

Mr. Pecora. That you regard as their moral duty, do you not?

Mr. Kahn. I do, yes; their moral and their social duty, and their self interest; but above all, their moral duty.

Mr. Pecora. Do you think that in the fulfillment of that duty they might make some attempt, based upon an evaluation of the listed securities, so as to see to it that the investing public is kept currently posted as to real values as distinguished from those values that result from artificial stimulation of the market through pool activities?

Mr. Kahn. The duty to keep the public posted is primarily upon the corporations whose stock is being traded in. To the extent that the stock exchange can see to it that information is fully given without any concealment of any kind whatsoever, and to the extent that they can say to the corporations, "If we catch you in the act of deceiving the public, out you go," I think they ought to do it by all means; but I do not see what more they can do than to insist upon those who have the privilege of supporting the exchange getting the fullest and fairest information; and if they recognize that, plus the action of the securities bill, I should hope that your purpose, with which I am in the fullest sympathy, will be accomplished. If it is not, then I think it is up to you to apply severer measures.

But, after all, this is a democracy. It is supposed to work by education, by enlightenment, by the decisive action of public opinion; and I hope and believe that there is no agency in this country which can evade that influence, and I hope that there is none which will seek to evade that influence.

Senator Barkley. Speaking of pools, to what extent, if at all, do pools which may be interested in the rise in prices on the stock market exceed those that may be interested in the decline of values?

Mr. Kahn. Sometimes one way and sometimes another. Of course, in 1930 and 1931, particularly in 1931, I think the pools that were working for a decline were much more potent than those working for the rise; but they had to have public sentiment with them.

Senator Barkley. They had to capitalize fear?

Mr. Kahn. Yes.

Senator Barkley. In order to bring about a decline which would result in profit to them?

Mr. Kahn. Yes.

Senator Barkley. Have you expressed or do you hold any opinion as to the propriety of what we know as short selling on the stock market?

Mr. Kahn. Again going into motives, if short selling is based not upon a cooperative movement deliberately intended to scare people, to spread rumors, to depress prices, to make somebody else's holdings less valuable, to cause him to throw his securities upon the market—if it is not based upon that, but is based upon a man's honest conviction that he can just as well invest, as some one has said, in being short of stocks as invest in being long of stocks—if that is his motive, I think it is quite legitimate; and I think if short selling takes the form of deliberately depressing prices it is even more wrong than the practice of artificially boosting prices. Both practices are wrong, but I think the practice of the short seller, of the combined short seller and short raider, is even more wrong, because it does harm to somebody else. It depreciates somebody else's property.

Senator Barkley. It has been testified here early in these hearings which really started out on the investigation of short selling in the stock market, but have taken a very much wider range, that it is customary among large commodity purchasers, like those who have to buy large quantities of cotton in advance of their needs, to order a certain amount of cotton at a given price and then they sell the same or any particular amount of cotton at a figure probably a little above what they had to pay for it, in order to protect themselves against inordinate rises in the future. They call it "hedging," I believe. The same process is indulged in among millers with reference to wheat.

Mr. Kahn. Yes.

Senator Barkley. It is defended on the ground that it is necessary to protect them against future contingencies, and I can well understand that.

Mr. Kahn. I think it is.

Senator Barkley. But do you recognize any difference between that sort of a procedure and the deliberate sales by one person or by a group of persons of that which they do not possess, purely upon the theory that it will go down and they can purchase it at a lower rate and thereby reap a profit out of the fact that they have sold something to somebody that they did not possess, and afterward buy it back and nobody gets possession of it, and in that transaction make a considerable profit and thereby exercise a considerable influence in the artificial depression of the price either of the commodity or of a stock? What is your view with reference to the comparative morality of the two kinds of transactions that I have described?

Mr. Kahn. I know, as you know, that it is the stock argument in favor of short sales that they provide a cushion for the market and that the man who has sold short has got to buy back, and therefore it provides in times of storm and stress a cushion, a resiliency to the market which would otherwise not exist; and that whenever it has been attempted, as it has been attempted as far back, I believe, as the time of Napoleon in France, to stop short selling by edict, it has had to be repealed ultimately because it was found that it weakened the resisting power of the market. I am prepared to attribute a good deal of weight to that argument, and yet my moral sense tells me that there is something inherently repellent to a right-thinking man about short-selling activities to the extent that they can depreciate another man's property or that they will induce fear or produce alarm to harm normal activities. The line is most difficult to draw, as you will readily see, Senator.

I will come back to my old favorite doctrine from which I have learned much, particularly since 1929. What was done then none of us would think of doing, law or no law, because public opinion has changed and we have all learned from public opinion. I come back to that, that public opinion ought to be watchful, and if it finds that there are activities on the short-selling side or otherwise which are socially harmful, some means ought to be found to supervise them and to exercise the weight of public opinion. By what kind of a mentor you can do that I don't know; nor do I know at present, without having as yet the opportunity of seeing how the various new laws which have been enacted will work in operation—nor do I know now what I would suggest; but the activities of some moral force which in England is defined by the Governor of the Bank of England; in France it is largely defined, though not to the same extent, by the Governor of the Bank of France; in Germany it is most definitely defined by Dr. Schacht, of the Reichsbank. The guiding by such a man, the calling attention by such a man or a body of men to activities which are socially or economically undesirable is the only thing which at present I could suggest, but I hope by next autumn I may possibly have evolved some theory more helpful than this one.

Senator Barkley. On yesterday you undertook to define the difference between gambling and speculation.

Mr. Kahn. Yes.

Senator Barkley. It is true, is it not, that short selling more numerously partakes of the qualities of gambling than long buying? Would that be your judgment?

Mr. Kahn. I know of a man who made a lot of money in 1929, and he said, "I have invested all my savings in short selling." And I think he was perfectly bona fide. That shows how much depends upon the psychology of the public at the time. These are times when the public actually thinks that the best way in which they can invest their money is in short selling. Personally it is most repellant to me. Personally I have never sold a share of stock short in my life, and I do not believe I ever shall—I know I never shall. But I must recognize that short selling does exercise a certain function and that it is probably impossible to stop the public from being guided by its impulses if it feels sufficiently strongly like investing in short selling. I do not like it, and I wish I could do away with it. I think all kinds of gambling are economically detrimental to the country. Speculation is different, but all kinds of gambling are economically detrimental to the country.

Senator Goldsborough. Would you differentiate between the "short sale" and the sale "against the box"?

Mr. Kahn. There is of course a distinct difference, in that a sale against the box is simply a deferred sale. It is a sale which is deferred. It is distinctly different from a short sale where the man has not got the securities that he sells and can only get them from some other man and where he hopes to get them at some other man's detriment. There is a distinct difference.

Mr. Pecora. Having in mind the distinction between gambling and speculation in stock-market operations, would you say that trading in puts and calls is a form of trading that partakes more of the nature of gambling than it does of speculation?

Mr. Kahn. Puts and calls are a mixture of the two. I think it is an attempt on the part of a man to avoid gambling and yet to do something which comes pretty close to it, but it is not direct gambling.

Mr. Pecora. Would you say it is an attempt on the part of the man to gamble, but with some limitation upon the losses he will sustain if the gamble goes against him?

Mr. Kahn. And also to salve his own conscience. He would probably not like to think of himself as a gambler. Consequently he says, "Well, if I put and call I am not a gambler, because I can get my stock and deliver my stock." I think to a large extent he puts a salve of good intentions upon something which comes pretty close to gambling, but which is not exactly gambling, and he does protect himself.

Mr. Pecora. Would you put any form of restriction upon or even eliminate trading on puts and calls?

Mr. Kahn. "Elimination" is to me a very disagreeable term, because I hope that these things which are inherently undesirable will be corrected by public opinion, and I am convinced that they will be, especially when the public's attention is called to these things as your committee and you are calling them to their attention. What is happening here? The tales which are being recited here, the matters which you are bringing to public knowledge, the recommendations which you will make ultimately are bound to have a very important effect upon public opinion.

Mr. Pecora. Do you think they will have a beneficial effect?

Mr. Kahn. I think it is bound to have a very important and very beneficial effect upon public opinion. I think the kind of thing which is being done and looked into and brought to the surface here, even though in some respects sometimes, according to the editor of the Evening Post and others, it may go a little further than the occasion necessitates, is a matter of the greatest statesmanlike importance and value, because I think nothing is more important for the welfare and for the satisfaction and for the absence of irritation and resentment and bitterness on the part of the people than to have pointed out to them in what way they ought to deal with that which is their all, upon which they and their family depend, and which they now think is frequently abstracted out of their pockets. If you can give them a guide, a code, and a protection, I think you will perform a public service not merely of economic importance but of great social importance.

Mr. Pecora. You recognize, don't you, that the vast majority of stock-market transactions participated in by the public are on a so-called "margin" basis?

Mr. Kahn. Yes.

Mr. Pecora. And in your dissertation or discussion of your views before this committee within the last 2 or 3 days on the differences between speculation and gambling in the stock market, at one point you made some observations that indicated to me that you felt that when trading was indulged in by the man of limited means to an extent that threatened his own complete financial ruin, it was a social evil?

Mr. Kahn. Yes.

Mr. Pecora. Would you say that marginal transactions in the stock market savor more of gambling as those transactions are permitted on a larger margin, as the margin basis is greater?

Mr. Kahn. I am not sure that I understand you correctly. I should have said it the other way.

Mr. Pecora. I meant, as the margin is smaller.

Mr. Kahn. Yes. There should be a very ample margin required from anyone who wants to gamble—no; I do not want to use that word—anyone who wants to invest on a marginal basis, because it is a legitimate form of investment. There is no reason why only the rich should be able to take advantage of their judgment as to the rise or fall, especially the rise, of securities.

There is every reason why everyone within his means should have that same opportunity, and within his means and within prudence he should not be confined to 4 percent for the rest of his life. If he believes he can do better and does not jeopardize his welfare and that of his family, I say it is in the public interest that the interest in securities of our corporations should be spread all over the country and that the benefit from their prosperity should be shared by the whole country as far as possible.

Mr. Pecora. If you cared to express an opinion, assuming that you have one at this moment on it, what would you say in the public interest would be a safe and proper marginal minimum?

Mr. Kahn. That varies according to circumstances. When there has been a violent upward movement, the margin ought to be increased. People ought not to be induced, as too many of our banks were induced, to make loans at a time when everything was booming. On the contrary, during such a time they ought to be particularly prudent and they ought to require a liberal and ample margin partly as a warning and partly for their protection and partly for the protection of their client.

On the other hand, as was the case in 1931, our securities were selling at prices which were manifestly absurd, considering the recuperative power of this country, the intrinsic wealth and the history of this country, then I think the public can be encouraged by somewhat more liberal terms to induce them to buy securities. When, for instance, the Union Pacific in June of last year, or early July, was paying a 6 percent dividend on its stock, with a magnificent record of performance behind it, located in one of the greatest parts of the United States, was selling below 30, the small man could legitimately be encouraged by liberal margin facilities to put some of his money into that stock. But when there has been a big boom, then I think the marginal requirements ought to be increased and ought to be increasingly stringent as the danger point is approached.

Mr. Pecora. To whose judgment should that determination be left, in your opinion?

Mr. Kahn. In the case of loans it should be left by the banks to our clearing houses which, under the Glass bill, are perhaps more strictly supervised than heretofore, and the Federal Reserve Board and the Controller of the Currency who are given pretty direct supervisory power and even responsibility to see that sane, wise, and conservative practices are performed; and in the case of our banks I think it is pretty safe to leave it as it is now.

Mr. Pecora. But it was not found safe to leave it to the judgment of the banks in 1928 and 1929, was it, speaking from the vantage point of hindsight that we now have?

Mr. Kahn. We were all sinners during that time, Mr. Pecora, or, if not sinners, we were all grossly mistaken or affected beyond our powers to resist by the then prevailing mania or greed. Put any blame you like upon all those who then had charge of the affairs of the country. I hope and believe they have all learned, and I hope and believe that those things will not in our generation occur again. But I do not mean to say that the policeman should not be around the corner, and that if we indulge again in practices that are socially, economically, and, from the point of view of the country, undesirable, I think the policeman ought to be ready to step in. I think he is, now, under the laws as they are.

In the case of the stock exchange itself, I think it is, as things are now, always subject to the possible interference of the policeman or to the watchdog who, not only can bark, but can also bite if necessary. I think it is safe to leave to the stock exchange what margin should be fixed for margin trading.

Mr. Pecora. Is the name of that policeman you have in mind the Congress of the United States?

Mr. Kahn. Of course, it is a superpoliceman who appoints all the subordinate policemen. It is that power of the United States and those to whom it delegates the power; and I think the power should always be latent and we should be always conscious of the fact that it is latent.

Senator Barkley. You also have a rather healthy pup in the New York Legislature that operates now and then?

Mr. Kahn. Yes.

Mr. Pecora. I would say that while an attempt has been made to brandish that club, to my personal knowledge, somehow or other the stock exchange seemed to either ward off the blow or dodge it.

Senator Barkley. You misunderstood my statement.

Senator Goldsborough. You did not even get a bark out of it, let alone bite.

Mr. Pecora. Now, Mr. Kahn, would you care to make any recommendations to this committee with regard to action which the Congress might take in respect of bringing about any improvement in the existing methods of investment banking?

Mr. Kahn. I have got to be particularly careful about what I say, because it affects me. [Laughter.]

Mr. Pecora. That is why I am asking you.

Mr. Kahn. And when I say "particularly careful," I hope it means that I have got to be leaning over backward in order not to claim something for us to which we are not justly entitled.

Mr. Pecora. All right.

Mr. Kahn. The test and the only justification which exists for the private banker is: What services can he render better than others to the industries of the country? To what extent is he better able by reason of his acquired knowledge, by reason of the fact that there is a kind of close-knit relationship between him and his clients, because a partner in a private banking house is necessarily different from a vice president in a bank and has necessarily a somewhat different spirit. The fact that there is necessarily something like a family spirit and a family preservation spirit prevailing in a private bank among private bankers, to what extent is that helpful in enabling him to render services to American industry in providing its long-range needs better than somebody else?

To what extent can he serve the public better? To what extent does his self-interest see to it that his client, the investment public, is given a fair deal, over that of the corporate entity, which necessarily does not feel these things as strongly as the private banker does, not by reason of virtue but because it is his self-interest. To what extent in this country, which is a democracy, based upon the education of public opinion, and by public opinion I mean submission to public opinion as it expresses itself; what extent should this, in this country, encourage private enterprise rather than encourage a system which makes everybody a hired man? If you do want to encourage private enterprise, to what extent can you afford to regiment things rather than to give a reasonable degree, consistent with public safety, of latitutde, and of freedom to the individual? All these things enter into this question, and I believe my questions have really given my answer. For if the private banker does render, as I believe he does, services which are necessarily better rendered by him than by a corporate entity, then I say let him go ahead. But impose upon him the strictest requirements of disclosure as to what he offers. Impose upon him the strictest requirements as to the profits he is to make. By that you will ipso facto limit those profits and prevent them from becoming exorbitant. The danger of exorbitant profits is always there with the temptation of making exorbitant profits.

But if you compel a man to disclose everything he is doing, and if you penalize him for anything which he deliberately or knowingly withholds; if you force him to disclose his profits in every transaction, then that, together with the workings of public opinion in staying away from the man who deals badly with it and going to the man who deals well with it, and together with the action of corporations in necessarily going to the man who gives them sound advice and a fair price rather than to the man who simply tries to gouge them, and who says, "I have made a lot out of them this time and that will do." I think that will pretty nearly accomplish your purpose.

Mr. Pecora. Now, Mr. Kahn, in the questionnaire that was sent to your firm in behalf of this committee—

The Chairman (interposing). Mr. Pecora, before you branch off on that, let me ask Mr. Kahn a question or two.

Mr. Pecora. Certainly, Mr. Chairman.

The Chairman. Mr. Kahn, you are familiar with the operations and practices of what are known as "investment trusts", I take it?

Mr. Kahn. Yes, sir.

The Chairman. Have you any observations to make with regard to any of their practices and operations, and whether or not some of them ought not to be corrected?

Mr. Kahn. A great many sins have been committed there, Senator Fletcher. Many things have been done which ought not to have been permitted; and I think, speaking generally, I would say that investment trusts, first of all, must not be controlled by a small group of people who happen to own one particular issue to which the voting power has been confided. Investment trusts must be controlled by their own people.

Secondly, investment trusts must deal at arm's length with every comer, including those that created it. They must not play favorites with those who are its originators. They are not children in the sense that I am my father's child. They are the public's child, and the public has provided the origination, and the public has provided the wherewithal that gave them their education. I think if you will make it the general rule that investment trusts must deal at arm's length with everybody, and must not be controlled by some small stock issue created for the purpose of providing control but must deal under the direction of their stockholders, and if you subject them, as you will subject them, to the same rule of profit disclosure, facts disclosure, to which the private banker is subjected, I think you will have done about all that can now be done or that should now be done.

The Chairman. All right. I thank you, Mr. Kahn.

ARTICLE BY ROBERT WINSMORE, "WALL STREET'S REPLY TO THE SENATE INVESTIGATION" JULY 22, 1933

The Literary Digest, July 22, 1933, 5; 31.

Wall Street is quite unashamed. For what the Senate's search-light re-cently revealed of principles and practises of American finance it is making no excuses. Some grim resentment of the search-light's glare and misdirection is still to be heard in the byways. Some indignation against the attendant ballyhoo still eddies in the lee of the Stock Exchange. But there are no apologies for what was disclosed, and one who asks why, is answered, "Why should there be?"

A trumpery mountain labored at Washington and brought forth—not even a mouse. That is how Wall Street shrugs and dismisses the Senate's inquisition. The House of Morgan was rigged out with horns and a tail and pilloried to make a New Deal holiday, but the show didn't half come off. Kuhn, Loeb & Company was paraded and frisked for evidence of sinister legerdemain in banking, but that number was also a palpable flop. More often than not Senatorial questionings lacked substance and intelligence, were far off their marks, were inept or inane.

There you have the Wall Street view. For all his license and support, the prosecuting Pecora quite failed to accomplish the inquisition's converted aims—to indict men and machinery of the market place for deliberately de-structive performance, and to brand the private banker, per se, as a malignant growth in the economic body. Pecora quite failed, says the Street, for no thinking man will vote a true bill on either count if he has read of the Senate committee's inquiry that was told in flashy newspaper captions.

Within earshot of Trinity's chimes that is the collective opinion. If it suggests smug complacency, however, the suggestion is misleading. Satisfied tho it is that its weighed institutions have not reasonably been found wanting. Wall Street is, nevertheless, well aware that its leaders and its whole self have once again been disadvantaged before the country. It is well aware that a great deal of misunderstanding has been created, a great deal of latent prejudice stirred up, a great deal of abiding hatred aroused to new snarling by the nation-wide bill-boarding of tax evasions, of "favored" lists, of millions once easily netted from the marketing of securities that have since cost the Ameri-can public its metaphorical shirt.

Quarrel With Methods

The Street is fully cognizant of all this, yet fully cognizant also of the futility of reasoning with the emotional unreason that it so largely represents. That is why there recently has been so little defensive explanation of the testimony at Washington to offset the distortions and exaggerations that were spread before the rank and file.

Such acceptance and reliance, then, is the attitude there at Mammon Four Corners, where Morgan House squats as solidly as ever in the shadow of the tall Stock Exchange and presents its cold shoulder to the emptied Subtreasury. There is no attendant complaining—at least none so loudly voiced as to carry beyond the neighborhood. And, indeed, if louder complaint were evoked it would not quarrel greatly with the presence of a State inquiry, since occasional State inquiries have come to be regarded as inevitable and not unjustified. The complaint would quarrel, rather, with the misdirection, the police-court methods, the undue emphasis upon extraneous matters which, as the market place thinks, characterized the recent Senatorial probing.

For instance, the matter of income taxes. What bearing—this is Wall Street asking—has the payment or non-payment of income taxes by an individual upon the question of the good or evil of private banking as an institution? None—this is Wall Street answering—except as it may serve to insinuate that one or another outstanding private banker is habitually a practitioner of evil, a sly evader of the law, and thus a true representative of a ruthlessly acquisitive financial machine.

Which insinuation, of course, is charlatanry. To pay no more taxes than the letter of the law demands is not only a settled universal custom, but an attribute of human nature. If it is knavery, then the United States is entirely a nation of knaves.

Note that this is one of Wall Street's still-voiced complaints. But note also that Wall Street is nowise sorry that the testimony of non-taxpaying bankers at Washington showed the present income-tax law to be faulty and inefficient. If one result of the Senate's probing is modification or elimination of the inclusion of capital gains and losses in income returns, no satisfaction will be more sincere than that of the financial community. Not only has it suffered much on its own account from that requirement of the law, but it fully agrees with Mr. Otto Kahn's opinion as to the artificial security market conditions periodically produced by its operation.

Even so, the Street considers the Pecora harping on individual tax statements to have been as foreign to the real purposes of the Senate committee's session as the introduction of the Ringling midget and the strangely privileged bombast of Huey Long. For his harping on bankers' lists of favored clients and friends, much greater relevancy is acknowledged, yet there is resentment of the false inferences drawn therefrom and boisterously hippodromed before an excitable, uninformed public.

The Sale of Stock

Why—it is Wall Street asking—should wholly sinister intent be imputed to a financing banker's sale of stock at less than public-market quotation to his present or prospective clientele and to those with whom he currently does or hopes to do business? Is this different from the very common practise whereby a manufacturer or jobber or merchant favors business and personal friends by selling them goods quietly at a lower price than the public currently has to pay at retail?

And has a banker an obligation, even an ethical one, to extract from a blindly gambling public in the open market a higher price for stock than he thinks it is worth and is willing to take for it? What material interest or moral right of the public was violated when J. P. Morgan & Company chose to ignore the unduly high market bid of $37 for Alleghany Corporation stock which had lately cost the firm but $20 a share, preferring to turn the stock over to its own clients at the cost price?

Preference to profit-producing clients and associates such as the Morgans and others freely disclosed at the Washington hearings is one of the most conventional practises in corporation financing. That it should have been placarded, by implication, as secret banking chicanery involving, among other evils, a purpose to secure political favor, is what Wall Street resents. It was almost ghoulish glee with which such names as Woodin, Raskob, Baker, Adams, Hilles, Mellon, McAdoo were plucked from the "preferred" lists and waved on high. There was no accompanying explanation that Morgan association with most, and perhaps all, of these men antedated their attainment to political eminence and power.

As an executive industrialist, the present Secretary of the Treasury had association with Morgan & Company for years before his Cabinet seat seemed even a remote possibility. John Raskob traded General Motors millions across the Morgan table years before he gave politics a thought—indeed, before he was a Democrat. And so on. Yet what was recently loud-pedaled at Washington was implication that sly subsidy of such political lights was the sole reason for the appearance of these names on the "preferred" lists of '28 and '29.

What Wall Street Admits

It is this seeming innuendo and unfair misrepresentation at the inquiry against which Wall Street mutters. In contrast, it is by no means lacking in respect for what attention was given to matters more pertinent to the official purposes of the inquisition. Self-interest naturally makes the market-place regard the whole investigation as unnecessary and unwisely provocative of hue and cry by an uninformed, emotional public. Nevertheless, it recognizes that, in the circumstances, exposure of details of the excessive exploitations and profits of the mad predepression period is not without justification.

Wall Street offers no objection to New Deal disclosure of the processes whereby capitalizations were then extravagantly pyramided with readily obtained banking aid to effect great combinations, such as the Van Sweringen railroad structure. It does not dispute the propriety of laying bare the steps whereby mammoth holding companies, like the Pennroad and United corporations, were banker-designed and banker-financed and perhaps held banker-controlled after ownership of them had been passed on to the furiously speculating public, at huge profit to the bankers. The Street's attitude, in fact, is quite in line with that shown at the Senate's inquest by the bankers who were its principal targets.

In one way or another, both J. P. Morgan and Otto Kahn acknowledged that for them, as for all men, the boom years were years of delusion; that they did much during that time which they now know to have been misconceived and would not repeat; that their great profits, astonishing even then and since vanished, were abnormal, not to say excessive. And Mr. Kahn, in connection of his defense of private banking as an honorable institution and highly valuable to the financing of business enterprise, seemed to go very far in agreement that governmental regulation, supervision and restriction are both justified and desirable. Yet, contrary to popular belief, that is the prevailing opinion in Wall Street.

TESTIMONY OF ALBERT H. WIGGIN
NOVEMBER 1, 1933

U.S. Senate, Stock Exchange Practices, *Hearings Before the Committee on Banking and Currency*, 73rd Congress, 1st Session, Part 6, 2969–78.

Mr. Pecora. Mr. Wiggin, as I recall the testimony you have given about these short sales made by the Shermar Corporation of Chase Bank stock, you said, in substance if not in words, that the making of those short sales is a good thing because it provides for purchasing power for the bank stock. Now, just what did you mean by that?

Mr. Wiggin. I meant that if there was a break in the stock that might be injurious to the bank there was somebody there to buy the stock and keep it from breaking further.

Mr. Pecora. Who was the somebody that you had in mind?

Mr. Wiggin. This company that was in a position to buy.

Mr. Pecora. The Shermar Co.?

Mr. Wiggin. Yes, sir.

Mr. Pecora. Now, as a matter of fact that furnishing of a purchasing power would not have been of avail for that purpose unless the stock was bought in the open market, would it?

Mr. Wiggin. Oh, I think so. No matter where it was bought it would have the same effect, would it not?

Mr. Pecora. I don't know. I am asking you.

Mr. Wiggin. I think it would have the same effect.

Mr. Pecora. Well, now, as a matter of fact, what really did happen was that the Murlyn Corporation bought 42,000 shares which had been sold short by the Shermar Corporation on December 11, 1929, from the affiliate of the bank.

Mr. Wiggin. Yes, sir.

Mr. Pecora. Well, how did that help to create a purchasing power for the stock that was beneficial to the market?

Mr. Wiggin. Well, it put the Metpotan Co. in a position to buy stock with the cash that they had if they wanted to.

Mr. Pecora. Did the Metpotan Co. do that?

Mr. Wiggin. I don't know. I would have to look that up in order to find out.

Mr. Pecora. When the Shermar Corporation made those short sales it did not know what the Metpotan Co. was going to do, did it?

Mr. Wiggin. No, sir.

Mr. Pecora. When the Metpotan Corporation made those short sales was it in the contemplation that the Shermar Corporation would cover its short position by purchasing the stock of the Metpotan Co.?

Mr. Wiggin. It had no definite plan.

Mr. Pecora. As a matter of fact you said among other things that another purpose you had in making those short sales for the Shermar Corporation was to enable your family to sell some of their holdings.

Mr. Wiggin. Yes, sir.

Mr. Pecora. That purpose was not accomplished either, was it?

Mr. Wiggin. Yes, sir. They did sell, and when the stock was repurchased it was at a lower price.

Mr. Pecora. Well, now, the stock was repurchased by the family interests, wasn't it?

Mr. Wiggin. Yes, sir.

Mr. Pecora. Through the Murlyn Corporation?

Mr. Wiggin. Yes, sir.

Mr. Pecora. And meanwhile the family had enough stock to enable the Shermar Corporation to deliver under its short sales without buying in the market, didn't it?

Mr. Wiggin. That is very true; yes, sir.

Mr. Pecora. So that did not help to provide a purchasing power for the stock, did it?

Mr. Wiggin. Why, I think it did.

Mr. Pecora. How?

Mr. Wiggin. Because they did buy back.

Mr. Pecora. They bought back, not in the market, but from the Metpotan Co.?

Mr. Wiggin. Yes, sir. They bought from the Metpotan Co.

Mr. Pecora. How did that improve the purchasing power in the market for the stock?

Mr. Wiggin. It put the Metpotan Co. in funds, with that cash in case they wanted to buy.

Mr. Pecora. But you said that the sales made by the Shermar Corporation were not made in combination with the Metpotan Co. In other words, you did not know that the covering was going to be done through purchases made from the Metpotan Co., did you?

Mr. Wiggin. No, sir.

Mr. Pecora. The Shermar Corporation would not have sold that stock short unless it expected to make a profit therefrom, would it?

Mr. Wiggin. Yes, sir; I think so. It reduced the holdings of the family that much. If the stock had gone up they would have had to cover at a loss, but they could have covered.

Mr. Pecora. Well, the family was not going to reduce its holdings at a loss if it could avoid doing so, was it? ·

Mr. Wiggin. Repeat that, please.

Mr. Pecora. The committee reporter will read it to you.

(The question was thereupon read by the reporter, as above recorded.)

Mr. Pecora. In other words, the family was not going to sell its holdings at a loss if it could avoid a loss, was it?

Mr. Wiggin. Probably not.

Mr. Pecora. The Shermar Corporation when it made those short sales expected to make a profit from them, didn't it?

Mr. Wiggin. I don't know whether they expected it or not. They hoped to.

Mr. Pecora. Well, did the Shermar Corporation consult any particular individual or individuals when it decided to make those short sales?

Mr. Wiggin. I don't think so.

Mr. Pecora. You made the decision for the Shermar Corporation with regard to making those short sales, didn't you?

Mr. Wiggin. Undoubtedly.

Mr. Pecora. What was in your mind at the time you made that decision? What object did you hope to accomplish or attain?

Mr. Wiggin. Just as I testified this morning.

Mr. Pecora. Well, this morning you said, among other things, that it would provide a broader purchasing power for the Chase Bank stock, and to that extent it would be beneficial to the bank.

Mr. Wiggin. It reduced the family holdings, and provided a purchasing power for the stock. I think those were the two reasons I gave.

Mr. Pecora. Those were the two reasons you gave?

Mr. Wiggin. I think so.

Mr. Pecora. Was the factor of selling either at a loss or a profit in your mind?

Mr. Wiggin. I have no doubt that I hoped I would make a profit on the transaction.

Mr. Pecora. And you thought you would make a profit by selling short?

Mr. Wiggin. I do not know what I thought at that time, Mr. Pecora.

Mr. Pecora. Well, you know what would animate you to make short sales of the security.

Mr. Wiggin. I might point out that if the stock had been bought back at a loss it would have been good business for the family to sell some of their stock at that time.

Mr. Pecora. Well, if you had thought you would have to buy that stock back at a loss you wouldn't have made those short sales, would you?

Mr. Wiggin. No; not if I had expected that.

Mr. Pecora. So it is a fair inference that you made the short sales because you thought it would result in profits?

Mr. Wiggin. I hoped it would; yes, sir. .

Mr. Pecora. Now, what prompted you to believe, in August, September, and October of 1929, that by selling the bank stock short profits would accrue to you?

Mr. Wiggin. I don't know.

Mr. Pecora. Well, if you don't know, who would know?

Mr. Wiggin. I probably had some definite reasoning at that time but I don't know today what it was. This was sometime ago, as you know.

Mr. Pecora. I know it, but there must have been some reason that led you to believe you might cover at a lower price and thereby make a profit.

Mr. Wiggin. Only the general reasoning that the market was very high on bank stocks.

Mr. Pecora. Did you believe that was the case at that time on Chase Bank stock?

Mr. Wiggin. I thought all bank stocks were high, and I thought Chase National Bank stock was selling in line with other stocks.

Mr. Pecora. That is, selling too high.

Mr. Wiggin. I don't know that—

Mr. Pecora (continuing). As compared with its real value.

Mr. Wiggin. I don't know whether I thought so or not.

Mr. Pecora. Haven't you just said in substance that that is what you thought?

Mr. Wiggin. Well, have I?

Mr. Pecora. You said all bank stocks, and Chase Bank Stock was a bank stock, and hence was included in the word "all," isn't that so?

Mr. Wiggin. I think that is a fair conclusion, yes, sir.

Mr. Pecora. In other words, that is a fair inference?

Mr. Wiggin. I think so.

Mr. Pecora. Now, if you thought Chase Bank stock was selling too high in the market in the summer and fall of 1929, why did you as the chief executive officer of the Chase Bank, and of its subsidiary, the Chase Securities Corporation, permit the Chase Securities Corporation and its wholly owned subsidiary, the Metpotan Corporation, to go into those various pools or syndicate accounts to stabilize the market, so to speak, or to keep up the price?

Mr. Wiggin. Well, did they at that time?

Mr. Pecora. Mr. Wiggin, I had nothing to do with those pools at that time, nor since. You did. That is why I am asking you the question and expecting you to answer it. I cannot tell. I do not know anything about those things.

Mr. Wiggin. Will you have the other question read to me?

Mr. Pecora. The committee reporter will read it to you.

(The question was thereupon read by the reporter as above recorded.)

Mr. Wiggin. Let me see. [Inquiring of an associate.]

Mr. Pecora. Do you have to get the answer to that question from Mr. Lynch?

Mr. Wiggin. I am trying to find out if they did do it. And I cannot find that they did.

Mr. Pecora. What is that?

Mr. Wiggin. I cannot find that they did do it at that time. If you have any information there, perhaps it will help me out.

Mr. Pecora. Well, you have given some testimony here—for instance, that the Chase Securities Corporation participated in a trading account managed by Dominick & Dominick, formed in July of 1929 and which continued to operate for several months thereafter; in fact that particular account was closed November 11, 1929. You have already given a lot of testimony about that trading account.

Mr. Wiggin. Well, I just wanted to identify the dates.

Mr. Pecora. Yes.

Mr. Wiggin. And the Metpotan Co. was selling stock, wasn't it?

Mr. Pecora. It was doing both. It was in this trading account which, as you have already testified, bought and sold, was in and out of the market practically every day during the life of that trading account.

Mr. Wiggin. And it sold stock. And the net result was a sale of stock, was it not?

Mr. Pecora. It both bought and sold. You said it was to stabilize the market. You said that was one of the purposes of that account and of other accounts of a similar character.

Mr. Wiggin. The net result was a sale of stock, wasn't it? And they did just what I did.

Mr. Pecora. Well, you did it for a profit. You sold short. You did not buy and sell. The Shermar Corporation sold short between August and December of 1929, didn't it?

Mr. Wiggin. That is right.

Mr. Pecora. Now, this trading account in which the Chase Securities Corporation, through the Metpotan, was a participant, and which was managed by Dominick & Dominick, was formed in July and operated until November 11. Now, you said they bought and sold, the Shermar Corporation sold short.

Mr. Wiggin. The net result was—

Mr. Pecora (interposing). So that the two accounts' operations were different.

Mr. Wiggin. The net result was the same to both corporations.

Mr. Pecora. Is that so, Mr. Wiggin, that the net result was the same?

Mr. Wiggin. The Metpotan sold.

Mr. Pecora. What was that net result you are speaking of?

Mr. Wiggin. On the options to Dominick & Dominick that they sold this large amount of stock.

Mr. Pecora. Did they not do both? They bought and sold, didn't they?

Mr. Wiggin. They bought and sold, but the net result was sales.

Mr. Pecora. Well, now, let us see if that is so. Let me look that up.

The Chairman. Mr. Wiggin, while Mr. Pecora is looking that up, do you know of any other officers of the Chase Bank who sold stock in the summer and fall of 1929 of the bank, bank stock?

Mr. Wiggin. Oh, I think a good many of them did.

Mr. Pecora. I am going to recall to your mind the testimony during the first week you were on the stand before this committee, which was the week before last, with regard to these Chase Bank stock syndicates. There were eight of them that you testified about.

Mr. Wiggin. There were quite a number.

Mr. Pecora. There were eight. The first one was formed on September 21, 1927, and terminated on April 18, 1928. During the life of that account, the account purchased 22,217 shares and sold that same number. So the amount of sales corresponded exactly to the number purchased in the open market.

Account no. 2 was formed on April 18, 1928, and terminated on April 9, 1929, and that account purchased 59,522 shares and sold that same amount.

The third account, being the first one managed by Dominick & Dominick, was formed on July 19, 1929, and terminated on November 11, 1929; and that also purchased 172,806 shares and sold that same number. So you see that the Metpotan and the Chase Securities Corporation, whichever one was the participant in those syndicate accounts or trading accounts, did not take a net short position in any of those accounts, whereas the Shermar Corporation's transactions gave it a net short position to the extent of 42,506 shares. So how could you say that the net result was the same?

Mr. Wiggin. The Metpotan Corporation reduced its holdings, didn't it?

Mr. Pecora. Not if the trading account sold the same number of shares it purchased.

Mr. Wiggin. I think it did, Mr. Pecora.

Mr. Pecora. That is not the evidence.

Mr. Wiggin. I do not think that that is inconsistent. They put a certain number of shares into the trading account and the trading account sold what it bought; but the Metpotan undoubtedly reduced its holdings.

Mr. Pecora. The Metpotan was not selling short in those accounts. It was selling stock that it actually owned?

Mr. Wiggin. Yes.

Mr. Pecora. The Shermar Corporation was selling short?

Mr. Wiggin. Yes, sir.

Mr. Pecora. It sold 42,000 shares it did not own?

Mr. Wiggin. Yes; but the Metpotan reduced its holdings on Chase stock. Let me point out another matter, too, that may be of interest to you. The Shermar Corporation, or any of the family corporations, never sold or bought a share of Chase stock except through the Chase Securities Co.; so that there could not be any interference with their interests.

Mr. Pecora. Now, was it the purpose of the Metpotan in going into those trading accounts to dispose of its shares of the bank stock, or was it its purpose to stabilize the market and obtain a wider distribution of the bank stock?

Mr. Wiggin. Both.

Mr. Pecora. What was the purpose of the Shermar Corporation in engaging in those short sales in the summer and fall of 1929?

Mr. Wiggin. To reduce the family holdings and to be in position to buy stock if it seemed advisable, or in the interest of the bank.

Mr. Pecora. In the interests of the bank? Will you be good enough to tell the committee how the bank's interests were served directly by the Shermar Corporation selling short 42 thousand shares? Just explain that in detail to the committee.

Mr. Wiggin. It gave them a purchasing power.

Mr. Pecora. When you say "they", whom do you mean?

Mr. Wiggin. The Shermar Corporation.

Mr. Pecora. To do what?

Mr. Wiggin. To purchase bank stock.

Mr. Pecora. From whom?

Mr. Wiggin. Anybody.

Mr. Pecora. How did it profit the bank?

Mr. Wiggin. It didn't profit the bank.

Mr. Pecora. How did it serve the bank's interests?

Mr. Wiggin. Because there were frequently occasions when a violent fluctuation in the stock, with no purchaser, was injurious to the bank, and it was wise to have somebody that could purchase stock.

Mr. Pecora. When the Shermar Corporation engaged in these short sales, was it making some contribution possibly to bringing about those wide fluctuations?

Mr. Wiggin. No, sir.

Mr. Pecora. Does not short selling operate to depress the value of a security, as a rule?

Mr. Wiggin. They would not have done it if it depressed the stock.

Mr. Pecora. Does not short selling as a rule have that effect, namely, to depress?

Mr. Wiggin. As a rule I cannot say, but perhaps it does.

Mr. Pecora. Is there any doubt about it in your mind that that is a distinct result of short selling?

Mr. Wiggin. It depends entirely on the particular transaction.

The Chairman. The purchasing power would not have been increased unless they had made a profit, would it?

Mr. Wiggin. Yes, sir. It gave them cash to buy with.

Mr. Pecora. If you thought, as an officer of the bank, apart from your relations to the Shermar Corporation with which the bank was not identified, that the market price of the stock of the bank in the summer and fall of 1929 was too high, why did you permit those high prices to be maintained through the participation in these trading accounts which dealt in the bank stock of the Chase Securities Corporation or the Metpotan Corporation?

Mr. Wiggin. The Metpotan was in a trading account with the right to buy and the right to sell. Its purpose was to reduce its holdings—one of its purposes.

Mr. Pecora. You are not forgetting the other purpose that you emphasized last week, or the week before—that of stabilizing the market—are you?

Mr. Wiggin. No, sir. The market price was entirely beyond my control.

Mr. Pecora. I do not think that answers my question, Mr. Wiggin.

Mr. Wiggin. Well, repeat the question and I will try to answer it.

(The question referred to was read by the reporter as above recorded.)

Mr. Wiggin. And the answer is?

(The reporter read the answer referred to as above recorded.)

Mr. Wiggin. That is the best answer I can make.

Mr. Pecora. You have said in the past that one of the main reasons you had the affiliate of the Chase Bank go into these trading accounts that dealt in the bank stock was to stabilize the market for the bank stock.

Mr. Wiggin. Yes, sir.

Mr. Pecora. And that is true, is it not?

Mr. Wiggin. Yes, sir.

Mr. Pecora. You have seen that one of these trading accounts, formed for the purpose, among other things, of stabilizing the market in the bank stock, was formed in July and operated until the 11th of November 1929, which period takes in the larger part of the period between August 8 and December 2, 1929, when your company, the Shermar Co., sold 42,506 shares short?

Mr. Wiggin. Yes, sir.

Mr. Pecora. Now you said one of the reasons for your company selling short was because you hoped to make a profit thereby. Is that correct?

Mr. Wiggin. I hoped it would make a profit.

Mr. Pecora. But you knew that it could not make a profit unless it could cover the short sales at a lower price; is that right?

Mr. Wiggin. That is the only way the Shermar Corporation could make a profit.

Mr. Pecora. You also said, in the course of your testimony here, that you thought in the summer and fall of 1929 all bank stocks, including the Chase Bank stocks, were selling too high?

Mr. Wiggin. Yes, sir.

Mr. Pecora. Now, keeping in mind all those elements, why did you, as the chief executive officer of the Chase Bank, as well as of its security affiliate, permit or sanction the security affiliate of the bank going into these trading accounts to stabilize the market or maintain the price for the bank stock?

Mr. Wiggin. Because they had the right to buy and also the right to sell, and they wanted to reduce their holdings.

Mr. Pecora. You did not permit them to do that in order that they might have the right to buy and the right to sell. That was simply an attribute of a trading account, was it not? It was not the reason for the trading account?

Mr. Wiggin. I think it was the reason for the trading account.

Mr. Pecora. You said the reasons for the trading account were to stabilize the market and enable the security affiliate to sell some of its holdings.

Mr. Wiggin. Yes, sir.

Mr. Pecora. You said, also, that in your opinion the market prices for the bank stock in that period of time were too high or, in other words, out of proportion to its real value.

Mr. Wiggin. I said I thought the market on bank stocks was high; yes, sir.

Mr. Pecora. And you, through your private corporation, the Shermar Corporation, acting upon the belief that you had that the market price for the bank stock was too high, and acting further upon the hope that you had that by selling the stock short your corporation would make profits, nevertheless permitted the security affiliate of the bank to go into trading accounts designed to stabilize the market at the time when you thought the market price was too high. Why did you do that?

Mr. Wiggin. I permitted them to go in to stabilize the market and buy and sell with the hope that they would reduce their holdings—the same purpose exactly.

Mr. Pecora. The Shermar Corporation had no holdings to reduce. They were engaged in a speculation, were they not?

Mr. Wiggin. The family had large holdings, and the interests were the same.

Mr. Pecora. And the family never let go of those holdings, because it caused the Murlyn Corporation to buy back the total amount of its short stock from the Metpotan Co. on December 11, 1929?

Mr. Wiggin. It did not buy it back until December.

Mr. Pecora. Who did not?

Mr. Wiggin. These family interests.

Mr. Pecora. The Murlyn Corporation bought it in December, did it not?

Mr. Wiggin. That is what I say: They did not buy it until December. You are speaking of August, I think.

Mr. Pecora. I am speaking of the whole period of time covered by the short sales, from August until December.

Mr. Wiggin. I understood that you were speaking of the Metpotan sales in August, or October, or whatever that date was. Am I right?

Mr. Pecora. I was asking you not about those sales at all. I asked you to tell the committee why you, as the chief executive officer of the bank and its security affiliates, permitted the security affiliate to go into market operations through the medium of these trading accounts to stabilize the market at a time when you thought the price of the stock was so high, so far out of proportion to value, that you, as the owner or one of the owners of the Shermar Corporation, operated in the market by selling short with a view of making a profit.

Mr. Wiggin. I think I have answered that question already, and the answer was that the Metpotan had the right to buy and the right to sell, and they hoped to reduce their holdings, and did.

Mr. Pecora. Do you know that the Metpotan reduced its holdings?

Mr. Wiggin. Yes, sir.

The Chairman. I understand the gist of the question is, Mr. Wiggin, why you should endeavor to stabilize the market and keep the price of the bank stock as it was, practically, when you realized and believed that the bank stock was too high?

Mr. Wiggin. Of course, any belief that I had that the bank stock was too high was purely a matter of opinion.

Mr. Pecora. It turned out that your opinion was pretty sound, did it not?

Mr. Wiggin. It happened so in that case.

Mr. Pecora. Did it not occur to you as an individual who owned large blocks of Chase Bank stock at a time when you thought the market price thereof was too high that it created a situation in the market that enabled you, by selling the stock short, to reap handsome profits through the Shermar Corporation's activities and that the affiliate of the bank of which you were the executive head at the same time was engaging in market operations that would keep this price up so as to enable you to sell short at the best possible profit to yourself?

Mr. Wiggin. Not at all, sir. They were both selling, and we never sold except in consultation with them, and let them handle the sales so that there would be no possible interference of their interests.

Mr. Pecora. Do you mean to say, by that, that during the time that the Shermar Corporation was making short sales of 42,506 shares of bank stock the Shermar Corporation's activities were coordinated with those of the bank and its security affiliate?

Mr. Wiggin. I mean to say that they never made a sale without doing it through the Chase Securities Corporation so it would not be allowed to interfere.

Mr. Pecora. How were these short sales that were made by the Shermar Corporation in the summer and fall of 1929 kept free from interfering?

Mr. Wiggin. Because we gave them to the Chase Securities Co. to handle and they did all the selling for us.

Mr. Pecora. You mean the Chase Securities Co. made these sales for the Shermar Corporation?

Mr. Wiggin. Yes, sir.

Mr. Pecora. How?

Mr. Wiggin. I don't know. Wherever the selling was. They did the whole thing.

Mr. Pecora. Were you using the security affiliate of the bank to promote the activities of your own private company?

Mr. Wiggin. No, sir. I was simply—

Mr. Pecora (interposing). It seems to me that is the inference from the testimony you have just given.

Mr. Wiggin. I don't think so. I was simply handling it in a way that would not be permitted to interfere with the interests of the company. Therefore I let them handle the whole thing. . . .

FRANKLIN D. ROOSEVELT TO DUNCAN U. FLETCHER MARCH 26, 1934

The Public Papers and Addresses of Franklin D. Roosevelt, III (New York, 1948), 169–70.

My dear Mr. Chairman:

Before I leave Washington for a few days' holiday, I want to write you about a matter which gives me some concern.

On February 9, 1934, I sent to the Congress a special message asking for Federal supervision of national traffic in securities.

It has come to my attention that a more definite and more highly organized drive is being made against effective legislation to this end than against any similar recommendation made by me during the past year. Letters and telegrams bearing all the earmarks of origin at some common source are pouring in to the White House and the Congress.

The people of this country are, in overwhelming majority, fully aware of the fact that unregulated speculation in securities and in commodities was one of the most important contributing factors in the artificial and unwarranted "boom" which had so much to do with the terrible conditions of the years following 1929.

I have been firmly committed to definite regulation of exchanges which deal in securities and commodities. In my message I stated, "It should be our national policy to restrict, as far as possible, the use of these exchanges for purely speculative operations."

I am certain that the country as a whole will not be satisfied with legislation unless such legislation has teeth in it. The two principal objectives are, as I see it:

First, the requirement of what is known as margins so high that speculation, even as it exists today, will of necessity be drastically curtailed; and

Second, vesting the Government with such definite powers of supervision over exchanges that it will be able itself to correct abuses which may arise in the future.

We must, of course, prevent, in so far as possible, manipulation of prices to the detriment of actual investors, but at the same time we must eliminate unnecessary, unwise and destructive speculation.

The Bill, as shown to me this afternoon by you, seems to meet the minimum requirements. I do not see how any of us could afford to have it weakened in any shape, manner or form.

Very sincerely,

Hon. Duncan U. Fletcher,
Chairman, Banking and Currency Committee,
Hon. Sam Rayburn,
Chairman, Interstate and Foreign Commerce Committee,
Washington, D.C.

SPEECH BY SENATOR DUNCAN FLETCHER INTRODUCING THE STOCK EXCHANGE BILL MAY 7, 1934

Congressional Record, 73rd Congress, 2nd Session, 8160–64; 8174–75.

Mr. Fletcher. I move that the Senate proceed to the consideration of Senate bill 3420, being the bill to regulate securities exchanges, and so forth.

The Vice President. The question is on the motion of the Senator from Florida.

The motion was agreed to; and the Senate proceeded to consider the bill (S. 3420) to provide for the regulation of securities exchanges and of over-the-counter markets operating in interstate and foreign commerce and through the mails, to prevent inequitable and unfair practices on such exchanges and markets, and for other purposes, which had been reported from the Committee on Banking and Currency without amendment.

Mr. Fletcher. Mr. President, I may be a little tedious in endeavoring to state the case to the Senate regarding a measure which is extremely complicated, difficult, and far-reaching. I shall be as brief as I can, and as fair as I may be in presenting the question of the need for the legislation, the demand for it, and what I concede to be the sound conclusions reached in the form of the bill now presented to the Senate.

On March 2, 1932, a resolution was introduced in this body by the Senator from Delaware [Mr. Townsend], at the request of his colleague [Mr. Hastings], and was approved on the calendar day of March 4, 1932. It provided that the Committee on Banking and Currency or any duly authorized subcommittee thereof was—

> Authorized and directed, first, to make a thorough and complete investigation of the practices with respect to the buying and selling and the borrowing and lending of listed securities upon the various stock exchanges, the values of such securities, and the effect of such practices upon interstate and foreign commerce, upon the operation of the national banking system and the Federal Reserve System, and upon the market for securities of the United States Government, and the desirability of the exercise of the taxing power of the United States with respect to any such securities—

And so forth.

Other resolutions were subsequently introduced looking in the same direction, among them being a resolution adopted on April 4, 1933, extending the powers of the committee and providing that the committee—

> Shall have authority and hereby is directed—
> (1) To make a thorough and complete investigation of the operation by any person, firm, copartnership, company, association, corporation, or other entity, of the business of banking, financing, and extending credit; and of the business of issuing, offering, or selling securities;
> (2) To make a thorough and complete investigation of the business conduct and practices of security exchanges and of the members thereof;
> (3) To make a thorough and complete investigation of the practices with respect to the buying and selling and the borrowing and lending of securities which are traded in upon the various security exchanges, or on the over-the-counter market, or on any other market; and of the values of such securities; and
> (4) To make a thorough and complete investigation of the effect of all such business operations and practices upon interstate and foreign commerce, upon the industrial and commercial credit structure of the United States, upon the operation of the national banking system and the Federal Reserve System, and upon the market for securities of the United States Government, and the desirability of the exercise of the taxing power of the United States—

And so forth.

In pursuance of those resolutions the Committee on Banking and Currency appointed a subcommittee. The subcommittee has been almost continuously engaged in the investigation.

There were a few weeks in 1932, during the summer vacation, and in 1933, when the committee were not holding hearings; but beginning October 3, 1933, practically every day, 4 or 5 days a week, hearings were held by the subcommittee. Every opportunity has been given the stock exchange, investment bankers, holding companies, industrialists, bankers, and what not, everybody interested in the subject, to be heard respecting the bill which was introduced and respecting the matters involved in the investigation. Subsequently there was introduced Senate bill 2693, and hearings were had upon that bill, and all persons interested were given opportunity to present their views to the committee.

Some 21 volumes of hearings have been printed. There probably will be two or three more volumes before we shall finish the final print, including the exhibits. In addition to the printed volumes a cross-reference index is being prepared, and is now practically complete. That will enable Senators to have access to the hearings with more convenience and speed, and will make the volumes all the more usable.

We expect later to make a report covering all the hearings, including the printed documents and the index, and to lay the whole subject before the Senate in response to the resolutions of the Senate.

Considerable results have already been attained. For instance, it may be mentioned that the National Bank Act of 1933 contains provisions based upon the developments before the committee, particularly with reference to the separation of commercial banks from affiliates. Another provision based upon the developments before the committee was the extension of the powers of the Federal Reserve Board so as to enable it to have a greater control over the flow of credit away from agriculture, industry, and commerce into speculation. As I say, that grew out of the hearings.

Another act which Congress passed last year, known as the "Securities Act", is the result of matters brought to light in connection with the hearings.

Now the final stage is reached. This bill, demanded by the country everywhere, is before the Senate. It undertakes to provide a system, plan, or method of Federal supervision of securities exchanges.

The hearings already printed are, of course, available to the Senate. As I stated, they are not entirely complete, because some of the work is now under way in the Government Printing Office. The last volumes of hearings and the index itself will be laid before the Senate shortly, so that all the data may be at the command of the Senate.

It may well be claimed that economic and social problems, and even legal problems, are approached under the influence, more or less, of our political and social philosophy. There is room for a difference of view. It may be conceded that legal principles must form a part of economic and social theories.

Events since the fall of 1929 have shown grievous errors of habits and practices in the past, and established universal demand for corrective measures and new methods. The demand was for a new deal, it being understood that this is a slogan, not a new political system or creed. It is a moral attitude in governmental action. Applying it to the measure now submitted, its cardinal principles I conceive to be, first, restoring as a rule of moral and economic conduct, a sense of fiduciary obligation; and, second, establishing social responsibility, as distinguished from individual gain, as the goal.

The President has three times in public messages and communications recommended legislation of the sort embodied in this bill. He has recognized that the stock exchanges of the country are not only a useful but an essential mechanism in our financial and economic structure, and serve a necessary public purpose. They are not private enterprises, free from a public interest or function.

In the hearings before the committee, representatives of the stock exchanges have conceded the principle of Federal regulation.

The objectives are appreciated by the stock exchanges and the administration.

Mr. Richard Whitney, president of the New York Stock Exchange, the giant among them all, said to our committee:

> It is the purpose of the New York Stock Exchange to assist in every possible way in the prevention of fraudulent practices affecting stock-exchange transactions, excessive speculation, and manipulation of security prices. We should be glad to see a regulatory body, constituted under Federal law, supervise the solution of these grave problems. We suggest in principle, and subject to the requirements of law and the constitutional power of Congress, an authority or board to consist of 7 members, 2 of whom are to be appointed by the President; 2 to be Cabinet officers, who may well be the Secretary of the Treasury and the Secretary of Commerce; and 1 to be appointed by the Open Market Committee of the Federal Reserve System; the 2 remaining members will be representative of stock exchanges, one to be designated by the New York Stock Exchange and the other to be elected by members of exchanges in the United States other than the New York Stock Exchange. Such a body would bring together a personnel which would be properly coordinated with the banking system and in other respects qualified to administer the broad supervisory power which our proposal would give. We suggest the inclusion in the power given to this body of authority to regulate the amount of margin which members of exchanges must require and maintain on customers' accounts; authority to require stock exchanges to adopt rules and regulations designed to prevent dishonest practices and all other practices which unfairly influence the prices of securities or unduly stimulate speculation; authority to fix requirements for listing of securities; authority to require stock exchanges to adopt rules and regulations tions intended or used to unfairly influence market prices; authority to penalize the circulation of rumors or statements calculated to induce speculative activity, and to control the use of advertising and the employment of customers' men or other employees of brokers who solicit business. This body should also have the power to study and, if need be, to adopt rules governing those instances where the exercise of the function of broker and dealer by the same person may not be compatible with fair dealing, as well as the power to adopt rules in regard to short selling, if the supervisory body should become convinced that such regulation is necessary.
>
> We believe that these regulatory measures will prevent abuses affecting transactions on exchanges, and will at the same time not interfere with the maintenance of free and open markets for securities.

This proposal represents the considered view of the New York Stock Exchange, adopted by its governing committee, which has given me authority to present it to you. I say to you confidently that the exchange will cooperate fully and by all the means in its power to assist in the prevention of unwise or excessive speculation and abuses or bad practices affecting the stock market.

That is a statement by the president of the New York Stock Exchange.
Mr. Norris. Mr. President—
The Presiding Officer (Mr. Copeland in the chair). Does the Senator from Florida yield to the Senator from Nebraska?
Mr. Fletcher. I do.
Mr. Norris. I should like to ask the Senator from Florida the date of the statement made by Mr. Whitney, particularly with reference to the time of taking testimony in the investigation conducted by the committee. Was it near the beginning of the investigation, or did he make the statement at its close?
Mr. Fletcher. Practically at the beginning. My recollection is that it was Mr. Whitney's opening statement to our committee; and it seems to me plainly, inescapably an admission that there are practices on the exchange which are vicious and unjustified and abuses and errors which ought to be corrected. We have not quite conformed to the mechanism of making corrections that Mr. Whitney suggests. In the bill we attempt, however, to accomplish precisely the reforms which he says ought to be accomplished. Every abuse and bad practice set forth in his statement we attempt to correct in the bill.

We do not agree that a commission of seven, such as Mr. Whitney suggests, ought to have the administration of the proposed act. We have provided in the bill now before the Senate for a special commission of five, to be appointed by the President and confirmed by the Senate. The proposed commission is to be similar to that which Mr. Whitney suggests, the original bill which was introduced having provided that the administration of the act should be under the Federal Reserve Board.

The bill has been amended three times, and in the form in which it is now before the Senate, it provides that it shall be administered by a special commission of five, to be selected by the President and confirmed by the Senate.

The bill does not provide that one of the commissioners shall be named by the New York Stock Exchange and one by the other exchanges of the country. What is the use of having a regulatory body controlled by those to be regulated? It provides for a separate commission, an independent commission, to be appointed by the President and confirmed by the Senate, to consist of five members instead of seven. In other respects the recommendations of Mr. Whitney himself are met, in my judgment, by the provisions of the bill.
Mr. Costigan. Mr. President, will the Senator yield?
Mr. Fletcher. I yield.
Mr. Costigan. As one member of the Committee on Banking and Currency who prefers using the Federal Trade Commission as a supervising agency, I feel that it might be helpful to the Senate if the able chairman of the committee will state the reasons why he prefers a separate commission.

Mr. Fletcher. Mr. President, frankly, I favored the measure being administered by the Federal Trade Commission and the Federal Reserve Board. I favored the original bill. However, there seemed to be strong demand on the part of the members of our committee for a separate commission, and by a majority vote provision to that end was placed in the bill.

I see no reason why the Federal Trade Commission should not administer the act. I think the Federal Trade Commission have done and are doing splendid work in connection with the Securities Act, and I have every confidence in that Commission; but it was argued before our committee by those representing the exchanges that that is a commission which has had no experience in the handling of securities and that sort of thing, and that this matter ought to be handled by people who have knowledge of transactions involving the distribution and issuance of securities, and so forth. So the committee finally reached the conclusion that it was advisable to have the proposed act administered by a separate commission in connection with the Federal Reserve Board, which has to do with the handling of credit matters.

Mr. Barkley. Mr. President, will the Senator yield to me?

Mr. Fletcher. I yield.

Mr. Barkley. It might be added, I think, that one of the reasons which actuated the committee, and also those outside of the committee who felt that an independent commission was preferable, was that, without any sort of reflection upon the good faith or the sincerity of the Federal Trade Commission or its ability to administer the law, necessarily it would have to be done under a subordinate bureau under the Federal Trade Commission; that it would be a sort of a lean-to under the Commission's original activities; while if a separate commission were appointed public attention would always be focused upon that separate commission.It was the theory also that the President could pick five men just as well qualified to administer the law separately as he could pick three additional men to be appointed to the Federal Trade Commission as a sort of a subcommittee of the Federal Trade Commission to administer the law.

I think those considerations had a good deal to do with the amendment substituting an independent commission for the Federal Trade Commission. It ought to be emphasized, however, that it was not done in any way through any lack of faith in the Federal Trade Commission, or any lack of appreciation of the fine work it has done heretofore; but the committee felt that a separate commission, whose duties would be centralized around the stock market and stock securities, would be in a better position to serve the public than a branch of the Federal Trade Commission.

Mr. Glass. Mr. President, will the Senator from Florida yield to me?

Mr. Fletcher. I yield.

Mr. Glass. The Senator from Kentucky has clearly stated the view of those members of the committee who prefer a separate commission, except that it may be added that to some of us it was inconceivable that either the Federal Trade Commission or the Federal Reserve Board could do the work as effectively as could a separate commission appointed for the purpose, in view of the fact that the Federal Reserve Board and the Federal Trade Commission have important and complex duties which to perform them effectively, now occupy all of their time and their ingenuity. There was no purpose and no word uttered which might be construed into a reflection upon the Federal Trade Commission.

Moreover, the distinguished chairman of the committee will recall that it was not done because at one time the stock exchange wanted a separate commission. The distinguished chairman will remember very well that the commission proposed by the stock exchange was as different from the commission embodied in the bill as day is from night. The stock exchange was to have material representation of its own upon the commission it proposed, and on this commission there is to be no member of the stock exchange, and the members of the commission are textually prohibited from having any connection whatsoever, direct or indirect, with any of the stock exchanges.

Furthermore, the stock exchange did not stay hitched to its own proposal for an independent commission. Its latest proposal was that the whole thing be turned over to the Federal Reserve Board, and there are those of us on the committee who think the Federal Reserve System ought to be kept as far away from the stock-gambling business as it possibly can be gotten, and its facilities denied to those engaged in stock gambling, or, to be rather more polite, in stock speculation.

It was for those as well as other reasons which might be mentioned, that the committee thought a commission picked for the purpose by the President, to be confirmed for the purpose by the Senate, subject to removal at any time, for reason, by the President, could very much more effectively perform these duties, than would be possible if they were divided up between the Federal Reserve Board and the Federal Trade Commission.

Mr. Borah. The Federal Reserve Board has demonstrated in the past that it was not very expert in dealing with this matter, has it not?

Mr. Glass. Exactly.

Mr. Costigan. Mr. President—

The Presiding Officer (Mr. Pope in the chair). Does the Senator from Florida yield to the Senator from Colorado?

Mr. Fletcher. I yield.

Mr. Costigan. In fairness should it not be said that much duplication of work will be required if a separate commission shall be established? It has been estimated that approximately half a million dollars a year may be saved if this work is carried on by the Federal Trade Commission.

Mr. Glass. Mr. President, will the Senator from Florida yield to me again?

Mr. Fletcher. I yield.

Mr. Glass. On the contrary, there would be infinite duplication if we adhered to the proposition presented to the committee to divide this work between the Federal Reserve Board and the Federal Trade Commission. In other words, the Federal Reserve Board has immediate and intimate access to all the reports of the Comptroller of the Currency, who is a member of the Federal Reserve Board. In addition to that, the Federal Reserve Board has its own examiners, supplementing the work of the examiners employed by the Comptroller of the Currency. What could be the sane reason for requiring reports to be made by members of the Federal Reserve Banking System to the Federal Trade Commission, when they are examined by these two sets of examiners, and are required to make reports current and at any time to the Federal Reserve Board?

The Federal Reserve Board should not have anything in the world to do with it except to see to it scrupulously and at all times that Federal Reserve member banks do not lend their facilities for stock-speculating purposes.

Mr. Costigan. Mr. President, will the Senator yield further?

Mr. Fletcher. I yield.

Mr. Costigan. I fear that there may be some misunderstanding of my suggestion, which was that a separate commission—my inquiry had no reference to the Federal Reserve Board—would necessarily duplicate much work relating to unfair practices and the administration of the Securities Act of 1933 now being carried on by the Federal Trade Commission. It was to the expense of that duplication alone that my remarks were directed.

Mr. Fletcher. Mr. President, in that connection I may say that, while the Federal Trade Commission has done a splendid work in connection with the Securities Act, I see no really serious objection or sound reason for supposing that a special commission, as provided in this bill, should not efficiently and satisfactorily administer the provisions of the Securities Act, and I have offered an amendment, since the bill carries with it the provision that the Securities Act shall be administered by the special commission, providing for the transfer to the commission to be set up under the terms of this bill of the administration of the Securities Act, so there will be no duplication if the Senate shall agree to my amendment.

The Securities Act itself, and the Securities Exchange Act, will be administered by this special commission. Of course, some delay would be involved. It would involve the turning over largely of the personnel and the set-up already established by the Federal Trade Commission, but these two acts, the Securities Act and this Securities Exchange Act, are so intimately connected that it seems to me advisable that they both should be administered by the same authority, and therefore I have provided in the amendment which I have offered, the transfer of the administration of the Securities Act, with all the records and everything pertaining to it, to this Commission.

Mr. Barkley. Mr. President, will the Senator yield?

Mr. Fletcher. I yield to the Senator from Kentucky.

Mr. Barkley. In view of the fact that the Securities Act, which has been very admirably administered by the Federal Trade Commission up to date, contemplated regulation with respect only to new securities issued after the passage of that act, and had very little relationship to securities already in existence, and in view of the fact that the bill under consideration sets up a regulation of the stock exchanges in all securities, whether old or new, the combination of the two acts under the administration of one commission would eliminate the duplication to which the Senator from Colorado has already adverted, and inasmuch as they are inseparably related, not only so far as the issue of securities may be concerned but the purchase and sale of those securities on a registered exchange, the logical thing is to have both administered by the same body.

Mr. Fletcher. That is the idea, I think, which was in the minds of the committee, and those who have done the longhand writing of this measure, and devoted weeks and weeks of study to it, and our final solution of it is that the two acts should be administered by the same body, which is provided in the amendment I referred to a moment ago. I did not intend now to go into that particular subject. I intended to give, if I could, a sort of general picture of the situation with respect to the bill itself.

Mr. King. Mr. President, will the Senator yield?

Mr. Fletcher. I yield to the Senator from Utah.

Mr. King. I may be asking a question as to a matter which has been covered by the Senator. The President some time ago appointed an inter-departmental committee of which the Secretary of Commerce, Mr. Ickes, was a member, for the purpose of studying the principles and policies involved in the measure now under consideration, and after an elaborate study the com-mittee reached the conclusion that the administration of the stock exchanges should be placed in the hands of an administrative commission to be ap-pointed by the President. I may add that, largely following their recommenda-tion, I offered an amendment before any was offered in the Senate committee, dealing with the subject, under which it was proposed to vest the administra-tion of the provisions of the law in an independent commission of three persons, to be appointed by the President.

Mr. Fletcher. The Senator from Utah is quite right. It was proposed in the Senator's amendment to vest authority in a separate commission, and we took advantage of his suggestion in that regard.

We are endeavoring, Mr. President, permanently to correct the evils and abuses which Mr. Whitney mentioned and which he admits should be and may be corrected. We may not fully succeed, but we are making an honest and fair effort in that direction, with every confidence there will result great improvement and real benefit.

We propose by this measure to establish, through Federal regulation of the methods and the mechanical functions and practices of the stock exchange, an efficient, adequate, open, and free market for the purchase and sale of securities; also to correct abuses we know of and others which may exist; to prohibit and prevent, if possible, their recurrence; to restore public confi-dence in the financial markets of the country; to prevent excessive speculation to the injury of agriculture, commerce, and industry; to outlaw manipulation and unfair practices and combinations by which to exploit the public and misrepresent values, such as pools, wash sales, fictitious transactions, and the like; to oblige disclosure of all material facts respecting securities traded in on the exchanges, which disclosure is essential to give the investor an adequate opportunity to evaluate his investment.

Criticism is made that we are calling upon corporations to make disclo-sures, and that we are thereby putting them to an enormous expense and trouble, and inquiring into affairs into which we have no business to examine. My suggestion is that if any corporation issues securities which are unfit to be certified because of what is back of them, the securities themselves are unfit to be offered to the public.

What right have brokers to appeal to the public to buy their securities if they are not willing to tell the truth about those securities? That is the whole proposition, and all we ask of them is to tell the truth.

They do not seem to want to tell the truth, in the first place, and, in the next place, they especially complain about liability for material misrepresenta-tions which have misled the public into buying securities. They are willing to expose, to some extent, the facts behind the securities, but they do not want to be liable in case they lie about them. That seems to be the basis of the objection. All we ask in the pending bill and in the Securities Act is that they tell the truth in their registration papers, so the public may know what is behind the securities.

We undertake generally to declare the intention of Congress, and enunciate specific principles as a guide to subsequent administration. That appears particularly in section 2. We lay the foundation for this legislation in section 2 of the bill.

The exchanges themselves, when they complained about our delegation of authority, proposed a bill, and advocated even greater delegation of power in the administrative body than is provided for in the pending bill.

In connection with the propaganda which has been broadcast over the country criticizing and objecting to the provisions of the bill, most of those who criticize say, "We object to the bill in its present form." The language in hundreds of thousands of letters which have come to the Members of Congress is, "We object to the bill in its present form."

This bill has been changed three times. The original bill was revised, and the committee then gave hearings upon the revised bill. The revised bill was introduced in the House. It was never introduced in the Senate, but we considered it in the Senate as a revision of the bill S. 2693. We had hearings on it. Finally that bill was revised. We agreed to certain amendments of that bill, and then the whole question was referred to a subcommittee, and that subcommittee met and considered every word, every line, every sentence in the bill, day after day, week after week, in an honest effort to be fair to all concerned and to eliminate any harsh features that were objected to by those opposing the bill and in endeavoring to satisfy any reasonable demand in connection with the legislation.

Some complained it was too drastic here, some complained it was too drastic there, and we endeavored to straighten that out, and then the subcommittee reported to the full committee a third revision of the bill. The Senate Committee on Banking and Currency unanimously substituted that revision for the original bill, and then by a vote of 11 to 3 ordered a favorable report upon the revised bill, which is the bill S. 3420, now before the Senate.

In the propaganda which was spread all over the country—and we received numerous letters about it—the statement was made: "We understand this bill was prepared by some inexperienced young men in the departments, sometimes called 'brain trusters.' " Such a charge, I believe, was made, as the Senator from Illinois [Mr. Lewis] suggests to me, in the chamber of commerce meeting. The question as to who were the authors of this bill is, I think, wholly irrelevant, immaterial, and impertinent. . . .

Mr. President, it will be remembered that the stock exchange claimed the right to make its own rules and regulations, and insisted that it could prevent abuses and correct errors and was willing to attempt it, and it claimed it had been doing so.

There have been some amendments to the rules and regulations. The officials gave us some assurance that they intended to continue to work out certain reforms and make certain revisions of their rules and regulations which would effect the correction of the abuses to which I have referred.

We appealed to them to do that. We hoped they would inaugurate rules and regulations and establish practices which would overcome what Mr. Whitney so clearly stated existed in connection with the stock exchanges, practices which needed to be reformed. They promised to do that, and they did adopt some amendments to their rules which I think were helpful. But evidently—and I believe this is their own view—they are powerless to accomplish all that should be accomplished. In the first place, they have no jurisdiction except over their own members. They have no jurisdiction over outside people issuing securities. In the next place, they have not the power or authority to accomplish what they would like to see accomplished. There is, therefore, need for some regulatory body with ample power to supervise these conditions.

Mr. President, this is shown by the experience, after they had assured us they were amending their rules and were working out reforms, in July and August of last year, in connection with the stocks to which I have referred, showing that these abuses, the formation of pools, the operations of the specialists, and all that sort of thing, were taking place as late as last summer, proving, I think, that the country cannot depend upon the stock exchange to bring about the reforms and the corrections which they themselves admit are necessary in order to correct vicious and unwise practices.

There are some people, of course, who say that the gambling propensity exists in nearly all men, and women as well, and that law should not interfere with its indulgence; in other words, that we cannot prevent people from gambling on the stock exchanges or anywhere else. To a large extent that is true. We cannot by law protect a fool against his folly. We cannot by law do away with gambling propensities. But we can take away the facilities and the attractions and the inducements to people to invest their money in speculative securities and really gamble. We can minimize that sort of thing.

The argument that people must gamble, that they have that impulse which they cannot control, and will gamble, simply leads to a reductio ad absurdum. If it is carried to its full extent, it means that we ought to repeal all laws against gambling in all the States; we ought to establish a lottery in the United States and let people gamble by means of a national lottery, because it is much less harmful than gambling on the stock exchange.

Mr. McKellar. Mr. President, will the Senator yield?

Mr. Fletcher. I yield.

Mr. McKellar. I was called out today just as the Senator reached the portion of his speech in which he was discussing the question of an independent commission or the Federal Trade Commission as an enforcer of the act. Is it not true that the Federal Trade Commission already has a set-up of experts, and has it not had quite an experience in the handling of other securities, and does not the Senator believe that we would really get a more efficient enforcement of the proposed act by having it administered by the Federal Trade Commission?

Mr. Fletcher. Mr. President, as I stated while the Senator from Tennessee was out of the Chamber, my personal view was expressed in the terms of the original bill, S. 2693, whereby the administration of the act was reposed in the Federal Trade Commission. I think that Commission has done splendidly in administering the Securities Act. It is a Commission in which I have the fullest confidence, and I have nothing but praise and commendation for what it has already accomplished.

Mr. McKellar. I feel the same way about it. I think it has done a wonderful work.

Mr. Fletcher. But in view of many objections raised to the Federal Trade Commission administering this proposed act on the ground, as was claimed, that its members were not bankers or financiers or acquainted with the handling of securities and that sort of thing, and that those charged with its administration ought to be specially qualified men, acquainted with such transactions and experienced in stock-exchange matters to a large extent, the prevailing sentiment seemed to be that there ought to be a special commission. That was the claim, and that was the demand—that there should be a commission. Partially, I think, in response to that, but in part independent thereof, there was a large sentiment in our committee in favor of a special commission.

To my mind it does not make very much difference one way or the other. If we shall have a special commission of five, appointed by the President and confirmed by the Senate, I think we will get a very efficient and capable body to administer this act; so we provided for such a commission.

Mr. McKellar. Mr. President, I have very great doubt about the appointment of experts in that line of business, because I am fearful that their enforcement of the act would not be so good as that of disinterested men, such as the members of the Federal Trade Commission. The House in its bill provided for the Federal Trade Commission as the enforcer of the act, and it seems to me that is a very wise provision to have contained in the bill. I have the greatest confidence in the honesty, the sincerity, and the ability of the Federal Trade Commission. I think it is a wonderful piece of machinery. It has done splendid work. In my judgment, this measure would be better enforced and more equitably enforced, if I may use that expression, in the hands of the Federal Trade Commission than if the enforcement were given over to a new commission. I have very great doubt about a new commission.

Mr. Fletcher. I am not disposed to disagree with the Senator about that. At the same time, a special commission seems to satisfy the demand and meet the approval of most people—at least, some of the critics of the original idea—and I think a special commission named by the President and approved by the Senate undoubtedly would give entire satisfaction.

Mr. McKellar. What was the vote of the Senate committee on this subject?

Mr. Fletcher. My recollection is that there was a vote of about 2 majority in favor of the special commission. I think the vote was 10 to 8.

I believe the special commission provided for in this bill would give satisfaction to the country and meet some objections; so, accordingly, I have offered an amendment which provides for the transfer of the administration of the Securities Act to the same commission.

Mr. Lewis. Does the Senator mean to the Federal Trade Commission?

Mr. Fletcher. No; to the special commission of five.

It is claimed and it has been argued that this proposed legislation would interfere with business. Business is based on confidence. Credit is the result of confidence. Let us insure confidence by giving securities an acknowledged status and recognition by requiring them to be registered and requiring exchanges where they are dealt in to be registered by a responsible agency. Inevitably that will help business, reassure capital, and increase investments.

It is claimed that pools or trading accounts are formed to stabilize prices and maintain a steady market. This is not what the broker wants. He wishes a gyrating market, because he makes commissions on its active movement up or down. Stabilization is the last thing he wants. He is after making money.

The Securities Act has saved millions of dollars to the people—the public.

This act will save billions of dollars—that is, prevent the loss of billions of dollars. Those whose money will thus be saved are some of the people for whom we are speaking.

It is testified that one out of six may win in stock speculation. These people I should like to serve.

It is said that 93 percent of the odd-lot traders lose.

It has been said this bill will put people out of business; will adversely affect business. What business?

There can be no interference with securities exempted from this bill. What are they? See paragraph 12, page 6, of the bill.

Uncontrolled and arbitrary management of security issues, security markets, speculative pitfalls for the unwary investor, selfish and individual management of large corporations affected with a public interest must come to an end.

The principle of trusteeship in all affairs so affected with the public interest must be made dominant and effective.

Mr. Lewis. Mr. President, will the Senator yield?

Mr. Fletcher. I yield.

Mr. Lewis. At this point I should like to ask the able Chairman of the Senate Banking and Currency Committee if he is not aware of the fact that England has had for a very long time a form of legislation carrying many provisions similar to those of the present bill and which have been recognized as working a most corrective benefit to and aiding the general welfare of the stock exchanges and the stock holdings in England? I should like to hear a little from the Senator on that subject.

Mr. Fletcher. Undoubtedly what the Senator says is true. The British companies act has been in effect for many years and is giving great satisfaction. Its provisions have been construed by the courts and form quite a body of precedent for our guidance. The British companies act is largely followed in this bill.

There is one thing I will mention. Under the practice on the London Exchange, there are no margin accounts. The allowance of margins and margin trading in this country has led to a great many abuses and to excessive speculation. That is not permitted in England. When a person is permitted to put up a few dollars on margin to buy stocks and take chances of winning or losing, he is tempted to do so. Margin operation, in my judgment, is responsible for the ruin of thousands and thousands of people.

Judge Clark, of New Jersey, who testified before us, advocated doing away entirely with margins. From his long experience he mentioned the fact that the penitentiaries are crowded with men who have been found guilty of embezzlement and other offenses, all by reason of their operations on the stock exchanges. Not only that, but men have lost their business, lost their property, lost their reputation and their good name by the hundred thousand in this country because they have been tempted to speculate on margin on the stock exchange.

I want to warn the people who have flooded this country with propaganda against this bill and against legislation of this kind, misrepresenting the alleged loss to business, the alleged harmful effect of this proposed legislation on business, the number of people who are going to lose their business, and all that sort of thing, that they will not be able to stem the tide of public opinion demanding this legislation in our country.

It has got to come. They are powerful, but they are not powerful enough to defy Congress. They are strong, but they are not strong enough to obstruct the Government. At least that is my hope and my belief, and I am convinced that unless we pass this proposed legislation now they will take on new strength and double their efforts and we will never pass it.

I feel like warning these gentlemen to this effect, "Continue your opposition and your fight and determination to have your own way, to be free absolutely from any supervision or regulation by anybody; regulate yourselves; I feel that if you persist in that struggle and that determination and that sort of fight and that sort of propaganda, the next movement that will come will be a determined and a successful effort to wipe away margins entirely from stock exchanges." That will take away from the exchanges 40 percent of their business. They will not like to see that; they will not enjoy that; but they are bringing that about, in my judgment, by their attitude respecting this proposed legislation.

Mr. Barkley. Mr. President—

The Presiding Officer. Does the Senator from Florida yield to the Senator from Kentucky?

Mr. Fletcher. I yield.

Mr. Barkley. In line with what the Senator just said, I wanted to suggest that, notwithstanding the Committee on Banking and Currency has been engaged in an investigation of this subject for more than 2 years, resulting in more than 21 volumes of printed testimony, notwithstanding the fact that it held open hearings for weeks on this particular measure, many of those who were given an opportunity but did not take advantage of it to come here and offer suggestions as to this proposed legislation, now that it is out of committee and on the calendar of the Senate, are taking advantage of every opportunity to persuade the Senate and the House not to pass any legislation at all on this subject, on the ground that we have not as yet investigated the subject sufficiently to know what sort of act to pass.

Mr. Fletcher. Precisely. They do not want any legislation at all; that is the whole story. As I said a while ago, I cannot understand why the director of any corporation, or the president or an officer of any corporation should object to a requirement that when he appeals to the public to buy the securities of his company it shall be exacted of him that he put upon the record the truth regarding those securities. Why should he not state the truth? And if he states the truth that is all that is required of him.

MAX LOWENTHAL TO FERDINAND PECORA MAY 12, 1934

Felix Frankfurter Papers, Library of Congress.

Rome

Dear Ferd:

A letter has come from Frank Meehan telling of the demobilization of your staff. I hope this is only temporary. Surely, the President's expression to Senator Fletcher and yourself that the investigation ought to go on was a wise one; and as you go on, you are entitled, by reason of the services you have already rendered to the nation as well as because of the stature of your understanding, to have full facilities for doing further noteworthy service.

You ought to have an opportunity for developing and presenting an organized and integrated body of facts on one of the biggest issues, the one Mr. Lamont brushed aside so airily; you referred to the issue at the time as the concentration of control over wealth. There is another subject almost equally calling for thorough search into the facts; your hearings have touched it from time to time, the matter of the relation between Wall Street and some of the biggest life insurance executives, and the consequences of that relation. Of course, there may be the cry that confidence will be hurt, the same cry raised to stop your inquiry into the big banking firms. Yet it was only by means of the inquiry and the changes it brought about that some confidence in the management of the biggest banks has been restored.

Another subject which you have already opened up is that of the manipulation of part of the country's railway system by financial careerists. In the last decade, as you and a comparatively small number of others know, almost the entire system became the football of a handful of such men. Are you not to be allowed to develop the picture as a whole, so that what you have already depicted is characteristic, not unusual, and so that they may guide themselves accordingly?

There is a field, involving the vast property under corporate trusteeship, that has thus far been examined hardly at all. Mr. Aldrich admitted, when he was on the stand, that it should be given further study. Guaranty Trust Company of New York, the biggest institution of the kind, is an outstanding example of the confusion of banking with trusteeship, and of the intermingling, under one roof, of wholly diverse kinds of trusteeship activities, with resultant paralysis of the corporate trustee's obligations. Not alone the merits, but also the undesirability of giving anyone opportunity to say later that, of all the big institutions, this one had immunity, point to the need for inquiry into its activities.

And, of course, as to banking firms, much remains to be done. There was an understanding that you would be permitted to complete the Morgan investigation, truncated by the firm's unwillingness to give you effective access to its records and by the serious time limitations under which you and your staff have been working. Then there are other banking firms, for example Hayden Stone and Seligman's, whose records are not merely cumulative to those you have already presented, but rather are illustrative of important phases which you have not yet had the time to develop.

Taking the high spots only (and of course the foregoing are only examples), there is far more to be done than could be completed within a year, even if you be given the ample staff and funds that you have never had.

To a great host of people, this investigation is a cherished cause, and promises much more even than that quickening of conscience in high places that you have brought forth wherever you have ploughed. They think, what you better than anyone know, that the continuance of the investigation insures the gathering of knowledge with the aid of which the country may achieve a fairer life. I hope you will be given every opportunity for carrying the task forward.

Sincerely yours,

Max Lowenthal

ARTICLE BY JOHN T. FLYNN, "THE MARINES LAND IN WALL STREET" JULY 1934

Harpers, CLXIX (July 1934), 148–55.

Before this makes its way into print the heavens will have fallen. The last and most direful of the catastrophes wrought by irresponsible meddlers will have overtaken the land. In short, the national act to regulate stock exchanges will have become a law. The marines will have landed in Wall Street. The place will be annexed to the United States. The government will have begun another experiment in the benevolent assimilation of a semi-civilized people. Can the federal government civilize Wall Street?

This is just a battle in a fifty-years war. But not the final one. The enemy is powerful, rich, vigilant, unscrupulous, and plays for vast stakes. Here, then, is a good moment to pause and survey the battlefield and estimate how much ground has been won in this long offensive.

The investigation from which this law was hatched was not a Roosevelt or New Deal design. It was the last gift of the New Era to the New Deal. When Mr.

Roosevelt came to power he found the investigation in full swing with Mr. Charlie Mitchell's head already in Mr. Pecora's basket. The sensations uncovered by Mr. Pecora were too lurid to permit anyone to stop his march. Of course Mr. Roosevelt never tried to stop it. But he did not do anything to press it forward. He did not put his position and influence behind it, as he did behind the NRA and the money farce and other acts in his shifting drama. He let it jog along. It certainly cannot be said to have constituted a dynamic part of *his* New Deal. Yet out of it have grown the only three measures which can be said to have any fundamental bearing on the great problem which he faced —the Securities Act, the Glass-Steagall Banking Act, and the National Securities Exchange Act of 1934. What is more, whatever teeth were drawn from the effective bill first introduced yielded to the forceps of Mr. Roosevelt's Treasury Department, Commerce Department, and his Federal Reserve Board, and not to the violent and boisterous wind and dust machine of the New York Stock Exchange. One word from Franklin D. Roosevelt, and the drastic first bill would have been passed with a whoop. Mr. Roosevelt made brave speeches about a bill "with teeth in it" while his departmental subordinates performed their dental depredations behind the scenes.

The investigation was provoked by Herbert Hoover. Hoover was saving the country by proclamations and forecasts. But Wall Street bears —Democratic bears too—were raiding the market, puncturing confidence. Hoover forced an investigation as a big bear trap. He planned to bring John J. Raskob, then Democratic national chairman, Barney Baruch, and a few others to Washington, pillory them as short-sellers (which they proved not to have been), adjourn the hearing in a few days, start the drums and trumpets again, and resume our upward march to the old prosperity of Coolidge and Mellon.

But, alas, Fate had planed one of its minions on the track in the person of Senator Peter Norbeck of South Dakota. He was chairman of the Senate Committee on Banking and Currency. Norbeck is one of those prairie Republicans—half Democrat, half other ingredients, but less than one-half of one per cent Republican. He too thought Wall Street had wicked bears. But he was convinced there was plenty more wrong there and that this was a grand chance to have a look at it. It was Norbeck, big, honest, calm, filled with common sense, who made this an investigation of Wall Street, who kept doggedly at the probe, who finally engaged Ferdinand Pecora, on the recommendation of Frank L. Polk, and who, more than any other man, gave to the investigation its tone, its character, and direction. He must come first in any distribution of awards for the results.

It was Wall Street's hard luck that Senator Fletcher of Florida succeeded Norbeck when the Democrats came into power. The old Senator stood like a stone wall for going ruthlessly through to the end. And despite his age he sat day after day through the greater part of fifteen months in sleepless vigilance at the hearings. Some day it will be possible to tell the inside story of the attempts made to end that investigation. They were continuous until Pecora's amazing revelations about the National City Bank. After that they weakened a little until the Morgan hearings, when the most powerful influences were set in motion to hamstring the whole enterprise. When the story is told it will be in order to speak specifically of the resoluteness, the patience, the calm and dignified surface which Mr. Pecora exposed to the most violent attacks and the most subtle underminings, the balance, intelligence, and fine sense of social purpose which he brought to his enormous task. All-day sessions in opening hearings; all-night sessions in preparation for the next day. I looked with astonishment at this man who, through the intricate mazes of banking, syndicates, market deals, chicanery of all sorts, and in a field new to him, never forgot a name, never made an error in a figure, and never lost his temper.

Mr. Pecora's investigation traveled two separate roads. He pursued the bad practices and the dishonest promotions of the bankers, investment houses, corporation executives ranging from the legerdemain of Mr. Insull in Chicago to the holding-company and affiliate-banking adventures of Cleveland, Detroit, and New York. The other phase involved a factual study of the stock exchanges of the country. The former occupied most of the open hearings. The latter went on behind the scenes and got little public notice.

In the flood of criticism which greeted the Exchange Control Bill every kind of voice was raised. Of course there had to be the voice of that cold and lofty being who affects an immense and overpowering intellectual superiority, a solemn pretension to calm philosophical detachment, unmoved by the small hatreds and partisanships of lesser men. Such a voice was supplied by the New York *Times*. It lost not an opportunity to play the game of the horde of parasites who prey upon the nation one day and hurry to its pages for the dope the following morning. It was shocked and saddened by the messy and immature methods of Mr. Pecora. It preferred the unprejudiced and selfless lucubrations of Mr. Richard Whitney. And finally it compared with unmasked irritation the deliberate and scientific proceedings of the Hughes Commission in 1907 with the unscientific and haphazard thrusts of Mr. Pecora.

The simple fact is that there has never been a greater travesty on an investigation than that supposed to have been conducted by the so-called Hughes Commission. It comprised a group of business men. What facts that commission based its findings on have never been vouchsafed to mortal eye. It sent a series of questions chiefly asking opinions to the Exchange. The governors sat in executive session and concocted the answers. The Commission agreed with most of them. Indeed, in one case at least its report was in almost the identical words of the Exchange's reply. It defended almost everything the Exchange stood for. It has been known as a whitewash, and Samuel Untermyer has denounced it repeatedly as a grim jest.

Contrast this with Pecora's method. He assembled a group of experts —accounting, economic, statistical, legal, trading. They set to work to collect, not opinions, but facts. Questionnaires were sent to every exchange asking, not for their views, but for data. Thousands of questionnaires were sent to every broker in the country, to bankers, to corporations. The answers were purely factual answers. The work of tabulating the replies occupied many months and a large staff. In addition, various exchange officials were interviewed in many conferences, brokers were questioned, bankers and corporation executives were examined. When it was all done the results, practically without the expression of an opinion, even by Mr. Pecora, were compiled in a series of reports and tables and submitted to the Senate Committee. That report is a mere collection of facts, open to anyone for any conclusions they can draw from it. It constitutes the first attempt ever made to bring to the surface the hitherto buried facts about operations on the exchanges. No future student of speculation can deal with the subject without digging into that report. And it was this report and its voluminous findings which shocked the *Times* into its comparison of Pecora's study with the Hughes Commission whitewash and brought from the *Times* editorial writer a bitter criticism before he had ever seen the report.

II

A great deal of pother has been made about the authorship of the Exchange Control Bill. It has been attributed to everyone from the "young adolescents in the Little Red House" in Georgetown to Trotsky and Lucifer. There is no mystery about it. It was drawn under the general direction of Mr. Pecora, who acted on the orders of Senator Fletcher, chairman of the Senate Committee. Mr. Pecora detailed a number of members of his staff and invited several others—Mr. Thomas Corcoran, counsel of the Reconstruction Finance Corporation; Mr. Ben Cohen, assistant counsel of the PWA, and Mr. Isaiah Stokes. Commissioner Landis, of the Federal Trade Commission, in charge of the securities division, interested himself at the suggestion of Senator Fletcher. Mr. Pecora's staff contributed, in addition to Mr. Pecora himself, his assistant counsel, Mr. Julius Silver, Mr. David Saperstein, and Mr. David Schenker; Mr. Frank J. Meehan, chief accountant of the Senate Committee, for many years in charge of the Wall Street investigations of the attorney-general's office in New York, Mr. Max Lowenthal, an expert in corporation finance, and myself.

The first draft, indeed the first three or four drafts of a bill, had been prepared by Messrs. Cohen, Corcoran, and Stokes, the actual writing being done by Mr. Cohen. Then, in conferences with the others mentioned above, this first draft served as an outline into which were fitted the various devices for meeting the variety of situations which the bill was designed to control. That first bill was a tremendously effective measure. I should like to have seen margin trading outlawed altogether. But aside from this, the measure on the whole would have dealt a real blow to a serious social and economic evil.

The President sent a message to Congress urging adoption of a market-control bill. But he carefully refrained from endorsing this measure. And then came that amazing and unparalleled storm of propaganda unloosed by the wounded beast in Broad Street. It might properly be called the Terror. That drive was designed to strike fear into the heart of every little and big business man, every bank, every investor, at the prospect of "upsetting the delicate mechanism of American business" by fooling with the mysterious machine of the exchanges. Somehow its operations, its gambling, its pools and syndicates, its manipulations, its chicanery, its greed had become the "heart of the Capitalist system." A bolshevist might have made such a charge against the Capitalist system. But this Terror succeeded in penetrating the inner circle of the President's official family, and the order came to revise the bill. Then the President directed the Secretary of the Treasury and the Governor of the Federal Reserve Board to collaborate with the framers of the bill in a revision. Mr. Thomas Smith, assistant secretary of the Treasury, Mr. Eugene Black, governor of the Reserve Board, Messrs. Pecora, Corcoran, and Cohen and a few others went into conference about this revision. It was at this point that Mr. Smith and Mr. Black did their work of emasculation on this bill while the President was talking for public consumption about a bill "with teeth in it." The chief fruit of these labors was to take out of the bill itself almost all of its teeth and lodge the almost complete discretionary control in a commission. The bill subsequently introduced followed this pattern. And at this point I considered the fight on the economic evils of speculation completely lost. The bill had degenerated to a collection of regulations to govern the game of speculation as between the speculators, with the United States sitting in as umpire. The deeper and more important economic evils of the game were left untouched.

It is fair to say that in some measure some of these protective clauses which had been deleted were put back. And for this credit is due to the incessant labors of Mr. Pecora before the Senate Committee, and Messrs. Corcoran and Cohen, along with the chairman, Mr. Rayburn, before the House Committee. The actual writing job throughout was done by Mr. Cohen. And when one considers the magnitude of the field covered and the variety of forces to be reached, an abler example of legislative writing has never made its way into our statute books.

But it is perfectly clear to me that a bill with real teeth in it could have been enacted if the President had been willing to make a fight for such a bill. I have not the slightest doubt, for instance, that had Mr. Roosevelt not opposed it, brokers could have been driven out of the money-lending business altogether. An amendment to the bill in the Senate, offered by the conservative and sane Senator Bulkley of Ohio, himself the head of a great corporation law firm, was almost passed by the Senate and would undoubtedly have been passed if the President had uttered a single word for it. Instead, throughout, the President was fixed in his position that margin requirements should not be made too high. The Exchange will turn upon Roosevelt with fury, I have no doubt. They should remember him with gratitude. He alone could have prevented a stronger bill.

III

From all this has emerged a bill which represents a definite advance. First of all, it is an assertion of the authority of the federal government over the whole field of security markets. This is, at least, a beginning. On the score of regulation the bill, while possessing much strength, fails in leaving too much to the discretion of a Commission. It remains to be seen what kind of a Commission Mr. Roosevelt will give us and how far such a body will go in dealing with the fundamental defects in the security markets. One need not speculate on the kind of regulation the nation will get under the kind of presidents we had in the three administrations preceding Mr. Roosevelt.

The theory underlying this law is that the whole question is not just a stock-exchange problem. In any kind of control of security speculation the marketplace must, of course, be severely scrutinized and supervised. But after all, the marketplace itself is nothing more than the gaming room. There remain the implements of the game, and these are securities and money. Intelligent and effective control, therefore, must reach, not merely the exchange and its members, but banks and others who lend money for the play and corporations which issue the certificates of stock which serve as counters.

The law does not put an end to exchanges. Anyone may organize an exchange. But the organization must be registered with the Commission. It must yield up full information about itself, must satisfy the Commission that it can enforce its rules and those of the Commission, and must make an agreement to abide by the Commission's regulations.

It is the intention that the immediate government of the market and the policing of it shall be in the hands of the exchange as at present. It may make its own rules, name its own officers, elect and expel its members, fix the dues, duties, functions, of members, provide for listings, delistings, hours of trading, terms of trading and settlement, reporting, and generally manage the marketplace as at present. But over this organization the Commission holds two potent weapons. One is the power of scrutiny, access to the records, the papers of the exchange and its members at all times. The other power resides in the Commission's right to compel the exchange, after hearing, to change almost any of its rules. The Commission can force changes in rules governing classification of members, methods of electing officers in order to give representation to every section of the market, suspensions, explusions, listing of stocks, striking them from the list, the carrying of fictitious accounts, reporting transactions, fixing commissions, odd-lot purchases, and so on.

Thus the Commission, if it desires, may do away with inactive memberships now used by bankers and large traders to enjoy special privileges in the matter of commissions. It can force proper trials of members instead of, as at present, trials of the complaining witness at his expense. It can enforce adequate investigation before listing, as contrasted with the loose and casual glance made by the Exchange when it admitted a mess of alcohol shares to the privilege of listing. It can do away with secret accounts under which bankers and corporation executives hide their raids on their own stocks. It can prevent the exchange or its members from evading the restrictions on margins by a resort to the foreign method of term settlements which would be a curse in this country. Hardly a law exists which cannot be nullified by the use of some of those corporate devices which now flourish in the laws of our charter-mongering States. The Commission is empowered to penetrate corporate fictions and check evasions by this stratagem. This section of the law is strong.

IV

What is to happen to that person who is awaiting the happy dawn when the joyous bull puts his nose once again round the corner of Broad and Wall Street? Thousands of hardy patriots look eargerly for the time when they will be able to recover the losses of the twenties by means of a little judicious margin trading. Can they do it? I am afraid they can. This is the great failure of the bill. Forty-five per cent margins will not stop it. Back in 1928, Mr. E. H. H. Simmons, then President of the New York Stock Exchange, declared that a survey revealed that the average margin was forty per cent. Enough loopholes are left in the bill and it is reasonably sure that the Commission, however composed, will not impose too severe a margin rule.

Margin trading involves a flow of funds from brokers to customers and from other lenders to brokers. This bill undertakes to lay the hands of the law on the movement of funds in both areas. The Commission can regulate the amount which they can lend. The Reserve bank, under the Glass-Steagall Act, can act to check the flow of Reserve member bank money into the market.

Money flows to brokers from various sources. The New York banks lend large sums. Out-of-town banks once loaned still larger sums. Large corporations put immense volumes of surplus cash into the call-money market. Individuals and institutions do the same thing. This bill undertakes to prevent brokers from borrowing from anyone save a member bank of the Federal Reserve System or a bank which agrees to abide by its rules. This, therefore, gives the Federal Reserve Board a chance to regulate the flow of loans to brokers. A good Federal Reserve Board can do much with this weapon. But apparently only God, the maker of trees, can make a good Federal Reserve Board. Moreover, the bill is weakened by provisions which enable the governing authority to loosen the requirements and to permit borrowing between brokers who are members and brokers who are not members of the exchange.

It will not be possible, apparently, for corporations to put their funds into the market as was done, for instance, by the Standard Oil Company of New Jersey, when in 1929 it loaned as much as $95,000,000 in a day to brokers. New York Clearing House banks have a rule also which will protect us from a renewal of bootleg loans for others. On the whole, loans to brokers do now come under some form of control and they will hardly rise to the 1929 levels again. New York banks, which will probably do this business, hardly expanded their market loans at all from 1926 to 1929, and there is hope for us in this moderation rather than in the bill itself. However, it is this provision of the bill which will bear the closest watching for evasions by the exchanges and weakness by the Commission.

V

The new law contains a number of provisions designed to strike at the evils of stock manipulation. But they amount chiefly to this, that the Commission is empowered to take the necessary measures to check the abuse. This differs from the original bill which specifically and directly outlawed certain practices essential to manipulation.

In two articles already printed in *Harper's* I undertook to prove that the chief economic evil of the Exchange was that it enabled promoters to load our corporations with huge burdens of debt and money claims, and that this was made possible through the device of issuing shares to outsiders, then listing them on the exchange and then, by "making a market" for them through manipulation, passing them on to uninformed investors. Many instances of this practice were brought out by Mr. Pecora to prove this point.

To end or at least check this abuse the chief aim must be, not so much to punish those who do it as to take out of their hands the weapons or tools with which they work. To rig the market the operator, whether acting alone or, as is usual, in a pool, must have an option. He must have the use of publicity, the privilege of creating an appearance of activity in the issue and thus running up its market price, an alliance with someone inside the exchange, the use of credit and generally the use of short-selling and the assistance of the specialist.

The original bill sought to take away forthwith all these dangerous implements from the brokers. That there should have been any hesitancy about this will give one an idea of the conservatism which dominated not Congress itself, but the leaders in Congress and particularly the responsible leaders of the administration. Only a short time ago Judge Woolsey of the Federal District Court for the Southern District of New York, held a pool operation and its creation of artificial activity to be a fraud and the use of the mails in furtherance of it a crime against the government, and the managers of that pool now stand convicted in a federal court. Still, with the soul of Mr. Casper Milquetoast dominating Congress from some quarter, these provisions were taken out of the bill and incorporated as grants of power to a Commission.

One of the worst surrenders was the elimination of the provisions which forbade specialists trading for their own account and which eliminated floor traders from the floor. The Commission can make rules on these points. But that leaves up to the Commission a fundamental evil which the law should have dealt with directly.

In the face of Mr. Pecora's revelations this was indeed an odd retreat. Mr. Whitney has persistently sought to make it appear that the Exchange floor is filled with busy commission brokers earnestly representing their clients, filling orders which pour in from all the hundred million people of the nation. Mr. Hamilton Fish, in a speech in Congress, told his colleagues that the Exchange was not in any way to blame for speculative excesses. They were just brokers on the Exchange. It was due to the greed of the plain people all over the country. Mr. Pecora showed that in July, 1933, 120,000,000 shares were traded in on the Stock Exchange and that one-fourth of these were bought by the members of the Exchange themselves for their own accounts and one-fourth sold by them; in other words, the members of the Exchange were on one side or the other of the market in practically one-half of the transactions. This did not include their tradings carried on in other names, the names of their wives (a popular device), the pools they were interested in. Nor did it include the trades of non-member professionals, like Thomas Bragg, Percy Rockefeller, Matthew Brush, and hundreds of others as well as corporation insiders. One specialist in July bought for his own account a million shares and sold a million shares for his own account—a single stock broker on one side or the other of the market in 1.65 per cent of all the trades. A specialist in eight months of 1933 made $200,000 in commissions and $2,000,000 in profits on his own speculations. The failure of the bill to outlaw these practices and to leave them to the mercy of the Commission was, in my humble judgment, a capital blunder.

VI

The chief strength of the bill lies in the provisions governing listed corporations. And it was this provision which brought down upon it the wrath of the embattled executives. The law abolishes unlisted security departments on exchanges and provides the Commission with power to exact complete and adequate information from all corporations seeking listing. The capital structure must be fully bared, including the terms on which all securities have been offered for the preceding three years. The share of directors, officers, large stockholders, their special agreements about bonuses, rights, salaries, and material contracts with the corporation must be disclosed. Had we had such a regulation before, Mr. Grace of Bethlehem Steel would have had to disclose his million-dollar-bonus cut; Mr. Dillon would have had to reveal the terms of his management contract with Goodyear Tire and Rubber and his twenty-cents apiece shares in United States and Foreign Securities Corporation; Mr. Brown would have had to unbosom himself of his strange option contracts in American Commercial Alcohol stock.

The Commission can exact periodical reports and an annual audited statement, may prescribe the forms of reports and, most important of all, can compel executives to report their own holdings and all changes in holdings each month, thus furnishing a check on the tradings of insiders in their own shares. There is much more to this effort to force corporation executives to respect their status of trustees. And while these powers, like others, are lodged with the Commission, there is every expectation that they will be invoked.

The whole matter now rests in the hands of the Commission, and the President must be held responsible for the kind of administration that is given of the act. The tendency this last year to acquit the President of every failure in his Administration and visit the guilt wholly upon the back of some subordinate is a little dangerous, to say nothing of its unfairness. The Commission will be composed of men of the President's choice. And it will be influenced in its action against the exchanges by the extent of the President's desire to curb them. As for the Exchange itself, it can be counted on to contest the painful struggle for reform every inch of the way. This foolish attitude, it may be assured, is the prime blunder which got it into its present straits. I have not seen in it throughout this long fight any real evidences of dawning wisdom.

BIBLIOGRAPHY

The twenty-odd volumes of Senate Banking Committee transcripts and reports provide the core of material on the Pecora investigations. Important supplementary information is also available in such contemporary sources as the *New York Times, New York Herald Tribune, New York American, Wall Street Journal, Washington Post, Literary Digest, Time, Business Week, The Nation,* and *The New Republic,* and in a series on "The Battle of the Market Place," by Joseph Alsop and Robert Kintner in *The Saturday Evening Post,* CCX (June 11, 1938 and June 25, 1938). I benefited from personal interviews with Benjamin V. Cohen, Thomas G. Corcoran, Telford Taylor, Louis Stephens, and Louis Pecora, as well as the oral histories of Ferdinand Pecora and James M. Landis at Columbia University. Pecora himself interpreted the hearings in *Wall Street Under Oath, The Story of Our Modern Money Changers* (New York, 1939, 1968). Other helpful sources include: Frederick Lewis Allen, *The Lords of Creation* (New York, 1935); Harry Barnard, *Independent Man: The Life of Senator James Couzens* (New York, 1958); Ralph F. DeBedts, *The New Deal's S.E.C., The Formative Years* (New York, 1964); John Kenneth Galbraith, *The Great Crash* (Boston, 1955); William H. Harbaugh, *Lawyer's Lawyer, The Life of John W. Davis* (New York, 1973); Matthew Josephson, *The Money Lords, The Great Finance Capitalists, 1925-1950* (New York, 1972); Raymond Moley, *After Seven Years, A Political Analysis of the New Deal* (New York, 1939); Michael E. Parrish, *Securities Regulation and the New Deal* (New Haven, 1970); and Arthur M. Schlesinger, jr., *The Coming of the New Deal* (Boston, 1959).

The Nye Munitions Committee
1934

The Nye Munitions Committee 1934

by John Edward Wiltz

If September 4, 1934, the Tuesday after Labor Day, seemed a typical late summer day in Washington—hot and humid—many individuals in the nation's capital were nevertheless astir. Representatives of the people, in the present instance a special committee of United States senators, after a fashion which had become (and would remain) a veritable ritual of American democracy, were about to begin the arduous business of exposing the awful merchants of death—greedy and conscienceless men, according to a popular view, who shamelessly took profit from the blood and misery of war. It mattered little that there was no air-conditioning in the white marble caucus room of the Senate Office Building, the scene of Teapot Dome hearings of recent memory, future site of such happenings as the Pearl Harbor, Army-McCarthy, and Watergate inquiries; and by mid-morning several hundred people had crowded through its doors. Some were lawyers, conservatively dressed, fidgeting with brief cases. About fifty were reporters, many in shirtsleeves, obviously enjoying the discomfort of certain of the distinguished principals in the spectacle about to unfold. Others were clerks, secretaries, security guards, photographers, cameramen, electricians. Still others were spectators, some of them tourists who rattled chairs and pointed out notable senators and titans of industry while preparing to witness a moment not apt to be lost in history.

The centers of activity in the caucus room that morning were several dark wooden tables—the altars about which the ritual of senatorial inquiry would be played out. The tables were littered with papers, pencils, cigarette packages, ash trays, flash bulb cartons, and four microphones stamped with the letters NBC. Taking a seat at the middle of the main table as 10:00 approached was the presiding official of the ritual, Senator Gerald Prentice Nye, chairman of the Special Senate Committee Investigating the Munitions Industry. Forty-two years old, Nye was a "progressive" Republican from North Dakota. Flanking the chairman were five older colleagues: W. Warren Barbour of New Jersey—a "regular" Republican, Walter F. George of Georgia, Bennett Champ Clark of Missouri, Homer T. Bone of Washington, and James P. Pope of Idaho—all Democrats of varying political colorations. Another Republican member of the committee, Arthur H. Vandenberg of Michigan, was absent. Facing the senators from a distance of barely fifteen feet, at the end of a short table which butted the middle of the main table, were officials of the Electric Boat Company, America's premier builder of submarines. Between the senators and industrialists, on opposite sides of the short table, were a committee investigator and thirty-eight-year-old Stephen Raushenbush, the investigative chief of the committee, who carried the unpretentious title of Secretary. (Senator Nye and his colleagues had no intention of letting Raushenbush, son of the well-known social gospeler Walter Raushenbusch, take the limelight as had Ferdinand Pecora in the investigation of financial malfeasance completed only a few weeks before.)

At 10:00 A.M. the chairman leaned forward and in a bell-like voice announced: "The Committee will come to order." The hum of electric fans became audible, movie cameras whirred. From Nye came no harangue, only a brief statement outlining procedures for the hearings. Still, the atmosphere was heavy with tension as senatorial inquisitors and the chieftains of Electric Boat peered at one another. For in the view of the senators and industrialists, not to mention uncounted millions of people across the world, the present affair, like many senatorial inquiries, seemed more than an investigation. It seemed a trial: *Peace-loving and Moral People* v. *Manufacturers and Salesmen of Implements of War.*

I

To borrow from Victor Hugo, the Senate's investigation of the munitions industry in the mid-1930s was an idea that had originated, for many Americans, in a time of peace, but had concluded in those years that businessmen of Europe and America were profiting from war. The logic seemed compelling. War or the threat of war offered a market for men who made and sold implements of death and destruction, hence it was in their interest to stir up tension and hostility among nations, and if war resulted, so much the better. Should the conclusion be valid, the time had come for Americans to do what they could about the munitions trade, perhaps by nationalizing their own armament industry. The obvious instrument for testing its validity and determining what if any action Congress should take was an inquiry by a committee of the United States Senate.

The idea that makers and salesmen of munitions were a cause of war had existed for many years. At The Hague, less than a hundred miles from the Western front, the First Congress of the Women's International League for Peace and Freedom in 1915 had found "in the private profits accruing from the great arms factories a powerful hindrance to the abolition of war." Delegates to the Paris Peace Conference of 1919 revealed a similar uneasiness about the munitions trade, and Article 8 of the Covenant of the League of Nations stated: "The Members of the League agree that the manufacture by private enterprise of munitions and implements of war is open to grave objections. The Council shall advise how the evil effects attendant upon such manufacture can be prevented, due regard being had to the necessities of those Members of the League which are not able to manufacture the munitions and implements of war necessary for their safety." Two years later a subcommittee of the League reported that munitions firms had fabricated war scares and bribed officials, organized international munitions combines, and exaggerated reports of military and naval programs. At the behest of the League an international conference in 1925 fashioned the Geneva Arms Traffic Convention, an innocuous document providing that each signatory government would regulate the munitions trade within its borders by a system of licenses.

The response in the United States? Americans had taken part in peace congresses which scored the munitions trade, helped write Article 8 of the League Covenant, and signed the Geneva Arms Traffic Convention. During the congressional debate over America's entry in the World War in 1917, Senator George W. Norris of Nebraska had charged that a vast propaganda effort was pressing the country to war to guarantee "the enormous profits of munition manufacturers, stockbrokers, and bond dealers." Appeals for regulations of the munitions trade, however, thus far created hardly a ripple in the United States. Even the piquant affair of William Baldwin Shearer in the latter 1920s aroused few Americans to the point of insisting on control of the builders and purveyors of armaments.

Brash and intolerant, Shearer in August 1929 filed suit against the three leading American shipbuilders, charging that they owed him more than $250,000 for advancing their interests over the past three years. Whereupon observers of the Geneva Naval Conference of 1927 recalled that Shearer, claiming to be a newsman, had attended the Conference, done what he could to stir discord, and received credit (or blame) in some quarters when delegates failed to agree on a naval disarmament treaty. For a few days Shearer commanded headlines, President Hoover expressed disbelief that shipbuilders might have tried to defeat the plans of the government, and a three-man subcommittee of the Senate undertook an investigation. Nine months later the chairman of the subcommittee, Samuel M. Shortridge of California, declared the affair closed. He reported that he and his colleagues had found no evidence that shipbuilders had dispatched Shearer to Geneva in 1927 to sabotage the naval conference. As for Shearer, Shortridge conceded that at Geneva he "may have been extravagant and assertive, but so far as I see it there is no reason for criticizing him."

Meanwhile another topic had caught the attention of many Americans: war profits. When talk turned to war profits in the 1920s and 1930s those discussing them were weighing a more pervasive, if less titillating, subject than the munitions trade, for in addition to the builder and seller of armaments, war profits touched all citizens—the manufacturer of nonmilitary commodities and Wall Street financier, farmer and worker—who stood to realize handsome returns, should the United States tumble into a new war, as in 1917–1918. People felt concern about war profits for two reasons. Applying logic similar to that used in sorting out the motives of munitions makers, Americans who were in rhythm with the assorted peace organizations which flourished at the time viewed potential war profits as a threat to peace. Not so lacking in conscience as dealers in munitions, general citizens who stood to profit in the event of American belligerency were not apt to wreck disarmament conferences or hatch conspiracies to move countries to war, so the argument went; but if it seemed that the United States was edging *toward* war they might be less than steadfast in the quest for peace and, on the contrary, might throw their influence toward the balance for hostilities.

Other Americans, particularly members of veterans' groups, thought it scandalous for citizens on the home front during wartime, as in 1917–1918, to realize bonanza returns while the men enduring the dangers and miseries of combat were drawing a dollar or two a day. So peace organizations and veterans' groups, which seldom agreed on anything, urged legislation to "equalize the burdens" should the United States again become a belligerent. The former thought such legislation would constitute a deterrent to war; the latter expected that the outcome would be justice for the fighting man.

Responding to appeals of pacifists and veterans, Congress in 1930 established the War Policies Commission comprising four members of President Hoover's cabinet, four senators, and four representatives. A few months later, in 1931, the commission in sixteen days of hearings took the testimony of a range of individuals who had thoughts about war profits. Few witnesses agreed with Richard Bartholdt, a former congressman from Missouri, that "war profits constitute a greater menace to peace than any other factor" and that "with the profits taken out of war, those who heretofore hugged war as their benefactor and friend, probably would not recognize it if they met it in the street." Most seemed to concur with Bernard M. Baruch who found it unthinkable "that any human could be persuaded by the prospect of personal gain, however magnificent, to invoke the horrors of modern war" and with General Douglas A. MacArthur, Army Chief of Staff, who believed that efficiency in war was desirable, effectiveness mandatory. (And effectiveness in his estimate required "normal" profits.) In its report, which Congress ignored, the commission recommended legislation for fixing prices and taxing "excessive" corporate profits in time of war.

The findings of the War Policies Commission faded quickly from the public consciousness. One need not search for an explanation for this. The new reality of life for Americans as they moved into the 1930s—the great overwhelming and bewildering problem commanding their attention—was the economic calamity known to history as the Great Depression. Still, as they sought a way out of their economic miseries, Americans of the early 1930s, if labeled "isolationist" by latter-day historians, were not oblivious to the undulations of politics and diplomacy across the world, and the threat of a new general war was never far from their thoughts. The threat seemed real enough, for it was manifest in those troubled years that the peace settlement worked out at Paris at the end of the "Great War" (as people continued to refer to the holocaust of 1914–1918) was coming apart. Seizing on an incident of their own manufacture, the Japanese in 1931–1933 swarmed over Manchuria and brought that sprawling territory, nominally a province of China, under the Rising Sun. Nobody could be sure where Japanese aggression might end.

The dictator, Benito Mussolini, meanwhile was haranguing throngs of Italians with talk about reviving the imperial grandeur of ancient Rome. And there was Adolf Hitler, an unimposing little man (in the American view, at any rate) who took power in Berlin in 1933 amid promises that he would restore the military might of Germany and right the wrongs which he claimed the victors in the Great War had inflicted on the Germans at Paris in 1919.

How should America respond in the event that the threat of general war became a reality? Anybody who has taken a freshman history course knows how Americans of the time answered that question. Disillusioned that their crusade of 1917–1918 had failed to accomplish its objective of making the world safe for democracy, touched by the assortment of books, plays, and movies depicting the horror of modern war which had appeared over the previous decade, moved by the pacifist contention that there was no such thing as a "just war," they began to insist that the United States should stay clear of any new hostilities. Let the peoples of Europe, Asia, and elsewhere strangle and mangle each other if they wished, but please excuse Americans from such insane, immoral, and fruitless enterprises.

As goings-on in Europe and Asia—and also in Latin America where Paraguayans and Bolivians were butchering one another for a trackless expanse of jungle called the Gran Chaco—strengthened the commitment of Americans to peace, such organizations as the National Council for Prevention of War; Women's International League for Peace and Freedom; and Stop Organized Slaughter (SOS, for short) stepped up their activities. For a variety of reasons they gave a fair part of their considerable energies to assailing manufacturers and salesmen of munitions. Like the slave traders of a century before, men who dealt in armaments offered unique opportunities for sensational disclosures. Whether these disclosures rested on evidence acceptable to lawyers or scholars was of no consequence. Consider the munitions merchant, slithering about the steaming Chaco peddling instruments of death to Paraguayans and Bolivians alike, and if the bloodletting and its profits seemed about to wane, spreading rumors in La Paz and then Asunción of new offensives by the other side. Or consider the dark-suited manufacturer of high explosives arriving at his skyscraper office building in a chauffeured limousine, secluding himself behind mahogany doors in a plush board room, and plotting destruction of a disarmament conference or arranging the secret sale of gunpowder to the enemy of his own government. Then many activists in the peace movement were political radicals, i.e., socialists of one sort or another, and attacks on what they often referred to as "the private traffic in arms," certain to stir popular sentiment for nationalization of the munitions industry, fell in with larger objectives. Not that such activists were cynical people trying to advance socialism by spreading monstrous lies about the munitions business. Far from it. Given their perception of capitalist ethics, they believed what they said about men who made and sold armaments.

2740 Congress Investigates

The effect of the attack on the munitions trade is hard to measure—before 1934, that is.

The effect of the attack on the munitions trade is hard to measure—before 1934, that is. In 1934 the attack escalated into a veritable barrage, and before the year was half over there was scarcely an American who did not know something about the misdeeds, real and alleged, of the men who trafficked in the paraphernalia of war.

An article entitled "Arms and the Men" appeared in March 1934, in *Fortune*, a magazine hardly reputed for anti-business pyrotechnics. It spun a sordid tale of intrigue and unconcern for human life by manufacturers and salesmen of munitions and reached millions of readers when Doubleday, Doran and Company published it as a pamphlet and *Reader's Digest* two months later brought it out in a condensed version. Asserted its unidentified authors, who were staff members of *Fortune*: "According to the best accountancy figures, it cost about $25,000 to kill a soldier during the World War. There is one class of Big Business Men in Europe that never rose up to denounce the extravagance of its governments in this regard—to point out that when death is left unhampered as an enterprise for the individual initiative of gangsters the cost of a single killing seldom exceeds $100. The reason for the silence of these Big Business Men is quite simple: killing is their business. Armaments are their stock in trade; governments are their customers; the ultimate consumers of their products are, historically, almost as often their compatriots as their enemies. That does not matter. The important point is that every time a burst shell fragment finds its way into the brain, the heart, or the intestines of a man in the front line, a great part of the $25,000, much of it profit, finds its way into the pocket of the armament maker."

The authors claimed that the "Armorers' Philosophy" was: "Publish periodical war scares. Impress governmental officials with the vital necessity of maintaining armaments against the 'aggressions' of neighbor states. Bribe as necessary. In every practical way create suspicion that security is threatened." They declared that "the armament leopards have never changed their spots. Detail upon detail, incident upon incident, illustrate how well the armament makers apply the two axioms of their business: When there are wars, prolong them; when there is peace, disturb it." The authors wrote that the Soviet Union "is today the only country in which there is no 'private' manufacture and sale of armaments." And a footnote observed: "Parenthetically it will be recalled by those who have followed the dreary course of disarmament conferences that Russia, in the mouth of Comrade Maxim Litvinov, has been the most consistent and the loudest advocate of disarmament."

At the same time that readers of *Fortune* were considering "Arms and the Men," booksellers began to advertise three key books: Otto Lehmann-Russbüldt, *War for Profit* (a new edition of a volume, originally published in Germany under the title *Die Blutige Internationale*, which had created a minor stir when first brought out in the United States in 1930); George Seldes, *Iron, Blood and Profits: An Exposure of the World-Wide Munitions Racket* (rated best of the three by the reviewer R. L. Duffus in the *New York Times*), and Helmuth C. Engelbrecht and Frank C. Hanighen's *Merchants of Death: A Study of the International Armament Industry* (perhaps as a consequence of its more imaginative title, the most influential of the three books).

In message and argument the books were indentical to "Arms and the Men." All essayed the evils associated with such names as Krupp and Skoda, Schneider-Creusot, and Vickers-Armstrong. All touched on the affair of William Shearer and presented chapters on Sir Basil Zaharoff, a shadowy munitions salesman *par excellence*, who for a half-century had moved about Europe's capitals peddling arms, and was variously labeled the "King of Armaments" (by Seldes), the "Supersalesman of Death" (by Engelbrecht and Hanighen), and the "Wickedest Man Alive," by a pamphleteer of 1934 who so designated Sir Basil because "he has given his life to an industry so vile and cruel, so fatal to the happiness and welfare of humankind, as to surpass the iniquity of the Inquisition, the slave trade, and the pogroms of the Jews." All three volumes devoted many pages to the alleged trading of strategic materials and munitions among corporations in the countries of opposing belligerents during the Great War. All found their sources in hearsay, tracts by assorted pacifist and socialist writers, and statistics and statements susceptible to varying interpretation.

Whatever their deficiencies, the effect of these articles and books was both immediate and dramatic. Remarks on the Senate floor by William E. Borah of Idaho denouncing munitions manufacturers ("international racketeers" in his phrase) received surprising publicity. The Foreign Policy Association and the American Academy of Political and Social Science invited Helmuth Engelbrecht to lecture their members on the evils of the munitions trade; the Book-of-the-Month Club made *Merchants of Death* a selection for April 1934. Rallies by peace organizations assailing armament makers attracted unprecedented attention. Editorials and cartoons on the arms trade blossomed in newspapers, new articles exposing the munitions business appeared in magazines: John Gunther's "Slaughter for Sale," in *Harper's* and Jonathan Mitchell's "The Armaments Scandal," in the *New Republic*, both appeared in May 1934. Even *Foreign Affairs*, a cautious—and in the view of some people, an almost stodgy—journal, offered an article, albeit a nonaccusative one, entitled "Arms Manufacturers and the Public" in its issue of July 1934. Most important, a resolution introduced by Senators Nye and Vandenberg providing for an investigation of the munitions industry and war profits won the consent of the Senate.

For the previous two years a congressional investigation of the munitions trade had been an object of one of the prominent peace organizations, the Women's International League for Peace and Freedom, and in 1933 the Executive Secretary of the American section of the WIL, Dorothy Detzer, had sought a senatorial sponsor of a resolution to bring about such an investigation. On the suggestion of Norris of Nebraska, too ill himself to get involved in a full-dress inquiry, she eventually turned to Nye of North Dakota.

A native of Wisconsin who found his way to North Dakota during the World War, Gerald Nye had drunk deeply of the ideas of Robert M. La Follette, and when he took on the editorship of a county newspaper in eastern North Dakota, he became an instant spokesman of those ideas. On appointment to the Senate in 1925 at the age of thirty-two, he slipped into alliance with such Republican progressives as Norris and Borah, and was one of those progressives whom Senator George H. Moses in the late 1920s labeled "sons of the wild jackass." His concerns in those early years in the Senate were not military affairs nor foreign policy. The great and overbearing problems of America in his view were monopoly and concentrated wealth—the oppressors, he was convinced, of farmers and small businessmen. As for his reputation as a senator, he had won minor acclaim before 1934 as the man who presided over the Continental Trading Company phase of the Teapot Dome investigation and played a part in sending Harry F. Sinclair to jail. He served as chairman of the special committee which had scrutinized tactics and expenditures in the senatorial elections of the 1930s (a precursor, of sorts, of the Watergate inquiry of 1973–1974), one aspect of which was exposure of the famous attempt to defeat Norris in Nebraska by placing on the same ballot the name of George W. Norris, a grocery clerk. At the time Detzer approached him Nye was attracting some attention, together with Borah, by attacking the National Recovery Administration, which he thought promoted monopoly and weakened small business.

Reluctant at first, Nye at length succumbed to Miss Detzer's appeal, and in the Senate chamber on February 8, 1934, snapped his fingers for a page and sent to the desk a resolution to investigate the munitions industry. At that moment he thought the resolution stood little chance of passage. But then came "Arms and the Men," which he inserted into the *Congressional Record* with the comment that "I think there has not been published in ages anything quite so enlightening as is this article appearing in *Fortune*." After that came Borah's remarks and the books purportedly exposing the munitions makers, particularly that by Engelbrecht and Hanighen. The Senate could not easily be oblivious to the increasing popular awareness of the alleged evils of the arms business.

Nye and Detzer meanwhile observed that earlier in the session Senator Vandenberg, urged on by the American Legion which continued to insist that the burdens of war be equalized, had introduced a resolution to review the findings of the War Policies Commission of 1930–1931. So they reasoned: Why not combine the Nye and Vandenberg Resolutions? By combining the resolutions, Detzer later recalled, "the measure would gain a double-barreled support from two diametrically opposed wings of public opinion—the peace movement and the Legion." Vandenberg was agreeable, and the outcome was S. Res. 206, authorizing the vice president to appoint a seven-member committee to investigate individuals, corporations, and agencies in the United States engaged in the munitions business; report on the adequacy of existing laws and treaties pertaining to the arms trade; review findings of the War Policies Commission; and submit recommendations on the desirability of nationalizing the country's armament industry. To carry out its mandate the special committee would have authority to subpoena witnesses and documents and would receive an appropriation of $15,000.

Without a word of dissent the Senate on April 12, 1934 approved S. Res. 206.

In view of the munitions inquiry's latter-day reputation as an exercise in demagoguery, the absence of criticism of S. Res. 206 in the spring of 1934, in retrospect, seems remarkable. No member of Congress or other individual of influence intimated that a munitions investigation might be inconsistent with the spirit of the general legislative power granted by the Federal Constitution, or that political considerations rather than legislative intent had moved Nye,

Vandenberg, and other proponents of the resolution. Nobody hinted that the special committee might infringe upon powers delegated to the judiciary, and from the White House came no laments that the special committee was about to embark on a fishing expedition which might weaken the national defense establishment or complicate the country's foreign relations.

Perhaps the mood of the moment received its most eloquent expression in a message to the Senate from President Franklin D. Roosevelt six days after the adoption of S. Res. 206. Even if not in complete agreement with all of his assertions (and there is no evidence to that effect), the fact that he felt constrained to make them testified to the national outrage over the munitions business. In his message the President expressed gratitude that the Senate was preparing to investigate the munitions industry, recommended that the Senate give generous support to the investigating committee, and charged the Executive branch to cooperate with the committee "to the fullest extent." Declared Roosevelt: "The private and uncontrolled manufacture of arms and munitions and the traffic therein has become a serious source of international discord and strife." He urged that the Senate consent to the Geneva Arms Traffic Convention of 1925, and appealed to the General Disarmament Conference, soon to reassemble in Geneva, to draft a more inclusive document regulating the munitions trade. He claimed that people in many countries were being taxed to the point of starvation to enable governments to engage in "a mad race in armaments" which if not stopped would result in war. "This grave menace to the peace of the world," he concluded, "is due in no small measure to the uncontrolled activities of the manufacturers and merchants of engines of destruction, and it must be met by the concerted action of the peoples of all nations."

The presidential message produced an instant response. Within an hour of its receipt Key Pittman of Nevada, chairman of the Senate Foreign Relations Committee, reported the Arms Traffic Convention of 1925 and introduced a joint resolution drawn up by the State Department prohibiting Americans to ship munitions to Paraguay and Bolivia; Senator Nye asked an additional $35,000 for the munitions investigation. In a matter of days the joint resolution had become law, and the munitions inquiry received the extra funds. Two months later the Arms Traffic Convention obtained the consent of the Senate—with the reservation that it would not bind the United States until approved by eight other nations and the British Empire.

Vice President John Nance Garner, meanwhile, had appointed Nye, Vandenberg, and five of their colleagues to the Special Committee Investigating the Munitions Industry, and on motion by Clark of Missouri the committee on April 23, 1934 named Nye chairman. For the senator from North Dakota the events of recent weeks had been exhilarating, and he found it impossible to await scrutiny of testimony and documents before deciding that the munitions makers were guilty, as Engelbrecht and others had charged. At New Haven on April 29 he declared, "I confidently predict that when the Senate investigation is over, we shall see that war and preparation for war is not a matter of national honor and national defense, but a matter of profit for few." Next day in New York he saw futility in trying to move out of the Great Depression when "we are preparing for new wars which will and

ought to be the end of our whole civilization," and after castigating armament expenditures as insane, proclaimed the time was at hand when it would
be understood "what monkeys the munitions makers can make of the otherwise intelligent people of America."

II

Not the product of a disciplined or ranging intellect, those words were
spoken in a clear, unpretentious accent, and came from a resonant baritone
voice. They also came from the heart, for Gerald Nye was an honest man who
meant what he said about merchants of death.

If often viewed from the vantage point of the present day as a demagogue
and a Neanderthal isolationist whose mark on history is best forgotten, Nye
was nevertheless an interesting person. Of average height, he was strong and
muscular. He also was handsome. And notwithstanding his reputation as a
man who spoke out in shockingly crude language against industrialists and
bankers and, after the onset of the Second World War in Europe, against
so-called "interventionists," he was a genial man who got on well with his
colleagues. His historical reputation as a bullwhip orator, relentless investigator, and crusader for peace via isolation, in truth, is misleading. Nye was
not an angry man. He did not pace the corridors and cloakrooms of the Capitol
haranguing fellow senators and newsmen. He did not have boundless confidence. Never having attended college, he stood in awe of university-educated
colleagues. He was reserved, and even shy. In the estimate of some observers
he presented the image of a rather ordinary Midwesterner. Comparing him
with colleagues on the munitions investigating committee, one reporter wrote
that "he looks less like a senator than any of them. . . . He has no flowing
mane, but a recent haircut. He has no senatorial bay window, but the lean
build of a second baseman." Fortunately Nye had assets: energy, zeal,
determination—and that magnetic voice.

For obvious reasons the Special Committee Investigating the Munitions
Industry, from the moment of Nye's election as chairman, came to be called
the Nye Committee. That was unfortunate, inasmuch as entitling the committee with the name of its chairman tended to exaggerate the chairman's part in
the munitions investigation. Nye's interest in the inquiry, to be sure, never
flagged. He spent many hours with colleagues and members of the committee
staff mapping the investigation and poring over documents. He attended
nearly every hearing. But if in that period Rudolf Hess was telling Germans
that "Hitler ist Deutschland und Deutschland Hitler ist," Senator Nye was not
the Nye Committee. Bennett Clark, for example, was as dedicated to the
inquiry as Nye, and almost as active. Clark, and to a lesser extent Vandenberg,
exercised nearly as much influence as the chairman in determining the direction of the inquiry. Clark, Vandenberg, and Homer Bone were much more
energetic in interrogating witnesses. And it was Raushenbush, the committee
secretary and a veteran critic and investigator of big business, who, in addition to helping the senators plan the investigation, supervised the crucial
business of the munitions inquiry, namely, the searching of the files of
such corporations as Du Pont and J. P. Morgan for incriminating or provoc-

ative documents, sifting through the piles of documents brought in by investigators, and drafting questions to be asked of witnesses.

The gathering and scrutiny of documents by Raushenbush's staff may have been the crucial business of the munitions inquiry, but it was the hearings in the caucus room, presided over by Nye, that attracted attention. There were ninety-three such hearings, and they concentrated on four topics: manufacture and sale of munitions (with emphasis on the international aspects of the arms trade); activities of the major shipbuilders of the United States; plans for removing, or at least reducing, corporate and individual returns in the event of American involvement in a new war; and finally, the economic circumstances of America's entry in the World War in 1917.

The first hearing, as mentioned, took place on September 4, 1934, the last, on February 20, 1936. Manufacture and sale of munitions was the focus of twenty-nine hearings in September and December 1934, and in February 1936. The shipbuilding industry was the subject of thirty-six hearings from January to April 1935; and in December 1934 and March and April 1935 the Nye Committee devoted eighteen hearings to war profits. After April 26, 1935, there were no hearings until January 7, 1936, when the committee held the first of ten hearings on loans to the Allied powers, industrial expansion, and neutrality during the World War—an attempt to discern whether the prompting of Wall Street financiers and other economic considerations had nudged the United States into war in 1917.

It was no accident that the Nye Committee elected to take up the munitions trade in the opening hearings. The trade was on the popular mind in 1934. People were anxious for the committee to expose the "merchants of death," and they would have felt a sense of letdown had hearings begun with consideration of such prosaic topics as collusive bidding among shipbuilders and excess-profits taxes in time of war. The public wanted to watch witnesses—unctuous and overfed tycoons of industry and sleazy arms salesmen—squirm when confronted with incriminating documents and accusative questions. The committee of course was anxious to satisfy the popular will, for it wanted to prevent any weakening of interest in the inquiry. The reasons were transparent. All of the members shared the national disgust with the arms trade, all were interested in other topics to be taken up during the investigation, notably corporate and individual profits, should America be drawn into the inevitable "next war," and they understood that any erosion of interest in what the committee was about would reduce chances of approval of legislation to bring the munitions makers to heel and equalize the economic burdens of American involvement in war. Then, too, the Nye Committee was operating on a parsimonious budget, and feared an early end to the inquiry if popular interest did not compel new appropriations. The inquiry's survival, then, seemed to depend on keeping interest at a high level. Finally, the senators were politicians, and if they made no public utterances to the effect that the munitions inquiry was apt to be a marvelous carriage for advancing political reputations, they must have thought as much. Should popular interest in the inquiry diminish, it went without saying, their coach would turn into a pumpkin.

The calculus of the senators proved accurate, for hearings on the munitions business produced a spate of sensational, or at least highly quotable, documents and testimonies which received front-page publicity. The Senate appropriated the funds necessary to keep the investigation going, and Nye *et al.*, remained in the spotlight.

There were two letters by Frank S. Jonas, an agent for such firms as the Remington Arms Company, Curtiss-Wright Export Corporation, and Federal Laboratories, Incorporated, who operated in South America. Jonas had written in late 1933: "The Paraguay and Bolivia fracas appears to be coming to a termination, so business from that end is probably finished. We certainly are in one hell of a business, where a fellow has to wish for trouble so as to make a living, the only consolation being, however, that if we don't get the business someone else will. It would be a terrible state of affairs if my conscience started to bother me now." In 1932, on a happier occasion (for him), Jonas had reported: "The unsettled conditions in South America has [sic] been a great thing for me, as I sold a large order for bombs to Brazil and also a fair cartridge order. I also sold very large bomb orders for Colombia, Peru, Ecuador, Bolivia, and now have made up all my losses, and I am back on my feet. It is an ill wind that does not blow someone some good." The first of those letters inspired Helmuth Engelbrecht to write another book, entitled *One Hell of a Business*.

If Frank Jonas was a small-bore arms salesman, authors of other documents put in evidence by the Nye Committee to prove the unconscionable character of the munitions trade were leaders of business. Such an individual was Vice President Lawrence Y. Spear of the Electric Boat Company who in 1928 had lamented that "it is too bad that the pernicious activities of our State Department have put the brake on armament orders from Peru by forcing the resumption of formal diplomatic relations with Chile." Asked by Senator Clark in 1934 if he indeed had regarded efforts by the State Department to improve relations among South American countries as pernicious, Spear had replied, "That is the word I used." Then there was Clarence W. Webster, President of Curtiss-Wright Export, who in 1933 had told an agent in Peru, "For your confidential information you might diplomatically inform interested parties that your neighbor to the extreme north [Colombia] is still purchasing [military equipment] in large quantities. Do not overlook such items as bombs, ammunition, machine guns . . . etc." Moved also by the prospect of profits to be taken from the war in the Gran Chaco, Webster in that same year had advised another agent in South America: "If we are able to sell them [the Paraguayans] anything, we will have to work very carefully and quietly . . . as the Bolivian Government would naturally raise 'merry hell' if they believed that we were dealing with their enemies." Webster's letters and kindred documents prompted Raushenbush to comment that the munitions business was "one in which the absence of moral judgment is a primary essential to success."

Still, the Nye Committee's attempt to prove the indictment of the munitions business drawn up by peace organizations and such authors as Engelbrecht and Seldes came to little. Raushenbush's investigators spent perhaps a thousand hours rifling through letters, reports, and memoranda in the files of sixteen corporations (and a few subsidiaries) in the United States which manufactured and distributed arms, ammunition, and other materials of war. They examined records of the Departments of State and Commerce and such private organizations as the Army Ordinance Association and Navy League. They found scattered documents indicating that at one time or another munitions makers and salesmen had committed many of the sins attributed to them by their critics: ignored the morality of customers, sold arms illegally, opposed disarmament schemes and arms embargoes. In aggregate, however, the evidence was paltry, and regarding most articles of the "gospel according to Engelbrecht" failed to support general conclusions. Most notably, documents and testimony failed to provide even the scantiest proof of the central contention of Engelbrecht *et al.*, namely, that there existed an international munitions "ring" composed of the principal arms makers of Europe (Krupp, Skoda, Vickers-Armstrong, Schneider-Creusot, Hotchkiss, Bofors) and America (Du Pont and possibly others) which, like a ubiquitous monster spreading its tentacles across the world—as cartoonists of the 1930s sometimes portrayed "the ring"—used bribery and whatever else might be necessary to prevent governments from negotiating disarmament treaties and imposing other restrictions on the munitions trade. The Nye Committee, of course, had no access to records of arament companies and chancelleries in Europe, Asia, and Latin America, and one can only speculate whether such records would have provided the proof of the Engelbrecht-Seldes-Detzer thesis on the munitions trade which the American Senate's special committee sought in vain in files in the United States.

All the Nye Committee affirmed about the munitions industry was that its overseas business depended to a large extent on "greasing the palms" of public officials in Latin America, the Near East, and China. Files of nearly every company scrutinized by Raushenbush's investigators yielded documents reporting payments to this or that functionary in return for arranging sale of a few airplane engines or cases of cartridges. At one point Senator Nye asked Clarence Webster, formerly of Curtiss-Wright Export, if it was not true that such a payment was called a commission. Webster replied, "That would be a very polite word for it, Mr. Chairman." "In fact," Nye asked, "it would be bribery, would it not?" "It would," answered Webster. "It is a rather harsh word, but it would be, strictly speaking." Bribery, however, was not a preserve of the munitions trade, so documents disclosing its use provided marginal reinforcement for the view that makers and sellers of arms were marked by special qualities of corruption. When the committee exhibited evidence that Du Pont had paid commissions to officials in China, Felix Du Pont explained that bribery was used "in most of the countries of the Orient in all walks of commercial life." "It is no different in the munitions business than it is in any other commercial business," he went on. "It is accepted; not talked about very much; but people in competition in those countries simply could not possibly carry on their trade if the customs of the country were not adhered to."

Failure of the Nye Committee to provide much support for the devil view of the munitions trade, however, was not readily apparent. That is understandable. Before the munitions hearings began many Americans had accepted the contention that arms makers were merchants of death, and scattered evidence supporting this or that particular of the Engelbrecht-Seldes indictment, some of it quite sensational (*e.g.*, the Jonas letters), buttressed such belief. Then there was the committee's procedure during hearings. If the committee had taken up the so-called "international munitions ring," exhibited all documents purporting to indicate the existence of a ring, and summoned witnesses from Du Pont and Remington and Electric Boat to answer questions about the ring, the paucity of evidence would have become apparent. People, accordingly, might have understood that the ring possibly was the creation of excited imaginations and in any event did not include American corporations. If the committee had focused on the contention that a standard practice of arms dealers was to make sales to one party to a conflict or dispute and then quietly advise the other belligerent or disputant that it had better keep abreast of its opponent, people would have seen that the two or three letters exhibited to the point scarcely supported a general conclusion. Instead of moving from topic to topic, the committee unfortunately moved from corporation to corporation. Documents indicated that this company had committed one type of indiscretion, that company another. Only a perceptive observer under such circumstances was apt to discern that on few occasions, bribery excepted, did abuses reappear.

Perhaps the perception of Americans and others would have been clearer had they grasped a message implicit in testimony given during hearings and in the thousands of pages of documents eventually published by the Nye Committee, namely, that the munitions industry in the United States in the mid-1930s was in pretty sad shape. Markets for its wares were scarce, its capacity for mischief was sorely restricted. Of the dozen or so companies (not including shipbuilders) which comprised the industry, only Du Pont, one of three or four producers of gunpowder in the country, seemed reasonably prosperous, and a mere fraction of Du Pont's manufacturing profits—two percent over the previous ten years—had come from sale of military products. As for the others, several of them shoestring operations, the larger ones only marginally involved in the business of making and distributing military arms, they were closed out of sales to the powers of Europe and Japan and their empires were unable to secure many orders from the government of the United States, which was spending little money on armament, save warships. Thus such companies were reduced to scrounging for sales in a few meager markets, mainly in Latin America.

The committee, one must assume, did become aware of the poverty level of America's munitions industry. Its investigative staff certainly did. After his first day at the Winchester Repeating Arms Company, the investigator, Robert Wohlforth, reported to Raushenbush: "In Winchester yesterday as per schedule. It is even more dismal a plant than Remington—a cross between an old ladies' home and a prison factory. This bunch are surely down in the mouth since the Olins took over; every department has been cut to the bone and the whole place seems to be wheezing along on one cylinder. . . . As far as I can make out, they use the Ix-nay system of filing. The old crone in the central filing room takes a bunch of papers marked 'U.S. government,' turns around three times with her eyes shut, says 'Ix-nay' and files the papers under 'Venezuela—commercial business.' . . . Needless to say I camped in Mr. Beebe's department [H. F. Beebe, Director of the Foreign Department]. . . . We fell to talking about the 1925 business [a meeting between government and arms company officials]. With another stroke of luck we discover he has all the papers on that little business in a folder, unbeknownst to Apple Annie of the filing room."

Still, the committee, perhaps sensing that its inquiry would lose its *raison d'être* if it blemished the popular portrait of munitions corporations wallowing in the profits of blood and gore while the rest of the world languished, gave no hint of the depressed state of America's merchants of death. And the merchants? They did not seem anxious to publicize their actual condition.

But alas, the truth more or less won out in the end. Without saying much about it, Americans gradually came to the conclusion that makers and salesmen of munitions were not such dangerous fellows after all. Perhaps people subconsciously understood that the Nye Committee had failed to prove the case against the manufacturers and sellers of arms. Perhaps they simply tired of pondering heady notions about merchants of death. After all, happenings other than the munitions inquiry were commanding their attention. There was the World Series of 1934 between the Cardinals and Tigers, an exciting affair dominated by the Dean brothers. By the year 1935, in any event, fewer individuals were issuing broadsides on the threat to peace and humanity presented by the munitions trade. And if Senator Nye, on Independence Day 1935, could shout that the "next war" ought to be called "a war to make the world safe for Du Pontcracy" and proclaim that munitions makers—he called them racketeers—"go out over this world and build up the hates, fears, and suspicions that build wars, that drive people into war, and then getting them there, they keep them there as long as they can," fewer people seemed to be listening than had listened the year before.

The erosion of faith in the truisms of 1934 never abated. When the Nye Committee in the spring of 1936 issued its report, only four members (Bone, Clark, Nye, and Pope) favored nationalization of the munitions industry, that elixir which in one grand swallow so many Americans and surely every certified pacifist had believed would eliminate the evils of the arms business and dramatically strengthen the cause of peace. Agreeing with the majority on every other point, the committee minority (Barbour, George, and Vandenberg) did not think the ills of the munitions trade warranted such drastic and unsettling medicine, the more so in light of the darkening state of world politics. In 1937 Philip Noel-Baker's book entitled *The Private Manufacture of Armaments,* a refined reiteration of information and themes set out by Engelbrecht and Seldes in 1934, created hardly a ripple. (Noel-Baker, however, would continue to toil in the vineyard of peace, and in 1959 receive his reward, a Nobel Peace Prize.) By 1938 scarcely anyone in America appeared to care a hoot about the comings and goings of such shadowy characters as Frank Jonas or the tactics of United Aircraft Export in selling a few planes in South America. By that time, it was true, the Yankees had become so dominant in baseball that the World Series no longer was very interesting, either. Still, Mussolini's conquest of Ethiopia, Hitler's remilitarization of the Rhineland, and the aftermath of the incident at the Marco Polo Bridge near Peiping seemed sufficient to prevent people from dreaming up new chapters in yesteryear's awful saga of the merchants of death. Twenty years later, even Gerald Nye, a man in the twilight of life, his career in the Senate having terminated in 1945, could say that he never had accepted the idea that munitions makers were a principal cause of war.

At the same time the senators were interrogating men who manufac-

tured and sold munitions and basking in the national spotlight, Raushenbush's investigators were assembling materials from the files of the country's
private shipbuilding industries. As everyone knew—or so it seemed—the
shipbuilders had dispatched William B. Shearer to the Geneva Naval Conference of 1927, and like other makers of implements of war were suspected
of conniving with federal departments and spending vast sums of money
to influence Congress. In the words of the National Council for Prevention of War: "Our shipbuilders are probably our most aggressive and sinister
propagandists of competitive naval building even if it brings war. They have
for years been ruthless in pursuit of profits."

The Nye Committee, however, treated shipbuilders apart from ordinary
makers of guns and amunition, for, unlike so-called merchants of death whose
prosperity depended on overseas markets, America's shipbuilding industry
constructed nearly all of its war vessels for the government of the United
States, and thus was not open to such accusations brought against the munitions trade as bribing foreign functionaries, stirring tensions in small countries, and violating arms embargoes. Some of the sins of which the committee
suspected shipbuilders, in truth, had little relation to questions of war and
peace. Most important, the senators thought, the "big three" of the shipbuilding industry—Bethlehem Shipbuilding Company, New York Shipbuilding
Company, and Newport News Shipbuilding & Dry Dock Company—had
come to dominate the industry, and that dominance had produced several
evils: attempts to freeze out smaller competitors; organization of elaborate
lobbies in Washington; and collusive bidding for naval contracts.

The Nye Committee's exhaustive study of the shipbuilding industry
proved another exercise in frustration. The senators proved that two shipbuilding executives had lied to the Shortridge Subcommittee during its investigation of the Shearer Affair in 1929, and established that the industry had
maintained an expensive lobby in Washington to influence legislation pertaining to merchant marine and naval construction. But they exhibited only
circumstantial evidence, effectively countered by representatives of the industry, that shipbuilders had engaged in collusive bidding—the aspect of the
study of the shipbuilding industry to which they gave the most time. And in
its re-examination of the Shearer episode the committee added nothing to
the findings of the Shortridge Inquiry of 1929–1930.

Equally frustrating no doubt, the lengthy examination of the shipbuilding industry, heavy with figures on cost estimates and bids, stirred little
popular interest and only rarely prompted city editors to think that copy
submitted by reporters deserved the front page. One of those rare instances
came when the committee aired a bizarre and inconclusive account of a union
official standing outside a hotel room while a representative of one of
Washington's "most influential citizens" and a "fixer" allegedly promised to
arrange a contract award to Gulf Industries, Incorporated, a small shipbuilder, in return for $250,000. Another titillation came when the committee
interrogated the volatile Shearer about a pamphlet he had written in 1928,
entitled *The Cloak of Benedict Arnold,* in which he had tagged several prominent Americans as "unpatriotic" because they did not share his Mahan-
ian views about a big navy. Senator Bone asked Shearer if he still considered
President Woodrow Wilson's Secretary of War, Newton D. Baker, as "unpa-

triotic." Shearer answered that he did. Bone asked about Harry A. Garfield, the son of the former President. Shearer explained that listing Garfield had been "a little bit of plagiarism on my part, taken from the Hearst papers." Bone told Shearer that "you ought not to admit plagiarism." Replied Shearer: "I am a plagiarist. I am in that case." What about former Attorney General George W. Wickersham? Claiming that he had served as an attorney for the Mitsubishi interests of Japan, Shearer said he still considered Wickersham "unpatriotic." Bone pointed out that Shearer had listed Franklin D. Roosevelt among the "unpatriotic." "Hearst," Shearer said. Retorted Bone: "Do you want to hide behind the skirts of a newspaper publisher?" "Let me tell you, Senator," Shearer exclaimed, "I do not hide behind anything, but Hearst published an article at that time that gave me the opportunity to use it, and I took it and put it in that pamphlet. I am opposed to all foreign entanglements and to being made an adjunct of the British." "Are you so cowardly," Bone asked a few moments later, "that you would not indict him [Roosevelt], if he required indictment, as a 'Benedict Arnold'? You told us you had lots of courage." "I have not mentioned my courage," Shearer spoke out, "and I do not like the implication about being a coward." "That is unfortunate," snapped Bone. Whereupon Shearer rose from his chair and began to move menacingly toward Bone. Nye pounded his gavel and shouted, "Go back to your seat as a witness and remain there." Shearer stopped short and returned to his chair.

III

In addition to the munitions trade and the shipbuilding industry the Nye Committee, as mentioned, took up war profits and economic influences on America's relations with Europe's belligerents in 1914–1917.

Abnormal returns in the form of dividends, wages, and bonuses when the United States was at war—all conveniently called war profits—were a subject which stirred popular emotions in the mid-1930s, as it had in some quarters as far back as 1920, the year the new veterans' organization, the American Legion, opened a campaign in behalf of legislation to curtail large civilian profits in time of national belligerency. In the view of many people it was manifestly unfair that a soldier at the front should be required to risk life and limb for a couple of dollars a day while workingmen, farmers, and industrialists (especially *industrialists*) at home realized bonanza returns, as in 1917–1918. Or as Senator Clark, an army officer in the World War, expressed it: "If a man is drafted . . . and is compelled to fight for the Old Flag for one-dollar-and-a-quarter a day [the wage of a private in the American Expeditionary Force in 1917–1918], why should not a man engaged in the industrial end of the game—which I agree is very essential, whether he be an executive or a laboring man—also make some sacrifice for the Old Flag?"

More than a spirit of fair play moved many Americans to deplore war profits. The prospect of huge returns in time of war, according to a popular belief, constituted a threat to peace. So the argument went, legions of Americans—workingmen, farmers, businessmen—recalling the returns of 1917–1918, might be tempted to view a new declaration of war by the government in Washington as a blessing, particularly in a time such as the present, *i.e.*, at a time of economic distress. Should large numbers of people—and especially captains of business who were assumed to have great influence in the councils of government—come to such a view, America's involvement in the next general war in Europe or Asia was inevitable. How might Americans be immunized against viewing war as a "positive good" (to borrow John C. Calhoun's famous estimate of slavery)? This was easy. Pass a law to "equalize the burdens of war," namely, a law which would guarantee that *no* American, workingman and industrialist as well as soldier and seaman, would realize large monetary returns during the period of hostilities. Such a law, the writer-economist John T. Flynn told the Nye Committee, would make war highly unpopular. Explained Flynn: "I rather think that the man who is disposed to be very sensitive, if some Japanese lieutenant fails to take his hat off in the presence of the American flag some place in Manchukuo, will not be so sensitive and will be more reasonable in his patriotism."

The Nye Committee shared popular emotions about war profits and determined to do something about them. The committee, in truth, viewed its investigation of war profits, if less apt to produce sensational documents and testimony, as more important than its scrutiny of the munitions trade. Its reasoning seemed logical. However shabby, the activities of a few arms companies in Peru and Paraguay were not likely to imperil America's peace. The profits to be taken in the aftermath of a new declaration of war appeared something else. These would touch virtually every citizen of a depression-weary republic, and if not foreclosed before eruption of that inevitable "next war" in Europe or Asia, the promise of such profits would dramatically reduce the chances of America staying clear of hostilities. The trick was to find a formula for restricting war profits which would pass muster with the national populace and its representatives in Washington.

This was a trick the Nye Committee failed to turn. Millions of Americans, it seemed evident when the committee began work in 1934, agreed that the prospect of untrammeled profits in time of war threatened America's peace. Thus, if the committee, then at the peak of its influence, had struck for a drastic war profits measure at that time the legislation might have passed. But it was apparent by the spring of 1935, when discussion of war profits came to a dramatic climax in Congress, that much of the citizenry was less fearful than the Nye Committee and its supporters in the peace movement that the expectation of abnormal returns would draw the country into war. Perhaps ordinary people, on reflection, had arrived at a "gut" feeling, beyond the comprehension of some men on Capitol Hill, not to mention quixotic crusaders of the peace organizations, that Americans would not betray their young men for uncounted pieces of silver. What bothered Americans by 1935 was the unfairness, and the scandal, of profiteering on the home front when American soldiers were facing death in the trenches. This meant that by that point the object of thoughtful citizens was, via price controls or excess profits taxes or both, to hold individual and corporate earnings in war to something approximating peacetime levels. Those same citizens, moreover, had come to sense that an extreme attack on the profit motive in time of hostilities might imperil the national war effort, and like General MacArthur, back in 1931, accepted the axiom that victory in *any* war in which the United States found itself must receive first priority. As for the Nye Committee, it remained intent on crushing any economic incentives Americans might have for going to war by making their involvement in war as economically unpalatable as possible.

More concerned with corporate than individual returns (large bonuses to corporate executives excepted), the Nye Committee began its public scrutiny of war profits by establishing what everybody already knew, namely, that American corporations had realized unprecedented returns in the time of the First World War. The picture was fuzzy, however, inasmuch as the committee made little distinction between the returns of corporations in 1914–1917, before America's entry into the conflict, and the year and a half following its declaration of war. Profits in the nearly three-year period before the Declaration of April 1917 of course hardly seemed germane to the committee's mandate to consider the matter of profits during national belligerency.

Whatever the confusion resulting from its approach to the subject, the Nye Committee made some unsettling disclosures during its hearings on war profits. There was the haggling between Du Pont and the government in 1917–1918 over construction of the Old Hickory smokeless powder plant near Nashville, Tennessee. The haggling had gone on for three months before the Du Pont corporation agreed to terms. As Lieutenant Colonel C. T. Harris, in the planning branch of the War Department in 1917–1918, told the committee, "three months were taken up in negotiations which finally led to the final agreement. . . . There were 3 months lost in the middle of the war by these negotiations. That had a very serious effect on the military effort. Fortunately it did not have a fatal effect, but it might have had." Evidence indicated that Du Pont, the only company in America capable of building and operating a smokeless powder plant of such dimensions, had delayed agreement in hopes of securing better terms. Or, as Pierre S. Du Pont had explained in a letter of November 1917, "We cannot assent to allowing our patriotism to interfere with our duties as trustees." Such reasoning seemed shocking in 1934, and Senator Clark expressed the Nye Committee's sentiments: "You take men to carry a gun and get jabbed up with bayonets without any consultation or negotiations or haggling." Then there was disclosure that during the war corporations had deferred tax payments when they disagreed with the government on the amounts to be paid. Evidence revealed that most such cases were not resolved until years later, and in nearly every instance the sum eventually paid was less than the liability originally calculated by the government. The Bureau of Internal Revenue, for example, had calculated the tax liability of the Phelps-Dodge Corporation for 1917–1918 at $16,378,000. The Corporation argued for $6,245,000, and deferred payment. When settlement of the case finally came in 1929 Phelps-Dodge had to pay only slightly more than $7,000,000.

In executing its mandate under S. Res. 206 to examine the findings of the War Policies Commission the Nye Committee, as indicated, hoped to provide a foundation for legislation that would restrict monetary gain and more or less equalize economic burdens when the United States went to war. Its views on what such legislation should entail were set out in a plan prepared by John T. Flynn and considered in hearings in March and April of 1935. The Flynn Plan was drastic. It urged that corporations in wartime be limited to annual profits of three percent of their real value. It called for confiscation of all annual individual earnings in excess of $10,000, a mind-boggling (and perhaps *mindless*) proposal which prompted Senator Pope to ask if such taxation would not be a serious matter. Replied Flynn: "It would not be a serious matter at all. It might be serious for them [persons whose life-style was geared to high incomes], but not for the Nation." Senator Clark interjected: "It is not as serious as being hit by a high-explosive shell, is it?" Flynn: "Not nearly." Flynn's plan also would require officials of industries declared essential by the President to register for the draft, whereupon the government could induct them into the industrial–management forces of the army at a rank no higher than colonel at pay appropriate to that rank, and then assign them to manage their own corporations. What about workers? Believing that there should be no exceptions, that the burdens of war must fall equally, Nye and Clark thought the plan should provide for conscription of labor as well as capital. But workers were too numerous and had too many friends on Capitol Hill, so the committee regretfully directed Flynn to make no recommendations for drafting labor.

Claiming that "the time has come to take the profit out of war," President Roosevelt meanwhile, in December 1934, had appointed a committee headed by Bernard M. Baruch and Hugh S. Johnson to draft legislation to eliminate excessive returns in time of war. The Baruch-Johnson Committee did not amount to much, and after cursory study reiterated the well-known views of Baruch. Then, in January 1935, Representative John McSwain of South Carolina, the author of many war profit resolutions over the years, introduced a new measure to curtail returns in wartime. An embodiment of Baruch's ideas, the McSwain Bill authorized the President, when the United States became a belligerent, to proclaim a ceiling on prices, rents, rates, commissions, and rewards, and granted the Chief Executive other powers over the economy intended to facilitate the national war effort.

The Nye Committee viewed the appointment of the Baruch-Johnson Committee and the introduction of the McSwain Bill as a crude maneuver by the White House to head off the drive for drastic legislation to eliminate war profits. Still, it felt compelled to invite Baruch to present his views at committee hearings. Baruch accepted the invitation. Of the McSwain Bill he exulted: "This is a great measure, not alone to prevent war, if there be people who desire profits in war, but to make certain this country will have the greatest war machine that we ever had, that the world has ever seen."

About the Flynn Plan Baruch held his peace during hearings, only to attack it a short time later in a statement filed with the committee: "I am not debating here whether the profit motive is right or wrong. I am only insisting that we recognize reality and what is here proposed. And I *am* saying that the advent of modern war and threatened national destruction, when the fate of the people, as at no other time, depends on the efficient operation at high-speed pressure, of its industrial system, is *not* the moment to select to switch from the fundamental base of our economic system to a new and wholly experimental system which was never adopted at any time in the world's history in peace or war without an immediate result of collapse and ruin."

If in the opinion of many people "Barney" Baruch was a "pompous ass," most Americans probably agreed with his estimate of the consequences of the sort of attack on war profits envisioned by the Nye Committee and its Flynn

Plan. In any event, when the issue of war profits came to a climax on Capitol Hill, in April 1935, the House of Representatives, returning to reality after a heady and tumultuous day during which it seemed to embrace the Nye Committee's ideas, approved the McSwain Bill by a vote of 367 to 19. Ignoring the obvious, *i.e.*, that legislation styled after Flynn's plan stood no chance of gaining consent of Congress or signature by the President, Nye determined to tilt against windmills and persuaded the Military Affairs Committee to accept Flynn–like amendments to the Senate's version of the McSwain Bill. This was to no avail. Only a handful of senators was interested in such an extreme remedy for the problem of profiteering in war, so the bill never came to a vote in the Upper Chamber, and by summer of 1935, in the face of concern over worsening relations between Ethiopia and Italy, the steam had gone out of the drive to enact war profits legislation.

Many months later, in January-February 1936, came the hearings on how economic considerations may have influenced the policy of the American government in 1914–1917.

To discern whether the munitions industry in any way was responsible for America's entry in the World War, the Nye Committee early in its inquiry determined to examine events of 1914–1917, whereupon investigators under the direction of Josephine Joan Burns began to assemble evidence from the State Department and other departments and agencies. Still, the Nye Committee, when it began its investigation in 1934, had no idea that it might become entangled in a great national debate over America's policy when other countries went to war—a debate over *neutrality*. At the time the Senate adopted S. Res. 206 the question of neutrality, in truth, did not seem urgent. The Far East was momentarily tranquil and the war in the Gran Chaco presented no threat to the United States. Congress, moreover, had considered neutrality the previous year, and the outcome had been an impasse which betrayed no sign of abating.

But then, in early 1935, the impending conflict in East Africa stirred new interest in neutrality, and in March of that year President Roosevelt, to the surprise of the senators and for reasons that remain unclear, suggested that the Nye Committee look into the matter of neutrality and draft relevant legislation. A few weeks later Nye and Clark, by then absorbed with the neutrality issue, introduced joint resolutions prohibiting loans to belligerent governments and their nationals, denying passports to Americans wishing to enter war zones, and prohibiting shipment of arms to belligerents, victims and aggressors alike—measures calculated to preclude activities and incidents of the sort which the senators believed had drawn the United States to war in 1914–1917. "Isolationists" (so-called) who wanted America to stay clear of foreign embroilments at almost any price, Nye and Clark agreed with a sentiment expressed in that period by the historian Charles A. Beard: "We tried once to right European wrongs, to make the world safe for democracy. Even in the rosiest view the experiment was not a great success. Mandatory neutrality may be no better, for aught anyone actually knows. But we nearly burnt our house down with one experiment; so it seems not wholly irrational to try another line."

The Nye Committee meanwhile announced plans for examining files and interrogating officers of J. P. Morgan & Company, the financial angel of the

Allied governments in 1914–1917. That announcement brought a thunder-clap from across the Atlantic, particularly from Great Britain, whose ambassador in Washington expressed fear that the committee would treat the British Government as a circus animal performing for spectators and deplored the consequences of such a spectacle on relations between Britain and the United States. The committee, as a result, did not gain access to Morgan's records until mid-August 1935, and it was not until January 1936 that Raushenbush's investigative staff had prepared the essential foundation for hearings. Too late to influence the debate which had culminated in the Neutrality Act of 1935, those hearings seemed certain to bear on discussion of what kind of legislation if any should be enacted upon expiration on February 29, 1936, of the neutrality measure of 1935.

If it put the Nye Committee back on "Page One" for a few days, the interrogation of J. P. Morgan and his partners on the subject of finance and foreign policy in 1914–1917 proved still another exercise in frustration. Equally distressing from the vantage of the committee—or, more accurately, the committee majority—an utterance by Senator Nye in the course of that interrogation brought an end to the entire munitions investigation.

Frustration and distress did not seem a probable outcome when on January 7, 1936, the Nye Committee faced the Morgan witnesses in the high-ceilinged Senate caucus room. Not since the first days of the munitions hearings had the committee attracted so much attention, the room being filled to capacity long before Nye called for order. The scene, if tense, was informal, almost unruly. Huddled at the witness table were J. P. Morgan (the younger), his pipe billowing smoke, and his partners, Thomas W. Lamont and George Whitney. Behind them was a corps of accountants, clerks, and publicists. Unlike during the Pecora Inquiry nearly three years before, the Morgan witnesses seemed anxious to submit their case to the public. Whenever the committee exhibited a document a Morgan functionary would extract a sheaf of copies from a brief case and distribute them to the forty or so reporters seated at two, long, flanking tables. And Morgan, wearing a high starched collar which made him appear a relic of another generation, talked with reporters and posed patiently for photographers.

When the hearings got underway the committee permitted Morgan to read a statement in which he conceded that, notwithstanding President Wilson's appeal of August 1914 urging Americans to be impartial in thought as well as action, the Morgan partners had found it "quite impossible to be impartial as between right and wrong." He explained that from the moment the war started "we, in common with many others, realized that if the Germans should obtain a quick and easy victory the freedom of the rest of the world would be lost." The Morgan partners therefore had "agreed that we should do all that was lawfully in our power to help the Allies win the war as soon as possible." That thought, he said, was "the fundamental idea underlying everything that we did from the beginning of the struggle till the Armistice of November 1918." Why did the United States eventually become a belligerent? "Germany drove the United States into the war by a series of insults and injuries, resulting in the loss of many American lives, any one of which injuries might have proved a cause of war had the United States not been so desirous of maintaining peace."

Morgan's statement did not satisfy the committee, for the senators wanted to know if his company out of affinity for the Allies or for its own advantage had prompted changes in President Wilson's policies which they suspected had drawn the United States closer to the war. Two happenings in particular, one in 1914 and another in 1915, sparked their interest. After letting investment bankers know in August 1914 that they should arrange neither loans nor credits to belligerents, Wilson two months later had given his consent to an extension of credits to the warring governments. Did Wall Street have a hand in persuading Wilson to make that change in his loan-credit policy? Conceding that there was no essential difference between loans and credits, only a technical one, J. P. Morgan denied any part in bringing the change, and the committee could produce no documents to contradict him. The second happening had occurred in August 1915 when the Morgan firm, which over the previous six months had supported the pound sterling in the international monetary market, withdrew support. The price of sterling plunged, and British purchases of American munitions, materials, and foodstuffs—purchases which in the past year had touched off an economic boom in the United States—seemed threatened. Whereupon Wilson revised his policy and sanctioned loans to belligerents (i.e., allowed bankers to float Allied securities in the United States), the pound recovered, and America's prosperity bounded forward. Did Morgan withdraw its support of sterling in August 1915 for the purpose of compelling the President to permit loans? No, the Morgan partners insisted. And again the committee had no documents with which to counter their denial.

If Morgan and other investment bankers had not conspired to persuade Wilson to pursue policies which in the Nye Committee's view had compromised America's neutrality and tended to draw the country in the war on the side of Britain and France, did not extensive trade with the Allies produce that result? In the words of Senator Vandenberg, "everybody that worked in one of these munitions plants was monetized, directly or indirectly, and all of these people [who] . . . had come to a realization of the tremendously important factor that this war trade was upon our economy had a sense of monetization."

In support of the view that trade with the Allies in 1914–1917 had weakened the determination of Americans and their leaders to stay neutral, the committee cited statements by a string of participants in the events of 1914–1917. After a conversation with Wilson's adviser, Edward M. House, in 1916, the German ambassador had reported House as saying that the President had lost the power to coerce the British because "American commerce was so completely tied up with the interests of the Entente that it was impossible for Wilson to disturb these commercial relations without calling forth such a storm of protest on the part of the public that he would not be able to carry out his intention." Britain's wartime Prime Minister David Lloyd George had recalled after the war that trade with the Allies "had its influence in holding back the hand of the American Government whenever excited to intense irritation by some new incident of the [British] blockade, it contemplated retaliatory measures." In his book *France and America,* Andre Tardieu, French High Commissioner in the United States in 1917–1918 and later the Premier of France, had written that on becoming economically bound with

Britain and France "the victory of the Allies became essential to the United States." More interesting was a cable to the State Department from the American ambassador in London, Walter Hines Page, dated March 5, 1917, claiming that the Allied financial situation was so desperate that termination of purchases in America was imminent. "This will, of course, cause a panic in the United States." Believing the crisis to be "too great and urgent for any private agency to meet," Page reported that only assistance by the government in Washington could save the situation. But such assistance presented a problem, inasmuch as the American government, as a neutral, could not legally aid belligerents, or as Page put it: "Unless we go to war with Germany, our Government, of course, cannot make such a direct grant of credit." He concluded that "perhaps our going to war is the only way in which our present prominent trade position can be maintained and a panic averted." Alas, there was no proof that President Wilson had read the Page cable, and the Nye Committee found not a shred of evidence indicating that Wilson had given even passing thought to economic considerations in taking the United States to war on the side of the Allies.

With its frequent suggestions that Wilson in 1914–1917 had fashioned policy for the benefit of the Allied powers while proclaiming neutrality, the Nye Committee meanwhile was stirring the anger of many Democrats for whom the wartime President remained a symbol of forthrightness and integrity. Indeed two Democratic members of the committee, George and Pope, had made themselves conspicuously absent during most of the interrogation of the Morgan partners. Then, on January 15, 1936, the committee considered evidence, circumstantial but persuasive, that before America's entry in the war Wilson had known of the secret treaties by which the Allies had agreed to a division of spoils, should they win the war. It also showed that Wilson and Secretary of State Robert Lansing in 1919 had told the Senate Foreign Relations Committee that they had not learned of the secret treaties until after the war. That discrepancy prompted Nye to remark that "both the President and Secretary Lansing falsified concerning this matter."

Wilsonians erupted. Tom Connally of Texas told the Senate: "I do not care how the charges were made; they are infamous. Some checker–playing, beer–drinking, back room of some low house is the only place fit for the kind of language which the Senator from North Dakota, the Chairman of the Committee, this Senator who is going to lead us out toward peace, puts into the *Record* about a dead man, a great man, a good man, a man who when alive had the courage to meet his enemies face to face and eye to eye." On January 17 Carter Glass of Virginia spoke out. Every seat on the Democratic side of the aisle in the Senate chamber was occupied, a large delegation of House Democrats was on hand, the galleries were filled. "From time to time," he rasped, "it has been suggested in the newspapers that the members of this committee were going to present the country shocking revelations. It remained until day before yesterday to present anything of a shocking nature; and that was the unspeakable accusation against a dead President—dirtdaubing the sepulcher of Woodrow Wilson." Of the committee's suspicion that Wall Street had influenced the wartime President, he shouted: "Oh, the miserable demagogy, the miserable and mendacious suggestion, that the house of Morgan altered the neutrality course of Woodrow Wilson." Pounding his desk until blood appeared on his knuckles, Glass concluded: "Now, Mr. President, lest I should infringe those rules which I always obey, perhaps I should better desist, because what I feel like saying here or anywhere else to the man who thus insults the memory of Woodrow Wilson is something which may not be spoken here, or printed in the newspapers, or uttered by a gentleman." Democrats were jubilant. They cheered and whistled and clapped, although one commentator later reported that it had been unclear whether Glass, a long-time friend of banking interests, was "more wroth for Morgan alive or Wilson dead."

Whatever his motives, Glass had signaled the sentiment of most Democrats when he promised that he would not vote another dollar to a committee whose members were "so insensible to every consideration of decency" that they would "bitterly assail two dead men who are honored by this entire Nation." And that was bad news for the Nye Committee, which was out of money and could not continue its inquiry without a new appropriation. To enable it to complete investigations in progress and prepare a report the Democratic majority in the Senate relented to the extent of voting a final $7,369, but the committee had to abandon long-range plans, and at 4:00 P.M. on the afternoon of February 20, 1936, Chairman Nye let his gavel fall and adjourned the munitions hearings for the last time.

From the vantage point of the writer of history it is too bad that the hearings did not end on February 5, the day the committee concluded its interrogation of the Morgan partners. When that interrogation had begun a month before, it seemed that the Nye Committee, out of the public eye for the better part of a year, was back on the main track and operating under a full head of steam. The outcome, the committee obviously anticipated, would be such popular support that the Senate, however grudgingly, would appropriate funds to enable it to continue and enlarge its investigation. But the documents and testimony did not prove sufficient to keep the steam pressure up; Connally and Glass threw obstacles on the track. And so it was that newsmen and photographers recorded the scene of February 5. There was Senator Nye, tired and discouraged if managing a weak smile, admitting forthrightly (and Nye was a forthright man) that his committee had proved nothing to the discredit of Morgan and his banking house in ten days of hearings on the firm's wartime and postwar operations. Then there was J. P. Morgan, jr., his briar pipe billowing smoke, his face beaming. Shaking hands with Nye, the titan of Wall Street said: "I have had a fine time; I would not have missed this investigation for the world."

IV

Investigations by committees of the United States Congress in the twentieth century have achieved varying historical reputations. Such inquires as those managed by Ferdinand Pecora in 1933–1934 and Harry S. Truman in 1941–1944 have received high marks as investigations conducted with a high sense of responsibility and in the best interests of the republic. Other inquiries, *e.g.*, the search for subversives by committees and subcommittees headed by the likes of Martin Dies and Joseph R. McCarthy, are generally viewed as deplorable exercises in demagoguery—or latter-day witch hunts

—fueled by popular hysteria resulting from frustration and warped under-
standings of national problems and ailments.

The Nye Committee inquiry of 1934–1936 has tended to fall in the second
category. The historian Arthur S. Link has written that the committee did not
conduct "a restrained inquiry but rather a ruthless investigation." In the view
of Dexter Perkins the munitions inquiry reinforced "the thesis that American
entry into the [World] War was the work of wicked Wall Street bankers, aided
and abetted by sinister arms barons." According to Thomas A. Bailey, the Nye
Committee aroused Americans "over the wrong things, and this state of mind
contributed powerfully to the passage of the heads-in-the-sands neutrality
legislation of the 1930s." Richard W. Leopold has written that "with an
astonishing display of oversimplification and a remarkable disregard for
causality, the committee argued that the United States had entered the Great
War to protect the arms traffic and save the bankers." In Leopold's estimate the
result "was to stimulate the resurgence of isolationism." In his memoirs
former Secretary of State Cordell Hull wrote that "the Nye Committee aroused
an isolationist sentiment that was to tie the hands of the [Roosevelt] Administration just at the very time when our hands should have been free to
place the weight of our influence in the scales where it would count." Former
Senator and President Harry S. Truman recalled that "the Nye Committee,
which was backed by isolationists and 'America Firsters,' was pure demagoguery in the guise of a congressional investigating committee." And
America's first Secretary of Defense, James V. Forrestal, recorded in his diary
in 1947 that "the Nye Committee . . . was staffed by Communist attorneys
and . . . had much to do with the curtailment of our own armaments industry in the period 1936 to 1939."

According to the prevailing historical estimate then—or historical
indictment—the Nye Committee, encouraged by political leftists who despised the capitalist economic system, set about to prove that munitions
makers were merchants of death and that greedy titans of Wall Street, to save
their huge investments in an Allied victory, had maneuvered the United
States into the World War. On proving its central assumptions, the estimate
continues, the committee expected to give America a leftward push toward
socialism and secure passage of legislation to assure America's isolation in
the event of a new general war. To achieve its grand purpose, the committee,
under the relentless leadership of Chairman Nye, intimidated witnesses and
ran roughshod over the rules of evidence, i.e., conducted "a ruthless investigation." What was worse, the Nye Committee, if failing to move the country
to the left, succeeded in its purpose of stirring isolationist impulses and encouraging anti-militarism in the United States at a time when the American republic should have been standing forthrightly against the aggression
of Italy, Japan, and Germany.

Like other historical estimates, that pertaining to the Nye Committee
contains a measure of truth. But the estimate is faulty on several counts, and
the image of the munitions inquiry which results from it is transparently
distorted.

It is true that Engelbrecht and Seldes and the spokesmen (and spokes-
women) of those peace organizations who roused Americans against the
munitions industry were decidedly leftist in political orientation and viewed

the alleged evils of the arms trade as proof of the rottenness of capitalism. Still, the munitions investigation, particularly in its early stages, received support from quarters not usually considered radical. The *Wall Street Journal*, in September 1934, while defending the work of the Nye Committee, declared of the international munitions trade: "It is a vicious system which both admits and tempts men to the commercial development of bad blood among neighboring peoples." Several months later the *Chicago Journal of Commerce* contended that "history has shown that the activities of munitions makers in times of peace are an important cause of war."

As for the committee, Stephen Raushenbush and some members of the investigative staff, including Alger Hiss, were opponents of big business and probably viewed the munitions inquiry as an instrument for moving the American republic in the general direction of socialism. Then observers of the Washington political scene often labeled Nye as an agrarian radical, and Senator Bone had an obvious affinity for socialist ideas. But Senator Pope was nothing more leftist than a faithful adherent of the New Deal (and few historians of the present day are inclined to view the New Deal as particularly radical). Clark's views were rather ill-defined. Suspicious of big business, he nonetheless looked on economic change with misgiving. In the main, Clark was a caustic man still consumed with bitterness because Woodrow Wilson had snatched the presidential nomination from his father, Beauchamp "Champ" Clark, at the Democratic National Convention in 1912. The other three members of the Nye Committee—Barbour, George, and Vandenberg—were well to the right of the center of the American political spectrum.

What of the committee's recommendations and hearing room behavior? Did they betray a leftist bias? The Nye Committee made only two recommendations which one might consider radical or leftist—and in both instances the obvious goal was advancement of the cause of peace, not socialism. Over the dissent of three of its seven members the committee recommended nationalization of the munitions industry (as did legions of non-radical Americans in the 1930s) and supported the drastic Flynn Plan for eliminating large economic returns in time of war. Otherwise the questions asked and statements made by senators and staff members during hearings were remarkably free of anticapitalist overtones. Even Alger Hiss, about whose "dad-bum" questions Carter Glass later complained, was a model of restraint and propriety on the two or three occasions when he interrogated witnesses, and asked nothing which seemed intended to discredit America's economic and social system.

The contention that the Nye Committee sought to bind the United States to an isolationist foreign policy by proving that J. P. Morgan & Company had maneuvered the United States to war in 1917—and that it succeeded—is a more difficult proposition.

Certainly there is nothing to indicate that when the munitions investigation got underway in 1934 the senators or staff members viewed it as an instrument for prompting legislation committing the American republic to noninvolvement—or isolation—when other countries went to war. At that time, as mentioned, America's policy vis-à-vis belligerents was not a pressing issue. That Senator Pope, one of Capitol Hill's most outspoken proponents of collective security via cooperation with the League of Nations, was an active and enthusiastic member of the committee in the inquiry's early stages is illustrative of the fact that few if any people thought exposure of the merchants of death might have large implications regarding America's relations with belligerents. But then, in early 1935, such relations commanded new attention, and the Nye Committee at Roosevelt's curious behest set about to examine the question of neutrality. To that end it announced its intention to investigate economic influences on America's policies toward Europe's belligerents in 1914–1917. Before the committee could conduct those hearings, so matters turned out, Congress in August 1935 passed the Neutrality Act, an isolationist measure providing for a mandatory embargo on arms shipments to belligerents, authorizing the President to prohibit Americans to sail on belligerent ships, restricting use of American ports by belligerent submarines, and establishing the National Munitions Control Board to license exporters and importers of munitions. When interrogation of J. P. Morgan and his partners finally took place, in January–February 1936, neutrality again was front and center as an issue—because of the imminent expiration of the Neutrality Act of 1935—and it was apparent that the Nye Committee's majority (Bone, Clark, Nye, and Vandenberg) was counting on those hearings to strengthen arguments for a more stringent neutrality law when the existing act expired.

And so one comes to the question: In what measure was the munitions investigation responsible for the impulses which resulted in the isolationist neutrality legislation of the mid-1930s? A precise answer of course is impossible, but it is difficult to escape the conclusion that historians and other observers have exaggerated the Nye Committee's responsibility for the neutrality laws of 1935–1937.

The overbearing commitment of Americans to peace—the veritable obsession of many Americans with the idea of peace at almost any price—surely antedated the Nye Committee. The committee held no hearings and issued no manifestoes on the subject of neutrality before passage of the first Neutrality Act of the period, that of 1935, and it was news in August 1935 that war in East Africa was imminent, not any revelations or appeals by the Nye Committee, that triggered the activity on Capitol Hill which resulted in that neutrality legislation. Then the Neutrality Act of 1936, enacted after the committee's hearings on economic influences on foreign policy in 1914–1917—hearings which one might have expected to exert large influence on subsequent legislation—fell so far short of the goals of the so-called Nye-Clark Neutrality Bloc that for a time Nye and his cohorts considered a filibuster to prevent its passage. Still, the Nye Committee, when doing nothing at all with the question of neutrality and concentrating only on munitions makers, shipbuilders, and war profits, was stirring America's will to peace, and it was the will to peace which produced the neutrality legislation of 1935–1937. The publicity which they received in connection with the munitions inquiry, moreover, probably strengthened the appeals of Bone, Clark, Nye, and Vandenberg when they spoke out in behalf of the legislation of 1935 (although that publicity did not prove sufficient to carry their ideas in 1936).

Fortunately the "ruthless investigation" charge against the Nye Committee is more easily disposed of: it is categorically untrue. In the opening hearings in September 1934 the committee showed a lack of sensitivity for the requirements of diplomacy when it exhibited documents implicating several Latin American dignitaries and King George V of Great Britain in assorted munitions dealings. In December 1934 it irresponsibly intimated that Du Pont had taken a profit of 39,321 percent in connection with construction and operation of the Old Hickory smokeless powder plant in 1918. In February 1935 Senator Clark, in a moment of pique, exhibited an unauthorized State Department document, and in January 1936 Nye and Clark referred to a sensitive British memorandum of 1917 (which memorandum, more embarrassing to admirers of President Wilson than to the British, then found its way into the press, probably by way of a member of the committee staff).

Otherwise, the committee in its handling of documents displayed a surprising sense of responsibility and admirable restraint, the more so in view of the high emotional state of Americans at the time when they pondered munitions makers, war profiteering, and neutrality. Chastened by its indiscretions of September 1934, particularly that of bringing the name of the King of England into the hearings, the committee worked out an arrangement with the State Department when setting about to scour the files of J. P. Morgan & Company for evidence pertaining to Wall Street's relations with the Allied governments in 1914–1917 and any attempts by investment bankers to influence American policy: The Department would maintain custody of Morgan's files during their scrutiny by committee investigators and the committee would publish no document without a State Department stamp and release. When the committee, in January 1936, found interesting wartime correspondence in the files of the National City Bank, whose records were not covered by the foregoing agreement, Chairman Nye thought it appropriate to secure the State Department's approval before using the material. He behaved in similar fashion a short time later when investigators turned up sensitive documents in the files of Colt's Patent Fire Arms Company.

As for treatment of witnesses, the Nye Committee's behavior was generally exemplary. On occasion a question or comment by Senator Clark, who had a reputation for public rudeness, contained a barb, and occasionally Senator Bone's temper seemed to rise, as during the aforementioned exchange with William Shearer. But there were no personal attacks after the fashion of "Joe" McCarthy's denunciation of Brigadier General Ralph Zwicker in 1954, when McCarthy accused Zwicker of being ignorant and a disgrace to the military uniform, or Senator John McClellan's badgering of union officials in hearings a few years later. Queried by the author in the latter 1950s, such Nye Committee witnesses as Charles W. Deeds of Pratt & Whitney, William S. Carpenter of Du Pont, George Whitney and Russell C. Leffingwell of J. P. Morgan, and William Flook of New York Ship, writing in a latter-day climate of opinion hostile to the committee when it would have been credible to claim intimidation, were surprisingly uncritical of the committee's behavior in commenting on their appearances at the munitions hearings. Flook said simply that "my treatment by the Committee was entirely courteous and unobjectionable." During interrogation of J. P. Morgan and his partners the *Wall Street Journal* observed that "on the whole, the Committee has not been too flagrantly unfair to any of them, the senatorial point of view being what it is." The committee allowed witnesses to make statements and exhibit documents even faintly relevant to the inquiry, and gave them ample opportunity to defend or explain their actions. Indeed it tended to treat representatives of such corporate giants as Du Pont and Morgan with considerable deference.

Contrary to an impression implicit in most commentaries on the munitions investigation, Senator Nye, moreover, was a model chairman—in the hearing room and during the committee's executive sessions. As the Du Pont public relations department reported in a memorandum to the author in 1958, "the Senator did not carry his platform eloquence over into the hearing room, at least during du Pont's appearance. By comparison, his conduct of the hearings was restrained. . . ." In the hearing room Nye spoke infrequently. Sometimes he interjected a question or opinion, or made a statement, but only rarely did he cross-examine. On occasion he cautioned that the committee must defer judgment until all evidence was in. During a dispute between Raushenbush and Thomas W. Lamont over the cause of American entry in the World War he interrupted: "Let us have a little agreement here that before we undertake, as members of the committee, spokesmen for the committee, or as witnesses, to declare whether or not it was the submarine which got us into the war, or industry and business and banking, that we will take the record of the documents on the subject into consideration, and then after that record has been completed, we can all have our say as to what the real cause was." When J. P. Morgan insisted on presenting a statement at the start of his appearance before the committee, Nye permitted him to do so, then interjected: "Mr. Morgan, thus far I fail to see that this is in anywise responsive to the question that was asked. However we will not quibble about this. Proceed with your statement."

But alas, the Nye of the hearing room was not the Nye of the speaker's rostrum. In the hearing room the senator was a gentleman, courteous and restrained, cognizant of his responsibilities. When he sat down before a radio microphone or, better still, stood face-to-face before a throng of admiring partisans, he cast restraint and responsibility to the winds and became a raving demagogue. An audience in truth seemed to do for him what the magical potion did to Doctor Jekyll. To make matters worse, he repeatedly intimated in 1934–1936 that the munitions investigation had substantiated his heady and extravagant assertions about arms makers, war profits, and neutrality. In most instances that simply was not true. Thus Nye, the model chairman in the hearing room, sorely abused his responsibility as chairman of the committee by rhetorical pyrotechnics. More than that, he contributed to the Nye Committee's latter-day reputation for ruthlessness. At least that was the estimate of Raushenbush, who many years later proposed to this author that historians and other observers, not inclined to work their way through 13,750 pages of testimony and exhibits published by the committee, had taken note of the chairman's speeches and concluded that they were indicative of the way the committee functioned. What prompted Nye to Jekyll-Hyde behavior? Perhaps one of the new psycho–historians now coming into vogue can answer that question. Raushenbush found an explanation in a mixture of Nye's feelings of personal inadequacy and his love of the roar of the crowd. By launching oratorical broadsides against the Du Ponts and Morgans the senator could generate roars from his audiences which crowded out feelings of inadequacy and persuaded him that he was a man of importance and courage leading people in the good fight for peace.

Whatever its investigative restraint and hearing room demeanor, did the Nye Committee stay within the bounds of its authority as a legislative investigating committee?

As shown elsewhere in the present series of books, the investigative authority of Congress was established in the first years of the Republic, and received reinforcement six years before the Nye Committee began its investigation when the Supreme Court in a unanimous opinion ruled that "the power of inquiry—with process to enforce it—is an essential and appropriate auxiliary to the legislative function." According to the justices, "a legislative body cannot legislate wisely or effectively in the absence of information respecting the conditions which the legislation is intended to affect or change; and where the legislative body does not itself possess the requisite information—which not infrequently is true—recourse must be had to others who do possess it." In the view of Woodrow Wilson, writing in the 1880s, enlightenment in the interest of wise and effective legislation was not the only justification for congressional investigations: "It is the proper duty of a representative body to look diligently into every affair of government and to talk much about what it sees. It is meant to be the eyes and the voice, and to embody the wisdom and will of its constituents. Unless Congress have and use every means of acquainting itself with the acts and the disposition of the administrative agents of the government, the country must be helpless to learn how it is being served; and unless Congress both scrutinize these things and sift them by every form of discussion, the country must remain in embarrassing, crippling ignorance of the very affairs which it is most important that it should understand and direct."

At the time of the Nye Committee's investigation, then, nobody seemed to doubt that committees of Congress had authority to conduct inquiries—and had authority to subpoena witnesses and documents—to gather information required for legislative discussion, serve as a brake on the Executive branch of the government, and alert the country to abuses and dangers.

When the munitions investigation got underway in 1934, as mentioned, no political figure or other observer of national affairs spoke out that the Nye Committee might abuse its authority. Nor did the committee later come under criticism on the ground that it had violated that authority. Even Senators Connally and Glass, in their crude assault on Senator Nye in January 1936 for his remarks about former President Wilson, did not charge the committee with ignoring constitutional restraints on congressional investigations. In those frenzied times of New Deal activity, of course, committees of Congress were continually investigating this or that aspect of national affairs, and in light of the work of the assorted committees and subcommittees which had exposed Teapot Dome and Pecora's uncovering of the manipulations of Wall Street, congressional investigating committees stood in high repute as instruments for promoting the public good. Unlike in the 1950s, in the aftermath of the nefarious activities of "Joe" McCarthy, there was no large opinion that the activities of congressional committees ought to be curtailed.

In retrospect it seems fair to say that the Nye Committee functioned in accord with the constitutional prerogatives of congressional investigating committees, and one might add parenthetically that Senator Nye and his colleagues never trampled on the constitutional rights of witnesses as subsequent congressional investigating committees were accused of doing. As if guided by the Supreme Court's opinion of 1927, the committee in every aspect of its investigation sought to prepare a foundation for possible legislation. In its study of the munitions industry it hoped to determine the desirability of nationalizing the munitions industry, and if a majority of the committee was persuaded in advance of the desirability and was seeking reinforcement of arguments in favor of nationalization, the committee in no way obstructed evidence and testimony supporting arguments against nationalization. In its inquiry of the shipbuilding industry the committee tried to determine if shipbuilders, in addition to being guilty of a variety of sins attributed to other producers of armament, required stricter control, via legislation, to prevent such abuses as collusive bidding for naval contracts. In its study of war profits the committee sought to determine what—if any—legislation should be enacted to restrict economic returns when America was at war, and to that end accepted arguments which opposed as well as supported its own views. In its investigation of economic circumstances surrounding America's entry in the World War in 1917 the committee contributed to the current congressional debate over neutrality legislation. One may add that the Nye Committee seldom if ever strayed from its legislative purpose. Documents exhibited and questions asked consistently seemed intended to enlighten Congress and the public about conditions which might require legislative attention, and in many instances sought to elicit information and ideas on the specifics of possible congressional enactments.

The Nye Committee, however, may have stretched its mandate under S. Res. 206.

The resolution clearly authorized investigation of the munitions industry and war profits, and it would seem that the authority to study the munitions industry gave the senators latitude to examine all aspects of naval shipbuilding. Whether it sanctioned the study of financial relationships and neutrality is questionable. Chairman Key Pittman of the Foreign Relations Committee certainly thought neutrality outside the Nye Committee's authority, and early in 1935 Senator Vandenberg, a sort of Midwestern windbag in the view of some people, but a man who during the munitions inquiry distinguished himself by judicious comments and questions, said that war profits were the only part of the neutrality question within the committee's jurisdiction. But the committee majority, citing Roosevelt's suggestion that the committee consider neutrality, determined to press on; and, on beginning the interrogation of the Morgan partners in January 1936, Chairman Nye quoted from S. Res. 206, including that passage authorizing the committee to investigate "the methods used in promoting or effecting the sale of arms, munitions, or other implements of war." He explained that "our investigations have shown us that, prior to our entry into the World War, a great deal of the sale, distribution, export, and also financing of arms and munitions of war was put into the hands of a few of our banking organizations." Thus it was "in accordance with this duty laid upon us that we propose during the course of the next days to examine into and secure information from witnesses regarding the matters which we were directed to investigate in this paragraph which I have just read." Whatever the merits of Nye's logic, nobody challenged the committee's authority to conduct that aspect of its inquiry, perhaps because there was so much interest in the question of the investment bankers and neutrality in 1914–1917, the more so in light of the debate on neutrality legislation then underway on Capitol Hill.

V

How does one, finally, assess the work of the Nye Committee? From its own perspective the committee must have viewed the munitions investigation as having come to little. Congress did not even consider, much less vote, nationalization of the arms industry, passed no legislation to restrict profits in time of war, and ignored two bills urged by the committee to prevent collusive bidding and limit profits by private shipbuilders on naval contracts. If Congress approved isolationist neutrality legislation, it turned aside the committee's contention that, when a neutral country becomes "an auxiliary arsenal" for foodstuffs and other nonmilitary supplies as well as arms for one set of belligerents (as the United States had become for the Allies in 1914–1917), it inevitably becomes an object of the military and naval strategy of the other belligerents—and when this happens any "neutral's" eventual involvement in the war becomes a virtual certainty. The neutrality laws passed during the period, as a result, were not as inclusive (or isolationist) as the committee majority thought they should be. About all the Nye Committee could show for its efforts, so the senators must have thought, was establishment of the National Munitions Control Board, an innocuous agency to watch over the arms trade (included in a provision tacked on to the Neutrality Act of 1935); a provision in the Neutrality Act of 1936 prohibiting loans to belligerents (already prohibited for most practical purposes under the Johnson Debt Default Act of 1934); and a provision in the Relief Appropriation Bill of 1935 that "no part of the appropriation shall be expended for munitions, warships, or military or naval matériel."

As matters turned out, however, the Nye Committee may have registered some achievements not readily apparent at the time. It inadvertently debunked a couple of notions which were distracting Americans in the mid-1930s: the proposition that American arms makers were part of an international munitions conspiracy, and that Wall Street had engineered America's entry in the World War. If Americans still faced the agonizing question of their place in world affairs—particularly their responsibilities when aggressor states went on rampages—they could face that question without having their thoughts muddled by arguments about merchants of death and Wall Street manipulations. It may then be that the committee's study of war profits, which touched the larger issue of wartime mobilization, saved the American people a great deal of money in the Second World War. The first federal price administrator during the War, Leon Henderson, at any rate thought it did. Henderson wrote the author in 1962 that "undoubtedly the Nye Committee findings helped us at OPA [the Office of Price Administration]. . . . I cannot put a dollar value on them—tho it was *high*."

Against its achievements or credits one of course must balance the Nye Committee's debits, notably its contribution to America's isolationist mood of the 1930s—assuming that isolationism was bad for the country and for the world at *that* time. Whether the committee's credits outweigh its debits will remain a matter of individual judgment.

"THE MARINE FOLLIES: GLORIFYING THE DANCE OF DEATH INSPIRED BY FANATICS WHO WORSHIP SELF-INFLICTED TORTURE" BY WILLIAM B. SHEARER 1935

Alleged Activities at the Geneva Convention: Hearings before a Sub-committee of the Committee on Naval Affairs, United States Senate, 71st Congress, 1st Session; pursuant to Senate Resolution 114, Appendix, 588–91.

In North Africa there lives a weird sect of people who believe in self-inflicted torture of many forms, including driving nails into their heads.

In North America a corresponding sect of people live that outdo their weird brothers; having completely lost their heads, they drive nails in their commercial coffin and inflict their punishment on the entire Nation.

Little children are taught how America was discovered by ships furnished by Spain, and then how America was lost to Spain through a new sea power, England. Then the English sea power defeated Holland and annexed her colonies. In turn the British defeated France and annexed all of North America east of the Mississippi. Then came the revolution, the battle of Lake Champlain, and the surrender of Burgoyne's army, followed by the battle of Yorktown, a victory of French ships under Admiral De Grasse who outwitted the British and cut the communications of Cornwallis which caused his surrender.

Shortly after the United States became a Nation.

In 1799, France seized our merchantmen, and our new Navy conveyed our ships and captured French cruisers, which forced Napoleon to make a new treaty of peace with us.

Several years later we defeated the Barbary pirates that had for centuries preyed on the commerce of all nations.

In 1812, when England began to seize American citizens from our merchant and naval vessels, we went to war, even though unprepared. We were blockaded and none of our vessels could appear on the Atlantic Ocean, forcing us inland to the Great Lakes. Here, Perry won his victory of Lake Erie. A year later, Macdonough won the second battle of Lake Champlain and forced the British Army into Canada. It was sea power that decided the war in our favor.

For 50 years afterwards, our clipper ships showed their heels to the world and carried 90 per cent of its commerce.

During the Civil War the north was able to blockade the south with over 250 ships, extending the blockade up the Mississippi River splitting the south in two. England reaped a harvest in the trade that gravitated to them by the

Civil War. England was quick to grant subsidies and build up a merchant marine of steel.

America turned toward the "Winning of the West" and left the sea, until we decreased in carrying commerce under the American flag from 90 per cent to 8 per cent.

In 1898, when the Spanish War came, we were without merchant ships to carry supplies or troops to our little army in Cuba and the Philippines. After the Spanish War, we brought back our troops in Spanish merchant ships that we had to charter. Secretary of the Navy Whitney had given us a Navy, but how?

We had to send abroad to England and Scotland in 1885, and for 22 years thereafter, naval constructors for education, having no schools or colleges of naval architecture in the United States. Our first battleship *Texas* was designed by an Englishman. In 1900 no American-flag ship sailed from our shores to Russia, Sweden, Norway, Denmark, Netherlands, Italy, Hungary, Greece, or Turkey. Only two small sailing ships sailed for France and returned in ballast, another small ship for Belgium returning in ballast.

When President Roosevelt sent the fleet around the world in 1908, we were compelled to use foreign-flag merchant ships to carry fuel and supplies for our naval vessels. We had 8 auxiliary vessels and had to charter 50. In case of war, we could not charter those 50 ships. All this Roosevelt knew and tried to drive it home to the American people, but the people were not interested; we continued to trust to luck.

Then came the Great War: Our export trade paralyzed for lack of ships, great lines of full freight cars blocked all tracks from Jersey City to Philadelphia, cotton and other products piled high on every pier, business and farmers in the hands of the banks.

When, in 1917, we entered the war, our troops sailed under foreign flags. Then came a mad orgy of building ships (a $3,500,000,000 orgy); steel ships, wooden ships, concrete ships, cargo ships, tankers, transports, tugs, shipyards, towns, railroads, dockyards, piers, terminals, and warehouses. We ordered ships everywhere, even Japan and China. Everybody had a contract. Men who had never seen a ship—watchmakers and barbers—were put in charge of building. We gave prizes and played music to this carnival of waste and inefficiency.

Admiral Sims sailed to take command; it took weeks and months before we could send our Navy overseas. We were totally unprepared. Plans were laid to manufacture 16-inch projectiles for 14-inch guns, airplane parts too large for the crankcase, railroads built to forests to gather timber, shoes made of paper, and rubber coats without rubber; untold millions spent for manufacturing nitrate, still unmanufactured; almost a billion went into the air force which only produced corruption, inefficiency, and profiteering.

The enemy submarines were sinking up to 900,000 tons of ships a month. The universal cry was "ships." America got into its stride. It launched ships backwards, frontwards, and sideways; some with rivets and some without rivets. At last the Navy got under way. Benson, Pratt, Schofield, Taylor, Griffen, Earl, Palmer, and others went to the mat with Daniels. The Navy was moving; Rodman to the North Sea, the convoy system effective, Strauss laying mines. McAdoo sold bonds while the bands played Over There; an allied victory, the armistice, and the world safe for democracy. The cheering over, scandal and investigations held the stage. The Sims inquiry stripped to the waist, they went into battle—Sims, Plunkett, Grant, and Lanning. Sims told the American people: "We of the Navy have decided never to go into another war under the same conditions as we entered the last war."

Who was interested in that? The carnage was over. Plots and profiteering, secret treaties and graft, like the cost plus contracts 50–10–10, came to an end. America was rich, millionaires on every corner to cheer our boys transported home under foreign flags. As the poppies grew over the graves of our youth in foreign soil, envy, hatred, and greed flared up. America's power, prestige, and influence was the danger.

The United States Navy, true to tradition, had built a mighty fleet to make the world safe for democracy. But America had not reckoned with its host. In 1919 Lloyd George and others demanded our naval strength. Failing in Paris they moved their publicity and propaganda batteries to America. The new administration was carefully led up to a disarmament conference. This British made and laid plan was in the hands of Balfour; the infallible British had discovered our weakness—sentiment, idealism, and self. Our marionnette statesmen were dangled before the world; human nature was to be changed, inoculated with the godly impulse. "It is better to give than to receive." The made-in-England plan was executed, our Navy sacrificed, and against the practical expert naval advice.

A new, fanatical sect of pigmies had usurped power. Petted and flattered into the British plan, they have, since 1922, consistently driven British nails of steel into America's commercial coffin. As a further justification of their folly and self-inflicted torture, they have nailed for-sale signs on our institutions, colleges, schools, and homes. Souls for sale, birthrights for sale, and national honor for sale, subsidized and slave thinking, they kneel in Bowling Green, their faces turned east like their oriental brother, worshipping the son of a prophet whose far-reaching tentacles long ago stretched out over the entire Nation.

A gusher of doctrines and policies poured forth from this new minaret of the prophet, the chug of the motor is his master's voice, every purr and thud pours into his coffers golden bricks to lay new foundations. Like the Rhodes Carnegie Foundations, they are built to supplant the foundations of free and popular government. Modern Babylon welcomes the superpower whose edict made the hip-pocket flask and dope household words. Forty tongues are high in their praise as they peddle their poison ware to the slaves of self-inflicted torture. But invisible and supergovernments, like the Frankenstein monster, will destroy in time their creators who have intrigued against the National Government.

As years roll on the voice of the prophet grows stronger: "Go ye into the world and preach internationalism, but only for America; debt cancellation, but only for America; unrestricted immigration, but only for America; disarm on land and sea, but only for America; and return not until the spirit of nationalism and patriotism is crushed. I am the prophet so ordained to pour oil on the troubled waters. Under the banner of pink, red, and yellow, you, Judas, will carry on and you, too, Brutus, will destroy the exclusion law—it is so written."

Strange and weird sounds come from every corner—over the radio, from the phonograph in homes, meeting places, and every temple of amusement. The slave thinking and low mentalities are being charmed and covered with a veneer of Ethiopian and oriental culture to build a modern Babylon of every fabric but pride.

A once great maritime power now converted to liberalism of thought and international control has reached its height. The pigmies, the sycophants, and the parasites of pleasure have joined hands in a new dance of death and self-inflicted torture, spiking the guns of sacred inheritance that could destroy a false prophet and deaden the rumble of their oriental god, the tom-tom.

The strong men of brain and sinew who built America are cherished memories to the faithful. Their majestic granite and bronze images rest in Statuary Hall under the dome of the Capitol of the United States. The faithful worship at their immortal shrine and pledge fidelity and guard the flag they gave us to defend. This mecca of American pilgrimage is often desecrated and disturbed with jabbering men and cackling women inoculated with the seditious germ of internationalism. These hyphenated Americans, high in their praise of the sturdy nationalism of the British, French, Italian, and others, decry any attempt at national solidarity at home. The much-heralded nationalistic spirit of China and Mexico receives their active approval, while American patriotism and nationalism are fought. Thus the inconsistent and destructive doctrine of Moscow is guiding the hand that reaches for the lanyards that fly the American flag.

As this strange sect of fanatics guide and teach our children that Washington was wrong, the endowed institutes and leaders hammer at the shield of national honor, driving nails into Americanism. Every blow is aimed at our independence; blows that have never ceased their monotonous thud since 1774.

The same formula of death is given America that was given every other maritime power in the world.

The crucible that once produced red blood and sturdy hearts will surely produce a Paul Revere, sounding the alarm and riding like hell over these Babylonian architects who would take us from the sea, and molding the younger generation for the dance of death—a self-inflicted torture of driving seditious nails into the cross of national crucifixion.

STATEMENT OF BERNARD M. BARUCH BEFORE WAR POLICIES COMMISSION MARCH 6, 1931

War Policies Commission: Hearing before the Commission Appointed Under Authority of Public Resolution 98, 71st Congress, 2nd Session, 30–37.

I thank you, Mr. Secretary. Mr. Secretary, the subject is rather a wide one and a broad one. In order to save the time of the commission, I have had my remarks printed and have presented to each member of the commission a copy of them, so that you can follow me in the reading. From time to time as I go ahead with my statement, I am sure a great many questions will arise in your minds. May I ask if any questions do arise, that you make a note of them on your copy and let me finish first. Then I shall be glad to answer any questions that may occur to you or any individuals present. During the course of my statement, I may have to ask a substitute to help me read; because I have one of the prevalent colds that are so widespread just now, and it will either be Gen. Hugh Johnson, who was connected with the draft under General Crowder and who was really responsible for the smooth working of it and who afterwards was associated with me as a representative of the United States Army, or Mr. Herbert Bayard Swope, who was an assistant to the chairman during the war.

I take it that we are of the common belief that war ought to be avoided if possible, but that we must plan in such a way that, if war comes, we shall meet the enemy with our maximum effectiveness, with the least possible injury and violence to our people, and in a manner which shall avoid inflation and waste. Our plans should eliminate war profiteering and they ought to provide that each man, thing, and dollar shall bear its just proportion of the burden. They should be designed to avoid the prostrating economic and social aftermath of war and, finally, they should be laid with full recognition that modern war is a death grapple between peoples and economic systems rather than conflict of armies alone and to that end we should merit for industrial America something of what Field Marshal Von Hindenburg in his retrospect of the World War had to say of its efforts in 1918:

> Her brilliant, if pitiless, war industry had entered the service of patriotism and had not failed it. Under the compulsion of military necessity a ruthless autocracy was at work and rightly, even in this land at the portals of which the Statue of Liberty flashes its blinding light across the seas. They understood war.

I. Scope of Inquiry and Feasibility of Its Purpose

The principal requirements of your organic joint resolution are that you consider and report whether a constitutional amendment is necessary, (1) to authorize Congress to take private property for public use during war; (2) to remove the profits of war; (3) to equalize the burdens of war; and (4) to consider and report policies to be pursued in war.

The committee is not to consider conscription of labor.

For purposes of discussion I venture to paraphrase the subject of inquiry thus:

> A plan to mobilize effectively the resources of the Nation for war which shall eliminate war profiteering, prevent war-time inflation, and equalize war-time burdens.

I assume that, if a constitutional amendment is not necessary to this end, a recommendation of policies is nevertheless desired and also that such policies should provide for war profits at a lower rate than peace profits.

Since there was never a war without inflation, profiteering, and unequal burdens, the resolution seems a large order, but it is with no hesitation that I can say from our own experience in the World War and from methods that were actually in practice here at its close that the ends sought are possible of attainment and that means to those ends are simple. This is neither dream nor theory. I shall recommend no principle that was not in actual practice and accomplishment in 1918.

II. Requirements of Modern War

Prior to 1870 nations hazarded their existence in reliance on small fractions of their strength. In the Franco-Prussian War, Germany showed some dim conception of what she called the "nation in arms" by which was meant that, in war, her entire resources of men, money, and things should suddenly become a compact instrument of destruction. The true intendment of this conception was fully grasped by none of the belligerents in 1914 and became clearly apparent only in the last months of the World War.

What it really means is that in the next major conflict the entire population must suddenly cease to be a congeries of individuals, each following a self-appointed course and become a vast unitary mechanism composed, in our case, of some 125,000,000 corelated moving parts all working to the end of directing practically all our material resources to the single purpose of victory. Modern war requires that the full power of the Nation be exerted in the shortest possible time, not only to the violent beating down of the enemy by any destructive material force we can invent or use, but also to every process of slow and often insiduous economic strangulation and political isolation that we can devise and administer.

The battlefield effort (while now only a part of what we shall be called upon to do) has become of itself a monstrous thing. Twentieth century means of transportation, communication, and supply have made possible—and therefore necessary—the massing of men in numbers never before deemed possible. The accelerating progress of science has created destructive forces which require for their use or for defense against them the products of practically the whole of industry in quantities many times those required for the uses of peace. Thus war requires that, at the very moment when productive effort is deprived of millions of men for military service, the country's facilities for production must be speeded up to disgorge unprecedented volumes of supplies. Civilian morale becomes as important as military morale, and it is necessary to make this cosmic change with the least practicable interference with the normal life of the Nation. Furthermore, the increasing dependence of each principal nation on uninterrupted contacts with practically all other nations entails the necessity—for both offense and defense—of an economic strategy and an intense economic tactics which must include practically every other nation—hostile or neutral—in its far-flung application.

No such results as these are at all possible without a sanction, control, and leadership in industry sufficient to organize and deal with it as practically a single unitary system instead of a highly competitive community. Once this unity is attained, however, experience has shown beyond question that the mobilized industry of America is a weapon of offense or defense far more potent than anything the world has ever seen—more terrible, I think, than the mind of any man has ever imagined.

War on this vast modern scale, has hitherto so violently disturbed the pattern of the normal economic structure of belligerent nations that, regardless of the side with which rests military victory, the aftermath of struggle prostrates both the conqueror and the conquered. With these most serious considerations you must deal. They depend on principles which we seem loath even to talk about—much less to provide for. These principles, while generally conceded in a vague, uncomprehending way, are hardly understood at all. Yet they are of such sinister and overwhelming importance that the neglect of them is, in my opinion at least, one of the most threatening aspects of our governmental policy. From my experience I am convinced that it is quite possible to prepare, in peace, plans that will make the transition from peace industry to war industry with minimum disruption, to carry on the feverish industrial activity of war with the least possible harm to civilian morale, to accomplish all in the economic struggle that we shall ever need to accomplish and, even with all this, to lessen the destructive aftereffects of major conflict. It is for these reasons that I regard the work of this commission very seriously and that I am much gratified to be able to lay before it the results of the experience of the War Industries Board in the World War.

III. Preventing War Inflation

The following sequence has attended every major conflict in history:

(1) Shortages of services and things develop rapidly.

(2) Competitive bidding among the procurement agencies of Government and, in the last war at least, other procurement agencies, and for the civil population send all prices into a rapidly ascending spiral.

(3) Expenses of government multiply. The abnormal need for money requires vast issues of certificates of governmental indebtedness. The inherent threat of destruction of government impairs national credit. The combination of all these things rapidly debases the exchange value of money thereby still further increasing the prices of things. The consequent destruction of buying power in the markets of the world begins almost immediately to impair the economic strength of the nation in the conflict. This sapping of economic strength will, in future wars, be the determining cause of defeat. As

Ludendorf has so bitterly complained, his military front remained impregnable long after what he called "the home front" had crumbled. Destruction of civil morale defeated Germany.

This process intensifies as time elapses with the following inevitable results:

(1) Destruction of domestic morale through a just and bitter resentment by soldiers, their families (and indeed by all persons of fixed income) at the spectacle of grotesquely exaggerated profits and income to those engaged in trade or in services for sale in competitive markets and the constantly increasing burden of bare existence to all those who are not so engaged. This is the greatest source of complaint of "unequal burdens." The present demands for "equalizing burdens" and "taking the profit out of war" both go back to this single phenomenon of war inflation. There is no more important problem to solve—whether we consider it purely as a means to maintain the solidarity and morale of our people, or as the basis of our economic strength for war purposes, or to avoid war's aftermath of economic prostration, or on the broader grounds of humanity and even-handed justice.

(2) The inflationary process affords opportunity to individuals and corporations to reap profits so large as to raise the suggestion of complacency if not of actual hospitality toward the idea of war. That any human being could be persuaded, by prospect of personal gain, however magnificent, to invoke the horrors of modern war is almost unthinkable; nevertheless the certainty that war could never result in the enrichment of any man would give us all security and comfort.

(3) Inflation enormously increases the cost of war and multiplies burdens on the backs of generations yet to come. The war debt of the nation is necessarily incurred in terms of debased dollar values. In the inevitable postwar deflation the debt, of course, remains at the inflated figure. Thus the bonds that our Government sold in the World War for 50-cent dollars must be paid through the years by taxes levied in 100-cent dollars. For example, our total war expenditure was $39,000,000,000 incurred in terms of 1917, 1918, 1919, and 1920 dollars. In terms of the purchasing power of 1913 dollars it would have been only $13,000,000,000, or in terms of 1930 dollars probably not more than $15,000,000,000. Such a grotesque result would be almost unbelievable were the figures not living facts. If anything can be done to avoid this practical doubling of the economic burden of war, certainly we should spare no effort to accomplish it.

When we entered the World War, the frantic demands and uncoordinated counterbidding of our future associates in war had already distorted our own price structure out of any semblance of its normal scheme. In other words, there was a robust inflation here before we ever entered the war. Furthermore, nearly 12 months elapsed after our declaration before we had evolved controls and organization capable of coordinating our own and our associates' procurement activities and of controlling price. Notwithstanding this delay and the dimness with which controlling principles were at first perceived, we did, in 1918, arrive at a method which checked the process of inflation in America and kept it in check until all controls were released in November, 1918. It is to this experience that I refer when I say that we have proved in practice a method to control inflation. That proof convinces me that it would also prevent inflation if applied at once upon the advent of war and before the inflationary process begins.

To measure inflation of price and profit we must have some norm. The obvious norm is the whole price structure as it existed on some antecedent date near to the declaration of war on which the normal operation of the natural law of supply and demand can be said to have controlled price. That determined, we need a method of freezing the whole price structure at that level. The obvious way to do this is simple—by proclamation to decree that every price in the whole national pattern as of that determined date shall be the maximum that may thenceforth be charged for anything—rents, wages, interest rates, commissions, fees—in short, the price for every item and service in commerce.

In these few words reside the basic principle of war control of national industry and of the present suggestion for elimination of war inflation in America. The superficial objection is, "You propose to repeal the law of supply and demand." We may as well take this bull by the horns. In modern war administrative control must replace the law of supply and demand.

In the national pattern of peace, all economic forces are operating under the work-a-day influences of that natural law. Prices, production, and finance all are factors of competition—in other words, of that law. But in peace the various parts of what will eventually be the economic engine for war are neither coordinated nor subject to any single guiding control. Indeed, to prevent such combination and control is the basic effort of peace-time administration. "Competition is the life of trade."

Suddenly war appears. The whole tempo, volume, and quality of the force of demand becomes distorted. Things that yesterday were of no great importance (e.g., toluol, picric acid, and sodium nitrate) suddenly become the aim of all endeavors. As to these, as well as to all other fundamental commodities, there is an almost instantaneous shortage. Now, in peace-time shortage, the highest bidder takes all. That is the law of supply and demand. In war—at least in major modern war—we can not permit this. The Government must assume control of the whole supply and ration and apportion it—not to the longest purse but to the most necessitous use. Furthermore, the distinguishing characteristic of peace-time economic operation is competition, and basic prices are largely determined thereby. Also it is literally the object of one great competitor to secure as great a proportion of all business as possible. Under war conditions the entire process is reversed. There is more business than all the facilities of the country can handle. Competitors must become cooperators in order to meet the very minimum demand for shortage items. Control of this cooperation rests in government. Thus both because governmental determination (and not price) controls demand, and because only complete cooperation (and not competition) can produce supply in sufficient quantity, the law of supply and demand adjourns itself.

These principles apply to shortage items. The crystallized price structure is a schedule of maxima. Items in ample supply are left free to fall below the fixed price level.

Furthermore, this provision, which places control of and responsibility for supply of shortage items in the hands of Government by no means solves the shortage problem. Under the law of supply and demand rapidly increasing demand (and consequent rising price) is the force relied upon to provide increased supply. In war we can not wait for this and we can not stand the waste and confusion incident to it. We must use other means such as were very fully developed in 1918. By way of introduction let us name them:

(1) Elimination of waste, loss, and unnecessary accumulation through frantic competition by all procurement agencies, which elimination is achieved by a rigorous control and coordination of them and the funneling of all demand through one central control agency.

(2) Rationing and allocation of shortage items in order that more necessitous uses (such as equipment and supply of field armies) may have priority in time with careful provision against undue hardship to the civil population.

(3) Conservation, by which is meant: Standardization of type and design; elimination of any but necessitous uses; prevention of hoarding and accumulation; postponement of all deferrable uses thus increasing supply by sharply curtailing demand.

(4) Substitution—by which is meant substitution of items of greater availability for shortage items.

(5) Discovery of new sources of supply.

The resiliency of a great people like ours—their capacity to "do without" or adapt themselves to new conditions makes the potentiality of the above expedients very great. No one who has not seen these expedients in operation would be likely to imagine the vast quantities of essential commodities, power, storage space, transportation, money, and labor which can be made available in this way. An explanatory word as to some of these expedients may be in order. Conservation is among the most effective of war-time expedients. Multiplicity of type and design in almost every commodity of commerce wastes a vast amount of component material. Had the war gone on another year our whole civil population would have gradually emerged (as wardrobes and inventories became exhausted) in cheap but serviceable uniform. Types of shoes were to be reduced to two or three. The manufacture of pleasure automobiles was to cease. Flaps from pockets and unnecessary trim in clothing would have disappeared. Steel had already been taken out of women's corsets.

The conservation program was, of course, much broader than this. It affected practically the whole field of commodities. We had instituted a deferment of every type of building construction except that indispensable to the prosecution of the war. We had gasless, meatless, sugarless, fuelless days and in ways and methods too numerous to mention, we were greatly increasing the supply for essential use by cutting off supply for nonessentials.

Yet, after all these things are done there will remain unavoidable necessity for adjusting the crystallized price structure upward in individual cases. We always have low-cost producers and high-cost producers. War requires all producers. This presents the most difficult aspect of the problem:

If we raise the price sufficiently high to pay a reasonable profit to the high-cost producer we will thereby create inordinately high profits to the low-cost producer.

There are only two alternatives—create a system of bonuses to the latter class or limit, by an excess-profit tax, the return on invested capital to the former class. After exhaustive study during the war, the former method was considered impracticable and the latter was adopted. The most cogent objection to it is the great variety of accounting systems and the consequent confusion and opportunity to conceal profit. Due to the income tax and the increasing ownership by the public of the securities of great corporations accounting is now much simpler. Some of the difficulty still remains but it is a hindrance—not an insuperable obstacle.

Besides the necessity of revising some prices upward there will also be a variety of occasions for revising others downward. A method must be devised to adjust the initial frozen-price pattern to the changing situation.

We did this during the war by a price fixing commission, which reported directly to the President, who passed final judgment and announced the price. There was nothing in the experience of that commission to suggest that a similar system would not be entirely effective in the future.

The frozen pattern of price will also have to be protected against the situation in export trade. If, as is almost certain, the inflationary process is in operation in the rest of the world, means will have to be applied to prevent extravagant foreign prices from upsetting our domestic schedule. Government, in its world economic strategy, must have almost plenary control over foreign trade. We shall see the agency for such control purchasing for export at the controlled domestic price, selling in export at world price and using the profit to buy necessitous imports at inflated world prices and sell to domestic needs at the controlled schedule.

Of course, the bases of the present suggestion is price fixing. The student of the economic history of war will say, "There is nothing new about this. Every nation with a debased currency has tried to force exceptance of it at a fiat figure. None ever succeeded."

One did succeed. It was the price-fixing policy of the World War. The distinction between that and previous attempts was that, for price fixing in 1918, the whole of industry was mobilized and under control of government in a sense never even imagined in any other country or in any other war. This I shall later demonstrate. Another distinction between all previous attempts with which I am familiar (including that of the World War) and the present suggestions is that what is here proposed is that we apply the organization and methods developed in 1918—not after rampant inflation has run away with our economic structure—but at the very outset.

As illustrative of these distinctions, New York, in the Revolution (1 Cook's New York Laws 1780, p. 210) enacted a law by which the profits of manufacturers, wages of mechanics and laborers, and the prices of a long list of commodities were fixed at a figure "not to exceed twentyfold of the prices paid in 1774"—the latter date was taken as reflecting the normal operation of the law of supply and demand and the "twentyfold" as measuring the debasement of the Continental currency. Here was an attempt to check inflation after it had occurred. The basic idea is the same as the one here suggested, except that we now propose to check inflation before it occurs.

Similarly, in the 1917 food control act, profits in July, 1914, were set as the maxima for war-time profits of bakeries. The New York price fixing was a failure. The food control act succeeded. Why? The former was a fiat with no adequate means of enforcing it. The latter was backed by the whole system of licensing, commandeering, and regulating powers slowly evolved by our war administration.

A recreation of that administration at the very outset of another war would insure the success of the suggestions here advanced. . . .

SIR CHARLES CRAVEN TO HENRY R. CARSE
OCTOBER 30, 1932 AND JANUARY 6, 1933

U.S. Senate, *Munitions Industry:* Hearings Before the Special Committee Investigating the Munitions Industry, Part 1, Exhibits 22 and 23, 332–33.

Naval Construction Works
Barrow-in-Furness
30th October, 1932

Henry R. Carse, Esq.
President, Electric Boat Company
40 Wall Street, New York
Dear Mr. Carse:

Very many thanks for your telegram reading as follows: "Referring to your letter of the 17th inst., we (I) accept your proposal."

I arrived back from Madrid yesterday and at once called at the admiralty. While I have been away, a good deal of technical information has been made available for my people, so I hope in a week or so to be able to requote. As a matter of fact, I should probably have quoted sooner but the director of contracts is away and I want to hand my figures in to him personally. I think the position will turn out as follows:

(1) We shall receive a firm contract for one submarine about the third week in November.

(2) At the same time we shall receive a letter telling us that the admiralty accept our price for the second submarine on the distinct understanding that if any circumstances arise between now and say March 1933 they can have the right to cancel the second one without any payment.

All that you and I gain by the transaction will be that we shall know that if the ship is built Vickers will get the order. If, on the other hand, Geneva or some other fancy convention decide that large submarines have to be abolished, no definite contract will be placed and the admiralty can retire gracefully without having to pay us anything. I cannot, of course, commence spending any money until say March, but, at any rate, our competitors will not receive the enquiry.

I much appreciate the prompt way you have met my request and all I can do now is to hope that we shall both have good fortune.

I had a very interesting visit to Spain. It was chiefly in connection with a large sum of money owing to my company by the sociedad. The political situation in Spain seems very confused but there seems a considerable prospect of our friends receiving orders for small craft on the pretext that they are purely defensive.

With all good wishes.

Yours very sincerely,

C. W. *Craven*

Naval Construction Works
Barrow-in-Furness
6th January, 1933

Henry R. Carse, Esq.
Electric Boat Company
40 Wall Street, New York
My Dear Mr. Carse:

You will be glad to know that I have now received a letter from the admiralty, saying that the contract for the H.M.S. *Severn* (the *Thames* repeat) will be placed with us, and I expect to receive it within a few days time. Immediately I do, I will credit your account here with the sum of $7,500 and send you a cable.

At the same time, the admiralty also promise us the order for H.M.S. *Clyde* (another repeat of the *Thames*), but in this latter case they will not give us a contract until after the end of March. In other words, they will have the right to withdraw their promised order for the second ship if Geneva or any other troublesome organization upsets the large submarine. In view of this, I am not saying anything publicly about the *Clyde*, and I would suggest that it would be wise that Spear should not let the information get into the hands of our Navy Department until after I can tell you that we really have a proper contract. Cammell Lairds will get the two small S boats. On the whole, I am very pleased, because it is impossible in these days of starvation of shipbuilding to get all the submarine orders.

With every good wish for 1933.

Yours very sincerely,

Charles W. Craven

"ARMS AND THE MEN"
MARCH 1934

Fortune, March 1934; reprinted in *Congressional Record,* 73rd Congress, 2nd Session, 3785–91.

(A primer on Europe's armament makers; their mines, their smelters, their banks, their holding companies, their ability to supply everything you need for a war from cannons to the casus belli; their axioms, which are (a) prolong war, (b) disturb peace.)

According to the best accountancy figures, it cost about $25,000 to kill a soldier during the World War. There is one class of big business men in Europe that never rose up to denounce the extravagance of its governments in this regard—to point out that when death is left unhampered as an enterprise for the individual initiative of gangsters the cost of a single killing seldom exceeds $100. The reason for the silence of these big business men is quite simple: The killing is their business; armaments are their stock in trade; governments are their customers; the ultimate consumers of their products are, historically, almost as often their compatriots as their enemies. That does not matter. The important point is that every time a burst shell fragment finds its way into the brain, the heart, or the intestines of a man in the front line, a great part of the $25,000, much of it profit, finds its way into the pocket of the armament maker.

The problem of European armaments is complex: If we are to get anywhere with it we must first park our emotions outside. Pacifists and militarists alike have indulged in a good deal of loose talk on the subject. Most pacifists are not sufficiently informed; their arguments and accusations frequently boil down to nothing more substantial than Sir Arthur Eddington's definition of the Quantum theory, that is, "Something unknown is doing we don't know what." Most militarists are insincere.

Furthermore, American business at its biggest and most secretive is today an open book compared with any European big business. Therefore what Fortune does not know about this subject would fill many a volume. But what Fortune does know is worth knowing; it is set down herein, not as argument or invective but as elementary data. Some time, not too far distant, Fortune hopes to inaugurate a greater campaign on this subject; let this article, then, be considered as no more than an opening gun.

Anyone who talks about European armaments and their makers must inevitably oversimplify. But to oversimplify is not to overgeneralize—and we should start by ridding ourselves of one generality that will give us trouble as long as it stays in our heads.

There is nothing that could, in any strict accuracy, be called an "armament ring" in Europe today. There is no perfectly homologous group of single-purposed individuals that sits down before a polished table in a soundproof room and plots new holocausts in Europe. Search through the armament makers as you will, you will find neither a Machiavelli nor a Dr. Fu Manchu. But that's all you won't find.

For without a shadow of a doubt there is at the moment in Europe a huge and subversive force that lies behind the arming and counterarming of nations: there are mines, smelters, armament works, holding companies, and banks, entangled in an international embrace, yet working inevitably for the destruction of such little internationalism as the world has achieved so far. The control of these myriad companies vests, finally, in not more than a handful of men whose power, in some ways, reaches above the power of the State itself. Thus, French interests not only sold arms to Hungary in fiat violation of the Treaty of Trianon, but when Hungary defaulted on the bill the armorers got the French Government to lend Hungary the money to pay the French armorers. Thus, too, the great Czechoslovakian armament company, controlled by Frenchmen, promoted the rise of Hitler in Germany and contributed millions of marks to Hitler's campaign. These same Frenchmen own newspapers that did more than any others to enrage France against Hitler. It is time we had a dramatis personæ of arms, and the men.

Krupp

Best known armament name in all the world is perhaps the name of Krupp. The Krupp who, despite early discouragements at the hands of his own government, built up the gigantic works at Essen and made his name a synonym for cannon was Alfred—a strange figure who wore wooden sabots when he visited his factory, opened the windows of his house only once a month, had a bathtub in his parlor, assembled his intimates in his home every few weeks to be weighed, for no discoverable reason, on scales of his own devising, and carried a steel walking stick. Alfred Krupp began as a humble petitioner of governments, coming hat in hand to ministers, kings, and emperors of assorted nationalities to beg orders for his guns. By the time of his death he was an intimate of Wilhelm I, the 1870 conqueror of France. He was also an officer of the French Legion of Honor (one of Napoleon III's earlier generosities) and a Knight of the Russian Order of Peter the Great. Under his son, Friedrich Alfred Krupp, the house rose to higher and higher glories. Yet Friedrich Alfred failed in one important respect: he left no male heir to carry on. It took Kaiser Wilhelm II to solve this difficulty. When big buxom Bertha, Friedrich Alfred's daughter, came of marriageable age Wilhelm II betrothed her to the protégé of his own selection and training, Gustav von Bohlen und Halbach—and it was the groom, not his bride, whose name was changed by the betrothal. He became then Krupp von Bohlen und Halbach. Under this new head of the house, who took command in 1909, Krupp went further still, supplied 52 countries with arms before the war, and stood all but single-handed against the world during it.

What of Krupp now? In theory, Krupp smelts only peaceful ore, and forges its steels only into such benign shapes as locomotives, rails, bridge girders, and others purely industrial. Actually, Krupp is rearming Germany—the discoverable portion of whose annual armament bill is now about $80,000,000. Germany, forbidden by the Treaty of Versailles to import armaments, receives generous supplies from Sweden (where Krupp controls the armament firm of Bofors) and Holland; forbidden to export armaments, she ships to South America, the Far East, or to any European nation that will violate its own treaty by ordering from her. Yet for all the might of the Krupp works we must look elsewhere today to find the real heart of the armament business.

Bethlehem Steel et al.

To the United States, perhaps? After all, we have our Du Ponts, who at least own the State of Delaware. We have an Army and Navy whose officers, according to the statement of a former Cabinet officer, are far and away more active than the officers of any other armed forces in the world against any sort of international understanding. We have an armament bill of over $200,000,000 a year. (When we say armaments we mean here, and hereafter, only the actual implements and materials of war—cannon, guns, ammunition, tanks, military aircraft, and naval vessels.) We once had our big bass drum, Mr. William B. Shearer, whose boast was that he wrecked the Naval Conference at Geneva in 1927. We have our Midvale Co. (controlled by the Baldwin Locomotive Works) which prospered mightily during the war and has continued the manufacture of guns and gun forgings, armor plate, and projectiles; our Colt's Patent Firearms Manufacturing Co., which supplies machine guns as well as squirrel rifles, which declared an extra dividend in 1933; our Remington Arms Co. (controlled by Du Pont) whose output of firearms and ammunition together is one third of United States production. And we have our Bethlehem Steel Co.

Bethlehem's Mr. Charles M. Schwab dismayed the cadets of West Point in 1927 by saying: "Today the Bethlehem Steel Co. has definitely abandoned any thought of ever again engaging in the manufacture of ordnance except in times of great national emergency." Such times are apparently with us now—have, in fact, been continually with us since Mr. Schwab unloosed this shaft of oratory. In the official listing of Bethlehem's products (you need only turn to Standard Statistics or Bethlehem's own most recent annual report) you will find armor plate, projectiles, gun and shell forgings, battleships, battle cruisers, scout cruisers, destroyers, submarines, and airplane carriers all listed as products of Bethlehem's plants. The site at Bethlehem where cannon and armor plate are made is separate from the rest of the plant. No outsiders are allowed, and it may be that Mr. Schwab has never been able to evade the vigilance of his watchmen. But if he could once get inside he would see a triumph of inventiveness—for Bethlehem not only makes armor-piercing projectiles, but nonpierceable armor plate—which must sometimes cause slight confusion on the proving ground when anyone attempts to demonstrate the virtues of both at the same time.

Our own country is not, then, quite so virginly innocent in this business as we might like to suppose. But despite the size of our armament bill and our armament and munitions exports to South and Central America and the Far East, we are essentially small fry in this game.

England's Vickers-Armstrongs

Much larger fry is England, where the firm of Vickers-Armstrongs is the brightest star in the armament firmament. The annual bills of Vickers-Armstrongs to nations for armaments purchased quite possibly amount to $100,000,000. For England's powerful position as one of the greatest exporters of the materials of war in the world, the bulk of the credit goes to Vickers-Armstrongs. It makes other things than armaments, true enough; such unwarlike products as sewing machines and golf clubs come from some of its factories. But its chairman, General the Honorable Sir Herbert Lawrence, G.C.B., one-time Chief of Staff of the B.E.F., has put himself on record as saying, "Vickers-Armstrongs, Ltd., relies very largely on armament orders for its existence." The Vickers research staffs work constantly to bring into mass production such bolsters to international comfort as the Vickers-Carden-Lloyd light amphibious tank, or the Vickers Vildebeest bombing machine.

The sun never sets upon Vickers. It has its factories in Rumania where, for greater convenience, Sir Herbert Lawrence is a director of the Bank of Rumania (and Vickers to some degree allies itself with the Czechoslovakian armament firm of Skoda). In Italy it latinizes its name to Società Vickers-Terni; in Japan it has as a subsidiary the Japan Steel Works, and thus allies itself with the Japanese armament and industrial firm of Mitsui. There are Vickers factories or subsidiary companies in Spain, Canada, Ireland, Holland (The Hague affords an appropriate site for some of the Vickers operations), and New Zealand.

Vickers directors are men of wide affairs. Sir Herbert Lawrence, besides being a director of the Bank of Rumania, is also a director of the Sun Insurance Office, Ltd., with which Vickers-Armstrongs had a curious agreement that "if the profits [of Vickers] in any year during the 5 years ending December 31, 1932, do not amount to £900,000, then a contribution not exceeding £200,000 will be made in each year." Sir Otto Niemeyer, the infant phenomenon of British finance, who first entered His Majesty's Treasury at the age of 23, is another Vickers director; he is, in addition, an officer of the Bank of England, a director of the Anglo-International Bank and the Bank of International Settlements.

Through these industrial and financial interlockings Vickers-Armstrongs conducts its affairs. They are profitable affairs—for, as the agreement with Sun Insurance indicates, a profit of some $4,500,000 a year is considered so unsatisfactory that insurance must be carried against it. And England's aristocracy takes pleasure in clipping its coupons. Among the more prominent shareholders of Vickers or allied concerns in 1932 were: Rt. Hon. Neville Chamberlain, chancellor of the exchequer; Sir Austen Chamberlain, M.P., winner of the Nobel peace prize in 1925; and Sir John Simon, secretary of state for foreign affairs (but who sold out his shares last year). In 1914 the list was even more imposing. It included that lofty philosopher, Lord Balfour; that glittering snob, Lord Curzon; and also Lord Kinnaird, president of the Y.M.C.A; three bishops; and Dean Inge, of St. Paul's. It was in that same year that Socialist Philip Snowden spoke in Parliament: "It would be impossible to throw a stone on the benches opposite without hitting a member who is a shareholder in one or other of these firms."

You will gather that England, peace-loving England, has been quite some time at the task of building up this organization. She has. The firm began in 1829. Slowly throughout the nineteenth century the firm grew, changed its name, cast its outworn skins, grew fat, prosperous, and highly multicellular through the acquisition of this torpedo works, of that heavy ordnance factory. And then there came along Mr. Basileios Zacharias.

He is known today as Sir Basil Zaharoff. He was an intimate of Lloyd George during the war; a few relatively mild revelations of the degree to which he influenced Great Britain's armament, military, and foreign policies during and after the war were enough, in 1922, to send Lloyd George, who did more than any other man to win the war, out of office forever. This strange character, the greatest armament salesman the world has ever known, struck a major spark in the world when he collided with an American of somewhat similar interests. Zaharoff at that time was a salesman for the Nordenfeldt Guns & Ammunition Co., Ltd., of England, and had done very well in profits out of the perpetual dog fights in the Balkans and the Near East, to which he was usually purveyor, and of which he was frequently (it was an easy trick once he learned it) instigator. The American that gladdened his heart was Hiram Maxim, whose new machine gun was incomparably the best killing machine Zaharoff had ever seen. Zaharoff took Maxim to his bosom, with reservations. First he used his wily, polyglot salesmanship to block the gun's sale in Austria as an impractical toy; then, when he had offered Maxim a partnership and got the sale of the gun firmly in his own hands, he swept over Europe and Asia selling such quantities that soon the new firm of the Maxim-Nordenfeldt Guns & Ammunition Co. was purchased for some $6,000,000 (the year was 1897) by Vickers interests and became Vickers Sons & Maxim. Sir Basil was established now as a power in armament affairs, hence in Great Britain's affairs, hence in world affairs. He already enjoyed the distinction of having sold the first practical submarine ever used in naval operations to his native Greece, and the further distinction of having used this sale to frighten Turkey into buying two submarines. The Boer War added to his laurels; Boers shot Englishmen with Vickers guns and ammunition. The Russo-Japanese War provided him with an even wider field for his gifts; Vickers sold as much war material (and possibly more) to Russia as it did to Japan, England's supposed ally.

But naturally it was the World War that gratified Sir Basil most. The profits of war-time armament manufacture were practically incalculable; by the end of the war Sir Basil had a personal fortune that was estimated as low as $100,000,000 or $200,000,000 and as high as a billion; and in 1917, when there seemed a possibility of peace through the intervention of the United States, Lord Bertie, British Ambassador to France, naively recorded in his diary: "Zaharoff is all for continuing the war jusqu'au bout. . . ."

So much for Germany and her Krupp, the United States and Bethlehem Steel, England and Vickers-Armstrongs, and the now withered and senile Sir Basil. Do these armament businesses seem big business? Then you must alter your sense of proportion before you go further. All the foregoing is a mere curtain raiser to the big show. The big show is France.

Schneider-Creusot

France stands at the very top. She stands at the top in the amount her government spends on armaments; at the top in the amount of arms she exports to other nations; at the top also by virtue of the billion francs she has spent to build a military Chinese wall of forts, many of them underground, along her eastern boundaries. But these mere quantitative details do not reveal the true significance of her position.

She stands today as a queer paradox: France, the democracy, a quiet pasture land for the world's most famous peasantry, coexisting with France, the greatest military power of modern times, with an army which all but equals in number and far surpasses in equipment Germany's vast militaristic machine of 1914.

At the head of this latter France stands the figure of Gen. Maxime Weygand (vice president of the higher war council, inspector general of the army, possessor of the grand cross of the legion of honor, member of the French Academy), ruling an army (including colonials) of 650,000 men. But, despite his decorations, his medals, his orders, and the power he has, once a new war begins, to order several million men to death, General Weygand, a devout Catholic, represents not the urge for war but, on the contrary, France's desire for peace—by means of security. The French threat to the peace of the world lies elsewhere—in France. For in France, and only in France, a new situation exists: The armament makers are no longer, like Alfred Krupp or Sir Basil Zaharoff, in his younger days, humble petitioners of government, hat-in-hand solicitors of orders—their influence is so infiltrated into the industrial, social, and political affairs of the nation that they have power in some ways beyond the state; a power so mighty that they are all but able, for their own individualistic reasons, to sweep the state along in a course of action against its own will. They are all but anonymous, these men. They are displeased by publicity and are well able to enforce their displeasure. But we must now displease one of them and present the figure of M. Charles Prosper Eugène Schneider.

Charles Prosper Eugène Schneider is a man of many offices—the executive head of hundreds of armament firms throughout Europe.[1] He is the president of the Schneider-Creusot Co., armament manufacturers, with mines, smelters, and foundries scattered throughout France. He is director of the Banque de l'Union Parisienne, one of whose most profitable sources of business is the financing of loans for armaments. In 1920 he founded and became the president of the Union Européenne Industriale et Financière, a holding company capitalized at 140,000,000 francs. Through it Schneider-Creusot controls 182 French companies that manufacture heavy ordnance, machine guns, tanks, shells, ammunition, and warfare chemicals. Out of the $300,000,000, which at the most conservative guess represents the annual

[1] One independent armament firm is the Anciens Etablissements Hotchkiss & Cie, founded by Benjamin Berkeley Hotchkiss, American engineer and inventor of the Hotchkiss machine gun, born in Watertown, Conn., in 1826. British, French, and American capital are intermingled in the company now, but the managing director is a self-expatriated ex-ensign of the United States Navy, Laurence Vincent Benét, uncle of Stephen Vincent Benét, the poet. His American citizenship did not stop him from selling tons of guns and other war materials to Japan at the same time that Secretary of State Stimson was vainly trying to keep the Japanese out of Manchuria.

billing of France's armament concerns, Schneider-Creusot or subsidiaries takes the lion's share.

Czech's Skoda

But the Union Européenne has an even more important function. Through it Schneider-Creusot reaches out to control 230 armament and allied enterprises outside France. The greatest of these concerns is that glittering jewel in the crown of the principal ideal state that came into being in 1919 as the result of the self-determination of oppressed peoples. The State is Czecho-slovakia and its jewel is Skoda.

Skoda, although its main works are in Brno (which was once on Austrian territory), has factories scattered not only over Czechoslovakia but over Po-land and Rumania as well. Upon the board of Skoda, which the Union Européenne controls through 56 percent of its stock, M. Schneider sits with his friend André Vicaire, director general of Schneider-Creusot; his brother-in-law, Arnaud de Saint-Sauveur; Eduard Benes, who, as Czechoslovakia's foreign minister, takes second place to no one in the vocal support he lends to the League of Nations; and two Czecho-Germans, Von Dutschnitz and Von Arthaber, who were, it is interesting to note in view of later facts, very heavy financial contributors to Hitler's political success. Political France and political Germany may be at constant swords' points, the Polish Corridor may inflame the Nazis, France may quiver at her lack of security from another northern invasion, but the lion and the lamb never lie down together with more good fellowship than these French, German, Czech, and Polish gentlemen when they come together to discuss, as fellow directors, the problems of increasing Europe's consumption of armaments. Thanks to the activities of Skoda and its allies, arms form a full 10 percent of all Czech exports—and 40 percent of all Skoda's products are exported—to the extent of $30,000,000 worth a year.

Back to Schneider

M. Schneider's nationality is capable of any supple manipulation that a political emergency may call for. The founder of his dynasty was his grand-father, also named Eugène, who, with a brother Adolph, left Bidestroff in the then German territory of the Saar and came to France in 1836. More particularly brothers Eugène and Adolph came to Le Creusot (literally "The Hollow" or "The Crucible") where, to the south of the Burgundy-wine district a small foundry has been making cannon from the days of Louis XVI. With perfect impartiality it had supplied first the monarchy, then the republic, and then Napoleon's Empire with its products. With the aid of the French banking house of Seillière these German brothers bought the foundry (La Société Générale des Hauts Fourneaux) for 2,500,000 francs—and were then forced to wait for almost 20 years for their first major war. War-promotion methods in those days were not what they were to become later in the century, but that gap was neatly bridged by the demands that the new steamboats and the even newer railroads were making on the producers of iron and steel. Then, in 1854, the Crimean War broke out and Eugène (alone now, following Adolph's death) converted Le Creusot almost exclusively to the manufacture of arms.

The family fortune was founded; the family tradition was established.

In the few years that followed the Crimean War, Eugène Schneider had time to look about him for parliamentary posts. First he became a member of the Chamber of Deputies; later he rose to be minister of agriculture, then of commerce. By 1865 he had become president of the Chamber of Deputies (analogous to the Speaker of the United States House of Representatives).

It was from this vantage point that he was able to watch the sweep of events that led to the Franco-Prussian War. Alfred Krupp saw it coming, too. He, like Schneider, was capable of an internationalism far above the confines of narrow patriotism and was anxious to equip Napoleon III's armies with his own cannon—a suggestion not entirely without its logic or, even, its sportsmanship, for Krupp had borrowed in Paris (from the same banking house of Seillière as had set Eugène Schneider up in business) the money with which he made the guns that later humbled France at Metz and Sedan.

But in those days Schneider was jealous of Krupp's mounting power and persuaded Napoleon III that his patronage of Le Creusot would be more enlightened. The inferiority of the French cannon in 1870 was one factor that brought about the catastrophic ruin of the Second Empire.

Nothing in the career of the Schneider dynasty is more remarkable than the fact that it was able to overcome this shocking disgrace and actually to get the job of re-equipping the new armies of the Republic. This time Eugène Schneider supplied France with cannon modeled upon the designs of the victorious Krupps. It was not until some 20 years later that he died, full of years and his own sort of wisdom, to be succeeded by his son Henri.

It was under Henri's son—the present Eugene Schneider, now 66 years old, that the Schneider-Creusot Co. began to work upon a gigantic, world-wide scale. Its real expansion began with the turn of the century. Eugene Schneider acquired iron mines in Lorraine and began a program of mill, foundry, and shipyard building at Bordeaux and Toulon. And then, opportunely, the Russo-Japanese War arrived.

Not until after the close of this war did the real genius of the living Eugene Schneider begin to manifest itself. Russia needed re-arming. The Krupps rushed in. The English firm of Vickers rushed in. Eugène Schneider rushed in. There ensued a brief jockeying for position among the three firms—and it was Schneider, perhaps, who captured the best. "Buy from us," he whispered gently into the proper ears, "and pay with French money." It was not hard to arrange. The French Ambassador to Imperial Russia was then Maurice Paléologue, who was likewise a director in the Schneider Banque de L'Union Parisienne. The Russians made a brief call on Paris and came back to St. Petersburg with money with which to pay for Schneider armaments. From that time until, in 1918, the Soviet Government of Russia expressed its official uninterest in paying the debts of the Czarist regime 16,000,000,000 gold francs drained slowly from the savings of the French people, were loaned to Russia, secured by bonds that have long since been tossed on the rubbish heap. Most of the profit in the 16,000,000,000 found its way back to Schneider-Creusot and is today in their foundries and their bank accounts.

Yet the Czar's Government was not wholly credulous. It seemed to have some qualms that so much Russian armament should be manufactured on foreign soil. This offered no problem to the armament makers. Schneider installed engineers and managers at the Putilov works in St. Petersburg. The Krupps did likewise. French newspapers screamed that the Krupps were spying. German newspapers screamed that the French were spying. But 1914 found Schneider and Krupp engineers side by side on terms of cordial friendship, overseeing ordnance manufacture on behalf of Nicholas II, Czar of all the Russias.

Eye Opener—Briey

If you have a naïveté about the war, shed it now; the war in no way interrupted the cordiality of the armament makers. Throughout the years from 1914 to 1918 they stayed on jolly terms, they even emerged from the war better friends than they were when they went into it. One major war-time episode in particular revealed their unshakable solidarity.

Before 1914 the great iron mines and smelters in the Briey Basin provided 70 percent of the ore used by France. The German advance wrested them from the political control of France—and quite naturally the German artillery chiefs saw to it that the mines were so protected from shellfire that they could be taken over intact. Thenceforth the mines of the Briey Basin were operated for the benefit of Germany—in association with other mines in Lorraine which had been in German hands since 1871 they supplied Germany with some three quarters of the ore she consumed during the war.

In 1916, some 2 years later, the Briey Basin came once again within the potential grasp of the French. Throughout the second battle of Verdun, Briey was within range of the operations of the French Second Army. The Briey mines and smelters were turning out tons of raw materials per day which were being continuously turned into weapons of death against French troops, and the naive civilian would therefore suppose that the French Second Army would now turn loose its bombing planes and blast out of existence a principal source of enemy supply.

The naïve civilian would be quite wrong. Bombs did not burst at Briey; nowhere near Briey did more than a few shells from either side fall during the entire course of the war. There were even line officers who shared civilian naïveté enough to question French general headquarters on the immunity of Briey. A reasonable explanation could have been that the French were withholding fire from Briey because they, in turn, hoped to recapture the basin and turn its products back to France. But this was not the explanation that emerged from headquarters; instead it was stated that if Briey were bombarded, the Germans, in reprisal, would turn their guns on Dombasle in Meurthe-et-Moselle, between the Argonne and Verdun, where equally large-scale mining operations were supplying the French with much of their own raw material for ordnance and ammunition. So long as the French left Briey alone the Germans would let Dombasle alone; what hothead was there who would want to upset the apple cart under these circumstances? Of course, if the French and Germans had each leveled the other's smelters the war would have ended sooner. And so would war-time profits. That was that. Briey and Dombasle came unscathed through the war.

Here the proof of the international operations of the armament makers is open to no question at all. In corroboration there is spread upon the records the testimony of Deputy Pierre Étienne Flandin (scarcely a flaming Bolshevist, for he was later finance minister under Tardieu) to the effect that he, an artillery officer during the war, knew of his own knowledge that the artillery of the French Second Army had been expressly forbidden to bombard Briey when the chance existed and when a 10-mile penetration of the sector would have come close to spelling German ruin. And the statement of his colleague, Deputy Barthe, in the chamber on January 24, 1919, lost little of its significance in the long, loud, vicious debates and investigations which followed it: "I affirm that either by the fact of the international solidarity of the great metal-lurgy companies, or in order to safeguard private business interests, our military chiefs were ordered not to bombard the establishments of the Briey Basin, which were being exploited by the enemy during the war. I affirm that our aviation service received instructions to respect the blast furnaces in which the enemy steel was being made, and that a general who wished to bombard them was reprimanded."

There is a quality of delirium about facts like these. Anyone who comes upon them for the first time is likely to feel a sense of incredulity that these can be facts at all; to feel that they must be, instead, some insane fiction of a super-Voltaire.

The sense of incredulity is quite excusable. Yet the facts are facts—and into the bargain they are quite easily explicable. In this present imperfect world nations have yet found no agreement upon practical methods of disarm-ing. So long as they refuse to, the easiest way for them to stay armed is to permit a full exploitation of the private profit system in the manufacture of armaments. By this device nations avoid the expense and annoyance of main-taining plants and inventories of armaments throughout a period of 20 years, when perhaps they may never be needed at all; the private armorer meanwhile is able to keep his plants oiled and humming by sales not only to his own government but to foreign markets in which he is able to foment enough suspicion to sell large bills of goods. Here is the rock upon which every private conference that precedes official disarmament conferences has split. Here the circle closes. So long as we must have armaments we must lend rein and scope to the business methods of the armorers. What happened at Briey, considered in this light, was very simple: the mere working out of the profit system in armaments to its perfect, logical, and ultimate conclusion.

Climax—the De Wendels

The episode of Briey brings us now to the pinnacle of the armament structure. Who held the impulsive line officers in check? Through whose influence was the general reprimanded?

We must look higher than to Schneider-Creusot for the final answer. For far overtopping Schneider-Creusot and its subsidiaries stands that great or-ganization of iron and steel manufacturers, the Comité des Forges de France.

The Comité des Forges is not, as it has frequently been called, the "French Steel Trust." It is not a cartel. Individual French iron and steel companies are bound together by rigid agreements covering quotas and prices into great groups like the Comptoir Sidérurgique de France or into lesser ones like the Comptoir des Rails or the Comptoir des Demi-Produits. The Comité cannot be said to combine these organizations; in actuality, however, it remains the most powerful iron and steel organization in France. It does not sell; it does not produce. Its activities are more subtle, more delicate than that. Essentially, its field is in the strategy and tactics of the iron and steel industries; accordingly, politics and propaganda are its principal concerns. It does not have subsidiaries; it has members that pay dues into its central treasury either upon a basis of their tonnage production or the number of their employees. Two hundred and fifty companies—mines, smelters, metallurgical establishments, foundries—make up its membership, and of these 250 companies, over 150 are armament concerns. The nominal capital stock of the member companies of the Comité totals some 7,500,000,000 francs, yet some accountants have placed the figure for a true valuation as high as 40,000,000,000 francs. The chief officer of the Comité, the president, is a man of whom we are to hear much more in just a moment. He derives his power not only from being president of the Comité but as one of the principal owners of his own iron and steel concerns. Beneath him and his administrative board on the Comité there spread out six regional committees: The Loire, Nord, l'Est, Minière d'Alsace-Lorraine, Forges de Lorraine, and Champagne. The total tonnage that the members of the Comité produce in France in a typical year are, for pig iron, some 10,000,000 tons, and for steel some 9,500,000 tons.

Membership begins with firms that may actually be as small and unimpressive as the capitalization would make them seem; it ends in the grand climax of member no. 1, Schneider-Creusot—whose capitalization of 100,000,000 francs reflects only a fraction of its true importance. The great and the little, thus bound together, make up the power and the glory of the Comité. It controls the press; it has the ear of the foreign office. Former President Millerand has been its legal defender; former President Doumer was a director of one subsidiary; present President Albert Lebrun is a former director of another. So—most significantly of all—is former Premier André Tardieu, great leader of the Right. There was no stronger influence upon former Premier Poincaré in his occupation of the Ruhr than the Comité; the present agitation over the Saar Basin springs from its headquarters. It is governed by a commission of directors, and upon this commission as president (we must now displease another lover of anonymity) there sits the misty and cloud-wreathed figure of François de Wendel.

François de Wendel comes legitimately by his present power and position; his family have been Europe's armorers since before the French Revolution—although the De Wendels have not always been French, nor, even, always the De Wendels. There was once a Johann Georg von Wendel, who in the seventeenth century was a colonel in the armies of Ferdinand III of Germany. Since his time, however, the family generally has preferred to remain out of uniform, on the theory that in uniform there is no higher title or power than that of general, whereas by the process of foregoing the title the power may be vastly increased. The members of this family have always been uniquely international. When their vast Lorraine estates lay upon soil politically German they attached to their name the prefix "von" and turned their eyes toward Berlin; when the political frontier shifted under their rich deposits of coal and iron they altered the prefix to "de" and looked to Paris.

Either capital was glad to claim them; the family was equally happy to serve either, or better, both. Today, for example, when political boundary lines throw most of their estates into France, but leave a few in Germany, the family consists preponderantly of De Wendels, but with a sufficient number of Von Wendels in reserve to manage its German affairs. (Being a De Wendel, however, is no necessary barrier to the perquisites and profits still obtainable from the German armament business, as will later appear.) In 1914 the ranking member of the family was Humbert von Wendel, a member of the German Reichstag, living at Hayange in Moselle, near the Saar Basin. After the Treaty of Versailles he became Humbert de Wendel. He still lives at Hayange, but he is no longer a member of the Reichstag. A younger brother, Guy, is a French Senator, however, and of his other brother, the François of the comitè, more later.

This international hermaphroditism is not a new family trait. The son of Johann Georg von Wendel, who fought for the German Ferdinand III, blossomed into Christian de Wendel, who was a follower of Charles IV of Lorraine. For a good period of years the family retained the prefix "de"; Christian's grandson, Ignace, was the true founder of the familys' fortune—and this, curiously enough, began when he established at Cruesot the works that the Schneiders were later to buy. When the Bastille fell Ignace's close relations with the monarchy drove him from the country. His properties were sequestered, but they were managed by his mother and were bought back through dummies for the account of his two sons. During this turbulent period the sequestered properties were arming the revolutionists, to the De Wendel profit, while the properties beyond the wabbling frontiers of the Republic were arming the monarchists, trying to regain power, and their allies—also to the De Wendel profit.

Then, with the Napoleonic Empire rearing its magnificance upon the ruins of the monarchy, an earlier François de Wendel (Ignace's son) returned to Paris to provide the armaments of the grande armée. The tragedy of Waterloo was no tragedy to the De Wendels; a cartoon of them going home after the battle to count their profit from it would not have been far-fetched.

Today's members of the family were, therefore, well equipped by wealth and heredity for the task of riding the political horses of France and Germany in the later years when Lorraine was to become one of the major circus rings for their virtuosity. Their long experience made Briey almost a minor episode to them. When a military advance turned a French possession into a German one, the De Wendels need have felt no great concern. Regardless of the national tag attached to these mines and smelters, they remained in the placid control of one or the other branches of the family.

The Francois de Wendel of the present day is a pooh-bah; his connections and directorships would fill this page. He is among other things a director not only of the French but of the German De Wendel companies. But that coincidence does not set forth his true qualities of being a pooh-bah. Is François de Wendel, president of the Comité des Forges, faced with a financial problem? Then let him consult François de Wendel, regent of the Banque de France. Is he in need of political support? François de Wendel, Member of the Chamber of Deputies for Meurthe-et-Moselle, intimate and supporter of André Tardieu, one time controller of some 60 deputies, is the man for him to see. Does this or the other piece of news need to be interpreted? He cannot do better than to consult that powerful journalist, François de Wendel, who owns a majority interest in Le Journal des Débats, is the head of the group that in October 1931 (jointly with the Comité des Houillères, the coal cartel) purchased the semiofficial newspaper of the French Government, Le Temps, controls the Journée Industrielle, and is a power in the management of Le Matin, L'Echo de Paris, and the Agence Havas, the newsgathering organization upon which the provincial press of France very largely depends. Yet for all the illustriousness of this multisided man the newspapers of France almost never mention his name. He does not like publicity.

Double-Edged Sword

Conspirators is not an unfair word to apply to the armament makers of France— yet it must not be used with any melodramatic connotations. Probably the conspirators are not bad men at all in their personal lives and their individual contacts with society. Sir Basil Zaharoff, the passion of whose declining years is orchid culture, would probably not be aghast at the suggestion that he was the greatest murderer the world has ever known. He has heard it too often. And he may even enjoy the irony of his gifts (they took a few millions of the hundreds of millions he made from the World War) for hospitalization of the war wounded. But probably Eugène Schneider and François de Wendel are lovable old gentlemen who weep at a Chopin ballade. If an advance angel of judgment should undertake today to quiz the de Wendels or Eugène Schneider on the ethics of their business, they would unquestionably answer: (a) They didn't invent the passions and cupidities that lead to war; (b) If they didn't supply the demand for armaments someone else would; and (c) They inherited the business, anyway.

All of which is perfectly true. Then why are these men conspirators? They are conspirators because they have no loyalties; because theirs is the sword that knows no brother. The rise of Hitler to power in Nazi Germany provides a neat example of this— and into the bargain shows what a double-edged sword it is that the armament makers wield.

In Germany the greatest steel company is the Vereinigte Stahlwerke A. G. and for its head it has Fritz Thyssen, king of the Ruhr. It was Thyssen who was Hitler's angel; who, as one move in a battle to retain control of his industrial affairs (dealt a desperate blow by Germany's banking crisis of 1931) began pouring money into the treasury of the Nazis to assure to himself the help of a friendly government. So far nothing improper; if Thyssen believed in the Nazi philosophy or the good it might do him, there was no real reason why he should not lend Hitler all the financial support he wanted to. In 1932 old Fritz Thyssen capped many previous generosities with a single contribution of 3,000,000 marks for the German presidential campaign. But old Fritz, despite his personally violent nationalism, was not at all hostile to the de Wendel-Schneider interests in France. He favored, in fact, a working compact with them so long as he could retain unhampered control of his own properties. We see, then, the spectacle of a Nazi supporter on the one hand breathing fire against France, and on the other sitting down on terms of thorough understanding with the principal armament firm that represented the implacable political enemy of his country.

But that does not complete the picture. The Comité des Forges and Schneider-Creusot were not at all unwilling to see Hitler gain ascendancy in

Germany. Here the documentary proof is lacking, but the inferential proof is close to inescapable. In 1933 Hitler sued a German journalist for having made the statement that Skoda (and, through Skoda, Schneider-Creusot) had contributed to his campaign expenses. When, however, he was challenged to make a direct denial that this was so, he stormed from the witness stand, cursed the opposing lawyer for a Jew, never specifically answered the question, and was subsequently fined 1,000 marks for contempt of court as a result. De Wendel and Schneider, according to their immemorial custom, said nothing, and nowhere has a denial of the accusation ever been made.

In other words, as the record stands, the leading munition makers not only in Germany but in France united in their support behind the one man most capable of stirring up a new outbreak of international anarchy in Europe. And by a curious coincidence (here is where the sword presents its other gleaming edge) the de Wendel-controlled newspapers in Paris immediately broke out in a fever of denunciation against the Hitler regime and called for fresh guaranties of security against the menace of rearming Germany. Awake, La Patrie!

Armorers' Philosophy

In that one example the whole philosophy of most armament makers reveals itself. Keep Europe in a constant state of nerves. Publish periodical war scares. Impress governmental officials with the vital necessity of maintaining armaments against the aggressions of neighbor states. Bribe as necessary.[2] In every practical way create suspicion that security is threatened. And if you do your job thoroughly enough you will be able to sink into your armchair and reecho the contented words of Eugène Schneider, announcing a dividend to his shareholders: "The defense of our country has brought us satisfactions which cannot be ignored."

For the armament industry operates with one curious advantage over any other business in the world; the greater the competition the greater the amount of business for all competitors. Perhaps it was Sir Basil Zaharoff who first discovered this economic fact when he played his one-submarine-two-submarine game with Greece and Turkey. At any rate, salesmen for the armament industry know the fact well and build on it today. If a Schneider-Creusot salesman sells 100,000 rifles to Yugoslavia he has already eased the path of the Vickers-Armstrongs salesman in selling 200,000 rifles to Italy. "Under this strange system", the French economist, Delaisi, wrote not long ago, "the war potential of a great country, or of a group of countries, is

---

[2] Scarcely a year old is the arms scandal in Rumania. In March 1933 the Rumanian Government discovered that the Skoda Works had evaded taxes to the extent of 65,000,000 lei (something over $600,000). It looked into the safe of Bruno Seletski, Skoda's agent in Rumania, and discovered that he had distributed more than 1,000,000,000 lei (close to $10,000,000) among the "right" officials of both the Government and the army, and their wives and mistresses, and that hundreds of thousands had gone to charity and entertainment because the beneficiaries will be used by us some day.

There was an intense amount of internal and international noise over the scandal, but it subsided in the general political turnover in Rumania last fall. And everything, including the bribes, is just about where it was except General Popescu who, in a fit of conscience, shot himself fatally through the head.

strengthened by the development of the adverse military power. The trade in arms is the only one in which an order obtained by a competitor increases that of his rivals. The great armament firms of hostile powers oppose one another like pillars supporting the same arch. And the opposition of their governments makes their common prosperity."

Who Holds the Bag?

A very handsome prosperity it has been; one that has endured as few others during the stormy days since 1929. As a result of the operations of these highly international concerns the world's yearly armament bill stands now in the vicinity of a billion and a half dollars. During the last few years the Far East in particular has contributed much to satisfy the MM. de Wendel and Schneider to say nothing of Vickers-Armstrongs' Sir Herbert Lawrence. Japan has been a highly profitable customer; the firm of Mitsui, allied to both Schneider-Creusot and Vickers-Armstrongs, served its country splendidly when Manchuria was flaming brightest. It also served China excellently. In 1930 China, the world's largest importer of arms, bought almost 40 percent of its war materials from Japan. The European armament makers who were supplying this trade found the free port of Hamburg convenient: during one famous week in 1932 there cleared from Hamburg two ships loaded with dynamite, grenades, and airplane parts; another with 1,000 cases of explosives, another with 1,700 cases of ammunition, and still another, bringing up a triumphal rear, with 100,000,000 francs' worth of French machine guns.

The world traffic in arms has continued unceasingly since the war; the armament leopards have never changed their spots. Detail upon detail, incident upon incident, illustrate how well the armament makers apply the two axioms of their business: when there are wars, prolong them; when there is peace, disturb it. Let one incident suffice here.

Inevitably, after the war, Hungary caught the itch to rearm. The Treaty of Trianon, by which she made peace with the Allies and associated powers, forbade it. Schneider-Creusot, however, was above treaties. Hungary got the money with which to place a larger order with Skoda, the Schneider-Creusot subsidiary in Czechoslovakia—got it through the Banque Générale de Crédit Hongrois, which in turn is financed by the Banque de L'Union Parisienne, of which Eugéne Schneider is a director. Thus it was that Schneider contrived once again to circumvent his government and rearm a nation that France had spent blood and treasure in the attempt to disarm.

But the story does not end here. When the Hungarian loan fell due it seemed inevitable that Hungary would default. Thereupon it was conveniently arranged that Hungary negotiate a loan from the French Government. The plan went through like clockwork. The French Government lent the Hungarian Government just enough money to repay the Schneider firm. The money was transmitted through M. Schneider's Banque de L'Union Parisienne, instead of, as one might have expected, through the Banque de France.

One voice crying in the wilderness was the voice of the French deputy from the Creusot district, Paul Faure. Several times in 1931 and 1932 M. Faure made speeches to the chamber. He raised the question of the Hungarian loan and asked, in essence, Who holds the bag? Obviously not Skoda; it had paid a dividend of 5 percent in 1920 and a dividend of 28½ percent in 1930, with never a recession in its steady year-by-year increases. He went further; he traced from the early days of the century the curious fashion in which French governmental loans insisted on relating themselves to Schneider-Creusot orders. Throughout these years France had made loans to Mexico, Greece, Japan, Russia, Spain, Italy, Rumania, Serbia, Bulgaria, and Turkey, and every one of these countries had thereupon placed armament orders with Schneider-Creusot. The last two countries had, in fact, pushed the return compliment as far as turning French guns, so bought, upon French troops at the outbreak of the war. Almost inevitably, M. Faure pointed out, there sat on the directorate of the financing bank of the country that bought the armaments a representative of Schneider-Creusot or some other member of the comité. This precaution did not, however, prevent most of these loans from being in default. Coming to the present, said M. Faure, "we find M. Schneider arming Bulgaria, M. Schneider arming Turkey, Skoda supporting Hitler, Franco-Japanese, Franco-Argentine, and Franco-Mexican banks. This is all"—he ended with a masterpiece of moderation—"extremely suspicious." Then, having made these revelations, M. Faure shortly after found himself defeated for reelection to the chamber; he was, after all, a deputy from the Creusot district, and M. Schneider found it more convenient to bring about his defeat than to listen to more of his speeches.

Ray of Hope

Have governments ever taken any steps to confiscate the business of the armament makers? Very few. In the early days after the war Europe's governments had small heart for proceeding against their betrayers, even though the waxen seals on the Treaty of Versailles were scarcely hard before they were once again busy disturbing the peace.

And although the conviction began later to grow among Europe's more enlightened statesmen that something had to be done about the De Wendels, the Schneiders, and their breed, governments were puzzled to know what it could be. A nation that suppresses or confiscates its private armament industry is faced with these alternatives: (a) It must disarm; (b) it must become exclusively an importer of arms; (c) it must make arms manufacturing a function of the state, which means, in effect, that the state must become (or inevitably thinks it must) a vast arsenal, since, having no opportunity to keep plants large and active by supplying an export trade, it must manufacture in quantities sufficiently large so that it could step overnight from a peace-time to a war-time production schedule.

Therein lay one difficulty. But why could concerted action toward disarmament make so little progress? One important reason was first laid bare by Lord Robert Cecil. "There is a very sinister feature," he said, "to all the disarmament discussions. I refer to the tremendous power wielded against all the proposals by armament firms. . . . We must aim at getting rid of this immense instrument in the maintenance of suspicion." Yet in 1932 the Disarmament Conference was enriched by the presence of M. Charles Dumont, of Schneider-Creusot, president of the Schneider-controlled Banque Franco-

Japonaise, on the French delegation. The British delegation was similarly benefited by the advice of Col. A. G. C. Dawnay, the brother of a director of Vickers-Armstrongs, and now the political supervisor of the British Broadcasting Corporation.

If the armament business were conducted by an outlawed band of international gangsters, the problem would be simple to define. The difficulty is that precisely the opposite is the case. The armament business is a part of the most essential industries of industrialized nations—steel and chemicals. But even so, the problem does not become acute until you have a nation in which the biggest part or a very, very large part of these essential industries is the manufacture of the actual munitions of war. Such is the case in France and also in Czechoslovakia and potentially in Germany.

No American would be shocked to hear that the steel business and the coal business of Pennsylvania, owners and workers together, exercised big political influence in Pennsylvania and, through Pennsylvania, upon the Nation. Now, put Detroit also in Pennsylvania. And then suppose that by far the most profitable part of the combined steel-coal-motor car industry were the manufacture of munitions. And then try to imagine a Senator from Pennsylvania convincing himself that there is no possible chance of war with Japan and that therefore both the American Navy and the American Army are much too big.

While this may make it easy to understand why Messrs. de Wendel and Schneider should be so influential in France, it brings us no nearer a solution. To deal with the general problem of disarmament in all its phases would be impossible within the limits of this article. Suffice it to say, the simplest solution is to have the State take over all the manufacturing of munitions. But to do that, the State would have to take over most of the essential industries of modern life. And for anyone but a 100-percent Socialist, that is not simple at all. Russia is today the only country in which there is no private manufacture and sale of armaments.[3]

Then is there no hope? Is Europe caught so tight in the steely grip of the armament makers that it can only do their bidding?

Well, the grip is pretty tight, yet there is some hope. Perhaps there is a war coming but first there is a fight coming.

And in recent months that fight has loomed most noticeably in France. The Comité des Forges has decidedly not been a popular name in France these last few months. To be exact, it never was a popular name. Just as a politician in the United States was always against Wall Street during his campaign, so in France many a political victory has been won by accusing the opposition of being in the pay of the Comité des Forges. Of late, as political tension in France has grown hotter, so resentment against the de Wendels and the Schneiders has grown more bitter.

No country has more to gain from peace and the sanctity of treaties than France. So it is not surprising to find that many Frenchmen are now saying that France made a tragic mistake in supporting Japan (in a backhand manner) in the Manchurian affair. And they note, with bitterness, that it was the de

[3] Parenthetically it will be recalled by those who have followed the dreary course of disarmament conferences that Russia, in the mouth of Comrade Maxim Litvinoff, has been the most consistent and the loudest advocate of disarmament.

Wendel press that wanted to let Japan have her imperial way.

To France's great credit it must also be said that, except in the Manchurian affair, France has been, for her own best interest, the stanchest supporter of the League. More than that, her Briand was unquestionably the greatest peace man of the post-war decade. Today, many a Frenchman is resentful of the fact that Briand's policies did not succeed in conciliating Germany, and while blaming Germany most, he wonders whether the failure was not helped along by the patriotic M. de Wendel.

By the time this is published France may have chosen her next major political direction. If Herriot should come to power again, it may well be that he will feel a mandate even more powerful than ever before to fight against the warriors of Europe—and to include among his enemies the armorers, greatest of whom are the greatest industrialists of his own land. For they are sometimes not too clever, these Schneiders and de Wendels. And they seem to miss one point: the fire trenches and shell holes that scar the countryside in war time are only the primary lesions of an international social disease. When the disease at last inevitably attacks the blood and bones of nations that have gone to war even De Wendels and Schneiders can suffer—suffer with their tottering banks, their dropsical holding companies, their shocked and collapsing industrial empires.

Within their long lives, however, neither François de Wendel nor Charles Prosper Eugene Schneider has ever let drop a word to indicate that he sees any connection between his business and an eventual ruin of his capitalistic industry. Only Sir Basil Zaharoff, doddering brokenly in his wheel chair, seems to give any outward evidence of disillusionment. That may be only because he gambled $20,000,000 of his personal fortune on the only war in which he ever took emotional sides—the Greco-Turkish war in 1921—and lost it.

Or it might be because he was always the cleverest, anyway.

APPENDIX: ARMS AND THE MEN

Love Thine Enemy

The armorers, after all, are the true internationalists. Regardless of their nationalities, they work in concert at the two axioms of their trade—prolong wars, disturb peace. Between 1914 and 1918 they practiced constantly a neat practical way of prolonging war.

It was this: If your enemy is in danger of running short of a basic raw material that he needs in the business of destroying your troops, sell him some out of your own surplus stocks.

Such interchanges went on constantly during the war—always, of course, through a neutral intermediary. (The amenities of warfare must be observed, even at some inconvenience.) Throughout the war English and French industries maintained to Germany a steady stream of glycerin (for explosives), nickel, copper, oil, and rubber. Germany even returned the compliment; she sent France iron and steel and magnetos for gasoline engines. This constant traffic went on during the war via Sweden, Norway, Denmark, Switzerland,

Spain, or Holland, by the simple process of transshipment—enemy to neutral to enemy.

It is no bristling Communist who supplies corroboration, but as conservative and well-considered a gentleman as Rear Admiral Montagu William Warcop Peter Consett, who was British naval attaché in Denmark between 1912 and 1917 and in Norway and Sweden between 1912 and 1919. He stated, in so many words, that if the blockade of Germany had been really effective during 1915 and 1916 Germany would have been forced to her knees long before the collapse of Russia permitted her to prolong the struggle by throwing more troops into the trenches of the western front. And it is her who is responsible for the following statement: "In 1915 England exported twice as much nickel to Sweden as in the 2 previous years put together. Of the total imports of 504 tons, 70 were reshipped to Germany. But it can be said that the total importation served the needs of Germany, for the remaining 434 tons were used in Sweden for the manufacture of munitions."

And so it went. Germany throughout the war had urgent need of nickel, aluminum, and chemicals like glycerin for explosives. France, because the rich Briey Basin and other sources were out of her control, had to scratch hard for iron and steel. Continuously, therefore, what one nation lacked, the armament manufacturers of an enemy nation did their urgent best to provide. Month after month, during the war, German heavy industries exported an average of 150,000 tons of scrap iron, steel, or barbed wire to Switzerland, where having been smelted to a more convenient form it was then transshipped to France. France, in her turn, shipped chemicals to the Lonza Co. (a Swiss industrial concern, German controlled, but with directors who were French, Italian, and Austrian as well) from which they reached munitions works in Germany. It was all very profitable—and the splendid war went on and on.

"THE PROFITS OF WAR AND PREPAREDNESS," RADIO ADDRESS BY SENATOR GERALD P. NYE APRIL 10, 1934

Records of the Special Committee Investigating the Munitions Industry, General Subject File, Box 20, Record Group 46, Records of the United States Senate, National Archives.

A restless mind exists throughout the world today. One naturally is concerned about our nation's preparedness for war. The cause of preparedness, however, has lent itself to abuses which amount to national scandal and in time will cause nations to bow their heads in shame of the frightful things done in its name.

To provide an adequate national defense is a positive duty of government. But what constitutes an *adequate* defense? Is it preparation to defend ourselves against aggressors? Or is it preparation to go to all quarters of the earth to carry on warfare? If the questions were left to the people there is not serious doubt as to what the answers would be. If the people, unhampered by interests with selfish purposes, had their way, *adequate* defense would involve alone preparation for war at home. Then, with no nation preparing to leave its own borders to make war there would quickly dawn a golden opportunity and invitation to further prune the expense of defensive preparation.

The sad facts are, though, that the people do not have their way upon matters involving ultimate war. Influences are constantly at work which disarm people of a feeling of security in what was once thought to be an adequate defense. These influences are by men who hold positions of great influence in our social and political order, men who have been highly success-ful in inducing others to accept as truth the baseless assertions of their false though profitable propaganda.

Americans left to their good sense and judgment will declare that never again will our country engage in war away from home. But never at any time is there let-up of that propaganda intended to convince us that other nations are more adequately prepared for war than are we. And the propaganda so effective with us is equally effective when used in other lands. The result is an increasing competition so insane in its accomplishment that the world finds itself completely forgetting what really is adequate in the way of national defense; a competition which witnesses nations launched upon preparation program on a scale never known to the world in peace times. Already the race is one which causes nations, including our own to spend two and three times more money now than before the late world war. And here we are, only fifteen years removed from that war with its painful and expensive economic and physical consequences, still upon us.

Under these circumstances it is fair to ask: Where does preparedness and national defense end? Viewing the insane trend of competition between nations it is equally fair to answer: It ends in war, war more terrible than any yet known; war, no one knows just where, when or for what cause, but war nevertheless. And to whose profit and satisfaction, pray tell? Certainly not to that of the men and boys who will be called upon to carry on, not to that of their loved ones; certainly not to the profit of the nation, for now, while still bleeding from the last war, we see that war gives, not profit, but debt —burdensome, crushing debt.

Is our civilization helplessly insane and laboring under a complex utterly suicidal? Who profits, who gains any satisfaction from this mad race of socalled preparedness?

The answer is not difficult of finding for those who will face facts.

Many studies are being made resulting in published articles on the subject of War and Profit. One of the most notable of these is to be found in the current number of Fortune Magazine. Here we find a most sordid tale of the scheming of European manufacturers to create a market for their instruments of war, of their perfect will of these manufacturers to supply the material to be used by enemy governments against their own, perhaps against the very factory workers whose labor created the munitions. These patriots have no prejudice. They perfect new death-dealing instruments and sell to whichever or however many governments will buy. There has been recorded the fact that

French soldiers were mowed down by French made guns in the hands of the enemy. German soldiers moving westward were killed by German made guns sold to Belgium while German-made machines sold to Russia visited death and destruction upon the men fighting for the Fatherland on the Eastern front. Mounted in monumental fashion in a small English community is a great gun captured from the Germans in an engagement which cost the lives of many of the young men of that British community. On one side of the gun are engraved the names of the sons of British who gave up their lives in that engagement before the machine was captured; on the other side is engraved the name of the British munitions maker who sold the instrument to Germany. The story of the commercialism of war and preparation for it is ugly, gruesome. It does no credit to European munition makers or to the countries which permitted these merchants to ply their trade.

But who are we to pity the poor souls with whom these European manufacturers play as with toys? Look at ourselves in America and the history of our own munitions makers who supply Uncle Sam's needs in "an adequate defense program" and rush their supersalesmen off to foreign lands to ply their trade at peace conferences!

Last Friday was Army Day, and past the Capitol and down the city's parade avenue there marched and rode five thousand of America's finest—America's defenders—strong splendidly uniformed men, beautiful, well matched steeds, shining steel helmets, rifles and mounted guns. All this, with the proudly waving colors, is at once inspiring. Hats off to these well-trained men prepared at a moment's notice to rush to the defense of country and flag! Yet, even in that inspiring moment, I could not fully restrain myself and be blind to the fact that those glistening steel helmets, for example, were the profit-returning products of American manufacturers, a product intended to protect those fine heads under the helmets against the shrapnel and shells which the same manufacturers had sold to the military departments of other nations which might some day be our foe in war! What madness! What rotten commercialism! Name a more inhuman trade! Was ever a more insane racket conceived in depraved mind or tolerated by an enlightened people?

After the adequate defensive needs of the American government have been provided for by the annual appropriations, it is said, off to South America go these manufacturers, breeding there suspicion and fear between countries while American statesmen strive to accomplish understanding and maintain peace. Incidentally, order books are carried along to record the orders for military needs which always grow out of suspicion and fear. China and Japan likewise seem to offer a fine market for our American merchants of death and destruction.

Just before the Civil War a leading financial figure conceived the idea of buying at auction thousands of rifles which the American Army was casting aside. The purchase was at a price of just over $3.00 per gun. The following year, when the Union forces desperately needed guns, this financier sold these same guns to the government at $22.00 each, a 700% profit. When Fremont's soldiers tried to fire these guns they shot off their own thumbs. But Morgan finally got his money, through court action, the court holding the contract was sacred. Is there profit for anyone in war?

But look out for Japan!——we are cautioned.

If we should, by some unbelievable chance find ourselves at war with Japan, it is safe to wager that our soldiers and sailors will find their enemy armed with and mowed down by instruments produced by American manufacturers—at a profit, of course.

In the name of "adequate defense" our American costs of maintaining the Army and Navy are now more than $700,000,000 annually compared with $343,000,000 just before we entered the World War—the war that was going to end war. From 1913 to 1930 Great Britain's cost of national defense increased 42%; France 30%; Italy 44%; Japan 142%; Russia 30%; while your Uncle Sam rushed to a 200% increase in his "defense" costs.

When will we cease this mad game? But, let us remember that the surest way to maintain peace is to prepare for war, we are urged.

I deny that there is any foundation in fact or historical experience for the claim that preparation for war maintains peace. The claim is a myth, sponsored and nursed by those whose unclean profits would vanish if ever they permitted the world to know that preparation for war is marvelously profitable for a few.

Between the United States and Canada there stretches a boundary of thousands of miles. During the lifetime of these two neighbors there has never been stationed a soldier, a mounted gun, or any evidence of military defense. It is encouraging to know that today fine minds in both countries are conceiving the establishment of a monument to commemorate these years of peace without demonstration of armed strength.

This monument is to take most unusual form. On each side of the boundary, in the Turtle Mountains of my state of North Dakota and Canada, hundreds of acres are being set aside to be developed and made known as the International Peace Garden. These acres will be landscaped and made a beautiful spot in commemoration of the peaceful relationship that has existed through all of these years without that common demonstration of "adequate" defense.

Oh, that there could be more such monuments!

There is a book about to come from the press which would save our nation billions and our people much of suffering if it could be read by every American. It is the story of profits and methods of munition makers, written by Engelbrecht and Hanighan, published by Dodd, Mead & Company, and chosen by the Book of the Month Club for May. And, what a title this work has: "Merchants of Death" is its name. It is packed full of worth-while facts about our munition makers. To this book I must credit some of the information I have offered tonight, and to it I am indebted for a reminder of that advertisement once published by an American munitions manufacturer. This manufacturer had developed a death-dealing instrument which it was anxious to sell and it advertised its accomplishment to the world as follows:

The material is high in tensile strength and very special. The timing of the fuse of this shell is similar to the shrapnel shell, but it differs in that two explosive acids are used to explode the shell in the large cavity. The combination of these two acids causes a terrific explosion, having more power than anything of its kind yet used. Fragments become coated with the acids in exploding and wounds

2804 Congress Investigates

caused by them mean death in terrible agony within four hours if not attended to immediately.

From what we are able to learn of conditions in the trenches, it is not possible to get medical assistance to anyone in time to prevent fatal results.

This is not a pleasant story with which to close my remarks. There ought to be something a little more cheering and I think that cheer is to be found in the prospect which is large that within the next few days the Senate will pass the resolution which has been offered by Senator Vandenberg and myself calling for a sweeping investigation of the activities and methods resorted to by our munitions makers to fatten thin bank accounts in the name of preparedness. I am sure that such an investigation will develop facts which will let people know how they are made monkeys of by profit-sundry, soulless madmen who are making lunatics of the people of the world by their incessant propaganda for ever-larger appropriations in the name of an "adequate defense". Truth always produces worth-while results. Truth concerning the methods and program of our munitions makers might fetch an awakening which would demand the removal of the element of profit from national defense and war. I am sure such action will not necessitate additional relief camps to accommodate those gentlemen who profit most largely when millions of men are giving their lives to the cause of flag and country. And it most assuredly will reduce the danger of more war and the terrific burdens of expense now required in the name of adequate defense.

MESSAGE OF FRANKLIN D. ROOSEVELT TO THE SENATE MAY 18, 1934

Congressional Record, 73rd Congress, 2nd Session, 9095.

I have been gratified to learn that, pursuant to a resolution of the Senate, a committee has been appointed to investigate the problems incident to the private manufacture of arms and munitions of war and the international traffic therein. I earnestly recommend that this committee receive the generous support of the Senate, in order that it may be enabled to pursue the investigation with which it is charged with a degree of thoroughness commensurate with the high importance of the questions at issue. The executive departments of the Government will be charged to cooperate with the committee to the fullest extent in furnishing it with any information in their possession which it may desire to receive, and their views upon the adequacy or inadequacy of existing legislation and of the treaties to which the United States is a party for the regulation and control of the manufacture of and traffic in arms.

The private and uncontrolled manufacture of arms and munitions and the traffic therein has become a serious source of international discord and strife.

It is not possible, however, effectively to control such an evil by the isolated action of any one country. The enlightened opinion of the world has long realized that this is a field in which international action is necessary. The negotiation of the Convention for the Supervision of the International Trade in Arms and Ammunition and in Implements of War, signed at Geneva, June 17, 1925, was an important step in the right direction. That convention is still before the Senate. I hope that the Senate may find it possible to give its advice and consent to its ratification. The ratification of that convention by this Government, which has been too long delayed, would be a concrete indication of the willingness of the American people to make their contribution toward the suppression of abuses which may have disastrous results for the entire world if they are permitted to continue unchecked.

It is my earnest hope that the representatives of the nations who will reassemble at Geneva on May 29 will be able to agree upon a convention containing provisions for the supervision and control of the traffic in arms much more far-reaching than those which were embodied in the convention of 1925. Some suitable international organization must and will take such action. The peoples of many countries are being taxed to the point of poverty and starvation in order to enable governments to engage in a mad race in armaments which, if permitted to continue, may well result in war. This grave menace to the peace of the world is due in no small measure to the uncontrolled activities of the manufacturers and merchants of engines of destruction, and it must be met by the concerted action of the peoples of all nations.

"ARMS MANUFACTURERS AND THE PUBLIC" BY "F" JULY 1934

Foreign Affairs, Vol. 12, No. 4, July 1934, 639–53.

On May 18, 1934, President Roosevelt sent a strongly worded Message to the Senate, recommending that it give generous support to the Special Committee which under the Chairmanship of Senator Nye has been charged with the investigation of the munitions industry. He further urged that the Senate give its advice and consent to the ratification of the Arms Traffic Convention of 1925, and expressed the hope that the General Disarmament Conference might find it possible to agree upon an international convention providing for more stringent regulation and control of the international traffic in arms than that agreed upon in 1925. Within an hour after the reading of this Message, Senator Pittman, Chairman of the Committee on Foreign Relations, presented to the Senate the unanimous report of the Committee in favor of the ratification of the Convention of 1925, and introduced a Joint Resolution, which he stated had the support of the Administration, authorizing the President to prohibit the sale of arms and munitions of war to Bolivia and Paraguay; and Senator Nye moved that $35,000 be added to the appropriation for the expenses of his Committee.

The events of that day served to focus public opinion upon a question in which various organizations have for years been attempting to awaken public interest, and for which opinion had been prepared by the appearance within the past few months of a number of widely-read articles and books.[1]

It would probably be impossible to determine just when it was first realized that the private manufacture of arms and the international trade in arms constituted serious dangers to the peace of the world, and that governmental supervision and control of those whom the President in his Message called "manufacturers and merchants of engines of destruction" must be a fundamental element in any program designed to restrict or abolish armed conflict among the nations. It first became a matter of world-wide discussion immediately after the Great War when men were seeking every possible means to prevent the recurrence of such a conflict. The statesmen who drafted the Covenant of the League of Nations were well aware of it when they included in it the following provision:

> The Members of the League agree that the manufacture by private enterprise of munitions and implements of war is open to grave objections. The Council shall advise how the evil effects attendant upon such manufacture can be prevented, due regard being had to the necessities of those Members of the League which are not able to manufacture the munitions and implements of war necessary for their safety.[2]

Within little more than two months after the signature of the Treaty of Versailles, a Convention for the Control of the Trade in Arms and Ammunition was signed at St. Germain-en-Laye and Paris on September 10, 1919, by the representatives of twenty-eight powers. Frank L. Polk, Henry White and General Tasker H. Bliss signed for the United States, but the failure of the Senate to give its advice and consent to the ratification of the Treaty of Versailles brought upon this Convention the same fate which met the other subsidiary treaties negotiated at the Peace Conference. It was not transmitted by the President to the Senate.

On numerous occasions from 1921 to 1923, the United States was urged by other signatory governments, and by the League of Nations, to ratify this Convention. They pointed out that as long as one of the principal manufacturing powers remained unfettered by its terms, other countries could not be expected to subject themselves to limitations which would result not in the control or the diminution of the trade in arms, but in the transfer of that trade to competitors of other nationalities to whom the Convention did not apply. The objections of this Government were, however, insuperable. The Convention was predicated upon the supposition that all the signatories would be members of the League, and certain functions of supervision and control were

[1] Among the most recent books and articles, some frankly sensational, others more sober, have been: "Merchants of Death," by H. C. Engelbrecht and F. C. Hanighen (New York: Dodd, Mead, 1934); "Iron, Blood and Profits," by George Seldes (New York: Harper, 1934); "Arms and the Men," *Fortune Magazine*, March 1934 (reprinted in pamphlet form by Doubleday, Doran); "Slaughter for Sale," by John Gunther, *Harper's Magazine*, May 1934; "The Armaments Scandal," by Jonathan Mitchell, *New Republic*, May 9 and 23, 1934.

[2] Article 8, Section 5.

placed in the hands of that organization. Thus ratification by the United States was, politically speaking, impossible. When this situation finally became clear to the other signatories to the Convention, and when they had come to realize that there was no likelihood that the United States would in the near future reverse the position which it had assumed in respect to the League, European statesmen came to the conclusion that the Convention of St. Germain could never be put into effect.

The Council of the League on April 21, 1923, adopted the following resolution:

> The Council, on the proposal of the Temporary Mixed Commission for the Reduction of Armaments, requests its President to ascertain whether the Government of the United States would be disposed to state its views as to the manner in which it would be willing to coöperate with other governments in the control both of the traffic in arms and the private manufacture of arms.

The reply of the United States Government to the communication transmitting this Resolution was such as to discourage all but the most persistent. The Council, however, was not discouraged. On December 14, 1923, an invitation was sent to the United States to participate in preparing the draft of a new convention. In the interval between these two communications, certain sections of public opinion in the United States had been aroused by the apparent unwillingness of the Government to coöperate with other nations in dealing with a problem so vital to the peace of the world. Perhaps the emphatic expression of this opinion had some effect in changing the attitude of the Government. In any case, the invitation of the Council was accepted and representatives of the United States participated in the drafting of a new convention. A conference to consider this draft was called by the League to meet in Geneva on May 4, 1925. The American delegates were Theodore E. Burton, former Senator from Ohio, at that time a Member of Congress; Hugh S. Gibson, then Minister to Switzerland; Rear Admiral Andrew T. Long, Allen W. Dulles, and Brigadier General Colden L. Ruggles. Throughout the negotiations, there was an evident desire on the part of the delegates of the other Powers to produce a convention which would encounter no difficulties in being ratified by the United States. Mr. Burton, in the report of the American Delegation of December 16, 1925, stated:

> The delegates at the Conference impressed upon the American Delegation their view that any international convention for the control of the trade in arms would be ineffective unless adhered to by the United States, one of the important arms-producing Powers. With a view to facilitating American adherence, the Conference did not press for the inclusion of any provision for the supervision or control of the arms trade by an international commission, recognizing that such control would be inacceptable to this Government. Further, the various proposals advanced from time to time by the American Delegation received the full and sympathetic consideration of the Conference and in every case where American principles and interests were involved, solutions which the American Delega-

tion considered acceptable were adopted. The American Delegation desire to record their recognition of this attitude and, in submitting the Treaty, to state that in their opinion the success or failure of the present Convention will in no small measure depend upon the position assumed by the American Government in the matter.

The Convention was transmitted by President Coolidge to the Senate for its advice and consent to ratification on January 11, 1926.

The signing of the Arms Traffic Convention of 1925 was hailed throughout the world as a great and signal victory. The evils arising from the private manufacture of arms and the international traffic in arms were now about to succumb to international supervision and control. Enlightened public opinion had triumphed—or so it seemed. But the proponents of the Convention were doomed, as a result of the indifference of the United States Senate, to a great disappointment. The Convention slumbered in the Committee on Foreign Relations from January 11, 1926, until May 18, 1934. It is difficult to determine why no action was taken on this Convention over such a long period. There are those who have not failed to discern in the inaction of the Senate the result of the nefarious machinations of American arms manufacturers. A much more probable explanation appears to be that, in the absence of an aroused public opinion in this country, the Senate did not feel impelled to act upon a Convention in which few of its members were particularly interested. No hearings were held by the Committee and no definite opposition developed. From time to time successive Secretaries of State attempted to prod the Committee into action. President Hoover sent a Message on January 10, 1933, urging that favorable action be taken. But this Message fell on stony ground. The immediate response of the Committee on Foreign Relations to the recent similar Message of President Roosevelt may probably be ascribed in no small part to the revival of public interest in questions relating to the munitions industry.

The ratification of the Convention by the United States would probably result in its coming into force within a reasonably brief interval. Other important Powers, remembering the Treaty of St. Germain, have waited action by the United States. The Convention provides that it will become effective when ratified by fourteen Powers. Twelve ratifications or accessions have already been deposited. Two other Powers have decided upon ratification, and one other Power upon accession, but ratification in these three cases has not been completed. Some of these ratifications are, however, conditional upon ratification by other specified powers. The Committee on Foreign Relations has recommended similar procedure for this Government by proposing a reservation to the effect that the Convention shall not come into force so far as the United States is concerned until it shall have come into force in respect to Belgium, the British Empire, Czechoslovakia, France, Germany, Italy, Japan, Sweden, and the Union of Soviet Socialist Republics.

The important provisions of the Arms Traffic Convention of 1925 limit the export of arms to those arms intended for the direct supply of the government of the importing state (or with the consent of such government for the supply of a public authority subordinate to it), and set up a machinery of licenses or export declarations for all arms exported or imported, and provide for full publicity for the arms traffic.

Ever since the end of the World War there have been two main currents of opinion as to the proper means of dealing with the evils arising from the private manufacture of arms and the international traffic therein. Some believe that the remedy lies in governmental supervision and control and full publicity; others are convinced that nothing short of the complete suppression of the private manufacture of arms and the nationalization of the whole armaments industry and the international traffic in arms and munitions will eradicate the evils inherent in the present system. The Arms Traffic Convention of 1925, following in general the lines laid down in the Convention of St. Germain, was an attempt to deal with the problem by the former method. The proponents of the latter method are still actively working for a solution in conformity with their views.

At the very beginning of its deliberations the General Commission of the General Disarmament Conference appointed a "Committee for the Regulation of the Trade in and the Private and State Manufacture of Arms and Implements of War" to canvass the opinions of the governments participating in the Conference, and to make recommendations with a view to the incorporation in a General Disarmament Convention of provisions dealing with this phase of the disarmament problem. The Committee met at intervals during 1932 and 1933 and discussed these matters at great length. Of all the Committees of this almost hopelessly deadlocked Conference, this Committee was perhaps the most hopelessly deadlocked. Its reports "on the progress of the work" are reports of lack of progress. Questions are posed, radical divisions of views recorded, and no conclusions of any consequence arrived at. Underlying the innumerable subsidiary differences of opinion which developed during the discussions of the Committee, was the fundamental divergence between the advocates of supervision and control and the advocates of suppression and nationalization. In the forefront of those advocating the former method of approach were the delegations of the United States, Great Britain, Belgium, Germany, Italy and Japan; the most energetic exponents of the latter method were the delegations of France, Poland, Denmark and Spain.

The position of the United States has remained unchanged since it was expressed by Mr. Burton during the negotiation of the Arms Traffic Convention of 1925, in part as follows:

> Many of those in Europe and America with whom I have coöperated for years past in movements for peace think that the solution of their problems rests in the prohibition of private manufacture. They argue, that so long as private manufacture continues, there will be a powerful industrial interest, the prosperity of which will be promoted by war, and this they consider to be a barrier in the way of peace. They consider also that these private manufacturers have also been extremely skilful in the circulation of propaganda unfavorable to peace. Thus, they say, the manufacture of arms, munitions and implements of war should be restricted to Governments.
>
> Let me point out to you the fallacy of this argument. The private

manufacture of arms and munitions is flexible and adapted both to peace and to war. It may consist of the manufacture of explosives and material for industrial purposes, of sporting arms which have nothing to do with war, to which can be added in time of conflict the manufacture of military arms. Take my own country as an example; the manufacture of munitions and military arms was negligible before the late Great War, but, during that period, private industry increased to enormous proportions; it has now fallen back to what it was before.

Government manufacture and control, on the other hand, are inflexible and look to a state of war. It involves the maintenance of a very considerable force, always engaged in the manufacture of implements of destruction. If that force is disbanded the nation is helpless, and there is always a strong interest in favor of maintaining in any form of Government activity a large force, expanding its operations to the maximum. Thus, I say that, at least in a country like the United States, the idea that the private manufacture of arms should be prohibited, and that such prohibition would promote peace, is a chimera. More than that, why should a Conference be called for the prohibition of private manufacture and leave the Governmental or public manufacture alone? Shall the respective Governments of the world, whether warlike or peaceful in their intentions, build huge structures to make arms, and at the same time prohibit the private manufacture? What of the private manufacturers, many of whom have the most pacific intentions? What have they done that there should be this discrimination against them? What hope have the lovers of peace in prohibiting private manufacture, if Governmental manufacture may still go on to an enormous and unlimited extent?

The opponents of nationalization of the munitions industry contend that such action would probably result in an increase in the production of arms and munitions and in an increase in the stocks maintained by the governments of the world. They argue that the governments of non-producing countries would be obliged to establish arsenals in order to supply their legitimate needs, and that their inability in an emergency to purchase arms and munitions from private producers abroad would probably lead them to maintain very large stocks on hand. They contend further that such a system would strengthen the strong and weaken the weak. The great majority of the nations of the world would be placed at the mercy of the ten or a dozen nations favored by nature with supplies of raw materials and possessed of the necessary industrial organization. There are many also who are strongly opposed to nationalization of the munitions industry because such a system would put governments into business on a scale unknown at present outside of the Union of the Soviet Socialist Republics.

As far as any tendency can be discerned in the recent discussions at Geneva, it would appear to be a tendency toward governmental supervision and control rather than toward nationalization. As the former solution is less extreme than the latter, there would appear to be more likelihood of its being agreed upon as a compromise, if any agreement is to be reached, than that the proponents of governmental supervision and control should be won over to the thesis of nationalization. Such an agreement might embody a reiteration of the provisions of the Arms Traffic Convention of 1925, modified in some non-essentials which have been subjected to criticism, together with provisions similar to those contained in the Draft Convention submitted to the Council of the League by a Special Commission in 1929. This Draft Convention provides for the setting up of a system of licenses for arms manufacture and a system of full publicity for the armaments industry, similar to the system of licenses and publicity provided for the traffic in arms by the Convention of 1925.

The Government of the United States has been more reluctant to accept the principle of supervision and control of the manufacture of arms than it was to accept this principle in respect to the international traffic. Until November 18, 1932, our delegates at Geneva had always met the proposal that governmental supervision and control be established by international agreement with the statement that the Constitution of the United States prevented the Federal Government from entering into a convention involving the control of manufacture in the several States. On that date, Mr. Hugh Wilson announced at a meeting of the Bureau of the Disarmament Conference that the United States was prepared to accept supervision of private manufacture provided that state manufacture was also supervised. This change of position had been foreshadowed by Mr. Stimson, who several days before was quoted in the press as stating that the Government had reached the conclusion that the position that the Federal Government lacked constitutional power to enter into such a convention was not well taken. In this statement, he referred to the case of Missouri *vs.* Holland as supporting the position that this Government could enter into such a convention and, having done so, would possess the constitutional authority to enact and enforce legislation pursuant to that convention. This statement in conjunction with the statement in President Roosevelt's Message of May 18, 1934, that it was his "earnest hope that the representatives of the nations who will reassemble at Geneva on May 29 will be able to agree upon a convention containing provisions for the supervision and control of the traffic in arms much more far reaching than those which were embodied in the Convention of 1925" would appear to indicate clearly that the Government of the United States is prepared to enter into an international convention providing for the most stringent supervision and control, both of the manufacture of arms and of the international traffic in arms, by the establishment of a system of licenses accompanied by full publicity.

It has been recognized by all students of the problem that no effective control of the munitions industry can be established except by international agreement. Nevertheless, some of the nations have independently enacted domestic legislation of the nature of that contemplated by the Arms Traffic Convention of 1925 and other proposals which have been made at Geneva. Great Britain and Sweden, for instance, require licenses for the export of arms and munitions, and permission to export is frequently withheld. Authority to prohibit the export of arms in particular cases is vested in the Executive of the governments of all of the important producing countries except Czechoslovakia, Switzerland and the United States.

The United States has lagged far behind other nations in legislation on this subject. Our Government has on several occasions expressed pious hopes and made pious gestures. The Department of State on December 27, 1923, issued a statement to the press, defending the position of this Government in regard to the Convention of St. Germain, and adding:

> The Executive Branch of the Government is not in a position to intervene in transactions which are wholly within the law; but not desiring to encourage other Powers to arm themselves for conflict, which is deemed contrary to the spirit of the country, this Government, in addition to adopting a strict policy with regard to the sale of surplus government army stores, has replied to the recent inquiries which it has received that it does not encourage the shipment of war material to the troubled areas of the world. This stand has been taken although this Government was not unmindful of the fact that intending purchasers would no doubt resort to other markets to supply their wants. It may also be added that under present conditions the Department would not favor the flotation of a foreign loan in this country for which the proceeds would be utilized for armament.

There is no evidence that the announcement of this policy had any practical effect in so far as the export of arms and munitions by private companies and individuals was concerned. Aside from the laws of the Federal Government and of the several States designed to prevent the sale of arms to criminals and minors and to protect the public against explosions, the only legislation relating to the traffic in arms is a series of Joint Resolutions which have been brought to public attention by recent debates in Congress.

The first of these Joint Resolutions was that approved on April 22, 1898,[3] which conferred upon the Executive the power to prohibit the export of war materials "within his discretion and with such limitations and exemptions as would seem to him expedient." Although this Resolution was a war measure passed in connection with the war with Spain, it remained on the statute books for fourteen years and the power conferred by it was used on October 14, 1905, when President Theodore Roosevelt issued a proclamation [4] in which "for good and sufficient reasons unto me appearing" he forbade the export of arms to any port in the Dominican Republic. This resolution was amended by the passage of the Joint Resolution of March 14, 1912,[5] as follows:

> Resolved by the Senate and House of Representatives of the United States of America in Congress assembled, That the joint resolution to prohibit the export of coal or other material used in war from any seaport of the United States, approved April twenty-second, eighteen hundred and ninety-eight, be, and hereby is, amended to read as follows:
>
> That whenever the President shall find that in any American country conditions of domestic violence exist which are promoted by the use of arms or munitions of war procured from the United States, and shall make proclamation thereof, it shall be unlawful to

[3] 30 Stat. 739.
[4] 34 Stat. 3183.
[5] 37 Stat. 630.

export except under such limitations and exceptions as the President shall prescribe any arms or munitions of war from any place in the United States to such country until otherwise ordered by the President or by Congress.

Sec. 2. That any shipment of material hereby declared unlawful after such a proclamation shall be punishable by fine not exceeding ten thousand dollars, or imprisonment not exceeding two years, or both.

By the Joint Resolution of January 31, 1922,[6] this authority was extended to include any country in which the United States exercises extraterritorial jurisdiction. These countries are, at present, China, Morocco, Egypt, Ethiopia, and some of the states of Arabia. Pursuant to the authority conferred by these two Resolutions, restrictions upon the export of arms have been proclaimed as follows: Brazil (proclaimed October 22, 1930; revoked March 2, 1931); China (proclaimed March 4, 1922; still in effect); Cuba (proclaimed May 2, 1924; revoked August 29, 1924); Honduras (proclaimed March 22, 1924; still in effect); Mexico (proclaimed March 14, 1912; revoked February 3, 1914; proclaimed October 19, 1915; revoked January 31, 1922; proclaimed January 7, 1924; revoked July 18, 1929); Nicaragua (proclaimed September 15, 1926; still in effect).

In enforcing the restrictions proclaimed under the Joint Resolutions of March 14, 1912 and January 31, 1922, the Secretaries of State have established a system of licenses for each individual shipment. These licenses have been granted or withheld in their discretion in accordance with the conditions existing at the moment in the countries for which the shipments were destined.

The principle underlying these resolutions was confirmed by the Convention relating to the Rights and Duties of States in the Event of Civil Strife, signed at Havana on February 20, 1928, under which the United States, as a party to the Convention, is obligated to prevent the export of arms intended for the use of rebels against the authorities of such Governments as have ratified that Convention.

It will be noted that the Joint Resolution of January 31, 1922, refers exclusively to "conditions of domestic violence." On January 10, 1933, President Hoover, in a Special Message, recommended that the authority of the Executive in this matter be extended to cover international conflicts. In pursuance of this recommendation, the Foreign Relations Committee of the Senate unanimously reported the so-called Arms Embargo Resolution, of which the vital portion reads as follows:

That whenever the President finds that in any part of the world conditions exist such that the shipment of arms or munitions of war from countries which produce these commodities may promote or encourage the employment of force in the course of a dispute or conflict between nations, and, after securing the coöperation of such governments as the President deems necessary, he makes proclamation thereof, it shall be unlawful to export, or sell for export, except under such limitations and exceptions as the Presi-

[6] 42 Stat. 361.

dent prescribes, any arms or munitions of war from any place in the United States to such country or countries as he may designate, until otherwise ordered by the President or by Congress.

This Resolution was passed without a dissenting vote by the Senate on January 11, 1933. A few days later, however, Senator Bingham of Connecticut moved to reconsider, explaining that it would take several hours for him to set forth his objections on constitutional grounds to the Resolution. As it was near the end of the session and as the Senate calendar was crowded, he found no opportunity to state his objections and no further action was taken by the Senate.

During the same session of Congress, the Resolution was debated at length by the House Committee on Foreign Affairs. At a series of hearings, it was supported by the Secretary of State, Mr. Stimson, and representatives of his department, and strenuously opposed by the representatives of a number of arms manufacturers. These latter attacked the Resolution as unconstitutional, as potentially harmful to American trade and as constituting a menace to the national defense. It was, however, voted out by the Committee with an amendment limiting its application to the Western Hemisphere. In view of the effective opposition of Senator Bingham to further consideration of the Resolution in the Senate, it was not deemed worth while to bring the amended Resolution to a vote in the House.

At the special session of Congress, which was called by President Roosevelt shortly after his inauguration, the Resolution was revived with the support of the new Administration. The Committee on Foreign Affairs of the House again discussed it at length and held further public hearings. The discussions now centered upon a statement which Mr. Stimson had made in support of the Resolution and, in particular upon the following portion of his statement that "one of two conditions would exist," namely that—

   a. The world would coöperate in refusing supplies to both nations. This would certainly involve no breach of neutrality by the United States as the movement would be general and the nations united in a common front.

   b. There might be a situation in which as a result of investigation and consultation on a large scale there was a clear definition agreed upon by all the coöperating powers that one side or the other was the aggressor. It is becoming evident in recent years that this condition is much easier to realize than used to be believed. The world-wide publicity afforded since the Great War on every international incident and army movement, and the means of investigation by international commissions which is rapidly gaining ground, all show that there are situations today in which there can be a general verdict far beyond previous anticipation. The verdict of the League of Nations on this point, for example, as shown by recent events, is a perfectly practicable procedure. If the League or any other comprehensive group of important states had mutually arrived at such a verdict, the participation of the United States in a general arms embargo would be not merely practical and sound but practically necessary to preserve our national dignity and standing as a peaceful nation.

This statement was hailed with enthusiasm by several well-known international lawyers who sensed in it an indication of a more coöperative attitude on the part of the United States, and it immediately drew the fire of other distinguished authorities on international law, including John Bassett Moore. The Arms Embargo Resolution suddenly became the center of a debate on the policy which the United States should adopt in relation to the whole structure of the machinery for peace which has been built up since the war. Out of the welter of arguments covering the Covenant of the League, the Briand-Kellogg Pact, Washington's Farewell Address, and the doctrine of neutrality as applied during the Napoleonic Wars, the chief point at issue clearly emerged. It was as follows: Was the President, in exercising the authority conferred upon him by the Resolution, to be bound to apply restrictions on the export of arms equally to all parties to an armed conflict, or might he be permitted discretion to apply them to a so-called "aggressor nation" in case aggression had been judicially or quasi-judicially determined, and in case the Government of the United States concurred in the decision, at the same time permitting the unrestricted sale of arms and munitions to the nations engaged in resisting the aggressor? The Democratic majority of the Committee, complying with the recommendations of Presidents Hoover and Roosevelt and their respective Secretaries of State, voted in support of the Resolution conferring discretionary power upon the President. The Republican minority presented an adverse report. After prolonged debate, the Resolution was carried in the House by an almost strictly partisan vote.

The Senate Committee on Foreign Relations adopted the position of the Republicans in the House and reported the Resolution to the Senate on May 30, 1933, with the so-called Johnson Amendment as follows:

> Provided, however, That any prohibition of export, or of sale for export, proclaimed under this resolution shall apply impartially to all the parties to the dispute or conflict to which it refers.

On the same day the Secretary of State was reported in the press as having stated that the Johnson Amendment did not conform to the views of the President or of himself, and, probably as a result of this statement, the Resolution was not brought to a vote in the Senate during the special session.

On February 28, 1934, the Resolution, with the addition of the Johnson Amendment, was unexpectedly called up in the Senate and passed without a dissenting vote. As the two Houses were in disagreement in regard to the amendment, it was returned to the House where at this writing it still reposes on the Speaker's desk. The Administration has, on several occasions, reiterated its opposition to the amendment. It has been pointed out that Mr. Norman H. Davis, on May 22, 1933, made a statement before the General Commission of the General Disarmament Conference in which, on behalf of the United States, he declared:

> In addition I wish to make it clear that we are ready not only to do our part toward the substantive reduction of armaments, but if this

is effected by general international agreement, we are also prepared to contribute in other ways to the organization of peace. In particular we are willing to consult the other states in case of a threat to peace with a view to averting conflict. Further than that, in the event that the states, in conference, determine that a state has been guilty of a breach of the peace in violation of its international obligations, and take measures against the violator, then, if we concur in the judgment rendered as to the responsible and guilty party, we will refrain from any action tending to defeat such collective effort which these states may thus make to restore peace.

The passage of the Resolution may not be necesary in order to permit the Government of the United States to carry out the terms of Mr. Davis's offer, although without the passage of such a Resolution the President would have no authority to prevent shipment of arms to both parties of a conflict and the shipment of arms to an aggressor nation might possibly be considered as action tending to defeat collective effort. The passage of the Resolution with the Johnson Amendment would obviously run counter to the principles and spirit underlying Mr. Davis's offer, as the prohibition of the shipment of arms to the nations engaging in collective action against an aggressor would undoubtedly tend to defeat such collective effort. From statements made in recent Congressional debates, it may be inferred that the proponents of the Johnson Amendment intended it as evidence of their disapproval of the disarmament policy of the President.

In view of the inability of two successive Administrations (of different political complexions) to secure the passage of the Arms Embargo Resolution, the prompt and unanimous action of Congress on the Resolution empowering the President to prohibit the sale of arms and munitions of war to Bolivia and Paraguay is little short of astounding. It was introduced in the Senate by Senator Pittman on May 18 and in the House by Mr. McReynolds on May 21. The respective Committees voted it out unanimously, and it was passed by the House without a dissenting vote on May 23, and by the Senate without a dissenting vote on May 24. At this writing, it seems probable that the President will within a few days approve the Resolution and issue the necessary Proclamation to make the prohibition effective. It is true that by the terms of this Resolution any prohibition on the sale of arms and munitions would apply equally to both parties to the conflict and that, therefore, the controversy which has raged about the Johnson Amendment did not arise. The Resolution has, however, the same "unconstitutional" character and offers the same "menace" to the national defense which were so eloquently denounced by the representatives of arms manufacturers in the public hearings on the Arms Embargo Resolution. This time no representatives of those manufacturers appeared at the Capitol. It may be surmised that they have sensed the trend of public opinion within the last few months and that they will no longer oppose, at least openly, legislation designed to control their activities in the public interest.

When Senator Nye introduced his Resolution, calling for a Senate investigation of all aspects of the munitions industry and the traffic in arms, it was freely predicted that he could not possibly secure favorable action by the Senate on such a Resolution. He has been quoted as having said at that time that, although he was introducing the Resolution in all good faith and would make every effort to secure its passage, he nevertheless had almost no hope of success. The Resolution has been passed. A Special Committee Investigating the Munitions Industry has been formed, consisting of seven Senators, with Senator Nye as Chairman. The President, in his Message of May 18, recommended that the Senate give its generous support to the Committee and promised the full coöperation of all the Executive Departments. The Committee is effecting an organization and has begun its labors.

It is to be hoped that the Nye Committee's investigation will be objective and thorough. It has an opportunity to present for the first time to the American people the facts in regard to an industry of which the activities are of the highest interest to the nation, and, on the basis of these facts, it will be in a position to recommend dispassionately and authoritatively legislation and policy in a field in which wise action by the American Government is imperatively necessary.

SENATE RESOLUTION 206
SEPTEMBER 4, 1934

U. S. Senate, *Munitions Industry:* Hearings Before the Special Committee Investigating the Munitions Industry, Part 1, 1–2.

Whereas the influence of the commercial motive is an inevitable factor in considerations involving the maintenance of the national defense; and

Whereas the influence of the commercial motive is one of the inevitable factors often believed to stimulate and sustain wars; and

Whereas the Seventy-first Congress, by Public Resolution No. 98, approved June 27, 1930, responding to the long-standing demands of American war veterans speaking through the American Legion for legislation "to take the profit out of war", created a War Policies Commission which reported recommendations on December 7, 1931, and on March 7, 1932, to decommercialize war and to equalize the burdens thereof; and

Whereas these recommendations never have been translated into the statutes:

Therefore be it

Resolved, That a special committee of the Senate shall be appointed by the Vice President to consist of seven Senators, and that said committee be, and is hereby, authorized and directed—

(a) To investigate the activities of individuals, firms, associations, and of corporations and all other agencies in the United States engaged in the manufacture, sale, distribution, import, or export of arms, munitions, or other implements of war; the nature of the industrial and commercial organizations

engaged in the manufacture of or traffic in arms, munitions, or other implements of war; the methods used in promoting or effecting the sale of arms,
munitions, or other implements of war; the quantities of arms, munitions, or
other implements of war imported into the United States and the countries of
origin thereof, and the quantities exported from the United States and the
countries of destination thereof; and

(b) To investigate and report upon the adequacy or inadequacy of existing legislation, and of the treaties to which the United States is a party, for the
regulation and control of the manufacture of and traffic in arms, munitions, or
other implements of war within the United States, and of the traffic therein
between the United States and other countries; and

(c) To review the findings of the War Policies Commission and to recommend such specific legislation as may be deemed desirable to accomplish the
purposes set forth in such findings and in the preamble to this resolution; and

(d) To inquire into the desirability of creating a Government monopoly
in respect to the manufacture of armaments and munitions and other implements of war, and to submit recommendations thereon.

For the purposes of this resolution the committee or any subcommittee
thereof is authorized to hold hearings, to sit and act at such times and places
during the sessions and recesses of the Congress until the final report is
submitted, to require by subpena or otherwise the attendance of such witnesses and the production of such books, papers, and documents, to administer such oaths, to take such testimony, and to make such expenditures, as it
deems advisable. The cost of stenographic services to report such hearings
shall not be in excess of 25 cents per hundred words. The expenses of the
committee, which shall not exceed $15,000, shall be paid from the contingent
fund of the Senate upon vouchers approved by the chairman.

NEW YORK TIMES REPORT
SEPTEMBER 2, 1934

"If we defeat the depression caused by the World War, and we accomplish
national recovery, what good will it do if we are moved into another war?"
Senator Nye asked a radio audience tonight, as he denounced munition
manufacturers into whose activities the Nye committee will start an intensive
investigation Tuesday.

Speaking over the Columbia Broadcasting System, he asserted that annual average profits of the Atlas Powder Company moved from $485,000 in
peace time to $2,374,000 in the World War years and gave increases for other
concerns as follows:

Hercules Powder Company—by $6,000,000.
General Motors Corporation—from $6,954,000 to $21,700,000.
Anaconda Copper Company—by $24,000,000.
United States Steel Corporation—from $105,331,000 to $239,653,000.
Bethlehem Steel Company—from $6,840,000 to $49,427,000.
Du Pont—from $6,092,000 to $58,076,000.

Scope of Investigation

The coming investigation, Senator Nye said just before he spoke on the radio, would constitute the disclosure of one of "the most amazing chapters" in the history of American manufacture of arms and munitions.

The list of over 100 witnesses, those called for next week to be made public tomorrow, would be a "Who's Who" of the industry, he added, and the inquiry would involve every angle of the war implements industry in this country and much of it that functions under other flags.

The first phase of the investigation will centre on submarines and other underwater weapons, the second will feature the traffic in anti-aircraft ordnance, while the third will enter upon the manufacture of ordnance in general.

Questions for Witnesses

Witnesses will be asked to disclose their past and present profits from manufacture of explosives, poison gas, airplanes, armor plate, heavy and light artillery, anti-aircraft ordnance, rifles, tanks and all implements of modern warfare.

They will also be called on to state what interest, understanding, or other relations exist between themselves, their firms or corporations and the manufacturers of arms and munitions in England, France, Germany or other foreign countries in which the industry is of major proportions.

Finally, the inquiry will take up alleged "lobbying" by agents of the industry in Washington and their role, if any, in disarmament conferences.

Senator Nye said that the investigation might result in a program comprising the following elements:

Establishment of a "peace department" on a par with the War and Navy Departments.

Government monopoly or control over the primary items entering into the conduct of war.

Legislation making it illegal for the American flag to fly over ships carrying cargoes to warring nations.

Taking the profit out of war by a revenue law amendment "which would automatically write new rates of income taxation with a declaration of war."

TESTIMONY ON "COOKY PUSHERS" OF THE STATE DEPARTMENT SEPTEMBER 13, 1934

U.S. Senate, *Munitions Industry:* Hearings Before the Special Committee Investigating the Munitions Industry, Part 5, 1134–35.

Senator Pope. Who is the president of the Federal Laboratories Co.? Do you know?

Mr. Casey. John Y. Young.

Senator Pope. John Y. Young. Where are they located?

Mr. Casey. John W. Young, I guess it is. At Pittsburgh.

Senator Pope. I offer in evidence a letter from Mr. Aiken Simons to Mr. Young, under date of December 28, 1932, just after Christmas, as "Exhibit No. 482."

(The letter referred to was marked "Exhibit No. 482", and appears in full in the text.)

Senator Pope. That letter reads as follows:

Mr. Dear John: Thank you for the very handsome dressing case which came to me on Christmas morning. I will find it very useful.

I spent a very quiet but very pleasant Christmas despite the rotten weather. Regarding the attempts of Mr. Hoover and the "cooky pushers" in the State Department to effect embargoes on munitions sent out of the country, I do not believe that there is the least occasion for alarm at present. The President and the State Department both lack authority to do anything now and in the spirit that Congress is in and with the large amount of oral business ahead I feel quite sure that no further authority will be granted.

Wishing you a very prosperous New Year.

And he signs:

Sincerely, Aiken Simons.

The Chairman. Senator Pope, does that particular letter carry a stamp revealing that upon instructions of the War and/or Navy Department it is of a confidential nature?

Senator Pope. I am interested in that rather "luscious" term, "cooky pushers." Do you know what Mr. Simons meant by "cooky pushers" in the State Department?

Mr. Casey. I have not the slightest idea, and I could not be responsible for a statement of that kind. That is a personal letter thanking him for a little brief case.

Senator Pope. Do you think it might have anything to do with those people who might have been favorable to embargo acts and similar legislation?

Mr. Casey. I could not tell.

Senator Pope. Do you know whether he included Secretary Stimson in that category?

Mr. Casey. I could not say.

Senator Pope. He mentioned Mr. Hoover and the "cooky pushers" in the same breath. Do you know whether he included Mr. Hoover in that category?

Mr. Casey. Again I cannot say. I have not the slightest idea.

Senator Pope. Did he ever talk to you about who were the "cooky pushers" up there?

Mr. Casey. No; in fact, I never heard the expression before, because I never saw the letter.

Senator Pope. You think, in the light of this statement here, just after Christmas Day, when he was at peace with the world and he said:

> I do not believe that there is the least occasion for alarm at present. The President and the State Department both lack authority to do anything now and in the spirit that Congress is in and with the large amount of oral business ahead I feel quite sure that no further authority will be granted—

that he was making that as a disinterested party, without knowledge of what Congress might do?

Mr. Casey. Yes, sir.

Senator Clark. Major, if this was a letter intended to promote "peace on earth, good will among men," do you know how it happened to get into the official files of the du Pont Co., from which it was taken by our investigators?

Mr. Casey. We opened everything, and that may have been in their personal files.

Mr. Irénée du Pont. The investigators did look through personal files in our corner of the building. I do not know whether they found anything.

Mr. Casey. Anything they wanted to see we gave them.

Senator Clark. Even though this was a personal letter, it contained a certain clear assurance on this embargo which had been placed by President Hoover.

MEMORANDUM OF LAMMOT DU PONT
TO GERALD P. NYE
NOVEMBER 14, 1934

U.S. Senate, *Munitions Industry;* Hearings Before the Special Committee Investigating the Munitions Industry, Part 5, 1411–14.

My Dear Senator Nye:

You have invited us to submit a memorandum for the consideration of your committee as it undertakes the formulation of a sound national policy with respect to munitions for presentation to the Congress. We welcome this opportunity to be of service. The subject is a very difficult one, having occupied the thoughtful attention of many minds over a long period of time, and we do not profess to be able to offer a complete solution for every question involved. We shall endeavor, however, to deal specifically and practically with some of the major questions as they are set forth in Senate Resolution #206.

We believe that two considerations must be paramount in any satisfactory national policy on munitions.

1. Adequate national defense must be assured.

2. The maintenance of peace must be encouraged and fostered.

Our thinking on each of the questions under discussion takes these two aims into account; answer to every question must be in harmony with both considerations: On the one hand the defense of the nation if it is attacked; on the other, the protection of the American people from the danger of war, with all its horrors and its malign consequences. There is no conflict here; a strong but forbearing America is the greatest guarantor of peace.

Necessity of Provision for the National Defense

No prudent nation can afford to be unarmed in the world today. Moreover, as modern wars are increasingly liable to be won or lost before the actual outbreak of hostilities, this country's preparation for defense needs to be wise and thorough. Its execution should be efficient, it must be effective.

The vital importance of your committee's investigations and recommendations must appeal to all thoughtful Americans, who are familiar with their country's history. In every one of its major conflicts the United States has sent its young men into battle without proper equipment, supplies, or support. Each war has been prolonged unnecessarily; each has cost thousands of lives that ought never to have been lost. The bravest, who volunteered first, have been sacrificed in the struggle to hold the line while the nation went through the slow, laborious, and terribly costly process of marshalling its resources.

Inadequacy of Government Monopoly

The attempt to limit this preparation to government monopoly in peace time and to confine the manufacture of munitions or ordnance to government plants and facilities in war time would, in our opinion, weaken and if carried far enough cripple our national defense. We are convinced that the problem requires maximum effort both by the Government and American industry. Neither one by itself can be relied upon to meet all requirements.

Munitions include all articles of every kind required for the supply of the Army and Navy; not only ordnance but uniforms, shoes, shelter, mess equipment, tools, fuel, automobiles, shipping, food, medicines, miscellaneous supplies. It is inconceivable that the government should undertake so vast a field of production either in peace or in war. All the resources of the country both public and private must be available for the productions essential to national defense.

Ordnance itself is also a field of tremendous scope. A partial list of implements of war as set forth by the Geneva Convention includes rifles, machine guns, ammunition, gun-sighting apparatus, cannon, projectiles, bombs, torpedoes, depth charges, grenades, mines, bayonets, tanks, armored cars, pistols, swords, warships and arms and ammunition therefor, aircraft, aircraft engines, gun powder, and explosives. The Ordnance Department of the United States Army had to deal in the World War with the production of over 200,000 separate components, among these some individual articles of ordnance comprising as high as 6,000 separate pieces. Nearly 8,000 industrial plants, including manufacturers of sewing machines, typewriters, boilers, radiators, electrical equipment, airbrakes, hardware, safes, etc., were engaged in the manufacture of ordnance in 1918; over 25,000 in all munitions. A modern nation fighting for its life requires practically all of its manufacturers to become munition makers.

It is estimated that private plants produced 95% and government arsenals 5% of this country's ordnance in the Great War. For example, the total output of the two long-established and well-equipped government smokeless powder plants during our participation in the World War, April 6th, 1917, to November 11th, 1918, was less than 2% of the powder made in the United States during that period; it would have sustained the fire of the American troops during the fall of 1918 for only nine days. Government cannot undertake the tasks enumerated above in time of war. It has then too much else to do. All the productive capacity of the nation must be called upon.

Since the War, government arsenals, although operating at only one-tenth of their capacities, have been supplying about 95% of Army ordnance, private manufacturers only 5%. But in the event of a major emergency experts estimate that government facilities would again only be able to furnish about 5% of the ordnance required. For adequate preparation for the defense of our country a policy of nationalization would thus call for the expansion of government arsenals forthwith to twenty times their present capacities. That would be a monstrous undertaking, advocated by no one. The cost would be colossal, ordnance appropriations would have to be increased over a hundred fold, operation would be extremely difficult if not impractical, the effect might be provocative.

If, lacking such facilities, we attempt to supply them after we are attacked we but court disaster. We were almost defenseless in some of these respects when we entered the World War in 1917. Every one who knows the facts will recall that over a year after our entrance into the War our troops had to be supplied throughout with British and French machine guns, cannons, and airplanes. Not until the autumn of 1918, just before the Armistice, was our production of ordnance becoming adequate. That experience which might have cost us so dear must not be disregarded and forgotten. The actual and potential facilities then revealed must not now be abandoned.

The Sound Plan for National Defense

We consider, therefore, that the only wise solution of the problem is just what has already been undertaken; the preparation of plans of defense, the survey and charting of industrial resources, the provisional enlistment of industry, so as to be ready to marshal the entire plant and personnel of the country immediately when the hour of danger arrives. This cooperation between government and industry for the defense of our country must be continued. And the maintenance in the fabric of American industry of effective nuclei for the rapid expansion of munitions production in an emergency is of vital importance.

Objections to Private Manufacture of Munitions

Two objections to private manufacture of munitions in general and ordnance in particular are raised; excess war profits, and abuses attending the traffic in arms. These we shall try to deal with in turn.

War Profits

We subscribe to the view that excess war profits should be eliminated. There is a popular demand, which is sound and just, that in the event of any such future national crisis as a major war the entire capital and productive resources of our country should be subjected to the national need without the prospect of extraordinary compensation. The national policy should be based on the principle that in a time of national emergency, when the country's man power is being mobilized, its material resources should be mobilized also.

A plan for carrying out this policy must consist of practical measures. It must be sure to succeed. It must harness every effort, employ every motive to insure speed, efficient operation, low costs, elimination of waste, conservation of materials, saving of labor. Further, it must be all inclusive in scope, extended throughout the whole fabric of our economic structure. Elimination of excessive earnings must apply to every business and every individual.

The formulation of a comprehensive and practical plan is a problem of tremendous difficulty. The Committee will appreciate that the elimination or recapture of profits in excess of peace-time earnings contemplates a new and drastic measure. The dangers of such a radical departure from normal economic habits may not be appreciated. We should be negligent if we failed to emphasize the national perils which would lurk in a superficial or unsound attempt at its solution. It can only be solved by able and exhaustive study. There is still available for this study the experienced judgment of the men who successfully conducted America's effort in the World War. To it should be applied the wisest minds of financiers, business executives, military experts, statesmen.

The time to make this study and elaborate a plan is now, when no immediate danger threatens our country. It would be too late when hostilities are imminent, for impromptu measures would surely be ineffective.

We recommend, therefore, that a thorough and detailed study of the problem be made by such agency as the Congress may determine with the view of developing a practical and effective plan of industrial mobilization for the national defense without excess profits to corporation or individual.

International Trade in Munitions

We believe that international trade in arms can be done away with, if that is a desirable aim, only by international agreement between all the producing nations, about twelve in number, to prohibit exports. Whether the cessation of this trade, which would tend towards the fixation of the status quo of oppressed and unarmed peoples, is desirable, is a question upon which we do not venture an opinion. It would seem likely that one prompt result would be the erection for their own defense of ordnance plants throughout the other countries of the world, imposing through excessive costs additional burdens upon them, and that a new competition in armament would thus spring up. If the United States alone were to forbid the export of munitions, our national defense would be impaired because such a policy of isolation might prompt reprisals and make it difficult or impossible in an emergency for this country to obtain essential materials from abroad.

In any case the question would arise, what constitutes munitions of war? Numerous harmless articles of peace-time commerce, the trade in which should not be inhibited, assume in war time greater military significance and strategic importance than many articles of ordnance. Prohibition of the traffic in arms might not be effective, and it would encourage illicit dealings.

Rather we feel that the international trade in arms should be subjected to strict governmental control, preferably by international agreement. At any rate the United States can immediately initiate its own policies in this respect. We suggest legislation permitting the export of arms from this country only after the visé of orders by a Federal Government bureau or commission as the Congress may determine. If this Commission made objection, shipment would not be permitted. Moreover, such legislation should require that upon consummation of an order full information must be reported to the Commission, including the amount and description of goods, their destination, and the complete financial settlement of the transaction.

Such a system of control, while permitting legitimate sales of arms for indispensible demands, would eliminate any abuses that may exist in the business, and would prevent improper sales where arms are desired for unlawful purposes.

We think it fundamental to distinguish between the causes and effects of war. Armament does not originate war; warfare brings forth arms. War is caused by economic and political rivalries. It is fomented by fanaticism, bad

2826   Congress Investigates

temper, suspicion of other people, criticism of their actions, sensational press dispatches, fraudulent or covetous practices. It is minimized by good-will, forbearance, self-control, honest statement, fair dealing. Fire-fighting apparatus is necessary, but it does not cause the fire; care and vigilance are required to prevent an outbreak of fire. International trade in any kind of material or product, if unwisely directed and improperly prosecuted, creates friction, animosity, hostility. On the other hand, international trade wisely and fairly conducted promotes closer association with other people, understanding and friendliness, a spirit of co-operation, good-will, peace.

Respectfully yours,

E. I. Du Pont de Nemours and Company,
Lammot Du Pont
President

THE McSWAIN BILL
JANUARY 3, 1935

U.S. Senate, *Munitions Industry:* Hearings Before the Special Committee Investigating the Munitions Industry, Part 21, 6145–46.

In the House of Representatives, January 3, 1935, Mr. McSwain introduced the following bill; which was referred to the Committee on Military Affairs and ordered to be printed.

A Bill To prevent profiteering in time of war and to equalize the burdens of war and thus to promote the national defense

Be it enacted by the Senate and House of Representatives of the United States of America in Congress assembled, That whenever Congress shall declare war or the existence of an emergency due to the imminence of war, then, from and after a date prior to such declaration which date the President is hereby authorized and directed to determine and announce, it shall be unlawful for any person to buy, sell, or otherwise contract for any article or thing at a higher rate, rent, price, commission, or reward than was in effect at the date so determined.

Sec. 2.
    Whenever in the sole discretion of the President he shall determine that any maximum price, rent, rate, commission, or reward should be adjusted either upward or downward he is hereby authorized to make and proclaim such adjustment, and such adjustment shall have the full force and effect under this statute of such price, wage, rent, rate, commission, or reward before such adjustment.

Sec. 3.

During the period of any war or emergency declared by Congress here-under the President is authorized to determine, and by proclamation announce, what classes of public service, or of dealers or manufacturers of any article or commodity, shall be required to operate under licenses, to fix the conditions of such licenses, and to grant licenses under such conditions. After such determination by the President it shall be unlawful for any public service, dealer, or manufacturer in such determined classes to engage in business without such license.

Sec. 4.

During the period of any war or emergency declared by Congress here-under the President is authorized to determine the order or priority in which any manufacturer, dealer, or public service in the United States shall fill customer's or other orders and after such determination it shall be unlawful for any such manufacturer, dealer, or public service to fill such orders in any other order of priority.

Sec. 5.

That during the period of any war or emergency declared by Congress hereunder the President is empowered to set up such agencies, boards, or commissions, or to designate such persons, to exercise such portion of his powers as he may deem necessary and proper to accomplish the purpose of this Act.

Sec. 6.

That any person violating any of the provisions of this Act, or violating any publicly proclaimed orders, rules, or regulations made by the President for executing the powers contained in this Act, is hereby declared to be guilty of a misdemeanor and shall be liable to indictment and trial therefor, and upon conviction thereof shall be sentenced to pay a fine, or to serve in prison, or both, at the discretion of the court, in such amount and for such time as the court shall see fit and proper, but in no single case shall the fine exceed $100,000 or the term of imprisonment one year.

"THE CRUSADING MR. NYE"
BY E. FRANCIS BROWN
FEBRUARY 1935

Current History and Forum, Vol. XLI, February 1935, 521–27.

Since the day Gerald P. Nye entered the United States Senate he has been a thorn in the side of all conservatives, of all who are content with the established ways of economic and political life. He has been a crusader and, like that famous American crusader of the nineteenth century, he will not equivocate and he will be heard. From North Dakota he has brought a deep-seated distrust of Wall Street finance and of large-scale industry and a sincere and abiding affection for the little fellow. Yet he is less a radical than an old-fashioned liberal, for his point of view is agrarian rather than industrial. The difference can be significant.

Senator Nye has been called, not inaptly, the "Wat Tyler of the prairies." In the face of agricultural disaster and a growing concentration of wealth, he stands forth as the champion of the farmer, the small shopkeeper and the consumer. This has led him into strange byways where fearsome dragons lie in wait; yet in every instance he has emerged, if not triumphant, at least bigger in stature. While opponents have sought to suppress him and called him names—"North Dakota hound of heaven" and "thunderbolt of war" are among the more complimentary—he has gained national influence and distinction.

Until the Fall of 1925 Nye was almost unknown. Then, not quite 33 years old, he sprang fully armed from his North Dakota prairie into the Senate chamber at Washington and suddenly became a political issue.

When Edwin F. Ladd, North Dakota's liberal-minded Senator, died in the Summer of 1925 there were many aspirants for the vacant seat. Should his successor be appointed by the Governor or chosen at a special election? In Washington the following December that question was argued on constitutional grounds, but in North Dakota it involved practical politics. The Governor, Arthur G. Sorlie, wanted to be Senator; obviously he could not appoint himself and a special election entailed risks. So he delayed until the prospective candidates and their supporters forced him to act. Then, by a manoeuvre which has never been satisfactorily explained, he sprang a surprise by giving the office to a man who had not been regarded as even in the running. This was Gerald P. Nye, editor of the *Sentinel Courier* at Cooperstown.

Nye's astonishment could hardly have exceeded that of his fellow-North Dakotans. His career had certainly not prepared him for a Senatorship. Born in Hortonville, Wis., on Dec. 19, 1892, he had passed his boyhood in another Wisconsin village, Wittenberg, where he graduated from its high school. These formative years coincided with the period during which Robert M. La Follette was awakening the social conscience of Wisconsin. Through his direct influence social and political reforms were adopted with startling rapidity. Income and inheritance taxes, workmen's compensation, railway-rate regulation and conservation of natural resources were only part of the "Wisconsin Idea" which was debated and discussed in every town and village of the State. Nye, an alert, wide-awake boy, could not escape the impact of the "Idea" nor fail to be aroused by the argument going on about him. That he was deeply influenced by this environment his later career abundantly testifies.

Before Nye was 20 he returned to Hortonville to take over a local newspaper. Thereafter, except for a few months on the *Des Moines Register*, he was continuously engaged in country journalism. By 1919 he had become editor and publisher of the Griggs County *Sentinel Courier* at Cooperstown, N. D.

Nye settled in North Dakota just as the Farmers Non-Partisan League approached its high noon. That organization of radical agrarianism dominated the State. At the legislative session of 1919 State supervision of the public grain elevators and flour mills and of the Bank of North Dakota was inaugurated. The league forced through a graduated income tax, an eight-hour day for women, workmen's compensation, State hail insurance and other liberal proposals. Though the league's program seemed radical, it was merely another phase of the farmers' prolonged struggle to escape the domination of great corporate interests. Radical though the farmer might be, he was after all a capitalist seeking only to protect himself against other and more powerful capitalists.

With his own rural background and his Wisconsin education, Nye responded naturally to Non-Partisan ideas. His editorials echoed them and he was also outspoken in his dislike of the Republican régime in Washington. Thus he wrote on one occasion: "This has been an age of buncombe, personified most materially since the advent of Calvin Coolidge." Such words did not endear the editor of the *Sentinel Courier* to Republicans, but they pleased the Non-Partisans, who, despite reverses, still ruled North Dakota. And they attracted attention to young Mr. Nye, who in 1924, while supporting La Follette for the Presidency, lost an election for Congressman. But defeat meant little. There would be other campaigns and his appearance on the hustings had won him some prominence. Then came the surprise.

Twelve days before his thirty-third birthday the new Progressive-Republican Senator from North Dakota prepared to take the oath of office, but for more than a month he had to cool his heels while the Senate Committee on Privileges and Elections examined his credentials and the Senate debated his eligibility. Had the Governor of North Dakota the power to fill a Senatorial vacancy by appointment? That was an issue which might never have been raised if Nye had been a Republican in good standing. For days the Senators quibbled—Tom Heflin of Alabama called them "technical lawyers who would amend the Lord's Prayer"—until on Jan. 12, 1926, by a majority of only two votes, they allowed Nye to take his seat. The Wichita *Eagle*, recalling that the new Senator was a nephew of Bill Nye, the humorist, believed that he would need "the family trait in his present job." After the Congressional elections in the following November he was Senator in his own right.

In Nye, whose appearance at that time was distinguished chiefly for a high-water haircut and yellow shoes, American small-town life had a representative who would fight monopoly and privilege with indomitable courage and religious zeal. By nature and association he sympathized with the plain, everyday people whom the rulers of America tended to forget. In his own State he had observed the far-reaching tentacles of modern finance. He had seen hard-working, honest neighbors ruined in 1920 and 1921 by the deflationary policy of the Federal Reserve; he could not forgive the bankers for that. Nor could he find much good in a tariff that bore harshly not only upon the wheat farmers of North Dakota but upon all American agriculture. Though the passing years have added to Nye's experience and knowledge, he remains loyal to the small town and its people. Their interests are still his interests. They can look up to him as a hometown boy who has made good.

Nye had little patience with Republican administrations. He laughingly suggested that the password for Cabinet meetings was "knub," which, he explained, was "bunk" spelled backward. He criticized the Coolidge-Mellon taxation policies and the lack of a farm policy. He attacked the war-debt settlements and insisted that in all fairness the farmers' debts should be scaled down, just as had been those of foreign debtors. Moreover, he declared in the Summer of 1926, the Coolidge administration was dominated by bankers and industrialists who did not want to see agriculture on "an even footing with protected industries." He had already given notice that he would "exert every effort for the relief of the farmer, who . . . is the only one who has not received what is coming to him since the war."

Once in the Senate Nye did exert every possible effort for farm relief. With his colleagues in the Progressive bloc—William E. Borah, Smith W. Brookhart, Lynn J. Frazier, George W. Norris and Robert M. La Follette Jr.—he agitated ceaselessly for a program that would lift the burden from the farmers' shoulders. In the late Twenties this meant the McNary-Haugen bill with its various measures for disposing of surplus farm products. Administration hostility and Presidential vetoes could not quiet Progressive pleading.

Farm relief became a campaign issue in 1928. At the Republican convention in Kansas City Nye opposed Mr. Hoover's nomination because of his apparent disregard for the American farmers' plight. "This man Hoover," wrote Nye, "whom some are trying to drive down our throats, believes that agriculture is improving. If agriculture is improving, it is dying of improvement." Nye's candidate, significantly enough, was Senator Norris of Nebraska. But in the end, Nye, apparently convinced that Mr. Hoover might after all do something for the people of the prairies, swung over to his support.

The Federal Farm Board, which the Hoover administration sponsored, won Nye's vote and allegiance. Those were honeymoon days when, after a White House meeting, he could say: "I came away satisfied that the President would name a farm board that was farm-minded and one which would not have the point of view of the grain men and capital." He was to be sorely disillusioned and to feel ultimately that the Farm Board had been deliberately sabotaged. That feeling helped to change him into one of President Hoover's bitterest opponents.

After 1929 the farmers had companions in misery. The paradox of poverty in the midst of plenty was at last recognized, and Nye wondered about a system that permits "a third of the population, that third resident upon the farms of America," to go without the necessities of life and to be unable to pay their debts because they have produced too much. Yet, at the same time, "another third of our population is in dire want of the very thing which those farmers have produced too much of."

Though the general depression made Nye more keenly conscious of the disadvantages of modern capitalism, they were not new to him. He had talked for years about "greedy capitalists." He had repeatedly challenged the strength of large-scale business and finance and he had indignantly pointed to the increasing concentration of capital which left the rich richer and the poor poorer. For his part, he had made it clear there could be no compromise with wealth. To iron out some of the inequalities, he supported all moves for higher inheritance and income taxes but, being always in opposition, he could do little.

He had acquired a hatred of monopoly capitalism from the elder La Follette. "Monopoly," Nye declared, "can lay scarce claim to creating anything. It reduces the number of persons employed and pays wages below a living scale. It is not creative of new business. It is the cancer that feeds upon the flesh of a living organism and threatens its life. Wherever it touches there is death, both to the town and individual enterprise. . . . When competition is destroyed the consumer and the producer suffer. . . . It must be admitted that a government is not worthy of the name unless it can protect its people against oppression and particularly oppression by the very creatures of which it is the creator."

No man with these views could be expected to show much affection for chain stores or branch banking, the two most obvious manifestations of monopoly in the Twenties. Both endangered the traditional small-scale enterprise which Nye favored, and so in Senate debate and on public platform he lashed out against them. When he sought to strengthen the Federal Trade Commission he did so in order to "free the channels of commerce from destructive 'cut-throat competition' and thus permit the continued existence of thousands of honest and efficient business establishments constantly threatened by giant monopolies."

This feeling for the little man led to Nye's voting against the National Industrial Recovery Act in 1933. He suspected that the act was not all it appeared to be and within five months of its passage his worst fears were confirmed. "The Blue Eagle," he insisted time and again, "is a bird of prey on the masses." The codes of fair competition he described as "swindles upon consumers"; he could not forbear adding that "the fact that the consumer has been at the mercy of the monopolies is the great weakness of the recovery system." With Senator Borah he assailed the NRA and its administration, for the NRA, he saw clearly, fostered monopoly and placed insuperable obstacles before firms which lack strong financial reserves and which are often unable to "enjoy the fruits of fixing prices resulting from the suspension of the anti-trust laws."

Though Nye and Borah were responsible for the sensational Darrow investigation of the NRA, the result can have been little to their liking. The little man's grievances were aired and he earned public sympathy. But monopoly continued to crush out his life.

Nye's dislike for big business was reinforced by his discovery of its political influence. He had long known vaguely about this, but he had no definite proof until 1927, when as chairman of the Senate Committee on Lands and Surveys he took part in the drawn-out drama of Teapot Dome. With Senator Thomas J. Walsh he washed before a curious public the dirty linen of the Continental Trading Company, a dummy corporation by which certain oil barons filled their own pockets at the expense of their stockholders. Indirectly the Continental entered the Teapot Dome scandal because through this dummy corporation had come the Liberty Loan bonds which enriched Secretary of the Interior Albert B. Fall. The Continental's profits were also used to buy still other bonds which found their way into various strange places, among them the treasury of the Republican party.

The steady succession of revelations about the Continental Trading Company kept Nye's name before the public. He began to be recognized as a crusader of the first rank. While politically this added prestige was worth a good deal to Nye, more important for him was the knowledge he was acquiring. Teapot Dome and the Continental Trading Company demonstrated to him "the frightful influence of money upon our political and economic life as a nation." The contributions from dubious sources to campaign funds distressed him greatly. "The great masses of people who are without great means," he declared, "can never hope to compete politically with influence which can pour unreasonable sums into partisan coffers."

Suspicion of the political influence of great wealth caused him in December, 1928, to oppose the confirmation of Roy O. West as Secretary of the Interior. West had been attorney for Samuel Insull and was too interested in the Insull properties to impress Nye as being desirable in a post which carried with it a place on the Federal Power Commission. Though West's appointment was easily confirmed, later events made Senator Nye's opposition understandable.

In 1930 Nye found an opportunity to go even more directly into the relation of money to elections when, as chairman of a Senate committee to investigate campaign expenses, he traveled up and down the country. In Pennsylvania, for example, he found that the Republicans spent more than $640,000 to elect their ticket, while Ruth Hanna McCormick spent $325,000 in the Illinois primaries alone. This revelation helped to defeat her Senatorial ambitions. Where did these vast sums come from and why were they given to party treasuries? Those were the questions that Nye was always asking. From the investigation he drew the lesson that the primaries were the "playthings of machine politicians," "the source of more evils than the regular elections." He advocated then, as he had earlier, a stricter Federal law for the regulation of elections and campaign expenses.

The investigation of Mrs. McCormick's expenditures led to a bitter quarrel between her and the Senator. Alleging that the agents had tapped her telephone, invaded her office and pried into affairs that were none of their concern, Mrs. McCormick set detectives on his trail in the hope of uncovering something that might drive him from public life. One of the detectives said later that he was sent to Fargo to gather "biographical" information about Nye, and that he had caused him to be shadowed at Glacier Park. The episode hurt only Mrs. McCormick, for the detectives found nothing that could be used against Nye.

While his career as a Senator and as an investigator won for Nye the respect, and in some instances the admiration, of many of his fellow-countrymen, it remained for his inquiry into the munitions industry in 1934 to make him a national figure. Though a believer in an adequate national defense, he has long been an enemy of militarism and imperialism, voting against all bills for naval expansion and opposing the protection of American foreign investments by armed forces. When, therefore, he offered on March 12, 1934, a resolution to investigate the munitions-makers' activities he was acting consistently.

Nye, there can be little doubt, is sincere in his attack upon the arms manufacturers. But he is also ambitious and he has known how to turn the investigation to his own advantage. There had been no hired prosecutors to steal the show; it has been all his. Nye, still handsomely boyish in appearance, a vigorous orator, poised and well groomed, has gone through the country telling uncomfortable truths about the munitions makers. To men and women who were hardly aware of his existence his name has become a household word. They have seen him on lecture platforms; they have heard his voice come through the ether, and they like him.

There are, however, those who find Senator Nye less attractive. To them he is a demagogue or a dangerous radical. Yet he is neither. His championship of the masses comes from the heart. Whenever he seeks their support it is done more in their interest than in his, and upon them is based the social philosophy which guides his thought and action.

He regards himself as a Progressive, but there are other Progressives who have done far more thinking upon a program for action than he has. After all, he is concerned less with the abstract than with the concrete; he is emotional rather than intellectual. And there lies his limitation.

With the general basis of Nye's work few liberals will disagree. It is extremely simple and fits the tradition of American liberalism. Commenting in 1931 upon a report that 80,000,000 Americans had annual incomes of $700 or less, he said: "Progressives believe that the first duty of government is concerned with the welfare of those 80,000,000 and of millions more who lack economic security." That is the first point in his creed. The second is the "determination that there shall be again in this land a government of the people, by the people and for the people." It is with the application of this creed that many will disagree.

Nye throughout his career has shown a hesitancy to go to the roots of the abuses he hates. Instead, like American liberals of an earlier time, he seeks to lop off the abuse, failing to see that unless the roots are destroyed a new and perhaps more virulent evil may spring up. Despite a generation of experience with government regulation of business practices, he does not admit that regulation has failed. He still supports, for example, the very anti-trust laws under which the monopolies he denounces have spread and flourished. For Nye there is a good and a bad capitalism. Though he does not stand alone in the belief that a beneficent capitalism can be realized, the teachings of history and experience lend little support to such a view.

In defending the little man, Nye is probably waging a losing battle. He is trying to turn back to the days of small-scale enterprise, whereas all signs of economic evolution point to the gradual extinction of the individual storekeeper or factory owner. Moreover, the rights of labor and the consumer have seldom been observed more scrupulously by the individual than by the corporate proprietor. There have been exceptions in both cases, but it is indeed a question whether the masses as a whole are better off under one than under the other. Seemingly, any clipping of the claws of big business must entail greater consideration for labor as labor than Nye has yet given or recognized the need for giving.

Though Nye opposes the growing concentration of wealth, he scarcely indicates that he grasps its full implications. He still lives in the age that tilts against great monopolies, despite the advent of finance capitalism. Today economic power rests in the hands of the few who through devices introduced into corporate organization determine the destiny of great undertakings, even if actual ownership and nominal control belong to unorganized stockholders. This great change puts a new complexion on economic and social problems, but Nye seems unaware of what has occurred.

Nye tends to simplify social questions. He believes, for example, that if the munitions makers are properly controlled, either through regulation or nationalization, the danger of wars will fade. Thus he has stated that "the profits of war and the preparation for it constitute the most serious challenge to world peace. . . . The removal of the element of profit from war would materially remove the danger of more war." In public, at least, he shows no appreciation of the fact that whatever the arms industry is or is not, it can be only one factor in the breeding of international conflict.

There is nothing in Nye's career to indicate a desire to destroy capitalism. His acts and utterances point to a belief that if corruption and evil-doing can be exposed they can be eliminated. Then all will be well. He is thus perhaps a real conservative in the sense that he wishes to retain the best, to heal only the ills of the system. On the other hand, his continuous attack upon the "octopus" of monopoly and his steady exposure of abuses serve to keep the public alive to the encroachment of the few upon the rights of the many. He leads people to consider the nature of the system under which they live. When viewed in this light he is far more the wrecker than the restorer.

Even if Nye's thinking appears more liberal than radical—and a little oldfashioned into the bargain—it is well to recall that even now he is only 42, and that he has come a long way in the past decade. Ten, twenty, maybe thirty years of public life stretch ahead of him. What will he be doing in that period? Will he develop greater constructive ideas? Will he, as have some of the Progressives already, analyze carefully the nature of American society and work out a definite program for its problems? Or will he champion and crusade alone? One thing is certain. Unless he develops a deeper social philosophy, unless he more fully comprehends changes in the body politic, he dooms himself to be only a critic, never a planner, and to remain until the end a member, not a leader, of the Progressives.

REPORT OF WAR POLICIES COMMISSION MARCH 5, 1935

U.S. Senate, *Munitions Industry:* Hearings Before the Special Committee Investigating the Munitions Industry, pursuant to Senate Resolution 206; 73rd Congress, 2nd Session, 74th Congress, 1st Session, and 74th Congress, 2nd Session, Part 21, 5990–91.

REPORT OF COMMISSION CREATED BY PUBLIC RESOLUTION NO. 98, SEVENTY-FIRST CONGRESS, APPROVED JUNE 27, 1930

To the President:

The Commission appointed under Public Resolution No. 98, Seventy-first Congress, entitled "Joint resolution to promote peace and to equalize the burdens and to minimize the profits of war," respectfully submits the following report and recommendations:

First. We recommend, in order to eliminate all doubt concerning the extent of the power of the Congress to prevent profiteering and to stabilize prices in time of war, that a proposed constitutional amendment clearly defining such power be submitted by the Congress to the States.

Second. We further recommend that until a constitutional amendment be adopted clearly defining the power of Congress to prevent profiteering and to stabilize prices in time of war, the following program be adopted as governmental policy in order effectively to minimize the profits of war and to distribute its burdens and sacrifices equitably:

(a) That the Congress should empower the President, in the event of war, to institute a program under which prices may be stabilized and thereafter adjusted at such levels as will minimize inflation and will secure to the Government the use of any private property needed in the prosecution of the war without affording the owner thereof profit due to the war. It should be clearly stated that such a program will not be placed in operation until Congress specifically directs it as a necessary measure in the conduct of the war.

(b) The Congress should empower the President to make, in war, such readjustments in, and additions to, the Executive departments of the Government as are necessary to assure adequate control of all national resources. The President should be empowered also to fix the status, for the period of the war, of personnel transferred under this authority, from one bureau or department of the Government to any other.

(c) Existing law empowering the President to compel acceptance of war orders and to commandeer property should be continued.

(d) In addition to all other plans to remove the profits of war, the revenue law should provide that, upon any declaration of war and during the period of such emergency, individuals and corporations shall be taxed 95 percent of all income above the previous 3-year average, with proper adjustments for capital expenditures for war purposes by existing or new industries.

(e) In time of peace continuous planning by the Federal Government, particularly by the War and Navy Departments, should be directed toward insuring:

(1) That upon declaration of war there shall be immediately available to the Congress accurate and detailed estimates concerning the man power and material needs of the military and naval services, together with detailed studies and recommendations concerning the most applicable methods for mobilizing the necessary men and procuring the required munitions.

(2) That there shall be no competitive bidding between Government agencies for the products of industry.

(3) There shall be no placing of contracts in excess of needs.

(4) That cost plus percentage methods of purchase shall be eliminated.

(5) That the munitions production load shall be distributed properly over the United States.

(6) That the governmental organizations required in the administration of war functions shall be set up promptly.

(7) That the necessry controls respecting prices, raw materials, transportation, priorities, war trade, finance, and related matters shall be continuously studied, so that in the event of war the will of Congress will be promptly and efficiently administered.

(f) Plans prepared in the War and Navy Departments for the accomplishment of the above should be continuously revised to meet changing national and international conditions and should be thoroughly examined and revised at least every two years by appropriate congressional committees.

Third. We recommend that no constitutional amendment to permit the taking of private property in time of war without compensation be considered by the Congress.

Respectfully submitted.

The report is signed by 10 of the 12 members of the Commission. It is signed by Patrick J. Hurley, chairman; David A. Reed, vice chairman; Jos. T. Robinson, John J. McSwain, Arthur H. Vandenberg, William D. Mitchell, C. F. Adams, R. P. Lamont, Wm. P. Holaday, Arthur M. Hyde, W. N. Doak, and Lindley H. Hadley.

One member of the Commission, the then Senator Swanson, now Secretary of the Navy, was absent in London at the time the Commission reported, but stated his concurrence in the report.

A minority report was submitted by Hon. Ross A. Collins, at that time a Congressman from Mississippi.

That concludes, Mr. Chairman, the recommendations made by the War Policies Commission.

EXTRACT OF TESTIMONY OF WILLIAM B. SHEARER ON SHIPBUILDING INDUSTRY MARCH 12, 1935

U.S. Senate, *Munitions Industry:* Hearings Before the Special Committee Investigating the Munitions Industry, Part 21, 5980–84.

Mr. Raushenbush. We want the list of names of those who you claim are persecuting you.

Mr. Shearer. I will give the three shipbuilders, to start out. I will give the Carnegie Foundation. I will give the peace organizations, Barney Baruch, and they have stopped me in everything I have tried to do. What is this racket going on in this country that an American citizen cannot speak? I saw this morning over here that a big foreign propagandist was heralding to the Nation, and in his own book he takes a crack at me, giving the plans for it.

Senator Clark. Who was that?

Mr. Shearer. Some big walrus-mustached looking guy who jumped off a steamer the other day. You know who it is.

Senator Clark. I do not know.

Mr. Shearer. I will get the name. They are coming in so fast I cannot keep up with them.

Senator Clark. You seem to have had the physiognomy in mind.

Mr. Shearer. My gosh.

Senator Bone. When did you write this pamphlet?

Mr. Shearer. The Cloak of Benedict Arnold?

Senator Bone. Yes.

Mr. Shearer. In 1928 I copyrighted it.

Senator Bone. Were you being persecuted then?

Mr. Shearer. I will tell you when that persecution started; in 1924, when I brought out the facts against the British Navy. It started in 1924, not 1928.

Senator Bone. I want to know if you catalog as unpatriotic citizens the men whose names I am going to read off to you. We will take them one at a time and you can say yes or no.

Newton D. Baker?

Mr. Shearer. Yes.

Senator Bone. You classify him as unpatriotic?

Mr. Shearer. Yes.

Senator Bone. And an undesirable citizen?

Mr. Shearer. I did not say that.

Senator Bone. Unpatriotic?

Mr. Shearer. In my way of thinking, yes; under the same way he thinks I am a jingoist, the same way I am all wrong.

Senator Bone. Dr. Harry A. Garfield, son of the former President?

Mr. Shearer. Incidentally, Senator, that is a little bit of plagiarism on my part, taken from the Hearst papers.

Senator Bone. You are the author.

Mr. Shearer. I simply copied it. It is a little plagiarism.

Senator Bone. You ought not to admit plagiarism.

Mr. Shearer. I am a plagiarist. I am in that case.

Senator Bone. You have original ideas, do you not?

Mr. Shearer. A couple of them.

Senator Bone. Dr. Ellen Pendleton, president of Wellesley? Do you consider her unpatriotic?

Mr. Shearer. Taken from Hearst.

Senator Bone. Ralph Pulitzer, president of the New York World?

Mr. Shearer. The whole New York World, until it cracked up.

Senator Bone. Chester Rowell, of California?

Mr. Shearer. Hearst.

Senator Bone. Henry Taft?

Mr. Shearer. Hearst.

Senator Bone. Mrs. Frank W. Vanderlip?

Mr. Shearer. They are all Hearst.

Senator Bone. What I am getting at, is your idea.

Mr. Shearer. I have got my idea on the front page of the back.

Senator Bone. I will bring this a little closer to you.

Mr. Shearer. All right.

Senator Bone. Henry W. Taft is unpatriotic, too?

Mr. Shearer. You are saying so.

Senator Bone. Not me. Here is the name right here.

Mr. Shearer. Hearst again.

Senator Bone. But this is a pamphlet entitled "The Cloak of Benedict Arnold", by W. B. Shearer.

Mr. Shearer. Yes, sir.

Senator Bone. What can be more blunt than that?

Mr. Shearer. Nothing.

Senator Bone. Who paid for the money to circulate this?

Mr. Shearer. Henry Hunter gave me the money.

Senator Bone. The shipbuilder?

Mr. Shearer. Yes.

Senator Bone. A shipbuilder furnished the money charging these people with being unpatriotic and like Benedict Arnold?

Mr. Shearer. Yes, sir; and there is a lot from the Department of Justice recorded about communistic activity.

Senator Bone. Are these people under the ban of the Department of Justice? That is another implication.

Mr. Shearer. That is from the Department of Justice, which I have.

Senator Bone. Let us leave the implication stand as you made it, that the Department of Justice viewed with disfavor the names I am reading.

Mr. Shearer. No; I did not say that.

Senator Bone. Make it plain.

Mr. Shearer. I said there are also in there names which I want you to read which are from the Department of Justice records.

Senator Bone. George W. Wickersham?

Mr. Shearer. Yes, sir; Mitsuibishi attorney, trying to break the exclusion law, and fought by McClatchey, of California, the man opposed by the Native Sons, opposed by Senator Jim Phelan, and tried to break down the exclusion law.

Senator Bone. Let us get him classified.

Mr. Shearer. Yes, sir.

Senator Bone. Dr. Mary Woolley, of Mount Holyoke College?

Mr. Shearer. Not only her.

Senator Bone. What do you say about Mary?

Mr. Shearer. Only what Hearst says. I never say anything about Mary.

Senator Bone. Colonel House.

Mr. Shearer. That is Hearst.

Senator Bone. That is Hearst.

Harvey Ingham, of the Des Moines State Register.

Mr. Shearer. Yes.

Senator Bone. Harold B. Johnson, of the Watertown (N. Y.) Times?

Mr. Shearer. Yes.

Senator Bone. He is undesirable, I take it?

Mr. Shearer. I did not say that.

Senator Bone. Tom Wallace, of the Louisville Times-Courier?

Mr. Shearer. Yes, sir; Hearst.

Senator Bone. Do you think he is an undesirable? You use the term "Benedict Arnold." I cannot approach the degree of contempt you used.

Mr. Shearer. Is there anything in there that is wrong?

Senator Bone. Then you wind up by setting out mention of these undesir- desirable and unpatriotic citizens, including the name of Franklin D. Roose-velt.

Mr. Shearer. Hearst.

Senator Bone. Do you want to hide behind the skirts of a newspaper publisher?

Mr. Shearer. Let me tell you, Senator, I do not hide behind anything, but Hearst published an article at that time that gave me the opportunity to use it, and I took it and put it in that pamphlet. I am opposed to all foreign entangle-ments and to being made an adjunct of the British. Why do you not read my letter to you? My letter will tell you about it.

The Chairman. Mr. Shearer, have you given Hearst the credit in this volume which you produced for these statements?

Mr. Shearer. Have I given Hearst credit for these statements?

The Chairman. Yes.

Mr. Shearer. You do not have to give Hearst any. Hearst takes credit.

The Chairman. You took credit for it?

Mr. Shearer. I got credit for nothing.

The Chairman. And copyrighted it?

Mr. Shearer. Yes; I copyrighted it; and the shipbuilders paid for it.

Senator Vandenberg. And likened Mr. Roosevelt to Benedict Arnold?

Mr. Shearer. I beg your pardon?

Senator Vandenberg. And likened Mr. Roosevelt to Benedict Arnold?

Mr. Shearer. If you will read the article—

Senator Vandenberg. That is the word.

Mr. Shearer. You read the article and see what it says.

Senator Vandenberg. That is the net result.

Mr. Shearer. It is a Hearst article, published, and describes just what Hearst said.

Senator Vandenberg. And you are taking the responsibility for it?

Mr. Shearer. I am taking the responsibility for it.

Senator Vandenberg. For likening Mr. Roosevelt to Benedict Arnold?

Mr. Shearer. I did not liken anybody, but published an article of Mr. Hearst's, and there is no criticism of Mr. Hearst. He is too big to reach.

Senator Vandenberg. And put your name on it?

Mr. Shearer. And put my name on it. I mean the heading; nothing but the front page.

Senator Bone. President Roosevelt's name appears under the caption in black type along with the others, under the caption of "Knaves or Fools." I am glad we have the President identified by a representative of a private ship-building company.

Mr. Shearer. Read the rest of the article. It does not apply to that. Do not turn the book upside down.

Senator Bone. The words "knaves or fools" are just above the name of President Roosevelt.

Mr. Shearer. All right, what does it say?

Senator Bone [reading]:

. . . the defeatists—

Mr. Roosevelt is a "defeatist"?

Mr. Shearer. Read the article as it is.

Senator Bone [reading]:

. . . the defeatists launch a mass attack to force the United States into the League Court.

Mr. Shearer. Yes.

Senator Bone [reading]:

It is notable that this new position bristles with names of prominent advocates of our entrance into the League . . .

This all appears under the caption "Knaves or Fools."

Mr. Shearer. Right.

Senator Bone. Let us get down to brass tacks and get the record right. You classify the President and Pearson as a fool?

Mr. Shearer. I would not classify Pearson along with the President.

Senator Bone. All these people are classified as "knaves or fools," because they do not agree with you, and not only that but as Benedict Arnolds.

Mr. Shearer. I have nothing to do with it. They do not agree with the majority of the people of the United States. They do not want foreign entanglements.

Senator Bone. A few of us voted for the World Court. Mr. Hearst's wholesome flattery almost embarrassed me, and the next day we were demagogues.

Mr. Shearer. That is because Hearst is a newspaper publisher and must have something to print.

Senator Bone. Why did you not take Mr. Hearst's name instead of allowing this to go out under your name, as a child of your own genius?

Mr. Shearer. Because everybody who read it knew there were just things in there which I could not possibly write—one, the article from the Hearst paper and the other from the Department of Justice records as to the Bridgeman situation. I did not compile it.

Mr. LaRouche. Did you not say you wrote it?

Mr. Shearer. Did you ever read a dictionary; who wrote it? You do not think every word in there is his.

Senator Clark. Was not the authorship of this pamphlet one of the items in your claim against the three shipbuilding companies?

Mr. Shearer. I beg your pardon?

Senator Clark. I say, was not this document one of the bases of your claims against the shipbuilding companies?

Mr. Shearer. In the bill of particulars I mentioned The Cloak of Benedict Arnold and having received two hundred odd dollars for my payment to the printer.

Senator Bone. You launched off on this indictment, including the President of the United States, under the head of The Cloak of Benedict Arnold?

Mr. Shearer. Yes.

Senator Bone. Do you want to be fair?

Mr. Shearer. That is right.

Senator Bone (reading):

A true story of idealism, intrigue, and treachery to destroy the United States as a sea power.

Mr. Shearer. That is true.

Senator Bone. You felt that the President, who had been an advocate of a big Navy, wanted to destroy us as a sea power?

Mr. Shearer. As long as you insist on bringing the President in——

Senator Bone. I did not bring him in. You brought him in.

Mr. Shearer. You mentioned his name.

Senator Bone. Wait a minute.

Mr. Shearer. Let us not split hairs. At that particular time, in 1928, when that was written, he was not President of the United States, in the first place.

Senator Bone. Are you so cowardly that you would not indict him, if he required indictment, as a "Benedict Arnold"? You told us you had lots of courage.

Mr. Shearer. I have not mentioned my courage, and I do not like the implication about being a coward.

Senator Bone. That is unfortunate.

The Chairman. Go back to your seat as a witness and remain there.

Mr. Shearer. Stop heralding this cowardly stuff, then.

Senator Bone. I withdraw it.

Mr. Shearer. It does not make any difference what you think I am, Senator Bone. I am still against the World Court, and I am still for the Navy.

Senator Bone (reading):

A lawyer-bound, slave-thinking people, under the lash of internationalism. Both parties are sacrificing America's welfare under the dictates of the invisible power.

Do you believe that we are lawyer-bound?

Mr. Shearer. Yes.

Senator Bone. Do you think we are slave-thinking?

Mr. Shearer. Yes, sir.

Senator Bone. You attack the American people as being slaves?

Mr. Shearer. At the present time.

Senator Bone. Whom are they slaves to, your shipbuilding crowd?

Mr. Shearer. My shipbuilding crowd?

Senator Bone. What crowd?

Mr. Shearer. The shipbuilding crowd has nothing to do with that statement. That respects the question of national defense, because of the internationalists, and you have read from it. Everybody is making speeches on it. Belgrano used it for making speeches. Why should not some American as well, just as Father Coughlin gave it to you last night, and others will give it to you? I do not agree with Coughlin on everything, and he does not with me, but there are certain people in the United States who are ready to go through with this thing. The only indictment I have in this case is I am an American born and I am a nationalist. That is all that is against me, and that is what is resented.

Senator Bone. Did you come down to Washington in 1927 or 1928 and obtain this house about which you have been telling us?

Mr. Shearer. No; I will tell you what I did. I went to a hotel and took a suite of rooms and told them to get me a house.

Senator Bone. Were you there when Mr. Wilder was carrying on his work for the Jones-White Act?

Mr. Shearer. Yes, sir.

Senator Bone. Did you participate in that?

Mr. Shearer. In a very small way.

Senator Bone. In what way?

Mr. Shearer. I was called in at their meetings.

Senator Clark. You participated to the extent of $10,000, did you not?

Mr. Shearer. Yes, sir. That is a good story. A man arrived at this time by the name of Capt. C. D. Burney, the designer of the R–100 and R–101, and stated in my presence that he came to this country to get mail contracts, and Mr. Hoover was the Secretary of Commerce, and an AP. dispatch blew into the paper that Burney was going to get the contracts, and I went to Senator Reed and Mr. Walter Brown, then Postmaster General, to get back of the United States and do it, and saw a man that was afterward Bascom Slemp's partner, and Senator Willis, a Republican Senator, who died, and I was asked to write the story, "What Price Hoover", opposing the British getting the mail contracts in this country.

Senator Bone. What do you think of these mail contracts?

Mr. Shearer. I do not know anything at all about them. I am talking about the time I stopped a foreigner from getting them. I am not interested in what Americans do. I have got enough trouble going after people who are trying to do things against us. . . .

EXPLANATION BY BERNARD M. BARUCH OF "PRICE CEILING PLAN" MARCH 27, 1935

U.S. Senate, *Munitions Industry:* Hearings Before the Special Committee Investigating the Munitions Industry, Part 22, 6269–83.

Senator Clark. Mr. Baruch, I was interested primarily in this hearing in the suggestions, the various suggestions, which have been made for fixing a ceiling for prices.

Mr. Baruch. Fixing a ceiling?

Senator Clark. Ceiling. You used the phrase a moment ago of a ceiling on prices at the outbreak of war and necessary price fixing during the war.

Mr. Baruch. Yes, sir.

Senator Clark. And in some of the questions I will ask you, it has to do with the price-fixing committee during the war, of which I understand you were not a member.

Mr. Baruch. Ex officio.

Senator Clark. But which I understand from your general memory you would be able to follow and express an opinion on.

Mr. Baruch. Senator, perhaps if I told you what I meant by putting a ceiling over prices, it would help.

Senator Clark. I was going to ask you that next. That is the first thing I was going to ask you.

Mr. Baruch. I do not know how familiar the members of this committee are with the testimony that I gave before the War Policies Commission, of which one of your members was a member. There we had a great deal of opposition to the plan and a great many ideas of how you could fix the prices this way, and you did not want to do this, and you did not want to do that, and the greatest opposition came from the Army and Navy, where it had always come from, because they did not understand it. There were various statisticians and economists and very distinguished people who thought you could do this piecemeal. But I sat through the execution of these plans, and I know very well, unless you have a ceiling, with its fixed relationship between activities of the people, that the prices are going to go up, and you put up the price of steel and copper and something else goes up, like shoes and rent, and that means wages must go up, and then other things go up. But if you put a ceiling over it, above which it cannot go, excepting after a particular investigation on any particular one, we have got something to start from. Otherwise you would have to fix prices so quickly, and you could not fix them quickly enough because they would be doing that [indicating]. I do not know whether I have made it clear.

Senator Clark. Yes. What I had in mind, Mr. Baruch, is this: If I understand the proposition correctly, you would fix a ceiling for prices at the outbreak of war.

Mr. Baruch. Or some day very near it. Suppose, for instance, war would break out within 30 days or 60 days, in which we were involved; the President might declare that today would be the day at which the ceiling would have to rest.

Senator Clark. But if we had a situation such as existed in 1917, when we got into the war, a situation in which a general world war existed nearly all over the world except in the United States, which had been in progress for 3 years, resulting in a very great rise of prices and expansion of production, and you were to fix a ceiling as of that date, the date we got into the war, or shortly before that, would not that have the effect of freezing prices at an abnormally high level?

Mr. Baruch. You do not freeze them. They cannot go above that but they can go down below, and the price-fixing committee can do just like they did in the war. The beauty about the ceiling idea is this, Senator: That it is due notice to every producer, every manufacturer, of what the policy of the Government is. I say that because I spent years—not years, but months—of study in what they call the constitutionality of this act, how you can fix these prices and whether you can do it or not. Hereby due notice of what the policy of the

Government is going to be is given. That means all the time that prices will be kept down. I think it will have a tendency to keep them down. In the instance to which you refer, it would not be as effective as it would be now, I am quite willing to admit, but it would not have the effect of freezing prices, Senator. That was an unfortunate expression I used in the beginning, by which I gave the wrong impression. It is like a balloon, getting up there [indicating].

Senator Clark. You would fix a top limit at the declaration of war, or shortly before it, and then put in your price-fixing machinery, and modify the prices either up or down as might seem best?

Mr. Baruch. Yes, sir. It does not mean fixation and stabilization. One of the points raised before the War Policies Commission was, a man said, "Why, wheat is 62 cents." I said, "That is too low. That would be raised accordingly."

But you would not have any bouncing up of these different prices. What I have got in my mind is the position of the ordinary individual in a community, who has wages, and they become unreal instead of real wages, when prices of food, clothing, and rent are going up. That got to be the most difficult public and social question with which we had to deal, and we never had an opportunity to tackle it. That is another thing in the back of my mind when making these recommendations.

Senator Vandenberg. Your ceiling is a maximum and not a fixed price?

Mr. Baruch. That is quite right, it is a maximum. I will admit that the misunderstanding of that was due to my inaptitude in phrasing the thought.

Senator Clark. We have had several theories that have been advanced here, and I wanted to find out what your suggestions have been on the question of price fixing. First, I would like to ask a question on something you referred to a moment ago. You said you had given a great deal of study and investigation to the subject of the constitutionality of price fixing. I noticed in the minutes of the War Industries Board that that question was a matter of considerable debate and considerable discussion during the war. Would you tell the committee briefly what your conclusions on that subject have been?

Mr. Baruch. I am satisfied from the expert information I got from legal authorities, which was buttressed by the fact that we had a battle royal in the last administration with the Attorney General there, and I have come to the conclusion that the bill, with slight modifications, as drawn up in the War Policies Commission hearing report, would be constitutional.

Senator Clark. That is, in time of war the Government has the authority?

Mr. Baruch. Yes, sir. As a matter of fact, we would not be helpless today, because, with the understanding that we have and with the right, which is undoubtedly the absolute right of the Government, to commandeer this plant, plus the priority which we learned to use, you can enforce any price regulation. There is not any doubt about that. We had that out in particular phases during the war. We intimated that in the steel regulation. I am afraid I lost my trend of thought by digressing.

Senator Clark. In other words, what I was trying to get at is, it is your conclusion that this would have some legal authority?

Mr. Baruch. That it is constitutional, such a one as is outlined there. There is no doubt that the exigencies of the Government can be used to fix a fair market price for the use of the things it needs. The situation which is created by war should not force the Government into fixing an unjust and unfair price. I think the decisions of the courts are all along that line.

Senator Clark. Now, Mr. Baruch, referring to the experiences of the Government during the last war, what is your general conclusion as to the matter of price fixing in that war, whether it was successful or unsuccessful?

Mr. Baruch. It was the best that could be done in the circumstances.

Senator Clark. I understand that you were constructing an organization as you went along, but as regards the matter of price fixing and the matter of excess-profits taxes, did you consider that it was profitable in the last war for the United States to buy as cheaply as possible, as might have been done, and to recover all the excess profits?

Mr. Baruch. You keep going higher than a cat's back all the time. If you did not have the excess-profits tax, if you did not have the fixed prices, and leave some kind of a ceiling, although it is a very uneven ceiling, you would never know where prices would have gone. Ship plates were selling at 14 cents a pound when we got the people to put in a cut, and they cut to three and a quarter cents, and Japan and other countries were willing to pay any price. Pig iron would have gone to any price. It was an emergency situation. The law of supply and demand was not operative because the law of supply and demand is always affected by time, which was the essential thing. You could not wait until day after tomorrow and it had to be done right there. You must have price fixing, and you cannot get away from it.

Senator Clark. What I want particularly to get at, Mr. Baruch, is this: There has been a great deal of talk in various speeches and newspapers about the spirit of cooperation by industrialists and the producers of raw commodities and other business enterprises during the war. I would like to find out whether or not they did actually sell to the Government during the war at cost plus a reasonable profit, or whether they did not, in many instances, more or less hold a gun at the head of the Government and force the price fixing committee and the War Industries Board to give them what was in effect an abnormal profit?

Mr. Baruch. I do not think in any instance in which the War Industries Board price-fixing committee fixed a price, they did that. You must take into consideration the problem as it was presented, the lack of knowledge, the great ignorance which we had of how to do the thing. We did not know. They always did the best they could, but if you will look into the records you will find we did pretty well. As a matter of fact, we persuaded some of the producers to agree to the prices that the price-fixing committee suggested, because I know in one instance I got a letter from President Wilson authorizing me to take over certain very large plants and when I suggested to the gentleman at the head of them that this might interest them, he then turned his back on me and said, "Well, you cannot make me work." I said, "No; you will be so busy explaining to your neighbors why you did not agree with us that we would not be able to get any work out of you." He said then, "Can't we fix this up?" And we did. In that instance we put the price down to about 22 percent of what was the price at that time prevailing. The largest proportion of the manufacturers did come along, just like the largest proportion of labor. There are always some chiselers. There are always a lot of men who can find some reason, moral or otherwise, why they should not accede to the will of the majority and the necessities of the case, but, by and large, they were all right. We did have to use some persuasive methods, the power to commandeer and the power of priority. Priority was more effective than commandeering, because I know in one instance, when the price-fixing committee could not get certain interests to do anything, I got Dr. Garfield to agree to commandeer the coal, and Mr. Baker to commandeer their steel, and McAdoo to stop all movements of traffic in and out of the factories. That was pretty persuasive. Then they acceded to our wishes.

But you have got to have the power, undoubtedly. You cannot leave any of these things to men's emotions or wishes at the time. The Government must have the power to fix these prices and to raise the taxes.

The Chairman. Mr. Baruch, was there any general knowledge during the war concerning the degree of bonus paying that we have learned since did enter largely into executive salaries during the war?

Mr. Baruch. The War Industries Board had nothing to do with contracts except a few that were specially referred or that we happened to hear about. As a matter of fact, we never saw that question—at least, I never heard of it. The things which this committee has so well brought out are indefensible from the standpoint of economics or business or morals. I did not hear of these, except one contract.

The Chairman. In other words——

Mr. Baruch. And in that contract I telephoned to the Secretary of War and said, "You cannot do this. This is going to break it up. If you carry out the bonus it will blow up the show. It is unsound in every way possible." The military always justified things to which we objected by saying "it is necessary to win the war." And I was on the spot. I said, "We are not going to lose the war, and you cannot make this contract, because it is unconscionable." It was brought out by Mr. Summers, one of the greatest men I know of developed in the war.

The Chairman. There was large secrecy about the bonus paying at those times?

Mr. Baruch. I do not know whether it was secret or not, but these contracts were written by the Ordnance Department or the Navy Department, the contracts about which we did not know anything. For instance, in the building of plants, it is only by chance that we would know about a plant which was going to be built. We would not know, except, for instance, when they came in with a requisition for priority.

That brings me to a very important point. There should be, in addition to what we have already now—and I think we ought to have it for peace time —what I call a "board of contract review." Some of the things which you brought out in this committee would not have been possible if there was a board of contract review before which that could have been taken. That would give an opportunity like we tried to do in the war—I admit its weaknesses and many of its errors—to give an opportunity for anybody who is interested to appear before a board whose only business it was to discuss those contracts or such things which they thought were unfair.

We had the most terrible difficulty in getting the Army, for instance, to get the 7 or 11 contracting agencies to agree among themselves. They fought each other as bad as they fought the Germans, and then they fought me just as hard, and fought the Navy just as hard. They had the right to make these contracts, and they had that entire right until the Overman Act commenced to work, and, of course, we had a year in there before it did commence to work, until sometime in 1918. The various departments of the Government had the right to commandeer. I found six men in one factory were commandeering one particular facility. Then we straightened that out because the President issued an order, an order synchronizing the work of the war, stating that no governmental agency could commandeer without the approval of the Chairman of the War Industries Board, but it came very late. But that is something which we hope we will put into effect now.

Senator George. Mr. Baruch, did you refer just now to the du Pont powder contract?

Mr. Baruch. Yes, sir.

Senator George. When did you first hear of that?

Mr. Baruch. As I say, Summers, I think, was the greatest man developed in the war, and he brought my attention to it. I did not know of it. That was developed in the Ordnance Department, a very fine lot of men, but you must not forget this about the Army: They want to get the stuff as quickly as possible.

Senator Clark. He does not care what it costs.

Mr. Baruch. He may care, but time is of the essence. Everybody was scared to death, and the Germans were almost in Pittsburgh. They used to talk about it, and they called upon us many times to the effect that munitions factories should be moved out West. Toward the end of the war we were doing that, but not because of that but because it was necessary to give other people of the country work.

Answering your question further, Senator, yes; that was brought to my attention. I was the one who called up the Secretary of War and told him the contract should be canceled. He did not give me the remaking of that. It was turned over and discussed with some other members of the War Industries Board. I would like to have had the doing of it myself, but the contract was changed very much indeed.

I want to be fair, and not necessarily defend anyone, but I do not think the du Ponts knew what they were doing. They had a man president of that company who was a hard fellow. He was thinking about the du Pont Co., and the du Ponts themselves were not running that company, and they had a stand-up knock-down fight, as a result of which many millions were saved, and I did not know anything about it beyond what has been brought out, Senator. But that was just an instance of many contracts of that kind with which we had to deal. I can outline a little of this thing. When the du Pont contract came about, I telephoned to the Secretary and had him break it. Baker was in a very difficult situation, and so were the Allies. They said, "If you do not get it, the Germans will be in Pittsburgh and maybe cross to the Pacific Ocean." It was a very delicate question as to how to get the thing done. They worked out something which may not have been perfect but was infinitely better than the one suggested.

"Price Ceiling Plan"—War-Profits Taxation

Senator George. Before Senator Clark goes on, Mr. Baruch, may I ask this to clarify the matter more in my mind: When you speak of the price ceiling, you also recognize the necessity for excess-profit taxes?

Mr. Baruch. Oh, yes. In this statement of mine I say that when you put your ceiling in, you proceed to do two things further:

One, to increase your peacetime taxes. Take the taxes of today and shove them up.

And, in addition, put on a tax which will skim off practically all of that which is due entirely to war.

Senator George. Now, Mr. Baruch, let me ask you this practical question: If you had a practical limitation on profits, by use of the taxing power—I do not refer to any effort simply to limit profits, but to tax all above a certain profit, take away all above a certain fixed profit for the war-time purpose—would it still be necessary, in your view, to maintain this price ceiling? Would it still be important to keep that?

Mr. Baruch. Oh, yes; and I will tell you why, Senator. You take a man who is a farmer or a man with wages. A man gets $50, $100, or $200 a month, and if you do not keep those prices from going up, his $200 becomes $50.

Senator Clark. In other words, his real wages will be constantly diminished as prices go up, unless you have a price ceiling?

Mr. Baruch. Exactly so.

Senator George. That situation will still have to be taken care of?

Mr. Baruch. Exactly so.

Senator George. Even though the profits which were being realized by the marketing of the things which we had to buy were ultimately taken away in taxes?

Mr. Baruch. Exactly. You are up here [indicating] as peace is declared, and you go down here [indicating]. That is like we did after our war, or after the World War. That is the official aftermath of the war. Then you keep the ceiling here [indicating] and it is not so bad, and only begins to get bad if you go down further. That is why I want to keep the ceiling low. There is no doubt in my mind it must be done. Prices would go anywhere otherwise.

Senator Vandenberg. Mr. Baruch, I notice you said something about excess-profits taxes above peace-time earnings, and your memorandum referred to placing the excess war-profits tax upon all earnings above peace-time earnings. Why should peace-time earnings be immune from this same sort of excess-profits taxes, when you are in a war?

Mr. Baruch. My suggestion was to take care of that by increasing peace-time taxes. It might be more than the other. This question of the taxes has got to be carefully studied. With a plan of that kind, we know the objective we want, but the experts who understand that question ought to start to work that out, and then let the men who have the objective in view criticize it.

One might take care of the other, but I want to be sure we cover them all.

Senator Vandenberg. I want to be sure that I understand your language, because, under your formula, as contained in your memorandum, all of the swollen earnings which exist in peace times would absolutely be ignored under your excess-profits scheme.

Mr. Baruch. I see what you mean. I propose two taxes, and you might put them in one, but I wanted to have it clearly in everybody's mind that we were going to increase the present-day earnings so that nobody can get any idea that he will get as much in war as in peace. I mean, we are going to increase the taxes of the present day, plus anything that may come in. I can very readily see that you can do it all in one tax.

Senator Vandenberg. Precisely. It seems to me that one of the errors we have made in our thinking is that we have talked about taxing away war profits on war activities, whereas there ought not to be any profits for anybody of any kind, peace or war profits during a war, that are immune to this tax system. Do you agree to that?

Mr. Baruch. Yes, sir. Of course, let us not go too far. But I am willing to go as far as possible in squeezing the thing down so that it won't interfere with the conduct of the war. I am with you on the road going down to that objective, with you or anybody else, but the thing is to work it out. I am not prepared to say how far you can go. It might be 100 percent.

Senator Vandenberg. All I wanted to be sure of was that your memorandum does not mean what it seems to say, that you are suggesting an excess-war profits tax on all earnings above peace-time earnings. You are not going to immunize peace-time earnings with this same sort of taxation?

Mr. Baruch. No.

The Chairman. Mr. Baruch, you are making it difficult for the reporter, when you move so far forward.

(At this point the witness withdrew from the bench and resumed the witness chair.)

Senator Clark. Mr. Baruch, does it not amount to this: That as to normal peace-time profits you must very heavily increase that tax to pay for the war; and, so far as profits entirely due to war are concerned, you want to take them all?

Mr. Baruch. Yes, sir.

Senator Clark. In other words, not only take all the war profits, but you must very heavily increase your normal peace-time taxes to pay for the war?

Mr. Baruch. Yes, sir; but the observation you make is quite correct; you can do it in one group, but when you sit down to draw up this taxation I think you will have to divide it into two.

Senator Clark. It is all a matter of detail to put it in 1 bill or 3 or 4 bills.

Mr. Baruch. That is right.

Senator Clark. I want to see if you agree with the proposition that normal profits from peace-time activities must have their tax heavily increased as a contribution on their part to pay for the war: and as to war profits, profits entirely due to existence of war, we ought to get them all.

Mr. Baruch. Yes, sir. And when I say that—and this observation comes from your suggestion, Senator—I mean, for instance, we will say the United States Steel Corporation is taken as an example. I think the steel company is doing about 40 percent. Without advancing the price, if they got 100 percent due to the war, or 60 percent more, instead of running even or in the red or a little way back, they would make a great deal of money. I think you ought to be careful and state your objections and then let the men work out this thing so that they will get your ideas complete. Otherwise you will find there is some escape.

Senator Bone. Mr. Baruch, what do you think the reaction of business in this country would be, and particularly the larger businesses, which would be normally expected to engage in the conduction of war munitions, to the proposal to not only take 100 percent of war profits or profits which might be attributable directly to war activity as well as a part of the normal peace-time profits; what do you think the reaction of the average business enterprise would be to that?

Mr. Baruch. I think they would come along all right.

Senator Bone. They did not evince any interest in that regard during the last war, did they?

Mr. Baruch. They did not know as much then.

Senator Vandenberg. And the country did not know as much.

Mr. Baruch. We also had the question of the Allies' purchases and things of that kind. I do not think you will have any difficulty about it, Senator. You must make up your mind what you do, and as soon as one gentleman does I think the others will come along.

Senator Bone. Suppose we translate those ideas into legislation and the country goes into war, and some gentlemen come down here and induce Congress to wipe them off the books. They can be wiped off in 24 hours.

Mr. Baruch. I have got a better opinion of Congress than that.

The Chairman. Even a war-time Congress?

Mr. Baruch. Yes, sir.

Senator Bone. You recall the bitter objections registered in the Senate of the United States against Senator La Follette's advocacy of taking all the war profits. He was almost expelled from the Senate for advocating it, and yet it was common knowledge that profits were being rolled up. There was bitter opposition aroused during the war against Senator La Follette on that. That is what inspired the question. How are you going to escape that sort of thing with these profits being offered and people seeing an opportunity to acquire them?

Mr. Baruch. I do not think they can do what you think.

Senator Bone. It is a difference of opinion.

Mr. Baruch. You may be right, and I may be wrong.

Senator Bone. I think these gentlemen would not surrender those profits without a bitter fight, which would be political in character.

Mr. Baruch. I do not see how they could help themselves.

Senator Bone. That is what we are trying to get at.

Mr. Baruch. You referred to Senator La Follette, and I think I called it to the attention of this body that there are two schools of thought, and one wanted to let the prices go where they would, and the other wanted to fix the prices, plus a profits tax.

Senator Bone. La Follette's proposals were said to be unfair, and in that way we should not capture those profits. You recall La Follette's proposal, supported by the members of the Senate at that time, was to capture all the war profits, or the major portion of them. There was very bitter opposition raised to that proposal at that time. You will recall that.

Mr. Baruch. I do not remember, but I can quite understand and I am sure it was so, but we are larger in numbers now than we were then.

Senator Bone. What do you mean?

Mr. Baruch. I mean on this side of the question. I do not think public opinion would permit such a thing. That is only one man's opinion.

The Chairman. The record has been such that the public would not be apt to tolerate a repetition of it in another war, would it?

Mr. Baruch. Yes, sir.

Senator Barbour. Mr. Baruch, do you not think the members of this committee have contributed in that respect, as far as general public opinion is concerned, and their being better advised, and otherwise they have helped in this whole philosophy, which is psychologically so important?

Mr. Baruch. Unquestionably so.

Senator Clark. If you ever get the law on the statute books, and it is repealed, that is the fault of Congress.

Mr. Baruch. Mr. Swope suggested that apropos of some of the questions which were asked, I read from this document, which I do not read from generally, because I presume people are more or less familiar with it.

(Reading from pamphlet entitled "Taking the Profit Out of War" by Bernard M. Baruch:)

> When we entered the World War, the frantic demands and un-coordinated counterbidding of our future associates in war had already distorted our own price structure out of any semblance of its normal scheme. In other words, there was a robust inflation here before we ever entered the war. Furthermore, nearly 12 months elapsed after our declaration before we had evolved controls and organizations capable of coordinating our own and our associates' procurement activities and of controlling price. Notwithstanding this delay and the dimness with which controlling principles were at first perceived we did, in 1918, arrive at a method which checked the process of inflation in America and kept it in check until all controls were released in November 1918.

It is different today because now they can do it.

> It is to this experience that I refer when I say that we have proved in practice a method to control inflation. That proof convinces me that it would also prevent inflation if applied at once upon the advent of war and before the inflationary process begins.

Senator Pope. What report are you reading from, Mr. Baruch?

Mr. Baruch. I am reading from the pamphlet "Taking the Profit Out of War," my testimony.

The Chairman. The War Policies Commission?

Mr. Baruch. The War Policies Commission (continuing reading):

> To measure inflation of price and profit we must have some norm. The obvious norm is the whole price structure as it existed on some antecedent date near to the declaration of war on which the normal operation of the natural law of supply and demand can be said to have controlled price. That determined, we need a method of putting a ceiling upon the whole price structure at that level. The obvious way to do this is simple: By proclamation to decree that every price in the whole national pattern as of that determined date shall be the maximum that may thenceforth be charged for

anything—rents, wages, interest rates, commissions, fees—in short, the price for every item and service in commerce.

In these few words reside the basic principle of war control of national industry and of the present suggestion for the elimination of war inflation in America. The superficial objection is, "You propose to repeal the law of supply and demand." We may as well take this bull by the horns. In modern war administrative control must replace the law of supply and demand.

Senator Vandenberg. Mr. Baruch, do you find your philosophy adequately translated in the McSwain bill?

Mr. Baruch. When the bill came out I asked McSwain, "What about the taxes?" because, as I shall show you here, he has gone as far on the road as anybody has.

He said, "The reason I did not couple up this thing"—I said the McSwain idea was all right, "but you have not said anything about taking out the profits of war."

He said, "The Military Affairs Committee have to deal with the method and manner of the military situation, but the Ways and Means Committee or the Appropriations Committee"—whichever body in which they originate taxes—"would be jealous of their prerogatives, and they would have to make the taxes."

May I just read you here something? Senator, it is the first time I have ever heard the expression "paying as you go" or "paying as you fight," which I think is a very good phrase, because it gets into the public mind exactly what you want to do, much better than "taking the profits out of war," which was first used by Mr. McSwain when he was a member of that committee. The reason I said I was for the McSwain bill was because in examination of me here the other day before his committee, he used this very expression, "pay as you go," if you will pardon me one second [examining papers].

Mr. McSwain said, "What do you say as to setting up a program"—he asked a question, and I am glad for the chance it gave me to answer it—Mr. McSwain said to me, and this leads up to the matter:

> Now, that leads up to this: What do you say as to setting up a program for conducting a war on the basis of pay as you fight, whereby, when the fighting is over, the paying would be finished, and the whole population could immediately resume its pre-war, normal activities—

And so forth. I go on to approve of this, and, when through with that testimony, he asked the question:

> We all assume that Mr. Baruch is an income-tax payer.

He was quite correct.

> How high would you say this income tax should go in time of war?

That was his question to me. [Continuing quotation:]

> I have in mind especially those incomes that are shown to be the

result of the dislocation of war, the war profits. How high would you say the tax rate should go for the purpose of reaching those?

I said:

Well, I was going to be funny and say as high as a cat's back. But I will say just as high as you can make it function. I think you should try to tax the profits that your price structures do not get.

The reason I was in favor of the McSwain bill was I thought it had coupled the taxation program with it when it came out.

It seems to me, Senator, that you are pretty close together.

Senator Vandenberg. I just wanted to raise a point in that connection. I hold great respect for Congressman McSwain, and I know he wants to go sled length in any program, but the McSwain bill by itself has been held out as a successful answer to the problem of taking the profit out of war, and I think the McSwain bill by itself is utterly inadequate. Is not that so?

Mr. Baruch. Quite so; because it must be accompanied by this tax program, or you do not get anywhere. You are where you were before. You might keep the prices from going up, but you won't keep the profits from going up.

Senator Pope. Are not you and Mr. Flynn pretty close together on your tax program?

Mr. Baruch. I have not seen the Flynn plan except in the newspapers. I would be glad if you will tell me what it is, or will give me a copy of it, to answer you, and I will study it and be glad to make observations on it.

The Chairman. In brief, the plan with respect to taxation is this: The first 6 percent of all corporation income or profit shall be subject to a tax of 50 percent. All profit in excess of that first 6 percent shall be subject to a 100-percent tax. As respects individuals, there will be an increase over the peace-time rates in all brackets, but after the $10,000 mark of income is reached, a tax of 100 percent is placed.

Mr. Baruch. Now, as to the first one, the 6-percent profit, I have given an instance in answer to that. The United States Steel Corporation, if they got one-half of 6 percent, would make a devil of a lot of money. If they did a 100-percent business, their earnings would be increased tremendously above normal.

Senator Vandenberg. I do not think you quite understand the chairman.

Senator Clark. We will get a copy of the minutes, Mr. Baruch, and will be glad to have you examine it.

Senator Vandenberg. It would probably be more advisable to submit the whole plan in writing.

Mr. Baruch. I would like to see it, because I would like to see how the thing dovetails in. I was not able to get it all, but there are a lot of things on which I can go along with him.

I can go along with him here down the road, and, perhaps, I can go all the way, but there are some things I want to discuss and get clearly in my mind. Have you a copy of the plan?

The Chairman. We have no tangible plan.

Senator Clark. We will furnish you the minutes of Mr. Flynn's testimony, and would be glad to have you look them over.

Mr. Baruch. I would be glad to.

The Chairman. Within a very few days, possibly within the day, there will be a definite draft of the plan which will be available.

Mr. Baruch. I want to say this in reference to the plan, or any other plan, or my plan: That I am as willing to go as far down the road for limiting profits as possible, and making ourselves just the most impregnable nation in the world in time of war that we can and still make ourselves safe. I do not want to interrupt the flow of industry. That is all I am interested in.

Senator Vandenberg. Do you care to consent to Mr. Flynn's philosophy to the extent of agreeing that, as far as it may be possible, we must pay as we fight?

Mr. Baruch. Yes, sir.

Senator Vandenberg. And if we pay as we fight, then do not we above everything else quarantine against post-war deflation, which is the greatest evil of all?

Mr. Baruch. It is the greatest loss of all war, the greatest loss in war. Nobody has gained anything out of this war. The winners lost and the losers lost.

Senator Vandenberg. You agree completely with that philosophy, as I understand it?

Mr. Baruch. Yes, sir.

Senator Bone. What do you think of the cost-plus contracts?

Mr. Baruch. Cost-plus contracts in the war were defensible because you could not fix the cost of things, because labor would be $3 a day, and the shipbuilder would make it $10, or the munition maker $12 a day. You did not have any ceiling then. The cost-plus in the present contract will be an entirely different one, because costs are fixed. Before they were not fixed. There were only a few things fixed in the World War. But today it would be an entirely different thing, where you know in advance what the cost of everything is. There they did not. They would say, "The cost will be $25,000 for this," and they said, "You boys better add another 10 percent, because you do not know what is going to happen."

In the present circumstances which we are discussing, you know what the cost will be exactly. It is an entirely different thing.

Senator Bone. Did the War Industries Board, or any agencies set up by the Government during the war to assume any sort of control over contracts, have anything to do with the preparation of the contracts for the Navy Department which were sent to these shipbuilding companies?

Mr. Baruch. No, sir.

Senator Bone. We have testimony here that cost-plus contracts were sent down to shipbuilding companies during the war that not only authorized a great many things which seem impossible at this time but they literally authorized the company to charge off income taxes as part of their operating expenses.

Mr. Baruch. The shipbuilding conduct was an entirely different division from mine. I might say we have never even allowed any fellow to have a taxicab ride free.

Senator Bone. Would you be in favor of drafting management of industry during war?

Mr. Baruch. What?

Senator Bone. Industrial management.

Mr. Baruch. You do not have to. Under this plan there they are in control of their plants and they are responsible. If you start out to draft management, then you have got to draft labor, and then you will get into a territory where you and I will have a stand-up and knock-down fight. It is not necessary, Senator.

Under the plan which you are all discussing, you do not have to draft them. You can say, "If you do not do that, we will commandeer the plant." He will not let anybody step in and take the plant, and that man will do better work than any new man. That is my personal reaction.

Senator Bone. Do you think that an organization in the nature of a war board should be set up in peace times?

Mr. Baruch. I think you should have your organization entirely planned and documented. For instance, ever since the World War there has been under The Assistant Secretary of War a planning division. The only fight there was was between them and myself because I wanted to take out of the hands of the military the conduct of civilian activities, and it was only at the last minute, Senator, that the Chief of Staff changed his testimony, just when I was about to argue against him, when I had to hurry to appear before that committee. I think the War Department is doing a good work now. Maybe I think they are doing that because I think they agreed with me, or we agreed. But they have been making a very intelligent study and a carefully set up plan, which I think should be carefully scrutinized, and I understand your committee has been looking at them.

The Chairman. Do you understand that that plan does anything to control profits?

Mr. Baruch. Sir?

The Chairman. Do you understand that that War Department plan does anything at all to control profits or to control costs in time of war?

Mr. Baruch. I flattered myself that they had agreed with this document which I had presented before the War Policies Commission, and I thought that they had rearranged their whole plan with the price ceiling and excess profits and with control generally of industry.

I have got some evidence of it in a document here.

Senator Bone. Where is this plan which the War Department has formulated? It has never been made public.

Mr. Baruch. I had an idea they were before your committee and that you cross-examined them pretty carefully.

The Chairman. There were certain bills recommended. Senator Clark has introduced those bills, not as his own but so that they will be before the committee. The committee has under consideration the legislation which the War Department has in mind as a part of its plan, but there is nothing about controlling profits, absolutely nothing.

Mr. Baruch. I thought they had adopted it.

Senator Clark. Some of the language in their pamphlet, Mr. Baruch, does go to the point of endorsing the policy of price fixing during war, but nothing in the legislation which they had prepared to be introduced in the event of war has to do with fixing prices, as I see it.

Mr. Baruch. I thought that they had in mind certain definite bills.

Senator Clark. They had in mind certain definite bills but none of them go to the point of price fixing, or have anything to do with it. I have introduced their bills, and they have been referred to this committee, but none of them go to the point of price fixing or regulating profits.

Mr. Baruch. They gave me to understand that they covered that. I do not know whether the bill came from them, but there was a price-fixing bill, covering the recommendations which I made in the War Policies Commission.

But you ought to have, Senator, answering your question, if you will permit me to say so, you ought to have, or this committee ought to see to it that there is set up, before you get through, as a part of your recommendations, the broad question of control of prices, allocations, taxes.

Senator Vandenberg. Mr. Baruch, when the War Policies Commission report was submitted to the Congress I introduced a resolution asking the Secretary of the Treasury to implement the tax regulation, and all that we got from Mr. Mills was a very short memorandum back, stating that it was not feasible to write a tax law until you got into war. Have you any sympathy with that point of view?

Mr. Baruch. No, sir.

Senator Vandenberg. Neither have I.

Senator Clark. Mr. Baruch——

Mr. Baruch. I have had my attention drawn to a little memorandum, answering your question, Senator.

The Chairman. Answering Senator George's question?

Mr. Baruch. Yes, sir. I think it was Senator George.

It has been said that fixation of prices—putting the ceiling over them, as I advocated—might mean the crystallization of profits. There may be something in this. It is a subject that requires specific approach. But you will forgive me if I point out one obvious phase of the situation that my experience and yours has taught me is of extreme importance to the civilian population; keeping the home fires burning without diminishing the morale. That point is seeing to it that adequate flow of food and other necessities of life is assured our population at reasonable prices, free from profiteering. Food is a universal necessity, as important to those at home as to the men at the front. I do not know how this essential element can be held from sky-rocketing except by price fixing. And what I say about food applies equally to all the other necessities of life.

In such a fixation of price there is bound to be an element of profit, but I see no difficulty in preventing this from becoming exorbitant, and recapture it by taxes. . . .

MEMORANDA OF JOSEPH C. GREEN, DIVISION OF WESTERN EUROPEAN AFFAIRS MARCH 30, APRIL 10, AND 12, 1935

Foreign Relations (1935), Vol. 1, 324–40.

Washington, March 30, 1935

In compliance with the Secretary's instructions, I called Mr. Raushenbush by telephone this morning. I told him that it had come to the attention of the Deparment that leading members of the Committee on Foreign Relations of both parties were irritated at the reports which have appeared in the press to the effect that the Nye Committee is contemplating the introduction of legislation modifying the Neutrality Policy of the United States. I said that they had pointed out that this was a subject which, under the standing rules of the Senate, came within the jurisdiction of the Committee on Foreign Relations. Mr. Raushenbush thanked me for the information but added that the Nye Committee had taken up the study of our Neutrality Policy at the specific request of the President.

Washington, April 10, 1935

Mr. Raushenbush called me by telephone this morning. He invited my attention to Article IV of the Committee's report of April 1 to the Senate, which reads as follows:

> The Committee is in substantial agreement on a principle to govern the export of munitions and contraband in case of a major war, and expects to make certain recommendations to the Senate on this subject in the immediate future and for action in the present session of Congress. This is the only phase of the neutrality problem which the Committee considers to be within its jurisdiction.

He told me in confidence that some members of the Committee wished to go even farther in limiting the sphere of the Committee's action and to have the Committee refrain from introducing any legislation in regard to contraband.

He said that Senators Nye and Clark [1] had, in their personal capacities, introduced into the Senate yesterday neutrality legislation in regard to passports and loans.[2] He explained that this legislation was *not* sponsored by the Committee.

[1] Bennett Champ Clark of Missouri, member of the Special Committee of the Senate Investigating the Munitions Industry.

[2] S. J. Res. 99 and S. J. Res. 100, *Congressional Record*, vol. 79, pt. 5, pp. 5286 and 5287.

I said that it was my understanding that the President, at his recent conference with the Committee, had requested the Committee not to introduce neutrality legislation without further conference with him, and that I felt that the introduction of such legislation by the Chairman of the Committee, without further conference with the President, might be misunderstood.

Mr. Raushenbush replied that I was correct in my understanding of the arrangement which had been reached with the President and that he saw that there was danger that such legislation introduced by Senators Nye and Clark might be considered to be Committee legislation. He assured me, however, that it was not.

Washington, April 12, 1935

In compliance with the Secretary's request, I called on Senator Nye in his office this morning. I found the Munitions Committee in executive session. All members of the Committee were present except Senator Vandenberg.

I told the Committee that when I had received from Mr. Raushenbush an intimation that the Committee was contemplating inviting the Secretary to appear before it in executive session to discuss neutrality legislation, I had informed the Secretary that such an invitation might be forthcoming. I said that the Secretary was anxious to cooperate with the Committee in every possible way, as he had ever since its organization, but that he had been informed that the Chairman and some members of the Foreign Relations Committee did not agree with the Munitions Committee's interpretation of its jurisdiction in respect to neutrality legislation, as expressed in Article IV of its report to the Senate. I said that, in these circumstances, the Secretary might be seriously embarrassed if the Committee were to invite him to appear before it to discuss neutrality legislation. I, therefore, suggested that the Committee might wish, through discussion with the Committee on Foreign Relations, to clear up this question of jurisdiction before sending any invitation to the Secretary.

Several members of the Committee replied. The substance of their remarks was identical. They all said that they thoroughly appreciated the embarrassment in which the Secretary would be placed if the contemplated invitation were sent to him, and that the Committee should refrain from sending such an invitation, at least until the question of jurisdiction was entirely settled to the satisfaction of the Committee on Foreign Relations. Senator Nye said that he wished that the Committee could wash its hands of the whole question of neutrality legislation; that the Committee had never contemplated dealing with such legislation until "the President laid it on our doorstep". He said that the Committee had plenty to do without attempting to deal with such a complicated matter and that he, for his part, would be glad to turn the whole thing over to the Committee on Foreign Relations. All of the members of the Committee present concurred in this view.

In regard to the question of jurisdiction, the Committee was unanimous in the opinion that the Resolution by which the Committee was created was sufficiently broad to justify it in presenting legislation on the question of neutrality if it so desired. Nevertheless, they felt that, as a matter of practical politics, it would be highly undesirable for the Committee to antagonize Senators Pittman and Borah. A motion was made and carried unanimously that Senator Nye should be directed to confer with Senators Pittman and Borah, with a view to settling the question of jurisdiction. The hope was expressed that he might be able to persuade them to undertake a discussion of neutrality questions in the Committee on Foreign Relations, and so relieve the Munitions Committee of all responsibility in this field.

I learned incidentally that the President had asked the Committee to confer with him, but that one of his secretaries had called up this morning and had postponed the conference, for which no date has as yet been fixed.

NEW YORK TIMES REPORT
APRIL 16, 1935

The Flynn plan to "take the profit out of war" would mean an "exaggerated inflation, far greater than if there were no plan at all," paralyze war production and render the United States practically helpless against a major attack, Bernard M. Baruch, former head of the War Industries Board, who at present is studying the war profits question for President Roosevelt, declared today in a statement filed with the Senate Munitions Committee.

Mr. Baruch's statement drew a sharp response from Senator Nye, chairman of the committee, who accused him of "hedging" from a previous position assumed in testimony.

The "pay-as-you-fight" plan drawn up by John T. Flynn, the writer, at the committee's request, provides for virtual confiscation of all incomes over $10,000 in time of war and for drafting the services of industrialists on a military basis. The committee is expected to back it in Congress as a substitute for the McSwain bill for the same purpose which has passed the House.

"It is clear that business and industry is in large part activated by the spending and investment of income, and that if a war government takes all of income, it will not have to worry about paying for the war," said Mr. Baruch. "Either its conquerors or the Commune will have that problem."

The statement was filed with the committee by Mr. Baruch largely to correct the record of his previous testimony on the same subject, which he said had been garbled.

At the same time the committee started its investigation into the sale in 1933 of the New York Shipbuilding Corporation, a bidder for many navy contracts, the true ownership of which was not disclosed until a few weeks ago, when evidence showed that a half interest in the company was held by Ben C. Smith and Thomas E. Bragg, Wall Street operators. They are represented on the board of the corporation by Gene Tunney, the former heavyweight boxing champion.

Of the Flynn plan, Mr. Baruch said:

"Plainly, the result would not be merely to skim off the profits due to war.

It is, with insignificant exception, to abolish the present economic system in war.

"I am not debating here whether the profit motive is right or wrong. I am only insisting that we recognize reality and what is here proposed. And I am saying that the advent of modern war and threatened national destruction, when the fate of the people, as at no other time, depends on the efficient operation at high-speed pressure of its industrial system, is not the moment to select to switch from the fundamental base of our economic system to a new and wholly experimental system which was never adopted at any time in the world's history in peace or war without an immediate result of collapse and ruin."

Redefining his plan, on which the McSwain bill is modeled, Mr. Baruch explained that it would establish a "ceiling" on prices, but would allow them to fluctuate beneath the ceiling. The plan would not fix or "freeze" prices, he said. It also provides 100 per cent taxation on all profit and income made in wartime above the average of the preceding three years of peace.

Speaking on the radio over an NBC hook-up on the National Radio Forum tonight, Senator Nye attacked Mr. Baruch's statement, charging that it was an attempt by business to "make harmless any legislative program that really tries to take the profits out of war."

"For days he appeared before our committee urging drastic programs to accomplish this," the Senator said.

"Now he says the bill is too drastic, that we would be defeated in another war under such legislation because business wouldn't do its share of fighting and helping to win the war when its profits were so restricted. May Heaven preserve us! I've expected some one to say that. But Mr. Baruch, I never expected it to come from you. So American business won't produce what is needed in war if it can't have its profits! So American business will not go into a war on the same basis that the boys go in when they are called!

"Well, if this be true it is high time America knew it. And double is my conviction tonight of the need of a constitutional amendment that will let the government in time of war commandeer such business as won't do its part, just as it commandeers the men who must make the fight with blood and life in the front lines."

Mr. Smith was present today when the committee began its hearings on the ownership of the New York Shipbuilding Corporation, but was not expected to testify before late tomorrow or early Wednesday. The witnesses today were Samuel H. Vallance of Vallance & Co., William Burden and Joseph W. Powell of New York and Henry H. Farley of Philadelphia, who, in July, 1933, cooperated in negotiations which, if successful, would have transferred control of the corporation to F. H. Prince of Boston and Newport.

Stock of the corporation was very active in the first nine months of 1933, ranging from a high of 4⅝ in January to 20⅞ in October, after which it sagged to 9⅝ in November. In 1934 it again took an upward trend, and was quoted at 23½ at the end of March.

The witnesses today said they had no knowledge of the facts behind these stock fluctuations and their testimony related entirely to the efforts of Mr. Prince to acquire 89,880 shares of Founders stock, the controlling stock, held at the time for $20 a share by the Chase Securities Company and Bancamerica-Blair corporation of New York.

Mr. Powell, who is president of United Drydocks, Inc., of New York City, and is a close friend of Mr. Prince, said that on July 5, 1933, the latter telephoned to him that he would like to discuss with him the possible purchase of the New York Shipbuilding Corporation. This was about a month before the corporation was sold to the Cord Company of Chicago and Mr. Smith and Mr. Bragg.

A meeting was held in New York a few days later, with Messrs. Prince, Powell, Vallance, Burden and Farley present. The facts were placed before Mr. Prince to the effect that the corporation was and had been making money for two years, and the outlook was unusually bright due to the government's announcement that the navy was to be built up to London treaty strength.

Mr. Prince was impressed, and said that if he acquired the corporation he would like to have Mr. Smith associated with him.

A conference to enable Mr. Smith to meet Mr. Powell was then arranged, and Mr. Smith was impressed so favorably with the proposal that he told Mr. Powell he would look into it and reply in two or three days.

On July 14 Mr. Smith said he had made an offer to the banks to buy the stock and would communicate with Mr. Powell as soon as he heard from the banks.

Mr. Powell said he heard nothing from him for several days, and on July 18 telephoned to him to inquire as to the progress of negotiations. He did not seem to be in a very good humor, said Mr. Powell.

"Smith said that he was proceeding in his own way and that if Mr. Prince was not satisfied he would drop the whole matter, and count him out and handle the negotiations with the Chase Bank himself," Mr. Powell continued. "When I told Mr. Prince this, he said he would do nothing more about making the purchase. I had no further connection, directly or indirectly, with the matter."

NEW YORK TIMES REPORT
APRIL 17, 1935

The story of the transfer of control of the New York Shipbuilding Corporation, one of the "big three" of the American industry, which for weeks has been a subject of speculation and suspicion on the part of the Senate Munitions Committee, was cleared up today.

The story was unfolded by men now in control of the Camden plant and others who failed in 1933 to gain control.

In the picture disclosed to the committee were New York brokerage houses, including Hornblower & Weeks, Thomson & McKinnon and J. R. Timmons & Co., and the Chase National Bank, the Cliffwood, an American, and Seven Oaks, a Canadian holding corporation, both owned entirely by Bernard E. Smith and Thomas W. Bragg of New York; Joseph W. Powell, president of United Drydocks, Inc., of New York; Bernard M. Baruch, Frederick H. Prince of Boston, chairman of the executive committee of Armour & Co.; Samuel P. Vallance of Vallance & Co., New York, and Gene Tunney, former heavyweight boxing champion of the world. Mr. Tunney became the Cord representative on the board of directors of the corporation.

Bernard Smith, who is "Ben" Smith in Wall Street, was the star witness. With Mr. Bragg, whom the committee has never been able to find for subpoena-serving purposes, Mr. Smith said he bought control of the New York Shipbuilding Corporation in July, 1933. So far as the records show, the sale was to the Cliffwood and the Seven Oaks corporations.

Subsequently, Mr. Smith asked the E. L. Cord Corporation to take half interest and sold to that company half the stock at $20 a share, at a profit to Smith and Bragg of $169,000.

The scramble for control of New York Shipbuilding began immediately after the announcement by the Roosevelt administration that it was going to build the navy to the maximum strength provided in the Treaty of London.

The stock began to jump and, according to Earle G. Hines, who participated in the sale transaction as a representative of the Chase Securities Corporation, from various quarters came proposals involving the purchase of the 90,000 "founder" shares held by the Chase and Bancamerica-Blair interests. This stock, which was controlling, was pooled, 53,000 shares being held in New York by the Chase, while the other 37,000 which Bancamerica-Blair owned were in Toronto.

The naval construction boom being definitely under way, the banks refused to take any options on the stock. It had to be a cash transaction and the price fixed by the banks as "a trading" starter was $20 a share. In July, 1933, with the allocation of the ships included in the $238,000,000 PWA naval program only a few weeks away, Mr. Prince decided to bid for the plant. Mr. Prince called in his friend, Mr. Powell of United Drydocks, and told him that if he bought the plant he desired Mr. Powell, who is a Naval Academy graduate and former president of the Bethlehem Shipbuilding Company, to take the presidency of the New York plant.

According to Mr. Smith, the insistence of Mr. Prince that Mr. Powell be the executive head of the corporation was "the straw that broke the camel's back." The only reason he gave was that Mr. Powell "annoyed" him. He never met Mr. Powell, he testified, until a short time before the deal was closed and the controlling ownership of the plant passed into the hands of the Cliffwood and Seven Oaks corporations.

Mr. Vallance, who preceded Mr. Smith in the witness chair, was associated with Mr. Powell in the negotiations on behalf of Mr. Prince. Mr. Vallance testified that, at Mr. Prince's suggestion, Mr. Smith, a friend of Mr. Prince, was informed of his ambition to enter the shipbuilding business.

The financier asked Mr. Smith to join him in the enterprise. Mr. Smith said Mr. Vallance then communicated with the Chase Securities Corporation and was told that control of the shipbuilding corporation would pass to any one willing and able to pay $20 a share for 90,000 shares.

Mr. Prince and Mr. Smith, declared that this was too much, in view of the fact that the stock was then selling on the Curb Exchange at about $12.50. The end of July was in sight and Mr. Vallance said that news of the purchase situation, so far as Smith was concerned, was hard to get. There were many telephone calls, but, he said, no worthwhile information as to how matters stood. A few more days passed and then came the news that the plant had been sold.

"It was a fine bit of double-crossing on the part of Smith," the witness charged. "Smith offered a bid on our behalf and a week later he bought the plant for himself."

Mr. Smith followed Mr. Vallance. He said he was a former partner of W. E. Hutton & Co., and that at 60 his principal business is the development of mining properties. In 1932 and early in 1933 he had been approached by various persons regarding the purchase of the controlling stock of the New York Shipbuilding Corporation, but had turned a deaf ear to all propositions.

"I told Prince," Mr. Smith testified, "that I would not consider the proposition if Powell was a part of it. Subsequently I told Prince if he was still considering Powell in it to forget it so far as I was concerned.

"Shortly thereafter Mitchell Tarabasch came to see me and suggested I go after the shares. I did and purchased them through Hornblower & Weeks, Timmons & Co., and Thomson & McKinnon. I purchased 30,000 shares outright at $15.50 and took an option on the remaining 60,000 shares in blocks and at prices up to $22. Then suddenly there was a substantial drop in the market and I decided to let the option go. However, we managed to get together and I bought the remaining 60,000 shares at $16.50."

Mr. Smith, in answer to questions, said that Bernard M. Baruch had agreed to buy 5,000 shares of the stock and it was delivered and paid for. Following a talk by telephone with Mr. Baruch, who was in Europe, Mr. Baruch asked him to cancel the purchase, since he, Mr. Baruch, did not care to be in business involving the government.

When the committee convened this morning, Senator Vandenberg, for the committee, made the following comment on Mr. Baruch's objections to the committee's "pay-as-you-go" war profits control bill:

"I flatly disagree with Mr. Baruch, and he disagrees with himself. He concurred with our committee that we should 'pay as we fight.' We simply propose to make that formula mean what it says. We practice what he has preached. We decline longer to pillage our children with war bills that ought to be 'C. O. D.'

"Mr. Baruch concurred with our committee that fighting wars on borrowed money is the root of post-war deflation from which our people still cruelly suffer. We propose to stop it—not just to talk about stopping it. The alternative is a real war-tax program from which Mr. Baruch promptly runs away, although it is entirely practical.

"He has earnestly talked for years about demonetizing war and has proposed partially effective plans in this direction. Even now, in the midst of his attack upon our prospectus, he still speaks about 'increasing taxes to the vanishing point.' Yet when we propose to do this precise thing, Mr. Baruch says we will wreck our economic system. He speaks in a confusion of riddles.

"There is nothing sacred about our tentative formula. It may need drastic amendment. But it is not the monster Mr. Baruch envisions as a threat to capitalism—and I speak as one who is everlastingly opposed to the collective state. On the contrary, God help capitalism if it won't defend a common national crisis without its pound of flesh. War itself is the monster of real menace.

"When Mr. Baruch asks me to believe that America's civilian population will not generally defend the Republic if temporarily forced to forego the normal profits motive, precisely as the soldier foregoes it, I decline to join him

in his low estimate of the national patriotism, and I decline to desert the
movement truly to equalize the burdens of war and truly to excise its commercial motive.

"I have not and shall not make any attack, on Mr. Baruch's war record in
1917–18. On the contrary, I applaud it as a fine, unselfish piece of work amid
frequently sordid conditions which we do not propose to have repeated."

SUMMARY FINDINGS AND RECOMMENDATIONS OF NYE COMMITTEE ON SHIPBUILDING INDUSTRY JUNE 1935

Senate Report 944, Part 1, 74th Congress, 2nd Session, 1–16.

The Special Committee on Investigation of the Munitions Industry, authorized by Senate Resolution 206 of the Seventy-third Congress to investigate
the munitions industry, to review the findings of the War Policies Commission, and to inquire into the desirability of creating a Government monopoly
in respect to the manufacture of munitions, submits the following report:

Findings

In submitting this preliminary report on naval shipbuilding, the committee wishes to emphasize that it is interested mainly in two things:

The first of these is that the naval defense shall be provided for without
profiteering or collusion.

The second of these is that the national necessity for a purely defensive
Navy shall not be confused with the private necessity of the shipbuilders for
continuing profits as a consequence of the present close interdependence of
the Navy Department and these private shipbuilders.

The Navy is an instrument of national policy. Its growth and activities are
watched abroad and take part in changing the foreign policy of other nations.
Such changes work back to reshape our own national policy. The growth of a
Navy contains within it the seeds of armament races and wars as well as the
legitimate seeds of a purely defensive national life insurance.

Because of this fact the naval shipbuilders are in a different position from
road or building contractors who may move in on a Government, hungry for
"plunder", as one shipbuilder's lobbyist described a naval appropriation.
These private shipbuilders are part of the private system of national defense
which has grown up. Their activities ultimately have a bearing on our foreign
policy.

Whenever the Navy becomes closely tied up to private shipbuilding interests and asks for and is dependent on their support either in the securing of appropriations or in the construction or designing of necessary ships or in the crippling of our foreign policy, a dangerous and delicate situation has been created, and one which the country should go to full lengths to avoid and stop.

The technical developments of the present years are rapidly making the armaments of this Nation, particularly in regard to naval vessels and naval aircraft, approach those of European countries in their effects. In Europe almost every major defensive weapon can be used offensively, and is regarded by other European nations as a distinctly offensive weapon. With recent developments we are rapidly approaching that situation ourselves.

This is an additional reason for providing for a cessation of any dependence by the Navy on those who may be primarily interested in their own profits and who may be unscrupulously glad to be in a position where they can wrap the flag around those private interests.

Congress must never allow the people of this Nation to let themselves be confused between the actual needs of the country in national defense and the needs of the private shipbuilding and supplying interests for continuing profits.

The record of our shipbuilders in the war, in the post-war period, and in the days from 1927 on, before and after the cruiser program was begun, has not been an entirely pleasant or wholesome story. Some of them are certainly not above suspicion of willingness to wave the flag or to circulate war scares in the plain and simple interest of their own pocketbooks, regardless of results.

It is clear that these results are not to be trifled with. Mr. Eugene Grace, president of Bethlehem Steel Corporation, questioned on the possible effect of another war on western civilization, testified:

> I should think it was possible to destroy it; if not in its entirety, certainly in its effectiveness. Just an anticipation of it is too terrible even to think of (galley 74 VW, Feb. 26).

With these possible results in mind, it is clear that the private shipbuilders should very definitely be policed in any and all moves made by them or through them to confuse public-defense needs with their private profits, or should be cut off entirely from the building of ships for the Navy.

The committee is not unmindful of the naval race prior to the World War between England and Germany and the self-interest part played in it by Krupp and other steel interests, and their *Flottenverein*. It is not unmindful of the fact, demonstrated in that naval race, that few elements of international competition can be used more effectively to scare other people into building larger fleets and spending more money on them than a Navy which has clearly outgrown the purposes of national defense. The committee is not unmindful of the part played by Vickers and the Electric Boat Co., an American company, in such a naval race in South America in the early twenties. (See vol. 1, Committee Hearings.) It is not particularly impressed with the thought that companies which have engaged in this sort of activity, or in the business of trying to make the United States Government remit just taxes or to pay admittedly exorbitant claims, are exactly the right people to allow to hang around very close to the powder keg of international relations.

If it were clear that the rush and pressure of the shipbuilders and their associated subcontractors and suppliers toward a constantly growing Navy had resulted in savings and economies to the Government in the construction of these cruisers and other naval ships, a case might be made for allowing them to live as close to the danger zone as they do now. While the evidence is not all in, the indications are, on the contrary, that the private yards cost the Government from one to two million dollars more per cruiser than the navy yards.

I. Agreements on Naval Bidding

Specifically, the committee finds, under the head of Agreements on Naval Bidding:

The Navy has become a big business. It is one of the largest governmental contractors in the world.

During the years 1933 and 1934 it gave out to private companies contracts totaling over $180,000,000.

The committee heard 9 companies, 67 witnesses, largely on the subject of these contracts. It spent 38 days, and took 4,036 pages of testimony.

The committee finds that the evidence indicates clearly that:

(1) In most cases the Navy wishes work to begin as soon as possible. The result of this is that there is often not time to prepare designs, let alone examine figures or to analyze the bids put before it by private companies.

(2) The rush has made it impossible for the Navy to use its own navy yards as current up-to-date yardsticks of private bids. The navy yards do not even know such essentials of the bids of private yards as the speed guarantees or oil guarantees until after the private bids are opened.

(3) The Navy has never examined the underlying costs or profits of the private builders. It makes no pretense of doing this. It has no staff for it. The figures studied by the Munitions Committee were all news to it.

The Navy makes no attempt to examine the costs of the private companies to determine whether the profit limitation of 11.1 percent in the Vinson-Trammell Act is enforced or evaded. That is left to the Treasury to do after 3 years, after a job is done.

(4) This rush, this lack of staff, this lack of acquaintanceship with the strange ups and downs of bidding by the private companies on the part of the Navy, leaves the Navy at the mercy of the shipbuilders. A series of bids are put before the Navy, and the Navy has to take the low one, and the taxpayers have to hope and pray that the low one is somewhere within a few million dollars of being reasonable and proper.

(5) The evidence presented to the committee showed that in 1933 on contracts worth $130,000,000 to the private shipbuilders, there was no hard-hitting competition among equally desirous bidders able to take on the work: On the aircraft carriers, worth $38,000,000; on the two light cruisers, worth $24,000,000; on the heavy cruiser, worth $12,000,000. There was no competition of that character on the heavy destroyer leaders, worth $30,000,000 nor on the light destroyers, worth $18,000,000. On the submarines there may have been honest competition, but one competitor possessed all the patents and would not tell the other company how much those patents would cost them. That is the way $130,000,000 worth of work was given out in 1933.

(6) From 1927 on when the cruiser program started, the record is the same. If there was no collusion, there was a sympathetic understanding among the big companies of each other's desires.

If there were no conversations about bidding among them, there was telepathy.

In 1927 the shipbuilders made profits of 35 and 25.4 and 36.9 percent on the cruisers. That was too good to spoil by hard competition. In 1929 the Navy asked for bids on two cruisers. Not one of the "Big Three" yards obliged. They bid on 1 each, and got 1 each. Their profits on these were around 22 percent.

The record is the same in 1931.

(7) In 1933 two shipbuilders knew and wrote down lists of the low bidders weeks in advance of the time the bids were opened. Mr. Bardo was one of them. Mr. Wilder was another. Mr. Bardo admitted discussing his desires for certain ships only with his two main competitors.

(8) The fact that many bids are submitted by shipbuilders does not mean that there is real competition. It does not mean lower prices. In fact, quite the contrary is true. When there is lots of work to go around the charges go up. The shipbuilders know that the Navy feels it has to have the ships, and they raise the prices. They admitted this frankly.

II. Excessive Profits

The committee finds, under the head of Excessive Profits, that the profit figures on the only naval vessels on which such figures are available were 35 percent (Newport News, 2 cruisers); 36.9 and 33.4 percent (New York Ship, 2 cruisers); 25.4 and 21.8 percent (Bethlehem Shipbuilding, 2 cruisers); 23.1 percent (Aircraft Carrier *Ranger*, Newport News).

III. Prices Increased with Big Navy

The committee finds, under the head Prices Increased with Big Navy, that the need of the Navy for many ships in 1933 was the main cause for the increase in prices charged by the private shipbuilders, and that they frankly admitted this, and that the Navy recognized the fact.

Q. They (the shipbuilders) were frank enough to say they were putting up prices because of the great amount of work at the time?—A. (Admiral Robinson) There is no question about that.

IV. Navy Yards as Yardsticks

The committee finds, under the head of Navy Yards as Yardsticks, that preliminary studies show the cost of building cruisers in navy yards to have been $2,116,304 lower than in private yards in 1927 and $1,569,090 lower in 1929. It also finds that in 1933 the low navy-yard estimate was $1,122,000 below the lowest private-yard fixed-price bid and $5,351,000 below the highest fixed-price bid. It also finds that the navy-yard estimates on the cost of building light destroyers averaged $1,240,459 lower than the average bids of the private yards and $943,460 below the lowest private-yard bid on a fixed-price basis.

The committee finds, further, that Navy officials have been transmitting to congressional committees figures on comparative costs of private and navy yards showing the profits on a privately built ship, the cruiser *Chester*, as $983,000, whereas the New York Shipbuilding Corporation informed the Munitions Committee that its profit on this cruiser was $2,946,706.

The committee finds, further, that the opposition of the private shipbuilders to navy-yard construction has been intense, reaching the point where the vice president of Newport News thought it better "to kill the Navy bill entirely" than to spend part of it in navy yards.

The committee notes the language used concerning a naval appropriation in 1931 by the Washington representative of Bath Iron Works:

> I understand the morning after the (appropriation) bill went through every East-coast yard had its representatives in Washington with their tongues hanging out and all teeth showing ready to fight for their share of the plunder, and the only thing that stopped the West-coast yards from being here was the fact that they couldn't come bodily by telegraph.

V. The Navy's Dependence on Private Yards

The committee finds, under the head of The Navy's Dependence on Private Yards, that at present light cruisers, aircraft carriers, light destroyers, destroyer leaders, and submarines are being built largely or entirely from the plans drawn by private companies, and that there are very definite disadvantages to a system in which the Navy has to depend on private companies for such an important part of the national defense.

The committee notes the awareness of several of the shipbuilding companies of the fact that the Navy is completely dependent on them for this work.

The committee notes the statement by Commander E. L. Cochrane:

> The Navy's developments of 15 years were—handed to the Electric Boat Co. on a silver platter, so to speak, on the conviction that it was desirable to keep at least one commercial company in the submarine game. . . .

and also notes the statements of Sun Shipbuilding officials who wanted to build submarines that they could not find out what the Electric Boat patents would cost them prior to entering a bid. The committee finds this apparent monopoly an unwholesome and unsatisfactory situation, especially in view of Electric Boat Co.'s foreign connections.

The committee finds further that a very considerable delay followed the allocation of $238,000,000 of P. W. A. money to the Navy in 1933, and that a large amount of this was due to delay in the planning work by these shipbuilding companies which had contracted to do this part of the work for the others and for the navy yards. The committee notes that this delay took place in spite of pledges by all shipbuilders to begin work as soon as possible for the benefit of the unemployed.

The committee finds, further, that while the Navy is dependent on the private shipbuilders for ways and plans, the private shipbuilders are dependent on the Navy for special favors, and have received a considerable number of them. Most notable among these are the adjusted price contracts of 1933 and 1934, the failure to use the navy yards as yardsticks, the failure to make itself independent of the private yards in planning work, and the Navy's opposition to profit limitation in 1934.

The committee finds indications of the use by the Navy of the shipbuilders as a lobby for its interests.

VI. Influence and Lobbying of Shipbuilders

The committee finds, under the head of Influence and Lobbying of Shipbuilders, that the Navy contractors, subcontractors, and suppliers constitute a very large and influential financial group.

The committee finds that three big shipbuilding companies had $53,744,000 of work at stake in the Geneva Disarmament Conference which the Navy had given to them a few months before the opening of the conference in 1927. It notes the admitted interest of the companies in the unfavorable outcome of that Conference. It notes Mr. Shearer's testimony that he was urged to go to the conference by Admiral Pratt, and was supplied with secret Navy information. It notes the secrecy of his employment by the shipbuilders, and the explanation for that secrecy. It notes his activities in the promotion of a war scare with England in 1928 and 1929, while being paid by the shipbuilders. It notes certain discrepancies between testimony given by the shipbuilders at the Shortridge hearings and the hearings of the Munitions Committee. It notes Mr. Shearer's claim that "as a result of my activities, eight 10,000-ton cruisers are under construction." Further, that owing to the failure of the tripower naval conference at Geneva, there is now before the Seventieth Congress a 71-ship building program costing $740,000,000. It notes Mr. Shearer's further testimony of his activities at the request of various Naval officials. It notes his description of his Geneva campaign as "fast and vicious." It notes his report at the "delight" of the shipbuilders at the result. It notes the payment by the shipbuilders of the costs of a pamphlet he wrote attacking certain private citizens, including Newton D. Baker and Franklin D. Roosevelt. It notes the payments he received from Mr. Hearst of $5,000 in 1929. It notes the spreading through a friendly newspaper syndicate of an alarmist story concerning alleged Japanese intentions by the president of the Bath Iron Works, with the intent and result of activity by a Senator and Representatives from Maine in connection with an appropriation bill in 1932.

The committee finds, on the basis of this and other testimony, that there is a clear and definite danger in allowing self-interested groups, such as the shipbuilders and their allied interests, to be in the close position of influence, as they are at present, to such an important instrument of national policy as the Navy is, and the danger in allowing them to remain in a position where it is to their financial interest to confuse public opinion between the needs of the country for a purely defensive Navy and their own continued needs for profits.

The committee finds, further, that there has been a large amount of bipartisan political activity on the part of the shipbuilders locally, in Congress, and also at the national headquarters of the two parties. It makes no claim to have gone into this field thoroughly. The committee notes the claims of the Washington representative of United Drydocks in 1934 that he could get a bill through Congress for $50,000, and that "there is no virtue in being Quixotic at this state." It notes the placing of Congressmen on certain committees at the request of the shipbuilders. It notes their claim to have helped the Navy on certain bills and to have elected Members to the House Rules Committee. It notes the reference to United Drydock Co. securing through Dave Hogan, secretary to Mr. McCooey, prominent Brooklyn democrat, the award of $6,800,000 in destroyers in 1933.

The committee finds that the matter of national defense should be above and separated from lobbying and the use of political influence by self-interested groups and that it has not been above or separated from either of them.

The committee finds, further, under this head, that the main lobby for the Merchant-Marine Act of 1928 was conducted by the shipbuilders under the leadership of Mr. Laurence R. Wilder, then president of American Brown Boveri (New York Shipbuilding Co.), and that a sum of over $140,000 was spent in putting that bill over.

The committee finds further that New York Shipbuilding Co. was acquired as a speculative investment by the Bragg-Smith-Cord interests just prior to the 1933 naval awards; that the present owners are not experienced shipbuilders and have since tried to divest themselves of the ownership, and that it is not a satisfactory situation to have such an important part of our potentially necessary national defense in the hands of people who are willing to sell it to the first bidder. Speculators and speculation should have no place in our national defense.

The success of the shipbuilders in securing an allocation of $238,000,000 for shipbuilding from P. W. A. funds has been their most recent demonstration of power. In this their purpose was aided by labor groups who later, when the expected employment failed to materialize, spoke of the matter as a "double cross" to the Navy officials who had solicited their support for the measure.

VII. Attempts to Limit Profits

The committee finds, under the head of Attempts to Limit Profits, that the failure of the Navy Department to turn the navy yards into effective yardsticks by which the charges of private shipyards could be measured and kept down has resulted in leaving the profits of the shipbuilders practically uncontrolled.

The committee finds that the Vinson-Trammell bill of 1934 limiting profits to 11.1 percent of cost cannot be enforced without a huge police force of accountants and that disputes concerning its interpretation, similar to those which delayed the payment of war-time taxes by the companies for 12 years may confidently be expected.

The committee finds that the Navy's grant of adjusted price contracts in 1933 with limitations on the amount of risk the Government assumed for the benefit of the shipbuilders and in 1934 without any limitation on the Government burden for increased costs has resulted, in effect, in cost-plus contracts. It finds these cost-plus contracts more profitable than the war-time contracts when only a 10-percent profit over cost was allowed.

The committee finds that in the case of the 1934 adjusted-price contracts on light cruisers, destroyer leaders, light destroyers, and submarines, the Government has assumed all the risk of increasing prices, and has lowered the risk for which the companies received 11.1-percent profit by an enormous amount.

The committee finds that the Navy, which has no responsibility for enforcing the act, and which has no reliable figures about private costs, is in a position to allow—and according to one company has actually allowed —increased overhead charges, which can invalidate the whole attempt by Congress to limit profits. The committee notes that it was by the allowance of such theoretical overheads during the war-years above actual overheads that New York Shipbuilding Corporation was paid $2,152, 976 more by the Government than it actually paid out itself.

The committee finds that the shipbuilding industry and its subcontractors and suppliers have united in efforts to find ways to avoid the incidence of this law, and that Mr. Gillmor, president of Sperry Gyroscope, Navy suppliers, told them, "If the shipbuilders, boiler manufacturers, and electrical manufacturers act in accordance with uniform rules, it will be so strong I think the Income Tax Bureau will have a hard time resisting it." The committee notes the unreliability of the shipbuilders' figures as indicated by the wide differences between their war-time reports and the audits of those reports by the Treasury (sec. VIII). It notes also in this matter of reliability the recent discrepancy of almost $2,000,000 out of a profit of $2,900,000 in the reports furnished by the New York Shipbuilding Co., passed on by the National Council of Shipbuilders and circulated recently among congressional committees by Navy officials. It also notes in this matter the evidence tending to show that the Bath Iron Works transferred an item of $60,000 incurred on a lighthouse tender to the costs of the destroyer *Dewey*.

The committee finds that there is no enforcement of the profit limitation law in effect until 4 years after the beginning of a cruiser. It finds, from war-time experience (sec. VIII) enough evidence of the difficulty of auditing thousands of old vouchers and of properly allocating overhead which the companies may have improperly saddled onto Navy vessels, to declare that there is no efffective profit-limitation law today.

It finds the price of real enforcement of the attempts of Congress to limit profits to be a costly policing force of accountants and auditors who would be in the yard for at least 3 years, and a series of costly lawsuits after those audits have been completed. It finds that the only way to prove that a company had not improperly allocated overheads from commercial jobs onto Navy jobs would be to audit all the commercial jobs being done by a private yard as well as the Navy work; in short, to audit all the work done by the yard and to establish uniform accounting.

The committee questions whether this additional cost for auditing and policing, plus the cost of lawsuits after such audits, on top of the 1 to 2 million dollars extra cost of private construction, and the $300,000 spent by the Navy for inspection of the privately built cruisers, justify the continuance of private yards as naval contractors. They have the appearance of being expensive luxuries.

The committee reserves decision on this phase of the matter until the completion of its investigation of the costs of governmental construction.

VIII. Wartime Attitude of Shipbuilders

The committee finds, under the head of War-Time Attitude of Ship-builders, that the record of the present shipbuilding companies during the war, wherever examined, was close to being disgraceful.

They made very considerable profits. On Treasury audits they showed up to 90 percent. They secured cost-plus contracts and added questionable charges to the costs. They took their profits on these ships after the war-time taxes had been repealed. They secured changes in contract dates to avoid war taxes. They bought from the Government, very cheaply, yards which had been built expensively at Government costs. In one case this was prearranged before the yard was built. One yard did not build necessary additions until it was threatened with being commandeered. Knowingly exorbitant claims were filed against the Government for cancelation. Huge bonuses were paid to officers. Profits were concealed as rentals.

After the war was over keels for $181,247,000 worth of destroyers were laid, which was probably the largest post-war favor done by any Government to any munitions group.

The committee finds no assurance in the war-time history of these companies to lead it to believe that they would suddenly change their spots in the case of another war.

After the committee's hearings on shipbuilding had closed, Gen. Hugh Johnson, at one time connected with the War Industries Board, later with B. M. Baruch, and later Director of the National Recovery Administration, explained that the N. R. A. had grown out of the plans developed by the War Department for the conduct of a future war. It was, he stated, developed directly from the war plans and was not shown to the industrialists for their approval until practically completed. In view of this statement, the committee finds significance in the testimony of a Department of Labor official concerning the unwillingness of the New York Shipbuilding Co. to observe the N. R. A. rules, with the result of a serious labor dispute in 1934. The company did not raise the question of constitutionality, and all that was involved was the question of observance or evasion of the law.

The committee finds in this evidence, taken together with the actual war-time experience of the Government with these companies, little hope for obedience by them of more stringent war-time provisions in the case of another emergency.

Recommendations

1. The committee postpones its final recommendations on the problem of removing or rendering harmless to the public interest the close interdependence of the Navy and the financially interested shipbuilding interests. The final report on this subject will be rendered immediately upon the completion of its study on Government costs in private and navy yards and on the cost of purchasing necessary private yards for public use.

In the interval the committee recommends an unusually strict reporting of the activities of all the representatives of the shipbuilders and allied interests. This is contained in section 2, paragraph 3, of the attached bill.

2. In the matter of collusion and profiteering, the committee recommends the immediate adoption by Congress of the following bills "to prevent collusion in the making of contracts for the construction of naval vessels in private shipyards, to safeguard military secrets of the United States, to make public the activities of the shipbuilding lobby, and for other purposes," and to prevent profiteering in the construction of naval vessels in private shipyards.

(S.3098)

The main purpose of the first bill (S. 3098) is to prevent collusion by the shipbuilders and to prevent their taking advantage of the Navy.

It does this by directing the Comptroller General to examine the navy yard estimates and the private yard estimates and bids before the Navy makes any awards. He is directed to analyze them on the basis of past bids and estimates and on the basis of the bids and estimates of all other companies and navy yards. (The studies of the Senate Munitions Committee on this subject are in this way to be utilized, maintained, and made permanent by the Comptroller General.) He is charged finally with the duty of recommending to the Navy whether bids shall be readvertised or not before any awards are made by the Navy Department.

This bill includes a provision for the registration of shipbuilding lobbyists and a statement of their income and expenditures. It includes a provision forbidding the sale abroad of naval inventions for a period of 5 years. It includes a provision to make the Navy independent of the private shipyards in the matter of designing and planning.

The committee recommends the adoption of all of the provisions in this bill as urgent and necessary to the public interest.

A copy of this bill (S. 3098), introduced June 19, is printed below as part of the committee's recommendations.

(S. 3099)

The main purpose of this second bill is to prevent profiteering.

It is provided in this bill that the Navy shall be allowed to pay to private shipyards a premium of no more than $500,000 per cruiser, $1,000,000 per aircraft carrier, or $300,000 per destroyer or submarine over and above the cost of building such a vessel in navy yards.

The committee believes that this is an adequate premium to pay to the shipbuilders, subject to its further studies of Government costs.

Since the Navy Department has at present assumed most of the risk of the shipbuilding industry in the form of adjusted-price contracts, and since the Vinson-Trammell Act was based on the assumption of risks by the industry instead of by the Government, the committee recommends that whenever the Government assumes the risk the profit be cut in half, i. e., to 5 percent instead of 10 percent of the total cost to the Government. The idea of having the Government assume all the risk of increasing prices for labor and material and in addition pay a profit of 11.1 percent on top of cost is preposterous.

This bill provides therefore that whenever the Government assumes all or a share of the business risk, as it does in the adjusted-price contracts of 1933 and 1934, that the shipbuilders, instead of being allowed a 11.1-percent profit as they are under the 1934 act, be allowed only one-half of that amount.

A copy of this bill (S. 3099) introduced June 19, is printed below, as part of the committee's recommendations.

3. The committee recommends further that Congress refuse in any way to weaken the provisions of the profit-limitation bill of 1934, but, on the contrary, strengthen them as much as possible.

The bills containing the constructive recommendations of the committee to effect these results were approved by the committee, and are as follows:

[S. 3098, 74TH CONG. 1ST SESS.]

A Bill, To prevent collusion in the making of contracts for the construction of naval vessels in private shipyards, to safeguard military secrets of the United States, to make public the activities of the shipbuilding lobby, and for other purposes.

Be it enacted by the Senate and House of Representatives of the United States of America in Congress assembled, That no vessel, the commencement of which is authorized by the Act entitled "An Act Making Appropriations for the Navy Department and the Naval Service for the Fiscal Year ending June 30, 1936, and for other purposes", approved ————, 1935, or by any subsequent Act, shall be built in any private shipyard unless (1) the Navy Department shall have prepared, prior to the advertising for any bid therefor, estimates of the cost of construction of such vessel in each of the navy yards; and (2) such private shipyard shall have agreed that all books, records, memoranda, documents, correspondence, and papers of such shipyard and of its subsidiaries and affiliates shall be subject to examination, during the usual hours of business, by representatives of the General Accounting Office and/or of the Navy Department. The word "subsidiary" as used in this subsection means any person, corporation, trust, or business unit over whom or over which such private shipyard has actual or legal control, whether by stock ownership, contractual relation, or otherwise; and the word "affiliate" means any person, corporation, trust, or business unit who or which has actual or legal control over such private shipyard whether by stock ownership, contractual relation, or otherwise.

Sec. 2.

No part of any appropriation made by such Act of 1935, or by any subsequent Act, shall be expended under any contract hereafter entered into with any private shipyard unless the bid of such private shipyard, upon the basis of which such contract was entered into, has been certified to by the Comptroller General as (I) fair, reasonable, and not excessive in amount, and (II) lower than any bid that could reasonably be anticipated upon readvertisement for bids. Such certification shall recite that it has been made after due consideration by the Comptroller General of (1) the Navy Department's estimates of the navyyard cost of construction of the vessel covered by such bid; (2) estimates and reports prepared by the Navy Department and by the Comptroller General of the costs of construction in navy yards and in private shipyards of similar vessels; (3) previous bids and estimates made by private shipyards for similar vessels; and (4) the likelihood of changing costs of construction during the period of construction contemplated by such bid. Nor shall any part of any appropriation made by such Act of 1935, or by any subsequent Act, be expended under any contract with any private shipyard unless the Comptroller General shall, prior to each payment under such contract, certify that such shipyard has complied with all applicable provisions of the Act of March 27, 1934 (Public, Numbered 135, Seventy-third Congress), and of all similar Acts hereafter enacted, relating to repayment of profits, insofar as previous contracts of such shipyards with the United States, or of any agency thereof, are concerned; and as a basis for such certification the Comptroller General shall cause examinations to be made of the books and records of such shipyard relating to actual costs of construction of the vessel or vessels built by such shipyard pursuant to such previous contracts, and such actual examination of such books and records as is made shall be recited in such certification.

Sec. 3.
No part of any appropriation made by the Act entitled "An Act making appropriations for the Navy Department and the Naval Service for the fiscal year ending June 30, 1936, and for other purposes", approved————, 1935, or by any subsequent Act, shall be available (1) for payment to any contractor of the Navy Department which sells, or in any way imparts, to any person not in the employ of such contractor or of a subcontractor thereof, any design, plan, patent, machinery, or other equipment used by the Navy Department at any time prior to five years after the first use thereof by the Navy Department; (2) for expenditure under any contract with any private shipyard unless such contract, and each modification thereof, shall have been approved by the Comptroller General; (3) for payment to any contractor of the Navy Department unless such contractor shall have filed with the Secretary of the Senate on July 1, 1935, and on each succeeding July 1, a list containing the names of all officials, agents, and representatives of (a) such contractor, (b) all subcontractors engaged by such contractor in the performance of any contract with the Navy Department, including insurance companies and insurance brokers, and (c) any association of which such contractor is a member or of which such subcontractors are members or to which such contractor or subcontractors contributes or contribute, who during the preceding year have interviewed, whether in person or by telephone, or corresponded with any Member of Congress or any employee or relative of any Member of Congress or any officer of the Navy or any official or employee of the Navy Department or of any other Government department or agency upon the subject of legislation relating to naval, military, or merchant marine matters, or upon the business of such contractor or of such subcontractor, such list shall contain statements of the subjects of such interviews and correspondence, the total compensation, itemized by sources, received by each such official, agent, or representative

during the preceding year from all sources, the itemized disbursements of such official, agent, or representative, including itemized statements of amounts expended for entertainment or for the benefit of any Member of Congress, or of any employee or relative of any Member of Congress, or of any naval officer or of any official or employee of any Government department or agency. The Navy Department shall also file on January 1 of each year with the Secretary of the Senate a list of the names of all officials, agents, and representatives of any private shipyard, and of any. subcontractor, including any insurance company or broker, of any private shipyard, which has submitted to the Navy Department a bid for the construction of any vessel, who have interviewed, whether in person or by telephone, or corresponded with any officer of the Navy or with any official or employee of the Navy Department with respect to legislation or to the business of such shipyard, or of such subcontractor, during the preceding year; such list shall contain statements of the subjects of such interviews and correspondence and shall include detailed accounts of all entertainment or benefit received by naval officers and by officials and employees of the Navy Department from any such official, agent, or representative; all such lists shall be published annually in full by the Secretary of the Senate as a Senate document; and (4) for payment to any private shipyard for plans and designs for vessels, whether as a part of the contract price for construction of a vessel or otherwise.

Sec. 4.

There shall be available for expenditure by the Secretary of the Navy from the appropriations under the caption "Increase of the Navy" in the Act entitled "An Act making appropriations for the Navy Department and the Naval Service for the fiscal year ending June 30, 1936, and for other purposes", approved ————, 1935, such sums as the Secretary of the Navy may from time to time determine to be necessary for the establishment in the Navy Department of a section of design and planning which shall prepare the plans and designs for vessels constructed by or for the United States; and the Secretary of the Navy is authorized to appoint and fix the compensation of such technical assistants, clerks, and employees, without regard to the provisions of other laws applicable to the employment and compensation of officers and employees of the United States, and to make such expenditures (including expenditures for personal services and technical services in the Navy Department and in the field, and for drafting and other supplies, printing and binding, books of reference, and periodicals), as he may deem necessary for carrying out the provisions of this section: *Provided*, That, notwithstanding any other provision of this section or of such Act of 1935, the President may by Executive order expend all or any part of the appropriations made under the caption "Increase of the Navy" in such Act for the expansion of existing navy yards.

[S. 3099, 74TH CONG., 1ST SESS.]

A Bill To prevent profiteering in the construction of naval vessels in private shipyards, and for other purposes.

Be it enacted by the Senate and House of Representatives of the United States of America in Congress assembled, That no vessel, the commencement of which is authorized by the Act entitled "An Act making appropriations for the Navy Department and the Naval Service for the fiscal year ending June 30, 1936, and for other purposes", approved ————, 1935, or by any subsequent Act, shall be built in any private shipyard unless such private shipyard shall have agreed to build such vessel for an amount not greater than the Navy Department's lowest estimate of the cost of construction of such vessel in a navy yard plus (a) $500,000, in the case of a cruiser, (b) $1,000,000, in the case of an aircraft carrier, and (c) $300,000, in the case of a destroyer or of a submarine; and unless in the contract for such vessel, except in the case of a fixed price contract, such private shipyard shall have agreed (A) to pay to the United States Treasury all profit in excess of five per centum of the total amount of the contract covering such vessel, such excess profit to become the property of the United States, and (B) to insert a like clause in all subcontracts, whether of purchase or of construction, in excess of $10,000 made by such private shipyard in the performance of such contract.

Not Covered

For lack of funds and because of the other duties laid upon it by the Senate, the committee reports no findings on the following subjects:

The possibility of monopoly and collusion among the big shipbuilders in the field of merchant-marine work was covered only in part by the committee. Inasmuch as the many millions of dollars that have been spent by the Government to build up its merchant marine, have been obtained largely on the basis of national-defense needs, this subject is germane to the investigation.

Some evidence is in the record showing the absence of competition on important merchant work, the probability of resulting high costs and inadequate ships. There was no opportunity for the committee to make a complete inquiry in this matter.

Tie-ups between shipbuilders and shipowners constitute one phase of the subject of collusion on merchant work. Preliminary studies indicate that such relationships exist and that they may not be for the best interests of the public.

The influence of the National Council of American Shipbuilders was not fully revealed. An examination of the files of the council were made by committee investigators and enough material was found to indicate that the council, in cooperation with the Steamship Owners Association, is able to influence public opinion in all parts of the country. The council is affiliated closely with powerful trade groups and has on its active membership list industrial groups with combined assets of several billions of dollars. The council maintains a statistical department which disseminates information of benefit to the shipping interests. Some of this information is turned over to the Navy and the Shipping Board, from whence it is sometimes issued as official data. Its accuracy is seriously open to question. Its influence on the public and on Congress can only be estimated.

Powerful interests other than shipbuilders are engaged in the business of supplying materials and parts for ship construction. These interests, which include United States Steel, Bethlehem Steel, Westinghouse Electric Co., General Electric, Sperry Gyroscope, Babcock & Wilcox, and many others, have much to gain by advancement of shipbuilding. Their part in the activities of the shipbuilding fraternity has been touched upon. A thorough examination of the files of the important subcontracting firms would add considerably to the sum of information already obtained. These subcontractors are members of the National Council and work in close harmony with the "Big Three" and certain of the smaller shipbuilders.

Only a preliminary examination was attempted in the field of ordnance supply. This includes armor, armament, and ammunition. In point of money the ordnance on a naval ship is equivalent to approximately one-third of the total cost. Thus it constitutes an important phase of the general problem of building and equipping ships of war.

In the field of ordnance it is interesting to note that the Government, shortly after the war, constructed a large armor plant to enable it to procure steel armor at a reasonable cost. This plant was abandoned after a comparatively short period of operation. It is within the scope of this committee's functions to determine the reason for this abandonment, particularly as to whether undue influence was brought to bear to attain that end.

Any investigation of armor, shell, and gun making would be incomplete without an analysis of the war orders; these materials, not only the war orders of the United States but also those of the European belligerents, made and filled before this country entered the war. This subject is one closely identified with the causes that led the United States to enter the war, partly by reason of the huge sums that were spent for ordnance during the years from 1914 to 1917, and partly by reason of the apparent influence of the steel manufacturers and their financial associates and backers.

Influence of the shipbuilders through campaign contributions was not investigated in full. There is reason to believe that all possible information on this subject was not unearthed. The reason for this is that few records of such contributions are kept by the shipbuilders. Witnesses, in at least two cases, were frank in saying (when not under oath) that these contributions were made by their firm in cash, and that no receipts were given.

Other "donations" by shipbuilders were in the form of jobs for constituents of public officials. Entertainment also provided a means of paying off obligations. This was especially true in connection with trial trips, keel layings, and launchings, the bills for which were included in the cost of the ship and hence were paid by the Government.

Proof of large-scale "influencing" could not be established without examination of the financial records of individuals and this the committee did not feel justified in attempting.

An important field of inquiry touched upon only lightly is that which concerns itself with the quality of the ships turned out under monopoly conditions. Evidence was introduced to show that the Government frequently receives inferior quality by reason of the absence of hard competition in the industry. Testimony on the faulty construction of the *Morro Castle* indicates that American shipbuilding might be improved, but no fair conclusions could be reached without far more thorough study.

Likewise, a comprehensive investigation was deemed impracticable in the field of labor conditions and wages in the shipyards of the "Big Three." Sufficient evidence was introduced to indicate that such a study might well be made. An incidental examination of the comparative treatment of men in Government yards and private yards indicated that the navy yards pay a higher wage than the private yards and that the conditions of employment in the navy yards are better. There is also evidence of concerted efforts by certain shipbuilders to bring down navy-yard wages.

STATEMENT OF J. P. MORGAN ON FINANCIAL OPERATIONS AT THE OUTBREAK OF WAR JANUARY 7, 1936

U.S. Senate, *Munitions Industry:* Hearings Before the Special Committee Investigating the Munitions Industry, 7483–85.

The Chairman. Mr. Morgan, July 30, 1914, found France entering what later on became the World War.

Mr. Morgan. Mr. Chairman, may I interrupt a moment?

The Chairman. Yes, sir.

Mr. Morgan. I have drawn up a little personal statement which I would like to make with regard to this matter, showing the general view of our position in the matter. It won't take 4 minutes to read.

The Chairman. Mr. Morgan, might it not be far wiser for us, in the light of the direction which the questioning is to take this morning, to pursue that line, and then if there is any part of the statement that has not been covered by the record to permit the statement then to be offered?

Mr. Lamont. You see, Mr. Chairman, if I may interrupt here, Mr. Morgan's statement is a very personal statement, which is entirely apropos of the question which you asked him.

The Chairman. It goes to this last question?

Mr. Lamont. Yes, sir; and it will take only 4 minutes to read it, and we would like very much to have it read.

Senator Barbour. I should think it would be fair to have Mr. Morgan read it.

The Chairman. Mr. Morgan, you may proceed, then.

Mr. Morgan. Considering the time that has elapsed since the war, and the difficulty of gathering from the voluminous records a complete view of our activities, it has seemed to me desirable to make a brief statement to the committee of the basic principles on which J. P. Morgan & Co. acted and the reasons for our action.

When in 1914 the war was begun by Germany by the unexpected and criminal invasion of Belgium in violation of a treaty which had been respected for 80 years, we were deeply shocked. None of us had expected such a course to be taken by any civilized nation, and in spite of President Wilson's urging impartiality "even in thought" we found it quite impossible to be impartial as between right and wrong. From that moment we, in common with many others, realized that if the Germans should obtain a quick and easy victory the freedom of the rest of the world would be lost. The whole German Nation had started out on the war with the cry of "world domination or annihilation," and we recognized that world domination by Germany would bring complete destruction of the liberties of the rest of the world.

We agreed that we should do all that was lawfully in our power to help the Allies win the war as soon as possible. That thought was the fundamental idea underlying everything that we did from the beginning of the struggle till the Armistice in November 1918.

The Chairman. Mr. Morgan, thus far I fail to see that this is in anywise responsive to the question that was asked. However, we will not quibble about this. Proceed with your statement.

Mr. Morgan. As the weeks went on we observed the difficulties of the allied governements, desiring to make purchases in this country, difficulties caused by a host of irresponsible agents who held themselves out as agents for various manufacturers, and the idea occurred to the late Mr. H. P. Davison that if one of us were to go to England it might be possible to show the British Government an advantage to it in using our services in coordinating the activities of its purchasing departments in this country. Davison went to London, and after a considerably prolonged discussion with the Government a contract was drawn up making us the purchasing agents for the British Government on certain terms. This contract is well known to the Committee and provided various things, among others, that it could be terminated at any time by either party without advance notice, and that we should make full disclosure of any interest any of us might have in any company with which we made a contract. This and the fact that the Government might buy directly without using our services, at its option, provided a complete answer for the Government to any criticism from outside that it had bound itself to one agent and had thereby lost the advantage of many agents.

In the spring of 1915 I went over to London to see that all was working satisfactorily. While there, M. Ribot, the then Minister of Finance of France, came on a visit to the Government. He sent for me and proposed that we should act for the French Government as well as the British. This question had been discussed earlier with both the British and French Governments, but no decision had been come to. On condition that the contract with the French Government should be exactly similar to that with the British, and that any changes in the latter should automatically become part of the contract with the former, and also that any competition between the Governments should be settled by them at home, so that we might never be put in the position of favoring either at the other's expense, I agreed.

The Committee and general public are acquainted with the facts that for the British and French Governments we ordered about $3,000,000,000 of materials of different sorts, they always having full knowledge of the details of the contract and we always having definite authority to sign each individual contract as their agents. For our services during the life of the contract we were paid the commission of, roughly, 1 percent, which was stipulated, amounting to approximately $30,000,000.

The agency agreements did not involve any commitment on our part to furnish or to find the funds required to pay for the goods ordered. The Allied Governments sent over immense sums in gold and securities to meet their outlays here. When questions of obtaining credit arose, we were consulted and we helped our clients find the money when we believed it could be done wisely and safely, but at no time were we committed to any guarantee that the money would be found for prompt payment. All questions of raising money to pay for materials ordered were taken up singly and from time to time either by the British and French Governments jointly, as in the case of the Anglo-French loan of October 1915, or separately, as in the case of other issues of obligations of these Governments issued by us in association with others prior to the end of the war. In this connection, I might say that subsequent to the Anglo-French loan of October 1915 there was collateral security for these loans.

When the U. S. A. came into the war it was not driven into it by any individual or individuals or any class. It came in because Germany had made it impossible for the United States to refrain any longer. Germany drove the United States into the war by a series of insults and injuries, resulting in the loss of many American lives, any one of which injuries might have proved a cause of war had the United States not been so desirous of maintaining peace. But there are some things it is better to die for than to live without, and a nation's self-respect and independence are two of them, as our country has proved once or twice before in its history. Germany, as I say, drove us into the war by a series of acts, beginning with the sinking of the *Lusitania* and ending in the crowning insult of suggesting to Mexico to make war on us, promising it should have assistance and the surrender of Texas, Arizona, and New Mexico as a reward. We certainly could not bear any more of such acts.

No one could hate war more than I do and always have done, but even with that hatred I was proud of my country when the President, on April 2, 1917, asked Congress to declare a state of war (which it did by a vote of about 8 to 1). In the speech asking for war, after reciting the violations of all the former rules of war which the German Government had committed to our detriment, the President said:

> There is one choice we cannot make, we are incapable of making—we will not choose the path of submission and suffer the most sacred rights of our Nation and our people to be ignored or violated. The wrongs against which we now array ourselves are no common wrongs; they cut to the very roots of human life.

In this I may say the President exactly expressed my own feeling in the matter.

As soon as the United States entered the war, we, against the expressed wish of our clients, moved to withdraw from the purchasing agency, as it seemed to us that any further purchases must be handled directly by the various governments, as the United States Government had taken over the control of all supplies.

The fact that the Allies found us useful and valued our assistance in their task is the fact of which I am most proud in all my business life of more than 45 years. Thank you, gentlemen.

The Chairman. Mr. Morgan, do you feel that your statement has covered everything that is relevant to the Committee's inquiry, or was that foreign to your purpose in the statement?

Mr. Morgan. My purpose in the statement was merely to give the Committee an idea of how we believed and how we stood, and how we got into the various things we did get into. . . .

SENATE DEBATE OVER NYE COMMITTEE'S WORK JANUARY 18, 1936

Congressional Record, 74th Congress, 2nd Session, 650–57.

Secret Treaties During World War

Mr. Clark. Mr. President, nothing could be further from my desire than unnecessarily or at any length to delay the consideration of the very important measure now before us in which I am so much interested. I feel, however, that certain remarks made yesterday by the senior Senator from Virginia [Mr. Glass] not only justify but make it necessary for me to take the time of the Senate for just a few moments in replying thereto.

Mr. President, more than 20 years ago I heard a very distinguished Member of the House of Representatives, on the floor of the House, refer to the present senior Senator from Virginia [Mr. Glass], then a Member of that body, as "the gentleman from Virginia who never speaks except in terms of intense indignation." The thought occurred to me yesterday, as I listened to the philippic delivery by the senior Senator from Virginia, that the Senator from North Dakota [Mr. Nye] was being added to the long list of distinguished gentlemen who in the last 25 years have been made the objects of the unbridled wrath of the Senator from Virginia.

Mr. Nye. Mr. President, will the Senator yield for the purpose of summoning a quorum?

Mr. Clark. No; I do not think that is necessary. I do not desire to delay consideration of the bill for that purpose.

Mr. President, I have known the Senator from Virginia for nearly 30 years. I not only have the deepest respect for his great ability, his integrity and force of character, but I entertain for him a feeling of deep personal affection and have for many years. However, I regret that the Senator from Virginia saw fit to pour the full force of his unrivaled power of vituperation, invective, and abuse upon an individual member of the Munitions Committee rather than to read dispassionately and soberly the record of the testimony which has been adduced in the hearings before the Munitions Committee with a view to learning therefrom what led to our unhappy experience in the past in being dragged into a war, with a view of keeping the United States out of war in the future. The purpose of the investigation which has been conducted since the convening of Congress early this month was not for the purpose of finding a basis for appraising criticism, giving laudation to the work of any man or even the course of any man, whether he be alive or whether he be dead.

Yesterday the Senator from Texas [Mr. Connally] inserted in the Record a long list of men whose names have been mentioned in the investigation and who have now passed to the Great Beyond. I submit that that is beside the point. I submit that any public man taking part in public affairs of great moment, going to influence the policy of a great nation in time of great stress, must know when he is doing so that he is making history and that his words, his letters, and his acts are the fair subject for investigation by his fellow countrymen or by anybody else in the world at a later time in the ascertainment of historic facts in connection with the events with which he was connected.

I submit that it is no reflection on the memory of President Wilson; that it is no reflection on the memory of Secretary Lansing; that it is no reflection on the memory of Secretary Bryan, or of any member of the House or Senate who supported or opposed the declaration of war in 1917, for us to soberly and dispassionately examine the facts in connection with the web of circumstances which finally brought us into the World War, a war in which victory was followed by calamity, a war which, viewed in the perspective of 20 years, can only be regarded as one of the greatest, if not the greatest, calamities that ever befell the United States in its entire history.

Mr. President, I desire for just a moment to review the course of the testimony adduced in the investigation which has been conducted by the Munitions Committee at this session of the Congress. That investigation has collected many facts already known. It has undertaken to assemble them in a perspective which could be presented from a new viewpoint. That testimony has shown that upon the outbreak of war in Europe in the summer of 1914 the President of the United States issued his neutrality proclamation, and in addition to the issuance of that neutrality proclamation he issued an official appeal, one of the most eloquent documents ever penned by Woodrow Wilson, in which he urged the people of the United States to be neutral in thought as well as in deed.

The record shows that very soon thereafter, upon an inquiry from J. P. Morgan & Co., international bankers of New York, the President officially expressed the opinion through his Secretary of State, Mr. Bryan, that it would be a violation of that principle of neutrality in thought as well as in deed for the United States Government to permit the flotation in this country of loans or credits by any of the belligerent nations, either of the entente group or of the Central Powers.

Contrary to the opinion expressed yesterday by the Senator from Virginia [Mr. Glass], who stated that an attempt had been made to make it appear that the United States Government had some legal authority to impose such a restriction on loans, the fact was that neither the President nor Secretary Bryan nor anybody else ever contended for a single moment that the Government of the United States had any legal authority to prevent such loans; but the fact also appeared from the testimony of Mr. Morgan and Mr. Lamont, and from the universal practice followed at that time and for more than a year later, that the request of the President, the expression of the President's opinion as to neutrality, had in fact the moral force of law. Mr. Morgan and Mr. Lamont testified that while they realized from the beginning of the war in 1914 that the President had no right under the law to prevent them from making loans to the Allies or from floating loans for the Allies in this country, the request of the President had such great moral force that they regarded it as if it had had the force of law.

The record shows that immediately after the outbreak of hostilities the firm of J. P. Morgan & Co., acting certainly well within their legal rights, entered into an arrangement with the Government of Great Britain by which they became the purchasing agents in this country for munitions, contraband, and various supplies, and that they purchased during the course of the war, prior to the entry of the United States into the struggle, some $3,000,000,000 worth of goods, for which they received a commission of $30,000,000.

The record shows that with the control of the seas by the British Navy our trade with the Central Powers fell away from a heavy normal trade to practically nothing, while our trade with the Entente Powers increased by leaps and bounds until it was more than tenfold what it had been prior to the outbreak of the war.

The record shows that from the very beginning of the struggle the neutral rights as to the freedom of the seas asserted by President Wilson and by Secretary Bryan and later by Secretary Lansing as the American position were flagrantly and deliberately and repeatedly violated by Great Britain. The record even goes to the extent of showing that on one occasion the American Ambassador to Great Britain actively participated in encouraging the seizure of an American ship bound with a cargo of cotton for a neutral port, in direct violation of the position taken by the Government of the United States.

The record further shows that during a number of months, for more than a year, the British Government, through the firm of J. P. Morgan & Co., had been actively and strongly supporting the exchange market—that is, supporting the value of the pound sterling—for the purpose of establishing credits of dollars in this country to pay for the various kinds of material, both munitions and otherwise, which were being purchased in this country.

The record shows that in August of 1915—on August 13, to be exact—the firm of J. P. Morgan & Co., as agents for the British Government, suddenly stepped out from under the support of the exchange market and the support of the pound sterling; that within a few days thereafter the pound sterling sold from $4.76 down to $4.50 and a fraction; and that immediately after the firm of Morgan & Co. had withdrawn from the exchange market, allowing it to slide off in that way, representations were made to various Government officials by Morgan & Co. as to the exchange crisis; the idea being created in the minds of some of those officials that a panic was likely to be caused in this country by the withdrawal of British purchases from our market.

The record shows that within 3 days after the withdrawal of the firm of J. P. Morgan & Co. from the exchange market, from the support of the pound sterling, a letter was written by the Secretary of the Treasury to the President emphasizing the crisis in exchange, and in the strongest possible terms urging the President to reverse the policy which had been adopted by the Government for more than a year of advising against, and as far as might be from a moral standpoint forbidding the flotation of allied loans in this country.

The record further shows that prior to the withdrawal of J. P. Morgan & Co. from the exchange market a British commission had already started to the United States for the purpose of negotiating an allied loan of $500,000,000. They intended at that time, as we were informed by the Morgan partners, to negotiate a loan for a billion dollars, and that at a time when our Government had not reversed its position as to the flotation of allied loans in this country.

The record further shows that after the Anglo-French loan of 1915 for $500,000,000 had been floated in this country, after the country had once been committed to the policy of permitting allied loans in this country, J. P. Morgan & Co., on instructions from the British Government, reentered the exchange market, pegging the pound sterling around $4.70, and maintained it there until the end of the war, clearly demonstrating the fact that there would have been no difficulty on the part of the British Government in maintaining the exchange market around $4.70 during the 2 months in the fall of 1915 when they had withdrawn from the market and when the first Anglo-French loan was being floated.

The record shows, furthermore, that during the whole war prior to 1917, when we entered the war, there had been repeated violations on the part of the British and French Governments of our neutral rights and of our contentions as to the freedom of the seas, and that President Wilson had not only protested bitterly to the British Government and the French Government but had in many ways evidenced his displeasure and his dissatisfaction with the course they were pursuing.

The record shows that after the beginning of unrestricted submarine warfare on the part of the German Government Secretary Lansing, who had succeeded Mr. Bryan as Secretary of State, proposed to the Allies a modus vivendi, as he called it, in which he pointed out very clearly and with unanswerable logic that there was merit in the German contention as to the use of submarines unless the British should abandon their illegal practice of arming merchant vessels with armament which would necessarily be offensive armament as against submarines, and should abandon their illegal practice of instructing such armed merchant ships to attack submarines on sight. The record shows that this representation on the part of Secretary Lansing was not only coldly received but was received with very scant courtesy on the part of the Allies, and thereafter it was dropped like a hot cake by our Government.

The record shows that after the *Lusitania* incident, the incident of the *Arabic*, and the sinking of the *Sussex*, when President Wilson sent a very severe note to Germany, the German Government replied in a note directed to the United States in which they agreed to stop their unrestricted submarine warfare, and that they did stop their unrestricted submarine warfare, but that in that note they attached as an addendum the statement that while they were stopping their illegal practices with regard to the use of the submarine, they depended on the good faith of the United States to see that the Allies also stopped their illegal practices which had given rise to the unrestricted use of the submarine by Germany. The record shows that the administration in Washington did endeavor to bring about this change in the illegal practices of the Allies, but entirely without success.

Then, Mr. President, the record shows something that is very significant. The record shows that during the summer of 1916, when the relationship between the American Government and the German Government was better than it had been at any prior time during the progress of the war, American public opinion was outraged, and President Wilson himself was outraged, by the publication by the British Government of a blacklist against scores of American firms, in which the subjects of the British Empire were forbidden not only to deal with the blacklisted firms but forbidden to deal with anybody who did deal with the blacklisted firms.

The record further shows that at that time the illegal British censorship of our mails and the mails of other neutrals, in which on occasion they even detained the diplomatic pouches en route to American embassies, aroused President Wilson to the point where he asked and obtained from the Congress authority for retaliatory measures against Great Britain, and considered putting into effect what amounted to an embargo, refusing clearance to ships armed with contraband of war.

The record further shows that at that time the Department of Commerce was requested for an opinion as to the most effective means to be taken by the Government of the United States to put into effect the retaliatory measures which had been authorized by Congress, and that the Secretary of Commerce replied that the United States had become so deeply involved in a commercial way by furnishing supplies to the Allies that to put in force any such retaliatory measures as those authorized by Congress would be likely to cause a panic in this country, and therefore that nothing was done about it, and nothing more was ever heard of the proposed retaliatory measures.

The record shows that during all that period the State Department had been repeatedly advised by our Ambassador to Germany, by our acting Ambassador to Germany, by our Chargé d'Affaires in Germany, and by the American Ambassador to Turkey, who was some time in Germany in transit, that unless the United States should compel the Allies to respect our contentions as to our neutral rights and our contentions as to existing international law, the Germans would be forced, under the exception contained in their *Sussex* note, again to employ unrestricted submarine warfare.

The record shows that in January the German Government did notify the American Government that they had reached an impasse where it was necessary for them again to resort to unrestricted submarine warfare.

The record further shows, not on my testimony, not on the testimony of the Senator from North Dakota, not on the testimony of any member of the Munitions Committee, but on the testimony of Secretary Lansing himself, that the notes of the United States to Great Britain as to their violations of international law, while quite severe in many cases, were deliberately involved in a sea of verbosity, in accordance with the extract from Secretary Lansing's war memoirs which I inserted in the Record yesterday, and I will read the last paragraph of it:

The notes that were sent (to Britain) were long and exhaustive treaties which opened up new subjects of discussion rather than closing those in controversy. Short and emphatic notes were dangerous. Everything was submerged in verbosity. It was done with a deliberate purpose.

I submit, Mr. President, that there cannot be any higher testimony as to the purpose and structure of the diplomatic notes which were sent by the United States to Great Britain than the testimony of the man who himself wrote those notes.

It should further be noted that the record discloses the fact that shortly after the outbreak of hostilities in Europe in 1914, and again in 1915, the suggestion was made in the American Congress that the shipment of munitions to one set of belligerents when access to our markets was forbidden to the other set of belligerents, by reason of the British control of the seas, was in itself an unneutral act; that is, unneutral in the definition which the President had laid down of being neutral in thought as well as in deed, although it was never contended on anybody's behalf, as far as I know, that the exportation of munitions in the existing state of the law was not entirely a legal performance, and the State Department, immediately after the outbreak of hostilities in 1914, rendered a public opinion to that effect. But at the time the suggestion was made in this body and in the body at the other end of the Capitol that the neutrality of the United States could best be preserved by forbidding the export of munitions to one set of belligerents when the other was shut out of our market, an official opinion was rendered at the State Department that to change the law after the outbreak of hostilities would in itself be an unneutral act. While that opinion has been questioned by very eminent international lawyers, who insist that it would not have been a violation of our neutrality to change the law after the outbreak of hostilities, I am of opinion from a reading of the Hague convention and other documents on the subject that the State Department was entirely justified and entirely within its rights in the views it then took.

Therefore, to answer the questions which were propounded here yesterday as to the purpose of this phase of our investigation, the purpose of the testimony put into the record was to study the events of those tragic years, to draw such lessons as may be possible from the perusal and scrutiny of those records and those events, with a view to taking steps at a proper time before the outbreak of another world-wide conflict to keep the United States from a web of circumstances similar to the web of circumstances which proved strong enough in 1914, 1915, 1916, and 1917 to draw even so self-reliant and strong willed an Executive as Woodrow Wilson, who undoubtedly desired to keep us out of war, into the struggle, and to precipitate upon the United States, as I said a moment ago, possibly the greatest calamity that ever befell it. That is the purpose of the investigation, and that is the purpose of the testimony produced before the committee.

The Munitions Committee is, of course, the creature of the Senate. The Senate created it. The Senate gave it all the authority which it has ever had. The Senate can take away that authority, or the Senate can refuse to appropriate for the conclusion of the hearings already scheduled. Nobody questions that. Senators may close their ears and shut their eyes to the historical records introduced before the committee, but I make bold to say that it will be impossible to wipe those records from the consciousness of the American people and from the scrutiny of future historians.

Mr. President, something was said here yesterday as to the action of the committee in availing itself of the services of men and women employed on a W. P. A. project.

The Senator from Arkansas went so far as to say that we had put the Senate on relief.

Mr. President, I am unable myself to see any impropriety in a governmental agency, whether it be a Senate committee or any other governmental agency, availing itself of the services of people whom the Government itself had desired and was seeking means to employ in some useful capacity. The project was a nonrelief project, employing white-collar workers of the city of New York on important clerical work, and otherwise it would have been necessary for the committee to have expended Government funds for the performance of that work.

I submit that it is better for the people on W. P. A. projects to be engaged in useful governmental work than to have them engaged in boondoggling, or in taking papers off one desk and carrying them across a room and putting them on another desk and then carrying them back and putting them on the first desk.

I further submit, Mr. President, that there is nothing either revolutionary or unusual in the use by the committee of a W. P. A. project. Many other governmental agencies have employed people employed on W. P. A. projects, and I am informed that one of the leading standing committees of this body, namely, the Committee on Interstate Commerce, which is presently engaged in a very important investigation of railroad receiverships, is itself at this moment availing itself of the services of people employed on W. P. A. projects, and I may say I think such employment by the Committee on Interstate Commerce is entirely proper and entirely fitting.

As far as the remarks of the Senator from South Carolina [Mr. Byrnes] on yesterday were concerned, as to his desire to terminate the work of the Munitions Committee, I may say that there is nothing new or unusual in the attitude of the Senator from South Carolina. Every appropriation which has been made for the Munitions Committee has been made after a struggle. It was originally the intention of the Senator from South Carolina to confine the appropriation to a paltry $15,000, which would have made it impossible even to start an outline of the work of the committee. Every additional appropriation, as I have said, has been secured after a struggle.

It may seem to the Senator from South Carolina that the appropriations made have been exorbitant. I submit to him that they are very small in comparison with the amount expended by a committee of which both he and the Senator from Virginia [Mr. Glass] are very prominent members—to wit, the committee conducting the Pecora investigation, which spent something in excess of $260,000.

Mr. President, before I conclude, may I be pardoned a personal word? For the past several days a studious effort has been made on the part of some newspapers in the United States to make it appear that my own part in the conduct of the examination of the Munitions Committee was actuated by personal animus because President Wilson defeated my father for the Democratic nomination for President in the Baltimore convention in 1912. That matter is very easily disposed of. There was never the slightest animosity between my father and President Wilson, or toward the memory of President Wilson by any member of my father's family. My father was a candidate at the Baltimore convention, as he had a right to be, and he received a majority of the votes cast on nine ballots. He was subsequently defeated by President Wilson, who was also a candidate, as he had a right to be, and who, so far as I have ever been informed, did nothing improper or blameworthy in connection with that fight.

Such animosity as my father had, such animosity as I have felt, and still feel, or as the other members of my family have felt, and still feel, was and is directed toward another man, a delegate instructed as a delegate for my father under a law which he drew himself, and who betrayed my father at the Baltimore convention, namely, William Jennings Bryan. It must be obvious, Mr. President, that if I were capable of being actuated in the slightest degree by my personal feeling in the performance of my official duty, that the last thing I should desire to do would be to introduce into the Record any testimony or any exhibits which would necessarily tend to justify the position taken by Mr. Bryan, as Secretary of State or as a private citizen, in contradistinction to the position taken by President Wilson or anybody else.

Mr. President, it seems to me that that is a proposition so plain, so obvious, and so concise that even such a lickspittle and sycophantic toady as Mr. Arthur Krock, of the New York Times, ought to be able to grasp.

Mr. Byrnes obtained the floor.

Mr. Connally. Mr. President——

The Presiding Officer. Does the Senator from South Carolina yield to the Senator from Texas?

Mr. Byrnes. I yield briefly.

Mr. Connally. Yesterday the Senator from North Dakota made the charge here that according to the proof, or what he called the proof, President Wilson and Mr. Lansing had falsified, and that they had knowledge of the secret treaties before we entered the war. Do I understand the Senator from Missouri to contend that, or does he contend——

Mr. Clark. Mr. President, the Senator from Texas does not understand me to contend that. I will state to the Senator that the other day in the committee I declined to agree with the Senator from North Dakota in his characterization of the testimony of President Wilson and Secretary Lansing. I do say, and I stated to the Senator day before yesterday, that there were in the State Department prior to the entrance of the United States into the war certain communications from Ambassador Walter Page at London, Ambassador Thomas Nelson Page at Rome, and Ambassador Francis in St. Petersburg which bore very considerably on those secret treaties. I further say that there were certain entries in the diary of Colonel House which indicated that Colonel House, who was President Wilson's unofficial diplomatic representative, had knowledge of the substance of the secret treaties.

So far as I am concerned, I have never said, and I do not say now, and I do not believe that President Wilson had personal knowledge of the treaties prior to the entrance of the United States into the war.

Mr. Connally. That is what I wanted to bring out, and I think my question was prompted as much by the desire to try to set the Senator correct before the Senate in that view as it was——

Mr. Clark. Mr. President, I never intimated or said that President Wilson had any such knowledge before entrance of the United States into the World War.

Mr. Connally. I desire to ask the Senator another question. The other day in the Munitions Committee, under the Senator's own leadership, he put into the record the so-called chronology of events leading up to the war. Is that correct?

Mr. Clark. Yes.

Mr. Connally. Why did not the Senator include in that the Zimmermann telegram, in which Germany proposed an alliance with Mexico conditioned on the fact that in the event of victory a number of the States, including Arizona, New Mexico, and Texas, and a great territory, should be given back to Mexico?

Mr. Clark. Because I did not think that that was any material contributing cause to the United States getting into the war. If the Senator wishes to include it, I shall be glad to include it.

Mr. Connally. No; I do not care. The Senator did not include that incident, which inflamed the people of this country very greatly. Why did not the Senator include in his chronology the action which Germany took after unrestricted submarine warfare was declared, after the declaration of which unrestricted warfare President Wilson stated that we must then wait for overt acts in the carrying out of that declaration?

Those overt acts were the sinking of the *Memphis*, the *Vigilancia*, and the *Illinois*, the *Vigilancia* having six Americans on board, and the sinking without warning of the American tanker *Healdton*. Why were they not included in the Senator's chronology?

Mr. Clark. There were a number of things which were not included in that chronology. I did not insert in that chronology the reply of President Wilson after the war was over to the question asked him by Senator McCumber, of North Dakota. Senator McCumber asked him whether it was his opinion that the United States would have gotten into the war if there had been no violations of American rights by Germany, in reply to which President Wilson said that he thought we would have gotten into the war anyway. There were a number of other things impossible to get into the simple chronology.

Mr. Connally. Let me ask another question. The Senator from North Dakota [Mr. Nye] yesterday, I think, made a statement regarding the private Lansing papers. I stated my understanding was that Mr. Lansing had left his private diaries with his wife with an injunction not to publish them within 20 years because of the living characters which were mentioned, and that Mrs. Lansing upon her death left them with Mr. Dulles, and he turned them over to the Library of Congress. The Senator from North Dakota stated that the committee had obtained control of those documents. Is it or not true that the committee subpenaed those documents from the Library of Congress?

Mr. Clark. I am unable to state to the Senator from Texas. So far as I am concerned, I have never seen the private Lansing documents.

Mr. Connally. If the committee subpenaed them, did the members not know at the time that it was in violation of the express wish of Secretary Lansing?

Mr. Clark. Let me say so far as that is concerned that Mr. Lansing——

Mr. Connally. If the committee did not do it, it does not make any difference.

Mr. Clark. I do not know whether we did or not, I am frank to say. The

Senator from North Dakota can answer that question. I am not familiar with the facts, and I did not see the papers.

Mr. Nye. Mr. President——

Mr. Clark. Let me say a word further before I yield to the Senator from North Dakota. If the Munitions Committee subpenaed the papers, I say with regard to any record or any data officially having to do with matters of great import to the United States, concerning so important a matter as the participation of the United States in the war, the Congress of the United States has the right to those papers if they are pertinent; and I submit to the Senator that no papers from that private collection have ever been placed in the records of the committee. The documents of Mr. Lansing which I placed in the record were other documents open to public inspection in the Library of Congress or else contained in the various writings of Mr. Lansing.

Mr. Connally. I make no quarrel with the Senator on the way he puts it. The acts of the public official which relate to his official duty are one thing, but the private personal diary of a dead man is another thing. That is what I am complaining of.

Mr. Clark. Mr. President, the private personal diary of a Secretary of State, who records in his diary underlying important events of the day, is not a private matter. It becomes a public matter.

Mr. Nye. Mr. President——

The Presiding Officer. Does the Senator from South Carolina yield to the Senator from North Dakota?

Mr. Byrnes. I yield.

Mr. Nye. The question is raised concerning the understanding by and through which we came into possession of the diary of Secretary Lansing. Before answering that I ought perhaps to make quite certain my ground. My recollection at this time, however, is, and I think it will be shared by the Senator from Missouri, that the response to our subpena for this record came only after the estate of Robert Lansing had indicated to the Library an agreement to permit that to be done. If I find myself mistaken in this assertion, I shall gladly report it to the Senate before the day is over.

Mr. Connally. Mr. President, will the Senator yield to me for a moment?

Mr. Byrnes. I yield.

Mr. Connally. Will the Senator from North Dakota state whether he has ready for the Record this morning the information regarding the lecture tours and compensation which he received?

Mr. Nye. No, Mr. President; I have not. I wonder if the Senator from Texas will join me in a few days in the introduction of a resolution calling upon all Members of the Senate to report annually their income? Will the Senator from Texas do that?

Mr. Connally. No; the Senator will not. The Senator will agree to put his own income into the Record if the Senator from North Dakota will put his in, however. It is none of my concern what is made by Senators in their private pursuits, such as practicing law and things of that kind. The Senator from Texas will agree, however, to put in under oath a detailed statement of his income if the Senator from North Dakota will do the same thing.

Mr. Nye. Mr. President, will the Senator yield further?

Mr. Byrnes. I yield.

Mr. Nye. Mr. President, if the Senator from Texas thinks that he is going to embarrass me to the extent of causing me to alter plans and programs which I have in mind, to convey to the people of this country the developments which have been the consequence of the munitions investigation, he is sadly mistaken. And if honorariums are offered for that service, I am going to accept them.

Mr. Connally. We know that.

Mr. Nye. If I can reach people who ought to know about these things, and no honorariums are paid, I shall, nevertheless, respond in each instance where I possibly can. If the Senator thinks he is going to alter that program, he is sadly mistaken. The Senator from North Dakota will be quite happy to join with the Senator, when he is prepared, in reporting accurately, precisely, and exactly what his income has been since the beginning of this investigation as the result of his lectures upon the munitions question.

Mr. Connally. Mr. President, we shall look forward with a great deal of pleasurable anticipation to that, and I think the Budget will be able to reduce its estimates on account of the increased income it will receive.

Mr. Byrnes. Mr. President, it was not my intention to say a word with reference to the discussion which has taken place between the Senator from Virginia [Mr. Glass], the Senator from Texas [Mr. Connally], the Senator from North Dakota [Mr. Nye], and the Senator from Missouri [Mr. Clark]. I intended to direct my remarks to the pending bill. The remarks of the Senator from Missouri, however, cause me to make a statement with reference to what has been said as to the appropriation for the Munitions Committee.

First, the Senator says that there is another committee, the Interstate Commerce Committee, which has had a work-relief project established in order to secure additional assistance in conducting an investigation authorized by that committee. I telephoned to the Director of the Federal Emergency Relief in order to ascertain the facts with reference to that matter. The cases are not parallel, according to the information given me, in that the City College of New York is making an investigation of certain statistics, railway figures, and it so happens that the information desired by the chairman of the Interstate Commerce Committee is of the same character as the information being compiled by the City College of New York, and that information has been made available to the Senator from Montana [Mr. Wheeler].

That at least is the information given to me by Mr. Baker, of the relief organization, and it is not comparable in any way with the action of the Munitions Committee in having the city of New York originate a work-relief project and have the city and State contribute $22,000 to carry on the work of a committee of the United States Senate with its employees on the relief roll, clothed with the power of the Senate of the United States. That is an entirely different proposal. The Senator said that when I referred to that on yesterday it was not surprising, because, in passing upon requests for appropriations heretofore, as chairman of the Committee to Audit and Control the Contingent Expenses of the Senate, I have been very liberal in recommending appropriations from that committee. It all depends on what one calls being liberal. When $125,000 was appropriated, $124,281 of which has been spent to date, I call it liberality to the extreme.

I wish to tell the Senate exactly how it occurred. When the first resolution was submitted and the Senator from North Dakota, and possibly the Senator from Missouri, came before the committee asking for an appropriation, $15,000 was granted. Then, only 2 months later, the Munitions Committee asked for $35,000 more, and the Committee to Audit and Control recommended $35,000. If the Senator from Missouri had been dissatisfied with that action of the committee, he had the right on the floor of the Senate to move to amend the resolution and suggest any sum he thought wise.

Mr. Clark. Mr. President, will the Senator yield?

Mr. Byrnes. Yes; I yield.

Mr. Clark. Mr. President, the Senator will undoubtedly recall that when the members of the Munitions Committee appeared before the Committee to Audit and Control the Contingent Expenses of the Senate and asked for an additional appropriation of $35,000, without which the work of the committee could not have been started, because the $15,000 which had been granted by the committee was so obviously inadequate, the Senator from South Carolina took such a hostile attitude toward the request for the additional grant of funds that I stated to him that I was going on the next day to rise in my place in this body and resign from the Munitions Committee for the reason that the Committee to Audit and Control the Contingent Expenses of the Senate was obviously making it impossible for the Munitions Committee to fulfill the duties imposed on them by the Senate. I came back to the Senate that afternoon and gave notice that the next day, as soon as the Senate met at 12 o'clock, it was my purpose to address the Senate on the subject of the Munitions Committee inquiry; that it was my purpose to state the facts which I have just stated. The next morning the Committee to Audit and Control the Contingent Expenses of the Senate met again and granted the Munitions Committee the additional $35,000. Obviously, I was not dissatisfied with the grant of $35,000, because that was exactly what the Senator from North Dakota [Mr. Nye] and, I think, the Senator from Idaho [Mr. Pope] and myself, who appeared before the committee, had requested.

Mr. Byrnes. The first resolution submitted requested $50,000, and the Committee to Audit and Control the Contingent Expenses of the Senate recommended $15,000. The Senator from Missouri could have arisen then and asked the Senate of the United States to increase the amount to $50,000, but the Senator from Missouri did not offer an amendment.

The Senator from Missouri makes a statement as to which I have no recollection, except that he did appear to advocate the adoption of the resolution. Again the Senator appeared and asked for $100,000, but the Committee to Audit and Control the Contingent Expenses of the Senate reported a resolution providing for $50,000. The Senator from Missouri could then have arisen at his seat on the floor of the Senate and moved to make it $100,000. He never offered an amendment.

Again I will say to the Senate at that time I told Senators on the Munitions Committee that ever since the armistice men had been parading over the country talking about taking the profits out of war. There was hardly a Member of the Senate who had not made speeches on the subject. We had investigated; we had appointed a congressional committee composed of Members of the House and the Senate. They had spent almost 2 years investigating; they had filed reports, but nothing had been done, and the Committee to Audit and Control the Contingent Expenses of the Senate believed it was time to legislate and not investigate; and we urged upon them, instead of asking for more money to continue an everlasting investigation, that they seek to legislate. We told them at that time—certainly I told the chairman of the committee—that certain matters had been brought out calling attention of the public to the investigation which would be helpful in securing legislation; that that was the time to ask for legislation; that if they did not do it, the matter would be forgotten and all the value of their investigation would be lost. I urged that upon the Senator who is now presiding over the Senate (Mr. Pope in the chair), as he well recalls.

Senators on the Munitions Committee agreed at that time with the statement I made; and when I look back I know that I was wise, because that report was made last year; and if the Committee on Munitions had followed it up and endeavored to secure legislation instead of continuing——

Mr. Clark. Mr. President, will the Senator yield?

Mr. Byrnes. I decline to yield now.

The Presiding Officer. The Senator from South Carolina declines to yield.

Mr. Byrnes. Instead of continuing the investigation and diverting the minds of the people to other subjects, today we would have made greater progress in the consideration of the measure to take the profits out of war. I want the Senate to act upon that measure. I want the Senate to legislate instead of investigate.

The Senator from Missouri wanted to investigate; the Senator from North Dakota wanted to investigate; and they continued their investigation until finally they shocked the Nation with the statement that a former President of the United States, Woodrow Wilson, had falsified the record.

Mr. Nye. Mr. President——

Mr. Byrnes. I share the resentment of the Senator from Virginia [Mr. Glass]. I will not attempt to express it as he did. I join in his expression of indignation that any Member of the United States Senate should make such a statement with reference to any President of the United States.

Mr. Nye. Mr. President, will the Senator yield?

The Presiding Officer. Does the Senator from South Carolina yield to the Senator from North Dakota?

Mr. Byrnes. Now I yield.

Mr. Nye. The Senator makes reference to the delay which the Munitions Committee has occasioned in the consideration of the bill to take the profits out of war.

Mr. Byrnes. No; I did not say any such thing. What I said was that if the Munitions Committee had devoted its time since last April, when they were working upon a report, to following up that report and securing legislation, instead of going into new fields, I believed they could have made a substantial contribution toward the enactment of such legislation.

Mr. Clark. Mr. President, will the Senator yield?

Mr. Nye. The Senator from South Carolina is not contending that the committee is asking for more time to consider the matter of taking the profits out of war?

Mr. Byrnes. Oh, no; the Senator can certainly understand plain English. I said that if the committee had consumed the time which has elapsed in following up its work along that line greater progress would have been made.

Mr. Nye. There are members of the Committee on Munitions who last spring and summer were striving as earnestly as they knew how to accomplish the hearings upon the war-profits bill. How unsuccessful they were only the record reveals.

Mr. Clark. Mr. President, will the Senator yield?

Mr. Byrnes. I know that measure is before the Committee on Military Affairs. The Senator is a member of that committee, is he not?

Mr. Nye. The bill is not before that committee. It has been reported out of that committee and is before the Finance Committee at the present time.

Mr. Clark. Mr. President, will the Senator yield?

Mr. Byrnes. The Senator from Missouri, then, is a member of the Finance Committee, and I hope he will devote his time to an effort to having the bill reported by the committee.

Mr. Clark. Mr. President, will the Senator yield?

Mr. Byrnes. I yield.

Mr. Clark. Let me say to the Senator that he has completely misstated the facts.

Mr. Byrnes. In what respect?

Mr. Clark. In regard to the bill for taking the profits out of war. That bill was reported from the Munitions Committee. It was then referred by the then Presiding Officer to the Committee on Military Affairs. The members of the Munitions Committee appeared before the Committee on Military Affairs. The bill was favorably reported from the Committee on Military Affairs, and then was referred to the Committee on Finance.

Mr. Byrnes. Mr. President, that statement——

Mr. Clark. Wait just a moment. Will the Senator let me complete my statement?

Mr. Byrnes. Very well.

Mr. Clark. Repeatedly I made representations in the Finance Committee looking to the consideration of the bill. The Senator from Wisconsin [Mr. La Follette] and other members of the committee requested consideration of the bill. We finally procured the appointment of a subcommittee headed by the Senator from Kentucky [Mr. Barkley], who will bear me out in what I am about to say; I am certain that I repeatedly spoke to him urging hearings on that bill with a view to taking it up; that the matter finally went to the extent that I served notice in committee that if the bill was not taken up by the subcommittee it was my purpose to offer that bill as an amendment to the revenue bill when it came in. Subsequently the Senator from Kentucky stated that he had been so busily engaged in his services on the Interstate Commerce Committee and other committees it had been impossible for him to take the matter up, and he resigned the chairmanship of the subcommittee.

The Senator from Texas [Mr. Connally] was then appointed chairman of the subcommittee; and the Senator from North Dakota and I repeatedly urged the Senator from Texas to take steps for the consideration of that bill. Finally—I think it was in June or July—a meeting was held by the subcommittee at which it was represented on the part of the experts in the Treasury Department that they had not been able to consider the taxable features in that bill on account of the work on the revenue bill, and an agreement was entered into with the

Senator from Texas and other Members interested in the measure by which it was understood that the matter would be taken up just as soon as it could possibly be done after the convening of Congress. Is not that true, I will ask the Senator from Texas?

Mr. Connally. In substance, the Senator is correct in that it was agreed by all, at the request of the Treasury experts, who stated they were not prepared to testify because of the revenue bill which was before us last year and its technical character, and that they could not give the committee information upon which to act until the present session of Congress. Yet the Senator from North Dakota, and the Senator from Missouri—not to the same extent, however—are seeming to blame the Finance Committee for not having taken action.

Mr. Clark. If the Senator will yield for just a moment, I should like to say that I have never blamed the Senator from Texas or the Senator from Kentucky.

Mr. Byrnes. Mr. President, I cannot yield further. The Senator from Missouri took the floor at about 1:15, and had all the time he wanted, and my time is now limited.

The fact remains that since November 17, 1918, the Congress of the United States has been talking about legislation to take the profits out of war. Prior to April 1 last year there was a resolution from the Munitions Committee, and in that resolution reported by the Committee to Audit and Control the Contingent Expenses of the Senate, I inserted a provision that on or before April 1, recommendations for legislation at this session of Congress based upon the inquiry to the date of such report should be made.

The Senator from Missouri says that he is not responsible; the Senator from North Dakota says he is not responsible. There are other members of that committee, and I cannot believe that the Committee on Finance will refuse to give consideration to the measure at any time the members of that committee demand consideration of the bill.

Then what happened? The Senator from Missouri and the Senator from North Dakota came before the Committee to Audit and Control the Contingent Expenses of the Senate and asked for an appropriation of $45,000. That was on June 7. The committee recommended an appropriation of $25,000, with this provision:

> Twenty-five thousand dollars, in addition to the amount heretofore authorized to be expended, to complete the investigation authorized in said resolution.

That resolution came upon the floor of the Senate. If the Senator from Missouri was displeased with the amount, if the Senator from Missouri was displeased with the language of the resolution which directed the committee to complete its investigation, he could have moved then to change the language of the resolution in order to suit his wishes. He never addressed the Chair, seeking to amend the resolution. The Committee to Audit and Control the Contingent Expenses of the Senate had a right to believe it was satisfactory to him.

Now, after having been directed by the Senate—for that resolution, although reported by the Committee to Audit and Control the Contingent

Expenses of the Senate, was adopted by the Senate and became the action of the Senate—after having been directed to complete the investigation with the $25,000, the Munitions Committee have established, or somebody for them has established, in New York City a works project to have the city of New York and the State of New York pay expenses incurred by the United States Senate.

I tell the Senate now that the Committee to Audit and Control the Contingent Expenses of the Senate has a very difficult task to perform. The appropriation bill which passed through the Congress gave to the committee $100,000 or $125,000 for all inquiries and investigations. There is a fight every year between the House and the Senate to retain that amount, because the House makes its investigations through members of its committees instead of employing people and clothing them with the powers of the House of Representatives. Consequently out of the $100,000 or $125,000 the Committee to Audit and Control has to determine which committees shall be given money to conduct investigations.

I say to the Senator from Missouri now that the Committee to Audit and Control should not be subject to criticism. I say to him that since he talked to me this morning I have prepared a resolution. I have left out the name of the introducing Senator. If he wants to introduce it, I want him to do so.

I have left out the amount. If he or the Senator from North Dakota will introduce the resolution, I promise to have it reported back immediately, because I have authority from other members of the committee to do so. I will report it back within 10 minutes after he has introduced it, and then we will let the Senate this afternoon, at the conclusion of the vote on the bonus bill, say whether the investigation committee is to be provided with any more money or whether it shall close in accordance with the language of the resolution adopted last May. I have the resolution prepared in that form, and I should be glad to have the Senator from North Dakota or the Senator from Missouri introduce it.

Mr. Walsh. Mr. President——

The Presiding Officer. Does the Senator from South Carolina yield to the Senator from Massachusetts?

Mr. Byrnes. I yield.

Mr. Walsh. The Senator has informed the Senate of various appropriations made for the use of this committee. It seems to me that before any action is taken on any further resolution we ought to be informed as to how that money has been spent, who received the money, for what purpose it has been spent, and that we should have a full itemized account of the expenditures of the investigating committee. I suggest to the chairman of the committee that he submit such a statement to the Senate.

Mr. Byrnes. It can be secured from the disbursing officer of the Senate. I have not the information. I know that the Senate directed this committee, in the resolution appropriating the last money for it, to complete the investigation. According to the disbursing officer of the Senate they have not more than $400 or $500 left and the work is going on. A resolution will doubtless be submitted asking for further funds. The Senator from North Dakota said he was going to submit such a resolution. If he wants to offer it now, I want him to do so and let the Senate take the responsibility of saying whether or not it wants this investigation to continue.

Mr. Nye. Mr. President——

The Presiding Officer. Does the Senator from South Carolina yield to the Senator from North Dakota?

Mr. Byrnes. I yield.

Mr. Nye. The Senator from North Dakota is quite confident that within a matter of hours the committee is going to be in position to determine accurately and exactly what its additional requirement is, and then it will be requesting that amount from the Senate.

Mr. Byrnes. That is all I desire. I say to the Senator that if he will submit the resolution this afternoon the Committee to Audit and Control has authorized me to report it back to the Senate before the Senate adjourns or recesses, so action may be had on it. We can ask unanimous consent for its immediate consideration.

Mr. Nye. I assure the Senator there is no prospect of it being offered this afternoon, because there is no chance of our knowing exactly what the need is.

Mr. Byrnes. Evidently that is true, because the committee has not been able to know accurately heretofore. I do not know what the committee has in mind, but I say to the chairman of the committee, if he cannot offer the resolution this afternoon, I hope he will introduce it Monday. If it is offered Monday, it will be reported to the Senate by the Committee to Audit and Control within 5 minutes after it is introduced.

Mr. President, after this excursion into the fighting of the war I wish to use the time I have left under the unanimous-consent agreement to say something in behalf of the bill providing for payment of the bonus to those who fought the war.

Mr. Glass. Mr. President, will my colleague submit to an interruption?

Mr. Byrnes. I am glad to yield to the Senator from Virginia.

Mr. Glass. I wish to say just a few words to the Senate. I do not need to pass compliments with the Senator from Missouri [Mr. Clark]. He knows perfectly well, because I have very often told him, of my affection for him. There has been nothing, so far as he is concerned, of a personal nature that I have said about him.

I feel constrained, however, to say now that I listened with the most intense interest to his summation of the record of his committee. According other Members of the Senate the same reasonable degree of intelligence that I claim for myself, I assert there is not a Member of this body who has not been familiar with every circumstance the Senator from Missouri cited as the record of his committee. I submit that it did not require the expenditure of $125,000 or of 25 cents to have made that record available to the Munitions Committee.

All of us followed the circumstances of that period. All of us discriminated the attitude of our Government as between the belligerent nations. All of us understood the intensely controversial nature of the diplomatic correspondence between the Government of the United States and the British Government and other governments.

I recall one of the outstanding incidents of that correspondence was that the skillful foreign minister of Great Britain put the United States Government on the spot by producing the record of the United States Government in the War between the States and showing that the United States Government, over and over again, did exactly the same thing that we were complaining of Great Britain doing.

That is not a revelation which should have cost the committee $125,000. There is not a fact stated in the summation of the record by the Senator from Missouri that Senators of reasonable intelligence were not fully aware of.

I do not care to add anything to the controversy.

SUMMARY FINDINGS AND RECOMMENDATIONS OF NYE COMMITTEE ON MUNITIONS INDUSTRY FEBRUARY 24, 1936

Senate Report 944, Part 3, 74th Congress, 2nd Session (9983), 3–17.

Findings

I. The Nature of the Munitions Companies

The committee finds, under the head of "the nature of the industrial and commercial organizations engaged in the manufacture of or traffic in arms, ammunitions, or other implements of war" that almost none of the munitions companies in this country confine themselves exclusively to the manufacture of military materials. Great numbers of the largest suppliers to the Army and Navy (Westinghouse, General Electric, du Pont, General Motors, Babcock & Wilcox, etc.) are predominantly manufacturers of materials for civilian life. Others, such as the aviation companies and Colt's Patent Firearms Co., supply the greatest portion of their output to the military services. In addition to the manufacturers there are several sales companies which act as agents for various manufacturers. There are also brokers dealing largely in old and second-hand supplies. In case of war, other companies, not at present producing any munitions, would be called upon to furnish them.

The Army manufactures its own rifles, cartridges, and field artillery. The Navy manufactures most of its own propellant powder, its own guns, and half of the battleships.

II. The Sales Methods of the Munitions Companies

The committee finds, under the head of sales methods of the munitions companies, that almost without exception, the American munitions companies investigated have at times resorted to such unusual approaches, questionable favors and commissions, and methods of "doing the needful" as to constitute, in effect, a form of bribery of foreign governmental officials or of their close friends in order to secure business.

The committee realizes that these were field practices by the agents of the companies, and were apparently in many cases part of a level of competition set by foreign companies, and that the heads of the American companies were, in cases, apparently unaware of their continued existence and shared the committee's distaste and disapprobation of such practices.

The committee accepts the evidence that the same practices are resorted to by European munitions companies, and that the whole process of selling arms abroad thus, in the words of a Colt agent, has "brought into play the most despicable side of human nature; lies, deceit, hypocrisy, greed, and graft occupying a most prominent part in the transactions."

The committe finds such practices on the part of any munitions company, domestic or foreign, to be highly unethical, a discredit to American business, and an unavoidable reflection upon those American governmental agencies which have unwittingly aided in the transactions so contaminated.

The committee finds such practices on the part of any munitions company, unethical, but that they carry within themselves the seeds of disturbance to the peace and stability of those nations in which they take place. In some nations, violent changes of administration might take place immediately upon the revelation of all details of such transactions. Mr. Lammot du Pont stated that the publication of certain du Pont telegrams (not entered in the record) might cause a political repercussion in a certain South American country. At its February 1936 hearings, the committee also suppressed a number of names of agents and the country in which they were operating, in order to avoid such repercussions.

The committee finds, further, that the intense competition among European and American munitions companies with the attendant bribery of governmental officials tends to create a corrupt officialdom, and thereby weaken the remaining democracies of the world at their head.

The committee finds, further, that the constant availability of munitions companies with competitive bribes ready in outstretched hands does not create a situation where the officials involved can, in the nature of things, be as much interested in peace and measures to secure peace as they are in increased armaments.

The committee finds also that there is a very considerable threat to the peace and civic progress of other nations in the success of the munitions makers and of their agents in corrupting the officials of any one nation and thereby selling to that one nation an armament out of proportion to its previous armaments. Whether such extraordinary sales are procured through bribery or through other forms of salesmanship, the effect of such sales is to produce fear, hostility, and greater munitions orders on the part of neighboring countries, culminating in economic strain and collapse or war.

The committee elsewhere takes note of the contempt of some of the munitions companies for those governmental departments and officials interested in securing peace, and finds here that continual or even occasional corruption of other governments naturally leads to a belief that all governments, including our own, must be controlled by economic forces entirely.

III. Their Activities Concerning Peace Efforts

The committee finds, under this head, that there is no record of any munitions company aiding any proposals for limitation of armaments, but that, on the contrary, there is a record of their active opposition by some to almost all such proposals, of resentment toward them, of contempt for those responsible for them, and of violation of such controls whenever established, and of rich profiting whenever such proposals failed.

Following the peaceful settlement of the Tacna-Arica dispute between Peru and Chile, L. Y. Spear, vice president of Electric Boat Co. (which supplied submarines to Peru) wrote to Commander C. W. Craven, of Vickers-Armstrong (which supplied material to Chile):

> It is too bad that the pernicious activities of our State Department have put the brake on armament orders from Peru by forcing resumption of formal diplomatic relations with Chile. . . .

When the proposal to control the international traffic in arms was made in 1924 the Colt licensee in Belgium wrote:

> It is, of course, understood that our general interest is to prevent the hatching up of a new agreement plan "under such a form" (as Sir Eric Drummond says) "that it may be accepted by the governments of all the countries who manufacture arms and munitions of war."

It then proposed methods of "lengthening the controversies" and to "wear out the bodies occupied with this question."

The first great peace effort after the war was incorporated in the Treaty of Versailles and in the treaty of peace between the United States and Germany in the form of a prohibition on the manufacture, import, and export of arms by Germany. The manufacture and export of military powder by German companies, in violation of these treaty provisions first took place in 1924 and was known to the Nobel Co. (predecessors of Imperial Chemical Industries) of England and to the du Pont Co., but was not brought to the attention of the Department of State. The du Pont officials explained that the violation was allowed because of the close commercial relations between the British and German chemical companies. Later, United Aircraft licensed a German company for the manufacture of its airplane engines. Sperry Gyroscope also licensed a German company for the manufacture of its equipment. Both the engines and the equipment were of military availability. (See part V, B, secs. II and III.)

The second peace effort was made in 1922, when the Washington Disarmament Conference took place, not long after the American shipbuilding companies had received post-war awards of destroyers at a cost of $149,000,000, and while battleships whose construction was left pending in 1917 were being completed. The naval part of that conference succeeded in stopping a naval race. There was, however, no effective action taken in regard to checking the use of poison gas, which was the other main subject for consideration. The committee's record is incomplete on the activities of the munitions companies in this connection, but does show their opposition to proposals for control of the chemical industry and their interest in the choice of chemical advisers to the American delegation. The conference had been preceded by the sale of all the German chemical patents to the American companies for a small sum, extensive propaganda and expenditures for high-tariff protection on grounds of national defense, and the instigation and writing of news stories from London and Paris designed to give the American public the impression that France and England were engaged in the construction of great poison-gas factories of their own to offset the German ones. Some of these were written by a du Pont agent under an assumed name. The Washington Conference operated in this atmosphere, and contented itself with repeating the declarations of The Hague conventions respecting the use of poisonous gases in warfare which had been violated during the war. Several delegations pointed out that this was no progress at all, but simply a reaffirmation of supposedly existing international law.

The embargo placed at the request of the Central (Nanking) Chinese Government on exports of arms to China was, according to the evidence, violated by American and European munitions companies. Shipments via Europe and Panama were frequently considered as a means of evading the embargo.

The Geneva Arms Control Conference of 1925 was watched carefully by the American and European munitions makers. They knew the American military delegates to the conference several weeks before the public was informed of their names, and one of them told the munitions makers that he believed a licensing system (the sine qua non of any control) to be undesirable. Du Pont representatives made known their objections to publicity. At a conference at the Department of Commerce (prior to the convening of the Geneva Conference) the objections of the munitions manufacturers were considered carefully and reservations to the draft convention to be discussed at Geneva were made. State Department documents, not entered into the record, give credit to the American delegation to the Geneva Conference for weakening the proposed draft convention in two important respects. The du Pont representatives (who attended the meeting at the Department of Commerce) later remarked of the final draft of the convention regarding the arms traffic signed at Geneva in 1925:

> There will be some few inconveniences to the manufacture of munitions in their export trade, but in the main they will not be hampered materially.

The draft convention was widely advertised as a large step forward in the direction of control of the traffic in arms. It has, in 1936, not yet been ratified by sufficient States to put it into effect.

The influence of American naval shipbuilding companies on the Geneva Disarmament Conference of 1927 has been described in the committee's report on Naval Shipbuilding (74th Cong., Rept. 944). Their agent at Geneva claimed credit for the failure of that conference, which came at a time when the Big Three shipyards had been given orders by the Navy for $53,744,000 in cruisers, which would have been cut materially in case the conference had been a success. He was paid by the shipbuilders into 1929. The Navy has not denied to the committee that this agent of the shipbuilders was in possession of confidential Navy Department documents during the time of his activity at Geneva.

Following the Geneva conference an arms embargo resolution was introduced in 1928 by the chairman of the American delegation to that conference, Representative Burton of Ohio. The munitions manufacturers, cocky with their success at Geneva, consulted with such allied interests as the Sporting Arms and Ammunition Manufacturers Institute, and found it unnecessary to appear in the front ranks of opposition to this resolution. In 1932 Representative Fish introduced a resolution for a multilateral agreement renouncing the sale and export of arms. Du Pont representatives were active in lining up War and Navy opposition to it. In 1932–33 President Hoover supported an arms embargo which drew the comment from a du Pont representative:

> Regarding the attempts of Mr. Hoover and the "cooky pushers" in the State Department to effect embargoes on munitions sent out of the country, I do not believe there is the least occasion for alarm at present.

The munitions people were active in opposition to the arms embargo proposal which was adopted in the Senate without opposition. Senator Bingham of Connecticut succeeded in killing the bill on reconsideration and received the thanks of the munitions people and of their organization, the Army Ordnance Association. The War Department also opposed the embargo.

In 1932, another disarmament conference was held at Geneva. By this time the failure to prevent the rearmament of Germany, described above, had resulted in great profits to the French steel industry which had received large orders for the building of the continuous line of fortifications across the north of France, to the French munitions companies, and profits were beginning to flow into the American and English pockets from German orders for aviation matériel. This in turn resulted in a French and English aviation race, and with Germany openly rearming the much-heralded disarmament conference which convened in 1932 has failed completely. It was pointed out by a committee member that du Pont representatives were aware that—

> the effect of the failure to check the [Versailles] treaty violation even goes to the extent of making a subsequent disarmament convention, if not improbable in its success, at least calculated to produce only an unworkable document.

In 1934, Congress adopted a joint resolution prohibiting, in effect, sales of munitions to Bolivia and Paraguay, then engaged in the Chaco War, for a period of almost 6 years. During these 6 years, the munitions companies had profited largely from the defeat of the Burton embargo proposal, offered in 1928.

The Chaco embargo, according to indictments issued by a Federal grand jury, was violated by the Curtiss-Wright Export Corporation and the Curtiss Aeroplane Motor Co. The lower court has held the embargo unconstitutional on the ground of delegation of power to the President.

Mayrink-Veiga, agents for many munitions companies in Brazil, suggested that the embargo could be evaded by the shipment of planes to Europe first, stating that to be the Curtis and Bellanca procedure.

In 1935, after a year of hearings by the special committee, a neutrality bill was passed including an embargo on arms, ammunition, and implements of war in the event of a state of war between two or more foreign states, and including a munitions-control board with power to issue export licenses. The Secretary of State has announced that not all the companies supposed to register under this law have done so. In 1936 an attempt was made to amend the neutrality law by holding the exports of necessary war materials (oil, copper, steel, etc.) to belligerents to normal quotas. This was defeated. Considerable quantities of those materials were already being exported to Italy, one of the belligerents in the Italo-Ethiopian War, and some of the exporting companies had connections and investments in Italy.

IV. The Effect of Armaments on Peace

The committee finds, under the head of the effect of armaments on peace, that some of the munitions companies have occasionally had opportunities to intensify the fears of people for their neighbors and have used them to their own profit.

The committee finds, further, that the very quality which in civilian life tends to lead toward progressive civilization, namely the improvements of machinery, has been used by the munitions makers to scare nations into a continued frantic expenditure for the latest improvements in devices of warfare. The constant message of the traveling salesman of the munitions companies to the rest of the world has been that they now had available for sale something new, more dangerous and more deadly than ever before and that the potential enemy was or would be buying it.

While the evidence before this committee does not show that wars have been started solely because of the activities of munitions makers and their agents, it is also true that wars rarely have one single cause, and the committee finds it to be against the peace of the world for selfishly interested organizations to be left free to goad and frighten nations into military activity.

The committee finds, further, that munitions companies engaged in bribery find themselves involved in the civil and military politics of other nations, and that this is an unwarranted form of intrusion into the affairs of other nations and undesirable representation of the character and methods of the people of the United States.

The export field of our munitions companies has been South America and China, with occasional excursions into Poland, Turkey, Siam, Italy, Japan, and other nations. There was less important dynamite loose in either South America or China than in western Europe. The activities of the munitions makers in Europe were of greater importance to the peace of the western world than their activities in either South America or China. It will remain for commissions with full powers in the large European nations to report on the provocative activities of their companies, particularly to investigate the statements made in the French Chamber of Deputies, that Skoda in Czechoslovakia, a subsidiary of Schneider-Creusot, financed the Hitler movement to power, which, more than any one other event, can be credited with causing the present huge rearmament race in Europe, so profitable to the European steel, airplane, and munitions companies.

In South America there have, in the post-war years, been moments of severe tension, occasionally breaking out into war. One of these moments apparently came directly after the World War, when Chile bought from Vickers a considerable battle fleet. This caused agitation in Brazil, Argentina, and Peru, with Vickers taking the lead in Chile and Argentina, and Electric Boat Co. in Peru and Brazil. The situation was apparently so delicate that an administration countermanded an offer from the United States Navy to sell destroyers to Peru inasmuch as the sale might encourage an outbreak of war between Chile and Peru (exhibits 54, 57).

Later tension developed between Peru and Chile over the Tacna-Arica matter and Aubry, the Electric Boat Co. agent, felt that if he brought the contracts for submarines for Peru—

> it would be a great blunder going to Argentina, for instance, via
> Chile (in this business we have to be tactful and a little diplomatist);
> and so in regard to Brazil as well as to the Argentine now that affairs
> are going to take place at the same time (exhibit 69).

Mr. Carse, president of Electric Boat, recognized the danger of armament when he pointed out in regard to financing Peruvian purchases "the armament which this money could purchase would not insure victory, as the other nation has much stronger armament and would tend more to bring conflict to a point than if they did not purchase the armament" (exhibit 61). It was sold, nevertheless.

The spreading effects of such fears were reported by Vice President Sutphen of Electric Boat:

> It appears that there has been quite an agitation in Bolivia, as you
> know, and a revolution has occurred there recently, and in the
> opinion of the bankers it has been instigated largely by Peru to have
> Bolivia join with her in opposition to Chile (ex. 60).

Chile was the country which bought the original increased armaments. It was in this connection that Spear wrote Craven of the "pernicious activities" of the United States Department of State in helping the resumption of diplomatic relations between Chile and Peru.

The naval armament had its military side. Evidence read into the record during the Colt Co. hearing in 1936 indicated an arms race with intense activity on the part of all machine-gun manufacturers. The country which was credited with starting military armament "out of all proportion with that of other countries in South America" was identified as a country whose officials were the most susceptible to bribes.

The Department of Commerce obligingly furnished Colts the information that the arms race was bringing about a cabinet crisis in one of the countries reluctant to participate in it.

The statement of a Federal Laboratories salesman that "the unsettled condition in South America has been a great thing for me" is the key, and also, "We are certainly in one hell of a business where a fellow has to wish for trouble to make a living."

Colombia and Peru, at the time of the Leticia incident, were each kept well informed by the munitions companies of the proposed purchases of the other nation. The evidence of the Colt agent in Peru was that the Vickers agent, after unloading a huge armament order on Peru, had boasted to the Peruvians that he would sell "double the amount, and more modern, to the Chilean Government." When a limited amount of matériel, such as machine guns, was available, Bolivia could be forced into ordering them on the threat that unless she acted quickly, Paraguay would get them. Killing the back-country Indians of South America with airplanes, bombs, and machine guns boiled down to an order to get busy because "these opera bouffe revolutions are usually short-lived, and we must make the most of the opportunity."

In China the munitions companies report that there was a certain amount of feeling between the Central (Nanking) Government and the Canton Government. The Boeing agent was able to sell 10 planes to the Canton Government. Referring to the Nanking (recognized) Government he wrote:

> Their anger at us in selling airplanes to the Cantonese is more than offset by the fact that the Cantonese have gotten ahead of them and will have better equipment than they will have. In other words, the Canton sale is quite a stimulant to the sale up here.

The company, interested in making sales also to the recognized Nanking Government, replied:

> If the present deal with the Cantonese can be put through, without unreasonable demands being made upon us, it is to our advantage to successfully conclude the business if for no other reason but for the effect it would have on the Nanking Government.

All this may be little more to the munitions people than a highly profitable game of bridge with special attention on all sides to the technique of the "squeeze" play, but to a considerble part of the world's inhabitants there is still something frightful in death by machinery, and the knowledge that neighboring governments have acquired the latest and fastest engines of destruction leads to suspicion that those engines are meant to be used, and are not simply for play and show.

At the time a naval bill for $617,000,000 was before Congress, the president of the Bath Iron Works in Maine asked the publisher of a string of newspapers to reprint a Japanese war-scare story, although the Chinese source of that story had been thoroughly discredited editorially by the newspaper originally publishing it, the New York Herald Tribune. He thanked the publisher for playing up the scare story (Report on Naval Shipbuilding).

Attempts to sell munitions frequently involve bribery, which, to be effective, must go to those high in authority. This is apt to involve the companies in the politics of foreign nations. Federal Laboratories, by putting itself at the disposal of the administration of Cuba and two opposing factions, all at the same time, is a case in point. The Colt agent in Peru reported on his helping overthrow the general in charge of ordnance orders. American airplane companies reported on the political influence of French and English airplane companies, in a certain European country. Sperry Gyroscope's representative reported on Vickers' (English) political influence in Spain, as did also Electric Boat Co. officials.

The political power of the companies is best indicated, however, by a letter from Mr. John Ball, director of the Soley Armament Co., Ltd., of England, in which he pointed out that "the stocks we control are of such magnitude that the sale of a big block of them could alter the political balance of power of the smaller States."

V. Their Relations with the United States Government

The committee first, under this head, repeats its report on naval shipbuilding, in which "the committee finds, under the head of influence and lobbying of shipbuilders, that the Navy contractors, subcontractors, and suppliers constitute a very large and influential financial group", and "the committee finds that the matter of national defense should be above and separated from lobbying and the use of political influence by self-interested groups and that it has not been above or separated from either of them."

The committee finds, further, that the munitions companies have secured the active support of the War, Navy, Commerce, and even State Departments in their sales abroad, even when the material was to be produced in England or Italy.

The committee finds that by their aid and assistance to munitions companies the War, Navy, and Commerce Departments condone, in effect, in the eyes of those foreign officials cognizant of the details of the transactions, the unethical practices of the companies which characterize their foreign sales efforts.

The committee finds that the munitions companies have constantly exerted pressure on the War Department to allow the exportation of the most recent American improvements in warfare, and have usually been successful in securing it, and have also furnished plans of important new machines of war to their foreign agents in advance of any release by the War Department.

The committee finds that the War Department encourages the sale of modern equipment abroad in order that the munitions companies may stay in business and be available in the event of another war, and that this consideration outranks the protection of secrets. (General Ruggles was quoted: "It was vastly more important to encourage the du Pont Co. to continue in the manufacture of propellants for military use, than to endeavor to protect secrets relating to the manufacture.")

The committee finds that as improvements are developed here, often with the cooperation of the military services, and these improvements presumably give the United States a military advantage, we are in the anomalous position of being forced to let the other nations have the advantages which we have obtained for ourselves, in order to keep the munitions manufacturers going, so that the United States can take advantage of the same improvements which its companies have sold abroad.

The committee finds, from official documents it has not entered into the record, that the United States naval missions to Brazil and Peru have been given considerable help to American munitions makers, and that their participation and leadership in war games directed at "a potential enemy" have not advanced the cause of peace in South America, and that their activity can be misinterpreted by neighboring countries as support of any military plans of the nations to which they are attached.

The committee finds, from official documents which it has not entered into the record, that the sales of munitions to certain South American nations in excess of their normal capacity to pay, was one of the causes for the defaults on certain South American bonds, and that the sales of the munitions was, in effect, financed by the American bond purchasers, and the loss on the bonds was borne by the same people.

The committee finds that the Army Ordnance Association, consisting of personnel from the munitions companies, constitutes a self-interested organization and has been active in War Department politics and promotions.

The committee finds that the Navy League of the United States has solicited and accepted contributions from steamship companies, the recipients of subsidy benefits, and that it has solicited contributions from companies with large foreign investments on the ground that these would profit from a large navy and that its contributors have at times been persons connected with Navy supplies. The committee also finds that the Navy League together with various Navy officials have engaged in political activity looking toward the defeat of Congressmen unfavorable to Navy League and Navy views.

The committee finds, further, that any close associations between munitions and supply companies on the one hand and the service departments on the other hand, of the kind which existed in Germany before the World War, constitutes an unhealthy alliance in that it brings into being a self-interested political power which operates in the name of patriotism and satisfies interests which are, in large part, purely selfish, and that such associations are an inevitable part of militarism, and are to be avoided in peacetime at all costs.

The committee finds, finally, that the neutrality bill of 1936, to which all its members gave their support and which provides for an embargo on the export of arms, ammunitions, and implements of war to belligerents, was a much needed forward step, and that the establishment of a Munitions Control Board, under the Department of State, should satisfactorily prevent the shipment of arms to other than recognized governments.

VI. International Agreements of Munitions Companies

The committee finds, under this head, that, among the companies investigated, the following have the most extensive foreign arrangements: E. I. du Pont de Nemours Co., Colt's Patent Firearms Co., Electric Boat Co., Sperry Gyroscope Co., Pratt & Whitney Aircraft Co.

The committee finds that the usual form of arrangement is a license to a foreign ally involving rights to manufacture and sell in certain parts of the world, together with more or less definite price-fixing agreements and occasionally profit-sharing arrangements, and that in effect the world is partitioned by parties at interest.

The committee finds that the granting of licenses to manufacture and sell to nations against which there were embargoes, such as Germany, was in practice a violation of the interest of such embargoes and nullified them.

The committee finds that the international commercial interests of such large organizations as du Pont and Imperial Chemical Industries may precede in the minds of those companies the importance of national policy as described publicly by the foreign office or State Department, and that such considerations of commercial interest were apparently foremost in the rearming of Germany beginning in 1924 and in the sale of a process which could be used to manufacture cheaper munitions in Japan in 1932, shortly after Secretary of State Stimson had taken steps to express the disapproval of this Nation for Japan's military activities in Manchuokuo. Several aviation companies also licensed Japan for the use of their material in Manchuokuo at a time when the United States Government refused recognition to it. Recognition by munitions companies may be far more important than diplomatic recognition.

The committee finds that the licensing of American inventions to allied companies in foreign nations is bound to involve in some form the recurrence of experiences similar to those in the last war in which Electric Boat Co. patents were used in German submarines and aided them in the destruction of American lives, and ships, and that in peacetime the licensing involves the manufacture abroad, at lower costs, of American material.

VII. The Chemical Industry and Munitions

The committee finds a general acknowledgment of the importance of the commercial chemical industry to the manufacture of such instruments of warfare as high explosives and gasses, that most of the large industrial nations have granted their chemical companies considerable measures of protection in the interests of national defense, and that no effective control has to date been established over these large military resources.

These findings were concurred in by all members of the committee.

Recommendations

The members of the committee are all agreed that, in view of these findings it is essential that the worst of these practices be stopped if it is possible to stop them, and that the nature of the foreign practices of American munitions companies and their profits on contracts for the military services of the United States should be strictly limited and controlled.

The committee majority (Senators Nye, Clark, Pope, Bone) recommends Government ownership of facilities adequate for the construction of all warships, by the United States Navy Department, also all gun forgings, projectiles, and armor plate, and of facilities adequate for the production of powder, rifles, pistols, and machine guns necessary for the United States War Department.

It does so because it believes that regulation is easily evaded, and cites the committee's unanimous findings on the profit limitation in the Vinson Act of 1934 incorporated in the committee's Report on Naval Shipbuilding. It is convinced that a thorough examination of the books of the naval contractors subject to that act will show greatly increased overhead and other methods of increasing apparent costs.

It does so also because any control over the foreign affairs of the companies, which is essential to the estoppel of present practices, will, in effect, amount to control of management, and cannot be effected successfully under the private ownership of these companies.

It does so also because of its findings that during the World War the munitions companies insisted throughout on their pound of flesh in the form of high profits for their production, and did not let their patriotism stand in the way of their "duty as trustees" to the stockholders.

In making its recommendations for Government ownership of certain facilities the committee majority believes that the War and Navy Departments can produce from their own ranks or employ sufficiently able technicians to operate these plants successfully.

The committee majority has noted the pressure on the service departments by the munitions and shipbuilding companies for orders and for help in foreign sales and for help in opposition to embargoes and other disarmament measures, and wishes the Army and Navy to be the masters in their own house, and free from outside pressure.

The committee majority believes that the manufacture of the material which it is proposed to have the Government manufacture (powder, projectiles, guns, armor plate, gun forgings, and naval vessels) can be carried on and improved on satisfactorily by the staff of the War and Navy Departments, and that the mobilization of the war-munitions industries in wartime for the wartime production of some or all of the necessary munitions can be carried out in the same way it is now proposed to do. Salaries for technicians should be made comparable with those in private industry. The Government plants should, in the event that new construction instead of purchase is decided upon, be located as close as possible to the present plants so that there may be a minimum of labor dislocation.

The committee majority believes the national defense will be greatly aided by the estoppel of the practice of selling American military inventions abroad, which can be accomplished effectively only in this manner.

The committee majority points out that the Government services already manufacture half of the naval vessels, their guns, their rifles, their ammunition, and, in the case of the Navy, their powder, and sees no change in principle to extend the present practice in regard to this material to the same or other material. If the Navy can manufacture powder, the Army can do so as well. The Army has made important contributions to machine-gun development and has at present no benefit of competition when it wishes to purchase machine guns. The Army has shown its ability in the development of the 75 field piece. The aircraft industry is at present exempted from these recommendations, although it is almost entirely dependent on Government orders or indirect subsidies, because airplane and engine construction are still rapidly developing arts and in that way different from the somewhat more standard articles for which it is proposed to have the Government acquire facilities.

The committee also recommends that the War Department be given sufficient appropriations to acquire the jigs, tools, and dies necessary for installation in private plants in time of war for the manufacture of munitions.

The plan as proposed by the committee majority looks forward to an adequate munitions plant to supply the peacetime needs only of the Army and Navy, and procurement by the military services of sufficient tools and equipment so that installation of them in private plants may be undertaken in time of war. This will be done under regulation or even in the absence of regulation upon the outbreak of war. It does not plan large munitions plants. In a later report on Government costs figures will be presented to show that the Navy could enlarge its facilities to produce all the ships necessary for a considerable naval race at a cost for those facilities of as little as $23,600,000, including sufficient machinery to modernize the yards and produce ships even more efficiently than at present.

The committee majority does not see any danger to overproduction in Government plants since the manufacture of the Army's guns and rifles and the Navy's powder and ships have not, according to any service officials, resulted in overloading the services with matériel.

At present the munitions companies charge into their costs to the Government all the overhead of idle plant, with resultant high costs to the Government. Carnegie Steel Co. made profits, according to its own figures, of 57.9, 43.4, and 42.7 percent on three typical Navy contracts between 1930 and 1934. Yet on the contract on which 57.9 percent profit was made Bethlehem Steel Co. had bid $130 a ton above Carnegie and Midvale had bid $110 a ton above Carnegie. It was admitted by the steel companies that their prices included overhead for idle time. (Compare Report on Government costs.) The committee majority believes that the idle Government armor plate plant should be brought into use and that the Government's own overhead can be cut down by its use.

The committee majority recommends strict control both in regard to profits and foreign and domestic activities for those parts of the industry not included in Government ownership.

The committee minority (Senators George, Vandenberg, and Barbour), supporting all other findings of the committee, questions the complete nationalization of certain defense commodities, because it doubts the advantage from the standpoint of (1) its effect upon disarmament, (2) its effect upon essential national defense, and (3) its effect upon Government costs. The committee minority believes that if large Government plants are erected to provide these commodities, there will be inevitable local, political pressure to maintain these plants at full capacity production regardless of actual defense needs, and the result will be to encourage armament rather than disarmament. The committee minority believes that if all production be thus concentrated in Government plants, furthermore, there will be no adequate corrolary reliance, through private manufacture, in the event of a war emergency unless the nationalized facilities are maintained at a needlessly extravagant and dangerous rate during peacetime. The committee minority believes, on the other hand, that unless these facilities are kept on a full-time production basis during peace years, the unit cost of production will increase to a point which will create higher costs to the Government than would be available through normal, private purchase. This could be another impulse to armament rather than disarmament through anxiety to maintain maximum arms production in order to maintain minimum costs. In other words, the committee minority believes that the public welfare, from the standpoint of peace, defense, and economy, can be better served by rigid and conclusive munitions control than by nationalization except in a few isolated instances.

W. C. CARPENTER, E. I. DUPONT DE NEMOURS AND CO., TO JOHN EDWARD WILTZ DECEMBER 24, 1958

Mr. John Edward Wiltz
Department of History
Indiana University
Bloomington, Indiana
Dear Mr. Wiltz:

On November 29th you addressed a letter to Mr. Irenee du Pont making some inquiries regarding the Nye Committee. It happens by coincidence that Mr. du Pont was 83 years old just a day or two ago and while he comes into the office for a short period each day he does not concern himself with the routine affairs of the Company and I am undertaking to reply to your letter in his stead.

I have had a memorandum prepared in response to your inquiries and I think this memorandum fairly expresses our recollections and our views on the subjects you have dealt with. You will, of course, realize the effect of the 25-year time interval since those hearings were held and that any attempt to reply in too much detail to questions would require a great deal of research and study and even then be perhaps rather unsatisfactory inasmuch as practically all of the people who were actively concerned with those hearings have either long since retired or have died.

The attached memorandum mentions a book "Appointment on the Hill" by Dorothy Detzer. You may have seen this but in any event I am having a copy sent along to you which you are welcome to keep. I certainly cannot vouch for its authenticity, but I am told that you might find it interesting in connection with your studies for whatever light it may throw upon the origins of the investigation.

Congressional investigations are certainly part of the machinery of government and may under proper circumstances serve a very useful purpose. In this particular case perhaps it proved a little disappointing that the investigation was undertaken in the first place. I think the subsequent reaction of the Senate itself indicated pretty clearly that the Senate felt that little if anything had been accomplished. Quite naturally the whole episode from our standpoint was an unhappy one. It required an enormous expenditure of time and substance to carry on our part but I think that our principal disappointment arose from the fact that we felt and in fact were confident that in connection with the War effort we had done a remarkable, outstanding and constructive job. The expressions of gratitude and praise from the Allied governments for our contributions were unqualified and this in spite of the fact that the large earnings made by the Company during that War period were made on contracts with these Allied governments prior to our own entrance into the War, at which time there was considerable readjustment of prices and profits. While the profits of the Company prior to our own entrance into the War were large in relation to our prewar earnings, they should more properly be related to the magnitude of the job done under conditions of greatest difficulty and under circumstances requiring commitments of unprecedented proportions on the part of our Company. The product of our efforts was frequently referred to as decisive in determining the fortunes of the War itself.

I hope that you may find the material which I am enclosing of value in your study and responsive to your inquiries.

Yours sincerely,

W. C. *Carpenter*
Chairman

Nye Committee Investigation
Memorandum for Professor Wiltz

1. Did you feel that the committee was unfair or abusive in its treatment of witnesses? Did you feel that by innuendo the committee attempted to distort the evidence exhibited and the testimony given by witnesses?

Congressional investigations, if conducted objectively, are extremely useful, if not indispensable. It is, therefore, all the more regrettable when they are abused for unworthy purposes, political or otherwise.

In the du Pont part of the Nye Committee investigation it seemed apparent at many points that objectivity was lacking. It could not be said that the committee was actually abusive in a personal way, but it seemed clear that the questioning was being shaped in a biased way and with an eye to the press. Of course, the press could only report what was observed and said. As a result many of the press accounts were injurious and misleading in that they magnified minor matters because these were magnified in the questioning; or the press accounts failed to place sufficient emphasis on important facts and explanations because of scant attention given in the hearings to this information presented by our witnesses.

As a sample, in the discussion of dividends paid by the du Pont Company, little attention was given to the enormous responsibilities and commitments assumed by the company in behalf of foreign governments—namely, the Allied powers—before the United States entered the war. This is merely a random sample of what seemed clearly to be unfairness and distortion.

2. Did you feel that the munitions investigators were consciously trying to discredit the American business community? Or did you feel, perhaps, that they were well-intentioned men who were attacking an alleged evil while having no thought of discrediting all of American business?

It is difficult to evaluate the motives of the committee or its staff. Certainly much of the questioning was not designed to reflect credit upon American industry. Yet it is hard to believe that a group of leading Senators would combine in a coldblooded effort to discredit American industry. The motives were probably very much mixed. Quite possibly some of the committee members, all skilled politicians, saw political advantage in the investigation, but this would not necessarily mean that they were not sincere.

Mere lack of understanding of industrial methods and requirements was perhaps a large factor. Erroneous notions as to the origins of war no doubt influenced some probably well-meaning people involved. The book "Appointment on the Hill" by Dorothy Detzer of the Women's International League for Peace and Freedom, is interesting in this connection, though one would hesitate to vouch for its completeness or accuracy since it does not purport to be anything more than the recollections of one person.

There was also a feeling that a subversive influence was at work, and that some of the protagonists were to some degree dupes of this influence. The recollection of this feeling is not based on the fact that Alger Hiss was one of the committee counsel; this fact may have significance for some people today, but it is inconclusive and, of course, nothing was known of his background at that time. The feeling was based rather on a sense that such subversive influences were quite active in Washington at the time, as was later revealed to be the fact.

3. Did you feel that the investigation was seriously damaging American war-making potential, American foreign relations, and American overseas commercial relations?

It seemed clear that the investigation at least threatened to damage American war-making potential in that it sought to arouse public opinion against manufacturers supplying the requirements of the Armed Forces, which result could only discourage the manufacturers in such important matters as research and expansion or modernization of plant capacity. This in turn could only have added to the confidence of any potential aggressor nation. It is purely a matter of speculation how much discouragement or hesitancy was produced in American industry. In the case of the du Pont Company, any such effect was not long-lived as was borne out by what happened just a few years later when war actually came. The company turned swiftly to its war production assignments, including the unprecedented atomic energy program, and discharged its responsibilities with an efficiency which has been widely recognized and of which we are, we think justly, proud.

The investigation is credited with resulting in the Neutrality Act. How much comfort and encouragement this gave to the Axis powers is a matter for historians to evaluate, as also it seems is the question of the effect on American foreign relations. As to American overseas commercial relations, there seems to have been no noticeable effect as far as the du Pont Company is concerned.

Senator Nye, in one of his speeches just before the investigation, pro-

posed making "the manufacture of the primary items entering into the conduct of war or preparation for it an outright government monopoly" or giving
the government "direct regulation over the munitions industry." It must be
remembered that there is hardly any manufactured product that is not in some
sense a "munition" in modern warfare. The Senator also proposed a wartime
tax of 98 per cent on all incomes over $10,000. (See text of speech, 9/1/34,
released by Columbia Broadcasting System, page 4.) Such proposals coming
from a leading Senator represented a threat that could not be ignored. If such
proposals had been put into effect they could have crippled what later was to
be acclaimed as the "Arsenal of Democracy."

The Senator did not carry his platform eloquence over into the hearing
room, at least during du Pont's appearance. By comparison, his conduct of the
hearing was restrained, although his lines of questioning left no doubt that he
felt that he was crusading against something sinister. Actually, he undertook
relatively little of the questioning as compared with other members of the
committee and its staff.

4. *Were you aware of any positive effort by any segments of the American
business community to curtail the Munitions Committee inquiry?*

We know of no effort by the business community to curtail the committee's investigation. As far as the du Pont Company is concerned, the fullest
cooperation was extended to the committee and its representatives.

DOROTHY DETZER DENNY TO
JOHN EDWARD WILTZ
SEPTEMBER 26, 1960

1661 Crescent Place, N.W.
Washington, D.C.

My dear Mr. Wiltz,

It is very nice indeed to know that Holman Hamilton suggested you write
me about the Munitions Investigation, and I hope very much that I may be of
some little help. Nevertheless, after an interval of 25 years, my memory is
somewhat foggy and so I am not sure how useful my answers will be.

However, before going to the questions, I should like to make a general
over-all observation which seems to me exceedingly important—namely, the
atmosphere, the tone—the spirit of the country at the time the investigation
took place. Just as today, everyone is aware that the current atmosphere is
charged with deep anti-communist feeling—so in the 1930's the national
atmosphere was charged with and saturated with emotion against those who
made "profits in death." If many citizens were uninformed and irrational,

nevertheless there was a general awareness of some kind of international conspiracy—secret, powerful, active.

Even tho the Peace Movement had hard going, in general there had been a good deal of hope on the part of common folk that an internationally organized world was in the making and, in time, the League of Nations would develop into an effective peace instrument. Then came the failure of the Naval Conf. and a new race in arms was on. At that time, there was no such attitude as holds today—that another war would be suicide.

Therefore, it seems to me that any study of the Munitions Investigation requires first of all a real comprehension of the tempers, tone, spirit of the country at that time. Russia was weak; the Fascists only in a nursing stage. It is orally in this context of the period, "that you will be able to understand the significance of the Investigation."

I recognize that all the above may be gratuitous, and that you are aware of all the factors and are able to capture the spirit & temper of the American people in the '30's. I have missed this point because I find that many young people have a tendency to scoff at the Investigation & to whitewash the Munition Industry and completely misunderstand the situation which then existed.

So forgive me if I have covered ground you are fully aware of. Now as to your questions:

1) I can not remember when the idea of an investigation was first projected. But there was general talk of it among peace leaders—tho I can't remember any specific suggestion until the H.I.L. Resolution in May 1933. My memory, however, is foggy on this point.

2) I have no doubt I was indebted to European colleagues for being made aware of the evils of the Munitions Industry. But I am sure they were in no way the instigators of the idea of an investigation by our Congress. I say this because no European Parliament provides for the investigation process as our Congress does, so they never thought in those terms.

You are right that there was more agitation abroad against the M.I. in the 1920's than in the U.S. However, I think the difference in the European and American criticism is this: The European peace movement began its attacks immediately *after* the 1st World War—and attempted to show that the Industry was chiefly responsible for that war. In America our effort was to expose the activities which might lead to a new war. So you are right about the timing—but I think, by and large, the emphasis abroad and in America was different.

3) a. It is difficult for me to answer the first part of this question accurately as I don't remember clearly. There was certainly a great deal of "support." However, this took the form chiefly of speeches; mailing campaigns etc. You see except for the Nat. Council for Prevention of War, no other organization (that is "active" organization) had headquarters or a lobbyist in Wash. (and the research organizations didn't "act"; they "studied.") Jeannette Rawkin, who lobbied for the Nat. Council, concentrated her efforts in the House but I

don't think she ever worked for a House Investigating Committee. So, in a sense, the Senate was almost my exclusive field! However, I sought and got advice from dozens of people—some in the Peace Movements whose organizations did not permit lobbying (Like the Foreign Policy Assoc.) or from newspaper men; even some young gov. officials.

b. Yes, I discussed the idea of an investigation with many senators; I should think about 20. It was when I became so discouraged not getting anywhere that I went back to Norris for help and advise. (See my book, *pg. 154*) As a matter of fact, I think it was Lud Denny to whom I am now married who supported I go back & lay the whole problem before "Uncle George"—as Norris was called.

c. (Again see Appointment on the H.7.I—page 154)

4) The *Fortune Article:* I had nothing to do with this. My memory is—tho I may be wrong—that William Stone of the Foreign Policy Assoc. was responsible for the article. It was certainly a major help primarily because it made the Investigation a much more "respectable" undertaking.

5) I have no idea if anyone in the Peace Movement suggested the writing of the 3 books you mention. Each of the authors I knew: I had talked to all of them—and they certainly must have discussed their manuscripts with many others. My guess is that each wrote his book because it was a "natural"; like someone writing on the space age or the Congo now. Neither subject would have to be "suggested" to anyone. It was quite obvious to a writer in the '30's that there would be a sale for books on the subject of Munitions.

6) I think Senator Nye has forgotten—or rather is confused re. what help I gave on the Committee and the staff. As indicated above, for a year I had "lobbied" for an investigation & therefore knew which Senators were at least interested in such an undertaking even if unwilling to initiate it. My memory is that I suggested Bone, Clark, Pope, Borah & Bob La Follette. However, it certainly is an unimportant point whether I suggested them or not. As to the staff: my book recounts how Steve Rauschenbush was appointed. But I suggested no other members of the staff. I had met Robert Wolforth & Floyd La Rouche; each had come to see me & it is possible I sent them to Steve—I don't remember. But the staff was up to Steve I felt, and should be left to him. Until after they were appointed to the staff, I had never met Weinple, Brown, Joe Burus or Alger! Of course, I came to know them all.

7 and 8) The last point (sentence) of your question #7 should perhaps be answered with the points you raise in #8.

As you point out, I was abroad when the Hearings began but after my return, I attended them day after day. I suppose that I had lunch with members of the staff & committee a couple of times a week. I was in a sense both an outsider and an insider at this time. That is as I had nothing to do with the direction & planning of the Hearing I could be a little more objective than either the Senators or staff on the effect the Hearings were having on those who attended. I think this was sometimes useful. Moreover, the staff of a Senate Investigating Committee, if it is really a good one, is primarily interested in getting the *facts* and not in promoting a Senator's ambition or desire for personal publicity. But being a staff, there are limits to which it can go in controlling the Senators—therefore, there were 2 or 3 of us (Bill Stone was one) who could discuss matters of "good taste"; wisdom; dignity; "understatement"; the mistakes of exaggeration; of color statements; of personal attacks etc., etc.—in a way the staff could not do. As far as the Hearings were concerned, this was my primary concern, my chief focus. I realized that probity was essential unless there was to be a bad reaction. Well, the reaction came. It was very unfortunate, but this is a matter impossible to write about. Someday, when you again come East, I should be glad to talk to you about it.

I believe Steve Rauschenbush did an outstanding job; I think he was a peerless investigator.

The chief purpose of an investigation committee is to recommend Legislation which it believes essential to curb some evil in the national Life. I believe that the interlocking legislation recommended by the committee was excellent. But it was important that the entire program be enacted. This was never done. I believe much of the "later day criticism" came from those who never knew or never took the trouble to find out about this Legislation program.

This is a very long rambling answer to your letter & I regret it is not typed. Unfortunately, I have no typewriter of my own & my husband's is constantly in use.

I'd like very much to talk to you about some phases of this subject which I think unwise to write about. Have you met Steve Rauschenbush? I think you should. If when you go to Swarthmiss, you could plan a stop-over here—and give me plenty of warning—I would be glad to arrange a joint session with Steve & his wife (Joe Burus) & perhaps Bill Stone—I think an hour's joint talk might give you more than any letters.

All good wishes on this project.

Dorothy Detzer Denny

BIBLIOGRAPHY

The reader who wishes to go beyond the present essay in examining the Nye Committee investigation might begin with my book *In Search of Peace: The Senate Munitions Inquiry, 1934–36* (Baton Rouge, 1963). The volume remains the only book-length study of the munitions investigation. For a somewhat different perspective, *e.g.*, the author believes the Nye Committee had larger responsibility for prompting isolationism in America in the 1930s than I do, there are the two chapters on the munitions inquiry in Wayne S. Cole's excellent book, *Senator Gerald P. Nye and American Foreign Relations* (Minneapolis, 1962). Cole's book has the additional advantage of placing the munitions investigation in the larger context of Nye's entire career in the Senate.

The more enterprising reader might wish to look at the committee hearings and report. When published the Nye Committee hearings and exhibits, in forty parts, filled 13,750 pages. Part 40, in a single volume, is an index of hearings, exhibits, and documents. More manageable is the report. Published in stages during 1935 and 1936, the report comprises seven thin volumes, and much of it consists of hearings and documents which the committee considered especially important. One might also examine the accounts of hearings which appeared in the *New York Times*. Unfortunately the reporters of the *Times* as well as other newsmen, if they caught the drama of the hearing room, seemed more intent on securing headlines than were the senators, and as a result their accounts sometimes emphasized documents and testimony to which the committee attached little importance.

There are of course some special books which might be of interest, notably Helmuth C. Engelbrecht and Frank C. Hanighen, *Merchants of Death* (New York, 1934), George Seldes, *Iron, Blood and Profits* (New York and London, 1934), and Philip Noel-Baker, *Private Manufacture of Armaments* (London, 1937). Then there is Dorothy Detzer's memoir *Appointment on the Hill* (New York, 1948) in which the author set out her recollections of the Nye inquiry.

The Dies Committee
1938

The Dies Committee
1938

by Michael Wreszin

From the passage of the Alien and Sedition laws in 1789 to the mid-twentieth century attempt to outlaw the Communist party, House and Senate committees have sporadically turned their attention to the activities of individuals and organizations charged with subversion. In 1919, during what is popularly known as the "Red Scare," a Senate committee was created to investigate the alleged propaganda activities of the brewery industry. Known as the Overman Committee, it quickly turned the main focus of its attention from German to Bolshevik propaganda. This shift from concern with the danger from the Right to that from the Left previewed the circumstances surrounding the creation of the Dies Committee, which was presumably fathered to expose Nazi and anti-Semitic propaganda, but quickly turned its attention to Communist and leftist activities. The Overman Committee was the first congressional committee to investigate alleged Communist activity, for even at that time it was customary for many Americans to link Bolshevism with "pro-Germanism" and to see both as alien, authoritarian ideologies.

Official concern with the Bolshevik menace died quickly in the 1920s and was replaced by a virulent racist xenophobia. Catholics, Jews, and blacks were lumped together with immigrants as a growing threat to the nation's Anglo-Saxon heritage. Demand for immigration restriction and the continued deportation of alien radicals occupied the minds of congressional defenders of Americanism. With the beginning of the Depression these racist and nativist anxieties were stimulated by a search for a scapegoat to explain the failures of the American system.

In May 1930 the House of Representatives was suddenly alarmed by New York Police Commissioner Grover Whalen's charge that the Russian Armtorg Trading Corporation was engaged in Communist propaganda. New York's aristocratic Republican representative, Hamilton Fish, was quickly appointed to chair the Special Committee to Investigate Communism in the United States. Fish, with an impeccable genealogy, was an appropriate choice to defend America against imported ideologies, but his direction of the committee revealed his scant knowledge of the subject. Although astonished by the very existence of avowed Communists in America, he treated the witnesses with the courtesy expected of a gentleman with his credentials. Congressman Carl Bachmann of West Virginia, on the other hand, played a role that became standard on such committees. Described by the hostile literary critic, Edmund Wilson, as the perfect caricature of the "lower type of Congressman . . . pot gutted . . . greasy looking . . . pig eyes . . . ," Bachmann's questions were designed to prove that communism was a weird belief held primarily by immigrants and other outcasts with no capacity to grasp the virtues of Americanism. His solution was to deport alien radicals and increase restrictions on immigration.

The findings of the Fish Committee were a potpourri of conflicting assertions and drastic recommendations. While it discovered that there were only 12,000 registered Communist party members in the United States, the committee estimated that there were also between 500,000 and 600,000 Communists and Communist sympathizers here. The American Civil Liberties Union was declared a bulwark of communism, passing itself off as a defender of the Bill of Rights. American labor unions, it charged, were Communist-infiltrated and in New York alone Communist youth camps were said to turn out 15,000 party members each year.

What should be done? The committee recommended outlawing the Communist party, registering all aliens determined to be radicals, and censoring the mail service to thwart publication of Communist propaganda. It also requested that the State Department obtain permission for Treasury agents to go to Russia to investigate their use of forced labor—a peculiarly quixotic proposal given America's continued resistance to recognition of the Soviet government.

The report and its recommendations were ridiculed by even the relatively conservative *Outlook* as both "stupid and dangerous." One critic charged that the "proposals of the Fish Committee may be far more dangerous to liberty and freedom than the pitiful handful of Communists in the United States have ever been." Fish warned about Communist promotion of class hatred and race mixing, and issued a proclamation asserting that America, with the fairest, most honorable government in the world, must stand ever vigilant against this alien menace.

This was the national atmosphere when Martin Dies came to Congress from Orange County, Texas, in 1931. He was to make it his mission each year to present bills labeled "Aliens, for the deportation of certain," or "Immigration, to further restrict." He soon gained a seat on the Committee on Immigration and Naturalization, a hotbed of nativist and anti-radical sentiment. In May 1932 Dies's bill, HR 12044, for the expulsion and exclusion of alien Communists, passed in the House over the vigorous opposition of Congressman Fiorello LaGuardia. It was, however, tabled in the Senate under the leadership of Robert La Follette, jr.

In these initial years Dies was not taken seriously. He was known for his leadership of the House "Demagogues Club," which was made up of younger members like himself who sarcastically pledged to vote for any appropriation bill and against any tax measure. Making a great display at roll call, they would dash into the chamber and register their votes to the accompaniment of loud guffaws and clowning antics. This "good ole boy" contingent of aspiring Dixie Demagogues was tolerated with general good humor. Dies appeared to be a simple country lawyer from Texas who was glad to be on the federal payroll and was quick to admit that it was "better than working." Marquis Childs, an astute observer of the congressional beat, recalled that he had never encountered a more cynical man who, despite his display of good humor, seemed to have nothing but "utter scorn for the whole institution of Congress."

How Dies became obsessively devoted to the issue of subversive activities is open to speculation. Childs suggests it may simply have been the developing political climate of the 1930s, the "frustration of obscurity and neglect," or some "gnawing force beneath the outer surface of cynicism" that awakened a latent zealotry which fed on itself and was encouraged by others. Allan Michie and Frank Ryhlick, in their study *Dixie Demagogues*, attribute it to a self-serving ambition aimed at pleasing Texas oil and utility interests opposed to all New Deal regulatory measures.

As a member of the Committee on Immigration and Naturalization, Dies soon encountered Samuel Dickstein, who represented a largely Jewish immigrant constituency on New York's lower East Side. Dickstein was devoted to the fight against anti-Semitism in extremist organizations which were encouraged by the rise of Hitler. If Martin Dies was to become an authority on Trojan horses designed to deceive God-fearing Americans, he found the right man for his purpose in this rabbi's son. He used Dickstein's concern with right wing propaganda groups as a cover to launch an assault on the entire spectrum of the Left in America and to smear the New Deal with a red brush. It was a shrewd political manipulation which was aided by the increasingly conservative congressional leadership.

In January 1934 Dickstein offered a resolution calling for an investigation of Nazi activities in the United States. After a rousing debate, during which opponents of the bill charged Dickstein with tarnishing the image of decent German Americans, the bill passed. Congressman John McCormack of Massachusetts was appointed chairman and Dickstein vice chairman of the investigating committee.

In light of subsequent investigations of subversive activity, the work of the McCormack-Dickstein Committee was relatively sane and judicious. It concentrated on such organizations as the German American Bund and the Friends of New Germany, but it also reviewed the evidence on communism gathered by the Fish Committee. It heard testimony from Earl Browder and

James Ford, two high officials of the American Communist party, and concluded that both Fascist organizations and the Communist party served the interests of foreign governments. Neither, however, presented an immediate threat, but both were potential dangers to the country.

The committee's procedures were unique in that all witnesses were interviewed first in executive sessions before undergoing public hearings, thereby eliminating wild charges and acrimonious debate. The committee retained the services of Thomas Hardwick, who had previously defended Communists during the Gastonia strike litigation, as its counsel. Later committees would have hardly found such a man acceptable.

The most significant legislation to emerge from the committee's recommendations were the McCormack Foreign Agents Registration Act of 1938 and a bill which permitted congressional committees investigating subversive activity to subpoena witnesses when conducting hearings outside of the District of Columbia. But before this legislation had been passed, McCormack, whose committee had been charged with having produced no legislation, presented a forceful argument that became the predominant justification for many subsequent investigating committees. McCormack asserted that legislation should not be the cardinal criterion for measuring the accomplishments of such committees. Their major purpose was to alert the public to an important problem and aid in the formation of public opinion. Dies was later to argue that "simple exposure was the most effective weapon" against subversive activities. "When the light of day is brought to bear we can trust public sentiment to do the rest." This was indeed a prophetic analysis.

Historically, there were three purposes for congressional investigating committees: to obtain information that would assist Congress in designing wise legislation; to supervise the Executive branch to see that the laws were faithfully executed; and, finally, to serve as a national forum—that is, to inform as well as shape public opinion. While the Supreme Court had only affirmed the first of these three purposes, it had generally agreed that the second and third were legitimate functions. The third, over the years, had broadened to mean the influencing of public opinion by the circulation of certain facts and ideas. This often became the sole defense of a committee's *raison d'être*.

In a defense of congressional investigations Woodrow Wilson pointed to the dire need for "instruction and guidance in political affairs" which the people might receive from a body which kept "all national concerns suffused in a broad light of discussion." He insisted that the "informing function of Congress should be preferred to its legislative function." The potential to abuse this "informing function" was quickly realized by astute politicians, sundry demagogues, and their victims.

During the twenties and thirties liberal reformers supported a host of congressional investigating committees which served to mobilize support for progressive social and economic legislation. In 1924 when Congress was investigating the moneyed interests and the Harding scandals, Felix Frankfurter, a champion of civil liberties, insisted that "the power of the investigative process should be left untrammeled." When conservatives attacked the committees as star chamber proceedings, liberals insisted on the "peoples' right to know."

It is not without significance, however, that the first hearings of the Dies Committee began in August 1938, just one day after what appeared to be the final hearings of the La Follette Committee, which concentrated on the violation of civil liberties by union-busting corporations. New Dealers were soon to discover that their effective weapon of securing favorable public opinion could also be used by a belligerent Congress to attack the New Deal Administration. Telford Taylor observes, in his fine history of investigating committees, that during the late thirties the "chickens came home to roost."

Throughout the Depression there had been a preoccupation with what Alistair Cooke called the "universal hobby of looking for a scapegoat." Conspiracy theories have not been the eminent domain of paranoid rural populists, as some recent historians have suggested. The liberal supporters of the New Deal, in their search for a simple explanation for the breakdown of the economy, had been delighted with the exposure of the "money changers," the "merchants of death" in the munitions industry, and the "economic royalists" of the corporate hierarchy. But despite the exposure of these villains, the Depression continued and soon the sophisticated "brain trusters" and social engineers of the New Deal bureaucracy found themselves in the rogue's gallery of scapegoats that marked the decade.

Southern Democrats, in league with vengeful Republicans, began to publicly voice their contempt for the wild schemes of the "lunatic professors." Others suggested a Machiavellian power play under the guise of fraudulent humanitarian rhetoric. From there it was only a short step to the old conservative charge that the New Deal program was a simple masquerade covering an alien and un-American conspiracy.

The Communist party line in the late thirties lent weight to this argument. During the earlier hard-line period, the party had reviled Roosevelt as a "social fascist" and the New Deal as a sugarcoated pill of reaction. This had guaranteed the party's isolation from the main thrust of American reform. But with the rise of powerful Fascist forces in Italy and Germany, the party had somersaulted and embraced democratic reform in its enthusiasm for a popular front against fascism. Now communism was defined by party spokesmen as nothing but twentieth century Americanism, and Communists as the "sons and daughters of the American Revolution." Many American reformers had been fascinated by the "Soviet experiment" and saw in Russia a unity of purpose and collective social consciousness lacking in the United States. It was not difficult to accept the Soviet Union or even American Communists as crusaders against Hitler and fascism abroad and bigotry and reaction at home. This apparent agreement between New Deal reformers and Communists on a program of social and economic reforms gave sustenance to the growing anti-New Deal coalition bent upon exposing the New Deal as the vehicle for an alien radical ideology.

By 1937 Martin Dies was on his way to becoming a leader in the anti-New Deal coalition. He had opposed the wages and hours legislation and had repeatedly called for an investigation of the "Communist instigated" sit-down strikes. Vice President Garner, who was beginning to make a sharp distinction between traditional Democrats and New Dealers, encouraged the young congressman. Big, boyish—an American to the core—Dies would make a perfect standard-bearer in defense of purity. He had all the qualifications—a fine-honed contempt for big city sophistication, a hatred for big labor law-lessness, and a suspicion of foreigners of any kind. In frequent speeches he recalled the example of his congressman father, who had bolted the party during the fight against the League of Nations because Wilson had been corrupted by "foreign advisors." Dies announced that he would always place the country before the party in a battle for true Americanism.

By the spring of 1938 the fortunes of the Roosevelt Administration were approaching their lowest point. The abortive attempt at court reform had seriously strained liberal loyalties and the sit-down strikes which accom-panied a downturn in the economy had undercut the President's authority in Congress. Democratic ranks were bitterly divided and Roosevelt had let it be known that he planned a purge of backsliding party members in the upcoming congressional election campaign. "Nothing," wrote the historian William Leuchtenburg, "divulged the sourish spirit of 1938 more than the creation of the House Committee on Un-American Activities."

Dies's bill (HR 282) had been in the works for nearly a year when it came up for debate again on May 26, 1938. It contained almost the same wording and provisons as the previous Dickstein resolutions for the investigation of sub-versive activities which had failed to pass. But Dies, according to Robert Strippling, had, unlike Dickstein, the tacit support of the House leadership and had been requested by the vice president to gather support for an Un-American Activities Committee that would have "substance and specific duties."

Contrary to the assumption of Walter Goodman, who labeled the Dies Committee "Dickstein's Monster," there is little irony in the bill initially proposed by Dickstein that resulted in the Dies Committee. That appears to have been the plan from the start, and partisans on both sides were aware of it. The son of a Russian rabbi would hardly be a fit leader for champions of American nativism. Nor is it likely that the Administration spokesmen in Congress had been caught napping as another analyst suggests. In the past, Roosevelt had been able to inspire friendly congressional committees and thwart hostile probes, but those days were gone. The Administration had lost much of its control of congressional leadership, and this had encouraged the ambitions of Martin Dies. New Dealers may have underestimated the subse-quent power and popularity of the committee, but the debate of May 26 must have warned them of the ultimate designs held by the bill's supporters. Dickstein's initial anti-Nazi preoccupations had only served as a shallow cover for a committee with much broader political ambitions.

Necessary support had been mustered well in advance, so Dies was able to assume a moderate and diplomatic role during the debate. To the charge that such a committee might endanger individual civil liberties, Dies elo-quently voiced his own fears. He warned that any "legislative attempt to prevent un-American activities . . . might jeopardize fundamental rights far more important than the objectives we seek." But that danger could be avoided simply by the way such a committee was chaired. Publicity-seeking politicians or sensation-mongers must, of course, be barred from serving on such a committee. This was a reference to Samuel Dickstein, who had been labeled as such by opponents of his anti-Nazi assaults.

In an indirect way, the public debate made several things clear to the politicians. Dies was assuring his colleagues that Dickstein would have no place on his committee. The exchange between Dies and John Cochran over appropriations for the committee revealed that Cochran understood that Dies was to be the chairman of the committee. And, as both John Rankin and J. Parnell Thomas had made it clear that no committee with Dickstein on it would receive their support, Dies was more than conciliatory on that point. He assured skeptical critics that the committee could achieve its modest goals during the remainder of the year and that it would not need a lavish appropriation. Evidence of Dies's calculated dissembling clearly supports Marquis Childs's opinion that the case history of Martin Dies is a story of "ambition, by Shakespeare, out of True Story Magazine."

If Dies took on the mantle of judicious statesmanship, a far cry from the earlier demagogue jeering at House protocol, the more flamboyant rhetoric demanded in such rituals was supplied by the traditional New Deal haters. Congressman Taylor of Tennessee was allotted an inordinate amount of time to defend the resolution, most of which he used to wrap himself in the flag, embrace red-blooded Americanism, and denounce the defilers of virtue who had only recently painted Plymouth Rock an unholy red. Scoundrels of this stripe, he shouted, should be "hunted down like rattlesnakes and kicked out of the country." Continuing on, he attacked Francis Perkins and the Department of Labor for their coddling of immigrants who "cared nothing about America."

J. Parnell Thomas pointed out that the Communist party was a greater threat than Nazi organizations since, according to his research, Communists outnumbered Nazis by more than five to one. Worse than both were the Communist-influenced agencies of the federal government; these were the real sources of un-Americanism and *they* must indeed be investigated.

It was left to F. Maury Maverick (D.–Texas), Gerald Boileau (D.–Wisconsin), and John Main Coffee (D.–Washington) to defend civil liberties and the integrity of the New Deal. They ridiculed the "pompous patriotism" of the bill's supporters and the potential spectacle of congressmen "swaggering around the country like inquisitors." The proposed committee was not designed to deal with fundamental problems facing the nation, but was a plot to dismantle the New Deal and harass liberal organizations. What constituted un-Americanism was a question which remained vague and ill defined. Dies argued that un-Americanism was simply the understanding that Americans derived their fundamental and inherent rights not from society or government but "from Almighty God." Maverick retorted that if one were for the wages and hours laws, for free speech, and for a living wage, he was apparently un-American, since these rights came from the determination of the courts and not from God. "Un-American is simply something that somebody else doesn't agree to," he concluded. Representative Harold Knutson (R.–Minnesota) won the prize for brevity. He repeatedly answered the question "What is un-American?" with the single word, "Goosestepping." What his colleagues thought about that is not recorded, but he did know the purpose of the committee. It was just another machination improvised to provide hard-pressed congressmen with "room and board during the summer months."

For all the "ballyhoo and bunk" the tally was an overwhelming 191 to 41 in favor of the resolution. Representative Cochran explained the lop-sided vote for an anti-New Deal measure in a House dominated by Democrats. Newspapers, he observed, would make it clear, if the resolution failed to pass, that the House had declined to investigate subversion. "I do not want to be accused of refusing to vote for legislation to investigate un-American activities." Eugene Lyons's later assertion that the Dies Committee grew out of a tiny congressional faction is simply erroneous. It was not a victory for the "Dies-Dickstein strategy" as Walter Goodman has observed. On the contrary, Dies had used Dickstein as his own Trojan horse upon which to ride the plains of anti-New Deal discontent. Dickstein, the reputed father of the committee, was not even permitted three minutes to address his colleagues at the end of the debate and was denied membership on the committee.

On June 6 Dies was predictably appointed chairman; the committee members, to no one's surprise, were five to two and often six to one against the Roosevelt Administration. Conservative Democrats Dies, Joe Starnes of Alabama, and Harold G. Mosier of Ohio were allied with the two Republicans, J. Parnell Thomas of New Jersey, and Noah Mason of Illinois. Only John J. Dempsey of New Mexico could be described as a New Deal Democrat, albeit a wavering one. The seventh member, Arthur Healey of Massachusetts, was a will o' the wisp Democrat who voted one way and then another but was usually absent at crucial junctures. Jerry Voorhis, the most dependable of New Deal liberals and a constant critic of the committee's conduct, was appointed to replace Mosier when he was defeated in the 1938 elections. Dies would later point to Voorhis's membership on the committee to counter charges of political partisanship.

While some observers persisted in believing the committee's main target was Nazi propaganda, ideologues on the Right and the Left were aware of the reality. Father Coughlin's *Social Justice* assured its readers that the anti-Communist block had backed the committee. The *New Republic* cited Dies's record against the New Deal and concluded that "if the principal energies of Mr. Dies are not given over to hounding Communists, it would be a miracle." But Dies was a knowledgeable performer and, as Walter Goodman has observed, he called upon anti-Nazi testimony intermittently during the investigations "like the comic who pops out between . . . skits with a broom and sets diligently to sweeping the stage until he is kicked off so the show may proceed."

During the months between the creation of the committee and its initial hearings in August 1938 Dies continued in his role with statesmanlike decorum. The committee, he informed the press, would conduct no "three ring circus." As chairman he would not permit "any individual or organization to use the Committee as a sounding board to obtain publicity." Dies's opening statement on August 12, 1938, was perhaps his most magnificent performance; it was as though it had been composed by the American Civil Liberties Union. The committee would conduct all hearings on a "dignified plane" and maintain a "judicial attitude." To the merriment of cynics, he insisted that the committee members held no preconceived views and that their single goal was to discover the truth. All witnesses would be treated with courtesy, fairness, and impartiality. There would be no "character assassination" nor "smearing of innocent people." Reckless charges would not be condoned, as the gathering of facts, not opinions, was the prime objective. "Charges unsupported by facts" were of no value. "It is easy," he warned, "to smear someone's name or reputation and very difficult to repair the damage that has been done." In the investigation of un-American activities it must be kept in mind that "because we do not agree with opinions or philosophies of others does not necessarily make such opinions or philosophies un-American." Too often partisans branded their opponents with a pejorative label rather than engaging in argument with "facts and logic." Conservatives were inclined to call all liberals Communists and "so-called liberals" stigmatized all conservative ideas as fascistic. The committee would take the utmost care to distinguish between what was "un-American and what was no more or less than an honest difference of opinion" on economic, political, or social questions.

Walter Goodman, after a study of subsequent hearings, wondered if "the lady of breeding" who had made such "a dignified entrance into town" had not in fact established "a bawdy house." But the charade was maintained by the first witness, John C. Metcalf, a German-American who had infiltrated the Bund and had gathered a file on their bizarre activities. The stage seemingly set for a thorough investigation of Nazi propaganda, Dies dropped the curtain the following day and introduced John P. Frey, president of the metal trades department of the American Federation of Labor, who immediately launched a sustained attack, charging Communist domination of the rival Congress of Industrial Organization. Here was the committee's response to the Senate's La Follette Committee, which had just ended its hearings on anti-union activities.

In three days, Frey provided 186 pages of testimony and accompanying documentation to support the A. F. of L. allegations. Frey was encouraged to make charges, and few CIO unions of any consequence escaped his condemnation. He named 210 union officials as "Communistic," but supplied little documentation to prove his allegations. He received no challenge from the committee, however. He also charged that the La Follette Committee investigators had close contacts with members of the Communist party; that charge proved to have some substance.

Frey's testimony received much attention in the press. *Communists Rule The CIO, La Follette Committee Linked to Communism* read the bold, black headlines. With roughly eighty-five percent of the press in opposition to the New Deal in 1938, Dies had little trouble monopolizing the front pages. Kenneth Crawford, a seasoned journalist, later declared that it was the "amazing success of the Frey testimony as an experiment in publicity that awakened Dies and his associates to a full realization of the . . . political gold mine they had struck. From Frey on it was catch as catch can with no holds barred."

The committee did not simply depend upon the hearings to produce publicity. It became standard practice for members and the staff to make statements outside of the public hearings; unfortunately, these often appeared in the press as part of the committee's findings. While Frey was testifying on August 14, Edward Sullivan, a committee investigator with a long history of labor spying and anti-Semitic associations, charged Harry Bridges, the longshoreman leader, with responsibility for sixty percent of the labor strife on the West Coast. In spite of his Communistic connections and inclination,

Sullivan continued, Bridges was being protected by an "outstanding official" in the Department of Labor.

Dies did not vouch for the authenticity of the charge. However, he soon joined with those calling for the impeachment of Frances Perkins, who refused to deport Bridges as an alien Communist organizer because the Bridges case was already being litigated in the courts and the Department of Labor had no legal grounds upon which to initiate deportation proceedings. Bridges was hounded by the Dies Committee and later by the whole House, which eventually passed a bill for his deportation on the grounds that it was "in the best interests of the United States." In 1945 Justice Murphy closed the case in Bridges's favor, with the observation that "seldom . . . in the history of the Nation has there been such a concentrated and relentless crusade to deport an individual because he dared exercise the freedom that belongs to him as a human being and that is guaranteed him by the Constitution."

Following Frey the committee offered a platform, in direct contradiction to Dies's opening day statement, to Walter S. Steele, a professional patriot and professional witness who made a career of testifying before subversive activities committees. Steele, claiming to represent 114 patriotic organizations and some 20 million Americans, named 640 organizations as Communistic and claimed that six and a half million Americans were engaged in some form of foreign propagandistic activity. Even the Boy Scouts and Campfire Girls were suspect for their pacifist inclinations and their faith in internationalism.

Dies anticipated the response of critics to such absurd testimony and occasionally interrupted to suggest that the testimony would not be admissible in a court, and thus the committee should be wary of causing injury to innocent persons. Dies's duty done, the witness would then be allowed to continue the harangue, urged on by friendly and leading questions from the committee members.

Day after day it went on. A legionnaire attacked the League for Peace and Freedom as Communist-dominated and committee member Noah Mason, picking up the cue, named eight government officials as members of the organization. J. Parnell Thomas initiated his crusade against the WPA with an assault on the Federal Theatre Project. The committee exposed its racist underpinnings by boldly pursuing the lurid story of a black project worker who had the temerity to ask a woman fellow worker for a date. Sally Saunders, the witness, disclosed that Communist workers "hob-nobbed indiscriminately" with blacks and "threw parties with them left and right." In answer to a question from Joe Starnes, she agreed that "social equality and race merging" were part of the Communist program.

The Frey and Steele testimonies established the general conduct and atmosphere of the hearings for the committee's first year. After the first month Dies violated nearly every code of conduct that he had initially announced. The committee was used as a platform by partisan witnesses, who, with few exceptions, were given free reign to make damaging accusations unsupported by corroborative evidence. If they were friendly witnesses, there was virtually no cross-examination. Committee members would put words into their mouths and urge them on with provocative and leading questions. Testimony which attacked organizations and reputations and offered no effective opportunity for rebuttal was constantly released to the press. Individuals were named and condemned on the basis of simple associations with organizations described as "Communistic." Paul Douglas, John Dewey, Reinhold Niebuhr, even H. L. Mencken, were referred to derogatorily, as the reporters scribbled on. If the hearings themselves failed to produce immediate headlines on any given day, members were free to take to the public podium to make further charges and to capture attention.

The witnesses were either "experts" who filed long, unexamined briefs, or rabid partisans. Particularly acceptable to the committee were disgruntled bureaucrats who had failed to find a home in some New Deal agency and sought an outlet for their animosity. D. A. Saunders of the *Public Opinion Quarterly* concluded in April 1939 that the witnesses had hardly inspired confidence in the investigation. A large number seemed "to have been professed patriots, vigilantes, political stool-pigeons, labor spies, anti-Semites, Nazi sympathizers and even criminals." One grieving member of the press covering the hearing complained that "the mixture of plausible testimony with fantasy, the practice of Committee members putting words in the witnesses' mouths, their almost universal failure to seek development of proof of startling accusations or to develop the backgrounds of possible animus of the accusers, makes covering the inquiry a headache of major proportions." Unfortunately, his conscientious concern was hardly typical.

If ignorance of the field of investigation and vagueness of direction characterized the initial hearings, they were saved, so to speak, by the evangelical proselytiser, J. B. Matthews. Shortly after a lengthy testimony on Communist-front organizations, Matthews was made an investigator for the committee, a job he held through the Hiss-Chambers hearings in 1949. He later served briefly as a staff director on the McCarthy Committee. Matthews was the classic American "seeker." He had traveled from evangelical fundamentalism to the humanitarianism of the Social Gospel, on down the road to the progressivism of the elder La Follette, through the pacifism of the Fellowship of Reconciliation, to the left wing of the Socialist party, into the Popular Front and militant consumerism, and, finally, back to the fundamentalism practiced by anti-Communist converts. There is some humor in the fact that Matthews's conversion to anti-communism occurred when, as an executive of Consumer's Research, he was outraged by a strike of its employees, charging that it was a Communist plot to take over the organization. Benjamin Gitlow saw him as a lightweight on Marxist social and economic theory, but Matthews could chart every twist and turn in the tortured history of fellow traveling.

This was the man for Dies. He lent respectability to the committee and was deferentially referred to as "Doctor" by some of its members. Whether he analyzed any situation as a witness or as an interrogator, his testimony was filled with the most minute details of popular front organizational structure, lists, names, dates, and places. He was a master archivist and his exhaustive knowledge made him invaluable to the committee because he could make connections between liberals, fellow travelers, and the hidden Communist conspiracy. Dies was out to slander the New Deal, and Matthews served his purpose well.

Matthews first appeared as a witness on August 22, 1938. He listed at least twenty Communist fronts with which he had been affiliated and recalled the most inconsequential episodes down to the last detail. Like so many anti-Communist witnesses, he inflated the Communist attributions of power and influence to organizations which were more accurately described by Murray Kempton as "structures of enormous pretension and pathetic foundation." But it was the meat and gristle of his life, and he did not believe that he had been on a feckless journey. He had heard the roar of the crowd in Madison Square Garden, as well as the mumblings in storefront temples.

It was Matthews who made the gaffe that the committee never lived down. In explaining how innocent, well-meaning people could be used by Communists, he noted that several movie stars such as Clark Gable, James Cagney, and Shirley Temple had been persuaded to send congratulations to a French Communist newspaper on its first anniversary. Matthews made a point of not saying they were Communists or Communist sympathizers but rather that their reputations had been exploited in the interest of Communist propaganda. But it was too late. Every critic of the committee leaped to the advantage. Harold Ickes conjured up visions of burly congressmen leading posses of investigators into Shirley Temple's nursery to gather evidence of Communist conspiracy. Frances Perkins thanked God that Shirley was a citizen and could not be deported.

By October 1938 the congressional election campaign was underway, and the political potential of the committee was apparent both to its chairman and to the Administration. Heated election struggles were already going on in the crucial swing states of Minnesota, Michigan, and California. On October 17, after protesting that the committee was only interested in communism and not political disputes, Dies produced Steve Gadler of St. Paul who testified that the Democratic candidate for governor of Minnesota, Elmer A. Benson, had been endorsed by Browder and the candidate had not repudiated the endorsement. Gadler went on to charge that the Farmer Labor party had been captured by the Communists, and six other nondescript witnesses testified to the same general information.

From Minnesota on to Michigan—the committee went to work on a Roosevelt favorite, Governor Frank Murphy, who was running for reelection. Returning to the sit-down strikes of two previous years, the committee recruited Paul V. Gadola, a Republican judge, to testify that the timid negotiating policy of Governor Murphy had contributed to the breakdown of law and order in that state. Murphy, Gadola charged, had become nothing more than a pawn in the hands of a crew of Communist lawyers and had refused to support the judge's injunction against lawless seizures of private property. After further damaging testimony from American Legionnaires and some local police officers, the committee heard from John M. Barringer, a former city manager and director of public safety in Flint, Michigan. Dies played on Barringer's testimony as though it were a musical instrument, leading the questions all the way. ". . . Would you say that [the sit-down strikes] would not have occurred if it had not been for the investigation and active leadership of the Communists?" Barringer obligingly replied, "No, it would not have occurred. And I can further answer that question—it would not have developed . . . if it had not been for the attitude of the members of the La Follette Committee, and Governor Murphy's treasonable action in not giving us help when we should have had it." Dies hit a bull's-eye which gained him headline dividends that surpassed even his wildest hopes.

Ignored during the questioning was the great potential for violence inherent in the organizing drive for industrial unionism. Murphy, under terrible pressure, had chosen the tactics of delay and negotiation over armed force, and the strike ended with no loss of life. From Murphy's perspective the situation had come close to civil war, with the American Legion at the head of assorted vigilante groups confronting a tough core of determined union militants.

Roosevelt, smarting under the steady attack on members of his Administration and angered by the blatant political partisanship of the committee's conduct, issued a public condemnation. The President described the witnesses as a "coterie of disgruntled Republican office holders," led by a "disgruntled Republican judge," a "discharged city manager," and a group of "officious" policemen who had been recruited to make "lurid" and unjustified charges that could not be verified. He eloquently defended Murphy as a "profoundly religious, able and law-abiding Governor" whose handling of the strike was such that "all peace loving Americans should praise him." The President indicted the committee for allowing itself to be used in a "flagrantly unfair and un-American attempt to influence an election." He hoped that the committee would abandon the practice of providing a forum for those who sought headlines.

Undaunted, Dies immediately reaffirmed all of the charges, insisting that despite the President's anger and opposition, he would continue to do his duty "undeterred and unafraid." Next to appear were two Californians who accused the Democratic candidate for governor, Culbert Olsen, of owing his nomination to Communist support. It was later asserted that these witnesses represented the interests of the Associated Farmers, a West Coast anti-union organization of fruit growers and packers which supported Republican candidates.

The Administration blamed the Dies Committee for the defeat of Murphy in Michigan, and Dies was delighted to accept the credit. Arthur Krock in the *New York Times* acknowledged the influence of the committee when he asserted that the election returns had emphatically rebuked the sit-down strikes and the Democratic-CIO alliance.

Dies and his committee were the beneficiaries of a growing disenchantment with the New Deal program and a fearful anxiety over what lay ahead. He had no intention of losing momentum, so he and his colleagues kept up a running assault on officials in the Executive bureaucracy. In an Armistice Day speech Dies accused Secretaries Ickes and Perkins of being purveyors of class hatred. Almost no agency or department head was immune from criticism as a collaborator or dupe of Communist design.

Harold Ickes was the only one to return the fire with any enthusiasm. In a press release he said that "anyone who wanted to get anything out of his system against any New Dealer" should apply to the accommodating Dies Committee. Dies, Ickes quipped, was the "outstanding zany of American political history." The following day Dies called for the resignation of Ickes and Perkins because no American could feel secure with an Administration staffed by Communists, Socialists, and the "ordinary garden variety of crackpots."

While this extracurricular activity went on, the committee conducted its final hearings in December 1938. They were designed to expose the criminal mismanagement of the Works Progress Administration (WPA) and particularly, the writer and theatre projects. With unerring instinct Dies and J. Parnell Thomas recognized that these projects constituted "the soft underbelly" of the WPA. Many Americans were indifferent or unsympathetic to a federal program providing employment for writers and actors whom they felt were, at best, loafers and, at worst, troublemakers. It was true, as Thomas repeatedly charged, that many Communists and fellow travelers of varying radical persuasions had found a home in the projects. This was notoriously true of the New York projects, which were frequently in a state of upheaval resulting from factional political struggles. In the eyes of middle-class respectability, the projects were composed of a motley crew of wild-eyed and frequently drunken poets, writers, and assorted bohemians whose life-style was an affront to all that was pure and decent. Imagine what the suffering, self-reliant taxpayer thought of a mystical raconteur like the legendary Joe Gould who, when not writing his mythical "Oral History of the World," rambled around his Greenwich Village turf flapping his arms like a seagull and disrobing at parties. Nor is it likely that the general populace could appreciate the genius of the Village bohemian-turned-Communist, Maxwell Bodenheim, who actually rose to the position of a supervisor in the writer's project until his penchant for spirits made it impossible for him to show up for work—even once a week.

This "gallery of grotesques," combined with the sectarian warfare between Stalinists and Trotskyites in the New York projects, gave the entire program a bad reputation and was a constant embarrassment to the Administration. As the hearings proceeded it was obvious that no major Administration official would exert much effort to protect this experiment in federal sponsorship of the arts, despite its many fine achievements.

The thrust of the attack on the projects rested on the testimony of disgruntled former employees. They charged that Communists controlled the employees' union, the Workers' Alliance, and used their power to intimidate and harass non-Communists. The editorial staff, they accused, was dominated by Communists who insidiously introduced propaganda into literary and theatrical productions. Critics complained that the famous state guidebooks invariably employed Communist phraseology, stressed the struggle between capital and labor, referred to blacks as the downtrodden, and championed the virtues and nobility of the "underprivileged." It was noted that the Massachusetts guide devoted more pages to the Sacco-Vanzetti case than it did to the Boston Tea Party.

Committee members followed their all too familiar practice of putting words into the mouths of witnesses.

> Congressman Mason: Would you say that the federal Writers Project is being used by a group of radicals to propagandize the states through the use of these guides?
> Witness: I do; and that is just the beginning.
> Chairman Dies: Do you think Mr. Alsberg (director of Writers Project) is bringing into the department as many radicals as he can?
> Witness: I don't know whether he is doing it under orders or voluntarily.
> Dies: But he is doing it?

Witness: It has seemed to us for a long while that he has been bringing in such persons.

Friendly witnesses were seldom cross-examined. However, when Ellen Woodward, the assistant administrator, testified in defense of the project, her testimony was challenged at every point, proof demanded of any generalizations, and her fitness as a witness discussed at length.

After a score of accusatory witnesses were heard, Mrs. Hallie Flanagan was finally permitted to defend the theatre projects. She was a spirited witness not intimidated by the committee. When asked what her duties were, she remarked that she worked to combat un-American activities by providing jobs for professional men and women. Dies refused to allow her to testify to anything she had not personally witnessed and no hearsay evidence was permitted. This was an astonishing switch from the usual procedure which had encouraged reams of unsupported hearsay evidence.

During her testimony, an old article by Mrs. Flanagan was dug up in which she referred to the "Marlowesque madness" of worker's theatres taking root in America. Congressman Starnes wanted to know who this Marlowe was. "Is he a Communist?" he asked. Mrs. Flanagan respectfully replied that she had been referring to Christopher Marlowe, but Starnes, unsatisfied, pressed on. "Tell us who Marlowe is. . . ." To this Mrs. Flanagan responded with delight: "Put in the record that he was the greatest dramatist in the period of Shakespeare, immediately preceding Shakespeare." A shout of laughter echoed through the chamber and out across the nation and every opponent of the committee was comforted by the knowledge that the red-necked Starnes knew as little about drama as he did about communism.

The theatre and writers projects had produced an amazing variety of material, some first rate and much of it little more than crude and inept political propaganda. But to the committee it was not so much Communist literary banality, as it was the abominable association of the government with these disreputable figures. It is a toss up as to who should be credited for ultimately killing these projects. The New Deal Administration found the experiment a political liability and gave it little support once under attack. The Dies Committee exploited every sensational facet of political and social nonconformity, thus damaging the reputation of the entire experiment, and the Communists' continuous, disruptive bickering and crude attempts at politicization made them vulnerable to ridicule.

The WPA hearings were a rehearsal for the first debate over the renewal of the committee. Dies had good reason to be optimistic, for despite the fact that a poll of journalists, solicited by Roosevelt, had declared the committee's conduct unfair and the Administration had hired Paul Anderson, a journalist, to attack it on a national network, a Gallup poll showed that it had wide popular support.

Harold Ickes insisted that the only way to deal with Dies was to confront him directly. He planned a nationwide speech entitled "Playing with Loaded Dies," which would inform the public of the outrageous conduct of the hearings. But the President, increasingly wary of Dies's political influence, especially after the decisive defeat in the congressional elections, was persuaded to cancel Ickes's speech. He continued to entertain the hope that congressional leadership could either curb the committee's longevity or the size of its appropriation through careful political maneuvering. He was advised that an Ickes attack would simply rally anti-New Deal support for Dies.

Ickes replied that Dies was making gains because the President and his Administration had refused to take the offensive. A number of cabinet sessions were turned over to a discussion of Ickes's strategy. He urged the Administration to encourage an additional appropriation for the La Follette Committee to counterbalance Dies's investigation, or to pack the Dies Committee with loyal New Dealers.

The President vacillated between these two proposals but refused to allow administrative officials to lobby on the Hill. The degree to which Roosevelt feared Dies may be seen in his request that Frank Murphy, whom he had only recently appointed attorney general, begin an investigation of the organizations that the committee daily attacked as subversive. This, however, gave substance and respectability to the charges of the committee.

Ickes was disconsolate when the committee was renewed in February and received a sizable increase in its appropriation, while the La Follette Committee's appropriation was cut in half in the Senate. He recorded in his diary that it was another example of "a complete falling down of Democratic leadership." They had "abjectly surrendered" to the demagogues. Sam Rayburn remarked: "Martin Dies could beat me right now in my own district."

When Congress convened in January 1939, Dies submitted the 125-page committee report. A considerable portion of the report was allotted to a defense of the investigation and an assault on the lack of cooperation from Roosevelt's Administration. Reflecting the opinion of its chairman, the committee report emphasized the notion that Americanism was the recognition that a citizen's fundamental rights came from God. The preaching of class conflict was un-American. The real danger of communism was not overt conspiracy, but the infiltration of organizations and the government itself. In its survey of the hearings, what evidence the committee chose to include was highly selective. It carefully detailed the testimony covering Communist influence in the WPA, but the hostile testimony of Hallie Flanagan was entirely omitted. Frey's charges of Communist domination of the National Labor Relations Board and the CIO were reasserted, as was the testimony attributing treasonous action to Governor Murphy during the sit-down strikes. Walter Steele's rambling testimony was constantly quoted to support charges against alleged Communist-front organizations. The American League for Peace and Freedom was cited as a prime example of a Communist front, and it obviously was. The Workers' Alliance, the American Student Union, and the National Negro Congress were all castigated as suspect organizations willingly serving the ends of Communist propaganda.

The general reception of the report in Congress and in the press was favorable. All agreed that the menace of un-American activities was a real threat to national security and that the committee's purpose had been justified. The problem was that the frequently shoddy conduct of the committee violated the American sense of fair play. Here was the beginning of that haunting refrain, "I believe in the objectives but I deplore the methods," which later became the basis of anti-Communist apologia during the next two decades.

The position of the *New York Times* was a classic of the genre. The committee, the newspaper asserted, had performed a useful service. It had exposed the deceit and hypocrisy of the so-called front organizations, the insidious nature of Communist tactics, and had correctly linked communism with nazism and fascism as another form of undemocratic authoritarianism. It was important that the public be alerted to propagandistic and subversive activities. On the other hand, the Dies Committee was not the perfect instrument to achieve these ends, the *Times* said. It had entertained "hysterical tosh," arrived at conclusions in advance of evidence, and was guilty of "red-baiting." Despite these failings, the newspaper endorsed the committee, felt it should be continued, and hoped for some reform of its personnel.

The *New Republic,* a strong supporter of the popular front, condemned the committee and its works. But the depth of their civil libertarian principles seemed to depend on certain conditions. They urged support for the La Follette Committee on the grounds that "nothing holds the forces of darkness in check like a Senatorial searchlight always in readiness to be turned upon their activities." Supporters of the Dies Committee held the same view with respect to a congressional searchlight on alleged subversive activities. One might agree that the power of union-busting corporations presented a greater threat to genuine democracy than that of the Communist Left during these years and that the conduct, research, and documentation of the La Follette investigation far surpassed the unfair and slip-shod methods of the Dies Committee, but this double vision, which accepted the political motivation of one committee while rejecting the other, set an example for the wavering integrity of some liberals who grew to accept the work of the un-American activities committees as a necessary evil in the fight against international communism.

While partisans of both sides discussed the needs, failings, and implications of the committee, *Colliers* magazine captured the popular attitude. In spite of some obvious theatrical flaws, phony witnesses, and fantastic stories, the public wished the show to go on, hoped for some improvement in the proceedings, and advocated a larger appropriation.

Dies was confident. In the congressional debate over renewal of the committee, the war horses of the opposition retreated. They no longer repudiated the committee's existence but simply demanded reform of committee conduct. Only one representative, Adolph Sabath, still angered over their neglect of anti-Semitic and Fascist groups, voted against renewal in the Rules Committee. After an hour of debate on the floor, Dies won an overwhelming vote of confidence, 344 to 35. Republicans supported the committee to a man; Democrats, reading public sentiment and noting the feeble opposition of the Administration, went along. The committee was awarded $100,000 and another year's tenure.

Dies was jubilant. "We've proved the job should be done." To conciliate critics and prove nonpartisanship, the liberal Californian, Jerry Voorhis, replaced Mosier, who had been defeated in the last election. For the next four years Voorhis played the role of the committee's conscience, invariably condemning its conduct while defending its continued existence.

In the spring of 1939 as the European horizon darkened, there was a lull in the headline accounts of the committee's activities. In the House, Dies continued to push for legislation to exclude and expel alien Communists, require registration of suspect, "Communist" organizations, and bar federal employment of known Fascists and Communists. The latter became law in August 1939, and it was not long before Dies would follow his triumph by exciting the House to attach riders demanding the dismissal of bureaucrats investigated by the committee to many appropriations bills.

The committee's first headlines of 1939 occurred on May 18. Committee investigators, a shadowy and elusive crew, had uncovered a Fascist, anti-Semitic plot allegedly threatening the entire nation. The plot involved the most bizarre of the right-wing fringe and a group of unknown red Jews. The story was shrouded in mystery, with secret sessions of the committee and unknown witnesses hidden from one another and the press. As details were leaked, it was learned that the anti-Semite, Dudley Pierrepont Gilbert, had discovered, through a waiter in a restaurant frequented by wealthy Jews, that there was a conspiracy afoot to take over the country. Gilbert had passed the information on to right-wing patriots who, in turn, planned a counterplot to rid the country of the Jewish menace.

As the story unfolded in the press the emphasis shifted from an exposure of anti-Semitism to an account of the Communist-Jewish plot. Anti-Semitic right-wing leaders, testifying before the committee, expounded upon the nature of the worldwide Communist-Jewish conspiracy. The effect was the revival of the flagging careers of those fringe groups who insisted that their main purpose was to protect the country from communism, a disease invariably carried by Jews. General George Van Horn Moseley, a retired army officer and leader of anti-Semitic groups, and George E. Deatherage, the national commander of the anti-Semitic, nativist Knights of the White Camelia, gave lengthy dissertations on the attempts his group had made to mobilize a counterforce against this conspiracy. Moseley's "astute" scholarship was summed up in his observation that "over two thousand years of recorded history shows very clearly that those traits which have made the Jew unwelcome every place he has domiciled cannot be bred out."

One is tempted to equate the fears of the Communist and Fascist menace as equally bizarre manifestations in American life during a period of hysteria. But if respectable institutions did not support the likes of Moseley and Deatherage, their tolerance of anti-Semitism was overt. Only a year later the genteel aristocrat Albert Jay Nock was commissioned to write an essay for the *Atlantic* on the "Jewish problem." In it he refined Moseley's message to assert that the Jew and the Gentile could never live amiably side by side and that some form of apartheid was necessary if the country was to survive. Neither could the press be excused for twisting this story and others so as to hang its headlines on the spectacle of an ancient Jewish conspiracy while playing down the anti-Semitic aspects of the affair. More than one historian of the committee has wondered why, with so much evidence of anti-Semitism, it failed to utilize its information to develop a full-scaled investigation of the native Fascist movement.

As was his practice, Dies delayed formal public hearings on this matter until the late summer and fall when Congress had adjourned. In August the approach of war in Europe brought the real menace of Hitler home to the American people. Dies obligingly investigated the German-American Bund and its national leader, Fritz Kuhn. The historian of nativist Fascist movements, Sandor Diamond, notes that in a "strange but understandable way"

Kuhn owed much to Martin Dies. Because "Dies was more concerned with the Communist threat to America than with the Nazi menace," Kuhn's only hope of reviving his waning movement was by "converting it into a militant anti-Communist and isolationist group." The Dies hearings on the Bund provided his platform but could not help but mobilize anti-Fascist feelings. It was not the Dies Committee, however, that was responsible for Kuhn's subsequent conviction on a tax evasion charge; it was the liberal Congressman La Guardia of New York.

The diverse and rambling hearings of the summer of 1939 simply could not sustain attention. The Nazi-Stalin Pact of August 24, 1939, was a lifesaver to the committee and its chairman, for they now had the documentation for their long-held contention that there was no difference between fascism and communism. Both were Godless forms of totalitarianism which would stop at no form of deceit. The subsequent invasions of Poland and Finland only confirmed the charge, which was immeasurably strengthened by the slavish servility of American Communists and fellow travelers who went to absurd lengths to defend these events. The apologetics of the Communist party, which involved the abandonment of their call for resistance to fascism and an espousal of pacifism and isolationism, proved to the committee and to most Americans that the party was nothing more than a vehicle of Soviet foreign policy. The stupidity of party spokesmen was more than many fellow travelers and former sympathizers could take. Granville Hicks, a literary critic who had eloquently defended the nobility of the popular front, submitted his farewell to the party to the *New Masses,* which refused to publish it; but the *New Republic,* still reeling from the shock of the Pact, did. Hicks lamented that the party had abandoned all pretense of independence from the Kremlin with its shameful claim that the Pact was a contribution to peace and democracy. He was chagrined that the party had not even bothered to defend the agreement as an act of political expediency necessary to gain time to prepare a defense against future Nazi aggression (which did become the rationale of many). He charged that since they were ill-equipped "to defend the Soviet Union intelligently, they would defend it stupidly."

For the less ideological and more romantic supporters of Communist goals, the Pact dealt a devastating blow to their idealistic commitments and principles. Irwin Edman's reaction is perhaps the most representative of many of the left-wing partisans who had marched with the Communists in worthy causes. There could be no rational reason for the Pact. The fact that there were such rationalizations, Edman wrote, "had eaten like a canker into the bloom of every value we enjoy and every ideal we cherish." It had made "a mockery of all their former hopes and knowledge." Even the "private joys" of former comradeship were made "shamefaced and precarious." Edman lamented that men in the nineteenth century had been saddened because they could no longer believe in God. But he and his friends were "more deeply saddened because they could no longer believe in man."

Such a lament tells more about the Communist menace than anything ever alleged by an un-American activities committee. The betrayal of political decency by the party struck a blow against the foundations of liberal optimism and soured a generation of well-meaning men and women on all forms of social commitment, encouraging many to retreat into private visions or a resigned acceptance of the irrational. Others enthusiastically embraced the status quo as the best of all possible worlds. Adopting a sophisticated Niebuhrian pessimism, they proclaimed a cynicism tantamount to political maturity. *This* was the most devastating legacy of the American flirtation with communism in the 1930s. It may also help to account for the conduct of jaded liberals during the cold war and in the 1960s when they, too, resorted to duplicity to justify actions beyond the understanding of reasonable men.

The undermining of liberal confidence and commitment was one of the goals of the Dies Committee and its chairman did not let the advantage offered by the Pact slip by. It provided an opportunity for the committee to exploit the more ludicrous dimensions of Communist logic. Earl Browder shamelessly declared that world peace would be the consequence of the agreement of Germany and Russia to refrain from mutual attack. William Z. Foster continued to insist that the American Communist party was independent of the Soviet Union. There were, he claimed, "tens of thousands" of times when the party had taken a stand independent of the Comintern. When pressed, however, he could think of no particular instance. He admitted that after a party member had been educated to a particular position but continued to oppose it, he would be expelled. None of this was startling information, but the committee presented it in such a way as to provide sardonic anti-Communists with unsurpassed examples of Communist sophistry.

At one point during Browder's hearing the Communist official broadened the definition of "transmission belt," a term used in Communist jargon to mean independent organizations used by the party to transmit their words to the masses, to include the A. F. of L. J. Parnell Thomas, right on cue, read off a list of liberal organizations to which high officials in the New Deal, including the President and his wife, had given addresses and asked if they were not also part of the transmission belt. When Browder conceded, Thomas commented with smug satisfaction that it seemed that the New Deal was working "hand in glove with the Communist Party."

During this period of daily revelations by Communist functionaries, Dies was shaping the strategy that would become his principal method of maligning the Roosevelt Administration. As early as 1938 Harold Ickes had confided in his diary that Dies had sent to the Department of State a long list of organizations which he insisted were "agents of a foreign government." Ickes had concluded then that Dies's strategy was "to put it up to the executive departments to take action." If they failed to respond, then Dies could go to the country urging the need for greater support and appropriations for his committee as the only defense against alien subversion.

In October 1939 the committee heard the testimony of the Reverend Harry Ward, one of the social gospelers who had found twentieth century Christianity in left-wing causes and was currently president of the American League for Peace and Democracy. During the Ward hearings committee investigators broke into the files of the Washington, D.C., chapter of the league. After some bickering with committee members Dempsey and Voorhis, the committee released to the press what was either a mailing or membership list. Major newspapers across the country gave their readers 563 names of citizens who were allegedly members of the league and at the same time government employees. Since the committee had already informed the public of the Communist-front nature of the organization, it concluded that these were defiant Communists or fellow travelers who had no business in the United States Government. When errors were corrected and names of people included who had no connection with the league or any knowledge of its activities, the committee blandly replied that the error was not theirs, but the league's. When others objected that many people named had long since left the league, committee members pointed out that they had had a full year to see that their names had been expunged from the list.

Through mass exposure, the Dies Committee investigations illustrated the power of publicity in punishing American citizens who were guilty of no crime but that of holding opinions contrary to those of the committee. The committee did not have to assert that the people listed were Communists, only that the league was a Communist-front organization. With publicity, the committee applied effective "moral suasion" forcing their resignations. It became clear that Dies was not interested in the Communist menace or the Fascist menace so much as he was in what he frankly described as the "left-wingers and radicals who do not believe in our system of private enterprise." This was a sweeping category encompassing all dissenters from the mildest liberal critics of *laissez-faire* orthodoxy to genuine revolutionaries. It obliterated all distinctions in opinion and victimized citizens guilty of nothing more than an association with unpopular causes.

Committee member Dempsey denounced the release of information as a damnable un-American act. Voorhis presented an eloquent but ambivalent appraisal of the situation: He denounced the committee for publishing the names but defended the sincere, if mistaken, motives of his colleagues. He argued that there were two real dangers to American democracy—"honest to goodness" subversive activities that had to be exposed at both extremes of the political spectrum, and the kind of political demagoguery of the moderate right and left, who branded their opponents with Fascist and Communist labels. He supported continued publicity concerning true subversives and defended the committee on the whole as having conducted itself "in a proper and fair way."

The President described the committee's action as a "sordid procedure," and Dies responded by denouncing the "sordid" policy of an administration which continued to hire and harbor Communist sympathizers. It was almost like a dress rehearsal for the McCarthy era, replete with lists, names, and an increasingly vulnerable administration.

Four days following the publication of the league's list of names the *St. Louis Post Dispatch* and the *Washington Sunday Star* printed an article based on an interview with Dies in which he boasted about the accomplishments of his committee thus far. Among a long list of achievements were the following: The committee had succeeded in "paralyzing the left-wing influence in the Administration," discredited the CIO, defeated Murphy for governor of Michigan, brought about an investigation of the National Labor Relations Board, encouraged the congressional abandonment of the federal writers and theatre projects, and stimulated the movement to cut the appropriation of the La Follette Committee. Dies never repudiated this article and later repeated most of the claims.

The last controversial event of the committee's activities in 1939 was the publication of J. B. Matthews's report on the Communist domination of the consumer movement. Matthews had been an executive official of Consumer's Research until its staff went on strike in 1935, when he abruptly lost his taste for Socialist militancy. Bent on personal revenge against his former associates, he founded the rival Consumer's Union. Matthews, now working with business interests, warned the country that many consumer organizations were determined to undermine the noble services of American advertising and manufacturing in order to support the Communist critique of decadent capitalism. Apart from fulfilling Matthews's vendetta against his former associates the report served to further Dies's growing political ambitions by encouraging the support of businessmen delighted with any attack on the consumer movement.

The Matthews report, released under the imprint of the committee, had never been discussed by its members. There had been no hearings, no witnesses called, and no vote taken. Matthews had simply aired his antagonism, courtesy of the official facilities of the committee.

It is astonishing that after a detailed account of such scurrilous violations of judicious procedure an historian of the committee, August R. Ogden, could still find praise for the "uniformly high plane" of the committee's performance during its second year. The conduct of the hearings had improved and now compared "favorably with the average run of investigations and exhibit[ed] only the faults common to this method of legislative procedure."

This tolerance reflected the apologetics of the time. With the exception of the leftist critique, no act of the committee seemed so nefarious as to suggest that the committee should be abolished. Walter Lippmann's appraisal of January 11, 1940, is a masterpiece of rhetorical ambivalence. The committee, he observed, was not "really a legislative committee at all." It was, on the contrary, a "committee of public safety" designed to repress activities condemned by the majority of the people, but which "are in themselves either not unlawful, or even if they were . . . could not be dealt with by the ordinary procedure of the law." In short, the Dies Committee, Lippmann conceded, was nothing more than a form of "official" vigilantism. Since its members operated in the absence of much needed legislation, they were, by necessity, often "lawless in spirit and disorderly in their methods."

But Lippmann was quick to insist that "only the very innocent and self-deluding have any doubt that the Dies Committee have been attacking a formidable evil in modern society. The menace is real. It is not imaginary," he warned. This posed the "ancient moral question of whether the end justifies the means." It was clear that Lippmann felt the seriousness of the problem simply had to be met and, while he went on almost routinely to indict the methods of the committee for their flagrant violations of "American morality," he conceded that the end, "which is to protect the American system," was being maintained by means which, "if used for some other end would be deplored by everyone . . . except . . . the revolutionists Mr. Dies is stalking."

According to Lippmann, the committee could not be abolished because the end did justify the means; it needed only to be reformed. He suggested the idea of adding "one or two learned lawyers" to the committee who "would make it their business to reform the procedure." He advocated a larger appropriation to insure the hiring of competent investigators so that the committee would cease to rely upon "dubious informers and crackpots who always gather about an inquiry of this sort."

This argument was repeated in one way or another by liberal and conservative politicians and commentators, and it has remained the basis for many subsequent evaluations of the committee. It goes a long way toward explaining how a committee whose means were its ends became an integral part of the American political process for the next three decades. It remains one of the curiosities of historical analysis that Lippmann's article was cited years later as "the soundest criticism . . . voiced at the time."

By late November 1939, Dies was preparing for the renewal debate coming up in January. A Gallup poll published in mid-December indicated strong popular support, but within the committee there was a deepening factional struggle. Voorhis, Dempsey, and Joseph E. Casey, a New Deal Democrat from Massachusetts who replaced Healey, were still furious over the publication of the ALPF list and the discovery that Dies and Matthews had already drafted the second annual report without consulting them. Stunned by the belligerent flamboyance of the report, largely the work of Matthews, they threatened to destroy the bipartisan image of the committee by issuing a minority report. Dies, ill and apparently fearful that a break in the ranks of House support was a possibility, agreed to support a new report prepared by Voorhis and unanimously signed by the other members.

The second annual report of the committee was published on January 3, 1940. It was described by the *New York Times* as an "astonishingly able and balanced document . . . a model of sound democratic reasoning." Even some of the committee's most persistent critics found it a judicious statement on the problem of subversive activities and the achievements of the committee in combating these forces. Others on the left, while conceding the change in tone, suspected that it was designed to weaken the resolve of the opposition.

The report was a classic liberal defense of the need for the committee. It began with the observation that the preservation of constitutional liberties and an adjustment of the nation's economic life were the two major problems facing America. It then offered a more precise definition of un-American activities, describing them as the work of organizations or groups "subsidized, directed or controlled by a foreign government" for the purpose of changing the American form of government in accordance with the "wishes of a foreign government." While it still left plenty of latitude for a broad interpretation, it was an improvement on the vague religiosity of earlier definitions.

The report outlined a solid case against the Communist party, U.S.A., proving that it was simply a branch of the Comintern, and associated with eleven front organizations serving Soviet propaganda interests. Noticeably lacking was a mention of the American Civil Liberties Union which Dies and Matthews had repeatedly charged with Communist infiltration.

In a section devoted to Communist influence in the union movement the report asserted that an overwhelming majority of CIO members and officers were neither Communists nor sympathizers and that at most the leadership of ten or twelve unions out of forty-eight were "more than tinged with Communism." But there was also encouraging evidence that the "leadership" of the CIO was making every effort to purge all Communist influence.

In marked contrast to the hysterical tone of its previous reports, the committee now argued that neither Communist nor Fascist organizations constituted much in the way of a direct threat to American institutions. The real danger was the possibility that totalitarian groups through deception might persuade a substantial number of citizens that their only defense lay in some form of violence against their opponents.

In its conclusion the committee listed the conviction of Earl Browder for traveling on a forged passport and the conviction of Fritz Kuhn for the mishandling of Bund funds among its achievements. However, in both cases, federal and state law enforcement agencies had begun investigations before the committee had held hearings, and it is dubious that the committee played any substantial role in their arrests and convictions. Defenders of congressional committees invariably make these kinds of claims, but Telford Taylor has observed that few congressional investigations have ever turned up evidence contributing to criminal prosecution that was not well known and acted upon by state and federal agencies.

Equal space in the report was given to summaries of Communist and Fascist propaganda, suggesting that a broad American consensus believed it was faced with a threat equal from the left as from the right. This illusion of balance, used to refute the charge that the committee's primary purpose was to harass the left, distorted the real political struggle of the 1930s, however. That conflict was not so much a confrontation between political extremists and the center as it was between the forces of reform and the defenders of the status quo. And it was not a struggle between equals. It is difficult to equate the power and influence of reform and leftist movements, even during this so called "red decade," with that of the conservative institutional forces opposed to fundamental changes in the American system. Surely the CIO, supported by the militant activism of many Communists and encouraged by members of the New Deal Administration, never had the strength of America's corporate hierarchy. It is unlikely that the liberal and leftist press had anything comparable to the power, influence, and circulation of the nation's conservative newspapers. The allegedly dangerous and subversive front organizations like the League for Peace and Freedom or the American Student Union, both weakened, had nowhere near the influence of the patriotic organizations—the veterans' associations, the Chambers of Commerce, the National Association of Manufacturers, or even the American Medical Association. Too often commentators, embroiled in what Telford Taylor calls the "Cold Civil War," have attributed far too much influence to the power of militant reform in this decade. Thus, even Voorhis's widely praised report hardly informed the people of the real issues at hand.

Once again, their report formed the basis for the defense of the committee's renewal during the debate in January 1940. That debate received a charge when Congressman Frank E. Hook, an ardent New Dealer from Michigan, fell victim to a clever hoax perpetrated by conservative supporters of the committee. Hook rose dramatically to offer documented evidence linking Dies with William Dudley Pelley of the anti-Semitic "Silver Shirts." The evidence consisted of an exchange of correspondence between Pelley and David Mayne, another official of the Silver Shirts, and confirmed charges made repeatedly by the radical press. However, within a week the letters proved to be forgeries sold to Gardiner Jackson, an agent of liberal opponents of the committee. The letters had then been turned over to Congress-man Hook, who had been, in the words of Mayne, "played for a sucker." Hook was forced to make a humiliating apology to the entire House, which exonerated Dies from any connection with the extreme right. However, the leftist press, which had taken the bait, continued to make the charge, claiming that the hoax failed to repudiate other solid evidence of Dies's warm associations with right-wing extremist organizations.

With the exception of this bizarre incident, in itself revealing of the atmosphere surrounding the committee's activities, the debate over renewal had become little more than a formality. Defenders championed the committee as the lone bulwark against all threats to the American way of life. Opponents damned it as an un-American violation of unpopular opinion. Representatives of labor remained silent, hoping that the committee would leave them alone. Liberal congressmen feared for their careers if they participated in an attack on Dies or the committee, but of course, Voorhis and Coffee played their standard roles; they continued to rebuke the committee for its conduct in certain particulars while eloquently insisting on the necessity for its continued existence. There was the usual talk of reform of committee procedure, but it was nothing more than talk. The committee had its own procedure.

The vote, 344 to 23, was another triumph for Dies. Voorhis's reasoned and moderate report had weakened what at one point looked like a faintly promising attack on the committee. Crawford, in the *Nation*, described the vote as Dies 344, Decency 23. Opponents of the committee feared that a vote against the committee would be widely interpreted as a vote for communism.

Dies started off the new year by announcing that there were seven million aliens in American industry who deserved serious investigation and exposure; Communist subversion in Hollywood was rampant; and there was a far flung Soviet secret police operation in the United States. It soon became apparent that his real attention this year was directed to middle-rung Communist party functionaries who, he announced, would be subpoenaed and requested to supply names, under threat of congressional contempt citations.

In March and April 1940 committee investigators, with the aid of local law officers, raided several party headquarters in various cities and absconded with party records. A federal judge in Pennsylvania, George A. Welsh, ordered the arrest of the raiders and enjoined Dies not to make use of the stolen documents, and in May the judge ruled the raid an illegal violation of the Fourteenth Amendment. Communists were an unpopular minority, but their rights had been violated, rights, the judge declared, that are sacred to all Americans regardless of their political persuasions. Dies, in response, fumed over the state of a society that would extend fundamental rights to "agents of a foreign dictator."

Apparently the documents proved worthless because the committee, when it did subpoena a number of Communists to demand membership lists and the names of friends and associates, for the first time, was defied by the Communists, who refused to answer questions. The committee, they charged, was establishing an illegal black list, their questions were prompted by the unlawful seizure of private property, and, more to the point, the committee was invading personal privacy by seeking information irrelevant to its stated investigative purpose.

Sol Cohn, the attorney for one of the witnesses, cited *Sinclair* v. *United States* (1929) as a defense of his client's right to refuse to answer questions regarding the Communist affiliations of members of his family. The limits of congressional inquiry had been raised in *McGrain* v. *Daugherty* as early as 1927, when the Court upheld the right of congressional investigations to demand information for the purpose of legislating, but also asserted that a witness "rightfully may refuse to answer questions . . . not relevant to the matter under inquiry." The *Sinclair* case was an elaboration on the *McGrain* case. The Court issued a ringing defense of civil liberties when it asserted in the majority decision that it had always been recognized that fewer rights were of greater importance than exemption from unauthorized, arbitrary, or unreasonable disclosures, in respect of "the citizens' personal and private affairs."

The committee's counsel insisted, however, that the only established grounds for refusal to respond to questions was "self-incrimination" under the Fifth Amendment. The committee preferred that plea because of the automatic inference of guilt it carried with it, the inference obviously serving the committee's purposes.

Dies did manage to have a number of witnesses cited for contempt, but only a few were ever convicted, and they received suspended sentences. The process involved court litigation and did not serve the publicity aims of the committee. Silent witnesses seldom produced headlines.

The first half of 1940 was chaotic, with the committee's seizure of worthless Communist records, hostile and unresponsive witnesses, and a rebuke by the courts for high-handed and illegal activities. In addition, the world's attention had become rooted on the German *blitzkrieg* of the low countries in May. The latter event gave strength to Dies's warnings against the threat of a fifth column and his case was further aided when the Smith Alien Registration Act was passed in July, making it a crime to "teach and advocate the overthrow of the United States Government by force and violence." There were only four votes against that measure, further evidence of the solid ground upon which Dies was now working.

Dies naturally understood these events as support for the committee's work and requested additional funds, which he received in September ($35,000). Dies was riding high; the committee had become synonymous with his name. It became the rule to conduct one-man hearings out of which information was released to the press. He, or one of his colleagues, seemed to be everywhere, holding closed meetings and releasing sensational disclosures concerning sabotage and fifth column conspiracies.

Dies had promised not to conduct hearings during the presidential election campaign in 1940, but on the eve of the election his first book, *The Trojan Horse in America*, was published. It proved to be little more than a lengthy polemic indicting the Administration: Public officials had deliberately harbored Communists; the President, Ickes, Wallace, Perkins, and countless lesser figures had served the evil designs of the "Trojan horse." Stalin, he charged, had "baited his hook with a 'progressive worm,'" and the New Deal suckers had "swallowed the bait—hook, line, and sinker." Mrs. Roosevelt had proved to be "one of the most valuable assets of the Trojan horse" because she had addressed countless subversive organizations, giving them prestige and respectability.

With Roosevelt's reelection in November 1940, Dies believed it was essential to transform the committee from a congressional investigative unit into a law enforcement body coequal with the Department of Justice and the Federal Bureau of Investigation. Such a grandiose ambition was sure to promote a direct confrontation with both and it was not long in coming.

Dies charged that the FBI's methods of fighting sabotage were not sufficient to cope with the present menacing situation. In October he claimed to have a list of over 300,000 active fifth columnists employed by the government, or by defense industries under contract to the government. He threatened to publish the list if the Administration did not initiate a more aggressive policy of screening suspected subversives.

On November 20, 1940, Dies's challenge to the Executive, the Department of Justice, and the FBI came to a head. The committee released a special report, the "White Paper," on alleged Nazi espionage and sabotage activities. Advertised weeks in advance, it proved to be an anticlimax; the information was widely known. The *Times* remarked that the report seemed to expose the "little schemes of little men" whose techniques hardly justified the extravagant claims made by the committee's chairman.

Two days after the publication of the White Paper Attorney General Robert H. Jackson publicly accused Dies and his committee of interfering with the work of the FBI. Jackson lectured the committee on the distinction between the responsibilities of an investigative committee and those of a law enforcement agency, a distinction which Dies was bent on ignoring. He charged that the publicity of the Dies Committee had jeopardized the department's attempt at apprehension and prosecution in several cases.

Jackson's criticism of the committee was a shrewd ploy not only because it pitted Dies against J. Edgar Hoover, but in choosing to fight over Nazis rather than Communists, the Administration also shifted the battlefield away from Dies's familiar stamping grounds. In late November the committee balanced its "White Paper" with the "Red Book" on Communist plans for sabotaging American industry. This was followed by a report from Hoover refuting Dies's claims to having exposed an extensive sabotage network in America. Hoover, while conceding the good work of the committee, insisted that it should not set itself up in competition with the FBI, thereby endangering the bureau's ongoing work.

Dies was aware that there was no political advantage in a dispute with Hoover. He requested a meeting with the President to work out a means of cooperation between his committee and the Executive departments. Roosevelt agreed, but pointed out that the administration of justice was an Executive responsibility and that "hasty seizure of evidence" and "premature disclosure of facts" were injurious to the Administration's pursuit of real subversives.

Dies met with the President on November 29. His account of the meeting suggests that Roosevelt lightheartedly belittled Dies's crusade. He reported later that the President had jocularly boasted that some of his "best friends were Communists." However, if Roosevelt treated Dies lightheartedly before the public, it is clear that he continued to view the chairman and his committee as a powerful threat that must be handled with kid gloves. Roosevelt supported a firm agreement among the committee, the Department of Justice, and the FBI. The committee agreed to cease publication of information until it had been cleared by the Department of Justice, which checked to see that it did not interfere with secret investigations which might lead to prosecution. The Department of Justice agreed to furnish the committee with all of its information on cases which it felt could not be successfully prosecuted in a court of law.

The effect of this conciliation was to enhance the committee's reputation as an integral branch of the law enforcement apparatus. In addition it amounted to an official recognition and a sanction of the committee's tactic of punishing people by proscriptive publicity, even if their actions were not unlawful. Roosevelt belittled Dies publicly, but the Administration accepted the committee and its methods as an established part of the system.

The committee's third annual report to Congress, published on January 3, 1942, defended the committee's existence by claiming to have been the "decisive force" in shaping the attitudes of the American people toward fifth column activity. The committee's work, it boasted, had been in the form of "public education," the importance of which could not be exaggerated. It noted that not a single country overrun by Hitler had had the protection of a similar committee preceding its downfall.

For the first time the annual report offered recommendations for legislation. The list was a veritable grab bag of restrictive prohibitions necessary to protect the nation. The committee called for the deportation of alien spies and saboteurs and all aliens who advocated "any basic change in the form of our government." (This supported Dies's assertion that attacks on capitalism were inherently un-American.) It insisted that the government withdraw all financial aid to educational institutions that permitted advocates of communism to remain on the faculty. It called for legislation barring immigration from countries refusing to accept the return of deported nationals. It called for new postal restrictions against "totalitarian propaganda," and asked for an extension of the statutory period during which citizenship might be revoked.

As a parting shot the committee closed its report with a hint as to its next major challenge to the Administration. It recommended that it become official policy to deny employment in the government or in national defense to any "person who has been and is now active in any political organizations found to be under the control and guidance of a foreign government." Since the committee would make that determination, it was clear that Dies intended to mount a legislative assault on the Executive by dictating his selection of Executive personnel. It was also, indirectly, an attack on the judiciary because the committee would be free to determine guilt outside of due process of law and, by mobilizing public opinion, they could punish the accused. This technique of exposure would become one of the most effective strategies of the committee in later years. Jerry Voorhis signed this report, objecting only to the proposed withdrawal of federal funds to educational institutions charged with harboring Communist faculty members. He felt such legislation would be impossible to administer fairly, but Voorhis's complaint was hardly a ringing defense of civil liberties.

The subsequent debate over renewal was a simple matter for the committee. Even Representative Coffee abandoned the opposition. Indeed, he had run for reelection in 1940 proudly endorsing the Dies Committee. Congressman Sabath, usually a critic, lavishly praised the committee's work when he reported the resolution for extension out of the Rules Committee. Only the hapless Samuel Dickstein and the eternally belligerent Vito Marcantonio vigorously fought against renewal. When Dickstein charged that Fascists had a key to the back door of the committee, the House, spurred on by Mississippi's John Rankin, ordered Dickstein's remark expunged from the record. Rankin made it clear that Dickstein did not speak for "the old line Americans." The vote was 354 to 6 and the committee was awarded its highest appropriation—$150,000.

The activities of the committee after 1941 are difficult to trace because it had become a one-man investigation that seldom held public hearings; Dies had transformed the committee into a one-man "denunciatory agency." From the summer of 1940 to the end of his tenure as chairman in 1944 Dies never appeared at a public hearing. His activities and those of most of the committee's members were reduced to speeches, articles, and the constant barrage of press releases informing the people of the committee's constant vigilance against subversion.

The German invasion of the Soviet Union on June 22, 1941, hardly served the interests of Chairman Dies, however. Once again the Communists' policy reversed itself and they presented themselves as comrades-in-arms against the Fascist menace. Although Dies never gave up the battle, he was driven to despair at the sight of Communists and their sympathizers masquerading as ardent patriots supporting the war effort. But, as the Administration mobilized for war, the Executive bureaucracy expanded and it hired men and women whose names were found in Dr. Matthews's encyclopedic files as members or supporters of suspicious organizations operating in the thirties.

Periodically, Dies released lists of names and renewed his demand that the Administration dismiss all persons remotely associated with alleged front organizations. Leon Henderson, head of the Office of Price Administration, was charged with membership in the Friends of Spanish Democracy. Robert Brady, Henderson's head consultant, had written a book critical of capitalism and was accused of being a Socialist and a destroyer of the church. Goodwin Watson, a broadcast analyst for the FCC, had been associated with a number of front organizations indicted by the committee and had supported Vito Marcantonio, a brazen and defiant fellow traveler who never lost an opportunity to denounce and ridicule Dies and his committee. Invariably, these charges were made without committee hearings or consultations. In fact, Voorhis and other members learned of these official findings in their daily papers.

When James L. Fly, chairman of the FCC, defended Watson and released a story revealing that Congressman Dies was repeatedly praised for his attack on to an FCC appropriation bill stipulating that Watson's salary be withheld. Malcolm Cowley, a former popular front literary critic, resigned his position as an analyst for the Office of Facts and Figures after Dies charged him with connections to seventy-two front organizations.

In March 1942 Dies accused Vice President Wallace of shoddy administration of the Board of Economic Warfare. Dies charged that thirty-five officials on the board had front affiliations, and, despite Wallace's outrage, he promised to see that the FBI checked all of the names on the list.

As ridiculous as Dies's activities appear, he was having a genuine impact on administrative policy. In the spring of 1941 Congress appropriated $100,000 to enable a willing Department of Justice to investigate federal employees accused by Dies. Attorney General Francis Biddle received a list of

1,121 names of suspects to investigate and indict if the sedition charges proved true. Biddle was under pressure from the President to follow through quickly in order to placate Dies's adherents. In September 1942 Biddle announced the results of his investigation. Only two persons were discharged as a result of information gathered by the Dies Committee, but Biddle took the occasion to censure the reckless methods of the committee. A large proportion of the complaints, he charged, were unfounded and never should have been submitted in the first place. He denounced the inquisitorial behavior of the committee for having sapped the time and energy of FBI investigators. Dies responded by accusing Biddle of hamstringing the FBI and insisting that the committee should see the reports, not the department heads.

In January 1943 when the committee published its fourth annual report, Voorhis refused to sign it, submitting a minority report critical of the unilateral action of the chairman. Dies's report was the product of no hearings and had been presented to committee members for signature on a "take it or leave it basis." Voorhis's complaint was of the chairman's autocratic conduct. He continued to insist that the committee, with proper leadership, could serve a useful purpose by stiffening American resistance to Nazi propaganda. When Voorhis finally resigned from the committee in 1943, he admitted that his efforts to reform the committee had been "one hundred per cent unsuccessful" and arrived at the "novel" notion that the committee had become "more and more a political instrument of definite conservative bias" and less and less a "dignified, important and effective congressional committee." Many observers might have wondered when it had ever served in a dignified manner.

Dies cared little about this dissent for he had discovered the old congressional weapon, the power of the purse. The attachment of riders to appropriation bills, insisting that suspected employees found guilty by verdict of the committee, i.e., Martin Dies, be dismissed or the department be denied its appropriation became a potent tool. This was perhaps the boldest attack on the Executive branch during the entire history of the committee.

On February 1, 1943, Dies rose in the House to defend himself against repeated charges that he was aiding the Axis powers by his unrelenting attacks on the Administration. The wartime alliance with the Soviet Union had made him and his committee vulnerable to criticism for hindering the war effort. In the course of his defense he came up with another list of names; this time it was thirty-nine government employees who were, according to Dies, irresponsible, unrepresentative, radical, and crackpots. He threatened the Administration: "If you do not get rid of these people, we will refuse to appropriate money for their salaries." It was no idle threat. The House, in the Goodwin Watson affair, had excluded his salary from an FCC appropriation, but the Senate had killed the bill.

The House, intent on pursuing the Dies strategy, created on February 9 a special subcommittee of the Committee on Appropriations to review the charges. It was an extraordinary situation. Dies would be the prosecuting agent, the new House committee would serve as a jury, and the whole House would constitute "the Lord's High Executioners." The obvious encroachments on the prerogatives of the Executive branch were ignored. Although the subcommittee dismissed the charges against most of the thirty-nine suspects, it did vote, after a heated debate, to demand that three be denied salaries before their respective departments received appropriations. The three victims were Goodwin Watson, William E. Dodd, jr., also of the FCC, and Robert Morss Lovett, formerly an eminent professor of English at the University of Chicago, a veteran of popular front causes, and presently the government secretary to the Virgin Islands. A House vote of 317 to 62 was unanimously rejected by the Senate, but during ensuing weeks Senate opposition weakened as the departments became pressed to meet their financial obligations.

The Administration and even conservative supporters of the Dies Committee denounced the act as a modern bill of attainder. The Administration kept the accused at work, but they were deprived of their salaries. Finally, the Supreme Court, in *Lovett* v. *United States*, rebuked the House for its illegal action. Justice Black, speaking for the majority, reminded the Congress that "when the Bill of Rights were written, our ancestors had ample reason to know that legislative trials and punishments were too dangerous to liberty to exist in the nation of free men they envisioned. And so they proscribed bills of attainder."

The last significant public hearings of the Dies Committee came in June and July of 1943 and, fittingly, were related to one of the most shoddy episodes in American history. In 1942 the Roosevelt Administration, bending before the hysteria following the attack on Pearl Harbor, inaugurated the evacuation of all persons of Japanese ancestry, citizens and aliens alike, from the West Coast. Hundreds of thousands of Japanese were transported to "relocation centers" under "protective custody," that is to say, concentration camps situated in the mountain and desert regions of Arizona and Wyoming. The reason for this flagrant violation of justice—military necessity.

There were other forces at work. For nearly fifty years prejudice against the Japanese had been prevalent on the coast. Nativist and racist sentiment was supported by hard economic interests. The efficient and hard-working Japanese farmers posed a constant threat of competition to Western growers and producers. Such organizations as the Sons of the Golden West and Legionnaires allied with the Chambers of Commerce and growers associations to pressure West Coast politicians to support evacuation. Among those supporting this movement was the attorney general of California, Earl Warren.

The camps were directed by the War Relocation Authority and staffed by men of good will who attempted to make the best of a bad situation. By 1943 they had mapped out a plan for the release of those evacuees whose "loyalty tests" showed they were of no danger to the nation. Those groups who had most enthusiastically championed evacuation, however, had never contemplated the return of the Japanese before the end of the war. Many had seen the program as the first step toward ultimate deportation. They immediately launched an attack on the WRA for faulty security, coddling of internees, failure to separate the loyal from the disloyal, and an ineffective Americanization program.

At this juncture the Dies Committee was called in to serve a purely political purpose. Dies had claimed shortly after Pearl Harbor that the Administration had thwarted a committee investigation of Japanese subversion by preventing the release of information that could have averted the sneak attack. The committee now leaped at the opportunity to further slander the Administration. For tactical reasons it was decided to create a subcommittee chaired by a native Californian, John Costello. Congressman Costello was a member in good standing of the nativist Sons of the Golden West, with close ties to the Los Angeles Chamber of Commerce. The old tactic of advance publicity was again employed to promote the hearings, and J. Parnell Thomas went to Los Angeles in May, a full month before the hearings were to begin. He bombarded the local press with inflammatory press releases which accommodating local editors turned into sensational headlines: *Rep. Thomas Reveals Jap Army in L.A.; Dies Prober Charges Relocation Plan is a Farce.* Thomas lamented the deplorable spectacle of "fat-waisted Japs" being released while "American boys" on Guadalcanal "were barely receiving enough food to keep alive"; but Thomas had yet to go near a relocation center. Robert Strippling, the chief investigator for the committee, authorized a statement from Washington asserting that the WRA was releasing "spies and saboteurs."

When the hearings began in early June, Costello had recruited a motley crew of nativists, Legionnaires, and a disgruntled former employee of the WRA to smear the program and its administrators. They raised the old saw, "once a Jap always a Jap," and ridiculed the notion that Orientals could ever be assimilated into a Caucasian society. These racist ruminations went unchallenged by the committee. Only Representative Herman P. Eberharter attempted to keep the hearings within the minimal bounds of judicious behavior. As was standard practice, the committee entertained accusatory witnesses before it would permit supporters of the program to rebut the charges, thus allowing the press to spread abroad the damaging testimony. Later rebuttals seldom attracted headlines.

Carey McWilliams observed that the committee conducted an inquisition rather than a hearing. It had deliberately encouraged scare stories about "dynamite caches" in the desert to inflame the local populace and to serve the racist, nativist, and economic interests determined to prevent the Japanese citizens from returning to their homes in California. It was an inexcusable performance, playing upon every tactic the committee had used throughout its career to exploit the worst instincts in the body politic and to serve the most reactionary political interests, while at the same time impugning the competence and loyalty of the Administration.

Despite the fanfare, the committee's final report was a relatively mild document calling for a more effective means of segregating the loyal from the disloyal prisoners, a more rapid Americanization program which did not bow to the ethnic eccentricities of the Japanese, and a review board that would investigate each evacuee who applied for release. Eberharter, in a minority statement, concluded that the report was marked by prejudice, and that its charges against the WRA were unsubstantiated.

It is no mitigation of the deplorable conduct of the committee to recall that many of its liberal critics supported the evacuation program. Few challenged the right of the government to imprison American citizens guilty of no crime. Thus, it is difficult to conclude that this latest travesty of the committee was the sole work of extremists. On the contrary, the conduct of the committee was simply the last episode in an act of injustice initiated and condoned by the established liberal community.

Despite the contemptuous performance of the committee, the House in January 1944 again renewed its contract and appropriated another $75,000 to facilitate its work, bringing the total appropriation to $625,000. Nevertheless, its activities and its dignity had been severely tarnished. Dies, who had abandoned public appearances before the committee, continued to use its files to launch attacks on the Administration, the labor movement, and organizations and individuals he deemed subversive. In the spring he engaged in a degrading public debate with Walter Winchell, a former ally. Winchell accused Dies, the committee, and other congressmen of hurting the war effort. So, even breast-beating patriots of Winchell's calibre came to the belated conclusion that the committee and its supporters no longer served the best interests of the nation. Dies, of course, demanded equal network time to call Winchell a liar.

By that time Martin Dies's days as chairman were numbered. He had lost a bid for a Senate seat in 1941 and faced stiff opposition for reelection in the fall of 1944. Militant labor groups in the Texas oil refineries had denounced him as a demagogue and were organizing to campaign against his reelection. Dies was tired and ill. He announced on May 12 that he would not seek reelection because he had "always had a dread of becoming a professional politician dependent upon the public" for his livelihood. One can fault his sincerity and integrity, but not his sense of humor.

Only a few weeks before the 1944 elections the committee published a report denouncing the Political Action Committee of the CIO and Dies promised to reveal more sensational documentation indicting the New Deal for disloyal collaboration with Communist forces. Dies ended his career as he had begun it, by using the committee's facilities for political purposes during an election campaign. The beneficial work of the Dies Committee was quickly recognized when Congressman Rankin, by careful political maneuvering, persuaded the House to make the Un-American Activities Committee a permanent standing committee. Even without Dies the committee would go on to bigger battles in the days ahead, until it was finally eliminated by the Ninety-Fourth Congress in January 1975.

August Ogden, author of the committee's most detailed history, leaves the reader with an ambivalent judgment about its performance. He laments that the committee failed to take advantage "of a wonderful opportunity to render real service to the country." He concludes that while the committee's work was not a total failure, it "stands in the history of the House of Representatives as an example of what an investigating committee should not be." Ogden's conclusion proceeds upon the assumption that the committee was created to render responsible service to the American people, and the evidence fails to support that notion.

If the Dies Committee and its successors were designed to serve such lofty ends, surely the House would not have appointed the likes of Fish, Dies, Thomas, Rankin, Velde, or Pool to chair such investigations. It is more reasonable to believe that the committees were designed to pander to popular fears during times of anxiety and to serve partisan political ends. Decent and responsible men were seldom persuaded to serve on these committees because they understood that the committee's conduct was rooted in the purpose for which it was created.

Too often commentators have presented the distorted notion that the liberal community constituted a united front against the committee. Evidence does not support such a self-serving interpretation. Liberals condemned the committee's questionable conduct but bowed before its political clout, justifying its continued existence. On occasion they tried to restrain the impact of the committee by supporting slightly weaker measures against the threat of subversion, as happened during the Truman Administration. At other times they tried to prove they were tougher on communism by increasing the penalties advocated by the committee, hoping to counteract the "soft on communism" charge made by their political opponents.

During the cold war the established liberal community seldom challenged the existence of the committee in any effective way. While tolerating its excesses, they shifted the blame for its existence on to rural reactionary elements in American life. When that was insufficient, they apologized for the committee's undemocratic methods by stressing the disreputable character of its victims. At times some suggested that the results of the committee's activities were not so horrendous since the targets of its wrath were kooks, Stalinist hacks, and people of no account. By denouncing the character of the victim, one could mitigate the iniquity of the committee's criminal conduct.

The basic argument which justified the committee's existence proceeded upon assumptions which, from the advantage of hindsight, seem dubious at best. It was widely accepted that the Communist menace constituted a genuine internal threat to the republic. This notion came to be held as sacred orthodoxy—to be challenged only at the price of self-incrimination. It was asserted that Communist influence and power pervaded the intellectual community, infiltrated the government, and controlled unions and the communications industry, thereby constituting a force equal to the country's established conservative institutions. This assumption appears more and more to have been a form of self-delusion. By such rationalizations the liberal community helped to inhibit sincere dissent and genuine reform, which is the lifeblood of a democratic society.

But self-delusion lived on. In 1953, after Dies had returned to the House, a Senate subcommittee investigating possible ways of reforming the conduct of congressional inquiries called on Dies for his expertise. He advised the senators: "Primarily, if you get a good chairman and a good committee you will have a good investigation. Outside of that all you need is a few general rules to see that the witness and the public get a fair break."

OPENING DEBATE OVER HOUSE RESOLUTION TO ESTABLISH UN-AMERICAN ACTIVITIES COMMITTEE MAY 26, 1938

Congressional Record, 75th Congress, 3rd Session, 7568–70.

The Clerk read the resolution, as follows:

House Resolution 282

Resolved, That the Speaker of the House of Representatives be, and he is hereby, authorized to appoint a special committee to be composed of seven members for the purpose of conducting an investigation of (1) the extent, character, and objects of un-American propaganda activities in the United States, (2) the diffusion within the United States of subversive and un-American propaganda that is instigated from foreign countries or of a domestic origin and attacks the principle of the form of government as guaranteed by our Constitution, and (3) all other questions in relation thereto that would aid Congress in any necessary remedial legislation.

That said special committee, or any subcommittee thereof, is hereby authorized to sit and act during the present Congress at such times and places within the United States, whether or not the House is sitting, has recessed, or has adjourned, to hold such hearings, to require the attendance of such witnesses and the production of such books, papers, and documents, by subpena or otherwise, and to take such testimony as it deems necessary. Subpenas shall be issued under the signature of the chairman and shall be served by any person designated by him. The chairman of the committee or any member thereof may administer oaths to witnesses. Every person who, having been summoned as a witness by authority of said committee, or any subcommittee thereof, willfully makes default, or who, having appeared, refuses to answer any question pertinent to the investigation heretofore authorized, shall be held to the penalties provided by section 102 of the Revised Statutes of the United States (U.S.C., title 2, sec. 192).

Mr. Dies. . . . Mr. Speaker, this resolution, as it shows on its face, is for the purpose of investigating un-American activities.

I desire to make it plain in the beginning of my remarks, Mr. Speaker, that this investigation is not directed at any race, and that the impression which has been created in some quarters that this investigation is directed at the German-American people is unfounded. I would not have anything to do with any investigation that sought to cast an aspersion upon the German-Americans of this country. I know of no more loyal citizens than the majority of German-Americans in this Nation. My own mother is of German descent. I desire to refute some of the unfounded charges that have been made to the effect that this investigation is aimed in that direction. This investigation is not directed at any race, for we all live in America, peoples of all races and of all creeds. While we may have our differences with regard to economic questions or methods that men use to achieve certain objectives, it seems to me that certainly all Americans of every political faith can agree upon those inherent and fundamental rights that distinguish this country from all foreign nations. I have often believed that the distinction between the American form of government and the forms of government which prevail in many European countries is the conception we have in America that we derive fundamental and inherent rights not from society, not from governments, but from Almighty God, and having derived those fundamental rights from God, no man or no majority of men can deprive us of the inherent right to worship God according to the dictates of our conscience or to speak our opinions and our convictions as we feel them. I can assure the House here and now that if I have anything to do with this investigation it will in no sense be an effort to abridge the undisputed right of every citizen in the United States to express his honest convictions and enjoy freedom of speech.

Mr. Warren. Mr. Speaker, will the gentleman yield?

Mr. Dies. I yield to the gentleman from North Carolina.

Mr. Warren. The wording of this resolution is most unusual. I do not recall a similar case. This resolution seeks to set up an investigating committee, but nowhere in the resolution do you provide for a report to Congress. This means that the lid is off. It would mean that you could come back here next January and ask for permission to file a report or to extend the inquiry over a period of years, if you cared to do so. I believe 7 months is long enough to investigate any subject on earth. The gentleman controls the previous question, and I am wondering if he would accept an amendment for a new section providing that the committee shall file its report to the House on January 3, 1939, or may file its report earlier, in case the House is not in session, with the Speaker of the House for printing as a public document. I may say this has nothing to do with whether or not I support the resolution. All I am asking is, Will the gentleman permit the filing of the report?

Mr. Dies. I may say to the gentleman it was my understanding and belief that any committee created by this Congress would terminate at the expiration of the Congress. I see no objection to the amendment, as far as I am concerned.

Mr. Warren. I hope the gentleman will accept the amendment. If not, we will just have to vote down the previous question so we can amend the resolution.

Mr. Dies. I see no objection to the acceptance of the amendment. It is perfectly all right with me, because I believe the committee ought to conclude its hearings by that date.

Mr. Maverick. Mr. Speaker, will the gentleman yield?

Mr. Dies. I yield.

Mr. Maverick. We do not want to be barred from offering other amendments, and if the resolution is to be open for one amendment, it ought to be opened for all amendments; and if the gentleman agrees that it may be opened for one amendment, would the gentleman agree to open it for all other amendments?

Mr. Dies. That is not a matter for me to agree to. That is a matter for the action of the House.

Mr. O'Connell of Montana. Mr. Speaker, will the gentleman yield?

Mr. Dies. I yield.

Mr. O'Connell of Montana. I have an amendment with respect to the Jersey City situation which I think ought to go in the resolution. [Laughter.]

Mr. Dies. As I was saying, Mr. Speaker, when I was interrupted, I have absolutely no patience with any effort in this country to abridge the rights of speech. I opposed a movement in my country which spread from one section to the other, and which was aimed at religious freedom and directed at certain races, and any effort in this country to create prejudice toward certain people on account of the fact that they happen to belong to certain racial groups is unworthy of the fundamental ideals of Americanism, as I understand them.

Now, I know the argument will be used, What is the value of an investigation? I have a mass of information that has been supplied to me that is shocking, information which shows the extent of the Nazi and Communist movements in the United States. I am not one of those who are inclined to be alarmists. I am not inclined to look under every bed for a Communist, but I can say to this House that there is in my possession a mass of information showing the establishment and operation of some 32 Nazi camps in the United States, that all of these camps have been paid for, that they claim a total membership of 480,000, that they assemble in these camps, and I have seen photographs that have been furnished from various sources showing the fact that in these camps men are marching and saluting the swastika, if that is the proper word for it. Not only is this true, but I have information in my posssession that certain individuals and groups in America have contributed funds for the purpose of encouraging the Fascist or Nazi movement in this country, and may I say in that connection that so far as I am concerned I regard communism and nazi-ism and facism as having one underlying principle—dictatorship —the theory that government should have the right to control the lives, the fortunes, the happiness, the beliefs, and every detail of the life of the human being, and that man is a pawn of the government, rather than the American conception that government is created for the benefit of mankind.

Mr. Johnson of Minnesota. Mr. Speaker, will the gentleman yield?

Mr. Dies. I yield.

Mr. Johnson of Minnesota. If the gentleman says he has positive information that there are 31 bund camps now organized in the United States, why does he not, as a member of the Rules Committee, see that the bill (H.R. 10003), the Voorhis bill, to forbid private military companies and organizations is passed by the House, rather than go on a fishing expedition all over the country when you have the information now?

Mr. Dies. I will say to the gentleman that I never knew there was such a bill until this morning, when it was shown to me, I believe, by the gentleman from Texas [Mr. Maverick].

Mr. Johnson of Minnesota. Will not the gentleman admit that when he knows the condition that exists in respect to Nazi activities in the United

States, that the thing to do is not to waste 7 months on that committee, but to pass an act immediately?

Mr. Dies. That is easy to talk about, but the most difficult matter in the world is to deal with this subject. In the first place neither the gentleman, nor I, nor any Member of this Congress would sanction any legislation that might have as its effect the abridgment of the right of free speech in America. I care not what the gentleman's views are, I care not what his economic or religious or political views are, and I respect every man in this House who believes in his views, but I do believe that every man's right to express those views should be safeguarded.

Mr. Harlan. Mr. Speaker, will the gentleman yield?

Mr. Dies. Yes.

Mr. Harlan. Is it not true also that there is a matter involved here that is a great deal more comprehensive than mere military drilling, in that it is to the interest of the people of the United States to find where these funds are coming from?

Mr. Dies. That is right.

Mr. Harlan. And what other activities they are engaged in, and who is the leader, and the general program of undermining our institutions. They would not be covered by a merely military organization.

Mr. Dies. The gentleman is absolutely correct.

The Speaker. The gentleman from Texas has used 10 minutes.

Mr. Dies. Mr. Speaker, I yield myself 5 minutes more. In connection with some of the information that has come to my attention. I have seen affidavits signed by supposedly reputable people, charging that in one of the principal Nazi camps only recently a speech was made by one member of this bund advocating the assassination of the President of the United States. In addition to that, on the other hand, I hold here a letter which was written to my colleague, the distinguished chairman of the Committee on Rules, the gentleman from New York [Mr. O'Connor]. I cannot read the name of the man who signed the letter, because I have been asked not to do that, but the charge is made in the letter that in the city of New York the Communists are preparing to picket the home of the gentleman from New York [Mr. O'Connor]—and I do not deny the right of men to picket industries where there is a labor dispute—and to harass and humiliate and to use every effort and purpose to bring about the political destruction of this Member of Congress.

Mr. Crawford. Mr. Speaker, will the gentleman yield?

Mr. Dies. Yes.

Mr. Crawford. The gentleman made such a clear-cut statement, with which I agree, a moment ago with reference to communistic activities, that I ask him whether he heard Browder's radio address last night, beginning at 10:30 and ending at 10:40 on this subject, and I suggest if the gentleman did not hear it, that he move heaven and earth to get a copy of it, because it was a hair-raiser.

Mr. Dies. I thank the gentleman.

Mr. Keller. Mr. Speaker, will the gentleman yield?

Mr. Dies. Yes.

Mr. Keller. How many committees or commissions have already been appointed by this House for a similar purpose?

Mr. Dies. There was one committee appointed some years ago headed by our distinguished colleague the gentleman from Massachusetts [Mr. McCormack] that performed a very useful function. Let me say to the gentleman that I believe all depends upon the way the committee is handled. I can conceive that a committee constituted or composed of men whose object it is to gain publicity, or whose object it is to arouse hatred against some race or creed, or to do things of that sort, might do more harm than good. On the other hand, investigations have a useful purpose. The other body creates committees constantly to investigate. I am not in a position to say whether we can legislate effectively in reference to this matter, but I do know that exposure in a democracy of subversive activities is the most effective weapon that we have in our possession. Always we must keep in mind that in any legislative attempt to prevent un-American activities, we might jeopardize fundamental rights far more important than the objective we seek, but when these activities are exposed, when the light of day is brought to bear upon them, we can trust public sentiment in this country to do the rest.

Mr. Keller. Was there not another committee headed by the gentleman from New York [Mr. Fish]?

Mr. Dies. I do not know about Mr. Fish's committee.

Mr. Keller. And did they not get about all the publicity possible before this country?

Mr. Dies. I know the gentleman from Illinois is a liberal-minded gentleman, but let me say to the gentleman that some of these groups, especially the Communists, are very strong in their advocacy of freedom of speech, and people throughout that great area are mere pawns in the hands of unscrupulous bureaucrats.

Mr. Keller. What was the recommendation of the McCormack committee and what have we done about it?

Mr. Dies. Oh, I have only a few minutes, and the gentleman must not ask me to go into that.

Mr. Cochran. Mr. Speaker, will the gentleman yield?

Mr. Dies. Yes.

Mr. Cochran. If this resolution passes, naturally the gentleman, or whoever is made chairman, will be appealing for an appropriation. Can the gentleman give us any idea as to the cost of this investigation?

Mr. Dies. Let me say to the gentleman that so far as I am concerned, I am opposed to lavish expenditure of money on these investigations. I shall oppose any effort to create an army of useless agents running around over the country, and I shall be opposed to any effort to pad any rolls, or to put any political friends on the pay roll, and so far as I am concerned, if the House votes this investigation I shall insist upon an economical investigation with sufficient funds to do the work.

As to the amount involved, I do not know; that is a matter that the Committee on Accounts will go into. I am sure it will be handled properly.

Mr. Cochran. As a member of the committee which will be required to vote this money—and, of course, the committee will consider it mandatory to vote the money if this resolution passes—I feel that the House should know now what sort of request is going to be made, how much money is going to be asked to carry out this resolution.

[Here the gavel fell.]

Mr. Dies. Mr. Speaker, I yield myself 5 additional minutes.

As I said a moment ago, the gentleman's committee will consider the matter, and that committee has shown a disposition in the past to be very careful about appropriating large sums.

Mr. Cochran. There is no limitation whatsoever in the resolution pending. There is nothing in the world to prevent the gentleman from Texas or anyone else offering an amendment to a resolution appropriating a certain amount to double, triple, or even quadruple the amount recommended by the committee.

Mr. Dies. I assure my distinguished friend from Missouri that that will not be done.

Mr. Cochran. I think the House should have some information as to whether it will cost $5,000, $10,000, $20,000, or $25,000.

Mr. Dies. I do not know. What does the gentleman think about it?

Mr. Cochran. I do not think we should spend more than $20,000 on the investigation. I would like an expression from the gentleman on that.

Mr. Dies. As I said, it is rather difficult for me to give an expression, because I do not know.

Mr. Cochran. The gentleman will have an idea just the minute this resolution passes.

Mr. Stefan. Mr. Speaker, will the gentleman yield?

Mr. Dies. I yield.

Mr. Stefan. I may say to the gentleman from Texas that while in his opening remarks he expressed deep sympathy to the patriotic German-Americans and that he is opposed to anything which would inflame Americans toward one particular race, I call the gentleman's attention to the fact that this country has been flooded with publicity regarding subversive activities. The gentleman's committee's investigation is going to be followed with a tremendous amount of publicity which I fear may inflame the American people against innocent but honest and good patriotic German-Americans. I caution the gentleman to use every effort in his power, if he is going to be chairman of this committee, to oppose anything that might be done in his committee to put publicity out into our country which will inflame one race against another.

Mr. Dies. I am in entire sympathy with the gentleman's statement. As I said a moment ago, there is no one who detests more sincerely or more deeply than I any attempt to inflame the American people against any group within our boundaries.

Mr. Stefan. I hope the gentleman will carry that attitude throughout the investigation.

Mr. Dies.   .   .   .   This resolution has been endorsed by the American Legion. I ask unanimous consent to incorporate the resolution of endorsement at this point in the Record.

The Speaker. Without objection, it is so ordered.

There was no objection.

OPENING STATEMENT OF MARTIN DIES
AUGUST 12, 1938

U.S. House of Representatives, 75th Congress, 3rd Session, Hearings before a Special Committee on Un-American Activities, Vol. 1, 1–3.

The Chairman. The committee will come to order.

I understand that it is customary for the chairman to make a preliminary statement before the committee begins to take evidence. The Chair will make his statement very brief.

This special committee was created by a resolution of the House of Representatives, House Resolution 282, for the purpose of conducting an investigation of the extent, character, and objects of un-American propaganda activities in the United States; the diffusion within the United States of subversive and un-American propaganda that is instigated from foreign countries or of domestic origin and attacks the principle of the form of government as guaranteed by our Constitution; and, all other questions in relation thereto that would aid Congress in any necessary remedial legislation. . . .

The Chair wishes to reiterate what he has stated many times—namely, that this committee is determined to conduct its investigation upon a dignified plane and to adopt and maintain throughout the course of the hearings a judicial attitude. The committee has no preconceived views of what the truth is respecting the subject matter of this inquiry. Its sole purpose is to discover the truth and report it as it is, with such recommendations, if any, as to legislation on these subjects as the situation may require and as the duty of Congress to the American people may demand.

We shall be fair and impartial at all times and treat every witness with fairness and courtesy. We shall expect every witness to treat us in the same way. This committee will not permit any "character assassination" or any "smearing" of innocent people. We wish to caution witnesses that reckless charges must not be made against any individual or organization.

The Chair wishes to make it plain that this committee is not "after anyone." All that we are concerned with is the ascertainment of the truth, whatever it is.

It is the hope of the committee that we can admit the public to the hearings. However, in the interest of a dignified and judicial hearing we cannot tolerate any demonstration, disorder, or interruption on the part of those who are the guests of the committee. If any such demonstration, disorder, or interruption occurs, the person or persons responsible for it will be immediately ejected by the police and denied further admittance.

The Chair wishes to emphasize that the committee is more concerned with facts than with opinions, and with specific proof than with generalities. Opinions, conclusions, and generalities have no probative force in any court of justice and they cannot be made the basis of any findings on the part of this committeee. It is the Chair's opinion that the usefulness or value of any investigation is measured by the fairness and impartiality of the committee conducting the investigation. Neither the public nor Congress will have any confidence in the findings of a committee which adopts a partisan or preconceived attitude. Statements and charges unsupported by facts have no evidentiary value and only tend to confuse the issue. It is easy to "smear" someone's name or reputation by unsupported charges or an unjustified attack, but it is difficult to repair the damage that has been done. As I previously stated, this committee is determined to be fair and just to everyone, and when any individual or organization is involved in any charge or attack made in the course of the hearings, that individual or organization will be accorded an opportunity to refute such charge or attack.

In investigating un-American activities it must be borne in mind that because we do not agree with opinions or philosophies of others does not necessarily make such opinions or philosophies un-American. The most common practice engaged in by some people is to brand their opponents with names when they are unable to refute their arguments with facts and logic. Therefore, we find a few people of conservative thought who are inclined to brand every liberal viewpoint as communistic. Likewise, we find some so-called liberals who stigmatize every conservative idea fascistic. The utmost care, therefore, must be observed to distinguish clearly between what is obviously un-American and what is no more or less than an honest difference of opinion with respect to some economic, political, or social question.

TESTIMONY OF WALTER STEELE
AUGUST 16, 1938

U.S. House of Representatives, 75th Congress, 3rd Session, Hearings before a Special Committee on Un-American Activities, Vol. 1, 424–28.

. . . Mr. Steel [National Republic Chairman of the American coalition Committee on National Security]. Now, while I am giving you later on the entire source of the birth of the American League, which you seem to be interested in, I am showing you who the Communists were who set it up and created it; but in addition to that, here is their own report—

Mr. Mason. A report from what organization?

Mr. Steele. The American League for Peace and Democracy. Now, they name in here their committees. They do not hesitate to name Earl Browder and the rest of the Communists in here.

Mr. Mason. In their committees, in their reports, they name these outstanding Communists as part of their organization?

Mr. Steele. In their report on their committees, they have, for instance, Earl Browder. This is a report of their last congress held in Pittsburgh,

November 26 to 28, 1937. This is not my printing. This is their printing. Their committee on resolutions, for instance, is headed by Elinor Brannon and has Earl Browder on it, who is the ranking member of it.

Mr. Mason. Would you say, sir, that a Government official who acts as a member of the League for Peace and Democracy would be entirely innocent of the fact that that organization is one of the organizations in the united front?

Mr. Steele. Well, I could not answer that.

Mr. Healey. Mr. Chairman, of course, that is a matter of opinion.

Mr. Steele. That would be a supposition on my part.

Mr. Healey. I do not think that has a great deal of value in this committee.

Mr. Steele. I could not say that.

The Chairman. You say here that a whispering campaign was launched against the banks during the period of the instability and uncertainty, and that this caused the bank runs in our country several years ago; that these people were instructed by Russia to prevent the restabilization of capitalism by keeping up a constant turmoil and strife. What evidence do you have on that point, for instance?

Mr. Steele. Here is a report by a party whom I will name to the committee, and give the address, who was in the bank-run organization in Flint, Mich.

Mr. Thomas. What do you mean by the bank-run organization?

Mr. Steele. They had that set up to create whispering campaigns all over the country.

Mr. Thomas. You mean a committee of the Communist Party?

Mr. Steele. That is right.

Mr. Healey. Against the banks?

Mr. Steele. Yes. It was during the period when the banks were in a critical state generally.

The Chairman. And this is this man's report of their organized effort?

Mr. Steele. That is right, of what he did, as well as what the rest of them did.

Mr. Healey. He is a Communist?

Mr. Steele. Yes.

Mr. Thomas. A member of the Communist Party?

Mr. Steele. He was.

Mr. Thomas. He was a member of the Communist Party?

Mr. Steele. Yes.

The Chairman. And he can testify directly as to these facts?

Mr. Steele. Yes. I will give the committee his name.

The Chairman. And that will support his testimony and sustain this statement in reference to a deliberate effort on their part to cause runs on the banks.

Mr. Steele. That is right.

The Chairman. Have you, in connection with these organizations that you say are fronts of the Communist Party, information to give the committee, such as the officers, and so forth?

Mr. Steele. Yes; I have these officers listed.

The Chairman. And the names of those who are known Communists?

Mr. Steele. No; I have not pointed that out, but I think in many instances I could tell you who they are.

The Chairman. Do you know, as a matter of fact, that in these organizations many of the officers and directors are known Communists?

Mr. Steele. Yes. For instance, I have given you a list of all the Communist Party leaders; that is, the national leaders and all the State leaders. I have already given you that. That information has been taken from their documents. Many of the same names will appear in the leadership of these other organizations which I am to submit.

We obtain that information in various ways. For instance, we obtain it from their own reports; in many instances from their own letterheads. But always from their own material, you understand. In other words, we will not call a person a Communist unless we can prove it by themselves, by the Communists themselves. We are not "red baiters."

The Chairman. I wonder if you could do this: Can you submit to this committee all of this evidence, to afford us an opportunity to go into it and then build up, as I have indicated, by direct testimony of witnesses, various phases of this work? I think that is the satisfactory and the best way to do it.

Mr. Steele. I agree with you, that is right.

The Chairman. Because otherwise it amounts to no more or less than hearsay testimony.

Mr. Steele. That is right.

The Chairman. Testimony of a kind which would not be accepted in court. I would suggest, Mr. Steele, if it is agreeable with you, that you submit all of this evidence that you have to the committee and let us work on it in connection with our investigation, and then, at a later time, when we have the opportunity, we will call for additional explanations that we may need and that you may have.

Mr. Steele. I would like very much to get what we have in the record, because we feel it is of value to the people throughout the country, especially the members of our organizations.

The Chairman. It furnishes a background.

Mr. Steele. Yes.

The Chairman. It gives the committee a picture of the situation. That is its prime value to the committee, to give the committee a picture of the movement and the historical significance of it, as well as a general outline.

Mr. Steele. Yes. I appreciate that you want it for a different purpose than why we want it. For instance, we want it so that we can inform the 6,000,000 members of these organizations, so they will not knowingly join any of these movements.

Mr. Healey. On that point, you contend that while many of these organizations have laudatory and legitimate purposes and objectives to attain, nevertheless these known Communists are attempting to use these organizations to further their own purpose?

Mr. Steele. That is right.

Mr. Healey. Namely, to bring about a revolution and establish a Soviet republic here in the United States?

Mr. Steele. That is right.

Mr. Healey. And they are only apparently working to achieve the known purposes of the organization?

Mr. Steele. That is right.

Mr. Healey. But in reality are trying to achieve communistic purposes?

Mr. Steele. That is right.

Mr. Healey. Is that your contention?

Mr. Steele. Yes, sir.

Mr. Mason. And, sir, would you not also contend that they are not only attempting to do it but they are actually doing it, so far as using these organizations is concerned?

Mr. Steele. Yes; I think that is true.

Mr. Healey. But many members of the organization are unaware of it?

Mr. Steele. Oh, yes.

Mr. Healey. Unaware of the fact that these people are merely using the organizations to attain their objectives.

Mr. Steele. I think you are right about that; yes, sir. But the purpose we have in mind in coming before you is not only to help your committee realize that, but to prepare, in a way, a document the wide circulation of which will later prevent others from making that mistake.

The Chairman. Of course, what we are primarily interested in is to get definite proof.

Mr. Steele. Yes.

The Chairman. We hear from representatives of organizations and they make such statements. Before we predicate any finding upon any statement, we want to know definitely that it is a proven fact. Otherwise, it would not be fair. It would not be fair for us to indulge in presumptions, merely imagine something. Someone charges an organization is a Communist organization. It is easy to make a general charge.

Mr. Steele. Surely.

The Chairman. But if we are going to be fair about this and conduct this investigation in a judicial way, we want definite proof. Otherwise you could cause a lot of injury. The same is true with reference to individuals. It is true that, over a long period of time beginning so far as my own recollection goes 10 years ago, when a man had certain views with reference to labor, other people would brand him as a Communist, using that as a general term. He would be a Communist because he had certain advanced views with regard to some social or economic problem. We have got to bear in mind always to make a clear distinction between those who use the term recklessly and those who have definite facts as to whether or not the man is a Communist.

Mr. Steele. That is right.

The Chairman. We all disagree with reference to many social and economic problems. But that does not make a man a Communist.

Mr. Steele. No.

The Chairman. Our committee, I am sure, will agree with me that our purpose is to go very carefully into these matters and establish the truth by competent testimony.

Mr. Steele. That is what we have tried to do, to stick to the facts. You cannot deny that the officers and the committeemen of these organizations are aware of what the organization is doing. Some of the membership, perhaps, but hardly the officers. If you belong to an organization and are an officer of that organization, you know pretty well what that organization stands for and what it is aiming to do.

The Chairman. That is true. Yet we do know of organizations—I know of one in particular—in which there are some good people who were led into it by false representations. I know of one in particular. I know the people personally. They got out when they found what the real objective was. I did not get into the organization. I was against it from the beginning. But there were those who were led into the organization believing that it was a good thing.

So when a sweeping declaration is made, we must be very careful to know that there are facts back of what is charged.

Mr. Steele. But you cannot get away from facts like these, unless they have misstated them themselves.

Mr. Mason. May I also make this suggestion? In connection with this witness's statement, the two purposes that actuate you in appearing before this committee are, one, to give us facts and proof of these certain things and to enlighten the public so as to protect the innocent members of these organizations and prospective members in the future.

Mr. Steele. You are right.

Mr. Mason. And you will accomplish the two things only if you produce facts and proof?

Mr. Steele. That is right. In other words, I disagree with some of that the more you speak the more you advertise these people. If the people do not know what is happening in this country, they are more apt to follow them than if they know what they are. That is my opinion about it. That is what we are trying to do here, to enlighten both the committee and the people.

The Chairman. Mr. Steele, we have a number of witnesses under subpena who are being brought here. We do not know just how many will be here tomorrow or whether they will not reach here until Thursday morning. We believe there will be some witnesses here tomorrow. You see, we have to pay their mileage and a per diem and we are anxious to finish with their testimony as quickly as possible. You could come here nevertheless, if you wish.

Mr. Steele. I want it understood that I should like to go very deeply into the Nazi and Fascist questions before I am through. I want to expose those, with photographs and testimony, and so forth.

TESTIMONY OF MISS SALLIE SAUNDERS
AUGUST 20, 1938

U.S. House of Representatives, 75th Congress, 3rd Session, Hearings before a Special Committee on Un-American Activities, Vol. 1, 857–60.

The Chairman. Before you testify, Miss Saunders, let me say we are not interested, as a committee, in the racial question, except only insofar as it forms a vital part of communistic teachings, practices, and doctrines. Later on it will be developed that Communists are working among the Negroes in certain sections of the country, and that their appeal is racial equality.

Miss Saunders. That is right.

The Chairman. Only as we link that in with Communist practices, doctrines, and methods—only to that extent, we are concerned with your testimony.

Miss Saunders. And only to that extent can I testify.

The Chairman. In your testimony I will ask certain questions, because we do not want to do anything that will stir up or increase any hatreds.

Miss Saunders. It has much to do with racial hatred, if it is explained clearly.

The Chairman. That is true. I will ask some questions, and you will limit yourself to answering the questions. This is a delicate matter, and I would like for you to answer the questions rather than make voluntary statements or get into a discussion of the fifteenth amendment, or something else than we have before us. I will ask certain pertinent questions, and I know you will cooperate in giving the material facts we want to develop by your testimony.

Miss Saunders. I will be glad to, Congressman Dies, but I feel very strongly about the fifteenth amendment.

The Chairman. But this is not the place nor the time to discuss the fifteenth amendment.

Miss Saunders. That is exactly the point the Communists are making.

The Chairman. We will reach that. Where were you from originally?

Miss Saunders. Originally from Vienna, Austria.

The Chairman. Are you a citizen of the United States?

Miss Saunders. Yes, sir; since 1920. I believe my father took out citizenship papers then.

The Chairman. How long have you been in New York?

Miss Saunders. Since 1930.

The Chairman. You have been employed by the Federal Theater Project; is that true?

Miss Saunders. Yes, sir.

The Chairman. When were you first employed?

Miss Saunders. March 3, 1936.

The Chairman. How long did you remain with the project?

Miss Saunders. Until October 8, 1937, when I took 90 days' leave of absence for private industry. I returned to the project January 7, 1938.

The Chairman. You are on the project now?

Miss Saunders. Yes, sir.

The Chairman. What is the work that you are doing now?

Miss Saunders. As an actress.

The Chairman. Have you seen with your eyes evidence of communistic or subversive activities on this particular project?

Miss Saunders. I can only say that literature has been sent around to me personally.

The Chairman. Do you know that Communist literature has been distributed on the premises?

Miss Saunders. Surely.

The Chairman. On one occasion you were called on the telephone. Will you go into the details of that without going too much into it?

Miss Saunders. Yes, sir. On Decoration Day I received a phone call from Mr. Van Cleave.

The Chairman. This year?

Miss Saunders. Yes, sir; and he asked me for a date. I lived at the Fraternity Club, and there are a great many men there. I thought it was someone I met at the Fraternity Club. I said, "Mr. Van Cleave, I do not remember you; when did I meet you?" He said, "I was the gentleman who sketched you in Sing for Your Supper." I said, "There were 289 people down there, and I do not know more than 25 of them." He said, "I am the fellow who was sketching you." The day before I had noticed a Negro making a sketch of me as I was dancing. He shoved the sketch in my face. I did not know his name, and did not know anything about him. All I knew was that a Negro had sketched me. I signed out and left the building. At first I thought it was someone trying to play a joke on me, and I became very angry about it and asked how he got my telephone number. He said that he took it from a petition blank or a petition to President Roosevelt, which we all signed regarding the $1,000 pay cut. He took my name and address from that petition.

Mr. Mosier. How did he know that was your address?

Miss Saunders. He was one of the committee passing it around.

The Chairman. After that time when he asked permission to make a date with you, did you report it to the supervisor?

Miss Saunders. I reported it to Mr. Hecht.

The Chairman. What did Mr. Hecht say to you?

Miss Saunders. He said, "Sallie, I am surprised at you. He has just as much right to life, liberty, and pursuit of happiness as you have." He said, "It is in the Constitution." I said, "Mr. Hecht, that happens to be in the preamble to the Constitution."

The Chairman. Let us not go into that. We know there is feeling in the matter, and we have to be very cautious about race feeling. You reported it to him, and he advised you, in effect, that he was in favor of social equality?

Miss Saunders. According to the Constitution, and there was some press clipping about equal social rights.

The Chairman. Did you report it to anyone else?

Miss Saunders. I talked it over with Miss Coonan, and she was appalled. I requested for an immediate transfer, which was granted. I then reported the matter through a personal friend to Senator Pat Harrison.

The Chairman. Who was Mr. Hecht?

Miss. Saunders. Mr. Hecht is in Sing for Your Supper.

The Chairman. An employee of the Federal project?

Miss Saunders. Yes, sir.

The Chairman. I think that is far enough. Is he connected with the Workers Alliance?

Miss Saunders. Mr. Hecht is of split nationality. He has a card in every organization which has the most power at the moment.

Mr. Mosier. What is his full name?

Miss Saunders. Harold Hecht.

The Chairman. Did you report it to Trudy Goodrich?

Miss Saunders. She is a secretary of a Workers Alliance division, and she came to me of her own accord. She said she felt very sorry that I felt that way about it, because she personally encouraged Negro attention on all occasions and went out with them or with any Negro who asked her to.

Mr. Starnes. Did she say that it was the policy of the Workers Alliance to do that?

Miss Saunders. She did not say that; but she is a representative of that party, and they hobnob indiscriminantly with them, throwing parties with them right and left.

Mr. Starnes. Is that a part of the Communist program?

Miss Saunders. Yes, sir; social equality and race merging.

The Chairman. I think that is all. I thank you for your testimony.

NEW YORK TIMES REPORT ON ROOSEVELT CRITIQUE OF COMMITTEE OCTOBER 25, 1938

At his press conference this afternoon one of the newspaper men present asked the President the following question:

"Mr. President, are you conerned with the testimony that has been given before the Dies committee, particularly in the case of Governor Murphy of Michigan? Testimony last week charged him with treasonable activities in the settlement of the sit-down strikes in Michigan two years ago."

The President:

"Yes, I certainly am concerned with that kind of testimony. I would like to say something about it but I think it probably would be better if I wrote something out instead of trying to talk extemporaneously."

Later the President dictated the following statement for the press:

"I was very much disturbed. I was disturbed, not because of the absurdly false charges made by a coterie of disgruntled Republican officeholders against a profoundly religious, able and law-abiding Governor, but because a Congressional committee charged with the responsibility of investigating un-American activities should have permitted itself to be used in a flagrantly unfair and un-American attempt to influence an election.

"At this hearing the Dies committee made no effort to get at the truth, either by calling for facts to support mere personal opinion or by allowing facts and personal opinion on the other side.

"On the threshold of a vitally important Gubernatorial election, they permitted a disgruntled Republican judge, a discharged Republican city manager and a couple of officious police officers to make lurid charges against Governor Frank Murphy, without attempting to elicit from them facts as to their undeniable bias and their charges and without attempting to obtain from the Governor or, for that matter, from any responsible motor manufacturer, their version of the events.

"Governor Murphy's painstaking and statesmanlike efforts to bring about a settlement of the sit-down strikes and to avert bloodshed and riot were not shrouded in secrecy. Every important move he made was communicated to the motor manufacturers and the union leaders affected, and was reported fully in the daily press. I received almost daily reports on the situation from the Governor.

"Governor Murphy never said a word in condonation of the sit-down strike or any illegal practice. But the Governor was informed by responsible officials of the National Guard that any attempt on the part of the National Guard forcibly to eject the sit-down strikers at Flint would result in bloodshed and riot. Knowing these facts the Governor labored in the open, in the American way, to bring about a prompt settlement of the labor trouble without resort to force.

"Governor Murphy always insisted that the lawful order of the court must be obeyed. But knowing that negotiations for settlement were proceeding and that precipitous efforts to enforce the court order would result in violence which would disrupt peaceful negotiations, he requested the Sheriff to postpone the enforcement of the court order over the week-end. For that act a few petty politicians accuse him of treason; for that act every peace-loving American should praise him.

"By Wednesday of the week following Governor Murphy's request for a temporary postponement of the enforcement of the court order, the strike —which was probably the most alarming strike which ever occurred in this country—was brought to an end without the loss of a single human life. That was a great achievement of a great American.

Cites Auto Men's Praise

"Governor Frank Murphy's great accomplishment elicited the commendation of all the important motor manufacturers involved, of Mr. Sloan and Mr. Knudsen of General Motors, of Mr. Chrysler of Chrysler Motors, and of the Fisher brothers of the Fisher Body Corporation, of Mr. Barrett of Hudson Motors and of Mr. Graham of Graham Motors.

"In handling the dangerous labor situation in Michigan in the dark days of 1937, Governor Murphy, as a true American, was concerned not only with the letter but the spirit of the law. Governor Murphy accordingly strove, and strove successfully, to effectuate a settlement not by force but by reason—a settlement which would satisfy not merely the letter of the law, but the community's sense of right and of justice.

"Most fair-minded Americans hope that the committee will abandon the practice of merely providing a forum to those who for political purposes, or otherwise, seek headlines which they could not otherwise obtain. Mere opinion evidence has been barred in court since the American system of legislative and judicial procedure was started.

"Three weeks ago the civilized world was threatened by the immediate outbreak of a world war. Cool heads pleaded for the continuance of negotiations. People may properly differ as to the result of such negotiations but the fact remains that bloodshed was averted.

"In the Winter of 1937 Governor Murphy was confronted with the same kind of a situation on a smaller scale. He knew that if negotiations were broken off bloodshed was inevitable. He worked successfully for the continuation of the negotiations. As a result of his fine leadership, there is no doubt that hundreds and even thousands of human lives were saved. That is the American ways of doing things."

DIES RESPONSE TO ROOSEVELT STATEMENT OCTOBER 26, 1938

U.S. House of Representatives, 75th Congress, 3rd Session, Hearings before a Special Committee on Un-American Activities, Vol. 3, 2019–20.

The Chairman. Before we proceed with the testimony this morning, the Chair wishes to read into the record the following statement:

After reading the President's statement, I desire to make a more detailed reply. As I stated last night, I have known from the beginning that neither the President nor his advisers favored this investigation. The Departments not only refused to comply with the request of Congress that our committee be supplied with adequate personnel, but they have thrown every obstacle in the way of a successful investigation. This campaign was aided by Members of the Cabinet. The Shirley Temple fabrication was conceived by certain radical writers whose sympathies for Soviet Russia are matters of common knowledge. Immediately, and as if by prearrangement, Secretary Perkins and Secretary Ickes repeated this crude and silly fabrication, thus hoping to lend the color of truth and respectability. Even the President was induced to refer to the Shirley Temple fabrication in one of his press conferences. When this campaign utterly failed and recoiled upon the heads of those who conceived and engineered it, the next move was to exert every conceivable pressure to stifle this investigation. When this likewise failed, as a last desperate move, the President was induced to permit the prestige of his great office to be used for the purpose of discrediting the investigation.

That the President has been wholly misinformed is obvious from his statement. Of course, the President did not hear the testimony and has not read the record. He is evidently relying upon reports that have reached him from prejudiced sources. Had he read the testimony he would have found that Democrats testified the same as Republicans, and that some of the testimony came from former officials of the U.A.W. He would have also found that the principal witness was Lieutenant Mulbar, chief of the State police, who holds a civil-service position and is absolutely nonpartisan. In this connection I wish to say that our investigator spent 2 months in Detroit with instructions to conduct a fearless investigation. As a result of 2 months' work on the ground, he subpenaed these witnesses independent of the question of politics, so that when the President states that the committee made no effort to get at the truth he is obviously misinformed. He is likewise misinformed when he says that we "did not call for facts to support personal opinion." The evidence which we received would be acceptable in any court, and if the President has any doubt about this I suggest that he appoint some experienced lawyer and I will do likewise. Then the two can appoint a third and together they can examine all of the evidence with reference to the Michigan situation and then report to the country as to whether or not this evidence was competent and admissible.

I have stated many times that every individual or organization against whom a charge or attack was made during the course of these hearings had a standing invitation to appear before the committee to disprove such charge or attack. In adopting this policy, the committee has shown itself absolutely fair.

The testimony with reference to the Michigan situation showed very clearly that the well-known Communists instigated and engineered the sit-down strike and the so-called Lansing holiday, when a mob of 15,000 people barricaded the State capitol and 2,000 of them, many of whom were armed with clubs, were ordered to march on the university and to bring part of it back with them. The evidence shows that the State police sat helplessly by for lack of instructions from the Governor in the face of open rebellion, while the Governor looked down upon the scene from a window in the capitol. It cannot be disputed that misdemeanors and felonies were committed on that disgraceful day under the very eyes of the Governor, who had sworn to uphold law and order. If open and undisguised rebellion is to be countenanced in the name of political expediency, then constitutional democracy will perish in America.

The people of this country are entitled to know the truth. As chairman of this committee, I have felt it my duty to conduct a fearless investigation, regardless of political expediency. Under my conception of public duty, it would have been wrong to shield Governor Murphy simply because he was a Democrat and a strong friend of the President. While I deeply regret the President's bitter attack on a congressional committee of an independent department of the Government, and while I regret that the President did not read the testimony before issuing this statement, I wish to make it plain that I shall continue to do my duty undeterred and unafraid. . . .

TESTIMONY OF MRS. HALLIE FLANAGAN
DECEMBER 6, 1938

U.S. House of Representatives, 75th Congress, 3rd Session, Hearings before a Special Committee on Un-American Activities, Vol. 4, 2856–85.

. . . Mrs. Flanagan. One of the great problems is that, while in the other art projects it is possible to establish them in every State in the Union, which we would also like to do here, it is not possible with us, because, while an artist can paint or a musician play or a writer write if there is no audience or only one or two people involved, we cannot set up theaters except in States where there are 25 or more people of satisfactory type on the relief rolls.

So that one of our problems is this centralization of the theater industry. Our big centers are New York, Los Angeles, and Chicago; and we, as much as possible, want to tour people out from those regions and want to set up small projects in the country.

However, it is very difficult to tour, because, as you know, it is very expensive business. We are touring a great deal out of the regional centers, covering the rural areas in Michigan and Illinois and so on. But we have not gone as extensively into touring as we would like to do.

May I go on for just a minute?

The Chairman. Where have your audiences been? What localities have you played mostly?

Mrs. Flanagan. We have played to, I think I am safe in saying, the widest variety of American audiences that any theater has ever played before.

The Chairman. In what localities, Mrs. Flanagan?

Mrs. Flanagan. The chief localities are, first, New York City, and next Los Angeles and Chicago, because that is where the greatest unemployment exists. They are the three largest centers. But if you are speaking now of the audiences themselves—I want to pick up that point, if you don't mind—

The Chairman. It is quite all right, but I merely want to know the places where you have played. But if you want to discuss audiences, it is all right.

Mrs. Flanagan. I do want to discuss them.

The Chairman. That is all right.

Mrs. Flanagan. Because that allegation was made here by one of your witnesses, which I would not like to remain in the minds of any of you around this table, because my impression is that you are trying to get at all the facts.

The Chairman. That is correct. And if this statement is untrue, we want you to refute it.

Mrs. Flanagan. I want to quote from her allegation. Miss Huffman says: "They couldn't get any audiences for anything except communistic plays."

Now, gentlemen, I absolutely deny that allegation, and I have here the proof that that is an absolutely false statement.

We have, as sponsoring bodies for the Federal Theater, lists of organizations covering 20 pages of this brief, which I intend to write into the record; and I will summarize them for you, if you like.

Two hundred and sixty-three social clubs and organizations, 264 welfare and civic organizations, 271 educational organizations, 95 religious organizations, 91 organizations from business industries, 16 mass organizations, 66 trade-unions, 62 professional unions, 17 consumers unions, 25 fraternal unions, and 15 political organizations.

Note, gentlemen, that every religious shade is covered and every political affiliation and every type of educational and civic body in the support of our theater. It is the widest and most American base that any theater has ever built upon; and I do request you not only to write that into the record, but to read the list of public schools and universities and churches and the civic and social groups that are supporting this Federal Theater.

Mr. Starnes. I want to quote finally from your article, "A Theater is Born," on page 915 of the Theater Arts Monthly, edition of November 1931.

Mrs. Flanagan. Is this the same article, Mr. Starnes?

Mr. Starnes. Yes. I want to quote this. This will be the final quotation. It is after you discuss the type of plays that are being used in this country at that particular time.

Mrs. Flanagan. By workers' unions.

Mr. Starnes. For instance they deal with unemployment and labor laws and those sort of things. This is your language that I am quoting.

> The power of these theaters springing up everywhere through-out the country lies in the fact that they know what they want. Their purpose—restricted, some will call it, though it is open to question whether any theater which attempts to create a class culture can be called restricted—is clear. This is important because there are only two theaters in the country today that are clear as to aim: one is the commercial theatre which wants to make money; the other is the workers' theater which wants to make a new social order.

> The workers' theaters are neither infirm nor divided in purpose. Unlike any art form existing in America today, the workers' theaters intend to shape the life of this country, socially, politically, and industrially. They intend to remake a social structure without the help of money—and this ambition alone invests their undertaking with a certain Marlowesque madness.

Mr. Starnes. You are quoting from this Marlowe. Is he a Communist?

Mrs. Flanagan. I am very sorry. I was quoting from Christopher Marlowe.

Mr. Starnes. Tell us who Marlowe is, so we can get the proper reference, because that is all that we want to do.

Mrs. Flanagan. Put in the record that he was the greatest dramatist in the period of Shakespeare, immediately preceding Shakespeare.

Mr. Starnes. Put that in the record, because the charge has been made that this article of yours is entirely communistic, and we want to help you.

Mrs. Flanagan. Thank you. That statement will go in the record.

Mr. Starnes. Of course, we had what some people call Communists back in the days of the Greek theater.

Mrs. Flanagan. Quite true.

Mr. Starnes. And I believe Mr. Euripedes was guilty of teaching class consciousness also, wasn't he?

Mrs. Flanagan. I believe that was alleged against all of the Greek dramatists.

Mr. Starnes. So we cannot say when it began.

Mrs. Flanagan. Wasn't it alleged also of Gibson and against practically every great dramatist?

Mr. Starnes. I think so. All right.

Now, I am quoting again:

> When we see, as we probably shall during the next year, their street plays and pageants, their performances on trucks and on

street corners, we shall doubtless find them crude, violent, child-
ish, and repetitious. Yet we must admit that here is a theater
which can afford to be supremely unconcerned with what we
think of it. It does not ask our advice, our interest, our advertising,
or our money. We need not deplore the lack of art in the workers'
theater for we shall not be invited to witness its performances. It is
only in the event of the success of its herculean aim—the reorganization of our social order—that we shall become involuntary audience.

Mrs. Flanagan. Well, you understand, Mr. Starnes, that that did not take
place, did it? The great hope of the workers' theater professionals landed
right in the lap of the United States Government; and I can again say that I
am concerned today, and have been for 3 years, with the rehabilitation of
those people.

Mr. Starnes. Of course you are, but this is what you said in this article.

If there are no communistic activities on your projects, we want to know
it. If there are, we think that that fact should be made public. And if the facts
are made public, we feel that surely you, as the directing head, will take the
necessary remedial action to rid the projects of such un-American activities.

Mrs. Flanagan. You are quite right. . . .

The Chairman. You have established the precedent of exhibiting a play
championing the cause of ownership of public utilities. You said that was
proper and you yourself thought you had a right to do that?

Mrs. Flanagan. I think so.

The Chairman. Now, what I am asking you is what would keep you or
the policy board from continuing that same type of plays so as to cover other
ranges of public ownership?

Mrs. Flanagan. Let me answer it this way: If someone came up with a
very good play proving that the private ownership of railroads was the best
possible thing, and the play was a good play, we would do it.

The Chairman. Then you would show it?

Mrs. Flanagan. Yes.

The Chairman. Then, on the other hand if the same play proved that the
public ownership of railroads was a good thing you would do it too, would
you not?

Mrs. Flanagan. Absolutely, and the test is is it a good play and within
the general range and the variety we have established.

The Chairman. And if someone came with a play showing the public
ownership of all the property in the United States, and it was a good play,
you would also exhibit that, would you not?

Mrs. Flanagan. Well, that is a very clever move on your part to maneuver me into a certain position.

The Chairman. I do not pretend to any cleverness. I would not undertake to match my cleverness with you on this subject because you are
thoroughly acquainted with it.

Mrs. Flanagan. No; I would not. We would stop with that, because
that would be recommending the overthrow of the United States Government, and I do not want that, gentlemen, whatever some of the witnesses
may have intimated.

The Chairman. In other words, you would favor doing it by degrees, but not all at once, isn't that right?

Mrs. Flanagan. Well, we probably would not agree——

The Chairman. Well, but you have said under oath the exhibition of a play championing the ownership of public utilities or railroads, if it were an entertaining play, that you would show it. You have said that yourself. Now, that is just the degree is it not?

Mrs. Flanagan. Well, it is a degree that the Congress of the United States has passed upon, isn't it?

The Chairman. Not yet; the question of public ownership of utilities, it has not passed on that.

Mrs. Flanagan. You did it one time.

The Chairman. Not that I know of.

Mrs. Flanagan. During the war.

The Chairman. Oh, well, you are going back now to emergency legislation.

Mrs. Flanagan. Of course, we have gone back into history and covered so much geographic range that perhaps I——

The Chairman. So, as I understand from your testimony, when a play is presented to you championing the public ownership of power, of railroads, if it is a good play you said you would exhibit it. Now, what I want to ask you and I want you to state is would you stop with those two forms of ownership, or would you go further and exhibit a play that would champion the cause of public ownership of other forms of private property?

Mrs. Flanagan. I can't go into these hypothetical questions. I came up here under the distinct understanding that I was to refute testimony given by witnesses before your committee. You are proposing a long series of hypothetical questions. . . .

The Chairman. You would not undertake to disprove that six of your supervisors on one project were Communists; would you?

Mrs. Flanagan. I would like to know what the names are. You mean the ones mentioned in the brief?

The Chairman. The ones in the testimony.

Mrs. Flanagan. We have every one of those cases listed here with accompanying affidavits.

The Chairman. That they are not Communists?

Mrs. Flanagan. No; on the charges.

The Chairman. Did you ever secure from any of the supervisors affidavits as to whether they were not Communists?

Mrs. Flanagan. No.

The Chairman. So you are not able to produce any evidence on the question as to whether they are not Communists?

Mrs. Flanagan. No.

The Chairman. So that it comes down to this, as a correct statement, does it not, that with reference to the plays themselves you can say unequivocally that none of them were communistic?

Mrs. Flanagan. Right.

The Chairman. That you have personal knowledge of?

Mrs. Flanagan. I do have personal knowledge of.

The Chairman. Because you have read each one of the plays, you supervised it, and so forth?

Mrs. Flanagan. Yes.

The Chairman. But outside of that you are not in a position to refute any of the testimony by any of the witnesses?

Mrs. Flanagan. Oh, yes; I am.

The Chairman. Dealing with the communistic activities charged on the project?

Mrs. Flanagan. Yes. For example, I quoted this morning Miss Huffman as saying we could not get any audiences except for communistic plays.

The Chairman. But that is not communistic activities on the project.

Mrs. Flanagan. Let us narrow it down specifically to the solicitation of funds, and the posting of notices on bulletin boards, and so forth.

The Chairman. In other words, we heard considerable testimony which forms an important part of this, that numerous people working on the project were Communists. We got that from one or two who are members of the Communist Party themselves. We got it from their own signatures, and statements that they were Communists, and received testimony that Communist literature was disseminated through the premises during project time, that they were printed on the bulletin board until this investigation began and it stopped, that meetings of the Communists units were held on project time in the premises, and other testimony.

I am just citing you some of the high lights. Now, that is the material fact involved here, as to whether that was done.

Mrs. Flanagan. May I ask is that all in the record which I have studied, or are you referring to other records?

The Chairman. I do not know what record you have studied, but that is in the record of the hearing, in all of the records.

Mrs. Flanagan. I think you must be confusing some of our testimony, because I have read it very carefully, because I have not found a single witness brought up before us that said he was a Communist.

The Chairman. Before us?

Mrs. Flanagan. Before you.

The Chairman. Well, Mr. DeSolo said he was a Communist.

Mrs. Flanagan. But he is not on the Federal Theater Project.

The Chairman. He is on the Writers Project.

Mrs. Flanagan. Yes; but not our project.

The Chairman. You are dealing with the Federal Theater Project.

Mrs. Flanagan. Because that is what I have jurisdiction over.

The Chairman. You do remember the statements with reference to dissemination of communistic literature on the premises?

Mrs. Flanagan. I would like to say something about that. I spent about half of my time the first year in the New York project, it is half of our project, and I have never seen these activities carried on. I have never seen subversive literature or communistic literature on the project bulletin boards, nor to my knowledge, have I ever known of Communist meeting being held on project property. So that, what I have to go on, is that your principal witnesses alleged that such things took place. I say I want this immediately traced and I want to find out about this. I have done that in every case.

The Chairman. What have you done?

Mrs. Flanagan. I have gone to the supervisor of the project, the administrative officer, Mr. Paul Edwards, and Mr. George Carnduff, head of the Theater Project, and asked them to trace every one of those allegations.

The Chairman. Have they done it for you?

Mrs. Flanagan. They have done it, and the affidavits are in the brief of the whole testimony that I had hoped to be allowed to read, but which, in any case, I wish to write into the record.

The Chairman. Now, they have all denied that communistic activities took place on the project as charged?

Mrs. Flanagan. Yes.

The Chairman. They did not cite a single instance where any of these things took place, did they?

Mrs. Flanagan. No.

The Chairman. So that, it was a complete denial on the part of all of the supervisors and everyone that reported to you that a single communistic activity had taken place on the premises?

Mrs. Flanagan. Yes, but this sounds, as you say it, as though 3,000 people testified. Ten people testified about some fifty other people. This is a project of 4,000 people.

The Chairman. What I am asking you is simply this, that all the reports you have——

Mrs. Flanagan (interposing). Have denied the allegation of communistic activities.

The Chairman. Denied them all?

Mrs. Flanagan. Yes.

Mr. Starnes. In view of the fact that we have testimony that Stevedore has been produced, I think that we should set out in the record here these excerpts which were referred to by the chairman a moment ago, that those excerpts should be set out in the record from Stevedore.

The Chairman. All right.

(The excerpts referred to are as follows:)

> (Page 24:) Lonnie. God damn dem, anyhow. Whey dey think I am? Do I look like some kind of animal? Do I look like somebody who'd jump over a back fence and rape a woman?
>
> (Page 29:) Walcott. You're too God damn uppity. . . . You black—— -of-a- —— you can't talk to me that way.
>
> (Page 42:) Rag Williams. Dat li'l skinny boy! Lawd, he couldn't rape nothing.
>
> Joe Crump. Why dey have to go and start dat rape stuff up again?
>
> (Page 43:) Rag Williams. He just a big hunk of horse rump, dat's
>
> Mrs. Flanagan. He turned over to me——
>
> (Page 53:) Lonnie. God damn you, let go.
>
> (Page 60:) Al. Well, I'll be God damned if you can use my car to help rape a nigger.
>
> Lem. Christ Almighty? Rape nigger.
>
> (Page 61:) Al. Well, by God some nigger raped her.

Marty. Rape, my eye.

Al. Yeah, rape. You let 'em get away with it, and no white woman will be safe on the streets anymore. Christ, if a nigger raped your woman in your back yard how would you feel if we helped him?

(Page 62:) Lem. Don't be such a God-damned fool.

Lem. Aw, for Christ's sake, Al.

Al. Yeah. Like a God-damned nigger-lover.

(Page 86:) Al. Yeah! That "red" bastard! Nigger-lover.

Mob. Let's get that bastard. Nigger-lover! Throw him out of here! God-damned nigger-lover.

(Page 90:) Mitch (looking her over leacherously). Um-m, I'll bet you're a hot mamma. Think I'm your size, brown sugar? Binnie. No. You couldn't handle me. You ain't man enough.

(Page 122:) Mitch. We'll kill every black bastard behind dat woodpile.

(Page 123:) Binnie. That red-headed——of a——, I got him!

The Chairman. Do you have any questions, Mr. Thomas?

Mr. Thomas. Just one. Mrs. Flanagan, following up Mr. Dies' questions relative to communistic activities on the project, did Paul Edwards, the administrator in New York City, tell you that there were no communistic activities on the project in New York City?

Mrs. Flanagan. No, he turned over to me a brief, part of which had been compiled on his project, that is, compiled in respect to things which he would know, and that his supervisors would know.

Mr. Thomas. In that brief did he deny that there were any communistic activities on the project in New York City?

Mrs. Flanagan. The brief does so deny, yes; point by point. Point by point it is refuted, point by point by affidavits.

Mr. Thomas. And that brief was sent to you by him and it is his statement?

Mrs. Flanagan. Not all of it, my own statement on anything relating to the plays and the chief of personnel running the project and the office, and of all charges made against me personally, I have written.

Mr. Thomas. What I am trying to find out is this: I want to know in response to your inquiry of the administrator in New York whether or not Paul Edwards admitted to you there were any communistic activities on the project in New York?

Mrs. Flanagan. He never did.

Mr. Thomas. He admitted that there were none?

Mrs. Flanagan. He turned over to me—

Mr. Thomas (interposing). He admitted that there were no communistic activities on the project in New York?

Mrs. Flanagan. He never said that there was communistic activity on the project.

The Chairman. What time is it, please?

Mr. Starnes. A quarter past one.

The Chairman. We will adjourn for 1 hour. Suppose we adjourn for an hour and then we will hear Mr. Alsberg.

Mr. Starnes. Have you finished, Mrs. Flanagan?

Mrs. Flanagan. Just a minute, gentlemen. Do I understand that this concludes my testimony?

The Chairman. We will see about it after lunch.

Mrs. Flanagan. I would like to make a final statement, if I may, Congressman Dies.

The Chairman. We will see about it after lunch.

(Thereupon, at 1:15 p.m., a recess was taken until 2:15 p.m. of the same day.)

AFTER RECESS

The committee reconvened, pursuant to the taking of recess, Hon. Martin Dies (chairman) presiding.

The Chairman. The committee will come to order. We are going to have to hurry along, because we have a number of witnesses here to be heard. We have two here from the west coast who have been waiting for 4 days, and we have the commander of the American Legion and a minister, and we have to hurry along as fast as we can. . . .

COMMITTEE DISCUSSION ON METHODS
AND RULES OF EVIDENCE
DECEMBER 14, 1938

U.S. House of Representatives, 75th Congress, 3rd Session, Hearings before a Special Committee on Un-American Activities, Vol. 4, 3060–64.

. . . Mr. Dempsey. Mr. Chairman, I would suggest, if it is proper, that any of these people who have statements to present, or who wish to get their views before this committee, be permitted to make their statement and, if in the opinion of the committee, it is a proper one, that we just incorporate it in the record, if not, that it be omitted from the record.

The Chairman. Why not permit people who want to deny, or advise people who want to deny allegations that have been made against them the same right to file statements, and give such statements to the press?

Mr. Dempsey. I think they are entitled to that right. I think that should be done, provided their statement is a proper statement.

The Chairman. That is, provided it is in answer to any charge that has been made against them.

Mr. Dempsey. Yes.

The Chairman. And incorporate that in the record?

Mr. Dempsey. I do not think, if they have not availed themselves of the opportunity to come here, that they should make charges against people who are not going to be in a position to deny the charges, but should simply make that statement in answer to statements already made.

The Chairman. What would be the objection to permitting, in absolute fairness, these people who want to do it—what is the objection to permitting them to do it? I want to make it clear there never was any request made of this committee by the Civil Liberties Union that they appear before the committee and answer any charge made against them in the course of the hearings.

Mr. Dempsey. Is that despite the statement that is made?

The Chairman. Despite the statement that is made, Mr. Clerk, is that right; is that a correct statement of the facts? I do not want incorrectly to state it.

In a speech made by me as an individual, over the radio, I made reference to the Civil Liberties Union, and they wanted to have an opportunity to deny my speech. Of course, they can deny it through the same facilities, over the air or through the press; but the statement is correct that there never has been any request by the Civil Liberties Union to appear before this committee to answer any charge made by any witness under oath, or otherwise, that involved the Civil Liberties Union. Of course, they were all made under oath.

I am sure the committee is going to be very careful, particularly when we make the report, not to base any conclusions on incomplete evidence.

But the point is, we wrote to the people, did we want to deny any charge, to send in a statement.

I think, in order to be absolutely fair about this thing, since it is manifest we cannot run here until January 3, because we have nothing to run on, unless we are prepared, as individuals, to pay these reporters for their expenses—I think it would be the fair thing to write these people and say to send in a statement in answer to any charge in this record. Of course, charges made on the air or in a speech have nothing in the world to do with this investigation. You might go out and make a statement, or I might go out and make a statement, and it would not have anything to do with the committee, but I mean in reply to some charges made in the record by some witness who has made a charge against somebody, that if he wants to deny that charge, in order to be absolutely fair and let the record show both sides, why not just write him a letter that he can answer that in a statement?

Mr. Mosier. Why not put it in affidavit form, Mr. Chairman?

Mr. Dempsey. I think that is objectionable.

Mr. Thomas. I do not think it is objectionable.

Mr. Dempsey. Let me finish.

Mr. Thomas. I thought you had finished.

Mr. Dempsey. The statements, I understand, they are going to make are coming to the committee and are to go into the record in their entirety, or after taking out such portions as might be objectionable? In other words, all the testimony of those witnesses should not go into that record—or did you mean in your report?

The Chairman. I did not.

Mr. Dempsey. All this testimony certainly is not going into the report?

The Chairman. Oh, no. Our report will be made just like any other report. The testimony in the record is not put in.

Mr. Mosier. Mr. Chairman, you are discussing now witnesses who go on the stand here and take an oath and testify before this committee, and one of them says that John Smith is a Communist, and John Smith wants to deny it, but we have not the facilities at the present time to accommodate John Smith and bring him here and put him on the stand. It seems to me that his denial, if we take it for any value at all, should be of the same grade as the testimony on the other side, which is under oath. I therefore suggest that his denial should be in affidavit form. If he does not care enough, if it is not serious enough for him to swear to an affidavit, it does not seem to me it ought to be considered seriously enough by us to receive it just in letter form.

The Chairman. Of course, the only object of the statement is to afford people an opportunity to have in this record their side of the story. But, so far as our findings are concerned——

Mr. Mosier. That has not anything to do with it. That is something else.

The Chairman. We are not going to predicate our findings on anything but the evidence.

Mr. Mosier. No.

The Chairman. I understand there are a very few who have requested an opportunity to be heard.

Mr. Dempsey. I am not speaking of the cases Mr. Mosier cited; I am speaking of cases where people come here and give you literature and say, "I believe this is a Communist organization." He does not say he knows, he says he believes. I think if a man write in and says, "I am not a Communist, insofar as I am concerned it is not a Communist organization; if it was, I would not be a member of it"—I do not think it is necessary for them to swear to it.

Mr. Thomas. But if the person who came here made his statement as a sworn statement?

Mr. Dempsey. That he believed such a thing; he did not know it, but he believed it.

Mr. Thomas. All right. He took an oath to it.

Mr. Dempsey. Yes.

Mr. Thomas. Consequently, I think anyone who was going to deny such a statement should also do it by taking an oath to an affidavit, just as Mr. Mosier says. I think if you are going to have the one under oath you should have the other.

The Chairman. I think we want the facts.

Mr. Mosier. Mr. Chairman, it only goes to the weight of the testimony, anyhow, so far as this committee is concerned.

The Chairman. Here is the point: Of course a man swearing under oath and then stating an opinion, that does not mean anything, because you could not get him for perjury.

Mr. Mosier. That is correct.

The Chairman. I mean an opinion stated under oath has no more validity than an opinion stated without an oath, because either one is opinion, except in the case of an expert.

As I say, I do not think but a very few have requested an opportunity to be heard. We have accommodated the most of them and, in accommodating

Government officials, they have put into the record a vast amount of material that is going to run up the cost tremendously. I mean the three Government officials who requested a right to be heard, have tendered large briefs and gone into the matter in detail, and for which this committee has to pay these reporters, as I understand, approximately 16 cents or 17 cents a page to transcribe this thing.

What I was thinking about is the people we have invited. Of course, we have a right to rescind that invitation, but the heads of those organizations will just have to understand that we cannot accommodate them, and the reason why we cannot do it. But as to the people who have been involved in any charge here, I think, in fairness, we ought to lean backward in order to give them an opportunity to make a statement because of the reference which has been made to them and incorporated in the record.

Mr. Dempsey. That is my opinion.

The Chairman. If someone of the witnesses on the stand swore to the fact, then ask the other one submit an affidavit.

Mr. Dempsey. My view of the difference is if this committee had confined itself to the rules of testimony that would be one thing, but we have been extremely generous in permitting people to make statements and sometimes members of the committee would ask questions which would take the witness far afield, into things we had nothing to do with, but the committee's desire to be generous to the witness has prompted them. And I quite agree with that; we cannot do anything else. But to make a man go and swear to that, I think would be unreasonable.

The Chairman. Suppose we do this: Where it is a question of evidentiary fact, as a statement of fact, if someone wants to deny it, let that denial be in the form of an affidavit.

Mr. Dempsey. Absolutely.

The Chairman. And at least such a witness has the advantage of not being subjected to cross-examination, so that he is at a great advantage over what he would be if he came here and denied it before the committee. Then we will incorporate that in the record as to each individual organization. But so far as we are concerned, we are not going to make any finding unless we have absolute proof in this record to sustain it.

Now, I want to make another statement as to the latitude this committee has granted. All that anyone need to do is to go and read the hearings of any other committee in this House, pick out any of your committees, and see the latitude that was granted in those cases. For instance, take the Monopoly Committee, which is going on right now, and see how much of that is pure opinion, and how much is just a conclusion of the witness.

Mr. Dempsey. You cannot get away from it.

The Chairman. You cannot get away from it; no; because a congressional committee is not governed by the rules of evidence, and never has been; because we are not like a court; we cannot pass judgment or sentence on anyone.

Mr. Dempsey. That is right.

The Chairman. All we can do is to undertake to report our collective action.

Mr. Dempsey. That is my point, exactly.

A man who appears here and swears "I sat in a Communist meeting with a certain man and he could not be there unless he was a Communist, and I have that knowledge," if a man wishes to deny that, he should deny it under oath.

The Chairman. That is right.

Mr. Thomas. But you are going to restrict this rebuttal, or whatever we call it, to a denial of the charges that have been made?

The Chairman. That have been made in the committee—not by a member, but in the committee by a witness.

Mr. Thomas. So that if the American Civil Liberties Union sends in a denial through their representative, they just cannot discuss every subject in the world, but they will have to confine their denial to the charges that have been made?

The Chairman. That is right, but to accord all of them a full opportunity to do it.

Now, it ought to be made clear that we undertook to get all of these people to come in here from the very beginning, repeatedly, and in spite of these invitations that have been carried over the air, that have been carried in the newspapers, carried even, in some cases, in letters, they did not see fit to come in. And now one or two of them toward the last, in the concluding days, when they read, evidently, that our money is nearly exhausted, and the committee is reaching an end, all of a sudden put up a cry, "I want to be heard." We want to be fair, because we have to be; that is our duty, to be fair, but we are now out of money and cannot continue and prolong this thing, and there is no way to do it unless we raise a contribution among ourselves to do it. So that the next best thing, and which will serve the same purpose, is to afford these people an opportunity to deny this in the way in which it is made. If it is a charge stated under oath, then let them confine their answer to the charge and swear to it in the form of an affidavit, and place it in the record. Then all sides will have a full opportunity.

I do not think anybody can take any exception to that, in view of the fact our money is gone, and now let it be thoroughly understood by these heads, and I want it to go out to the organizations, that the reason we are not carrying this through is because we cannot pay their expenses to come here, nor can we continue to run this thing and run up the bills for stenographers. And the reason we cannot is because of the financial difficulties we are facing. I want that thoroughly understood, because the statement is going to be made that we heard certain people and certain organizations, but other people and other organizations we would not hear. . . .

FIRST ANNUAL REPORT OF DIES COMMITTEE JANUARY 4, 1939

U.S. House of Representatives, 76th Congress, 1st Session, House Report No. 2, Report of the Special Committee on Un-American Activities pursuant to House Resolution 282 (75th Congress), 8–11; 118–24.

. . . The committee did not appoint any investigators until after the department heads refused to cooperate with the committee in accordance with the resolution of Congress. This is important to remember in view of the charges that have been made to the effect that the committee sought to discredit the New Deal. If the committee had ever had any such intention, it would certainly not have offered to let the New Deal appointees do the investigating.

Most of the hearings were held in the city of Washington, but subcommittee hearings were conducted in New York and Detroit. More than a hundred witnesses from various States and towns were heard by the committee and a vast quantity of documents and written and printed evidence was submitted. With the exception of a few witnesses who appeared at the request of certain national organizations, all of the witnesses who appeared before the committee were located by our investigators and subpenaed. These witnesses were furnished transportation by the committee and paid the usual fee which the law allows in such cases.

While there have been a large number of offers of financial assistance from individuals throughout the country, out of consideration of public policy, the committee has refused such offers in every case and has not accepted any contribution from any source. The contributions that were sent to the committee in the form of cash and checks were promptly returned.

We have heard over 100 witnesses from nearly every section of the country and from nearly every walk of life. We have heard from officials and members of the American Federation of Labor and the Congress for Industrial Organization. Ministers, lawyers, judges, college professors, newspaper reporters and editors, laboring people, policemen, national guardsmen, merchants, and the heads of such great organizations as the American Legion, the Veterans of Foreign Wars, the Daughters of the American Revolution, the Boy Scouts of America, and many others have appeared as sworn witnesses before our committee. Some of the witnesses have been Democrats, some Republicans; others have been Communists, Progressives, Socialists, and Farmer Laborites. We have heard from Jews and Gentiles, and from Protestants and Catholics.

We know of no committee which has heard a more representative group of American citizens than we have, although we do not assume responsibility for the credibility of every witness any more than a court. Some of the testimony may be discarded because of bias or the tendency to exaggerate. None of our findings are predicated upon such testimony or upon opinions or hearsay. We have also received a mass of documentary evidence, most of which is absolutely authentic and would be admissible in any court.

We have devoted considerable time and effort to the investigation of Nazi and Fascist activities in the United States. A large part of the $25,000 placed at our disposal has been spent to uncover Nazi and Fascist activities. We secured a mass of documentary evidence with reference to Nazi and Fascist activities and propaganda. After much difficulty we finally secured from the Department of Justice its report on Nazi activities in the United States. While there was very little in this report that we did not have, we were able to secure some leads, which we developed so that the record of hearings and this report will give the public the benefit of the combined investigation of Nazi activities conducted by our committee and by the Department of Justice.

There is one astonishing fact which we have discovered. Witnesses from widely separated areas corroborate each other, and the oral testimony of some witnesses is supported by documentary evidence which they have never seen. While Homer Martin, president of the United Automobile Workers of America, branded Ralph Knox, an official of that union, as a "screwball," when you read the testimony of both you will find that they testified to substantially the same facts and described the same situation. We further find that witnesses like Martin, Dobrzynski, Eagar, McCartney, and others who are either bona fide members or officials of the C. I. O. and, therefore, cannot be accused of being prejudiced against the C. I. O., corroborate the testimony of other witnesses.

In the beginning, the committee employed six investigators, but, due to diminishing funds, the committee was compelled to discharge three of these investigators. This left three investigators to do the work. The committee has never employed any lawyer, and most of the work has been done with a minimum of stenographic help.

While the committee has unearthed some startling facts, it has been greatly handicapped in its work, due to insufficient funds and the refusal of the heads of the respective departments to comply with the request of the House. The committee has been able to hear only a few of the numerous witnesses that can be subpenaed. In fact, the committee has only scratched the surface, and what we have already proved is merely a preface to what can be proved if we are given a fair and decent opportunity. Much of the oral testimony is supported by documentary proof. It is interesting to note that many of the facts found by the committee were also found by the United Mine Workers and Mr. John L. Lewis in 1924 when they investigated un-American activities, as will be shown by their published report which will appear in the record of our hearings.

The committee has largely confined its investigation to communism, fascism, and nazi-ism. In connection with its investigation of communism, the committee has given careful consideration to the numerous front organizations of the Communist Party which are under the control or influence of the Communist Party of the United States. The committee has also heard considerable evidence with reference to the permeation of labor unions by Communists and their seizure of strategic positions in such labor unions. In its consideration of nazi-ism and fascism the committee has heard evidence with reference to other organizations which preach and advocate racial and religious hatred.

It must be emphasized that this committee is nonpartisan. It has not been deterred by partisan or political consideration from the fearless performance of its duty and functions. The committee has felt that it is its sworn duty and solemn obligation to the people of this country to focus the spotlight of publicity upon every individual and organization engaged in subversive activities regardless of politics or partisanship.

WHAT ARE UN-AMERICAN ACTIVITIES?

(A) Americanism Defined

In order to determine what activities and propaganda are un-American, we must first define Americanism. No scientific definition will be attempted, but we will undertake to set forth in simple and understandable language what some of the chief principles of Americanism are. In the first place, Americanism is the recognition of the truth that the inherent and fundamental rights of man are derived from God and not from governments, societies, dictators, kings, or majorities. This basic principle of Americanism is expressed in the Declaration of Independence, where our immortal forefathers said that all men are created equal and that they are endowed by their Creator with certain inalienable rights, chief among which are life, liberty, and the pursuit of happiness. From this declaration and the well-established interpretations that have been put upon it from the beginning of the Republic down to the present moment, it is clear that Americanism recognizes the existence of a God and the all-important fact that the fundamental rights of man are derived from God and not from any other source. Among these inalienable rights which are the gifts of man from his Creator are: (1) Freedom of worship; (2) freedom of speech, (3) freedom of press; (4) freedom of assemblage; (5) freedom to work in such occupation as the experience, training, and qualifications of a man may enable him to secure and hold; (6) freedom to enjoy the fruits of his work, which means the protection of property rights; (7) the right to pursue his happiness with the necessary implication that he does not harm or injure others in the pursuit of this happiness. Upon this basic principle, the whole structure of the American Government was constructed. The system of checks and balances in the Constitution was wisely conceived and ingeniously constructed to provide every possible guaranty that every citizen of the United States would enjoy and retain his God-given rights. First, the Federal Government was specifically enjoined from exercising any power that was not expressly or by necessary implication granted to it in the Constitution. Second, such powers as the Federal Government was authorized to wield were wisely distributed between the three great departments, the executive, the legislative, and the judicial. The essence of Americanism is therefore class, religious, and racial tolerance. It should be emphasized in the strongest language possible that the maintenance of these three forms of tolerance is essential to the preservation of Americanism. They constitute the three great pillars upon which our Constitutional Republic rests, and if any one of these pillars is destroyed, the whole structure of the American system of government will crumble to the earth. Therefore, the man who advocates class hatred is plainly un-American even if he professes racial and religious tolerance. The converse of this proposition is equally true. It is as un-American to hate one's neighbor [sic] he has more of this world's material goods as it is to hate him because he was born into another race or worships God according to a different faith.

The American Government was established to guarantee the enjoyment of these fundamental rights. It therefore follows that in America the Government is the servant of the people. The rights of the people are protected through laws and their strict enforcement. For this reason, law and order are essential to the preservation of Americanism while lawlessness and violence are distinctly un-American.

Americanism means the recognition of the God-given rights of man and the protection of those rights under the Constitution through the instrumentality of an independent Congress, an untrammelled judiciary, and a fair and impartial Executive operating under the American system of checks and balances. Americanism likewise means the protection of an unorganized majority from an organized minority as well as the protection of a helpless minority from an inconsiderate and thoughtless majority.

The characteristic which distinguishes our Republic from the dictatorships of the world is not majority rule but the treatment of minorities. Dictatorships muster huge majorities at the polls, through intimidation and high-powered government propaganda, but these majorities are used for ruthless tyranny over minorities. The majority rule of the American form of government is distinguished by its recognition of certain rights of minorities which majorities cannot alienate.

All of these definitions of Americanism are based upon the Declaration of Independence and the Constitution.

(B) Americanism Contrasted with Communism, Fascism, and Nazi-ism

The simplest and at the same time the most correct definition of communism, fascism, and nazi-ism is that they all represent forms of dictatorship which deny the divine origin of the fundamental rights of man. Since all of these forms of dictatorship deny the divine origin of the rights of man, they assume and exercise the power to abridge or take away any or all of these rights as they see fit. In Germany, Italy, and Russia, the state is everything; the individual nothing. The people are puppets in the hands of the ruling dictators. Rights which we have come to regard as elementary, such as freedom in its sevenfold aspect, either do not exist or if they do exist to any degree are subject to the whims and caprice of the ruling dictators. In all of these countries where these philosophies of government hold sway, the citizen has no rights that the government is required to respect or protect. While the foundation of Americanism is class, racial, and religious tolerance, and the foundation of nazi-ism and fascism is racial and religious hatred, the foundation of communism is class hatred. Americanism is a philosophy of government based upon the belief in God as the Supreme Ruler of the Universe; nazi-ism, fascism, and communism are pagan philosophies of government which either deny, as in the case of the communist, or ignore as in the case of the fascist and nazi, the existence and divine authority of God. Since nazi-ism, fascism, and communism are materialistic and pagan, hatred is encouraged. Since Americanism is religious, tolerance is the very essence of its being. . . .

SUMMARY OF FINDINGS

While it is true that our committee has only scratched the surface of the un-American and subversive activities of those who are invading America with their alien ideologies, it is also true that we have received abundant evidence to support the following findings with reference to the Communist Party:

It is an integral part of a world revolutionary movement for proletarian internationalism.

It is under direct control of the Third International which has its headquarters in Moscow.

It looks upon Russia as the "fatherland of the revolutionary workers," and cannot claim, therefore, any degree of loyalty to the American form of government.

Whereas it once employed the frank slogan of "the Defense of the Soviet

Union," it works today to embroil this country in a foreign war by the propagation of the doctrine of "collective security."

It seeks ultimately the overthrow of the American form of government as established by the Constitution of the United States.

It aims to set up a dictatorship of the proletariat in this country, notwithstanding its present tactical silence on this fundamental tenet of communism.

It rests upon brutal violence despite its present dishonest profession of belief in the processes of democracy.

It is bound by no ordinary ethical limitations in seeking to advance its program.

It aims at the complete confiscation of private property in the means of production, including the socialization of the land.

It hides behind civil liberties in pursuing ends which will destroy civil liberties for all but the ruling few of the proletarian dictatorship.

It works on the principle of leverage in accomplishing its purposes, depending not upon a majority of voters but upon a highly disciplined minority.

It is energetically applying the Trojan Horse tactic of penetrating other organizations for the purpose of seeking to control them or, failing that, to destroy them.

It is unusually active in our schools, both openly and subtly insinuating its propaganda into the minds of students.

It is boring from within the two major political parties.

During the next 2 years, it will concentrate much of its effort in the formation of a national farmer-labor party which it will seek to dominate.

It is the enemy of all forms of religion and looks upon faith in God as an outworn superstition.

It is, nevertheless, doing its utmost to make inroads into numerous religious organizations.

In the masquerade of science, it offers the most unscientific approach to human problems which the world has seen since the Dark Ages.

It stifles the creative impulses of the individual by its deadening regimentation.

It is basically a philosophy of hatred which seeks to promote class war.

It is boring from within labor unions on a wide scale, seeking to dominate or wreck the unions for purposes that are alien to the interests of organized wage earners.

It deliberately provokes violence in labor disputes for the purpose of training a revolutionary group in the tactics of civil war.

It seeks to sabotage and cripple our economy on every possible front, with a view to its profiting by the resulting economic crises.

It alines itself with every crack-pot scheme to undermine our system of free enterprise and private initiative.

It has penetrated the Government itself, with the result that some Communists hold key positions in Federal agencies and projects.

It has induced and financed many volunteers to go from this country to fight on the side of the Spanish Loyalist Government.

It aims to incite race war by its special agitation among the Negro population of this country.

It fears to have the spotlight of publicity turned upon its real aims and methods, and will stop at nothing to discredit, if possible, those who fearlessly expose its program and activities.

It seeks to silence all hostile criticism by charging its critics with red-baiting, while, at the same time, it viciously baits those who dare to oppose it.

It resorts to organized campaigns of character assassination wherever the charge of red-baiting does not suffice to silence its critics.

It tries to exploit any existing discontent for the purpose of building a revolutionary movement which has nothing to do with the solving of the problems from which discontent arises.

It dangles the promise of economic security before the victims of economic distress, offering them a new slavery in the name of emancipation.

It systematically and deliberately deceives many of our people by the use of high-sounding names for organizations which profess laudable objectives, but which, underneath, are designed solely to advance the cause of communism.

It exercises extensive influence among several millions in this country through the device known as the united front.

It persuades thousands of careless or innocent Americans to lend their names for the propaganda purposes of the Communist Party.

It employs numerous "fellow travelers" who outnumber its card-holding membership, and by the use of these "fellow travelers" extends its influence into organizations and institutions of every description.

Finally, it is diametrically opposed to the principles of Americanism, as set forth in the Constitution and the Declaration of Independence.

Our committee has received abundant evidence to support these findings with reference to the nature, program, and activities of the Communist Party. We have also probed into the activities of the Nazi-Fascist groups which are operating in this country under instructions from Germany and Italy. The Nazi-Fascist groups gave their own special techniques, but they, like the Communist Party, aim ultimately at the destruction of our free institutions. Communism differs from nazi-ism and fascism in details, but in the larger fundamentals these three forms of dictatorship become more and more alike with every passing year. Both the Nazis and the Fascists have shown themselves to be apt students of the Communist tactics of propaganda as well as able imitators of the Communist form of dictatorship in government.

We believe that the failure of the Labor Department to carry out the laws with respect to deportation is a contributing factor to the widespread activities and propaganda carried on by un-American elements in the United States.

This committee believes that the National Labor Relations Board should be subjected to a thorough investigation for the purpose of determining to what extent the members of the Board and its employees approve of the Communist views expressed by Mr. David J. Saposs, chief economist.

Communists seized strategic positions in certain unions affiliated with the C. I. O.

Communist documents and records presented to the committee indicate that the Communist leaders assumed great credit for the organizing of steel, automobile, and other industries and the direction of the strikes which followed.

This committee has established, on the basis of the Communist Party's own literature, that Communists are actively boring from within churches, schools, youth organizations, and every other organization and institution into which they can find entrance.

A courageous stand on the part of all public officials involved—with reference to sit-down and unauthorized strikes and Lansing Holiday incident—would have prevented these disgraceful occurrences and would have avoided the loss of millions of dollars to both labor and capital, which resulted from the stoppage of work and the inability of thousands of employees to work. This committee feels it would be derelict in its duty to the people if it did not denounce this lawlessness as distinctly and clearly un-American.

The sit-down strike technique was largely imported from abroad and was put into effect in this country for the purpose of paralyzing industry and producing a revolution.

It would be hard to estimate the total loss sustained by the Nation as a result of the numerous acts of violence and lawlessness that occurred during this period. Most of it can be attributed to the activities of the Communists in instigating and conducting unauthorized strikes and sit-down strikes.

The evidence indicates very clearly that the Communists had succeeded in penetrating the Farmer-Labor Party of Minnesota and seizing many strategic positions; that they were using the Farmer-Labor Party to promote communism and class warfare.

From the information before the committee, we feel convinced that a thorough investigation of the west coast will show that the Communists have enjoyed greater success there than in any other section of the country; that they have seized many important positions in the labor movement, and are directing many labor and political activities. The loss in money and man-hours directly traceable to Communist activity is tremendous.

The Communist Party has never found it necessary to have a majority of the members of the united front on its side in order to exercise a dominant control in their affairs and activities.

The aim of the united front is to extend the influence of the Communist Party far beyond the circle of its own membership, and even far beyond the periphery of the fellow travelers.

By the utilization of discontent, the Communist Party undertakes to transform any degree or kind of protest into petty hatred, and from this to fashion the instruments of class war.

The largest of the Communist front movements in the United States is the American League for Peace and Democracy, formerly known as the League Against War and Fascism.

Second in size and importance, from the Communist standpoint and, therefore, a menace to our country, is the Workers Alliance of America.

According to documents published by the International Labor Defense, it is the American section of the M. O. P. R., or the Red International of Labor Defense, often referred to as the Red International Aid.

The Friends of the Soviet Union is possibly one of the most open Communist fronts in the United States.

Possibly one of the most effective and closely knitted organizations among the Communist front movements is the International Workers Order.

As a section of the World Student Association for Peace, Freedom and Culture, the American Student Union is the result of a united front gathering of young Socialists and Communists.

The Communist front movement in the United States among Negroes is known as the National Negro Congress.

The American Youth Congress was not originally set up by Communists but it was penetrated by them, as shown by the reports of its first congress, which was held in Washington, D. C.

From the evidence before us we are not in a position to definitely state whether or not the Civil Liberties Union can properly be classed as a Communist organization. But the statement of the United Mine Workers to the effect that the Civil Liberties Union is serving as a forerunner and trail blazer for the active and insidious activities of the Communist is borne out by the evidence we have heard thus far. We strongly urge that this organization be investigated.

A large part of un-American activities is inspired by Communists, Nazis, and Fascists, aliens in the United States. Some of them are direct representatives and agents of foreign governments. Some of them occupy important positions in other organizations and are able to wield considerable political influence.

There is no excuse for the failure of the Labor Department to deport these aliens.

In the opinion of the committee the *Strecker case* does not have any important bearing on the *Bridges case* because the facts in the *Bridges case* are much stronger than in the *Strecker case*.

In the record of these hearings will be found considerable evidence, arguments, and citations of legal authorities which, in our judgment, definitely establish that the Department of Labor is without justification in postponing deportation proceedings against Harry Bridges.

The testimony reveals that the Communists have conducted a systematic and well-organized campaign to secure volunteers for the loyalist cause; that they have a central office in New York City where all volunteers are directed to report; that they have sufficient funds to finance the transportation of these volunteers to Spain and that they have been able to circumvent the law and operate illegally in getting these volunteers to Spain.

It was definitely shown that the Nazi activities in the United States have their counterpart in everything that has been done and is being done by similar movements of Nazis in other countries.

These Nazi activities in the United States are traceable to and linked with government-controlled agencies in Nazi Germany and it is not unreasonable to suppose that unless checked immediately an American-Nazi force may cause great unrest and serious repercussions in the United States.

From its membership, the German-American Bund can muster within its own ranks a uniformed force of 5,000 storm troops.

In this correspondence (correspondence secured by an investigator of the committee from the Chicago Bund post) it was definitely shown that the foreign institute of the Nazi Government at Stuttgart was one of the instruments used in assisting the German-American Bund in spreading propaganda in this country. Throughout this entire correspondence there is definite evidence and proof that the groups operated in this country are directed by organizations in Germany and get their support and directions from the German Government itself.

Some German-American children are being Hitlerized by the leaders of the German-American Bund, despite the fact that under the American law every child born in this country is an American citizen.

Denials to the contrary notwithstanding, this committee was greatly impressed with the evidence presented showing that there is a relationship existing between the German Government and the German-American Bund through the activity of Nazi consuls in this country.

Propaganda direct from the German Ministry of Propaganda and Enlightenment is distributed by bund officials and evidence was introduced showing definitely that printed propaganda material was shipped from Germany to the United States.

Pistol and rifle ranges for all storm troops of the German-American Bund were to be set up according to plans formulated at the conference of the bund in New York City in July 1937, according to testimony heard by this committee on October 5, 1938.

The Amerika Deutscher Volksbund, United States voice of nazi-ism, has been seeking to consolidate their varicolored shirts into one great movement which the Hitler-inspired bund is to lead.

American-Italian Black Shirt Legions, 10,000 strong are marching in America with the same resounding tread as those of the goose-stepping detachments of German-American Bund storm troops, testimony before the committee revealed.

Many of the antiracial organizations that have come under our scrutiny were created for the pecuniary and selfish aggrandizement of crackpots whose offspring they are.

From the testimony we heard we are convinced that a rather large number of the employees on the Federal Theater Project are either members of the Communist Party or are sympathetic with the Communist Party. It is also clear that certain employees felt under compulsion to join the Workers' Alliance of America in order to retain their positions. The evidence is very clear that certain employees carried on communistic activities openly in the Federal Writers' Project.

The real influence of Communists must be measured in terms of their ability to direct or influence other organizations and groups who have many times the membership that the Communist Party claims. It cannot be too strongly emphasized that the great majority of citizens of the United States of every race, religion, social, or economic condition in life are loyal and patriotic Americans, that the great majority of laboring people, both organized and unorganized, are opposed to communism.

RECOMMENDATIONS

Although this committee has worked continuously since the adjournment of Congress and has done everything within its power to get as many facts as possible to the people we have only skimmed the surface. We were able only to hold brief hearings in New York and Detroit. We were urged to conduct hearings in many other cities, such as Chicago, Philadelphia, Pittsburgh, Minneapolis, Milwaukee, Birmingham, Atlanta, New Orleans, San Antonio, Los Angeles, San Francisco, Seattle, and Portland, but due to limited time and funds we were unable to comply with these requests. We had hoped and planned to conduct extensive hearings on the west coast because the evidence before the committee indicates that this area ranks first in the extent of un-American activities and propaganda. We received numerous letters from citizens and public officials in the west coast area urging us to hold hearings there. We have approximately 150 witnesses in the west coast section that should have been heard. However, due to a lack of funds we were unable to devote any extensive consideration to west coast activities of Communist, Nazi, and Fascist groups. The situation is so serious on the west coast that it would require 6 months of preparatory investigation before a committee would be ready to conduct hearings, and it is probable that hearings would last 3 or 4 months.

Not only were we unable to investigate un-American activities and propaganda in many important sections of the country, but as a matter of fact, we found it impossible to investigate many of the important phases of un-American activities. Even as to those that we did investigate, we only scratched the surface.

In view of the foregoing, we do not think that the investigation has proceeded far enough to justify us in recommending legislation to Congress. We need and can secure much more information not only from sections of the country that we have investigated but also from the larger areas that we have not even touched before recommending legislation to Congress. Even after we are supplied with full and complete information and facts several months of consideration must be devoted to the question of legislation. This will require expert assistance and thorough research.

It is our recommendation that the House of Representatives adopt a resolution continuing this committee and investigation for a period of 2 years, and that the House of Representatives place at the disposal of the committee not less than $150,000; that the committee continue its investigation along nonpartisan and courageous lines because any investigation conducted along any other line would be more harmful than helpful; that unless the committee is supplied with adequate funds upon the definite understanding that the investigation shall continue along nonpartisan lines, without regard to any other question except the discovery of the truth, the investigation should not be continued. No individual or organization engaged in un-American activities should be shielded because of political expediency. The Congress should also require the appropriate departments to cooperate with the committee. The continued success of the investigation will depend solely upon the courage, fearlessness, and the thoroughness with which it is conducted, and upon the assumption and maintenance throughout the investigation of a strictly non-partisan attitude and policy.

> *Martin Dies*
> Chairman
> *Joe Starnes*
> *John J. Dempsey*
> *Harold G. Mosier*
> *Arthur D. Healey*
> N. M. Mason
> *J. Parnell Thomas*
> Special Committee on Un-
> American Activities

Attest:
    Robert E. Stripling, Secretary

HOUSE DEBATE OVER COMMITTEE RENEWAL
FEBRUARY 3, 1939

Congressional Record, 76th Congress, 1st Session, 1098–1127.

Mr. Cox. Mr. Speaker, by direction of the Committee on Rules, I call up House Resolution 26 for immediate consideration.

The Clerk read as follows:

House Resolution 26

Resolved, That the Special Committee to Investigate Un-American Propaganda and Activities is authorized to continue the investigation begun under authority of House Resolution 282 of the Seventy-fifth Congress, and for such purposes said committee shall have the same power and authority as that conferred upon it by said House Resolution 282 of the Seventy-fifth Congress and shall report to the House as soon as practicable, but not later than January 3, 1941, the results of its investigations, together with its recommendations for necessary legislation.

Mr. Sabath. . . . For 32 years it has been my contention that Members of this House should have the privilege given them in the Constitution of voting on bills and resolutions, rather than having legislation buried in committees. I have likewise always insisted that Members be given a fair and equal chance to state their position and express themselves on legislation before the House. That conviction has guided me in my consideration of the resolution now before us. Insisting that those in favor of it have the right to be heard, I reserve the right to speak against it.

I maintain that the special committee created by the original resolution, for which I voted in a firm belief that there should be a thorough investigation of un-American activities, has used the prestige of this Congress to become a medium for partisan attacks upon the Democratic administration, members of the Cabinet, organized labor, and many respected and outstanding citizens. The gentleman from Tennessee stated that the special committee had been smeared. If anyone was undeservedly smeared it was the thousands of loyal and patriotic American citizens who were given no slight opportunity to defend themselves before this committee. I have in my possession as chairman of the Committee on Rules thousands of telegrams and letters from preachers, teachers, organized labor leaders, civic leaders, public officials, veteran leaders, and others against whose organizations and themselves the most vicious insinuations have been made by unreliable and discredited investigators and witnesses of the special committee. I say the use of a congressional committee to give credence and publicity to such baseless

charges has been unfair to these thousands of Americans and their organizations. Unfortunately, from the very outset this committee has been led astray
and has given widespread publicity to charges made by men who have been
later discharged by the committee itself because it was learned that these
persons were untrustworthy and undeserving of belief.

Mr. Speaker, for reasons unknown to me, the majority of the Rules
Committee have seen fit to disregard the storm of protest raised against
continuation of the committee and, ignoring the thousands of pleas for a
sober, careful, and deliberate consideration of the resolution now before us,
they have insisted upon a hasty and, to my mind, ill-considered report and
vote by the House. Even my suggestion that the committee's membership be
increased to avoid repetition of the charge of one-man dictatorship was
rejected by the gentleman from Texas and a majority of the Rules Committee
for reasons I cannot ascertain. I think increased membership would be a
healthy thing for the committee and help accomplish all the work the chairman says is unfinished. Is it possible that increased membership might
upset the program that the committee has already planned in advance of the
action of the House in continuing it?

In all my congressional experience of 32 years, I know of no committee so
broadly condemned because of its conduct by people in all stages of life and
from all parts of the Nation. No one denies the necessity for a complete
investigation into un-American activities as was contemplated when the
Congress originally created this committee. But thousands of reliable and
outstanding people insist that the committee has been solely a medium to
smear political and civic leaders whose views, while being far from communistic, differ from those of the chairman of the committee. I recall a proposal often made by a gentleman in this House in the cloakroom that a demagogue club be formed in Congress and he be the president. I thought this
was just humor, but I am seriously wondering now if it was not meant in
dead earnest. Certainly thousands of law-abiding citizens and liberal-
minded and progressive people who support the President, and even the
President himself, have been exposed to the rankest kind of demagoguery by
the actions of this committee. And not only that, but in every section of the
country Democratic candidates for high office have been falsely and mali-
ciously accused of communistic alinements without a shred of evidence or
justification for such baseless charges. Men made these charges while on the
pay roll of a committee of Congress and who were later found to be labor
spies connected with strikebreaking organizations and groups specializing
in the lowest type of character assassination; men whose recklessness with
the truth and general unreliability should have been ascertained by the special committee before they were permitted to fill hundreds of pages of the
record with their outrageous charges and statements. This was bad enough,
but when the special committee permitted itself to be used to allow veiled
insinuations against the President to be made, their conduct not only dis-
gusted but was resented by millions of fair-minded citizens of our country.

There is no need to explain why the Republicans favor continuation of
the committee. I notice that they are unanimous in their support of this
resolution and will undoubtedly vote for it to a man. I cannot wholly blame
them for this strictly partisan attitude of utilizing the best opportunity they

have had in years for what they hope will continue to cast discredit upon the Democratic Party, its officials, and a Democratic President. But I regret extremely that the Democrats are so short-sighted as to permit themselves to be used for such an unsavory purpose and to have Democratic legislators go to the extent of even refusing a fair chance and opportunity to Members of this House to express their views and submit evidence as to why this instrument of attack on organized labor and the Democratic Party should be stopped now.

Mr. Speaker, I originally supported and voted for the resolution that created this special committee in the belief that I was helping to bring about a real investigation of all the un-American and subversive activities in this country. I was therefore amazed to find out during the course of the hearings before the Committee on Rules that little or none of the original intent of the House had been carried out. Instead I became convinced that this committee had spent its time and money on little less than a "smearing campaign" against all who have tried to promote liberal government and aid in supporting the great humanitarian principles of your President and mine. What about un-American organizations that spread bigotry, class prejudice, and racial hatred throughout this fair land of ours? Were they investigated by the committee? Was there any attempt made to find out who finances them and for what purpose? Was Mr. Pelley, of North Carolina, and his Silver Shirts, subpenaed and investigated? Was the Republican candidate for Governor of Kansas, Mr. Winrod, investigated? Was Fritz Kuhn brought in and investigated? Were the Black Shirts of Michigan investigated? Oh, no; the committee could not get around to them before their money ran out, and I am wondering why.

It is a strange and distressing coincidence that the enemies of President Roosevelt and the administration will stop at nothing and use any kind of instrument at hand to undermine and try to destroy the confidence of our people in the administration. This is not the first time it has been tried, but it will fail like the others when the people realize who and what is back of these vicious smearing campaigns. How very much like the campaign against our American President now being carried in the Nazi press in Germany, how nearly in the same language are these vicious attacks by the agents of fascism, silver shirtism, nazi-ism, and other "isms" which are given credence and publicity by our ill-advised and misguided special committee. Only today newspapers report our President being called a "Bolshevist tool." Read the special committee's hearings and the press reports about them and see if that does not sound to you like the ravings now being carried in the Hitler press. The headlines in reactionary newspapers accompanying every hearing of this special committee have echoed in substance the vituperations of the German Nazi directed against our great President. I know the administration would not have uttered one word of criticism of the committee if it had felt its work and real purpose was to investigate and expose un-American activities, instead of attacking, libeling, and attempting to intimidate every liberal, progressive, and humanitarian group and person in sympathy with the objectives of our administration to better the conditions and lives of the masses of our people.

History repeats itself sometimes, and I know the future will justify my position and that of all others in this House who refuse to submit to partisan prejudice and political hysteria. No number of attacks on the President and his administration, no matter how cleverly masqueraded or concealed, will detract from his fine reputation and the noble and humane efforts he is making in behalf of our democratic form of government and especially in behalf of the needy and downtrodden for whose condition the greedy and avaricious special interests are responsible and whose agents howl gleefully at every attempt to smear him or those who support him.

In conclusion, Mr. Speaker, I want to say that neither my conscience nor my sense of decency will permit me to vote for this resolution. . . .

Mr. Blackney. Mr. Speaker, I am emphatically in favor of House Resolution 26 and the report of the Special Committee to Investigate Un-American Activities and Propaganda in the United States. This is in pursuance of House Resolution 282 of the Seventy-fifth Congress, and the committee was authorized to investigate, first, the extent, character, and objects of un-American propaganda activities in the United States; second, the diffusion within the United States of subversive and un-American propaganda that is instigated from foreign countries or of a domestic origin and attacks the principle of the form of government as guaranteed by our Constitution; and, third, all other questions in relation thereto that would aid Congress in any necessary remedial legislation.

I am particularly interested in this subject because the district of which I have the honor to represent, namely, the Sixth Congressional District of Michigan, during the last 2 years has been subjected to subversive activities on the part of outside radicals who came to Michigan in great numbers at the time of the labor difficulties, particularly in the city of Flint and the city of Lansing, both of which are in my district.

Let me say, first, that the great mass of industrial workers in Flint and Lansing and throughout my district are law-abiding citizens, believers in the Constitution and believers in the fundamental principles of America. The major difficulty during the strikes occurring in Michigan, and particularly in my district, was due to the propaganda spread by these outside radicals.

I never thought the time would come in my life when the laws of my city and of my State would be ruthlessly set aside, when disorder would prevail, when radicalism would be heard on every hand, and yet that time did come in the strikes of 2 years ago.

Loud-voiced radicals appealed to the masses to assert their authority, to disobey the law, to hold in contempt the courts of our State, and carried their activities so far that the local authorities, particularly in the city of Flint, were unable to cope with the situation and the State authorities did not interfere in this radicalism nor did anything to protect the law-abiding citizens, or to protect life and property.

The testimony of the witnesses from Flint who appeared before the Dies investigating committee, under oath, stated conclusively that the great trouble was the presence and the activities of outside Communists and radicals who were using the local situation as a means of spreading their un-American doctrine. Had it not been that the law-abiding citizens of Flint were in the great majority, believing in the enforcement of the law, believing in the integrity of the courts, then the radicals would have gained greater power than they otherwise did.

We hear a great deal on the floor of Congress in favor of freedom of speech. I know full well the constitutional provision which guarantees to each one freedom of speech. But I wish to call the attention of the House to this thought: That there is a vast difference between the freedom of speech guaranteed by the Constitution, and unbridled license of speech as used by the Communists and radicals who do not believe in American principles.

I think the time has come in America when, instead of shedding useless tears in favor of those who do not believe in American institutions, we should pay some attention to the great mass of honest citizens who do believe in the Constitution and who do believe in the orderly processes of government.

In my judgment, one of the great causes of the spread of subversive doctrines in America has been the loose administration of our immigration laws. I believe in immigration properly regulated, but I do not believe in letting down the bars of immigration so that radicals from foreign countries who believe in every other "ism" but Americanism should be allowed to come to this country and spread their nauseating doctrine of hate.

I have every respect for those from foreign lands who came to the United States with the intent of making this country their home, of becoming attached to American institutions and who learn to love the Constitution of the United States and who are willing to become American citizens and do become law-abiding American citizens. For these people I have the utmost respect, but for those who come from foreign soils, unwilling to become citizens of the United States, unwilling to take the constitutional oath as citizens, but who come here for the sole purpose of undermining the principles of our Government, for these people I have the utmost contempt.

I think the quicker we put teeth in the immigration laws the better for us. I think the quicker we deport aliens illegally here, the better for America. In other words, if aliens come from foreign soil, unwilling to adapt themselves to American principles and to become law-abiding citizens, let them be sent back to the land of their birth. America has no use for such people.

I can honestly state that the Dies investigating committee has done much to alleviate the radical situation in my home city, and the effect of this committee's activities, particularly in my home State, has been greatly beneficial and salutary. I am constantly receiving letters, letters by the hundreds, from patriotic citizens of my district, who stress the thought that the United States should free themselves from those radicals who do not believe in our form of government; that those who are here illegally should be deported; that the immigration laws should be greatly strengthened and then rigidly enforced. If we are to preserve the great heritage of American institutions and love of country, then this must be done, otherwise the great sacrifice made by loyal American soldiers who were willing to give their lives for the preservation of the Constitution and the American form of government was in vain. The great majority of Legionnaires, of Spanish War veterans, and of other soldier organizations are preponderantly in favor of the continued investigation by this committee.

I think this appropriation should be granted and the committee authorized to proceed fearlessly in their investigation, and let the chips fall where they may. There are no politics in this resolution. Every Republican, every Democrat, every man loyal to American institutions should stand back of this committee. I think the committee should be congratulated upon the splendid work that they have done.

I know full well the obstacles that have been placed in the committee's progress from certain sources, but again I state that if we are to preserve America, as you and I have been taught to believe in America, if the America of the future is to protect our boys and girls as we have been protected, then this committee should be authorized to proceed further.

I shall vote for this appropriation gladly, knowing full well that should it carry, as I believe it will, that it will strike a death knell to the ruthless and subversive group whose sole purpose is the destruction of America as you and I know it, and the substitution in its place of a government that will not conform to the great American ideal which has made America the leader of the world. . . .

Mr. Fish. . . . The gentleman from Texas [Mr. Dies] and his committee need not be surprised at the virulent attacks and the attempts of the Communists and their friends of the United Front to smear the committee, as that is the usual tactics of the Communist Party and its allies and subsidiaries.

The Communists and other radicals are again up to their old tricks of trying to smear every investigation by Congress into un-American and seditious activities in the United States. Every known device of ridicule, distortion, and falsehood is being unloosed by skillful radical propagandists to undermine and destroy public confidence in the Dies committee. The congressional committee deserves the support of all American citizens, irrespective of party affiliations.

The deplorable fact is that not a single alien Communist has been deported to Soviet Russia since Miss Perkins took office, and I doubt if any will be as long as she holds office.

I hope the Dies committee will continue its investigation of the political link between the Workers' Alliance, a Communist controlled group, and the W. P. A., particularly in New York City. I hold in my hand a telegram from the Workers' Alliance that probably was sent to other Members of the House. It reads:

> On behalf of Workers' Alliance of America representing four hundred thousand unemployed and W. P. A. workers, we urge Rules Committee do not extend life or vote funds to Dies committee.

And so forth. This telegram is signed by David Lasser, national president, and Herbert Benjamin, general secretary-treasurer, two of the most notorious Communists in the United States of America. These men claim to be speaking for 400,000 unemployed and W. P. A. workers. I say to the gentlewoman from New Jersey [Mrs. Norton] that if we appropriate $100,000 for the Dies committee and that $100,000 is spent alone on exposing the Workers' Alliance and showing the wage earners of America that it is a 100-percent Communist-controlled organization, the money will be well spent. [Applause.]

We are talking about appropriating $2,000,000,000 for national defense. I say we have more to fear from our enemies within than from our enemies from without. [Applause.] Yet there are those who question the advisability of spending $100,000 to preserve our own American system—our free institu- [Applause.]

I love the Dies committee for the enemies it has made. . . .

Mr. Celler. Mr. Speaker, the purposes of this committee called the Dies committee are laudable and proper. My hatred of Communists is as great as my hatred of Fascists and Nazis. It is hoped that all influence making for converts to those "isms" can be ripped out root and branch. But some of the methods pursued by this committee heretofore make for increased rather than lessened communism, nazi-ism, and fascism.

I shall vote down the previous question so that we may have an opportunity to offer amendments to the resolution.

The personnel of the committee should be increased. Some of its personnel have been most intolerant and have been guilty of practices that have a tendency to create the very radicalism they seek to destroy. I would want the Speaker to appoint as additional members of that committee, men of poise and understanding, of judicial temperament, of fairness in thought and speech.

I shall vote for the final resolution primarily because recently, in a conversation I had with the gentleman from Texas [Mr. Dies], he agreed specifically that he had made errors and that he would not repeat them. I asked him a series of questions in order to bring out his future plans for the conduct of his committee. His answers were satisfactory.

Firstly, I asked him: "Are you going to make the same fiery and unbalanced speeches over the radio that you have made heretofore?" His answer was "No." I explained that as chairman of the committee he was more like a judge; that it was improper for him to prejudice his witnesses by making intolerant speeches against them. He agreed.

Secondly, I asked him, "Are you going to hire a skillful and adroit lawyer to sift fact from fiction, wheat from chaff, and are you going to follow his advice and counsel? He said "Yes." Heretofore he and his committee members have refrained from hiring counsel. They probably did not have money to do so. But many a worthy member of the bar would have been glad to donate his services. A committee of this important character cannot successfully function without the aid of good counsel. Again the gentleman from Texas agreed.

Thirdly, I asked him, "Will you continue to allow your committee to be a sounding board for crackpots and professional agitators?" He said he would not.

Lastly, I asked him, "In your reports, are you going to come to strained and violent conclusions based on flimsy and insufficient evidence?" He said he would exercise the greatest care and vigilance before making any pronouncements, and that he would be as cautious as possible.

It must be remembered that the leadership of the House has put its imprimatur of approval on this resolution. It apparently is going to carry overwhelmingly. The gentleman from Texas [Mr. Dies] has been cautioned against intemperate remarks against the administration, and I understand further that he has agreed not to attack the administration.

In the light of these questions and answers and the pledges of Mr. Dies, I am constrained to vote for the resolution, after voting against taking the previous question. . . .

Mr. Dies. This committee spent a large part of its funds investigating Nazi and Fascist activities in this country. We sent an investigator all over the United States, and during the last days, when our money was being rapidly exhausted, nevertheless, we investigated numerous so-called Nazi and Fascist organizations. In spite of bona fide and honest efforts to investigate nazi-ism, nevertheless, those who are opposed to an investigation of communism began to disseminate propaganda all over this country that the committee was sympathetic with the Nazis, sympathetic with the Fascists. Why did they do this? What is there about this thing that brings about such a hue and cry? We Democrats do not fear an honest and fearless exposure of communism. Everybody knows the Democratic Party is not in sympathy with communism. The Democrats of this Nation are Americans. [Applause.] And I resent this misrepresentation; I resent it; I resent it.

I did not attack a Cabinet officer until certain Cabinet officers went out of their way to attack an independent agency of this Congress. I love this Congress. My father served in this House for 10 years. [Applause.] And during all the time he was here he defended the integrity, the dignity, and the prerogatives of this House. When, therefore, Cabinet officers—appointive officials of the Government—went out of their way not merely to attack me, for I am merely an humble and insignificant member of a great body—when they attacked this committee they attacked the greatest deliberative body on earth, and I resented such action. [Applause.] I say this in justification.

May I also express my deep gratitude to the members of this committee for their loyalty and their courage. There was a time when our backs were against the wall, when radical writers were trying to besmear us with deliberate lies and misrepresentation. There was a time when powerful forces were turned loose for the deliberate purpose of destroying an investigation that was honestly and sincerely undertaking to do a patriotic service to the people of this country. Let me say further that the real liberals have nothing to fear from an honest investigation, for true liberals are as much opposed to communism as are the conservatives.

Mr. Celler. Mr. Speaker, will the gentleman yield briefly?

Mr. Dies. Yes; I yield to the gentleman from New York.

Mr. Celler. I am glad to note that the gentleman says he will rectify some of the errors. Will he retain skillful and adroit counsel and will he follow counsel's advice to sift facts from fiction?

Mr. Dies. The chairman of this committee will do what he did before, everything in his power to render an honest and patriotic service. [Applause.]

Let me say this to the gentleman and let me say it to other Members of this House, that no one can deny that the intolerant ideologies of Europe have been transplanted to our shores. The quarrels and the feuds of the Old World have been transferred to America. No one can deny that insidious forces are seeking to change the structure of this Government by intrigue and by violence. Yet I hear Members of Congress accuse me of seeking to hurt my administration, or to hurt my party.

I am thinking of one whose memory will ever dwell in my heart and for whom I entertained profound love and devotion. He left me as a priceless heritage a record in this House which was distinguished by courage and patriotism. No man loved the Democratic Party more than he did. And yet at a moment of crisis he did not hesitate to place his country above partisanship. I would be unworthy of him and the heritage of unselfish service which he left me if I did not place the interest of our beloved country above what some misguided partisans conceive to be the interest of the party.

As a matter of fact, this is not a partisan question. Here we are dealing with the life of America, with the fundamentals, with that concerning which all men of all parties, of all races, and of all creeds can unite in a common defense.

Mr. Celler. The gentleman has not answered the question. Will the gentleman hire a lawyer to help him?

Mr. May. Will the gentleman yield?

Mr. Dies. I yield to the gentleman from Kentucky.

Mr. May. If, as a matter of fact, there is anything wrong within the councils of the Government of the United States and the Democratic Party is in charge of the Government, is it not the duty of our party to see that it comes out, and is that not the only purpose of this committee?

Mr. Dies. I would rather the Democrats take the initiative and show courage than to leave it to some other party to do.

Mr. Speaker, can it be said that we have erred in exposing men prominent in this Government who by their own admissions subscribe to communism? Can it be said that we erred in going into certain labor unions and showing by uncontradicted evidence, by the testimony of officials and members of the union itself, that here were Communists who had infiltrated the legitimate labor unions, had seized strategic positions, and were converting those labor unions into instrumentalities of class warfare? Were we being partisan when we gave to the American people facts with respect to those matters? Were we being partisan when we exposed one situation in the city of New York on the Federal Writers project whereby, through their own admission, 103 out of 300 employees being supported by the money of loyal American citizens, were members of the Communist Party?

Mr. Speaker, I submit that America comes before all questions of partisanship. [Applause.]

TIME ARTICLE
MAY 29, 1939

If ham-fisted Congressman Martin Dies had been able to call Orson Welles's Martians before his Committee to Investigate Un-American Activities he could not have extracted a more lurid story than he got last week. Witnesses testified in all seriousness to their belief in:

1) A Jewish-Communist plot to overthrow the U. S. Government next August by the ingenious means of bringing in 150,000 Communists, mostly ex-Loyalist Spaniards. The importees would seize U. S. arsenals, take over public utilities and transportation facilities. Meanwhile, rich Jewish conspirators would unload their securities, creating financial chaos.

2) A counter-revolutionary scheme by fascistic anti-Semites who intended to crush Revolution No. 1 before it got under way, set up a dictatorship in Atlanta under a retired U. S. Army General.

No Communists were produced by the Dies Committee. They apparently existed only in the vast credulousness of some people like a Manhattan socialite named Dudley Pierrepont Gilbert, who had nothing better to do after he lost his money (but not his wife's) in the depression than to organize something called American Nationalists, Inc., which he endowed with a Fascist salute. After that petered out, Mr. Gilbert told the committee, he met a "medium-sized" man named George Rice who said he was a bodyguard-waiter for the Communistic plotters within Manhattan's Harmonie Club (for rich Jews).[1] "George Rice" told Dudley Gilbert eye-popping stories about the coming revolution. Dudley Gilbert hastened to build himself a retreat in the fastnesses of the Kentucky mountains, a place to hide himself and family from the dread Communists.

Frightened Dudley Gilbert passed the dire information on to two men of action: James Erwin Campbell, Army reserve captain and V. F. W. official of Owensboro, Ky., and George E. Deatherage, a St. Albans, W. Va., house painter with a Hitleresque mustache who calls himself "national commander of the Knights of the White Camellia." Messrs. Campbell and Deatherage decided to set up a sort of Hitler to whom they would play Göring and Goebbels. For their Führer they chose sympathetic Major General George Van Horn Moseley, who retired as commander of the U. S. Army's Fourth Corps Area last year with a blast against the New Deal, followed up with frightening speeches about the dastardly Jews, warnings that the time might come when the Army would have to "take over." General Moseley had started his own investigation of "isms" which called for considerable travel. "If the Jews bump me off," he wrote in a spirit of martyrdom to Captain Campbell, "be sure to see they get credit for it from coast to coast. It will help our cause."

Having found their Hitler, Knight Deatherage ("Judaism and Com-

---

[1] A search of the club's records failed to reveal any such employe as George Rice.

munism are synonymous") proposed to Captain Campbell that they go about organization, contact "leaders of main groups throughout the nation" —Father Coughlin, Kansas' anti-Semite Gerald Winrod, John Frey of the A. F. of L.'s Metal Trades Department, the American Legion's Americanism Commission Director Homer Chaillaux,[2] Louis John Taber, master of the National Grange, Walter Garrison of the Associated Farmers of California —"in all, men who are heads of large groups on our side of the fence." George Deatherage's meeting to bring these leaders together never came off.

With his customary bull-in-china-shop finesse Mr. Dies managed to kick the chairman of the Republican National Committee, redheaded John Hamilton, out of the subversive bag. Mr. Hamilton, it seems, had been in correspondence with Fascist Campbell to the extent of sending him a copy of the Republican National Committee list when he asked for it. Another potent Republican was revealed to be Mr. Campbell's correspondent. Chairman Dies introduced a letter from paunchy, cigar-smoking Banker Felix McWhirter, treasurer of the Indiana Republican State Committee, who asked Mr. Campbell if any of three persons were of Jewish blood: Alf Landon, William Allen White, Mrs. Cordell Hull.

At week's end the U. S. had not yet been overthrown by anyone.

TESTIMONY OF EARL BROWDER
SEPTEMBER 6, 1939

U.S. House of Representatives, 76th Congress, 1st Session, Hearings before a Special Committee on Un-American Activities, Vol. 7, 4482–84.

. . . Mr. Voorhis. If you say there was no act of friendship between Germany and Russia in this pact, why should it have broken the axis? Is there not an implication in what you said that Germany sacrificed all her close ties that she had?

Mr. Browder. I did not say this was not an act of friendship with Germany. It most certainly was an act of friendship between the German and Russian people, and we have to distinguish between friendship between peoples and alliances between governments. It was an act of friendship between these peoples and in no way an alliance between governments.

Mr. Thomas. Just a few moments ago you referred to some individuals who were closest to the picture and you said you were making a comparison between those in Washington closest to the picture and others who were farthest away from the picture. Who were you referring to as being closest to the picture and who would think that was a good pact?

---

[2] Himself a star witness on Communists before the Dies Committee last year.

Mr. Browder. I was merely suggesting to you a method of putting to the test this question. I have no personal acquaintance with any of the people who handle these questions.

Mr. Thomas. You did not have any one particularly in mind?

Mr. Browder. No.

Mr. Thomas. Here is another question I want to ask you, which has to do with the testimony you gave this afternoon.

You were referring to the utilization of transmission belts, and I inferred from what was said that the transmission belts were what were formerly known as the united front organizations; is that correct?

Mr. Browder. Yes; that is all organizations for the masses of workers, in which we would unite people with various views.

Mr. Thomas. At one time in your testimony you referred to them as the united front, and at another time you referred to the same organizations as transmission belts. Are those two terms as used by the Communists synonymous?

Mr. Browder. No.

Mr. Thomas. You mentioned specifically the Workers Alliance as being one of the transmission belts.

Mr. Browder. Transmission belts refer entirely to the Communists' approach to the problems of reaching the masses. Transmission belts mean having Communists work among the masses in the various organizations. If you say that the leaders of the organizations are transmission belts that makes it senseless.

Mr. Thomas. As I understand it, some of those organizations are the Workers Alliance of America, The American League for Peace and Democracy, and the American Youth Congress. Those are three mentioned here this afternoon.

I also want to know whether these organizations can be included: The International Congress of American Democracies. That is one. Is it all right to include that?

Mr. Browder. I am not familiar with that particular name. If you will name the various organizations, I will tell you.

Mr. Thomas. There is the International Congress of American Democracies.

Mr. Browder. I am not familiar with the name. I would say there have been those along this line that could go under that head.

Mr. Thomas. How about the National Lawyers' Guild?

Mr. Browder. Yes; they are one of the organizations.

Mr. Thomas. And the American Students Union?

Mr. Browder. Yes.

Mr. Thomas. And the National Negro Congress?

Mr. Browder. Yes.

Mr. Thomas. And the World Youth Congress?

Mr. Browder. Yes.

Mr. Thomas. And the Southern Conference for Human Welfare?

Mr. Browder. Yes.

Mr. Thomas. And the Negro Youth Congress.

Mr. Browder. Yes.

Mr. Thomas. And the Consumers' National Federation?

Mr. Browder. Yes.

Mr. Thomas. And the American Civil Liberties Union?

Mr. Browder. Yes.

Mr. Thomas. Now, I have here a list of all these organizations which you—

Mr. Browder. I could add to that considerably.

Mr. Thomas. I know you can, but I just have this list, and it is interesting to note, that at the national convention of each of these organizations last year the following governmental officials either gave the opening address of welcome, or made the opening address. At the International Congress of American Democracies, they were greeted at the opening by Secretary Henry A. Wallace. At the convention of the National Lawyers' Guild the opening address was delivered by Secretary Harold Ickes.

At the convention of the American League for Peace and Democracy, there were opening greetings in writing from Secretary Ickes, who was forced by pressure to cancel a personal appearance.

At the convention of the American Students' Union, it was opened by written greetings from President Roosevelt.

At the National Negro Congress, the opening address was delivered by Secretary Ickes.

At the opening of the World Youth Congress, the opening address was delivered by Mrs. Roosevelt.

At the convention of the Workers' Alliance, it was opened by addresses by Mr. Aubrey Williams and Mr. Robert Bulkley.

The American Youth Congress was opened by Mrs. Roosevelt.

The Southern Conference for Human Welfare was opened by greetings from President Roosevelt.

The Negro Youth Congress was opened by greetings from Secretary Ickes.

The Consumers' National Federation convention was opened by an address by Secretary Henry A. Wallace; and at the convention of the American Civil Liberties Union, the opening address was delivered by Secretary Ickes.

Of course, that may have been just a coincidence, but it seems to me to be more than a coincidence. It seems as though the New Deal was hand in glove with the Communist Party. . . .

ATTACK ON COMMITTEE BY JOHN J. DEMPSEY NOVEMBER 1939

U.S. House of Representatives, 76th Congress, 1st Session, Hearings before a Special Committee on Un-American Activities, Vol. 10, 6432–34.

. . . Mr. Dempsey. . . . I understand that in executive session the committee adopted a resolution, to release to the press and the public the names of the members of the American League for Peace and Democracy. I am afraid in doing that, you have released not only the names of members but you have released the names of people who have contributed, for instance, to the Spanish refugee fund, but who are not members of the League for Peace and Democracy at all.

So far as I am concerned, I want to protest against any such action. I think it is most un-American. And as a member of this committee, I am not here to be a party to injuring anybody who is innocent or who has joined an organization, not knowing the purpose of the organization, and who has resigned after finding out the purpose of the organization. I think it is most reprehensible for this committee to pass any such resolution and release the names of 800 people, many of whom will be accused of being Communists when, as a matter of fact, there is no member of the committee who is any better an American than many of the people who are now going to be charged with being affiliated with the Communist Party.

As a member of this committee, at no time am I going to smear anybody. No politics is going to be injected into this. There is not going to be any politics so far as I am concerned. I think what we have done is the most damnable thing, and I just want to go on record to that effect. . . . It is my feeling that a Communist should not be employed in the Government service at all. And that goes for the Nazi as well; I mean, those whose loyalty is to the German Government rather than to the American Government. It is my opinion that a Communist's first loyalty is to the Russian Government and not to the American Government. So do not misunderstand me on that.

But I am not in favor of smearing a lot of good American citizens just because they inadvertently contributed to something that had a very patriotic sounding name—and that is what many of them have done.

Mr. Mason. The statement issued by the chairman under orders of the majority of the committee definitely clears any suspicion of the fact that these people are all Communists.

Mr. Dempsey. Mr. Mason, you do this. You published 800 names, and let us assume that the committee were to say that 95 percent of these people are not Communists, but 5 percent of them are. Unless you point out those that are, then you reflect upon every other one of the 95 percent who are not.

Mr. Mason. More than a year ago we found, by a majority of this committee, that this was a Communist-front organization, and we notified the world in our report of that. That was followed by action on the part of this local chapter of putting on a campaign for increased membership as a defy of that report. It seems to me we have no reason to protect such people.

Mr. Dempsey. Mr. Mason, we did point out, as you say—

Mr. Starnes (interposing). I want to be courteous to the gentlemen, but I do not think it helps the committee or the conduct of the investigation to debate this matter after it is closed. If any member wishes to make a statement to the press expressing his views, he is at liberty to do so. But I do not think it is proper procedure for the members of the committee to engage in a controversy on a matter that is already a closed chapter.

Mr. Dempsey. It is not a controversy so far as I am concerned. I am simply stating my position.

Mr. Starnes. Which you have a perfect right to do.

Mr. Dempsey. If you will allow me to continue for a minute: This committee did point out that this American League for Peace and Democracy was a front organization. As a result of that, I have personal knowledge of many, many withdrawals. Yet their names will appear in the press as members of this organization. That is what I am taking exception to. . . .

NEW YORK TIMES REPORT OF ROOSEVELT ATTACK ON DIES COMMITTEE OCTOBER 27, 1939

Publication by the House Committee to Investigate Un-American Activities of a list of purported members of the local branch of the American League for Peace and Democracy was declared today by President Roosevelt to be a "sordid procedure."

His description was given at a press conference in response to a question as to his opinion on the action by the committee, which was taken on Wednesday on the ground that the league is a Communist "front."

The President replied that he was not sufficiently acquainted with the details to discuss this "sordid procedure," but when reporters asked if they might quote his description he said they might.

(Later in the day Representative Martin Dies, chairman of the committee, defended the action of the committee in an address given before the annual convention of the New York City Federation of Women's Clubs in New York. While refusing to enter into a controversy with the President, Mr. Dies said that "government employes who belong to organizations controlled by a foreign power ought to be exposed.")

The President's remark served principally, for the time being, to accent Republican efforts in the House to make a direct issue of the alleged Communist control of the league in the political campaigns next year.

In carrying forward this program, Representatives Mason of Illinois and Hoffman of Michigan took the floor today to suggest courses of action to clear this alleged "Communist influence" from the government.

Mr. Mason, who started the movement to publish the league list, called on Federal employes to resign from the league or resign from government positions.

Hoffman Would Stop Pay

Mr. Hoffman introduced a bill to forbid payment of government salaries to persons "belonging to any organization which is affiliated with any organization which advocates the overthrow of the government by force, or which is controlled in whole or in part by any foreign government or any agency of any foreign government."

The speeches and the bill were predicated upon a complicated argument embodied yesterday by Chairman Dies in a letter requesting the Attorney General to proceed against the league for alleged violation of American laws requiring the registration of agents of foreign governments.

Chairman Dies, Mr. Mason and other committee members maintain that evidence taken by the committee shows the league to have been an agent of the Communist party, although possibly an unwilling one as far as many members were concerned.

On the basis of that decision, the committee published the names of 563 persons who are or have been on the government payroll.

The list was made public as "a membership list." Many of the persons so named denied they were members. Others defended the league against the reports of Communist control.

Mr. Mason told the House, in which were about a score of members, that the President's description "undoubtedly is his opinion," but, he added:

"It is not my opinion, and neither do I believe it to be the opinion of the great majority of the nation.

"The publication of this list at my insistence is the culmination of a campaign of 'moral suasion' that the committee has conducted for more than a year for the purpose of securing:

"1. The resignation of the innocent government employes that are members of the local chapter, and

"2. The resignation from government service of those members who are not innocent, but who sympathize with and are willing to aid the Communists in their efforts to overthrow the very government they are working for, and if the resignations from the government service are not forthcoming, then to separate them forcibly from the public payroll."

Representative Mason indicated that forced dismissal could be accomplished by Congress only through legislation affecting appropriation bills, and this conclusion was believed to have prompted the introduction of Mr. Hoffman's bill.

Mr. Hoffman made it clear that his bill was aimed directly at the league, although it was drafted in general terms.

In the midst of this debate, Representative Dempsey of New Mexico, a committee member who fought to stop publication of the league list, placed in the Record a letter from a woman named in the list who, he said, had been subjected to demands for her resignation from a teaching position because of this publication.

The woman, Mr. Dempsey said, "had never even heard of the league."

The action of the committee was denounced by Mr. Dempsey as "assassinating character."

NEW YORK TIMES REPORT OF DIES RESPONSE TO ROOSEVELT ATTACK OCTOBER 28, 1939

Grieved and pained, he said, by President Roosevelt's criticism of, and "continued unfriendliness" toward, the House Committee on Un-American Activities, Chairman Dies declared tonight in a radio address that nothing would stop him from exposing to the public the presence of Communists in the Federal Government.

Refusing to enter into a controversy with the President, Mr. Dies "served notice upon the country and the Administration" that should the investigation continue, he would not stop from investigating the "tax-supported officialdom of the nation's capital."

"If we are not free to reveal the identity of the parlor pets of Moscow who plot the overthrow of our government over their teacups, then we can have no investigation worthy of the name," he asserted in his speech over the Columbia Broadcasting System.

The chairman's remarks were made as a reply to the accusation of "sordid procedure" with which President Roosevelt recently characterized the release by the committee of the list of members and mailing list of the American League for Peace and Democracy. That organization, Mr. Dies said tonight, had always served the interests of the Soviet regime.

Asks Letters From Public

The investigation, said the chairman, would be greatly hampered if the Administration did not change its attitude, but, he added, he would rather see the committee die than be "party to a cowardly white-wash."

Then, appealing to the American people, he suggested that they write their "servants in Washington" if they wished the investigation to go on as now conducted.

"I know," said Mr. Dies, "that you will understand me when I say that I have been deeply grieved by the President's characterization of the procedures of our committee as 'sordid.' I have not sought and will not now enter into controversy with the Chief Executive of my government. Neither will I say that my wisdom and judgment are superior to his, but I do know that the Federal Government has Communists in key positions, and nothing will deter me from exposing them to the people.

"I know, furthermore, that there are hundreds, yes thousands, of members of the Communist-controlled organizations, scattered throughout the departments and agencies of our Federal Government and nothing will deter me from apprising the American people of this fact.

"When a list of leaders of the German-American Bund was made public by our committee, there was no charge of 'sordid procedures.' When a mailing list of William Dudley Pelley's Silver Shirts was spread upon the record, there was no charge of 'sordid procedures.' Why then this sudden fury of attack upon the procedures of our committee when the membership of more than 500 officials and employes of the Federal Government in the Communist-controlled American League for Peace and Democracy is disclosed to the American people?"

Mr. Dies said that his committee did not assert that the Peace League members were Communists.

"Can it be true that some of the names on that membership list were too big for release to the public?" he inquired.

"There is nothing new about this latest attack by the Administration upon the work of our committee, nothing new except the occasion which prompted it. I profoundly regret that the President and all the members of his Cabinet have not from the beginning supported our committee with that same unanimity of support which we have received from the people of this country.

"I am as pained as the Communists and their fellow-travelers are pleased at the President's continued unfriendliness toward our committee. I wish it were otherwise, and I am compelled to state that, unless there is a change in the Administration's attitude, it will be extremely difficult, if not impossible, for our committee to produce the results which the country has every reason to expect.

Not to Spare Officials, He Says

"Can it be true that any one wants the American people kept in the dark with respect to the connections, innocent or otherwise, of high-salaried executives with organizations which the Communist party has set up for purposes that are utterly un-American?

"I wish to serve notice upon the country and upon the Administration that if I am to remain as chairman of this investigation into un-American activities, and if this investigation is to be continued, which is necessary, I will not stop in the pursuit of the facts at the outskirts of official Washington. I, for one, will have no part in an inquiry which spends all of its time on the subversive activities of private citizens and is afraid to enter the tax-supported officialdom of the nation's capital."

After a lengthy argument designed to show the connection of the league with Communist influence, Mr. Dies added:

"Conceived in Moscow, delivered in Amsterdam, nourished in its infancy in America by the famous French Communist, Henri Barbusse, the American League for Peace and Democracy has from its beginning served the interests of the Soviet Government."

The time had come, said the chairman, when the future of his investigation must be considered.

"In urging that we begin to consider the necessity for continuing this investigation. I wish to make it clear that great as is the necessity for continuation I had rather see the committee expire on Jan. 3 than to be a party to a cowardly whitewash," he asserted.

"I think, therefore, that the time has come when the country and those in control of the government should determine whether or not we shall be permitted to continue the investigation along fearless and nonpartisan lines or be constantly handicapped, embarrassed and thwarted by Washington officialdom.

"In order to make the issue perfectly clear, I here and now declare that I will have no part in any other kind of investigation, I do not want the House of Representatives and the Administration to continue the investigation on any other assumption.

"To the people of America I refer my case. If you agree with me that this is no time for concealment or soft-pedaling on account of partisan interests you have but to make known your views and wishes to your servants in Washington. As for me, I shall not swerve from the path of duty as God gives me the light to see it."

Representative Dempsey [said] today a suggestion that he retire from the Dies committee was "rather presumptuous." The suggestion was made by Thomas L. Harris, national secretary of the American League for Peace and Democracy, after Mr. Dempsey criticized the committee's release of the list of names.

"Your telegram suggesting that I resign from the Dies committee indicates a misconception on your part that I am friendly in my attitude toward the American League for Peace and Democracy," Mr. Dempsey wrote Mr. Harris.

"For your information, I hold no brief in any way for that organization, I am merely trying to protect the reputations of the good citizens who have been erroneously included in a list of names associated by the Dies committee with the league. Your suggestion that I resign appears to me to be rather presumptuous."

SECOND ANNUAL REPORT
JANUARY 3, 1940

U.S. House of Representatives, 76th Congress, 3rd Session, House Report No. 1476, Investigation of Un-American Propaganda Activities in the United States, 1–25.

Mr. Starnes of Alabama, from the Special Committee on Un-American Activities, submitted the following

REPORT

Introduction

Every modern democratic nation is confronted by two pressing problems. The first is the preservation of the constitutional liberties which their people have gained through the years of struggle. The second is the problem of adjusting their economic life to the difficulties of the machine age. Throughout all ages there have existed groups of people who have sought power and influence through the exploitation of the economic difficulties of the people of various nations. The more difficult economic circumstances become, the greater the opportunities for groups of this character. There is at present taking place in the world a struggle between democracy on the one hand and dictatorship on the other, upon the outcome of which the future of human liberties in the next few centuries may well depend.

As long as this struggle continues the American Nation, along with other true democracies in the world, faces a serious dilemma. It is of primary importance to prevent the growth or spread of influence of any organization or group which seeks to undermine democracy and substitute dictatorship of whatever sort for it. But it is at least equally important that in combating subversive groups of this character nothing be done which would undermine the fundamental structure of constitutional liberty itself.

One method which can and should from time to time be used is the method of investigation to inform the American people of the activities of any such organizations in their nation. This is the real purpose of the House Committee to Investigate un-American Activities. By un-American activities we mean organizations or groups existing in the United States which are directed, controlled or subsidized by foreign governments or agencies and which seek to change the policies and form of government of the United States in accordance with the wishes of such foreign governments.

For almost a year and a half, the committee has taken testimony from scores of witnesses, most of whom have had first-hand knowledge of subversive and un-American activities. This testimony fills some 7,000 printed pages. In addition vast amounts of documented evidence have been made part of the committee's record. As source books of first-hand or primary evidence on the workings of the Communist, Nazi, and Fascist organizations, these volumes of testimony given at the public hearings of the Special Committee on un-American Activities are without equal.

It has happened that in certain European nations dictatorships have been set up in recent years. The most noteworthy examples of such dictatorships are the Communist dictatorship of Stalin in Russia and the National Socialist or Nazi dictatorship of Hitler in Germany. Starting out with ideals which apparently differed widely from one another, these two dictatorships have converged upon one another, not only in the matter of their foreign policy but also with regard to their domestic programs, until today we find little to distinguish one from the other and even find that these two dictatorships are cooperating together in Europe for their supposed mutual benefit.

Both Stalin's communism and Hitler's nazi-ism pursue the policy of attempting to build up in other nations groups of followers who could be depended upon to protect the interests of the European dictators under every circumstance. There is evidence of similar efforts by the Italian Fascists. The primary representatives of these efforts in the United States have been the Communist Partys on the one hand and the German-American Bund on the other. Up until the time of the signing of the pact between Stalin and Hitler, the Communist Party on its part was about to gain its greatest influence in the United States by attempting to represent itself as the spearhead of an "anti-Fascist" movement, and the German-American Bund on the other hand was about to make its most effective appeal by representing itself as the spearhead of an "anti-Communist" movement. Significantly enough, in the first case the movement was supposed to be anti-Fascist on the one hand, but not anti-Communist, and in the second case to be anti-Communist, but not anti-Fascist.

At the present time, with the signing of the Soviet-Nazi pact, these movements have been severely crippled and this tactic is far less effective than formerly. The committee finds that criticism of Adolph Hitler has practically disappeared from the columns of the Communist press, while criticism of the Soviet Union is likewise conspicuous by its absence in the Nazi press. The Communist Party has even gone so far as to lift the boycott which it had declared on German-made goods. (Announcement by William Z. Foster, chairman, Daily Worker, December 12, 1939.) It is important, therefore, to understand that the difference between various kinds of totalitarian governments is much more apparent than real, and it is essential to approach the problem of studying their activities in the United States with this idea clearly in mind.

As further background for an adequate understanding of the findings of the Committee on Un-American Activities, a brief outline of changes in the "party line" or tactics of the Communist Party is important. Essentially, communism is an international revolutionary movement seeking to replace democratic government by a so-called dictatorship of the proletariat. This is the aim and goal of all true Communists and fundamentally it never changes. The greatest danger to a movement of this kind is obviously the existence of successful efforts to peacefully and progressively solve the economic problems of a people within the framework of a constitutional democratic government. Progressive reform movements, therefore, must always be eliminated in order for a communistic movement to be ultimately successful, and such movements can never expect to benefit from "united front" activities with Communists.

Beginning in 1935, however, the Soviet Government of Russia attempted a policy of cooperation with the capitalistic democracies in attempting to build what was known as "collective security" against fascist and nazi nations. In accord with this, the tactics of the Communist Party in the United States were changed and for approximately 4 years the party pursued a policy of pretending to cooperate with all progressive and liberal forces with the primary idea in mind of gaining greater and greater influence within, and ultimate control of such forces, and thus being able to influence the policy of the United States in accordance with Soviet interests. It is in this 4-year period, while pursuing this particular line or policy, that the Communist Party in the United States has succeeded in extending its influence among so-called "front" organizations and in some labor organizations as well. It is important to remember in this connection that the Communist Party at this time was deliberately refraining from preaching communism in any real sense of that term.

Beginning with the time of the signing of the Nazi-Soviet Pact, the Communist line and tactics in the United States have changed once again and the policy now being pursued is the true and traditional Communist Party policy of outright revolutionary agitation. Under these circumstances, and particularly in view of the recent Soviet attack on Finland, the arrest of certain outstanding Communist leaders in the United States for violations of Federal law and a variety of other factors, it is reasonable to expect that there will take place a sharp reduction not only in the influence exerted by the Communist Party in the United States but also in the number of people adhering to it.

In somewhat similar fashion the Nazi or Fascist movement has at the moment suffered certain severe set-backs, due largely to the present international situation. It has already been pointed out that the most effective appeal of such groups has been an attempt to rally those who were for obvious reasons ready to enlist in an "anti-Communist" movement. With the demonstration of the similarity of purpose and method between Stalin's communism and Hitler's nazi-ism, this tactic, as has already been pointed out, became less effective.

The committee conceives its principal task to have been the revelation of the attempts now being made by extreme groups in this country to deceive the great mass of earnest and devoted American citizens. The committee finds that the danger to American democracy lies not only in the rather remote possibility that Communists, Nazis, or Fascists will succeed in a frontal attack on our Constitutional government and overthrow it, but also in the much greater chance that each extreme totalitarian group seeking by deception to advance its own cause and pad its ranks will succeed in convincing a really substantial number of people that their only defense against violence from the opposite extreme is to accept the violence of the one they find least objectionable.

The committee condemns without reservation the evident willingness of some supposedly responsible people to endanger the very civil peace of their country by encouraging, for purely political purposes, suspicion, fear, and bigotry of the worst sort. Those on the right of political center cannot in the long run be benefited nor can they save their country by attempting to brand as Communists all those on the left of that center. Conversely, those on the left cannot advance their cause nor save their country by leveling the charge of fascism and attempting to brand as tools of Hitler all who would proceed more slowly than themselves.

The committee's work should result in freeing the progressive and labor movements from Communist control or domination and in preventing sincere conservatives from temporizing with essentially Fascist or Nazi groups or philosophies. If the findings of this committee were to be used as a pretext for the building of an un-American movement of any sort on the excuse that such movement were "necessary to combat such-and-such a danger to the country" clearly a disservice to our democratic institutions would have been done. The committee wishes to state emphatically that the only proper and democratic method whereby un-American activities can be effectively combatted is by the duly constituted law-enforcing bodies of America operating under our Constitution and with the support of an informed public opinion.

The Communist Party as a Branch of the Soviet Government

Hundreds of pages of testimony have established the fact that the Communist Party of the United States can make no more than a superficial claim that it is a "political party" in the sense in which the American people understand those words. It is, on the contrary, a constituent member of the Communist International and is its agent in the United States. The Communist International in turn is completely dominated by the Communist Party of Soviet Russia.

The committee feels that a careful examination of the facts justifies the assertion that the Communist Party in the United States is a foreign conspiracy masked as a political party.

The committee is forced to conclude that in practice, the Communist Party is actually functioning as a "border patrol" on American shores for a foreign power—The Soviet Union.

Since the Communist Party of the United States has the avowed purpose of drastically changing the form of government of the United States, it is the opinion of the committee that the party's activities constitute a violation of the Treaty of Recognition entered into between the Government of the United States and the Government of the U. S. S. R. in 1933.

The evidence for these conclusions come from three sources: (1) Admissions drawn from the present leaders of the Party, including Earl Browder, William Z. Foster, Max Bedacht, William Weiner, and Alexander Trachtenberg.

(2) Testimony of former leaders of the party who had themselves engaged in all the operations of this international conspiracy, including Ben Gitlow, Jay Lovestone, Fred E. Beal, Joseph Zack, and W. G. Krivitsky.

(3) The official literature and publications of the Communist Party and of the Comintern (the Communist International).

The evidence for our conclusion with respect to the true nature of the Communist Party is both direct and cumulative. It falls into the following subdivisions:

(1) *History of the Comintern.*

The Communist Party of the United States is an admitted section or affiliate of the Communist International. The Communist International was founded in 1919 on the initiative of the Communist Party of the Soviet Union and under the personal leadership of Lenin. The Communist Party of the Soviet Union rules the U. S. S. R., and according to the testimony of numerous witnesses who appeared before the committee, it likewise rules, unchallenged, the Communist International of which the American Communist Party is an affiliate.

(2) *Statutes of the Comintern.*

The basic law governing the workings of the Communist International makes it clear that all constituent national parties in the Comintern are completely subservient to the will of its real leaders in Moscow. All witnesses, whether past or present leaders, on the Communist Party of the United States, testified that *obedience or expulsion* is the law governing the relations of national parties to the Comintern.

(3) *The "model" party.*

Present leaders of the Communist Party of the United States, such as Browder and Foster, admitted that the Communist Party of the Soviet Union is the "model" after which all other Communist parties are patterned. At the present time, the American Communist Party is engaged in a systematic study of the History of the Communist Party of the Soviet Union, which has as its avowed aim the inculcation of the idea that the CPSU is the true "model" party for all other Communist parties.

(4) *The "Fatherland."*

Present leaders of the American Communist Party admitted that they look upon and have spoken about the Soviet Union as the "Fatherland of the working class of the world."

(5) *Primary loyalty.*

It was clear from the testimony of every present member of the Communist Party who appeared before the committee that his primary loyalty, in the event of any conflict between the United States and the U. S. S. R., would force him to choose the side of the U. S. S. R. And the head of the party, Earl Browder, general secretary, admitted in the following testimony before the committee that he would attempt to turn an aggressive war into a civil war:

> Mr. Matthews (examining the witness) . . . Assuming that it (the United States) should attack the Soviet Government, or become involved in war against the Soviet Union, what then?
>
> Mr. Browder. If it were possible for the American Government to do that, or if we assume that the American Government should make an aggressive war against the Soviet Union, I would stand as absolutely opposing such a war, and as doing everything possible to stop it.
>
> Mr. Matthews. Even to turning such a war into a civil war?
>
> Mr. Browder. Yes, sir; in every way I could to stop it. I cannot conceive, however, of America being an aggressor nation.

(6) *Representatives in Moscow.*

The Communist Party of the United States has consistently maintained a number of official representatives in Moscow for the purpose of interlocking the American party with the ruling party of the U.S.S.R. Witnesses, such as Joseph Zack, who had once served in the capacity of representative to Moscow were among those who gave testimony before the committee.

(7) *Representatives from Moscow.*

According to the statutes of the Comintern and also according to numerous witnesses with first-hand knowledge of the facts, the Communist International has from time to time sent representatives to the United States armed with complete authority over the affairs of the American Communist Party. Among these Comintern representatives here have been Harry Pollitt, Dengel, and S. Gussev.

(8) *OGPU agents.*

The Soviet Government maintains a far-flung system of secret-service agents engaged in espionage throughout the world. These OGPU agents, according to the testimony of Krivitsky, former head of the Soviet Union's western European military intelligence, have looked upon the United States as one of the countries in which their work has been done with least interference from governmental agencies. The work of these OGPU agents is, furthermore, closely interlocked with the work of the Communist Party itself. Among the OGPU agents identified by witnesses was Nicholas Dozenberg, who has since been indicted and apprehended by Federal authorities. Former high leaders of the Communist Party in this country described members of the party as persons possessing the "OGPU mind." In other words, while only a comparatively few party members actually become OGPU agents, all of them are in a position where they can be used to furnish information to the secret service of the Russian Government, and where they may at any time be called upon to either act under Russian instructions or be expelled from the Communist Party.

(9) *Training of leaders.*

For many years, the Russian Government maintained in Moscow a school for the training of leaders of foreign communist parties. Scores of the leaders of the American Communist Party, such as Clarance Hathaway, have passed through this school, and some of its graduates have been among the committee's witnesses, such as William Nowell. The training which these leaders have received in Moscow has included preparation for eventual uprisings and civil war in the United States.

(10) *Visits of party leaders to Moscow.*

Without exception the leaders of the American Communist Party have made repeated visits to Moscow. In official documents introduced as evidence, it appears that Moscow has been described as "Mecca" in the parlance of the Communist Party of the United States.

(11) *Reports to Moscow.*

All high officials of the American Communist Party have made periodic reports to Moscow on their activities in the United States. These reports have been subjected to the criticism of the officials of the Comintern who are at the same time officials of the Soviet Government.

(12) *Moscow's supervision of publications.*

According to documentary evidence, the authenticity of which was conceded by Earl Browder, general secretary of the Communist Party, issues of the Daily Worker (official newspaper of the Communist Party in the United States) have been analyzed and criticized by official Moscow agencies, and changes in the Daily Worker's policy have been dictated from Moscow as the result of this analysis and criticism.

(13) *Moscow's permission necessary.*

When the Communist Party of the United States moved its headquarters from Chicago to New York, it was necessary to obtain the permission of Moscow for the move. Likewise, whenever the Communist Party of the United States has desired to hold a convention, it has been necessary to obtain the permission, in advance, of authorities in Moscow.

(14) *Leadership and advise of Stalin.*

The present head of the Communist Party in the United States, Earl Browder, acknowledged that he and his party have accepted the leadership and advice of Stalin on matters that pertain to the work of the Communist Party in this country. Furthermore, the tenth convention of the American Communist Party formally acknowledged the leadership of Stalin and Dimitrov, the latter being the head of the Communist International.

(15) *Directives.*

Scattered throughout the proceedings and literature of the American Communist Party and the Comintern are numerous examples of actual instructions given by the Comintern to the American party. These were introduced into evidence before the committee.

(16) *Parallel policies.*

From numerous documentary sources, as well as from the first-hand knowledge of witnesses, it was shown that the basic policies of the Communist Party of the United States closely parallel the policies of the Government of the U. S. S. R. When shifts of policy have occurred in the Soviet Union, based upon its internal situation alone, these shifts have been mechanically reflected in similar shifts by the party in the United States without any regard for the situation confronting the Communist Party here.

(17) *Defense of the Soviet Union.*

For many years the Communist Party of the United States used as one of its principal slogans "The Defense of the Soviet Union." A revolution of the Seventh World Congress of the Communist International, to which Browder and Foster and other leaders of the American Communist Party declared their allegiance, described the defense of the Soviet Union as "the paramount duty" of Communists throughout the world.

(18) *Support of Stalin's foreign policy.*

One of the most striking attributes of the American Communist Party in the present world situation is the complete support which its leaders and publications give to the foreign policies of Stalin. For years the American party conducted its most energetic propaganda campaigns around the issue of antifascism. With the signing of the Stalin-Hitler Pact, all this has changed, and the American party has launched an equally energetic propaganda campaign against Great Britain and France. For years the American party was quick to organize rallies and front organizations around the issues of Hitler's various aggressions against small European countries. Today the party has lapsed into silence on the subject of Hitler's aggressions and has been quick to organize its propaganda campaigns in defense of Stalin's aggressions against Poland, Estonia, and Finland.

(19) *Illegality on behalf of Moscow.*

In demonstrating its unswerving loyalty to the Soviet Government, the Communist Party of the United States, under instructions from the Comintern, has from time to time pursued policies in direct violation of the laws of the United States. These violations have included the obtaining of fraudulent passports, counterfeiting of American currency, the maintenance of a secret espionage apparatus, and violation of injunctions.

(20) *Financial support from Moscow.*

Numerous witnesses testified before the committee that Moscow has from the very beginning of the Communist Party in the United States supplied the party here with funds for its subversive activities. Some of these witnesses, such as Gitlow and Lovestone, have in the past themselves brought these funds from Moscow to the United States.

(21) *Soviet Government agencies in the United States.*

The interlocking of Soviet Government agencies in the United States with the American Communist Party was established through the testimony of several witnesses. The Soviet embassy, the Amtorg Trading Corporation, the Bookkniga (propaganda literature agency) and the Amkino (propaganda movie distributors) were involved in this interrelationship of the American Communist Party with official Soviet agencies.

(22) *Soviet literature.*

Through the medium of the International publishers, whose head, Alexander Trachtenberg, was a witness before the committee, extensive Soviet propaganda is subsidized in the United States. Both the American Communist Party and the Soviet Government are involved in this ostensibly commercial concern which distributes foreign-subsidized books and pamphlets in the United States.

(23) *Press agencies.*

The tie between the Soviet Government and the American Communist Party is expressed in numerous propaganda services, masking as news agencies and involving cable tolls and other forms of subsidy which effectively aid the Stalin conspiracy on American soil.

(24) *Moscow control over party leadership.*

Through numerous witnesses and documents it was established that Stalin and Molotov have personally intervened to change and determine the leadership of the American Communist Party. The confidential versions of Stalin's speeches on the situation in the American Communist Party were introduced into evidence before the committee. They reveal beyond any possibility of dispute the fact that Joseph Stalin is the dictator not only in Russia but also of the American Communist Party.

(25) *The Moscow "solar system."*

Indisputable evidence was introduced to show that the interference of the Soviet Government in American affairs goes far beyond the confines of the American Communist Party itself. Organized and maintained under strict Communist Party control are organizations having direct connections with Moscow as well as indirect connections through the American Communist Party. As an example of this type of organization, we cite the now defunct Trade Union Unity League which was under the control of the American Communist Party and which was also affiliated with the Profintern, the Red International of Labor Unions, having its world headquarters in Moscow. The committee also received evidence placing the International Labor Defense and the Young Communist League in this category.

Communist technique in "transmission belts" and "united
    fronts."

Numerous witnesses support the testimony of Benjamin Gitlow, former secretary of the Communist Party, who described the party's technique in the organization and control of its "front organizations" in the following language:

> First, a number of sympathizers who are close to the party and who the party knows can be depended upon to carry out party orders are gotten together and formed into a nucleus which issues a call for the organization of a particular front organization which the party wants to establish. And generally after that is done a program is drawn up by the party, which this provisional committee adopts. Then, on the basis of this provisional program, all kinds of individuals are canvassed to become sponsors of the organization, which is to be launched in the very near future. A secretary is appointed, a provisional secretary is appointed before the organization is launched and in every instance in our day the secretary who was appointed was a member of the Communist Party, because the secretary has access to the letters and to the files and to the organization. And as president of the organization, we would put up some prominent public figure who was willing to accept the presidency of the organization, generally making sure that, if that public figure was one who would not go along with the Communists, he was of such a type that he would be too busy to pay attention to the affairs of the organization, and therefore would represent no problem to the organization.
>
> On the committee that would be drawn together, a sufficient number of communists and Communist Party sympathizers who will carry out party orders, was included, and out of this number a small executive committee is organized, or acting committee, which carries on the affairs of the organization, so called, and this small executive committee, with the secretary, really run the organization. And this small committee and the secretary are the instruments of the Communist Party, with the result that when

manifestoes or decisions on campaigns are made, these campaigns are ordered by the Communist Party.

Communist Party "fronts."

The committee finds that the following organizations are properly classified as "front organizations" of the Communist Party:

American League for Peace and Democracy.
International Workers Order.
American Student Union.
Friends of the Soviet Union.
National Negro Congress.
Southern Negro Youth Congress.
League of American Writers.
Workers Alliance.
Spanish Refugee Relief Campaign.
North American Committee to Aid Spanish Democracy.
Friends of the Abraham Lincoln Brigade.

In the case of the International Labor Defense, although some non-Communists have undoubtedly lent support to its efforts and perhaps even cooperated with it, the committee has established that it is, essentially, the legal defense arm of the Communist Party of the United States.

In the case of the American Youth Congress, the committee finds a central organization which has no membership of its own, but which attempts to affiliate together the largest possible number of organizations of American young people, the vast majority of whom have no connection with communism, nazi-ism, or any movement of that sort, but are members of some of the most necessary and valuable organizations which our country possesses. The Young Communist League, as well as certain other organizations in which Communists have played an important part, is affiliated with the American Youth Congress and testimony has been presented to the committee to indicate that this minority group has at times exerted an influence on the American Youth Congress out of all proportion to its size. The committee is unable to see how it is possible for this or any other organization of American young people claiming to preserve and vitalize the American institutions and life of America to expect to promote that work by including within its ranks those who do not believe in democracy, but in a contrary philosophy of life and form of government.

Due to its extraordinary size and influence, we give a summary of the evidence concerning the American League for Peace and Democracy. For the evidence concerning the other aforementioned "fronts," or "transmission belts," we refer readers to the full transcript of testimony given in public hearings.

American League for Peace and Democracy.

The committee finds on the basis of overwhelming and conclusive evidence that the American League for Peace and Democracy is a Communist "front" organization.

According to its own publications, the American League was organized at the Amsterdam World Congress Against War in 1932. That congress was convened on the call of the famous French Communist, Henri Barbusse, acting under instructions of the Communist International. It was attended by 2,196 delegates of whom 830 were avowed members of the Communist parties of the world. In addition to these avowed Communists, there were 291 delegates who styled themselves "Social Democrats" but whose position, according to their own proclamation, was in complete agreement with the Communists. These self-styled Social Democrats pledged themselves to work for civil war in their respective countries in the event of another international conflict. The Amsterdam congress unanimously adopted a program which declared that it would not allow the Soviet Union "to be touched." This program was adopted as its own by the American Section of the world committee which was set up at Amsterdam. Of the 32 American delegates to the Amsterdam congress, a large majority were well-known Communist Party members or came from organizations such as the John Reed clubs whose affiliation with the Communist Party is clear beyond dispute.

The American section of the Amsterdam movement first called itself the American Committee for the Struggle Against War. Its secretaries, Oakley Johnson and Donald Henderson, were well-known Communists. It was this committee which called the First United States Congress Against War, at which the founding of the American League Against War and Fascism took place. Donald Henderson became the first secretary of the organization.

In three successive programs adopted by the annual congresses of the American League, the organization boldly declared its first objective to be the work of interfering with the preparation of our national defense. Point 1 in these programs stated this purpose in the following language:

> To work toward the stopping of the manufacture and transport of munitions and all other materials essential to the conduct of war.

At its second annual congress, Harry F. Ward, present national chairman of the American League, declared this program to be "sound." Earl Browder, one of the main speakers at that Congress and vice president of the American League at that time, joined Harry F. Ward in this declaration concerning the League's program. Shortly before that, Browder, who was also secretary of the Communist Party, had gone in person to Moscow to report to the Executive Committee of the Communist International that the program of the American League was "politically satisfactory." Browder also declared in Moscow that the Communist Party had led the First United States Congress Against War "quite openly" and that the American League represented the Communist Party's "most successful application of the United Front."

In 1937 the American League Against War and Fascism changed its name to the American League for Peace and Democracy. This was in keeping with the Communist Party's new "line" on the People's Front.

According to one of the recent minutes of the Washington, D. C., branch of the American League, it was decided "to set up League committees in the units of Government agencies with our present membership in those agencies as a nucleus." These nuclei of the League are now formed in more than a score of Government agencies. H. C. Lamberton, chairman of the Washington branch of the League, testified under oath before the committee that there are 700 Government employees who are members of the American League for Peace and Democracy.

Both the financial secretary of the Communist Party, William Weiner (indicted since his testimony before the committee as an impostor falsely posing as an American citizen in obtaining a passport), and the national chairman of the American League for Peace and Democracy, Harry F. Ward, testified under oath that the Communist Party is the only national organization which contributes any appreciable sum of money to the work of the American League. According to these two witnesses, this amounts to the sum of two or three thousand dollars annually and represents approximately 15 percent of the total annual budget of the American League. This financial contribution from the Communist Party has continued down to the present time, despite the fact that the Communist Party formally severed, for tactical reasons, its affiliation with the American League more than 2 years ago.

The Chicago branch of the American League for Peace and Democracy sent out a letter in 1938 in which its executive secretary boosted the Communist Party's newspaper, the *Midwest Daily Record*. The secretary wrote:

> I have sent you about a dozen copies of the May 10 Record under separate cover. I am sending copies of this issue to all of our branches calling attention to the invaluable role of the Midwest Record in this important phase of our activity and urging their support by subscriptions, etc. It is a shame that the Midwest Record does not have one hundred times its present circulation.

When the American League backs an avowed Communist Party publication in that manner, it is clear that the league and the Communist Party have a link with each other that the leaders of these two organizations have attempted to conceal from the public.

A member of the national committee of the American League, Mrs. Clinton A. Barr, appeared as a witness before the committee and told how a radio address which she had been asked to deliver under the auspices of the American League since the signing of the Soviet-Nazi pact, was completely revised by the secretary of the Communist Party of the State of Wisconsin. The committee finds it significant that among the changes which the secretary of the Wisconsin Communist Party made in this radio address of the national committee-woman of the American League was the deletion of uncomplimentary references to Adolph Hitler. Mrs. Barr refused to deliver the revised radio address and resigned.

The committee finds that the league's record on the Soviet-Nazi pact stamps it as an organization subservient to the Communist Party. A statement prepared by the executive committee of the Washington branch of the American League reads, in part, as follows:

> This pact is a real contribution to world peace and to the peace and security of the United States. . . . The signing of the nonaggression pact between the U. S. S. R. and Germany is not a war alliance between the two powers. It is not an agreement for the partition of Poland. . . . In this sense the pact between the U. S. S. R. and Germany is the only real contribution to the security of Poland that has been made to date. . . . In doing this, the Soviet Union has made a real contribution to an understanding of the present crisis in Europe. It has made a real contribution to the peace and security of Europe, the world, and the United States.

The committee believes that earnest Americans who seek the solution of their country's problems within the framework of our constitutional government should either refrain from lending their names to organizations with which they are not completely familiar or else should be sufficiently active in such organizations to make sure that they, and not any foreign-dominated group, control its activities. The committee believes it is especially important that such a policy be pursued by persons employed by the Government of the Nation.

The committee finds that the American League for Peace and Democracy has probably been the most effective of all the united front organizations in drawing innocent and earnest people into activities cooperative with the Communist Party. We fully realize that the vast majority of the membership of the League consists of people that simply believe in peace and democracy, and we find it difficult to understand why this majority has not asserted itself with greater vigor in connection with the activities of the League.

The Problem of the Labor Movement

Up until the year 1934 the Communist Party pursued the policy of dual unionism, setting up rival labor organizations in the same industries as were organized by affiliates of the American Federation of Labor. In that year, however, this policy was dropped and the attempt was made by Communists to bore from within the American Federation of Labor. On the whole this effort met with but slight success.

With the formation of the C. I. O. the price efforts of the Communists were turned in the direction of that organization. It is unmistakably clear that the overwhelming majority of the members of the C. I. O. as well as its president are not Communists or Communist sympathizers, but sincere American workers seeking to improve their lot in life in perfectly legitimate American fashion. The evidence before the committee indicates, however, that the leadership of some 10 or 12 of the constituent unions of the C. I. O. out of a total of some 48 unions is more than tinged with communism. The evidence shows that some of their leaders are either card-holding members of the Communist Party or subservient followers of that party's "line." In the rank and file membership of these unions, on the contrary, the proportion of Communists and Communist sympathizers is very small indeed. There is encouraging evidence of an attempt on the part of the C. I. O. leadership to remove this Communist influence and it is a matter of record that most of its largest organizations are free of any Communist control, domination, or even serious influence. It is plain to this committee that the situation which does pertain in the organizations listed below is the most serious one, both from the standpoint of American industries and from the standpoint of the organized labor movement itself.

On the basis of the evidence submitted, we find Communist leadership entrenched in the following organizations: National Maritime Union; United Cannery, Packing, and Allied Workers; Federation of Architects, Engineers, Chemists and Technicians; Fur Workers International Union; International Longshoremen's and Warehousemen's Union; Transport Workers Union; United Office and Professional Workers Union; American Communications Association; United Electrical, Radio and Mechanical Workers of America; and the United Furniture Workers of America.

American labor has borne the brunt of the Communist efforts to pursue the policy of penetration of mass organizations in the past 4 years and, to the degree that that effort has been successful, American labor has a task of great seriousness and importance on its hands. The serious factor in the situation, from the standpoint of the Nation as a whole, lies not so much in the purely economic views which the members of labor organizations may hold, as in the foreign control over Communist Party members, which might in time of stress lead to sabotage and to espionage, and in the Communist rule-or-ruin policy so disruptive to the labor organizations themselves.

The committee believes that the American labor movement must, and will, as speedily as possible, free itself of Communist leadership and control wherever it exists.

The committee is emphatic in its belief that a strong and vigorous labor movement is an element of strength in the life of our democracy. But the committee must assert that the Communist Party is interested in trade-unions primarily for the purpose of attempting to utilize those labor organizations for the benefit of the Russian dictatorship and its foreign policies.

Nazi-Fascist Organizations

The committee heard numerous witnesses and received a large volume of documentary evidence concerning the extent, nature and activities of a number of Nazi-Fascist groups, individuals and organizations which are presently operating in the United States, or which have recently been active in this country. Some of the principal witnesses who testified before the committee regarding such activities were:

James E. Campbell, captain, Engineer Corps, United States Army Reserve; Commander, Veterans of Foreign Wars Post, Owensboro, Ky.; Americanism Chairman of the Department of Kentucky of the Veterans of Foreign Wars.

George E. Deatherage, National Commander, Knights of the White Camellia.

Dudley Pierrepont Gilbert, organizer and leader of the American Nationalists, Inc.

Felix McWhirter, treasurer, Indiana Republican State Committee; president, Peoples Bank, Indianapolis, Ind.

General George Van Horn Moseley, United States Army, retired.

Henry D. Allen, former member of the Silver Shirt Legion of America.

Robert B. Barker, Investigator for the Special Committee on Un-American Activities.

Fritz Kuhn, leader of the German-American Bund.

John C. Metcalfe, former member of the German-American Bund.

Dr. John Harvey Sherman, president, University of Tampa.

Helen Vooros, former member and leader of the German-American Bund Youth Movement.

Gerhardt Heinrich Seger, former member of the German Reichstag and a member of its Foreign Relations Committee.

Emil Revyuk, associate editor of "Svoboda," Ukrainian Daily newspaper; President of the United Ukrainian Organizations of the United States.

Richard Forbes, former member of the German-American Bund.

Fritz Heberling, clerk, German Consulate, Chicago, Ill., and head of the German Bund.

James J. Metcalfe, special agent, Investigation Division, Farm Security Administration, United States Department of Agriculture.

Neil Ness, former member of the German-American Bund.

From the evidence which has been heard, the primary aims of these groups appear to be (1) a radical change in the American form of government, and (2) the collection of dues from such misguided citizens as will contribute to their support. The evidence also reflects that these various groups are engaged in a form of racketeering as well as in subversive activities. When the money ceases to flow into the coffers of one organization they abandon it and start another one. These groups and organizations make their chief appeal to the basest forms of religious and racial hatred. They promise to deliver this country from the menace of communism; they heap scorn upon the institutions of democracy; and they urge the short cuts of force and violence.

The German-American Bund

Fritz Kuhn, the fuehrer of the German-American Bund, claims that his organization is nothing more than a political group whose primary purpose is to promote the welfare and best interests of the citizens of the United States and to assist in a solution of their problems. Testimony before the committee, however, both from hostile and friendly witnesses, establishes conclusively that the German-American Bund receives its inspiration, program, and direction from the Nazi Government of Germany through the various propaganda organizations which have been set up by that Government and which function under the control and supervision of the Nazi Ministry of Propaganda and Enlightenment.

The bund presently has three major administrative divisions in the United States—the eastern, the midwestern, and the far western—each under the direction of a division leader who takes his orders from Fritz Kuhn, the National Fuehrer. There are in the three divisions 47 districts and in the districts are a total of 69 local posts or units. It has been impossible to accurately determine the extent of the bund's membership due to the secrecy with which it operates and the fact that all membership lists, correspondence, and other records have been destroyed by order of the national leader, an admission he made on the witness stand to this committee. In the absence of membership lists, the committee has had to accept as the best available figure the statement of Fritz Kuhn concerning the bund's membership. He testified that the bund has a membership of approximately 20,000 to 25,000. (A Department of Justice investigation made of the bund in 1937 placed the membership at 6,500.) In addition to the regular membership, it has what is known as the sympathizer or "fellow traveler" group, consisting of those who are sympathetic to the bund but do not actively participate in its proceedings. He testified that the sympathizer group is composed of approximately 80,000 to 100,000 individuals.

It was established that the German-American Bund operating in the United States is similar to the Nazi groups which were built up in Austria and Czechoslovakia prior to their annexation by Germany. The August 31, 1939, issue of the Deutscher Weckruf and Beobachter, official newspaper of the bund, printed an article written in German under the following title:

> Fritz Kuhn, America's Henlein. German-American Bund, the organization of which he is the leader, eight to ten thousand uniformed storm troops. The duel, Kuhn versus Dewey.

It was established that the program and the activities of the German-American Bund are similar to Nazi organizations in Germany and in other countries. The bund newspaper makes frequent use of material emanating from Nazi propaganda sources, such as "World Service." The emblem of the National Socialist Party, the swastika, also is the emblem of the German-American Bund.

Fritz Kuhn, in defending the position that the bund is strictly an American political organization, claims that members of the bund must be American citizens. The following is a quotation from the "Weckruf," official organ of the bund, which is illustrative of the bund's attitude with reference to citizenship:

We may have lying in the closet different citizenship papers and yet we are all German men and links of a big German community of hundreds of millions.

In 1936 Fritz Kuhn accompanied a large delegation of bund members to Germany ostensibly for the purpose of visiting the Olympic games. The group paraded in uniform of the Orderly Division (storm troops), and the parade was reviewed by Adolf Hitler. Following the parade, Fritz Kuhn and other officials of the German-American Bund were received by the German Feuhrer, at which time they presented him with a golden book containing autographs of bund members and delivered to him a contribution of $3,000 for the German winter relief fund. This money had been solicited from bund members, some of whom, according to Kuhn's testimony, were unemployed and on relief.

In his testimony with reference to the meeting with Hitler, Kuhn stated that no report was made by him concerning bund activities in the United States and that the subject was not mentioned during the interview. However, the December 10, 1936, issue of the official bund newspaper carried an article concerning a speech which Kuhn made in San Francisco following his return from Germany. According to the article, Kuhn stated in his speech that Chancellor Hitler advised him, "Go back and carry on your fight."

It was established through the testimony of Fritz Kuhn that the bund had worked sympathetically with other organizations throughout the United States and cooperates with them. Kuhn testified that some of these groups are the Christian Front, the Christian Mobilizers, the Christian Crusaders, the Social Justice Society, the Silver Shirt Legion of America, the Knights of the White Camellia and various Italian Fascist, White Russian, and Ukrainian organizations. Kuhn testified that some of the leaders of these groups had addressed meetings sponsored by the bund and that representatives of the bund in turn frequently appeared as speakers at meetings and gatherings sponsored by the above-named groups. It was also established that the bund cooperated with some of these organizations and their leaders by exchanging literature and publications with them and by publishing material emanating from them in the official organ of the bund. Numerous articles have appeared in the bund newspaper expressing the bund's approval of the activities of the organizations already mentioned. The literature put out by the various groups and individuals named is distributed or sold at the bund camps, meetings, and other gatherings.

The following excerpt from the testimony of Fritz Kuhn is indicative of his attitude:

> Mr. Whitley (examining the witness). Mr. Kuhn, what are the relations between Mr. Joe McWilliams and his Christian Mobilizers and the German-American Bund?
>
> Mr. Kuhn. They are very friendly to each other, because the Christian Front, the Christian Mobilizers, really have ideas which we sponsor 100 percent.

With reference to the exchange of literature and propaganda material between the bund and various Fascist groups, the committee received testimony that the following are standard reading in bund camps: Hitler's Mein Kampf, Pelley's booklets and publication, Liberation, the books of Julius Streicher (German propagandist), and the Rev. Charles E. Coughlin's publication, Social Justice.

The German-American Bund, like the National Socialist Party in Germany, pays particular attention to the training of its youth. Testimony was heard that members of the youth movement were taught nothing concerning American institutions or ideals, and that they were encouraged to be extremely critical of the United States and its Government. It was also found that the uniforms worn by the members of the youth groups, their camps and program of activities were similar in every respect to those of the Hitler youth movement, and that the Nazi salute was the accepted gesture of greeting.

It was established that groups of leaders of the German-American Bund youth movement are frequently sent to Germany for special training. Testimony was received from a witness who was a member of a group of 15 boys and 15 girls from various parts of the United States who were selected by the bund to be sent to Germany for special training. According to the witness, all instructions concerning arrangements and the trip came from V. D. A. (League of Germans Living Abroad), one of the Nazi propaganda agencies; and all plans and arrangements with reference to the trip were carried out with the utmost secrecy.

It was established through the two witnesses, both former bund members, that there is a political agent on all German ships and that these political agents maintain contact with the Nazi representatives in foreign countries. They are intermediaries for transmission of instructions to the bund leaders in the United States and they receive reports from these leaders concerning the bund's activities, according to the witnesses.

A former bund member on the west coast testified that German agents engaged in espionage activities, contacted bund leaders in the United States and sought and received their cooperation. This witness also testified that he had heard discussions among bund leaders with reference to the manner in which the bund, through its members in various industrial plants, could effectively carry out a program of sabotage in case such action became necessary.

Evidence was heard by the committee that members of the bund had assisted German agents whose arrests were sought by officials in the United States in avoiding apprehension and had helped get them out of the United States with the cooperation of German ships.

Evidence also was taken indicating that Nazi propaganda agencies, through officials of the German Government in the United States, have attempted to propagandize educational institutions in this country. It was testified that a German consul general had offered, on behalf of the German

Government to subsidize German departments in American universities provided the professors were "acceptable" to the Nazis.

Cooperating Groups.

The committee has found abundant evidence of the cooperation of certain other organizations with the German-American Bund. This is a more serious matter than is the direct strength or influence of the bund itself. For example, in August 1938 a so-called anti-Communist convention was held at the bund headquarters in Los Angeles at which Hermann Schwinn, leader of the bund on the west coast, was one of the principal speakers; and Arno Risse, bund leader, who has since fled the country, was one of the two or three persons most active in promoting and making arrangements for the convention. According to the testimony of Henry D. Allen, one-time Silver Shirt leader, organizer of the American White Guard, and prominent figure in Fascist circles generally, the following persons participated in this convention:

Kenneth Alexander, Southern California leader of the Silver Shirts; J. H. Peyton, of the American Rangers; Chas. B. Hudson, of Omaha, Nebr., organizer and leader of America Awake, who accompanied General Moseley when he appeared before the committee; Mrs. Leslie Fry, alias Paquita Louise De Shishmareff, mysterious international figure who has since fled the country, then leader of the Militant Christian Patriots; representatives of Italian Fascist and White Russian organizations; and a number of others of similar point of view.

Bund literature mingled with that of William Dudley Pelley, Robert Edmondson, Mrs. Fry, and George Deatherage on the tables of this convention.

It is clear to the committee that this convention was in no real sense an anti-Communist convention but rather another of a series of attempts to unite some of the various forces of intolerance, racial hatred, Naziism and Fascism in order to achieve greater influence in the United States. This effort like others of its kind yielded no apparent results.

Allen further testified that he was sent out by Mrs. Fry on an extended trip throughout the country, and that all his expenses were paid by Mrs. Fry, but Allen did not know her source of the money. During the course of this trip Allen visited George Deatherage, leader of the Knights of the White Camellia, James True of Washington, D. C., publisher of the so-called Industrial Control Reports, Gerald B. Winrod, Kansas preacher, Nazi protagonist, and unsuccessful candidate for the Senate, Robert Edmondson, disseminator of Fascist literature, and Fritz Kuhn. On this same trip Allen went to Atlanta, Ga., to attempt to "buy the Ku Klux Klan" for Mrs. Fry for the sum of $75,000. He testified that he talked to Hiram W. Evans, head of the Klan, but that Evans "was not interested in the idea."

In releasing this report on the activities of Nazi agents in the United States the committee wishes to make the emphatic statement that neither the committee as a whole nor any of its individual members entertains the slightest doubt of the unswerving loyalty to the United States of our fellow citizens of German descent. In a number of cases it was their cooperation which made disclosures of bund activities possible. They felt that it was as much in their interest as in that of the Nation as a whole that the committee endeavored to bring to light some of the facts concerning the operations of Nazi agents and the leaders of the German-American Bund.

The question of the form of government of the German or any other nation is not one that concerns either this committee or the American people. But attempts by any foreign agency to influence American citizens in favor of a foreign form of government and against American democracy is quite a different matter and one concerning which the Committee on Un-American Activities has immediate and great concern.

Fascist Groups.

In recent years a large number of organizations and individuals sympathetic to Nazi and Fascist ideals and forms of government have been extremely active in the United States. There is no way to determine accurately exactly how many such organizations are presently active or have been existant in recent years. They are conceived in the minds of would-be "Fuehrers" and spring up overnight with alarming frequency. They often operate only for a short time and then are replaced by some other organizations with a name which is thought to have a popular appeal. For the same reason, it is impossible to determine the total membership of these groups, but it is safe to estimate that the actual membership plus sympathizers and potential supporters is many thousands.

Many of these so-called organizations are nothing more than letterhead or "name" organizations and have little or no actual membership. In some instances one individual will create and be the self-designated "dictator" of several such groups at the same time. The words "patriotic," "Christian" and "American" frequently are used in the names of the various organizations for the purpose of attracting followers. Needless to say, the use of these words by such organizations is a gross misrepresentation and entirely inconsistent with the actual purposes for which the organizations stand.

The evidence received by the committee, both verbal and documentary, establishes that all of these organizations receive their inspiration from the Nazi and Fascist forms of dictatorship, although they all profess to be strictly American and interested only in the institutions and problems of this country.

One witness, Dudley Pierrepont Gilbert, who appeared before the committee had written to one of his associates, James E. Campbell, frankly describing his own destiny in terms of the careers of Mussolini and Hitler. "Remember," Gilbert wrote, "those who are finally successful always suffer much before victory. You and I are no exception to that rule. Mussolini was insulted, stoned, and driven from town to town. . . . Hitler was jailed and persecuted for years. . . . It is that very suffering that has welded together the strong type of men that have led Nationalism to victory in other countries. The same will be so here. . . . You and I are destined to lead America to that greatness."

It was established that these groups and individuals receive literature from the various propaganda agencies of the Nazi and Fascist governments and that they frequently reprint portions of this material in their own publications without indicating its source. They have expressed their admiration for the Nazi or Fascist forms of government. They advocate similar forms of government for the United States.

Some of the organizations which have been brought to the committee's attention frankly describe themselves as "Fascist." One publication introduced into evidence states: "This issue carries at the masthead our newly selected emblem—the swastika."

They advocate as a part of their program the accomplishment of a change in our present form of government by force and violence. "Frankly," Campbell wrote to Deatherage, "I say to you that this thing has gone so far that there is only one remedy, and that is a military action which will put a military court in charge of the United States Federal Government and each State government. . . ."

If not actually advocating such methods, they repeatedly profess to believe that military action will be necessary in order to combat the influence and activities of minority groups. "I believe as you do," wrote Deatherage on one occasion, "that it will take military action to get this gang out and the organization must be built around a propaganda organization, now, that can in a few hours be turned into a militant fighting force."

The leaders of some of the organizations have worked out elaborate plans and charts for developing the various groups into a propaganda machine which could quickly be converted into a military organization. They have also concerned themselves with the problems of securing arms to be used when the expected military action was undertaken.

Probably the largest, best financed, and certainly the best publicized of such groups is the Silver Shirt Legion of America, whose leader is William Dudley Pelley of Asheville, N. C. For those reasons, the committee feels that he and his organization serve best as an example of this type of subversive activity.

In his own book titled "The Door to Revelation," Mr. Pelley describes how he launched his Silver Shirts on January 31, 1933, the day after Hitler took power in Germany, and how he regards himself as the American Hitler. But, as a matter of fact, documentary evidence from the records of the United States district court at Asheville, presented to the committee at public hearings, showed that Mr. Pelley, on January 14, 1934, from Hollywood, Calif., wired Harry F. Sieber, one of his associates in Asheville, to destroy all records of the Galahad Press, Mr. Pelley's defunct publishing company, the insolvency of which had been brought about by the diversion of over $100,000 in funds to other accounts; $29,497.42 of this amount having been deposited in Mr. Pelley's personal account in the Franklin National Bank, Washington, D. C., and $81,366.97 having been deposited in two Asheville banks to credit of the "Foundation for Christian Economics," a dummy corporation set up by Pelley. The Galahad Press, later, on May 1, 1934, was adjudicated a bankrupt with losses of over $13,000 to the preferred stockholders and over $20,000 to creditors. It was further shown that the Silver Shirt Legion of America was actually incorporated on March 17, 1934, by a Delaware charter. Mr. Pelley and three of his associates were subsequently indicted in North Carolina and Pelley and one of his lieutenants were tried and convicted, Pelley being fined $1,719.50 and placed on probation of continuous good behavior for 5 years from and after February 18, 1935.

On September 2, 1939, as a result of false testimony under oath before the committee on August 23, 1939, a paid secret agent of Pelley's was indicted by a Grand Jury in the District of Columbia for perjury committed by said agent in his efforts to secure employment as an investigator with this committee.

It was Pelley who repeatedly in his weekly publication "Liberation" challenged the committee to call him before it but who when summoned by the committee to appear and testify attempted to enjoin the committee in an abortive suit in Federal court at Asheville which was dismissed on August 29, 1939. Thereupon, Pelley disappeared.

Subsequent efforts by committee agents and the United States marshal at Asheville to serve a subpena on Pelley have been unavailing and Pelley is still in hiding somewhere—either in or out of the United States.

A careful investigation of Pelley's bank accounts, and books and the records of the post office at Asheville has established the fact that thousands of dollars in funds coming into Pelley's hands from his organization and publishing house now known as Skyland Press, have been disposed of in a way so devious as to defy accounting.

These facts may explain the desperate efforts, so far successful, of this self-styled Hitler and superpatriot to avoid an appearance before the committee and answer questions.

On September 3, 1939, Pelley sued six members of the committee and an investigator for the committee for $3,150,000 damage, but it is believed that this suit will, like numerous suits filed by Pelley against public officials in the past, be dismissed on motion.

On October 19, 1939, Hon. Zeb Nettles, judge of the Superior Court of Buncombe County, N. C., in directing the Clerk to issue a capias to the Sheriff for the arrest of Pelley on a citation to show cause why his parole should not be revoked, made the following statement in open court:

> It is not those from without that we must watch, but those so-called saviors of mankind who are preaching a doctrine deadly to American institutions. This defendant who has been moving in our midst seeking to further the cause of nazi-ism with himself as

the dictator, seeking to destroy justice and liberty and abolish all laws, living under the very protection of that law—he is seeking to overthrow and trying to undermine our system of government. Such a man cannot deserve the blessings of a Government like ours. He is a menace to our society. Gratitude is one of the most beautiful attributes of human character. This man "smites" the hand that feeds him and has the unenviable record and distinction of being a contemptible ingrate.

We do not have to defend this system of government of ours from such an individual. For 3 weeks I sat here in this very courtroom and helped unravel a course of crooked dealing, thievery, and stealing sufficient to damn any man, much less this contemptible seeker after notoriety, W. D. Pelley, so-called and self-styled leader of the Silver Shirts—convicted felon—not even a citizen. A Bumcombe County jury says he is not, yet he would be our dictator and would tell our county what to do.

The capias for Pelley's arrest to answer the citation to show cause why his parole should not be revoked is still outstanding and unserved.

From the documentary evidence and testimony before the committee concerning the activities of Pelley, the conclusion that he is a racketeer engaged in mulcting thousands of dollars annually from his fanatical and misled followers and credulous people all over the United States, Canada and certain foreign countries, is inescapable.

Pelley provides the typical case, but his methods differ little from others in the same field.

The committee's evidence shows that virtually all these organizations and individuals make the common use of racial and religious hatred to enlist members and secure financial support. It was found that these groups and individuals cooperate to the extent of lending moral support to one another. They also attend meetings and conventions together, and exchange literature and speakers. They apparently do not cooperate where finances are involved and each is jealous of his own sources of income.

Each would-be Caesar has hopes of bringing about a permanent national organization or federation with himself as the supreme leader. Such an organization would include all or most of the smaller groups. Numerous attempts have been made by the leaders active in the various groups to bring about such a consolidation. National conventions have been held at which representatives of many of the groups have been present and plans for one large national organization have been discussed. None of these attempts has as yet been successful due primarily to the jealousy which exists among the leaders and the desire of each to be the "Fuehrer" of the consolidated organization.

The evidence reflects that no person engaged in this type of activity has as yet achieved sufficient prominence and prestige to enable him to receive the support of all organizations and individuals as a national leader. From the testimony heard, it appears that Gen. George Van Horn Moseley was being seriously considered as the national leader prior to the time such plans were exposed and the general was called as a witness before the committee. However, the unending quest for the "man on horseback" continues.

The testimony reflects that the German-American Bund, as well as the Nazi propaganda agencies in Germany, cooperate with the groups and individuals named and give them their full sympathy and support.

It is apparent that one of the principal concerns of the "dictators" of these organizations is the collection of money through the sale of literature and from contributions. It is clear from the testimony received that many of the organizations were set up primarily for the purpose of selling religious and racial hatred and that their leaders are nothing more than racketeers.

The groups and individuals engaged in this particular type of activity have turned out an almost unprecedented volume of literature of the most vicious kind with which they have flooded the United States in their efforts to secure supporters. They have also exchanged this literature with foreign organizations of a similar nature in practically every country. Their efforts in this direction have been ably supplemented by the mass of literature sent to them for redistribution by foreign propaganda agencies, such as the Fichte-Bund of Hamburg, Germany, the "World Service" of Stuttgart and others.

The leaders of the various groups are extremely active as speakers, and meetings, rallies and conventions are constantly being held at which these professional purveyors of hate attempt to spread their doctrines, recruit followers, secure financial support and encourage the use of force and violence.

As stated above, the committee has established that numerous of these essentially Fascist groups in America have sought from time to time to effect a unity. The outstanding effort of this kind was known as the American Nationalist Confederation which was headed by George Deatherage, at that time, but no more, the leader of the Knights of the White Camellia. The official emblem of the American Nationalist Confederation was the swastika.

The following organizations and individuals took part in one way or another in this attempt to create a united Fascist movement:

> Knights of the White Camellia (George Deatherage).
> Militant Christian Patriots (Mrs. Leslie Fry).
> William Dudley Pelley.
> Gerald B. Winrod.
> Charles B. Hudson.
> James True.
> National Liberty Party (Frank W. Clark).
> E. N. Sanctuary.
> Robert E. Edmondson.
> The American Rangers (J. H. Peyton).
> The American White Guard (Henry D. Allen).
> The Constitutional Crusaders of America.

Examination of testimony and evidence received can only leave the committee with the conclusion that the German-American Bund must be classified with the Communist Party as an agent of a foreign government.

Although at the present time it is difficult to establish the international ties of the Bund as clearly as in the case of the Communist Party, no reasonable person can read the testimony on the Bund and believe other than that the Bund is operating primarily in the interest of Germany.

It is noteworthy that there is an additional parallel between the bund and the Communist Party in the employment of "united front" tactics. The willingness and eagerness of the bund to encourage establishment of Fascist-minded organizations in this country is strikingly similar to the "front" policies pursued by the Communists and is to be equally condemned.

It is the urgent recommendation of this committee that the proper authorities enforce most vigorously and conscientiously all laws applying to organizations whose obvious objectives can be no other than to destroy the American form of government at the direction and in the interests of foreign powers.

Continuation of the Investigation.

The question of continuation of this investigation into subversive and un-American activities and propaganda lies, of course, with the House of Representatives. We feel that the following in this connection merits the attention of the House:

1. The continually changing international situation—with its direct bearing on the activities of these un-American groups in this country—warrants the constant vigilance of a special investigating committee of the House in the immediate future.

2. With these un-American groups—both on the right and on the left—in a state of confusion as a result of the disclosures by this committee, the events abroad, and recent prosecutions by various governmental agencies, it becomes doubly important that such an inquiry be continued to make certain that the aforementioned confusion is turned into complete rout.

3. Since the advent of the European war, the committee has been deluged with offers of evidence and testimony of extreme importance to the American public and damning to the cause of subversive groups, but which could not be accepted because of the shortness of time for preparation of the cases before the life of the committee expired, and because of the press of cases already prepared.

4. Because of several reasons beyond this committee's control, numerous important cases were prepared and scores of witnesses obtained, particularly on the west coast, whose testimony is yet to be heard. The west coast cases alone would require from a month to 2 months to hear.

The committee believes that its efforts to expose un-American activities should keep pace with an active campaign of prosecution by the various agencies of government to the end that America and American institutions may successfully repel these insidious forms of attack by foreign powers.

Accomplishments of the Committee and Conclusion

The purpose of this committee is the task of protecting our constitutional democracy by turning the light of pitiless publicity on the activities of organizations seeking to work the will of foreign dictators in the United States or to destroy our constitutional democracy and set up a totalitarian regime of some sort in its place. The committee's objectives have been advanced to a remarkable degree in a brief 12 months. The Soviet-Nazi pact has helped by making more clear the real nature of all dictatorships and by revealing the similarity between Hitler's naziism and Stalin's communism. The attacks on Poland and Finland have caused a revulsion of feeling in America against the nations which were responsible.

The work of the committee has unquestionably been an important factor in bringing about the following results:

(1) Fritz Kuhn, styled "fuehrer" of the German-American Bund, has been sent to prison as a man unable to be trusted with the custody of the funds of his own organization;

(2) Earl Browder, general secretary of the Communist Party, and William Weiner, party treasurer, have been indicted on the charge of falsifying American passports, and the Department of Justice is understood to be preparing further cases of a similar sort against other leaders of that organization;

(3) Nicholas Dozenberg has been charged with counterfeiting of American money on orders from the Communist International;

(4) William Dudley Pelley, self-styled "leader of men," disappeared from view completely a couple of months ago rather than appear "like a man" before the committee or appear in court in his own county in North Carolina to answer to a citation from the superior court to show cause why his parole should not be revoked for violation of his probation. Pelley is a fugitive from justice and this fact is very apparently having a serious effect on his Silver Shirt organization;

(5) Officials of Bookniga, Soviet propaganda agency, have pleaded guilty to the charge of failure to register with the State Department as foreign agents and similar cases are in preparation by the Justice Department;

(6) Arno Rissi and Mrs. Leslie Fry, west coast Nazi and Fascist leaders, have fled the country for good and sufficient reason.

(7) Many bills of a corrective nature have been introduced and passed by the House as a result of the testimony produced by this committee.

Speaking more generally, the German-American Bund, the Communist Party, the Silver Shirts and some other similar organizations have fallen upon the darkest days they have seen yet. They are losing both membership and prestige and the time may speedily come when they will cease to be seriously regarded by anyone in the United States. If this result is to be achieved, however, the earnest effort of all groups of people in the United States will be required, as well as vigorous action to enforce the laws we now have on our statute books.

We believe that the committee would render a disservice to the Nation if it left the impression in its report that there is anything in the present situation to cause anyone to lose faith in the American people as a whole or their devotion to their basic institutions. Indeed, one of the greatest facts of all that should be recorded in the report of this committee is that on the basis of evidence presented to the committee, not over 1,000,000 people in the United States can be said to have been seriously affected by these essentially foreign or un-American activities. That leaves about 131,000,000 Americans who in spite of the efforts of Nazis, Fascists, Communists, self-styled saviors of America and all the rest, and in spite of the suffering and distress of 10 years of unemployment and depression, are still as sound and loyal to American institutions and the democratic way of life as they ever were. We owe something to these 131,000,000 people—especially to the poor, the unemployed, the distressed among them. We owe something to our farmers, our workers, our business and professional people who have so nobly stood by America, her institutions and ideals through these difficult years. We owe them a solution of the economic and social problem of unnecessary poverty in the midst of possible plenty.

> *Martin Dies,*
> Chairman
> *Joe Starnes*
> *Joseph E. Casey*
> *Jerry Voorhis*
> *John J. Dempsey*
> *N. M. Mason*
> *J. Parnell Thomas*

Attest:
  Robert E. Stripling, Secretary

CRITIQUE OF COMMITTEE
BY WALTER LIPPMANN
JANUARY 11, 1940

New York Post, January 11, 1940; reprinted in *Congressional Record,*
76th Congress, 3rd Session, January 23, 1940, 597.

The Dies committee are not really a legislative committee. They are a kind of committee of public safety set up by Congress to suppress activities which, though detested by the great majority of the people, are in themselves either not unlawful, or, even if they were outlawed, could not be dealt with by the ordinary procedure of the law. The Dies committee are official vigilantes operating in an area, that of the political underworld, where there is as yet no effective law and there is, therefore, no order. The committeemen, like their vigilante predecessors on the American frontier, are therefore themselves often lawless in spirit and disorderly in their methods.

This accounts for the somewhat shamefaced approval which thoughtful men have given to the work of the committee. The public is confronted with the ancient moral question of whether the end justifies the means. Thus, only the very innocent and self-deluding have any doubt that the Dies committee have been attacking a formidable evil in modern society. The menace is real. It is not imaginary. And it must be met. Yet there is no doubt also that the procedure of the Dies committee is itself a violation of American morality; it is a pillory in which reputations are ruined, often without proof and always without the legal safeguards that protect the ordinary criminal; it is a tribunal before which men are arraigned and charged with acts that are, as a matter of fact, lawful.

End is Attained by Deplorable Means

Therefore the end, which is to protect the American system, is attained by means which, if used for some other end, would be deplored by everyone, by everyone, except, of course, the revolutionists whom Mr. Dies is stalking.

It is plain that the Dies committee cannot be abolished and must be continued since it offers a center of resistance to evils which could not otherwise be brought to light and checked. It is equally plain that the committee needs to be reformed, so that its methods will in spirit, at least, be lawful, and, therefore, capable of commanding the respect of law-abiding citizens.

I do not know how this can be done except by subjecting the procedure of the committee to public criticism, and by adding to the membership one or two learned and respected lawyers who will make it their business to reform the procedure, and by giving the committee enough money to hire competent investigators so that they may cease to rely upon dubious informers and the crackpots who always gather about an inquiry of this sort.

SOL COHN'S DEFENSE OF WITNESS'S REFUSAL TO ANSWER APRIL 3, 1940

U.S. House of Representatives, 76th Congress, 2nd Session, Hearings before a Special Committee on Un-American Activities, 7561–62.

. . . Mr. Matthews. Who is the secretary of the Harvard Young Communist League?

Mr. O'Dea. I refuse to answer that question because I believe that by answering that question I will expose this person to economic persecution. He will be unable to get a job, and getting a job is the only way he will be able to live, and I think under the fourteenth amendment, that is due process, his only property will be his scholarship and his job, and he will lose that.

The Chairman. Then you decline to answer?

Mr. Lynch. I think that that should be stricken from the record, all of the witness's statement except the statement that he refuses to answer, on the ground that it is entirely immaterial. The only right that he has to refuse to answer is one, that his answer might tend to incriminate him; and if he objects on that ground why, of course, that is all right, but otherwise he has absolutely no right to refuse.

Mr. Cohn. I think that is an incorrect statement of the law handed down by the United States Supreme Court in the case of Sinclair against the United States and other cases. I think that the objection of the witness is well taken.

Mr. Casey. What is the *Sinclair case?*

Mr. Cohn. In that case the Supreme Court said that the witness had other rights to object in addition to the one, the privilege against self-incrimination. It said that, for example, the committee had no right to delve into matters that were personal or private matters affecting the witness, and other cases held that the committee may only ask questions, and the witness has the right to refuse to answer questions which are not material to the investigation, questions that are not relevant to the investigation, questions that are not within the scope of the investigation.

The committee is limited by those decisions of the United States Supreme Court in addition to the constitutional provision against self-incrimination.

May I further say that it is my belief that the witness has a full right to explain his refusal to answer.

Mr. Lynch. I submit that none of the reasons advanced by Mr. Cohn are applicable to this witness. In other words, this witness does not say that they are not material, this witness does not say that they are personal to him, but he says that they are personal to someone else, and, of course, he has no right to attempt to protect somebody else.

Mr. Cohn. We are going to bring to the United States Supreme Court the question of whether a witness has a right to decline to answer questions, in view of what the chairman has already stated in the record, that he proposes to use any names of Communist members for a blacklist to see to it that those—

The Chairman (interposing). That is stricken from the record; that is incorrect and will be stricken.

Mr. Cohn. That was the testimony when Mr. Cooes was examined. If my recollection is correct, the chairman then said that that was his purpose, and I said under those circumstances that the witness has a right to decline to answer.

The Chairman. That is stricken from the record; you are incorrect.

Mr. Cohn. I respectfully object.

The Chairman. The Chair will take under advisement the question of whether a witness can state the reasons for his declining to answer. The Chair is not familiar with the decisions with respect to that, but for the time being we will take that under advisement. The Chair now directs you to answer the question that was asked you. Do you decline to do so?

Mr. O'Dea. I do, for the reasons stated.

The Chairman. You have already said that. You decline to answer the question?

Mr. O'Dea. I do, for the reasons stated. . . .

SPEECH OF MARTIN DIES, "TROJAN HORSE" MAY 17, 1940

Congressional Record, 76th Congress, 3rd Session, 6295–6304.

Mr. Chairman, democracy and the principles for which it stands are seriously challenged throughout the world today. Both as a form of government and as the spirit of free peoples, democracy is still young in the world. Democracy is everywhere threatened more seriously than it has been during the century and a half since our fathers drafted and proclaimed the Declaration of Independence. No man knows what new crisis for democracy each succeeding week holds. The paramount duty and the principal concern of every American must be the preservation of liberty and constitutional democracy.

We in America are not now in danger of any invasion of foreign enemies. Fundamentally no power or combination of powers could ever successfully invade our country even if they dare to try, so long as we are adequately prepared and stand united in allegiance to the God of our fathers and the Constitution upon which our economic and political institutions are founded. This confidence that we are invulnerable to attack rests only in part upon the strength of our armed forces, which we must maintain at maximum efficiency according to our defensive needs.

This confidence—if it is to be an enduring trust in our capacity for self-protection—must rest even more upon that strength of unity which we derive from the sacred commitment of all of our people to the principles of Americanism. It is this unity of our commitment to Americanism which the "fifth column," through Trojan-horse tactics, is now seeking to undermine. It is this unity of our commitment to Americanism whose strength we have not properly valued as a measure of national defense.

The safety of a modern republic lies, first of all, in ideological and spiritual defense erected throughout the length and breadth of its territory, in the hearts and minds of its people. It is this fundamental national defense which we have been far less diligent in building than we have been in preparing to stop armies and navies at our borders and coasts.

The experience of this generation, more than that of any other, has demonstrated that the enemies within a country constitute its greatest menace. Treason from within rather than invasion from without has been the cause of the speed with which modern governments have collapsed in the face of totalitarian assaults. Stalin and Hitler have pushed their Trojan-horse tactics to the point of perfection.

This Trojan-horse policy was adopted at the Seventh Congress of the Communist International held in Moscow. It was described by George Dimitrov in an address to the congress on August 20, 1935, in the following language:

> Comrades, you remember the ancient tale of the capture of Troy. Troy was inaccessible to the armies attacking her, thanks to her impregnable walls; and the attacking army, after suffering many sacrifices, was unable to achieve victory until with the aid of the famous Trojan horse it managed to penetrate to the very heart of the enemies' camp. We revolutionary workers, it appears to me, should not be shy about using the same tactics.

Years ago Adolf Hitler described in detail this new and diabolical method of destroying the governments and liberties of other countries. I ask you to ponder his words:

> When I wage war, troops will suddenly appear. . . . They will march through the streets in broad daylight. . . . No one will stop them. Everything has been thought out to the last detail. They will march to the headquarters of the general staff. . . . The confusion will be beyond belief. But I shall long have had relations with the men who will form a new government—a government to suit me. We will find such men; we shall find them in every country; we shall not need to bribe them. They will come of their own accord. Ambition and delusion, party squabbles and self-seeking arrogance will drive them. . . . Our strategy is to destroy the enemy from within, to conquer him through himself.

The Trojan-horse minorities within Austria, Czechoslovakia, Poland, Finland, and Holland made it impossible for these countries to offer any serious resistance to foreign invasion. The subversive work of Nazi and Communist sympathizers in the countries overrun by Hitler and Stalin has everywhere constituted a major factor in the spectacular success of the German war machine. In Czechoslovakia the Government permitted the formation of a Nazi organization of 1,500,000 citizens and noncitizens residing in Czechoslovakia. The fuehrer of this organization was Comrade Henline, a traitor to his own country and an agent of Adolf Hitler.

During the early stages of this Nazi movement in Czechoslovakia a few wise and patriotic statesmen of that Republic warned the Government that this movement was disloyal to the Republic and that Henline was contemplating the betrayal of his country.

The world has not yet appreciated the important role played by this Nazi organization in the easy conquest of Czechoslovakia by the Nazi legions. It is a fact, however, that this treasonable organization delivered the Republic into the hands of Hitler.

The next victim of the "fifth column" was Poland, with a population of 35,000,000 people and a standing army in excess of 1,000,000 soldiers. Polish officers now in exile have testified to the fact that there were so many Nazi and Communist agents and sympathizers in Poland, and their aid to Hitler and Stalin was so valuable and important, that the Polish Army, with thousands of traitors in its rear and with the ruthless war machine of Hitler in its front, virtually collapsed.

After the easy conquest of Poland, Hitler admitted in a public statement that he knew the military plans of the Polish high command 6 weeks before he gave the order to invade Poland.

In Finland we see another example of the success of Trojan-horse tactics. The Communist Party in Finland, which had been tolerated under the free institutions of that heroic country, set up a puppet government and furnished the pretext for the Communist invasion. Their treasonable cooperation with Stalin seriously handicapped the brave people of Finland in their immortal defense.

American correspondents who witnessed the working of this new combination of internal revolution and foreign invasion in Norway have reported its shocking details for our American newspapers. Editors all over the country have commented upon its despicable character. It has not been generally reported, however, that the Communist Party of Norway fully supported the invasion by Hitler's troops, and that the Communists of Norway, like the Nazi sympathizers in the country, welcomed the setting up of the Nazi totalitarian regime in Oslo. The Daily Worker, official Communist Party newspaper in the United States, even points with pride to this treasonable role of the Norwegian Communists. The Daily Worker of April 17 publishes in full a manifesto of the Norwegian Communist Party. In this manifesto there is not one line of criticism of Hitler's invasion. On the contrary, the entire blame for the present fate of Norway is laid at the door of England, which the Norwegian Communists accuse of violating the country's neutrality. The Communist Party of the United States has itself taken exactly the same line as that taken by the Norwegian Communist Party, and both act as Trojan-horse traitors for Stalin.

The most recent example of the fifth-column strategy is the case of Holland. It is not generally known, but it is a fact, that a Nazi organization composed largely of Dutch citizens and to some extent augmented by noncitizens of Holland, with a membership of 60,000, cooperated with the German soldiers in the conquest of that great country.

In the year 1935 the strategy of the Nazis, the Communists, and the Fascists underwent certain fundamental changes designed to perfect the Trojan-horse tactics. It is sometimes overlooked that nazi-ism, fascism, and communism were promulgated as world theories. In Mein Kampf Adolf Hitler advances his cult of nazi-ism as a world theory to be embraced and spread throughout the world with the zeal which characterized the early disciples of Christianity. The same thing is true with reference to fascism. In his book What is Fascism? Mussolini describes it as a world theory which cannot, and should not, be compressed within the narrow boundaries of any one country. In the many speeches and writing of Lenin, Karl Marx, and the other founders of communism it is stressed repeatedly that communism is a world theory, not to be confined to any one country, but to embrace the proletariat of every country. This being true, Italy, Germany, and Russia established organizations throughout the world which masked themselves as political parties in some instances, and in other instances as social, patriotic, or fraternal societies.

In France, Moscow played an important part in the formation of the Popular Front. The Communists were the most militant and aggressive group which comprised the Popular Front; and as a result of this militancy they exercised a preponderant influence in the front. They elected many members of the party to the Parliament, and they became so powerful that they were able to prevent France from adopting adequate measures of national defense. In the face of German aggression, the Communists and their allies threatened a general strike. And it was only by resort to oppressive and democratic methods that France was finally able, though too late, to prepare herself to resist the war machine of Adolf Hitler.

I stress the experience of France in order to illustrate the danger and effectiveness of a program which is able to go into a country and enlist the support and sympathy of some of its citizens in order to destroy the liberties and freedom of that country. I also desire to emphasize another truth that is sometimes overlooked. For 2 years I have been stressing the fact that communism, nazi-ism, and fascism are fundamentally alike. When Mussolini approved the definition of fascism—"Everything for the state, nothing against the state, nothing outside the state"—he was expressing in different language the philosophy of Adolf Hitler, who declared that the highest duty of the individual is to subordinate himself to the state. This declaration was not original with Mussolini and Hitler; it was merely an expression of Marxian theory predicated upon the erroneous premise that the individual should be nothing and the state should be everything; that the individual should lose his dignity and identity as a human being and become a cog in a collectivistic system.

Now, what I propose to do—and I wish I had more time to go into it— what I first propose to do is to show you that the Communist, Nazi, and Fascist organizations in this country are not political parties as some of them pretend to be; that they are not social or fraternal socieities as others pretend to be, but that, as a matter of fact they are foreign conspiracies under the control of foreign dictators.

Lenin, who is the undisputed authority on which the Communist Party bases its teachings and tactics, describes the Communist Party as—

> A small kernel consisting of reliable, experienced, and steeled workers with responsible agents in the chief districts and connected by all the rules of strict conspiracy.

In that same book on organization Lenin mentions the word "conspiracy" 20 times. Not only does he emphasize the fact that the Communist Party is a conspiratorial organization, but in the program of the Communist Internationale, under which the American Communist Party operates, it states bluntly that legal methods must unfailingly be combined with illegal methods. That accounts for the fact that leaders of the American Communist Party, such as Browder, Wiener, Dozenburg, and others, have recently been indicted and convicted for violation of our laws as a result of one investigation. That accounts for the fact that the Communist Party in the United States openly violated the laws of this country when it enlisted and sent to Spain some 5,000 recruits.

In the city of Detroit indictments were returned against 17 of them for a violation of the passport laws, but, as a matter of fact, the committee received evidence from other sections of the country showing that the Communist Party as an organization, and in obedience to orders from Moscow, recruited American boys and sent them to Spain, often under phony passports, and paid their expenses to Spain in many instances.

Lenin said, "Revolutionaries who are unable to combine illegal forms of struggle with every form of legal struggle are very poor revolutionaries."

Earl Browder, the present head of the Communist Party in the United States, has himself estimated that there are nearly 2,000,000 Americans who go with the Communist Party all the way to its full program. Let me analyze the growth of the Communist Party, the German-American Bund, and the various Fascist organizations in the United States.

The Communist Party, according to Earl Browder, has 5,000 branches in the United States, members in 42 States, district organizations in 36 districts. In 1929 the party claimed 7,000 members; in 1935, 25,000; and from 1935 to 1939, the membership, according to Browder, grew from 25,000 to 100,000 members. The party claims 28,000 members in New York City, 7,000 in Chicago, 6,000 in California, and 4,000 in Washington and Oregon. But let me caution you not to accept—at face value—the statement of Communist leaders with reference to their full membership. When the committee obtained certain documents and files in Chicago it found membership books with membership numbers in excess of 100,000. In the spring of the revolution in Russia the Communist Party claimed to have had 60,000 paid members, and yet they were able to seize the Government of Russia.

In China the party claimed to have 416,000 members and yet they were able to control one-fifth of China.

In Germany the Communists were claiming 220,000 members in the fall before the Hitler election and at election they polled nearly 6,000,000 votes in Germany.

In Spain, according to their own documents, the Communists claimed, in 1933, 800 paid members in the party, and yet that fall they polled 400,000 votes.

I mention these facts to illustrate that it is the policy on the part of the Communist organizations, as well as the Fascists and Nazis, to underestimate their strength, in order to lull the people into a sense of false security. . . .

Let me make myself clear. The committee has said, and properly so, that the great majority of working people in both unions are loyal, patriotic American citizens, but the committee has unanimously designated 10 national unions as being under the control of Communist leadership, or, rather, that Communist leadership was intrenched in those unions.

Not only did the Communist Party by their policy seek to gain a foothold in the trade-union movement in the United States, but likewise it established a number of so-called front organizations. What do we mean by "front organizations"?

We can take the International Workers Order as an illustration, although there are numerous other organizations that this committee has unanimously found to be under the control of Communists. What evidence do we have to support such statements? I merely want to illustrate the type of evidence in order to convince you that the question is not even open to serious debate.

Here is the International Workers Order that now has 165,000 members in the United States, 1,900 branches or lodges scattered throughout this country. It maintains a school for the training of youth. This organization grew from 5,000 members in about 1930 to 165,000 members today. Who is the president of it? William Weiner, the financial secretary or treasurer of the Communist Party of the United States.

Who is secretary of the International Workers Order? Max Bedacht, who is a high functionary in the Communist Party, head of the International Publishers Association, which prints and distributes Communist literature and books in the United States. Here is one of the pamphlets issued by the International Workers Order. It was issued by the campaign committee of the International Workers Order in 1932. In this pamphlet they openly advocate the election of Communist candidates for office. I cannot take the time to read excerpts from this, but it is a document prepared by the International Workers Order openly sponsoring Communist candidates.

We charged the American League for Peace and Democracy with being one of the organizations under the control of the Communist Party. There was a great hue and cry throughout the United States. We based that charge upon documentary evidence, upon printed and verbal admissions, and upon what I conceive to be absolutely indisputable evidence. The American League, in obedience to the Trojan horse policy dictated by Dimitrov in 1935, succeeded in obtaining recruits or members throughout the United States and at one time during the height of its power in this country it claimed 4,000,000 members, directly and indirectly affiliated with it. Of course, no one is intimating that those 4,000,000 members were all Communists. The great majority of them were not Communists.

I wish to illustrate for the benefit of the House the cleverness, the subtlety, the intrigue, and the strategy of the Communists in setting up so-called liberal organizations in the country for the purpose of deceiving many gullible people who otherwise would not associate with the Communist movement.

As I said a moment ago, according to the report of our committee, Communist leadership is entrenched in 10 of the labor unions affiliated with the C. I. O. Do you know that a trade union of technical men led by the Communist Party has a unit in every navy yard in the United States and that the total membership of this union of technicians is 7,000?

In the confidential minutes of the Communist Party of New York is the following statement:

> At the present time, while all are not functioning perfectly, we
> have, nevertheless, some 300 fractions in the trade-unions, and in
> about 150 trade-unions there are party comrades who are either
> fully or partially in the leadership of these unions.

Fred Howe, secretary of Local No. 2 of the American Communications Association, recently testified that there were 150 radio operators in our merchant marine in the Communist Party, and that it was an easy task for these operators to transmit messages to Moscow or Berlin. . . .

It may be interesting to the Members of this House to know that as a result of the audit of the bank accounts of the Communist Party and their controlled organizations—I am speaking now of organizations where they are in control through secretaryships and presidencies of the organization or through the executive committees which they control—the audit that our committee made of their books shows that their receipts in the United States total about $10,000,000 a year. You are dealing with an organization that is able to collect $10,000,000 and to distribute some 600 publications throughout the United States. Let us take certain typical examples of it. Here was William Browder, brother of Earl Browder, who was secretary of the Communist Party of the State of New York.

The audit of his bank account showed that he ran an account in one New York bank of $1,300,000 for 1 year and 11 months. He testified before the committee that the funds belonged to the Communist Party. But, as a matter of fact, there was nothing in the record of the bank deposit to indicate that the funds belonged to the party. I asked him the question: "Did you render an income-tax return, did you pay an income tax on this?" And he said he had not. I then called this fact to the attention of the Internal Revenue Department. Now, let us inquire somewhat further into their financial transactions in the United States, because I want to convince you that you are not dealing with a small and poorly financed movement. According to Earl Browder in his testimony before our committee much of their revenue comes from thousands of contributors and the contributions range from $10 to $3,000. Some of the men who are the backbone of this movement in the United States, are men like A. A. Heller, who is a wealthy man in New York and who has financed the International Publishing Co. since the day of its inception by subsidizing it.

These contributors are not people who are in dire financial straits; they are people who are able to make contributions from $10 to $3,000, according to the testimony of the head of the Communist Party; and, according to Earl Browder's statement, something like 50,000 members of the party are now members of labor organizations in the United States. He said further that two-thirds of that number are in the C. I. O. and one-third in the A. F. of L., as I recall his testimony. Let us consider the financial transaction in the case of Sam Carp, who, according to his own admission, went to Moscow to see his brother-in-law, Molotov (Premier of Russia), and there received a commission to spend $100,000,000 in the United States for supplies, largely military equipment. He is a citizen of this country through naturalization, and he returned to the United States from Russia with $100,000 in $1,000 bills, according to his testimony. But when we checked his bank account we found that he had made other cash deposits totaling about $400,000. We traced $52,000 of it and found that this amount had been spent to buy political influence. We have not yet traced the remainder of the cash brought from Russia, although I have information where that money went, and I hope before long we shall be able to show the country where at least some of it went.

I think I have shown you that the Communist Party is not a political organization, that its members, according to the testimony of Earl Browder, William Weiner, and the other leaders, must obey the decisions of the party leadership upon penalty of expulsion. Communist leaders have also admitted in their testimony before the committee that the Communist Party of the United States must obey the decisions and follow the policies of the Communist International if it is to continue its affiliation with the International.

The Communist International is controlled by the Presidium, a small group that governs when the Congress is not in session. This Presidium is completely controlled by Joseph Stalin. For a period of 7 years the Congress of the International did not meet and during that interval the dictator of Russia, Joseph Stalin, was not only in absolute control of the Communist Party in the United States but of every other country.

We asked a Communist leader, James Dolsen, who, by the way, was lecturing on a W. P. A. project in Pittsburgh, whether it would be the duty of a Communist to give information to his party leadership, and, in answer to the question, he frankly said that it would be the duty of a Communist to give such information. This means, in effect, that we have an espionage system in the United States which Russia does not have to pay for. This new method has many new advantages over the orthodox system employed by other countries. In the first place, Stalin and Hitler are able to enlist the services of many sincere and fanatical followers who can be depended upon to be loyal, faithful, and zealous. In the second place, the system can be operated at a profit to Stalin and Hitler. Through it they have been able to obtain financial aid. In addition to these advantages, the espionage agency is able to carry on its activities and propaganda under the cloak of legality. While the primary function of this espionage system is to gather important industrial and military information to transmit to Russia, the ultimate objective is to promote class hatred and overthrow the free institutions of America by force and violence and, in the interim, to undermine the unity of this country as the Communists and Nazis were able to do in France and Poland, and as they have been able to do in every other country in order to prevent adequate preparedness.

The Communists have formed many "front" organizations in the United States. For 2 years our committee has repeatedly warned everyone with reference to the identity and aims of these "front" organizations. When we expose one organization like the American League for Peace and Democracy and it dissolves, immediately another organization is established. . . .

In the case of the Communist Party of California, its report shows that one half of the membership was born abroad and the other half in the United States. In the case of the German-American Bund, I venture to say that 95 percent of the 100,000 members of that organization are Germans who came to the United States after the World War and have become citizens of the United States through naturalization. Many of them served in the German Army during the World War.

Let us take up that organization. What is its constitution?

> To be and remain worthy of our Germanic blood, our German motherland, our German brothers and sisters, and to cultivate our German language, customs, and ideals, and to be outstandingly proud of these principles.

This organization has in the United States 100 units, and a unit must have not less than 20 members, according to the testimony of the head of that organization. It has 47 districts in the United States. It has a membership composed of regular members who have voting privileges and sympathizing members who do not have voting privileges but who pay dues without any record being kept of their affiliation with the organization.

New York City has 5 bund units and New York State has 15 bund units;

New Jersey has 4 bund units; New England has 7 units; California 9 units; Philadelphia 1 unit; Pittsburgh 1 unit; Wheeling, W. Va., 1 unit. There are units in Chicago, Detroit, and Flint. The application blank, written in German, calls for a person who will vouch for the applicant in Germany. In other words, the applicant has to furnish a German witness, living in Germany, for reference. Initiation fee is $1, and monthly dues amount to 75 cents per month per member. One-third of the fees that the members pay their local units goes to the headquarters. Voluntary contributions from members and outsiders for the last half of 1938 and the first half of 1939 amounted to $18,000. The German-American Business League is a separate organization but closely affiliated with the bund. It is composed of German-American merchants who pay $3 a year to be registered in a special book which the Business League puts out. The league has a membership of 800 in New York. There are similar German-American business leagues located in 11 other States. The Prospective Citizens' League is affiliated with the bund. To be eligible for membership the applicant must have first papers and establish a residence of at least 2 years in this country. The bund cooperates with the Christian Front, Christian Mobilizers, and the Christian Crusaders. The head of the bund states that its purpose was to establish a separate political party. The bund maintains summer camps, and the youth movement where boys and girls are trained.

In the Weckruf, dated May May 12, 1937, page 3, is an article which includes a reprint of literature which was sent in by George Deatherage, president of the American Nationalist Confederation. In the issue of June 23, 1938, is a report from the Los Angeles chapter of the bund, stating that Roy Zachary, field marshal of the Silver Shirts, declared in an address to the bund that the Silver Shirts were similar to the bund. The Weckruf published James True's material. In the Weckruf, dated May 26, 1938, is an article by Edmondson. And it was also admitted by bund leaders that the Italian Fascist groups cooperated with the bund. Seven different Italian groups and organizations met with the bund upon different occasions. On June 18, 1937, at Camp Nordland, a large group of Italian black shirts were present and participated in a demonstration. The Weckruf for May 26, 1938, contains an item from the Los Angeles bund paper concerning a meeting of 100 Italian Fascists, attended by a man by the name of Ferri, who spoke to the organizations of the bund, and at the close of the meeting there were three cheers for Hitler and three for Mussolini.

The Committee received evidence with reference to an organization in Chicago composed entirely of German citizens with a total membership of approximately 1,000. We discovered that most of them were working in the important industries in and about Chicago. As a matter of fact, the 100,000 members of the German-American Bund in the United States are, for the most part, working in basic industries, and many of the members of the bund are skilled workmen, such as chemists and technicians.

In the 1937 yearbook of the German-American Bund is a statement from Adolf Hitler to the bund members of the United States in which he uses the expression, as translated:

> Your fatherland is Germany; love it more than anything in words and in accomplishments.

The German-American Bund sent a delegation of its members to Berlin. This delegation carried $3,000 in cash, which was donated to the winter relief campaign in Germany. These delegates were American citizens. They saluted and marched under the swastika. They were addressed by Goebbels and upon their return they published the special message to them of Adolf Hitler. Let me make it clear that the great majority of the people of German descent in America, are loyal and patriotic Americans, let us make no mistake about that. We are dealing with minority groups with respect to nationalities and labor unions. But the people who compose these minority groups are so imbued with zeal and enthusiasm for Nazi Germany or Communist Russia or Fascist Italy that they cannot conceal it.

I do not mean to imply that all the members of the Communist Party and the German-American Bund are traitors to this country, but fifth-column technique is to use innocent and sympathetic people for the purpose of obtaining valuable military and industrial information, and to support the foreign policies of the dictatorships and to undermine national unity.

Fascist Italy has used the same tactics in this country. The committee received evidence that there are Fascist organizations in this country; that these organizations are seeking to train and indoctrinate American boys and girls in Fascist ideology; that they have raised funds to aid the Fascist regime in Rome; and that they have cooperated with the German-American Bund. For instance, the committee received in evidence a letter written by Consul Decicco, of New Haven, Conn., addressed to all Italian-American fraternal societies. In this letter the consul says:

> There are a big number of Italian-American societies in the State of Connecticut. It is necessary that this office be in possession of the names and addresses of all those who belong to such societies. Therefore, I would appreciate it very much if you would send me the names and the addresses of those who belong to your society.

The committee also received evidence that there is a branch of the Italian Government secret service known as the O. V. R. A., which corresponds to the G. P. U. of Nazi Germany. There are letters from other members of the Italian consular service, which may be found in volume 2 of the committee's hearings.

I have examined some of the textbooks used in the Italian schools which glorify the Fascist regime in Italy. American children of Italian descent have been sent to Italy as guests of the Italian Government. These children were given Fascist uniforms and taken to training camps. They have participated in services, meetings, and parades on the streets of Rome, Genoa, and other cities.

It is clear from the evidence that there are in the United States certain Italian organizations which are Fascist in principle and belief.

Now, what are we going to do about these organizations? There has been a demand that we suggest legislation, and the committee is undertaking to do so. The gentleman from California [Mr. Voorhis], a very sincere and tireless worker on the committee, as is indeed true of every member of our committee, has conferred with the State Department and the Justice Department with reference to the preparation of a bill requiring the registration of these organizations, but I would not be honest and truthful with you if I led you to believe that the solution of this problem is through new legislation. The first thing you have to do is to enforce existing law. [Applause.]

Now, we might as well be frank about this. I wrote letters to the State and Justice Departments about a year ago naming organizations in this country that are the agents of foreign governments, and recommending that these organizations be prosecuted for failure to register in accordance with the provisions of existing laws.

If the Government of the United States and the States in which the Trojan-horse agencies are incorporated will enforce existing laws without fear or favor, we can go a long way toward solving this problem. In the enforcement of these laws, however, the Federal Government and the States must be prepared for the opposition which they will encounter from certain influences in the C. I. O. Before we had any hearings of the committee, we invited Mr. John L. Lewis to appear before the committee and give us the benefit of any information which he had. Mr. Lewis did not see fit to accept this invitation. At a later date, when the testimony of certain witnesses who appeared before our committee was challenged by Labor's Non-Partisan League, I invited the representatives of that organization to appear before the committee and deny under oath this testimony. They declined to do so. The committee unanimously found that on the basis of the evidence submitted Communist leadership is entrenched in the following organizations: National Maritime Union; United Cannery, Packing, and Allied Workers; Federation of Architects, Engineers, Chemists, and Technicians; Fur Workers' International Union; International Longshoremen's and Warehousemen's Union; Transport Workers' Union; United Office and Professional Workers' Union; American Communications Association; United Electrical, Radio, and Mechanical Workers of America; and the United Furniture Workers of America.

These unions exist in and largely control vital and basic industries in America that affect our whole national defense. I hope that the Members of this House can read the testimony of witnesses dealing with these unions, and especially the testimony of the heads of these unions, such as Joe Curran, Michael Quill, and Merwyn Rathbourne. It cannot be stressed too often that the enforcement of existing laws is absolutely essential if we are to check these undemocratic minorities in our midst. We must enforce our laws dealing with immigration, deportation, income-tax evasion, registration of foreign agents, passport requirements, and so forth.

I recognize the fact that many people in this country have been deceived by the insidious wiles of foreign influence. There were some sincere liberals in the United States who were deceived by the pretensions of the Communist Party that it was a democratic organization. On the other hand, there were some so-called patriots who, on account of racial and religious prejudice, joined organizations that were used by foreign governments for their own purpose and benefit in the United States. There is no longer any excuse for these misguided people to continue their affiliation with organizations which our committee has exposed as agents of foreign countries.

It is true that we can supplement existing laws by making more stringent our deportation and immigration requirements and by requiring registration and full publicity of Fascist, Communist, and Nazi organizations in this country. I hope and believe that our committee can offer legislation along these lines at an early date. However, I am now pleading for positive and vigorous action on the part of the Federal Government of the United States in the enforcement of existing laws. I do this not in the spirit of rancor but because the national welfare requires it without further delay. The strengthening of our national defense is necessary and urgent, but it will be wholly inadequate if we fail to check the progress of the enemy within our country and the "Trojan horse" organizations under which he masks his treasonable designs and activities.

This committee has been fair to John L. Lewis. It has found in its report that a great majority of the members of his organization are patriotic Americans. It has specifically exonerated Mr. Lewis of being a Communist. But I say to Mr. Lewis that it is his patriotic duty to expel men like Quill, Joe Curran, and Harry Bridges, and certain other leaders in these vital unions and thereby make known to the American people that there is no place for such men in the American trade-union movement. If Mr. Lewis will accept this challenge, the C. I. O. can clean its own house, and when it does this committee will give it a clean bill of health. We are dealing here with a vital question—a question as to whether or not we shall permit agents of foreign governments and their dupes, who are masquerading under high-sounding titles and objectives, to do in the United States what they did in Poland and what they did in Czechoslovakia and other European countries, or whether through democratic processes and in accordance with the Constitution of the United States we will here and now reckon with them and say to them: "At least it is not a violation of the Bill of Rights to enforce the laws of this country."

This Government should have deported Harry Bridges. [Applause.] There was sufficient evidence before our committee to justify his deportation, and in justice to the American people it should have been ordered.

There are some mistaken ideas and misunderstandings in official Washington but I plead with those in control, first of all let us enforce the laws of this country. This committee will submit supplemental legislation, but you must remember that in dealing with this question in peacetime it is not an easy matter. There is always the charge that if we undertake in the slightest manner to expose these subversive organizations we are violating the Bill of Rights. We subpena them to bring their records, and they arrogantly defy the committee. We have sat there for 2 years and endured the insulting remarks, arrogance, defiance, evasions, and perjury of these groups not because we wanted to, but in order that we might make a record of who these people are and what they are doing, so that in the event of a great national emergency we will at least have some means to check them and to deal with them.

Our great mistake was to sit idly by during the period in which they increased from a few thousand to the several million that now comprise, either wittingly or unwittingly, the Fascist, Nazi, and Communist movements in the United States.

There was a time when these organizations operated so openly and boldly that it would have been easy for the Department of Justice to obtain the names of all of their officers and make a permanent record. I am sorry to say that was not done. Five months ago when a representative of the Department of Justice came to my office and when I tendered him our fullest cooperation—he was a friend of mine, a former Member of this House—he frankly admitted to me that they knew very little about the subject, and had no valuable or dependable information.

I say that, although I run the danger of having someone charge that I am attacking the Department of Justice. I am not. This is a new problem that has baffled the peoples of every country. It has deceived England, it has deceived France, and it has deceived all the countries. All I am asking as a Member of this House, in a spirit of good will and harmony, is that the Government of the United States here and now cooperate with this committee to the fullest extent possible. We are now in such a critical condition throughout the world that there is no justification for the slightest feeling between any agencies of government. We need the help of this Government. We have never had more than seven or eight investigators.

In dealing with the most difficult problem that the Government can deal with we have been handicapped in every conceivable manner. I say to this House and to our Government that we need your help. We need the help of the F. B. I. We need trained men in order that we may do a full and complete job, and for that help I now plead.

I appreciate very much the opportunity I have had to bring some of these facts to the attention of the House. I want to make myself perfectly clear, that there is no indictment or intended indictment of a great majority of the American people. But minority movements, highly organized, constitute the greatest threat to modern democratic governments. We have seen the ability of a small group, tightly organized as a kernel, holding strategic and vital jobs in utilities, in shipping, in transportation, and in communications, to deliver a whole country over to an invading host.

We have seen their ability to promote strife and hatred in a country in order to divide it into hostile camps either along racial, religious, or class lines. We have seen the disastrous results that have come to other republics and other democracies by such a course.

If we are to be preserved as a democracy we must match the brains, the ingenuity, the patriotism of men who believe in democracy against this new and sinister influence. We must revitalize democracy and offer it as a challenge to the fanatical followers of Hitler, Stalin, and Mussolini. I believe that democracy can develop a tremendous enthusiasm for the principles of freedom and constitutional government. I believe that through voluntary and cooperative union on the part of all classes in America, labor and capital, all races and all creeds, that we can meet the challenge that has been flung at every democracy on the face of the earth; and, as one people under one God, regardless of our differences of race, religion, or class, we can unite in the defense of the greatest democracy the world has ever seen. . . .

NEW YORK TIMES REPORT
DECEMBER 11, 1940

An agreement by the Dies Committee and the Department of Justice to work together to combat subversive elements was disclosed through correspondence made public today.

Letters exchanged by Attorney General Jackson and Representative Jerry Voorhis of the committee declared that while the department and the committee had separate functions, there was no reason why they should not coordinate their activities. Under the arrangements set forth in the letters, the committee would furnish secretly to the department information which it believed might lead to prosecutions and the department would give to the committee information regarding fifth columnists and other elements when this information seemed not to involve possible prosecutions.

Clashes between the department and the committee brought from President Roosevelt late last month a warning to Mr. Dies that injudicious disclosures might defeat the ends of justice. In a telegram conveying this warning the President suggested that Mr. Dies confer with Mr. Jackson. As a development Mr. Voorhis, as representative of the committee, met Mr. Jackson a day or so ago for a private talk.

President's Telegram Cited

In his letter to Mr. Voorhis, Mr. Jackson expressed his pleasure that "we are agreed that the department and your committee are not in any sense competitors or rivals." The functions of each, Mr. Jackson added, could not be better stated than in the Roosevelt telegram, with which, he stated, Mr. Voorhis seemed to agree completely.

"On that basis," Mr. Jackson went on, "I suggest the following working arrangement to effectuate the general principles stated in your letter:

"I will be satisfied to have your committee determine for itself whether a set of facts which it has developed should be referred to this department for prosecution or should be disclosed in aid of formulation of legislation to better meet the situation.

"In the cases which you decide to expose it is not unlikely that as you proceed conflicts may appear between your investigation and some of the work of this department. I do not think that we can, or need to, work out in advance a formula which will cover such unpredictable situations, but I am confident that you and I can settle such conflicts informally between us as they arise.

"In determining whether to refer cases for prosecution it will be helpful to bear in mind that no convictions can be obtained in the courts because of activities, however objectionable and injurious to the public interest, unless they also violate a specific Federal statute and can be established by technically admissible evidence legally obtained.

"If the case on these tests is one that you consider proper for prosecution, we ask you not to disclose it or even to disclose that you are referring it to us. This mere announcement is a tip-off that often leads to destruction of evidence or the 'fixing' or removal, or silencing of witnesses.

"If we are to prosecute a case, it should be developed in the secrecy of the grand jury, which is the lawful forum for the purpose. If the case is developed by the committee in public, the whole case is put in the hands of the defense. Witnesses called before your committee also get certain immunities which complicate cases.

"The Department of Justice will be glad to comply with your request to furnish the committee information which it may obtain which is not involved in probable prosecutive action. Of course you understand why reports of the Federal Bureau of Investigation always have been held highly confidential so long as prosecution is at all likely. The information is often from confidential sources and reports often contain 'leads' that are ultimately found to be elusive.

"While the bureau's activities are confined to investigating probable violations of Federal law or acts so closely associated with violations as to indicate probable connection therewith, there is at times information which can properly be made available. Specific information has been given, when asked by yourself, by Congressman Starnes, Congressman Dempsey and perhaps others. Any limitations that we have asked on publicity have in each instance been faithfully observed.

"I suggest, therefore, that matters of this kind be handled informally between yourself or other appropriate members of the committee and this department. Whenever you feel that a conference between us will be helpful to the general understanding I shall be glad to arrange it."

NEW YORK TIMES REPORT
DECEMBER 17, 1940

A long report by the Federal Bureau of Investigation on Harry Bridges, West Coast labor leader, which has been submitted to Attorney General Jackson, declares that Bridges is a Communist and that the Communist party advocates the overthrow of the United States Government, J. Edgar Hoover, director of the FBI, said in an interview today.

The report was sent to Mr. Jackson by Mr. Hoover on Nov. 28. At the time its contents were described as "confidential" and "factual." No further description was given. It was said that no recommendations were contained in it.

Mr. Hoover declined to divulge the exact nature of the "factual evidence" about communism he said the report contained, and he would not predict what action would be taken in Mr. Bridges's case.

Mr. Bridges, head of the C.I.O. Longshoremen's Unions on the Pacific

Coast, has been the center of a controversy in and out of Congress for many months and the status of his citizenship has been investigated by the Labor and Justice Departments.

Mr. Hoover said the Federal Bureau of Investigation had no authority to order his deporation. Neither can it arrest any person for merely holding membership in the Communist party, he explained, adding that only Congress can outlaw any group.

"We are an investigating agency, and all we can do is investigate and report," he continued.

The Attorney General probably will call public hearings on the report, Mr. Hoover predicted.

16,000 Fifth Column Reports

The F.B.I. is checking on 16,000 reports of fifth column activity, he reported, and the G-men have assembled a "defense index" of 6,000 names of "potential enemies of the nation." The index, he explained, contains the names of every Communist leader and every member of the German-American Bund.

Although the F.B.I. has not uncovered any evidence of sabotage in American industry, Mr. Hoover said, 1,200 plants which produce war materials have been surveyed and plans drawn to prevent any future trouble in this direction.

He believes, the director reported, that there is a definite place for such a group as the Dies Committee on Un-American Activities, but added that it should not be in competition with the F.B.I. He asserted that if Mr. Dies had any charges to make against the bureau they should be "specific rather than in generalities."

"Our report confirms the belief that Bridges is a Communist and that the Communist party advocates overthrow of the United States Government," Mr. Hoover said.

He added that the public had a misconception of F.B.I.'s activities in connection with communism. "I am often asked why we don't outlaw it." he said. "Only Congress could outlaw the party. By being investigated it has in effect been outlawed.

"The F.B.I. can't deport Harry Bridges. That's up to the imigration service."

Mr. Hoover, here for a vacation, said the Attorney General probably will call for public hearings on the report on communism prepared by his bureau.

The Dies Committee on Un-American Activities, he said, should "be more specific" in criticizing the F.B.I.

"It is unfortunate," he continued, "that the chairman of the Dies Committee has sought to center attention on his committee by holding the F.B.I. up to ridicule. If he has charges to make against the bureau, he should do so specifically by giving us frank and outright charges rather than generalities."

Mr. Hoover said that as far as the F.B.I. had been able to discover, there had been no concentrated or ordered sabotage in the United States, Canadian or English industry.

THIRD ANNUAL REPORT
JANUARY 3, 1941

U. S. House of Representatives, 77th Congress, 1st Session, House Report No. 1, Investigation of Un-American Propaganda Activities in the United States, 1–25.

Mr. Dies, chairman of the Special Committee on Un-American Activities, submitted the following

REPORT

Introduction

The work of the committee has been carried on during the past year against a back drop of war in Europe and Asia on the one hand and a greatly heightened concern over national defense here at home on the other hand. In these circumstances, it is almost inevitable that feeling among people of all sorts should be intensified. Many people who were formerly indifferent to the activities of foreign-controlled, antidemocratic, and un-American groups are now fully aroused. Many others who were, through a misconception of these un-American activities, hostile to the work of the committee in exposing the identities and programs of these un-American groups have now come to understand the importance of the committee's work.

The committee are fully aware that the present circumstances of aroused public opinion call for great care and discrimination in its work. The committee have followed a policy of sharp differentiation between those foreign-controlled agencies and forces which are dangerous to the future of our country on the one hand and those American groups and individuals who hold minority views concerning social and economic questions on the other hand. The committee's view is that a great gulf lies between those who, because of attachments to foreign powers and dictators, are basically disloyal to America and those who simply hold unorthodox economic views and hence advocate changes in the status quo which they sincerely believe would benefit the majority of the American people. The right to individual liberties of free Americans must be preserved as zealously as the efforts of totalitarian agents are combated. It is one thing for loyal Americans, exercising their own constitutional freedom of thought and speech, to advocate changes which the majority may consider radical. It is an entirely different thing for the controlled agents of totalitarian powers to try to exploit that freedom in the interests of Moscow, Berlin, Rome, and Tokyo.

In short, the committee warns against the possibility that a wave of hysteria may supersede an informed public opinion on matters which have to do with the subjects of its investigation. Such a situation would do much to defeat the very ends and workings of democracy which the committee's inquiry is calculated to serve.

In preventing the development of an undiscriminating and undemocratic attitude which degenerates into hysteria, special groups within our population bear a special responsibility. Throughout the 3 years of the committee's work, we have noted that some special-interest groups have failed to make their positions unequivocally clear by speaking out in defense of democracy against all the totalitarian systems alike. These special-interest groups have been quick enough to condemn some one of the totalitarian systems while remaining silent with respect to the others. Inasmuch as Communists have customarily tried to hide behind the pretext of being strongly progressive and prolabor, the committee believes that a special responsibility rests upon all genuinely progressive and prolabor groups—the overwhelming majority—to dissociate themselves with all possible emphasis from those who follow Moscow's leadership and principles. Inasmuch as Nazis and Fascists have customarily tried to hide behind the pretext of being strongly patriotic and conservative, the committee believes that a special responsibility rests upon all genuinely patriotic and conservative groups—the overwhelming majority—to dissociate themselves with all possible emphasis from those who follow Axis leadership and principles. The evidence before the committee shows clearly that the agents of Moscow have, for the most part, tried to bore from within labor and progressive movements, just as the agents of the Axis Powers have, for the most part, tried to bore from within patriotic, conservative, and business groups. These respective groups will, therefore, most effectively serve the interests of their country and themselves by promptly and energetically purging themselves of whatever foreign-controlled, totalitarian "borers" that would use them as covers for their un-American activities.

Certain aspects of the European picture have served to clarify the nature and purpose of the chief totalitarian regimes, i. e., Stalin's and Hitler's. This clarification has now reached a point where no justification can be found for those who persist in remaining attached to the Communist and Nazi movements or their front organizations. The illusion that Stalin's regime was a progressive one and that his leadership was the world's best protection against the spread of nazi-ism has now been exploded by Stalin himself. His government today stands forth as one of naked opportunism, conquest, and power politics. The illusion that Hitler's regime was a conservative barricade against the spread of communism has been effectively dispelled by the fuehrer himself. His government, too, stands forth as one of brute military force aiming at unlimited expansion of the Third Reich, and ready to employ whatever appeals to class hatred suit his program. Three aspects of the European picture are worth noting in this connection. The Stalin-Hitler Pact of August 1939 dealt a shattering blow to whatever prestige their respective agents and followers enjoyed in the United States. It remained only for Stalin to attack Finland and to annex the whole or large portions of five other neighboring countries to show unmistakably that Stalin is no better than Hitler. Finally, we have the spectacle of Hitler's attempt to place himself at the head of the European proletariat as the champion of the "have-nots" against the "haves." Mussolini's and the Mikado's wars of aggression long ago stamped them as second-rate international bandits. Today, the four totalitarian dictators are revealed clearly for what they have been from the beginning, a combined threat to the democratic way of life throughout the world. Those who believe unreservedly in the democratic form of government, whether they look upon themselves as progressive and prolabor or as conservatives and pro-business, will not hesitate to separate themselves from the totalitarian movements and their numerous front organizations.

Indeed, upon their doing this will depend in large part America's chance to achieve a real unity of all groups and to proceed with a united effort not only to build an impregnable defense but also to solve our pressing domestic problems.

I. Totalitarian Designs Against the United States

It is a striking characteristic of the totalitarian dictators that they have not attempted to conceal their designs for conquest. Many years ago, they put their programs for imperialistic expansion down in writing where all the world could read them. To a very large extent, they have translated their words into deeds. Not a single country which has been overrun by the totalitarian armies during the past year had any reason to be surprised at its fate. All had been forewarned by the dictators themselves.

The official program of the Communist International has for years declared that "the ultimate aim of the Communist International is to replace world capitalist economy by a world system of communism." The United States has been accorded no exception in this avowed program. On the contrary, Stalin, in an address to delegates of the American Communist Party in Moscow in 1929, called special attention to the strategic position of the United States in his scheme for world revolution. "When a revolutionary crisis develops in America," said Stalin, "that will be the beginning of the end of world capitalism as a whole." In the same declaration Stalin commanded his agents of the American Communist Party to remember that their party was "one of the few Communist parties in the world upon which history had laid tasks of a decisive character from the viewpoint of the world revolutionary movement." Stalin left no doubt in the minds of these American delegates to Moscow about who controlled the Communist Party of the United States. "The American comrades," he said, "will unhesitatingly submit to the decisions of the executive committee of the Communist International and actively carry them into effect."

Hitler's plans for the United States are fully as clear as Stalin's. "National Socialism alone," said Hitler (in 1934), "is destined to liberate the American people from their ruling clique and give them back the means of becoming a great nation." Elaborating his intentions with respect to the United States, the Nazi fuehrer said: "I shall undertake this task simultaneously with the restoration of Germany to her leading position in America."

Mussolini too has made an effort to spread among people of Italian ancestry in America the idea that their first loyalty is to Fascist Italy. The faithful Fascist, whether or not he be an American citizen, is now required to take the following oath which speaks for itself:

> In the name of God and of Italy I swear to accomplish the orders of the duce and to serve with all my strength and if necessary with my blood, the course of the Fascist revolution.

Both Stalin and Hitler have made it plain that their strategy in achieving their objectives in the United States includes the use of Trojan horses or "fifth columns."

The committee has received a vast amount of evidence which shows that hundreds of organizations are operating in the United States today for the purpose of carrying out the wishes of the totalitarian dictators. Most of these organizations are thinly veiled fronts whose methods, purposes, and personnel have been fully exposed in testimony given before the committee. In addition to these numerous front organizations, there are agents of totalitarian espionage whose trails have been found again and again in the course of the committee's investigations.

During the 3 years of its existence, the committee has heard voluminous testimony and compiled a vast amount of evidence which clearly points to the existence in this country of scores of organizations whose common characteristic is the propagation of Nazi ideology. These groups or organizations differ from each other in the directness of their tie-up with the government of Nazi Germany, in the measure of the financial support which they receive from Hitler's Reich, in the degree of their subservience to foreign dictation, and in the extent to which they draw their inspiration directly from Nazi sources. The committee is compelled to conclude, however, that together they constitute an un-American bloc in our population.

As in the case of the Nazi front organizations, so in the case of the Communist front organizations it is impossible to determine the precise degree to which these groups are subservient to foreign agencies. The committee has compiled a vast amount of evidence which indicates that there are scores of organizations whose common characteristic is strict adherence to the "line" of the Communist Party. In almost all cases, these organizations are composed of party members, persons whom the party calls Non-Party Bolsheviks, Communist sympathizers, and thousands of innocents who have been hoodwinked into joining by appeals to worthy sympathies.

From the very beginning of the Communist movement in this country, it has been the practice of the Communist Party to utilize a great diversity of 'organizations with frequently changing names. The theses and statutes of the Third International explicitly stated:

> It is also necessary, in all cases without exception, not to limit oneself to unlawful work, but to carry on also lawful work overcoming all difficulties, founding a lawful press and lawful organizations under the most diverse, and in case of need, frequently changing names.

II. Preliminary Report on Nazi Organizations

The committee recently published a report entitled "A Preliminary Digest and Report on the Un-American Activities of Various Nazi Organizations and Individuals in the United States, including Diplomatic and Consular Agents of the German Government."

This report, as the title indicates, reflects the results of the committee's investigation into the activities of certain Nazi front organizations and individuals who are engaged in the task of furthering the interests of the Nazi government in the Western Hemisphere. The report, fully substantiated by documentary evidence, reveals that the Nazi government, for a number of years, has set up in the Western Hemisphere various organizations which at all times are under the control of the foreign ministry in Berlin. The report reveals that these organizations have a preordained program to fulfill, one of the objectives of which is the conducting of a virulent propaganda campaign, which in the United States takes the form of glorifying nazi-ism and which in Central and South America is strongly anti-American.

The report reflects the activities of the Transocean News Service and the individual activities of Dr. Manfred Zapp. The German Government, according to documentary evidence, set up these organizations, which while shrouded with all the accouterments of a legitimate press organization are able to carry on the work of propaganda and which, by virtue of their accepted position in press circles, are able to operate as centers about which revolves the working of German agents. Prior to the publication of this report, investigations had failed to disclose in any detail the modus operandi of the Nazi government. The documentary evidence contained in this report gives a partial answer to the reason why it has been impossible to uncover evidence which would show this program. The evidence reveals that much, if not all, of the operations of these Nazi-controlled agencies in the Western Hemisphere are carried out through the direction of the German consulates and embassies with the consequent result that all such activities are insulated with diplomatic immunity. For example, the evidence disclosed that the German Embassy and the consulates in the United States have acted as soliciting and collecting agencies for the Transocean News Service, that the embassy and the consulates have also transmitted instructions and exercised direct control of the Transocean's operating policy, which at all times is in conformity with the wishes of Berlin. Consul General Kapp, of Cleveland, Ohio, Consul General Herbert Scholz, of Boston, Mass., Consul General Fritz Wiedemann, of San Francisco, Calif., and Chargé d'Affaires Hans Thomsen, of Washington, D.C., are among the German consular agents who have acted as soliciting and collecting agents for the Transocean News Service. The evidence further reflects that the official German representatives in this country have not only lent their active aid and support to the dissemination of this propaganda but have also contributed financial aid and support to the Transocean News Service.

The report further shows that the anti-American propaganda that is disseminated in the Central and South American countries is controlled and in part broadcast from the United States through the agency of the Transocean News Service.

The investigation further discloses that the Nazi government has set up in this country organizations which are countenanced as bona fide academic, cultural, and commercial organizations, but which in effect are nothing more than outlets for the spreading of Nazi ideology. This phase of the investigation includes the German Library of Information, the German Railroads Information Office, the American Fellowship Forum, and individual German agents.

The report reveals that the German Library of Information in New York City has grown by leaps and bounds since the outbreak of the war in Europe. The organization which is controlled by the German Embassy and the New York consulate also receives all of its direct financial support from Berlin. This organization works in close cooperation with the Transocean News Service. It has built up a mailing list of over 70,000 persons in the United States and periodically sends Nazi publications to all of these people.

The German Railroads Information Office—which has expended over a million dollars in the last few years in the United States—and which, according to its director, is affiliated with the Rome-Berlin Axis, comprises one of the more subtle sections of the foreign division of the Nazi Party. It, too, has built up a tremendous mailing list and regularly sends its publications, which are prepared in Germany, to the persons on this list.

The American Fellowship Forum, which is a typical front organization, has attempted to prey upon the emotions of the millions of German-Americans in this country as being a legitimate organization for the advancement of German-American relations. However, the results of a full investigation of this organization reveal that thousands of real American citizens have been duped into joining an organization which, in reality, has as its purpose the advancement of Nazi influence in the United States.

The report further reveals that the guiding light of the American Fellowship Forum was Dr. Frederic Ernest Ferdinand Auhagen. Investigation disclosed that Dr. Auhagen, from the time that the Forum was brought into existence, regularly received financial aid direct from Germany.

The report points out that the investigative branchos of the Government have made many investigations into the activities of organizations which were alleged to be affiliated with the Nazi government, but, due to diplomatic immunity, it was never disclosed that the membership of any organization was under the direct control of officials of the German Government until the records of the Transocean News Service were subpenaed. These records disclose that there is in operation in this country an organization known as the foreign division of the National Socialist Party, which is under the leadership of Dr. F. Draeger who is attached to the German Consulate in New York City.

The report further shows that the activities of the German Government in this country were not devoted solely toward propaganda and so-called military espionage but also reflected the fact that the German Government over a period of years has been engaged in a far-sighted program of penetrating the economic structure of this country and those of Central and South America. The evidence discloses that Dr. Ferdinand A. Kertess, president of the Chemical Marketing Co. of New York, is one of the agents of the German Government in this country and is actively engaged in maintaining an increasing German economic strength in this country and in Central and South America. Dr. Kertess is an American citizen, but the evidence discloses that he has engaged in activities that amount to military espionage for the German Government. In addition to the above activities, Dr. Kertess formulated plans for the establishing of an organization known as "The Organization of German Industry in America After the War," and also for an organization entitled "The Founding of a German Banking Institute in New York After the War."

The Congress is advised that investigations into several aspects of the foregoing matters are still in process, and that since the rendition of the above report the committee's investigators have uncovered additional facts of importance which will require intensive research before a full and complete report can be made to the Congress.

III. Kyffhauserbund

During the past year, the committee has made a thorough investigation of an organization known as the Kyffhauserbund. Originally, the organization bore the name Stahlhelm. Its English name is the League of German War Veterans.

The Kyffhauserbund was organized in the summer of 1937, in Philadelphia. From there it spread to New York, New Jersey, Massachusetts, Connecticut, Michigan, Illinois, and Texas.

The New York organization of the Kyffhauserbund shared office space with the German-American Vocational League, an organization which sponsored lectures in this country by the Nazi agent, Dr. Colin Ross.

The committee found that the Kyffhauserbund is affiliated with the Kriegesbund which has its international headquarters in Germany. In the organization's membership book it is stated:

In our fatherland, the Kyffhauserbund has become the standard bearer of all inactive German veterans and veterans' organizations, and it is hoped that this bund here in America will accomplish the same results.

The membership book of the organization stresses rifle and pistol practice. The membership book also bears a line which reads "Recommendation of Organization Leader as to Member's ability of being trusted with confidential work." The committee is forced to conclude that there is no place in this country for any organization which has foreign ties and which asks its members to do confidential work or to promote rifle and pistol practice.

The State commander of the Kyffhauserbund in Texas wrote a memorandum which includes the following declaration of political allegiance: "We did not need to unlearn anything when Hitler came to power in Germany. We were already Nazis when he took up the reins of government Reich."

In pursuing its investigation of the Kyffhauserbund, the committee discovered other facts of the greatest importance. These included the fact that editors of German language newspapers in the United States have been sent to Germany, with all expenses paid, for purely propaganda purposes. One such editor, Hans Ackerman of the Texas Herald, returned from his subsidized trip to Germany to sing the praises of Hitler in the columns of his newspaper.

The committee further discovered that the Nazi consul general in New Orleans, Baron Edgar Von Spiegel, was supplying the editors of German language newspapers in the United States with material from the Transocean News Service. Elsewhere in this report the committee calls attention to the fact that the Transocean News Service is one of the propaganda media of Nazi Germany in the United States. . . .

IV. The Problem of the Labor Movement and of Industry

The evidence which the committee has gathered bears abundant testimony to the fact that throughout the years there has been a major purpose of the Communist Party to attempt to bore from within the ranks of the American labor in an effort either to turn labor organizations into its political tools or to disrupt and destroy them. The Nazis tactic on the contrary has been to have their members gain as many important positions as possible in the industries of America and to gain favor with management rather than work within the ranks of organized labor.

It is of basic importance to understand the exactly opposite purposes of the American labor movement on the one hand and the Communist Party on the other. The aims of the American labor movement are to improve the conditions of the American workers and over a period of time to secure for them a better and fuller life and a place of partnership in the industrial life of the United States. The purposes of the Communists on the other hand are in the words of Stalin to make the unions a school of communism, to increase in every possible way the antagonism between wage earners and other sections of the population and to prostitute the labor movement for the use of the party in carrying out various of its international plans even if in so doing the welfare of the particular group of workers in question may suffer as a consequence. Hence, wherever Communists have gained a foothold in the labor movement they have sought by every means at their command to remove from office any leader however devoted to the welfare of the rank and file workers he might be who has refused to cooperate with the party line.

Only by the most determined and consistent effort such as has been put forth recently by such organizations as the American Federation of Labor generally, the Amalgamated Clothing Workers of America, and the United Rubber Workers of America can this situation be cured. It is incumbent upon other elements in the population to support with the utmost vigor the efforts of responsible leaders and constructive groups within the ranks of labor to root out Communist influence and control. For the future of the labor movement itself which forms so important a factor in the social and economic life of the United States depends upon the success of these efforts. As an example of the kind of action that some labor organizations are taking, the committee quotes paragraph adopted to the constitution of the United Rubber Workers at their recent convention:

> Membership shall be denied to any individual who has proven a member of or affiliated with the Communist, Fascist, or Nazi Parties or any other organization that has for its purpose the overthrow of our democratic form of government.

Wherever the conditions of life of any group of workers are most distressing there is presented the very sort of opportunity which the Communist desires; for example, the neglect on the part of other sections of the population of the plight of many thousands of migratory agricultural workers coupled with the fact that many of these people had recently suffered the experience of being driven from their farms constituted the fertile soil in which it was possible for the Communist Party to become a moving force in the organization of the United Cannery Agricultural Packing and Allied Workers Union of which Donald Henderson, an avowed member of the Communist Party, is the head. . . .

We find that the program of the Communist Party calls for determined opposition to the national-defense program and for a concentration of efforts in basic and war industries. The committee's records show that from the Communist standpoint the main purpose of a strike is political and in order to further in some way or another the program of Moscow. Clearly, this could be served by the bringing about and prolonging of strikes in defense industries. Thus we see again how diametrically opposite are the aims and purposes of the American labor movement on the one hand and the Communist Party on the other.

The committee has evidence of the fact that many members of the

German-American Bund, German National Alliance, and other similar pro-Nazi organizations are employed in important chemical and mechanical positions in our industries and that people having definite Nazi sympathies held some important jobs in the aircraft industry. It is important to point out the difference between their technique and that of the Communists. As a rule, the Nazi sympathizer is not a member of any labor organization at all. Due to the natural and altogether admirable proficiency of the German, he is usually a highly skilled workman. Thus it is possible for him to make his appeal to the employer and to attempt to become his confidante and trusted lieutenant.

The committee wishes to state, however, that in its confident judgment the vast majority of Americans of German name and lineage are loyal Americans—nazi-ism and the German people are by no means synonymous.

Persistent active membership in the German-American Bund or a similar organization would seem to the committee to indicate that a person's primary loyalty is to the German dictator rather than to the United States. . . .

V. Communist Party Election Petitions

In May of this year, the committee obtained some evidence indicating the possible existence of trickery, fraud, and misrepresentation in getting signatures to the Communist Party's nominating petitions. There seemed to be a clear lead to an investigation of the extent of the party's corruption of the ballot.

Immediately, the committee instituted an investigation in a number of States—in Maryland, in West Virginia, in Pennsylvania, in Kentucky, in New Jersey, and in Ohio. We obtained photostatic copies of the Communist Party's nominating petitions which had been filed with the various secretaries of state.

Acting upon the partial evidence in our possession—evidence which showed the existence of fraud and misrepresentation—we addressed a letter, over the signature of the chairman of the committee, to every individual in Pennsylvania whose name appeared on one of these nominating petitions. We inquired of him whether he had actually signed the petition himself, or whether his name had been placed on the petition without his knowledge and consent.

Within 24 hours after the mailing of these letters, the committee's offices in Washington were deluged with thousands of replies from the people of Pennsylvania. These letters advised the committee that thousands of people had never actually signed such a petition, that they had no knowledge whatsoever of the petition, and that they were at a loss to understand why their names appeared thereon. Other thousands of replies stated that the writers had signed a petition but that it had been misrepresented to them, and that at the time of signing they had been led to believe that it was a petition for better housing, for playgrounds, for the lowering of gas rates, for the third term, or for scores of other causes.

Letters similar to the one sent to the petition "signers" in Pennsylvania were then sent to other States.

The evidence is plain that hundreds of names were written on these petitions in the same handwriting. For example, there appeared on the petitions filed with the secretary of state in Kentucky 658 cases of duplication of handwriting. In other words, forgery was compounded 658 times over, within the limits of a relatively small number of "signatures."

The committee's investigation also shows that the names of people who have been dead 10 to 15 years appear on the petitions—deceased persons who had probably never heard of the Communist Party or certainly would not have subscribed to its program if they had ever heard of it.

In some instances, the names of children not over 2 years of age were placed on these petitions.

Furthermore, some 15,000 letters which the committee sent out have been returned unclaimed—no such persons, no such addresses.

The committee's investigation has disclosed that the same frauds were practiced by the Communist Party in Pennsylvania, West Virginia, Kentucky, Maryland, and the other States. The committee is able to report to the House that this gigantic fraud of the Communist Party has not gone unchallenged in these States. The State law enforcement agencies have responded promptly to Moscow's challenge of our democratic processes. Following the committee's exposé in Pennsylvania, the local prosecuting authorities and the grand juries began a series of investigations.

As a result of these local investigations in Allegheny County, in Pennsylvania, a grand jury early in July indicted 43 persons who had circulated these Communist Party petitions, charging deceit, false statements under oath, and fraudulent representation. These indictments charged 31 with perjury, 32 with conspiracy, and 20 with obtaining signatures on false pretenses. Similar indictments were handed down in other counties in Pennsylvania. In most, if not all, of these cases, convictions have already been obtained.

In one county in Pennsylvania, the Communist Party raised overnight $100,000 in cash and in property forfeits, to bail out 36 men and women who were under indictment in connection with obtaining the signatures to these petitions.

In the State of West Virginia, as a result of the committee's exposure of the petition frauds, Oscar Wheeler, the Communist Party's gubernatorial candidate, was sentenced to from 6 to 15 years in the penitentiary for fraud in failing to reveal the identity of the political party for which he was collecting signatures on the nominating petitions. Six others were indicted with Wheeler on the same charge. One hundred and fifty were indicted for voting in a primary after signing the Communist Party petition.

On August 29 the committee made public the results of its investigation of the Communist petitions in Maryland. Immediately following this, Gov. Herbert O'Conor and State's Attorney J. Bernard Wells began an investigation based upon the evidence which the committee had compiled. Governor O'Conor ordered a further inquiry into the alleged Communist fraud and ordered the certification of the Communist Party on the Maryland ballot held up, pending the outcome of his inquiry.

In Maryland, the Communist Party had worked mostly among the Negro population. The committee received hundreds of letters from these Negro people denying that they had signed the petitions, or, in cases where they had signed, advising that they had done so on the representation that it was for better housing, the abolition of lynching, etc. The same kind of fraud and misrepresentation appeared in Maryland as in the other States. The matter was presented to the grand jury in Baltimore, and, as in other States, convictions have been obtained.

In Ohio, the Communist Party filed petitions containing the names of some 34,000 persons. The secretary of state in Ohio furnished the committee with copies of the petitions. Thousands of people from that State wrote the committee repudiating their signatures, on the ground that they were induced to sign by fraudulent means.

In several States, the Communist Party was ruled off the ballot, largely as a result of the committee's investigation and exposure of the fraud involved in these Communist Party petitions.

Since the committee's exposure of these frauds perpetrated by the Communist Party, there has been much shouting about persecutions, the violation of civil liberties, and the intimidation of minority parties. The committee points out the obvious fact that civil liberties are one thing, while fraud and misrepresentation are another.

Communist front organizations and Communist-sympathizing groups attempted to make it appear that the Communist Party was being persecuted for its beliefs.

The National Lawyers' Guild addressed a communication to the Attorney General of the United States, suggesting an injunction against the committee to restrain it from conducting the investigation into these petition frauds. During the year several prominent lawyers resigned from the National Lawyers' Guild on the ground that the organization was unwilling to take any action contrary to the Communist Party "line."

Despite the clearest evidence of crime, the Communist Party has, through its various "Trojan horse" organizations and through the media of its own publications, raised the cry of the denial of civil liberties. The party's principal medium for this purpose was the National Federation for Constitutional Liberties. Every member of the House received from that organization a letter accompanied by a circular which had a section setting forth alleged "Violations of Rights of Minority Parties." That identical document appeared in the Communist Party's newspaper, the Daily Worker, and not elsewhere in the press, on the same day, September 6, that it was forwarded to the Members of the House.

VI. Communist Party on Violence

During the year, the committee has published "A Compilation of Original Sources Used as Exhibits to Show the Nature and Aims of the Communist Party, Its Connections With the U. S. S. R. and Its Advocacy of Force and Violence." Among other things, the authoritative documents included in this compilation show conclusively that the Communist Party has throughout its entire existence maintained that its objectives can be achieved only through a resort to force and violence. In these documents, the party speaks for itself. The following are not the words of the party's critics but the doctrines of its own recognized spokesman:

> In depicting the most general phases of the development of the proletariat, we traced the more or less veiled civil war, raging within existing society, up to the point where that war breaks out into open revolution, and where the violent overthrow of the bourgeoisie lays the foundation for the sway of the proletariat (p. 91,[1] Manifesto of the Communist Party, 1848).
>
> They openly declare that their ends can be attained only by the forcible overthrow of all existing social conditions (p. 19, Manifesto of the Communist Party, 1848).
>
> The epoch of imperialism is an epoch of open clashes between classes, of direct preparations by the working class for the overthrow of the bourgeoisie, and of proletarian revolutions (p. 27, Otto Kuusinen, 1934).
>
> "Turning the imperalist war into a civil war," such is the correct slogan (p. 32, Otto Kuusinen, 1934).
>
> Expressing the historical need for an international organization of revolutionary proletarians—the gravediggers of the capitalist order—the Communist International is the only international force that has for its program the dictatorship of the proletariat and communism, and that openly comes out as the "organizer of the international proletarian revolution" (p. 36, Program of the Communist International, together with its Constitution, 1936).
>
> The conquest of power by the proletariat is the violent overthrow of bourgeois power, the destruction of the capitalist state apparatus (bourgeois armies, police, bureaucratic hierarchy, the judiciary, paraliaments, etc.), and substituting in its place new organs of proletarian power, to serve primarily as instruments for the suppression of the exploiters (p. 47, Ibid.).
>
> This mass action includes: A combination of strikes and demonstrations, a combination of strikes and armed demonstrations, and finally, the general strike conjointly with armed insurrection against the state power of the bourgeoisie (p. 67, Ibid.).
>
> The fundamental slogans of the Communist International in this connection must be the following: Convert imperialist war into

[1] Page numbers in parentheses refer to appendix, pt. I of the Special Committee on Un-American Activities.

civil war; defeat "your own" imperialist government. . . . (p. 68, Ibid.).

"The Communists disdain to conceal their views and aims. They openly declare that their aims can be attained only by the forcible overthrow of all the existing social conditions" (p. 69, Ibid.).

The revolution confronts us directly with the problem of armed insurrection. And to speak of this without proper technical preparations is merely to mouth empty phrases. He who wants the revolution must systematically prepare for it the broad masses, who will, in the process of preparation, create the necessary organs of the struggle (p. 78, A. Losovsky, 1924).

Lenin also knew that the establishment of the proletarian power is impossible without a violent revolution. . . . (p. 82, Ibid.).

For the class struggle in revolutionary times has always inevitably and in every country taken on the form of a "civil war," and civil war is unthinkable without the worst kind of destruction, without terror and limitations of formal democracy in the interests of the war (p. 104, Lenin, 1918).

The Communist International makes its aim to put up an armed struggle for the overthrow of the international bourgeoisie and to create an International Soviet Republic as a transition stage to the complete abolition of the State (p. 111, theses and statutes of the Third International, 1920).

It is especially necessary to carry on unlawful work in the army, navy, and police, . . . (p. 118, ibid.).

The class struggle in almost every country of Europe and America is entering the phase of civil war. Under such conditions the Communists can have no confidence in bourgeois laws. They should create everywhere a parallel illegal apparatus, which at the decisive moment should do its duty by the party, and in every way possible assist the revolution (p. 122, ibid.).

The working class cannot achieve the victory over the bourgeoisie by means of the general strike alone and by the policy of folded arms. The proletariat must resort to an armed uprising (p. 126, Ibid.).

"The best guarantee, the best security for freedom, is a bayonet in the hands of the workers" (p. 191, N. Bucharin, 1920).

The overthrow of imperialist governments by means of armed insurrection and the organization of the international Soviet Republic, such is the way to an international dictatorship of the working class (p. 196, Ibid.).

Neither can the Communist International admit into its ranks those organizations which have inscribed in their program the dictatorship of the proletariat, but which at the same time continue to rely in their tactics upon a peaceful solution of the historical crisis (p. 213, Manifesto of the Second Congress of the Third Communist International, 1920).

Armed insurrection of the proletariat, resulting in victorious revolution, as in Russia; and a series of open armed conflicts with the state power of the bourgeoisie, as in Germany. This is typical of the conditions throughout the world (p. 215, Constitution and Program of the Communist Party of America, 1921).

By the use of force, the proletariat destroys the machinery of the bourgeois state and establishes the proletarian dictatorship based on Soviet power (p. 217, ibid.).

The Communist Party will keep in the foreground the idea of the necessity of violent revolution for the destruction of the capitalist state and the establishment of the dictatorship of the proletariat based on Soviet power (p. 219, ibid.).

The Communist Party must in this manner convince the widest circles of the proletariat by word and deed, that every economic or political conflict, given the necessary combination of circumstances, may develop into civil war, in the course of which it will become the task of the proletariat to conquer the power of the state (p. 256, Theses and Resolutions of the Third World Congress of the Communist International, 1921).

Under "direct action" we mean all forms of direct pressure of the workers upon the employers and the State: Boycott, strike, street demonstrations, seizure of the factories, armed uprisings, and other revolutionary activity, which tend to unite the working class in the fight for socialism (p. 284, ibid.).

The imperialist war must be turned into the civil war, through which the power of the exploiting class shall be broken (p. 408, J. Louis Engdahl and William F. Dunne, 1924).

The American workers, when called upon to go into this war against the Soviet Union, must refuse to fight the Russian workers, and go over on the side of the Red Army. The American workers, like the Russian workers in 1917, must turn the imperialist war into a civil war against their real enemies—the capitalist class of the United States which exploits and oppresses the American working class (p. 466, Leon Platt, 1929).

The means of struggle are—all the forms of mass struggle, including the highest form, armed insurrection (p. 471, I. Komar, Ten Years of the Communist International, 1929).

We explain to the workers, and we teach the workers that only by violence finally can a revolution be accomplished. All revolutions have been accomplished by force and violence (p. 482, William Z. Foster, 1930).

"Orderly revolution" means no revolution. The whole international experience of the working class, immeasurably enriched by the Russian Revolution, proves this beyond question (p. 497, William F. Dunne, 1932).

Let us take root in the factories, let us work thoroughly in the reformist trade-unions, let us work among the mass of unemployed, let us penetrate into Fascist trade-union organizations, into the Army, into the Navy (p. 505, Executive Committee of the Communist International, 1933).

In the midst of imperialist war, the revolutionary working class must put forward the slogan, "Defeat of our own imperialism" (p. 546, Earl Browder, 1933).

Those who accept the class struggle must accept civil wars, which, under certain circumstances, are a natural and inevitable continuance, development, and accentuation of the class struggle in every society based on class divisions . . . To deny or to overlook civil wars would mean becoming a victim of the most hopeless opportunism and abandoning the social revolution (p. 548, Lenin, published in the Daily Worker, 1933).

The proletariat fights against the wars between imperialist states with a program of defeatism and the transformation of the war into a civil war against the bourgeoisie (p. 568, Sixth World Congress of the Communist International, 1928).

It is the bounden duty of Communists strongly to combat all peace phrase-mongering; for at a certain moment in the war, this can be utilized by the bourgeoisie as an extremely important ideological weapon to prevent the imperialist war from being transformed into civil war (p. 573, Ibid.).

The Communists' attitude toward the question of the general strike against war is determined by the same point of view, viz, the transformation of imperialist war into civil war (p. 573, Ibid.).

Side by side with other revolutionary mass actions (demonstrations, strikes in munition works, transport strikes, etc.), the general strike—as the supreme form of the mass strike movement —is an extremely important weapon, and as a transition to the armed uprising it constitutes a stage in the transformation of imperialist war into civil war (p. 573, ibid.).

If the general situation is favorable for it, Communists must utilize such mass movements for the formation of guerilla forces, and for the immediate development of civil war (p. 574, ibid.).

An extremely important point in the matter of transforming imperialist war into civil war is revolutionary work at the front (p. 575, ibid.).

The Communists in the army must organize fraternization and give it a clear, political color, particularly in regard to the question of peace and the organization of the revolutionary forces in the army (p. 575, ibid.).

All this makes it incumbent upon the Communists, primarily in connection with struggle against imperialist and counterrevolutionary wars, to put the question of proletarian civil war openly to the masses and to study the lessons of the above-mentioned uprisings (p. 575, ibid.).

There is an art in rebellion; but rebellion is not purely a military problem, it is primarily a political problem. Only a revolutionary party can lead a rebellion. On the outbreak of the rebellion the party must subordinate the whole of its activity to the requirements of the armed struggle (p. 576, ibid.).

Revolutionary war of the proletarian dictatorship is but a continuation of revolutionary peace policy "by other means" (p. 578, ibid.).

Unless the significance of the revolutionary policy in the war question is explained to the broad masses, and unless work is carried on in the army, the struggle against imperialist war and attempts to prepare for revolutionary wars will never reach beyond the stage of theory (p. 580, ibid.).

These demands will have revolutionary significance only if they are linked up with a distinct political program for revolutionizing the bourgeois army (p. 584, ibid.).

Revolutionary work in the army must be linked up with the general revolutionary movement of the masses of the proletariat and poor peasantry (p. 584, ibid.).

The slogan "transform imperialist war into civil war," must already become the leading idea in our propaganda, before imperialist war breaks out (p. 592, ibid.).

. . . . The dictatorship of the proletariat cannot come about as a result of the peaceful development of bourgeois society and of bourgeois democracy; it can come only as the result of the destruction of the bourgeois state machine, of the bourgeois army, of the bourgeois civil administration, and of the bourgeois police (p. 597, Stalin, 1934).

Lenin is therefore right in saying: "The proletarian revolution is impossible without the violent destruction of the bourgeois state machine and its replacement by a new one" (p. 597, Ibid.).

But along with the growth of revolutionary mass actions, such as demonstrations, strikes in basic industries, munitions works, waterside, rail transport, etc., the general strike—as the supreme form of the mass strike movement—can be a mighty weapon, and "as a transition to the armed uprising it constitutes a stage in the transformation of the imperialist war into civil war" (p. 599, H. M. Wicks, The Communist, 1934).

In fighting against war, the Communists must prepare even now for the transformation of the imperialist war into civil war, concentrate their forces in each country, at the vital parts of the war machine of imperialism (p. 606, Executive Committee of the Communist International, 1934).

Should a new imperialist world war break out, despite all efforts of the working class to prevent it, the Communists will strive to lead the opponents of war, organized in the struggle for peace, to the struggle for the transformation of the imperialist war into civil war against the Fascist instigators of war, against the bourgeoisie, for the overthrow of capitalism (p. 646, Seventh Congress of the Communist International, 1935).

The revolutionary overthrow of the capitalist system is the historic mission of the working class (p. 694, The Communist—A Manual on Organization, 1935).

We Communists say that there is one way to abolish the capitalist state, and that is to smash it by force. To make communism possible the workers must take hold of the state machinery of capitalism and destroy it (p. 740, M. J. Olgin, Why Communism? 1935).

"But this is force and violence," somebody will contend. "Don't you Communists know that the use of force and violence is wrong?" We reply to this, first, that if being a "red-blooded American" means anything, it means that you must not take punishment lying down, that you must offer resistance (p. 742, ibid.).

But at the same time we emphasize that capitalism cannot be done away with by the ballot (p. 749, James W. Ford and James S. Allen, The Negroes in a Soviet America, 1935).

But any one who tells you to depend upon the ballot and civil rights for your defense is betraying you (p. 750, ibid.).

You will be given a gun. Take it and learn well the art of war. This is necessary for the proletarians, not in order to shoot your brothers, the workers of other countries . . . but in order to fight against the bourgeoisie of your own country, in order to put an end to exploitation, poverty, and war, not by means of good intentions, but by a victory over the bourgeoisie and by disarming them (p. 754, Otto Kuusinen, 1935).

The replacement of the bourgeois by the proletarian state is impossible without a violent revolution (p. 762, Lenin, published by the Communist Party of America, 1935).

History does not show a single example in which state power was transferred from one class to another by peaceful means, whether in the form of voting or some other method of formal democracy (p. 766, Earl Browder, 1936).

VII. Totalitarian Propaganda

Recently the committee compiled a preliminary report on totalitarian propaganda in the United States. From the evidence in the committee's possession, the following things appear:

1. The totalitarian regimes of Germany, Russia, Italy, and Japan are flooding the United States with propaganda.

2. A high official in the United States Customs Service has made the following observation within the past 10 days:

> All of the propaganda comes from Germany via Russia and Japan, and has been increasing in quantity steadily since the war began. A Japanese boat which arrived yesterday discharged nearly 400 sacks of this propaganda literature, weighing nearly five tons. . . . Even greater quantities are being received at Seattle and San Francisco.

The foregoing paragraph referred only to the propaganda which is emanating from Germany, and, as the context clearly shows, did not mean to imply that large quantities of propaganda are not being mailed to the United States from the other totalitarian countries.

Five tons of propaganda arriving on a single boat is typical of what has been happening during the past year.

According to the same official of the United States Customs Service, this propaganda is "addressed to thousands of individuals, schools, colleges, institutions, business houses, etc. . . ."

3. Under the Universal Postal Union Convention, to which the United States is a signatory, the taxpayers of the United States must bear the full cost of distributing this totalitarian propaganda from the time it is landed on our shores until it is delivered to the addressees.

4. Even larger quantities of totalitarian printed propaganda are put out in the United States. Much of it enjoys the privilege of second-class mail, which, in effect, is another subsidy paid for by the taxpayers of the United States.

It is the committee's view that no process of democracy nor any constitutional right requires the American people as a whole to meet the costs of this totalitarian propaganda which is inimical to the interests of this country.

The committee is of the opinion that added legislation is necessary at this time to place restrictions on the distribution of totalitarian propaganda when that distribution involves any cost to the American taxpayers, and when such propaganda emanates from a foreign source.

It is therefore respectfully recommended to the standing committees of both Houses of Congress on Post Offices and Post Roads, that the evidence contained in this report be carefully examined with a view to proposing legislation that will exclude, from the benefits of the Universal Postal Union Agreement, propaganda that is directed against the United States.

VIII. National Defense and Subversive Activities

The importance of national defense requires the most careful consideration on all sides of the menace to our national security which arises from subversive activities.

Perhaps the most serious danger which threatens the security of a people in the face of an attack from one of the totalitarian regimes is the lack of national unity. This would seem to be the lesson which we should draw from the experiences of certain European countries which have been conquered by the dictators. It is also for this reason that the great bulk of subversive activity directed and inspired from the totalitarian countries aims precisely at the destruction of our national unity, the breaking down of our national morale. This subversive aim has come to be known as the "softening process."

The committee is of the opinion that the dangers of sabotage are also great, even though in sheer bulk they may constitute a more limited area of operation than is true in the case of the "softening process." The committee has found that Nazis and Communists are present in all of the industries vital to national defense. This is a situation which calls for the utmost vigilance. The committee readily recognizes that, in the very nature of the case, this is a situation which must be handled by the Department of Justice, the Federal Bureau of Investigation, the Naval Intelligence, the Military Intelligence, the United States Secret Service, and other appropriate law-enforcing agencies. The committee earnestly desires to cooperate with these agencies in this work in every way that it can.

There are two aspects to the danger of Communist influence in the labor situation. One is the obvious danger to the labor movement itself as well as to the Nation, arising from the necessarily irresponsible (except of course for the responsibility which the Communist Party must bear) actions of Communists in attempting to lead American workers into situations of conflict for conflict's sake. The second aspect of the danger of Communist influence in labor situations is one which industrial management itself must handle in the interests of national defense. There can be no justification whatever for industrial management anywhere in utilizing the national emergency as an excuse for permitting or perpetuating conditions in which their employees have real grievances. The committee points out that Communists make the most of such situations. Lacking any real grounds for "sharpening the lines of class conflict" in labor relations, even the most clever Communist propaganda will find it difficult, if not impossible, particularly in these grave times, to induce the great rank and file of American labor to strike in defense industries or to engage in any other activities which might serve the purposes of the Communist Party.

IX. Summary of Committee's Work

One accomplishment will, by universal consent, be credited to the committee: We have educated and awakened the American people to a far better understanding of the sinister character and wide extent of subversive activities. We may justly claim to have been the decisive force in shaping the present attitudes of the American people toward the activities of the "fifth columns" which aim at our destruction. Our work has been a type of public education whose importance cannot be exaggerated. Not a single one of the countries of Europe which have been overrun by Stalin and Hitler had the protection of a committee like ours during the years that preceded its supreme crisis.

When we began our work, the German-American Bund had a hundred thousand followers who were pledged to its fuehrer, Fritz Kuhn. The very first exposure which our committee undertook in the summer of 1938 was that of the German-American Bund. The first volume of our hearings opens with a hundred pages of detailed testimony on the un-American and subversive character of the bund.

During the past week the committee published a translation of the official, confidential Manual of the Storm Troopers of the German-American Bund. That document proves conclusively that the German-American Bund is an organization which is highly militarized, and which requires absolute loyalty on the part of its members.

Today Fritz Kuhn is in Sing Sing prison and the German-American Bund has been thoroughly discredited. James Wheeler-Hill, former secretary-treasurer of the bund, is also in prison. Our exposures have provided thousands of innocent people with adequate protection against the false claims of the bund. Its drastically reduced membership and following may now be held to consist only of those whose loyalty is to Hitler.

When we began our work, the bund and a score of Nazi-minded American groups were laying plans for an impressive united front federation—a federation which would be able to launch a first-rate Nazi movement in the United States. By our exposure of these plans, we smashed that Nazi movement even before it was able to get under way.

In like manner, the committee had a large part in breaking up the People's Front. This was more difficult than the breaking up of the Nazi Front. The People's Front was composed of several million adherents and scores of organizations, which bore high-sounding names. The People's Front exercised real political influence. But one by one we took its component organizations and showed by incontrovertible evidence that each was a tool of Stalin's revolutionary conspiracy. It is true that Stalin helped greatly by his alliance with Hitler to bring the People's Front into general disrepute; but, even in that, Stalin was only confirming the committee's indictment of his movement. Long before the Nazi-Soviet pact, we had exposed the hypocrisy of the People's Front in its pretended espousal of democracy.

The largest unit of the People's Front movement was the American League for Peace and Democracy. When we began our work, the American League boasted of 7,000,000 adherents. We kept the spotlight of publicity turned upon this organization until it finally gave up in despair and went out of existence. It was killed by exposure. It would have been a great thing for the protection of our country if our disclosures about the league could have been made in 1933 instead of in 1938 and 1939. Our exposure of the league was not premature; it was long overdue.

Other organizations which formed units in the People's Front movement have been greatly crippled in their effectiveness as a result of our exposures. The American Youth Congress once enjoyed a very considerable prestige and an impressive following among the youth of our country. Today many of its distinguished former sponsors refuse to be found in its company. Best of all, it has been deserted by American youth. We kept the spotlight of publicity focused upon the American Youth Congress, and today it is clear to all that, in spite of a degree of participation in its activities by many fine young people, it was never at its core anything less than a tool of Moscow.

Another of the important People's Front units was the Workers Alliance. At one time in its history, the alliance had an actual dues-paying membership of 600,000. It had an influential lobby in Washington, and claimed to be the only Government-recognized bargaining agency for the unemployed. The alliance became so bold that it took physical possession of the State capitols in New Jersey and Wisconsin. Our committee kept the spotlight of publicity turned upon the Workers Alliance. Finally, its influence was destroyed when it became apparent to all that its control was in the hands of the agents of Moscow. Its non-Communist element withdrew under the leadership of David Lasser in June of this year, and today the Workers Alliance is a mere shadow of its former self—without influence anywhere and completely discredited.

In 1938 William Dudley Pelley was spreading a million pieces of literature over the country. The religious bigots organized in Pelley's Silver Shirts have now lost their leader. Immediately after Pelley was placed on the stand before our committee, he ordered the dissolution of his silver-shirted band. We had exposed it out of existence. One of Pelley's agents who tried to secure a job with our committee by falsely representing himself before us while under oath was tried and convicted for perjury.

Deatherage and his Knights of the White Camellia, who tried to make themselves the nucleus of an American Nazi group, under the name of the American Nationalist Confederation, have likewise gone the way of those who could not bear up under the full exposure of their true purposes. Our committee heard all that Deatherage could say for himself under questioning, and that was enough to put an end to his propaganda of religious bigotry.

The same thing happened to Gilbert and Campbell when we obtained their records under the authority of our congressional subpena, and exposed the falsity of their propaganda of religious hatred.

The country did not know that Earl Browder had traveled on false passports until our committee placed him on the stand and obtained the damaging admission from his own lips. After that exposure, Browder was successfully prosecuted and now awaits a prison term.

The case of Nicholas Dozenberg was fully aired before our committee. The whole country was apprised of the fact that this former leader of the American Communist Party had entered the espionage branch of Stalin's machine. Three months later, Dozenberg was apprehended by the Secret Service of the Treasury Department. He was then tried, convicted, and sentenced. The American public learned through our exposure of Dozenberg's case that members of the Communist Party are subject to draft into Stalin's espionage ring.

For 2 years our committee piled proof upon proof that the Communist Party was nothing more or less than a foreign conspiracy masked as a political party. In our annual report at the beginning of the present year, we showed in detail how the Communist Party was tied to Moscow. One of our members introduced legislation which will require such foreign-controlled agencies as the Communist Party and the German-American Bund to make a public record of all pertinent facts concerning themselves. His bill was passed unanimously by both Houses of Congress. In its effort to evade the provisions of the Voorhis Act, the Communist Party has now made the gesture of severing its connections with Moscow. Our relentless exposure of the party has it on the run.

Recently, our committee gave to the country the clearest picture it has yet received of the technique and aims of Hitler's subsidized propaganda in the United States. Because the German diplomatic and consular agents were involved in this un-American propaganda campaign, our committee took every possible precaution not to embarrass the State Department in its conduct of our foreign relations.

During the recent election campaign our committee obtained the names of more than 200,000 persons who had signed the election petitions of the Communist Party. We made an extensive investigation and exposed the fact that these election petitions were tainted with wholesale fraud, perjury, and misrepresentation. On the basis of our exposures, local law-enforcement authorities have obtained more than a hundred indictments and from 50 to 60 convictions. Without a single exception throughout the United States, we have found State and local authorities prepared to cooperate to the fullest with our committee.

In addition to all these things, the committee has built up very complete files on "fifth column" organizations. These files contain the names and records of several hundred thousand individuals. They contain many thousands of pieces of literature and practically all of the publications which "fifth column" organizations have put out during the past 20 years. They also contain thousands of signed letters which have passed between "fifth columnists." These files cannot be duplicated anywhere else in the world today.

Finally, the committee has shown that there is a way to combat the "fifth column" without creating a Gestapo. It is the way of exposure—a way which conforms to the letter and the spirit of a democracy, and is at the same time more effective than a Gestapo. In both Russia and Germany, half the population spies on the other half. That is the logical end of a system which depends exclusively on methods of counterespionage.

X. Legislative Recommendations

The committee realizes the difficulty of reaching and curbing certain phases of un-American and subversive propaganda and activities through legislative action. In view of our findings and the origin of these activities, we submit the following recommendations as a partial legislative program:

1. The enactment of legislation to bring about the immediate mandatory deportation of alien spies and saboteurs.

2. The mandatory deportation of aliens who advocate any basic change in the form of our Government.

3. The enactment of legislation requiring that all employees and officials of our Federal Government be American citizens.

4. Withhold all Federal financial support from any educational institution which permits members of its faculty to advocate communism, fascism, or nazi-ism as a substitute for our form of government to the student body of

these educational institutions. (This particular recommendation is not concurred in by Mr. Voorhis, not because of disagreement with the principle involved but on the ground that the administration of such an act is impossible without risking grave injustice being done to people seeking merely to explain the principles involved in totalitarian philosophy.)

5. The enactment of legislation to outlaw every political organization which is shown to be under the control of a foreign government. As long as these organizations have a legal status in the United States, it will be difficult for any agency of the Government to deal with them. We now know that they furnish the legal apparatus for the operations of saboteurs, and the window dressing for espionage. The committee believes that legislation can be worked out to outlaw such organizations, and that this will in no sense constitute a violation of the Bill of Rights, since such legislation would only affect organizations controlled or directed by foreign countries.

6. The enactment of legislation to stop all immigration from foreign countries that refuse to accept the return of their nationals found under American law to be deportable from this country. This legislation is made necessary by the fact that some foreign governments have refused to accept their own citizens who have been ordered deported by the United States Government.

7. As previously stated in the body of the report, the committee recommends the passage of added legislation to place restrictions on the distribution of totalitarian propaganda, when that distribution involves any cost to the American taxpayers, and when such propaganda emanates and is shipped from foreign sources.

8. We recommend that the statutory period during which citizenship papers can be revoked under existing law be extended to at least 10 years.

9. Due to the fact that the committee has discovered that many members of foreign controlled organizations have traveled on American passports which have been fraudulently obtained, the committee feels that, the statute of limitations should be extended from 3 to 7 years. This is made necessary because of the unusual difficulty in apprehending those who resort to the use of fraudulent passports within the period of 3 years.

Recommendations

1. We recommend the continuation of this committee for a period of 2 years with an adequate appropriation. This committee is the only agency of Government that has the power of exposure. No other agency can require witnesses to appear before it and testify under oath with respect to un-American activities and subversive propaganda. No other agency of Government has the power to subpena records and documents of un-American organizations, and individuals, except under unusual circumstances. There are many phases of un-American activities that cannot be reached by legislation or administrative action. We believe that the committee has shown that

fearless exposure, coupled with effective enforcement of the laws that are on the statute books, is the democratic answer to the "fifth column." The committee believes that it should have at least 2 years in order to formulate and put into effect a long-range program.

2. The committee recommends as a policy that employment in national-defense industries or the Government service be denied to any person who has been and is now active in any political organization which is found to be under the control and guidance of a foreign government.

> *Martin Dies*
> Chairman
> *Joe Starnes*
> *N. M. Mason*
> *John J. Dempsey*
> *Jerry Voorhis*
> *J. Parnell Thomas*

FIFTH ANNUAL REPORT
JANUARY 2, 1943

U.S. House of Representatives, 77th Congress, 2nd Session, House Report No. 2748, Special Report on Subversive Activities Aimed at Destroying our Representative Form of Government, 1–16.

Mr. Dies, chairman, from the Special Committee on Un-American Activities, submitted the following

REPORT

Subversive Activities Aimed at Destroying our Form of Government

I

Since the last report of this committee to the House on January 5, 1941, our country has been plunged into a global war on whose outcome hangs no less an issue than that of our national survival.

Of our ultimate victory in this war, we can entertain no doubt. Nevertheless, we do not hold—and we caution our people not to hold—this faith in the eventual triumph of our arms lightly; for there may yet be exacted of us a price in life and treasure which we cannot, at this stage of the struggle, begin to comprehend. But, however great the sacrifice still required for victory, we must, as a people, grimly resolve that no part thereof shall be the loss of that human liberty which is the essence of Americanism. To this end, we must guard, as never before in any wars of the past, our internal safety against the machinations of fifth columns.

By common consent, we are engaged in a global war against the existence and spread of totalitarianism. A world which is half totalitarian will forever menace our liberties and challenge our way of life. This global war is unique not only in the use of new physical weapons but even more unique in the use by our totalitarian foes of saboteurs whose work is to spread both physical and spiritual destruction within our borders. The systematic sowing of rumors, the calculated whispers of defeatism, and the treacherous campaigns to create internal disunity by un-American hatreds may be as dangerous as the saboteur's bomb and flame.

This committee has defined its special function, in accordance with the terms of the mandate given by the House, as the discovery and exposure of those enemy groups which fight with nonphysical weapons as a fifth column on our home front.

Our committee decided many months ago, after the entrance of the United States into the war, to refrain from holding any public hearings which might involve the activities of Axis saboteurs, so as not to run any risk of premature disclosures which might embarrass those whose responsibility it is to prosecute those guilty of espionage and sabotage.

Assistance Furnished Government Agencies

This committee came into existence at about the time Hitler and his Axis partners were sending their armies out for world conquest. When we began our investigation in 1938, our hearings and exposures were not received in certain official quarters with the attention that they deserved. Fortunately, however, the members of our committee and a great majority of the Members of the House and the American people saw and realized that this committee had put its finger on a dangerous condition existing in this country which threatened to become increasingly worse.

In 1938, the German-American Bund had many posts throughout the Nation and boasted 100,000 members. The Communist Party and its Popular Front, claiming the support of "millions," were approaching their highest peak. The Japanese "treaty merchants" were busy throughout our Nation gathering information for Hirohito. The Silver Shirt Legion of America, under Pelley, was flourishing and other native Fascists were operating unmolested.

The pattern was not entirely clear, but the members of this committee had heard and seen enough to convince them that it was time some agency of our Government should equip itself to deal with this approaching threat. It was for this reason that the committee, late in 1938, began to assemble and organize all available information on so-called subversive activities in America. The committee points out that at that time there was no agency of the Government engaged in checking on so-called subversive groups for the very simple reason that they had no authority to do so under the law; and the Communists, the Nazis, the Fascists, and all their stooges had long ago learned that it was easy enough to carry on much of their work within the law.

In 1938, only two file cabinets were required to hold the files of this committee, whereas today the committee's files and records on subversive activities fill 135 file cabinets. The index to these files contains over 1,000,000 cards, each containing information on individuals and organizations engaged in subversive activities. All of these cards are based upon documentary evidence in the possession of the committee and so filed that it is readily available to any Government agency desiring it.

This material has been obtained during the past 5 years in various ways but principally through the use of the congressional subpena, an authority which no other Government agency possesses. Therein lies the advantage and necessity of congressional investigating committees. Had it not been for this authority of subpena, our committee could never have built up these irreplaceable files on subversive activities which have served as the chief source of information on un-American individuals, groups, and organizations for the many agencies of this Government.

From the time Hitler marched into the lowlands and the people and Government of this country were shocked into the realization that there *was* a fifth column in America, the files of this committee have served as a veritable fountainhead of information for the various agencies of the Government charged with the internal safety of the United States.

As evidence of this service to Government agencies, the committee reports to the House that during the past 14 months some 1,600 agents from the various Intelligence units of the Army, the Navy, the Federal Bureau of Investigation, Secret Service, and others have called at the committee's office in Washington alone for information. Hundreds of agents from the same agencies have called at the committee's branch offices in New York, Philadelphia, Los Angeles, and Chicago for similar information.

In addition to the above, the following agencies have detailed liaison agents to work daily at the committee's offices checking and obtaining information from the committee's files: Civil Service, Intelligence Unit of the Treasury, Military Intelligence, Naval Intelligence, State Department, Federal Bureau of Investigation, Work Projects Administration, Secret Service, and Office for Emergency Management. The branch offices of the committee have been used in a similar manner.

Numerous requests for information which the committee has received from Government departments have involved the committee's turning over large files of documents. For example, the committee on February 3, 1942, supplied the Office of the Coordinator of Information with 210 documents on Nazi propaganda. Somewhat earlier, the committee turned over to the Department of Justice hundreds of original documents which provided the Department with the basis of its cases against Auhagen, Zapp, and Tonn.

On August 15, 1942, the committee forwarded to the President a list of approximately 17,000 individuals who had been identified or affiliated with the Nazi movements in this country and suggested at the time to the President that some form of surveillance should be kept over these people.

This committee has also assisted various State committees which have been investigating un-American activities, particularly in New York and California, and supplied the special committee of the Argentine Chamber of Deputies, investigating subversive activities, headed by Sr. Damonte Taborda, with considerable information and furnished them at their request with a memo on how to proceed in making such an investigation. Early this year when Senor Taborda was in the United States he examined the files of the committee and was very complimentary of the committee's set-up and surprised at the amount of information contained in its files.

The committee has taken 11,725 printed pages of testimony and has issued reports comprising 3,000 printed pages, and the information contained in these hearings and reports has been of immeasurable value not only to the Government agencies but has served to enlighten the people of this country and the Americas of the workings of the Communists, the Nazis, the Japanese, and their sympathizers and agents. . . .

II

Communists in the Government

The committee would like to state at the outset that it has never investigated the personnel of the Federal Government to determine how many of its employees were Communists or so-called fellow travelers. However, since the committee's creation in 1938, there has come to its attention from time to time the presence in the Federal Government of high-salaried employees who were prominently and definitely identified with communism and its front organizations. Many of these cases were promptly called to the attention of the President, the Congress, and the departmental head concerned by either the committee or its members. At this point, the committee would like to cite a number of examples where this procedure has been followed.

On October 25, 1939, the committee made public the names, positions, and salaries of some 563 Government employees located in Washington, D. C., who were members of the American League for Peace and Democracy. In three reports which this committee has made to the House, it has found the American League for Peace and Democracy to be a Communist front organization. It will be recalled that Earl Browder was vice president of the organization. Furthermore, the Attorney General, Mr. Francis Biddle, has branded the American League a subversive organization, in language as strong as any used by this committee in its characterizations. In making public this list, the committee issued an accompanying statement which made clear that it did not consider all of the people on that list or any one of them in particular to be Communists, but in view of the fact that these Government employees were members of a Communist front organization and continued their membership long after the organization was exposed as being communistic, the committee felt that the Congress and the people were entitled to know who they were. This was an authentic membership list obtained from the headquarters of the American League for Peace and Democracy by due process of subpena, which was served upon the secretary of the organization.

On September 6, 1941, the chairman of this committee wrote the President a letter, accompanied by 43 exhibits, detailing the Communist affiliation and background of the following officials of the Office of Price Administration and suggested that they be dismissed from their positions:

Robert A. Brady, head consultant of Office of Price Administration and Civilian Supply, salary, $7,500.

Tom Tippett, Assistant Chief of Rent Section of Office of Price Administration and Civilian Supply, salary, $5,600.

Mildred Edie Brady, principal specialist in consumer education, Office of Price Administration and Civilian Supply, salary, $5,600.

Dewey H. Palmer, consultant of Office of Price Administration and Civilian Supply, salary, $20 a day.

At the time, Mr. Leon Henderson, head of the Office of Price Administration, issued a public statement in which he said that he would refer the cases to the Civil Service Commission and abide by their decision. Subsequently, the chairman was advised by the President that the matter had been referred to the Civil Service Commission. After several months of investigation, the Civil Service Commission recommended to Mr. Henderson the dismissal of his chief consultant, Robert A. Brady, and his wife, Mildred Edie Brady. Mildred Edie Brady resigned. In the case of Robert A. Brady, Mr. Henderson refused to abide by the decision of the Civil Service Commission even though he had previously stated he would do so. Mr. Brady is still employed in the Office of Price Administration. The Commission's recommendation was issued over a year ago.

On November 18, 1941, the chairman of the committee wrote a letter to James Lawrence Fly, Chairman of the Federal Communications Commission, calling his attention to the fact that the committee had a considerable file revealing the Communist affiliations of one Goodwin Watson who had just been appointed Chief Broadcast Analyst of the Federal Communications Commission. Chairman Fly, without availing himself of the evidence, replied that he had personally investigated Mr. Watson's case and found the committee's charges to be baseless. In the meantime the agency of the Government charged with investigating employees of the Federal Communications Commission had called at the committee's offices and requested all information in its files on Goodwin Watson. The committee furnished the information, which consisted of over 100 exhibits. The Federal Communications Commission was also furnished a copy of this material. No action was taken. However, when the appropriation bill for the Federal Communications Commission was before the House for consideration, an amendment was adopted which prohibited Goodwin Watson from receiving any of the funds appropriated. This amendment was subsequently eliminated when the bill was sent to conference, and Goodwin Watson is still on the Federal pay roll of the Federal Communications Commission.

On January 15, 1942, the chairman of the committee, in a speech on the floor of the House, called attention to the presence in the Office of Facts and Figures of one Malcolm Cowley, chief information analyst, at a salary of $8,000 per annum. The chairman inserted in his speech the record of Malcolm Cowley, which showed 72 affiliations with the Communist Party and its front organizations. Several weeks later Mr. Cowley resigned his position with the Federal Government.

On November 28, 1941, in a speech on the floor of the House, the chairman called the attention of the members to the case of Gardner Jackson, principal economist in the Department of Agriculture at a salary of $5,600 a year, and included in his speech the Communist record of Gardner Jackson. Jackson will be remembered as the same individual who in 1939 paid $110 for fraudulent letters which sought to discredit the chairman of this committee. Mr. Jackson is still in the Department of Agriculture.

On March 28, 1942, the chairman wrote a letter to the Honorable Henry A. Wallace, Chairman of the Board of Economic Warfare, and called his attention to the Communist affiliations of eight of its employees and made particular reference to one Maurice Parmelee, principal economist at a salary of $5,600 a year, who had written several books advocating the practice of nudism in America. He also called attention to the presence of C. Hartley Grattan, economic analyst of the Bureau of Economic Warfare, at a salary of $5,600 a year, who had written a foreword to the notorious German White Paper which was circulated by the Nazi Government, and which sought to place the blame of the war on the United States. The following week, Mr. Parmelee was dismissed from the Board of Economic Warfare, and Mr. Grattan resigned.

In the act, making appropriations for the Department of Justice for the fiscal year 1941 (Public Law No. 135 of the 77th Cong., 1st sess., approved June 28, 1941), there was contained a provision which specified that of the amount appropriated for the use of the Federal Bureau of Investigation—

> at least $100,000 shall be available exclusively to investigate the employees of every department, agency, and independent establishment of the Federal Government who are members of subversive organizations or advocate the overthrow of the Federal Government and report its findings to Congress.

The Department of Justice sought to have this amendment stricken from the appropriation bill when it was before the Senate Finance Committee but failed. On October 17, 1941, Attorney General Biddle wrote the chairman of our committee a letter, in which he stated—

> I should be pleased to receive from you any information in the possession of your committee or its investigators which bears upon

the membership of any employee of the Federal Government in subversive organizations, or such employee's advocacy of the overthrow of the Government of the United States.

Pursuant to this request, the committee, on October 17, sent to the Attorney General the names of 1,124 Federal Government employees who were members of organizations which this committee had found to be subversive. These membership lists had been obtained largely by subpena and had been identified and authenticated by the officials of the organization involved. All of the committee's files were immediately made available to the Attorney General and his investigators who were charged with carrying out the mandate of Congress as contained in this act.

On September 2, 1942, Attorney General Biddle laid before the Speaker of the House his report on the investigation called for in Public Law No. 135 of the Seventy-seventh Congress. The following day the chairman of our committee wrote a letter to the Speaker of the House in which he said—

I am compelled to charge that the Attorney General has utterly failed to carry out the mandate of the Congress as expressed in Public Law No. 135 of the Seventy-seventh Congress. Instead of fulfilling the mandate of Congress, the Attorney General has issued a meaningless conglomeration of statistics set in a framework of general conclusions which are either totally irrelevant to the issues involved or dangerous to the internal safety of this country as applied to employment in the Federal Government.

According to the Attorney General's report, the first procedure adopted by his office in making this investigation was to forward all complaints involving the subversive affiliations of a Federal employee to the departmental head concerned. If he requested an investigation, the Federal Bureau of Investigation was then authorized to make such an investigation and file its report with the departmental head for whatever action he deemed necessary. The Attorney General, in his report to Congress, however, explained that this procedure proved most ineffective in that out of 1,597 complaints received and forwarded to the departmental heads only 193 requests for investigation were returned. It was then that the Attorney General reported he had adopted the procedure of having the Federal Bureau of Investigation investigate all complaints received. After investigation, the Federal Bureau of Investigation report was forwarded without conclusions or recommendation to the departmental head for whatever action he might wish to take. The Attorney General also brought out in his report that, in order to follow this procedure, it was necessary to determine which organizations were subversive. To determine this he caused to be set up an inter-departmental committee to review the evidence against all organizations concerned and then to submit a memorandum and finding to the Attorney General who in turn was to transmit it to the departmental heads to serve as a guide for them in considering the cases which would come before them.

This committee's report is primarily concerned with the manner in which the Attorney General dealt with, or rather failed to deal with, the 1,124 cases which were submitted to him by the committee at his request. Of the 1,124 names submitted, according to the Attorney General's report, the Federal Bureau of Investigation actually investigated only 601 cases. Of these 601, the Attorney General stated that he had received replies from departmental heads on only 501 out of the 601, and that action had been taken in only 3 cases—2 dismissals and 1 disciplinary action. The Attorney General did not enlighten the Congress as to how many of the Federal employees included in the original list of 1,124 had resigned, or what disposition had been made of the 100 cases which had not been heard from. On September 24, 1942, the chairman of this committee addressed the House for 2 hours at which time he covered every phase of the Attorney General's report and established the fact that hundreds of Federal employees who were on the committee's list are still in the Government service even though they belong to organizations which the Attorney General himself has held to be subversive. In a number of cases these Government employees belong to 3 or more such organizations. In the opinion of this committee, the Attorney General did not carry out the mandate of Congress, which was simply that an investigation be made and a report to Congress be filed, that would show how many Federal Government employees belonged to subversive organizations, knowingly or unknowingly, in order that the Congress might determine for itself the extent of the inroads being made by subversive groups into the Federal service. This the Attorney General did not do.

In the Chairman's speech of September 24 he also presented to the House the names of 19 officials of the Government, together with their connections with organizations which the Attorney General himself, according to his own memorandum, had found to be subversive. Yet, to the committee's knowledge, no action has been taken in the cases of the 19 officials.

III

Since the committee's last report to the House on January 5, 1941, seven major subjects have been covered in our investigations, hearings, and special reports. These investigations, hearings, and special reports have dealt more or less exhaustively with the following: (1) The American Peace Mobilization; (2) sabotage strikes in our defense industries; (3) Japanese activities in the United States; (4) anti-Semitic propaganda; (5) the Union for Democratic Action; (6) the National Federation for Constitutional Liberties; and (7) the Axis Front movement in the United States.

(1) *The American Peace Mobilization*

The committee employed two investigators whose full time was devoted to an exhaustive inquiry into the nature, aims, and activities of the American Peace Mobilization.

On May 21, 1941, a subcommittee of the committee under the chairman-ship of the Honorable Joe Starnes began public hearings on the American Peace Mobilization. In our investigations and hearings on this organization, the following facts were established:

(a) The American Peace Mobilization was the direct successor of the American League for Peace and Democracy and was, like the latter organiza-tion, completely under the control of the Communist Party.

(b) The American Peace Mobilization picketed the White House for many weeks prior to Hitler's invasion of Russia, and, in fact, maintained that picket line right down to the very day of Hitler's attack upon the Soviet Union.

(c) The avowed objects of the American Peace Mobilization's White House picket line were vicious by every test of American patriotism.

(d) The American Peace Mobilization attempted to penetrate and in-fluence the armed forces of the United States for clearly treasonable purposes.

(e) The American Peace Mobilization openly aided and abetted wide-spread sabotage strikes in the most important American defense industries, thereby seriously hampering our Nation's preparedness to meet just such military crises as that of Pearl Harbor.

(f) The American Peace Mobilization denounced the President as a war-mongering tool of Wall Street bankers and the whole American defense pro-gram as a Wall Street plot to aid British imperialism.

(g) The American Peace Mobilization echoed the Communist Party's line that Great Britain was engaged in an imperialistic war for her own im-perialistic ends.

(h) The American Peace Mobilization did all within its power to oppose our lend-lease aid to the nations which were embattled against the Axis Powers.

(i) The American Peace Mobilization denounced the conscription of American manpower as an invasion of civil liberties.

(j) The published propaganda of the American Peace Mobilization was replete with statements which were deliberately calculated to sabotage the American defense program, the following being a typical example of state-ments issued over the names of the organization's leaders:

> But even if we don't approve of England's war, isn't her side still preferable to Hitler's: and isn't it better to fight and beat Hitler with England than without her? No. An English victory will result in the same sort of imperialist, anti-democratic peace as will a Nazi vic-tory.

(k) Immediately after Hitler's invasion of Russia, the American Peace Mobilization changed its name to the American People's Mobilization, and reversed all of its former positions in exact accordance with the changes which Hitler's invasion of the Soviet Union occasioned in the line of the Communist Party.

(2) *Sabotage Strikes in our Defense Industries*

In the early part of 1941, a wave of sabotage strikes in American defense industries reached its highest point. From the very beginning of these strikes, this committee pointed out that these menacing work-stoppages were led by known Communists and that the Communist Party's program called for just such treasonable interference with this country's military and industrial preparedness. The damage done by these strikes was incalculable. In every instance, the union involved in these interruptions of production was affiliated with the Congress of Industrial Organizations. A brief summary of the more serious situations which the committee investigated is as follows:

(a) *Allis-Chalmers.*—One of the most damaging of the sabotage strikes was that at the Allis-Chalmers plant in Milwaukee which lasted for many weeks. The strike was conducted by the United Automobile Workers of America, whose leader at the plant was Harold Christoffel. The committee's investigation left no doubt about Christoffel's Communist affiliations. Among other Communist connections, he was one of the leaders of the American Peace Mobilization and of the National Federation for Constitutional Liberties.

(b) *Harvill.*—The committee made a thorough investigation of the strike leadership at the Harvill plant in Los Angeles, Calif. There the striking union was the National Association of Die Casters, and the leader of the strike was Kenneth Eggert. Although Eggert slipped into California under an alias for the purpose of tying up the Harvill plant, the committee promptly identified him and exposed him as Kenneth Eggert, former Communist Party secretary in Toledo, Ohio.

(c) *Vultee.*—The committee exposed the Communist leadership of the disastrous work stoppage at the Vultee aircraft plant in Los Angeles, Calif. The union involved was the United Automobile Workers of America, and among the more important Communist leaders of the strike was Wyndham Mortimer.

(d) *International Harvester.*—For weeks, the International Harvester plant at Chicago was tied up by the Farm Equipment Organizing Committee under the leadership of Grant Oakes whose Communist record included prominent activity in the American Peace Mobilization.

(e) *Aluminum.*—In April 1941, the National Association of Die Casters tied up the plants of the Aluminum Co. of America in Cleveland, Ohio, The committee's investigations turned up the fact that Alex Balint, leader of the strike, was an alien, an ex-convict, and an old-time Communist Party member who had used the name "Al Barry."

(f) *North American.*—The strike at the North American Aviation in Inglewood, Calif., led to an order by the President for the United States Army to take over the plant. In this instance also, the committee established the fact that the strike leadership was Communist. The president of the local of the United Automobile Workers which conducted the strike was Elmer J. Freitag. Freitag vehemently denied all Communist connections until confronted with indisputable documentary evidence in the committee's possession.

(g) *New York Transport.*—In March 1941, the Transport Workers' Union called a strike which seriously interrupted the facilities of the transportation system in New York City. The committee published a special report, known as appendix V, which established the far-reaching Communist control of the Transport Workers' Union under the leadership of Michael J. Quill.

(h) *Lumber.*—The International Wood Workers of America called and continued a disastrous strike in the lumber industry in defiance of governmental agencies. The union's leader, O. M. Orton, was exposed by the committee as a Communist who occupied a place of foremost leadership in the American Peace Mobilization.

(i) *Trona.*—The Mine, Mill, and Smelter Workers' Union, headed by Reid Robinson, brought about a particularly serious work stoppage at Trona, Calif. The committee's investigation clearly established the fact of the Communist motives and leadership of the strike. Reid Robinson was vice president of the American Peace Mobilization.

(3) *Japanese Activities in the United States*

In February 1942, the committee published a special report, known as appendix part VI, which dealt comprehensively with the subversive activities of the Japanese in the United States. For more than a year the committee had employed special investigators to make a thorough study and investigation of the Japanese who were living on our west coast.

Among the committee's findings, prior to Pearl Harbor, were the following:

(a) The Japanese had a map showing in great detail the fleet positions and battle formations of the United States Navy around Pearl Harbor. This map also included vital military information on the Panama Canal, Alaska, and the Philippine Islands.

(b) The Japanese were in possession of the most detailed information concerning all the naval craft of the United States.

(c) A former attaché of the Japanese consulate in Honolulu was prepared to testify that an elaborately organized fifth column of Japanese was being drilled for collaboration with the armed forces of Japan when the latter should attack Pearl Harbor.

(d) The Japanese Government was using front organizations in this country for the compiling of an elaborate census of Japanese who were residing in the United States.

(e) Japanese fishing vessels on our west coast, as well as in Hawaii and the Philippine Islands, were an important arm of espionage for the Japanese Navy.

(f) A police officer on Terminal Island in Los Angeles Harbor was prepared to testify that numerous conferences had been held between officers of the Imperial Japanese Navy and Japanese residents on the island.

(g) Japanese-language schools in California and in Hawaii were inculcating traitorous attitudes toward the United States in the minds of American-

(h) Japanese civic organizations in the United States, such as the Central Japanese Association, were loudly pretending their loyalty to the United States Government while surreptitiously serving the deified Emperor of Japan.

(i) Japanese civic organizations were collecting funds in this country which they were sending to Japan for the Empire's war chest to be used for purchasing bombers.

(j) In California, there were Japanese veterans' organizations composed of men with military training and experience who vowed allegiance only to the Japanese Emperor whether they were American- or Japanese-born.

(k) Japanese treaty merchants, abusing the hospitality of the United States and using their merchant status as a subterfuge, were engaged in espionage activities for the Japanese Government.

(l) Japanese in California were occupying large tracts of lands which were militarily but not agriculturally useful.

(m) Many Japanese had taken up residence adjacent to highly important defense plants.

(n) Having failed through diplomatic channels to obtain important information concerning the water-supply system and other public utility services of Los Angeles, Japanese had obtained employment in these places where they were in positions to do incalculable fifth-column damage.

(o) Japanese espionage agents had obtained detailed information on the location of California's airports and were in possession of aerial photographs of every important city on our west coast as well as of the vital Gatun locks in the Panama Canal.

A direct result of the committee's report on Japanese subversive activities in this country was the removal of the Japanese population from vital west-coast areas.

(4) *Anti-Semitic Propaganda*

In January 1942, this committee brought a score of witnesses to Washington for a probe into their alleged anti-Semitic activities. All of these witnesses were heard by the committee in executive session. The character of the testimony given was, by and large, of such extreme and fanatical tenor that in the opinion of this committee no good purpose could have been served by taking it in public.

This committee has held from its very beginning that antiracial and antireligious propaganda is un-American per se. It has always been so, and it may be said to have a particularly vicious form of un-Americanism in this period when one of the chief characteristics of the Axis Powers has been the dissemination and practice of anti-racial hatred.

The hearings in executive session last January were a continuation of the committee's investigations into antiracial hatreds, which from the very first day of the committee's life down to the present have been concentrated upon such un-American propagandists as William Dudley Pelley and his ilk.

(5) *Union for Democratic Action*

In June, 1942, this committee published a special report to the House on the Union for Democratic Action. The Union is one of a considerable number of agencies which form a widespread movement in this country looking toward the discrediting of the legislative branch of government.

The Union for Democratic Action, in conjunction with the New Republic, circulated something like a million copies of an elaborately prepared smear-Congress bulletin. It will probably be conceded in all quarters that this committee's exposure of the aims and activities of the Union for Democratic Action went far toward nullifying its effectiveness in the recent political campaign.

Since the publication of our report on the Union for Democratic Action last June, the committee has come into possession of a large amount of evidence which will—when and if published—constitute a final exposure of that organization as an un-American sham.

(6) *National Federation for Constitutional Liberties*

During the past year, the committee made an extensive investigation into the nature and activities of the National Federation for Constitutional Liberties.

The committee found that to a very large extent the persons who were guilty of the treasonable conduct under the auspices of the American Peace Mobilization, which has been described in section (1) above, are today the very same persons who constitute the National Federation for Constitutional Liberties. The committee found, for example, that 52 of the leading figures in the present National Federation for Constitutional Liberties were also among the outstanding leaders in the American Peace Mobilization.

On September 24, 1942, the chairman of this committee delivered a 2-hour address to the House in which he outlined in detail the nature, aims, and activities of the National Federation for Constitutional Liberties.

(7) *The Axis Front Movement in the United States*

For several months, the committee has been preparing a comprehensive report on the Axis Front movement in this country.

This report covers the activities and propaganda of 298 organizations and several thousand individual leaders who were connected with these organizations. In the main, the committee found the following broad types of Axis agents and propagandists in this country: *(a)* Organizations and individuals known to have been financed in whole or in part from Nazi Germany; *(b)* organizations owing complete allegiance to the Emperor of Japan; *(c)* organizations which have been carrying on Mussolini's Fascist propaganda among the Italians and Italian-Americans in this country; *(d)* organizations composed primarily of German nationals and Americans of German descent which were distinctly pro-Nazi in their activities and propaganda; and *(e)* native Fascist groups having both antiracial and pro-Nazi characteristics.

In May 1941, this committee published a special report, known as appendix part IV, on the German American Bund. This report consisted largely of original documents taken from the personal effects of G. Wilhelm Kunze, national fuehrer of the bund, which finally exposed the bund as a dangerous Nazi front organized along military lines. This report was used by the prosecution in the recent trial and conviction of Kunze and his bund associates.

It is unnecessary at this time to give a lengthy enumeration of all the cases where the Government has successfully prosecuted agents of the Axis Powers on the basis of clues and documentary evidence provided by this committee. A few examples, however, will indicate the importance of the investigations which the committee has made in this field and the manner in which the prosecuting authorities have been dependent upon the committee's work. Auhagen, Zapp, and Tonn were convicted on the basis of documentary evidence turned over by this committee to the Department of Justice. Ralph Townsend, recently convicted as a Japanese agent, was first exposed as such by this committee in August, 1939. Several hundred cases of denaturalization of Germans have been brought before the courts as a result of the exposures made by this committee. Among these denaturalization cases are those of Hans Ackermann, his wife, and his wife's brother whose trials are scheduled for January in Austin, Tex., and all of whom were exposed as pro-Nazi propagandists by this committee in August, 1940.

> *Martin Dies*
> Chairman
> *Joe Starnes*
> *J. Parnell Thomas*
> *Noah M. Mason*

Minority Views

It is impossible for me to give unqualified approval to the Annual Report of the Committee on Un-American Activities for the Year 1942. This is the first time I have taken such a position on an annual report since I have been a member of the committee, having heretofore signed each annual report. My reasons for dissenting from certain aspects of the majority report on this occasion are as follows:

1. There has been no opportunity for discussion or amendment of the report or for committee members to do any work upon it. No meeting has been held for its consideration. The report was presented to members on a "take it or leave it" basis. It is, in my judgment, wrong for such a document as an annual report of this committee to be treated in this manner, particularly at the present time.

2. Beyond this I have one major point and several of lesser importance which I am impelled to make. The major reason for my dissent is this. Amer-

ica is at war against Germany, Japan, and Italy. The very existence of freedom, democratic government, and all America has stood for hinges upon the
outcome of that war. It is perfectly clear to me that under circumstances of
this sort, the primary task of a committee on un-American activities, is the
exposure of the activities and propaganda of forces friendly to enemy countries and of groups in this country who witting, or unwittingly promote their
cause. In speaking in the House on March 11, 1942, in favor of continuance of
the committee, I made the following statement:

> In my judgment the future of the committee should be devoted
> primarily and with every bit of major emphasis at its command to
> the doing of a job of exposing and combating the work of people
> who attempt to create confusion in our country and to build up
> sympathy with the Nazi philosophy of government. Thus they seek
> to weaken America's war effort. I believe the whole effort of the
> committee will stand or fall on the basis of how well it does that job.

That was my position then and it is my position now.

This annual report should, in my judgment, have consisted in large part at
least of guidance to the American people as to how they might identify, avoid,
and combat the propaganda and activities of agents and friends of enemy
nations of the United States in the current war. For all will agree I am sure that
it is the primary duty of any governmental group to contribute to the maximum possible extent to the winning of that war. I believe these things should
have constituted, but unfortunately do not constitute, the major emphasis of
this annual report.

It is true that within the past couple of months considerable work has
been done, at the request of the chairman, by myself and members of the
committee staff, on a report on organizations and individuals carrying on
propaganda and other activities favorable to the Axis cause and the Axis
philosophy of government. That report has not yet been approved by the
committee and there appears to be some doubt even that it will be approved.
In any case most of the material upon which it is based has been in the
committee's possession for months and such a report should have been issued
long ago. This reason (No. 2) is the weightiest reason by far for my dissent
from the majority report.

There are, however, other considerations as well which have prompted
my action.

3. Much of the material contained in this report bearing upon the question of alleged "Communist affiliations" of certain individuals deals not with
matters upon which there was any committee action whatsoever, but only
individual action taken by the chairman. On at least two occasions, notably
the one affecting employees of the Board of Economic Warfare, when I protested that the committee had given no consideration to the charges made, the
point was made in reply that this was the chairman's personal action and the
committee was not involved. And yet such material appears here in an annual
report of the committee as a whole. In my opinion it has no place there.

4. With the general position of the majority of this Committee that Communists should not be employed by our Government, I am of course in full agreement. I no more believe a Communist should be so employed than I do that a sympathizer with the Axis cause should be so employed. I am also in agreement that where the head of an agency has requested a report from the Civil Service Commission and where that report has recommended the dismissal of an employee, the recommendation of the Commission should be followed.

The question is not, however, whether Communists or Fascists should be employed by the Government, but whether individuals in question really are "subversive" on the one hand or whether they are simply people whose views don't agree with the majority on the other hand. There is at present all too much tendency in America for so-called "left-wingers" to shout "Fascist" at every conservative who holds an important position in the War Production Board, for example, and for "right-wingers" to shout "Communist" at liberals or progressives who hold positions in some department or agency. This sort of thing is doing America no good. In some respects it is positively dangerous. For it associates in the public mind the words "Fascist" and "Communist," not with those to whom they can properly and accurately opponents toward their particular views on particular subjects may be.

There is no doubt that Communists did use as "Fronts" the four organizations from which the committee compiled the list of 1,124 Federal employees concerning which so much has been made and to which this report again refers. But the annual report is inaccurate when it states that "these membership lists had been obtained largely by subpena and had been identified by the officials of the organizations involved." For at least in the case of the Washington Committee for Democratic action my information is that the list was obtained in toto by the committee from a non-Federal agency and that no identification or authentication was made. And I am certain in my own mind that it was nothing more nor less than a mailing list. Therefore the fact that a person's name was carried on its list by one of these organizations seems to me to constitute no substantial evidence of "subversive" activity, especially since in many instances the person's name was included without any action on his part or even without his knowledge. For these reasons it is not surprising to me that investigation by the Department of Justice failed to disclose that there was any substantial evidence of "subversive" activity or point of view in the case of more than a very small fraction of the people contained on these lists.

To attempt to indicate that everyone whose name was carried on the list of the Washington Committee for Democratic Action, the Washington Cooperative Bookshop, or the Washington Committee to Aid China, is thereby to be regarded as per se subversive is, in my opinion, as false an implication as it would be to attempt to say that every member of the America First Committee was sympathetic with fascism or the Nazi cause. The latter statement no thoughtful American would make, even though we know that attempts were made in certain sections of the country to use the America First Committee as a vehicle for pro-Axis propaganda and activities.

5. The section of the report on Japanese activities deals, of course, with one of the subjects which is of greatest importance at the present time. But when the committee states in conclusion of this section that the removal of the Japanese from west coast areas was "a direct result of the committee's report on Japanese subversive activities in this country," I believe it is making an extravagant claim. The committee report could accurately have been described as one among many factors which brought about Japanese relocation.

Japan is as relentless an enemy of America at the present time as our country has ever had. All reports from the fighting fronts bear this out, and America must be guided accordingly in her action and policy. I believe it no more than fair to point out that there are some citizens of Japanese descent —how many I do not know—who have resisted the tremendous pressure of the Japanese system and the Emperor-worship pattern of Japanese tradition, and have maintained a loyalty to the United States. The relocation program, however, was and is the only safe policy to be pursued from the standpoint of all concerned.

6. It is my view that there should have been appended to the section dealing with "Sabotage strikes of 1941" a statement pointing out the unquestioned loyalty and record of outstanding production of the great rank and file of American workers.

In concluding this statement, I wish to say that I do not subscribe to the attacks made on the Committee on Un-American Activities by those who have claimed that it never has investigated Nazi and Fascist groups in this country. The committee has made such investigation and in the case of certain of these groups has done a very good job. But this report fails to place its major emphasis on the primary importance at this time of exposing the propaganda and activities of Axis agents and those who wittingly or unwittingly serve that cause. I would no more include in this group people who at one time or another have attended meetings or even been members of organizations which later were discovered to be Axis Front organizations, than I would do in the case of persons over whom Communists have taken similar advantage. But I feel very profoundly that the main excuse for this committee's existence at the present time is that it may contribute to the maximum possible extent to stiffening of the resistance of the American people to open or covert pro-Axis propaganda and to the building of a vigorous and unified democratic sentiment in the United States. Its annual report offered an opportunity to strike a blow in that direction. That opportunity has been neglected.

Jerry Voorhis

CRITIQUE OF COMMITTEE
BY JERRY VOORHIS
FEBRUARY 8 AND 10, 1943

Congressional Record, 78th Congress, 1st Session, 723–24; 807.

. . . One of the cornerstones upon which our country has been built is that of the right of political minorities to exist and express their opinions. In speaking of political minorities, I am not talking about groups which seek by unconstitutional methods to undermine and destroy the structure of constitutional government and to impose a dictatorship by a class or group. I am talking about people who believe either in the necessity of very much more conservative policies than those being pursued by the Government or very much more progressive policies than those being pursued by the Government.

And I would like to state at this point that the course of my own political experience has led to the strong belief that progress for the common man is not by any means necessarily to be associated with increased power on the part of a central government, although in the case of certain types of problems governmental action seems to me to be absolutely necessary, if the weak are to be fairly protected and the strong appropriately restrained. The issue here, however, is one which becomes of tremendous consequence in time of war, for at that time the effort of every one of us should be to bind together the efforts of every American who is loyal and devoted to his country's cause.

The war has not yet burned deeply enough into the consciousness of many of us to scorch away the superficial differences which have existed in the past and to make us feel that kinship with other loyal Americans which we shall need before this struggle is over, and which above all we shall need in the reconstruction of our country and the finding of her proper place in the world after the war has been won. In England the experiences of the war have apparently led to that very result. It has for the time being at least obliterated many old antagonisms, has caused people to cling to one another regardless of their differences much more closely than ever before, and it has made people there welcome rather than scoff at proposals that offer substantial hope for a happier day tomorrow for the heroes who will come back from battle. The men who win this war will, as the gentleman from Texas said, want the basic structure of our constitutional Government to remain—they will want us to protect while they are gone a precious heritage of free institutions that no other large nation ever has known. But those men will also demand a chance, a full big fair chance, at a good job with opportunity to grow and develop. And they are going to get it.

The crux of this portion of my speech is a question. Once we depart from the standard of loyalty to our country in passing judgment on people, what standard are we to use? Are we to use the standard of who is a "crackpot" in the judgment of the gentleman from Texas, or in the judgment of the Department of Justice, or in the judgment of the gentleman from California who is now addressing the House? In every case that standard would obviously be different and in every case I submit it would be wrong. The whole future hope of America lies in not dividing ourselves politically between two bitterly hostile groups, one calling the other Fascist and the other calling the one Communist, when neither epithet is true or accurate. Our hope lies rather in our drawing political lines as nearly as we can between the real totalitarians of each extreme and the vast majority of us in the middle fighting out our political battles in the traditional American way.

I come now to a discussion of the necessity of national unity in America. I submit such unity can only be established around a certain point of view which stresses big issues and not little ones. Our greatest issue is the defeat of our enemies in this war. Another issue of importance is the place of the Congress in our National Government. And the third is the winning of the peace and the establishment of a condition of prosperity in our own country after the war.

In order to achieve unity around these issues it is necessary that we combat with all the effort at our command those forces abroad and at home who would give aid and comfort to our enemy. That enemy today is Germany, Japan, and Italy—the Fascist powers of the world. It is for this reason that I have tried to emphasize the importance of this committee's contributing to national unity by laying its major emphasis upon the problem of exposing the propaganda efforts of these powers and their friends and agents. In saying that, however, I want to completely disavow statements which have been made over the air to the effect that pre-Pearl Harbor isolationists were supposed to be included in such a category of people. I do not think there is any more right to saying that a man is sympathetic to Nazis or Fascists because he was isolationist than it is to say he is a friend of the Communists because he entertains progressive political views. My own personal opinion is that the pursuit of an isolationist policy after this war will be dangerous to the future peace of this Nation and the world. But this certainly does not lead me to feel that anybody advocating such a policy is any more un-American than I am.

Concern has been expressed over the difficulty of determining what constitutes a person who is a Fascist or a Nazi in America. I want to say on this point in the first place that I deplore quite as much the tendency on the part of certain groups to shout Fascist at every conservative, as I do the tendency on the part of other groups to shout Communist at people who are not Communist at all. But when people ask "What is a Fascist?" I would reply by asking them "What is a Communist?" If to that question it is replied that a Communist is a member of the Communist Party, then I would set up a standard that a Fascist or a Nazi is a person who is a member of the German-American Bund or an Italian or a Japanese organization and who takes his line from such foreign sources. But if people are going to define a Communist in some big category of people who somehow seem to be too far to the left, then inevitably the corresponding definition of Fascist moves over to include people who in some other people's judgment are too far to the right.

How we can achieve national unity if we are going to use definitions of this sort I am unable to see.

The thing we must look for is efforts on the part of the Axis Powers to break down America's will to victory by various propaganda devices. Undoubtedly this is being attempted every day.

These are some of the forms that Axis propaganda will take:

First. "Germany and Japan can never be defeated, the least we can hope for is a draw. There is no use to count upon a real victory."

Second. "The American cause is being betrayed by our country's own leadership."

Third. "This war is not a battle for democracy, but is the result of a plot by international big business or the Jews or somebody else. Hitler and Hirohito are really not such bad fellows."

Fourth. "Ameica cannot trust her allies so we had better not give any aid to them but instead keep all our material in this country to protect ourselves against invasion."

Fifth. "The President deliberately steered America into the war when it could have been avoided."

Sixth. "The American Government is honeycombed with disloyal people."

Seventh. "There is a plot being developed by capital or labor or new dealers or reactionaries or somebody to take over the country after the war is over. It is more important to prevent this than to defeat Hitler."

Eighth. "America cannot win the war without going bankrupt."

Ninth. "England is not doing her share of the fighting, so why should we?"

Tenth. "The only purpose of this war is to protect the British Empire."

Eleventh. "The war does not need to interfere with the normal way of living of Americans, but the Government deliberately creates shortages, maladjustments, and difficulties just so it can increase its power."

These 11 false ideas are some of the ones which our enemies will try to get the American people to believe.

This is not to say that those who make such statements are necessarily disloyal to the United States. But it does mean that this type of propaganda should be combated by all of us who are devoted to a real victory on the part of our Nation.

Achievement of national unity then calls above all things for the application of a test of loyalty about which I have already spoken, before we pass judgment on any of our fellow citizens.

Young people throughout all history have been inclined to venture farther into fields of new and progressive thought about mankind and its problems than have old people. In my opinion a terrific loss would be sustained by our country and by its free institutions if by the action of this Congress, or a committee thereof, young people were rendered fearful of thinking along progressive lines. I say this particularly because I anticipate that the men now fighting this war will want to have something to say about a constructive solution of the problems of the peace.

For the past 4 years I have been a member of the Dies committee.

As a progressive in my political beliefs, I believe the committee has rendered a service to the cause of true American progressives by exposing the methods used by Communists to attempt either to dominate, use, or destroy progressive organizations. I believe it has rendered a service to the labor movement by pointing out who the Communists in its ranks are. To a lesser extent the committee has rendered a service to sincere conservatives by pointing out how Nazi and Fascist individuals and philosophies have attempted to infiltrate into, to use, and, if possible, to dominate conservative organizations.

A committee of this sort can serve a useful purpose.

But during the past year, in addition to several dissents from personal statements of other members, I have twice dissented from reports of the committee. One of these occasions was that of the last annual report. I did not sign it but appended a statement of minority views to it instead. The New York Herald Tribune, among other established newspapers, agreed editorially and without qualification with the position I took on that occasion.

My position has been, and is, that the committee's work should constitute exposure of all types of prototalitarian activities, Communist, Fascist, or Nazi, and especially to expose disloyalty to the United States and propaganda seeking to undermine that loyalty. I do not believe it is in the committee's province to sit in judgment on the political views of any loyal American, be he reactionary or radical. With the outbreak of war between our country and the Fascist powers, I believed the major task of the committee lay in the field of exposure of activities friendly or helpful to our enemies, and the philosophies they represent.

It has been no particularly easy task to constitute a minority of one on a committee of this sort.

In previous years I have proposed rules of procedure to guide the committee's work and action. I have been 100 percent unsuccessful in getting any of them adopted. I shall attempt at this time to tell neither the House nor myself that such rules will be adopted by the committee. It just is not in the cards.

I believe there are things such a committee should do: first, to investigate with equal zeal all totalitarian movements; second, to avoid accusation against persons in the absence of either substantial documentary evidence or an opportunity to be heard; third, to act as a committee and to afford to all members an opportunity to carry out their responsibilities to the House and to the country as members; and so forth, and most important, to avoid so far as possible domestic political controversy and to give—so long as this war shall last—major emphasis in its work to the defeat of the propaganda of enemy powers.

As I have worked on this speech and thought about the whole matter of my own relationship to the committee I have naturally been confronted with the decision as to whether or not I should remain a member of it. I have told one or two people that I would stay on the committee and do the best job I could along the lines just outlined. But I want in all honesty to say to these people and to the House that as I think about this question it becomes more and more difficult for me to see my way clear to follow that course.

I should like to close by stating that I am devoted to this Congress. My service in it has been the greatest privilege I have ever known. I like to see congressional committees independent of influence from the Executive or any other place. Because, however, I am thus devoted to the Congress, I am at all times concerned that its work be dignified and effective, and I do not want anything done by us here to be recorded in the chronicles of the future as narrowminded, bigoted, foolish, or unfair.

[Here the gavel fell.] . . .

Mr. Speaker, for 4 years I have been a member of this committee. Three times before today I have come into the Well of the House, on similar occasions, and have made speeches in which I said that I believe, as I do now, that a committee of this kind could render a useful service; that I believed that this committee had done work which was important and valuable, that I had certain convictions about the mistakes that such a committee could make which would very seriously weaken if not ruin its effectiveness, and that so far as I was concerned I would pledge the House that I would use my best efforts to see that those mistakes were not repeated and that rules of procedure were adopted that would prevent their being made. It has been my conception that a committee of this kind should investigate all types of activity which were subversive of constitutional government with equal force and vigor. It has been my conviction that a committee of this kind should in time of war direct its efforts primarily against agents and propaganda of enemy powers. I believe a committee of this kind should act as a committee, and as a group; should consider carefully every public statement before it was made by any member. It is my conviction, deepest of all, that the effectiveness of the battle by any democracy against communism on the one hand and fascism on the other is to be won first and foremost by the kind of fairness, justice, and opportunity of which the gentleman from New York [Mr. Baldwin] spoke, and that democracy is not helped if those charged with the task of investigating such matters are not very careful indeed to distinguish those who fundamentally do not believe in constitutional government from all those who are fundamentally loyal to constitutional government regardless of their political opinions.

The events of the last few months and especially those of the past week have impelled me to recognize that the direction in which this committee is now veering is away from and by no means toward my conception of the way this job ought to be done. I have seen it becoming more and more a political instrument of definite conservative bias, and less and less a dignified, impartial, and effective congressional committee. For when a committee or one member of a committee includes people, loyal to their country but whose opinions simply disagree with those of a majority of that committee on a list of those to be proscribed, and accused, then such action becomes dangerous to democracy itself instead of an exposure of un-American activities.

It seems obvious to me, in time of war especially, it becomes of fundamental importance that the emphasis of such a committee's work should be against the efforts of enemy powers and their agents to weaken our nation's war effort. I do not say the committee has done nothing in this field, for it has, but the real impact and emphasis of its work falls more and more in the field of domestic political controversy, less and less where, in my judgment, it belongs if our Nation's cause is to be served. I voted three times to continue the committee; I cannot do it this time. I am impelled by my own conviction and by the fact that I know perfectly well from my experience, that although I might try to urge that certain changes be made in the methods of the committee so mistakes might be avoided, I should not succeed. For this reason it seems to me that the only thing for me to do, is to vote against its continuance, and I shall do so when the roll is called. Under these circumstances, of course, I should not expect that I would be named as a member of it in the future.

Two reports of this committee, the reports of 1940 and 1941, carry my signature. Those reports I helped to prepare along with other members of the committee. I stand on what was said in those reports. The last annual report I could not sign. My minority views are appended thereto and represent, together with my speech of Monday last, my further reasons why I cannot vote to continue this committee.

[Here the gavel fell.]

BIBLIOGRAPHY

Auerbach, Jerold S. *Labor and Liberty: The LaFollette Committee and the New Deal*. New York, 1966.

Barth, Alan. *Government by Investigation*. New York, 1955.

———. *The Loyalty of Free Men*. New York, 1951.

Bentley, Eric. *Thirty Years of Treason*. New York, 1971.

Buckley, William, and the editors of *The National Review*. *The Committee and its Critics: A Calm Review of the House Committee on Un-American Activities*. New York, 1962.

Burns, James M. *Roosevelt: The Lion and the Fox*. New York, 1956.

Carr, Robert K. *The Constitution and Congressional Investigating Committees*. New York, 1954.

———. *The House Committee on Un-American Activities, 1945–1950*. Ithaca, 1952.

Cooke, Alistair. *A Generation on Trial*. New York, 1950.

Dies, Martin. *The Trojan Horse in America*. New York, 1940.

Goodman, Walter. *The Committee: The Extraordinary Career of the House Committee on Un-American Activities*. New York, 1964.

Gurke, Leo. *The Angry Decade*. New York, 1947.

Ickes, Harold. *The Secret Diary of Harold Ickes*. New York, 1954.

Kempton, Murray. *Part of Our Time: Some Ruins and Monuments of the Thirties*. New York, 1955.

Latham, Earl. *The Communist Controversy in Washington*. Cambridge, Mass., 1966.

Leuchtenburg, William. *Franklin D. Roosevelt and the New Deal*. New York, 1963.

Lyons, Eugene. *The Red Decade: The Stalinist Penetration of America*. New York, 1941.

3112   Congress Investigates

McGeary, M. Nelson. *The Development of Congressional Investigative Power.* New York, 1940.

McWilliams, Carey. *Prejudice: Japanese-Americans, Symbol of Racial Intolerance,* New York, 1944.

Mangione, Jerry. *The Dream and The Deal: The Federal Writers Project, 1935.* Boston, 1943.

Michie, Allan A., and Ryhlick, Frank. *Dixie Demagogues.* New York, 1939.

Ogden, August Raymond. *The Dies Committee: A Study of the Special House Committee for the Investigation of Un-American Activities, 1938–1944.* Washington, D.C., 1945.

Seldes, George. *Witch Hunt: The Technique and Profits of Redbaiting.* New York, 1940.

Taylor, Telford. *Grand Inquest: The Story of Congressional Investigations.* New York, 1955.

Voorhis, Jerry. *Confessions of a Congressman.* New York, 1947.

Wilson, Edmund. *American Jitters.* New York, 1932.

The Truman Committee
1941

The Truman Committee 1941

by Theodore Wilson

The Senate Special Committee to Investigate the National Defense Program (popularly known as the Truman Committee) is often characterized as the most successful congressional investigative effort in United
States history. Whether or not this is correct, this committee certainly
played an important role in the ebb and flow of Executive-Legislative relations which shaped the mobilization effort of the United States during the
Second World War. The Truman Committee, created to satisfy a junior
senator's pique regarding the allocation of defense contracts, evolved into
the dominant congressional body scrutinizing the defense program. As
such, it became enmeshed in numerous critical questions—constitutional,
political, economic, and ethical—regarding the organization and administration of America's wartime mobilization efforts. Although the committee
and its chairman did not resolve certain of these questions (and, indeed,
refused to confront certain of them), its record of responsible, restrained
investigation established an admirable standard.

In times of national crisis, especially in time of war, the constitutional
demarcations of authority between the Legislative and Executive branches
of government have wavered and shifted dramatically. During the
nineteenth century and into the twentieth, Congress and the President

struggled periodically for supreme control over the process of war-making and its attendant responsibilities. This struggle was a result of the ambiguous language of the Constitution regarding Executive and Legislative responsibilities for declaring, prosecuting, and concluding wars. Each branch possessed strong claims to primacy. Certainly, the Constitution's grant of authority was great: "The executive power shall be vested in a President of the United States of America"; he shall recommend "such measures to Congress as he shall judge necessary and expedient"; and, most important, "the President shall be Commander-in-Chief of the Army and Navy." On the other hand, the Constitution empowered Congress "to provide for the common defense and general welfare of the United States, . . . to declare war, . . . to raise and support armies," and "to provide and maintain a navy." Further, Congress was given authority "to make all laws which shall be necessary and proper for carrying into execution the foregoing powers, and all other powers vested by this Constitution in the government of the United States, or in any department or officer thereof." These phrases, ambiguous in content, would appear to make possible a titanic struggle for domination should the two branches find themselves disagreeing about the necessity for military action or the manner of conducting a war.

On the basis of explicit constitutional authority, Congress would appear to have the upper hand in any such conflict. It possessed power over both the purse and the sword, it guarded the sole authority to declare war, and the Executive's war power was but rhetoric unless Congress bestowed its approval via appropriations and other legislation. That the President, by virtue of his role as supreme military commander and other powers which have accrued to him, has come to dominate almost all phases of the nation's activities in time of war was the result of Executive aggrandizement and, equally, of Legislative ineptitude and abdication. It is, nevertheless, the central fact in any analysis of Executive-Legislative relations during wartime.

Before the Civil War, Congress held the upper hand in both constitutional theory and practice. The Commander in Chief clause, upon which expansion of Executive authority was later based, was viewed only as stating the obvious fact that the President was "top general and top admiral" of the armed forces. As Chief Justice Taney observed of the President in 1850:

> His duty and his power are purely military. As commander-in-chief, he is authorized to direct the movements of the naval and military forces placed by law at his command, and to employ them in the manner he may deem most effectual to harass and conquer and subdue the enemy. . . . But his conquests do not enlarge the boundaries of this Union, nor extend the operation of our institutions and laws beyond the limits before assigned to them by the legislative power.

President Abraham Lincoln interpreted his role as Commander in Chief as authorizing Executive intervention in areas previously reserved to Congress. On his own, during the period after Fort Sumter, Lincoln created an enormous army, paid it out of Treasury funds without authorization or appropriation, proclaimed a blockade of Southern ports, suspended the writ of habeas corpus, and undertook various other actions without statutory authorization. He justified these measures by claiming that his position as Commander in Chief, combined with the President's duty "to take care that the laws be faithfully executed," produced a war power sufficient to carry out all necessary steps. Taken together, these acts amounted to an assertion that the President has, as Edward S. Corwin wrote, "for the first time in our history, an initiative of indefinite scope and legislative in effect in meeting the domestic aspects of a war emergency." President Lincoln "had laid hold upon vast emergency powers not describable in the usual terms of military command, the results of which, nevertheless, Congress had accepted, willy-nilly; and in these regards the Civil War was the prototype of both the First World War and the Second." But Congress did not accede to the President's actions without a struggle.

Indeed, the Joint Committee on the Conduct of the War, an intensely partisan investigatory committee which harassed the President throughout the war, did assert a powerful check on presidential authority. The committee was established on December 9, 1861, following the Union defeats at Bull Run and Balls Bluff, to "inquire into the conduct of the present war." Dominated by Radical Republicans and chaired by a leading radical senator, Benjamin F. Wade, the Joint Committee claimed the right not only to investigate Executive acts and advise the President, but attempted to take over direction of the war effort. Hearings were convened in late December 1861 and continued until early 1865. At these sessions, the committee discussed past and future battles and strategic plans, disloyal employees, and war supplies and contracts. In this effort the committee was partly successful, for the Confederate leader Robert E. Lee commented that "the Committee was worth about two divisions of Confederate troops." The committee repeatedly questioned the strategy and tactics of the Union, establishing a standard for meddling to which later congressional investigations might aspire, though the more responsible ones, such as the Truman Committee, consciously rejected the presumptions and behavior of the Joint Committee on the Conduct of the War. Senator Truman and his colleagues would have agreed with one later writer who shuddered at the War Committee's "undocumented insinuations, loud publicity against the reputations of men who were not permitted to defend themselves, its suppression of testimony which did not support the official thesis about the war, its star chamber atmosphere, and its general disregard of the rules of fair procedure." The Joint Committee played a powerful role in the conduct of the Civil War, but its power derived from political not constitutional sources. Thus, its influence was of brief duration and, by any estimate, the presidency emerged the victor.

The experience of the First World War further strengthened the hand of the President, though Congress also acquired enormous, hitherto unimagined, authority over personal and property rights. Edward S. Corwin has written: "First and foremost of the constitutional problems that confronted the President and Congress in 1917 . . . was that of adapting legislative power to the needs of 'total war.' Congress was suddenly called on to extend its power to a vast new range of complex subject matter that had hitherto existed outside the national orbit, and at the same time to give its legislation a form capable of keeping it easily responsive to the ever changing requirements of a fluid war situation. The problem was solved by the delegation to the President of the broadest discretion." The President received and, in some cases, merely took authority over a wide range of activities. While Congress might have originally bestowed these powers, the active role of the President in implementing them, and the pattern of delegating powers to persons and agencies acting solely in his name tended to exclude Congress from any meaningful part in directing the war effort.

To meet the challenge of rearmament during the Second World War, as early as 1938 President Franklin D. Roosevelt began to establish Executive offices responsible for the nation's defense. Shortly after the bombing of Pearl Harbor, a White House organization chart listed forty-two Executive agencies, of which thirty-five had been created by Executive order rather than by statute. The agencies which were given congressional authorization, such as Selective Service and the Office of Lend-Lease Administration, were staffed and operated with little regard for the sensibilities of Congress.

Despite the broad latitude permitted the President, the nation's defense mobilization moved forward slowly because of inadequate planning. The War and Navy Departments assumed, that prior to a declaration of war, "it was unlikely that an appreciable mobilization, either in manpower or materials, could be expected." There was no provision for gradual mobilization, and the Industrial Mobilization Plan, a sketchy document drafted without consultation of civilian leaders, would go into effect only when war was imminent. Because of congressional indifference, as late as March 1940, the House Appropriations Committee reduced a War Department request for replacement airplanes from 496 to 57, denied funds for an air base in Alaska, and discouraged any rapid expansion of the armed services.

The German blitzkrieg in the Low Countries and France during May 1940 reversed congressional opposition to rearmament and opened the floodgates for extensive defense expenditures. On May 16, 1940 the President requested an urgent appropriation of $1.2 billion for the armed services; two weeks later he requested another billion. Congress quickly authorized these sums. On July 10 Roosevelt proposed further authorizations and appropriations totaling almost five billion dollars which were approved in less than two months. Altogether, between June 1 and December 1, almost $10.5 billion in defense-related contracts were awarded.

At this point, however, the lack of careful preparation and the peculiar administrative philosophy of President Roosevelt became critically important. The President could request billions for defense and Congress could appropriate funds, but production of weapons and munitions remained largely beyond their control in a country that was officially at peace. Factory production capacity, still at depression levels, could be quickly increased, but the nation's resources were not unlimited, and priorities had to be established.

The Roosevelt Administration's penchant for overlapping organization, the growth of competing bureaucracies, and the President's inability to delegate authority realistically produced conflicts between existing defense agencies and the President's newly-created organizations. No organization had complete control of any defense program; instead, each agency had partial control of many operations. On May 26 FDR created a National Defense Advisory Commission, with members drawn from business, labor, and government. Though the NDAC acquired a staff and assorted responsibilities (including approval of defense contracts), it never overcame its administrative deficiencies. Individual members acquired considerable power (in 1940 Donald Nelson became administrator of priorities; William S. Knudsen, industrial production; and Sidney Hillman, manpower), but coordination proved impossible. In December 1940 FDR responded to the clamor for unified direction of the defense program by establishing another new agency, the Office of Production Management. Although OPM had only two chairmen, Knudsen and Hillman, their ability to coordinate the war effort was impaired as they were not given the authority to establish priorities, place orders, or allocate resources.

Despite the Administration's failure to achieve internal cohesion, once the United States entered the war, the President and his subordinates accepted responsibility for the conduct of the war. Indeed, President Roosevelt, in an address to Congress on September 7, 1942, asserted his right to ignore an act of Congress if necessary to win the war.

By 1941, Congress had accepted (and by its acceptance given tacit approval to) the Executive's claim to major authority in conducting the war effort. Given the political situation of 1941–1945, an inordinately skilled politician occupying the White House and his party dominating both houses of Congress, it appeared that the wartime role of Congress would be passive. Executive predominance was based on claims of superior knowledge; since this knowledge was derived from the Executive's accessibility to vital elements of information and organization which were denied to Congress, Congress could only acquiesce, thus excluding itself from meaningful participation in directing the war effort.

Executive control of America's participation in the Second World War was not questioned until March 1941, when the Senate Special Committee to Investigate the National Defense Program was created. Indeed, the investigatory power of Congress, hallowed by a great tradition of Legislative practice in English and American history, appeared to offer Congress an effective means of challenging claims of Executive preeminence: "We are called the Grand Inquest of the Nation, and as such it is our duty to inquire into every step of publick management, either Abroad or at Home, in order to see that nothing has been done amiss," William Pitt had informed the House of Commons in 1742. No one seriously questioned the right of Congress to conduct investigations for, as Donald H. Riddle has noted, "the purpose of informing itself, controlling the executive branch, or informing the public."

Senator Truman and his colleagues could not match the President's domination of the mechanisms of government, especially his control over information vital to a public challenge to his authority. Also, Truman did not intend to duplicate the shoddy work of the Civil War investigation. Therefore, much of the potential for Legislative-Executive conflict, embodied in the Truman Committee's charge to make a full and complete study of the national defense program, was siphoned off at the outset.

The creation of the Senate Special Committee to Investigate the National Defense Program is an undramatic story, perhaps befitting the sober mien of its chief sponsor and first chairman. In early 1941, Harry S. Truman, newly reelected junior senator from Missouri, was returning to work after an exhausting campaign. As a strong supporter of the Roosevelt Administration, Senator Truman was naturally interested in the measures then underway to achieve the President's "arsenal of democracy" program. Truman, a member of the Military Affairs Committee and the Military Subcommittee of the Appropriations Committee, possessed a life-long interest in military issues. He had visited a number of army installations and had become alarmed about the waste, favoritism, and lack of direction which he found in the defense program. Letters from constituents made him aware of the enormous economic benefits to be gained from the assignment of defense plants and military installations, and he was determined that Missouri communities should receive a fair share of this lucrative defense business.

On August 15, 1940, Senator Truman wrote confidently to his friend, Lou E. Holland, president of the Mid-Central War Resources Board in Kansas City, that Missouri possessed a great opportunity to obtain defense plants and defense-related contracts. "I have been interviewing the people here who are at the source of the fountain, and I believe that with proper organization Missouri can get its proper place in the set-up," Truman told his friend. He went on to describe the mobilization program, as army and administration officials had explained it to him: The key was decentralization. "The program, as outlined, contemplates the location of Government plants and key industries in five different sections between the Appalachians and the Rocky Mountains. . . . We are in Area C, which consists of southern Indiana and southern Illinois, Missouri and Kansas. The plan is to make each area a complete unit, with every sort of set-up needed in the National Defense program. Powder plants, loading plants, small arms factories, and so forth will be in each one of these areas. They are urging factories to decentralize all over the whole area. . . . This is our opportunity, if we ever had it." Within a few months, however, Truman recognized the favoritism given to Eastern states. "I think they are working with a little private clique of their own and not giving the local people a chance to do the work," he charged the War Department. Although Missouri had received fifty-five percent of all defense expenditures between the Mississippi River and Rocky Mountains by mid-1941, Truman decided that he had to defend the interests of the mid-West and the little businessman.

On February 10, 1941, after weeks of preparation, Truman rose in the Senate to address the problems he had identified in the defense program. This speech, a rare event for Truman, was given before a small but increasingly interested audience of colleagues, journalists, and professional gallery-sitters. Truman had previously stated that his purpose was "heading off scandals before they started." This speech dealt mainly with possibilities for corruption and the geographical and economic injustices which the present system of letting war contracts perpetrated. "There seems to be a policy in the national-defense set-up to concentrate all contracts and nearly all manufacturing that has to do with the national defense in a very small area," he observed indignantly. "I am reliably informed that from 70 to 90 percent of the contracts let have been concentrated in an area smaller than England." Such concentration was militarily unwise and also unfair to those regions which were being denied an opportunity to participate in the defense program, a result of the federal bureaucracy's preference for dealing with large corporations located in a few heavily industrialized areas. "The little manufacturer, the little contractor, and the little machine shop have been left entirely out in the cold. The policy seems to be to make the big man bigger and to put the little man completely out of business."

Personal favoritism, the sort of palm-greasing, "do a favor for a friend" attitude that had produced so much waste and graft during the First World War was wide-spread. For example, a Detroit company had won an ammunition plant contract from equally qualified construction firms in Missouri. Was it accidental that a partner in the Detroit firm was a good friend of a member of the War Department's Construction Advisory Board? Similarly, non-local companies had obtained contracts for the St. Louis Ordnance Plant and Ft. Leonard Wood and, in the latter case, the firm awarded this huge contract possessed no construction experience. This was simply not fair, Truman concluded, especially since the War Department was blatantly ignoring suggestions from members of Congress. "It is considered a sin for a United States Senator from a State to make a recommendation for contractors, although he may be more familiar with the efficiency and ability of our contractors than is anybody in the War Department," he said.

One means of correcting this deplorable situation, Senator Truman proposed, was to establish a committee to investigate the manner in which defense contracts were being awarded. Since tax money was being spent, the Senate should make use of "every safeguard possible to prevent their being misused and mishandled." Such a committee, empowered to ascertain the facts, would perform an important service in maintaining public confidence in the defense program. To that end, Truman announced his intention to introduce a resolution calling for such an investigation: "I am merely stating what I believe to be conditions that deserve investigation. If nothing is wrong, there will be no harm done. If something is wrong, it ought to be brought to light." He introduced Senate Resolution 71 three days later and had it referred immediately to the Committee on Military Affairs. On February 22, the committee unanimously reported the resolution to the Senate. At this point, however, Truman's proposal was frozen, being referred back to another committee, the Senate Committee to Audit and Control the Contingent Expenses of the Senate, chaired by James F. Byrnes, a confidant of President Roosevelt.

The Administration naturally was concerned about any proposal for a congressional investigation of the defense program. Congressional snooping into such sensitive matters as contracts and the progress of the mobilization effort might produce unwelcome publicity, thus upsetting the President's carefully orchestrated campaign to swing public opinion in favor of America's support of Great Britain. A call for such a committee in May 1940 by Republican Senator Arthur H. Vandenberg had been immediately scotched, but by early 1941 pressures for a congressional inquiry were mounting. In January two such resolutions had been introduced in the

House of Representatives. One, by Representative Eugene Cox, a conservative Georgian hostile to organized labor, called for a joint committee "to investigate and keep itself currently informed on all activities of the Federal Government in connection with the national defense." As well, a young Republican congressman, Henry Cabot Lodge, jr., had introduced a resolution that proposed a congressional committee with authority "to formulate and develop a consistent and complete defense policy for the United States." Lodge's proposal "amounted to a committee to conduct the war." No one in the Administration wanted either of these probes, and the only other alternative appeared to be the comparatively mild investigation proposed by Senator Truman. When the Cox resolution was discussed at a White House meeting, Byrnes informed the President: "I can fix that by putting the investigation into friendly hands." Truman later implied that he had given such assurances to the White House; "I couldn't get Jimmy Byrnes to act. Everybody thought I wanted to set up a headline business like the Dies Committee. . . . After much haggling and delay he recommended that I be given the magnificent sum of $15,000 with which I started the activities of that committee." Byrnes permitted Senate Resolution 71 to be reported on March 1, 1941. It was unanimously adopted the same day, with two alterations: an increase in the size of the committee from five to seven members, and, as noted above, a reduction of Truman's funds from $25,000 to $15,000.

Senator Truman, sponsor of the resolution, became committee chairman. His proposal had been authorized by the Senate (and tacitly, at least, by the Administration); he had $15,000 to spend, and, if he and the committee proved themselves worthy of the Senate's trust, the prospect of additional funds and a renewed authorization at some point in the near future.

Although initially it proved difficult to persuade senatorial colleagues to serve on the committee, within a week all seven had been selected. On March 8, the committee's membership was officially appointed: Truman as chairman; Joseph H. Ball (R.–Minn.); Owen Brewster (R.–Me.); Tom Connally (D.–Az.); Carl Hayden, James M. Mead (D.–N.Y.); and Monrad C. Wallgren (D.–Wash.). Carl A. Hatch (D.–N.M.) soon replaced Hayden, who resigned on April 15, 1941, and perhaps should be considered an original member. The committee was comprised of five Democrats and two Republicans, probably a reflection of the Administration's anxiety that it not spawn a political vendetta. The membership reflected impressive geographical balance and considerable diversity of background and political outlook. Notably, however, all save Connally, Hatch, and Truman were serving their first terms in the Senate.

At the time he became chairman of the Special Committee, Harry S. Truman was fifty-seven years old. The junior senator from Missouri had been in the Senate since 1934, but was virtually unknown outside his home state and the Senate chambers. A quiet, hardworking, physically unprepossessing man, Truman had served a long political apprenticeship. When he first came to Washington, he was identified with the political organization of Kansas City boss Thomas Pendergast; he gradually made a name for himself by supporting the New Deal. In 1941, Truman was just coming into his own, having won a tight battle for reelection with almost no assistance from the Administration. Intelligent, pragmatic, and deeply conscious of the historical dimension of the committee's work, Truman was determined to make a success of this assignment, the most important he had been given during his tenure. Nevertheless, no one would have predicted that he would demonstrate great ability, and that his dedicated and crusty leadership of the investigation would make his name a household word within a few months.

Ball had been appointed to the Senate in 1940 and won reelection in 1942. An ardent internationalist, Ball strongly supported FDR's program in foreign affairs (he would co-author the B_2H_2 resolution), and accepted the Administration's conduct of the war. The committee's senior Republican, Brewster, had also entered the Senate in 1940. Connally was the ranking Democrat on the committee. Connally had enjoyed a long career in Texas and national politics and was by 1941 one of the most powerful men in the Senate. Hatch did not attend committee sessions regularly, but he had served in the Senate since 1933 and could be counted an Administration loyalist. One of the most active members of the committee, Mead had served nineteen years in the House, was then appointed to the Senate in 1938, and elected in his own right in 1940. Mead was an Administration regular and perhaps the most liberal among the committee members. Elected in 1940, Wallgren was a little-known Democrat interested primarily in problems affecting his home state, such as lumber, light metals, and aircraft.

The membership of the committee was remarkably stable and these seven members served throughout Truman's chairmanship. The group was enlarged to ten members in November 1941, when Styles Bridges (R.–N.H.), Harley M. Kilgore (D.–W.Va.), and Clyde L. Herring (D.–Ia.) were appointed. Bridges resigned from the committee, pleading other responsibilities, in March 1942. He was replaced by Harold H. Burton (R.–Oh.), who took an active part in the committee's inquiries until he was appointed to the Supreme Court in 1945. Becuase Herring was defeated in the 1942 elections, Homer Ferguson (R.–Mich.) was appointed and became an aggressive critic of the military, particularly interested in the administration of the defense program.

Senator Truman once said of his colleagues on the committee: "I have . . . been extremely lucky in having associates who are sound thinkers and honest men." From small towns and middle class in background, the committee members appeared to share Truman's pragmatic approach to their job, viewing it as a vehicle for exposure and correction of abuses (especially where big business was concerned) rather than a platform for ideological disputation. Although every member had at least six committee assignments (Truman served on seven committees), the seven freshman senators were less heavily burdened than their elders and, undoubtedly, considered the Truman Committee a superb opportunity to gain quick recognition. As a whole, the committee established a standard of participation and knowledgability considerably above the norm.

The committee's second urgent chore was to obtain a qualified staff. On the recommendation of Attorney General Robert Jackson, Truman appointed Hugh Fulton, a young lawyer who had served as a United States attorney, as chief counsel. After a second appropriation in August 1941, Truman and Fulton then recruited the remainder of the staff, consisting of an associate counsel, an assistant counsel, a chief investigator, twelve to eighteen investigators, and various clerical persons. Matthew Connelly, who later became President Truman's appointment secretary, was the first chief investigator, and he recommended many of the other investigators, mostly young lawyers or accountants. For a time the committee, following a tradition of some years, co-opted employees from various Executive agencies (such as the Justice Department, Labor, the U.S. Housing Authority, Federal Power Commission, and the Office of Price Administration) as investigators.

In all, between 1941 and 1948, the Truman Committee held 432 public hearings at which 1,798 witnesses appeared (giving 27,568 pages of testimony), and another 300 Executive sessions that produced 25,000 additional pages of transcript. Fifty-one reports totaling 1,946 pages were published; and, as a result of the committee's careful attention to relations with the media, thousands of press releases were issued. All this was the end product of uncounted hours of research, hundreds of field trips, and thousands of interviews. Throughout its existence, the committee was almost never embarrassed by sloppy or inaccurate staff work. Indeed, the Truman Committee's thoroughness soon became so highly regarded that other congressional committees which became involved with defense issues often borrowed the committee's documentation, tacking on their own conclusions.

Together, Truman and Fulton decided upon guidelines for staff investigations and committee sessions. The Truman Committee asked only for the right to subpoena witnesses, as they normally dealt with readily available information and cooperative witnesses. The committee received thousands of letters during its existence, many describing alleged graft or waste; but it usually made independent decisions to launch investigations. Hearings were but a small part of the committee's activities; Truman and the staff often arranged numerous private meetings before deciding whether to schedule a hearing on a particular topic.

These public hearings (and the Executive sessions which were convened if issues directly affecting the national security or the individuals' reputations were involved) were conducted by explicit though unwritten rules. Although Truman was not always able to control the conduct of his colleagues, he insisted upon a modicum of fairness and objectivity. The committee decided not to act as a court of law and witnesses were accorded an impressive range of legal protections. They were permitted to submit prepared statements, to be attended by counsel, to place in the record documents supporting their views, and to review the pertinent hearing transcripts. The committee stated that it recognized, without prejudice, recourse to the Fifth Amendment, though a careful search of the record suggests that no witness ever invoked this provision. In sum, the Truman Committee followed a code of procedures that was rational, fair, and efficient; perhaps as objective as such an agency—which, after all, was created and conducted by politicians for political purposes—can be.

Overlapping jurisdiction greatly worried Truman, for the committee faced potential friction from standing committees and other investigatory groups. Fortunately, the Truman Committee encountered little hostility from the Senate establishment. Neither Naval Affairs nor Military Affairs evinced any interest in procurement and contract procedures; the Small Business Committee did have certain interests in common, but Truman and its chairman worked out a compromise. Truman kept his colleagues informed of the committee's work senators were welcome at committee hearings and were invited to take part in examination of witnesses. Further, the members of the Truman Committee, via service on other committees, strengthened the committee's position.

Two House committees, Naval Affairs and Military Affairs, occasionally grumbled about the Truman Committee's intrusions into their spheres. Their dissatisfaction may have been caused by the favorable headlines earned by Truman and his colleagues. An army officer stated as much in September 1941: "Confidentially I sat in on a meeting . . . where the House Naval Affairs Committee were bemoaning the fact that the Truman Committee has grabbed all the glory, has received the maximum of publicity, and has dampened the efforts of the other investigatory committees." Fortunately, relations with the House Select Committee to Investigate Defense Migration, which under the leadership of Representative John Tolan looked at a variety of defense-related problems, were quite friendly. The Tolan Committee might be termed the House equivalent of Truman's inquiry, though it never received the public recognition accorded its Senate counterpart.

The resolution that created the committee bestowed it with a remarkably broad grant of authority. Empowered to investigate all phases of the national defense program, the committee was specifically requested to study the following:

1. the types and terms of contracts awarded by the government;
2. methods by which such contracts are awarded and grantees selected;
3. use of small business facilities, through subcontracts or otherwise;
4. geographic distribution of contracts and location of plants and facilities;
5. effects of the defense program on labor and the migration of labor;
6. the performance of contracts and the accountings required of contractors;
7. benefits accruing to contractors;
8. practices of management or labor, and prices, fees, and charges which interfere with the defense program or unduly increase its cost;
9. such other matters as the committee deems appropriate.

Again and again, Truman and other members stated that their aim was to serve as a watchdog, a "benevolent policeman," to dig out the facts and present them to the American people. Originally, the Truman Committee was concerned with possible corruption and waste stemming from the rapid and enormous expansion of the defense production program. "I have had considerable experience in letting public contracts," Truman observed in an early speech, "and I have never yet found a contractor who, if not watched, would not leave the Government holding the bag. We are not doing him a favor if we do not watch him." The deplorable experiences of the aftermath of the First World War, during which numerous investigations uncovered widespread corruption and waste in the government's war production activities, was a powerful argument for careful scrutiny while contracts were being awarded and weapons manufactured.

The Truman Committee fulfilled this assignment with admirable efficiency and fairness. During the most active period of its existence—from summer 1941 to spring 1944—the committee investigated an incredible list of problems alleged to be retarding progress of the nation's domestic war effort and hundreds of cases of supposed graft and corruption. They maintained close scrutiny over the government's policies with regard to the award of contracts, labor-management relations, the geographical distribution of war plants, and the treatment of small business (Truman's pet concern). The committee held hearings and issued reports on such diverse problems as the aluminum shortage, camp and cantonment construction, light metals, aircraft, rubber, the conversion program of the War Production Board, Senator Albert B. Chandler's swimming pool, manpower, gasoline rationing, barges, farm machinery and equipment, renegotiation of war contracts, fake inspections of steel plate by Carnegie-Illinois Steel Corporation, shipbuilding and shipping, the comparative merits of rayon and cotton tire cord, magnesium, Ream General Hospital, conditions at Curtiss-Wright Corporation, and transactions between Senator Theodore G. Bilbo and various contractors. Its watchfulness certainly resulted in diminished graft, since potential wheeler-dealers were deterred from engaging in shady activities. One estimate of the actual monetary savings for which the Truman Committee was responsible is fifteen billion dollars. More important, perhaps, thousands of lives were saved as a result of the committee's success in ferreting out cases of production of defective weapons, aircraft, and other war supplies.

Nevertheless, the work of the Truman Committee, judged in historical perspective, was to prove not entirely successful. Increasingly, as mobilization picked up speed, it became apparent that the greatest threat to full production and to efficient and equitable use of the nation's resources was the chaotic administrative situation in Washington. The Truman Committee, as with previous investigatory committees in similar circumstances, found itself in a quandary regarding the issue of governmental waste and inefficiency. Should the committee have wished to do so, it might have found a justification in its grant of authority (especially its charge to investigate "such other matters as the Committee deems appropriate") to undertake a full inquiry into the Roosevelt Administration's conduct of the war. Such a step was repugnant to Truman, the other Democrats on the committee, and even to their Republican colleagues, for they sincerely desired to "help the President to win the war." They feared that public exposure of the full dimensions of bureaucratic confusion and conflict in Washington—and of its effects on the defense effort—would weaken and, perhaps, destroy public confidence in the Administration. That, in turn, might have caused the United States to lose the war.

Senator Truman clearly was aware of this conflict and of the dangers it posed. During a Senate debate in August 1941, he was pressed by Senator Vandenberg to admit that the President was culpable.

> "In other words," Vandenberg challenged Truman, "the Senator is now saying that the chief bottleneck which the defense program confronts is the lack of adequate organization and coordination in the administration of defense. . . . Who is responsible for that situation?"
>
> Truman: "There is only one place where the responsibility can be put."
>
> Vandenberg: "Where is that—the White House?"
>
> Truman: "Yes, sir."
>
> Vandenberg: "I thank the Senator."

To face this problem squarely, however, would be to open a Pandora's box. Truman and his Democratic colleagues certainly wished to avoid doing political injury to the President. At the same time, no one on the committee wanted to risk charges of whitewash because they ducked legitimate questions. Even if the committee had raised the issue of presidential responsibility directly, Truman must have doubted whether his committee—or even Congress as a whole—possessed sufficient clout to force the sort of changes that were necessary. Above all, Truman wished to avoid the kind of disgusting spectacle evoked by the internecine warfare carried on between 1861 and 1865 by the Joint Committee on the Conduct of the War. The Truman Committee stated repeatedly that it would not concern itself with matters of strategy and tactics. Whenever Truman was informed that a committee inquiry threatened to enter this realm (as defined by the Executive branch), he abandoned that line of investigation. This, of course, proved a source of continuing frustration, for strategy and even tactics were even more intimately connected with matters of production and the allocation of resources during the Second World War than they had been during the Civil War.

At almost every turn, the Truman Committee, pursuing legitimate and seemingly innocuous inquiries, found itself in potential conflict with Executive prerogatives and policies. It may be that the value of tracing the committee's route is not so much in measuring their boldness under fire, not even in discovering how far they traveled; rather, any benefit may derive from recognition of the dangers they faced and being better prepared to avoid or defuse them if ever the nation again undertakes such a journey.

At its first meeting on March 12, 1941, the Truman Committee decided that it should not undertake the investigation of any controversial subjects until it had established its legitimacy before the Senate and the American people. For the time being, Truman eschewed study of such sensitive topics as the location of defense facilities and racial discrimination in hiring at these plants. Public relations, the members correctly recognized, was of foremost importance for any congressional investigatory committee; without popular acceptance, its efforts would be worthless. Thus, the committee agreed that "its first duty would be to give to Congress and the public a clear picture of the present state of the program." On April 15, the committee convened hearings on this subject and sat back to hear Secretary of War Henry L. Stimson, Under Secretary of War Robert P. Patterson (soon to be a familiar visitor), Secretary of the Navy Frank Knox, and OPM's Hillman and Knudsen discourse on how smoothly the program was proceeding. The session gained favorable publicity for the committee and introduced it to certain of the complex issues to be dealt with in the next few years.

The committee's next target in this preliminary phase was the camp and cantonment construction program, a matter of great interest to the public. Some 229 projects had been started at an estimated cost of slightly over 500 million dollars; thus, the likelihood of waste and chicanery was large. Investigators of the Truman Committee failed to uncover corruption, but they did raise further questions about the concentration of contracts and they discovered that the construction program was far in excess of its original estimated cost. Ultimately, the cost was $828,424,000, over $300 million above the original estimates. General Brehon Somervell, the arrogant chief of the army's Services of Supply, bitterly complained about the Truman Committee's meddling, a forewarning of other clashes. Somervell admitted increased expenditures of over 100 million dollars but justified them on grounds of the urgency of the situation. This, too, would become a familiar refrain. The committee gave the army a fair opportunity to rebut its findings, sending Somervell a copy of its draft report and expressing willingness to reevaluate its conclusions. The report, released on August 14, 1941, placed blame for the enormous cost of the construction program on the cost-plus contract scheme (whereby a contractor received all costs incurred in fulfilling a contract, plus a percentage profit) and the inability of the Quartermaster Corps (which was responsible for all construction) to administer efficiently such projects. The committee did not recommend outright abolition of cost-plus contracts. It did, however, suggest that responsibility for construction be shifted to the Engineers Corps. Some months later the War Department accepted this recommendation, a decision which greatly enhanced the Truman Committee's reputation.

Two other investigations in the committee's first months of operation—a one-day session on labor problems in the coal industry and a careful look at aluminum shortages—were typical of the watchdog dimension of its activities. In April the committee decided reluctantly that it should take a hand in the bitter dispute between the United Mine Workers and the coal operators. Concerned about the effects of the coal strike on steel production, Truman convened a one-day hearing which accomplished little aside from giving UMW chief John L. Lewis a forum for some flamboyant oratory. However, a settlement was reached a few hours after the committee adjourned.

A study of the critical shortages of aluminum which had come to light during the spring was much more serious. The Aluminum Company of America, which possessed a virtual monopoly over production of aluminum, had repeatedly given assurances that it could supply the needs of both the defense program and the private sector. However, in recent months demand had outstripped Alcoa's production by more than one hundred percent. The Truman Committee held hearings during May-June 1941, responding with impressive speed once the bottleneck was brought to its attention. In the June 26 report the committee criticized Alcoa for acting selfishly to protect its monopoly and blasted the Office of Production Management's handling of the situation. Faulting OPM for underestimating aluminum requirements and for indecision once the problem had been discovered, the Truman Committee pressed for better coordination of the defense program. Truman commented: "We rapped some knuckles to be sure, but we tried to do it in a constructive way. We didn't take the easy course and blame the President. We want aluminum, not excuses." Unfortunately, the only way to obtain more aluminum immediately was to let Alcoa off the hook. This would not be the last time the Truman Committee would encounter this sort of genteel blackmail: the necessity to ignore principle in order to obtain immediate production.

The Truman Committee, particularly its inexperienced chairman and staff, performed with the skill of veterans. Truman was greatly encouraged, believing that "we have justified the existence of the Committee." He wrote a friend: "I don't believe there will be any serious difficulty for us to get the necessary funds from now on to carry out our work." His confidence was justified, for in August 1941 the Senate increased the committee's budget and authorized use of facilities and personnel drawn from the Executive branch. Thereafter, the Truman Committee's position never was seriously challenged, and its mandate was routinely renewed each year.

Senator Truman, as committee chairman, was receiving favorable recognition as well, as he was eager to dig into what he believed to be glaring inequities regarding the location of defense plants and the treatment of small business. In part, this resulted from an emotional distrust of "bigness" in any form. Writing in a populist vein to a Missouri friend, Truman stated:

> I am trying my best to carry on my investigation of the . . . contract racket as fairly as I possibly can. It is a most difficult job to perform but I believe we are getting some results. . . . It has been the policy of the Army and Navy to let contracts to big contractors and to big business because it is the easiest way out. A half a dozen big construction companies and manufacturers have more than seventy-five per cent of all the contracts. They obtained all the priorities on basic metal, and the little manufacturers like Chapman Brothers there in Independence are simply being put out of business.

Bringing every sort of pressure at the committee's command to bear on this problem, Truman and his colleagues obtained a measure of improvement. However, the War Department, concerned with getting as much production as quickly as possible, persisted in dealing mainly with large firms. All through the war, unhappy constituents deluged Congress with complaints. Truman himself admitted: "If you should see my correspondence, you would think that every little businessman in the country is going out of business." Frustrated by its inability to correct the problem, the Truman Committee gradually realized that the government's method of awarding contracts was not solely responsible, but that the total approach to defense production, including such problems as cost-plus contracts, allocation of scarce materials, reliance on dollar-a-year men, and the stubborn impassivity of the War Department, was also involved. Exerting pressure on OPM to correct these inequities was futile, since OPM was helpless to bring into line the agencies which it supposedly managed.

This realization caused the Truman Committee to confront the most important issues it would deal with during the war. Fearful for the defense program if the current state of administrative chaos in Washington was permitted to continue, the committee faced awkward alternatives: it could blow the whistle and subject OPM and the entire Administration—including, if necessary, the President—to indictment and trial in the forum of public opinion; or the committee could work behind the scenes, hoping to force the administrative *apparat* to pull together for the common good. Neither strategy was very appealing, and either course entailed considerable risk for the committee's members and for the nation. Not surprisingly, the committee adopted a compromise strategy, borrowing from both of the above alternatives as the situation warranted. None of its members wanted to run the war, a possible outcome if a publicity barrage attacking the Administration had been totally effective. "The Committee," its first annual report affirmed, "has not and does not intend to substitute or attempt to substitute its judgment . . . for the judgment of the executive agencies involved." Its proper role, Senator Truman stressed again and again, was "auditor of the national defense program," not dictator. But, at the very least, OPM must be replaced by a new agency with real power over the assorted satrapies that had sprung up. If that were done, the committee could provide powerful support for the Administration, using its publicity leverage against recalcitrant bureaucrats instead of the President.

Senator Truman unveiled the committee's plan in his presentation of the first annual report to the Senate on January 15, 1942, just five weeks after Pearl Harbor had propelled the United States into war. There was little drama in Truman's awkward summary of the committee's findings; but the conclusions he diffidently offered had a dramatic effect on his audience. The report was, clearly, a devastating indictment of the Office of Production Management. "Its record has not been impressive," the report began. "Its mistakes of commission have been legion; and its mistakes of omission have been even greater. It has all too often done nothing when it should have realized that problems cannot be avoided by refusing to admit that they exist." The report criticized the practice of using dollar-a-year men and lambasted OPM for ignoring the tremendous contribution which small companies could make. "Fundamentally," Truman observed, "the disappointing record of the Office of Production Management is not so much due to its lack of power as to its failure to perform the functions for which it was created." Cynically, one might view this as an attempt to absolve the President of blame by placing that blame on ineffective subordinates. Nonetheless, Truman sincerely believed in this explanation. The report also blasted selfish interests, especially organized labor, concerned solely with their own aggrandizement; but it returned repeatedly to OPM as the chief bottleneck in the defense program. The report recommended that a single person be appointed to direct the production and supply program, and that OPM be abolished and a new agency be created.

The Truman Committee's major proposal already had been implemented when Truman spoke. Two days before, on January 13, President Roosevelt had announced the creation of a new super agency, the War Production Board, which would "exercise general direction over the war procurement and production program." He appointed as its head Donald Nelson, the experienced and highly regarded former Sears Roebuck executive.

While the President was being pressed from all quarters to straighten out the administration of the domestic war effort, Truman's submission, some days before its formal release, of the committee report to FDR may well have prodded him into a decision. Certainly, the press credited the Truman Committee with a major role in this reorganization of defense programs.

It appeared that the committee's efforts to obtain central direction of the war production program had been amply rewarded. Nelson, who had been permitted to draft the Executive order that set up the War Production Board, had inscribed therein sweeping powers for himself. The chairman's authority over other agencies was explicitly stated: "Federal departments, establishments, and agencies shall comply with the policies, plans, methods, and procedures in respect to war production and procurement as determined by the Chairman." However, Nelson's authority was seriously circumscribed, for it depended, as did all such administrative arrangements under the New Deal, on his personal relationship with FDR and the coterie of presidential intimates surrounding the President. Nelson did not possess the complete confidence of the White House. Lacking this, officials of agencies theoretically subordinate to Nelson's authority could (and did) go over his head, taking their objections to Roosevelt or one of his advisers. Further, Nelson was no "production czar" but rather a super-coordinator. His decisions had to be enforced on those agencies which negotiated procurement contracts and supervised the production of war supplies. As the Truman Committee was soon to learn, Nelson simply was not aggressive enough to protect and extend his authority. Preferring persuasion to coercion, Nelson avoided confrontations with imperious representatives of other government departments. This defect was obvious in his relations with General Somervell, chief of the Army Services Forces. Somervell's procurement activities clearly placed him under Nelson's authority, but he operated the agency with almost total private freedom. "Nelson was not aggressive about his jurisdiction and his powers," the historian of WPB admitted. "He allowed [the Army-Navy Munitions Board] to elude his group, although it was subordinate to him, and he permitted the War Department's Services of Supply, over which he said he had control, to become something decidedly other than what he thought it ought to be." In Nelson's favor were his flexibility, openness, and enthusiasm.

These latter qualities favorably impressed the Truman Committee. Nelson quickly gained good relations with committee members and, in particular, with Truman. The WPB was careful to keep the committee fully informed and normally dealt with Congress through Truman. In response, the committee adopted a proprietary attitude toward WPB. At Nelson's first appearance before the committee in late January, Truman stated: "Mr. Nelson, this Committee has been working for seven months to get the responsibility for the war effort centered in one man, with the power to act. . . . We have fought to get you this job. We are going to fight to support you now in carrying it out." Nelson had come to discuss the dollar-a-year men issue, and the committee objected vehemently to his statements in support of the practice. However, Senator Truman's comments revealed the situation in which the committee found itself following Nelson's appointment. Truman first remarked:

> We want you to understand . . . that we want the war won as quickly as possible. If you have to have dollar-a-year men to win the war, this Committee is not going to interfere with that procedure on your part, because we want the war won, but we still have some ideas on dollar-a-year men and the ethics and things that are brought to bear on that subject. But this committee does not want to hamper you in carrying out your job. That comes first. . . . Here is the situation. Whether you are right or wrong under the present circumstances, this Committee feels . . . that your idea ought to prevail, because we have to win the war.

Arranging Truman's emotional statement in a roughly logical sequence demonstrates the committee's helplessness. Although the committee believed that reliance on dollar-a-year men, favoritism of big business, et al were ethically wrong and boded ill for the future, they had to be accepted if they contributed to the war effort. The committee accepted the sole competence of the Executive branch to judge whether something did or did not contribute to winning the war. The Truman Committee certainly never gave automatic approval of WPB decisions. During the next twelve months, the committee objected strenuously to a number of WPB policies and decisions, and relations between Nelson and Truman were at times decidedly strained. The possibility of a total break was minimal, for Nelson recognized that the Truman Committee was his strongest ally and the committee believed WPB was its best hope for centralized control and, thus, protection of civilian interests.

The fatal defect in this strategy was that the Truman Committee could not force Nelson to use the powers he had been given. It could only offer encouragement, as Truman stressed during Nelson's first appearance before the committee: "If you meet any obstacles . . . where this committee can turn the light of publicity on the subject or call attention to legislation that should be enacted to give you the necessary means to carry the job out, we want to be informed, and we are at your service"; but what if Nelson refused to fight, what if the process of bureaucratic imperialism continued unabated, what if the President permitted these quarrels to persist? Truman and his colleagues were obligated by their own definition of the proper role of an investigatory committee in wartime not to mutiny. Notably, the Truman Committee first opposed proposals that were introduced to Congress in mid-1942 for the creation of a top-level liaison committee between Congress and the Executive branch. Many congressmen were unhappy about their lack of knowledge of the defense program. "All is not well with us. . . . We do not always have the information which we should have," lamented one senator in October 1942. FDR rejected the liaison proposal, and the Truman Committee at this time also opposed it, largely because its members believed the committee served this function.

Of course, Harry Truman was psychologically incapable of restraining his irritation and repressing frustration with WPB's failures. Throughout 1942 and into early 1943, the Truman Committee held hearings on critical areas where production bottlenecks had developed. The rubber program (which proved a source of great embarrassment for Nelson), defense housing, steel shortages, and gasoline rationing were some of the topics it examined. The committee criticized the greedy actions of both large corporations and the unions, and gained enormous support for this position. Truman's outspoken statements regarding those who used the war as an opportunity for private profit made him one of the most popular figures in America.

Increasingly, however, Truman and the committee zeroed in on the War Department as the greatest source of difficulties in the war effort. This resulted from the committee's bitterness about the army and navy procurement agencies' role in destroying the effectiveness of Nelson and the War Production Board. It certainly was possible to date the downfall of WPB to March 12, 1942, when an agreement setting forth the relationship between WPB and War Department purchasing agencies was signed by Nelson and Under Secretary of War Robert Patterson. In effect, WPB abdicated to the armed services full responsibility for military procurement and, given shortages, tight production schedules, and conflicting priorities regarding military and civilian needs, that inevitably produced further conflict.

The Truman Committee remained steadfastly loyal to Nelson; but it could not tolerate the erosion of his authority. Other agencies asserted their independence, leading eventually to a reorganization of WPB in September. Further rebellions during the fall culminated in February 1943 in a decision by FDR to replace Nelson with the World War I "czar," Bernard Baruch. The Truman Committee regretfully abandoned Nelson and began to speak in favor of a legislative solution to the need for centralized authority. A bill to establish a Department of Supply, long advocated by Senator Kilgore, a committee member, was introduced and received Truman's support. In April the committee scheduled hearings on "conflicting war programs" and its report on this subject, released on May 6, stated forcefully: "Today discussion of the overall legal authority of the War Production Board is mere pedantry. Although the authority may exist it has not been exercised." Four days later, the Senate enthusiastically approved a bill to establish an independent, civilian-dominated supply agency. White House alarm at this threatened congressional revolt led to FDR's appointment of his "assistant president," James Byrnes, to the post of director of an Office of War Mobilization. Byrnes was given essentially the powers to coordinate the procurement and production programs that WPB had possessed.

This decision ended the struggle for primacy over war production. The Truman Committee applauded Byrnes's appointment and justifiably claimed that the congressional and popular pressure it had mobilized was a major cause of FDR's decision. Certainly, the committee had played an important role throughout the struggle, although the objectives for which it originally had entered the fray—favoritism toward big business, wasteful procedures regarding contracts, over-emphasis on military needs, and so forth—had not been achieved. Nor would they receive significant attention in the future, for Byrnes, a conservative Southerner who was sympathetic to the military's viewpoint, had no need to look for support to the Truman Committee.

The committee's involvement in overall control of the domestic war effort did, however, continue, though its emphasis shifted. As the battle for

domination of the domestic war effort progressed, Truman and several
other members began referring to the critical issue not as centralized administration but in terms of a struggle for civilian control of the war effort.
This concern emerged quite early though it was largely obscured by other
problems until WPB's disintegration. On November 26, 1942, for example,
Truman took part in a "March of Time" interview. Responding to a question about the problem of civil-military relations, Truman bluntly stated:

> That is the most important question of the day. The function of
> generals and admirals is to fight battles, and to tell us what they
> need to fight battles with. They have no experience in business
> and industry, and the job of producing what they ask for should
> be left to business men under the direction of experienced
> civilians. I am firmly convinced that any attempt on the part of
> these ambitious generals and admirals to take complete control
> over the nation's economy would not only place vital functions in
> inexperienced hands, but would present a definite threat to our
> postwar political and economic structure.

He was referring specifically to the conflict then raging over utilization of
manpower but the threat, as perceived by Truman and others, involved
every phase of American economic and social life. The generals and admirals in no way pursued a calculated plan to take over the country, though
they might have succeeded had they made a serious effort. They were interested solely in obtaining everything necessary to win the war, and they
approached the wartime economy from this narrow perspective. Military
bureaucrats such as General Somervell, who once described the Truman
Committee as "formed in iniquity for political purposes," had no patience
with arguments that the people at home required a fair share of rubber,
aluminum, gasoline, and other scarce materials. Civilians had to make do;
military requirements—which often reflected an assessment of actual needs
and all possible contingencies—came first.

The Truman Committee cooperated with other groups to resist the War
Department's efforts to impose its priorities on the nation. Where the
military's challenge of civilian control was blatant—the manpower issue,
stockpiling of truck tires, or the conflict between the army program and
legitimate domestic requirements—resistance was remarkably effective. The
principle of civilian authority was maintained, though the pervasiveness of
the military in domestic matters continued to increase until the end of the
war.

As noted previously, the Truman Committee repeatedly renounced any
desire to meddle in strategy or tactics. But that did not resolve the problem
of civil-military relations, for what was a legitimate military program and
what represented an illegitimate military effort to overturn civilian rule?
There were no clear guidelines, and the committee did not possess sufficient information—or the power to compel the military to make such information available—to devise effective rules. Access to information was crucial: With junior officers, the committee believed that it possessed the
power to force military representatives to testify. Writing to Patterson in
March 1943, Truman strongly objected to a War Department claim that Ex-

ecutive privilege excused Colonel John H. Amen from responding to the committee's questions. "Since the Committee obtained from other officers of the Army the information which it expected to obtain from Colonel Amen," Truman informed Patterson, "it will not take the necessary steps to cite him for contempt. But the Committee desires to make it clear that in so doing it does not in any sense acquiesce in your contention that any officer in the Army has the right to refuse to divulge to the Committee within the scope of its powers of investigation." However, when principal officers of the War Department refused information on the ground of military necessity, the committee willingly complied. Undoubtedly the most significant case of this sort arose when committee investigators ran across enormous and unexplained expenditures for something identified only as the Manhattan Project. Truman telephoned Secretary of War Henry L. Stimson, who told him: "Now that's a matter which I know all about personally, and I am only one of the group of two or three men in the whole world who know about it."

Truman: "I see."
Stimson: "It's part of a very important secret development."
Truman: "Well, all right then &"
Stimson: "And I—"
Truman: "I herewith see the situation, Mr. Secretary, and you won't have to say another word to me. Whenever you say that to me that's all I want to hear."

Truman was not to learn the Manhattan Project's purpose until the day he became President.

More typical of the information imbroglio was the ill-starred Canol Project, a scheme to supply high-octane gasoline, using locally-produced and refined petroleum, for the Alcan Highway and U.S. airfields in the region. The project was clearly impractical and required enormous expenditures of manpower and scarce goods. Nevertheless, the War Department and, specifically, General Somervell, forged ahead, ignoring the question of cost-effectiveness and practicality. "Military necessity requires that the Canol Project be completed as rapidly as possible," was Somervell's stock answer when objections were raised by civilian agencies.

The Truman Committee launched an investigation of the Canol Project in summer 1943 and in September a subcommittee looked at the site and convened hearings. Gathering a huge amount of evidence, the committee soon decided that the scheme was indefensible, and should be closed down. WPB, the Department of Interior, and various other civilian agencies supported this recommendation. Although $100 million already had been spent, an immediate shutdown would save $30 million already authorized but not expended. The War Department flatly ignored the committee's judgment, stating without elaboration that Canol was "necessary to the war effort." Since no Executive agency was able to overrule the army, the Truman Committee's only recourse was to place the facts in the record. This was done via public hearings in late 1943 and a report by Truman to the Senate. Despite continued pressure from members of the committee, the army obtained a further appropriation from Congress and completed all phases of the project in October 1944. The fifth annual report of the Truman Committee, released in September 1946, reported that Canol had cost $134 million and had produced about as much fuel as could have been transported by one medium tanker in a period of three months. The Canol Project, though certainly not typical of wartime development programs, showed the limits of the Truman Committee's influence.

The committee performed splendidly in its principal role as production watchdog. Perhaps the greatest of the committee's accomplishments was the high level of public confidence in the Roosevelt Administration's conduct of the war. The committee served as an important source of information on what the government was doing to win the war, and most Americans accepted its assurances that the domestic war effort, despite administrative tangles and bureaucrative incompetence, was going well. Notably, the public seemed little concerned about the committee's reluctance to investigate charges of congressional graft and influence-peddling. Only three such inquiries took place (only one, involving Senator "Happy" Chandler's swimming pool, during Truman's tenure) in almost seven years.

In April 1942 Truman wrote his friend, Lou Holland: "We have the political campaign coming on, and with the Republican Committee endorsing the war program the campaign will be made of course on the efficiency of the conduct of that program. So unless the Democrats whole-heartedly endorse what my Committee is trying to do I fear very much I will become a political issue, and then the fat will be in the fire sure enough." Truman's anxieties proved unwarranted, for the committee attained such recognition and public acceptance that it became virtually invulnerable to political attack. Ironically, the committee's unique status largely stemmed from Truman's request that the committee's deliberations be conducted as impartially and reasonably as possible.

It may be said that Truman's resignation on August 4, 1944, to accept the Democratic Party's vice presidential nomination, was a watershed in the history of the committee. Although it was to continue in existence until April 1948, after Truman's departure there occurred a large turnover in the committee's membership, erosion of its prestige, and growth of partisan bickering. The committee, headed by James M. Mead, Harley Kilgore, and then Owen Brewster, conducted some forty-five public hearings. It issued reports on such important topics as reconversion, disposal of surplus property, the proposed loan to Great Britain, and the renegotiations of war contracts. However, if "congressional investigations are essentially exercises in the creation of public opinion," the heyday of the Senate Special Committee to Investigate the National Defense Program ended with Truman's resignation. Indeed, recognition of the feisty Missourian's centrality to all that the committee accomplished—and failed to do—perhaps is the most useful insight to be gained from study of its activities.

SENATOR HARRY S. TRUMAN TO LOU HOLLAND, PRESIDENT, MID-CENTRAL WAR RESOURCES BOARD AUGUST 15, 1940

Papers of Harry S. Truman, Senatorial and Vice-Presidential Files,
Harry S. Truman Library, Independence, Missouri.

Dear Lou:

It was a very great pleasure to get your good letter. I have tried every time I have been at home to get in touch with you, because I have some most important matters to discuss with you.

I have been interviewing the people here who are at the source of the fountain, and I believe that with proper organization Missouri can get its proper place in the set-up. In the last few days I have talked with Mr. Knudsen, Mr. Stettinius, and the Army Board personally and with a committee of Senators, and I know now exactly what's going on here.

Nichols is here promoting himself, and not doing much else. He has no national outlook and is thinking most all the time about how he can place something so as to help his own housing projects.

What we need is a first class dollar-a-year man who knows what it's all about, who can devote his time exclusively to getting concrete surveys of our whole State situation in a form so that these fellows back here can easily understand it. He ought to have a State-wide outlook and he ought to have the national welfare in view first.

The program, as outlined, contemplates the location of Government plants and key industries in five different sections between the Appalachians and the Rocky Mountains, and three hundred miles south of the Canadian border and three hundred miles north of the Gulf of Mexico and the Mexican border.

We are in Area C, which consists of southern Indiana and southern Illinois, Missouri and Kansas. The plan is to make each area a complete unit, with every sort of set-up needed in the National Defense Program. Powder plants, loading plants, small arms factories, and so forth will be in each one of these areas. They are urging factories to decentralize all over the whole area which I named in the beginning.

A man with the right perspective and the personality and energy could get everything we need for Missouri.

A large powder plant was contemplated for the St. Louis area, principally because the materials are available immediately in St. Louis. Mr. Nichols put forth all the energy he had, trying to prevent that plant from going to St. Louis.

Of course, Clark and the St. Louis Congressmen heard about it, and you know how much cooperation he is going to get out of them now. It was a perfectly asinine thing to do.

The industries that are to be located in our area must be sold on the fact that our area is the place for them to come. For instance, Boeing is being urged to increase its facilities at Wichita, rather than enlarge its Washington plant on the Coast. Douglas and Lockheed are both being urged to move into the Central area with new plants. Douglas is adamant and won't move. Lockheed, I am informed this morning, is moving to Dallas, Texas.

These people are not instructed where to locate within this great area I mentioned to you. It is the business of the local communities to get that done themselves. The number of Government plants is comparatively small, and there isn't a chance in the world of getting more than one or two in an immediate neighborhood.

I must see you and discuss the whole thing through with you, because we are losing opportunity, due to the fact that we only have a promoter back here when what we need is a super-salesman to work among the industries themselves.

It is the policy of everybody connected with this set-up, and the policy of the Army and the Navy Boards, to decentralize in the central area. They are not encouraging the enlargement of plants on the Coast. This is our opportunity, if we ever had it. I wish we had a Mayor with vision, and Lou Holland at the head of the Chamber of Commerce.

Sincerely yours,

Harry S. Truman

SPEECH OF SENATOR TRUMAN TO THE SENATE FEBRUARY 10, 1941

Congressional Record, 77th Congress, 1st Session, 830–38.

Mr. President, I expect to submit a resolution asking for an investigation of the national-defense program and the handling of contracts.

I feel that it is my duty at this time to place before the Senate certain information which I have, and which I am sure is of vital importance to the success of the national-defense program.

There seems to be a policy in the national-defense set-up to concentrate all contracts and nearly all the manufacturing that has to do with the national defense in a very small area. This area is entirely outside the location which the Army survey, itself, has shown to be safe. The little manufacturer, the little contractor, and the little machine shop have been left entirely out in the cold. The policy seems to be to make the big man bigger and to put the little man completely out of business. There is no reason for this that will stand up, because plans have been presented to the National Defense Committee which would solve the condition of the little manufacturer and the little machine-shop owner.

A perfectly practical and concrete plan was presented by the Mid-Central War Resources Board. A survey of the region within 100 miles of Kansas City was made by this Board, and 160 small machine shops and manufacturing plants were located. It was proposed to combine the facilities of these little machine shops and allow them to take a contract, or contracts, which they could, working as a unit, carry out successfully.

Under this program there would be no housing problem. The shops are in the small towns. The people already have their houses. They are the best workmen and the most loyal citizens in the whole country.

The same sort of a survey was made in St. Louis and the immediate surrounding territory, and the same conditions exist there. I have no doubt that these conditions exist in Iowa, Illinois, and Indiana.

When this matter was put up to the Defense Committee, an effort was made to find out where the machines in these small shops were located so that the big fellows could go and buy them and move them. They are buying these machines wherever they can find them, shipping them to Detroit, Philadelphia, Norfolk, and industrial cities in Massachusetts and Connecticut. They are hiring our young men and moving them to the Atlantic and Pacific seaboards and to Detroit, leaving us denuded of manpower as well as machines. This makes a double housing problem. It leaves our cities with vacant property which is rapidly depreciating in value, and creates a condition at Norfolk, Philadelphia, Detroit, Hartford, Conn., and Los Angeles, Calif., where housing problems have to be met. It just does not make sense. The policy seems to be to make the big men bigger and let the little men go out of business or starve to death, and they do not seem to care what becomes of these little fellows. . . .

Now I wish to read a few extracts from a confidential letter which I received just the other day. This letter is from a man who knows what he is talking about.

> I think I can say that enough evidence is accumulating here in Washington of the "dog in the manger" attitude of the big fellows to provide the tinder for a rather serious blow-up a little later on. In the last analysis, of course, the Government itself is to blame. Unless the matter can be policed at the time and place where contracts are given out, i. e., unless the Government intervenes to exercise some supervision over new plant installation, it is almost certain to result in the prime contractor "tooling up" to handle the bulk of the business himself. As I see it, here is more or less the attitude the Government should take when it gives out a contract (for example) to Westinghouse Electric & Manufacturing Co. for the construction of two big ordnance plants—one at Louisville, Ky., the other at Canton, Ohio. "We are ready to give you a contract. That contract provides for the amortization of indispensable new plant equipment and buildings over a 5-year term, in 60 monthly install-

ments, in accordance with the law. Now, let us see just what new capital investment your corporation proposes to amortize." At this point Westinghouse presumably submits a list of what it will provide in the way of new plant facilities. Somewhere along the line of scrutiny, the Government should say, "Sorry, but you cannot include in your price for the finished articles any amortization charge for this and this and this item of equipment. Our surveys indicate beyond the possibility of a doubt that the facilities already exist in the following plants, which we are satisfied will be in a position to collaborate with your concern as subcontractors on a farming-out basis." My guess is that if it were feasible to look into the situation in any large contract that has been given out recently, it would be disclosed that the Government's agreement to amortize new plant facilities covered machine-shop and metal-working facilities already available in other plants.

Now, it is essential to the functioning of this idea, however, that when the Government in Washington says, "We know the facilities are available," it should be in position to cite chapter and verse. This is where our regional pooling associations (Mid-Central War Resources Board, etc.) come into the picture. Or, to put it another way: When the Government is in negotiation with Westinghouse for the construction of the two new ordnance plants, it should start with the proposition: "Where do you propose to locate these plants?" In the discussion as to location, the Government should raise its voice in terms of the availability of facilities in different regions that could supplement the new ordnance plants to the best advantage. Really, the office for production management should take the lead in determining where new Government-owned plants are to be located. It should start out by asserting that a certain plant is to be located in a certain place, because, among other reasons, there are facilities in smaller shops in the area tributary to that location which could effectively supplement the new plant. This is really national-defense planning. Of course, nothing like this point of view exists anywhere in official Washington, and I don't see any signs of such an attitude developing anywhere in the new set-up.

To illustrate a little further: One of the reasons why North American's new assembly plant is to be located in Kansas City is that in the region tributary to your metropolis there are so many plants that can effectively supplement the facilities of North American as "subcontractors."

So long as the present "let the big fellows do it" attitude governs in the national-defense set-up, you can be sure that they will tool up in order to do everything possible under their own roofs—why not, there's more money in it that way. There is no risk for the prime contractor. He knows this national-defense show is going on for several years; it probably signifies the entry of our Nation on a totally different path of destiny than it has ever trod before. In any case, the prime contractor is protected. At the end of 5 years he has gotten back all of his capital expenditure.

If, for any reason, he wants the plant, he has an option to buy it. If he doesn't want it, well, let the taxpayers have it as scrap iron. The same thing happened in 1919 in the liquidation of war plants.

The position we are in, as I see it, is this: The forces of the times run more and more strongly in the direction of bigger and bigger business. Unless the Government intervenes to reverse this trend, there will be no stopping the concentration of business in fewer and fewer hands. Under separate cover we send you our bulletin 3, a list of 650 corporations classified as to State and locality, that have something like $6,000,000,000 of war contracts. But something like 114 of them have the bulk of the business. This simply will not do. . . .

Similarly, with regard to the new shipyards. Something like 50 new ways are to be constructed in about 10 years. Assuming 2 ships per way per year, the 200 ships would be turned out by December 31, 1942. Query: Is the Maritime Commission permitting the ships constructors to duplicate facilities which already exist in other plants inland? Incidentally, these 200 new ships are to be 100 percent welded. You might inquire of the boys in K.C. Structural what effect this decision has on the availability of the inland fabricating shops for collaboration in this program. . . .

Mr. President, under the War Department there are three types of contracts—the lump-sum contract, the purchase-and-hire contract, and the fixed-fee contract. Under the lump-sum contract the contractor is awarded the contract for the work, either on a low-bid basis or on a negotiated lump-sum basis. The purchase-and-hire form of contract is, as it would imply, a straight cost-plus contract. With the cost-plus-a-fixed-fee contract, under which most of the present construction work is being performed, the contractor is selected and a fee for his work fixed. The fixed fee amounts to approximately 3.2 percent. All costs allied with the construction work, including all overhead, blue prints, telephone calls, stenographers, clerks, field inspectors, labor, and material, are paid for by the Government. The fee can be interpreted as a profit to the contractor for the use of his services and his organization.

I do not pretend to be entirely familiar with the workings of any of these departments. However, the fixed-fee branch is now in the process of being reorganized. General Hartman has been retired, due to overwork. Colonel Somervell, former P.W.A. chieftain of New York City, is now at the head of the fixed-fee branch. Mr. Loving was formerly the construction chief. Colonel Groves is now very important in the construction branch.

Fixed-fee contracts are also being awarded to large industrialists, such as Chrysler, Du Pont, Remington, Atlas, and Hercules. These industrialists are given a fixed fee for the use of their engineering facilities. After the building has been erected and the plant completed by Government money, these industrialists lease the plant and supply the Government with the product of the plant at a fixed cost per unit.

On August 15, the Chrysler Corporation was awarded a contract in the amount of $53,000,000. The fee for construction which is paid by the Government to Chrysler is in the amount of $1. This looks exceedingly patriotic.

Nevertheless, during the 1-year period of the Chrysler Corporation's lease of the factory facilities they will produce 1,000 tanks at a cost to the United States Government in the amount of $33,000,000. I doubt if anyone could give the method by which the cost of $33,000 per tank was fixed. Chrysler has full jurisdiction over the spending of all money and the inspection of all work at the job. I am sure the constructing quartermaster at the job is sincere in his effort to guard every penny of the United States Government's money; but with Chrysler having full control, it is almost impossible to do anything else but what Chrysler wants. I do not say that the Chrysler Corporation is performing anything other than its patriotic duty, but I do feel that even the large corporation should be subject to a full accounting for every nickel spent and the profit accrued on every task.

The same procedure followed in the award of the contract to the Chrysler Corporation has been pursued in awarding all contracts to the large corporations. The Remington Co. get $600,000 for acting as advisers to the Government. No one knows what this advice is or what it is worth. In addition to the $600,000, they will receive a profit of no one knows how much for each 30-caliber and 50-caliber shell they produce in a factory which has been financed by the United States Government. After the operating company—the large industrialist—has been selected, an architect, an engineer, and a construction contractor are selected.

Every contractor in the country, with but few exceptions, and every architect and engineer have registered with the Quartermaster General and with the Navy. Each firm presents a portfolio including a statement of Government fixed-fee contracts.

The information which the contractor, the architect, and the engineer furnish the Quartermaster General is turned over to the Construction Advisory Board.

The Construction Advisory Board consists of three men: Messrs. F. Blossom, F. Harvey, and F. Dresser. Mr. Blossom is a member of the firm of Sanderson & Porter, engineers and contractors of New York City. Mr. Dresser is a former civil-service employee who was employed by the U. S. H. A., has been in business for himself in the Middle West, and has had considerable interest in the Association of General Contractors.

After the information is submitted to the Quartermaster General, it is reviewed by the Board, which interviews the prospective contractor or engineer. The contractor is then given a rating which is filed for future use. The Board could really be considered an indexing committee of contractors and architects throughout the country.

The contractor is supposed to be financially sound. He should have an organization equipped to do the work. He should have done work of a similar character, or at least of similar size. Because he is a local contractor, he is considered conversant with local labor conditions and material markets; and, being in the vicinity of the project, he can serve better than one who is removed from the project because of geographical location. Were these requirements religiously carried out, no one could find fault with them; but the rules do not fit with the facts.

If there is a job in St. Louis after the operating company has been selected, the Board is requested to submit the names of those who, in its judgment, are the most competent contractor and architect for the job. The Board usually selects three.

In selecting the contractor for the job in question, the Board is supposed to bear in mind the geographical location of the contractor with reference to the job.

The name of the contractor selected by the Board is then submitted to Mr. Loving. Mr. Loving, after perusing the files of the contractor, requests that the contractor come to Washington for negotiations. Contractor No. 1 selected by the Board is then called into conference with Mr. Loving, Mr. O'Brien, and Captain Kirkpatrick and one of the section chiefs. Negotiations then take place, and generally at that meeting the contractor is informed, confidentially, that he has the job.

After negotiations a proceed order, in the form of a letter, is sent to the contractor. Final contracts are drawn up and submitted to the office of the Under Secretary of War for final signature.

One of the first jobs awarded was an $18,115,000 project at Fayetteville, N. C. This contract, strange as it may seem, was awarded to T. A. Loving & Co., at Charlotte, N. C. Mr. Loving, former construction branch chief, bears the same name and is from the same town. It is said that no relationship whatsoever exists between the two Mr. Lovings. Another instance occurred where a contractor and an architect had been selected because they have special merit for a reasonably small project. The Philadelphia quartermaster depot was awarded to the Ballinger Co. and Wark & Co. in the amount of $700,000. Within a month's time this same group received an additional contract in the amount of $9,911,000 as an extra. There were no negotiations. The same thing occurred at Camp Blanding, Fla., Camp Edwards, Mass., and at Camp Meade, Md.

Many of the contracts which have been awarded have been traced to a connection between a member of the contractor's firm and Mr. Dresser, namely, they have been personal friends in the past. This, however, should not effect any criticism. Friends may have been made because of their quality performance. Friendship should not be a handicap to anyone seeking work in the War Department. When a friendship, however, dominates the selection of an inferior contractor, then that selection is wrong. Colonel Wahlbridg of Wahlbridg and Aldinger was a personal friend of Mr. Dresser, so I am told. Wahlbridg & Aldinger of Detroit, and Foley Bros. of St. Paul, Minn., were awarded the $8,000,000 Remington small arms ammunition plant at Lake City, Mo. The two firms were neither geographically located in regard to the job, nor were they in any way better equipped than local contractors of Kansas and Missouri.

The same policy was followed in letting the contract at Camp Leonard Wood at Rolla, Mo. I am told that the gentlemen who got this contract were dirt movers and had never had a construction job in their lives. They are having much trouble getting organized and are having a great deal of difficulty with local labor conditions.

Smith, Hitchman & Grylls, architects and engineers, of Detroit, were awarded the architectural work at Lake City. Smith, Hitchman & Grylls are personal friends of Mr. Harrison, who is in the Housing Section of the National Defense Council. Mr. Harrison, I believe, and from what I am told, was the booster of Smith, Hitchman & Grylls. Smith, Hitchman & Grylls, after having had the contract since September 23, were unable to produce a suitable plot plan for a reasonably simple project until December 31, and it was not until the section chief handling the particular project forced construction, whether right or wrong, and against the wishes of both Remington and Smith, Hitchman & Grylls. Smith, Hitchman & Grylls were considered for the second Remington Arms plant in Denver.

On the Western Cartridge small-arms ammunition plant, to be known as the St. Louis ordnance plant, negotiations were held with two firms who were combined by the Dresser committee. Albert P. Greensfelder, of the Fruco Construction Co., formerly known as the Fruin-Colon Contracting Co., is a personal friend, so I am told, of Mr. Dresser. The Fruco Co. was combined with the Massman Construction Co. Massman is a river contractor. The particular project on which he was selected to be the contractor is within the city limits of St. Louis, and all the barges which Massman may own would serve no useful purpose for this project. The Fruco Co. had, a month prior to the negotiations, so I am told, a B rating. The second choice for the St. Louis job was Winston, or Winston & Turner, of New York. For some reason Winston has been pushed into practically every job in the Middle West by the Advisory Committee. A short time ago they were awarded, as co-contractors with Sollit Construction Co., the bag-loading plant, at Charlestown, Ind. The operators of this plant were intent on using a contractor close to the job, the H. K. Fergeson Co., of Cleveland. Winston, however, seems to have gotten the job.

At Camp Blanding, Fla., Starrett Bros. & Eakin, Inc., general contractors, of New York City, were awarded a $9,000,000 project, and 8 days later, awarded an additional $8,000,000 project—a total of $17,463,777 in construction. This particular job was supposed to be completed January 15, 1941, but as of December 27, 1940, was but 48 percent completed. There has been much discussion on this particular project. Fischbach & Moore, electrical contractors, of New York City, received the contract for the electrical work. So, too, did a New York contracting firm, J. L. Murphy, for all the plumbing work on the project. No one knows why Starrett Bros. & Eakin, of New York City, should have received the contract for this particular project.

One of the first projects that was awarded was the Ellwood ordnance plant at Wilmington, Ill. This project was in the amount of $11,564,000, and was awarded to Mr. Blossom's firm, Sanderson & Porter. Mr. Blossom is on the committee.

I have been informed—and this also needs verification—that John Griffiths & Son Construction Co., of Chicago, were bankrupt 5 years ago, but through a Colonel Paddock, chief Washington representative of the firm, they were awarded a $6,268,669 contract for the construction of Camp Grant in Illinois. At Falmouth, Mass., the Walsh Construction Co., of Boston, a tunnel contractor, received the contract for the construction of Camp Edwards in the amount of $7,000,000 first and $12,000,000 second, a total of $19,697,948 for construction. Fischback-Moore, electrical contractor of New York, is in on this job. The estimated date of completion was February 1 and December 20. To date they are about 70 percent complete. On this particular job, I have been told on good authority that there was a local union consisting of about 100 members who so organized the labor on this job that the 5,000 men employed would have to pay $50 apiece to the local union before they set foot on the job. Labor conditions similar to this have existed on many of the camp jobs, including Fort Dix, Fort Meade, Lake City, St. Louis and Rolla, Mo.

Maureen, Russell, Crowell & Mullgardt were awarded, as associated with Giffels & Vallet, the contract for the design of the $30,000,000 St. Louis Ammunition Plant. Russell, again, is a personal friend of Mr. Dresser, so I have been informed. Russell's firm has never done this type of work before. It is said that this firm received approximately $76,000,000 worth of national-defense construction. There has been good reason for criticism of the Fixed Fee Branch of the War Department.

It is also said that Albert Kahn, Associated Architects & Engineers, Inc., have received between three hundred and five hundred millions of dollars in engineering and architectural contracts. Giffels & Vallet are, I am told, an offshoot of Albert Kahn. The Senate will remember what a tremendous fuss was raised when it was discovered that Chip Robert and his engineering firm in Atlanta, Ga., had received engineering and architectural contracts to the sum of $76,000,000. It looks as if Chip has been a piker and was not in at the right time.

I do not believe that any contracts should be let on the basis of friendship or political affiliation. We are facing a national emergency. Patriotism would require that these contracts be let to the man best fitted to carry out the contracts. I believe the Senate ought to go to the bottom of the whole procedure.

It is my opinion, from things I have heard, that the violations of ethics and common-sense procedure are just as flagrant in the lettering of contracts for the Navy.

They say the selection of a contractor and architect is based on their financial stability and their past experience. If the contractor and the architect were selected on the basis of their familiarity with labor and local material markets, and if the contractors were provided with a suitable method of reimbursement, and if the red tape connected with the payments were removed, smaller contracting firms would be judged on the same basis as the larger firms are now judged. Past performance is really no guide for judging a contractor today. In the past 11 years there has been little, if any, industrial expansion. The building industry throughout the United States, as we all know, has suffered for the want of work. The only work that contractors have been performing has been P.W.A. and W.P.A. projects. The firms who were good prior to 1929 are not necessarily the firms who are good today.

I am calling the attention of the Senate to these things because I believe most sincerely that they need looking into. I consider public funds to be sacred funds, and I think they ought to have every safeguard possible to prevent their being misused and mishandled. . . .

I think the Senate ought to create a special committee with authority to examine every contract that has been let, with authority to find out if the rumors rife in this city have any foundation in fact. This will be a protection to the men who are responsible for letting these contracts, and will also insure a more efficient carrying out of the contract itself.

I have had considerable experience in letting public contracts; and I have never yet found a contractor who, if not watched, would not leave the Government holding the bag. We are not doing him a favor if we do not watch him.

When safeguards are removed from a man who is entrusted with funds it does him a disservice, for the simple reason that it is much better to place the necessary guards around public funds and keep men from embezzling them than it is to prosecute men after embezzlement has taken place. When a bank teller is permitted to run loose without bond and without the necessary supervision, in the long run he gets his money mixed up with the money of the bank. The same thing happens in letting Government contracts. I do not like a cost-plus contract. I think it is an abomination; but, under the present conditions, I do not see how else this situation could have been met, although in the time that has been wasted as this matter has been handled, plans and specifications could have been drawn and contracts could have been let to the lowest and best bidder, which is the only proper way to let contracts.

I am particularly alarmed at the concentration of national-defense industrial plants. I am reliably informed that from 70 to 90 percent of the contracts let have been concentrated in an area smaller than England. It undoubtedly is the plan to make the big manufacturers bigger, and let the little men shift for themselves.

I think the "educational order" program ought to be gone into thoroughly. If it is necessary to give Henry Ford and Chrysler and General Motors millions of dollars for educational purposes for mass production, then we are certainly out on a limb. I understand that they have been given $11,000,000 apiece for educational purposes. The educational-order program was instituted along in the 1920's and 1930's by the War Department and the Navy Department to educate certain manufacturers in what the Army and the Navy might need in case an emergency should arise. Those educational orders are things of the past, and ought now to be abandoned. They are merely a gift. That phase of our national-defense program should be thoroughly gone into.

I am merely stating what I believe to be conditions that deserve investigation. If nothing is wrong, there will be no harm done. If something is wrong, it ought to be brought to light. The location of these national-defense plants and the profits that are supposed to be made on tanks, planes, and small arms should be a matter of public record, unless we are to have the same old profiteering situation that we had in the last war.

Everyone connected with the national-defense program should have a patriotic interest in seeing that it is properly carried out; and the Senate ought to know whether such persons have this interest, whether they be manufacturers or laboring men. . . .

SENATE RESOLUTION 71
MARCH 1, 1941

Congressional Record, 77th Congress, 1st Session, 1615.

Resolved. That a special committee of seven Senators, to be appointed by the President of the Senate, is authorized and directed to make a full and complete study and investigation of the operation of the program for the procurement and construction of supplies, materials, munitions, vehicles, aircraft, vessels, plants, camps, and other articles and facilities in connection with the national defense, including (1) the types and terms of contracts awarded on behalf of the United States; (2) the methods by which such contracts are awarded and contractors selected; (3) the utilization of the facilities of small business concerns, through subcontracts or otherwise; (4) the geographic distribution of contracts and location of plants and facilities; (5) the effect of such program with respect to labor and the migration of labor; (6) the performance of contracts and the accountings required of contractors; (7) benefits accruing to contractors with respect to amortization for the purposes of taxation or otherwise; (8) practices of management or labor, and prices, fees, and charges, which interfere with such program or unduly increase its cost; and (9) such other matters as the committee deems appropriate. The committee shall report to the Senate, as soon as practicable, the results of its study and investigation, together with its recommendations.

For the purpose of this resolution the committee, or any duly authorized subcommittee thereof, is authorized to hold such hearings, to sit and act at such times and places during the sessions, recesses, and adjourned periods of the Seventy-seventh and succeeding Congresses, to employ such clerical and other assistance, to require by subpena, or otherwise, the attendance of such witnesses and the production of such correspondence, books, papers, and documents, to make such investigations, to administer such oaths, to take such testimony, and to incur such expenditures as it deems advisable. The cost of stenographic services to report such hearings shall not be in excess of 25 cents per hundred words. The expenses of the committee, which shall not exceed $15,000, shall be paid from the contingent fund of the Senate upon vouchers approved by the chairman of the committee.

TRUMAN COMMITTEE NEWS RELEASE
APRIL 18, 1941

Papers of Harry S. Truman, Senatorial and Vice-Presidential Files, Harry S. Truman Library, Independence, Missouri.

The Senate Special Committee investigating the National Defense Program had just finished its first week's sessions. The Committee heard the Secretary of War, Mr. Stimson, the Under Secretary of War, Mr. Patterson, the Secretary of the Navy, Mr. Knox, and William S. Knudsen, Office of Production Management.

Each witness reviewed the difficulties and handicaps encountered in their several departments at the beginning of the National Defense program, due to the government's lack of facilities to execute it, and to provide equipment. Contrast was made between the conditions prevailing in 1917 and those at the time our defense program began. Then, England and France were intact and we purchased most of our heavy weapons from them; now every weapon must be built in this country.

In overcoming the obstacles it was pointed out that the government was obliged to develop and expand many private plants at great cost. The Selective Draft Act, Secretary Stimson said necessitates planning a program of training which may last for five years. He discussed cantonment construction and explained the methods and operation of contracts and told of the present status of the projects. The percentage of those behind schedule was small and steadily diminishing while others were being completed ahead of the time expected.

He emphasized the fact that the Army places orders but that business must fill them. In doing so the principal contractors had entered into many subcontracts which scattered the work widely in different parts of the country.

The Lease-Lend bill, he said had superimposed a vast new program to cover the needs of other nations, over our own requirements. It is proceeding with even greater speed and efficiency than marked the programs which were instituted last summer.

Testimony of Mr. Patterson

Mr. Patterson took up the subject of procurement with which he is charged. Of the $6,623,000,000 made available, ninety-five per cent has been obligated. Under a decentralized system purchases in a large measure had been made in the field. pursuing further the subject of contracts touched upon by Mr. Stimson, the Under Secretary told of contracts awarded "with and without advertising", and under the "cost-plus-fixed-fee" method. These negotiated contracts were made to expedite the program. From July 1, 1940 to March 1, 1941, the Department had entered into approximately 739,000 such contracts at an aggregate cost of $6,062,000,000. He denied that any political or personal favoritism had been exercised in making the awards. The industrial mobilization plan he said had worked well in emergency and months of valuable time had been saved. Fixed fees on construction at military posts never exceeded six per cent and in practice ranged down to two per cent. Architect-engineer fees averaged ¾ per cent. By the end of November, 1940, the Quartermaster Corps had made contracts aggregating $900,000,000. He deplored intermediaries in obtaining contracts, a pernicious practice, but the Department was using its efforts to prevent the abuse.

Summarizing, Mr. Patterson said the shelter, clothing and rations provided for troops are the best the army has ever provided. Barracks are comfortable and built to last for years. The armament is of advanced design and thoroughly efficient; tanks are superior to those of any other army. Combat planes, bombers and pursuit are of advanced designs and incorporate meritorious features developed from the European war.

The program is huge and mistakes have been made; errors have been discovered and corrected and the work prosecuted with skill and vigor.

Testimony of Secretary Knox

Secretary Knox told of the navy's expansion following a steady decline in the shipbuilding and munitions industry from 1920 to 1936. No battleships were laid down after the World War until 1937. The Navy now has 2,226,950 tons of combat ships under construction and 282,507 tons of auxiliaries. Nearly all yards are working on three shifts. Future difficulties which may cause a hold up lie in the production of structural steel, aluminum, steel forgings and armor.

Of aircraft, 840 planes were contracted for in 1940 and 6,038 in 1941. The program of expansion calls for 15,000 planes. The work is proceeding with rapidity and training capacity for pilots has increased to thousands a year. Formerly all major purchases were made on a competitive basis, but the practice was not adapted to speed nor a rational plan to utilize industrial resources. It became necessary to expand capacity and the government had given aid to manufacturers who in turn gave subcontracts to many hundreds of smaller manufacturers for parts.

In supplying material to Great Britain, Mr. Knox said allocations had been received from the President for $128,963,000 and $272,422,000 have been requested. It is on its way but shipping orders are not publicly known. Mr. Knox said of the OPM "it works" and he would not change its character to "a one-man outfit".

Of price fixing he said he wanted "to hold up a bit" but thought some price control must be exercised. He did not think it would seriously affect the cooperative attitude of industry. He considered the designation of Harry Hopkins as a clearing house under Lease-Lend procurement, a very desirable setup. Mr. Knox expressed much concern over a possible shortage of aluminum. Ultimately we may have to come to commandeering aluminum of every character in private hands. The cartel control of magnesium he considered an indefensible monopoly.

Testimony of William S. Knudsen

Mr. Knudsen said planes were his first consideration when he took up his present work. There were then 7,000 on order; the number was pushed up to 33,000 in July, of which 19,000 were for our own needs, and 14,000 for the British. Next came the machine tool problem. The industry's production had been quadrupled.

Seven plants are now making tanks, medium and light. They will be in full production by October 1st, and bomber plants by the latter part of this year. Last month 1,400 planes were delivered, three times the number produced last June.

Describing the procedure under the Lease-Lend bill Mr. Knudsen said the specifications came from the Army and Navy and were handled as if they were for these services. He does not deal directly with Mr. Hopkins.

"When we get going" Mr. Knudsen declared, "we will have more production capacity than any two European countries" and he was "not afraid". Around 2,800,000 men have been placed in defense work since last June and the number may go to four million more before the close of the year. He did not think anything more would be heard of unemployment.

Mr. Knudsen said that his committee had gone over the action taken by Mr. Henderson in the matter of price fixing. He did not think it would cut down production. There had been some howls, but he added "A howl never hurts anybody".

He felt better about the labor situation than he did a year ago.

None of the witnesses dwelt upon strike conditions but insisted that capital and labor would work together to accomplish the job undertaken.

TRUMAN COMMITTEE NEWS RELEASE MAY 13, 1941

Papers of Harry S. Truman, Senatorial and Vice-Presidential Files,
Harry S. Truman Library, Independence, Missouri.

For the past month a special committee of the United States Senate, of which Senator Truman of Missouri is chairman, has been investigating the National Defense Program and officials, engineers and contractors have offered testimony and submitted to questioning with respect to our condition of military preparedness and what has been done and is being done to improve it.

Many interesting facts have been brought out and some of them may prove to be a bit startling to the public unacquainted with and unappreciative of the enormity of the task involved in providing adequate defense.

Aside from the statement of Secretary of the Navy Knox, the committee's inquiry has been devoted to the Army branch of the service. It first heard Secretary of War Stimson, and he was followed by his assistant, Mr. Patterson, in charge of procurement. Both presented carefully prepared statements setting forth the situation in the Army when the present emergency developed and told what had been accomplished and is being accomplished to bring the fighting force up to the required state of efficiency.

Details affecting cantonment construction to which the committee has devoted much attention have been supplied by their subordinates and by contractors. While there has been nothing in the evidence thus far which would indicate any collusion or graft on the part either of officials or contractors, there has been a mass of testimony showing that with respect to certain camps, the War Department's estimates of cost have been exceeded by actual costs, in some cases by more than 100 per cent.

In extentuation of the errors of these officers in making their estimates, it has repeatedly been pointed out that physical conditions prevailing, the changes made in the methods of warfare and the reluctance of the public and of Congress to provide the means to enable the Army to prepare adequate plans, have been responsible for their temporary failure to supply them. Although the question of a selective draft has been discussed by Army officers, more or less secretly, for fifteen years, none of them really expected that Congress would enact such a law in time of peace. In consequence, their plans for speedy mobilization in most cases were sadly inadequate. They had not anticipated that an army of nearly a million and a quarter men requiring accommodations, equipment and training would be assembled when the country was not at war. Moreover, the character of warfare, as shown on the battlefields of Europe has undergone a radical change. Officials had been advised of Hitler's warlike preparations, especially in the air, but the weight of his tanks and their use to supplement the air forces were a part of his military secret.

The coordination of air and ground forces, and the employment of ground troops with mechanized and armored vehicles was a new application of a fundamental principle, as General Marshall, Chief of Staff, said. Hitler's Polish campaign was merely a dress rehearsal—a training affair—and enabled the Germans to approach the next operation with tremendous effectiveness. Observers were not permitted with either the German or the Polish army until the campaign was at its end.

These and other developments necessitated the introduction of radical departure from our plans involving expense and delay. The combination of air and mechanized troops had previously been considered, but the Air Corps believed it to be impractical.

Estimates as to equipment in some instances went very much wrong, especially as to aluminum which constitutes from 54 to 80 per cent of an airplane. The Aluminum Company of America, the sole makers of the product gave the assurance that there would be sufficient aluminum to supply both the Army and private needs. It was not long before the demand exceeded the manufacture by more than one hundred per cent, making necessary the elimination of its use for private purposes, even that made from a secondary raw material at increased cost, and still there is possibility that the Government may have to erect its own plant which probably will not be producing for a year. Developments were so rapid that the estimators could not even make a good guess.

Aluminum was only one instance of grossly inaccurate estimates. Specifically they were equally glaring with respect to two large cantonments which the committee had been investigating—Fort Mead, Maryland, and the Leonard Wood camp at Rolla Missouri. For Fort Mead the department's estimates called for an expenditure of $10,000,000. Ultimately, it will cost $21,000,000. More than a million dollars of this increased cost was chargeable to the fact that the large hospital was not erected where the engineers, the contractors and most of the Army officials concerned with the cantonment believed it should have been and where it was originally intended to be placed. The intimation that it was placed where it now is in order to preserve an Army golf course, has not been sustained.

General Palmer, the Post Commander, accepted full responsibility for its location as well as for the entire camp which he said he knew more about than anyone else. The arrangements which he made were for the purpose of affording adequate training facilities which was the prime object for which the camp was built, although changes necessitated by reason of making water and sewer connections and other provisions greatly added to the cost. Officers on the ground did not advise War Department officials of many of these changes because it was said they were presumed to know of them and of the additional cost.

Labor troubles played a part in the increased costs at Fort Meade although elsewhere it has not been shown that they were particularly burdensome. At Fort Mead where 18,000 men were employed at the peak there was a turnover, amounting to 60 per cent. The Carpenters Union of Baltimore, although with a membership of less than 1,100, apparently dominated the labor situation for the contractors ran a closed shop. Many men were employed who were not carpenters and the union protested, but finally allowed a three days probation period to determine their fitness and to enable them to join the union whose membership fees were considered excessive. There was an intimation that in some cases after the fees had been paid the men were disqualified.

With respect to Fort Leonard Wood an extraordinary situation developed. The site for the training of the Seventh Corps Area was originally intended to be in Decatur County, Iowa. Before the present emergency arose authorization had been made by Congress for the acquisition of 40,000 acres of land. A survey was made to determine its water supply. It was reported to be adequate and a joint contract for the erection of the camp was signed with four comparatively small Iowa contractors with the War Department's approval of the combination. Six weeks after the contract was signed their organization comprised only 200 men. In the meantime an "assistant professor" in the Iowa State College who came in as a reserve officer "discovered" that the water supply would not be sufficient even with the estimated expenditure of $1,200,000 to empound the water of the Grand River in a reservoir and bring it in. The Department then moved the camp to Mark Twain Forest at Rolla, Missouri, where it was necessary to construct a railroad, at about three times its estimated cost, and to make extensive and costly highway improvements.

Because of the transfer of the camp and, as the contractors insisted, the failure of the Department to supply plans, the work was begun with only about 600 men. Subsequently, they employed 30,000 at their peak, and according to their statement, had no labor troubles whatever although they ran an open shop. They did have, however, a large amount of labor overtime which was costly, as was also the case at Fort Mead. The camp will cost approximately $35,000,000. The original estimated cost made by the Department was $15,000,000.

No other large camps have been under investigation by the committee thus far, but there are intimations that the cantonment at Fort Blanding, Florida, may be subjected to its quiz. It is said to be located on land which is largely swampy but capable of draining. It was one of six sites examined in the State.

The committee devoted a day to the effect of the coal strike on national defenses. It was shown that steel production was being slowed up by reason of the failure of the operators and the miners to reach an agreement. Its inquiry was concluded with an oratorical speech by John L. Lewis devoted largely to denunciation of the southern operators. On the following day a temporary truce was effected and the committee thereupon dropped its consideration of that subject.

It has been announced that investigation will be made into the machine tool situation, the matter of subcontracts and other factors which may have a bearing upon production of war materials.

Mr. Fulton, the Chief Counsel for the committee, who has interrogated most of the witnesses, has demonstrated a remarkable insight into cantonment construction conditions, and a careful study of contractual requirements which has resulted in the development of the information sought by the committee.

Contracts were made upon the cost-plus basis and while six per cent was allowable most of them were figured down to a much less amount, in one instance, at least, to 1.7 per cent.

Increased costs have been attributed to erroneous estimates, overtime, increased cost of material in some instances, unfavorable weather conditions and various changes of plans. All of these elements have contributed to delay, although on the whole the showing has been that substantial progress has been made.

On the part of the committee Senator Wallgren has been the principal inquisitor, although all members have at times taken part in the examinations.

SENATOR TRUMAN TO BRIGADIER GENERAL L. H. CAMPBELL, JR., ORDNANCE DEPARTMENT JUNE 18, 1941

Papers of Harry S. Truman, Senatorial and Vice-Presidential Files,
Harry S. Truman Library, Independence, Missouri.

Dear General Campbell:

I have been informed again that there is undoubtedly discrimination against Midwestern contractors in obtaining contracts from your Department. I have no special pet contractors or any one else I am anxious to see get jobs down there, but I do know there are construction men from the Rocky Mountains to the Mississippi River who are able and capable of doing some of this construction work for the War Department, and they are not getting fair treatment.

It has just come to my attention that an organization of several contractors and the General Tire and Rubber Company has been broken up simply because the contractors are not in good with the War Department, and by "in good" I mean they don't come from Detroit, New York, Boston, or Baltimore.

The policy of the War Department also seems to be to give all their engineering and architectural work to one or two firms. That is a perfectly asinine procedure. There are architects and engineers all over the United States who are perfectly capable of doing some of this work. I can specifically point out to you where it has been reported to me that a billion dollars' worth of work has been given to a firm in Detroit, and one in New York has been equally favored. I have no objection in seeing these gentlemen have a reasonable part of the architectural and engineering work but it not only doesn't help the standing of the War Department with the general public but it is absolutely contrary to the efforts of the National Defense Program to concentrate this work in the hands of a few people.

Sincerely yours,

Harry S. Truman

TRANSCRIPT OF C.B.S. RADIO PROGRAM, "THE CONGRESSIONAL MAILBAG" JULY 22, 1941

Appendix to the Congressional Record, 77th Congress, 1st Session, A3628–30.

Announcer. The Columbia Broadcasting System presents tonight the Congressional Mailbag in cooperation with the Committee of Americans. This is the third in a series of broadcasts brought to you from Washington by the Committee of Americans. Tonight we look at the mail of two members of the Special Senate Committee Investigating the National Defense Program, and of a member of the Senate Military Affairs Committee. What is the concensus of American opinion about the various aspects of national defense? Let's have a look at the contents of the Congressional Mailbag and see. Presiding over the letter opening will be Royce Powell, of the Committee of Americans.

Mr. Powell. This is Royce Powell in Washington about to open the Congressional Mailbag. Tonight the Committee of Americans presents two United States Senators, members of committees especially concerned with national defense. They obligingly have agreed to let us have a look at their mail from back home and hear their comments upon it. It is a pleasure to announce the following guest speakers: Senator Harry S. Truman, of Missouri, chairman of the Special Defense Committee; Hugh Fulton, chief counsel for the Special Defense Committee, who is pinch hitting tonight for Senator Mead, of New York, a committee member, who has been unavoidably detained; and Senator Styles Bridges, of New Hampshire, a member of the Senate Military Affairs Committee. In the order named, I am going to ask each of these gentlemen to give us the general contents of his mail from back home. Senator Truman, as chairman of the special committee, generally known as the Truman committee, you're from Missouri. So will you, therefore, lead off by showing us your mail and what it shows you?

Senator Truman. Yes, Mr. Powell, I'm from Missouri, both actually and in the sense that I have to be shown. In that sense, all of us concerned with national defense should be from Missouri. Each day the mail bags bring letters from all over the country to me and to my defense committee; we not only welcome these letters, we need them. It gives us a feel of the pulse of America. For instance, a worried mother writes to complain of conditions in her son's Army camp. Another is a penciled note from a man in Texas. He owns a small but well-equipped machine shop. He has tools needed for defense, and he knows how to use them, but he can't seem to get a Government contract. Priority regulations prevent him from getting materials to make every-day civilian things. He may have to close his shop. I get many, many letters like that one. Here's a telegram from my own State of Missouri. It reads in part, "there are thousands of small shops such as ours with idle equipment because we can't get defense work on the one hand nor material to make nondefense products on the other." In this connection, Mr. Powell, I would like to assure this Nation-wide audience that the whole question of defense contracts is a paramount consideration of the National Defense Committee. We are going to make sure that the defense contracts are so drawn and so executed that Mr. Taxpayer gets his money's worth.

Mr. Powell. I'm sure all we taxpayers are happy to hear that promise, Senator Truman, for we will soon get the tax bill. Thank you, Senator Truman. Before asking you for a further outline of your mail and your opinions on it, I would like to ask Mr. Fulton about what the postman drops on the desk of the Senator from New York. Mr. Fulton?

Mr. Fulton. Mr. Powell, during his 22 years in Congress Senator Mead has observed great changes in both the mood and volume of his mail. There was a time when he could personally attend to each item of correspondence. Not any more. Whereas mail used to arrive in pouches it now comes in carloads. For every one letter received before the war and before we launched our national-defense program, there are now hundreds of letters. Everybody seems to be Government-conscious. The cry is "Write your Senator!" And believe me they do. During one particular week his office was smothered with 20,000 letters and telegrams every day. To handle such bulk we need an electric gadget just for opening envelopes and two special clerks working at top speed. Even so Senator Mead cannot begin to acknowledge all of it. There are such extraordinary demands on his time these days that he can personally read only a few hundred a week. His assistants must read the rest and tell him their contents. Nevertheless, he warmly welcomes all this mail from home. By that, he means however, that he welcomes the honest, straightforward, and constructive type of mail because very often criticisms, suggestions, and ideas offered by constituents prove most helpful. Unfortunately though, he gets barrels of the other kind, too—letters obviously inspired by pressure groups, letters that are abusive or threatening or demanding.

Mr. Powell. Mr. Fulton, just what is Senator Mead's run-of-mine mail all about?

Mr. Fulton. Well, Mr. Powell, when you consider that the State of New York has more than 13,000,000 inhabitants representing just about every race, creed, and walk of life, you can well imagine that the contents of Senator Mead's mail runs the gamut of what people want, think about, and worry over. Flood control, droughts, the milk strike, defense contracts, jobs, taxes, airports, and harbors. Those are but a few of the subjects. And there are the more bizarre requests. Senator Mead has been asked to review poetry, to settle bets, to advise the lovelorn, to sign notes, and to lend money. One morning he even received a crate containing an ailing dejected-looking chicken. The owner wanted the Senator to diagnose the illness.

Mr. Powell. I presume that chicken had merely mislaid an egg. But seriously, Mr. Fulton, what about the mail dealing with defense?

Mr. Fulton. This mail Senator Mead feels to be the most important of all during this crucial hour for America. Senator Truman just a moment ago referred to these letters and he has mentioned how much the defense committee is concerned over them. I mean the letters from businessmen and manufacturers who can no longer get the raw materials to make the things they have all along been making . . . for the reason these raw materials are needed for tanks, bombers, helmets, and hand grenades.

Mr. Powell. I believe the congressional mailbag audience would like to hear about this in some detail, if you will. But first, if I may, I would like to call on Senator Styles Bridges, of New Hampshire, for a brief index of his daily mail. Will Mr. Fulton yield?

Mr. Fulton. Gladly, Mr. Powell.

Mr. Powell. Thank you, Mr. Fulton. Then, to hear next from Senator Bridges, of New Hampshire.

Senator Bridges. My experience has been identical with Senator Mead's. My mail from New Hampshire and New England simply pours in nowadays. To be sure the people back home are profoundly concerned with the violent events in Europe, but they are even more concerned with the huge defense effort here in America. And being hard-headed New England Yankees they want the facts about this defense job, and they want their facts undiluted. Furthermore, they want action, not excuses or promises. You'll have to admit that we have seen lots of promises made and broken, and lots of excuses offered as substitutes for efficiency.

My friends in New England aren't easily fooled, and if I do say so they are past masters at reading between the lines. For example, all sorts of optimistic reports have appeared in the papers and over the radio. One official says our tank program is well ahead of schedule. Another says the same thing about our airplane production. These announcements listen well, but they're too pat for comfort.

Mr. Powell. Thank you, Senator Bridges, for these introductory remarks which promise some very interesting listening a bit later. At the moment and for the benefit of many, perhaps like yourself, who are not fully acquainted with work of the Senate Defense Committee, I would like to call again on its chairman, Senator Truman. Senator, would you briefly sketch the character and work of this special committee?

Senator Truman. Well, Mr. Powell, we who are on the Special Defense Committee are assigned to the job of finding the logs that jam the flow on our vast river of national defense. When we find these logs we try to discover how they got there. And then we try to ascertain the best and quickest way to pry them loose and dig them out.

Mr. Powell. As a matter of fact, Senator, didn't this committee play a principal part in the settlement of the April coal strike?

Senator Truman. Well, Mr. Powell, it took the participation and cooperation of a lot of persons and agencies to effect that settlement. Our committee acted as a sort of clearing house of information where opinions were crystal-lized and issues threshed out in the open. Several hours following the close of a stormy public hearing, we received word from the White House that terms of agreement had been reached. So the answer to your question, Mr. Powell, is that the committee did not directly settle the strike. But it helped to get those miners back to their digging. And that's the important thing.

And right here, Mr. Powell, I would like to point out that the national-defense committee does not seek to substitute its judgment for that of other governmental departments or agencies of defense. They have their own jobs to do. However, we can and will and do ascertain the facts about what they are doing and why they are doing it. And we bring these facts to light and suggest that they consider changes or different courses of action whenever we think it necessary to the effective working of the defense program. We leave the determination up to them, but we want to be very certain that no stone is left unturned. And, Mr. Powell, every citizen in this great Nation during this great emergency has a stake in that. And furthermore, these defense contracts must be distributed in such a way that every person who can do his share, gets his share of the work. This defense job includes everybody, big and small, the plain, unvarnished people as well as the wealthy and influential.

Mr. Powell. Senator Truman, would it be possible to sum up in a single definition the character of this committee? That is, is it a dictatorial oligarchy of legislative punitive powers vested in a hierarchy of bureaucratic solons, or is it——

Senator Truman. Whoa, Mr. Powell.

Mr. Powell. Thanks for stopping me.

Senator Truman. Briefly put, you might say our committee is a benevolent policeman. We play no favorites, and we don't propose to whitewash the walls of any office. Ours is the painstaking labor of sifting the truth from the masses of evidence. We must be circumspect in our attitude and fair in our judgment. As important considerations present themselves we hold public hearings. Also from time to time the committee Senators make speeches explaining their findings from the Senate floor. Periodically, too, the committee submits re-ports to the Senate. For example, we did that in the case of aluminum. We heard all sides of that situation. And when we got through we realized that there was not only a serious shortage of that light, precious metal, but also that there was delay and lack of cooperation right down the line. Senator Mead spoke out sharply about aluminum from his Senate desk. And in our report we reemphasized the need for greater speed and better teamwork. We rapped some knuckles to be sure, but we tried to do it in a constructive way. We didn't take the easy course and blame the President. We want aluminum, not ex-cuses. The same goes for anything else that's not coming down the river of defense. The goods either will come down or we'll know the reason why. Mr. Powell, I'm from Missouri.

Mr. Powell. So is the whole country, Senator. And thank you very much. I would now like to ask Mr. Fulton if he would resume his earlier discussion of the problems facing business hit by priority rulings involving shut plants and unemployment.

Mr. Fulton. Yes; I was pointing out that some business, long engaged in peace industry, can no longer get raw material now going into implements of war. Fortunately some of these businessmen and manufacturers have been able to convert their machines and equipment. This makes them eligible for defense contracts and raw materials. Thus they can help make the helmets and hand grenades. However, many—all too many—seem unable or unequipped to do that. What happens then? Well, let's take a hypothetical case. Here is a small, peaceful, and prosperous community. The one large factory in this little town makes, let us say, garden implements. Many hundreds of the town's inhabitants work in that factory. Now along comes the defense program and priority regulations. The factory in the little town can no longer get all the steel needed to make garden implements. Rakes, trowels, and sprinklers aren't needed very much for defense.

At first gradually, and then in increasing numbers, men are laid off. Soon the factory shuts down altogether. Whole families of good Americans face a perilous future. And at a time, moreover, when their skills and determination are needed most.

Mr. Powell. I gather, Mr. Fulton, that Senator Mead's concern over this perplexing dilemma is occasioned in good measure by what he hears from home.

Mr. Fulton. Yes, indeed, Mr. Powell. He's getting letters in increasing numbers from people facing this tragic possibility. They all ask their Senator for a quick, fair solution. It isn't one easily arrived at. It will be reached; however, because America must finish this defense job and still stay in business when the war is over. For instance, we are locating the bottlenecks caused by defense demands, so they can be opened, thus holding the defense plan at express-train speed. We are studying how we can quickly put to work available tools and machines usable for defense. In other words, we want to see to it that this big job is so spread out that everyone can roll up his sleeves, spit on his hands, and pitch in. In that way our imagianary little town will be saved. The machinery and tools in the factory will be readjusted. Instead of rakes and trowels it will produce actuating pins for hand grenades and buckles for helmet straps. Gradually the workers will return to their jobs and life in our little community will go busily on.

With it all, Mr. Powell, Senator Mead's mail does include a chuckle now and then. The man with his chicken, and then there's always the ingenious scientist who secretly tells us about a mysterious, all-powerful, death-dealing device almost ready for sale. Yes; the mail bag is always full and he'll probably never get caught up with it. He's still glad to get it. It's part of the way of life we're striving so hard to maintain.

Mr. Powell. Thank you kindly, Mr. Fulton. And now to hear further from Senator Bridges, of New Hampshire, who indicated earlier in the program that his people back home were a bit skeptical about optimistic reports and head-lines on the defense program. How about it, Senator?

Senator Bridges. Yes; they are skeptical and there are reasons, despite the fact we seem to have a booming defense industry. To get an accurate, over-all picture, we must realize that for this year we are planning to produce only $17,000,000,000 of defense materials, or about one-fifth of our total income. At best this is a modest schedule. But we're even 20 to 30 percent behind on that. And remember Hitler turns more than 45 percent of German capacity to war use. Yet only last week our Under Secretary of War made the statement that—and I quote him—"I doubt that more than 15 percent of America's productive endeavor is devoted to defense work." There's your true situation and it's not one to write home about. But you can readily see why people write to me about it here in Washington. Here is a typical letter. I quote: "Why aren't we moving faster? Why are we still so far behind on all our effort, when a year has passed since we started on this major program? Billions have been spent, but with insufficient result. Senator Bridges, what is the answer to this—that's what we people here in New Hampshire want to know."

Mr. Powell. And Senator, what is the answer to that letter?

Senator Bridges. The answer, I am convinced, and I'm not injecting a partisan note here, lies in the lack of a single unifying agency responsible directly to the President, yet having full power to get this job done right. All too many Government units are now operating and often at cross purposes. If we don't adopt some intelligent way of pulling this whole thing together, America is heading for trouble. Let me refer to the situation on aluminum. I understand that when all the evidence placed before the Truman committee had been gathered, separated, and weighed they found that there was no one individual or agency upon whom the blame could be placed. All they knew was that there was a serious shortage with no one responsible for seeing to it that the shortage was made up. The same holds true of our machine-tool capacity. Fifty percent of such capacity is still idle this very day. That couldn't happen with responsible administration.

Mr. Powell. Senator Bridges, do you not find that your constituents feel that the national program is not a thing apart, but very much an integral element of their daily budget? That is to say, Senator, that the people back home, the taxpayer, if you please, wants to be reassured that his extra tax dollars are not being spent for those things which are not basically part of our defense program?

Senator Bridges. Yes, Mr. Powell; the mail I receive which does not directly deal with Government contracts for defense orders, reflects a genuine concern on the part of the average voter as to whether there is not room for economy even in a super super spending program.

Mr. Powell. You mean, Senator, to put it another way, that the rank and file of America has billions for defense business, but not one cent for monkey business.

Senator Bridges. Put it that way if you will, Mr. Powell, but in the words of those from whom I hear, America wants an accounting of its tax dollars.

Mr. Powell. I see, sir. And what do you think the Congress ought to do in this respect?

Senator Bridges. It is hard to say, with the new revenue bill not yet out of the House Ways and Means Committee, but I am convinced that the new revenue bill should directly call upon the executive branch of the Government to specify wherein cuts can be made in Federal expenditures to the benefit of both taxpayer and the defense program.

Mr. Powell. In other words, you feel the President himself should indicate to Congress how it can prune and where?

Senator Bridges. I do, indeed.

Mr. Powell. Well, if I'm not talking out of turn, those are exactly the sentiments of the large membership of the Committee of Americans. And, in fact, the membership of this committee, individually and collectively, has urged upon the House Ways and Means Committee that a resolution accompany the new three and a half billion dollar revenue bill calling for a restriction of spending on all items not directly contributing to national defense.

Senator Bridges. Mr. Powell, I hope you're right, and I don't think your group or anyone intelligently seeking a cut in nondefense spending is talking out of turn.

Mr. Powell. Thank you, Senator. What do people up your way consider as a typical nondefense expenditure?

Senator Bridges. No. 1 on the list of unnecessary things should be the proposed St. Lawrence waterway. This project would probably cost around $1,000,000,000. It would require from 6 to 8 years to complete. It would divert to a questionable project men and material vitally needed to build planes, ships, tanks and guns.

Mr. Powell. Aside from the vast cost of this project, do you feel, as a member of the Military Affairs Committee, that it might turn out to be a military liability instead of a military advantage?

Senator Bridges. I do feel it would be a liability. I have sat in committees and listened to the testimony of experts. I have talked with our military leaders, who have stated that if this country were invaded the best way for a foreign power to invade it would be down the St. Lawrence, splitting this country in two. In other words, if we should build the St. Lawrence waterway, we should be offering to any hostile invading power a paved highway to the heart of America.

Mr. Powell. Thank you very much Senator Bridges. We have a few minutes left and in this interval, I would like to recall the chairman of the Special Committee Investigating National Defense, Senator Harry Truman, of Missouri. Senator Truman, you said that your mail brought an inquiry from a mother who wondered whether her boy was comfortable at camp.

Senator Truman. Yes, Mr. Powell, I have received not one, but many such letters.

Mr. Powell. Fact is, Senator Truman, I understand that your committee has been conducting an extensive investigation into Army-camp construction and partly because of the pressure from back home. Just what do you and your defense committee hear from back home in this respect?

Senator Truman. I have been hearing plenty, Mr. Powell. I have received a surprising number of communications from persons who are shocked at some of the waste and negligence that they have seen. Also, I have personally inspected several of the camps and talked to the soldiers themselves. After all you can't expect an electrician, for example, who has been drafted at $21 a month to find pleasure in watching an Army camp building being completely wired three times. And you can't blame soldiers who were professional carpenters before the Army got them, for being indignant when they see a gang of highly paid novices standing around leaning on their ladders.

I do think that we all have to expect a certain amount of waste because of the tremendous emphasis on speed. But I for one have been amazed at the extent of this waste. In fact at the present time Senator Wallgren, of Washington, a member of our defense committee, and Charles P. Clark, the committee's associate chief counsel, are out on the West coast investigating the defense situation out there.

I attribute this waste largely to the lack of proper planning. The Army had 20 years to prepare for this emergency, and, like most other Americans, I had always thought that when M-day came around the Army would simply open its files, take out carefully prepared plans, and quickly provide the necessary construction along lines predetermined long ago.

Mr. Powell. But that wasn't the case, Senator Truman?

Senator Truman. No; the fact is that M-day or mobilization day came and they didn't even know it until several months later. And then it turned out that the plans available were all based on assumed facts. The assumed facts proved false, and hastily improvised plans had to be substituted.

Mr. Powell. If you please, Senator Truman, give us just one "for instance" to illustrate what you mean.

Senator Truman. Very well. For instance, one camp site was presumably chosen because it was in an area having an adequate supply of water. It developed subsequently, though, that the same site had to be abandoned because of the actual inadequacy of the water supply.

Mr. Powell. It certainly is no joking matter, but it would seem the situation you describe practically turned M-day into thirst day.

Senator Truman. I can't exactly subscribe to that, Mr. Powell. But it was just one of those things which you are bound to find in a democracy which overnight girds itself to meet dictatorship. We start slowly, but we finish fast.

Mr. Powell. I know you are perfectly right there, Senator.

Senator Truman. Moreover, Mr. Powell, I am glad to be able to say that the Army did get the camps constructed in time; that they were in fact very good camps; and that the soldiers, furthermore, are today well housed, well fed, and well taken care of.

Mr. Powell. Then your criticism, Senator Truman, is what?

Senator Truman. My criticism of camp construction is limited to criticism of the high cost, the waste, and the inefficiency. And you and I are going to have to pay for the cost, the waste, and the inefficiency in the form of increased taxation for years to come.

Mr. Powell. Senator Truman, the clock tells me I must forbear asking you and Senator Bridges and Mr. Fulton any further questions with respect to our national-defense program. But I see I have a few seconds to pay my grateful respects to you all. In this connection, and on behalf of Dean Emeritus Roscoe Pound, of Harvard, who is chairman of the Committee of Americans, I wish to thank you most appreciatively for your joint contribution of this third presentation of the Congressional Mailbag. Joining with me in this expression of gratitude are Prof. Edwin Kemmerer, of Princeton, and Berkley Thomas, who are respectively vice chairman and president of the Committee of Americans.

Senator Truman. Mr. Powell, if I may have a second, I wish to say that we on Capitol Hill who have followed these programs of the Committee of Americans, bringing the legislative branch closer to its constituents back home, are happy to have the opportunity offered.

Mr. Powell. Very kind of you, Senator Truman, and thank you, Senator Bridges and Mr. Fulton for your part in the development of this program, the Congressional Mailbag. This is Royce Powell saying good night.

Announcer. You have just heard from two United States Senators appearing on a presentation of the Committee of Americans entitled "The Congressional Mailbag." This program marked a third in a series of programs brought to you from Washington and featuring Members of both Houses of Congress who read from and comment on the mail they receive from back home. On tonight's program were Senator Styles Bridges, of New Hampshire, a member of the Senate Military Affairs Committee, and Senator Harry S. Truman, of Missouri, chairman of the Special Senate Committee Investigating the National Defense Program, and Hugh A. Fulton, who spoke in behalf of Senator Mead, of New York, a member of that committee. Royce Powell, acting for the Committee of Americans, presided over the opening of the Congressional Mailbag. For copies of this broadcast, write to Committee of Americans, 122 East Forty-second Street, New York City.

TRUMAN COMMITTEE STATEMENT OF POLICY DECEMBER 10, 1941

Congressional Record, 77th Congress, 1st Session, 9600–01.

Mr. Truman. Mr. President, I ask unanimous consent to make a brief report from the Special Committee to Investigate the national-defense program. The committee held an executive session this morning for the purpose of determining how the committee could best contribute to the defense of the Nation.

The committee never has investigated, and it still believes that it should not investigate, military and naval strategy or tactics. Such matters should be handled strictly by the Military and Naval Affairs Committees of the Congress.

From its inception the special committee has concerned itself with the nonmilitary aspects of the defense program—that is to say, with seeing to it that the defense articles which the Army and Navy have determined that they need are produced in a minimum of time at a minimum of cost and with as little disruption of the civilian economy as possible.

During the 8 months in which the special committee has operated, it has noted and called attention to many things which have adversely affected production, particularly the failure to increase the production of strategic materials soon enough and fast enough, and the failure to utilize in the defense program the existing facilities of the intermediate and small manufacturing establishments. By its action, the special committee believes that it has forced a greater attention to these problems; it believes that the various defense agencies are giving now more adequate attention to them; but it believes also that it is necessary to continue a constant watch for the purpose of assuring that such problems are met head-on and solved.

The special committee has no doubt of the ability of the United

States to win this war. It is simply a question of when and at what cost the war will be won, but that is a most important question. The committee is determined the war should not continue weeks or months longer because of the failure to get the production which we need as soon as possible. An unnecessary prolongation of war, caused by failure to produce as fast, efficiently, and economically as possible, would cause an unnecessary loss of life and property.

There were present at the meeting of the committee this morning 9 of the 10 members, and it was the unanimous opinion that what I have outlined should be the continuing policy of the committee.

SENATE DEBATE OVER TRUMAN COMMITTEE REPORT
JANUARY 15, 1942

Congressional Record, 77th Congress, 2nd Session, 380–91.

Mr. Truman. Mr. President, the special committee of 10 Members of the Senate, appointed pursuant to Senate Resolution 71 to make a full and complete study and investigation of the operation of the national defense program, herewith submits an interim report (Rept. No. 480, pt. 5) covering the matters which have been considered by it during the year 1941.

The Vice President. The report will be received and printed.

Mr. Truman. Mr. President, the committee has held public hearings, commencing April 14, 1941. To date, 252 witnesses have testified, some of them on a number of different occasions. The printed record of such testimony comprises more than 3,000 pages. The committee also privately considered a number of matters as to which the committee was unable to schedule public hearings.

The committee's principal purpose is to ascertain that the billions of dollars being allocated to the national defense program are being efficiently and economically expended so as to obtain a maximum of production with a minimum of expense and a minimum of dislocation to the civilian economy.

The committee believes that the war and defense program not only will produce sufficient supplies for the defense of the Nation, but that it will produce enough supplies to enable the United States to take the offensive and to win the war. We must take the offensive, because wars are not won on the defensive. The committee, however, wants the war to be won as soon as possible, and at a minimum expenditure of life and property. Carelessness and inefficiency have already cost us a great deal, and, if continued, may cost us much more, even though in the long run we shall win the war because of the sheer extent of our resources.

We are only just commencing to receive the benefits of the national defense program, and can confidently expect that each month will find us becoming stronger.

The committee, in the investigations which it has already conducted, has found numerous instances of gross inefficiency, and still more instances in which the private interests of those concerned have hindered and delayed the defense program. A considerable quantity of supplies and material which we should have today has not been produced, and as a result the war effort has been seriously handicapped.

Many of the inefficiencies and wastes which have been brought before the committee have been eliminated; still others have been partially corrected; but all too many others, the committee is sorry to say, continue. The committee believes that no constructive purpose would be served by investigations after the war for no other reason than assessing the blame. Numerous such investigations were conducted after World War I, as a result of which a great deal of valuable information was obtained as to how not to conduct a war; but little heed was paid thereto. For this reason the committee believes that a constant check should be made into the activities of the defense agencies during the actual course of the war when it is possible for the Congress to require remedial action to be taken before it is too late. The very fact that such a check is being made is of incalculable value. It restrains and modifies the more intemperate and unjustified requests of business or labor for special treatment to which they are not entitled. Public officials constantly have before them the knowledge that their acts or failures to act may be subjected to public scrutiny. This has already prevented the doing of many things which otherwise might have been done.

A defense and war program by its very nature requires a tremendous dislocation in the business economy of the Nation and in the relations between business and government. The Government in war must determine what is to be produced, the quantities and the materials to be used, and even the exact methods by which the articles are to be produced. In order to insure adequate supplies of war materials it is necessary for the Government to go even further and to determine the quantities and kinds of raw materials which should be produced, and the extent to which such materials can be used for civilian economy.

The civilian economy cannot be treated as a separate problem. There are certain minimum and basic needs of the civilian population which must be met in order to keep up morale and the ability to continue producing war materials in the quantities needed.

Moreover, government cannot neglect the fact that fundamentally the whole defense and war program was embarked upon for the purpose of preserving from Fascist aggressors the American way of living and that little will be gained if in winning the war we destroy the ability of the country to readjust itself and to resume the American way of living.

To do this we must preserve to as great an extent as possible a sound civilian economy. But the civilian population must be prepared to make sacrifices. Those of us behind the lines must remember that ships, guns, tanks, food, and clothing have to reach the fighting front, and reach it promptly. That fighting front is world-wide, and it will take an all-out effort to win the victory. We have been so in the habit of expecting the Federal Government to pick us up every time we fall downstairs that we shall find it difficult to become the stoics that it will be necessary to become in order to win this war. When we reach the point of expending 50 percent of our national income for war purposes everybody in the Nation will feel the pinch. We must relearn the fundamental lesson that the Government is to be supported, and supported with all we have, if we are to win; and win we must.

Under a war program the Government also has the responsibility for making long-range plans to cope with the emergencies which may arise, so that the shifts that are made necessary by the defense and war program may take place, to the end that plants and labor may be transferred from civilian work to defense work with a minumum of dislocation and unemployment.

Office of Production Management

The task of correlating and administering most of the defense and war production program has been entrusted to the Office of Production Management, which was especially created for that purpose. Its record has not been impressive; its mistakes of commission have been legion, and its mistakes of omission have been even greater. It has all too often done nothing when it should have realized that problems cannot be avoided by refusing to admit that they exist.

Apologists for the Office of Production Management have stressed the lack of authority on its part to require the other agencies of Government with whom it must deal to follow its decisions. There has been a very real effort to cooperate, even though such cooperation has required tremendous sacrifices on the part of tens of thousands of small businessmen. The public has wholeheartedly supported the defense program, and has considered no sacrifice to be too great, when all have been treated alike. The Office of Production Management, therefore, has had at its disposal at all times the most effective weapon which could be given to it, namely, the weapon of public opinion.

In those instances where it has failed the failure has not been due so much to the lack of power as to the ineptitude of the officials of the Office of Production Management and their unwillingness to use the weapon which they had. The usual procedure was to refrain from raising the issue and to avoid responsibility by claiming lack of authority, and, if possible, by referring the matter to some other agency of Government. Fundamentally the disappointing record of the Office of Production Management is not so much due to its lack of power as to its failure to perform the functions for which it was created.

The principal positions of the Office of Production Management were assigned to persons holding important positions with large companies who were willing and anxious to serve on a dollar per year, or without compensation—W. O. C.—basis. They usually did not sever their business connections, but, instead, obtained leave of absence. In many instances they continued to act for their companies, publicly announcing that their Government work was part-time work only. Their companies continued to pay their salaries. In some cases their compensation was even increased.

Although the contracts obtained by the companies loaning the services of dollar-a-year and without-compensation men are not passed upon by the men so loaned, such companies do obtain very substantial benefits from the practice. The dollar-a-year and without-compensation men so loaned spend a considerable portion of their time during office hours in familiarizing themselves with the defense program. They are, therefore, in a much better position than the ordinary man in the street to know what type of contracts the Government is about to let and how their companies may best proceed to obtain consideration. They also are in an excellent position to know what shortages are imminent and to advise their companies on how best to proceed, either to build up inventories against future shortages, or to apply for early consideration for priorities. They can even advise them as to how to phrase their requests for priorities. In addition, such men are frequently close personal friends and social intimates of the dollar-a-year and without-compensation men who do pass upon the contracts in which their companies are interested.

It is only natural that such men should believe that only companies of the size and type with which they were associated have the ability to perform defense contracts; that small and intermediate companies ought not to be given prime contracts; that the urgencies of the defense program are such that they have no time to consider small companies for defense contracts; that the large companies ought not to be required to subcontract items which they could profitably manufacture and as to which they express lack of confidence in the productive facilities of smaller concerns; that the procedure of strategic materials should not be expected or required to increase their capacities, even at Government expense, where that might result in excess capacity after the war and adversely affect their post-war profits; and that large companies should not be expected or required to convert their existing facilities into defense plants, where they prefer to use their plants to make the profits from their civilian business and, at the same time, to have additional plants directly or indirectly paid for by the Government, which they can operate profitably on terms dictated by themselves.

The committee has been trying for months to force a greater use of our existing facilities, of both large and small plants, and believes that a belated but serious effort has been made to make progress in this direction. The past cannot be undone, but it is vitally important that the same mistakes should not be repeated in the future. . . .

Aluminum

With respect to aluminum, the committee held hearings at which for the first time it was developed that we would be short more than 600,000,000 pounds of aluminum per year, and that this shortage exists despite a drastic civilian curtailment. Efforts since then to increase the aluminum capacity have been unsatisfactory.

The committee criticized, as taking undue advantage of the Government, the contract made between the Defense Plant Corporation and the Aluminum Co. of America. After the committee had made this criticism, Alcoa and the Defense Plant Corporation negotiated a supplemental agreement dated December 12, 1941, which corrected many but not all of the defects in the original contract.

The committee believes that its efforts have resulted in a substantial improvement of the contract.

More important, in the committee's opinion, is the realization by business interests seeking contracts of this kind that their acts may be subjected to investigation, and that they may be called upon to explain why they drive such hard bargains with the Government at a time when most people are making substantial sacrifices for the prosecution of the war.

Copper, Lead, and Zinc

The committee has examined into the situation with respect to the principal nonferrous metals, namely, copper, lead, and zinc. The actual production of the three metals—lead, copper, and zinc—has been most disappointing.

The committee concludes that the Office of Production Management failed to realize the necessity of increasing the production of copper, lead, and zinc until long after the probability of shortage was apparent, and that it did not then take, and has not yet taken, adequate steps to increase the production so as to assure (1) sufficient quantities for military use, and (2) as great a quantity as possible for the civilian economy. In the opinion of the committee, the Office of Production Management should have acted much more expeditiously in this matter, instead of taking the position that there could never be a shortage of materials, and that small businesses by the thousands would not have to close their doors and discharge their employees for lack of materials with which to operate. However, the least that the Government owed to such businessmen and their employees was an early and vigorous attempt to increase the production of the materials upon which they were dependent. This duty was not fulfilled.

Steel

With reference to steel, a sharply divergent view was evidenced within the Office of Production Management as to need for increasing existing steel capacity. Eventually, the Office of Production Management embarked on a program for increasing existing capacity by 10,000,000 tons per year.

The contract proposed by the Bethlehem Steel Corporation to the Defense Plant Corporation to obtain financing for steel expansion is outrageous.

I desire to urge the Members of the Senate to read this report. It will be in print in a day or two, and copies of it will be sent to the office of every Senator, together with the appendixes which go with it. I hope Senators will look at it and at least glance through it. It is a voluminous thing, but it covers the activities of the committee, and I think the suggestions made are at least constructive so far as the war effort is concerned.

Automobile Industry

Automobile companies have scarcely even begun to produce defense articles. Automobile companies were not required to utilize their existing plants for the defense program, but were permitted not only to continue but to increase their regular production of automobiles. Before the actual declaration of war the automobile industry took the position that their tooling facilities that could be used were about 10 percent of the gross total. Now, when it is impossible to make automobiles, they take the position that the plants can be converted in a relatively short time. The committee believes that the latter position was correct all the time.

Small Business

One of the problems that have given the committee the most concern is the plight of the small businessmen. They have been almost completely ignored in awarding defense contracts. Their existing facilities have not been utilized. They have been unable to obtain the necessary materials to continue in business because of priority restrictions, and they have been put in competition for labor with large contractors who operate with Government contracts.

Mr. Floyd Odlum, Director of the Division of Contract Distribution of the Office of Production Management, testified before the committee shortly after assuming his duties, and requested its forbearance until he had time to complete his staff. The time he stated would be required has almost elapsed, and the committee plans to hold hearings within the next few weeks to ascertain the progress made by the contract services of the War and Navy Departments, and by the Division of Contract Distribution of the Office of Production Management.

Tax Amortization

The committee has been engaged in a study of the methods by which the Army and Navy have allowed tax-amortization deductions to manufacturers who build new plant facilities for defense production.

The committee informed Mr. Odlum on October 27, 1941, that it thought his Division of Contract Distribution should take care to see to it that no necessity certificates should be issued to duplicate existing facilities that are not in use. Mr. Odlum assured the committee that this would be done.

During the committee's study it has become apparent that in many cases certifying authorities have approved applications for certificates of necessity without sufficient investigation. The committee feels that reviewing officials not only should be careful to consider the desirability and necessity of expansion of production capacity within an industry, but should examine the necessity of the construction of particular facilities in order to expand such capacity.

Labor

The committee believes that when labor matters affect the defense program, and when there is indication that the executive agencies have been unable to deal satisfactorily with the matter, the committee should afford such assistance as it can and develop the facts with respect to the labor question and attempt to ascertain whether there is any fair means of settling the dipute that has not been fully explored.

In connection with its investigation of the War Department's camp and cantonment construction program, the committee checked into the labor situation as it affected the construction of camps and cantonments, primarily practices with respect to the collection of permit fees. The committee's interest in this matter was to explore the income to the various locals as a result of work-permit fees, and the extent to which this affected the excessive labor turn-over found in camp construction. In many instances large amounts were collected. Union locals should be required to show what became of these large collections, and they should be made publicly to account therefor. No man should be required to pay a racketeer a fee for the privilege of working for the Government. . . .

Aviation Program

The committee for several months has been engaged in an inquiry into the adequacy of the aviation program and its administration. At the outbreak of the war our production of aircraft was such that the armed forces possessed only enough airplanes to furnish skeleton forces with equipment, a great deal of which was of inferior quality. We have not had a great quantity of planes in action, and many of the ships used were of types long considered to be obsolete.

We investigated every plane-manufacturing company in the country. The committee visited the plane factories in California and elsewhere on the west coast, the Martin plant near Baltimore, and the Wright engine plant at Buffalo, and went into the subject in some detail; so I think the committee is informed when it speaks.

Our services have merely purchased what the manufacturers had to offer, instead of planning to use available facilities to produce what they needed at maximum capacity. There is no planned and coordinated program for the production of aircraft.

All the aircraft manufacturers complained that they would no sooner get a plane in production than some man would come running down and change the specifications; and in one specific instance 165 planes were held up while some little piddling thing was done to a carbuertor, which ought to have been figured out in the first place.

Though it was created to organize and manage production facilities, including aircraft, the Office of Production Management has acted as a rubber stamp for the service agencies, allowing them to follow their own policies of procurement.

Many manufacturers and experienced groups, because of priorities or official indifference to their possibilities, are entirely idle, or are operating as technical schools, repair stations, parts manufacturers, experimental plants, and so forth, despite the fact that facilities of these companies are already existing and available.

There are in this country at least 20 or 25 little airplane companies that could make at least 1 or 2 airplanes a week, but that are not being utilized at all. The same policy is being followed as with contracts; the authorities are letting the big men get bigger, and putting the little fellows out of business. The mere fact that these companies exist is of no importance to the country unless they are actually producing military airplanes or parts therefor.

Plant Financing

One method of financing new-plant construction for the defense program is through the Defense Plant Corporation, a subsidiary of the Reconstruction Finance Corporation.

The Defense Plant Corporation has had an enormous task before it, and has been placed in a very bad bargaining position. It has been very difficult for the Defense Plant Corporation to protect the Government's interests, and at the same time to make certain that money is provided as quickly as possible for plant expansion which the Office of Production Management has found to be necessary. The committee is critical of some of the contracts that were entered into, but appreciates the difficulty involved, and believes that in spite of the circumstances under which it has had to work, the Defense Plant Corporation has made a valuable contribution to the defense program.

Lobbying

The spending of billions of dollars necessarily attracts those who seek to use influence or friendship to obtain contracts. Big business has had its lobbyists in the form of dollar-a-year and W.O.C. men. Small and intermediate businessmen have sought to obtain the same benefits by hiring those who they think have influence. In some cases the persons are hired to render legitimate services, and are paid so handsomely as to lead many to think that their employers must have expected to receive added benefits. In others, no legitimate services are rendered, and the payments that are made can be treated only as compensation for influence.

Sometimes those seeking contracts take the initiative, and employ persons, who they expect to use influence in their behalf. For obvious reasons, no contract is made between them, and in most instances there is no express conversation with respect to the use of influence. Those who seek to take unfair advantage of their Government are no more likely to say so, even to their intimates, than criminals are likely to admit their crimes or to characterize their acts. Consequently, they frequently pay for what is neither promised nor delivered to them. In many such cases they get only what they would have been entitled to had they not resorted to lobbying; but their actions in attempting to purchase influence weaken the public confidence in the integrity of Government officials, and cannot be too severely condemned.

A direct result thereof is the widespread belief, especially among small and intermediate businessmen, that Government officials can be "reached," which makes them credulous dupes of "peddlers of influence," who approach them furtively with stories of their close connections in Washington and promises of contracts if they are paid a commission, usually 5 or 10 percent of the contract price. In most instances the Washington connections are nonexistent, and the "peddlers of influence" are simply acting on the chance that the businessman in question could obtain a contract without help if he would make a serious and determined effort. In many instances, all the peddlers do is to disclose information as to contracts about to be negotiated, which they have gleaned from Government sources available to all. The practice is difficult to expose and eliminate, because the businessmen who are duped by it hate to admit that their avarice led them to attempt what they thought was bribery of Government procurement officers. In cases in which they obtain no contracts, they seldom have a way of proving the attempted extortion.

The committee suggests that when businessmen are approached by such peddlers the committee be informed, so that the exact facts with respect to such peddlers and their activities can be obtained, and appropriate action taken.

The committee believes that legislation to alleviate the evils inherent in lobbying should be carefully considered.

Navy Shipbuilding

As of September 1, 1940, the Navy had made arrangements for about $4,000,000,000 of shipbuilding, at a ratio of 70 percent in private yards and 30 percent in naval yards. The scope of the program has since been increased. Before the emergency the ratio had been about 50-50; but Admiral Robinson testified that it had not been possible to increase naval-yard capacity as much as that of the private shipyards. One of the principal reasons was that the navy yards were located many generations ago, and are mostly in congested areas where it is impossible, except at very high cost, to acquire more land.

Admiral Robinson stated that it was almost impossible to compare the costs of private with navy-yard shipbuilding because of the Navy's method of keeping its books. The committee believes that in a matter of this importance the Navy should take steps to ascertain the actual facts. The Navy should be able to build ships as efficiently as private enterprise is able to do so; and if there is a wide disparity between the cost of building ships in Navy yards and the prices charged for similar ships in private yards, the Navy should require a reduction of profit to a reasonable amount.

There is pending in the Committee on the Judiciary proposed legislation introduced by the Senator from New Mexico [Mr. Hatch], who is a member of our committee. The committee believes that legislation to alleviate the evil inherent in lobbying should be carefully considered. By the way, at this point I desire to say that the committee is not through with its lobby hearings as yet, and some of the prime lobbyists have not been before it.

The Navy was extremely liberal with private shipbuilders. Nine of the 13 companies which had cost-plus-fixed-fee contracts are entitled to receive fees plus possible bonuses which exceed the amount of their net worth on December 31, 1939, as estimated by them.

The fees plus possible bonuses bore no relation whatever to the average net profits of the companies during the period from 1936 to 1940. In one case they exceeded by nearly 800 times the average annual net profits, in other cases by 20, 30, and 40 times the average annual net profits.

The committee believes that these fees and bonuses are excessive, and that it should not have been necessary to give so huge a reward to the private shipbuilding companies. . . .

Camp Construction

In order to analyze the reasons for increased cost of camp facilities over that originally estimated, the committee made a study of the camp-construction progrram.

Various officials of the War Department have testified on general-construction procedure and policies, particularly with respect to nine camps which were subjected to special study. These were chosen not as an average group of camps, but because they most graphically present a picture of the factors to be avoided in future construction. All nine of these camps were erected on the cost-plus-fixed-fee contract method. Those cantonments which the War Department let upon lump-sum contracts were erected more cheaply and with less difficulties.

In the selection of sites, investigation disclosed that the War Department had given little or no attention to probable camp sites until after the Department decided to undertake the expansion of camp facilities and until after the bill to provide for camp construction was actually before the Congress. In its investigation of possible camp sites the War Department failed to utilize engineering and topographical data which could have been developed by the Corps of Engineers or obtained from other governmental agencies.

In the acquisition of land the War Department was found to have had no well-developed plan for leasing or purchasing camp sites. This caused considerable delay in acquiring the land and also delayed construction.

In the construction of the camps, speed was necessary in order that the housing could be ready for the troops as they were inducted into service.

In the nine camps investigated by the committee, the contracts were all of the cost-plus-a-fixed-fee type. After the contracts were awarded, the architect-engineers and contractors were required to make preliminary surveys and tentative lay-out plans before new work could be started. This required a delay of some weeks, and resulted in construction being delayed until the attendant difficulties of winter construction were encountered. It also contributed to the contractors paying time and a half and double time for overtime, and the employment of very large numbers of men who could not be used efficiently.

The architect-engineers and contractors were provided with little or no information as to the problems they faced until they had already arrived at the sites of the proposed camps. The architect-engineers had little knowledge of the tactical requirements, which resulted in considerable confusion when troops arrived at the camp.

In the selection of architect-engineers and contractors for cost-plus-a-fixed-fee contract, a contract advisory committee was formed by the Construction Division of the Quartermaster Corps, which was guided by information submitted by those firms desiring fixed-fee contracts.

The fees applicable to the contracts were determined by referring to a set of figures which has been prepared by the Construction Advisory Committee to the Army and Navy Munitions Board. This method of fixing fees completely deprived the Government of any possible competition between competitors for the contract, and no effort was made to determine the minimum amounts for which responsible firms could be induced to take the contracts.

In its original report on camp construction, released on August 14, 1941, the committee made the recommendation that authority should be granted to the Secretary of War to assign additional construction work to the Corps of Engineers. Air Corps construction had been so assigned previously.

The committee believed that this would enable the Quartermaster Corps to concentrate on the problems of obtaining supplies for the Army for which it was originally organized. Acting on the recommendations of the committee in this regard, a bill was introduced in the Congress which authorized the Secretary of War to direct the Chief of Engineers of the Army to assume direction of all construction. This bill was passed by the Congress and approved on December 1, 1941.

At the present time the transfer of officers and civilians in the Quartermaster Corps Construction Division is being carried out in accordance with the above-described legislation and the Corps of Engineers has assumed complete jurisdiction over all present and contemplated construction. The committee believes that this transfer of jurisdiction will bring about considerable improvement in the construction program and will make possible greater efficiency in the operation thereof.

The committee believes that the personnel of the Corps of Engineers will be better qualified to cope with problems involved in a construction program of such magnitude due to more specialized training of the officers of the corps and to the experience the engineers have had in construction work. There were many able men in the Construction Division of the Quartermaster Corps, but there were many others who should never have been assigned to the positions which they held. There was also too great a tendency to protect such persons when in the interests of efficiency they should have been weeded out.

I have mentioned, in a general way, some of the matters covered in the report which the Special Senate Defense Committee is submitting herewith. We believe that the very existence of the committee has led to greater efficiency and economy in the operation of the defense program.

Now that we are in war we believe that the committee can perform a very valuable function by attempting to assure that the necessary implements of war are produced speedily and efficiently and that each dollar expended for war purposes will produce a dollar's worth of the necessary war supplies. . . .

Mr. La Follette. I should like to say, if the Senator will permit me, that having had some little experience in the conduct of investigations in the past, I think it is nothing short of remarkable that with the comparatively small sums of money which the Senator's committee has had, and the consequent shortage in adequate staff, the committee has been able to accomplish what it has accomplished. Speaking for myself, I feel certain that the welfare of the country and the morale of the country make it imperative that the committee be given an adequate appropriation and that it have an adequate staff in order to be able to perform its work more speedily and more thoroughly and keep more nearly abreast of the developments of the war procurement programs, thereby rendering a great service to this body and to the country.

I hope the Senator will submit his resolution, and that on the basis of the present showing, which is really in the nature of a preliminary report of the committee, the Committee to Audit and Control the Contingent Expenses of the Senate will speedily give consideration to it, and that the Senate will act promptly.

Mr. Truman. I thank the Senator very sincerely.

Mr. President, I submit a resolution, which I ask to have referred to the Committee on Printing, providing that 3,000 copies of the report be printed for the use of the Senate.

The resolution (S. Res. 217) was referred to the Committee on Printing, as follows:

> *Resolved,* That 3,000 additional copies of Senate Report No. 480, part 5, current Congress, as submitted to the Senate pursuant to the resolution (S. Res. 71, 77th Cong.) directing an investigation of the national defense program, be printed for the use of the Special Committee to Investigate the National Defense Program.

Mr. Truman. I also submit a resolution asking for funds to continue the work of the committee, which I ask to have referred to the Committee to Audit and Control the Contingent Expenses of the Senate.

Let me say to the Senator from Wisconsin that the committee has had only $40,000 to expend over the past year. The committee was organized in March. We started to hold hearings on the 15th of April. We have had only four or five investigators, and only enough stenographers to take down what they brought in. We have only touched the edges. I hope the Senate will allow us sufficient funds so that we may continue adequately to perform the duty which the Senate has imposed upon us.

The resolution (S. Res. 218) was referred to the Committee to Audit and Control the Contingent Expenses of the Senate, as follows:

> *Resolved,* That the limit of expenditures under Senate Resolution 71, Seventy-seventh Congress, first session, relating to the investigation of the national defense program, agreed to on March 1, 1941, is hereby increased by $100,000.

Mr. Lee. Mr. President, will the Senator yield?

Mr. Truman. I yield.

Mr. Lee. I desire to add my word of approval and congratulation to the Senator's committee for the work it has done, and to assure the chairman of my enthusiastic support of his request for more funds with which to continue the investigation. I believe it much wiser that we now have an investigation to reveal the efforts at profiteering in this country in order that we can prevent them, rather than after the war have a hearing which will show what has happened after it is too late to do anything about it.

Mr. Truman. I thank the Senator.

Mr. Mead. Mr. President, will the Senator yield?

Mr. Truman. I yield the floor.

Mr. Mead. I wish to make a brief comment or two on the report which has been submitted to the Senate by the chairman of our committee. I desire to say to my colleagues in the Senate that the able chairman of the committee, the distinguished junior Senator from Missouri, has been conscientious and diligent in the discharge of his duties. He has worked tirelessly, and has made every effort to conform to the wishes of the Senate as set forth in the resolution creating our committee.

I desire to say to the Members of the Senate that, in reading the report, I hope they will bear in mind the province of our committee. It is not a committee to investigate monopoly; it is not directed at the labor organizations of the country; it is not specifically and primarily a committee to aid small business. We have had, and still have, committees whose specific tasks are the responsibilities I have just mentioned.

However, the defense program and its expeditious progress have been the responsibility of our committee, a responsibility capably discharged by the committee under the leadership of its distinguished chairman. I believe the record will prove that our work has resulted in economy of construction, dissemination of contracts to a marked degree, elimination of certain shortages, and the reduction of other shortages. In a word, Mr. President, it has speeded the program. Surely we are not satisfied with the speed, nor will we overlook the fault of those who in the past have been guilty of neglecting the program. But I may say that directives have been issued by both the Army and the Navy calling for the dissemination of contracts, and insisting that small business be given some consideration. A new defense contracts distribution service has been created by Executive order. It has more power than that possessed by the agency which preceded it, but, in the estimation of our committee, it does not have sufficient power.

I believe, Mr. President, that until Mr. Odlum's division is able to exercise authority to the extent of granting educational orders and making loans and grants for the conversion of idle plants, we shall not have an all-out, Nationwide mustering of industry in the defense program.

Therefore our committee, and, I am sure, the committee headed by the able junior Senator from Montana [Mr. Murray] will study the problem of dissemination of contracts, so that every small enterprise in the country will be able pridefully to take its position in the defense program.

In reading the report, Mr. President, it will be found that there is a statement that, as a result of strikes, a certain number of workdays have been lost to the defense program. However, as I said a moment ago, the committee is not a special committee created to investigate labor and labor organizations. One must remember that whatever happened, occurred in what is now known as the prewar period. But since Pearl Harbor all that has changed. We are united and labor and industry are going forward, arm in arm, doing their full share of the job.

There will probably be found in the record the statement that big business has been favored through fixed fees, liberal loans by the R. F. C., tax exemptions by the Congress, and the safeguarding of monopoly by those who are in responsible positions in emergency defense units. There will be charges that labor went on strike altogether too frequently. But we should have in mind the fact some of the strikes were caused by wages and working conditions so low and so contrary to the policy announced by Congress as to represent a disgrace in American industry.

When Senators read in the report a statement regarding the North-South coal controversy, I trust that they will remember that there was no justification for the conditions which existed in some of the coal fields of the country and also will remember that in the North-South coal fields South may be North and North may be South; the name is a misnomer, and it has no geographical justification.

In connection with the Currier case, mention of which will be found in the Record, it will be well to bear in mind that Currier has been a notorious labor baiter all his life, and that it was hard, difficult—perhaps impossible—for Mr. Hillman, of O. P. M., or Mr. Carmody, of F. W. A., to agree to approve or to sanction a contract with Mr. Currier at a time when he was in the courts in response to charges of violation of the wage and hour law and when he was known to be a violent objector to the policy enacted by Congress, as set forth in the National Labor Relations Act.

So, while we regret that there was even one strike, while we regret that any favoritism was shown to monopoly or big business, we must bear in mind the fact that the committee was not appointed for the purpose of investigating monopoly or wages but, rather, was created by the Senate to consider the defense program in its over-all picture and to do whatever it possibly could do to expedite the program. Having in mind the authority contained in the resolution creating the committee, I am sure the committee's report will be found to be of very great interest.

Mr. Ball. Mr. President, I shall not detain the Senate long, but I desire, as a member of the Truman committee, to express my appreciation for the fine job done by the chairman of the committee. I think he has been scrupulously fair to all members of the committee, to all witnesses, and to all agencies which have appeared before us.

Before the committee began its hearings we met and decided on a policy and approach to the investigation. We decided that we did not want to make it either a smear committee or a whitewash committee, and, while we would pull no punches in exposing shortcomings of the defense efforts wherever found, we would try always to combine our criticisms with constructive suggestions designed to improve the program. I believe that policy and approach have been followed out largely because of the hard work put in by the chairman of the committee, the Senator from Missouri [Mr. Truman], and by the fact that he has always considered the matter immediately before the committee in its true perspective, having in mind the immensity of the defense program.

In one consideration I would go a little further than the report filed today. The section on O. P. M. quite rightly criticizes the officials of O. P. M. for their many sins of omission and commission. They certainly failed, and failed miserably, to foresee the shortages of raw materials which are now plaguing us; and there are many things that they could have done which they did not do. I make no apology for them, but I believe that the most fundamental weakness, the greatest mistake in our defense effort, as revealed by the months of hearings held by the committee, was less the shortcoming of any individual than the inherent error in the set-up itself, in that no one agency or individual was given the authority to make decisions and to see that things were done that needed to be done. As an example, when they finally realized we were facing a shortage of aluminum, various projects for increasing production were kicked around from pillar to post, from the War Department to the Federal Power Commission, to the O. P. M., to the T. V. A., and back again, and nobody had the authority to cut through departmental differences and red tape and see that aluminum was produced.

The same condition has hampered the effective work of the contract-distribution division of the O. P. M., which was set up to see that a greater number of small plants participated in the defense program. The officials of that agency have worked out policies and procedures which they think will accomplish that end, but then they have to "sell" them to half a dozen other agencies, and when they finally get through, unless they can overcome the prejudice of the two services against dealing with small business, they get nowhere.

Therefore it has been perfectly obvious that what was needed was one "over-all" authority to make decisions, so that all the various disputes between departments and divisions and various agencies would not all have to go to the President's desk to be decided.

I think the report, to some degree, overemphasizes the failures of individuals in O. P. M. and does not sufficiently criticize the fundamental weakness in an administrative sense of the set-up itself.

So far as I am concerned, the best news I have read since the attack on Pearl Harbor was that in the newspapers on Wednesday morning announcing that the President was creating a War Production Board with Don Nelson as chairman, and that, according to the press release, Nelson's "decisions as to questions of procurement and production will be final." I hope the Executive order creating the Board will fully implement that statement.

I may add that of all the officials concerned in the defense program who have appeared before the committee I think Don Nelson has impressed many of us the most favorably. From the beginning he has realized what a tremendous program it was, and he has had the drive and the energy, and has fought for more authority to do the job. But the personality of the individual who is appointed chairman of that Board is far less important than that the chairman be given the authority and responsibility to do the job. Then if Don Nelson does not do it, there is no way the responsibility for failure can be dodged; and, in that event, we can soon get someone else who will do the job. . . .

Mr. Brewster. Mr. President, I desire to supplement what the Senator from Minnesota [Mr. Ball] has just said regarding the fine work of the Senator from Missouri [Mr. Truman], chairman of the committee investigating defense activities. It will stand, I feel, as a monument to his devotion to the very great responsibility placed upon him by the Senate at this time in the exercise of its investigatory function, which has usually followed a war, but in this instance is being carried on while the war itself is in progress.

The Senator has at no time been enticed by the idea that the function of the committee went beyond the scope of investigating primarily the domestic activities incident to defense. I believe this is of very great importance, because the responsibility of the President as the Commander in Chief and as the one charged with the conduct of foreign relations must be jealous of the undue intervention of Congress in the conduct of the war. History records what happened in the War between the States, so far as the North was concerned by reason of the activities of the committee called the Committee on the Conduct of the War that constantly harassed President Lincoln, summoning generals before it to determine the strategy of the campaign. Whether any Members of the Senate conceive an activity of that character to be appropriate, it certainly has not seemed the purpose of this committee of which the Senator from Missouri is the chairman, and I feel that in any continuation of the committee powers such a limitation may very well be recognized as the scope within which the committee will seek to function.

The committee and its agents cannot enter any contest for popularity. Over the doorway of the Truman committee, as it has sometimes been properly called, is inscribed the motto, "All hope abandon, ye who enter here," because it is constantly our necessity to ask agencies of the Government and outside interests concerned with contracts to give us information which they always conceive to be not a matter of our immediate concern. In all this conflict which necessarily arises with administrative agencies and with outside contractors, the chairman of the committee on the part of the Senate has never, in my observation, yielded one iota to influence of any character, however high. That, to my mind, is a tribute to the character of the work that he has tried to carry on. . . .

U. S. DISTRICT JUDGE LEWIS B. SCHWELLENBACH TO SENATOR TRUMAN JANUARY 23, 1942

Papers of Harry S. Truman, Senatorial and Vice-Presidential Files, Harry S. Truman Library, Independence, Missouri.

Dear Harry:

Harold McGrath sent me the mimeographed copy of your speech which I have studied carefully. I think it is splendid. I was particularly pleased with the fact that you used such simple and understandable language. I think you covered the field very well. I am glad that the War Department found you too feeble to command an artillery battery. You are worth more than half a dozen Generals in the conduct of the war. Last night I enjoyed reading the Congressional Record and noting the number of Senators who praised you and the committee, I am sure that each member of the committee feels proud of his connection with it.

Having said that, I wonder if you would permit me to make a few suggestions. I realize that I am far away and that there are many angles of your problems with which I am unfamiliar. On the other hand, I have studied your report carefully and I have the advantage of a far-away perspective without all of the confusion of the Washington, D.C., scene. I also have the advantage of a purely local reaction to your activities. Generally speaking, that reaction has been highly favorable. You are given the credit for having forced the acceptance by the President of the one-man control and the appointment of Donald Nelson. On the other hand, there is the criticism that your report was too general and that it pointed the finger of suspicion towards everyone without differentiating between those who had been derelict and those who had not. A comparison has been made between your report and the report of the Naval Affairs Committee of the House along this line. I am satisfied that such a comparison and criticism is entirely unfounded. It seems to me it is an expression, generally, of the same point of view as was evidenced on the Senate floor by a number of the Senators, particularly Senator Vandenburg. I refer to the questions asked by him and others as to when those to blame were to be brought to prosecution or as to what specific pieces of legislation are to grow out of your committee investigations. Such questions indicate a complete lack of understanding of the fundamental purposes of your committee. Of course, there has always existed the fiction that the justification for Senatorial investigations is legislation. Everybody knows that that is merely fiction and that, by and large, the investigatorial power of the Senate is exercised largely for the purpose of the investigation itself. I think you can well afford to openly acknowledge the purpose of your committee. Most other committees haven't dared to do this. They have been compelled to hide behind the fiction. Your committee has acquired such a standing that I think you can dare to do it. It seems to me that the results to be accomplished by taking an open stand justify you in doing it. Such a stand would completely eliminate the criticism of the report you have just filed.

You can't take time out now to insist upon individual prosecutions. Neither can you attempt to lay down broad policies for legislation. It is possible for you, from time to time, to make specific suggestions as to legislation. However, if you did attempt to draw up a legislative program, it would take you so long to get the legislation through and that effort would consume so much of your time that you'd have to neglect the investigatory work in the meantime. On the other hand, you run the risk of letting the attitude expressed by Senator Vandenburg and others be continued too far. What I am afraid of, Harry, is that, after a time, the Senators and the public are going to say: "The Truman Committee is fine but nothing ever comes of its work. We want somebody prosecuted or we want to pass a law about something." You can't afford to risk the possibility that your work will be discounted and negatived by that sort of an attitude. Senatorial investigating committees have to be particularly careful to keep building up a body of public sentiment in their favor at the same time as they are carrying on their work of investigation. I know this by experience on the Lobby Investigating Committee. We got along fine at first but because we neglected public attitude, the last half of the work that we did was completely nullified by the public sentiment which had been built up against us while we were too busily absorbed with our task to pay any attention to it. Having these facts in mind, I wonder if you would object if I make a few specific suggestions.

1. That you make perfectly clear that the sole purpose of your task is to

make sure that our conduct of the war is at all times subject to the "white light of piteous publicity." Make clear that you don't intend to become a prosecuting agency. That is someone else's job. Make clear that there isn't time in this emergency for your committee to be formulating the legislative program. If you make certain that everyone understands that your task is a preventive one rather than a curative one, you won't run the risk of losing the force which your investigation deserves. I know that Senator Vandenburg was perfectly sincere when he asked the questions about when and where the individuals were to be selected for prosecution. Unfortunately, however, the A. P. Dispatch gave that statement almost as much importance as your report itself. That was extremely unfortunate in the public mind. Both the Senate and the public have to understand what you are supposed to do.

2. I think you could strengthen your position upon the question of O.P.M., Dollar-a-Year and W.O.C. employees if you'd put it upon the question of responsibility. Everyone understands that a man is responsible to that organization from which he draws his pay. Naturally, if a corporation is paying him twenty-five or fifty thousand dollars a year and the Government is paying him nothing, he is going to recognize his responsibility towards that corporation. Prior to the declaration of war, it was perfectly all right for these men to be permitted to draw their salaries. Most of them were receiving much more than the ten or twelve thousand dollars a year the Government could pay them. Their living standards were such that they could not be expected to work for the amount the Government could pay. Once war was declared, however, the situation changed. The Government has an absolute right to ask every man possessing special training and ability to go into Government service at pay according to Government standards even though he has to sacrifice his own and his family's mode of living. It is inconceivable that justification can be made for these men continuing their allegiance and responsibility to private corporations now that we are at war. They should be compelled to work for the Government at a pay in conformity with Government standards. This is a problem which should be dealt with immediately. Unless it is solved within the next month or so, we will drift along throughout the entire war with no solution. That cannot be permitted to happen.

3. I think you'd strengthen your reports by a little more detail in the way of examples. I don't mean to pick out particular concerns and put them on the rack. I wouldn't make use of the most flagrant of the cases. I would, however, add to the strength of the report by giving a few more details. For example, you refer to the Bethlehem Steel Company and you say that its proposed contract was outrageous. Having gone that far, I think you should, in a brief paragraph, explain why it happens to be outrageous. You refer to the requirement of labor unions for the payment of initiation fees. It seems to me you could have strengthened that by giving a few of the facts concerning such requirements. In giving these examples, you must be careful not to be intemperate. One of the strong points in your report is the temperate tone in

which it is written. Temperateness, however, doesn't require the elimination of sharp facts used for illustrative purposes.

4. I think you'd find value, from time to time, in praising individual manufacturers or concerns who are doing a good job. The faults of one may ofttimes be as well illustrated by pointing out the merits of another as by the criticism of the faults themselves. For example, in the matter of the selfishness of most large manufacturers evidenced by their unwillingness to share the work with small manufacturers, the citation of a few exceptions would be extremely valuable. The one that comes to my mind is the York Safe and Lock Company at York, Pennsylvania. A brief recital of what Mr. Laucks did there would put the other manufacturers as much to shame as would the direct recital of their faults. Furthermore, the dropping of a word of praise here and there if the praise is deserved is the best evidence of fairness and lack of bias on the part of the committee.

5. I am wondering, now that you have your sixty thousand dollars, if you might consider the more elaborate task of setting up a rather complete record so that everyone would know at the end of the war just what your committee has done and would know that, in that record, there could be found a complete history of the war production during this period. The knowledge that such a record was being evolved would be of extreme value to you in your task as a preventive organization. In addition, it would mean that when you got through you'd have something of permanent value. There is nothing less valuable than several volumes of testimony before a senatorial committee. They have no continuity. They are not properly documented. Usually they just become a part of the archives. That, of course, can't be done at the conclusion of committees' tasks, it has to be built up as the work of the committee is going along in order that each one of the pieces of evidence may be documented and dovetailed into a complete picture. I should think that the money required for this portion of the work would be negligible.

Well, Harry, having given you all this gratuitous advice, I trust that you won't think that I have a too unlimited nerve. You know how anxious I am that you make a success of this job. Give my best regards to Mon and the rest of the boys.

Yours very Truly,

Lewis B. Schwellenbach

TESTIMONY OF DONALD M. NELSON, CHAIRMAN, WAR PRODUCTION BOARD, ON DOLLAR-A-YEAR MEN JANUARY 28, 1942

U.S. Senate, Investigation of the National Defense Program Hearings Before a Special Committee Investigating the National Defense Program, 77th Congress, 2nd Session, 4025–43.

Mr. Nelson. As you know, Congress —but successive statutes beginning in June 1940—expressly adopted the policy of authorizing employment of dollar-a-year men in times of national emergency. This policy was extended by Congress to all governmental departments and agencies concerned with defense. And, as you know, an identical policy was followed during the last war.

We have heard much comment on this policy recently on all sides. It was criticized in the report of this committee on January 15—and may I say here that I was gratified to note that after months of scrutiny of O. P. M. by your lawyers and investigators, you did not report a single specific case of impropriety? However, that does not eliminate all the grounds for criticism, so I want to discuss with you these questions:

Should the policy of Congress with respect to dollar-a-year men be changed?

If the policy is to be continued, how should it be administered?

I have one over-all standard for passing on these questions. It is quite simple, and it is as follows: What will contribute most toward winning the war in the shortest possible time? That is the test I apply, and I am confident it is the test your committee and Congress will also apply.

On this job we must get the maximum results from American industry. To do that we must have down here men who understand and can deal with industry's intricate structure and operation. In other words, we must have men with expert business and technical knowledge. For the most part we have to get them from industry itself. But no matter where we get them or how we get them we simply must have them in the places they are needed, when they are needed.

All things being equal, these men ought to be brought in to serve on a regular Government salary. I wish that were possible. It isn't. You can't get all the help you need of the kind you need on that basis. The reason is simple: most of these men, many of them specialists, have been getting salaries much higher than those which can be paid Government employees. Since they have been getting such salaries, they naturally have incurred extensive financial obligations over the years—mortgages, life insurance, income taxes which they have to pay this year, and so on—so that it is extremely hard for them to adjust themselves abruptly to a much lower income. In many cases it is literally true that the man in question simply can't make the change to a Government pay roll without extreme hardship to his family.

Furthermore, when we bring these men in for this war effort, we are not offering permanent careers to them. In the very nature of things we are offering them temporary jobs. So if we did not have any provision for dollar-a-year men, we should in every case be forced to ask these men to sever their old connections entirely to take temporary jobs at salaries which might not enable them to meet their fixed obligations. In practice, then, we would usually get from industry only older men who were independently wealthy and who could therefore afford to make the break, or those who have already retired. I do not think the Congress could approve the principle of such an arrangement, and I do not think the Congress would like to limit the War Production Board to the ranks of the very wealthy in the selection of personnel.

All these factors, I am sure, were in the minds of Congress which, in two wars, has provided for the employment of dollar-a-year men.

Now the dollar-a-year policy can of course be abused. It must be administered with great care and restraint. If it is so administered, it is in my judgment an extremely useful adjunct—possibly even an indispensable one—to the war program.

Sound administration, of course, requires a carefully determined administrative policy within the limits of congressional policy. With this in mind, I have laid down the following rules and limitations for the War Production Board to govern employment of dollar-a-year men:

1. No person shall be appointed on a dollar-a-year basis unless he is a man of outstanding business or technical ability, of unimpeachable integrity, and especially qualified for the work for which he is chosen.

2. No dollar-a-year man shall be appointed to any position if, with reasonable effort, a man equally qualified can be found and induced to come here to fill such position on a regular Government salary.

3. No person shall be employed in any position in which he will make decisions directly affecting the affairs of his own company.

4. No appointment shall be made except after a thorough investigation of the proposed appointee by one of the investigating agencies of the Government.

These are the rules which will be followed with respect to all future employment of dollar-a-year men by the War Production Board.

In addition, I have instructed the various directors of divisions within the War Production Board to reexamine all past appointments of dollar-a-year men to see whether they conform. If these requirements are not satisfied in the case of any dollar-a-year man now engaged by the War Production Board, he will be asked to leave.

I would like to spend a moment on a more specific discussion of the dollar-a-year men now with the War Production Board. There are some 300 of them. Every one came here at the request of the Government. Every one was carefully investigated by the Federal Bureau of Investigation or one of the other Federal investigatory services. Of the 225 appointed up to August 30, every one received the personal, signed approval of the President. On August

30, 1941, the President delegated this power of approval to the heads of the various departments and agencies concerned, including the Director General and the Associate Director General of the O. P. M. Since August 30, 73 appointments have been thus approved. The power of approval has now been delegated to me.

Of all of these men, substantially over 70 percent were operating men, plant superintendents, technical engineers, research experts, division managers, and the like, rather than heads of companies. These are the men who have actually run the production machinery within their own industries.

About 15 percent were heads of companies, and their skill as overall executives and their experience in large affairs have been very helpful to us. There are, in addition, a number of dollar-a-year men drawn from university faculties, some of the professions, and some from labor unions.

As a group, these men have worked hard and rendered valuable service. Those who have should be commended. Those who have not will be removed. But any member of our organization failing to deliver will be removed, whether he is here on a regular Government salary, a dollar-a-year basis, or under any other circumstances. In the last analysis, it is the integrity, capacity, and zeal of men which should govern their selection, and not the accident of their financial position and need.

In conclusion, I want to thank you for what I think this committee has done. It has rendered a very valuable public service. I am having the committee's recent report analyzed by members of my staff in order that any errors or abuses which I have occurred in the war effort may be corrected.

It is my hope, sir, that from time to time I may meet with this committee so that I may have the advantage of such counsel and advice as you gentlemen will be able to give us.

I thank you.

The Chairman. Mr. Nelson, this committee has been working for 7 months to get the responsibility for the war effort centered in one man, with the power to act. We are informed that you have that power.

Mr. Nelson. I am so informed, too, sir.

The Chairman. And this committee under no circumstances wants in any way to hamper your effort to win this war, for every day that is saved on the end of this war means the saving of lives and of millions of dollars. The lives, of course, are the important thing. Whether you are right or wrong, this committee is going to back you up in what you want to do.

Nevertheless, the committee, I think, has different views from those expressed in your statement, but as I say, the committee is not going to hamper you about the carrying out of your program.

I don't think that there should be any special class. I just received a letter this morning from a young man who is getting $25,000 a year. He is a Reserve officer. He is going to get $140 a month, and he can't draw his $25,000 while he is gone. He is satisfied to do that because he wants to win the war, just as you do and just as I do, by every means possible, no matter what it costs him, because if he doesn't win it, his $25,000 won't be worth a cent.

I am laboring, and have been, under the delusion, maybe, that if the Government has the power to take these young men away from their jobs and their outlook on life for the purpose of this emergency, the dollar-a-year men could face the same situation and face it adequately and would be glad to do it. However, if that is not the case, and their morale won't stand it—and you say it won't—we want to win the war. Therefore, we are not going to hamper you in that effort and in your manner of handling it.

We have fought to get you this job. We are going to fight to support you now in carrying it out. If you meet any obstacles in the carrying out of this job where this committee can turn the light of publicity on the subject or call attention to legislation that should be enacted to give you the necessary means to carry the job out, we want to be informed, and we are at your service.

Now, I am sure that some of these gentlemen will want to ask you some questions, and I hope that you will be willing to submit to that ordeal.

Mr. Nelson. I shall be glad to do that.

Before doing that, I want to tell you how much I appreciate that, Mr. Senator. I knew that was the attitude that your committee would take, and I want to assure you that anything we are doing at any time is open to your scrutiny, sir.

The Chairman. We appreciate that.

Mr. Nelson. We are on this job, working in a gold-fish bowl, just for one objective, and, sir, anything we do that we can give you information on, it is at your disposal. . . .

Senator Ball. Mr. Nelson, in the committee's criticism of these dollar-a-year men, I don't think any of us wanted to question the integrity of these men, but it would seem to me and, I believe, to most of us, that they kept an unconscious bias toward preserving as much as possible the status quo and of avoiding disruption of the present industrial set-up. I think you have been on the other side of that picture and have argued from the beginning that we had to make an all-out effort.

Mr. Nelson. That is right.

Senator Ball. And that business as usual was out the window. I am wondering just how many of these 300 dollar-a-year men are in key positions in your organization, where they would influence the broad policy and where this unconscious bias—and you can't blame them for having it—might play quite an important effect. Are most of your division heads, for instance, dollar-a-year men?

Mr. Nelson. Yes, sir; they are. Among my division heads, as you know, are Mr. William Batt, who I think has been on record for an all-out effort for some little time; and Mr. William Harrison, whom you perhaps don't know as well, a man in whom I have a great deal of confidence. He has been given the responsibility for and is literally going to town on this production job.

Mr. Knowlson—Jim Knowlson—came into our organization quite recently from Stewart-Warner; a man with a great record of production in Chicago, a man of unusual ability, in my opinion, who, I think, will certainly be interested in conversion 100 percent. He was in charge of the industrial branches where most of this conversion will take place, because he sees that it can be done. He ran a small factory himself, and a larger one. He was a small businessman before he was a large businessman; and I think he sees the problem quite clearly.

I believe, sir, that the men whom I have picked in most of the key jobs are men who believe, just as I do, that we must go out and do an all-out job in this whole picture. I should unqualifiedly say to you, sir, that the men I have picked as my first assistants are men who have exactly the same opinion about this job as you and I have.

Senator Ball. I take it you agree that that is the chief trouble with dollar-a-year men, that their whole way of life is dependent upon the economic system as it is now set up and that, consequently, unconsciously or otherwise, they kind of hate to——

Mr. Nelson (interposing). Mr. Senator, may I analyze that a little bit? There is a great deal of confusion in the mind of the public in their attitude toward dollar-a-year men. Isn't that really an attitude you are expressing toward businessmen rather than dollar-a-year men? And whether they were on salary or not, that would not necessarily change that particular bias of a lifelong experience. I think, sir, there is a difference in that picture. There are many businessmen, of course, who believe in the status quo. There are many labor men, many university professors; there are many from all walks of life. There are probably many Senators and Congressmen, and many of all types. I think that that is true.

Our job now is to try to pick the man who knows how to do that job and who will throw his whole heart and soul into it and, in a patriotic motive, do the job. Certainly it is my policy to see that there are no others around there except that type of man.

Senator Ball. Fine. One more question, Mr. Nelson.

Mr. Nelson. If, in the opinion of the committee, there are any obstructionists anywhere in this picture at any time I should be glad to have counsel or any member or Senator talk to me about it and should be glad to have it carefully reviewed.

Senator Ball. I think we have all felt that the failure to expand steel production and aluminum production as soon as it should have been done was due partly to that subconscious holdback.

Mr. Nelson. That was partly true. Of course, partly it was due to a lack of imagination on the part of all of us in seeing what the problem really was.

Senator Ball. And because they didn't have one man with authority to do it.

I remember that last summer you told us about your ideas as to how we could speed up production and force more subcontracting and, as I recall, you suggested two things: One, to revise existing contracts possibly to require, in certain cases where it was feasible, that a certain percentage of the work be sublet; and the other, arbitrarily to move up delivery schedules on them and force them to speed up, to work 24 hours a day, and to subcontract everything they could. Are you moving in that direction?

Mr. Nelson. I haven't changed my mind a particle on that, sir. Of course, we haven't had much time yet to go into that thoroughly, except that I know now that it is the attitude of the Army that that be done also, because we have got a tremendous procurement program to put through in this year and next.

Senator Ball. And what we will get chiefly in the next 6 months will be from existing contracts?

Mr. Nelson. That is right, sir.

Senator Ball. So, are you taking steps toward revising those contracts?

Mr. Nelson. Yes, sir; toward speeding them up; getting them on a 24-hour basis. I want this field organization to go more energetically than ever into subcontracting. A great deal has been done. I think Mr. Odlum and the field organization made a great contribution to that subcontracting. I view it as largely a local proposition, working out the subcontracting within that, and having regions communicate with each other and work out rather than having everything come back here and then go back out into the field.

Senator Ball. That is all, Mr. Chairman.

The Chairman. Senator Brewster?

Senator Brewster. I am very happy at your asking to appear. It is recognition that in some measure you represent the voice of America that is concerned. I read in the paper yesterday that one Senator said that he found the War Department with 350 of their men employed answering questions of committees. I was happy to find that was a year and a half ago, before our committee started.

I assume that your appearance recognizes that we do have a function to perform?

Mr. Nelson. I do, sir; very definitely.

Senator Brewster. We can't take all your time, and I don't think we ought to have more than one-tenth of 1 percent of it for the next year or two while we are winning this war. But we have to have liaison. This committee—and I think I speak for it—has had more difficulty with O. P. M. than with any of the others—War Department or Navy Department or any of them—in getting information and cooperation, and I take it your coming here shows that perhaps we are going to have a "new deal" in that regard.

Mr. Nelson. Sir, I want our organization to work closely with this committee.

Senator Brewster. You contemplate the designation of a man of considerable caliber as liaison?

Mr. Nelson. Yes, sir; definitely.

Senator Brewster. I think that is very important. The Army and Navy have both done that, and it has been extremely helpful. We can't constantly ask you, but if you have some man designated in your organization who can go to any branch of your organization and get the information we desire, rather than a mere clerical assistant, I think it would be helpful. And you do contemplate that step?

Mr. Nelson. I do, sir.

Senator Brewster. Now, about the dollar-a-year men. You also have men without compensation?

Mr. Nelson. Yes, sir.

Senator Brewster. What is the distinction, aside from the dollar?

Mr. Nelson. The distinction in my mind, sir, is this, and I don't know that it has been fully carried out. But it is my policy and will be fully carried out, that no man on the W. O. C. basis will be other than a consultant. He will not be given administrative or executive authority. He will be drawn in as a consultant. Many of these W. O. C. men are men who have been brought in by the Labor Division in panels in the various communities, as consultants on their training programs.

Senator Brewster. In many cases, part time?

Mr. Nelson. Just an hour or two a day, or 1 or 2 days a week.

Mr. O'Brian. There are over 400 of the W. O. C.'s, as we call them in the Labor Division. They are engaged only a day or two a week. They serve on these panels to aid in the training in industry. The Labor Division has about 44 dollar-a-year men in addition. The War Production Board, separating it from the Labor Division, has about 214 W. O. C. men who are usually in the nature of technicians or engineers or specialists.

Senator Ball. Do the dollar-a-year men work full time? Is that the idea?

Mr. O'Brian. Yes; as I understand it.

Mr. Nelson. And a man in an administrative and executive capacity in this picture must work full time.

Senator Brewster. What is the relation on the approval of contracts now under this new doctrine of infiltration?

Mr. Nelson. Of course, contracts are made by the Army and by the Navy—by the military services and the Maritime Commission. They have had approval through contract clearance in the office of O. P. M.

Senator Brewster. On anything over $500,000?

Mr. Nelson. On anything over $500,000. Now, in order to speed this up and not delay it, we are setting up methods by which that approval can go along concurrently, instead of consecutively. Consecutive approvals always slow up a thing, and my policy is to have concurrent approvals where necessary, rather than consecutive ones, because the consecutive one is quite apt to be merely a veto power. It is my experience that it always slows it up.

The contract approvals now are made by the War Department out in their own offices up to as much as $5,000,000, but those contracts come in and, after they are made, will be reviewed, and if we find they are bad, they will be renegotiated.

Senator Brewster. You do recognize that that presents a duality of executive function with two men sitting in, one your representative and the other the executive department, each of whom have coordinate authority?

Senator Brewster. How are you going to stop it?

Mr. Nelson. In this way, sir—and the War Department and the Navy are quite cooperative and see the necessity for taking in trained civilians who will actually do the work as their employees. The main thing——

Senator Brewster (interposing). As whose employees?

Mr. Nelson. As the War Department or Navy employees. I don't intend to set up, sir, any commissar system of dual authority or responsibility. I believe it to be bad.

Senator Brewster. You have seen Pearl Harbor.

Mr. Nelson. I have seen a lot of administration, too.

Senator Brewster. Well, I don't want to press this thing at all to an embarrassing point as I can understand it is a matter of some delicacy, but you have said that you understand you possess practically unlimited authority, subject only to the President, to run this production and procurement program. Is that right?

Mr. Nelson. That is right, sir.

Senator Brewster. That must mean that your men must, let us say, be responsible.

Mr. Nelson. No, sir; not at all. I do not think that at all. I mean the Army and the Navy men still are responsible. They can be held just as responsible for doing the job and for doing it under right policies, and so forth. They are responsible for doing a job. I am not considering, sir, that I have to have a group of men, all of whom take responsibility for everything that is done. Responsibility can be delegated, sir, and it is delegated. It is delegated by the President. It is delegated properly so. That doesn't mean, sir, at all that I would not consider it very bad administration if I felt that everything that was done had to be done either by one of my men or approved by one of my men.

Senator Brewster. Then do I understand that 6 months from today, if this thing isn't working, you are going to tell us that you can't be blamed?

Mr. Nelson. I do not, sir; no, sir.

Senator Brewster. I mean either you have got to be responsible or you are not.

Mr. Nelson. Sir, I have no alibis to make now or 6 months from now under the authorities which have been granted me by the President. If they fail, it is my failure solely and not because of any alibi I can give you, sir.

Senator Brewster. And you will be responsible for the elimination of anything savoring of friction as between your representatives and your department?

Mr. Nelson. Yes, sir; and there will not be friction, sir.

Senator Brewster. That is all we want to know.

Mr. Nelson. Because friction means delay. There will be differences of opinion——

Senator Brewster. Of course.

Mr. Nelson. As there will be between members of your committee.

Senator Brewster. But there will be decisions?

Mr. Nelson. But there will be decisions, sir.

Senator Brewster. Now, on the matter of placing the contracts, all the departments, as you know, now are under serious question on the matter of profits, the limitation of profits. Our various legislative committees are considering the possibility of legislation. To what extent do you consider it is practical in your program to have restrictions as to the profits on your contracts, as distinct from tax legislation which would reach whatever might be excess profits, if you would give an opinion on that?

Mr. Nelson. Yes, sir. I haven't thought this through carefully yet, of course, but I feel that no manufacturer is entitled to unconscionable profits on a war contract. I think a manufacturer, a workman—anybody connected with it—as long as we have the profit system in this country, is entitled to a fair profit for his labor or his management, and that it should be a fair profit. It is my opinion that where excessive profits occur in a contract, that contract ought to be renegotiated. That occurs at times, because we are dealing in new territories.

Senator Brewster. And with vast volume.

Mr. Nelson. Vast volume; vastly increased volume. And there is no one wise enough today to know what the cost will be when a plant gets working full on repeat business and when they learn how to make that economy. I hope that we will get an interchange of ideas as between manufacturers making an item, so that economies brought about in one plant can be brought about in another, and that we can get economy primarily of time, of course, but of cost, too. While I think the cost is secondary in this effort, and that time is primary, I think we should not waste money in getting the time element.

Senator Brewster. You said before our committee sometime ago that you felt America was ready to make any necessary sacrifice to win this war as long as they were each assured that the burden was equitably distributed.

Mr. Nelson. That is right, sir. I said they would as long as, first, they thought it was necessary and, second, if they thought it was being shared alike by all.

Senator Brewster. And you do consider it is a part of your responsibility in the tremendous powers given you, to achieve as far as possible those two goals?

Mr. Nelson. Yes, sir; I think they are fundamental in having morale in this country.

Senator Brewster. And it will be your endeavor to educate all agencies of procurement, business, and labor and everyone else to that philosophy?

Mr. Nelson. Yes, sir; because I believe that an absolute, fundamental conception of economy in a democratic system.

Senator Brewster. You do recognize, taking the two big fields in connection with your dollar-a-year men, two groups of industries, the monopoly groups and the competitive groups? When you have a dollar-a-year man from a monopoly group like aluminum, for instance—possibly automobiles, but aluminum—there has, of course, been the feeling, warranted or not, that their advice must be affected by the tremendous concern with which they are associated. Senator Ball raised the question about the matter of competitive solution of that problem. How are you going to liberate yourself from any possible bias of that character?

Mr. Nelson. Well, of course, you are pointing out one of the most difficult jobs of administration in my big job. That is a difficult job of administration, I will grant you. I think it can be eliminated, first, in the man you select for the job and, secondly, of course, in the type of supervision and policies that he works under and the care that is exercised in seeing to it that everybody who has an idea in the picture gets a fair and considered hearing on that idea.

Senator Brewster. Perhaps you would say that the problem would be solved if it is recognized?

Mr. Nelson. I think that is a very fair way of putting it, sir.

Senator Brewster. And you do recognize it?

Mr. Nelson. I recognize, sir, that in all of us there are biases.

Senator Brewster. Yes. In the competitive industries, in the highly competitive smaller industries, you have the peril of favoritism in allocation, and you recognize that also, that is, that a man who is carrying on a business and finds a dollar-a-year man in charge here, being paid a salary by a competitor, isn't going to be very happy about it. Is there any way by which you can reassure those fellows that they are going to get a fair break?

Mr. Nelson. You ask the mechanism by which they do it. I don't know at the moment. I can assure you that——

Senator Brewster (interposing). Again you recognize it?

Mr. Nelson. I recognize it, sir, but I would also like to point out that that would be equally true if that man severed his connection and worked on a Government salary. I don't believe that the difference between the dollar you pay him and the $8,000 which you can pay him under the regulations would change that bias if it is there, sir. I think that is the important difference that is in my mind about this.

Senator Brewster. You mean his bias as between concerns?

Mr. Nelson. Well——

The Chairman (interposing). Isn't it true, Mr. Nelson, that the probabilities are that the most biased ones will probably go home because they are more interested in the money than they are in the country? You recognize these problems and, when you go to solve them, the chances are that those fellows who feel that they can't under any circumstances sever their connections on account of the fact that they have to have that much money to live, will in all probability go home, and you won't be bothered with them. Then you can get somebody who can agree with your policy and carry this thing out.

Mr. Nelson. Mr. Senator, of course. I don't feel that those criteria necessarily apply. That is the difference, I think. I don't believe that the amount of money you pay or whether a man has severed his connection——

The Chairman (interposing). I was just remembering the statement that you made that these fellows had created for themselves a standard of living which they couldn't forgo for $8,000 a year.

Mr. Nelson. Well, sir, it isn't quite the standard of living which they don't forgo—it is a question of their obligations, the debts and other things they have, and their families could not live. True, you say they would do it if they went into the Army. Well, in the Army you take mostly younger men who haven't reached that stage where they have big income taxes to pay. When I say "big income taxes," there is no criticism of it. I believe that everybody should pay it and pay according to his ability, sir.

The Chairman. That is true, but you must also remember that many of these Army boys are on the other end of the string and are probably leaving a lot of debts which will be harassing them when they get back from this emergency. That is just the other point of view.

I am not going to argue this question with you, because I have certain views on it and you have certain views. We are behind you to win this war, and I say, whether you are right or wrong, we are going to get behind you and help you win it.

Mr. Nelson. I appreciate that attitude more than I can tell you. . . .

SENATOR TRUMAN TO JUDGE SCHWELLENBACH
APRIL 21, 1942

Papers of Harry S. Truman, Senatorial and Vice-Presidential Files,
Harry S. Truman Library, Independence, Missouri.

Dear Lew:

It was certainly a pleasure to get your good letter of the Ninth, and I have had so many things to do and so much work piled up on me I have not had a chance to answer it. . . .

I think you are entirely correct in saying that it is about time for us to get mad at the Japs instead of quarreling among ourselves. My Committee has had so much publicity in the last sixty days that its work is not nearly as efficient as it was before that time. We are in a situation where the slightest mistake will cause us serious difficulty. I have tried to conduct the program in such a way that the facts could speak for themselves.

Just the other day I refused an offer to make ten speeches for a fee of $4,000.00 and expenses. Of course Martin Dies has followed a program of that sort but I think when he does he sells the country down the river. No one cares about hearing me speak, and the Chairman of this Committee is not for sale.

The program is slowly and gradually approaching a serious and difficult bogdown. The Government has financed hundreds of plants for magnesium, aluminum, steel, rubber, and everything else that is necessary to win the war, and very shortly these plants are going to be in production. In the meantime truck tires are going to begin to give out. The ship-building program is not up to schedule and we are going to have all our docks loaded with materials, and freight cars are going to be standing by waiting to be unloaded, and I fear a very serious situation will develop unless we can get it untangled. Synthetic rubber of course is the answer, but it is going to take almost a year and a half before we can even begin to produce it in any quantity unless by some miracle the plants are completed far ahead of schedule, and it is going to be an experimental program even then and will probably take trial after trial to obtain an efficient result.

On top of that situation which is staring the Committee in the face and one which we must take some action, we have the political campaign coming on, and with the Republican Committee endorsing the war program the campaign will be made of course on the efficiency of the conduct of that program. So unless the Democrats whole-heartedly endorse what my Comitee is trying to do I fear very much I will become a political issue, and then the fat will be in the fire sure enough, but I am going to keep on trying to get efficiency. I don't see how any one can quarrel over a program to obtain efficiency.

Sincerely yours,

Harry S. Truman

TRUMAN COMMITTEE REPORT ON SENATOR ALBERT B. CHANDLER'S SWIMMING POOL JULY 16, 1942

U.S. Senate, 77th Congress, 2nd Session, Report 480, Part 10, 1–5.

On July 1, 1942, Senator Albert B. Chandler, of Kentucky, informed Senator Truman, the chairman of this committee, that an issue was being raised in Kentucky concerning his swimming pool and requested an immediate investigation into certain charges concerning himself made by a Mr. John Young Brown, his opponent in the forthcoming United States senatorial primary election in Kentucky. Thereafter Senator Truman received a written communication from Mr. Brown, stating he was in a position to furnish information which would convince the committee of the truth of the following accusations against Senator Chandler and Mr. Collings:

1. That Senator Chandler had used his office as United States Senator to assist a Mr. Ben H. Collings, a Louisville contractor, in obtaining prime war contracts as well as subcontracts.

2. That as consideration for such assistance, Senator Chandler was the beneficiary of a $10,000 swimming pool constructed at his home in Versailles, Ky., by Mr. Collings.

3. That in the construction of this pool Mr. Collings had violated certain priority regulations in that steel and brass went into the construction without a priority rating being obtained.

4. That the construction of this pool violated War Production Board Order L-41, which order prohibits certain new construction after April 9, 1942.

Pursuant to these requests and because of the grave nature of Mr. Brown's accusations, in that they pertained to the letting and prices of defense contracts which are within the jurisdiction of the committee, the chairman of this committee on July 7 sent an investigator to Kentucky to ascertain the facts and report them to the committee.

Mr. Brown, in addition to the allegations above set out, charged orally that irregularities had occurred in the awarding of a contract to one of Mr. Collings' firms for the supplying of ready-mixed concrete for a powder plant constructed for the Government by the E. I. du Pont de Nemours Co., prime contractors at Charlestown, Ind., in 1940. Mr. Brown alleged that the Colonial Co. was awarded a contract for 209,000 cubic yards of ready-mixed concrete by the du Pont Co. despite the fact that Colonial was high bidder. He also charged that the price of $8.30 per cubic yard alleged by him to have been paid to Colonial was exorbitant, in view of the fact that on a similar project for the construction of a powder bag plant, also located in Charlestown, the Central Ready Mixed Concrete Co., of Milwaukee, Wis., was awarded a contract for 75,000 cubic yards at a bid price of $6.17 per cubic yard. This company, according to Mr. Brown, was the low bidder on the Charlestown powder plant but its bid as well as that of another vendor, the American Builders Supply Co. of Louisville, Ky., was ignored in favor of the Colonial Co.

Mr. Brown was asked if he would furnish the committee an affidavit setting forth the charges he had made both written and oral. Mr. Brown declined, giving as his reason the fact that he had no proof to support his charges and that they were based completely on hearsay.

Mr. Brown, the complainant, and Mr. Collings, one of the owners of the Colonial Supply Co., as well as other parties in interest, were interviewed in Kentucky. Records of the Colonial Supply Co., the Andrews-Collings Asphalt Co., the Louisville Sand & Gravel Co., and the Charles E. Cannell Co., in all of which companies Mr. Collings has a financial interest, were examined.

Mr. Collings categorically denied Mr. Brown's charges. He stated that on no occasion had Senator Chandler, either gratuitously or otherwise, interceded in his behalf, directly or indirectly, to obtain any contracts involving Government work for any of the companies in which he had a financial interest, and that he had never approached Senator Chandler, directly or indirectly, to solicit his assistance in obtaining such contracts.

Mr. Collings stated that he had been an intimate personal friend of Senator Chandler and his family for many years and that the swimming pool constructed for Senator Chandler's family was a gift which grew out of this friendship.

Mr. Collings stated that the total cost of the pool was less than $3,500. Mr. Collings contended that the charges of Mr. Brown that Mr. Collings had violated War Production Board orders relating to priorities and new construction were entirely without foundation and were moreover made for political purposes in order to embarrass Senator Chandler, who, according to Mr. Collings, had nothing to do with the construction of the pool. As noted before, Mr. Brown was unwilling to make any affidavit with respect to them. The committee has referred this portion of the charges to the War Production Board, because they involve the interpretation and application of the War Production Board's orders. The War Production Board has advised the committee that it is conducting an investigation on this point and will shortly reach its conclusions.

Records of the Colonial Supply Co., the Andrews-Collings Asphalt Co., the Louisville Sand & Gravel Co., and the Charles E. Cannell Co., in all of which companies Mr. Collings has a financial interest, were examined. This examination disclosed that the Andrews-Collings Co. received one contract in April 1941 from the Procurement Division of the United States Treasury Department for the delivery of approximately 12,000 cubic yards of concrete to a Work Projects Administration project at Fort Knox, Ky. The Andrews-Collings Co. was the low bidder on this contract.

The Louisville Sand & Gravel Co. received numerous Government orders from the Treasury Department, in each case on written bids submitted in connection with formal invitations. The largest of these contracts was for 120 tons of sand in July 1941, amounting to $258.

The C. E. Cannell Co. was awarded a drainage contract approximating $300,000, in connection with the construction of the War Aid Depot in Louisville. This contract was likewise awarded on a competitive bid basis with the C. E. Cannell Co. being the lowest bidder.

The records of the Colonial Supply Co. disclosed that up to the year 1941 the company did an annual business ranging between $1,500,000 and $2,000,000. In that year the company concentrated on supplying materials, principally mixed concrete and steel, directly to the Government and to prime contractors engaged by the Government in the performance of war work. During 1941 the company business approximated $3,200,000. For the 4 months ending March 31, 1942, the net sales of the company, largely in connection with war work, totaled $832,607.

The only negotiated contract received by this company since the inception of the defense program provided for the furnishing of ready-mixed concrete to the United States area engineer at Fort Knox, Ky. This contract presently in force calls for the delivery of approximately 1,000 cubic yards of ready-mixed concrete at an estimated cost of from $6,000 to $8,280. Regarding this contract, evidence shows that quotations were requested from three suppliers and that the Colonial Supply Co. was the lowest of the three.

In addition to direct sales to the Government, the Colonial Supply Co. received orders from various prime contractors performing war work. One such contractor from whom orders were received was the E. I. du Pont de Nemours Co., engaged in constructing a powder plant at Charlestown, Ind.

Mr. Brown charged publicly that the Colonial Co. was not entitled to these orders from du Pont inasmuch as two bidders were lower. He further charged that Colonial received the contract through the intercession of Senator Chandler.

The records show that in August 1940, invitations were issued and bids were received by the du Pont Co. for an estimated 30,000 cubic yards of ready-mixed concrete. The lowest bidder was the Central Ready Mixed Concrete Co. of Milwaukee, Wis. The next lowest bidder was the Colonial Supply Co. Central's bid, although lower, was rejected by du Pont because it did not conform with the specifications which required the furnishing of electrical power. This rejection was upheld by the War Department.

Following this rejection of the low bid, the du Pont Co., after making an inspection of Colonial's plant, equipment, and organization immediately available and after investigating its financial structure, issued a purchase order to this company for approximately 30,000 cubic yards of concrete at $8.35 per yard. The volume of orders later increased and commensurate with this increase in May 1941 Colonial reduced its price to $7.65 per cubic yard. On January 15, 1942, a further reduction was made to $7.35 per cubic yard. A total of approximately 210,000 cubic yards has been delivered to the project by the Colonial Co. since September 3, 1940.

The president of the Central Ready Mixed Concrete Co., Mr. James Kolinski, stated in a letter dated July 6, 1942, to Mr. Collings that—

> 15 minutes ago, a Mr. Brown, of Lexington, called me stating he was investigating the du Pont contract at Charlestown in 1940. I told him I did not know what you got, only heard that my bid was irregular because of an electric power stipulation. I mentioned that

stipulations in bids are common and can have bids regarded as irregular.

It was also alleged by Mr. Brown that the Central Ready Mixed Concrete Co. furnished 75,000 cubic yards of concrete to the prime contractors on the bag-loading plant at Charlestown, Ind., at a price of $6.17 per cubic yard as compared with a price of $8.30 paid to Colonial for concrete furnished the powder plant, although both projects were in close proximity.

With respect to this allegation, evidence shows that bids were invited by the prime contractors on the bag-loading plant for an estimated 127,000 yards. The low bidder was the Central Co. which quoted a price of $6.19 per cubic yard. Several factors contributed to the variance in prices at the two plants. In the case of the powder plant, the estimated requirement was 30,000 yards as compared with the original estimated requirement for the bag-loading plant of 127,000 yards. It is usual that a great volume results in a lower price.

According to Mr. Collings, the powder plant job was begun at the beginning of the winter season and he included in his costs additional expenses which would be incurred in heating the concrete to be furnished. Mr. Collings said that the bag-loading job, on the other hand, got under way at the beginning of the summer under more favorable weather conditions and such additional expense was not included in prices bid by the Central Co. Furthermore, at the time the powder-plant construction was begun, Mr. Collings said that he took into consideration that no access roads had been built, which increased the hauling cost and the depreciation of equipment, and these factors affected his estimates. The bag-loading plant construction was not begun until about 1 year later, at which time adequate access roads had been built.

Mr. James Kolinski, president of the Central Co., stated to the committee's investigator that he was familiar with the operations of both projects at Charlestown. He recalled that the powder plant was a much more difficult and costly operation than the bag plant. In his opinion, the prices quoted by the Colonial Supply Co. were fair and reasonable; the price for which he contracted with the prime contractor on the bag-loading plant was too low; and the operation warranted a minimum price of $6.79 per yard.

Upon completion of his work at the bag-loading plant, Mr. Kolinski entered a new contract at the Lone Star shell-loading plant at Texarkana, Tex., which presented similar problems to those encountered at the powder plant in Charlestown. On this project on an estimated requirement of 202,000 yards Mr. Kolinski was the successful bidder at a price of $8.46½ per cubic yard. This price should be compared with the price of $8.35 a yard paid to the Colonial Co. for an initially estimated 25,000 yards at Charlestown later reduced by Mr. Collings to $7.35 per yard when a larger volume was obtained.

Mr. Kolinski stated he was completely satisfied that the sole reason for the rejection of the bid submitted by him in behalf of his company was a stipulation in the bid which made it irregular.

The E. I. du Pont de Nemours Co. has informed the committee that Senator Chandler never contacted it with respect to the Charlestown, Ind., powder plant or Mr. Collings and his companies.

The War Department and the Navy Department have informed the committee that they have no knowledge of intercession or attempted intecession by Senator Chandler in behalf of Mr. Collings or his companies.

The committee has found no evidence and Mr. Brown has supplied no evidence in any way indicating that Senator Chandler interceded with anyone to assist Mr. Collings or his companies to obtain any contracts.

All matters affecting elections should properly be referred to the duly constituted committees of the Senate, such as the Committee on Campaign Expenditures or the Committee on Privileges and Elections. The jurisdiction of this committee is limited to matters involving the war effort.

SENATOR TRUMAN TO JUDGE SCHWELLENBACH JULY 29, 1942

Papers of Harry S. Truman, Senatorial and Vice-Presidential Files, Harry S. Truman Library, Independence, Missouri.

Dear Lew:

I envy those three members of the Special Committee their visit with you. I wanted to come very badly, but the situation in Missouri and the steel situation here in Washington kept me on the job.

Senator Hatch, I think, is probably doing too much, but you know how these Senators are. It is hard to keep them from working when the country is in an emergency such as it is now, and Hatch's judgment is certainly needed at this time.

You are very kind to say that the Committee is doing a good job. We are in a much more delicate position now, so far as the reputation of the Committee is concerned, than we were when I was lucky enough to be able to pay you a visit last year. We have created a feeling of confidence, both in the Senate and with the public, that we must make every effort to maintain. One bad tactical error, political or otherwise, can ruin the whole structure much more easily now than it could have done when we were first starting.

I am always glad to have your views on any subject, and I will be particularly pleased if you will frankly tell me what your reaction, and the general reaction as you get it, is to the things which we are trying to do as a Committee.

The steel situation is much worse than the aluminum or copper or lead. We have been sending tremendous quantities, of course, to Russia for their plane program, and we have had immense amounts of that cargo steel buried at the bottom of the Atlantic. That actually is the main reason for our domestic shortage right at this time. The fundamental reason is, however, that the steel people used the same tactics to maintain control as the aluminum and copper people did.

United States Steel and Bethlehem and the group known as Little Steel were very reluctant to do any expanding, and they are extremely anxious not to open any new ore beds for the reason that they fear competition when the war is over. The aluminum people were very frank on that score, as were the big three who control copper.

We must take some action on this situation, but you can see that from the standpoint of unity and whole-hearted support of the Commander-in-Chief, a blow-up in steel at this time might be extremely bad for the war effort. Yet I can't sit idly by and let the country lose the war because of a lack of facilities for making steel when we have all the necessary raw materials with which to produce it. . . .

Sincerely yours,

Harry S. Truman

"WE CAN LOSE THE WAR IN WASHINGTON" BY SENATOR TRUMAN NOVEMBER 1942

American Magazine (November 1942).

We are in danger of losing this war in Washington.

We are in danger of losing it because of red tape and bureaucratic waste, because of conflicts between military and civilian agencies, because of overlapping jurisdictions and the failure to delegate authority.

A mere shake-up in the production high command will not remedy the situation. Beheading certain generals and admirals offers no solution. In too many instances, after such an official execution, the same old faces turn up again in other positions of authority. Nor will the creation of a super-gigantic war agency to "co-ordinate" the work of all the existing boards and bureaus provide the answer.

What we must have is unity of leadership on the home front, just as we must have unity of leadership at the battle front. That leadership can be achieved only if there is a clear delegation of authority to a single man to run the show and produce the weapons to beat the Axis.

Chaotic conditions in war production are by no means a thing for which the administration or the men in charge are alone to blame. Leadership implies "followship." And up to now we, who have been free in finding fault, have shown ourselves poor followers. If we wish to correct the situation, the power lies with us.

As chairman of the special Senate committee investigating the national defense program, I have listened to witness after witness testify to the manner in which ambition, personal conniving, and business-as-usual have been permitted to spike the guns of national security. From their stories I have pieced together an alarming picture of the threatened breakdown of our war effort here at home.

The examples which I shall give are offered in no spirit of carping criticism. They are offered in the hope that an enlightened public will force the adoption of drastic measures to save us from disaster.

We are in danger of losing this war on the home front because authority over vital sectors of the battle has been parceled out into too many hands.

When our committee tried to find out what was being done to solve the rubber shortage, we had to go to no less than *seven* separate government agencies—the War Production Board, the Reconstruction Finance Corporation, the Office of Petroleum Co-ordinator, the Office of Defense Transportation, the Price Administrator, the Board of Economic Warfare, and the Department of Agriculture.

We are in danger of losing this war on the home front because the various military and civilian boards and bureaus have failed to work together.

As I write, thousands of pounds of virgin copper are piled to the rafters inside a certain naval warehouse, awaiting future use in ships. A near-by factory is threatened with imminent shutdown on a vital army contract—for want of the selfsame metal. Yet the Navy refuses to loosen up with any of its hoard.

Again, a motortruck producer notified the Army early this spring that he would be unable to obtain engines until October. Nevertheless, the War Department told him to keep on stockpiling parts and building motorless chassis—thereby tying up materials and equipment which the Navy urgently required to complete its small-boat construction program.

We are in danger of losing this war on the home front for lack of adequate planning.

Consider the case of vanadium, one of the rarer metals used in alloy steel. Early in 1942 the Army–Navy Munitions Board forecast our military consumption of this strategic metal for the year as between 50 and 60 million pounds. However, 50,000,000 pounds happens to be just about 10 times the entire annual output of vanadium for all the countries of the world.

In this lack of planning, the civilian war agencies have been just as negligent as the military.

The old Office of Production Management considered it had done its job when it let contracts for so many thousand guns or planes or tanks, totally ignoring where the materials for those orders were to come from, or whether the same productive facilities might not be contracted for twice over.

The present War Production Board has avoided these mistakes. But it has been guilty of some bloomers of its own. Last March, for instance, WPB issued an order for conserving steel which would have limited safety-razor manufacturers to an output equivalent to one blade per week for each adult male in the United States. However, it was quickly discovered that America's razor-blade consumption had never exceeded that amount. When this fact was called to their attention WPB officials hastily amended their order, stating that lawn mowers, not razor blades, were what they really had in mind. This left the unfortunate impression that Washington was unable to distinguish between devices for harvesting grass and whiskers.

Another way in which we are in danger of losing the war is by reason of military old-fogyism and resistance to every sort of change. I came across a word in the dictionary the other day which seems to describe the affliction of certain of our generals and admirals. That word is "neophobia." It means the fear of new things or new ideas. I suggest that until recently a large proportion of our Army and Navy high commands have been suffering from neophobia.

It was neophobia—the fear of innovation—which caused the brass hats of the Air Force to receive the Republic Thunderbolt pursuit plane "without enthusiasm" when it was first submitted to them back in 1937, and to pigeonhole the design. The Air Force was then committed to liquid-cooled motors in pursuit ships, a principle which the P-35, as it was then known, violated in favor of the air-cooled engine. Now that the Japanese "Zero" fighter and the Nazi Focke-Wulf 190 have proved conclusively the case for the latter type of power plant, the Air Force commanders have ceremoniously disinterred the Thunderbolt (rechristened the P-47), and hailed it as the wonder plane it truly is. As a result of five years' delay, we have far too few of these fighters with which to challenge the enemy.

Please do not jump to the conclusion that the vision of our military leaders has been uniformly bad. It has not. Army and navy chiefs have cleared out much of the dead wood which encumbered the higher branches of the services during the long years of peace.

We are in danger of losing the war on the home front by reason of bureaucratic wastefulness and red tape.

In our investigation of camp construction we unearthed example after example of how red tape clogs the gears and tangles the threads of America's war program. In one instance, the contractor at Fort Leonard Wood, Missouri, got tired of waiting for the blueprints of certain buildings. Knowing from previous experience precisely what was wanted, he went ahead without them. Weeks after the job was finished, government draftsmen were still working on the plans.

Washington has become a city where a large proportion of the population makes its living, not by taking in one another's washing, but by unreeling one another's red tape. Every request for immediate action must be accompanied by several pounds of supporting documents.

Red tape makes it necessary for many companies with war contracts to employ clerks and bookkeepers who do nothing but fill out government forms and questionnaires—forms for the War Department and the Navy, for the War Production Board, the Bureau of Internal Revenue, the Office of Price Administration, the Social Security Board, and many more besides.

In peacetime, red tape represents a necessary evil, keeping public servants from straying too far out of bounds. During the war emergency, however, we need administrators with the moral courage to slash through and get things done—and get them done on time.

The current salvage campaign offers innumerable illustrations of red tape, duplicated effort, and working at cross purposes on the part of government agencies.

With the country's steel furnaces pleading for more scrap, the War Production Board early in the summer launched a publicity campaign to persuade the public to turn in its old metal. So far the results have been disappointing from the Government's point of view, and the public feels that it's been bilked.

For example, one citizen reports to me that he patriotically collected every ounce of unused steel or iron on his country place—old rakes, mowers, cultivator blades, and the like—until he had upwards of a thousand pounds. Then followed weeks of fruitless telephoning for some agency to come and get it. Finally he paid his garbage man $2 to cart it all away.

One reason for this unfortunate situation is that the scrap dealers have been subjected to a welter of confusing and often contradictory orders issued by the Iron and Steel Branch, Scrap Section, of the War Production Board, by the Bureau of Industrial Conservation, by the Office of Price Administration, by the Office of Defense Transportation, and by the local scrap-collection agencies.

There are 15,000,000 tons of steel lying around the countryside in abandoned bridges, mines, and railroad tracks which cannot be collected, for the sole reason that the price ceiling set by OPA makes salvage operations unprofitable. Then again, the junk peddler, with his rickety old wagon and a single horse, used to form the first and vital link in the scrap-collection chain. But price ceilings, plus unfamiliar "paper work," are rapidly driving the junkman from the field.

With the peddler disappearing, the dealer is forced by necessity to go out and collect the scrap himself. But here he runs up against the regulations of the Office of Defense Transportation, which has ruled that driving must be cut by 25 per cent, and which further states that only full truckloads may be carried. In one instance, a farmer had 8 tons of metal in the form of old farm machinery he wanted to dispose of. However, the dealer couldn't go and get it, because 8 tons wouldn't constitute a "full load" for his 10-ton truck.

We are in danger of losing this war if we continue to permit personal self-seeking and business-as-usual to interfere with all-out production schedules.

Monopoly practices seriously impeded our war production in its early stages, and they still account for threatened shortages of steel, aluminum, and other vital metals.

The reluctance of big business to pass out sub-contracts has written the death warrant for many smaller firms. This has meant unemployment for their workers, and has deprived the Government of extra output.

It is unfortunate that, out of more than 184,000 manufacturing establishments in the United States, a mere handful has obtained three-quarters of all the army and navy contracts, while the remaining quarter of the Government's war business has been divided among less than 6,000 concerns.

Even more serious, from the national viewpoint, has been the long delay in converting entire industries to defense work.

For the first 6 months of the current year, factories were permitted to chew up quantities of steel, copper, tin, and lead, and turn it into toy soldiers, electric trains, go-carts, and mechanical games.

For this failure to convert to war work the businesses in question are not entirely to blame. The president of a typewriter company would be considered crazy if he shut down his plant, discharged his employees, retooled his factory to make small arms or machine-gun parts, and then waited for the Government to come through with a contract. And yet that is what the Army and the Navy apparently expected industrialists to do. Then again, the board of directors of a motor corporation is merely being prudent when it asks for some assurance that its competitors will not monopolize civilian markets during the interval when its own output is being devoted to the war.

The only fair and practical way to convert an industry is by an over-all order which affects all members equally and at the same time. This sort of general conversion WPB and other officials have, so far, been hesitant about invoking.

It was to investigate these and similar shortcomings of our war-production program that the defense investigating committee was created by the Senate on March 1, 1941. Since that date the members have held more than 120 hearings, listened to 400 witnesses, taken 6,000 pages of testimony, and issued 11 reports. The members of the special committee have made investigations all the way from Maine to California, and from Washington State to Florida. The Secretary of War and the Secretary of the Navy have appeared before us in executive sessions. So have aircraft workers and garage mechanics.

As a direct result of our investigations into the high cost of war, several war contracts have been reviewed and renegotiated, at a saving to the Government of more than $150,000,000. The indirect economies which the committee has achieved are conservatively reckoned at between 2 and 3 billion dollars.

The reasons for the waste and confusion, the committee found, were everywhere the same; the lack of courageous, unified leadership and centralized direction at the top.

The need for a strong hand at the helm of America's war production finds fresh confirmation in each new batch of mail that lands on my desk. Here, for example, is a letter from a shoe manufacturer in New England. He tells me that he has 30,000 pairs of military boots, loaded on freight cars standing in his yard. They have been there, he asserts, for several weeks. The shoes were originally ordered by the Lease-Lend Office, and were intended for one of our allies. Owing to the military and shipping situations, they cannot be delivered immediately. The Army would very much like to have those shoes; the railroad is crying for the cars; and the manufacturer, my correspondent, is eager for his money.

With one man in complete control, that situation could be straightened out in a jiffy. However, for lack of co-ordination among Lease-Lend, the Army Quartermaster Corps, the Office of Defense Transportation, and the War Production Board—all of whom have to be consulted—it has so far been impossible to ship the shoes, unload the cars, or authorize a payment.

Then again, consider the situation with regard to steel. The record plainly shows that from the outset we badly underestimated our steel requirements and grossly overcalculated our ability to meet them. Captains of the iron and steel industry, apparently fearful that their postwar profits would be menaced by an increase in ingot capacity, insisted that they could and would fulfill every demand of the defense program.

The steel men buttressed their position by pointing to the smallness of the orders which the War and Navy Departments then estimated their war orders would consume. Consequently, a considerable portion of the blame for the current pinch in steel must fall upon our military planners, who failed to anticipate the vast quantities of all raw materials required for waging total war.

But the want of strong leadership at the top is responsible for the fact that certain "dollar-a-year men" delayed the construction of new furnaces. I refer to those representatives of the steel industry who, while serving the Government without compensation, have been unable to divorce their viewpoint completely from that of their former companies—to which, incidentally, they still look for payment of their salaries.

Some people have gathered the impression that my opposition to this type of dollar-a-year man in the employ of Uncle Sam is a matter of "New Deal antipathy to successful businessmen." That is not the case.

We want more businessmen in government, and especially in the war effort. However, it is no more than human that a steel man, for example, who has been loaned to the war administration, should suffer some qualms about ordering any action which might injure the postwar standing of the company or the industry to which he hopes eventually to return, even though the immediate, military need may be for ruthless action.

Britain went through the same experience a couple of years ago. It was only after a newspaper publisher had been drafted to supervise the aircraft industry—and after there had been a general switching around of jobs, so that steel men were placed in charge of textiles, and textile men in charge of steel, that Britain's war output began really to hit its stride.

Fundamentally, England's production crisis was a crisis of leadership. And the same thing holds true for the United States today.

Leadership is what we Americans are crying for. We aren't complacent. We are by no means downcast. We are fighting mad, and ready to tackle any job and to make any sacrifice that will contribute to the defeat of our Axis enemies. All we ask is that we be intelligently and resolutely led.

With the world going up in flames about us, we owe it to ourselves to insist that the President act promptly to halt the selfish fights for power, the endless bickering and dissension, which have so far blocked the complete utilization of our productive energies.

Already the people are demanding that there be an end to divided power, timid counsels, and halfway measures. Moreover, unless I fail to understand the public's temper, they are adamantly opposed to the appointment of any army officer to supervise production on the civilian front. In this country we abhor the notion of a military czar.

The leader of our production effort must be a man who can stand up to the generals and the admirals and tell them where to head in. He must have the authority required to rule the industrial roost, and the determination to use that power.

He must have the imagination and industrial daring to conjure up unheard-of ways of doing things instead of reasons why they can't be done.

The American people are ready to spend blood and sweat and tears to buy victory. American industry must be ready to sacrifice, too. There can be no holding back of productive energy to protect postwar profits. Without victory there will be no profit for anyone but Hitler and the Japs.

TRUMAN COMMITTEE REPORT ON GASOLINE RATIONING DECEMBER 11, 1942

U.S. Senate, 77th Congress, 2nd Session, Report 480, Part 13, 1–16.

General Discussion

For several years the increasingly frequent showers of increasingly complicated questionnaires have been driving small businessmen to despair and larger concerns to the creation of increasingly complicated organizations devoted solely to the preparation of governmental forms.

Into this scene there now comes the proposal to restrict by formula the supplies of oil products to millions of Americans everywhere.

The farmer with a small truck working 12 hours a day to keep body and soul together and to contribute perhaps in some small measure to the war effort finds himself suddenly obliged to digest a 32-page pamphlet of instructions and to fill out an elaborate questionnaire requiring detailed data on activities long past from entirely nonexistent records.

The practical experience of men of intelligence and integrity familiar with the problem of the small farmer and truck operator should have been called to the council table in far greater degree when determining how to proceed.

Sharing confidences with the Congress as representative of the country would have insured something of that measure of public understanding and confidence that is vital in a republic where widespread cooperation is essential to the success of any rationing program.

Lack of confidence between business and Government wherever it arises is a serious handicap in our war effort. Lack of confidence by the people generally in the intelligence, reasonableness, or integrity of their Government can mean disaster.

Reorientation of rationing along simpler lines, together with the cooperation of all agencies concerned in forming public opinion will provide insurance that the vast majority of our people understand what it is all about. The rest will then willingly fall in line.

No challenge is required of the sincerity of those in authority in urging a far closer and more sympathetic contact with the problems of those everywhere in America who are bearing the burden of the war effort.

This is no time for epithets or name calling. A democracy must demonstrate its capacity to mobilize one hundred million Americans. Their united strength is irresistible if used against the enemy.

Nation-wide gasoline rationing to conserve rubber seems abundantly justified by the developments of every passing day. The Baruch report on rubber in September and the recent report of William Jeffers as Rubber Director have confirmed the recommendation of this committee last May that the rubber situation was extremely critical and that every possible measure of conservation should be immediately adopted.

The committee at the same time stressed the importance of a simple and sensible approach and emphasis on local responsibility so far as practicable.

The truck regulations on rationing constitute an outstanding illustration of the present difficulty. Early modification and simplification is essential to avoid a crisis in our productive economy this coming year.

Pleasure driving should pass out for the duration. When William Jeffers as Rubber Director advises the American people that only a miracle can produce the rubber essential to keep our military machine functioning and that any break-down such as ordinarily is anticipated might mean the paralysis of our military and civilian economy it is high time for America to stop, look, and listen.

Fuel-oil rationing on our east coast is absolutely essential and must grow more and more stringent. Fuel-oil rationing in the Midwest can be justified only on the ground that it will release essential transportation that will help the East. The authorities are moving to make this possible. Community cooperation in accepting all reasonable restrictions and in making conversions to coal will be of tremendous benefit to the war effort. Compulsory conversion, wherever practicable, may soon be essential.

A more practical approach by local rationing boards in cutting red tape and making sure that minimum requirements for home heating are satisfied is imperative. No Americans must freeze. War production must not be impeded by epidemics.

As America moves into the valley of regimentation in food and manpower those in authority must keep their gaze on the peaks and not lose their way in a forest of detail.

Americans realize that in war we cannot expect absolute equality of individual sacrifice. That is not the way of war. Americans expect only simple common sense. With complete faith in the loyalty, reasonableness, and intelligence of the American people, this committee seeks only to assist in applying simplicity, faith, and common sense to the entire program of rationing.

Rationing of gasoline for passenger automobile use should be made Nation-wide as a rubber-conservation measure. Rationing should apply even to those areas where gasoline is plentiful.

Such rationing should be administered locally by local boards that are familiar with local needs and have authority to provide gasoline for those needs. Certain conditions exist in the West and Middle West, such as the great distances involved, that do not exist in the East. Full consideration should be given to those differences when determining the amount of gas to be allowed.

The applications which farmers and other truck operators were asked to fill out to obtain certificates of necessity for gasoline for trucks were unnecessarily complex. The Office of Defense Transportation should not have attempted to handle the allocation of gasoline on a national basis for Detroit. The matter should be handled by local boards which should include, in their membership, farmers and other truck owners familiar with truck operations. Truck operators found guilty of black-market operations should be punished.

Fuel for farm tractors should not be rationed, but the amounts used should be reported to local boards charged with the duty of examining and correcting those cases where the use appears to be excessive.

There is a shortage of fuel oil in the territory east of the Rocky Mountains, which was caused by the increased requirements of the war program and by the inability to obtain huge supplies of fuel oil which were formerly shipped to east coast ports by tanker from the Caribbean area. Tankers are not available in sufficient number because of the diversion of many of them to other routes for military purposes and because of the submarine menace. The lack of tankers forces us to transport petroleum products from the Gulf region and the Middle West to east coast terminals by railroad tank cars. It is not possible greatly to increase the number of tank cars in that service, so it is important to obtain as much as possible from the Middle West instead of the Gulf region because of the shorter haul. Two tank cars moving from the Middle West to east coast terminals can transport as much as three tank cars originating from Texas.

Great quantities of oil could have been transported by barges which could have been converted to haul petroleum and for which adequate hauling power could have been made available. The committee advocated last spring that this be done, but a plethora of Government agencies working at cross purposes failed to get the program under way soon enough.

The shortage of fuel oil and the shortage of transportation make it necessary to ration the use of fuel oil for residential heating in the Middle West as well as in the East. Every possible effort should be made to produce more crude oil and utilize idle refinery capacity in the Middle West, even if there is no transportation available to send it to the east coast. Such fuel oil should be used locally to lessen the extent of the rationing necessary. Wherever possible, the requirements of fuel oil for military and industrial uses as well as for residential heating uses should be reduced by using coal instead of oil.

The fuel-oil shortage will be greater in 1943 and 1944 than in 1942, and all homeowners in rationed areas where coal is available who have grates and furnaces capable of conversion to coal should do so just as soon as they can get the means of conversion.

Attention should be given now to providing the necessary materials and labor to produce the amount of coal which will be needed next year, because the mines cannot store huge quantities of coal and the railroads are better able to transport it in the summer months.

The rationing of fuel oil for residential heating purposes should have been done in the first instance by determining the percentage by which consumption would have to be reduced in each area and announcing a straight-line cut of that amount of last year's consumption. This would have produced some inequities. Local boards should have members familiar with local heating problems and should have authority to allow more oil to those who need it. Such boards could also have examined those cases where the amount of oil used per person appeared to be excessive and required the home owner to make whatever changes in heating practices could be made to reduce the consumption of fuel oil.

The formula which was used to determine the amount of fuel oil to be allowed was complicated, and in many cases produced unworkable results. We should not attempt to administer rationing programs from Washington through complicated formulas which cannot easily be understood, unless they produce proper results in almost all cases. There should be more confidence in the ability of the American people to handle such matters locally through persons familiar with local problems who have obtained the facts from the persons they are rationing. General principles should be determined to guide such local boards in their decisions, and they should be removed if they do not achieve the over-all savings which are to be realized from their areas, but within those limits they should have authority to allocate the materials to be rationed in accordance with the facts as to each situation as they find it.

The American people will enforce rationing in themselves whenever the need is demonstrated and the program is reasonably simple, clear, and fair. A great majority of them will welcome the opportunity and will respond cordially to responsibility placed upon them.

National Gasoline Rationing of Passenger Automobiles

Last May this committee reported to the Nation that the rubber shortage was so acute that the use of automobiles would have to be substantially reduced in order to conserve rubber. The committee concluded that:

> Driving must be curtailed on the basis of the present rubber outlook. Therefore national gasoline rationing on a sensible basis must be given consideration.

The committee referred to five different measures to be considered for the curtailment of rubber consumption by motorists. They were:

1. A Federal speed law regulating maximum speed at 40 miles per hour.
2. A law prohibiting the purchase or holding of any tires over five per car.
3. Over-all gasoline rationing to minimize nonessential driving.
4. Organization of compulsory pick-up systems to obtain maximum utilization of privately owned vehicles.
5. Power to requisition any transportation vehicle, including private automobiles, where it appears that such vehicle is necessary for the purpose of transporting either goods or passengers essential to the war program.

Most of these measures have since been adopted with the exception that the speed limit has been set at 35 miles-per-hour instead of 40.

The committee's recommendations were not based on the shortage of gasoline but on the shortage of rubber.

The committee's report on the rubber situation was made after an extended study, and its conclusions were reached only after all the principal public officials who had knowledge of the facts had been consulted and had been shown copies of the committee's report and requested to make suggestions with respect thereto. However, at that time, many people were not sufficiently aware of the extent of the rubber shortage to be concerned about it, and unfortunately action was not taken. On September 10, 1942, $3\frac{1}{2}$ months after the committee had rendered its report, the Baruch Committee restudied the rubber situation and reached substantially the same conclusions.

More recently, this committee has reexamined the rubber situation, and it agrees entirely with the position of Mr. William Jeffers, the Rubber Administrator, that gasoline rationing on a national basis is essential to conserve rubber. The committee believes that Mr. Jeffers is doing a good job.

Mr. Jeffers' function is to determine the amount of rubber which has to be saved. The task of devising and putting into effect a rationing system for passenger autos which will conserve the rubber to the extent directed by Mr. Jeffers is the duty of the Office of Price Administration under the direction of Mr. Leon Henderson. The task of rationing trucks is under the jurisdiction of the Office of Defense Transportation under the direction of Mr. Joseph Eastman.

When the committee advocated last May that national gasoline rationing be given serious consideration it was careful to stress the following consideration:

> However, in considering the question of requisitioning, as well as the question of rationing, we should be sensible. There is no virtue in sacrifice for sacrifice's sake. Automobile tires wear out almost as fast when held in reserve as spare tires. Almost as much rubber will be saved by permitting sensibly restricted necessary driving as by indiscriminately forcing the automobiles off the roads. The latter course would not only be wasteful, but it would jeopardize maximum production for the war effort. The problem is one of intelligent restrictions on the part of public officials and care in driving and maintenance on the part of motorists.

Both Mr. Jeffers and Mr. Henderson testified before this committee that they were going to see to it that steps would be taken to effect a common-sense administration of gas rationing for the sole purpose of conserving rubber.

They made it plain that all the gasoline required would be given to those who could prove to a committee of their neighbors that the uses to which they proposed to put their automobiles were reasonably essential.

Both Mr. Jeffers and Mr. Henderson stated that they were aware that certain conditions exist in the West and the Midwest, such as the great distances involved, that do not exist in the East and that they were prepared to give full consideration to those differences. They also both agreed that the determination of individual needs should be made locally by boards or committees composed of farmers and other local representatives familiar with local needs and who would have the power to administer gas rationing on a sensible basis. The committee believes that such action is essential to the success of any national gas rationing program.

The committee's attention has also been called to the fact that it is difficult, especially in the West, where great distances are involved, for traveling salesmen and other businessmen to pool their cars for rubber conservation purposes because they are not permitted to pool their gas tickets. The committee therefore recommends that permission be granted to persons pooling their cars for business purposes to use the gasoline tickets of those participating in the pool.

Trucks

As to trucks, the committee found that 3,000,000 owners of about 5,000,000 trucks, including more than a million farmers, were forced to apply to the Office of Defense Transportation in Detroit, Mich., for certificates of necessity in order to obtain gasoline for their trucks. Many farmers and other owners of trucks had difficulty in obtaining the applications and even greater difficulty in understanding the 32-page printed booklet of instructions for preparing the application which was issued by the Office of Defense Transportation.

Even where they obtained and understood the proper application blank they usually did not have the information requested in the blank which was unnecessarily detailed. For example, for each 3 months' period, farmers were required to specify the amount of gasoline used, the miles operated, the number of trips operated, the average loads in tons of freight or cubic feet, the average capacity of the truck in tons or cubic feet, which of the orders of the Office of Defense Transportation were applicable to their operations, the steps they had taken to conserve tires and other information. Most farmers and other owners of only one or two trucks did not keep records which would enable them to supply such information.

The committee believes that the truck application was unnecessarily complex and that it was most undesirable to attempt to obtain from 3,000,000 separate owners detailed figures with respect to 5,000,000 trucks. Perhaps the information was useful, but the intelligent analysis of 3,000,000 applications by a hastily recruited clerical force in Detroit presented an almost impossible task. Mr. Eastman stated that he adopted this complex method of rationing truck gasoline because local rationing boards in the East, who were unfamiliar with truck operations, had largely given truck owners what they asked for, with the result that many got more than was necessary, and black markets were created. The committee believes that such a situation should have been remedied by putting farmers and other truck owners on the local boards and punishing those found guilty of black market operations. The Office of Defense Transportation has assured the committee that gas rationing of trucks will be handled on a local basis, with minimum operational records by persons familiar with the needs of farmers and other truck operators, and that the mistakes which have been made will be rectified so that the work of the truck which is essential both to industry and agriculture can be carried on.

Tractors

The committee recommends that there be no rationing of gasoline or other fuel for tractors. To the extent that tractors use gasoline there is and will continue to be plenty of gasoline except in the East and to the extent that they use kerosene and other light distillates the principal drain will be in the summer months. The need to conserve gasoline in the East and kerosene and other light distillates in both the East and the Middle West must be recognized, but the need for unhampered use of tractors by farmers to produce vitally needed food must also be recognized. Farmers are patriotic citizens, and they can be depended upon not to waste tractor fuel that they know is scarce. Those who do should be severely punished, but farm production should not be hampered by devising a complicated application blank which will not prevent a dishonest use of tractor fuel by the few who would resort to it and which will hamper the honest majority.

The committee recommends instead that local rationing boards issue to farmers coupons to be turned in on all purchases of gasoline or other fuel for tractors and farm equipment other than trucks so that a record will be available of all such purchases. The local boards should then be charged with the duty of investigating those cases where the purchases appear to be excessive Thus the local boards composed of persons having knowledge of local farm problems and fuel consumption in general can do the vital policing job after giving the individual farmer a chance to explain his own peculiar problem.

Fuel Oil

Crude Oil

The committee finds that there is no current shortage of crude oil productive capacity when the country is considered as a whole. However, the productive capacity of certain important producing areas, such as Illinois and Oklahoma, has been and is now decreasing on account of the lack of continued discovery of new fields needed to offset the depletion of older developed producing fields in these areas. With the declining production of Illinois and Oklahoma, it has been necessary to draw more heavily on the available productive capacity of other areas such as Kansas, Texas, Louisiana, New Mexico, and Mississippi, most of which are more distant from the heavy consuming centers in the East and Midwest, to the extent that transportation facilities will permit. In order to provide an adequate continuous supply of crude oil, from which the necessary quantities of petroleum products required for war and for essential industrial and civilian activities can be manufactured, it is essential that new oil fields be discovered and developed in an orderly manner and new reserves thus made available in volume at least sufficient to balance consumption. This means that exploratory and development activities must be continued with whatever intensity is required to locate new fields and to develop properly the reserves thereby discovered and that the materials, equipment, and personnel required for the purpose must be made available to the petroleum industry, to the extent that they can be supplied in the light of other urgent war needs.

Fuel Oil

Fuel oil for the heating of residences has been rationed for the purpose of obtaining a 25-percent cut in last year's consumption in the rationed area. The necessity for rationing and the extent of the saving to be made were determined by the Office of the Petroleum Coordinator, and the manner in which the rationing was to be effected was determined by the War Production Board.

Historically it has been necessary to transport fuel oil to the east-coast region of the United States, because the quantities of fuel oil used there were so great that if sufficient crude oil had been refined to supply the fuel oil, it would have produced other byproducts such as gasoline in quantities greater than could be used on the east coast. Consequently, in order to keep refinery operations in balance, for many years prior to the war there were heavy importations of fuel oil from the Caribbean area. That source of fuel oil has not been available since the beginning of the war because of the shortage of tankers and the need for such fuel oil elsewhere.

There is large refinery capacity in the eastern part of the United States, referred to by the Petroleum Administrator as petroleum district No. 1, but the quantity of crude oil produced there is only a small fraction of the amount consumed.

The production of crude oil per day in district No. 1 is approximately 80,000 barrels per day and the expected consumption in district No. 1 after giving effect to the rationing program and to increased offshore consumption will be from approximately 1,200,000 to more than 1,400,000 barrels per day.

The production of fuel oil in district No. 1 will be approximately 250,000 barrels per day, and the estimated consumption after giving effect to rationing will be 845,000 barrels per day.

This means that it is necessary and will continue to be necessary to transport into District No. 1 huge quantities of crude oil and fuel oil. This transportation was formerly accomplished by the use of tankers from Gulf ports. Transportation by tanker was cheaper than transportation by pipe line, and had the advantage of flexibility in that tankers could receive oil at any Gulf terminal and deliver it to any Atlantic coast terminal. With the advent of war it became impossible to continue these normal tanker operations because of the need for tankers to supply oil for military uses at distant points and because of the inability of the Navy to prevent the sinking of tankers.

This made it imperative that all means of transporting oil by pipe line, barge, or railroad tank cars should be utilized to a maximum.

It is unfortunate that the original pipe line proposals were not hastened to completion. The reason assigned for the failure to do so was the scarcity of steel, which in turn was itself due to the failure of the former Office of Production Management and the armed forces to realize the necessity of increasing all basic commodities. Very little if any steel was saved because enormous quantities of steel were lost in the tankers which were sunk, attempting to supply oil which could have been carried by pipe line.

Similarly it is most unfortunate that the oil barge program has been the subject of such continued and unreasonable delays. Huge quantities of crude oil and petroleum products could have been transported from the Gulf coast region where they are plentiful, to the east coast region where they are exceedingly scarce, if proper attention had been given (1) to converting existing barges, and (2) to building new barges of wood and other materials.

This committee held hearings last spring at which time it ascertained that there were numerous agencies participating in or which had to be considered with respect to the barge program. They included the Office of Petroleum Coordinator, the Office of Defense Transportation, the War Production Board, the Army Engineer Corps, the Maritime Commission, and Reconstruction Finance Corporation. The committee was informed that barges would be converted wherever possible and shortly thereafter in July the President approved the recommendation of his Emergency Committee for East Coast Supply urging that all available barges be converted.

Originally 259 barges with an approximate capacity of 2,500,000 barrels were to be converted. The number to be converted was later reduced to 130, with a total capacity of 1,500,000 barrels. Power has been made available for the 130 barges, but less than 15 have been converted and only 52 are expected to be completed by the 1st of March. It is expected that they will be largely utilized in the Gulf area but by relieving other forms of transportation they will indirectly lessen the burden on districts Nos. 1 and 2.

Therefore, we will not get the substantial benefit from the barge program which this committee was led to believe would be achieved and which this committee believes could have been realized during this coming winter. The committee expects Mr. Ickes, the Petroleum Administrator, to use the new authority conferred upon him to give immediate attention to this problem. The decision with respect thereto should be made strictly on the basis of the war emergency and should not be affected by the views of any refinery operators as to the effect of such barges on their post-war operations or their preference for pipe lines or other forms of transportation.

The committee also desired to have as many new barges as possible built and was particularly interested in the possibility of building them of wood either for oil transportation or to replace steel barges now carrying other cargoes which could be converted to oil carriers. The committee realized that the barge program would require the building of tugs which in turn would require engines, but there was no evidence then and there is no evidence now that it was not possible to build barges and tugboats and to equip them with the necessary engines, and it is the considered opinion of the committee that the failure of the numerous agencies to formulate a plan acceptable to all of them and put it into effect for the production of such barges and towboats has greatly injured the oil situation.

For lack of adequate pipe-line and barge facilities it became necessary either to shut down the operations of many of the large refineries in the East or to attempt to supply crude oil to them by railroad tank car. Since those refineries use approximately 6 percent of the crude oil shipped to them as a fuel to refine the balance of the crude oil, the committee has asked for detailed evidence that such refinery operations should have been continued. Six percent of the 400,000 barrels per day of crude oil being transported to the East by tank car for these purposes is equivalent to almost one-sixth of the fuel oil which will be saved by rationing fuel oil for residential purposes.

The principal reasons cited for continuing the operation of these large refineries in the East instead of refining the crude oil at Gulf ports and shipping only the refined products, thereby eliminating the transportation of the 6 percent used for refining operations, are that (1) ultimately all refining capacity will be needed wherever located, (2) the large refineries in the East are equipped to produce articles for which there is great military need such as military lubricants, asphalt for air bases and the components of 100-octane gasoline, and (3) that some of the products such as heavy fuel oils present loading and shipping problems which reduce the quantity that can be delivered per railroad tank car.

The weight to be given to these points can be determined only by an examination of detailed data which is in course of preparation for the committee.

If transportation were available, it would be desirable to obtain the fuel oil and other petroleum products which we need in district No. 1 (east coast region) from district No. 3 (the Gulf region). District No. 3 produces approximately 1,900,000 barrels of crude oil per day and 600,000 barrels of fuel oil per day and will have a local demand of only 700,000 barrels per day of crude oil, out of which 280,000 barrels per day of fuel oil are obtained. Such a transfer would very greatly alleviate the critical shortage of fuel oil in district No. 1, the east coast region, but a substantial shortage would still exist there because we can no longer obtain fuel oil from the Carribean region and because of the increased use of fuel oil for military and other reasons connected with the war effort.

But the amount of oil which can be transported to the east coast from the Gulf region is, and will continue to be, limited by the number of railroad tank cars which can be put into that service, until and unless we get additional pipe-line and barge facilities.

There are approximately 143,000 tank cars of all types and descriptions in the United States, of which 112,000 are presently assigned to petroleum service, exclusive of some 10,000 used by the railroads for their own particular needs. Many are needed for other essential services which can be supplied only by tank cars. The number of tank cars now in service for transporting oil to the east-coast region is about 68,500, and it will be difficult to make any substantial increase. So it appears that we cannot increase the number of tank cars in the service, and therefore must direct our efforts toward the most efficient use of tank cars. It takes approximately 18 days for a tank car to make a round trip from a Gulf terminal to an east-coast terminal, so that it is desirable to obtain as much crude oil or fuel oil as possible from the Middle West where the turn-around time is much lower. Stated simply, 2 tank cars moving from the Middle West to east coast terminals can transport as much as 3 tank cars originating from Texas. For that reason and because of the great need for oil in the east-coast region, heavy drains will be made upon the Middle West region.

The Middle West from Ohio to the Rocky Mountains and from North Dakota to Oklahoma constitutes petroleum district No. 2, which, taken as a whole, has a daily supply of crude oil and fuel oil of approximately 1,000,000 barrels and 475,000 barrels, respectively, and a daily consumption of 1,100,000 barrels and 473,000 barrels, respectively. Taken as a whole district No. 2 has a shortage, but one of much smaller proportions than the shortage in district No. 1 (the east coast). The area included in district No. 2 is immense, and if it were subdivided, as perhaps it should be, into several districts some of them, taken separately, would not have any shortage at all. This would apply for example to the area comprising the five States of Nebraska, Kansas, Oklahoma, Missouri and Iowa. But even though such areas taken separately have sufficient oil they must be and are prepared, because of the emergency due to the lack of transportation facilities, to share their oil on an equitable and common sense basis with the east coast region.

The Office of the Petroleum Administrator estimates that even if all the crude oil produced or now in above ground storage in districts No. 1, 2, and 3 (everything east of the Rocky Mountains) could be pooled without transportation difficulties, there would be an over-all shortage during the 4 winter months of 39,000,000 barrels which would reduce our 69,000,000 barrels of crude oil in storage to only 30,000,000 barrels. The 30,000,000 barrels would be held in reserve to meet possible additional military requirements and to enable the refineries to operate efficiently.

This critical situation is not temporary. The production of crude oil in districts No. 1 and 2 is expected to decrease in 1943 and in 1944, and the requirements of fuel oil for new installations and for additional military purposes are expected to increase. We may therefore expect that our fuel oil situation will be more critical in the winters of 1943 and 1944 than it now is and that the necessity for rationing its use for residential heating will be greater then than now. It is therefore necessary to increase as much as possible the production of crude oil.

Some substantial increase in production can be obtained by modifying Government restrictions upon the drilling of new wells and upon the operation of existing wells. Before new wells can be drilled in the number needed, it will be necessary for the Government to make available the necessary drilling supplies, to permit the expert drillers and other oil men to continue at oil work and to provide sufficiently high prices for products to induce the necessary exploitation and development work. Increased production from existing wells undoubtedly could be obtained by simply removing governmental restrictions. For example, the chairman of the Corporation Commission of the State of Kansas, which is charged with the administration of the State proration law, testified before the committee that Kansas could produce an additional 20,000 barrels of crude oil a day without danger to its wells, but the Office of the Petroleum Administrator, following the recommendations of a production committee for district No. 2, composed of oil company representatives, directed his agency to permit the production of only 300,000 barrels instead of 320,000 barrels per day. The importance of this can be estimated by contrasting that 20,000 barrels per day of crude oil with the 52,000 barrels of fuel oil which are expected to be saved by rationing fuel oil for residential heating purposes in the whole of district No. 2.

There is sufficient unutilized refinery capacity in the Middle West to refine a considerably greater quantity of crude oil if it were produced. This is evidenced by the fact that the Office of the Petroleum Administrator on November 20, 1942, issued instructions to refineries in the Middle West, with a few exceptions, to reduce their production by 5 percent, although many such refineries were not then producing at full capacity. Of course, the increase in crude oil production should be obtained as far as possible in places where there are already sufficient feeders and pipe lines to transport the crude oil to refineries. Mr. Edward B. Swanson, head of the Research Division of the Petroleum Administrator's Office and Mr. Wirt Franklin, regional head of the Office of the Petroleum Administrator of district No. 2, indicated in testimony before the committee that at least some of the increased production of fuel oil could not be transported to the east coast because it would be produced at points where transportation facilities could not be made available on an efficient basis.

The committee recommends that such increased production be obtained and made available locally for the purpose of limiting or eliminating the necessity for fuel-oil rationing for residential purposes in such local areas. The committee recommends that local officials study their own local situations to ascertain whether there is a possibility for such an increase in their area, and, if so, they should bring the facts to the attention of the Office of the Petroleum Administrator.

The committee recommends that wherever possible industrial users and large residential users, such as hotels and apartment houses, be required to convert from oil to coal and that home owners who have the necessary grates and furnaces capable of conversion to coal should do so as soon as they can get the means of conversion, except in those regions where it is no easier to obtain coal than fuel oil.

The committee also recommends that the Petroleum Administrator consult the War Production Board and ascertain whether grates can be made available for the conversion of furnaces for home owners who do not have grates. In the event that they can be made available for the conversion of furnaces for home owners who can obtain coal but do not have grates the committee recommends that consideration be given to requiring such home owners to convert with grates furnished to them at Government expense but installed at their own expense. The committee believes that in that event there is just as much reason for the Government furnishing grates to home owners as there is for the Government paying the large eastern oil refineries the difference between the cost of transporting oil to their refineries in tank cars and the cost of transporting it by tankers.

The extent of the fuel-oil shortage is due not only to the lack of transportation formerly available but to increased demands for new installations and uses. Such increases in use should not have been permitted where coal could have been used.

On March 14 of this year the War Production Board issued a directive which prevented those who continued to install oil-burning equipment from obtaining fuel oil. That directive applied only to district No. 1 and should have applied to both district No. 1 and district No. 2. On June 15, it was made applicable to both districts.

The committee believe that it is the duty of the Army and Navy and other war agencies to use the utmost care not to increase unnecessarily the military demands for articles to which a shortage exists.

The committee found that early attention was given to the necessity of increasing coal production and of utilizing the summer months to transport and stock pile quantities both for residential and industrial use, and commends that policy, without which we would be in very great trouble today.

Coal production increased from 514,000,000 tons of bituminous and 54,107,222 tons of anthracite in 1941 to 565,000,000 tons of bituminous and 58,000,000 tons of anthracite estimated in 1942.

It is now proposed to increase coal production to 600,000,000 tons of bituminous and 60,000,000 tons of anthracite in 1943. To do this the miner will have to work longer hours; absenteeism will have to be greatly reduced and the mine operators will have to be supplied with sufficient repair parts. Also their manpower must be maintained.

In most areas sufficient coal can be produced and transported provided a large proportion of the transportation occurs in the summer months and home owners fill their bins, and provided also that the mine operators get the men and materials they need to work with.

In certain areas the production and transportation of coal presents serious difficulties which will have to be given immediate attention if we are to have sufficient coal during the winters of 1943 and 1944. District No. 15 is such an area. The marketing area of that district includes major portions of Missouri, Kansas, Oklahoma, and Texas, and smaller portions of other States. It is expected that the coal consumption in that district in 1942 will be 9,180,000 tons, and that in 1943 it will be 11,289,000 tons, whereas the coal produced in that district in 1941 was only 8,360,000 tons. Some new mines which started production in 1942 will contribute to increased production in 1943. One mine producing 320,000 tons in 1942 has exhausted its coal supply and will be out of production in 1943. It is expected that production can be increased in 1943 to approximately 10,220,000 tons without the opening of new mines, in which event the district will be short more than 1,000,000 tons of coal, which would have to be obtained from points as far east as West Virginia.

That would involve a heavy burden on the railroads which would then be hauling oil east from the Middle West and returning with empty tank cars while coal was being hauled in the opposite direction by cars returning empty.

The committee does not believe that we can safely rely upon the optimistic expectation of Thomas J. Thomas of the Office of Solid Fuels that 30 percent more coal could be produced in district No. 15 with 10 percent less labor and without any new materials except repair parts, and without opening any new mines.

Moreover, the heating problems in that territory will be increased by the inability of the Cities Service Gas Co. to meet the fuel demand in 1943 of its present customers unless it is permitted to install additional pipe-line facilities. It estimates that the deficiency in gas will be equivalent to about 1,650,000 tons of coal, which would create a deficiency even if we accept the most optimistic estimates of production possible in 1943 from existing mines.

The committee therefore recommends that immediate steps be taken to open up new coal mines in district No. 15 to provide emergency fuel for Iowa, Missouri, Nebraska, and the adjoining States. The committee also recommends that similar studies be made as to the other areas where a coal shortage is possible and that action be taken in advance to insure that fuel is obtained in places where transportation is available.

The amount of fuel oil that must be obtained for other uses by rationing fuel oil for residential heating purposes east of the Rocky Mountains, is estimated to be approximately 157,000 barrels per day, of which 52,000 are to be saved in district No. 2 (Middle West) and 105,000 in district No. 1 (east coast). The saving so made will constitute only about 13 percent of the fuel oil to be consumed in those districts so that an increase of 1⅓ percent in the supply of fuel oil or a similar decrease in the consumption of fuel oil would enable home owners to receive back one-tenth of the 25 percent they were cut.

The average cut in the use of fuel oil for residential heating purposes which will have to be made in order to save 157,000 barrels of fuel oil per day during the winter heating period will be 25 percent. The necessity for a cut of this amount was determined by the Office of the Petroleum Administrator, and the means by which such cut was to be effected were determined by the War Production Board under the direction of Mr. Leon Henderson.

The committee has examined the instructions of the Office of Price Administration, the forms of applications for heating oil prepared by it, and the formulas by which they are resolved. The committee is of the opinion that they were unnecessarily complex, and that such complexity has not only created confusion in the public mind but has resulted in an inequitable and unworkable determination of fuel-oil needs.

The committee believes that the American people, when informed of the facts as to shortages such as this, are willing to make the necessary sacrifices and that they can be trusted to play fair with each other for the mutual benefit of all. It is neither necessary nor desirable to approach the problem of rationing with the opinion that the American people are going to do everything possible to escape the burdens of rationing and that it is necessary to devise application blanks and formulas so complex that it is thought that they will take care of every possible attempt to avoid the effect of rationing.

In all except rare instances home owners knew or were able to ascertain how much fuel oil they used last year. Since it must be assumed that they did not desire to waste their own money by purchasing fuel oil they did not need, the Office of Price Administration should have assumed that they purchased it because they needed it. Consequently the committee is of the opinion that if the Office of Price Administration had concluded that a straight line cut could be made without rendering the home uninhabitable, it should have proceeded in the first instance to make a flat percentage cut in each area with provision for application by individual home owners for more fuel oil where they could prove a necessity by reason of special circumstances and with provision for review by local boards of those situations where by reason of special circumstances less fuel oil would be sufficient.

Instead of doing that the Office of Price Administration, through its experts, has examined the temperature statistics for the last 43 years in each of the thousands of counties involved to ascertain an average temperature for each county; has then determined the number of square feet that its experts think should be allowed for each individual, which number differs with the number in the family, and then has determined the number of gallons of fuel oil which its experts believe should be consumed in heating that many square feet to the temperature which the experts expect to have prevail in that particular county. All of these figures have been reduced to complicated tables which are consulted by volunteer clerical workers to determine the amount of fuel oil which each householder is to receive. Such a system not only insures misunderstanding by the home owner and numerous clerical errors in the computations both by the home owner and by the inexperienced volunteer assistants, but it also fails to take into account many important factors, and therefore necessarily results in many ridiculous allowances which are not only inequitable but which are in many cases unworkable. Although temperature may be the most important single factor governing the amount of fuel oil used, it is by no means the only important factor. Everyone knows that both humidity and wind velocity have a very great deal to do with the amount of fuel used. The extent of exposure of homes to the wind differs with almost every home, and the effect of the exposure is dependent upon the manner in which and the materials of which the house is constructed. Another factor of great importance is the number and size of windows.

The use of the number of square feet as the determining factor also gives no effect whatever to either the outside wall exposure or the height of the ceilings. For example, it is obvious that a bungalow containing 2,000 square feet has much more outside wall and roof exposure than a two-story house containing the same number of square feet, and rooms with 10-foot ceilings require more heat than rooms with the same floor area with 7- or 8-foot ceilings, yet the formula devised by the Office of Price Administration makes no allowance whatever for these factors.

Many of the allowances when computed in this manner are so low that it would be absolutely impossible to heat the homes with the existing heating system, even where rooms could be shut off. To date, no provision has been made and the scarcity of materials makes it difficult to make provision to install new heating systems which would produce the necessary heat through the use of other fuels. The allowances therefore are equivalent to an order to such persons to get out of their homes unless they have a furnace capable of conversion to coal, or can use a heating stove or space heater.

The committee realizes that a straight line percentage cut of the fuel oil to be permitted to users for residential heating purposes would not be equitable in all cases and would require some adjustment by local boards familiar with the premises to be heated. But, the committee believes that no complicated formula should be devised and substituted for a straight line percentage cut unless the formula actually operates to furnish a workable result in nearly every instance. Procedure by formula always has the disadvantage that the public does not know how the formula was devised. Americans are willing to make necessary sacrifices, but they want to be able to understand the reasons for the sacrifice and the fairness of the burden sought to be laid on them.

Since many of the results obtained by applying the formula devised for heating would not be workable or equitable, the committee believes there should not have been an attempt to handle the matter from Washington with a cut and dried formula. Instead of consuming many weeks and months in the development of the formula, the committee believes that the Office of Price Administration should have notified home owners to fill out simple application blanks setting forth the number of people in the home, the size of the home, and the number of gallons of fuel oil consumed in each of the last 3 years. It should also have informed them that they would receive the average number of gallons which they had used less the percentage of the cut. Home owners who by reason of special circumstances thought that they required more oil could have applied personally to their local boards, which after informing themselves of the actual facts could have decided whether an increase was justified or could have advised the home owner that it would be necessary for him to convert to coal or provide additional heat from space heaters or to insulate or otherwise improve his home where he was found financially able to do so. Similarly, the local boards could have been instructed to call in for review for possible decreases those home owners who would obtain by the straight line percentage cut method a high amount of oil per person. In that manner the decision would have been made locally by persons familiar with local conditions and after home owners at least had had an opportunity to discuss their problems with those who made the decisions.

DONALD M. NELSON TO SENATOR TRUMAN
JANUARY 4, 1943

Papers of Harry S. Truman, Senatorial and Vice-Presidential Files,
Harry S. Truman Library, Independence, Missouri.

My dear Senator Truman:

As our nation enters upon a year in which war production must expand to greater and entirely unprecedented volume, involving as it inevitably will problems of great complexity and difficulty, I wish to express the hope that your Special Committee Investigating the National Defense Program may continue to serve the same high purpose that it has comprehended so well since its creation. That purpose, as I see it, has been to obtain the best possible results in our march toward total economic mobilization for war.

Both from personal experience with your committee and from regular study of its extensive activities, I should like briefly to express my deep appreciation and approval of its work. My appreciation becomes the deeper when I consider that your task, which is so often thankless, has been pursued by you and your associates with courage and perseverance.

First, your work has been broad in scope and has provided a needed incentive for the fullest coordination of our war effort. Such coordination has been most helpful, because of the fact that all war agencies are inescapably affected by the plans and operations of any one agency. By making available to these agencies, through formal reports, public or private hearings and in other ways, a variety of approaches to war production problems, your committee has brought vigor and freshness of viewpoint to their solution.

Second, the quality of your analysis has been kept at a high level, noticeably avoiding personalities, minor issues, and biased or incomplete collection of evidence.

Third, the clear and unequivocal character of your conclusions has stimulated plans for improvements and has been especially helpful because of the care and thoroughness with which your supporting reasons and data have been marshalled.

Finally, perhaps the most conspicuous single characteristic of your work from the viewpoint of an administrative agency, has been the constant emphasis you have placed upon the need for foresight—upon anticipating coming events and upon making adequate plans and taking appropriate action to meet them.

In short, I believe the committee has made a substantial contribution to the war effort and with it to the work of the War Production Board.

Sincerely,

Donald M. Nelson

TRUMAN COMMITTEE MEMORANDUM ON EXECUTIVE SESSION, JANUARY 20, 1943

Papers of Harry S. Truman, Senatorial and Vice-Presidential Files,
Harry S. Truman Library, Independence, Missouri.

An Executive Session of the Committee was held on January 20, 1943, at 11:00 a.m. in Senator Truman's office, with Senators Truman, Hatch, Mead, Brewster, and Burton, and Assistant Counsel Halley, Boyle, and Russell present. The Session was attended by Mr. Donald M. Nelson, Chairman of the War Production Board, and Mr. Edward A. Locke, Mr. Nelson's Assistant.

Senator Truman stated that the purpose of the session was to obtain information concerning the conflict between the Army, Navy, and Rubber Administrator on the 100 octane gasoline, the escort vessel, and the rubber programs.

Mr. Nelson explained that after the Baruch report had confirmed the Truman Committee's report, it was agreed that some way had to be found to replace the country's dwindling rubber supply, because the national economy would break down without rubber. The only source available was synthetic rubber. One of the reasons for the delay in the synthetic rubber program was the clash of personalities involved in the program—individuals hating each other with a violent hate. For example the Madigan-Dewey feud. In any event, the program lagged, and Mr. Jeffers reported that the rubber production plants were not being built. On December 1, Mr. Nelson decided that steps had to be taken to get the synthetic plants built or else there would be no rubber. Some of the problems were involved in engineering, disorganization, etc. In addition, there was too much expediting. Thirty-four component parts were vital in all three programs. A bad job was being done on the production of these components by the Army, Navy, and others. It must be remembered that the component parts were not purchased directly by the Army and the Navy, but by contractors to use in finished products for delivery to the services. The services had gotten in the habit of conflicting with each other on their expediting programs so that the manufacturer might be in the position of rescheduling and re-arranging his production program on one item several times.

Mr. Nelson explained that in view of these conditions he had to step in as the only alternative and issue directives on the production of the component parts to assure that at least part of the program came through on time. Conceding that this was a violent method of handling the matter, he issued a directive (the first directive) on 20% of the uncompleted portion of the rubber program. Since the escort vessel program was not so far along, his approach was to re-arrange the program itself inside the manufacturing plants. Both the Army and Navy opposed the first directive, but in Mr. Nelson's opinion it was the only way to insure the completion of a portion of the rubber program, and at the same time carry along the high octane and escort vessel program. Naturally, Mr. Jeffers wanted to obtain completion of the entire rubber program on directives, but it was Mr. Nelson's decision to issue the first directive on only 20% thereof. A copy of the first directive is to be furnished to the Committee.

Mr. Nelson then explained how the directive operated. The manufacturer was instructed to produce a specified amount of component parts on definite delivery dates, which were synchronized with the building of the synthetic rubber plants, with further instructions to advise in what manner the directive conflicted with his existing schedule. Mr. Nelson was of the opinion that the directive often impelled manufacturers to do a proper scheduling job themselves so as not to have some of their contracts taken away. For example when Babcock & Wilcox, with contracts for Navy boilers and catalyst cases received the directive, it first advised that it could not manufacture the cases. With the prospect of losing the contract for the cases, the contractor managed to schedule both production programs properly by re-arranging its schedules and sub-contracting. Similarly, on heat exchangers requiring high alloy drawn steel tubing there were real conflicts between the Army and the Navy, since each wanted its production first. The supply was very tight because quantities had to be sent to Russia as well. The War Production Board stepped into the picture and obtained proper scheduling by arranging and re-arranging the program. It took the production of 105mm. guns out of a tubing factory owned by Alcoa, and the factory went back to tubing production.

Mr. Nelson further explained that the first directive did not provide enough rubber plants to keep the rubber supply at a point which Mr. Jeffers felt was the minimum safety factor. Consequently, Mr. Nelson formulated a second directive to provide for completion of 55% of the Baruch rubber program on the basis that this percentage was necessary to prevent a breakdown of the national economy, including essential Army and Navy transportation. The 55% equaled approximately 500,000 tons of Buna-S rubber. One important factor in his consideration is that the rest of the world, except the Axis, depends on us for rubber.

The Army opposed this second directive, Mr. Nelson explained, on the ground that there was enough rubber for what the Army considered essential civilian uses and it did not need the additional supply. The Army laid stress on airplane and 100 octane gasoline production. Furthermore, the Navy wanted to complete its escort vessel program and opposed the second directive.

Mr. Nelson took no exception to the Army's or Navy's position concerning their needs, but felt that it was his job to provide a sufficient rubber supply to keep the economy going and decided that with orderly production, all programs could be brought through much faster. He emphasized that this decision did not result from any pressure applied on him. It was simply a matter of fact because of the dissipation of the rubber supply.

He further explained that the Army wanted to save 3,000 tons of rubber by cutting out non-essential deliveries to civilians, as of soft drinks and tobacco. He felt that this was a red herring compared with the 500,000 ton program which was essential. He also compared the use of tires by civilian trucks and busses and by the Army. As the Army ruins tires, it can use reclaimed rubber because the life of Army tires is not long anyway. Civilian uses wear tires out, and using a cheaper rubber would, as he is advised, require the use of more crude in the long run. An additional factor is the plentiful supply of reclaimed rubber for all Army uses so that the Army does not have to concern itself with synthetic rubber too much.

Mr. Nelson's goal was to provide sufficient rubber production to prevent the bankruptcy point in October or November, which would be reached then unless steps were taken now. He says that he is getting an orderly program on the production of components. With Mr. Gibbs on the escort vessel program, the War Production Board cannot find that it has hurt the escort vessel program, because every interference with that program which has come to the knowledge of the War Production Board has been solved. His opinion is that the second directive will not hold back the escort vessel program more than a month or two, and then only on a very few vessels, whereas, the first directive has not hurt at all.

He explained that the second directive is in the President's hands for action with plenty of heat but little light being cast on the subject by the military. The Navy's position is that they will be hurt, not that they have been hurt.

One of the retarding factors has been the lack of standardization in the escort vessel and the shipbuilding program. With the many different kinds of the same type of ships being built, naturally the program is retarded. The Maritime Commission opposed the appointment of Gibbs, but Mr. Nelson over-ruled them so that orderly programing could be worked out. He added that the Army and the Navy now seem to be reconciled to the orderly scheduling of the production of the component parts.

It was his opinion that everything came along so fast and at the same time that all the production was crammed into the first 5 months of this year. Although there might be production facilities to supply enough valves for a year, all competing demands could not be supplied at once.

His approach has been on a 3 point basis—first, to obtain enough manpower to increase the supply of the component parts; second, to obtain more orderly scheduling and increase production by not disturbing schedules frequently; and third, to get orders in for the various programs.

On the third point, he interjected that much of the escort vessel program has not been ordered as yet and past policy has been to wait until the last minute. To correct this the War Production Board has ordered the Army and Navy to put its orders in for the first six months of 1943 by February 15, and for the next six months by March 15, under penalty of not getting on the manufacturers production program without specific authorization on any particular item from the War Production Board.

Mr. Nelson's emphasis was on the orderly production side with three top-flight men (Wilson, Gibbs and Cordner) getting order into the picture.

Discussion was then had concerning the scheduling of production of component parts under the first directive, with Mr. Nelson explaining how sequence scheduling worked.

In this connection, he said on the second directive that the only point of uncertainty was whether more butadiene should be provided for.

Senator Mead asked about the adequacy of the 55% completion of the

Baruch report recommendations. Mr. Nelson explained that everything he had done had been done after careful consultation with Mr. Baruch who consulted with his committee, and that Mr. Baruch agreed that the proper procedure was to finish the 55% and let the 45% come along later.

Discussion was then had concerning the butylene aspect with Senator Truman taking the lead, but Mr. Nelson could not answer about the conflicts over its use or whether the supply would be adequate.

In answer to Senator Brewster's question concerning Army and Navy propaganda in support of their views, Mr. Nelson stated that Mr. Byrnes had the matter in hand and was stopping it. Mr. Nelson was violently opposed to the services' appeal to the public on a matter in the hands of the President for decision. He agreed with Senator Brewster that cognizance should be taken of the constantly inspired propaganda put out by the services.

Senator Truman inquired about the Houdry plants which might produce gasoline better than the 100 octane type, and Mr. Nelson said that some of the plants in the program were Houdry plants. Senator Mead asked about progress on the escort vessel program. According to Mr. Nelson, this program is coming along slowly. He felt that the Navy did not accept their necessity soon enough and that there were too many designs.

Referring again to the first directive, Mr. Nelson felt that the lessons learned had furnished sufficient basis for doing many things which could be accomplished by the second directive. The Navy's position is that the second directive will interfere so much more than the first directive that it should not be put into effect. The Army's position is that the second directive should not be put into effect because there is enough rubber, and if the Rubber Administrator drastically curtailed use there would be no need for so much synthetic rubber production. The Army wanted Mr. Jeffers to cut the issuance of crude rubber by 15%, to which Mr. Nelson is opposed, pointing out by way of illustration the effect of such a cut on the Russian offensive.

TIME MAGAZINE ARTICLE, "BILLION-DOLLAR WATCHDOG" MARCH 8, 1943

Anywhere but in a democracy, the Senate's irreverent Truman Committee would be fair game for liquidation. In a perfect state, free from butterfingers and human frailty, it would be unnecessary. In the U.S., democratic but far from perfect, the Truman Committee this week celebrated its second successful birthday as one of the most useful Government agencies of World War II.

Had they had time, its ten members might have toasted their accomplishments all night. They had served as watchdog, spotlight, conscience and spark plug to the economic war-behind-the-lines. They had prodded Commerce Secretary Jesse Jones into building synthetic-rubber plants, bludgeoned the President into killing off doddering old SPAB and setting up WPB.

They had called the turn on raw-materials shortages, had laid down the facts of the rubber famine four months before the famed Baruch report. One single investigation, of graft and waste in Army camp building, had saved the U.S. $250,000,000 (according to the Army's own Lieut. General Brehon B. Somervell). Their total savings ran into billions, partly because of what their agents had ferreted out in the sprawling war program, partly because their hooting curiosity was a great deterrent to waste.

The Truman Committee was too busy to celebrate. In its 16th month of war, the U.S. had still not digested some of war's first readers. The first annual Truman report, with its shocking evidence of all-around bungling, had not spelled the end of bungling. This week the Committee worked on its second annual report, which would have to recite much the same story, chastise many of the same men, pose some of the same old problems. How big should the Army be? How could the manpower tangle be solved? Where would the nation get its food this year? What was wrong with WPB?

Over these basic questions, which the Truman Committee, on behalf of all American citizens, had hoped would be solved two years ago, the committee still sweated, glowed and tried to shed light.

The bigger the U.S. arsenal grew, the more important the Truman Committee became. As the arsenal turned into a modern-day Great Pyramid, most Washington officials still lugged just one stone, and many carried it in the wrong direction.

The closest thing yet to a domestic high command was the Truman Committee. Its members had no power to act or order. But, using Congress's old prerogative to look, criticize and recommend, they had focused the strength of public opinion on the men who had the power. They had a fund of only $200,000 (some still unspent) only twelve investigators, 18 clerks and stenographers. But it was an obscure war plant that had never been visited by the committee. Its members had heard hundreds of witnesses, taken 4,000,000 words of testimony. With battle-royal impartiality, they had given thick ears and red faces to Cabinet members, war agency heads, generals, admirals, big businessmen, little businessmen, labor leaders.

In wartime, even more than in peace, a democracy must keep an eye on itself. This eye the Truman Committee has kept unblinkingly and, by & large, well. It has made mistakes. Some of its data have been gathered too quickly, then reduced to generalities that glittered without illuminating. Its members, including Chairman Harry S. Truman, have sometimes failed to look before they leaped to conclusions. But it has never strayed too far off the beam, nor stayed there too long.

Said one Washingtonian last week: "There's only one thing that worries me more than the present state of the war effort. That's to think what it would be like by now without Truman." For a Congressional committee to be considered the first line of defense—especially in a nation which does not tend to admire its representatives, in Congress assembled—is encouraging to believers in democracy. So is the sudden emergence of Harry Truman, whose presence in the Senate is a queer accident of democracy, as the committee's energetic generalissimo.

Neat, grey Harry Shippe Truman was sworn in as Senator from Missouri in 1934. The only men seen to smile during the ceremony were two husky lieutenants of Boss Tom Pendergast's notorious Kansas City Democratic machine, who sat beaming in the gallery.

In a perfect democracy, free from bosses, string-pulling and finagling at the polls, Harry Truman would probably never have reached Washington. He was Tom Pendergast's hand-picked candidate, yanked out of obscurity so deep that few Missouri voters had ever heard of him. He was nominated, over two more deserving candidates, largely by a vast plurality rolled up in Boss Pendergast's Jackson County, whose registration lists were loaded with dead men and men who had never lived. Thanks to the Boss's great power and the New Deal's 1934 popularity, his election was then automatic.

No one yet knows exactly why Boss Pendergast picked Truman for the Senate. One theory: the Boss was in the whimsical mood of a socialite sneaking a pet Pekingese into the *Social Register*. A better theory: the Boss was impressed by the Midwestern adage that every manure pile should sprout one rose—he saw in Truman a personally honest, courageous man whose respectability would disguise the odors of the Pendergast mob. Certainly Truman was no statesman in 1934. Neither had he ever been touched by scandal.

Truman grew up on a Jackson County farm 15 miles from Kansas City. He tried for West Point, was rejected for one weak eye, gave up the thought of college and went to work instead. He dusted bottles in a drugstore, wrapped papers for the Kansas City *Star*, clerked in Kansas City banks. Five years out of high school he was droning along at $100 a month and ready to go back to his father's farm for good.

World War I pulled him off the farm again. He went to France a lieutenant, became captain of the 129th Field Artillery's rough-&-tumble Battery D. He was shy, reserved, wore big shell-rimmed glasses: to his pugnacious Irish privates he looked like something of a milquetoast. At the start he was perhaps the most unpopular captain in France. But he led his men doggedly through St. Mihiel and the Argonne, spiked a panic when German artillery once drew a bead on his battery, lost only one soldier killed and one wounded, was promoted to major. On the ship back from France his men took a cut out of all crap games, bought him a monstrous loving cup four feet high and big enough to hold ten gallons.

The war, brightest spot in Truman's pre-Senate record, was soon followed by the saddest. With a soldier buddy and $15,000 saved and borrowed, he opened a haberdashery on Kansas City's sporty Twelfth Street, roamed behind the counters selling socks, neckties and garters. In twelve months the store went broke, with debts it took years to pay off.

At 37, Harry Truman, bottle duster, bank clerk and would-be haberdasher, was bogged deep in failure. All he had to show for his career was an old army uniform and a loving cup too ostentatious to keep on the mantel.

Most U.S. political machines, however disreputable, have two saving graces to their credit: 1) they are close enough to the people to know basic human desires, tragedies and needs; 2) their bosses, earthy and disillusioned men, have sometimes found talent where more snobbish souls would never have thought to look. In 1921, with his haberdashery under the hammer and black days ahead, Truman looked up some old servicemen friends in the

Pendergast organization. Truman was a veteran, a farmer, a Mason, a Democrat from three generations back; he had friends all over Jackson County. The
machine made him road overseer, then country judge (an administrative
post), finally U.S. Senator.

Truman was no ball of fire in his first term. He sat meekly in the freshman
row, blinked when critics called him Pendergast's "errand boy," was second
only to Pennsylvania's Joseph Guffey (whose vote for New Deal measures was
pure automatic reflex) in unswerving support of Administration policies.

On Burt Wheeler's Interstate Commerce Committee, he showed unexpected talents as an investigator of railroad high shenanigans. (He and canny
Burt Wheeler are still good friends, despite their schism on foreign policy.) But
this was too esoteric an assignment to impress many voters back home. They
saw him chiefly in another light.

A young U.S. attorney named Maurice M. Milligan was cleaning up
Kansas City, sending one Pendergast henchman after another to jail for vote
frauds, getting closer & closer to the Big Boss himself. When Milligan came up
for reappointment, Truman did his best to ease him out, made one of the
bitterest speeches ever heard on the Senate floor. Milligan got the reappointment anyway, promptly sent Pendergast to prison for evading income taxes on
some of his slush money. Truman shouted: "Purely political. . . . I won't
desert a ship in distress. . . ."

In a perfect democracy, run without hitch, Truman would never have
been returned to the Senate in 1940. A majority of Missouri Democrats, in full
revolt against the machine, opposed him in the primary. But Attorney Milligan and ex-Governor Lloyd Crow Stark split the opposition vote, and Truman slipped in with an 8,000-vote plurality. For a nation whose Administration, army and war contractors are not perfect either, it has turned out to be a
good thing.

The Senate Committee Investigating National Defense was Truman's
own idea. As country judge he had awarded $60,000,000 in contracts; he knew
how hard it had been to get honest performance. Up rose the Senator to
demand that Congress keep an eye on war expenditures: he had never yet
found a contractor who, left unwatched, "wouldn't leave the Government
holding the bag."

At first nobody took the Truman Committee seriously. The Senate gave
him $15,000 (about as much as the Dies Committee spends every seven weeks)
and a group of colleagues chosen mostly from junior Senators, such as
Minnesota's young Joseph Ball, Washington's first-terming Mon C. Wallgren,
New York's busy James M. Mead. Also on the committee went cagey old Tom
Connally of Texas, to see that the juniors kept their heads. For its first assignment, the Committee chose a modest chore: delving into the more flagrant
charges of graft in camp and war-plant construction, plugging some of the
more open sewers down which Government money drained.

But Truman had bigger ideas. In selecting the Committee's chief counsel,
he rejected all political recommendations, went instead to Attorney General
(now Justice) Robert H. Jackson for advice. Thus he got a top-flight investigator: rotund, brilliant, young Hugh Fulton, a Justice Department prosecutor who had sent Howard C. Hopson, head of Associated Gas & Electric
Corp., to prison.

Truman's junior Senators, hungry for tough assignments, went to work with a will. Harry Truman, a shrewd politician, a maker of friends, a great man for shooting trouble, always kept his committee happy and on the ball. It got more money, branched out, found itself deep in every phase of the war. Today few committees, and few men, wield such power.

Harry Truman would rather be fighting the war than policing it. At 58, he still goes solemnly through his setting up exercises every morning, can still get into his World War I uniform. In 1939, like any old soldier, he dug out his old artillery maps, hung them on his office wall to help follow the fighting. He applied for active duty after Pearl Harbor, still likes to think the Army was wrong to say no. When Senate office building janitors began marking off air-raid shelters, he fetched his two rusty World War I helmets to his office, announced that he was ready to serve as warden. No planes came over Washington, so he finally stacked the helmets in his office fireplace and redoubled his efforts on the committee.

To a man once called errand boy, those efforts have produced gratifying results. The St. Louis *Post-Dispatch,* which once threw at him everything its angry editors thought fit to print, recently called him "one of the most useful and at the same time one of the most forthright and fearless" of today's Senators. In Kansas City he was feted by the Chamber of Commerce, which once fought him tooth & nail. A naturally shy and self-effacing man, Harry Truman brushes off the praise: instead of speaking himself in Kansas City, he introduced the members of his committee, let them talk. But even a perfect democrat could not have helped being pleased.

Truman is still a politician, would be loyal to the Pendergast machine today if it still existed. "Tom Pendergast never asked me to do a dishonest deed," he says. "He knew I wouldn't do it if he had asked me. He was always my friend. He was always honest with me, and when he made a promise he kept it. I wouldn't kick a friend when he was down."

But Harry Truman has many another quality not usually associated with machine politicians. He is scrupulously honest: when a magazine paid him $750 for an article on his committee, he added the money to the committee's funds. His only vices are small-stakes poker, an occasional drink of bourbon.

As committee chairman he is a man with a crusade: he says, "The goal of every man on the committee is to promote the war effort to the limit of efficiency and exertion. It doesn't do any good to go around digging up dead horses after the war is over, like the last time. The thing to do is dig this stuff up now, and correct it. If we run this war program efficiently, there won't be any opportunity for someone to stir up a lot of investigations after the war —and cause a wave of revulsion that will start the country on the downhill road to unpreparedness and put us in another war in 20 years. . . ."

In many ways Harry Truman and his committee, celebrating their anniversary this week by poring over another report, seemed the best living proof that democracy, even when imperfect, can be a success.

TRUMAN COMMITTEE REPORT ON CONFLICTING WAR PROGRAMS MAY 6, 1943

U.S. Senate, 78th Congress, 1st Session, Report No. 10, Part 9, 1–5.

The committee held an executive session for the purpose of determining how they could best contribute to the defense of the Nation.

The committee never have investigated, and they still believe that they should not investigate, military and naval strategy or tactics.

From their inception the special committee have concerned themselves with the nonmilitary aspects of the defense program, that is to say, with seeing to it that the defense articles which the Army and Navy have determined that they need are produced in a minimum of time at a minimum of cost and with as little disruption of the civilian economy as possible.

The committee have the utmost confidence in Admiral King, Chief of Operations of the Navy, and General Marshall, Chief of Staff of the Army, and we believe that matters of tactics and strategy should be entirely in their hands.

The conflict between the synthetic rubber, aviation-gasoline, and escort-vessel programs has been relieved and largely removed by bringing the respective loyal, competent, and aggressive disputants face to face. This should have occurred days ago in the ordinary quiet process of administration.

It shows the need for the following procedure recommended on March 11, 1943, on page 3 of this committee's second annual report:

> During the coming year attention must continue to be focused on the primary need for clearly defined authority in the administration of our domestic war program. This authority should be centralized in a few officials—each solely responsible for the administration of certain activities. Each should be of high ability. *In addition to doing their administrative work they should meet frequently to eliminate all conflicts of jurisdiction and be ready to advise with the President on important questions of policy while relieving him completely of purely administrative work.*

On April 22 the newspapers reported that the Under Secretary of War had accused the persons responsible for the synthetic-rubber program of delaying the production of aviation gasoline to the serious detriment of the war effort. The Petroleum Administrator was reported to second the charges, although the fact appears to be that the newspapers correctly stated his opinions without authorization. The Under Secretary of the Navy entered the fracas, towing into the scene the long-delayed escort-vessel program. Finally, the newspapers reported that the Rubber Director had demanded an investigation, and suggested the resignation of the losing combatant.

This committee announced hearings when it became evident that some of the Nation's key officials had publicly worked themselves into an impossible position. The democratic right of public expression had passed the point of useful exchange. The problems of balancing complex programs involving the high strategy of war cannot be solved in an open forum. The difficulties of such a procedure were demonstrated at this committee's hearings. In several cases, witnesses were constrained and properly so, to present vital facts to the committee privately. The public, which in effect was originally invited by the disputants to judge the issue, cannot know all the facts at this time.

More important, the tenor of the alleged public statements was such that further controversy of this character might seriously impair the effectiveness of able leaders. We cannot afford unnecessarily to lose any men who have proved their ability to cope with intricate problems.

Energetic, aggressive men, striving to meet war needs, will tend to clash when their duties bring them into conflict. But destructive, wasteful feuding must be suppressed.

The task of control and guidance is of utmost importance. Clear leadership in strong hands is required. The influence from above must be always towards unity. Where necessary, heads must be knocked together.

The issues in this dispute, involving war strategy, can and should be resolved by the agency established for that purpose, the War Production Board. This report is directed, not at these issues, but at the weaknesses in administration of the war effort which permit such disputes to reach the point of public controversy.

After Pearl Harbor we found ourselves woefully unprepared for war. This committee reported on the rubber situation and warned that supplies were dangerously low; that erection of synthetic rubber facilities was essential; that there would probably be no new rubber for civilians until 1944. Precious months were wasted in discussion after our findings were made public. Finally, after the President's Baruch committee arrived at the same conclusion, synthetic rubber got under way. To accomplish this a rubber czar was set up, within the War Production Board to be sure, but still more or less autonomous. For a few more months the rubber program seemed stalled, hampered by a clash of personalities and by inability to obtain sufficiently high priorities ratings. In the fall of 1942, for instance, the Navy and Maritime Commission had tied up practically all of the Nation's valve-making facilities.

To break the priorities jam the War Production Board instituted in December a program expediting 20 percent of the rubber and 20 percent of the aviation gasoline programs. This amount proved insufficient and in January of 1943, a total of approximately 55 percent of the Buna S rubber program and a somewhat smaller percentage of the aviation gasoline program were expedited.

It is significant that the contest between rubber and aviation gasoline at that time proved too hot for the War Production Board to handle, and it was finally decided after an appeal to higher authority. Even after the decision, the battle flared up publicly from time to time.

Shortly after Pearl Harbor the committee studied the aviation gasoline situation, and, as in the case of rubber, followed later developments. The armed forces failed by a wide margin to anticipate wartime needs for aviation gasoline. A year after Pearl Harbor, the armed forces were still raising their sights. Their estimates made last September will apparently be met by production this summer. But during last fall and winter—after almost a year of war—these estimates were tremendously increased. This, of course, intensified the priorities jam.

Throughout last winter the Navy was not in a position to build escort vessels in large numbers due to a strategic decision to devote available facilities to another product. Until February of 1943 the Navy was not in a position to place the bulk of its orders and therefore the War Production Board could not begin scheduling.

To expedite the rubber and 100-octane programs certain of the rubber plants and aviation gasoline plants were given precedence over other claimants. This, of course, put the Rubber Director in the driver's seat for at least part of the trip. It resulted in unfortunate personality clashes, as it required other claimants to go to the Rubber Director instead of to the War Production Board for some very important and sorely needed items. On the other hand, it was a method determined after consultation with the various agencies, and after prolonged, if not too prolonged consideration. Efforts were made to relieve the impact of the expediting directives where collisions resulted with varying success.

At the present time the order of expediting the various programs is considered settled by the War Production Board. A vigorous effort to schedule production is under way, apparently with the hearty approval of all concerned. The Chairman of the War Production Board has declared that no new issue was presented to him before the present public flare-up, and his statement was sustained by the other testimony.

Vigorous, able men are now at work on these programs attempting to make up ground lost because of our failure to set our sights high enough. There is a perfectly normal and healthy tendency on the part of each leader to view his program as the most important. Each has complained to the committee that his program has been treated inequitably. It is perfectly clear today, as it was a year ago, that these three competing programs, synthetic rubber, 100-octane gasoline, and escort vessels, are essential to win the war.

The precise balancing of these programs in point of quantity and of time is crucial. A serious error could spell disaster. The deciding agency must have the facts relating to all three programs before it. Its decisions must stick. Confusion in planning today will cut production a year hence. It defeats strategy. Weakness in enforcing decisions will breed confusion.

The job of balancing the conflicting programs has been done and is being done by the War Production Board. The task is one of tremendous magnitude. It can no more be accomplished by discussion before a committee than by castigation in the press.

The present conflict is a result of basic weaknesses in the control of the war effort. In its report of January 15, 1942, this committee called for a strong over-all planning agency. The committee and the Nation believed that these weaknesses had been eliminated by the subsequent creation of the War Production Board. The Chairman of the War Production Board was given sweeping powers, which at least on paper appeared broad enough to enable him to direct war production under the Commander in Chief.

The Chairman was empowered to:

(a) Exercise general direction over the war procurement and production program.

(b) Determine the policies, plans, procedures, and methods of the several Federal departments, establishments, and agencies in respect to war procurement and production, including purchasing, contracting, specifications, and construction; and including conversion, requisitioning, plant expansion, and the financing thereof; and issue such directives in respect thereto as he may deem necessary or appropriate.

(c) Perform the functions and exercise the powers vested in the Supply Priorities and Allocations Board by Executive Order No. 8875 of August 28, 1941.

(d) Supervise the Office of Production Management in the performance of its responsibilities and duties, and direct such changes in its organization as he may deem necessary.

(e) Report from time to time to the President the progress of war procurement and production; and perform such other duties as the President may direct.

Federal departments, establishments and agencies were ordered to comply with the policies, plans, methods, and procedures with respect to war procurement and production as determined by the Chairman. The Chairman was empowered to exercise his authority through such officials or agencies and in such manner as he might determine. His decisions were, by the terms of the order, to be final.

Here is a clear and unequivocal delegation of authority. Why then, was it not exercised? At least part of the answer is to be found in the history of some of the major problems of 1942. The past year has seen several disputes which called for exercise of the Chairman's power to issue "such directives . . . as he may deem necessary and appropriate" and to make "final decisions."

The determination of the Nation's rubber requirements was made on a plane superior to the War Production Board. The findings of the President's Rubber Committee were ordered to be executed by a Rubber Director. This official was declared to be responsible to the Chairman of the War Production Board, but was given power himself to issue directives to the various agencies. The Chairman of the War Production Board was requested by the Commander in Chief to divest himself of concern with the rubber program. Therefore, practically speaking, the Chairman of the War Production Board has had only tenuous authority over the Rubber Director although technically he is the boss.

An Administrator was placed in charge of petroleum programs, including aviation gasoline. The Executive order declares that he "shall be directly responsible to the President." On the other hand, he exercises the "powers, authority, and discretion conferred upon the Chairman of the War Production Board" with respect to the petroleum industry, "subject to the direction of the Chairman of the War Production Board." The lines of authority are confusing even on paper. As a practical matter they breed disputes such as that under consideration.

Today discussion of the over-all legal authority of the War Production Board is mere pedantry. Although the authority may exist it has not been exercised. But the Chairman of the War Production Board has exercised the power to allocate materials and to schedule the production programs of the various departments, and to resolve conflicts between these programs.

Even in the matter of scheduling, when the conflict between the rubber and aviation gasoline programs reached major proportions, the dispute was carried from the Chairman of the War Production Board to the Commander in Chief, who upheld the Chairman.

The War Production Board is serving well as a scheduling and allocating agency. It has succeeded in deciding between claimant programs and in providing materials within the limitations of the conditions under which it has been forced to work. In this field the War Production Board and its Chairman have been successful, and his authority should be sustained.

Two things must be accomplished. First, the strong over-all authority of the War Production Board must be made a living reality. This authority must be ready to make decisions and to enforce them over the objections of aggressive department heads. It must operate in such manner that the various men responsible for individual programs will feel that they have been fairly treated and fully heard.

Second, without dilution of the power of the Chairman, the War Production Board should function as a board. The persons in charge of each major program should sit on it and discuss their problems together regularly and frequently. Each must be made to feel a great sense of responsibility for the entire program with no diminution of his responsibility for that part directly under his control.

RADIO ADDRESS BY SENATOR TRUMAN, SHENANDOAH, IOWA OCTOBER 4, 1943

Congressional Record, 78th Congress, 1st Session, A4145–48.

Today we are engaged in total war. Victory or defeat depends upon our armed forces, but they, in turn, are dependent upon what we give them with which to fight. They are risking their lives. They are entitled to the best that we can give them.

Their needs are determined by the procurement officers of the Army and Navy. The Army and Navy specify what war materials they want, and ask business to produce them in accordance with the Army and Navy specifications.

Business contracts to supply materials that conform to these specifications. Common honesty requires that business should not foist off upon the Government materials that do not conform to contract. But more than honesty is involved here. Our soldiers and sailors are dependent upon those materials for their lives, and our Nation is dependent upon them for its liberty, and even for its continued existence.

For these reasons, the committee of the Senate, of which I have the honor to be the chairman, has considered itself obligated to check charges that come to it from Government inspectors that certain corporations are delivering war material that does not meet specifications. These Government inspectors are patriotic men. They are honest and conscientious. They make no profit from the sale of the war materials. They gain nothing by making unfounded charges, and by complaining at all, they risk their jobs.

The committee has investigated a number of such charges. Unfortunately, it has found several outstanding examples in which they were true. In all such cases, the committee has insisted that the corporation involved should correct the situation, and that it should either produce material according to specifications, or obtain the approval of the armed service using the material for the delivery of substandard items to be paid for as substandard material and used only where it can safely be used.

The committee will continue this policy. It will not accept excuses from management, except where it is convinced that management is acting promptly, and in good faith, to remedy the situation and to discharge those responsible for the fraud upon the Government. By the latter, the committee does not mean the little fellows at the plant who pass the materials, but the plant superintendents who, through carelessness and incapacity, are responsible for the existence of the situation.

Such a policy seemed to the committee to be so clearly right and necessary that it expected that the press and radio would join it in requiring management to conform to Government specifications, and in telling defense workers that they would receive support in their efforts to make good war material.

This is not asking too much. Practically all of industry is producing good, high-grade material. The great mass of companies are giving our Government what it pays for. Only a very few of our large corporations have strayed from the path. And honest business and industry have been unanimous in condemning such practices. I want it perfectly clear that I have no criticism of industry or business in general. The few whom I have had to criticize are the exceptions and not the rule.

By and large the committee's efforts have received such support. The press and radio deserve a great deal of credit for this, because the companies which have had to be corrected include several of the largest corporations in the United States. They spend millions of dollars for advertising, which the press and radio risk if they publicize their mistakes.

These corporations also employ staffs of publicity men, who occupy themselves in attempts to confuse the issues and obtain public comment favorable to the companies based on a misunderstanding by the press or radio of the underlying facts.

A few of our better known newspapers and one popular radio news columnist have misunderstood the situation and by their reports to the public have unwittingly assisted in creating a false impression.

For example, the committee found that the Carnegie-Illinois Steel Corporation, the principal subsidiary of the United States Steel Corporation, was producing steel plate for the Navy and the Maritime Commission and Lend-Lease in its Irvin Works, and that the physical tests to which the finished steel plates were subjected to determine their tensile strength were faked and falsified. The company men in charge of the operation of the testing machines testified that about 5 percent or more of the tests were deliberately faked for the purpose of falsely reporting that the steel plate was in accordance with specifications. To do this they instructed the testers under them to cheat.

The case required particular emphasis because of the improper and obstructive attitude which was taken as to it by the Carnegie-Illinois Corporation when the matter was first brought to its attention. Instead of cooperating in an investigation of a serious situation, which had arisen by reason of the carelessness and negligence of the management, it attempted to delay and obstruct the investigation by refusing access to records and an opportunity to examine witnesses. When it became impossible to continue such tactics, it resorted to attempts to minimize the importance of the dishonesty which it was forced to admit had been practiced by its employees. The presentation of its case before the committee was marked by a lack of frankness and candor.

The situation was so bad that Mr. Fairless, the president of the United States Steel Corporation, stated to the committee: "We are just as shocked to get these facts as you and we are just as desirous of correcting them as you are," and "I consider it was very, very poor management."

Mr. Charles E. Wilson, executive vice chairman of the War Production Board informed the United States Steel Corporation that:

> Although the evidence adduced to date does not prove that the culpability for the falsification goes higher than the chief metallurgist, Mr. McGarrity, it does nevertheless indicate, in our opinion, poor management on the part of the officials of the Carnegie-Illinois Steel Corporation.
>
> Needless to say, this entire situation has deeply disturbed us at the War Production Board, and we are determined, as we feel certain you are, too, that immediate steps shall be taken to put an end to all falsifications, to take appropriate disciplinary action with regard to those responsible for such practices, no matter how high in the organization they may be, and finally so to readjust your organization that, in the future, we can look forward with the fullest confidence to effective, efficient, and straightforward operation of your corporation and its subsidiaries.

Mr. Wilson could not have used plainer language, and he acted only after consulting with the Navy Department and the Maritime Commission and being assured that they concurred in his opinion.

This was not the first time that Carnegie-Illinois Steel Corporation had been guilty of faking tests on steel supplied to the Navy. Forty-nine years ago, in 1894, the House Naval Affairs Committee investigated charges against the Carnegie Steel Co. and found the following charges to have been proven:

> False reports of the treatment of the plates were systematically made to the Government inspectors.
> Specimens taken from the plates both before and after treatment

to ascertain the tensile strength of each plate were stretched without the knowledge of the Government inspectors, so as to increase their apparent tensile strength when actually tested.

False specimens taken from other plates were substituted for the specimens selected by the Government inspectors.

The testing machine was repeatedly manipulated by order of the superintendent of the armor-plate mill so as to increase the apparent tensile strength of the specimens.

The similarity between the frauds practiced today and the frauds practiced 50 years ago is so striking that a single report might well have served to summarize both investigations.

The committee believed that it was time that such practices should stop and was extremely surprised when a leading Pittsburgh paper ran a scare head all the way across the front of its paper as follows: "Steel slump blamed on Truman—Committee's bungling slows war output."

The story referred to an exhaustive independent inquiry just completed by that newspaper. In all this exhaustive inquiry the newspaper had not once contacted the committee for any information. The article proceeded to say that although official production figures for April were not available:

Preliminary and informal reports to the W. P. B. on production trends show that instead of April being the month in which all records for steel-plate production would have been broken, this month's production may fall seriously below previous months —possibly fall off as much as 35 percent.

As I understand the newspaper article, it was a charge that because the Senate had dared to require the United States Steel Corporation to be honest we were going to lose up to 35 percent of our steel-plate production, and that that loss should be attributed to the committee's bungling.

This article with its prediction of a 35-percent slump for April was published on April 16, after half the month had expired.

The fact is that after the month had ended and the figures were in, the War Production Board announced that April was a record-breaking month, and that the steel industry produced more steel plate than it had ever before produced in a similar month.

I wonder, and I think you will wonder, who told that newspaper that there was going to be a steel slump and why was such a ridiculous rumor circulated.

Shortly afterward the committee found that the Wright Aeronautical Corporation, a subsidiary of the Curtiss-Wright Corporation, was guilty of selling for installation in Army and Navy planes airplane engines that were not in accordance with specifications.

The engines in question were made at Lockland, Ohio, near Cincinnati, in a plant designed by Curtiss-Wright, but built by the Government at a cost of more than $140,000,000.

I want to tell you just how this investigation started and was conducted. In order to make sure that the engines being produced could properly be used in our military aircraft, both Curtiss-Wright and the Government employed many inspectors, at a total cost of several million dollars a year. The committee received letters from a number of these inspectors, particularly the Government inspectors, complaining that they were being forced to pass parts and engines which were not in accordance with the specifications. Now, these specifications were prepared by Curtiss-Wright itself, and approved by the War Department. Curtiss-Wright has never claimed that the specifications were needlessly made too strict.

A committee investigator was sent to Cincinnati. He found that the majority of the Government inspectors looked to the Senate to correct a situation which they had lost hope of having corrected by Curtiss-Wright. In fact, one of the inspectors broke down and cried as he told his story, saying that he had two nephews in the Air Forces. Before our investigator had finished, not only a majority of the Government inspectors, but also a number of the Curtiss-Wright inspectors made the same charge, namely, that the inspectors were not being permitted to reject parts and engines that failed to conform to specifications.

These men had come to the committee only as a last resort. They had tried to tell their story to Curtiss-Wright. They had tried to tell their story to their own superiors in the United States Army. The only reward of those who attempted to do this was that they were transferred under a cloud, or otherwise penalized. Morale was almost completely destroyed.

Their complaints were unanimous. There were no discrepancies. They had been forced to accept bad materials. In many cases, where they attempted to reject material which was clearly bad, Curtiss-Wright succeeded in having them overruled by appealing, over their heads, to their superiors.

They did not charge their superiors with dishonesty—they simply pointed out that, again and again, material which was clearly and dangerously bad, had been accepted. They were able to show our investigator defective parts which had been accepted. They were able to point out engines which had been accepted with defects.

The committee did not make any public announcement of the conditions which its investigator had found, because it wanted to be absolutely sure that it was fair to Curtiss-Wright and to the Army. What the committee did do was to call in both Curtiss-Wright and the Army, and give them each a week or two within which to make their own investigation of the inspection procedures at the Lockland plant. Both later reported to the committee that they had found nothing. Some of the Curtiss-Wright personnel, who claimed to have made an investigation, have since been discharged or removed from their jobs, and the Army has instituted court-martial proceedings against some of the officers upon whom it relied for an investigation.

A subcommittee of the Truman committee then went to Cincinnati to inspect the plant and to hold hearings. Before it finished, it had heard scores of witnesses. One witness would suggest several others. A group of inspectors would go out, voluntarily, and dig up a number of other inspectors who had the same story to tell. The subcommittee took 1,200 pages of testimony, and found a situation which was appalling.

At the subcommittee's invitation, an Army officer accompanied it, and was at its hearings. At his request, the testimony taken by the subcommittee was made available to the Army, which also made a further investigation of its own. The Army and the committee are in substantial agreement that the situation at the Lockland plant was extremely bad, and required drastic corrective action.

General Arnold, commander of the Army Air Force, recently complimented me on the accomplishments of the committee at Lockland and informed me that the committee's action has been of great value and assistance to the Army Air Force.

Maj. Gen. Charles Branshaw, commanding general, matériel command, at Wright Field, recently informed Senator Wallgren, the chairman of the Subcommittee on Aircraft, that in his opinion the situation was three times worse than the committee had said it was.

The committee leaned over backward in this case to be certain that it was fair to Curtiss-Wright. It even submitted its report to Curtiss-Wright, as well as to the Army, in advance, so that both would have an opportunity to present any evidence they desired, and to suggest any changes which they thought might merit the approval of the committee. I do not know how we could have been more fair.

Very significantly, Curtiss-Wright confined itself to a few generalities. It could not discuss the detailed facts themselves because they did not admit of argument.

The committee issued a report to the Senate to force Curtiss-Wright and the Army to take further additional corrective action, and to take it promptly.

In its report, the committee specifically called attention to the fact that Curtiss-Wright, through the Wright Aeronautical Corporation, was producing and causing the Government to accept defective and sub-standard material and that this was accomplished in the following ways:

1. By the falsification of tests.
2. By destruction of records.
3. By improperly recording results of tests.
4. By forging inspection reports.
5. By failing to segregate substandard and defective material.
6. By failing to promptly destroy or mutilate such defective and substandard material.
7. By orally changing tolerances allowed on parts.
8. By circumventing the salvage committee set up to pass on the usability of parts outside of tolerances.
9. By allowing production to override the inspection force, thereby destroying morale of both company and Army inspectors.
10. By skipping inspection operations.

The committee found no evidence that Curtiss-Wright was deliberately disregarding the specifications for the purpose of sabotage. We understood that the reason why some of its officials wanted lax inspection was that they were not able to produce engines in quantity that conformed to the specifications. For these reasons, the committee expected that the rate of production of engines would fall off when the plant was required to produce engines which conformed to Curtiss-Wright's own specifications. In other words, to get the quality which both the company and the War Department thought was necessary for engines going into military aircraft, it would be necessary to sacrifice quantity until Curtiss-Wright could improve the management and the procedures at the Lockland plant. Of course, this was distasteful to the plant managers whose negligence and incapacity were being demonstrated, and to Curtiss-Wright which would suffer a financial loss because less engines would be accepted and paid for by the Government.

Most newspapers and radio commentators thoroughly understood this situation, but a few of them allowed themselves to be confused by Curtiss-Wright officials who wanted to make it appear that it was the Senate, and not themselves, who should be censured for their inability or unwillingness to produce airplane parts and engines in accordance with their own specifications.

These newspaper articles and radio talks insinuated and, in some cases, stated: First, that the loss of production at the Lockland plant was due to bungling by the Truman committee which had caused inspectors to reject parts that should have been passed; second, that the committee's report was unnecessary and issued only for sensational purposes because Curtiss-Wright had already corrected the situation; third, that in any event, all the defective parts had been found before the engines were finally accepted for use in airplanes; fourth, that the quality of the engines was demonstrated by the job they were supposed to have done in the Tokyo raid; and fifth, that airplane production was going to suffer for lack of these engines.

You may be interested to know that the same man who predicted for the Pittsburgh paper the steel slump that never materialized somehow got himself substituted for a well-known radio commentator. For several days he attacked the Truman committee over the radio for daring to call Curtiss-Wright to account.

If these reporters were not duped, I suggest that they were, themselves, the sensation mongers. It is very significant that no official of Curtiss-Wright has ever publicly to you, or privately to the Senate committee, made any such statements as these.

Let us look at what Mr. Guy Vaughan, president of Curtiss-Wright, had to say as to the charge that production was lowered because the inspection procedures were too rigid:

> Question. The stoppages you refer to are your own stoppages which you have had to instigate to correct a situation that was not right?
> Mr. Vaughan. That is right. . . .
> Question. Does the company, through you now, publicly take the position that the reason for your reduction in production is the fact that the Army inspection service is blocking production by its inspection procedure?
> Mr. Vaughan. No; it could not. . . .
> Question. And any articles to that effect you would repudiate as not being in accordance with the facts?
> Mr. Vaughan. Publicly, internationally, any other way.

Mr. Vaughan could not take any other position because Major LaVista, resident representative of the Army for the Lockland plant had just testified that he had contacted three of the principal officials of the Lockland plant and that they had been unable to point out any cases where their production had been held up by being forced to comply with inspection procedures.

The suggestion that Curtiss-Wright had taken full corrective action before the committee's report was equally unfounded.

Question. You do not disagree with General Echols in his conclusion that the management of the company at present is not satisfactory.

Mr. Vaughan. I will agree to the fact that we have had a number of things that are not called good management, but I won't agree that the people who have been building up this thing have done a bad job. I think it can be made better as time goes on. It has got to be made better.

Major General Echols, in charge of matériel for the Army Air Force, officially testified on behalf of the War Department that:

General Echols. In my opinion, the management which has been there for the past several months has not shown itself qualified to accomplish the job as laid out by that plant.

General Echols further testified that:

General Echols. The Government has had discussions with the top management of the Wright Aeronautical Corporation with regard to getting men to strengthen the management in this plant.

Question. You mean by that, I take it, General, that in addition to the question of the top man in the plant you are dissatisfied with what you might term the management group in the highest brackets in the plant and have desired that they be strengthened by the addition of other qualified men.

General Echols. This is my opinion. They should be.

Question. Why has not the Wright Aeronautical Corporation, of its own volition, provided that kind of management?

General Echols. I don't know.

Question. What reasons have they given you for their failure to do it?

General Echols. The reasons they have given me were that they believed that the present management could work the problem out.

Thus, 6 weeks after the committee had issued its aircraft report, Curtiss-Wright had still failed to provide good management at the Lockland plant, and the situation was still so bad as to require both the Army and the Truman committee to give the company the ultimatum "produce or get out."

As to the suggestion that the engines produced were not defective, Major LaVista testified:

Three engines which were on the shipping dock, finally inspected and sealed, ready to ship to the destination, were brought back, disassembled, and reinspected 100 percent. Everyone of the three engines were found to be in such a condition that they could not have been installed in an airplane. In fact, the conditions found were bad enough that the company immediately ordered 89 engines, which were ready to ship, returned to the assembly department to be completely disassembled and reinspected 100 percent.

Major LaVista also testified that over 400 engines were turned down on final run due to high oil flow because no effort had been made to maintain a close tolerance on the connecting-rod bearings. When 33 engines out of these 400 were reassembled with a proper fitting, all 33 went through the penalty run without trouble. Major LaVista also testified that parts which had been rejected and which had not been found suitable for salvage were discovered in the so-called green assembly line ready to be assembled into engines.

Major LaVista concluded, and I quote:

> It can be readily seen from the above facts that production could be completely bottled up until such time as these engines and parts are out of the way.

Since the Cincinnati hearing the Army has torn down and reexamined 64 of the 89 engines referred to by Major LaVista. It has also called in 100 engines as a sample selection of the engines produced from January to April prior to the committee's report. So far 10 of these have been torn down and reexamined. The results were were obtained from the Army by the committee, in confidence, and I would like to set them forth here for your information as a direct, final, and conclusive answer to the contention that the engines produced were not defective and were fit for use in airplanes.

However, Under Secretary of War Patterson has specifically requested that this information not be made public. Without his consent, I will not make it public.

Since this speech was announced, further conferences have been had with officials of the Army, including Under Secretary of War Patterson. The Under Secretary stated to the committee on Saturday, "Investigations made by the Army confirm the findings made by the Truman committee as to the construction and inspection of engines." I am happy to say that the Army officials have reiterated their views that the Truman committee has performed the most worthwhile service in connection with the Curtiss-Wright plant at Lockland.

Under Secretary of War Patterson and other officials of the War Department agree with us that the results of the investigation made by the Truman committee, the matters about which we complained and which we pointed out, were matters of serious import and concern. We also agree that, happily, through vigorous efforts of the Army and the Truman committee, these conditions recently have been largely corrected. Since the committee's report the Curtiss-Wright Co. has installed much better management and procedures of every kind. Rigid inspection is now required, not only by the War Department but also by the company itself. Fathers and mothers of American boys who are pilots, and the boys themselves, can be assured that the Truman committee, the Army, and all branches of the armed forces will continue the most careful scrutiny of every plant in order that the lives and safety of our boys may be protected as far as it is humanly possible.

As to the contention that the Lockland plant must be good because its engines powered the Tokyo raiders, the fact is that Mr. Vaughan, president of Curtiss-Wright, has written the committee apologizing for that assertion. When he checked up—and it is to his credit that he checked up—he found that none of the planes raiding Tokyo had an engine manufactured at Lock-land.

The suggestion that the requirement that these engines be made properly in conformance to Curtiss-Wright's own specifications is holding up airplane production is likewise unfounded. The War Production Board informs the committee that these engines are used in eight types of planes, and that deliveries of completed aircraft have been affected in only one instance, a Navy flying boat.

Let me repeat, I am very glad to be able to tell you that since our report Curtiss-Wright has taken drastic action and recently has made real progress. It has obtained some experienced personnel from other industries. Curtiss-Wright has hired a new senior vice president, who is giving all of his attention to correcting the situation. It has obtained a new manager for the Lockland plant and has relegated the former manager to other work. It has fired some of the principal assistants. It has sought and obtained outside advice as to how to better its inspection and production procedures. The improvements have borne fruit. Production is better and is expected to become much better.

These steps are all to the good, and the committee will support fully every effort of Curtiss-Wright to produce good planes and engines. It will unhesitatingly call attention to any failures where it believes that Curtiss-Wright or any other company is failing to produce good material and is slow or unwilling to take action to correct its failure.

A constructive and timely investigation of failure to conform to Government specifications may be painful to the businessmen involved, but it may also be very useful even to them. Some weeks ago there was a most unfortunate accident to a glider, which resulted in the loss of a number of lives, including that of the mayor of St. Louis and the president of the company manufacturing the glider. I checked on the cause of this glider crash and was informed that it was due to a strut fitting which had been improperly machined down to a point far below Government specifications. As a result it broke under stress and caused the glider to crash. Had we checked earlier and criticized the company for installing these defective parts the president of the glider company might, like United States Steel and Curtiss-Wright officials, have resented it. But he would have been alive today.

The committee will disregard newspaper articles and radio programs which confuse the issues and seek to absolve corporations for their failures. The next time you read such an article or hear such a program, I would appreciate it if you would write me. I will send you a copy of the report of the public hearings in question. After you have read them, if you disagree with the committee, I would appreciate your writing and telling me so. If you disagree with the newspaper or radio commentator, I would appreciate your writing him and telling him so.

TESTIMONY OF LT. GEN. BREHON B. SOMERVELL ON CANOL PROJECT DECEMBER 20, 1943

U.S. Senate, Investigation of the National Defense Program Hearings Before a Special Committee Investigating the National Defense Program, 78th Congress, 2nd Session, 9655–74.

. . . there was urgent and even desperate need for oil in the general location of the Alcan Highway; the oil was at the Norman wells; it was of excellent quality, but in an indeterminate amount. Strategically, we were on the defense. Our shipping was dwindling rapidly and there was no relief in sight for an indeterminate period. I was sure of the final outcome of the war, but there was certainly no conclusive evidence even to that effect at that time. With all of the facts at one's disposal, the conclusion that the project should have been adopted at the time, even on hindsight, seems inescapable.

Now the next question is, Is the project feasible?

I am reminded, and I don't know whether I told you that New Zealand was decided upon the same day that this other project was decided upon. If I didn't tell you that, I should have. The whole thing was being carried along as a general consideration in the whole line from Alaska to the Far East.

The question is, Is the project feasible? We were told there wouldn't be any oil. We were told there was no oil supply. We were told that the oil wouldn't flow through the pipes after we built the pipe line; and we were told we couldn't build a pipe line, and we couldn't maintain it even if we did build it.

Senator Hatch. You mean that before you started the project, you were told these things?

General Somervell. I was told the latter right afterward, along in May and June. On the question of oil flow, it was before the project; but on the question of our not being able to do it, it was after. In other words, the hazards of the project were played up to us very vividly during the weeks and months that followed the decision.

Senator Hatch. Would you mind telling us who played up those hazards?

General Somervell. Mr. Ickes called our attention to them sometime later. The question of oil was played up by the oil companies themselves. Everybody who had ever run a cigar store in Alaska said we couldn't build a project, that the climate was too severe. In other words, we had counsels of that kind from a good many sources.

Now let's take up the question of oil supply. There is no question about our anxiety regarding the oil supply. I told you that so far as we knew, there was a limited amount of oil, and my memory is now refreshed to the fact that about 8,000,000 barrels was the figure which was given to us as a sure thing by the oil company at that time. Our anxiety was, Would there be enough oil?

And suppose there was not enough oil, what should we do about it? Of course, there was only one thing to do, and that would have been just to fold up. It would have been another defeat. That is exactly what did happen in New Zealand and we did fold up.

Fortunately, the oil is present in the Norman fields, not only in the quantities that we hoped for, which jumped from 2,000,000 to 8,000,000 barrels, but in quantities far in excess of our wildest expectation. This is not an 8,000,000-barrel field; it is at least a 58,000,000-barrel field, and probably a 100,000,000-barrel field. There are geological and geophysical conditions that indicate that other fields which we have discovered since in this general location will also bring in tremendous amounts of oil. In other words, what we have discovered is the biggest oil field that has been uncovered in the last 15 years. If that is a crime, we are guilty of it.

Senator Brewster. In the world, you mean?

General Somervell. On the North American Continent.

It was alleged that the oil would not flow through the pipes. Now, obviously, if we built a pipe line and the oil wouldn't flow through it, it would be a very unwise undertaking. However, we knew that the oil was of exceptional quality. We have had the oil analyzed as we have gone along, and we find that it has a pour point of something like −72°. Now, the lowest temperature that has ever been experienced up there is higher than that, and the mean minimum run around only about 25° below zero. We had this looked into by a number of organizations, including the Bureau of Mines in the Department of the Interior, and their report is that it is an oil of unusually fine characteristics.

The next thing that was supposed to happen was that when the oil was pumped through the line, paraffin would be deposited in such quantities as to clog the line, and consequently it wouldn't operate. Paraffin, of course, is present in many lines. There are customary ways of removing it which are available here. In addition to that, we have unusual facilities in that we have a small refinery at Norman wells and we can put a slug of gasoline into the line at any time we want, to supplement all the other methods. We have sedimentation and the usual scrapers and go-devils that are used for that purpose; but I think we can dismiss all these fears and stop worrying about them, because we are pumping oil through the line now.

Senator Ferguson. General, what part of the line are you pumping oil through?

General Somervell. From Norman wells. We started to fill the line on the 18th, and it is now 29 miles from Norman wells.

Senator Ferguson. What is the temperature today?

General Somervell. Fifteen degrees below zero.

It has likewise been alleged that the line couldn't be constructed. Well, it is practically finished.

Next, it has been alleged that the line couldn't be maintained, once it was constructed. I would like to invite the committee's attention to the fact that the line from Skagway to Whitehorse, which is through the most rugged of all the territory, has been in use for over a year.

Mr. Fulton. That is a gasoline line.

General Somervell. It makes no difference, Mr. Fulton, what goes through the line. The point I am discussing is whether the line could be maintained intact. There is a heavy list of experts that say it will be maintained. That is in addition to the fact that it has been maintained for a year. We expect the customary difficulties. We have them in northern United States, in Montana and Idaho with temperatures far below the mean minima encountered in this field.

I think, and most of the oil experts think, that the dangers to be expected from floods and things of that kind, which are encountered along all pipe lines, are probably more hazardous than what we have to expect up there. I would like to invite the committee's attention to the fact that our most recent and most spectacular pipe line, the Big Inch pipe line, which was built from Texas to the East, happens to run through my home town, Little Rock, Ark., and that the line was completely wiped out in Little Rock last year, and the Army went in and built the by-pass to get the oil through the line. It is something to be expected, and we can expect breaks in any oil line. However, we certainly do not anticipate any great difficulty maintaining this line, and our year's experience proves it.

We weren't content, however, to trust our own opinion. We have got expert, disinterested opinion which is available.

Senator Brewster. Has it been maintained through an Alaskan winter yet?

General Somervell. Yes, sir; spring is the time when you expect trouble, and it has been maintained through the spring and winter.

Mr. Fulton. You don't mean the Whitehorse-Fairbanks pipe line which isn't finished yet?

General Somervell. I do not. I mean the part of the lines from Skagway to Whitehorse, which is in the worst part of the country, both in regard to weather and with regard to the land itself, has been maintained.

Mr. Fulton. That is along a railroad line, is it not?

General Somervell. Most of it. But the people who are concerned about it are concerned about ground movements and things of that kind, which are alleged to tear the pipe apart.

Senator Kilgore. How many breaks did you have last year from contraction and expansion.

Brig. Gen. L. D. Worsham (division engineer, Northwest Division, United States Army). The first was in May of this year, May of '42.

Senator Kilgore. You had one?

General Worsham. Yes, sir; the first break.

Senator Kilgore. When did you start operating?

General Worsham. January 20, 1943.

General Somervell. I think we can dispose of these things. All of these hazards have been successively razed: First, "we will have no oil" (we have struck a bonanza); secondly, "the oil won't flow through the pipe" (it is flowing through the pipe); third, "you can't build the line" (it is being built, practically finished); and fourth, "you can't maintain it" (and we have maintained it for this length of time). And our contractor, the California Standard Oil Co., has no qualms whatever about operating the line.

The next question, "Has the work been done competently?" It hardly seems necessary for me to mention this. The job along the Alcan Highway and many others that we have undertaken were rated as impossible. Well, they have been done, and they have been done, I may say, with admiration of professional and lay groups. This job, from the point of view of engineering accomplishment, ranks along with a lot of others. It certainly is no less noteworthy as a bit of engineering skill and daring and ingenuity and organization.

It has been done by the Corps of Engineers of the Army, and there is no organization in this country or elsewhere with a record to excel it.

We could have finished this job sooner. There were, as you know, a number of changes in the local and in the general situation which made it unnecessary for us to have pushed the job to the extent which we would have, had the Japanese been successful in Alaska. We could have shoved the refinery in sooner, and we could have left some troops along the route which we removed for more urgent work elsewhere. However, a very workmanlike job has been done under extremely difficult conditions, and it has been done in an extremely short time. And I should say that all of the people who have been engaged in the construction (I haven't, so I can say this freely) deserve the very highest praise.

The next question is whether the decision was right or wrong. We have got this project to the point we have. Should we finish it or should we enlarge it?

Now, whatever may be the right or wrong of the original decision—and it seems abundantly clear to me that we were right—we have to answer that question, "Shall we finish it or shall we enlarge it?"

We are no longer on the defensive. We are no longer being crowded against the wall. We are pushing the offensive in all parts of the globe, and that is due to a number of things—among others, to the leadership of our Chiefs of Staff and our leaders in the field, and to their well-equipped troops in every corner of the globe.

Now we are on the offensive and no stone must be left unturned to make it possible for us to move against the enemy everything we can in overwhelming force.

The Chiefs of Staff have considered the position of the Northwest in the strategy they are pursuing, and they have considered the position of this project in the Northwest, and we have decided that the project is essential. Since that decision, they have had an opportunity to review their strategy with that of our Allies during the last month. That review has served only to strengthen the position which they had previously taken. . . .

It is going to go all the way to Whitehorse. It will be 81 miles on Christmas Day, and it will keep on going until it gets to Whitehorse, where it will be put in the refinery and refined.

Senator Ferguson. Is that just filling the line?

General Somervell. Yes sir; filling and testing.

Senator Ferguson. Just filling the line?

General Somervell. Filling and testing.

Mr. Fulton. When will the pipe line be finished and the first drop of oil reach Whitehorse?

General Somervell. Would you mind if I finished the statement?

Mr. Fulton. No; but I couldn't understand. Why put oil in a pipe line that wouldn't be finished for many months?

General Somervell. That isn't true. The line will be finished before many months.

The Chairman. How soon will it be finished?

General Somervell. I will give you the figure. The pipe line is expected to be completely welded by the 15th of January. Filling by crude to start by the 18th of December, with crude arriving in Whitehorse early in March, allowing for adjustments and repairs.

Mr. Fulton. That was in accordance with our information, that it would be the spring before the pumping station would be ready.

General Somervell. You must remember that you have to fill the line before you can take anything out of the opposite end.

Mr. Fulton. Oh, yes. But you have to keep pumping it while it is in the line in order to keep it from settling down, don't you.

General Somervell. I couldn't hear you. Would you repeat that?

Mr. Fulton. And you have to keep pumping it all the time that it is in the line, do you not?

General Somervell. Oh, absolutely; if you want anything to come out the other end.

Mr. Fulton. No; but I mean if you don't want to clog up your line with paraffin you have to keep pumping your oil.

Senator Kilgore. Keep the oil moving.

General Somervell. We expect to keep the oil moving. We have large stores in Whitehorse.

Mr. Fulton. In other words, you will pump it back and forth.

General Somervell. No, No.

Mr. Fulton. You can't get it to Whitehorse until March.

General Somervell. We are testing the line from the east, as I told you, and from the west with gasoline. The line will be tested, and the oil will be pumped through there and we will deliver oil to the refinery for refining purposes early in May.

Senator Kilgore. In other words, what is being pumped and put in it now is gasoline.

General Somervell. No, sir. It is oil, crude oil.

Senator Ferguson. Is the oil merely being put in the pipe line today for testing purposes?

General Somervell. Testing purposes and filling.

Senator Ferguson. Filling.

General Somervell. On the money side of the project aside from the distribution lines, which haven't been questioned, as far as I know, there is about $24,000,000 still on the books to be spent, and of this there is about eight and one-half million for further exploration of the field. If we stop, we could save about seven million of that. We have $7,000,000 in there for demobilization. That will be spent whether we stop tomorrow or stop when the project is finished. That leaves only $10,000,000 really which is in connection with this project as it stands now. In other words, $10,000,000 is the figure that we are talking about.

Senator Ball. What is that seven million for demobilization?

General Somervell. That means getting all the men and equipment out of there, returning them to the United States and their homes, and all the other expenses necessary for the clean-up of the job.

Senator Ball. That is an awfully large item for that. How many men have you up there?

General Somervell. There are about 10,000 men.

Senator Kilgore. Does that figure include civilians and soldiers or just civilians?

General Somervell. All civilians now, no soldiers up there now. At least, to answer your question, Senator Ball, whether we spent it or not, that amount is set up in the estimates for that purpose, and this $7,000,000 isn't involved in any consideration that we have of whether or not to finish the job. That is the point I am trying to make.

So, we have $10,000,000 to talk about.

The War Department has been asked to join in prospecting in Alaska with the Department of the Interior and a figure of $5,500,000 has been set up as the cost of the exploration. If we went in there and if we spent the 5½ million dollars, and if we were successful, at a minimum it would be 12 to 18 months before we would get any oil. It probably would take a lot longer time than that actually to develop any field there which would be producing in quantity.

Now, the difficulties to be expected are comparable with those on this job. Remember, this is in Alaska.

Now, instead of getting oil for this 5½ million dollars, we may get nothing but dry holes. We want to do it—

Senator Brewster (interposing). In the Point Barrow area, do you mean?

General Somervell. No. Point Barrow is way down on the list, priority 6 or something of that kind. Most of it is in the southern part of Alaska.

Now, we want to do this prospecting. We want to go into it. We want to develop all the oil we can. We want to get all the oil we can for this war. I don't know how soon the war is going to be over, and we also want a reserve for our use when the war is over. So we think the prospecting is all right. But considering it solely now on the basis of the 5½ million, we are going up there, we are not going to get anything for at least 12 to 18 months, if we get it at all. What we want is oil now, and we want a certainty and not a promise and have it in this project.

We are urging developments in Persia, and Arabia, and Burma, and the East Indies. We want oil in all those places. We have lend-leased to the Russians and the British $125,000,000 to get oil.

Senator Brewster. You mean that in equipment?

General Somervell. Yes, sir. This project gives us oil and gives it to us right now, and it gives it to us where we want it and it holds promise backed by the most convincing geological and geophysical facts that it will be a tremendous field. To me, there is no question of completing the project. The only question is one of expansion.

Now, for the reason that I have given you, I won't ask your approval now for the expansion, but I think it is quite probable that approval for this expansion will be sought within a relatively short time. . . .

Now, to sum up what I have said, gentlemen, when the project was adopted, no other course of action seems even now to have been possible. The job has been courageously executed, and all the hazards, all the timid counsel that have been offered have proved to have been wrong. Not by counter arguments, but by actual physical demonstration.

Oil greatly in excess of what was expected has been discovered. The project, as originally proposed for a much smaller prospect, is virtually complete. It will deliver oil where and when we want. It requires no more material. It is declared a military necessity by the highest military authorities, and, I might say, while I was out of the country. These man are the directing heads of your armed forces in the field. That decision has been reinforced during the last month. The project holds promise and even certainty of much greater usefulness. Its completion should be unquestioned, and its expansion should only await the completion of negotiations and the finishing of certain data that we are now collecting.

How is it possible for anyone to conceive of refusing oil under the present conditions from any source is beyond me.

That is all I want to say, Senator.

The Chairman. Senator Kilgore was chairman of the subcommittee which went into this Canol project. Have you any questions, Senator Kilgore?

Senator Kilgore. Yes, Mr. Chairman.

From the discussion in here I want to know the exact conception under which you are treating this. In other words, is this being treated as a post-war project for World War No. 3 as you expressed it, or is it being treated as a project for the current war?

General Somervell. First of all, we want oil now. We want it for this war. Secondly, we have discovered what is apparently a very valuable asset. Should we, after making that discovery, make the most of it or not? That is, for the next war.

Senator Kilgore. Then the project to date is not a post-war feature. It is a current war feature that we have been discussing and has been discussed up to the present time, is that right?

General Somervell. It is both, of course, I don't know how—

Senator Kilgore (interposing). If it is both, why couldn't it have been protected in this contract? You have spoken of a contract. The contract is merely a proposal by the United States which was acceded to by the Canadian Government and by Imperial Oil Co., isn't that right?

General Somervell. No, sir.

Senator Kilgore. In other words, they made no proposal. We made the proposal and they accepted it, isn't that right?

General Somervell. Well, there are two things: One is the contract, sir, which is a—

Senator Kilgore. Well, it amounted to a contract.

General Somervell. One is a contract with the Imperial Oil Co. and the other is an agreement with the Canadian Government.

Senator Kilgore. Yes.

General Somervell. Now in the contract with the Imperial Oil we put in a proviso which permitted renegotiation. Of course, our arrangements with Canada are subject to change at any time.

Senator Ferguson. General, would you have your aide find whether or not that contract has been modified?

General Somervell. Yes, sir.

Senator Kilgore. And that was the provision made in your contract then—the right to renegotiate as far as this 3,000-acre lease of Imperial Oil Co. is concerned?

General Somervell. Yes, sir.

Senator Kilgore. And it was a proposal by the Government in both cases, by our Government?

General Somervell. That is true. Most decidedly.

Senator Kilgore. And they accepted our terms.

General Somervell. Most decidedly; yes, sir.

Senator Kilgore. Now, a large part of your discussion both in this public hearing and in the private hearing related to the need for petroleum. Now, at the outset this is what I want to bear down on, what did you expect to add to this picture by spending $135,000,000 to get 479 barrels of aviation gasoline a day, and at the same time in that critical period using 300,000 tons of vital shipping and 300,000 tons of critical material.

General Somervell. Well, sir, in the first place we are not spending it to get 470 barrels of aviation gasoline a day. That is only a part of the product. In the second place, we haven't spent 300,000 tons of material up there.

Senator Kilgore. 479 barrels a day is all of the aviation gasoline that is expected to be produced from the present plant, isn't it?

General Somervell. As I explained to you, Senator, we are not seeking to get aviation gasoline alone.

Senator Kilgore. All right, then we still get a thousand barrels of truck gasoline on top of that.

General Somervell. And certain other distillates come out.

Senator Kilgore. Isn't it a fact, also, that in that place you are going to have to use all your other distillates and probably part of your gasoline to get heat to maintain the refinery?

General Somervell. I don't think so.

Senator Kilgore. It takes a tremendous amount of heat to maintain a refinery in Texas, and I imagine at 25 below it would take still more heat.

General Somervell. Let me give you the output. The output amounts to 2,220 barrels.

Senator Kilgore. Consisting of what?

General Somervell. Wait a second. That was the original figure that you are talking about. That was the 2,220 barrels. Of that, there were to be 479 barrels of 100-octane, 1,048 of—

Senator Kilgore (interposing). Truck gasoline.

General Somervell. Truck gasoline, 400 of Diesel oil, and 293 of recharging stock and residual fuel.

Senator Kilgore, Is that net, without importing additional components from the United States to step that gasoline up?

General Somervell. That is the net, with the exception of a little tetraethyl lead; yes, sir.

Senator Kilgore. Have you deducted anything to take care of the material necessary to operate that refinery?

General Somervell. Yes, sir. We deducted 800 barrels. We get a 3,000-barrel input and a 2,200-barrel output.

Senator Kilgore. That 800 barrels you maintain will operate the refinery?

General Somervell. Yes, sir.

Senator Kilgore. At the time this project was planned, was that considered enough to justify this material expenditure?

General Somervell. At that time it was, most decidedly. Our backs were to the wall. We were driven practically out of every outpost. We didn't know where we were going to turn next. Any amount of oil would have been justified.

Senator Kilgore. Any amount of oil, no matter where placed, would have been justified?

General Somervell. Well, within the realms of reason; yes, sir. . . .

MEMORANDUM OF HUGH FULTON, CHIEF COUNSEL, TRUMAN COMMITTEE MAY 26, 1944

Papers of Harry S. Truman, Senatorial and Vice-Presidential Files,
Harry S. Truman Library, Independence, Missouri.

To All the Members of the Truman Committee:

The Committee has obtained a copy of a press release, prepared by the United States Steel Corporation, with respect to the acquittal of the Corporation in the criminal proceedings brought in Pittsburgh. A copy of the release is attached.

After discussion with several members of the Committee, Senator Truman requested that I inform the members of the Committee as to the facts in case any of them should have occasion at any time to discuss the Carnegie-Illinois case with persons who might not understand the true situation. Senator Truman suggested that in the next annual report of the Committee the situation could be reviewed. He was of the opinion, however, that no release in answer to the United States Steel Corporation was necessary.

The Corporation was the only defendant. A verdict was directed as to the charge that records had been destroyed, because the Judge was of the opinion that the Corporation could not be held criminally responsible unless it was established that the destruction of the records had been made by a company policy-making official. He was of the opinion that the chief metallurgist of the Plant was not a company policy-making official.

With respect to the second charge concerning the faking of inspections of steel plate and the testing of steel beneath the standard of the Government in the purchase contracts, the Corporation made no attempt to deny those facts, but instead assured that there was no criminal intent on the part of the Corporation, and that the steel, although substandard, was not defective because there was no proof that it had failed to stand up under the uses to which it was put. The Department of Justice states that it was given no cooperation whatever by the Navy Department and Maritime Commission on this point. In addition, some of the witnesses who testified before the Committee as to the faking and forging of tests, did not testify at the trial because they claimed their constitutional privilege against self-incrimination.

Under these circumstances, the Corporation of course is entirely inaccurate in inferring that it was cleared of "unfair and unsubstantiated accusations made by the Truman Committee" because it admitted at the trial that the accusations the Truman Committee made were that records had been falsified and substandard steel furnished.

In addition, a verdict of acquittal in a criminal proceeding is not an exoneration of anyone, and merely means that the Judge was not convinced beyond a reasonable doubt that the Government had proved every point in its case.

Hugh Fulton

News Release of U.S. Steel Corporation
May 23, 1944

"We are happy to have the public know that the unfair and unsubstantiated accusations made by the Truman Committee of the delivery by Carnegie-Illinois of defective plates have been completely refuted," J. L. Perry, President of Carnegie-Illinois Steel Corporation, a U.S. Steel subsidiary, said in commenting upon today's acquittal of Carnegie-Illiniois in the criminal suit prosecuted by the Government against it in the Federal Court at Pittsburgh.

"No witness" Mr. Perry continued "testified either before the Truman Committee or before the Federal Court at Pittsburgh that any defective steel plates were ever supplied by Carnegie-Illinois Steel Corporation from Irvin Works or elsewhere."

Mr. Perry added:

"About a year ago, when indictments were found against Carnegie-Illinois Steel Corporation, relative to alleged false reports of tests of steel plates at Irvin Works, I stated that Carnegie-Illinois was confident that when it was afforded the opportunity to present in court the full facts, the outcome would be complete exoneration. Such statement reflected my firm conviction that none of the plates supplied by Irvin Works were either defective or inferior, and that any irregularities in test reports which might have occurred concerned relatively unimportant variations from the specifications. My statement has since been proved to have been entirely accurate.

"After an exhaustive three week's trial, just concluded before Judge Robert M. Gibson in the United States District Court at Pittsburgh, such complete exoneration has been obtained. Today the jury in that case acquitted Carnegie-Illinois of the charges contained in 47 counts of an indictment, that it had falsely certified tests on certain plates furnished to or for various government agencies. During the trial, Carnegie-Illinois introduced evidence to establish the actual heat numbers of the steel involved in each of these 47 counts, as well as evidence to prove that all of the steel in question had, in fact, been properly tested and had met the chemical and physical requirements of the contract specifications.

"Federal Judge Gibson directed a verdict of acquittal on another indictment, charging Carnegie-Illinois with the destruction of pertinent records. The Government was unable to present any evidence connecting Carnegie-Illinois with destruction of records.

"Carnegie-Illinois is justly proud of its outstanding productive record in support of our country's great war effort, including the delivery of more than 10 million tons of steel plates of all kinds since Pearl Harbor. About one-sixth of these very considerable plate deliveries came from Irvin Works."

TRUMAN COMMITTEE NEWS RELEASE
JUNE 15, 1944

Papers of Harry S. Truman, Senatorial and Vice-Presidential Files,
Harry S. Truman Library, Independence, Missouri.

Senator Harry S. Truman, Chairman of the Special Senate Committee Investigating the National Defense Program, announced today:

In its Third Annual Report issued in March, the Truman Committee emphasized the necessity of declaring materials free for the manufacture of civilian articles as soon as it became clear that there was a surplus of such materials over and above the quantity necessary for the production of war materials. The Committee foresaw that there soon would be sufficient supplies of many articles of war, and that it would be necessary to cutback or cease production in many lines. In November 1943 the Committee had recommended that the Armed Services analyze their needs and give notice of expected termination as far in advance as possible.

There has been much discussion recently of creating adequate machinery to distribute contracts for whatever war material is still needed among manufacturers whose contracts have been cut back. That work is important but, at best, it is only a stop-gap. Obviously, as the cutbacks begin to involve more and larger contracts, it will become impossible for any agency, however efficient it might be, to parcel out new contracts to the companies affected. If the Government should attempt to provide contracts for those affected, the Government would be assuming a control of civilian business that would be a major step towards regimentation of industry.

American business is so complicated that I do not believe that there is or can be any substitute for the individual initiative and experience of American manufacturers. They should be told when and to what extent their contracts are expected to be cutback; the materials which are in surplus should be made free and available for any use to which they want to put them except in areas of manpower shortages; and they not only should be allowed but should be encouraged to place orders now for the acquisition of plants, machine tools and dies necessary to resume production of any articles that they can make out of the materials that are free, in any design and quantity that they see fit.

It is particularly important that progress along these lines be made now because cutbacks and cancellations of major proportions already are contemplated, and it is reasonably certain that the necessity for still others will be ascertained within the near future.

Mr. Donald Nelson, Chairman of the War Production Board, has assured the Committee that he is prepared to end general restrictions on materials that are in surplus, as recommended by the Committee, and to substitute specific restrictions which will apply only to the materials or semi-finished articles as to which there is still a scarcity. I am convinced that that is the most effective action that can be taken, and that it should be taken right away. The only way to begin any job is to start doing it.

Mr. Nelson will explain his views in further detail at a public hearing in Room 318 in the Senate Office Building at 10:00 o'clock A. M. on Monday, June 19.

For a number of months there has been a surplus of aluminum and magnesium. It has even been necessary to shut down a number of production units. Yet, the general limitation orders have been continued. These, undoubtedly, will be among the first to be eliminated.

It is now up to the aluminum industry to take the initiative and to show what uses it can make of aluminum and magnesium and, if possible, of the facilities for the production of aluminum and magnesium built by the Government at a cost of more than a billion dollars.

At the public hearing on Monday the Committee will ask the Aluminum Company of America and the Reynolds Metals Company, the two principal manufacturers of aluminum and principal fabricators and users of magnesium and aluminum products, to inform the Committee as to what they think can be done with respect to those metals.

I believe that all other manufacturers should be thinking along these lines and making preparations that will enable them to provide employment for their workers when their war contracts are cut back or terminated.

There are some industrialists who want to control their competitors and who think in terms of industry planning, whereby those who run out of war contracts will be restricted as to what they can make. Such plans are dangerous because of the self interest involved and because no one is intelligent enough to make worthwhile plans for the future of entire industries. The best way is the American way of encouraging individual initiative.

HARPER'S MAGAZINE ARTICLE, "THE JOB THAT MADE TRUMAN PRESIDENT" BY WESLEY McCUNE AND JOHN R. BEAL
JUNE 1945

With all due allowance for the accidents of mortality and politics, it is clear that Harry S. Truman was lifted into the White House by his performance as an investigator. In 1941 he was just another obscure junior Senator with no visible political future. Three years later he had made himself known, and respected, as the chairman of a special committee investigating war production and, in consequence, the almost inevitable choice of his party as a compromise candidate for the Vice Presidency.

Truman's handling of that investigation throws a good deal of light on his character, methods, and capabilities. It also provides a noteworthy lesson in the handling of Congress' investigating power, one of the sharpest (and most hazardous) tools in the whole arsenal of government.

Plenty of other Senators and Representatives were running investigations at about the same time, in fields as important as Truman's. Most of them had greater political experience, and at least as much money and staff. Yet none was able to build himself into a national political figure. On the contrary, some—notably among the members of the Dies Committee—cut their political throats with spectacular thoroughness. Obviously Truman had learned, somehow, to wield his investigating tool with uncommon adroitness.

II

His training in the highly specialized business of Congressional inquiry began in 1936 under a master of the craft, Senator Burton K. Wheeler of Montana. Because Wheeler's isolationist views have dimmed his reputation during the war years, many people have forgotten that he earned fame as one of the most able, honest, and thorough of Senate investigators. He and Truman sat together on the Interstate Commerce Committee and he chose the younger Senator to serve as his lieutenant in a special study of railway holding companies.

For two years this inquiry plodded along through some of the dullest hearings ever recorded at the Capitol. During the early months, Truman seldom opened his mouth. He watched the Montana maestro question an endless procession of witnesses; and he studied railway finance and corporate organization with a dogged intentness which his colleagues considered rather eccentric.

The public's indifference to the railroad inquiry was simply deafening. As the hearings dragged on, the other members (including Wheeler) lost interest, and Truman frequently was the only Senator who showed up for public sessions. Before no audience except his own counsel, the witness and his lawyers, and one or two weary newspapermen, he conducted the questioning with meticulous fairness and a growing knowledge of the nation's transport system. He made no reputation; indeed, his fellow Senators sometimes hinted that he was wasting time. But the investigation did result in a few important though obscure reforms. And a handful of industrialists and financiers began to speak of Truman as a strange sort of politician—a New Dealer who showed no desire to persecute business, a man who dug for his facts, used them surely, and tolerated no wool over his eyes.

This tedious schooling paid off handsomely when Truman decided early in 1941 to organize an investigation of his own. It was to be his first venture into the big-time political arena and its possibilities were not immediately apparent. There was no rivalry for the chairmanship, nor any stampede for seats on the committee. Consequently, Truman had an unusually free hand in indicating to the Senate leaders the men he wanted. His choices, together with the subsequent hiring of the committee's staff, perhaps can be taken as some indication of the course Truman may follow in making Presidential appointments.

The distinguishing mark of the original committee members—five Democrats and four Republicans—was a sort of unspectacular competence. All were junior senators from their respective states, with the exception of Tom Connally of Texas. They obviously were picked with an eye to their special knowledge of various phases of the war production program, and to the desirability of a balanced representation from every section of the country.

Carl A. Hatch, a wiry little man with a face tanned to leather by the New Mexico sun, is a crony of Truman.

Mon C. Wallgren, a ruddy, grey-haired jeweler from Everett, Washington, was the committee's lumber and aircraft man. He has since resigned to become governor of his state.

James M. Mead of New York and Harley M. Kilgore of West Virginia are generally regarded as spokesmen for labor and the little businessman. Kilgore has carried a heavy share of the load in the steel and shipbuilding phases of the inquiry.

Ralph O. Brewster of Maine, one of the ablest and hardest-working members, is particularly interested in the naval program because of his membership on the Senate Naval Affairs Committee.

Joseph H. Ball, young ex-newspaperman, came to the Senate as a Willkie-Stassen internationalist from supposedly isolationist Minnesota.

Harold H. Burton, former Cleveland mayor, has shown a marked ability in the analytical questioning of witnesses.

Homer A. Ferguson, the one-man grand jury from Michigan, is an experienced sleuth for facts, with some background in the automotive industry.

In one way or another, each of these men has demonstrated another characteristic—an uncommon degree of courage. Ball defied his party to support Roosevelt in the last election. Both Ferguson and Burton had chalked up records of unterrified independence in local politics before they came to the Senate. Mead, who was elected as a "labor Senator," and Kilgore, in whose state the coal miners are the strongest single political factor, risked their careers when the committee tangled with John L. Lewis. And so on. This phenomenon may have some significance; Truman has shown the same quality, and it may be that he has an intuition for discovering it in other men.

III

Truman's selection of the committee's staff was even more revealing. Such jobs are luscious patronage plums, and swarms of political job-hunters were drooling in his outside office. But Truman had learned from the old railway inquiry—and perhaps, too, from watching the embarrassingly inept performance of the Dies Committee—that the technical staff can make or break a Congressional investigation. He decided that he simply could not afford to take a chance on patronage appointments.

Instead he paid a visit to Robert H. Jackson, then Attorney General, to ask him to recommend a good lawyer who might serve as counsel for the new committee. The request must have surprised Jackson; he was more accustomed to hearing Senators demand jobs in the Justice Department for their own henchmen. Yes, he told Truman, he knew a good man—a young fellow recently out of Michigan Law School who was at work in New York as a special assistant to the attorney general. He had successfully prosecuted the utilities magnate, Howard C. Hopson, in the celebrated Associated Gas & Electric case and was even then preparing to indict a judge. Jackson promised to tell the young lawyer to drop around.

A few days later Hugh Alfred Fulton called at Truman's office. Neither had seen the other before, but they got along well from the beginning. Truman outlined his plan for the committee, and emphasized the mistakes in the history of past investigations which he wanted to avoid. He did not conceive his job to be that of running the defense program; a Committee on the Conduct of the War had tried that during the Civil War, and had caused President Lincoln and the Union much grief. He did not want to sit by until scandals developed, and then try to assess the blame after it was too late to do any good; that had been tried after World War I, in 116 post mortem investigations (one lasting as late as 1935) which dug into everything in sight for every conceivable partisan purpose.

Both these pitfalls might be avoided, he believed, if the new committee tried an entirely new technique. It would undertake a current, continuing checkup on each major war program as it developed. The aim would be to keep an alert watch for bottlenecks, graft, waste, bureaucratic deadlocks, and other weaknesses, and to remedy them promptly before they could grow to ominous dimensions. What he wanted above all, he told Fulton, was facts. "I don't want to whitewash and I don't want to smear," he explained.

Fulton decided it was the kind of job he wanted to tackle. The thick-set, chubby-faced young lawyer was no typical committee counsel. Usually such jobs go to a man who is either (1) a political creditor of the chairman; (2) a lawyer borrowed from an interested pressure group or government department; or (3) a big-name attorney who works only part time and lets the inquiry flounder for want of tight direction. Fulton had no political strings, no axes to grind, and no objections to working all hours of the day and night. Moreover, he quickly developed an ability to make his subordinates work the same man-killing hours—and love it.

In his method of conducting a hearing Fulton also varied from the conventional pattern. He never tried to entrap or bully a witness, or to over-dramatize a line of questioning purely for the sake of the headlines. He brought into each session a carefully prepared list of questions, designed to lead the witness into the heart of his story with a minimum of lost motion. The questioning itself often was done by the chairman or the Senator with a special interest in the subject at issue.

Truman and Fulton together assembled a staff of some 15 investigators, who have been largely responsible for the high quality and sweeping range of information the committee has brought to light. Of necessity the crew was relatively small; Truman's request for an initial appropriation of $25,000 was pared by the Senate to $15,000. Later appropriations also were modest in comparison with those, for example, of the Dies Committee or a dozen others.

In general the investigators were of the Fulton type—relatively young, no experience in war production, no private connections, no closed minds. The theory was that if, say, shipbuilding was to be scrutinized, it was better to have the fact-gathering done by someone who had never seen a ship than by an expert with preconceived views. Later the experts could make their contribution from the witness stand.

One of the ablest of the crew was Matthew Connelly, a professional Congressional investigator—or what is sometimes described in Washington as a "committee dick." At the age of 35 he had worked for five Congressional inquiries, and he knew all the twists and pitfalls of the trade. He also had acquired a tight-lipped discretion, and a thorough knowledge of the shifting, complex web of Washington pressures and power relationships.

Near the bottom of the list of investigators appeared the name of Walter Hehmeyer. He actually did some leg-work, but his primary job was that of press agent. He handled the committee's publicity quietly and honestly, with none of the synthetic fireworks which characterized some other Congressional investigations.

Several of these investigators seem likely to play an important part in the Truman administration. Five days after the new President took office he called Connelly to the White House to serve as his confidential secretary—a position considerably more important than the title may imply. Fulton had breakfast with Truman the morning after Roosevelt's death, and has been close at hand ever since. At this writing he has received no formal appointment; but it appears probable that he may come closer than any other man to filling the uniquely personal status which Harry Hopkins held during the Roosevelt regime—although Truman is far less inclined than his predecessor to operate through personal deputies with nebulous assignments.

Other members of the old committee staff are standing by. Truman knows their capabilities and is used to working with them. It would not be surprising if a number of them eventually sift into responsible administrative posts.

IV

Through the door of Room 449 in the Senate Office Building, the committee headquarters, flowed a strange assortment of mail and people. A typical day might bring an eccentric inventor with a gadget; he said the Army and Navy had given him the brush-off. He would be followed by a manufacturer who thought his product had been discriminated against by the Quartermaster General. A maker of mouthwash for the Army couldn't get priorities for alcohol; a dry kiln owner couldn't get a government contract for his lumber; or an industrialist accused a competitor, now holding a dollar-a-year job in

WPB, of using his official position for private ends. And every day there was an assortment of government officials, labor representatives, lobbyists, and occasionally a plain citizen with an idea he hoped might help the war effort. Some came in search of a new shoulder to cry on; others looked to Truman as a court of last resort.

None was turned away coldly, although the crackpots and whiners were dispatched as quickly as politeness would permit. Complaints with a color of merit were submitted to pertinent agencies for information. If they were urgent, a few well-placed telephone calls often got results—as they did when Fulton called WPB to see why a priority for sprinkling pipes had not been delivered to the manager of a rubber-seedling nursery.

Both visitors and correspondence, which ran to more than a hundred letters a day, were screened by the investigating staff. The promising tips and scraps of information were passed immediately to Fulton, who decided whether to act at once, shelve the project, or order a further investigation. Many of the committee's best leads were uncovered in this fashion. Other lines of inquiry were developed on the committee's own initiative, and investigators were assigned to dig up all available data on such broad subjects as steel, shipbuilding, and rubber.

Basic strategy was developed in a series of early morning meetings. Truman rose at farmers' hours, and Fulton ate no breakfast; so between eight and nine each morning the two would comb over a stack of memos, reports, and letters which had been bundled up the night before for the Senator's evening reading.

Their tentative decisions, on matters of importance, were then taken up with the rest of the committee in private sessions held once or twice a week in Truman's "dog house," a small room behind his office. Sometimes the Senators invited some big-shot who seemed headed for trouble to sit in. Donald Nelson, Rubber Czar William Jeffers, Undersecretary Robert Patterson of the War Department, and Manpower Chief Paul McNutt were among those who told their sides of some confused story—thereby either crystallizing or averting a public hearing.

By such methods the committee and its staff accomplished at least half of their work without any publicity whatever. It may, indeed, have been the more important half. The committee's informal conferences often pried open bureaucratic logjams, which had come about because the White House had been unwilling (or too busy) to knock stubborn heads together. Army, Navy, and WPB appointed high-ranking liaison men to expedite action on the committee's requests. And in many cases the mere knowledge that Truman's people were interested in a particular subject was enough to galvanize everyone concerned—bureaucrats, generals, manufacturers, and labor—into special efforts to avoid mismanagement or delay.

V

The results of Truman's unorthodox formula for running a Congressional inquiry surprised everyone—including the committee members. The performance differed in four important respects from that of most such investigations.

First of all, it got results. The accomplishments of the typical Congressional committee are at best minor, and at worst a sheer waste of time and money. All too often such inquiries begin with a fanfare of publicity, and then dribble away into confusion, bickering, and impotence. The Truman Committee, on the other hand, started modestly—and then proceeded to produce. One of its earliest projects, which uncovered waste and extravagance in the construction of Army camps, led to an overhaul of the contract-letting system with savings estimated at well over a hundred million dollars. Its investigations of aluminum, steel, and other shortages spurred officials into finding ways to increase production; its rubber inquiry built a fire under Jesse Jones. The Committee insisted on the spreading of war contracts among smaller plants, at a time when both the Army and Navy tended to concentrate their orders with a handful of giant corporations. Its discovery of outright incompetence in the Navy's Bureau of Ships led to a reorganization, although publication of the report was withheld at the request of Navy Secretary Knox.

Most spectacular of all, its first annual report. condemning bungling by the Office of Production Management, needled President Roosevelt into an eleventh-hour shakeup which created the War Production Board with Donald Nelson at its head. Mr. Roosevelt beat the committee to the draw by a scant 24 hours because of his advance knowledge of the report; that was all right with Truman, who wanted action more than credit.

Perhaps the best evidence of the committee's effectiveness was the wry testimony of Undersecretary of War Robert Patterson, more than a year ago, that the investigators' recommendations often irritated him, but that they invariably turned out to be constructive. "Some of the very best features of our war program have had their origin from the investigations made by this committee," he concluded.

This does not mean that the committee's record was perfect. Its investigation of Senator A. B. Chandler's swimming pool, built free on the grounds of his home by a contractor, reeked strongly of politics. Twice the committee hauled John L. Lewis on the carpet in connection with threatened coal strikes, and came off second best. After watching the operations of OPM, Truman became convinced that the government was not getting its money's worth from dollar-a-year men; but he permitted Nelson to call him off that line of inquiry, on the plea that they were needed to help him do his new job with WPB.

On the whole, however, the committee built a record of accomplishment seldom surpassed in Congressional history.

A second distinguishing mark of the Truman group was its good administration. All investigation of this sort presents a more serious administrative problem than is generally recognized; while the number of people involved is relatively small, the committee members are likely to be prima donnas who are notoriously hard to handle.

Truman handled his colleagues with unobtrusive skill. Unlike many investigations, his did not turn into a one-man show; all, or nearly all, of the Senators contributed an uncommon amount of hard work. Truman carefully apportioned the fields to be covered among the members, so they did not get into each other's hair. He also made a point of spreading the credit and publicity, while he himself kept in the background as far as possible; as a result, internal jealousies never flared into open friction.

It is particularly significant that in four years of operation no committee member ever dissented from any report. Truman achieved this surprising unanimity by tireless search for all the facts, and then by consultation—no matter how tedious—until a set of conclusions was hammered out on which everyone could agree. Once a member objected when the committee prepared to spank an official from his own state for bungling one of the major war material programs. But after reviewing the case, the member decided against a minority report—the facts just couldn't be disputed. Senator Brewster summed it up in these words: "Reasonable men don't differ much when they have the facts."

In addition, Truman did a good job in administering the committee staff. He picked competent men; he gave a precise assignment to each, and made sure it did not overlap anyone else's job; and then he left them alone to do their work without undue interference.

Already there are indications that Truman has carried over these habits of administration to the infinitely more complex task of Chief Executive. He has made an emphatic point of frequent consultations with Congressional leaders. And his early decisions from the White House tend toward more clear-cut allocation of responsibility than has been customary in Washington in recent years.

In the third place, the Truman committee demonstrated a sense of fairness and responsibility which inspired widespread confidence.

All too frequently Congressional investigators have set out to smear somebody, by fair means or foul and without giving their victims a chance for rebuttal. In contrast, Truman's group went to unheard-of lengths to make sure its facts were right, and that everyone concerned had a chance to check up on them. Its shipbuilding report, for example, was eighteen months in preparation. Several months before its release, the conclusions were circulated in draft to the WPB, Maritime Commission, and the Navy. All private shipbuilders mentioned in the document were consulted by telegram, and the maritime unions also were checked. Even the widow of a seaman was given opportunity to check the printer's proofs of her late husband's testimony. When the newspapers finally got the 75-page report, it was established as gospel.

It is noteworthy that Secretary Forrestal, whose Navy Department has come under frequent committee scrutiny, once remarked that the investigation was "as objective as I think possible." His view is shared by virtually all other government agencies; and in addition, both management and labor have been generally satisfied with the committee's impartiality.

Finally, the committee displayed a brand of courage rare among politicians. It did not hesitate to criticize labor, when plainly at fault. Similarly, it pulled no punches in its reports on the misbehavior of several of the most powerful of industrial corporations. Truman went after some of the biggest brass hats, including General Somervell himself, at a time when no other civilian dared raise a voice against military encroachment into control of the civilian economy. Many a government agency—not excepting the White House—smarted under his blunt comments, at a time when Truman must have known he was being discussed as a possible vice presidential candidate.

Such apparently foolhardy behavior turned out, of course, to be good politics. It nearly always does. It is curious that most politicians still believe implicitly in the myth that conspicuous valor in the face of entrenched pressure groups means political suicide—in spite of contrary evidence piled up by scores of public men from Lincoln to George Norris. In the performance of his investigating committee, Truman proved once more that a politician can make honesty and courage pay off. Perhaps it is not too much to hope that in the White House he will remember his own lesson.

BIBLIOGRAPHY

The official records of the Special Committee to Investigate the National Defense Program, approximately 400 linear feet, are located in the National Archives. An almost equally valuable source is Truman's senatorial files, which fully document his role on the committee. These papers are at the Truman Library, Independence, Missouri. The published hearings and reports of the Truman Committee are also essential. Publications of various war agencies, especially the Budget Bureau's *The United States at War* (Washington, D.C., 1946), are informative. Also see the relevant volumes of the Department of the Army's history of the war.

Surprisingly, few historians have tapped this store of information. Donald Riddle, *The Truman Committee: A Study in Congressional Responsibility* (New Brunswick, 1963), remains the most helpful analysis. Roger Willson has written an impressively researched study, "The Truman Committee" (unpublished Ph.D. dissertation, Cambridge, 1966). See also Harry A. Toulmin, jr., *Diary of Democracy: The Senate War Investigating Committee* (New York, 1947), an uncritical account. Herman M. Somers, *Presidential Agency: OWMR, Office of War Mobilization and Reconversion* (Cambridge, Mass., 1950), Harry Lever and Joseph Young, *Wartime Racketeers* (New York, 1945), and Leslie R. Groves, *Now It Can Be Told: The Story of the Manhattan Project* (New York, 1962) treat important issues. Studies of the larger context in which the Truman Committee operated include Elias Huzar, *The Purse and the Sword* (Ithaca, 1950), Walter Millis, et al, *Arms and the State* (New York, 1958), Edward S. Corwin, *The President: Office and Powers* (New York, 1958), Roland Young, *Congressional Politics in the Second World War* (New York, 1956), and Alan Barth's excellent *Government By Investigation* (New York, 1955). Also useful are *War and Society: The United States, 1941–1945* (New York, 1972), by Richard Polenberg, and the prejudiced but insightful work by Eliot Janeway, *The Struggle for Survival: A Chronicle of Economic Mobilization in World War II* (New Haven, 1951).

Books by and about the personalities who struggled for power in wartime Washington include Harry S. Truman, *Memoirs: Year of Decisions* (Garden city, 1955), Margaret Truman, *Harry S. Truman* (New York, 1973), Merle Miller, *Plain Speaking: An Oral Biography of Harry S. Truman* (New York, 1973), Jonathan Daniels, *The Man of Independence* (Philadelphia, 1950), James McGregor Burns, *Roosevelt: The Soldier of Freedom, 1940–1945* (New York, 1970), Donald Nelson, *Arsenal of Democracy* (New York, 1946), and James M. Mead, *Tell the Folks Back Home* (New York, 1944). Additionally, men such as Harold Ickes, Henry Wallace, Jesse Jones, Harry Hopkins, and James Byrnes are described in numerous biographies and memoirs. Bruce Catton, *The War Lords of Washington* (New York, 1948) effectively captures the atmosphere of those times.